GW00383019

The
Golf Guide
2004
Where to play, Where to stay

Over 2800 courses and hundreds
of hotels throughout Britain and Ireland including
a selection in holiday areas abroad

PLUS Golf Tours and Products Section

Contents   Page 6

In Association with

GOLF
MONTHLY

 Publications
Paisley

COUNTRY
&LEISURE   Part of IPC Country and Leisure Media
MEDIA

Other FHG Publications

• Recommended Country Hotels of Britain • Recommended Country Inns & Pubs of Britain • Pets Welcome!
• Britain's Best Holidays • Bed and Breakfast Stops • Self-Catering Holidays in Britain
• Farm Holiday Guide to Coast & Country Holidays • Recommended Short Break Holidays in Britain
• Guide to Caravan and Camping Holidays • Children Welcome! Family Holiday and Days Out Guide

Acknowledgements

The Publishers wish to acknowledge the assistance of Jane Carter of GOLF MONTHLY and The Professional Golfers' Association regional golfing correspondents in the preparation of this 27th edition of THE GOLF GUIDE. For colour photographs we wish to thank Dartmouth Golf & Country Club (p1), Jane Carter (p7), Peter Godsiff for The Dorset Golf & Country Club (p10) and St Enodoc (p17), Old Thorns Hotel, Golf & Country Club (p21), Aldenham Golf & Country Club (p29), West Midlands Golf Club (p35), Wellingborough Golf Club (p41), Houghwood Golf Club (p43), The Cliff Hotel at Cardigan Golf Club (p52), East of Scotland Golf Alliance for Carnoustie Golf Club (p61) and The Old Course, St. Andrews (p68), Failte Ireland for Royal Portrush Golf Club (p86), Connemara Golf Club (p90), The Kildare Hotel & Golf Club (p93), Michael Gedye for Chateau des Sept Tours (p104), Golf Vilamoura (p106), and The Rose Garden Golf Club (p109), Golf Platja de Pals (p108), Loch Palm Golf Club (p110), Pelican's Nest Golf Club (p112), Drivetime Golf Centre (p656).

We wish to thank all our advertisers and, finally, the Club Secretaries, Professionals and others who have co-operated in the annual updating of the golf club directory entries which are the essential ingredients of THE GOLF GUIDE: Where To Play/Where To Stay.

Cover design: Focus Network with thanks to Macdonald Cardrona Hotel

ISBN 1 85055 354 8 © IPC Media Ltd. 2004

Whilst every care has been taken to obtain and compile accurate and reliable information, the Publishers cannot accept liability for any errors or omissions in this publication.

Published by FHG Publications, Abbey Mill Business Centre, Seedhill, Paisley PA1 1TJ
Tel: 0141 887 0428; Fax: 0141 889 7204; E-mail: FHG@ipc.media.com

Distribution: Book Trade: Plymbridge House, Estover Road, Plymouth PL6 7PY
Tel: 01752 202300; Fax: 01752 202333
NewsTrade: Market Force (UK) Ltd, 5th Floor Low Rise, King's Reach Tower
Stamford Street, London SE1 9LS
Tel: 0207 633 3450; Fax: 0207 633 3572

US ISBN 1 58843 364 -1
Distributed in the United States by Hunter Publishing Inc. 130 Campus Drive, Edison, NJ. 08818, USA

Typeset by FHG Publications, Paisley

Printed and bound in Great Britain by William Clowes, Beccles, Suffolk

The Golf Guide; Where to Play/ Where to Stay is an FHG Publication, published by IPC Country & Leisure Media Ltd, part of the IPC Media Group of Companies

PRINTED AND PUBLISHED IN BRITAIN

WHEREVER YOU'RE PLAYING

PICK UP A GUIDE MAP
TO WHAT'S BEST IN THE AREA

From all leading
Tourist Information Centres
or with the compliments of
participating hotels & golf clubs

TOURIST PUBLICATIONS
5 Eglinton Crescent, Edinburgh EH12 5DH.
Tel: 0131 225 4547. Fax: 0131 220 6789.

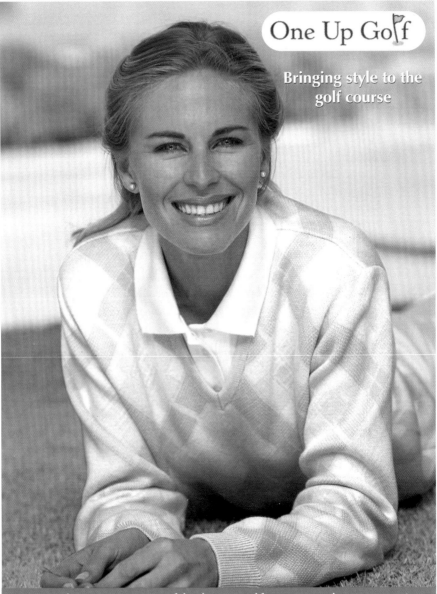

Contents

Foreword

by Jane Carter
Editor of

GOLF
MONTHLY

The 2004 edition of *The Golf Guide* gives all golfers the opportunity to visit a large variety of courses and stay in accommodation convenient for golfers. I am pleased to again discover the delights contained in this comprehensive guide to courses throughout the UK and Ireland, with a selection in holiday destinations abroad.

The range of courses included in the guide is only equalled by the variety of people taking up the game of golf, with juniors and lady golfers in particular making up an ever increasing percentage of new players.

High profile tournaments such as The Solheim Cup encourage everyone to venture onto the course and with 2003 being a 'back to back' year for this tournament the European Ladies certainly gave us something to cheer about with a victory at the Bar Seback Club near Malmo.

This 'doubling up' of the Solheim Cup leaves the stage clear for the Ryder Cup in 2004 when the Americans will have home advantage.

Be sure to make full use of The Golf Guide this year. Make a point of trying some different types of courses in areas you may not have visited before and to get the most enjoyment out of the game make sure you take your copy of *The Golf Guide* with you.

Jane Carter

Golfing National Regions

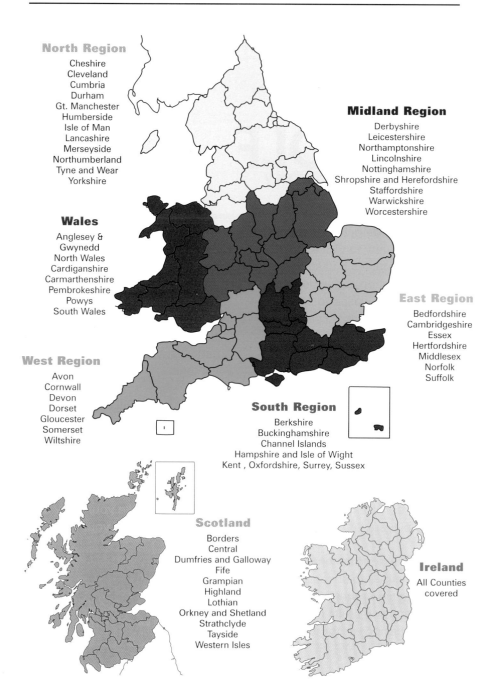

North Region
Cheshire
Cleveland
Cumbria
Durham
Gt. Manchester
Humberside
Isle of Man
Lancashire
Merseyside
Northumberland
Tyne and Wear
Yorkshire

Midland Region
Derbyshire
Leicestershire
Northamptonshire
Lincolnshire
Nottinghamshire
Shropshire and Herefordshire
Staffordshire
Warwickshire
Worcestershire

Wales
Anglesey &
Gwynedd
North Wales
Cardiganshire
Carmarthenshire
Pembrokeshire
Powys
South Wales

East Region
Bedfordshire
Cambridgeshire
Essex
Hertfordshire
Middlesex
Norfolk
Suffolk

West Region
Avon
Cornwall
Devon
Dorset
Gloucester
Somerset
Wiltshire

South Region
Berkshire
Buckinghamshire
Channel Islands
Hampshire and Isle of Wight
Kent , Oxfordshire, Surrey, Sussex

Scotland
Borders
Central
Dumfries and Galloway
Fife
Grampian
Highland
Lothian
Orkney and Shetland
Strathclyde
Tayside
Western Isles

Ireland
All Counties
covered

Golfing around Britain and Abroad

Where to Play and Where to Stay around the Golfing Regions

A recent survey has shown that while golf is still most popular amongst 'middle aged, middle class men the spread of golf has been fairly rapid and almost half the people who play golf are now under age 45, with a large percentage under 20. This, along with the increase of women in the game, can only be healthy for the sport. In the past few years there has been a steady rise in the number of people who watch golf on TV and this is reflected by over 10% of the non-golfers surveyed saying that although they had never played golf in the past, they were likely to try it in the future.

This increase in popularity of casual golf shows up in the mix of golf members compared with 'occasional' players. In total there are just under 1.2 million club members with about three times that number who play on a pay-per-play basis or only play with friends, colleagues or on holiday.

This book hopefully caters for every type of golfer, male, female, young, old, serious or casual. It gives details of the almost 3,000 courses spread throughout the UK, Ireland and selected holiday destinations.

With details of accommodation convenient for golf courses and recommended by golfers for golfers, there is no reason not to try as many different types of course as possible, moving from the challenge of a seaside links course to an inland parkland, moorland or heathland course.

Each offers its own unique blend of difficulty and enjoyment, which keeps the golfer coming back for more.

British golfers are particularly fortunate in having the largest variety of courses anywhere in the world with the greatest number of courses per head of population.

When visiting different courses, do always remember that to be welcomed back you should behave as you would like visitors to your own course to behave. Everyone knows that they should rake bunkers, repair pitch marks and replace divots; but remember that the bane of most golfers' lives is slow play - the holiday mood can cause even experienced golfers to walk more slowly, talk more and forget about the job in hand. All this is fine if the course is quiet, but will not be appreciated if there are members behind looking to fit in a quick 9 holes.

Remember also that golf need not be purely a summer game. There is a lot of pleasure to be had from an early start on a crisp winter morning when the course is quieter, the greens are softer and there is not as much chance of the ball shooting off into the rough, which is less dense in winter.

No matter when you go, or where you go in the UK or abroad, don't forget to take your copy of **The Golf Guide** and we are sure you will enjoy the accommodation and courses featured throughout this guide.

GOLF IN THE WEST

Peter Godsiff

The Dorset Golf & Country Club, Wareham, Dorset

The West Country is the prime holiday destination in Britain and has numerous classic golf courses and hotel-golf complexes.

Everyone knows the principal championship venues and travelling Americans will always head for places they know and have read about.

Saunton's East and West courses in North Devon come high on anyone's must-play list. St Enodoc, the glorious links in North Cornwall, is another.

Somerset's prime links is at Burnham and Berrow, where a dormy house also offers accommodation on site. Minehead and West Somerset is another links well worth checking out. The holiday town of Weston-super-Mare has two courses and several more within a few miles.

Jack Nicklaus designed only one course in the West and his masterpiece is the championship layout at St Mellion, the former home of the Benson and Hedges European Tour event.

The latest tour venue is Woodbury Park, owned by motor racing ace Nigel Mansell. He hosted the first of three annual Nigel Mansell Classics on the European Tour last August.

His impeccable 27 hole golf complex complete with 58-room hotel, leisure complex, football field, dining facilities and the owner's motor racing museum has earned worldwide recognition, yet remains affordable.

Cornwall may boast picture-postcard villages and hamlets wending their way down to the sea, but there is an abundance of golf packages available to suit all pockets.

China Fleet at Saltash, the gateway to Cornwall, has strong naval connections. On the opposite coast the thriving seaside town of Newquay is a perfect golfing centre for those who like a lively nightlife.

Moving northwards from Newquay, Trevose remains my favourite venue with its charming course, ample self-catering villa and apartment accommodation and superb (if a little pricey) restaurant.

Bowood Park has accommodation to complement a fast maturing course with an exciting back nine. Bude and North Cornwall, a half links, half parkland course, dominates the town, and every hotel and guest house can produce attractive stay-and-play deals.

Devon is the largest county and features more than 40 clubs, ranging from the imperious Manor House Hotel at Moretonhampstead, with its tight but beautiful course, to Elfordleigh, now with an 18-hole hotel course that is earning a high reputation.

The Manor House and Ashbury Hotels at Okehampton in the heart of Devon provides a carefree holiday centre that offers incredible value.

Situated on the fringe of Dartmoor, the hotel offers free golf on its 63 holes to all residents, who can also indulge in a host

of other activities, including arts and crafts, not forgetting croquet.

Torbay is another bustling centre, with quality courses on the coast and just inland. Historic Exeter is a fine city to visit, and a number of courses, like Downes Crediton inland and the stretch, taking in the wonderful East Devon coast at Budleigh Salterton, Sidmouth, Dawlish and Axe Cliff, lead to Dorset.

Apart from the seaside town of Weymouth, close to the rolling Came Down course at Dorchester, The Dorset Golf and Country Club near Wareham is a 27 hole layout with superior clubhouse and an adjoining hotel that offers superb stay-and-play deals for couples and groups.

Sophisticated Bournemouth features quality courses like Broadstone, Parkstone, Ferndown and the fast-improving Dudsbury, that hosts the PGA Wood-BMW Classic each year.

Meyrick Park, like Queens Park a

municipal course of the highest quality, features a 17-suite lodge.

Back into Wiltshire, the Marquis of Lansdowne's Bowood at Calne is a course that ranks among the best in the region, adjacent to the country estate.

The Manor House at Castle Combe offers perhaps the highest quality hotel and restaurant with the adjoining golf course to match.

The Georgian city of Bath is perhaps the most visited city in the West and, amid the sightseeing, there is time to play the local courses.

Bristol also has an abundance of golf and Thornbury's 36 hole site on the outskirts offers accommodation to suit all golfers, either passing through or making a dedicated visit.

Gloucestershire features many top-notch courses, like Minchinhampton, where Open qualifying is held. Gloucester's Ramada complex on Robinswood Hill, Hilton Puckrup Hall at Tewkesbury, the friendly Bells Hotel at Coleford and Speech House Hotel next to the Forest Hills club in the heart of the Forest of Dean all have much to offer the golfing traveller.

You can be assured of a warm welcome from golfers in every part of the West Country.

FHG

Finding a particular club or course is easy with our website

www.UK-GolfGuide.com

ELFORDLEIGH
HOTEL : GOLF : LEISURE

Colebrook, Plympton,
Plymouth, Devon PL7 5EB
Tel: 01752 336428
Fax: 01752 344581
e-mail: elfordleigh@btinternet.com
website: www.elfordleigh.co.uk

Elfordleigh offers the peace, calm & tranquillity of an English Country House, to a privately owned hotel with an atmosphere of warmth, ease & charm. The acres of glorious parkland perfectly positioned for exploring the timeless elegance of Devon yet only minutes away from the heart of Plymouth. Whether on business or taking a short break you are welcome at Elfordleigh. Only 7 miles from the centre of Plymouth and within easy reach of the sea and Dartmoor. Plymouth is on the main intercity rail network, airlink to London and totally accessible by main road links and ferry port serving connections between France, Spain and the UK.

The beauty which surrounds Elfordleigh influences the character of the hotel & its rooms. Bedrooms are light and airy with spacious bathrooms and splendid views of the green tranquillity of the golf course & beyond.

Churchill's Restaurant offers good food, excellent wines, outstanding service, exquisite conservatory, wonderful location – *need we say more!* With our growing reputation, it is advisable to book before coming. Civil wedding ceremonies are also on offer.

Our country bar serves bar meals and light snacks throughout the day and evening to cater for an impromptu visit.

- Squash Court
- Two Spas
- Sauna
- Steam Room
- Swimming Pool
- Separate Children's Pool
- Fully Equipped Gym

- Large Sun Terrace & BBQ area
- Dance Studio
- Three Tennis Courts
- Solarium
- Beauty Therapy
- Hairdresser
- Jogging Track

All this from under £1 per day.

One of the special features of Elfordleigh is our 18-hole golf course. Although the course is the home of a thriving members community it is also open to visiting golfers and hotel residents. Elfordleigh offers residential golfing breaks, society day packages (available from £20) and the unique opportunity to play golf – whatever the weather – through the smart golf indoor golf simulator, with over 33 world famous courses to choose from.

In addition we also offer practice facilities and expert tuition from PGA golf professional Scott Macaskill.

ELFORDLEIGH OFFERS A CHARMING WAY TO COMBINE BUSINESS WITH PLEASURE

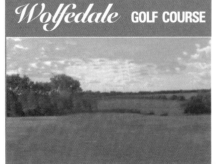

St Enodoc links course, North Cornwall

Old Thorns Hotel, Golf & Country Club, Liphook, Hampshire

GOLF IN THE SOUTH
Peter Ward

Entering my sixth year in the South, I still find it extremely difficult to fully appreciate the magnificent golf courses that lie within a short drive of the P.G.A. offices based at Clandon Regis.

As an Association, we are privileged to visit many of the world acclaimed establishments, as well as Clubs that have celebrated 100 years of golf and also the many new facilities that provide for the playing of the game across the South. There are in excess of 500 venues within the Counties of Berkshire, Buckinghamshire,Oxfordshire, Hants, Kent, Surrey and Sussex.

A Spring break in the Channel Islands is the perfect start to your golfing year with the challenging Royal Jersey, La Moye, Les Mielles, Wheatlands and Royal Guernsey to whet your appetite for the year. Travelling with your car on the regular service allows you time to explore the wonderful scenery that is unique to the Islands.

Royal St Georges, the host Club of the 2003 Open, is just one of the truly great links courses to be found on the Kent coast. Prince's Golf Club, with its 27 hole complex, Littlestone and Royal Cinque Ports are as good as anywhere in the world and are at the top of the list for the golfing enthusiast.

Le Meridien Selsdon Park Hotel is one option as a base for your party, its location presenting an opportunity to experience the variety of golf courses within approximately an hour's drive. Your family can enjoy the luxury of the Hotel whilst you explore courses that are both challenging and fair. The P.G.A. Order of Merit holds events at The Drift, Wildwood Golf & Country Club, Sweetwoods and at Selsdon Park itself and are recommended for a warm welcome. A suggested base for the following few days would be the Old Thorns Golf Course and Hotel, which provides facilities to suit the whole family

and lies within a short drive of Cowdray Park, the host of our Championship. It celebrates its Centenary in 2004 and with the new Golf Club and Lodge accommodation, is a must. Dale Hill and Chart Hills, designed by Ian Woosnam and Nick Faldo respectively, are superb in their layout, as is the nearby Burgess Hill complex, host of the Par 3 Championship.

Continue your journey into Berkshire where, with the award-winning Donnington Valley Hotel and Golf Club as a base, you can complete your tour with visits to the superb courses of Parasampra Golf and Country Club, Magnolia Park, Beaconsfield, Sandford Springs or The Oxfordshire Golf Club among others, all renowned not only for their golf but also for the hospitality extended.

Enjoy the game wherever you play.

NOTE

All the information regarding Golf Clubs in this guide is given in good faith in the belief that it is correct. However, the publishers cannot guarantee the facts given in these pages, neither are they responsible for changes in ownership or facilities, such as green fees, that may take place after the date of going to press. Readers should always satisfy themselves that the facilities they require are available and that the terms, if quoted, still apply.

Aldenham Golf & Country Club, Watford, Hertfordshire

GOLF IN THE EAST
John H. Smith
PGA East Region Secretary

The East Region, which encompasses seven counties and over 350 golf courses, offers an abundance of opportunity for all golfers. Whether for a day's golf, a short golfing break or something a bit longer, the variety of courses allows you the diversity you've always been looking for.

From the top of the Region, Norfolk, Hunstanton and King's Lynn Golf Clubs, the host venues of the PGA Searles Spring Classic, provide something very special, with a selection of very fast greens, deep bunkers, blind shots and pine tree-lined fairways. In addition, Royal Cromer Golf Club and Sheringham Golf Club further complement Norfolk with heritage and tradition.

Travelling south to the City of Norwich you'll find Weston Park and Eaton Golf Clubs and a little further on Thetford Golf Club, all three very different and near enough to enjoy one in the morning and one in the afternoon.

Moving into Suffolk and Cambridgeshire, Aldeburgh Golf Club beckons, a wonderful course, a club rich in history and where foursomes golf is very much part of regular play. Adjoining Aldeburgh is Thorpeness Golf Club, just a few miles down the road; here we have a course designed by James Braid, but don't let the first few holes lull you into a false sense of security. This is a very challenging golf course even without the wind! Good accommodation is available here, book early to avoid disappointment. Both these venues host our PGA Autumn Classic sponsored by St James's Place Partnership.

Links Golf Club at Newmarket is developing well. This course offers a fine test of golf for the high and low handicapper alike. Woodbridge and Fynn Valley Golf Clubs are close to hand, both very different but worth a visit.

With Ely Cathedral in sight for some quick sightseeing, Ely golf course, with lush fairways and quick greens, is set in true Cambridgeshire countryside . The Cambridge Moat House offers a championship course of some reputation; this venue hosts the PGA East Anglian Open which is sponsored by Queens Moat House. Saffron Walden Golf Club, a short trip from Cambridge, offers an excellent golf course coupled with stunning views of Dudley End. Brampton Park Golf Club, falling on the borders of Cambridgeshire and Bedfordshire, is a course which predominantly winds between tree-lined fairways, where you need to hit straight, a true test of golf. John O'Gaunt Club affords two quality courses, always in excellent condition, where you will be tested for length and accuracy. Leighton Buzzard Golf Club takes us to our furthest point west; you'll be pleased if you play within your handicap here, a very friendly club with warm hospitality.

On the last lap of our journey we travel south towards London, taking in the remaining three counties, Essex, Hertfordshire and Middlesex. Colchester, Chelmsford and Braintree Golf Clubs extend perfect venues for a day's golf, Braintree hosting the PGA EEIBA Charity Championship. For supreme tranquillity try Stock Brook Manor Golf Club, which hosts our PGA East Region Freedom Leisure Golf Classic and provides a championship golf course complemented by a luxurious country club.

Our remaining PGA Order of Merit Championship course in Essex is Nazeing Golf Club, where some wide open fairways give you the opportunity to open your shoulders, but watch those tricky par threes. Romford, West Essex and Wanstead Golf Clubs all complement the county and are worthy of a day's golf.

FHG

Finding a particular club or course is easy with our website

www.UK-GolfGuide.com

Perched on the borders of Essex and Hertfordshire is Bishop's Stortford Golf Club, an undiscovered gem. Excellent location, a superb golf course, you are assured of a friendly welcome in the Clubhouse, where the catering is generous. A day's golf is a must here.

Within easy reach of London you are spoilt for choice – Panshanger Golf Complex where we hold our GA Trainees' Championship, East Herts which stages the PGA Rimex Championship and Verulam Golf Club in St Albans, the home of the Ryder Cup. Just down the road South Herts Golf Club is always worth a visit. Also in Hertfordshire is the venue for the PGA Stocks Charity Classic, the former Playboy mansion, Stocks, with its 5-star facilities offering you that stay you have always promised yourself.

Enfield, Bush Hill Park, Crews Hill and Hampstead Golf Clubs take us very nearly into London and our trip around the region is complete. In fact, with the London Underground system servicing the many golf clubs around the London area, there is a great deal of choice for the discerning golfer.

NOTE

All the information in this guide is given in good faith in the belief that it is correct. However, the publishers cannot guarantee the facts given in these pages, neither are they responsible for changes in ownership or facilities that may take place after the date of going to press. Readers should always satisfy themselves that the facilities they require are available and that the terms, if quoted, still apply.

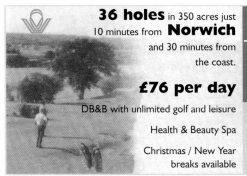

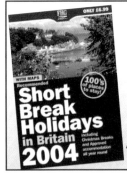

GOLF IN THE MIDLANDS

Jennifer Prentice

West Midlands Golf Club, Solihull, West Midlands

Middle England is just the core of the Midlands. Golfers heading to the region as a whole are able to choose to play a heady mix of widely differing courses. They are spread over a vast area and offer a range of challenges to golfers of all abilities. At the heart are world-famous venues like The Belfry and the Forest of Arden. But the choice stretches from the hills and valleys butting on to the Welsh border, to the bracing East coast, and all points in between. Transport links are good for those seeking a short or longer break. Europe's triumph at the De Vere Belfry over the Brabazon course in the 2002 Ryder Cup against the United States of America may have been delayed from the originally scheduled encounter date, but was no less sweet for the postponement. The Cup match was contested there for the fourth time. Golfers can tackle for themselves the tests posed by this fine course and capture at least some of the atmosphere of a great, truly memorable sporting occasion. The

Brabazon is undoubtedly the best known of the three Belfry courses, but the PGA National and the Derby also have their own special appeal. It is a fine golfing resort with off-course facilities of an exceptionally high standard, whether for putting in intensive practice on your game, or for more relaxed pursuits. The Benson and Hedges International Open 2003, over the Brabazon, produced an inspiring tournament and a worthy winner in Paul Casey, one of the rising stars of the professional game. Magical memories pervade the extensive estate at the Marriott Forest of Arden, where the Daily Telegraph Damovo British Masters was contested in 2003. There was a maiden European Tour victory for a Midlander – Greg Owen from Nottinghamshire. This is truly Shakespeare's country, with the playwright said to have set 'As You Like It' among the mediaeval woodland, some of which still forms a highly attractive feature of this golfing stage.

Professionals are always warm in their acclaim of the Arden course and it is a delight for all golfers willing to accept the questions it poses, or those set by the shorter Aylesford, the second 18 holes here. Less enthusiastic golfing family members can enjoy other delights if they prefer, all within easy reach, as well as the top class amenities within the hotel complex itself.

The Midland region of the PGA hosted two of its 2003 Order of Merit Championships at hotel venues. The Midland Professional Championship was played at the De Vere Belton Woods. This is the oldest title anywhere in the world in professional golf, so is always greatly coveted. There are two 18 hole courses – The Lakes and Woodside, as well as the 9 hole Red Arrows – along with other recreational opportunities. These range from clay pigeon shooting, go-karting and horse riding to quad biking, tennis and fishing. A few days later, the Midland PGA

staged the CPD 2003 Forest Pines Classic Championship in North Lincolnshire over the widely praised John Morgan designed course which features three loops among splendid mature trees. The Briggate Lodge Country House Hotel on site has well appointed luxury bedrooms and has become a popular venue with golfers. Other stopping-off spots for the Midland PGA regularly include Hawkstone Park, Hill Valley and Patshull Park, all with accommodation for golfers on a break. The Marriott Breadsall Priory, a Grade II Listed building, parts of which date from the 13th century, was the scene for a competitive EuroPro Tour event. There are two courses, both with stunning views. The Priory twists through undulating parkland, while the Moorland is deep in the Derbyshire countryside. All this is just a few miles from the spectacular Peak District. The Hotel combines a sense of history with all the modern features a golfing guest could desire.

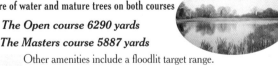

WELLINGBOROUGH
GOLF 🦌 CLUB

Harrowden Hall, Great Harrowden
Wellingborough,
Northamptonshire NN9 5AD
TELEPHONE 01933 677234
FACSIMILE 01933 679379

'The house rebuilt in 1719, has been in recent years restored and is now home to Wellingborough Golf Club, a private members club and one of the best in the country. Wellingborough Golf Club, situated at Harrowden Hall in the heart of the English countryside, presents a magnificent golf course with facilities for conferences, business meetings and private functions. We cater for numbers from 4 to 80 at competitive inclusive rates.'

★ **All facilities within a short distance of the main motorway network.**

★ **Telephone and fax available.** ★ **Easy parking available.**

★ **Coffee on arrival.** ★ **Snack available throughout the day.** ★ **Full lunch and dinner menus daily.**

Situated 2 miles from Wellingborough on the A509, 68 miles from London and 3 miles from A1/M1 link.

– For further details contact: The Secretary/Manager on 01933 677234 –

Church Stretton
Golf Club

Come and enjoy the magnificent scenery, play to permanent greens all year round, walk on springy, well-drained turf and marvel at the buzzards and red kites.

Winter Packages, including food, from £18 per person per day.

For more information (and more photographs) visit our website:

www.churchstrettongolfclub.co.uk

or ring John Povall, Hon. Secretary, on

01743 860679

e-mail: secretary@churchstrettongolfclub.co.uk
or James Townsend, PGA Professional on 01694 722281

Hunters Moon, Trevor Hill,
Church Stretton, Shropshire SY6 6JH

FHG   Publisher's Note

While every effort is made to ensure accuracy, we regret that FHG Publications cannot accept responsibility for errors, omissions or misrepresentations in our entries or any consequences thereof. Prices in particular should be checked because we go to press early. We will follow up complaints but cannot act as arbiters or agents for either party.

NOTE

All the information regarding Golf Clubs in this guide is given in good faith in the belief that it is correct. However, the publishers cannot guarantee the facts given in these pages, neither are they responsible for changes in ownership or facilities, such as green fees, that may take place after the date of going to press. Readers should always satisfy themselves that the facilities they require are available and that the terms, if quoted, still apply.

Wellingborough Golf Club, Great Harrowden, Northamptonshire

GOLF IN THE NORTH
David Birtill

Houghwood, St Helens, Lancashire

So, what's all the fuss about the North-South divide? We don't have a problem with it up here.

You can still buy a terrace house for less than £50,000 and get some change out of a couple of quid for a pint of the local brew. The quality of life is also better because the only rat race is in the sewers, and the natives are friendly. Oh, in case you didn't know already, we have some of the best golf courses in the world and you won't need a second mortgage to play them. And you can also take it as fact that no other region in the United Kingdom can match the North for variety. There are more than 500 clubs in an area stretching from coast to coast and from the Midlands northwards to the Scottish border. Throw in a couple of islands and you have a veritable golfing paradise.

We also boast three Open Championship venues all, of course, having the Royal Seal of Approval – Lytham, Birkdale and Hoylake, where the action returns in 2006, the first time since Argentinian Roberto De Vincenzo won 37 years ago. All great links courses to rival

those in Scotland, and all within an hour of so of each other. Is it so surprising, therefore, that the region is home to countless golfers? The sport rivals that other "beautiful game" in the football strongholds of Manchester, Liverpool, Leeds and Newcastle. In fact, the two often complement each other. Many soccer stars relax on the fairways between playing and training, and at venues such as Mottram Hall and Marriott Worsley Park there are even full size soccer pitches to make them feel at home! They are, for the most part, used by visiting teams who book into the adjoining hotels. When Real Madrid came over to face Sir Alex Ferguson's Reds in the Champions League last season, half their players squeezed in a few holes at Worsley, where dozens of fans camped outside the gates.

Let's return to Royal Liverpool for a moment. It is not only one of the most challenging links in the country, but the club is such a treasure house of golfing history you could spend a whole day there absorbing it all. Now the

43

infrastructure is firmly in place, huge crowds are expected for the championship but that's nothing new in these parts. Last year, attendance records were broken for the Weetabix British Women's Open at Royal Lytham where Annika Sorenstam, the winner, was one of the main attractions. Southport, meanwhile, is justifiably promoting itself as Britain's top golfing resort. Apart from Birkdale, there's Hillside, Hesketh, Formby, Southport and Ainsdale, and West Lancs. Being next door neighbour, Hillside shares many similarities with Birkdale, regarded as possibly the best of the Open venues. Southport and Ainsdale, like Formby, though not as rugged, is nevertheless a tough test, but if you really want to find out what links golf is all about then try pegging up at West Lancs when the prevailing wind whistles across the dunes. Hesketh, especially on the seaboard side, can be a real tiger, too, but it does afford shelter on most of the closing holes. We are not sure when the Open will be back at Lytham, but the course defended itself well for the Weetabix. Visitors are guaranteed as typical a warm Lancashire welcome there as they are at Fairhaven, St Anne's Old Links, De Vere Heron's Reach and the many courses along the coastline. It's also worth pitching up at Blackpool North Shore, close to the famous tower and home to the James Brearley Lancashire Open.

De Vere are big supporters of golf nationwide but especially in this area. Oulton Hall, where the City of Leeds Cup has been played for the last eight years, is the only five star hotel in the North of England and overlooks the 27 hole course. Mottram Hall, near Macclesfield, where the Manchester Evening News Manchester Open is staged, has a golf course to match the opulence of the hotel. Here Dave Thomas has skilfully blended the relatively flat front nine with

the contrasting, more demanding inward holes. And Slaley Hall has become established as a major championship location. Not far from there is Matfen Hall, a majestic hotel refurbished and extended last year and venue for the Northern Rock North East Masters.

If you are in this most scenic part of the country, try Wynyard and The Ramside. They complement the well established clubs such as Newbiggin, Whitley Bay, Prudhoe in Northumberland, and Seaton Carew, South Shields, Bishop Auckland and Barnard Castle in Durham.

Back down the M6, you will have to go a long way to find better courses than those at Stockport, Ormskirk, Pleasington and Prestbury, the latter two taking over from the former for Open Championship regional qualifying this year.

A short flight from any of the region's airports will take you to the Isle of Man but

you might consider playing the rugged links courses at Bull Bay and Holyhead on Anglesey before boarding the super-fast Seacat service to Douglas. Either way, the Isle of Man can been reached in 90 minutes from Liverpool by the hover service, 30 minutes or so by plane and a little longer by the more traditional sea routes from Heysham and Fleetwood. But whichever way you choose, there's a treat at the other end with Castletown, home of the HSBC Manx Classic, the jewel in the island's crown. This is links golf at its best. Mount Murray, some eight miles away, is also worth a visit and its hotel has excellent conference facilities. For something completely different, pop up to Jurby and play Glen Truan, carved out of natural links land, and which opened last year.

Back on the mainland, drive over the Pennines and into Yorkshire - God's golfing county - and Humberside, where you are spoiled for choice by a vast array of courses. Few can rival Ganton, near Scarborough, one of the country's greatest inland links, where the Walker Cup was played last year and the Curtis Cup this summer. Fulford, Sand Moor, Moor Allerton, Pannal, Lindrick, Catterick - the list is almost endless. Rudding Park, near Harrogate, also has a superb hotel and there's always a warm welcome at the parkland course which stages the PGA Super 60s Seniors' Tournament.

GOLF IN WALES
Chris Smart

The Cliff Hotel at Cardigan Golf Club, Cardigan

Two words can sum up the current boom that golf in Wales is enjoying – Ryder Cup. The Celtic Manor Resort's successful bid to host the 2010 Ryder Cup matches has created an unprecedented level of interest in the sport. And that interest is extending far and wide as the Ryder Cup Wales committee ensures that every corner of the Principality benefits. The Celtic Manor Resort itself is the jewel in the crown - Sir Terry Mathews' multi-million pound development in Newport now attracting visitors from all over the world. The five star hotel, leisure club and stunning surroundings appeal to those who just want to enjoy being pampered.

And then there is the golf.

From the award-winning Coldra Woods short course, through the challenging Roman Road layout to the Robert Trent Jones Wentwood Hills championship course, there is something for everyone. Changes to the Wentwood Hills layout, including several new holes and a brand-new clubhouse down in the Usk Valley

basin, are in their initial stages. Various special packages are available to golfers throughout the year.

But Celtic Manor is not the only golf resort in Wales that is setting new standards. The Vale of Glamorgan complex at Hensol, like Celtic Manor just a few minutes off the M4 motorway, is another luxurious setting.The adopted home of the Wales national rugby and soccer teams, the Vale boasts impressive leisure and golf facilities. The Lakes course has already hosted the Welsh PGA Championship and the recently opened Wales National course, designed by Peter Johnson, has received critical acclaim.

Right in between the Celtic Manor and the Vale is Europe's most rapidly expanding capital city - Cardiff. As such the city now offers a huge variety of accommodation and attraction for visiting golfers. And you don't have to venture too far out of the City to find good golf.

Llanishen, Radyr, Whitchurch and

Cardiff golf clubs are all within a Tiger Woods' drive.

In fact, for those who want a real test there is the opportunity to try out all four courses in one day, as they stage the annual Longest Day Challenge each June. In the shadows of Celtic Manor to the East the glorious setting of the Newport club at Rogerstone is always a popular venue, while the Monmouthshire club at Abergavenny and the spectacular Rolls of Monmouth are also well worth a visit

It almost goes without saying that any golfing trip to Wales would be incomplete without a visit to the famed Mid Glamorgan triumvirate of Royal Porthcawl, Pyle and Kenfig, and Southerndown.

Three of Britain's finest links courses, they offer the ultimate golfing test - not to mention some quite stunning panoramas.

Further west Swansea Bay and the Gower peninsula offer plenty of tourist and golf attractions.

And heading ever further West there is now the chance to sample Jack Nicklaus' first Welsh course at Machynys in the beautiful Millennium Coastal Park near Llanelli.

Mid and north Wales are equally well blessed with fine golf courses and accommodation to suit all pockets. Royal St David's at Harlech, now home to the Wales Seniors' Open on the European Tour, remains one of the country's toughest links. And nearby Aberdovey is a gem also.

Conwy, Llandudno (Maesdu), North Wales, Rhuddlan, Prestatyn, host to W.G.U. Championship and many other national events, and Northop Country Park all span the length of the A55 coastal road. Golfers and non-golfers alike are now spoilt for choice.

NOTE

All the information regarding Golf Clubs in this guide is given in good faith in the belief that it is correct. However, the publishers cannot guarantee the facts given in these pages, neither are they responsible for changes in ownership or facilities, such as green fees, that may take place after the date of going to press. Readers should always satisfy themselves that the facilities they require are available and that the terms, if quoted, still apply.

NORTH WALES GOLF CLUB, West Shore, Llandudno

Join us at the North Wales • Par 71 •

Enjoy the infinite variety of this true links championship course with its natural beauty, undulating fairways and slick greens.

• Visitors and societies welcome •
• No entrance fee payable for membership •
• Full and Country Membership available – Country Membership mileage restriction now 50 miles •
• Full catering facilities available •
• Golf Shop Golf Professional •
• Electric buggies, trolleys and clubs for hire •
• Summer and Winter Specials available •

e-mail: golf@nwgc.freeserve.co.uk
website: www.northwales.uk.com/nwgc

Tel: 01492 875325 • Fax: 01492 873355

MOSS VALLEY GOLF CLUB
Moss Road, Moss, Wrexham LL11 6HA • Fax/Tel: 01978 720518

Established in the late 1980's the 9 hole course was designed by Golf Architects in a beautiful parkland setting just 5 minutes' drive from the centre of Wrexham. The scenery can be compared with any part of North Wales and some of the views from the course are quite breathtaking. Every hole is different in character, providing a good test of golf for both beginners and the experienced. Various categories of membership are available and the club actively encourages youngsters to become involved in the club. 9/18 Holes. Twin Tees on every hole.

e-mail: info@mossvalleygolf.com
website: www.mossvalleygolf.com

Charming Victorian country house hotel set in a natural amphitheatre with spectacular sea and mountain views. All rooms are en suite and well equipped. Excellent cuisine, fine wines and a characterful bar await you.
Ideal for walkers, golfers (breaks arranged) and enthusiasts of historic buildings. Enjoy the many attractions within easy reach and then return to the peace and quiet of Caerlyr Hall.

WTB ★★★

CAERLYR HALL HOTEL
Conwy Old Road,
Dwygyfylchi, Conwy,
North Wales LL34 6SW
Tel: 01492 623518
Fax: 01492 622070
www.caerlyrhallhotel.co.uk

TENBY
GOLF CLUB
Est 1888

The Burrows, Tenby,
Pembrokeshire SA70 7NP

Telephone/Fax: 01834 842978
e-mail: tenbygolfclub@uku.co.uk
website: www.tenbygolf.co.uk

*Visiting Golfers and Societies
are welcome to play
the oldest affiliated
course in Wales*

The Rose & Crown Heol-y-Capel, Nottage, Porthcawl, Bridgend CF36 3ST
Tel: 01656 784850 • Fax: 01656 772345 • Hosts: Sue and Mike

• Quaint 16th century pub with en suite
accommodation • Separate Restaurant with
Carvery at weekends • Easy access to several
local golf courses including Royal Porthcawl
(recent venue of the Walker Cup) • Ideal
location for visits to Cardiff and Swansea.

*From £35 Single, £45 Double or Twin
(includes Breakfast)*

RAGLAN PARC GOLF CLUB
A challenging 6604 yard Par 73 parkland course in historic
surroundings, combined with a friendly and welcoming club
atmosphere. Beginners and experienced golfers welcome.

*Professional – Gareth Gage. For further details about membership
or visitor and society bookings, please contact:*

**RAGLAN PARC GOLF CLUB
PARC LODGE, RAGLAN, MONMOUTHSHIRE NP5 2ER**
TEL: 01291 690077 • FAX: 01291 690075
e-mail: golf@raglanparc.freeserve.co.uk

INDIVIDUAL DAILY GREEN FEES £16; WEEKENDS £24
SOCIETY & GROUP PACKAGES AVAILABLE

GOLF IN SCOTLAND
Nick Roger

Carnoustie Golf Club, Fife

All golfing roads lead to Royal Troon this year, as the venerable Ayrshire links welcomes back the Open Championship for the first time since 1997. The 132nd chapter of the world's greatest tournament will unfold from July 15-18 and will provide the centrepiece to another mouth-watering season of golf north of the border.

As one of Scotland's great golfing strongholds, Ayrshire, with its abundance of courses and accommodation, is well geared to handling vast legions of players and followers alike and that capacity will be tested to the full in July when the Open bandwagon trundles into Burns Country.

Drama is always guaranteed over Troon's classic, undulating and imaginative terrain and should this year's battle for the Claret Jug serve up the same excitement as it did seven years ago, then spectators are in for a special treat. Eager observers expected Tiger Woods to follow up his runaway success in the Masters three months earlier with another victory on Scottish soil, but it was fellow American Justin Leonard who stole the headlines on a frantic final day as he

Relax

Set in over 150 acres of grounds, on the outskirts of Gatehouse of Fleet, Cally Palace is a traditional luxury hotel where you can relax. The hotel boasts an indoor swimming pool, sauna, jacuzzi, as well as an all-weather tennis court and a putting green.

Golf

You can, of course, spend your holiday on the exclusive 18-hole golf course which starts just outside the hotel front door and finishes, quite conveniently, at the conservatory bar.

Dining

Only first-class fresh produce is used to create mouth-watering dishes each evening. A pianist will accompany your meal, while our attentive and friendly staff will try to anticipate your every need.

Cally Palace

Gatehouse of Fleet DG7 2DL • 01557 814341

www.callypalace.co.uk

HISTORIC HOTELS
with great golf on your doorstep

If you're looking for great golf in superb surroundings, head for Macdonald Hotels in Scotland's magnificent North East corner, home to some of the country's best courses.

Four of our finest hotels blend history and character with every modern luxury and offer superb facilities including award-winning restaurants and exclusive health and leisure spas.

Choose from Ardoe House on the banks of the River Dee upstream from Balmoral Castle, or 17th century Pittodrie House set in 2,000 glorious acres. Head for the rural hideaway of Thainstone House in private parkland, or the more modern comforts of Waterside Inn on the banks of the River Ugie a few miles from Peterhead.

Whatever your choice, the warmest hospitality is guaranteed with unrivalled golf on your doorstep. Welcome to golf at Macdonald Hotels.

For information and reservations call
Ardoe House - 01224 860 600
Pittodrie House - 01467 681 444
Thainstone House - 01467 621 643
Waterside Inn - 01779 471 121

MACDONALD
HOTELS

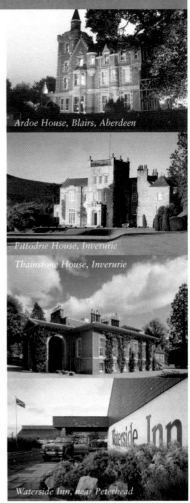

Ardoe House, Blairs, Aberdeen

Pittodrie House, Inverurie

Thainstone House, Inverurie

Waterside Inn, near Peterhead

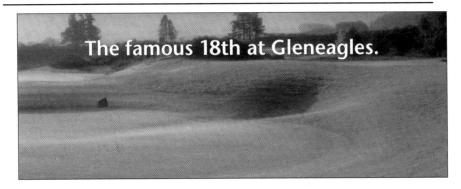

The famous 18th at Gleneagles.

And the other one.

And the other one.

There is only one place in Scotland that can boast three championship golf courses. It's a place where you don't even have to stay to play; a place where there's a spa, riding, fishing, shooting and off-road driving all available amongst some of Scotland's most stunning scenery. Not to mention a choice of four restaurants including the Michelin starred 'Andrew Fairlie at Gleneagles'. That place is Gleneagles. (There is no other like it.) Book online or call us free on 0800 328 4010 for more information.

THE GLENEAGLES HOTEL

Auchterarder, Perthshire, Scotland PH3 1NF. Just 1 hour from Edinburgh/Glasgow.

Telephone +44 (0) 1764 662231 Fax +44 (0) 1764 662134   www.gleneagles.com

The GLENEAGLES word and EAGLE Device are trade marks.   A member of *The Leading Hotels of the World*   Ref: GOLF GUIDE

Inchmarlo Royal Deeside

Inchmarlo Royal Deeside, Banchory, is a relatively new golf attraction to the North East of Scotland.

Inchmarlo Royal Deeside

Ponds, meandering burns and even dry stone walls, combine with the more traditional bunkers to test the skill of even the most accomplished player, at the same time rewarding the accuracy of the short game expert. The Laird's Course opened for play in July 2001 and at 6218 yards, this championship standard par 71 course is set to be one of Scotland's most sought after golfing venues, complementing the existing nine-hole course and the Centre's other facilities, including tuition from a team of PGA professionals.

View from 2nd Tee

Catering for all age groups, the recently refurbished Golf Professional's shop is stocked with all the latest in golf fashion.
Cuisine of the highest standard is available in our various bars and restaurant, and a warm and friendly welcome is assured.

Golf Professional's Shop

Classic Golf Course design, stunning scenery, excellent facilities....
The Laird's at Inchmarlo Royal Deeside is ready for the challenge - are you?
For further details contact Hector Emslie
Tel: 01330 826424
e-mail: info@inchmarlo.com • www.inchmarlo.com

Portpatrick Holiday Cottages

Heugh Road, Portpatrick, Dumfries & Galloway DG9 8TQ

Portpatrick Holiday Cottages are the perfect choice as a base for golfing, walking or simply getting away from it all. Close to the picturesque harbour village of Portpatrick with its good variety of restaurants, pubs, gift and craft shops, the cottages offer very comfortable accommodation and outstanding value.

• Each cottage has private bathroom facilities, lounge/dining area.
• TV. • Fully equipped kitchen. • 2 and 3 bedrooms with accommodation for up to 6.
• Towels and bed linen provided. • Electricity and heating. • Free car parking.
• Daily maid service. • Pets welcome by prior arrangement. • Open all year.
• Accommodation from 2 to 40 guests.

The historic village of Portpatrick is located at the most westerly point of Dumfries and Galloway, in which sub-tropical plants and trees flourish in the equable local climate. In summer the harbour becomes home to a myriad of fishing and recreational boats.

There is plenty to see and do in this part of Scotland. The scenery is breathtaking and walking is a must to fully appreciate its magnificence.

Attractions vary from castles, abbeys and museums to gardens and visitor theme parks.

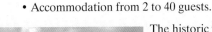

For more details contact:

| Choice of many local courses | Portpatrick Holiday Cottages Ltd. 37 Cable Depot Road, Riverside Estate, Clydebank, West Dunbartonshire G81 1UY Tel: 0141 941 3800 • Fax: 0141 941 3800 or visit our website at www.portpatrickholidays.co.uk | Golf & Accommodation from £25 p/p |

overhauled Swede, Jesper Parnevik's, commanding five-shot lead to win the title by three strokes.

The Open may be taking centre stage in Scotland this year, but the support acts on offer in the months building up to the main event could not be better.

In late June, the Gleneagles Hotel, one of the world's premier resorts and host venue of the 2014 Ryder Cup, will again play host to the blossoming Diageo Championship. Won by Denmark's Soren Kjeldsen last year - the Scandinavian's maiden European Tour victory - the Diageo Championship, played over the Jack Nicklaus-designed PGA Centenary course, continues to grow in stature. Just ask the 40,000 enthusiasts who treaded the fairways over four days of closely fought competition last year.

Unfortunately for those keen followers of the game, only one thing has been missing from the tournament in recent years - a home winner. It's not been through the lack of effort from the local heroes however. Edinburgh's Raymond Russell claimed second place behind runaway winner Adam Scott in 2002, while last year, Alastair Forsyth of Paisley chased Kjeldsen all the way, but finished

two shots adrift of the triumphant Dane in the runners-up spot. In 2004, it may well be third time lucky for the tartan contingent.

Barely three weeks after the Diageo Championship, the strongest field of the season in Europe, outside the Open itself, will tee up in Scotland again at Loch Lomond as the world's finest warm up for the battle for the Claret Jug in the Barclays Scottish Open. As ever in Scotland, the amateur game holds huge appeal and 2004 will be a particularly special year as the Royal and Ancient Golf Club of St Andrews celebrates its 250th anniversary. The 'Auld Grey Toon' will be very much the place to be for golf enthusiasts as, from May 28 to June 13, a series of local and international events to mark the occasion are being held.

Amid the festivities, the world's leading amateur golfers will contest the 109th Amateur Championship over the Old Course from May 31 to June 5. It will be the first time the famous old links has staged the tournament since 1981. Team competition is very much to the fore north of the border this year, with three of the biggest competitions on the amateur calendar returning to Scottish soil. In late

The Old Course, St. Andrews

August, Nairn, host venue to the 1999 Walker Cup, will be the setting for the St Andrews Trophy match between the leading male amateurs from Great Britain, Ireland and Europe, as well as the boys' equivalent, the Jacques Leglise Trophy.

Two weeks later, in early September, the cream of the talent from Scotland, England, Wales and Ireland will do battle for the Raymond Trophy in the Home Internationals at Prestwick, the birthplace of the Open Championship. With an abundance of splendid competitions taking place in some of Scotland's great golfing heartlands, 2004 promises to be another exciting and memorable year.

FHG

Publisher's Note

While every effort is made to ensure accuracy, we regret that FHG Publications cannot accept responsibility for errors, omissions or misrepresentations in our entries or any consequences thereof. Prices in particular should be checked because we go to press early. We will follow up complaints but cannot act as arbiters or agents for either party.

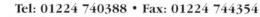

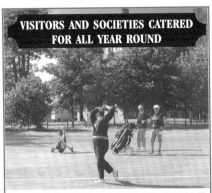
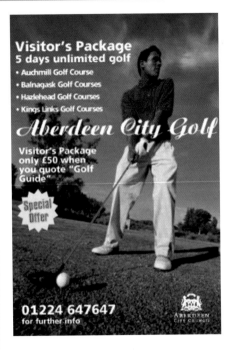

DUNS GOLF CLUB

TEL: 01361 882194

The course is 6,209 yards from the medal tees, SS70. Visitors play from the yellow tees 5,763 yards, ladies from the red tees 5,405 yards. The Wellrig burn runs through the course and comes into play on several of the holes. There are two or three short climbs but otherwise the course has gentle slopes and gives lovely views of the countryside around Duns and towards the Cheviot Hills to the south. Full Bar & Catering. Parties and visitors very welcome at any time.

HARDEN ROAD, DUNS,
BERWICKSHIRE TD11 3NR

Hirsel Golf Club   Coldstream

The First and Last course in Scotland. A parkland course of great natural beauty and breathtaking views of the Cheviot Hills and surrounding countryside. Nestling in the beautiful and historic Scottish Borders.18 very different holes designed to make the most of the hills, valleys and natural hazards. Recently voted "The Friendliest Course in the Borders", you are assured of a warm welcome from our members. Excellent bar and restaurant facilities. Golf societies welcome.

Hirsel Golf Club, Kelso Road, Coldstream TD12 4NJ Tel: 01890 882678

---

18 holes, 6021 yards, par 69, SSS 70

• lunch • dinner • club bar • bar snacks
• tea & coffee • club hire • cart hire
• trolley hire • changing room

Situated just one mile north of Galashiels on the A7

Visitors welcome daily
Voted "The Most Visitor Friendly Golf Club" 2001

Torwoodlee GOLF CLUB

Edinburgh Road, Galashiels TD1 2NE • Tel & Fax: 01896 752260

Photo: David J. Whyte

Kirriemuir is a pleasant mixture of heathland and parkland, situated within some beautiful Angus countryside and is renowned for its superb panoramic views across the Glens. The course was the work of the famous James Braid who was also the inspiration behind Gleneagles.

At 5510 yards, this Par 68 makes for some low scoring. Heathers and whins wind their way strategically along the fairways, making direction, not length, the priority, with fast rolling greens demanding accurate approach play.

We guarantee an enjoyable day at Kirriemuir, with full bar and catering facilities available.

KIRRIEMUIR GOLF CLUB
NORTHMUIR, KIRRIEMUIR
ANGUS DD8 4LN
01575 573317

Visit the FHG website

www.holidayguides.com

for details of the

wide choice of

accommodation

featured in

the full range of

FHG titles

Located four miles from Carnoustie and ½ hour from St Andrews. Two courses offer golf for all levels with the Medal being used as an Open Championship Qualifier. These beautiful links courses also feature tree-lined fairways in many places.

Medal Course £35, Ashludie Course £17; a package includes a round of golf on each course, coffee, bacon roll, soup and sandwiches, and high tea at the day's end. All for £55!

For bookings call the Links Secretary on
01382 532767
The Starter's Box, Monifieth Links,
Princess Street, Monifieth DD5 4AN
monifiethgolf@freeuk.com

The hidden gem in Angus

Monifieth Golf Links

Panmure Arms Hotel   52 High Street, Edzell, Angus DD9 7TA

Ideally situated in the picturesque village of Edzell, minutes from the local 18 hole golf course. The large level of varied clubs in close proximity makes the Panmure Arms Hotel the perfect destination for your golfing holiday. Refurbished to the Scottish Tourist Board three star level, with family rooms, twin rooms, double rooms and singles, all en suite. Here the emphasis is on quality and service. The Panmure Arms Hotel provides quality meals at competitive prices, warm and clean surroundings, pleasant and attentive staff and of course, a plentiful selection of wines, beers and spirits.

For rates and availability telephone David on 01356 648950 • Fax: 01356 648000
e-mail: david@panmurearmshotel.co.uk • website: www.panmurearmshotel.co.uk

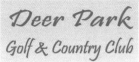

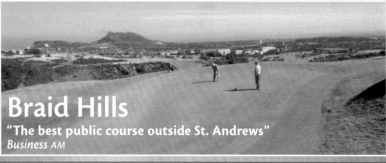

GLENCORSE GOLF CLUB
MILTON BRIDGE, PENICUIK EH26 0RD

An extremely picturesque 18 hole parkland course of 5217 yards with an SSS of 66. Green fees are **£25** per round on weekdays and **£32** at weekends and public holidays. A day ticket is also available for **£32**. Packages available on request. Outings are welcome from Monday to Thursday and Sunday afternoons only.

Please contact: W. Oliver (*Secretary*)
Tel: 01968 677189 Fax: 01968 674399
Professional: Cliff Jones 01968 676481

Eden House Hotel

2 Pitscottie Road, Cupar, Fife KY15 4HF

The hotel is a Victorian Town House dating from 1876, enjoying a truly superb elevated position overlooking the Haugh Park in the centre of Cupar, one of the oldest burghs in Scotland. Personal care, attention and the warmest of welcomes awaits.

Tel: 01334 652510 • Fax: 01334 652277
E-mail: info@edenhousehotel.com
Web: www.glenfarghotel.co.uk

Exclusive for guests at the Glenfarg and Eden House Hotels, our private minibus, capable of seating 8 people, is available 24 hours a day for transport to golf course, airport, city... in fact anywhere in the UK. It can be booked at either reception.

Set in the popular historic town of St Andrews on the east coast of Scotland, commanding magnificent views of St Andrews Bay and the clubhouse of the Royal and Ancient Golf Club.

• 30 bedrooms, all individually decorated
• Two restaurants
• Scorecard Lounge Bar • Chariots Bar
• Open all year • Major credit cards accepted

76 The Scores, St Andrews KY16 9BB
Tel: 01334 472451 • Fax: 01334 473947
e-mail: office @scoreshotel.co.uk

Scores Hotel, St Andrews

Balbirnie Park Golf Club
Balbirnie Park, Markinch, Glenrothes KY7 6NR
Tel: 01592 612095 • Fax: 01592 612383

Balbirnie Park is a fine example of the best in traditional parkland design – the natural contours being the inspiration behind the layout. With a par of 71 and measuring 6200 yards from the Gents' Back Tees, it is a good challenge for golfers of all abilities.

It is immediately apparent to any visitor that the course is blessed with a truly superb and picturesque site, situated in the heart of the magnificent Balbirnie Park. The park has the finest collection of rhododendrons and azaleas adjacent to the golf course. Visitors and parties always welcome. Individual packages arranged. Excellent cuisine. Well stocked golf shop.

Leven Links, in part one of the oldest pieces of golfing ground in the world, is a true seaside links course. It has hosted many national and international events and is used as a final qualifying course for the Open Championship when it is held at St Andrews. The strength of Leven Links lies in its fine variety of links-type holes combined with large greens; turning into the prevailing west wind at the 13th leaves the golfer with a lot of work to do before reaching one of the finest finishing holes in golf.

**Leven Links, The Promenade,
Leven, Fife KY8 4HS**
Tel/Fax: 01333 428859
e-mail: secretary@leven-links.com

Situated on The Scores overlooking St Andrews Bay, this small friendly hotel, personally run by Gordon and Fiona De Vries offers good food and comfortable accommodation. 10 twin/double rooms, all with private facilities, satellite TV, telephone and tea/coffee making. Just two minutes' walk from the Old Course and equally convenient for town centre and beaches. The Russell has acquired a fine reputation for excellent cuisine and exceptional service. Major credit cards accepted.

The Russell Hotel
The Scores, St Andrews, Fife KY16 9AS
Tel: 01334 473447 • Fax: 01334 478279
e-mail: Russellhotel@talk21.com • www.russellhotelstandrews.co.uk

AA

Improvements to roads have helped **Royal Dornoch** to continue to be one of the most popular golf courses in Scotland. Magazine polls across the world regularly have it in their top twenty. It is well worth the extra miles it takes to get there.

As golfers walk over the headlands to the third tee they get the sense of this striking golf course. Wondrous swards of fairway and green, with clusters of players dotting the beachfront, unfold a mile in each direction. Raised or sloping greens are characteristic, as well as elevated tees

Royal Dornoch's second links, the Struie, has been improved by the construction of five new holes and some existing holes have been extended with new tees/greens. Now Par 72, 6276yds, the new layout will require the use of all clubs in the bag. Equally important, golfers will be able to enjoy the views of the Dornoch Firth – as some of the new holes lie alongside the shoreline – the Struie Hill and the further mountains to the west.

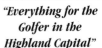

Golf in Ireland
Great Courses...Great Hospitality

Damian Ryan
Director of Golf, Failte Ireland

Royal Portrush Golf Club, Co. Antrim

Beauty, they say, is in the eye of the beholder; and when it comes to golf, Ireland has many suitors. The attraction, of course, is obvious, and infatuating. For this is an island that possesses great links courses, strewn like green emeralds, which dot each nook and cranny of the thousands of miles of Irish coastline. These are courses where the sound of the sea crashing off rocks and the salty taste of seaspray, are constant companions.

And there's more.

Of course, there are the famous courses. On Ireland's East Coast, there are Portmarnock and The European. On the Northern shoreline – along the Causeway coast where the legendary giant Finn McCool reputedly left his mark with the basalt columns of the Giant's Causeway - awaits Royal Portrush and, under the shadows of the mountains of Mourne, lies Royal County Down.

In the North-West, there is the great links course of Ballyliffin and Rosses Point and, further south, along the west coast lie Lahinch old course and Doonbeg. Then, along the South West seaboard, there is the magnificent links

at Ballybunion – which runs along the cliffs into the mouth of the River Shannon where it meets the Atlantic ocean, and the equally magnificent links at Waterville, which is on the beautiful Ring of Kerry. And along the South Coast, awaits the cliff top setting of the Old Head of Kinsale. It's a seemingly endless necklace of one jewel after another.

The hidden gems are not just confined to seaside courses, either. In the past decade or so, a number of fine parkland courses – among them The K Club, which will stage the Ryder Cup in 2006; Mount Juliet, which held the American Express world golf championship won by Tiger Woods in 2002 and will host the event again in 2004; and Druids Glen, where the Seve Trophy was played in 2002 – have been built.

The fact of the matter is that there is a start and no end to an Irish golfing odyssey, for the journey is never complete. One treasure after another awaits, and it would take a lifetime to savour it all. The best we can ask is that you savour most of it, for Ireland truly is a golfing destination beyond compare.

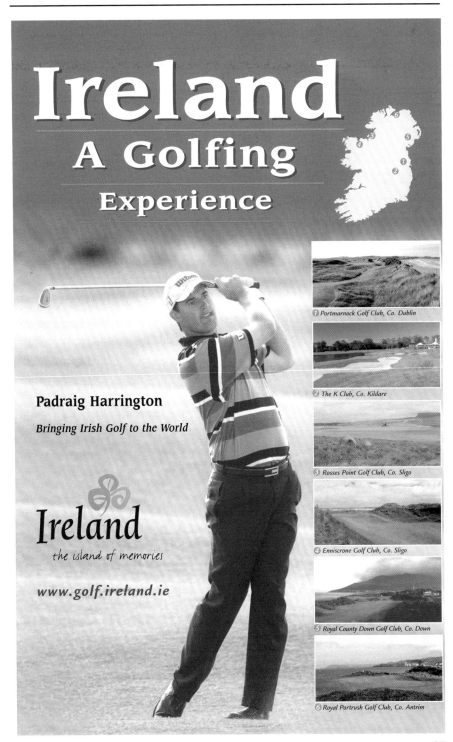

Ireland
A Golfing
Experience

Padraig Harrington

Bringing Irish Golf to the World

Ireland
the island of memories

www.golf.ireland.ie

① *Portmarnock Golf Club, Co. Dublin*

② *The K Club, Co. Kildare*

③ *Rosses Point Golf Club, Co. Sligo*

④ *Enniscrone Golf Club, Co. Sligo*

⑤ *Royal County Down Golf Club, Co. Down*

⑥ *Royal Portrush Golf Club, Co. Antrim*

87

SEAFIELD
GOLF & COUNTRY CLUB

Ballymoney, Gorey, Co. Wexford, Ireland
Tel: 055 24777 • Fax: 055 24837
Web: www.seafieldgolf.com • E-mail: Info@seafieldgolf.com

In life as in golf there are some shots which you only play once. The chance to play 18 Holes at Seafield Golf and Country Club is one of those shots. Set in rolling park and woodland by the sea in the sun-kissed south-east of Ireland, the course is built to the highest standards with a new Clubhouse opened in June 2003.

Golf-pros and amateurs alike will find much to challenge and delight during long rounds at Seafield

PERFECTION

Sumptuous five star surroundings in the Clubhouse

SEAFIELD GOLF & COUNTRY CLUB, the newest addition to the long list of spectacular Irish golf courses, marked the opening of their stunning new clubhouse in suitable style. For the second year running the Wexford property development played host to the Canon Pro Golf Series featuring some of the biggest names in the game. Last year Retief Goosen, Padraig Harrington and Barry Lane graced the course's opening. This year it was the turn of Open champion Paul Lawrie, English Star Justin Rose and South African Trevor Immelman to mark the historic opening of the stunning new clubhouse.

The three stars took a break after the European Open at the K-Club to visit Seafield where they entertained leading Canon customers and Seafield members. The day began with a nine hole pro-am where the amateurs played three holes with each of the pros. This was followed by a prize giving luncheon and a one hour golf clinic. The clinic was followed by a nine hole shoot-out between the three players

over Seafield's picturesque but demanding back nine. Justin Rose played spectacular golf posting a two under par thirty-four, which included a bogey on the par four index one, fifteenth hole, proving himself to be far superior than both Immelman and Open champion Lawrie who finished five strokes behind at three over par.

The new clubhouse played a major role in attracting the Canon event for the second time, a massive undertaking by Seafield considering the project only began in January and was completed by the July 7th deadline. Situated in the heart of the golf course the glass and granite structure features spectacular panoramic views of the Irish sea and the back nine of the McEvoy designed course. An exterior deck surrounds three sides of the clubhouse offering a fantastic viewing place for golfers to unwind and take in the relaxed atmosphere. Excellent caterers provide a first class menu, and the clubhouse is open to the public for dining.

GOLF IN IRELAND
Tony McGee

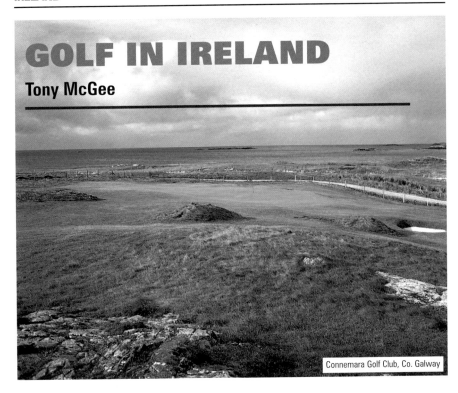

Connemara Golf Club, Co. Galway

Ireland is bulging with golf courses of all standards, from the plush fairways of the likes of Mount Juliet and The K Club to the modest nine-holes that are dotted all around the country. Some may argue that we have too many courses in the Emerald Isle but that, surely, is a fable. In recent years many more have been added. In July 2003 the tapes were cut on The Heritage Golf & Country Club at Portlaoise in Co Laois, the first course designed in Ireland by Seve Ballesteros. Colin Montgomerie's Carton House at Maynooth is also a pretty new addition to the top market, while Doonbeg in Co Clare is set to be one of the most prestigious places in Europe, if not further afield. Not content with his now well-established North Course at The K club, in Co Kildare, Michael Smurfit has added a twin - the South Course, designed by Arnold Palmer. It also opened in July 2003.

But Irish golf is not all about the top class and serious player who wants to include these courses along with Portmarnock, Mount Juliet, Killarney, Waterville, The Old Head at Kinsale, Royal County Down and Royal Portrush on his (or her) CV. There is much more to golfing in Ireland than that. Apart from the outdoor game there is the craic in the evenings that attracts as many visitors as the golf does. Everywhere, the visitor will find Irish traditional entertainment with some of the world's best-known artists in full flow in some instances. Like Westport where, after a day's sporting action on the scenic golf course in the shadows of the majestic Croagh Patrick, one will find excellent music, song and beverage in Matt Molloy's Pub. Matt is the flute player with the world-renowned Chieftains and will often, when not on tour, entertain his customers in the back room. In all, Ireland has well in excess of 400 clubs spread out

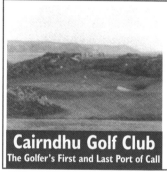
all over the land, with a fine mixture of links and parkland tracks. Indeed, the country has the highest ratio of links courses in Europe.

It's reckoned that Doonbeg, already mentioned, may be the last true links course to be built in either Ireland or Britain. The architect was Greg Norman, but the layout was really designed by nature as the course is along 1.5 miles of crescent-shaped beach and dunes. The ocean is visible from the green, fairway or tee at 16 of the 18 holes, something akin to Ballyliffin, Ireland's most northerly course on the top tip of Donegal.

Co Clare is well known for its craic, with festivals held at various times of the year and where traditional Irish music, song and dance is a way of life. Anyone who drops into the little village of Doolin, for example, just a few miles from famed Lahinch, will hear the music pouring out from the various establishments. That,

of course, is common in many parts of the land where the 'craic and porter black', as the Dubliners sang about, is the food of the day.

Irish roads are constantly improving so travel throughout the country is becoming easier all the time. Lots of big towns are now being by-passed with new motorways, so the visitor travelling by car can experience beautiful scenery in an uncluttered countryside between the rounds of golf. It is possible in many parts of Ireland to play at least three different courses in the same day, if stamina allows it, and then have a relaxing meal and entertainment in one of the thousands of hostelries around. Accommodation, too, is plentiful with Ireland noted for its friendly B&Bs - not bread and bacon but bed and breakfast houses. For the more discerning there are also hundreds upon hundreds of hotels ranging from two-star to five-star.

If one wishes, there are various ways of booking a golf holiday before leaving the fireside, and nowadays some golf clubs have teamed up together to provide a complete holiday tour of different courses. One such organisation is the *North & West Coast Links,* known as the *10 Links of Heaven*, full details of which can be had on www.westcoastlinks.com or by e-mail from wcgolf@iol.ie. The scheme began 14 years ago with a group of clubs in the west, but last year (2003) the three "jewels" of the north coast, Castlerock, Portstewart and Royal Portrush joined up to strengthen the chain and give the customer a wide choice. The other courses are Connemara, Carne at Belmullet, Enniscrone, Co Sligo, popularly known as

Rosses Point, Donegal at Murvagh, Rosapenna and Ballylifffin. "This trip has become very popular and we have worked hard at marketing these *10 Links of Heaven,"* says Linda Barrett, who is kept extremely busy in the organisation's Galway office in between her trips abroad. "The addition of the three northern clubs adds great variety to the tour. While marketing golf is the primary objective, it follows that our brochure provides a full range of guest houses, hotels and Manor Houses that are available. Services like accommodation, food and hospitality are integral elements in the whole golf experience."

Of course, there are many other clubs in the west and north that are not included in this project. Like Bundoran

When touring the Causeway Coast it would be unthinkable not to visit the geological phenomenon of the Giant's Causeway, a World Heritage site noted for its honeycomb rock and the giant Finn McCool. Just two miles inland lies the village of Bushmills home of the world's oldest licensed distillery where visitors are welcome for a tour and a 'wee tot'.

The village is also famous for its hotel, the legendary **Bushmills Inn**

which, despite not having its own Golf course, was voted Ireland's Golf Hotel of the year in 2003. Described as a 'living museum of Ulster hospitality" its new rooms are so skilfully designed that it's difficult to work out where the original ends and the new begins.

Try the Inn's busy Restaurant (and adjoining garden patio) – it's open all day, every day for a full meal or a light snack.

The K Club , Straffan, Co. Kildare

overlooking the wild and wonderful Atlantic where the Roghey Links is wrapped around the Great Northern Hotel. Bundoran is the scene of a major professional tournament each year and also the headquarters of the West Coast Amateur Open Challenge Trophy in September. The competitors also play Donegal, Strandhill and Enniscrone. If your holiday happens to be during the first week in September then you could do worse than enter this 72 hole event.

There are many other such tournaments during the year in Ireland and either the Northern Ireland Tourist Board or Bord Failte could supply details.

Taking a wider look at the scene in the north, easily reached from Scotland by ferry, one could spend months playing the dozens of different style courses available. Belfast offers 13 with excellent parkland terrain at Shandon Park, Malone, Belvoir Park and Knock. Just seven miles north on the motorway is

The Hilton Templepatrick, set to host a major event in the not-too-distant future, I understand. Designed by David Jones, this is a testing track among both mature and young trees with water very much in evidence. There is the flat Massereene at Antrim on the edge of Lough Neagh, and further north at Ballymena is Galgorm Castle, built on an historic site around the Rivers Maine and Braid and designed by Englishman Simon Gidman. An ancestral home of Jacobean architecture has been turned into first-rate club premises housing a variety of facilities, including conference rooms and restaurant. The owner, the Honourable Christopher Brooke, spent millions reroofing and decorating the property.

Various stops can be made before reaching Portrush, with a trip out east to Ballycastle, taking in the Giant's Causeway, well worthwhile. Darren Clarke's father Geoffrey is Greenkeeper at Ballycastle and has transformed the

Cork Golf Club was founded in 1888 and designed in 1927 by Alister MacKenzie. It has matured to become one of the finest courses in the country. Many Amateur and Professional championships have been hosted here. The course is always in immaculate condition and playable all year round.

For further information regarding green fees, please contact Matt Sands, General Manager, at:

CORK GOLF CLUB

Little Island, Co. Cork, Ireland
Tel: 00 353 21 4353451 • Fax: 00 353 21 4353410
e-mail: corkgolfclub@eircom.net
www.corkgolfclub.ie

Call now for your free copy of the West Cork Holiday brochure, Golf brochure or Conference brochure.

WEST CORK TOURISM
turasóireacht iarthar chorcaí

Town Council Offices,
North St, Skibbereen, West Cork
Tel: +353 28 22812
Callsave 1850 250 999
Email: info@westcork.ie

www.westcork.ie   Supported by West Cork Leader Co-op Society

course since moving there from Dungannon. After visiting Royal Portrush, Portstewart and Castlerock, a stop at Roe Park is a must. Steeped in history this complex includes a golf course overlooking the town of Limavady, a magnificent five-star Radisson Hotel, leisure centre, Courtyard Restaurant and Golf Academy run by professional Seamus Duffy. This area should be of special interest to Scottish visitors as it was here in 575AD that St Columba, after sailing from Scotland, addressed the High Kings of Ireland and Scotland, on the subject of taxes, at the Convention of Drumceatt. The meeting was held on a plateau right in the middle of the golf course - a spot preserved in history.

City of Derry Golf Club is at hilltop Prehen, just outside the city, and across the Foyle into Donegal one finds clubs spread all over the county.

Mid-Ulster has many attractive courses as well, the most illustrious being Slieve Russell in the heart of Cavan Drumlin Country. Now 12 years old, this is an oasis in the countryside, a mile from the village of Ballyconnell, with a magnificent hotel attached. Apart from the place itself, one of the attractions is that it is equidistant from Dublin and Derry, with Belfast only around 90 minutes away by car.

Co Down has a host of clubs, including Royal County Down, and recently Ardglass has become a busy place. Out on the coast with a backdrop of the Mourne Mountains and overlooking Coney Island, Ardglass boasts the oldest building converted into a clubhouse in the world. The history of what was Ardglass Castle can be traced back to the 14th century. The three new holes, designed by David Jones and opened last year, have been described as "the most beautiful holes to be found anywhere in the world." This is a true holidaymaker's golf course.

Moving further south the Co Louth Club is a few miles north of Drogheda at Baltray. Here a qualifying round for the British Open Championship is played. Just "over the hedge" is Seapoint while further down the coast is Laytown & Bettystown, three sandy tracks suited to the reasonable holiday golfer. Portmarnock Links, designed by Bernhard Langer, Portmarnock and Royal Dublin, in the north of the capital, are well known - the 'no women' rule attracts attention, especially to Portmarnock - with Woodbrook and Hermitage the most popular of the south city courses. However, there are 27 courses in Dublin City and many more in the surroundings, all of merit. It would be easy to spend a month or more playing golf around Dublin without travelling very many miles. Less than an hour away from the Capital is Druid's Glen with its 36 holes at Kilcoole in Co Wicklow, the village that was made famous by the RTE Soap Glenroe. Druid's Glen has hosted the Irish Open on quite a few occasions and also staged the Seve Trophy event in 2002. Like Portmarnock and The K Club, Druid's Glen is not for the high handicap golfer, nor is Mount Juliet at Thomastown in Co Kilkenny. Still they are beautiful courses that attract thousands of visitors, many from America, each year.

More suited to the casual player would be the likes of Arklow in Co Wicklow, St Helen's Bay in Co Wexford or nearby Courtown. The fact that Rosslare Harbour is convenient to these clubs makes for easy access from abroad for visitors bringing their own transport. There is also a beautiful course at Blessington, 12 miles south of Dublin. Tulfarris is the club's name and, set in deep countryside on the shore of the magnificent Blessington Lakes, it is a haven of peace and tranquillity. A hotel

and leisure centre is part of the set-up.

Moving inland from the East Coast, Headfort at Kells, Royal Tara and Glasson at Athlone in the hub of Ireland are places to visit. The province of Munster has 88 clubs ranging from the likes of Killarney, Waterville, Ballybunion, Fota Island outside Cork City, Lahinch and Doonbeg to the more sedate middle-to-high handicap players' favourites. Douglas, a few miles from Cork City, and the Cork Golf Club would be among these. So are the two Limerick clubs - Limerick and Limerick County. Faithlegg in Co Waterford, Tramore and Waterford Castle are notables, while the Co Tipperary Golf Club at Dundrum House has been attracting a lot of attention recently. Tucked in beside the lovely quaint village of Adare is Adare Manor Golf Club, another of the luxurious clubs dotted around Ireland. The Robert Trent Jones-

designed track is set among mature trees with three lakes included. There is a 14-acre lake anchoring the front nine so this course is certainly a test for the best. Of course, while in Munster golf is not the only attraction, with the famous Ring of Kerry, the Cliffs of Moher and Blarney Castle proving major magnets for the tourist. Why not take a cruise on the Shannon as well and bring the golf clubs? One can travel all the way from Co Clare to Lough Erne in Co Fermanagh by cruiser, hopping off at various places to have a round of golf. That's attractive, you must agree

Anyhow, wherever you travel in Ireland you can be assured that there is going to be 'A Welcome on the Mat' and that you are never very far from a golf course or from accommodation ranging from the superior to the modest.

Why not see for yourself?

When making postal enquiries, remember that a stamped, addressed envelope is always appreciated

NOTE

All the information regarding Golf Clubs in this guide is given in good faith in the belief that it is correct. However, the publishers cannot guarantee the facts given in these pages, neither are they responsible for changes in ownership or facilities, such as green fees, that may take place after the date of going to press. Readers should always satisfy themselves that the facilities they require are available and that the terms, if quoted, still apply.

★ ★ ★ ★ ★

THE KILDARE HOTEL & GOLF CLUB

at Straffan, Co. Kildare, Ireland

The 4th Green of the new South Course,
opened July 2003

"Luxurious comfort, superb facilities"

The 550-acre grounds of The K Club are nestled amid lush
green woodlands, just 17 miles from Dublin, Ireland's capital city.
Already acclaimed as one of the finest in the world, this magnificent 5 star Hotel
offers you the highest standards of comfort and service combined with the elegance
and unique charm of an Irish country house.

You can relax and be lavishly pampered or indulge in any of the quality leisure
activities available, including our two championship golf courses,
both designed by Arnold Palmer.

95 bedrooms, all individually appointed to the highest standard.
Be it for business or pleasure, The K Club is the most rewarding place to stay.

For further information and Reservations:

Hotel Tel: 353 (0)1 601 7200 • Fax: 353 (0)1 601 7299 Reservations

Golf Tel: 353 (0)1 601 7300 • Fax: 353 (0)1 601 7399 Golf Reservations

E-mail: golf@kclub.ie E-mail: sales@kclub.ie • Web: www.kclub.ie

Home to The Smurfit European Open

HOST TO THE RYDER CUP IN 2006

Chateau des Sept Tours in the Loire Valley

HOLIDAY GOLF IN FRANCE
Michael Gedye

This guide looks at several overseas countries for holiday golf – each with quite distinct attitudes to the game, different histories and cultures, varying levels of local interest – in short, an exciting selection of new golfing experiences. There are distinct holiday choices - relaxed or busy; organised or laid back; manicured or natural; with full service or self-service; smiling caddies or carry your own. Winter or summer there are locations for all seasons, all tastes and all budgets. Although the recommendations include some members' clubs which welcome visitors, we have concentrated on the wealth of purpose-built vacation courses set in attractive holiday locations.

The largest and most popular country is France, with considerable regional variations of location and climate plus a long golfing history. It can boast continental Europe's oldest golf club

(Pau in 1856), the first non-British winner of the Open (Arnaud Massey of La Boulie at Hoylake in 1907) and 520 golf courses, more than any other European country. Many of the earlier courses, created by the British, are linked to such elegant seaside resorts as Dinard, Deauville, Le Touquet, Biarritz and Cannes. A visit to any of these is a journey back in time, when the wealthy and well-connected chose to holiday there.

Much of the well-established golf in France will seem familiar – classic designs running over natural terrain, friendly clubs that are laid back, low key and refreshingly underplayed. But look out also for the new breed of resort course, mostly built around the coast, offering international style golf of high quality, well-maintained and created solely for holiday visitors.

One of France's primary virtues is ease of access. With numerous car ferries, the Channel tunnel and cheap flights, golfers can visit for a day, a long weekend or an extended stay. The most favoured season runs from spring to autumn, with warmer weather the further south you venture towards the Mediterranean. France is great for touring, with clubs offering visitors a warm welcome and room to play. There are comparatively few local golfers, despite the large number of courses, which contributes to open fairways and comparatively low green fees. One useful tip - the French traditionally flee to the seaside during August, leaving inland courses empty. Some clubs even offer discounted visitor rates during the peak summer months.

Nowhere else in Europe does the term apres golf have such significance. Whether it is lunch in the clubhouse or dining out under the stars, appreciation of cuisine and the wealth of fine wines are a natural part of daily life. One club even has an annual competition, where consumption of gourmet food and wine completes every hole. Another has every one of its 36 holes sponsored by a 'grand cru' chateau, the holes then being replicated on the clubhouse wine list. This is a country steeped in history and culture, with much to see and do off the course. Chateaux, boutiques, museums, music festivals and much more compete for your time. Prices are relatively low and an exacting public ensures quality.

Golf in France can be found in a wide variety of locations. From sandy coastal links to thickly wooded parkland; rolling hills to narrow valleys under towering snowcapped peaks. The choice is broad; golf to suit all skill levels and pockets. One region, however, stands out from the rest. Aquitaine in the south-west, stretching from Bordeaux east past Perigeux and south along the Atlantic coast to the Spanish border, has it all. Forty-four golf clubs, some rich in history, others amongst the best in the land offer their charms against a background of pine forests, sandy beaches, fertile vineyards, ancient chateaux, foie gras, Arcachon oysters, Roquefort cheese, and some of the world's greatest wines. A gourmet golfing paradise.

HOLIDAY GOLF IN PORTUGAL
Michael Gedye

Portugal has become synonymous with holiday golf to most players, in no small part because virtually all the courses popular with visitors are of relatively recent construction and created purely for an overseas holiday market. Blessed with a mild and generally sunny winter climate and only a couple of hours south by jet, the country has come to represent the ideal location for a winter golfing getaway. Added bonuses are an ancient historic culture, fresh Atlantic fish and seafood, a wealth of little-travelled but most enjoyable wines, especially from the Douro and Alentejo, plus the courteous charm of the friendly Portuguese themselves. From small beginnings in the southern Algarve nearly forty years ago, modern holiday resort golf has grown and flourished, in line with a growing demand for off-season sunshine play from European countries further north.

One should not think, however, that the game arrived in the country comparatively recently. Expatriate British wine shippers established a

The Old Course, Club de Golf, Vilamoura, Algarve

course by the sea just south of Oporto in 1890 and the British were also responsible for further courses at Belas and Estoril near Lisbon, created for their own recreation. Portuguese involvement in the game is still relatively small. Out of the million rounds played annually on the courses throughout the country, Portuguese players accounted for only 8%. The rest were by visitors, led by the British (60%), Germans, Scandinavians and Dutch.

The focal point for holiday players and those companies producing golfing travel packages, is the southern coastal strip of the Algarve. No less than twenty-eight courses run like an emerald necklace right along the extent of the coast, offering rolling green fairways lined with umbrella pine, cork oak and almond, a few seaside links holes, and others edging sheer red cliffs plus some spectacular views. From major championship venues to humble nine-holers, there is plenty of golfing choice for all.

For those who prefer the advantages of being close to a sophisticated and historic city, the courses around Lisbon have much to offer. Less busy and generally better value than the Algarve, they offer fine golf in often extremely scenic locations. A number of courses, both old and new, lie near the seaside spa town of Estoril and further north past Obidos. Alternatively, seek out the Costa Azul just to the south of the city, where some superb golf, still relatively unknown, runs through tall pinewoods or on sandy land by the sea and demands attention.

There are now sixty-five golf courses in Portugal and its islands, with more under construction or being planned. Golf can be found on mountain slopes in the north, in rural farmland, by the sea amongst sandy dunes, even atop extinct volcanos. Many are of true championship specification and have been designed by such notable golf architects as Robert Trent Jones, Ronald Fream, Rocky Roquemore, Donald Steel, Frank Pennink and Martin Hawtree. Be assured of modern, well-drained construction coupled with high levels of maintenance and the promise of warm, restorative winter sunshine on your back, whatever your score.

With most of the recommended golf courses laid out around the coasts, ably supported by good hotels and local restaurants, there is ample opportunity to sample the 'fruits of the sea'. Be prepared to be surprised by the quality of many relatively little-known wines and the country's prime export, port, the white version of which is often served chilled as an aperitif. Take time to explore some of the monuments and museums that record a historic and adventurous past as well as enjoying the colourful local festivals that perpetuate a unique culture. Visiting Portugal for golf, from the warm welcome onwards, can be a memorable experience.

HOLIDAY GOLF IN SPAIN

Michael Gedye

The first forms of holiday golf revolved around wealth and privilege. In the early 20th Century, royalty and the rich and famous assembled at select seaside resorts to indulge in a variety of leisure pursuits – casinos, horse racing, polo and, importantly, golf. Following fashion and the sun, they frequented northern France in the summer and travelled further south, to Biarritz and Cannes, in the winter. Early golf links were either created to cater to this elite minority or were built by isolated groups of expatriate British far from the sport they enjoyed. In both cases, this ensured that the game around the coasts of Europe remained, for many decades, a pursuit for an exclusive minority.

Golf Platja de Pals, Pals, Costa Brava, Spain

A major change came in the 1950s, with the introduction of charter flights and inexpensive package holidays, initially to Spain. This travel revolution opened up overseas holiday travel to a broader and more cosmopolitan market, and created new demands on local facilities and infrastructure, including the provision of golf. An added bonus was that, whereas family beach holidays were inevitably a summer affair, sunshine golf could be comfortably played through the Iberian winter season, creating a new market to keep the hotels, shops and restaurants open. The initial trickle became a flood, with most new golf developments geared to

foreign players on vacation. Spain now has more than two hundred golf courses, mostly situated around its attractive Mediterranean coastline in resort areas, including the largest number of pure holiday golf courses of any country in the Western hemisphere.

Spain is a major player in the market for winter golf breaks. Steadily increasing demand by players from Great Britain, Germany and Sweden among others, lured south by off-season sun and the prospect of a wide selection of world-class places to play, has created a world apart. Prime passions amongst locals are football and bullfighting; the resort golf courses are

essentially for holiday visitors. Developers were quick to realise that the warm weather, moderate costs and relaxed lifestyle could tempt many visitors to invest in holiday or retirement homes. An essential ingredient would be golf courses, designed to international standards and maintained to perfection. Designers have included Robert Trent Jones, Jack Nicklaus, Gary Player and Cabell Robinson, while the home front has produced fine work from Javier Arana, Pepe Gancedo and Spain's most successful player, Severiano Ballesteros. Such is the high standard of these courses, that they have regularly hosted European Tour events, two World Cups and the 1997 Ryder Cup at Valderrama.

Primary focus is on the southern Costa del Sol (termed the 'Costa del Golf'), with forty-plus courses in play along its coastline, more inland in Andalucia and a number under construction. One of the most concentrated stretches of resort golf in the world, it has been called the 'Palm Springs of Europe'. All around the coast, from the Portuguese border past the Costa Blanca and Valencia to the Costa Brava and the Balearic Islands, exciting golf lies waiting. This proud, dynamic, colourful country, home of Picasso, Dali, flamenco and paella, offers a warm welcome to all.

HOLIDAY GOLF IN THAILAND
Michael Gedye

Talk of Thailand and images emerge of delicate Bhuddist temples, palm-fringed sunbathed beaches, shimmering silks, exotic cuisine and a colourful ancient culture. Few, if any, would immediately consider this country as a serious competitor in the world of long-haul holiday golf. Yet Thailand, a similar flying time away to California or South Africa, has roughly three times as many great

10th tee at The Rose Garden Golf Club near Bangkok

Loch Palm Golf Club, near Phuket , Southern Thailand

golf courses as the Algarve and Costa del Sol put together at a fraction of the price. This is as near to golfing paradise as one may ever find. Green fees that equate to the cost of a round of drinks; armies of smiling young lady caddies who will look after you for 18 holes for the price of a golf ball, and more courses of true world class than you can possibly hope to play. The winter season, from November through to March, offers constant sunshine, no rain, superb playing conditions and comfortable temperatures, especially in the north. The real bonus is that no-one should visit Thailand for golf alone. This beautiful country with a rich culture has so much more to offer the visitor, to make his visit truly memorable.

The Kingdom of Thailand has nearly 200 courses currently in play, many in holiday resort locations. Most were created during the last thirty years and particularly in the last decade, ensuring the latest design and construction techniques. You can play rolling palm-lined tests backed by wooded mountains or follow beachside holes edging the Andaman Sea; from the outskirts of urban Bangkok, the capital city (where the World Cup was held in 1975) to tackling demanding layouts dominated by strategic water and a wealth of colourful flowers. Thailand has three distinct seasons - hot (from April to June), rain (from July to October) and cool (from November to March). The latter is best for golf, although the game is playable on well-drained and automatically irrigated courses all year round.

The most popular tourist areas, with the largest selection of good hotels and related facilities, are also where to find most of the best resort golf. The most temperate winter climate and some of the finest courses lie in the north, near Chiang Mai and Chiang Rai, close to the picturesque Golden Triangle on the Mekong River. This is a fascinating mountain region noted for colourful hill tribes, elephant treks, fine handicrafts and rich cuisine. Centrally-sited Bangkok has much to see and admire plus access to Kanchanaburi on the River Kwai as well as the excellent beach resorts of Cha-Am and Hua Hin to the west. To the east, you will find the mountainous Khao Yai national park as well as the Chonburi coast, including the bustling seaside resort of Pattaya, which has a wide selection of courses to choose from. Phuket Island, in the far south, is a popular tropical world apart with palm-fringed white beaches, craggy hills and a well-developed tourist infrastructure.

The game has been played in Thailand since 1898, initially as a recreation for British expatriates in northern Chiang Mai. Later a few courses were added for use by the royal family and their friends. It is only recently, since the early 1970s, that the game has really taken off, fuelled by a realisation of the great tourist potential of world class resort golf. This in turn has created a burgeoning domestic market (more than 300,000 Thais play the game). Top international golf architects were employed – Jack Nicklaus, Ronald Fream, Robert Trent Jones Jr., Arnold Palmer, Pete Dye and Dennis Griffiths among others - to create a succession of excellent tests of the game, often in the most spectacular natural settings.

Playing the game in Thailand will open your eyes to a new experience, one you will want to repeat. The clubhouses, often more like luxury hotels, have superb facilities with air-conditioned restaurants offering Thai, Chinese, Japanese and Western menus. You can rent golf clubs and electric carts plus enjoy the benefit of drink and snack shelters every three holes around the course. All golf clubs offer the services of well trained young lady caddies who will look after your clubs, help you make a better score, shelter you from the sun with your umbrella and even tote a folding chair should you wish to rest between shots. This is luxury golf at bargain rates supported by the legendary service for which Thailand is famous. Do also find time to explore this ancient and exotic land off the course; with its colourful culture and ready smiles, you cannot fail to be enchanted.

HOLIDAY GOLF IN USA

Michael Gedye

The game in the USA is a matter of superlatives. There are more courses, more players, more top tournament professionals and greater expenditure than anywhere else on earth. In many aspects, such as course architecture and equipment design, the United States leads the world. The nation dominates the game internationally and sets the standard. However, visitors should be aware that the American way of holiday golf is a world of its own, entirely geared to its own vast domestic market.

Such a large country, with so many places to play, can offer a wide choice of often stunning locations to choose from. Because of this, few golfers need ever consider playing abroad and, in fact, most Americans do not even own a passport. The holiday golf scenario has been refined to meet the needs and demands of the huge domestic market and, like the fast food industry, rates high for consistency and service but low on originality. The US golfer on holiday tends to be social rather than serious,

Pelican's Nest Golf Club, Fort Myers, Florida

most often a high-handicapper who seldom plays at other times, looking for level, not too demanding courses with a high level of maintenance and overall service. Since the market is entirely customer led and highly competitive, with the player knowing exactly what he likes and expecting more of the same, there is a certain bland sameness to American vacation resort courses. But they are beautifully presented, well-organised and offer attractively low prices plus an assurance of consistent quality.

The levels of service and organisation may surprise you. On arrival at a typical resort course, your golf bag is taken away to be returned on a normally mandatory golf cart, often kitted out with scorecard, pencil, tees, a full ice bucket and seed mixture for divots. The cart will be lined up with others to correspond to a pre-arranged tee time. Pro shops and clubhouses offer every conceivable facility with a smile. You will find regular drink and snack shelters around the course or else a roving refreshment vehicle, often driven by a stunning blonde.

Clubs tend not to need your handicap certificate; only proof you can pay. Rounds, therefore, tend to be slow by European standards, particularly as locals will take full advantage of the periodic drink stops; golf tends to be more social than serious. But the sun will shine, the views can be sensational, the course will be magnificently manicured, with perfect fairway lies and you may just shoot the score of your life. Do things the American way and enjoy a golfing experience unlike any other.

We have chosen a selection of reliable courses for the guide, located in Florida, the Carolinas and Palm Springs in California – three fabled vacation areas with guaranteed sunshine and much more besides.

Golfing around Britain and Abroad

Where to Play and Where to Stay around the Golfing Regions

With the widest variety of courses in the world to choose from, British golfers are particularly fortunate in being able to enjoy different types of courses within close proximity of each other. The challenges are different and equally enjoyable on seaside links, parkland, moorland or heathland. Why not plan a journey taking in as wide a range as possible and stopping off at some of the excellent accommodation featured in the guide?

The beauty of the game of golf, compared with any other sport, is that even when playing the same venue on a regular basis, it presents new difficulties each time, as the course is subject to the vagaries of the weather. The nature of a hole can change dramatically when coping with windy or wet conditions compared with a breezeless sunny day. It is this variety that golfers thrive on, and the best way to experience this is to take a break in accommodation recommended for golfers and try out as many of the local courses as possible.

The best way to enjoy golf at any level is to ensure that you have the right equipment. The game is constantly evolving, and modern equipment allows even average players to achieve their full potential. A selection of golfing products and tour operators is shown at the back of this guide. If you are looking for buggies and trolleys to make light work of hilly courses, golfwear for comfort and style, or golf bags and equipment, all this and more can be found in this section.

Do try to make full use of this guide by visiting as many clubs as possible. This has become easier, with discount schemes such as 'Golfpoints' run by *Golf Monthly* which allow golfers to benefit from reductions in green fees.

When visiting different courses, do always remember that to be welcomed back you should behave as you would like visitors to your own course to behave. Everyone knows that they should rake bunkers, repair pitch marks and replace divots; but remember that the bane of most golfers' lives is slow play – the holiday mood can cause even experienced golfers to walk more slowly, talk more and forget about the job in hand. All this is fine if the course is quiet, but will not be appreciated if there are members behind looking to fit in a quick 9 holes.

Wherever you go in the UK or abroad, don't forget to take your copy of *The Golf Guide* – we are sure you will enjoy the golf courses you visit and the accommodation you stay in.

How to use the Golf Guide

THE GOLF GUIDE *Where to Play* • *Where to Stay* contains up to date basic information on every course (as far as we know) in Britain and Northern Ireland. Details are provided by the clubs themselves. You will also find sections on the Irish Republic plus holiday golf in Spain and Majorca, Portugal, France, the USA, South Africa, Dubai and Thailand.

The guide carries entries from hotels, guest houses and other accommodation convenient to specific courses or areas. These are generally 'paid' entries and usually follow a recommendation from a club. THE GOLF GUIDE, in association with Golf Monthly, is usually available for sale in golf clubs through the Professional and/or the Secretary, as well as bookshops etc.

Golf Course Information

For virtually every course you will find the following details, updated annually:

1. Name, address and telephone number.   2. Location.   3. Brief description.

4. Number of holes. length and Standard Scratch Score.   5. Green fees.

6. Details of facilities for visitors – individuals, groups and societies.

7. Name and telephone number of the Professional and the Secretary.

The accuracy of details published depends on the response of the clubs and to our best knowledge is correct at the time of going to press (November 2003). Where entry details have not been confirmed an asterisk (*) is shown.

Choosing a Course

The golf clubs and courses are listed alphabetically by nearest town or village within the appropriate county section for England, Scotland, Wales, Ireland, the Isle of Man and the Channel Islands. Courses overseas are also listed by region. We have chosen to classify by place-name rather than club or course name since this seems more straightforward and recognisable to the majority.

If you want to find a club or course by its name, you should simply refer to the Index where you will see the page number of the listing. In each entry the name of the club or course is always shown in bold type after the place-name heading.

Accommodation

Accommodation entries are placed as near a particular club or course as possible and there are also hotel displays in the front colour section. Most of the accommodation advertised has been recommended by the local golf club. A full index is provided.

Maps

At the back of THE GOLF GUIDE you will find a set of maps showing cities, towns and villages in Britain with counties, motorways and main roads. Although many of the place-names under which the courses are classified are on the maps, please note that the maps are not golf course or club location maps.

The location details supplied with each entry should get you there and if you are in any doubt at all you should ask directions from the club itself.

Please mention THE GOLF GUIDE *Where to Play* • *Where to Stay* when you make a hotel booking or play at courses after using our guide.

Publisher's Note

With the addition of new courses and ones not previously covered, the 27th edition of THE GOLF GUIDE *Where to Play • Where to Stay* now features over 2,800 UK and Irish courses, along with a small taster of golf available in other countries including France, Spain, Portugal, South Africa, Thailand and the USA.

Golf is a game which is increasing in popularity and is attracting a wider range of people than ever. It is a game for all ages with juniors trying to be the next Tiger Woods while senior members still try to emulate Ben Hogan or Arnold Palmer.

With so many courses to choose from it is difficult for a new golfer to know where to start. Each course has its own character and each hole presents its own unique challenge and this, the definitive guide to courses, gives you the opportunity to try, and enjoy, as many as possible. As usual, we offer the following advice to readers.

Enquiries and Bookings. It is quite normal to confirm a booking in writing and also to receive written confirmation – and a receipt for any advance payment. You should check prices and also any special requirements.

Cancellations. Any booking is a form of contract for both parties. If you have to cancel, try to give maximum notice. With reasonable notice the hotel should normally refund any advance payment but on short notice a full refund is not necessarily a legal entitlement.

Complaints. Most owners/managers are anxious to sort out problems on the spot so that you are a satisfied customer. If a problem persists you can get advice from a Citizens' Advice Bureau, Consumers' Association, Trading Standards Office, Tourist Board or indeed your own solicitor.

Serious complaints are unlikely to arise with the kind of accommodation you'll find on our pages. FHG Publications Ltd. do not inspect accommodation and an entry does not imply a firm recommendation. However, most of the advertisers have been recommended or proposed by local golf clubs and have standards which satisfy and in many cases far exceed those expected by inspecting authorities. In addition we will be pleased to hear from you if you have a serious complaint and although we cannot act as intermediaries or accept responsibility for our advertisers. we will record the complaint and follow it up with the advertiser in question.

We are grateful to all Club Secretaries and Club Professionals who assist in the supply and revision of entries and to the PGA for editorial support. We are happy to hear from any Club which for some reason does not already have an entry. We also thank our advertisers for the wide range of accommodation choices for golfers. their families, friends and colleagues available in this edition and welcome suggestions for the future. We are particularly keen to receive accommodation recommendations from clubs and golfers themselves.

When you make enquiries and bookings for golf, accommodation or both, please mention this latest edition of THE GOLF GUIDE: *Where to Play • Where to Stay.*

George Pratt
Publishing Director

1. INVERCLYDE
2. WEST DUNBARTONSHIRE
3. NORTH AYRSHIRE
4. RENFREWSHIRE
5. EAST RENFREWSHIRE
6. CITY OF GLASGOW
7. EAST DUNBARTONSHIRE
8. NORTH LANARKSHIRE
9. FALKIRK
10. CLACKMANNANSHIRE
11. WEST LOTHIAN
12. CITY OF EDINBURGH
13. MIDLOTHIAN
14. SOUTH LANARKSHIRE
15. EAST AYRSHIRE
16. SOUTH AYRSHIRE

17. GREATER MANCHESTER
18. MERSEYSIDE

19. FLINTSHIRE
20. DENBIGHSHIRE
21. WREXHAM

22. WEST MIDLANDS

23. SWANSEA
24. NEATH AND PORT TALBOT
25. BRIDGEND
26. RHONDDA CYNON TAFF
27. VALE OF GLAMORGAN
28. MERTHYR TYDFIL
29. BLAENAU GWENT
30. CAERPHILLY
31. CARDIFF
32. NEWPORT
33. TORFAEN
34. MONMOUTHSHIRE

GREAT BRITAIN COUNTIES

A selection of Golf Events in 2004

•APRIL

West of Ireland Amateur Open Championship, Portumna, *April 9-13*

Peter McEvoy Trophy, Copt Heath, *April 14-15*

Munster Youth's Amateur Open Championship , Royal Dublin, *April 16-18*

Lytham Trophy, Royal Lytham St Annes, *April 30-May 2*

•MAY

Irish Amateur Open Championship, Royal Dublin, *May 7-9*

Clwyd Open, Wrexham/Prestatyn, *May 8-9*

Brabazon Trophy, West Lancs, *May 14-16*

English Ladies Close Amateur Championship, Northants, *May 18-22*

Scottish Open Amateur Stroke Play Championship, Lundin Links, *May 21-23*

Irish Seniors' Amateur Open Championship, Roscommon, *May 27-28*

Amateur Championship, St Andrews, *May 31 – 05 June*

•JUNE

East of Ireland Amateur Open Championship, Co Louth, *June 5-7*

St Andrews Links Trophy, St Andrews, *June 11-13*

Irish Amateur Close Championship, Donegal, *June 12-16*

Scottish Open Mid Amateur Championship, Hamilton, *June 18-20*

Scottish Youths' Open Amateur Championship, Brunston Castle, *June 18-20*

Ladies British Open Amateur Championship, Gullane, *June 22-26*

•JULY

Ladies British Open Mid Amateur Championship, Hunstanton, *July 2-4*

Junior Open Championship, Kilmarnock (Barassie), *July 12-14*

English Ladies Stroke Play Championship, Woodhall Spa, *July 12-15*

Open Championship, Royal Troon, *July 15-18*

Scottish Amateur Championship, Gullane, *July 26-31*

Weetabix Women's British Open, Sunningdale, *July 29 – 1 August*

•SEPTEMBER

English Ladies County Finals,
High Post, *September 1-3*

LGU Home Internationals,
Royal Porthcawl, *September 8-10*

Home Internationals, Ballybunion,
September 8-10

Senior Ladies British Open Amateur
Championships, Port Stewart,
September 21-23

Ladies British Open Amateur S.P.
Championship, Alwoodley,
September 25-27

Scottish Club Championship, Erskine,
September 26

Seniors' Home Internationals, Wales,
September 28-30

•OCTOBER

Scottish Area Team Championship
Finals, Cardross, *October 2-3*

•AUGUST

Boys' Home Internationals,
Royal Dublin, *August 3-5*

Seniors' Open Amateur
Championship, The Berkshire,
August 4-6

Girls' British Open Amateur
Championship, Lanark, *August 4-8*

Girls' Home International Matches,
Strathaven, *August 11-13*

British Mid Amateur Championship,
Royal Liverpool, *August 11-15*

Jaques Leglise Trophy, Nairn,
August 27-28

For full details of
clubs and courses,
plus convenient
accommodation,
visit the

 FHG golf website

London (Greater & Central)

ASHFORD. **Ashford Manor Golf Club,** Fordbridge Road, Ashford, Middlesex TW15 3RT (01784 424644; Fax: 01784 424649). Parkland course, flat with narrow fairways. 18 holes, 6352 yards. S.S.S. 71. *Green Fees:* weekdays £35.00 per round, £40.00 per day. *Eating facilities:* dining room and snacks. *Visitors:* welcome weekdays; it is advisable to ring in advance, Handicap Certificate required. May not play at weekends other than with a member. *Society Meetings:* welcome. Professional: I. Partington (01784 255940). Manager: Ian Buchan (01784 424644; Fax: 01784 424649).

BARNET. **North Middlesex Golf Club,** The Manor House, Friern Barnet Lane, Whetstone N20 0NL (020 8445 1732; Fax: 020 8445 5023). *Location:* five miles south of Junction 23 of M25. 18 holes, 5594 yards. S.S.S. 67. *Green Fees:* weekday per round £25.00, per day £30.00; weekends and Bank Holidays £30.00. *Eating facilities:* luncheons, snacks and dining facilities. *Visitors:* welcome (with Official Handicap), weekends playing with a member and in possession of Official Handicap. Advisable to telephone Professional to book time. *Society Meetings:* catered for. Professional: Freddy George (020 8445 3060). General Manager: Miss Alex McDonald (020 8445 1604; Fax: 020 8445 5023).

BARNET. **Old Fold Manor Golf Club,** Old Fold Lane, Hadley Green, Barnet, Herts EN5 4QN (020 8449 1650). *Location:* Junction 23 M25 - A1000 one mile north of Barnet. Heathland course. 18 holes, 6447 yards. S.S.S. 71. Practice ground and putting green. *Green Fees:* weekdays £25.00 per round (with a member £12.00), £35.00 per day (with a member £20.00); weekends £15.00 with member only. *Eating facilities:* restaurant and bar except Mondays and Wednesdays when cafeteria/snack bar is available. *Visitors:* welcome weekdays, public days Monday/ Wednesday £16 per round; special visitors' concessions at weekends by arrangement. *Society Meetings:* catered for Thursdays and Fridays. Professional: Peter McEvoy (020 8440 7488). Manager: Brian Cullen (020 8440 9185; Fax: 020 8441 4863). website: www.oldfoldmanor.co.uk

BEXLEYHEATH. **Barnehurst Public Pay and Play Golf Course,** Mayplace Road East, Bexleyheath, Kent DA7 6JU (01322 523746; Fax: 01322 523860). *Location:* 10 minutes from M25, follow signs for Erith. Mature inland course in traditional woodland setting. 9 holes, 2737 yards. S.S.S. 68 (for 18 holes). Designed by five times Open Champion James Braid in 1903. Practice ground. *Green Fees:* Direct Debit scheme available. *Eating facilities:* fully licensed bar with catering facilities. *Visitors:* welcome, no restrictions. Newly refurbished club house. *Society Meetings:* catered for. Large function rooms. Golf Manager: Freda Sunley.

BROMLEY. **Bromley Golf Club,** Magpie Hall Lane, Bromley, Kent BR2 8JF. *Location:* off A21 Bromley to Farnborough road. Open course with many trees and water. 9 holes, 2397 yards. S.S.S. 67. Putting green and teaching facilities. *Green Fees:* £6.10 weekdays, £8.00 weekends. Concessions £3.70 weekdays only. *Eating facilities:* food available. *Visitors:* no booking required as this is a public course. Professional: Alan Hodgson (0208 462 7014).

CHINGFORD. **Chingford Golf Club,** 158 Station Road, Chingford E4 (020 8529 2107). 18 holes, 6342 yards. S.S.S. 70. *Green Fees:* information not available. *Visitors:* welcome weekdays only, an article of red must be worn. Pro shop: 020 8529 5708. Professional: Andy Traynor. Secretary: Bryan Sinden.

CHINGFORD. **Royal Epping Forest Golf Club,** Forest Approach, Chingford, London E4 7AZ (020 8529 2195). *Location:* 200 yards east of Chingford (BR) Station. A private club on a public course. Wooded. 18 holes, 6342 yards. S.S.S. 71. *Green Fees:* information not available. *Eating facilities:* public snack bar. *Visitors:* may play course but may not use clubhouse. Must wear red garment (trousers or shirt/sweater). Professional: Andy Traynor (020 8529 5708). Secretary: Mr D Bright - Thomas (020 8529 2195).

CHINGFORD. **West Essex Golf Club,** Bury Road, Sewardstonebury, Chingford, London E4 7QL (020 8529 7558; Fax: 020 8524 7870). *Location:* two miles north of Chingford BR Station. M25 (Junction 26) and Waltham Abbey follow directions to Chingford (Daws Hill on left). Parkland, wooded, hilly. 18 holes, 6289 yards. S.S.S. 70. Driving range (for members, members' guests and societies). *Green Fees:* weekdays £32.00 per round, £37.00 per day; weekends with member only. *Eating facilities:* restaurant and bar facilities. *Visitors:* welcome weekdays except Tuesday mornings and Thursday afternoons. Phone first. *Society Meetings:* catered for by arrangement Mondays, Wednesdays and Fridays. Professional: Robert Joyce (Tel & Fax: 020 8529 4367). Secretary: (020 8529 7558; Fax: 020 8524 7870).
e-mail: sec@westessexgolfclub.co.uk
website: www.westessexgolfclub.co.uk

DULWICH. **Dulwich and Sydenham Hill Golf Club,** Grange Lane, College Road, London SE21 7LH (020 8693 3961). *Location:* off South Circular, Dulwich Common. 18 holes, 6051 yards. S.S.S. 69. *Green Fees:* information not available. *Eating facilities:* lunch every day. *Visitors:* welcome, prior arrangement advised. *Society Meetings:* catered for. Professional: David Baillie. Secretary: Mr Brian O'Farrell.

EDMONTON. **Leaside Golf Club,** Lee Valley Leisure Centre, Pickett's Lock Lane, Edmonton N9 0AS (020 8803 3611; Fax: 020 8884 4975). *Location:* M25 Juntion 25, nearest town Enfield. Flat parkland course, lake on first 9 holes, good drainage; short but challenging course. 18 holes, 4811 yards (yellow). S.S.S. 64 (yellow). 20 bay driving range, practice ground. *Green Fees:* information not available. *Eating facilities:* cafe and bar. *Visitors:* welcome everyday. Trolleys available. Professional: Richard Gerken (020 8803 3611). Membership/Secretary: David Campbell (020 8364 7782).*

EDMONTON. **Lee Valley Leisure Golf Course,** Picketts Lock Lane, Edmonton N9 0AS. (020 8803 3611). *Location:* off Meridian Way between north Circular Road and Ponders End. Flat parkland course with lake and River Lea as water hazards. Short but challenging. 18 holes, 4902 yards. S.S.S. 66. 20 bay covered driving range. *Green Fees:* information not available. Senior Citizens/Junior weekday concessions. *Visitors:* welcome, pay and play everyday. *Society Meetings:* small societies welcome, prior booking. Professional: R.G. Gerken (020 8803 3611).

ELTHAM. **Eltham Warren Golf Club,** Bexley Road, Eltham SE9 2PE (020 8850 1166). *Location:* off East Rochester Way (A2) at Falconwood, then onto A210 Bexley Road. Parkland course, narrow fairways. 9 holes, 5840 yards. S.S.S. 68. Practice ground. *Green Fees:* £28.00 per day; with member £14.00. *Eating facilities:* dining room and bar. *Visitors:* welcome weekdays only, weekends with member only. *Society Meetings:* welcome Thursdays only. Professional: Gary Brett (020 8859 7909). Secretary: D.J. Clare (020 8850 4477).

ELTHAM. **Royal Blackheath Golf Club,** The Clubhouse, Court Road, Eltham SE9 5AF. *Location:* M25, A20 exit London bound, second set of traffic lights turn right, 600 yards up hill on right. Parkland, wooded with water. 18 holes, 6219 yards. S.S.S. 70. Practice area. *Green fees:* £45.00 per round, £65.00 per day. *Eating facilities:* excellent dining room and two bars. *Visitors:* welcome weekdays, weekends only if introduced by and playing with member. Museum. *Society Meetings:* catered for midweek, prior booking essential. Professional: Richard Harrison (020 8850 1763). Secretary: A. G. Dunlop (020 8850 1795; Fax: 020 8859 0150). e-mail: info@rbgc.com   website: www.rbgc.com

ENFIELD. **Crews Hill Golf Club,** Cattlegate Road, Crews Hill, Enfield EN2 8AZ (020 8363 0787). *Location:* off Junction 24 M25, follow directions to Enfield. Parkland. 18 holes, 6230 yards. S.S.S. 70. Practice area. *Green Fees:* on application. *Eating facilities:* full bar and snacks available, restaurant by arrangement. No catering Mondays. *Visitors:* welcome weekdays. Handicap Certificate required. Weekends by invitation of member. *Society Meetings:* by arrangement. Professional: N. Wichelow (020 8366 7422). General Manager: A. Stewart (020 8363 6674; Fax: 020 8363 2343).

ENFIELD. **Enfield Golf Club,** Old Park Road South, Enfield, Middlesex EN2 7DA (020 8363 3970; Fax: 020 8342 0381). *Location:* off Junction 24, M25; follow directions to Enfield. Parkland; designed by James Braid. 18 holes, 6200 yards. S.S.S. 70. *Green Fees:* on request. *Eating facilities:* full bar and catering facilities. *Visitors:* welcome weekdays, limited availability at weekends. It is essential to telephone Professional Shop before travelling. *Society Meetings:* welcome weekdays only by prior arrangement. Professional: Lee Fickling (020 8366 4492). Secretary: Jacqueline North (020 8363 3970; Fax: 020 8342 0381). e-mail: enfieldgolfclub@dial.pipex.com website: www.enfieldgolfclub.co.uk

ENFIELD. **Whitewebbs Golf Club,** Clay Hill, Beggars Hollow, Enfield EN2 9JN (020 8363 2951). *Location:* A10 off M25, north of Enfield. Parkland course. 18 holes, 5863 yards. S.S.S. 68. Practice area, separate 9 hole pitch and putt. *Green Fees:* information not available. *Eating facilities:* public cafe on site. *Visitors:* welcome, public course, no restrictions. *Society Meetings:* contact the Secretary. Professional: Gary Sherrif (020 8363 4454). Secretary: Stephen Pyke (020 8363 2951). *

FINCHLEY. **Finchley Golf Club,** Nether Court, Frith Lane, Mill Hill NW7 1PU (020 8346 2436; Fax: 020 8343 4205). *Location:* close A1/M1, near Mill Hill East underground station. Parkland course, tree lined, designed by James Braid. 18 holes, 6411 yards. S.S.S. 71. *Green Fees:* weekdays £28.00 per round, £35.00 per day; weekends £37.00 per round. *Eating facilities:* two bars and catering. *Visitors:* welcome weekdays except Tuesdays, Thursdays and weekend mornings. Clubs, shoes, trolleys and carts for hire. Excellent 19th century Manor House. *Society Meetings:* catered for Mondays, Wednesdays and Fridays. Professional: David Brown (020 8346 5086). Secretary: J. Seatter (020 8346 2436). e-mail: secretary@finchleygolfclub.co.uk

GREENFORD. **Ealing Golf Club,** Perivale Lane, Greenford, Middlesex UB6 8SS. *Location:* on Western Avenue A40 half a mile from Hanger Lane Gyratory System. Flat parkland. 18 holes, 6216 yards. S.S.S. 70. *Green Fees:* information not available. *Eating facilities:* spike bar, mixed lounge, restaurant - lunch, dinner and bar snacks. Conference room. *Visitors:* welcome weekdays with reservation through Professional Shop. *Society Meetings:* catered for on Monday, Wednesday and Thursday only. Professional: David Barton (020 8997 3959). General Manager: June Mackison (020 8997 0937; Fax: 020 8998 0756).

GREENFORD. **Horsenden Hill Golf Club,** , Greenford, Middlesex UB6 0RD. *Location:* two miles from A40; off Whitton Avenue East, next door to Sudbury Golf Course. Situated on Horsenden Hill Conservation Area. Undulating parkland course, eight Par 3, one Par 4. 9 holes, 1632 yards. S.S.S. 28. Practice area, nets and putting green. *Green Fees:* £7.00 for 9 holes. *Eating facilities:* bar/cafe. *Visitors:*

welcome at all times, public course. Membership available. Trolley hire. *Society Meetings:* welcome. Professional: Jeff Quarshie (020 8902 4555). Golf Course Manager: Ray Peters (07989 243219).

GREENFORD. **Perivale Park Golf Club,** Stockdove Way, Argyle Road, Greenford, Middlesex. *Location:* A40, turn off at sign for Ealing and Perivale. Entrance to golf club is at Stockdove Way, Perivale. Flat, riverside course set amongst the meadows of Brent River Park. Internal out of bounds areas. 9 holes (18 holes), 2733 yards (white tees). S.S.S. 65. Practice area. *Green Fees:* information on request. *Eating facilities:* cafeteria. *Visitors:* welcome at all times. Public course. Membership available. Professional: P. Bryant (020 8575 7116). Golf Course Manager: Ray Peters: (07989 243219).

HAMPSTEAD. **Hampstead Golf Club,** Winnington Road, London N2 0TU (020 8455 6420). *Location:* off Hampstead Lane adjacent to Spaniards Inn. Undulating parkland with mature trees. 9 holes, 5812 yards. S.S.S. 68. *Green Fees:* £30.00 (£40.00 per day) weekdays; weekends £35.00. *Eating facilities:* bar meals/snacks and afternoon teas. *Visitors:* welcome weekdays (not Tuesdays); limited at weekends, telephone Professional. Professional: P J. Brown (020 8455 7089). Secretary: (020 8455 0203; Fax: 020 8731 6194).

HAMPTON HILL. **The Fulwell Golf Club,** Wellington Road, Hampton Hill, Middlesex TW12 1JY. *Location:* opposite Fulwell Railway Station and bus garage. Flat parkland course. 18 holes, 6544 yards. S.S.S. 71. Practice ground. *Green Fees:* weekdays £30.00 per round, £40.00 per day; weekends £35.00, £15.00 with member. *Eating facilities:* lunches and teas. *Visitors:* welcome weekdays, weekends by prior arrangement. *Society Meetings:* welcome Monday, Thursday and Friday. Professional: Nigel Turner (Tel & Fax: 020 8977 3844). Secretary: Peter Butcher (020 8977 2733; Fax: 020 8977 7732).
e-mail: secretary@fulwellgolfclub.co.uk
website: www.fulwellgolfclub.co.uk

HAMPTON WICK. **Hampton Court Palace Golf Club,** Hampton Wick, Kingston-upon-Thames KT1 4AD (020 8977 2658). *Location:* between Hampton Court and Kingston Bridge, entrance at Kingston Bridge roundabout. Flat parkland. 18 holes, 6513 yards. S.S.S. 71. *Green Fees:* information not available. *Eating facilities:* full bar and dining facilities. *Visitors:* welcome; booking one week in advance through Pro Shop. *Society Meetings:* catered for by arrangement. Professional: Adam Smith (020 8977 2658).

HANWELL. **Brent Valley Golf Club,** Church Road, Hanwell, London W7. *Location:* one mile from Uxbridge Road, off Greenford Avenue, entrance at Church Road. Situated in a picturesque valley in the Brent River Park, 18 holes, 5446 yards. S.S.S. 67. Pay and Play. Nets and practice area. *Green Fees:* information on request. *Eating facilities:* bar/cafe. *Visitors :* welcome at all times. Membership available Public course. *Society Meetings:* welcome. Professional: V. Santos (020 8567 1287). Golf Course Manager: Ray Peters (07989 243219).

HENDON. **Hendon Golf Club,** Ashley Walk, Devonshire Road, Mill Hill, London NW7 1DG (020 8346 6023) *Location:* leave M1 southbound at Junction 2. Turn off A1 into Holders Hill Road, first circle , take first left into Devonshire Road, golf club approx. 50 metres on the left. 10 miles north of London. Parkland, wooded, well bunkered. 18 holes, 6289 yards. S.S.S. 70. *Green Fees:* weekdays £30.00 per round, £35.00 per day; weekends £35.00 per round. *Eating facilities:* full bar and catering facilities. *Visitors:* welcome weekdays (limited at weekends and Bank Holidays), book through Pro Shop. *Society Meetings:* catered for by arrangement Tuesdays to Fridays, book through Secretary's office. Professional: Matt Deal (020 8346 8990). Secretary: Chris Bishop (020 8346 6023; Fax: 020 8343 1974). e-mail: hendongolf@globalnet.co.uk

HIGHGATE. **Highgate Golf Club,** Denewood Road, Highgate, London N6 4AH (020 8340 1906). Founded 1904. *Location:* near A1, turn down Sheldon Avenue, opposite Kenwood House and first left. Parkland. 18 holes, 5985 yards. S.S.S. 69. *Green Fees:* £30.00. *Eating facilities:* bar, restaurant. *Visitors:* welcome weekdays except Wednesdays from 9.30 am. *Society Meetings:* catered for Thursdays/Fridays. Professional: Robin Turner (020 8340 5467). Secretary: Nigel Challis (020 8340 3745).

HILLINGDON. **Hillingdon Golf Club**, 18 Dorset Way, Hillingdon, Uxbridge, Middlesex UB10 0JR (01895 239810). *Location:* near A40, adjacent to RAF Uxbridge. Gently undulating wooded parkland course sloping down to river. 9 holes, 5490 yards, 5068 metres. S.S.S. 67. *Green Fees:* information not available. *Eating facilities:* bar meals available Tuesday to Friday. *Visitors:* welcome Mondays, Tuesdays and Fridays; Thursdays - Ladies' Day. *Society Meetings:* catered for by special arrangement only with Committee through Club Secretary. Professional: Phil Smith (01895 460035). Secretary: B.L. Russell (01895 233956).*

HOUNSLOW. **Airlinks Golf Club,** Southall Lane, Hounslow, Middlesex TW5 9PE (020 8561 1418; Fax: 020 8813 6284). *Location:* Junction 3 on M4, A312 to Hayes. Same entrance as D. Lloyd Tennis Centre. Parkland course with water holes and doglegs. 18 holes, 6000 yards. S.S.S. 68. Floodlit driving range. *Green Fees:* information not available. *Eating facilities:* full catering and bar facilities/restaurant area. *Visitors:* weekdays no restrictions, some restrictions weekends, bookings advised seven days in advance. Membership, including 5 and 7 day, now open. *Society Meetings:* catered for all week. Professional: Tony Martin. Secretary: Stefan Brewster.*

HOUNSLOW. **Hounslow Heath Municipal Golf Course,** Staines Road, Hounslow TW4 5DS (020 8570 5271). *Location:* Staines Road A315 between Hounslow and Bedfont. Heathland course with water hazards, tight fairways. 18 holes, 5901 yards. S.S.S. 68. Practice area. *Green Fees:* information not available. *Eating facilities:* snacks; teas and coffee. *Visitors:* welcome at all times, bookings seven days in advance for weekends and Bank Holidays. *Society Meetings:* by arrangement.

ISLEWORTH. **Wyke Green Golf Club,** Syon Lane, Osterley, Isleworth, Middlesex TW7 5PT (020 8560 8777). *Location:* situated half-a-mile north of A4 near Gillettes Corner. Fairly flat parkland. 18 holes, 6182 yards. S.S.S. 70. *Green Fees:* Monday to Thursday £40.00 per day, £20.00 after 5pm; Monday to Friday £17.00 with a member. *Eating facilities:* full catering restaurant and halfway house. *Visitors:* welcome; weekends only with member until after 4pm. *Society Meetings:* catered for on Tuesdays and Thursdays by arrangement, minimum 12. Professional: Neil Smith (020 8847 0685) Secretary: David Pearson (020 8560 8777; Fax: 020 8569 8392).

LONDON. **Dukes Meadows Golf Club,** Dukes Meadows, Great Chertsey Road, London W4 2SH (020 8995 0537 Fax: 020 8995 5326). *Location:* next to Chiswick Bridge on the A316, one mile south

Hogarth roundabout. Parkland course, greens to USGA standard. 50 bay floodlit driving range.6 hole Academy Course for young players acccompanied by adult golfers. *Green Fees:* information not available. *Eating facilities:* bar/restaurant area available. *Visitors:* welcome, tee times up to 48 hours advance booking. 12 teaching PGA professionals, trolleys available. *Society Meetings:* welcome by arrangement. Professional: Malcolm Henbery (020 8995 0537). General Manager/PGA Professional: Scott Margetts. (020 8994 3314). *

LONDON. **London Scottish Golf Club**, Windmill Enclosure, Wimbledon Common SW19 5NQ (020 8788 0135). *Location:* just off A3 – Tibbetts Corner – just south of Putney SW15. Wooded commonland. 18 holes, 5458 yards. S.S.S. 66. *Green Fees:* Monday £10.00, Tuesday to Friday £15.00. *Eating facilities:* bar and catering. *Visitors:* welcome weekdays only. Check with Professional recommended. Red top must be worn, no jeans or sweatshirts. *Society Meetings:* welcome. Professional/Secretary: Stephen Barr (020 8789 1207/7517).

LONDON. **Mill Hill Golf Club,** 100 Barnet Way, Mill Hill, London NW7 3AL (020 8959 2282). Est. 1925. *Location:* A1, south half a mile before Apex Corner left into clubhouse car park – signposted. Wooded parkland. 18 holes, 6247 yards, 5697 metres. S.S.S. 70. Practice ground. *Green Fees:* weekdays £25.00; weekends £30.00. *Eating facilities:* restaurant and bar. *Visitors:* welcome Monday to Friday; weekends and Bank Holidays prior bookings recommended. Two snooker tables. *Society Meetings:* welcome weekdays with prior booking. For green fees ring the Pro Shop (020 8959 7261); for society and membership enquiries ring Club Office (020 8959 2339). Professional: D. Beal. Secretary: R. Haslehurst.

LONDON. **Richmond Park Golf Club,** Roehampton Gate, Richmond Park, London SW15 5JR (020 8876 1795; Fax: 020 8878 1354). *Location:* set within parkland in Richmond. Two courses (36 holes), 6036 yards and 5868 yards. S.S.S. 68/68/67. Driving range. *Green Fees:* information not available. *Visitors:* welcome every day. *Society Meetings:* all welcome. Secretary: Tony Gourvish (020 8876 3205).*

LONDON. **Thamesview Golf Centre,** Fairway Drive (off Summerton Way), Thamesmead North, London SE28 8PP (020 8310 7975; Fax: 020 8312 0546). Delightful, undulating Public Pay & Play Course, founded 1991. Water hazards and a mixture of new and mature trees. The 4th hole is a challenging 515 yards down a narrow fairway. 9 holes, 5462 yards, par 70. S.S.S. 67. Floodlit 30 bay driving range, putting green. *Green Fees:* information not available. *Eating*

facilities: restaurant, bars and function room. *Visitors*: no restriction. Fully stocked Pro Shop, club hire. *Society Meetings*: welcome, book by telephone or in writing. Professional: Graeme Wilson. Club Secretary: Sarah Springham.*
e-mail: enquiries@thamesview-golf.fsnet.co.uk
website: www.thamesview-golf.fsnet.co.uk

LONDON. **Trent Park Public Golf Course,** Bramley Road, Southgate, London N14 (020 8367 4653). *Location:* opposite Oakwood Tube Station. Undulating parkland. 18 holes, 6176 yards. S.S.S. 69. Modern heated, floodlit 36 bay driving range. *Green Fees:* information not available. *Eating facilities:* restaurant and snacks. *Visitors:* open to public at all times. Bookings advised on weekdays and necessary at weekends. Golf superstore. *Society Meetings:* welcome any day. Professional: Ray Stocker. Secretary: Richard Flint. *

NORTHWOOD. **Northwood Golf Club Ltd,** Rickmansworth Road, Northwood, Middlesex HA6 2QW (01923 821384; 01923 840150). *Location:* on A404 between Pinner and Rickmansworth. Parkland/ wooded course. 18 holes, 6535 yards. S.S.S. 71. *Green Fees:* weekdays £35.00 per round; £45.00 per day. *Eating facilities:* restaurant and bar snacks, lounge bar. *Visitors:* welcome weekdays, except Tuesdays; with members only at weekends. *Society Meetings:* by arrangement, details from the Secretary. Professional: C.J. Holdsworth (01923 820112). Secretary: T. N. Collingwood (01923 821384).

NORTHWOOD. **Sandy Lodge Golf Club**, Sandy Lodge Lane, Northwood, Middlesex HA6 2JD. *Location:* adjacent to Moor Park Underground Station. Sandy Lodge Golf Club is a member of the Hertfordshire Golf Union and situated on the Moor Park Estate close to Moor Park, Batchworth Park. Chorleywood and Rickmansworth. Inland links. 18 holes, 6328 yards. S.S.S. 71 (white). *Green Fees:* on application. *Eating facilities:* full catering and bar service available. *Visitors:* weekdays only, please telephone in advance. Handicap Certificate required. *Society Meetings:* by prior written arrangement. Professional: Jeff Pinsent (01923 825321). Secretary: John C. Coombes (01923 825429; Fax: 01923 824319).*

PINNER. **Grim's Dyke Golf Club**, Oxhey Lane, Hatch End, Pinner, Middlesex HA5 4AL (020 8421 1286). *Location:* on A4008 Watford to Harrow (2 miles west of Harrow). Undulating parkland, tree lined, testing greens. 18 holes, 5600 yards. S.S.S. 67. Practice area. *Green Fees:* weekdays £30.00 per round, £35.00 per day; weekends only with a member. *Eating facilities:* bar snacks, lunches available on request. *Visitors:* must produce Certificate of Handicap. Buggies available. *Society Meetings:* catered for Mondays to Fridays. Professional: Nathan Stephens (020 8428 7484). Secretary: Bob Millard (020 8428 4539; Fax: 020 8421 5494).

PINNER. **Pinner Hill Golf Club,** Southview Road, Pinner Hill HA5 3YA (020 8866 0963; Fax: 020 8868 4817). *Location:* one mile west Pinner Green. Parkland course with magnificent views over

London. 18 holes, 6392 yards. S.S.S. 71. *Green Fees:* £33.00 weekdays, £38.50 weekends by prior arrangement. *Eating facilities:* bar and catering available at all times; parties by prior arrangement please. *Visitors:* welcome with Handicap Certificate. *Society Meetings:* weekdays. Professional: Mr Mark Grieve (020 8866 2109). General Manager: Ian Prentice (020 8866 0963).
e-mail: pinnerhillgc@uk2.net
website: www.pinnerhillgc.co.uk

ROEHAMPTON. **Roehampton Club Ltd,** Roehampton Lane, London SW15 5LR (020 8480 4200; Fax: 020 8480 4265). *Location:* just off South Circular Road between Sheen and Putney. Parkland. 18 holes, 6065 yards. S.S.S. 69. *Green Fees:* weekdays £24.00; weekends £32.00. *Eating facilities:* restaurant, bistro. *Visitors:* welcome as members' guest only, Handicap Certificate required at weekends. *Society Meetings:* catered for by arrangement. Professional: Alan L. Scott (020 8876 3858). Chief Executive: Mark Wilson (020 8480 4205). Games Manager: James Tucker (020 8480 4200).

RUISLIP. **Ruislip Golf Club,** King's End, Ickenham Road, Ruislip, Middlesex HA4 7OQ (01895 638081). *Location:* two and a half miles from Junction 1, M40, first left after M40/A40 merge, onto B467, then left at T-Junction onto B466. Parkland course. 18 holes, 5571 yards. S.S.S. 67. Driving range (40 bays). *Green Fees:* information not available. *Eating facilities:* full restaurant facilities. *Visitors:* welcome, booking system at all times. *Society Meetings:* welcome by arrangement. Professional: Paul Glozier (01895 638835). Secretary: P.C. Thornton (01895 638081).

SHEPPERTON. **Sunbury Golf Club,** Charlton Lane, Shepperton TW17 8QA (01932 772898). *Location:* two miles south-west of M3 Junction 1; south-east of Queen Mary Reservoir between villages of Charlton and Upper Halliford. Two parkland courses. 18 holes, 5103 yards. S.S.S. 65, Par 68. 9 holes, 2444 yards, Par 33. 32 bay floodlit driving range (8am to 10pm), practice puttting green. *Green Fees:* information not available. *Eating facilities:* snacks, meals and bar. *Visitors:* welcome, no restrictions. Booking up to one week in advance essential. Buggies and trolleys for hire. *Society Meetings:* welcome at all times; advance booking required; special packages available. Professional: Alistair Hardaway (01932 772898). General Manager: Richard Pilbury (01932 771414; Fax: 01932 789300).*

SHOOTERS HILL. **Shooters Hill Golf Club Ltd,** "Lowood", Eaglesfield Road, Shooters Hill, London SE18 3DA (020 8854 6368; Fax: 020 8854 0469). *Location:* off A207 between Blackheath and Welling. Hilly wooded course with fine views. 18 holes, 5721 yards. S.S.S. 68. *Green Fees:* weekdays £22.00 per round, £27.00 per day; weekends with a member only, £15.00 per round or day. *Eating facilities:* bar and diningroom; jacket and tie required. *Visitors:* members of other clubs welcome weekdays on production of letter of introduction, or official Handicap Certificate. Buggies available. *Society Meetings:* catered for Tuesdays and Thursdays only. Professional: David Brotherton (020 8854 0073). Secretary: Martin Bond (020 8854 6368).

SOUTHALL. **West Middlesex Golf Club,** Greenford Road, Southall, Middlesex UB1 3EE (020 8574 3450). *Location:* junction of Uxbridge Road (A4020) and Greenford Road. 18 holes, 6119 yards. S.S.S. 69. *Green Fees:* please telephone the Pro Shop on 020 8574 1800. *Visitors:* welcome weekdays and at weekends after 3.00pm, except on competition days. *Society Meetings:* catered for by prior arrangement. Professional: T. Talbot. Secretary: E. Marper (020 8574 3450; Fax: 020 8574 2383).

SOUTHWARK. **Aquarius Golf Club**, Beachcroft Reservoir, Marmora Road, Honor Oak SE22 0RY (020 8693 1626). *Location:* nearest main road - Forest Hill Road. The course is situated on and around a reservoir, testing first and eighth holes. 9 holes, 5246 yards. S.S.S. 66. *Green Fees:* information not available. *Eating facilities:* limited. *Visitors:* welcome with member only. Professional: F. Private. Secretary: Jim Halliday.
e-mail: aquariusgolfclub@btopenworld.com

STANMORE. **Brockley Hill Golf Park,** Brockley Hill, Stanmore HA7 4LR (020 8420 6222; Fax: 020 8420 6333). *Location:* Junction 4 M1, A41. Parkland course. 9 holes, 1102 yards, 1007 metres. S.S.S. 27. Covered and floodlit 2 tier driving range. *Green Fees:* information and prices please telephone for details. *Eating facilities:* "Inspiration" catering hot and cold food available all day. *Visitors:* welcome anytime - pay as you play. *Society Meetings:* welcome on application. Professionals: James Reynolds (Head), Pat Winston.*

STANMORE. **Stanmore Golf Club,** 29 Gordon Avenue, Stanmore, Middlesex HA7 2RL (Tel & Fax: 020 8954 2599). *Location:* turn off A410 by church to Old Church Lane, Gordon Avenue is to the right. Wooded, parkland course. 18 holes, 5879 yards. S.S.S. 68. Practice and putting areas. *Green Fees:* from £15.00. *Eating facilities:* restaurant facilities available *Visitors:* welcome. No jeans or trainers. Jacket and tie after 7pm. *Society Meetings:* catered for Wednesday and Thursday by prior booking only. Professional: James Reynolds. Secretary: Maria Bateman. Caterer: (020 8954 4661).
e-mail: secretary@stanmoregolfclub.co.uk
website: www.stanmoregolfclub.co.uk

SUNBURY ON THAMES. **Hazelwood Golf Club**, Croysdale Avenue, Sunbury on Thames TW16 6QU (01932 770932; Fax: 01932 770933). *Location:* Junction 1 of M3. Parkland course. 9 holes, 2785 yards. Practice putting green, 36 bay driving range, bunker and chipping practice. *Green Fees:* information not available. *Eating facilities:* Bunkers Cafe/Bar. *Visitors:* welcome every day. *Society Meetings:* welcome. Professional: FrancisSheridan.*

TOTTERIDGE. **South Herts Golf Club,** Links Drive, Totteridge N20 8QU (020 8445 0117). *Location:* off Totteridge Lane N20, one mile from Whetstone, nearest underground station Totteridge & Whetstone. Parkland. 18 holes, 6432 yards. S.S.S. 71. *Green Fees:* on request. *Eating facilities:* lunch, high tea

(breakfast and dinner by arrangement). *Visitors:* welcome with reservation Mon to Fri and Sun pm. *Society & Corporate Meetings:* welcome Monday to Friday. Professional: R.V. Mitchell (020 8445 4633). Secretary: (020 8445 2035; Fax: 020 8445 7569). website: www.southhertsgolfclub.co.uk

TWICKENHAM. **Strawberry Hill Golf Club,** Wellesley Road, Strawberry Hill, Twickenham TW2 5SD (020 8894 0165). *Location:* A316; 200 yards Strawberry Hill Station. Flat parkland. 9 holes, 4762 yards. S.S.S. 63. *Green Fees:* £20.00; with a member £10.00. *Eating facilities:* restaurant and bar. *Visitors:* welcome, restrictions weekends and competition days. *Society Meetings:* welcome weekdays, small parties only. Professional: Peter Buchan (020 8898 2082). Secretary: Paul Astbury (020 8894 0165; Fax: 020 8898 0786).

TWICKENHAM. **Twickenham Park Golf Centre,** Staines Road, Twickenham TW2 5JD (020 8783 1698; Fax: 020 8941 9134). *Location:* at end of M3, on A305 near its junction with A312 and A316. Interesting tree-lined parkland course with water feature. 9 holes, 3109 yards. S.S.S 35. 27 bay floodlit driving range. *Green Fees:* information not available. *Eating facilities:* Pavilion Bar and cafe. *Visitors:* play and pay. Function room available. *Society Meetings:* welcome. Professional: Suzy Watt (020 8783 1698; Fax: 020 8941 9134). Secretary: Norman Harnett (020 8783 1748).*

UPMINSTER. **Upminster Golf Club**, 114 Hall Lane, Upminster RM14 1AU (01708 222788). *Location:* one mile (north) Upminster Station, one and a half miles west M25/A127 junction. Parkland/wooded – River Ingrebourne runs through the course. Beautiful Grade II Listed Clubhouse, rebuilt in 1654, with an official ghost – listed in the British Book of Ghosts. 18 holes, 6076 yards. S.S.S. 69. *Green Fees:* information on request. *Eating facilities:* full catering service every day. *Visitors*: welcome weekdays by arrangement except Tuesday mornings. *Society Meetings:* catered for Wednesdays, Thursdays and Fridays (max 40). Professional: Steven Cipa (01708 220000). Secretary: Geoff Scott (Tel & Fax: 01708 222788).

UXBRIDGE. **Stockley Park Golf Club**, Stockley Park, Uxbridge UB11 1AQ (020 8813 5700; Fax: 020 8813 5655). *Location:* Junction 4 M4, Heathrow Airport turnoff, A408 to Uxbridge. Parkland course, designed by Robert Trent Jones Snr. 18 holes, 6754 yards. S.S.S. 71. Practice nets, chipping and putting greens. *Green Fees:* on application. *Eating facilities:* balcony restaurant and bar. *Visitors:* all welcome. Trolleys available. *Society Meetings:* welcome. Professional: Alex Knox. Adminstration: Lucy Newell.*

UXBRIDGE. **Uxbridge Golf Course**, The drive, Harefield Place, Uxbridge UB10 8AQ (01895 237287; Fax: 01895 810262). *Location*: off Swalkelys Junction - M40. Undulating parkland. 18 holes, 5753 yards. S.S.S. 68. *Green Fees*: information not available.

Eating facilities: bars, carvery restaurant. *Visitors*: welcome anytime, booking required at weekends. Function suite. *Society Meetings*: welcome. Professional: Phil Howard (01895 237287). Secretary: Tom Atkins (01895 272457).*

WANDSWORTH. **Central London Golf Centre,** Burntwood Lane, Wandsworth SW17 0AT (020 8871 2468; Fax: 020 8874 7447). *Location:* turn right through the Wandsworth town centre into Garrat Lane, Burntwood Lane is off Garrat Lane. Short course with three good Par 3s and several good Par 4s. 9 holes, 2223 yards. S.S.S. 31. Large practice putting green. 14 bay driving range. *Green Fees:* weekdays £10.00 for 9 holes, £18.00 for 18 holes; weekends £12.50 for 9 holes, £23.00 for 18 holes. £1.00 reduction for Senior Citizens and Juniors. *Eating facilities:* full bar and restaurant; function room. *Visitors:* welcome, no restrictions. Special disabled putting green. Trolleys for hire. *Society Meetings:* welcome, special terms on request. Professional: Jeremy Robson (020 8871 2468). e-mail: golf@clgc.co.uk
website: www.clgc.co.uk

WANSTEAD. **Wanstead Golf Club,** Overton Drive, Wanstead E11 2LW (020 8989 3938; Fax: 020 8532 9138). *Location:* one mile from junction of A12 and A406. Parkland bordering Epping Forest with featured lake. 18 holes, 6109 yards. S.S.S. 69. *Green Fees:* £30.00 per day weekdays; weekends as member's guest only. *Eating facilities:* dining room and bars. *Visitors:* welcome Mondays, Tuesdays and Fridays by prior arrangement with the Secretary. Handicap Certificate required. Weekends with member only. *Society Meetings:* welcome, apply Secretary. Professional: David Hawkins (020 8989 9876). Secretary: Keith Jones (020 8989 3938; Fax: 020 8532 9138).

WEMBLEY. **Sudbury Golf Club Ltd,** Bridgewater Road, Wembley, Middlesex HA0 1AL (020 8902 3713). *Location:* junction of A4005 (Bridgewater Road) and A4090 (Whitton Ave East). Undulating parkland. 18 holes, 6282 yards. S.S.S. 70. *Green Fees:* information on request. *Eating facilities:* dining room and bars. *Visitors:* welcome weekdays with Handicap Certificate. *Society Meetings:* catered for. Professional: Neil Jordan (020 8902 7910). General Manager: Neil Cropley.

WEST DRAYTON. **Heathpark Golf Club**, Stockley Road, West Drayton, Middlesex UB7 9NA (01895 444232; Fax: 01895 444323). *Location:* in grounds of Crown Plaza Hotel, Junction 4 M40. Undulating parkland course. 9 holes, 3856 yards. S.S.S. 64. *Green Fees:* call for information. *Eating facilities:* catering and bars. *Visitors:* welcome, dress code. *Society Meetings:* welcome at all times. Contact: B. Sharma.*

WIMBLEDON. **Royal Wimbledon Golf Club,** 29 Camp Road, Wimbledon SW19 4UW. *Location:* one mile west of War Memorial in Wimbledon Village. 18 holes, 6348 yards. S.S.S. 70. *Visitors:* Weekdays by prior arrangement. *Society Meetings:* Wednesdays

and Thursdays only, by arrangement. Professional: David Jones (020 8946 4606). Secretary: Norman Smith (020 8946 2125; Fax: 020 8944 8652).

WIMBLEDON. **Wimbledon Common Golf Club,** 19 Camp Road, Wimbledon Common, Wimbledon SW19 4UW (020 8946 0294; Fax: 020 8947 8697). *Location:* Wimbledon Common. Wooded course. 18 holes, 5438 yards. S.S.S. 66. *Green Fees:* Monday £10.00, Tuesday to Friday £13.00. Four or more £13.00. *Eating facilities:* bar, full catering every day except Mondays. *Visitors:* welcome weekdays, only with a member at weekends. Dress code – pillar box red upper garment must be worn. *Society Meetings:* welcome, groups of up to 50 catered for. Professional: J.S. Jukes (020 8946 0294; Fax: 020 8947 8697). Secretary: Ray Pierce (020 8946 7571).

WIMBLEDON. **Wimbledon Park Golf Club,** Home Park Road, Wimbledon, London SW19 7HR (020 8946 1002; Fax: 020 8944 8688). *Location:* Church Road, Arthur Road and Home Park Road from Wimbledon High Street, or by District Line to Wimbledon Park Station where signposted. Parkland, wooded around a lake. 18 holes, 5492 yards. S.S.S. 66. *Green Fees:* £50.00. *Eating facilities:* dining room and bar snacks each day. *Visitors:* welcome on production of letter of introduction or Handicap Certificate. *Society Meetings:* welcome. Special rate 36 holes, morning coffee, Ploughmans, three-course meal £65.00; Winter Package – bacon roll, 18 holes, three-course meal £35.00. Professional: Dean Wingrove (020 8946 4053). Secretary: Eileen Inwood (020 8946 1250; 020 8944 8688).
e-mail: secretary@wpgc.co.uk
website: www.wpgc.co.uk

WINCHMORE HILL. **Bush Hill Park Golf Club,** Bush Hill, Winchmore Hill, London N21 2BU (020 8360 5738; Fax: 020 8360 5583). *Location:* half a mile south of Enfield town (off London Road). Parkland. 18 holes, 5825 yards. S.S.S. 68. Practice ground and nets. *Green Fees:* weekdays £28.50 per round, weekends only with member. *Eating facilities:* restaurant, bar, bar snacks. *Visitors:* welcome weekdays except Wednesday mornings, Handicap Certificate required. *Society Meetings:* catered for Tuesdays, Thursdays and Fridays. Professional: Adrian Andrews (020 8360 4103). Secretary: Rachael Meade (020 8360 5738; Fax: 020 8360 5583).

WOOD GREEN. **Muswell Hill Golf Club**, Rhodes Avenue, Wood Green, London N22 7UT (020 8888 2044; Fax: 020 8889 9380). *Location:* North Circular/Bounds Green tube station one mile. Mature parkland. 18 holes, 6438 yards. S.S.S. 71. Practice ground. *Green Fees:* weekdays £32.00 per round, £45.00 per day; weekends £35.00 by prior arrangement. Bookings through Secretary and Professional. *Eating facilities:* restaurant open seven days. *Visitors:* welcome weekdays, weekends pre-booked with Professional. *Society Meetings:* welcome weekdays; terms on request. Professional: D. Wilton (020 8888 8046). Secretary: Mrs J. Underhill (020 8888 1764).

Bedfordshire

AMPTHILL. **The Millbrook Golf Club,** Millbrook, Ampthill MK45 2JB (01525 840252; Fax: 01525 406249). *Location:* just off A507 Ampthill to Woburn Road, near Junction 13 of M1. Rolling links situated on the Greensand Ridge overlooking Bedfordshire. 18 holes, 7021 yards. S.S.S. 73. Two practice areas. *Green Fees:* weekdays £22.00 18 holes; weekends only after 12 noon £28.00. *Eating facilities:* bar/restaurant, breakfasts, lunches, dinners. *Visitors:* welcome midweek. *Society Meetings:* by invitation only. Professional & Tee Time bookings: Geraint W. Dixon (01525 402269). Manager: Derek Cooke (01525 840252; Fax: 01525 406249).

ASPLEY GUISE. **Aspley Guise and Woburn Sands Golf Club,** West Hill, Aspley Guise MK17 8DX (01908 583596; Fax: 01908 583596). *Location:* two miles west of Junction 13 M1, between Aspley Guise and Woburn Sands. Undulating parkland, 18 holes, 6079 yards. S.S.S. 70. *Green Fees:* weekdays £28.00 per round, £38.00 per day; weekends by prior arrangement. *Eating facilities:* catering service, bar. *Visitors:* welcome weekdays with bona fide handicaps - check with Secretary. *Society Meetings:* Wednesdays and Fridays. Professional: Colin Clingan (01908 582974). Secretary: Richard Norris (01908 583596; Fax 01908 583596).

BEADLOW. **Beadlow Manor Hotel, Golf and Country Club,** Beadlow, Near Shefford SG17 5PH (01525 861292). *Location:* from M1 (J12) take A5120 east to Ampthill, then A507 to Shefford. From A1 (J10) take A507 west to Ampthill. Challenging, rolling parkland with water hazards. Two courses (Baron and Baroness): 18 holes, 6819 yards. S.S.S. 72; 18 holes, 6072 yards. S.S.S 69. Covered 25 bay floodlit driving range, practice area. *Green Fees:* information not available. *Eating facilities:* restaurant, three bars, snacks, refreshments, two function rooms. *Visitors:* welcome at all times. Residential Golf Breaks available. Professional academy and shop. Special mid-week and weekend Breaks for Society and Company Groups. All reservations through Sales and Marketing Office. Golf Manager: Geoff Swain. *

BEDFORD. **Bedford and County Golf Club,** Green Lane, Clapham, Bedford MK41 6ET (01234 354010). *Location:* off A6 north of Bedford before Clapham Village. Parkland. 18 holes, 6420 yards. S.S.S. 70. *Green Fees:* information not available. *Eating facilities:* full catering facilities and bar. *Visitors:* welcome without reservation except weekends. *Society Meetings:* catered for Mondays, Tuesdays, Thursdays and Fridays. Professional: Mr R Tattersall (01234 359189). Manager: Mr R Walker (01234 352617; Fax: 01234 357195). website: www.bedfordandcountygolfclub.co.uk

BEDFORD. **Bedfordshire Golf Club,**Spring Lane, Stagsden, Bedford MK43 8SR (01234 822555; Fax: 01234 825052). *Location:* one mile west of Bedford town centre on the A422. Wooded parkland, flat. 18 holes, 6565 yards. S.S.S. 72. 9-hole course. 24-bay driving range. *Green Fees:* information not available. *Eating facilities:* bar and catering; evening meals by arrangement. *Visitors:* welcome on weekdays, must be with members at weekends. *Society Meetings:* catered for weekdays. Professional: Peter Saunders (01234 826100). Manager: D.E. Romans (01234 822555).*

BEDFORD. **Mowsbury Golf Club,** Cleat Hill, Kimbolton Road, Bedford MK41 8DQ (01234 771403). *Location:* on B660 at northern limit of city boundary. 18 holes, 6510 yards. S.S.S. 71. Driving range. *Green Fees:* on request. *Eating facilities:* meals and bar snacks until 2pm; evening meals if booked in advance. *Visitors:* welcome. Squash courts. *Society Meetings:* by arrangement with the Professional. Professional: Malcolm Summers (01234 216374), for tee reservations and fees. Secretary: B.E. Edwards (01234 771041).

BEDFORD. **Pavenham Park Golf Club,** Pavenham, Bedford MK43 7PE (01234 822202; Fax: 01234 826602). *Location:* take the A6 out of North Bedford, from Clapham follow signs to Pavenham. Parkland course with fast and contoured greens. 18 holes, 6400 yards. S.S.S. 71. Practice ground. *Green Fees:* information not available. *Eating facilities:* bars, snacks and course refreshments. *Visitors:* welcome midweek only, must adhere to dress code. Buggies and carts available. Part of the Kolven Golf Group. *Society Meetings:* welcome, excellent rates. Professional: Zac Thompson. Secretary: Mario Rizzi.* e-mail: kolvengolf@ukonline.co.uk website: www.kolvengolf.com

BEDFORD. **The Bedford Golf Club,** Great Denham Golf Village, Biddenham, Bedford MK40 4FF (01234 320022; Fax: 01234 320023). *Location:* two miles west of Bedford on A428. American-style course with 90 bunkers and eight water features, built on free-draining sandy soil. 18 holes, 6478 yards. S.S.S. 72. Practice area. *Green Fees:* weekdays £30.00, weekends £40.00. *Eating facilities:* restaurant and bar meals; course refreshments. *Visitors:* always welcome - excellent rates. Buggies for hire. Part of the Kolven Golf Group. *Society Meetings:* welcome. Manager: Simon Pepper. e-mail: thebedford@btopenworld.com website: www.kolvengolf.com

CADDINGTON. **Griffin Golf Club,** Chaul End Road, Caddington LU1 4AX (01582 415573 Fax: 01582 415314). *Location:* Ten minutes from Junctions 9 or 11 M1. Gently undulating parkland. 18 holes, 6240 yards. S.S.S.70. *Green Fees:* £14.00 Monday to Thursday, £17.00 Friday, £20.00 weekends (after 2pm). *Eating facilities:* bar with catering available. *Visitors:* welcome anytime midweek; weekends by arrangement. *Society Meetings:* welcome, special deals available. Manager: Dave Sweetnam. e-mail: griffin@griffingolfclub.fsbusiness.co.uk

COLMWORTH. **Colmworth and North Bedfordshire Golf Club,** New Road, Colmworth MK44 2NN (01234 378181; Fax: 01234 376678). *Location:* north of Bedford just off B660 and only 10 minutes from the A1 at Wyboston. Fast maturing, well drained course in its 10th year offering easy walking yet challenging golf all year round. 18 holes, 6459 yards. S.S.S. 71. 9-hole Par 3 course. 8 bay driving range. *Green Fees:* weekdays £13.00; weekends and Bank Holidays £20.00. *Eating facilities:* licensed clubhouse with bar. *Visitors:* no restrictions. Self-catering cottages offer base to play numerous courses in the area, play this well-maintained course, or for "learn to play golf or swim' holidays.

DUNSTABLE. **Dunstable Downs Golf Club,** Whipsnade Road, Dunstable LU6 2NB (01582 604472; Fax: 01582 478700). *Location:* on B4541; one and a half miles from town centre. Downland course with exceptional views. 18 holes, 5903 yards. S.S.S. 70. Practice ground. *Green Fees:* information not available. *Eating facilities:* bar and restaurant. *Visitors:* welcome weekdays, weekends with member only. Handicap Certificate required. Carts for hire. *Society Meetings:* Mondays, Tuesdays and Thursdays, limited availability on Fridays. Professional: Michael Weldon (01582 662806). Secretary/Manager: Brian Woodcock (01582 604472; Fax: 01582 478700).

DUNSTABLE. **Tilsworth Golf Centre,** Dunstable Road, Tilsworth, Leighton Buzzard LU7 9PU (01525 210721; Fax: 01525 210465). *Location:* two miles north of Dunstable off A5, Tilsworth turn-off. Parkland course, water hazards on three holes! 18 holes, 5306 yards. S.S.S. 67, Par 69. 30 bay floodlit driving range. *Green Fees:* weekdays £15.00 per round; weekends £17.50 per round. *Eating facilities:* bar snacks and restaurant available. *Visitors:* welcome any time except Sundays before 10am. Bookings taken up to seven days in advance. *Society Meetings:* welcome by prior arrangement. Professional: Nick Webb.

HENLOW. **Mount Pleasant Golf Course,** Station Road, Lower Stondon, Henlow SG16 6JL (01462 850999). *Location:* three-quarters of a mile west of A600 (Hitchin to Bedford) at Henlow Camp roundabout. Undulating meadowland. 9 holes (alternative tees for second 9 holes), 6003 yards, 5487 metres. S.S.S. 69. Practice chipping, putting and nets. *Green Fees:* weekdays £8.00 for 9 holes, £14.00 for 18 holes; weekends £10.50 for 9 holes, £18.00 for 18 holes. Reductions for Senior Citizens

and Juniors. *Eating facilities:* spike bar, dining room. Group catering by prior arrangement. *Visitors:* welcome anytime, booking required for weekends and summer evenings. *Society Meetings:* welcome Mondays to Thursdays. Professional: Mike Roberts. Proprietor: David Simkins. website: www.mountpleasantgolfclub.co.uk

LEIGHTON BUZZARD. **Aylesbury Vale Golf Club,** Stewkley Road, Wing, Leighton Buzzard LU7 0UJ (01525 240196). *Location:* four miles west of Leighton Buzzard on Stewkley to Wing road. Gently undulating course with water hazards. 18 holes, 6622 yards, S.S.S. 72. 9-bay driving range. Green Fees: weekdays £16.00; for weekends telephone 01525 240196. Weekend twilight tickets available. Senior Citizens £6.50 Tuesdays. *Eating facilities:* first floor bar and balcony, ground floor bar and restaurant. *Visitors:* welcome any time, no restrictions apart from correct dress. Telephone in advance. Individual lessons from £15.00. *Society Meetings:* welcome, competitive rates, Monday to Friday only. Professional: James Pugh (07771 752143). Secretary: Chris Wright (01525 240196).

LEIGHTON BUZZARD. **Leighton Buzzard Golf Club,** Plantation Road, Leighton Buzzard LU7 7JF (01525 244800). *Location:* off A5 between Dunstable and Milton Keynes at village of Heath and Reach. Wooded parkland course. 18 holes, 6101 yards. S.S.S. 70. Practice ground. *Green Fees:* weekdays £34.00 per round, £36.00 per day; weekends with member only, £16.00. *Eating facilities:* available - dining room and three bars. *Visitors:* welcome weekdays with Handicap Certificate only. (Tuesday Ladies' Day). Weekends and Bank Holidays with member only. *Society Meetings:* catered for weekdays only, except Tuesdays. Professional: M. Campbell (01525 244815). Secretary: D. Mutton (01525 244800; Fax: 01525 244801).

LEIGHTON BUZZARD near. **Ivinghoe Golf Club,** Wellcroft, Ivinghoe, Near Leighton Buzzard LU7 9EF (01296 668696; Fax: 01296 662755). *Location:* leave A41 at Tring and take B488 to Ivinghoe. When approaching the village, the church is on the left, and Vicarage Lane is on the right. Go down the lane to the Rose & Crown pub and turn right up to the club. Gently rolling parkland course in lee of Ivinghoe Beacon. 9 holes, 4508 yards. S.S.S. 62. Pro shop, tuition available. *Green Fees:* weekdays: 9 holes £6.00, 18 holes £9.00; weekends: 18 holes £9.00 (9 holes £6.00 after 12 noon). *Eating facilities:* bar meals anytime. *Visitors:* welcome except before 8am weekends; dress code in operation. *Society Meetings:* catered for. Professional: Bill Garrad (01296 668696). Secretary: Mrs S.E. Garrad (01296 668696). Steward: Mr R. Barden (01296 661186).

THE APPEARANCE OF AN ASTERISK (*) AT THE END OF A CLUB OR COURSE ENTRY INDICATES THAT UP-TO-DATE INFORMATION HAS NOT BEEN SUPPLIED

LEIGHTON BUZZARD near. **Mentmore Golf and Country Club,** Mentmore, Near Leighton Buzzard LU7 0UA (01296 662020; Fax: 01296 662592). *Location:* between Leighton Buzzard and Aylesbury in village of Mentmore. Rolling parkland, mature trees and with many water features. Two courses - Rothschild and Rosebery. 36 holes, 6777 and 6763 yards. S.S.S. 72. Driving range. *Green Fees:* information not available. *Eating facilities:* restaurant, two bars, spike bar; function room. *Visitors:* welcome. Also available swimming pool, sauna, jacuzzi and steam room, two tennis courts, full gymnasium and aerobics studio. *Society Meetings:* welcome everyday, please telephone for details. General Manager: Kevin Whitehouse. Sales Manager: Matthew Darley. Professional: Robert Davies. *

LUTON. **South Beds Golf Club,** Warden Hill Road, Luton LU2 7AE (01582 591500). *Location:* on east side A6, two and a half miles north of Luton. Undulating downland course. 18 holes, 6438 yards. S.S.S. 71. Also 9 holes, 4914 yards. S.S.S. 64. Practice fairway and chipping area. *Green Fees:* weekdays 9 hole course £12.00, 18 hole course £23.00; weekends 9 hole course £14.00, 18 hole course £32.00. *Eating facilities:* three-course meals (must be booked), snacks at all times. *Visitors:* welcome anytime on 9-hole course, weekdays and limited weekends on 18-hole course. Handicap Certificate essential for 18-hole course. Tuesday is Ladies' Day. *Society Meetings:* catered for by arrangement on Mondays, Wednesdays and Thursdays. Professional: Eddie Cogle (01582 591209). Secretary: Ray Wright (01582 591500; Fax: 01582 495381).

LUTON. **Stockwood Park Golf Club,** London Road, Luton LU1 4LX (01582 431788). *Location:* adjacent Exit 10 of M1 exit Luton Airport. Parkland. 18 holes, 6049 yards. S.S.S. 69. Driving range, mini golf course and pitch and putt. *Green Fees:* information not available. *Eating facilities:* two bars and restaurant. *Visitors:* always welcome, municipal club. *Society Meetings:* catered for Mondays, Tuesdays and Thursdays by prior arrangement. Professional: G. McCarthy (01582 413704). Secretary: Mrs R. McMillan (01582 431788).

SANDY. **John O'Gaunt Golf Club,** Sutton Park, Sandy SG19 2LY (01767 260252; Fax: 01767 262834). *Location:* on B1040 off A1 two miles north of Biggleswade. Parkland courses. Two 18 hole courses: John O'Gaunt Course 6513 yards S.S.S. 71 and Carthagena Course 5869 yards S.S.S. 69. Small practice area. *Green Fees:* £50.00 weekdays, £60.00 weekends (2003). *Eating facilities:* restaurant and bar. *Visitors:* welcome weekdays, Handicap Certificate required. *Society Meetings:* welcome weekdays. Professional: L. Scarbrow (01767 260094). Secretary: S. Anthony (01767 260360).

SHARNBROOK. **Colworth Golf Club,** Unilever Research, Sharnbrook MK44 1LQ (01933 353269). *Location:* off A6 between Bedford and Rushden through Sharnbrook village. Parkland course, narrow fairways, tree lined. 9 holes, 5210 yards. S.S.S. 66. *Green Fees:* information not available. *Eating facilities:* none. *Visitors:* with members only. Secretary: E.W. Thompson (01933 353269).

TODDINGTON. **Chalgrave Manor Golf Club,** Dunstable Road, Toddington, Near Dunstable LU5 6JN (Tel & Fax: 01525 876556). *Location:* two minutes from Junction 12 M1 (Toddington Services), on main A5120 between Toddington and Houghton Regis. Rolling, open course with many natural undulations; four holes with water features. 18 holes, 6417 yards, 5892 metres. S.S.S. 71. Practice areas. *Green Fees:* weekdays £20.00 per round, weekends and Bank Holidays £30.00 per round. Day tickets available. *Eating facilities:* meals available Tuesday to Sundays inclusive, licensed bar. *Visitors:* booking not required. No starting times before 11am weekends and Bank Holidays, no restrictions midweek. *Society Meetings:* welcome weekdays by prior arrangement. Secretary: Steve Rumball (01525 876554).

WYBOSTON. **Wyboston Lakes Golf Course,** Great North Road, Wyboston Lakes, Wyboston MK44 3AL (01480 223004). *Location:* one mile south of St Neots at the junction of the A1 and the A428 east. Flat parkland with five lakes. 18 holes, 5955 yards. S.S.S. 69. Driving range. Putting green. *Green Fees:* weekdays £13.50 per 18 holes; weekends £16.50 per 18 holes. Juniors £6.50 weekdays and £8.50 weekends. Subject to review. *Eating facilities:* available. *Visitors:* welcome, bookings required for weekends and Bank Holidays. Motel on site. *Society Meetings:* catered for seven days. Professional: P.G. Ashwell (01480 223004; Fax: 01480 407330). Secretary: D. Little(01480 223004). Society Secretary: Simon Smith (01480 212625; Fax: 01480 223000).

Berkshire

ASCOT. **The Berkshire Golf Club**, Swinley Road, Ascot SL5 8AY (01344 621495). *Location*: on A332 between Bagshot and Ascot. Heathland (wooded) course. 36 holes. Blue Course: 6260 yards, S.S.S. 71, Par 71. Red Course: 6369 yards, S.S.S. 71, Par 72. Practice facilities. *Green Fees*: information not available. *Eating facilities*: dining room open daily except Monday, snack bar open daily; bar open every day. *Visitors*: welcome weekdays only by application to the Secretary. *Society Meetings*: catered for by prior bookings. Professional: P. Anderson (01344 622351). Secretary: Lt. Col. J.C.F. Hunt (01344 621496).

ASCOT. **Lavender Park Golf Centre**, Swinley Road, Ascot SL5 8BD (01344 893344). *Location*: Ascot to Bracknell Road, half a mile from racecourse. Very pleasant flat 9 hole, Executive course, 8 Par 3's and one Par 4. 9 holes, 1104 yards. S.S.S. 28. 23-bay driving range. *Green Fees*: information not available. *Eating facilities*: bar snacks. *Visitors*: welcome at all times; pay and play. 8 table snooker hall. *Society Meetings*: welcome. Director of Golf/Senior Professional: David Johnson (01344 893344). *

ASCOT. **Mill Ride Golf Club**, Mill Ride Estate, Ascot SL5 8LT (01344 891494; Fax: 01344 886820). *Location*: off Junction 3 of M3 or Junction 6 of M4, one mile west Ascot Racecourse. Parkland, links course, seven lakes in play on 11 holes; designed by Donald Steel. 18 holes, 6807 yards. S.S.S. 72. Driving range. *Green Fees*: on application. *Eating facilities*: bar food. *Visitors*: welcome on application. Accommodation available in four overnight rooms and luxury apartments. *Society Meetings*: individual and corporate membership available; contact Archie Gillies. Professional: Terry Wild (01344 886777; Fax: 01344 886820). Manager: Gordon Irvine (01344 891494; Fax: 01344 886820).
e-mail: golf@mill-ride.com
website: www.mill-ride.com

ASCOT. **Royal Ascot Golf Club**, Winkfield Road, Ascot SL5 7LJ (01344 622923; Fax: 01344 872330). *Location*: Winkfield Road is off Ascot High Street (A329). Heathland. 18 holes, 5716 yards. S.S.S. 68. *Green Fees*: weekdays £15.00 as member's guest; weekends £18.50 as member's guest. *Eating facilities*: full catering available. *Visitors*: welcome only as guests of members. *Society Meetings*: catered for Wednesdays and Thursdays, maximum 40. Professional: Alistair White (01344 624656). Secretary: Mrs Sheila Thompson (01344 625175).
e-mail: golf@royalascotgc.fsnet.co.uk

ASCOT. **Swinley Forest Golf Club**, Coronation Road, Ascot SL5 9LE (01344 620197). *Location*: between Ascot and Bagshot. Wooded heathland course. 18 holes, 6001 yards. S.S.S. 69. *Green Fees*: information not available. *Eating facilities*: lunches served. *Visitors*: welcome only with a member. *Society Meetings*: catered for. Professional: Stuart Hill (01344 874811). Secretary: I.L. Pearce (01344 874979; Fax: 01344 874733). *

BINFIELD. **Blue Mountain Golf Centre**, Wood Lane, Binfield, Bracknell RG42 4EX (01344 300220; Fax: 01344 360960). *Location*: two miles from M4 near Bracknell/Wokingham. Parkland course with numerous lakes. 18 holes, 6097 yards. S.S.S 70. 33 bay covered floodlit range. *Green Fees*: information not available. *Eating facilities*: fully licensed restaurant/bar New Blues Bar with live jazz and food. *Visitors*: welcome any time. *Society Meetings*: always welcome, please call for details. Professional: Jez Henry (01344 300220).

BURNHAM. **Huntswood Golf Club**, Taplow Common Road, Burnham SL1 8LS (01628 667144). *Location*: Junction 7 of M4, at roundabout turn left onto A4, then at Sainsburys roundabout turn right. Go straight over next two roundabouts, Huntswood Golf Club is quarter of a mile on the left. Only 18 hole Pay & Play course in Burnham. 18 holes, Par 68. *Green Fees*: information not available. *Eating facilities*: bar and dining facilities after 7am. Professional: Neil Pagett.

CROWTHORNE. **East Berkshire Golf Club**, Ravenswood Avenue, Crowthorne RG45 6BD (01344 772041; Fax: 01344 777378). *Location*: M3 Junction 3 - Bracknell turn off, follow signs to Crowthorne, Ravenswood Avenue opposite Railway Station. Heathland course. 18 holes, 6344 yards. S.S.S. 70. *Green Fees*: information not available. *Eating facilities*: bar snacks. *Visitors*: welcome weekdays by prior notification. *Society Meetings*: Thursdays and Fridays only. Professional: Jason Brant (01344 774112). Secretary: David Kelly (01344 772041; Fax: 01344 777378).

MAIDENHEAD. **Maidenhead Golf Club,** Shoppenhangers Road, Maidenhead SL6 2PZ (Tel & Fax: 01628 624693). *Location:* adjacent to Maidenhead Station (south side), one mile from M4. Flat parkland course. 18 holes, 6364 yards. S.S.S. 70. *Green Fees:* weekdays £35.00. *Eating facilities:* restaurant and bar meals Monday to Friday. *Visitors:* welcome weekdays, no visitors after 12 noon Fridays. Handicap Certificate required. *Society Meetings:* welcome, main days Wednesdays and Thursdays. Professional: Steve Geary (01628 624067). Secretary: T.P. Jackson (Tel & Fax: 01628 624693). e-mail: manager@maidenheadgolf.co.uk website: www.maidenheadgolf.co.uk

MAIDENHEAD. **Temple Golf Club,** Henley Road, Hurley, Near Maidenhead SL6 5LH (01628 824248; Fax: 01628 828119). *Location:* exit M4 Junction 8/9 or M40 at Junction 4. From M4 or M40 take A404 then A4130 signposted Henley. Chalk Downland course - exceptional drainage. 18 holes, 6266 yards. S.S.S. 70. Excellent practice area, putting and chipping green. *Green Fees:* information not available. *Eating facilities:* bar and restaurant seven days a week. *Visitors:* welcome by prior arrangement. Handicap Certificate required. *Society Meetings:* welcome weekdays by prior arrangement; booking accepted one year in advance; minimum number 20, maximum 40. Professional: James Whiteley (01628 824254; Fax: 01628 828119). Secretary: Keith G.M. Adderley (01628 824795; Fax: 01628 828119).

MAIDENHEAD. **Winter Hill Golf Club,** Grange Lane, Cookham SL6 9RP (01628 527613). *Location:* M4 Junction 8/9, four miles from Maidenhead. Parkland with extensive views of the Thames. 18 holes, 6408 yards - white tees, 6228 yards - yellow tees. S.S.S. 71. Large practice area. *Green Fees:* £31.00 per day weekdays; £21.50 from 2pm BST Monday to Friday. £18.50 from 12pm GMT Monday to Friday. *Eating facilities:* lunches and snacks available every day. *Visitors:* welcome weekdays; preliminary enquiries advisable, and with member at weekends. *Society Meetings:* may be accepted by application to the Secretary; minimum number 16, maximum 40. Dress rules: strictly no jeans, trainers on course or in clubhouse. PGA Club and Teaching Professional: Mr Roger Frost (01628 527610). Secretary: Mr Mick Goodenough (01628 527613).

MAIDENHEAD. near. **Bird Hills (UK) Ltd.,** Drift Road, Hawthorn Hill, Near Maidenhead SL6 3ST (01628 771030; Fax: 01628 31023). *Location:* M4 Junction 8/9, take A308 then A330 to Bracknell. Flat parkland course. 18 holes, 6176 yards. S.S.S. 69. 36 bay driving range. *Green Fees:* information not available. Juniors/Senior Citizens concessionary rates. *Eating facilities:* club bar, restaurant, members bar, barbecue, private function hall. *Visitors:* always welcome, open every day except Christmas Day. Large Pro shop, Conference facilities. *Society Meetings:* always welcome. Professional: Mr Nick Slimming. Secretary: Mrs Eve Lane. *

NEWBURY. **Deanwood Park Golf Club,** Stockcross, Newbury RG20 8JS (Tel & Fax: 01635 48772). *Location:* 200 yards off the A4 west of Newbury towards Stockcross village. Two miles from Newbury town centre. Undulating parkland/wooded course. 9 holes, 2114 yards, 1932 metres. S.S.S. 60 (18 holes). 7 bay driving range, practice net, practice bunker and putting green. *Green Fees:* weekdays £8.50 9 holes, £14.50 18 holes; weekends £10.50 9 holes, £17.50 18 holes. Discounts for fourballs. Earlybird and Senior Citizen rates £6.00 9 holes. *Eating facilities:* Lounge/bar/restaurant facilities; food served all day. *Visitors:* welcome at all times but must book in advance. Standard golf dress code applies, no jeans allowed on the course. Trolley/club hire available. *Society Meetings:* Society/Company groups welcome at all times - mix and match price structuring for golf and catering. Professional: James Purton. Secretary: John Bowness (Tel & Fax: 01635 48772). e-mail: deanwood@newburyweb.net website: www.newbury.net//deanwood

NEWBURY. **Donnington Valley Hotel & Golf Club,** Snelsmore House, Snelsmore Common, Newbury RG14 3BG (01635 568140; Fax: 01635 568141). *Location:* Junction 13 of M4, then A34 towards Newbury. Take first exit off A34, follow signs to Donnington Castle, entrance on the right. 18 holes, 6353 metres. Practice net, computer analysis of swing. *Green Fees:* information not available. *Eating facilities:* two bars and a restaurant. *Visitors:* welcome, must have own shoes. Accommodation in 4-star 58-bedroom hotel. *Society Meetings:* welcome. Professional: Martin Balfour (01635 568142; Fax: 01635 568141). Secretary: Lorraine Storey (01635 568140; Fax: 01635 568141).* e-mail: golf@donningtonvalley.co.uk website: www.donningtonvalley.co.uk

NEWBURY. **Newbury and Crookham Golf Club Ltd,** Bury's Bank Road, Greenham, Newbury RG19 8BZ (01635 40035; Fax: 01635 40045). *Location:* on south side of Newbury; Junction 13 on M4. Varied and interesting with woods or trees on almost every hole. 18 holes, 5949 yards. S.S.S. 69. *Green Fees:* weekdays £30.00 per round. *Eating facilities:* restaurant/bar. *Visitors:* welcome, except weekends and Bank Holidays unless with a member. *Society Meetings:* welcome Wednesdays, Thursdays and Fridays. Professional: Mr David Harris (01635 31201). Club Manager: Mr Stephen Myers M.B.E (01635 40035).

NEWBURY. **Newbury Racecourse Golf Centre,** The Racecourse, Newbury RG14 7NZ (01635 551464; Fax: 01635 528354). *Location:* one mile south east of Newbury. Challenging flat links course for all standards. Good conditions throughout the year. 18 holes, 6500 yards, S.S.S. 71. Pro Shop, Driving range, practice area and green. *Green Fees:* information not available. *Eating facilities:* bar food. *Visitors:* welcome to pay and play. *Society Meetings:* all welcome. Professional: Nick Mitchell (01635 551464). Manager: R. Osgood (01635 40015; Fax: 01635 528354).*

NEWBURY. **Parasampia Golf and Country Club,** Donnington Grove, Grove Road, Donnington, Newbury RG14 2LA (01635 581000; Fax: 01635 552259). *Location:* M4, Junction 13. Head for Donnington, straight over first mini roundabout, right at second into Grove Road, 200 yards on right. Dave Thomas designed, USGA specification greens, championship standard course. Parkland with lakes and other features. 18 holes, 7045 yards. S.S.S. 74. *Green Fees:* information not available. *Eating facilities:* bar snacks and restaurant. *Visitors:* welcome anytime weekdays, after 11am weekends. Tennis courts, sauna, Japanese bath, hotel. *Society Meetings:* catered for; many packages available. Please telephone for information. Professional: Gareth Williams (01635 551975; Fax: 01635 552259). * e-mail: enquiries@parasampia.com website: www.parasampia.com

NEWBURY. **The West Berkshire Golf Course,** Chaddleworth, Newbury RG20 7DU (01488 638574). *Location:* M4 Junction 14. A338 towards Wantage, then follow signposts to RAF Welford. Downland. 18 holes, 7001 yards. S.S.S. 74. Two practice grounds, tuition available. *Green Fees:* £35.00 per day, £25.00 per round weekdays; weekends p.m. only £35.00 per round. *Eating facilities:* full catering available. *Visitors:* welcome weekdays; restricted to afternoons weekends, reservation required. Trolleys and buggies available. *Society Meetings:* welcome by arrangement. Professional: Paul Simpson (01488 638851). Secretary: Mrs C.M. Clayton (01488 638574; Fax: 01488 638781).

READING. **Calcot Park Golf Club,** Bath Road, Calcot, Reading RG31 7RN (0118 9427124; Fax: 0118 945 3373). *Location:* off Exit 12, M4 along A4 towards Reading, approximately one and a half miles. Undulating wooded parkland. 18 holes, 6216 yards. S.S.S. 70. Limited practice areas. *Green Fees:* weekdays £40.00. *Eating facilities:* fully licensed restaurant, snacks available, three bars. *Visitors:* welcome on provision of Handicap Certificate. Not weekends or Bank Holidays. Advisable to ring first to check availability. *Society Meetings:* catered for midweek. Professional: Ian Campbell (0118 942 7797; Fax: 0118 945 3373). Secretary: J.R. Cox (0118 942 7124; Fax: 0118 945 3373). e-mail: info@calcotpark.com website: www.calcotpark.com

READING. **Castle Royle Golf and Country Club,** Knowl Hill, Reading RG10 9XA (01628 820700; Fax: 01628 829299). *Location:* alongside A4 between Maidenhead and Reading. Junction 8/9 M4. Parkland, links course. 18 holes, 6828 yards. S.S.S. 73. Practice ground. *Green Fees:* restricted access club. *Visitors:* members' guests only. Health and fitness club, 20x10m swimming pool, jacuzzi, sauna, gym, health and beauty and dance studio. *Eating facilities:* Full restaurant facilities and spike bar. Professional: Robert Watts. Golf Operations Manager: Nick Roberts. General Manager: Simon Jones.*

READING. **Hurst Golf Club,** Sandford Lane, Hurst, Reading RG10 0SU (01189 344355). *Location:* five miles Reading towards Wokingham. Parkland by the side of a large lake. 9 holes, 3154 yards. S.S.S. 70. *Green Fees:* Adult weekdays £6.50, weekends £8.00 Reduction for Seniors/Juniors. *Eating facilities:* bar and restaurant seating for 30. *Visitors:* unrestricted, bookings accepted. *Society Meetings:* welcome. Manager: Mr P. Priddle.

READING. **Pincents Manor Golf,** Pincents Lane, Calcot, Reading RG31 4UQ (01734 323511; Fax: 01734 323503). *Location:* Junction 12 M4 behind Savacentre. Parkland. Two courses: Manor Course - 18 holes, 6028 yards. S.S.S. 69; Lodge Course - 9 holes, 2600 yards. S.S.S. 68. Par 3 course. *Green Fees:* information not available. *Eating facilities:* Orchard Restaurant, Oak Bar, cruck barn. *Visitors:* welcome on Lodge Course, members only on Manor Course. Accommodation available in three bedrooms. *Society Meetings:* welcome. Professional: Alistair Thatcher.*

READING. **Reading Golf Club,** 17 Kidmore End Road, Emmer Green, Reading RG4 8SG (0118 947 2909). *Location:* two miles north of Reading off the Peppard Road (B481). Parkland. 18 holes, 6212 yards. S.S.S. 70. Practice facilities. *Green Fees:* information not available. *Eating facilities:* available. *Visitors:* welcome Monday to Thursday if member of recognised club, with handicap of 28 or less. Friday to Sunday with member only. *Society Meetings:* catered for by arrangement Tuesdays, Wednesdays and Thursdays. Professional: Scott Fotheringham (0118 947 6115). Secretary: Roy Brown (0118 947 2909).* website: www.readinggolfclub.com

READING. **Sonning Golf Club,** Duffield Road, Sonning RG4 6GJ (01189 693332; Fax: 01189 448409). *Location:* left off A4 at Sonning Roundabout, then left again. Parkland. 18 holes, 6366 yards. S.S.S. 70. *Green Fees:* on application. *Eating facilities:* new restaurant - phone for booking 01189 272055. *Visitors:* welcome, must be member of a recognised golf club with an official handicap; weekends with members only. *Society Meetings:* catered for Wednesdays. Professional: R. McDougall (01189 692910). Secretary: A.J. Tanner.

READING. **Wokefield Park Golf Club,** Mortimer, Reading RG7 3AE (0118 9334018; Fax: 0118 9334031). *Location:* 10 minutes Junction 11 M4, 20 minutes Junction 5 M3. Championship parkland course with winding streams, 9 lakes and large bunkers. 18 holes, 6961 yards. S.S.S. 73. Practice facilities. *Green Fees:* weekdays £30.00, weekends £45.00. Seasonal special offers. *Eating facilities:* bar and two restaurants. *Visitors:* welcome at all times. Hotel with 322 en suite bedrooms; leisure facilities. *Society Meetings:* contact Golf Sales Team (0118 933 4018). Professional: Gary Smith (0118 9334078; Fax: 0118 9334162). Secretary: David Luffrum.

SINDLESHAM. **Bearwood Golf Club**, Mole Road, Sindlesham RG41 5DB (0118 976 0060). *Location*: on B3030 from Winnersh to Arborfield. Flat, wooded course. 9 holes, 2802 yards. S.S.S. 68 (18 holes). Driving range 7.30am to 7.30pm every day. *Green Fees*: information not available. *Eating facilities*: food available all day. *Visitors*: welcome weekdays and weekends after 3pm. *Society Meetings*: maximum of 21 catered for. Thursday only. Professional: Bayley Tustin; Manager: Barry Tustin (0118 976 0060). Shop: 0118 976 0156.

SLOUGH. **Datchet Golf Club**, Buccleuch Road, Datchet SL3 9BP (Tel & Fax: 01753 541872; Clubhouse: 01753 543887). *Location*: within two miles of both Windsor and Slough. 9 holes, 6087 yards. S.S.S. 69. *Green Fees*: £20.00 per round, £27.00 per day. Subject to review. *Visitors*: welcome weekdays until 3pm. *Society Meetings*: small societies welcome, maximum 24 players. Professional: Ian Godleman (01753 545222) Secretary/Manager: Keith Smith (Tel & Fax: 01753 541872). e-mail: secretary@datchetgolfclub.co.uk website: www.datchetgolfclub.co.uk

STREATLEY ON THAMES. **Goring and Streatley Golf Club**, Rectory Road, Streatley on Thames RG8 9QA (01491 873229; Fax: 01491 875224). *Location*: 10 miles north west of Reading off A417 Wantage Road. Downland course on Berkshire Downs. 18 holes, 6355 yards. S.S.S. 70. *Green Fees*: £30.00 per round, £40.00 per day. *Eating facilities*: full restaurant and bar meals. Restaurant (01491 875122). *Visitors*: welcome on weekdays by telephone booking. *Society Meetings*: catered for. Professional: Jason Hadland (01491 873715). Secretary: Mrs Val Jones (01491 873229). website: www.goringgc.org

SUNNINGDALE. **Sunningdale Ladies' Golf Club**, Cross Road, Sunningdale SL5 9RX (01344 620507). *Location*: second left going west on A30, past Sunningdale level crossing. Heathland. 18 holes, 3622 yards. (Designed for Ladies' Golf). S.S.S. 60. *Green Fees*: weekdays £22.00, weekends and Bank Holidays £25.00. *Eating facilities*: snack lunches available except Sundays. *Visitors*: welcome, telephone first. Must have Handicap Certificate. *Society Meetings*: catered for. Secretary: Stephen Harris.

WARGRAVE. **Hennerton Golf Club,** Crazies Hill Road, Wargrave RG10 8LT (0118 940 1000; Fax: 0118 940 1042). *Location*: halfway between Maidenhead and Reading off the A321 to Henley, follow "Golf Club" signs from Wargrave High Street. Scenic course overlooking the Thames Valley. 9 holes, 5460 yards. S.S.S. 67. Driving range. *Green Fees*: on application. *Eating facilities*: clubhouse with full facilities. *Visitors*: welcome most times, phone Pro Shop. *Society Meetings*: telephone for details. Professional/Manager: William Farrow (0118 940 4778; Fax: 0118 940 1402).

WOKINGHAM. **Bearwood Lakes Golf Club,** Bearwood Road, near Sindlesham, Wokingham RG41 4SJ (0118 979 7900; Fax: 0118 979 2911). *Location*: just off M4 at Reading. Wooded 18 hole golf course. 6800 yards, S.S.S. 72. *Green Fees*: information not available. *Eating facilities*: restaurant, bar, function room, dining club. *Visitors*: must be the guest of a member. Practice ground available. Professional: Tim Waldron (0118 978 3030). General Manager: Scott Evans (0118 979 7900).

WOKINGHAM. **Downshire Golf Course**, Easthampstead Park, Wokingham RG40 3DH (01344 302030; Fax: 01344 301020). *Location*: off Nine Mile Ride/Easthampstead Road Bracknell. Parkland course, water on 14 holes. 18 holes, 5988 yards. S.S.S. 69. 9 hole pitch and putt, 30 bay floodlit driving range. *Green Fees*: weekdays £17.00, weekends £21.00. *Eating facilities*: new clubhouse. Function room available. *Visitors*: welcome. *Society Meetings*: welcome. Large Pro Shop. Professional: Wayne Owers (01344 302030; Fax: 01344 301020). Golf Manager: Paul Stanwick. e-mail: downshiregc@bracknell-forest.gov.uk website: bracknell-forest.gov.uk/downshiregc/

WOKINGHAM. **Sand Martins Golf Club,** Finchampstead Road, Wokingham RG40 3RQ (0118 9792711; Fax: 0118 9770282). *Location*: off Nine Mile Ride, two miles from Wokingham town centre. Parkland, links/wooded course. 18 holes, 6204 yards. S.S.S. 70. Practice area including bunker/pitching area. *Green Fees*: information not available. *Eating facilities*: bar, bar food and restaurant. *Visitors*: welcome weekdays, weekends with a member. *Society Meetings*: welcome weekdays. Professional: Andrew Hall (0118 9770265). Club Secretary: Elizabeth Roginski (0118 9792711; Fax: 0118 9770282). *

Buckinghamshire

AYLESBURY. **Aylesbury Golf Centre**, Hulcott Lane, Bierton, Aylesbury HP22 5GA (01296 393644). *Location:* north of Aylesbury on the A418 Leighton Buzzard road. 18 holes. 30 bay covered floodlit driving range. *Green Fees:* 18 holes £10.00 midweek, £14.00 weekends. *Eating facilities:* bar, bar snacks 11am to 11pm. *Visitors:* welcome. *Society Meetings:* catered for. Professional coaching available. General Manager: Kevin Partington. Professional: R. Wooster

AYLESBURY. **Aylesbury Park Golf Club,** Oxford Road, Aylesbury HP17 8QQ (01296 399196; Fax: 01296 336830). Location: Just outside Aylesbury town centre off the A418. Historic parkland course. 18 holes, 6146 yards. S.S.S. 69. 9 hole short course now open. *Green Fees:* £16.00 midweek, £21.00 weekends. 9 hole short course £5.00 per round. Numerous green fee special offers take place throughout the year - call for details. *Visitors:* welcome at all times. No Handicap Certificate required. *Society Meetings:* welcome at all times.

AYLESBURY. **Chiltern Forest Golf Club,** Aston Hill, Halton, Aylesbury HP22 5NQ (Tel & Fax: 01296 631267). *Location:* five miles south-east of Aylesbury, signposted St. Leonards. Wooded, hilly course. 18 holes, 5765 yards. S.S.S. 69. *Green Fees:* £30.00 weekdays; £15.00 with a member weekends. *Visitors:* weekdays unrestricted, weekends with a member. *Society Meetings:* welcome, preferably Wednesdays. Professional: Andy Lavers (01296 631817). Secretary: Bob Clift (01296 631267; Fax: 01296 632709).
e-mail: secretary@chilternforest.co.uk
website: www.chilternforest.co.uk.

AYLESBURY. **Ellesborough Golf Club,** Butlers Cross, Aylesbury HP17 0TZ (01296 622375). *Location:* on B4010 one-and-a-half miles from Wendover. Chiltern Hills course. Undulating links. 18 holes, 6360 yards, 5815 metres. S.S.S. 71. Practice net/ground. *Green Fees:* information not available. *Eating facilities:* full catering available. *Visitors:* welcome except Tuesday mornings and competition days, weekends with a member only. Must provide Handicap Certificate. *Society Meetings:* catered for Wednesdays and Thursdays only by arrangement. Professional: Mark Squire (Tel & Fax: 01296 623126). General Manager: (Tel & Fax: 01296 622114).

AYLESBURY. **Weston Turville Golf Club,** New Road, Weston Turville, Near Aylesbury HP22 5QT (01296 424084; Fax: 01296 395376). *Location:* two miles south east of Aylesbury off A41. Easy walking course at the foot of the Chiltern Hills. 18 holes, 6008 yards. S.S.S. 69. *Green Fees:* information not available. *Eating facilities:* meals, snacks and visitors' bar. *Visitors:* truly welcome. *Society Meetings:* especially catered for. Professional: Gary George (01296 425949; Fax: 01296 395376). General Manager: David Allen (01296 424084; Fax: 01296 395376). *

BEACONSFIELD. **Beaconsfield Golf Club,** Seer Green, Near Beaconsfield HP9 2UR (01494 681180; Fax: 01494 681148). *Location:* from A40 at Beaconsfield, A355 Amersham Road, one mile turn right to Jordans, one mile signposted. Parkland course. 18 holes, 6493 yards, Par 72. Large practice ground, driving range. *Green Fees:* £36.00 per round, £50.00 per day. Subject to review. *Eating facilities:* dining room or bar menu; two bars. *Visitors:* welcome weekdays with accredited introduction – check with Pro. Handicap Certificate required. *Society Meetings:* catered for Tuesdays and Wednesdays. Professional: Mike Brothers (01494 676616). Secretary: K.R. Wilcox (01494 676545).
e-mail: secretary@beaconsfieldgolfclub.co.uk

BUCKINGHAM. **Buckingham Golf Club,** Tingewick Road, Buckingham MK18 4AE (01280 815566; Fax: 01280 821812). *Location:* two miles south west of Buckingham on A421. Undulating parkland - eight holes affected by river. 18 holes, 6082 yards. S.S.S. 69. Practice ground. *Green Fees:* weekdays £30.00; weekends as members' guests only. *Eating facilities:* seven day catering - bars, lunch and evening. Tel: 01280 813282. *Visitors:* welcome weekdays only. Pro shop (01280 815210). *Society Meetings:* pre-booked on Tuesdays or Thursdays. General Manager: Tom Gates (01280 815566; Fax: 01280 821812). Professional: Gregor Hannah (01280 815210).

BURNHAM. **Burnham Beeches Golf Club,** Green Lane, Burnham, Slough SL1 8EG (01628 661448; Fax: 01628 668968). *Location:* Junction 7 on M4. Parkland/wooded course. 18 holes, 6449 yards. S.S.S. 71. *Green Fees:* weekdays 18 holes £38.00, 36 holes £56.00 (2003 rates subject to review). *Eating facilities:* bar and restaurant. *Visitors:* welcome weekdays, Handicap Certificate required. *Society Meetings:* welcome Wednesdays to Fridays April to October. Professional: R. Bolton (01628 661661). Secretary: T.P. Jackson (01628 661448).

BURNHAM. **The Lambourne Golf Club,** Dropmore Road, Burnham SL1 8NF (01628 666755; Fax: 01628 663301). *Location:* take M4 to Exit 7; take M40 to Exit 2. Parkland course, six lakes. 18 holes, 6771 yards. S.S.S. 73. Practice facilities available. *Green Fees:* information not available. *Eating facilities:* snack bar, half-way hatch, restaurant. *Visitors:* welcome. Handicap Certificate required. Golf Director: (01628 662936). Professional: David Hart (01628 662936; Fax: 01628 663301). General Manager: Brian Sparks.*

Please mention
'The Golf Guide' when
enquiring about clubs
or accommodation.

CHALFONT ST GILES. **Harewood Downs Golf Club,** Cokes Lane, Chalfont St Giles HP8 4TA (01494 762308; Fax: 01494 766869). *Location:* off A413, two miles east of Amersham. Rolling, tree lined. 18 holes, 5958 yards, 5448 metres. S.S.S. 69. Practice ground. *Green Fees:* weekdays £30.00 per round, £40.00 per day; weekends £35.00 per round, £45.00 per day. Special rates, winter golf. *Eating facilities:* full restaurant and bar. *Visitors:* welcome on weekdays with current Handicap, weekends by prior arrangement only. *Society Meetings:* welcome, mainly Thursdays and Fridays. Professional: G. Morris (01494 764102). Secretary: S. Thornton (01494 762184).

CHALFONT ST GILES. **Oakland Park Golf Club,** Bowles Farm, Threehouseholds, Chalfont St Giles HP8 4LW (01494 871277 Office). *Location*: off main A413 towards Amersham. Parkland course. 18 holes, 5246 yards. S.S.S. 66. Practice range, green and bunkers. *Green Fees*: weekdays £25.00. Twilight fees during Winter. *Eating facilities*: clubhouse bar, full catering all week. *Visitors*: welcome weekdays only. *Society Meetings*: welcome. Professional: Alistair Thatcher (01494 877333; Fax: 01494 874692). General Manager: Adam King.

CHESHAM. **Chartridge Park Golf Club,** Chartridge, Chesham HP5 2TF (01494 791772). *Location*: M25 Junction 18, Amersham, Chesham, three miles from roundabout by pond. Flat parkland course with wooded areas, two water holes and views over the Chiltern Valley. 18 holes, 5510 yards, 5061 metres. S.S.S. 68. Small chipping and putting area, driving nets. *Green Fees*: weekdays £30.00; weekends £40.00. *Eating facilities*: snacks and cooked food available seven days a week; bar. *Visitors*: always welcome, please ring to book tee times. *Society Meetings*: always welcome but please book in advance. Professional: Peter Gibbins. Secretary: Anita Gibbins.

CHESHAM. **Chesham and Ley Hill Golf Club,** Ley Hill, Chesham HP5 1UZ (01494 784541). *Location:* off A41 on B4504 to Ley Hill, nearest town - Chesham. Wooded parkland. 9 holes, 5296 yards. S.S.S. 65. *Green Fees:* information not available. *Eating facilities:* licensed bar, food available at certain times. *Visitors:* welcome Mondays and Thursdays all day; Wednesdays after 12 noon; Fridays up to 4pm.

Society Meetings: Thursdays only by prior arrangement. Secretary: B.E. Durand (01494 784541).

DENHAM. **Buckinghamshire Golf Club,** Denham Court, Denham Court Drive, Denham UB9 5PG (01895 835777; Fax: 01895 835210). *Location:* Junction 1 M40 off Denham roundabout, follow signs to Denham Country Park. Gently undulating parkland, River Colne and River Misbourne run through course. 18 holes, 6880 yards. S.S.S. 73. Practice range with ball dispenser and collection. *Green Fees:* weekdays £80.00; weekends £90.00. *Eating facilities:* Heron Restaurant, spike bar; lunches and menu. *Visitors:* welcome Mondays to Thursdays; advance bookings only. *Society Meetings:* welcome, golf company days up to 80 – details on application. Professional: John O'Leary. Enquiries: Dubravka Dartnell.

DENHAM. **Denham Golf Club,** Tilehouse Lane, Denham UB9 5DE (01895 832022; Fax: 01895 835340). *Location:* off A412 near Uxbridge. Parkland - undulating. 18 holes, 6462 yards, 5903 metres. S.S.S. 71. Practice ground. *Green Fees:* information not available. *Eating facilities:* diningroom, bar snacks. *Visitors:* welcome Monday to Thursday by prior arrangement only. Handicap Certificate. *Society Meetings:* catered for Tuesdays, Wednesdays and Thursdays. Professional: Stuart Campbell (01895 832801). Secretary: M.J. Miller (01895 832022; Fax: 01895 835340).
e-mail: club.secretary@denhamgolfclub.co.uk
website: www.denhamgolfclub.co.uk

GERRARDS CROSS. **Gerrards Cross Golf Club,** Chalfont Park, Gerrards Cross SL9 0QA (01753 278500; Fax: 01753 883593). *Location:* alongside A413 (to Amersham) about three miles from junction with A40 (London to Oxford road). Wooded parkland course. 18 holes, 6295 yards. S.S.S. 70. Practice nets and putting green. *Green Fees:* weekdays £38.00 per round, £52.00 per day. Subject to review. *Eating facilities:* lunch, bar snacks, afternoon tea always available, evening meals to order. *Visitors:* welcome except at weekends and Public Holidays but must produce a letter of introduction or current Handicap Certificate. Tuesday is Ladies' Day. *Society Meetings:* catered for Thursdays and Fridays, maximum number 100. Professional: M. Barr (01753 885300). Secretary/Manager: B.F. Cable MBE (01753 883263).

HIGH WYCOMBE. **Flackwell Heath Golf Club Limited,** Treadaway Road, Flackwell Heath, High Wycombe HP10 9PE (01628 520929; Fax: 01628 530040). *Location:* M40 Exit 3 from London, Exit 4 from Oxford. 2 miles High Wycombe. Undulating heath and woodland. 18 holes, 6211 yards. S.S.S. 70. *Green Fees:* weekdays £25.00 per round, £38.00 per day; weekends with member only - £16.00. Eating facilities: restaurant and bars daily (limited catering Mondays). *Visitors:* welcome weekdays with Handicap Certificate, weekends with member only. *Society Meetings:* catered for by arrangement Wednesdays and Thursdays - contact the Secretary. Professional: Paul Watson (01628 523017). Secretary: S. J. Chandler (01628 520929).

HIGH WYCOMBE. **Hazlemere Golf Club,** Penn Road, Hazlemere, Near High Wycombe HP15 7LR (01494 719300; Fax: 01494 713914). *Location:* from M40 North: Junction 2, via Beaconsfield and Penn on B474; from M40 South; Junction 4, through High Wycombe on A404. Undulating parkland course with a number of feature water holes. Practice area. 18 holes, 5810 yards. S.S.S. 69. *Green Fees:* weekdays £20.00; weekends £30.00. *Eating facilities:* coffee shop and bar. *Visitors:* welcome 7 days a week (after midday weekends). *Society Meetings:* welcome weekdays. Professional: Paul Harrison (01494 719306). Secretary: (01494 719303).

HIGH WYCOMBE. **Wycombe Heights Golf Centre,** Rayners Avenue, Loudwater, High Wycombe HP10 9SW (01494 816686; Fax: 01494 816728). *Location:* one mile south-east of High Wycombe off A40. Impressive tree-lined parkland course with panoramic views of Chilterns. Challenging final loop from 15th to 18th. 18 holes, 6265 yards, Par 70, S.S.S. 72. 18-hole, Par 3 course, practice green and bunker, 24-bay floodlit driving range. *Green Fees:* weekdays £14.00; weekends £19.50. *Eating facilties:* full clubhouse facilities. *Visitors:* welcome, booking in advance advisable. *Society Meetings:* welcome 7 days, telephone or write for details. Professional: Cranfield Golf Academy. Manager: Christopher Benson.

IVER. **Iver Golf Club,** Hollow Hill Lane, Off Langley Park Road, Iver SL0 0JJ (01753 655615; Fax: 01753 654225). *Location:* near Slough. Situated on the right off Langley Park Road leaving the town of Langley and heading towards Iver. Flat parkland, easy walking with natural ditches and ponds. 9 holes, 5628 yards. S.S.S. 67. 18 bay driving range, practice area, putting green, bunker area onto a green. Plus NEW 9 hole short course OPENING September 2003. *Green Fees:* weekdays £8.00 for 9 holes, £14.00 for 18; weekends £9.50 for 9 holes, £17.00 for 18. Special rates available, please enquire. *Eating facilities:* bar lunches 11:30am until 6:30pm seven days. *Visitors:* always welcome, best to phone on day of play for booking. We have a new Junior section, a vet society every Tuesday and are willing to accommodate most requests. Senior Members' competitions Thursday mornings. *Society Meetings:* always welcome. Professional: Jim Lynch (01753 655615).

IVER. **Richings Park Golf and Country Club,** North Park, Iver SL0 9DL (01753 655370; Fax: 01753 655409). *Location:* M4 Junction 5. Flat parkland. 18 holes, 6209 yards. S.S.S. 68. 5 hole par 3 course, practice area, two putting greens, bunker and chipping area. *Green Fees:* information not available. *Eating facilities:* bar, restaurant, and spike bar. *Visitors:* welcome with restrictions at weekend. *Society Meetings:* welcome, minimum 12. Professional: Sean Kelly (01753 655352). Secretary: Adam Garland. General Manager: Gill Dutfield. *

LITTLE CHALFONT. **Little Chalfont Golf Club,** Lodge Lane, Little Chalfont HP8 4AJ (01494 764877; Fax: 01494 762860). *Location:* Junction 18 M25, two miles towards Amersham on A404, first left past garden centre. Undulating parkland. 9 holes, 5752 yards S.S.S. 68. *Green Fees:* information not available. *Eating facilities:* full bar and restaurant. *Visitors:* always welcome. *Society Meetings:* welcome mid-week. Professional: J.M. Dunne (01494 762942). Secretary: Michael Dunne.

MARLOW. **Harleyford Golf Club,** Harleyford Estate, Henley Road, Marlow SL7 2SP (01628 816161; Fax: 01628 816160). *Location:* two miles from Marlow on the A4155 to Henley. Parkland course designed by Donald Steel. 18 holes, 6809 yards, S.S.S. 72. *Green fees:* midweek £45.00, weekends £65.00. *Eating facilities:* restaurant, lounge and bar. *Visitors:* book via Pro Shop. Handicap certificate required. *Society Meetings:* welcome by arrangement Tuesday, Wednesday and Friday - contact events office (01628 816163). Excellent practice range and green available. Soft spikes only, no metal spikes allowed. Professional: Lee Jackson (01628 816162). General Manager: Marc Newey (01628 816167).
e-mail: info@harleyfordgolf.co.uk
website: www.harleyfordgolf.co.uk

MILTON KEYNES. **Abbey Hill Golf Centre,** Monks Way, Two Mile Ash, Milton Keynes MK8 8AA (01908 563845; Fax: 01908 569538). *Location:* 2 miles west of town centre, just off the A5 on the H3. Undulating parkland course with mature trees and impressive backdrops. Water comes into play on seven holes. 18 holes, 5996 yards. S.S.S. 69, Par 71. Additional Par 3 course, putting green, 24 bay floodlit driving range. *Green Fees:* information not available. *Eating facilities:* full clubhouse facilities. *Visitors:* welcome, booking in advance advisable. *Society Meetings:* welcome, telephone or write for details. Professional: Cranfield Golf Academy. Manager: Jonathan Gale. *

MILTON KEYNES. **Kingfisher Country Club,** Buckingham Road, Deanshanger, Milton Keynes MK19 6DG (01908 560354; Fax: 01908 260857). *Location:* twixt Milton Keynes/Buckingham on A422. Mature course setting - wooded - lakes and ponds major feature. 9 holes, 5471 yards. S.S.S. 67. Full 9 hole floodlit. 10 bay covered range. *Green Fees:* weekdays £8.00, weekends £11.00. *Eating facilities:* full club house and separate spike lodge both overlooking lake. *Visitors:* welcome, some weekend restrictions on Sundays and Public Holidays. *Society Meetings:* welcome. Director: D.M. Barraclough.

MILTON KEYNES. **Three Locks Golf Club,** Great Brickhill, Milton Keynes MK17 9BH (01525 270050 golf; Tel & Fax: 01525 270470 accommodation). *Location:* A4146 Bletchley to Leighton Buzzard. Parkland with lakes and water hazards. 18 holes, 6400 yards. S.S.S. 71. Practice ground. *Green Fees:* weekdays £18.50 per round, £30.00 per day; weekends £23.00 per round. After 3.30pm twilight fees £12.00. *Eating facilities:* dining room and bar. *Visitors:* welcome every day. Golf buggies for hire. *Society Meetings:* all welcome. Professional: Visiting Professional. Secretary: Maureen Darby (01525 270470).

MILTON KEYNES. **Wavendon Golf Centre,** Lower End Road, Wavendon, Milton Keynes MK17 8DA (01908 281811; Fax: 01908 281257). *Location:* from Junction 13 M1, A421, follow signs to Woburn Sands. Parkland with six small lakes as hazards. Three courses: 18 holes, 5608 yards. S.S.S. 69. 9 holes, 1424 yards. S.S.S. 27, pitch and putt course, Par 26, 536 yards. 36 bay driving range, practice, putting and bunker. *Green Fees:* information not available. *Eating facilities:* fully licensed bar and carvery restaurant. *Visitors:* always welcome. Buggies. *Society Meetings:* welcome. Professional: Greg Iron (01908 281811). Secretary: Greg Iron (01908 281005). *

MILTON KEYNES. **Windmill Hill Golf Club,** The New Clubhouse, Windmill Hill Golf Course, Tattenhoe Lane, Bletchley, Milton Keynes MK3 7RB (01908 367398; Tee reservations 01908 631113 7 days in advance). *Location:* M1 South Junction 14/M1 North Junction 13 A421 towards Buckingham. Flat parkland championship course, Henry Cotton design. 18 holes, 6773 yards. S.S.S. 72. 23 bay covered floodlit driving range, seven grassed bays. *Green Fees:* weekdays £13.00, weekends £18.00. *Eating facilities:* adjoining carvery restaurant, cafeteria and two bars, function room. *Visitors:* welcome at any time, booking seven days in advance. *Society Meetings:* welcome (after 11am weekends and Bank Holidays). Professional: C. Clingan (01908 378623; Fax: 01908 271478). Secretary: Steve Walton (Tel & Fax: 01908 501233).

MILTON KEYNES. **Woburn Golf and Country Club,** Little Brickhill, Milton Keynes MK17 9LJ (01908 370756; Fax: 01908 378436). *Location:* four miles west of Junction 13 M1. Three courses, 54 holes: Duke's Course 6976 yards, S.S.S. 74; Duchess' Course 6651 yards, S.S.S. 72; Marquess Course 7214 yards, S.S.S. 74. Three practice grounds. *Green Fees:* information not available. *Eating facilities:* two restaurants; breakfasts, lunches and dinners. *Visitors:* welcome weekdays with prior arrangement. Members' guests only at weekends. *Society Meetings:* catered for, details on application. Professional: L. Blacklock (01908 626600). Secretary: Mrs G. Beasley (01908 370756).

PRINCES RISBOROUGH. **Princes Risborough Golf Club,** Lee Road, Saunderton Lee, Princes Risborough HP27 9NX (01844 346989. Fax: 01844 274938). *Location:* A4010, Princes Risborough, turn off at Rose and Crown Inn, 1 mile on right. Parkland course, slightly undulating, water hazards and has beautiful views. 9 holes, 5552 yards. S.S.S. 67. Practice area and nets. *Green Fees:* 9 holes weekdays £12.00; weekends £14.00, 18 holes weekdays £16.00; weekends £21.00. *Eating facilities:* restaurant and bar. *Visitors:* always welcome properly attired. *Society Meetings:* welcome. Outside functions catered for. Professional: Simon Lowry (01844 274567). Secretary/Proprietor: J.F. Tubb.

PRINCES RISBOROUGH. **Whiteleaf Golf Club Ltd,** Upper Icknield Way, Whiteleaf HP27 0LY (01844 274058/343097). Location: A4010 from Princes Risborough turn off at signpost for Whiteleaf into Upper Icknield Way. Hilly course with beautiful Chiltern views. 9 holes, 5391 yards. S.S.S. 66. Practice area. *Green Fees:* weekdays £20.00; weekends £12.00 with a member. *Eating facilities:* full catering facilities, except Mondays. *Visitors:* always welcome; probably better to phone Secretary in case of disappointment. *Society Meetings:* on Thursdays – apply to Secretary. Professional: Ken Ward (01844 345472). Secretary Derek Hill (01844 274058).

THE APPEARANCE OF AN ASTERISK * AT THE END OF A CLUB OR COURSE ENTRY INDICATES THAT UP-TO-DATE INFORMATION HAS NOT BEEN SUPPLIED

SLOUGH. **Farnham Park Pay and Play Golf Course,** Park Road, Stoke Poges, Slough SL2 4PJ (Tel & Fax: 01753 643332). *Location:* just off A355, two miles north of A4. Challenging parkland course with water. 18 holes, 6172 yards. S.S.S. 71. Short game practice facilities, 20 bay driving range at our nearby golfing academy (one mile away). *Green Fees:* information not available. *Eating facilities:* hot and cold food always available. *Visitors:* welcome, hire facilities available. Pro shop with hire facilities. *Society Meetings:* welcome, special packages available, from as little as £20.00 per person. Professiona: Paul Warner (01753 643332). Operated by South Bucks District Council. Contact: Mr K Simpkins (01753 533333). Secretary: Mrs M Brooker (01753 647065).

STOKE POGES. **Lanes Golfing Academy,** Stoke Road, Stoke Poges SL2 4NL (01753 554840). *Location:* half-a-mile from Slough Railway Station in direction of Stoke Poges. Parkland course ideal for the less experienced player. 9 holes. 2400 yds. S.S.S. 62 (18 holes). 18 bay driving range. *Green Fees:* information not available. *Eating facilities:* small lounge area with snack facilities. *Visitors:* open to the public seven days a week. Clubs for hire. Expert tuition available. The Tiger Club for under 12's with 12 monthly competitions held. *Society Meetings:* ideal for company tuition days. A Golf Foundation starter centre. Professional: Paul Warner (01753 554840). Operated by South Bucks District Council Contact: Mr K Simpkins (01753 5333333).*

STOKE POGES. **Stoke Park Club,** North Drive, Park Road, Stoke Poges SL2 4PG (01753 717171; Fax: 01753 717181). *Location:* one mile north of Slough, eight miles from Heathrow. Parkland course - voted Golf Club of the Year. 27 holes, 6670 yards. S.S.S. 72. Practice ground (tokens available from Club Shop). *Green Fees:* information not available. *Eating facilities:* Orangery, dining room, President's Bar and Park Restaurant. *Visitors:* welcome weekdays with Handicap Certificate or letter of introduction; weekends subject to availability. 21 bedrooms now available, conference facilities. *Society Meetings:* catered for. Club Director: Mark Fagan (01753 717171; Fax: 01753 717181). Professional: Stuart Collier. Club Shop: 01753 717184. website: www.stokeparkclub.com

STOWE. **Silverstone Golf Club,** Silverstone Road, Stowe MK18 5LH (01280 850005; Fax: 01280 850156). *Location:* A43 half mile south of Silverstone Grand Prix Circuit. Flat, maturing copses bordered by woodland. 18 holes, Par 72. 6558 yards. S.S.S. 71. Putting area, covered driving range. *Green Fees:* £18.00 weekdays, £25.00 weekends. *Eating facilities:* meals at all times, licensed bar. *Visitors:* welcome, booking seven days in advance. Conference facilities. Coporate days with motorsport activities and golf. *Society Meetings:* welcome. Professional: Rodney Holt. Manager: Bryan Major.

STOWE. **Stowe Golf Club,** Stowe, Buckingham MK18 5EH (01280 816264). *Location:* situated at Stowe School, four miles north of Buckingham. Parkland course with follies and lakes. 9 holes, 2189 yards. S.S.S. 63. *Green Fees:* £10.00. *Visitors:* only as a guest of a member. *Society Meetings:* catered for by appointment. Secretary: Bill Kemp (01280 818282).

WEXHAM. **Wexham Park Golf Course,** Wexham Street, Wexham, Slough SL3 6ND (01753 663271; Fax: 01753 663318). *Location:* M40 to Beaconsfield, A40 to Gerrards Cross, direction Fulmer on right hand side, near Wexham Park Hospital. Undulating parkland courses. 18 holes, 5251 yards. S.S.S. 66. Also 9 hole course, 2727 yards, par 34; and 9 hole course, 2219 yards, par 32. Driving range and short game practice area. *Green Fees:* weekdays £12.50 for 18 holes, £7.00 for 9 holes; weekends £16.50 for 18 holes, £9.50 for 9 holes. Veterans weekday £8.00 18 holes, £5.00 9 holes. *Eating facilities:* clubhouse bar and full kitchen facilities. *Visitors:* welcome, Pay and Play, open to all. *Society Meetings:* 7 days a week by prior arrangement. Professional: John Kennedy (01753 663271). Secretary: J. Dunne.

WOOBURN COMMON. **Hedsor Golf Course,** Pay & Play, Broad Lane, Wooburn Common HP10 0JW (01628 851285). *Location:* from Junction 2 of M40, take A355 to Slough, turn right at Hedsor Golf Course sign, then follow golf arrows to course. Easy walking course in mature parkland; many water hazards. 9 holes. Par 34. 18 holes S.S.S 64. *Green Fees:* special rates for senior citizens. *Eating facilities:* bar and catering available. Professional: Stuart Cannon.

N O T E All the information regarding Golf Clubs in this guide is given in good faith in the belief that it is correct. However, the publishers cannot guarantee the facts given in these pages, neither are they responsible for changes in ownership or facilities, such as green fees, that may take place after the date of going to press. Readers should always satisfy themselves that the facilities they require are available and that the terms, if quoted, still apply.

Cambridgeshire

CAMBRIDGE. **Cambridge Golf Club,** Station Road, Longstanton, Cambridge CB4 5DR (01954 789388). *Location:* 10 minutes from city, off A14 at Bar Hill, turn right to Longstanton B1050. Parkland course. 18 holes, 6736 yards, S.S.S. 73. 9 bay floodlit grassed driving range, 9 holes pitch and putt. *Green Fees:* weekdays: 9 holes £8.00, 18 holes £12.00; weekends: 9 holes £10.00, 18 holes £16.00. All day £20.00. *Eating facilities:* clubhouse; 50-seat function room available for hire. *Visitors:* welcome, may need to book on competition days. Coaching by appointment. *Society Meetings:* catered for. Professionals: Adrienne Engleman, Geoff Hugget.

CAMBRIDGE. **Cambridge National Golf (Home of Cambridge Meridian Golf Club),** Comberton Road, Toft, Cambridge CB3 7RY (01223 264700; Fax: 01223 264701). *Location:* 5 minutes from Junction 12 of M11 onto B1046. Heavily landscaped championship design set in 250 acres with six lakes and 108 bunkers. 18 holes, 6707 yards. S.S.S. 72. Practice ground and putting green. *Green Fees:* weekdays £15.00 round, £25.00 day; weekends £20.00 round, £35.00 day. Subject to review. *Eating facilities:* available all day. *Visitors:* welcome at all times (subject to availability). Buggies and trolleys for hire. *Society Meetings:* corporate and society golf days catered for. Professional: John Saxon-Mills (01223 264702). Golf Administrator: Ingrid Van Rooyen.
e-mail: meridian@golfsocieties.com

CAMBRIDGE. **Cambridgeshire Moat House Hotel Golf Club,** Bar Hill, Cambridge CB3 8EU (01954 249988). *Location:* five miles north from Cambridge on A14 Huntingdon Road, Junction 29. Well established parkland course with many mature trees. 18 holes, 6750 yards (newly extended 18th tee). S.S.S. 73. Practice grounds. *Green Fees:* 18 holes weekdays £24.00; weekends £30.00. Reduced rates for hotel residents. Daily and weekend golf packages. *Eating facilities:* two restaurants and three bars (Mon-Fri lunch). *Visitors:* welcome anytime by prior phone call. 134 Bedroom Hotel including 35 air-conditioned executive bedrooms. Full leisure facilities including gym, heated pool, sauna, solarium, steam rooms and tennis courts. *Society Meetings:* welcome weekdays. Professional: Paul Simpson (01954 780098). Golf Co-ordinator: (01954 249971; Fax: 01954 780010).

CAMBRIDGE. **Girton Golf Club,** Dodford Lane, Girton, Cambridge CB3 0QE (01223 276169; Fax: 01223 277150). *Location:* two miles north of Cambridge. Flat parkland. 18 holes, 6012 yards. S.S.S. 69. Large practice area. *Green Fees:* information not available. *Eating facilities:* diningroom, lounge and bar. *Visitors:* weekdays only. *Society Meetings:* welcome Tuesdays to Fridays. Professional: S. Thomson (01223 276991). Secretary: (01223 276169; Fax: 01223 277150).*
website: www.girtongolfclub.co.uk

CAMBRIDGE. **Gog Magog Golf Club,** Shelford Bottom, Cambridge CB2 4AB (01223 247626; Fax: 01223 414990). *Location:* Two miles from the A11-A1307 roundabout, Colchester - Cambridge Road A604. Open, undulating chalkland hill course. Old Course - 18 holes, 6400 yards, S.S.S. 70. Wandlebury Course - 18 holes, 6750 yards, S.S.S. 72. Large driving range and practice areas, with ball hire available. *Green Fees:* weekdays £37.00 per round. *Eating facilities:* diningroom, bar meals, large bar area with lounge and spike bar. *Visitors:* only with members at weekends and Bank Holidays, Handicap Certificate required. *Society Meetings:* catered for Tuesdays and Thursdays. Professional: I. Bamborough (01223 246058). Secretary: I.M. Simpson (01223 247626).
e-mail: secretary@gogmagog.co.uk
website: www.gogmagog.co.uk

ELY. **Ely City Golf Course Ltd,** 107 Cambridge Road, Ely CB7 4HX (01353 662751). *Location:* on southern outskirts of city on A10 if heading towards Cambridge. Parkland course, undulating, magnificent views of the 12th century cathedral. 18 holes, 6627 yards. S.S.S. 72. Practice area. *Green Fees:* weekdays £32.00 per day; weekends and Bank Holidays £38.00 per day. 50% reduction as a member's guest. Twilight rates also available. *Eating facilities:* full bar, catering and restaurant facilities. *Visitors:* welcome anytime with a member or in possession of a valid Handicap Certificate. Jeans, T-shirts and trainers not allowed. Well equipped Pro Shop. Snooker. *Society Meetings:* welcome Tuesday to Friday inclusive by arrangement. Professional: Andrew George (01353 663317). General Manager: Michael Hoare (01353 662751; Fax: 01353 668636) e-mail: elygolf@lineone.net website: www.elygolf.co.uk

HUNTINGDON. **Brampton Park Golf Club,** Buckden Road, Brampton, Huntingdon PE28 4NF (01480 434705). *Location:* three-quarters of a mile off A1, travelling north take first Huntingdon turn, south take second sign for "RAF Brampton". Picturesque with many water hazards, wooded areas and prolific wildlife – swans, badgers, muntjac deer, Canada geese, water fowl, etc. 18 holes, 6300 yards. S.S.S. 72. 10 bay driving range. *Green Fees:* weekdays £20.00 per round, £25.00 per day; weekends £35.00 per day/round. *Eating facilities:* bar snacks, restaurant, two bars. *Visitors:* welcome at all times, no restrictions save telephone for tee reservations prior to arrival. Accommodation and business conference facilities and banqueting for up to 120 available. *Society Meetings:* welcome. Professional: Alisdair Currie (Tel & Fax: 01480 434705). Secretary: Richard Oakes (01480 434700; Fax: 01480 411145).

HUNTINGDON. **Hemingford Abbots Golf Club,** Cambridge Road, Hemingford Abbots, Huntingdon PE28 9HQ (01480 495000; Fax: 01480 496000). *Location:* two miles south of Huntingdon on the A14. Gently undulating parkland with trees. 9 holes, 2680 yards. S.S.S.68. *Green Fees:* weekdays £9.00 for 9 holes, £13.00 for 18 holes; weekends £11.00 for 9 holes, £16.00 for 18 holes. *Eating facilities:* comfortable clubhouse with bar. *Visitors:* welcome, no restrictions. New conference facility for meetings and private functions. *Society Meetings:* welcome. 'The Friendly One' , all standards welcome. Alternative tee positions on back nine. Secretary: Sonja McCabe.

HUNTINGDON. **Lakeside Lodge Golf Centre,** Fen Road, Pidley, Huntingdon PE28 3DF (01487 740540; Fax: 01487 740852). *Location:* on the B1040 St Ives to Warboys Road. Course has 8 lakes and considerable landscaping. Three courses - Lodge Course: 18 holes, 6437 yards. S.S.S. 73; Manor Course: 9 holes, 2601 yards; Church Course: 6 holes, 1645 yards. Driving range and Teaching Academy. *Green Fees:* weekdays £14.00 for 18 holes, £7.00 for 9 holes; weekends £22.00 for 18 holes, £9.50 for 9 holes. After 12 noon weekends £17.00. *Eating facilities:* full bar serving all day snacks and meals. *Visitors:* welcome but best to book. Ten Pin Bowling. Accommodation available in seventeen twin en suite bedrooms adjoining the course. *Society Meetings:* all welcome. Professional: Mr Scott Waterman PGA (01487 741541). Secretary: Mrs Jane Hopkins (01487 740540; Fax: 01487 740852).

visit the FHG golf website on

www.uk-golfguide.com

HUNTINGDON. **Ramsey Golf and Bowls Club,** 4 Abbey Terrace, Ramsey, Huntingdon PE26 1DD (01487 812600: Fax: 01487 815746). *Location:* 20 minutes from A1, 12 miles south of Peterborough, 10 miles north of Huntingdon. Flat parkland with a river running full length which comes into play on many holes. 18 holes, 6163 yards. S.S.S. 70. Two practice grounds, chipping area. *Green Fees:* information not available. *Eating facilities:* bar and full catering service available. *Visitors:* welcome weekdays, with member weekends. Six rink county standard bowling green. *Society Meetings:* welcome by prior arrangement. Professional: Stuart Scott (01487 813022). Secretary/Administrator: M. Kjenstad (01487 812600; Fax: 01487 815746). e-mail: admin@ramseygolf.com website: www.ramseygolf.com

MARCH. **March Golf Club,** Frogs Abbey, Grange Road, March PE15 0YH (01354 652364). *Location:* quarter of a mile west of March bypass (A141). Flat parkland. 9 holes, 6204 yards. S.S.S. 70. Six acre practice area. *Green Fees:* £17.50 per day midweek. *Eating facilities:* bar, dining facilities bookable in advance. *Visitors:* welcome. *Society Meetings:* welcome mid week only. Professional: Mark Pond (01354 657255). Secretary: A.P. Cranstoun.

PETERBOROUGH. **Elton Furze Golf Club,** Bullock Road, Haddon, Peterborough PE7 3TT (01832 280189; Fax: 01832 280299). *Location:* four miles west of Peterborough on old A605 Oundle to Peterborough road. Opened April 1993. Scenic parkland, wooded. 18 holes, 6279 yards, 5715 metres. S.S.S. 70. Driving range. *Green Fees:* weekdays £30.00 per round; weekends £34.00 per round. Subject to review. *Eating facilities:* new spacious bar and restaurant (holds 120). *Visitors:* welcome any time. Buggies available for hire £14.00 for 18 holes, £20.00 all day. *Society Meetings:* welcome Monday to Friday - small groups only on Friday - need to pre-book. Contact: Helen Barron. Bar/Restaurant (01832 280118). Professional: Glyn Krause (01832 280614). Managing Partner: Ben Martin.

PETERBOROUGH. **Orton Meadows Golf Course,** Ham Lane, Orton Waterville, Peterborough PE2 5UU (01733 237478). *Location:* three miles west of Peterborough on A605, at entrance to Nene Park. Parkland, lakes. 18 holes, 5613 yards. S.S.S. 68. with 12 hole pitch and putt course adjoining. *Green Fees:* weekdays £11.90, Concessions; £7.10, Juniors; £5.20. Weekends and Bank Holidays £15.70, Concessions £15.70, Juniors £5.20. Pitch and Putt weekends and Bank Holidays £3.50, Juniors £2.60; weekdays £2.90, Juniors £2.30. *Visitors:* welcome; unrestricted – Pay as you Play course. Catering at adjoining pub/restaurant. Bookings taken seven days in advance. *Society Meetings:* Golf Societies welcome, contact Pro Shop (01733 237478). Head Professional: Ashley Howard (01733 237478). Director of Golf: Roger Fitton. e-mail: enquiries@ortonmeadowsgolfcourse.co.uk website: www.ortonmeadowsgolfcourse.co.uk

PETERBOROUGH. **Peterborough Milton Golf Club,** Milton Ferry, Peterborough PE6 7AG. *Location:* on A47 west of Peterborough, three miles east of A1. Parkland. 18 holes, 6505 yards. S.S.S. 72. *Green Fees:* £30.00 per round, £40.00 per day. Societies £37.50 per day. *Eating facilities:* available daily except Mondays. *Society Meetings:* available by arrangement with Secretary. Professional: Mike Gallagher (01733 380793). Secretary: Andy Izod (01733 380489).

PETERBOROUGH. **Thorney Golf Centre,** English Drove, Thorney, Peterborough PE6 0TJ (01733 270570). *Location:* left at traffic lights in Thorney off A47 Peterborough to Wisbech road out of village. Fen Course - flat, ideal for beginners; Lakes Course - challenging links with lakes. 36 holes: Fen 18 holes, 6104 yards, S.S.S. 69; Lakes 18 holes, 6402 yards, S.S.S. 71. Driving range. *Green Fees:* weekdays Fen £7.75, Lakes £12.50; weekends Fen £9.75, Lakes £20.00. *Eating facilities:* three bars and restaurant. *Visitors:* welcome, no restrictions on Fen Course, Lakes Course contact in advance at weekends. *Society Meetings:* all welcome. Professional: Mark Templeman. Secretary: Jane Hind (01733 270842).

Two Great Courses – Two Great Choices

Orton Meadows Golf Course
Orton Waterville, Peterborough
Tel: 01733 237478
website: www.ortonmeadowsgolfcourse.co.uk

Thorpe Wood Golf Course
Thorpe Wood, Peterborough
Tel: 01733 267701
website: www.thorpewoodgolfcourse.co.uk

☑ Pay as you play at affordable prices   ☑ Club and Trolley Hire available

☑ You do not have to be a member or have a handicap to play

☑ Large well-stocked Golf Shops   ☑ 12-hole Pitch and Putt Course at Orton Meadows

☑ Golf Societies welcome   ☑ Catering available at adjoining pub restaurants

PETERBOROUGH. **Thorpe Wood Golf Course,** Thorpe Wood, Peterborough PE3 6SE (01733 267701). *Location*: two miles west of Peterborough on A47. Parkland. 18 holes, 7086 yards. S.S.S. 74. Practice ground. *Green Fees*: weekdays £11.90; Concessions; £7.10; Juniors £5.20 weekends and Bank Holidays £15.70, Concessions £15.70, Juniors £5.20. Weekdays and Bank Holidays £15.70, Concessions, Juniors £5.20 *Visitors*: welcome, unrestricted - Pay as you Play course. Catering at adjoining pub/restaurant. Bookings taken 7 days in advance. *Society Meetings*: Golf societies welcome – contact Jenny Walters (01733 267701). Head Coach: Gary Casey (01733 267701). Director of Golf: Roger Fitton.
e-mail: enquiries@thorpewoodgolfcourse.co.uk
website: www.thorpewoodgolfcourse.co.uk

RAMSEY. **Old Nene Golf Club,** Muchwood Lane, Bodsey, Ramsey PE26 2XQ (01487 813519 or 815622). *Location*: three-quarters of a mile north of Ramsey towards Peterborough, halfway between Ramsey and Ramsey Mereside and half mile from Rainbow Superstore. Easy walking course with water hazards, quiet with wildlife – herons, swans, pheasants, partridges. 1996 Eastern Area Environmental Winner. 9 holes, 5605 yards, S.S.S. 68. Edrich driving range on site. *Green Fees:* information not available. *Eating facilities:* in clubhouse, open to all, fully licensed bar; bar snacks always available, meals to order.. *Visitors:* welcome, telephone to avoid club tee closures. *Society Meetings:* welcome. Driving Range. Professional: Ian Galloway. Secretary: Mrs P.B. Cade (01487 813519). Clubhouse: (01487 815622).*

ST IVES. **St Ives (Hunts) Golf Club,** Westwood Road, St Ives PE27 6DH (01480 464459). *Location:* B1040 off A14. 9 holes, 6180 yards. S.S.S. 70. *Green Fees:* £20.00 per day weekdays; members' guests only at weekends. *Eating facilities:* full catering. *Visitors:* welcome weekdays. *Society Meetings:* welcome. Professional: Darren Glasby (Tel & Fax: 01480 466067). Manager: Vince Benson (Tel & Fax: 01480 468392).

ST NEOTS. **Abbotsley Golf Club and Hotel,** Eynesbury Hardwicke, St Neots PE19 4XN (01480 474000; Fax: 01480 471018). *Location:* A428 St Neots Way, turn towards St. Neots at Tesco's follow signs to Eynesbury Hardwicke and Abbotsley. Pleasantly undulating, parkland course with several water features. Two courses, 36 holes - Abbotsley 6311 yards, S.S.S. 72; Cromwell 6087 yards, S.S.S. 69. Floodlit covered driving range, 300 yard grass practice area. 9 hole Par 3 course. *Green Fees:* information not available. *Eating facilities:* 90 cover restaurant, three bars. *Visitors:* always welcome. 42 bedroom hotel. *Society Meetings:* welcome. General Manager: Jonathan Tubb. Professional: Tim Hudson. Sales Manager: Sharon Brown (01480 474000; Fax: 01480 471018).*

ST NEOTS. **St Neots Golf Club,** Crosshall Road, St Neots PE19 7GE (01480 472363). *Location:* just off the A1, Junction B1048 heading for St. Neots. Picturesque, undulating parkland course with water hazards and challenging greens. 18 holes, 6033 yards. S.S.S. 69. Practice ground, putting green. *Green Fees:* weekdays £30.00. *Eating facilities:* full catering and bar. *Visitors:* welcome, with Handicap Certificates; weekends with a member only. *Society Meetings:* welcome weekdays. Club Secretary: Frank Thorpe (Manager: 01480 472363; Pro shop: 01480 476513).

WISBECH. **Tydd St Giles Golf Centre,** Kirkgate, Tydd St Giles, Wisbech PE13 5NZ (01945 871007; Fax: 01945 870566). *Location:* A1101 from Wisbech to Long Sutton to Tydd Gate and follow the river to Tydd St Giles, one mile from this junction on right hand side. Slightly undulating course, fenland Grade 1 silt/loam free draining. Course always open. 18 holes, 6226 yards, S.S.S. 70. Indoor/outdoor floodlit driving range. *Green Fees:* weekdays £11.00, Seniors £9.00; weekends £14.00. *Eating facilities:* all day snacks/grills. Full Pub licence - everyone welcome. *Visitors:* welcome, please ring for a tee off time, dress code applies. Tuition available daily. *Society Meetings:* welcome, packages available. Professionals: Martin Perkins (07944 974011); Alison Johns (07887 594313). e-mail: enquiries@tyddgolf.co.uk
website: www.tyddgolf.co.uk

Cheshire

ALDERLEY EDGE. **Alderley Edge Golf Club,** Brook Lane, Alderley Edge SK9 7RU (01625 585583). *Location:* off A34. 9 holes, 5836 yards. S.S.S. 68. *Green Fees:* weekdays £12.00 9 holes, £22.00 18 holes, weekends £15.00 9 holes, £27.50 18 holes. 2-fore-1 vouchers accepted. *Eating facilities:* meals served in clubhouse. *Visitors:* subject to restrictions on Tuesday mornings, Wednesday afternoons and weekends. *Society Meetings:* welcome on Thursdays. Professional: P. Bowring (01625 584493). Secretary: R.C. Harrison.

ALSAGER. **Alsager Golf and Country Club,** Audley Road, Alsager, Stoke-on-Trent ST7 2UR (01270 875700; Fax: 01270 882207). *Location:* off M6 at Junction 16 onto A500 to Stoke, first left to Alsager, course is one and a half miles on right. Parkland. 18 holes, 6201 yards. S.S.S. 70. *Green Fees:* £25.00 Mondays to Fridays. *Eating facilities:* restaurant and bar snacks. *Visitors:* welcome Mondays, to Thursdays and Fridays 8am to 12pm, without reservation. Wedding, conference and banqueting facilities. Bowls. *Society Meetings:* welcome Mondays, Wednesdays and Thursdays, packages arranged. Professional: Richard Brown (01270 877432; Fax: 01270 882207). Administration Manager: Margaret Davenport (01270 875700). e-mail: business@alsagergolfclub.com

APPLETON. **Warrington Golf Club,** Hill Warren, London Road, Appleton, Near Warrington WA4 5HR (01925 261620). *Location:* M56 Junction 10, A49 Warrington one and a half miles on left. Parkland course. 18 holes, 6210 yards. S.S.S. 70. Practice ground. *Green Fees:* information not available. *Eating facilities:* available every day. *Visitors:* welcome with booking through Professional. *Society Meetings:* Wednesdays only, booked through Secretary. Professional: R. MacKay (01925 265431). Secretary: N.F. Morrall (01925 261775; Fax: 01925 265933). *
e-mail: secretary@warrington-golf-club.co.uk

CHEADLE. **Cheadle Golf Club,** Cheadle Road, Cheadle SK8 1HW (0161-428 2160). *Location:* one-and-a-half miles Junction 11 M63. Parkland. 9 holes, 5006 yards. S.S.S. 65. *Green Fees:* on application. *Eating facilities:* by arrangement with the Steward. *Visitors:* welcome, must be members of a bona fide golf club; current Handicap Certificate to be produced; no visitors on Tuesdays or Saturdays. *Society Meetings:* catered for by arrangement with the Secretary. Professional: S. Booth (0161-428 9878). Secretary: C.T. Openshaw (0161-491 4452).

CHEADLE. **Gatley Golf Club Ltd,** Waterfall Farm, Styal Road, Heald Green, Cheadle SK8 3TW (0161-437 2091). *Location:* from Gatley village to South down Styal Road and follow directions into Yew Tree Grove, then Motcombe Grove to Club entrance. Parkland course. 9 holes, 5934 yards. S.S.S. 68. *Green Fees:* information not available. Special rates by arrangement. *Eating facilities:* available except Monday, bar. *Visitors:* welcome Mondays, Wednesdays and Thursdays. *Society Meetings:* welcome Thursdays. Professional: James Matterson (0161-436 2830). Secretary: R.W.R. Salt (0161-437 2091).

CHESTER. **Aldersey Green Golf Club,** Aldersey, Near Chester CH3 9EH (01829 782157). *Location:* on A41 Chester to Whitchurch road five minutes from Broxton roundabout. Flat wooded parkland. 18 holes, 6159 yards. S.S.S. 69. Practice area. *Green Fees:* weekdays £15.00 per round, weekends £20.00 per round. *Eating facilities:* bar with meals available. *Visitors:* welcome. *Society meetings:* welcome. Professional and Secretary: Stephen Bradbury.

CHESTER. **Carden Park Hotel Golf Resort & Spa,** Carden, near Chester CH3 9DQ (01829 731000; Fax: 01829 731032). *Location:* take A41 from Chester to Broxton roundabout, turn right onto A534 (Wrexham). Parkland courses with trees and superb views over the Cheshire countryside. Cheshire Course, 18 holes, 6824 yards. Par 72. Nicklaus Course, 18 holes, 7045 yards, Par 72. Par 3 Azalea Course. Driving range. *Green Fees:* £40.00 Cheshire Course, £60.00 Nicklaus Course. *Eating facilities:* Clubhouse; brasserie within hotel. *Visitors:* welcome, some restriction on certain competition and members' days. No metal spikes allowed. Accommodation in 192 bedroom hotel. *Society Meetings:* welcome. Professional: Paul Hodgson. e-mail: enquiries.carden@devere-hotels.com

CHESTER. **Chester Golf Club,** Curzon Park, Chester CH4 8AR (01244 675130). *Location:* one mile south west of city centre. From Chester Castle take A483 (Wrexham) to first roundabout over Grovesnor Bridge. Turn right into Curzon Park North and follow signs. Parkland on two levels overlooking the River Dee. 18 holes, 6508 yards. S.S.S. 71. *Green Fees:* weekdays £30.00 per day; weekends £35.00. Reductions if playing with a member. *Eating facilities:* full restaurant and bar facilities. *Visitors:* welcome most days but advisable to telephone first. *Society Meetings:* catered for by prior arrangement. Professional: George Parton (01244 671185). Secretary: V.F.C. Wood (01244 677760).

CHESTER. **Eaton Golf Club,** Guy Lane, Waverton, Chester CH3 7PH (01244 335885). *Location*: three miles south east of Chester off A41. 18 holes, 6562 yards. S.S.S. 71. Substantial practice area. *Green Fees*: weekdays £30.00, weekends £35.00. *Eating facilities*: catering available seven days. *Visitors:* welcome at all times but with Handicap Certificate and prior checking with either Secretary or Professional. *Society Meetings*: welcome except Wednesdays. Society rates available on request. Professional: Bill Tye (01244 335826). Secretary: Kerry Brown (01244 335885; Fax: 01244 335782).

CHESTER. **Mollington Grange Golf Club**, Townfield Lane, Mollington, Chester CH1 6NJ (01244 851185; Fax: 01244 851349). *Location:* A 540, 5 minutes from end of M56 and two miles from Chester City. A superb undulating course with five lakes, 16 ponds and a Par 3 island green, providing a challenge for the advanced player while remaining friendly to the average player or beginner. 18 holes, 6400 yards. Par 71. Driving range. *Green Fees:* information not available. *Eating facilities:* club house with warm and friendly atmosphere, lounge and bar area, restaurant and sports lounge/bar situated on the first floor. *Visitors:* welcome. Membership open, details on request. Fully stocked golf shop and comfortable changing facilities. *Society Meetings:* welcome. Corporate days and corporate membership catered for. Details available on request. Director of Golf: Ben Keegan. Secretary: Gail Matthews.*

CHESTER. **Pryors Hayes Golf Club,** Willington Road, Oscroft, Near Tarvin CH3 8NL (01829 741250; Fax: 01829 749077). *Location:* situated between A41 and A51 at Oscroft, near Tarvin. Flat, parkland course. 18 holes, 6054 yards. S.S.S. 69. Practice area. *Green Fees:* £20.00 weekdays, £30.00 weekends. *Eating facilities:* restaurant and bar. *Visitors:* welcome every day subject to availability. *Society Meetings:* Societies/ Companies/ Groups all welcome. Professional: Martin Redrup (01829 740140; Fax: 01829 749077). Secretary: Joan Quinn (01829 741250; Fax: 01829 749077).

CHESTER. **Upton-by-Chester Golf Club,** Upton Lane, Chester CH2 1EE (01244 381183; Fax: 01244 376955). *Location:* off A41, near Zoo turn-off traffic lights. Flat parkland course. 18 holes, 5808 yards. S.S.S. 68. *Green Fees:* £30.00 per day, £20.00 per round. *Eating facilities:* large restaurant and bar. *Visitors:* no restrictions except Competition Days. *Society Meetings:* welcome except Mondays, Tuesdays and weekends. Minimum number 16. All day packages £39.00. Professional: Stephen Dewhurst (01244 381183). Secretary: Fred Hopley (01244 381183; Fax: 01244 376955).

CHESTER. **Vicars Cross Golf Club,** Tarvin Road, Great Barrow, Chester CH3 7HN (01244 335174; Fax: 01244 335686). *Location:* four miles east of Chester on the A51. Undulating parkland course, wooded. 18 holes, 6446 yards. S.S.S. 71. Practice grounds/ covered bays. *Green Fees:* £30.00 per day, £20.00 after 3pm. Subject to review. *Eating facilities:* restaurant and bar snacks. *Visitors:* welcome every day except competition days - phone Secretary or Professional beforehand. *Society Meetings:* welcome Tuesday/Thursday. Conference facilities, lounge/ dining rooms available for hire. Professional: John Forsythe (01244 335595). Secretary: Mrs Katrina Hunt.
e-mail: secretary@vcgc.fsnet.co.uk

CONGLETON. **Astbury Golf Club**, Peel Lane, Astbury, Near Congleton CW12 4RE (01260 272772). *Location:* on outskirts south of Congleton, leave A34 Congleton to Newcastle Road at Astbury Village. Parkland/meadowland, water feature on four holes. 18 holes, 6178 yards. S.S.S. 69. Large practice area. *Green Fees:* weekdays £30.00, £12.00 with member; weekends £15.00 with member only. *Eating facilities:* dining room and bar. *Visitors:* welcome weekdays, weekend with a member only. Must be members of recognised golf club with bona fide Handicap. Smart casual dress in clubhouse, jackets expected when meal/presentation held. *Society Meetings:* Thursdays only April to November £25.00 per player. Professional: Ashley Salt (01260 272772). Secretary: Fred Reed (01260 272772). Caterer: (01260 299266).

CONGLETON. **Congleton Golf Club**, Biddulph Road, Congleton CW12 3LZ (01260 273540). *Location:* one mile south of Congleton Railway Station on Biddulph Road. Parkland. 9 holes, 5119 yards. S.S.S. 65. *Green Fees:* weekdays £21.00, weekends £31.00. *Eating facilities:* lunches and evening meals served if ordered in advance. Snacks available. *Visitors:* welcome. *Society Meetings:* welcome Mondays and Thursdays by prior arrangement. Professional: John Colclough (01260 273540). Secretary: R. Brindley (01260 273540).

CREWE. **Crewe Golf Club Ltd,** Fields Road, Haslington, Crewe CW1 5TB (01270 584099). *Location:* off A534 between Crewe and Sandbach in the village of Haslington. Parkland course. 18 holes, 6424 yards. S.S.S. 71. *Green Fees:* £24.00 after 1pm, £30.00 before 1pm. Subject to review. *Eating facilities:* bar, diningroom. *Visitors:* welcome weekdays only, not Bank Holidays. Snooker room. *Society Meetings:* Tuesdays only. Catering (01270 584227). Professional: David Wheeler (01270 585032). Secretary: Alan Whittingham (01270 584099; Fax: 01270 256482).

CREWE. **Onneley Golf Club**, Barr Hill Road, Onneley, Near Crewe (01782 750577). *Location:* one mile from Woore on A525, 12 miles from Stoke-on-Trent. Parkland on gentle slope. 13 holes, 5781 yards. S.S.S. 68. *Green Fees:* weekdays £20.00 (£10.00 with member); Saturdays and Bank Holidays with member only. Juniors half normal price. *Eating facilities:* Dining-room and bar snacks *Visitors:* welcome weekdays unrestricted. *Society Meetings:* welcome, except Tuesdays and Fridays (£20.00 per round including meal). Secretary: Peter Ball (01782 846759).

CREWE. **Queens Park Golf Course**, Queens Park Drive, Crewe CW2 7SB (01270 662378). *Location:* next to Queens Park, one mile from Crewe Station. Parkland. 9 holes x 2, 4920 yards. S.S.S. 64. *Green Fees:* weekdays £6.50 per round; weekends £8.50 per round. *Eating facilities:* bar with excellent bar snacks. *Visitors:* welcome, restrictions Sunday mornings to 11am. *Society Meetings:* welcome. Professional: Jamie Lowe (01270 666724). Secretary: Tom Weston (01270 662887).

DISLEY. **Disley Golf Club Ltd**, Stanley Hall Lane, Disley, Stockport SK12 2JX (01663 762071). *Location:* off A6 at Disley Village. Open hillside/parkland course. 18 holes, 6015 yards, 5832 metres. S.S.S. 69. *Green Fees:* information not available. *Eating facilities:* available. *Visitors:* welcome weekdays. *Society Meetings:* catered for by arrangement. Professional: A.G. Esplin (01663 762884). Secretary: Mrs D. Bradley (01663 764001). *

FRODSHAM. **Frodsham Golf Club**, Simons Lane, Frodsham WA6 6HE (01928 732159); Fax: 01928 734070). *Location:* 10 minutes from Junction 12 M56. Parkland with views over Mersey estuary. 18 holes, 6328 yards. S.S.S. 70 (gents), 70 (ladies). Two practice areas, putting green, bunker and net. *Green Fees:* information not available. *Eating facilities:* clubhouse: dining room, lounge bar, spike bar, snooker room. *Visitors:* welcome weekdays only, guests of members only at weekends. *Society Meetings:* welcome weekdays. Professional: Graham Tonge (01928 739442; Fax: 01928 739037). Secretary: Mr E.I Roylance (01928 732159; Fax: 01928 734070). e-mail: office@frodshamgc.golfagent.co.uk website: www.frodshamgolfclub.co.uk

HELSBY. **Helsby Golf Club**, Towers Lane, Helsby WA6 0JB (01928 722021; Fax: 01928 725384). *Location:* 7 miles south of Chester. M56 Junction 14 take B5117 to Helsby. Through traffic lights one mile, first right into Primrose Lane, then first right into Towers Lane (400 yards). James Braid designed parkland course. 18 holes, 6229 yards. S.S.S. 70. Practice area available. *Green Fees:* £25.00 weekdays; £17.00 with a member weekends. Subject to review. *Eating facilities:* full restaurant facilities. *Visitors:* welcome weekdays, weekends must play with a member. Snooker facilities. *Society Meetings:* welcome Tuesdays and Thursdays by arrangement. Professional: M. Jones (Tel & Fax: 01928 725457). Secretary: L.J. Norbury (01928 722021).

KNUTSFORD. **Heyrose Golf Club,** Budworth Road, Tabley, Knutsford WA16 0HZ (Tel & Fax: 01565 733664). *Location:* Junction 19 on M6 right at Windmill Pub to Pickmere, three-quarters of a mile right fork, half a mile further on right. Undulating parkland, wooded course. 18 holes, 6513 yards. S.S.S. 71. New 12 bay driving range, net and bunker, putting green, indoor teaching room. *Green Fees:* weekdays £25.00 per round; weekends £30.00 per round. Subject to review. *Eating facilities:* bar and restaurant. *Visitors:* no visitors on Saturdays before 3.30pm, Ladies priority Wednesdays, Seniors priority Thursdays. *Society Meetings:* welcome weekdays. Professional: Paul Affleck (Tel & Fax: 01565 734267). General Manager: Mrs Elizabeth Bridge (Tel & Fax: 01565 733664). e-mail: secretary@heyrosegolfclub.com website: www.heyrosegolfclub.com

KNUTSFORD. **Knutsford Golf Club,** Mereheath Lane, Knutsford WA16 6HS (01565 633355). *Location:* quarter of a mile from town centre. 9 holes, 6200 yards. S.S.S. 70. *Green Fees:* weekdays £25.00. weekends and Bank Holidays £30.00. *Eating facilities:* bar snacks, other meals by prior arrangement. *Visitors:* welcome with reservation except Wednesdays and Saturdays and Sundays before 10:00am. *Society Meetings:* catered for by prior arrangement. Professional: Granville Ogden. Secretary: Danny Burgess.

KNUTSFORD. **Mere Golf and Country Club**, Chester Road, Mere, Knutsford WA16 6LJ (01565 830155; Fax: 01565 830713). *Location*: one mile east of Junction 19 M6 and two miles west of Junction 7 M56. Parkland Championship course. 18 holes, 6817 yards. S.S.S. 73. Short game practice area, one 18 hole putting green, driving range (April to October). *Green Fees:* information not available. *Eating facilities:* informal atrium spike bar and brasserie. *Visitors:* welcome by prior arrangement only. *Society Meetings:* Mondays, Tuesdays and Thursdays only by arrangement. Professional: Peter Eyre (01565 830219). Golf Bookings: Karen Gallagher (01565 830155). Secretary: S. Janvier.

KNUTSFORD. **Mobberley Golf Club**, Burleyhurst Lane, Mobberley, Knutsford WA16 7JZ (01565 880188; Fax: 01565 880178). *Location*: exit 6 M56 to A538 Wilmslow, turn right at Mobberley Road. 9 hole course set in rolling Cheshire countryside. 5542 yards, S.S.S. 67. *Green Fees:* information not available. *Eating facilities*: fully licensed facilities available. *Visitors*: welcome at all times. Dress code must be adhered to. No denims, tracksuits, collarless shirts. Golf shoes must be worn. *Society Meetings*: welcome at all times. Professional: John Cheetham. Secretary: Nicholas Donaghy (Tel & Fax: 01565 880178).

KNUTSFORD. **The Wilmslow Golf Club**, Great Warford, Mobberley, Knutsford WA16 7AY (01565 872148). *Location:* two miles from Wilmslow off the Knutsford Road. Parkland course. 18 holes, 6607 yards. S.S.S. 72. Practice facility. *Green Fees:* weekdays £40.00 per round, £50.00 per day; weekends £50.00 per round, £60.00 per day. *Eating facilities:* full catering except Monday, two bars. *Visitors:* welcome, Ladies' Day Wednesday. *Society Meetings:* Tuesdays and Thursdays only. Professional: L.J. Nowicki (01565 873620). Secretary: Mrs M.I. Padfield (01565 872148; Fax: 01565 872172). e-mail: wilmslowgolfclub@ukf.net website: www.wilmslowgolfclub.ukf.net

KNUTSFORD near. Peover Golf Club, Plumley Moor Road, Lower Peover, Near Knutsford WA16 9SE (01565 723337; Fax: 01565 723311). *Location*: Junction 19 of M6, A556, Knutsford. Parkland course, 18 holes, 6702 yards. S.S.S. 72. Practice area, putting green. *Green Fees:* £23.00 weekdays, £30.00 weekends. Subject to change. *Eating facilities*: bar food and function room. *Visitors*:

always welcome. Please ring for a tee time. Buggy and trolley hire. *Society Meetings*: welcome, except weekends.
e-mail: email@peovergolfclub.co.uk
website: www.peovergolfclub.co.uk

LYMM. **Lymm Golf Club,** Whitbarrow Road, Lymm WA13 9AN (Tel & Fax: 01925 755020). *Location:* five miles south east of Warrington, two and a half miles from Junction 20 on M6 and Junction 9 on M56. Parkland. 18 holes, 6304 yards. S.S.S. 70. Practice ground. *Green Fees:* weekdays £26.00. *Eating facilities:* coffee, bar snacks, lunches and dinner, bar. *Visitors:* welcome with Handicap Certificates, no visitors at weekends, Bank Holidays or Thursdays until 2.30pm. *Society Meetings:* catered for Wednesdays with reservations. Professional: Steve McCarthy (01925 755054). Secretary: Mrs S. Nash (Tel & Fax: 01925 755020). Clubhouse (01925 752177). website: www.lymm-golf-club.co.uk

MACCLESFIELD. **Macclesfield Golf Club,** The Hollins, Macclesfield SK11 7EA (01625 423227). *Location:* turn off A523 Leek Road into Windmill Street, half a mile fork right. Hillside course with extensive views. 18 holes, 5769 yards. S.S.S. 68. *Green Fees:* £30.00 weekdays; £40.00 weekends and Bank Holidays. *Eating facilities:* full catering and bars. *Visitors:* welcome by arrangement. *Society Meetings:* welcome weekdays except Thursdays. Professional: Tony Taylor (01625 616952). Secretary: David English (01625 615845; Fax: 01625 260061). e-mail: secretary@Macgolfclub.co.uk website: Macgolfclub.co.uk

MACCLESFIELD. **The Tytherington Club,** Dorchester Way, Tytherington, Macclesfield SK10 2JP (01625 506000; Fax: 01625 506040). *Location:* one mile north of Macclesfield off A523. Undulating parkland with numerous water features and ample woodland. 18 holes, 6765 yards. S.S.S. 74. Driving range, short game area. *Green Fees:* £34.00 weekdays; £40.00 weekends. *Eating facilities:* bar with Brasserie-style food and private function rooms available. *Visitors:* welcome, by prior arrangement. Buggies available. *Society Meetings:* welcome weekdays only. Highly competitive packages available. Professional: Gavin Beddow (01625 506013). General Manager: Daniel Sheratte. e-mail: tytherington.events@clubhaus.com

NANTWICH. **Alvaston Hall Golf Club**, Alvaston Hall Hotel, Middlewich Road, Nantwich CW59 6PD (01270 628473; Fax: 01270 623395). *Location*: A530 Middlewich Road. Parkland course. 9 holes. S.S.S. 59. *Green Fees*: information not available. Professional: Kevin Valentine. Secretary: Nick Perkins.

NANTWICH. **Reaseheath College Golf Club,** Reaseheath College, Reaseheath, Nantwich CW5 6DF. *Location*: A500 north of Nantwich. Flat parkland. 9 holes, 1772 yards. S.S.S. 58. Reaseheath College Golf Club is primarily a 9 hole college golf course principally for the training of greenkeepers throughout the UK. *Green Fees*: £7.00. Only playing with a member as small parties. *Visitors*: subject to approval. *Society Meetings*: subject to approval. Secretary: Chris Bishop (01270 625131; Fax: 01270 625665).

NORTHWICH. **Antrobus Golf Club,** Foggs Lane, Antrobus, Northwich (01925 730890; Fax: 01925 730100). *Location*: two minutes from Junction 10 of M56 between Northwich and Warrington. Parkland course with lakes. 18 holes, 6220 yards. S.S.S. 72. Putting green and driving range. *Green Fees:* weekdays £22.00; weekends £25.00 (same prices for 2004). Cheshire Cards accepted. *Eating facilities:* available. *Visitors:* welcome every day, except Saturdays. *Society Meetings:* welcome any day except Saturday. Ring for discounted rates. Professional: Paul Farrance (01925 730900). Secretary: Celia Axford (01925 730890; Fax: 01925 730100).

NORTHWICH. **Delamere Forest Golf Club,** Station Road, Delamere, Northwich CW8 2JE (01606 883264). *Location*: opposite Delamere Station on the B5152 Tarporley to Frodsham road. Undulating heathland course suitable for play winter or summer. 18 holes, 6305 yards. S.S.S. 71. Two practice grounds. *Green Fees*: weekdays £35.00 18 holes; £50.00 per day, weekends £60.00 *Eating facilities:* bar meals, diningroom. *Visitors:* welcome most weekdays if no large parties booked. Some restrictions on four balls on Sundays. Prior booking with Pro advisable. *Society Meetings:* societies, corporate days, parties and small groups catered for. Professional: E.B. Jones (01606 883307). Secretary: J.J Mulder (Tel: 01606 883800; Fax: 01606 889444). e-mail: info@delameregolf.co.uk website: www.dfgc.co.uk

NORTHWICH. **Hartford Golf Club**, Burrows Hill, Hartford, Northwich CW8 3AP (01606 871162; Fax: 01606 872182). *Location*: Just off A49 and A556 near ICI at Winnington. Undulating parkland course with numerous water hazards. 9 holes, 2780 yards, Par 35. 26 bay driving range. *Green Fees*: 18 holes £10.50 weekdays; 18 holes £12.50 weekends. Pay as you play and membership available. *Eating facilities*: clubhouse open spring 2004. Large golf shop, tuition available. *Society Meetings*: welcome. Professional: L. Percival (01606 871162; Fax: 01606 872182). Secretary: C. Maddock.

NORTHWICH. **Sandiway Golf Club**, Chester Road, Sandiway, Northwich CW8 2DJ (01606 883247). *Location*: off A556, Northwich by-pass. Undulating heavily wooded parkland. 18 holes, 6404 yards. S.S.S. 72. *Green Fees*: information not available. *Eating facilities:* lunches and teas served daily, full restaurant facilities. *Visitors:* welcome on weekdays with letter of introduction and Handicap Certificate from home club. *Society Meetings:* restricted to Tuesdays, parties up to 40; Wednesday and Friday; parties up to 20. Professional: William Laird (01606 883180). Secretary: R.H. Owens (01606 883247; Fax: 01606 888548). Caterer: (01606 882606).*

NORTHWICH. **Vale Royal Abbey Golf Club,** Whitegate, Northwich CW8 2BA (01606 301291; Fax: 01606 301414). Parkland championship course. 18 holes, 6463 yards, S.S.S. 71. Short game practice area, putting green, chipping green, practice range. *Green Fees*: on application. *Eating facilities*: informal spike bar. *Visitors:* welcome by arrangement only. *Society Meetings*: welcome by arrangement. Professional: Richard Stockdale (golf bookings at Pro Shop 01606 301702).

POYNTON. **Davenport Golf Club,** Worth Hall, Middlewood Road, Poynton SK12 1TS (01625 876951; Fax: 01625 877489). *Location*: A6 from Stockport, Macclesfield Road at Hazel Grove, left at Poynton Church. Undulating parkland course. 18 holes, 6027 yards. S.S.S. 69. Putting green and practice ground. *Green Fees*: weekdays £30.00 (£12.50 with member), weekends £40.00 (£15.00 with a member). *Eating facilities:* bar snacks daily except Mondays, full meals by arrangement. *Visitors:* welcome, advisable to check with the Professional for availability of first tee. *Society Meetings:* catered for Tuesdays and Thursdays only. Professional: Gary Norcott (01625 877319). Secretary: Brian Sandham (01625 876951; Fax: 01625 877489).

POYNTON. **Shrigley Hall Hotel, Golf & Country Club,** Shrigley Park, Pott Shrigley, Near Macclesfield SK10 5SB (01625 575757; Fax: 01625 575437). *Location*: easily accessible from the M56, M62,M60, M6,A523 and A6, only 10 minutes from Manchester Airport. Parkland course with magnificent views. 18 holes, 6305 yards. S.S.S 71. *Green Fees:* information on request. *Eating facilities:* private rooms catering 16-250 people plus hotel Orangery Restaurant. *Visitors:* corporate, society and resident golfers welcome. Hotel 156 bedroomed four star hotel. Professional: Tony A. Stevens (01625 575626). Secretary: Sally Bowker (01625 576681).

PRESTBURY. **De Vere Mottram Hall Golf Course,** Wilmslow Road, Mottram St. Andrew, Prestbury SK10 4QT (01625 820064). *Location*: M56 and M6. Flat parkland/woodland course. 18 holes, 7006 yards, 6250 metres. S.S.S. 72. Practice area. *Green Fees*: information not available. *Eating facilities*: golf centre bar and restaurant. *Visitors*: no restrictions. Accommodation in 132 bedrooms. *Society Meetings*: no restrictions except at weekends. Professional: Tim Rastall.

PRESTBURY. **Prestbury Golf Club,** Macclesfield Road, Prestbury, Cheshire (01625 828241). *Location*: in between Wilmslow and Macclesfield. 18 holes, 6359 yards, 5812 metres. S.S.S. 71. Practice ground. *Green Fees:* to be arranged. *Eating facilities:* snacks, lunches, teas and dinners. *Visitors:* welcome on weekdays 9.30am to 11.30am and after 2.30pm; Tuesdays Ladies' Day until 2.30pm. Wednesdays Gentlemen members only until 3pm. Bank Holidays and weekends only with a member. *Society Meetings:* Thursdays only. Professional: Nick Summerfield (01625 828242). Secretary: (Tel & Fax: 01625 828241).
e-mail: office@prestburygolfclub.com
website: www.prestburygolfclub.com

RUNCORN. **Runcorn Golf Club,** Clifton Road, Runcorn WA7 4SU (01928 572093). *Location:* signposted The Heath, A557; M56 Junction 12. High parkland, easy walking course. 18 holes, 6035 yards, 5514 metres. S.S.S. 69. *Green Fees:* weekdays £24.00. *Eating facilities:* bar snacks, lunches; dinner by arrangement. *Visitors:* welcome weekdays, Tuesday is Ladies' Day. No visitors weekends or Bank Holidays except with a member. Handicap Certificate required. *Society Meetings:* by arrangement Mondays and Fridays. Professional: D. Ingman (01928 564791). Secretary: A. Booth (Tel & Fax: 01928 574214).

SANDBACH. **Malkins Bank Municipal Golf Course**, Betchton Road, Malkins Bank, Sandbach CW11 4XN (01270 765931). *Location:* M6, Junction 17 west on A534 for one mile, south on A533 for 400 metres, turn into Hassall Road (signposted). Parkland course. 18 holes, 5971 yards, S.S.S. 69. Practice area. *Green Fees:* weekdays from £8.80; weekends from £10.30 subject to review. Weekday concessions for Senior Citizens and Juniors. *Eating facilities:* bar and food available. *Visitors:* welcome at all times, please pre-book (01270 765931). *Society Meetings:* welcome, please pre-book (01270 765931). Professional: Davron Hackney (01270 765931; Fax: 01270 764730).

SANDBACH. **Sandbach Golf Club,** 117 Middlewich Road, Sandbach CW11 1FH (01270 762117). *Location*: two miles from Junction 17 of M6 on Middlewich Road. Meadowland course. 9 holes, 5397 yards. S.S.S. 67. Practice field. *Green Fees:* weekdays £20.00 per day, £10.00 with member; weekends and Bank Holidays must be accompanied by a member. *Eating facilities:* available except Mondays and Thursdays. *Visitors:* welcome weekdays, weekends by invitation only. *Society Meetings:* catered for only by advance arrangement with Hon. Secretary. Secretary: P.R. O'Harro.

SOUTH WIRRAL. **Ellesmere Port Golf Centre,** Chester Road, Childer, Thornton, South Wirral CH66 1QF (0151-339 7689). *Location*: approximately six miles north of Chester on main A41 trunk road to Birkenhead. Wooded parkland with a lot of ponds. 18 holes, 6296 yards. S.S.S. 70. Practice ground with green and Smart Golf Simulator (£6.00). *Green fees:* information not available. Eating facilities: bar and catering facilities. *Visitors:* welcome anytime. *Society Meetings:* by arrangement with Professional. Professional: Danny Youd (0151-339 7689). Secretary: Colin Craggs (0151-334 6579).

STALYBRIDGE. **Stamford (Stalybridge) Golf Club,** Oakfield House, Huddersfield Road, Carrbrook, Stalybridge SK15 3PY (01457 832126). *Location:* on B6175 off A6018. Moorland course. 18 holes, 5701 yards. S.S.S. 68. *Green Fees:* weekdays £20.00; weekends after 3pm £25.00. Special rates for golf societies. *Eating facilities:* full meals except Monday (bar available). *Visitors:* welcome without restrictions. *Society Meetings:* catered for by appointment only. Golf Shop: (01457 834829). Secretary: Mr B.D. Matthews (0161-633 5721).
e-mail: stamford.golfclub@totalise.co.uk

STYAL. **Styal Golf Club,** Station Road, Styal SK9 4JN. (01625 530063). *Location:* Station Road, Styal, five minutes from Manchester Airport, Junction 5 M56, five minutes from Wilmslow. Flat, parkland course with many water hazards and interesting features. 18 holes, 6194 yards, 5760 metres. S.S.S. 70. 9 hole, par 3 course, 1242 yards, Par 27. 24 bay deluxe driving range and short game academy. New 12 bay outdoor range. *Green Fees:* 18-hole course: weekdays £20.00, weekends £24.00; 9 hole course: £8.00 for 9 holes, £12.00 for 18 holes. *Eating facilities:* fully equipped restaurant and bar. *Visitors:* welcome. *Society Meetings:* welcome; packages available. Professional: Simon Forrest (01625 528910). Director of Golf: Glynn Traynor (01625 530063). Golf booking line (01625 531359).
e-mail: gtraynor@styalgolf.co.uk
website: www.styalgolf.co.uk

SUTTON WEAVER (NEAR RUNCORN). **Sutton Hall Golf Club,** Aston Lane, Sutton Weaver WA7 3ED (01928 790747; Fax: 01928 759174). *Location:* M56, Junction 12 signposted Frodsham. Wooded, parkland course. 18 holes, 6608 yards. S.S.S. 71. Full practice ground, putting green. *Green Fees;* weekdays £20.00, weekends £24.00. *Eating facilities:* Club House catering available all day. *Visitors:* welcome weekdays; by arrangement only at weekends. *Society Meetings:* welcome. Professional: Jamie Hope (01928 714872; Fax: 01928 759174). Secretary: Maxwell Faulkner.

Visit the FHG website
www.holidayguides.com
for details of the wide choice of accommodation featured in the full range of FHG titles

TARPORLEY. **Portal Golf and Country Club**, The Championship Course, Cobblers Cross Lane, Tarporley CW6 0DJ (01829 733933; Fax: 01829 733928). *Location*: half-a-mile from Tarporley on A49. Near Oulton Park. Donald Steel Championship course set in scenic parkland in the heartland of Cheshire with breathtaking panoramic views – lots of water! 18 holes, 7037 yards. S.S.S. 74. Driving range, practice facilities, putting green. Indoor golf academy. *Green Fees:* information not available. *Eating facilities:* excellent facilities with large banquet suite and bar area. *Visitors:* all visitors are required to book tee times in advance - seven day availability. Golf Shop, locker rooms, buggies. *Society Meetings:* welcome. Professional: Adrian Hill. Director of Golf: David Wills.*

TARPORLEY. **Portal, The Premier Course,** Forest Road, Tarporley CW6 0JA (01829 733884). *Location:* half a mile from Tarporley on A49. Undulating parkland with scenic views of Cheshire Plains. 18 holes, 6600 yards. S.S.S. 71. Practice area and putting green. *Green Fees:* information not available. *Eating facilities:* bar and restaurant. *Visitors:* welcome. *Society Meetings:* welcome, except weekends. Professional: Judy Statham (01829 733703). Director of Golf: David Wills.

For full details of clubs and courses, plus convenient accommodation, visit the FHG golf website

www.uk-golfguide.com

WARRINGTON. **Alder Root Golf Club,** Alder Root Lane, Winwick, Warrington WA2 8RZ (Tel & Fax: 01925 291919). *Location*: M6 Junction 22, A49 2 miles north of Warrington. Flat, parkland 10 holes, 5834 yards. S.S.S. 68. Putting green. Practice ground. Lessons available. *Green Fees:* £12.00 weekdays; £14.00 weekends. Two "Fore" one rates available. *Eating facilities: Visitors:* no restrictions weekdays, ring at weekends for details. *Society Meetings:* welcome. Professional: C. McKevitt (Tel & Fax: 01925 291932). Secretary: Mr E. Lander (Tel & Fax: 01925 291919).

WARRINGTON. **Birchwood Golf Club,** Kelvin Close, Science Park North, Birchwood, Warrington WA3 4ES (01925 818819; Fax: 01925 822403). *Location*: Junction 11 off M62, follow A574 signs for Risley then Science Park North signs. Flat parkland course with numerous natural ponds and streams. 18 holes, 6727 yards. S.S.S. 73. Practice ground, putting green. *Green Fees:* information not available. *Eating facilities:* bar snacks throughout the day; restaurant facilities on request. *Visitors:* welcome on weekdays. Conference and banqueting facilities. Trolleys for hire. *Society Meetings:* Societies, companies and groups are welcome Mondays and Wednesdays if booked in advance. Professional: Paul McEwan (01925 825216; Fax: 01925 822403). Secretary: Mike Cullen (01925 818819; Fax: 01925 822403).

WARRINGTON. **Leigh Golf Club,** Kenyon Hall, Broseley Lane, Culcheth, Warrington WA3 4BG (01925 763130). *Location:* off A580 East Lancs Road to Culcheth Village. Parkland with tree-lined fairways. 18 holes, 5876 yards. S.S.S. 68. Three practice areas, practice nets. *Green Fees:* information not available. *Eating facilities:* two bars and restaurant. *Visitors:* check with Professional. *Society Meetings:* catered for Mondays (except Bank Holidays) and Tuesdays. Professional: Andrew Baguley (01925 762013). Secretary: D.A. Taylor (01925 762943; Fax: 01925 765097).

WARRINGTON. **Poulton Park Golf Club Ltd**, Dig Lane, Cinnamon Brow, Warrington WA2 0SH (01925 812034). *Location*: M6 (Junction 21), off A574 (Warrington/Leigh) Crab Lane. 9 holes, 4798 metres. S.S.S. 69. Practice ground. *Green Fees:* on application. *Eating facilities*: available except Mondays. *Visitors:* welcome most days, restricted at weekends. *Society Meetings*: catered for except weekends, maximum 24. Golf Society Packages available. Professional: Andrew Matthews. (01925 825220). Secretary: E. Caise (01925 822802).

WARRINGTON. **Walton Hall Golf Club**, Warrington Road, Higher Walton, Warrington WA4 5LU (01925 266775). *Location*: two miles south of Warrington off A56. Wooded parkland. 18 holes, 6801 yards. S.S.S. 73, Par 72. Practice ground. *Green Fees*: information not available. *Eating facilities*: licensed clubhouse, meals and bar snacks. *Visitors:* unrestricted. *Society Meetings:* welcome, weekends after 1pm. Professional: J. Jackson (01925 263061). Secretary: Dave Johnson (01925 230860 or 07765 451541).

WIDNES. **Mersey Valley Golf Club**, Warrington Road, Bold Heath, Widnes WA8 3XL (0151-424 6060; Fax: 015i 257 9097). *Location*: two miles from Junction 7 off M62, on the A57 towards Warrington. Flat parkland course. 18 holes, 6511 yards. S.S.S. 71, Par 72. *Green Fees*: weekdays £20.00; weekends £25.00. *Eating facilities*: full facilities available. *Visitors*: welcome at all times. Tuition available. Non members welcome. *Society Meetings*: very welcome, special rates apply. Contact General Manager. Professional: Andy Stevenson PGA. General Manager: Chris Gerrard.

WIDNES. **St. Michaels Jubilee Golf Club**, Dundalk Road, Widnes WA8 8BS (0151-424 6230). Parkland course. 18 holes, 5638 yards. S.S.S. 67, Par 69. *Visitors*: unrestricted. Professional: D.Chapman (0151-424 6230). Secretary: A.J. Woodall (01695 726953).*

WIDNES. **Widnes Golf Club**, Highfield Road, Widnes WA8 7DT (0151-424 2440; Fax: 0151-495 2849). *Location*: near town centre, five miles from M56 and M62. Parkland course. 18 holes, 5729 yards. S.S.S. 68 White, 69 Ladies. *Green Fees:* weekdays £19.00; weekends £25.00. *Eating facilities:* two bars and full catering service. *Visitors:* welcome, normally Thursday. *Society Meetings:* catered for by arrangement Thursdays. Professional: Mr Jason O'Brien (0151-420 7467). Secretary: Mr V.A. Rudder (0151-424 2995).

WINSFORD. **Knights Grange Sports Complex,** Grange Lane, Winsford CW7 2PT (01606 552780). *Location:* signposted "Outdoor Sports Complex" from traffic lights Winsford Town Centre. 6 miles from M6, 16 miles from Chester. Set in beautiful Cheshire countryside on the outskirts of Winsford. A challenging course for golfers of all abilities. 18 holes - front 9 mainly flat but with water, ditches and other hazards. Back 9 take players deep into the countryside with many tees giving panoramic views of the course. There is also a lake and many mature woodland areas. Red Tees 5137 yards, S.S.S. 70; yellow tees 5270 yards, S.S.S. 66; white tees 5921 yards, S.S.S. 70. *Green Fees:* information available from Reception. *Eating facilities:* snacks and hot drinks available from Complex. Public house adjacent. *Visitors:* unrestricted, advance booking (01606 552780). Tennis, football, athletics. *Society Meetings:* welcomed - booking in writing in advance to Manager. Society packages available, run in conjunction with "Knights Grange Pub". Professional: Graham Moore. Manager: Mrs P. Littler (01606 552780).

> THE APPEARANCE OF AN ASTERISK (*)
> AT THE END OF A CLUB OR COURSE
> ENTRY INDICATES THAT
> UP-TO-DATE INFORMATION
> HAS NOT BEEN SUPPLIED

Widnes Golf Club

Highfield Road, Widnes WA8 7DT
- 18-hole parkland course five miles from M56 and M62
- Green Fees: weekdays £19, weekends £25.
- Visitors welcome (normally Thursdays).

Tel: 0151-424 2440 • Fax: 0151-495 2849

Recommended

Country Inns & Pubs of Britain

FHG

Where to enjoy the best of traditional British hospitality – a large selection of pubs, inns and small hotels, with separate supplements for pet-friendly and family-friendly establishments. *Available from bookshops and larger newsagents for £6.99*

FHG PUBLICATIONS LTD
Abbey Mill Business Centre, Seedhill, Paisley PAI 1TJ
www.holidayguides.com

PLEASE MENTION THE GOLF GUIDE WHEN YOU WRITE OR PHONE TO ENQUIRE ABOUT CLUBS OR ACCOMMODATION.

Cornwall

BODMIN. **Lanhydrock Golf Club,** Lostwithiel Road, Bodmin PL30 5AQ (01208 73600; Fax: 01208 77325). *Location:* one-and-a-half miles outside Bodmin on B3269. Parkland with generous tees and greens, easy walking, with many natural water features. 18 holes, 6100 yards, 5600 metres, Par 70, S.S.S. 70. Practice range. *Green Fees:* on application. One week unlimited golf pass available. *Eating facilities:* full catering facilities available, two bars. *Visitors:* welcome all week, booking advised. Large Pro shop, golf buggies available. *Society Meetings:* welcome by arrangement, private suite available. Professional: Jason Broadway. Manager: Graham Bond.
e-mail: golfing@lanhydrock-golf.co.uk
website: www.lanhydrock-golf.co.uk

BUDE. **Bude and North Cornwall Golf Club,** Burn View, Bude EX23 8DA (01288 352006; Fax: 01288 356855). *Location:* seaside links course situated in the centre of the town adjacent to beaches. 18 holes, 6205 yards. S.S.S. 70. Practice net and grounds. *Green Fees:* weekdays £27.00 per day; weekends £32.00 per day. *Eating facilities:* restaurant and bar snacks. *Visitors:* welcome without reservation. Snooker, billiards and pool. *Society Meetings:* catered for by bookings. Professional: John Yeo (01288 353635). Secretary: Mrs Pauline Ralph (01288 352006).

visit the FHG golf website on
www.uk-golfguide.com

CAMBORNE. **Tehidy Park Golf Club,** Camborne TR14 0HH (01209 842208; Fax: 01209 843680). *Location:* A30 via Blackwater and Camborne by-passes to sign for Portreath. Parkland, wooded, 3 new lakes. 18 holes, 6241 yards. S.S.S. 71. *Green Fees:* information not available. *Eating facilities:* bar snacks, à la carte restaurant except Mondays. *Visitors:* welcome with Handicap Certificate. *Society Meetings:* by arrangement; early booking essential. Catering Manager: (01209 842557). Professional: J. Dumbreck (01209 842914). Secretary/Manager Ray Parker (01209 842208; Fax: 01209 843680).*

CAMELFORD. **Bowood Park Hotel & Golf Course,** Lanteglos, Camelford PL32 9RF (01840 213017; Fax: 01840 212622). *Location:* M4, M5, A30, A39 through Camelford, turn right to Boscastle/ Tintagel before BP garage, then left after Park Lane Motors. Well groomed, parkland course set in 230 acres of rolling hills and woodland with 26 ponds and lakes. 18 hole, par 72. Covered driving range and Golf School. *Green Fees:* price on application. *Eating facilities:* full restaurant and bar facilities. *Visitors:* welcome. Large, well-stocked Pro Shop. Buggies for hire. Hotel accommodation available in 31 spacious en suite rooms, most with golf views, from £45.00 per person per night dinner, bed, breakfast and Golf. *Society Meetings:* society and corporate days welcome by arrangement. Professional: John Phillips. Secretary/ General Manager: Colin Willis (01840 213017).
e-mail: golf@bowoodpark.com
website: www.bowoodpark.com

To Let - Luxury House on Golf Course, Bowood Park Golf Course, Cornwall. Overlooking 15th Fairway. Spectacular view over the course. Enjoy playing your favourite sport in a superb holiday location for all the family. • Close to the beautiful North Coast and all amenities • Sleeps 6 persons • Available 7 or 14 nights, Sunday to Saturday bookings only. Reduced Green Fees.
Tel: 01934 823815 (please quote No.11 Bowood Park)
Bowood Park Golf Course, Lanteglos, Camelford, Cornwall

See also Colour Advertisement on page 13

This renowned inn is situated in an unspoilt fishing cove on the rugged North Coast of Cornwall. With its 17th century origins the inn provides comfortable bedrooms (all en suite) with tea and coffee making facilities.

The beach is just 50 yards from the front door and the Coastal Path offers miles of breathtaking scenery.

Our chef prides himself in serving good local food, seafood being a particular speciality of his.

If you are looking for a relaxing break with a friendly atmosphere you need look no further.

Golf, fishing, sailing and riding are all nearby.

Port Gaverne Hotel
Near Port Isaac, Cornwall PL29 3SQ
Tel: 01208 880244
Fax: 01208 880151

Pets welcome in the Inn and Self Catering Accommodation

See also Colour Advertisement on page 12

FALMOUTH. **Budock Vean Golf and Country House Hotel,** Near Mawnan Smith, Falmouth TR11 5LG (01326 250288; Fax: 01326 250892). *Location:* near Mawnan Smith, Falmouth – area of Helford River. 9 holes/18 tees, 5227 yards. Par 68. S.S.S. 65. *Green Fees:* information not available. *Eating facilities:* two bars, two restaurants, lunchtime bar menu. *Visitors:* daily only for outside visitors who are most welcome, but must have Handicap Certificate and book start time. Hotel accommodation. Secretary: R.M. Whitwam (Tel & Fax: 01326 252102). Golf Manager: A. Ramsden.*

FALMOUTH. **Falmouth Golf Club,** Swanpool Road, Falmouth TR11 5BQ (01326 314296; Fax: 01326 317783). *Location:* quarter of a mile west of Swanpool Beach, Falmouth, on the road to Maenporth. Wooded parkland course with magnificent views. 18 holes, 6037 yards. S.S.S. 70, Par 71. Driving range. *Green Fees:* £30.00 per 18 holes. *Eating facilities:* catering and bar all year round. *Visitors:* welcome at all times, except during major competitions. *Society Meetings:* always welcome. Professional: Bryan Patterson. Secretary: R. Wooldridge.

HELSTON. **Helston Golf and Leisure,** Redruth Road, Wendron, Helston TR13 0LX (Golf: 01326 572228; Restaurant: 01326 565103). *Location:* one mile out of Helston on B3297 Redruth Road. Parkland course. 18 holes, 2000 yards. S.S.S. 54. Nets and practice green. *Green Fees:* £6 per 18 holes, day card £9.00. *Eating facilities:* licensed bar with meals and snacks. *Visitors:* welcome; family course, all ages

welcome, pay and play; playable all weather. Club and ball hire £1. Other leisure facilities for all the family include crazy golf, boules. *Society Meetings:* all welcome, please book. Secretary/Owner: A. Burns.

HELSTON. **Mullion Golf Club,** Cury, Helston TR12 7BP (01326 241176). *Location:* from Helston on the A3083 past Culdrose Air Station, take first right past roundabout; signposted three miles. Cliff top and links. Indoor Golf Teaching Academy. 18 holes, 6037 yards. S.S.S. 70. *Green Fees:*£25.00 weekdays, £30.00 weekends and Bank Holidays. *Eating facilities:* bar and catering available each day. Caterers: (01326 241231). *Visitors:* welcome, with Handicap only. *Society Meetings:* by prior arrangement. Professional: Ian Harris (01326 241176). Secretary/Treasurer: G. Fitter (01326 240685)

HELSTON. **RNAS Culdrose Golf Club**, Royal Naval Air Station, Helston TR12 7RH (01326 552413). *Location:* A3083 one mile from Helston towards Lizard. Flat parkland course built around part of the airfield. 18 holes, 6132 yards. S.S.S. 70. Large practice area. *Visitors:* members only. Captain: G. Arthur.

LAUNCESTON. **Launceston Golf Club,** St Stephens, Launceston PL15 8HF (01556 773442). *Location:* one mile north of town on Bude road (B3254). Parkland. 18 holes, 6407 yards. S.S.S. 71. *Green Fees:* weekdays £25.00 per round, £28.00 per day. *Eating facilities:* available. *Visitors:* welcome. *Society Meetings:* catered for. Professional: J. Tozer (01566 775359). Secretary: C.S. Hicks (01566 773442; Fax: 01566 777506).

LAUNCESTON. **Trethorne Golf Club,** Kennards House, Launceston PL15 8QE (01566 86903). *Location:* 200 yards off A30. Set in a picturesque valley with mature trees and water. 18 holes, 6432 yards. S.S.S. 68/69/71. Driving range, putting green. *Green Fees:* £28.00. Winter rates on application. Groups of over 10 players £17.00. *Eating facilities:* bar, lounge bar and restaurant seating 150. *Visitors:* welcome, please ring for tee times. Non-handicap players welcome after 1pm. Accommodation available in 29 en suite bedrooms at the Club. Driving range available. Voted by "Fore" magazine as the best 2 fore 1 course in 2000. *Society Meetings:* welcome, rates on application. Professional/ Secretary/Golf Manager: Mark Boundy.

LOOE. **Looe Golf Club,** Bindown, Looe PL13 1PX (01503 240239; Fax: 01503 240864). *Location:* three miles east of Looe on A387. Downland/parkland, panoramic views over countryside to sea; designed by Harry Vardon. 18 holes, 5940 yards. S.S.S. 69. Large practice ground. *Green Fees:* on application. *Eating facilities:* catering available. *Visitors:* most welcome, phone for tee reservations. Clubs buggies for hire. Golf tuition available. *Society Meetings:* welcome by arrangement. Professional/Golf Manager: Alistair MacDonald. Secretary: Peter Street, Tony Day.

LOSTWITHIEL. **Lostwithiel Hotel, Golf and Country Club,** Lower Polscoe, Lostwithiel PL22 0HQ (01208 873550; Fax: 01208 873479). *Location:* off A390, Lostwithiel. Parkland course. 18 holes, 5984 yards. S.S.S. 71. Driving range and practice area. *Green Fees:* information not available. *Eating facilities:* bar and restaurant. Visitors: welcome by prior arrangement. 21 bedroomed 3 Star Hotel. *Society Meetings:* welcome by prior arrangement. Professional: Tony Nash (01208 873822).*
e-mail: reception@golf-hotel.co.uk
website: www.golf-hotel.co.uk

NEWQUAY. **Merlin Golf Club and Driving Range,** Mawgan Porth, Newquay TR8 4DN (01841 540222; Fax: 01841 541031). *Location:* on coast road between Newquay and Padstow, after Mawgan Porth take St. Eval Road, golf course on right. Heathland, fairly flat course. 18 holes, 6210 yards. S.S.S. 71.

Covered driving range. *Green Fees:* £15.00 subject to review. Special rates for groups/societies of 8 or more. *Eating facilities:* catering and bar all year round. *Visitors:* very welcome, some restrictions during club competitions. Buggies, carts and clubs for hire. *Society meetings:* very welcome. Proprietor: Mr Ross Oliver. Secretary: Mrs Margaret Oliver.

NEWQUAY. **Newquay Golf Club,** Tower Road, Newquay TR7 1LT (01637 874066). *Location:* 400 yards from Newquay Town Centre. Gently undulating seaside course running parallel to the beach and open to wind. Breathtaking views. 18 holes, 6155 yards, S.S.S. 69. *Green Fees:* information not available. *Eating facilities:* lunches and bar snacks, evening meal by arrangement with the caterer on 01637 872091. *Visitors:* welcome at all times, please telephone. *Society Meetings:* catered for except Saturdays and Sundays. Professional: Mark Bevan (01637 874830). Secretary: G. Binney (01637 874354; Fax: 01637 874066).*

NEWQUAY. **Treloy Golf Club,** Newquay TR7 4JN (01637 878554). *Location:* five minutes' drive from Newquay on the A3059 Newquay to St. Columb Major road. Parkland. 9 hole Executive golf course. First of its kind in Cornwall - sculptured greens, American Pencross grass, extensive mouldings and bunkers. 9 holes, 2143 yards, 1955 metres. Par 32. Practice green. *Green Fees:* 9 holes £9.00, 18 holes £13.50. *Eating facilities:* available, bar. *Visitors:* welcome. *Society Meetings:* welcome. Changing facilities, golf shop, club hire and buggy hire. Secretary: Jane Paull.

NEWQUAY near. **Carvynick Golf and Country Club,** Carvynick, Summercourt, Near Newquay (01872 510716; Fax: 01872 510172). *Location:* turn off the A30 at Summercourt then take B3058 towards Newquay. Half a mile on left. Parkland and wooded course. 9 holes, 1246 yards. S.S.S. 27. *Green Fees:* weekdays £7.00; weekends £9.00. *Eating facilities:* at 16th century village inn and restaurant. *Visitors:* welcome all year. Sauna, gym, indoor swimming pool and badminton court. Luxury holiday cottages available.
e-mail: info@carvynick.co.uk
website: www.carvynick.co.uk

NEWQUAY near. **Holywell Bay Golf Park,** Holywell Bay, Near Newquay (01637 830095; Fax: 01637 831000). *Location:* take A3075 out of Newquay then follow signs to Holywell Bay and Cubert. Par 3 Links course. 18 holes, 2755 yards. Pitch and putt. *Green Fees:* £10.00. *Eating facilities:* bar and club house available April to October. *Visitors:* welcome at all times. Excellent value - all players welcome. No Handicap required. No dress code. Fun Park with go-karts, boats etc. Tourist Park. *Society Meetings:* all welcome, ring for special prices. Secretary: Mr Hartley (01637 830095).

PADSTOW. **Trevose Golf and Country Club,** Constantine Bay, Padstow PL28 8JB (01841 520208; Fax: 01841 521057). *Location:* M5 to A30 to A39 to B3274. At St Merryn turn right for golf club. Links course, superb test of golf in lovely coastal setting. H. Colt designed Championship course 18 holes, 6608 yards. S.S.S. 72. 9 hole full length course (Par 35) and one 9 hole short course (Par 29). *Green Fees:* main course £25.00 to £38.00, other courses £10.00 to £25.00 depending on season. Reduced rates if staying in our accommodation. *Eating facilities:* lunchtime snacks and evening dinners, bar open 11am to 11pm. *Visitors:* welcome if checked by telephone beforehand; Handicap Certificate required. Accommodation, three tennis courts, heated swimming pool in summer. *Society Meetings:* welcome if arrangements have been made. Professional: G. Alliss (01841 520261). Secretary: Nick Gammon (01841 520733). e-mail: admin@trevose-gc.co.uk website: www.trevose-gc.co.uk

PENZANCE. **Cape Cornwall Golf & Country Club,** Cape Cornwall, St Just, Penzance TR19 7NL (Tel & Fax: 01736 788611). *Location:* A30 to Land's End, A3071 from Penzance to St Just, turn left at clock tower to Cape Cornwall. Cliff top course with spectacular coastal views. 18 holes, 5650 yards. S.S.S. 68, Par 70. Practice putting green and golf area. *Green Fees:* adults from £20.00 for 18 holes. *Eating facilities:* restaurant open daily; extensive à la carte evening menu Wed-Sat evenings incl. *Visitors:* welcome anytime. Accommodation available on site. Leisure facilities: gymnasium, indoor heated swimming pool, sauna, tanning suite. *Society Meetings:* welcome; prior booking advisable. Club Managers: E. Keddie, U. Handley. e-mail: info@capecornwall.com website: www.capecornwall.com

PENZANCE. **Praa Sands Golf Club,** Germoe Crossroads, Near Penzance TR20 9TQ (01736 763445; Fax: 01736 763399). *Location:* midway between Helston and Penzance on A394. Parkland - beautiful sea views from all holes. 9 holes, 4122 yards. S.S.S. 60 men, 63 ladies, Par 62. Putting green and net. *Green Fees:* information not available. *Eating facilities:* restaurant, bar snacks. *Visitors:* welcome at all times without Handicap Certificate except Sunday mornings. Clubs and trolleys for hire. *Society Meetings:* catered for by arrangement. Secretary: Simon Edwards. Proprietors: Kate and David Phillips. * e-mail: praasandsgolf@aol.com

PERRANPORTH: **Perranporth Golf Club,** Budnic Hill, Perranporth TR6 0AB. Seaside links course overlooking Perranporth and beach. 18 holes, 6252 yards. S.S.S. 72. Par 72. Practice green. *Green Fees:* weekdays £25.00; weekends £30.00. *Eating facilities:* lunch and dinner. *Visitors:* welcome without reservation. Concessionary rates from selected holiday accommodation. *Society Meetings:* catered for with advance notice; concessionary rates. Professional: D. Michell (01872 572317). Secretary: David Mugford (01872 573701). website: www.perranporthgolfclub.com

REDRUTH. **Radnor Golf and Ski Centre**, Radnor Road, Treleigh, Redruth TR16 5EL (01209 211059). *Location:* two miles north east of Redruth, signposted from A3047 at Treleigh and North Country crossroads. Purpose-built Par 3 - interesting layout. 9 holes, 1312 yards. S.S.S. 52. Covered driving range. *Green Fees:* information not available. *Eating facilities:* coffee, tea etc. *Visitors:* welcome. Indoor ski training machine. Small touring caravan site. Professional: Gordon Wallbank.*

ST AUSTELL. **Carlyon Bay Hotel Golf Course,** Beach Road, Carlyon Bay, St Austell PL25 3RD (Hotel: 01726 812304; Golf Club: 01726 814250). *Location:* St Austell A390. Clifftop course running into parkland. 18 holes, 6597 yards. S.S.S. 71. Six acre practice ground. *Green Fees:* £25.00 to £39.00 depending on season. *Eating facilities:* bar open 11am to 11pm, food available during high season 10am to 9pm Tuesday to Friday, 10am to 6pm Saturday to Monday. *Visitors:* welcome, must phone Professional for starting times. Accommodation available in 4 star hotel. *Society Meetings:* catered for by arrangement. Professional: Mark Rowe (01726 814228). Manager: Yvonne Lister (01726 814250).

ST AUSTELL. **St Austell Golf Club,** Tregongeeves, Tregongeeves Lane, St Austell PL26 7DS (01726 74756; Fax: 01726 71978). *Location:* one mile west of St Austell on A390 St Austell to Truro road. Parkland course. 18 holes, 6091 yards. S.S.S. 69. Floodlit driving range. *Green Fees:* weekdays £20.00; weekends £22.00. Reduction when playing with member. *Eating facilities:* bar and restaurant – meals can be arranged. *Visitors:* welcome with reservation, must be club members and hold Handicap Certificate. *Society Meetings:* catered for weekdays by arrangement. Professional: Tony Pitts (01726 62681). Secretary: K. Trahair (01726 74756; Fax: 01726 71978).

ST IVES. **Tregenna Castle Hotel Golf and Country Club,** St Ives TR26 2DE (01736 797381). *Location:* on the main road between Carbis Bay and St Ives, half a mile from town centre. Parkland, 73 acres of grounds with beautiful sea views overlooking St Ives Harbour and Atlantic coast – a very tricky course. 18 holes, 3478 yards. Par 60. *Green Fees:* information not available. *Visitors:* welcome. Accommodation available in the hotel if booked. *Society Meetings:* welcome. Golf Supervisor: Ian Pleasants.*

ST IVES. **West Cornwall Golf Club,** Church Lane, Lelant, St Ives TR26 3DZ (Tel & Fax: 01736 753401). *Location:* two miles from St Ives - in village of Lelant - take Church Road, course situated approximately quarter of a mile past Lelant Church. True links course - wonderful coastal views. 18 holes, 5884 yards. S.S.S. 69. Practice ground, putting green. *Green Fees:* weekdays £25.00 per day; weekends £30.00. Five Day ticket £90.00, Seven Day ticket £100.00. *Eating facilities:* bar with bar menus and à la carte dining room. *Visitors:* must be golf club members with Handicap Certificate. Trolleys for hire. Snooker table. Home of "Long" Jim Barnes - first American Professional Champ 1916, Open Champion USA 1921, British Open Champion 1925 and World Champion of Golf 1921–1925. *Society Meetings:* welcome, written application required. Professional: Paul Atherton (01736 753177). Secretary: Ian Veale (01736 753401).

SALTASH. **China Fleet Country Club,** Saltash PL12 6LJ (01752 848668). *Location:* one mile from Tamar Bridge. Parkland course with beautiful river views. 18 holes, 6551 yards, S.S.S. 72. 28 bay floodlit driving range. *Green Fees:* information on request. *Eating facilities:* bars and bar meals, full restaurant facilities, coffee shop. *Visitors:* welcome, Handicap Certificate required. Other facilities include large Pro Shop, full leisure facilities and 42 self contained apartments. *Society Meetings:* welcome, minimum number 12 persons. Professional: Nick Cook (01752 854665; Fax: 01752 848456). Golf Manager: Linda Goddard (01752 854657; Fax: 01752 848456).

SALTASH. **St Mellion Hotel, Golf and Country Club,** Near Saltash PL12 6SD (01579 351351; Fax: 01579 350537). *Location:* A38 to Saltash, A388 from Saltash to Callington. Parkland. Nicklaus Course: 18 holes, 6651 yards, par 72, S.S.S. 72 - designer Jack Nicklaus. Venue of the Benson & Hedges International Open 1990-1995. Old Course: 18 holes, 5782 yards, par 68. S.S.S. 68 - designer J. Hamilton-Stutt. Practice range. *Green Fees:* Old Course £35.00 per round. Nicklaus Course £50.00 per round, £70.00 per day. *Eating facilities:* full restaurant (awarded AA Rosette) and The Gallery Brasserie. *Visitors:* welcome at all times. Leisure club includes two indoor swimming pools, gymnasium, dance studio, sauna, steam room, spa pool, sports hall, creche. Skincare and spa centre. Founder member of the

Set in 180 acres of beautiful Cornish countryside, with views of the River Tamar and Dartmoor, China Fleet's golf course boasts some of the best scenery in the South West.

• 18 Hole Par 72 Golf Course
• 28 Bay Floodlit Driving Range • Europro Golf Shop
• Expert Tuition • Extensive Fitness & Leisure Facilities

For further information call 01752 848668

China Fleet Country Club, Saltash, PL12 6LJ
Fax:(01752) 848456 E-mail: sales@china-fleet.co.uk Website: www.china-fleet.co.uk

See also Colour Advertisement on page 13

Premier Golf Clubs of Great Britain. *Society Meetings:* welcome. Accommodation available in Hotel overlooking 18th fairway, and in Fairway Lodges in the grounds. Head Professional: David Moon (01579 352002).

TORPOINT. **Whitsand Bay Hotel Golf Club,** Portwrinkle, Torpoint PL11 3BU (01503 30276). Location: on coast six miles from Torpoint. Clifftop course. 18 holes, 5953 yards. S.S.S. 69. *Green Fees:* £25.00. *Eating facilities:* hotel. *Visitors:* welcome at all times with Handicap Certificate. Swimming/leisure complex. *Society Meetings:* catered for and hotel accommodation arranged on application to hotel. Professional: D.S. Poole (01503 30778). Acting Secretary: B. Cranch (01752 829173). Hotel: (Tel & Fax: 01503 230276).

TRURO. **Killiow Golf Club & Driving Range,** Kea, Near Truro TR3 6AG (01872 270246; Fax: 01872 240915). *Location:* take A39 Truro to Falmouth road, turn right into club at first playing place roundabout (2½ miles). 18 holes, Par 69. All-weather floodlit driving range open 8am to 9pm weekdays (weekends until 6pm). *Green Fees:* information on request. *Eating facilities:* bar and restaurant. *Visitors:* only restricted by competitions; phone for availability. Secretary: John Crowson (01872 266876).

TRURO. **Truro Golf Club,** Treliske, Truro TR1 3LG (01872 272640). *Location:* two miles west of Truro on A390 to Redruth. Undulating parkland with magnificent views. 18 holes, 5357 yards. S.S.S. 66. *Green Fees:* weekdays £20.00 per day or round, weekends and Bank Holidays £25.00 per day or round. *Eating facilities:* restaurant and bar snacks available. *Visitors:* welcome with Handicap Certificates. Buggies and carts available. *Society Meetings:* welcome - special rates on application. Professional: N. Bicknell (01872 276595). Secretary: H.W.D. Leicester (Tel & Fax: 01872 278684).

WADEBRIDGE. **Roserrow Golf and Country Club,** Roserrow, St Minver, Near Wadebridge PL27 6QT. *Location:* between Wadebridge and Polzeath off the B3314. Undulating wooded valley. 18 holes, 6507 yards, 5951 metres. S.S.S. 71. 15 bay driving range with indoor swing-analysis studio, practice putting green. *Green Fees:* £30.00 (£35.00 July to September). Discounts for large groups. *Eating*

facilities: restaurant, bar food available. *Visitors:* always welcome, phone for tee times. Luxury self-catering accommodation on site. Indoor swimming pool, fitness suite, sauna, jacuzzi, steam room, solarium, outdoor tennis courts. Buggies, electric trolleys, carts for hire. *Society Meetings:* welcome by arrangement. Club Secretary: Joe Blewitt (01208 863000; Fax: 01208 863002). website: www.roserrow.co.uk

WADEBRIDGE. **St Enodoc Golf Club,** Rock, Wadebridge PL27 6LD (01208 863216; Fax: 01208 862976). *Location:* take the B3314 from Wadebridge, signposted Rock (three miles). Seaside links. Two courses: Church Course 18 holes, 6243 yards. S.S.S. 69; Holywell Course 18 holes, 4103 yards. S.S.S. 61. Practice range, putting greens, etc. *Green Fees:* information not available. *Eating facilities:* restaurant and bar snacks. *Visitors:* Handicap Certificates (24 and below) required for Church Course; no restrictions for Holywell Course. *Society Meetings:* all welcome by arrangement with the Secretary. Professional: Nick Williams (01208 862402). Secretary: Mr. T.D. Clagett (01208 862200).

WADEBRIDGE. **St Kew Golf Club,** St Kew Highway, Near Wadebridge, Bodmin PL30 3EF (Tel & Fax: 01208 841500). *Location:* on the main A39, two-and-a-half miles from Wadebridge towards Camelford. Parkland course, 9 holes (18 tees), 4543 yards. S.S.S. 62. Covered driving range, practice chipping/bunker area. *Green Fees:* adults 9 holes £10.00, 18 holes: £15.00; juniors 9 holes £5.00, 18 holes £8.00. *Eating facilities:* coffee shop and restaurant; licensed bar. *Visitors:* welcome. No restrictions. *Society Meetings:* discounts for eight or more. Professional: Nick Rogers (Tel & Fax: 01208 841500). Secretary: John Brown.

ISLES OF SCILLY

ST MARY'S. **Isles Of Scilly Golf Club,** St Mary's, Isles of Scilly (01720 422692). *Location:* one mile from Hugh Town, St Mary's. Heathland links course with magnificent views. 9 holes, 18 tees, 6001 yards, 5537 metres. S.S.S. 69. Par 73. *Green Fees:* £22.00 per day. *Eating facilities:* lunches and evening meals available. *Visitors:* welcome. Secretary: Steve Watt (01720 423371; Fax: 01720 423782).

Cumbria

ALSTON. **Alston Moor Golf Club,** The Hermitage, Middleton in Teesdale Road, Alston CA9 3DB (Tel & Fax: 01434 381675; Fax: 01434 381675). *Location:* one and three quarter miles from Alston on B6277 to Barnard Castle. Penrith, Hexham, Carlisle all within 30 miles. Parkland with panoramic views (highest golf course in England). 10 holes (18 tees), 5456 yards. S.S.S. 66. Practice ground. *Green Fees:* weekdays: £11.00 per day, after 5pm £6.00 per day, with a member £6.00; Saturdays and Bank Holidays £13.00 per day, Sundays with a member £8.00. *Eating facilities:* 19th Hole bar, catering at weekends May to October. *Visitors:* welcome anytime, prior notice required for groups. Competitions most Sundays, tee reserved 9am to 10am and 1pm to 2.30pm. *Society Meetings:* welcome by arrangement. Secretary: Mr H. Robinson (01434 381354).

APPLEBY. **Appleby Golf Club,** Brackenber Moor, Appleby-in-Westmorland CA16 6LP (017683 51432). *Location:* off A66 at Coupland Beck, two miles east of Appleby. Moorland course. 18 holes, 5901 yards. S.S.S. 68. *Green Fees:* weekdays £19.00 per round, £21.00 per day; weekends and Bank Holidays £22.00 per round, £26.00 per day. *Eating facilities:* meals available each day; reduced catering on Tuesdays. *Visitors:* welcome with Handicap Certificate without reservation. *Society Meetings:* 12 or more catered for by prior arrangement. Handicap Certificate required. Professional: Gary Key (017683 52922). Secretary: J.M.F. Doig.

ASKAM-IN-FURNESS. **Dunnerholme Golf Club,** Duddon Road, Askam-in-Furness LA16 7AW (01229 462675/467421). *Location:* A595 Askam-in-Furness, over level crossing. Seaside links with stream on four holes, spectacular views from elevated 6th green. 10 holes (18 tees), 6154 yards. S.S.S. 70 White, 70 Red, 69 Yellow. Practice ground. *Green Fees:* £15.00 per day. *Eating facilities:* bar in evenings; meals not available. *Visitors:* welcome without reservation, excluding competition days. Competitions Saturday mornings and Sundays May to October. Sky TV. *Society Meetings:* catered for by prior arrangement. Secretary: Mr A. Haines (01229 462675 day, 01229 826198 evenings).

ASPATRIA. **Brayton Park Golf Club,** Lakeside Inn, Brayton, Aspatria CA7 3TD (016973 20840). *Location:* one mile east of Aspatria. Parkland course. 9 holes. S.S.S. 65 (18 holes). *Green Fees:* £7.00 for 18 holes £5.00 for 9 holes (all week, including weekends). *Eating facilities:* available at Lakeside Inn. *Visitors:* always welcome. *Society Meetings:* welcome. Coarse fishing pond. Secretary: David Warwick (016973 71708).

BARROW-IN-FURNESS. **Barrow Golf Club,** Rakesmoor Lane, Hawcoat, Barrow-in-Furness LA14 4QB (01229 825444). *Location:* one mile from Barrow town centre, approach via Dalton bypass, turn left at Bank Lane opposite "Kimberley Clarke" paper mill. Clubhouse at top of hill on left hand side. 18 holes, 6184 yards, 5679 metres. S.S.S. 70. *Green Fees:* £20.00 per day; County Cards/2 for 1 accepted. Ladies' Day - Fridays. *Eating facilities:* catering available Tuesday to Sunday inclusive. *Visitors:* welcome without formal reservation. *Society Meetings:* welcome by prior arrangement, call Club Administrator or Secretary. Club Administrator: E. Payne (01229 825444). Secretary: J. Slater (01229 826968). e-mail: barrowgolf@supanet.com

BARROW-IN-FURNESS. **Furness Golf Club,** Central Drive, Walney Island, Barrow-in-Furness LA14 3LN (01229 471232). *Location*: A590 into Barrow via Dalton by-pass, follow sign to Walney Island, over bridge, straight on at lights. Clubhouse half-a-mile on right hand side. Seaside links. 18 holes, 6363 yards. S.S.S. 71. Practice area. *Green Fees:* weekdays £20.00 (£10.00 with member) weekends and Bank Holidays £25.00 (£17.00 with member). *Eating facilities*: full catering (except Mondays), licensed bar. *Visitors*: parties by prior arrangement, others without reservation; must hold current Handicap Certificate. Ladies' Day - Wednesdays; Competition Days - Saturdays or Sundays in summer. *Society Meetings*: welcome (tee reservation by prior arrangement). Secretary: J.W. Anderson. e-mail: jimanderson@talkgas.net

BRAMPTON. **Brampton Golf Club**, Talkin Tarn, Brampton CA8 1HN (016977 2255). *Location*: situated on the Brampton-Castle Carrock road (B6413), approximately one and a half miles from Brampton. Rolling fell countryside, excellent views. 18 holes, 6407 yards. S.S.S. 71. *Green Fees*: weekdays £22.00, weekends and Bank Holidays £30.00. Practice facilities available plus snooker and pool tables. *Eating facilities*: catering available every day during playing season and on most days during winter period. *Visitors*: welcome without reservation but pre-booking is advisable. *Society Meetings*: catered for, limited numbers at weekends. Secretary and contact for visiting societies/party bookings: I.J. Meldrum (01900 827985). Professional: S. Wilkinson (016977 2000; Fax: 016977 41487). e-mail: secretary@bramptongolfclub.com website: www.bramptongolfclub.com

CARLISLE. **Carlisle Golf Club**, Aglionby, Carlisle CA4 8AG (01228 513029). *Location*: on A69 Newcastle Road, half a mile from Junction 43 of M6. Parkland course with wide variety of trees, strategic hazards, etc. 18 holes, 6278 yards. S.S.S. 70. Practice area. *Green Fees*: weekdays £30.00 per round, £45.00 per day; £45.00 per round Sundays only; Saturdays with member only. Subject to review. Package deals for parties of 12 or more. *Eating facilities*: bar meals, restaurant, two bars, etc. *Visitors*: welcome except on a Saturday (unless with

a member), unless tee is reserved; visitor bookings (01228 510164). Trolley hire. *Society Meetings*: catered for Mondays, Wednesdays and Fridays. Professional: Mr M. Heggie (01228 513241). Secretary: Roger Johnson (01228 513029; Fax: 01228 513303).

CARLISLE. **Dalston Hall Golf Club,** Dalston Hall, Dalston, Carlisle CA5 7JX (01228 710165). *Location:* leave M6 at Exit 42, take road to Dalston; at Dalston turn onto B5299, course on the right after one mile. Scenic parkland course. 9 holes, 5294 yards. S.S.S. 67. Practice area. *Green Fees:* information not available. *Eating facilities:* full catering and bar facilities. *Visitors:* welcome, tee reservation is required at weekends and after 4pm during the week. *Society Meetings:* welcome by prior arrangement. Secretary: Jane Simpson (01228 710165).*

CARLISLE. **Stoney Holme Municipal Golf Course,** St Aidans Road, Carlisle (01228 33208). *Location:* off A69 between M6 Junction 42 and town. Parkland course, 18 holes, 6000 yards. S.S.S. 68. Large practice area, changing rooms. *Green Fees:* information not available. *Eating facilities:* bar and restaurant. *Visitors:* welcome without reservation, but booking advisable weekends and Bank Holidays. *Society Meetings:* welcome by prior arrangement. Professional: Stephen Ling (01228 625511). *

CARLISLE. **The Eden Golf Course**, Crosby-on-Eden, Carlisle CA6 4RA (01228 573003). *Location*: M6 Junction 44, A689 to Low Crosby. Parkland course incorporating lakes, streams and River Eden. 18 holes, 6368 yards. S.S.S. 72. *Green Fees*: weekdays £28.00, weekends £32.00. Special offers for large visiting parties. *Eating facilities*: full restaurant and bar meals. *Visitors*: welcome at all times, telephone booking requested. *Society Meetings*: welcome at all times, telephone booking requested. 16 bay floodlit driving range and practice facilities. Professional: Steven Harrison.*
website: www.edengolf.co.uk.

EMBLETON. **Cockermouth Golf Club,** The Clubhouse, Embleton, Near Cockermouth CA13 9SG (017687 76223/76941; Fax: 017687 76941). *Location*: three miles east of Cockermouth. Scenic fell land course. 18 holes, 5496 yards, S.S.S. 67. *Green Fees:* weekdays £18.00; weekends and Bank Holidays £22.00. Concessionary rates parties of 10 or more (includes food): £25.00 weekdays, £30.00 weekends. *Eating facilities:* bar, meals by arrangement with Secretary. *Visitors:* welcome except Wednesdays between 3.30pm and 6pm, some restrictions at weekends. Some trolleys for hire. *Society Meetings:* welcome as per visitors. Secretary: R.D. Pollard (Tel & Fax: 017687 76941 mornings only weekdays).

GRANGE-OVER-SANDS. **Grange Fell Golf Club,** Fell Road, Grange-over-Sands LA11 6HB (015395 32536). *Location:* Cartmel Road from Grange one mile. Hillside course with panoramic views. 9 holes, 4840 metres. S.S.S. 66. *Green Fees:* weekdays £15.00, weekends and Bank Holidays £20.00. *Eating facilities:* bar. *Visitors:* welcome without reservation, closed most Sundays until 4pm during season. *Society Meetings:* not catered for. Secretary: M. Higginson (015395 34098).

GRANGE-OVER-SANDS. **Grange-over-Sands Golf Club,** Meathop Road, Grange-over-Sands LA11 6QX (015395 33180; Fax: 015395 33754). *Location:* leave the A590 at roundabout signposted Grange, take the B5277 for approximately three miles. Flat parkland. 18 holes, 5958 yards, 5422 metres. S.S.S. 69. Practice area, bunker, green. *Green Fees:* weekdays £20.00 per round, £25.00 per day; weekends and Bank Holidays £25.00 per round, £30.00 per day. *Eating facilities:* dining room open every day; bar snacks and bar every day. *Visitors:* welcome without reservation weekdays and most weekends. *Society Meetings:* by arrangement with Secretary. Professional: Andrew J. Pickering (015395 35937). Secretary: S.D. Wright (015395 33754).

KENDAL. **Carus Green Golf Club**, Burneside Road, Kendal LA9 6EB (Tel & Fax: 01539 721097). *Location:* one mile north-east of Kendal on Burneside Road. Flat parkland course. 18 holes, 5716 yards, S.S.S. 68. 160 yard practice ground, putting green, net. *Green Fees:* weekdays £15.00, with member £10.00; weekends £19.00, with member £15.00. *Eating facilities:* light snacks available, licensed. *Visitors:* welcome anytime, restrictions on competition days. Tuition available. Clubs, buggy and trolley hire. *Society Meetings:* welcome anytime, please call for details. Professional: David Turner (Tel & Fax: 01539 721097). Secretary: Bryan Lumsden.

KENDAL. **Kendal Golf Club**, The Heights, Kendal LA9 4PQ (01539 723499). *Location:* off A6 at Town Hall, signposted. Undulating parkland course with magnificent views in all directions. 18 holes, 5769 yards. S.S.S. 68. *Green Fees:* weekdays £22.00 per round, £26.00 per day; weekends £27.50 per round, £32.50 per day. *Eating facilities:* meals available all day; bar. *Visitors:* welcome with reservation. Buggy hire available. Professional: Peter Scott (01539 723499).

KESWICK. **Keswick Golf Club,** Threlkeld Hall, Threlkeld, Keswick CA12 4SX (017687 79324; Fax: 017687 79861). *Location:* four miles from Keswick on A66 road to Penrith. Scenic fell and parkland course. 18 holes, 6225 yards. S.S.S. 72, Par 71. Extensive practice area. *Green Fees:* weekdays £23.00; weekends and Bank Holidays £28.00. *Eating facilities:* daily by arrangement (Caterer: (017687 79013); bar. *Visitors:* welcome, Ladies' Day Thursdays 11am to 2pm. *Society Meetings:* welcome by arrangement, unrestricted weekdays, 11.30am to 12.30pm weekends. Professional: Gary Watson (017687 79010). Secretary: Robert C. Jackson (017687 79324).

KIRKBY LONSDALE. **Kirkby Lonsdale Golf Club,** Scaleber Lane, Barbon, Kirkby Lonsdale, Carnforth, Lancs LA6 2LJ (015242 76365). *Location:* three and a half miles from Kirkby Lonsdale on the A683 Sedbergh Road. Parkland course in Lune Valley crossing Barbon Beck and along the banks of the River Lune. 18 holes, 6538 yards. S.S.S. 71. Par 72. Practice area, lessons. *Green Fees:* weekdays £25.00; weekends £30.00. Subject to review. *Eating facilities:* full facilities. *Visitors:* welcome, no restrictions except on competition days. Handicap Certificate required or certificate of competence. *Society Meetings:* welcome by arrangement. Package deals available for groups of eight or more. Professional: Chris Barrett (015242 76366). Secretary: Geoffrey Hall (015242 76365). e-mail: KLGolf@Dial.Pipex.com website: www.klgolf.dial.pipex.com

KIRKBY LONSDALE near. **Casterton Golf Course,** Sedbergh Road, Casterton, Near Kirkby Lonsdale, via Carnforth LA6 2LA (015242 71592; Fax: 015242 74387). Location: from Junction 36 of M6 take A65 to Skipton, five miles to Kirkby Lonsdale, one mile north on A683. Undulating parkland course, scenic with wonderful views. 9 holes, 5726 yards. S.S.S. 68. Practice area and driving net. *Green Fees:* weekdays £10.00; weekends and Bank Holidays £14.00. *Eating facilities:* light refreshments and shop in clubhouse (licensed). *Visitors:* always welcome. Booking advisable at weekends. Clubhouse has well-stocked Pro Shop, changing facilities and toilets. Clubs and trolleys available for hire. Two holiday flats sleeping two/four. *Society Meetings:* parties of under 20 persons only. Professional: Roy Williamson. Secretary: Elizabeth Makinson. Course Manager: John Makinson. e-mail: castertongc@hotmail.com website: www.castertongolf.co.uk

MARYPORT. **Maryport Golf Club Ltd.,** Bankend, Maryport (01900 812605). *Location:* approximately one mile north of Maryport on B5300 towards Silloth. 9 holes links extended to 18 with new holes parkland type, exposed, relatively flat. 18 holes, 6088 yards. S.S.S. 69. *Green Fees:* weekdays £17.00, weekends £22.00. *Eating facilities:* available. *Visitors:* welcome, no restrictions. *Society Meetings:* catered for by prior arrangement. Chairman: H.L Hayston. Secretary: Mrs M. Skinner.

PENRITH. **Penrith Golf Club,** Salkeld Road, Penrith CA11 8SG (01768 891919). *Location:* off Junction 41 M6 motorway, towards Penrith, golf course signposted. Parkland course. 18 holes, 6026 yards. S.S.S. 69. Range facilities. *Green Fees:* weekdays £24.00/£29.00 weekends £29.00/£34.00. *Eating facilities:* all day catering seven days a week. *Visitors:* welcome, book through Professional shop, tee times required at weekends. *Society Meetings:* by appointment with Secretary. Professional: Mr Garry Key (Tel & Fax: 01768 891919). Secretary: Mr David Noble (Tel & Fax: 01768 891919).

ST BEES. **St Bees Golf Club,** Peckmill, Beach Road, St Bees (01946 824300). *Location:* four miles south of Whitehaven off A595. Hilly, seaside course. 9 holes, 5392 yards. S.S.S. 66. *Green Fees:* £12.00. *Visitors:* welcome weekdays (except after 4pm Wednesdays). Only after 3.00pm weekends. Bar available April to September between 12pm and 8pm. Secretary: B. G. Ritson (01946 822515).

SEASCALE. **Seascale Golf Club,** Seascale CA20 1QL (Tel & Fax: 019467 28202). *Location:* B5344 off A595 to north of village. Links. 18 holes, 6416 yards. S.S.S. 71. 16-acre practice ground. *Green Fees:* weekdays £24.00 per round, £29.00 per day; weekends £27.00 per round, £32.00 per day. Three-day rate £70.00. 10% reduction for parties of 12 or more. *Eating facilities:* catering available every day. *Visitors:* welcome when no tee reservations in force. *Society Meetings:* catered for by arrangement with Secretary. Professional: Sean Rudd (019467 21799). Secretary: David Stobart (019467 28202).

SEDBERGH. **Sedbergh Golf Club,** Sedbergh LA10 5SS (015396 21551). *Location:* five miles J37, M6, one mile out of Sedbergh on road to Dent, well signposted. Superbly scenic course in Yorkshire Dales National Park. 9 holes, 5588 yards. S.S.S. 68. *Green Fees:* weekdays £18.00 per round; weekends and Bank Holidays £20.00 per round. *Eating facilities:* full bar and catering facilities. *Visitors:* welcome, but prior booking advisable (essential at weekends). Various packages available. Golf shop; hire trolleys. *Society Meetings:* very welcome by prior arrangement. Secretary: David Lord (015396 20993).

SEASCALE GOLF CLUB

Play our challenging links course

Superb 6,416 yards traditional links. Reduced terms for daily parties of 8 or more. Any three consecutive days golf for £70. Bookings now being taken for 2004. Both midweek and weekend dates available. Societies and groups assured of a warm and friendly welcome.
For further details contact: David Stobart, The Secretary,
Seascale Golf Club, Seascale, Cumbria or phone 0194 672 8202

See also Colour Advertisement on page 44

SILECROFT. **Silecroft Golf Club**, Silecroft, Near Millom LA18 4NX (01229 774250). *Location:* three miles north of Millom on the coast. Near junction of A595 and A5093, eight miles west of Broughton-in-Furness. Seaside links course with good greens. 9 holes (18 tees), 5877 yards. S.S.S. 68 (67 off Yellow tees). *Green Fees:* £15.00 per day Monday to Friday, £20.00 per day weekends and Bank Holidays. *Eating facilities:* catering available at nearby public house (Silecroft Miners Arms), bar at club. *Visitors:* welcome, although access to the course may be restricted on Bank Holidays or on competition days. Secretary: Mr D.L.A. MacLardie (01229 774342).

SILLOTH. **Silloth on Solway Golf Club,** The Clubhouse, Silloth, Carlisle CA7 4BL (016973 31304). *Location:* from south - M6 Junction 41 B5305 Wigton, B5302 Silloth. From north and east - M6 Junction 43 A69 Carlisle, A595/596 Wigton, B5302 Silloth. Seaside links, rated in the best five links courses in England. 18 holes, 6618 yards. S.S.S. 73. Practice facilities. *Green Fees:* weekdays £32.00 per day, weekends and Bank Holidays £43.00 per round. Subject to review. Restriction, only one round allowed per day at weekends. *Eating facilities:* full bar and catering. *Visitors:* welcome without reservation. *Society Meetings:* welcome midweek, weekend times available on request. Professional: J. Graham (016973 32404; Fax: 016973 31782). Secretary: John Hill (016973 31304; Fax: 016973 31782).

ULVERSTON. **Ulverston Golf Club Ltd,** Bardsea Park, Ulverston LA12 9QJ (01229 582824). *Location:* Exit 36, M6. A590 to Barrow then A5087 to Bardsea village. Wooded parkland. 18 holes, 6194 yards. S.S.S. 70. *Green Fees:* information not available. *Eating facilities:* lunch and bar snacks. *Visitors:* welcome except Saturdays (competition day), and Tuesdays (Ladies' Day). Must be members of accredited golf club and have a Handicap. *Society Meetings:* welcome, write with reservation to the Match Secretary. Professional: M.R. Smith (01229 582806). Secretary: K. Oliver.

WHITEHAVEN. **Whitehaven Golf Club,** Red Lonning, Whitehaven CA28 8UD (01946 591177). *Location:* set in parkland above Whitehaven. Parkland course with spectacular views of the Lakeland fells. 18 holes, 6079 yards, Par 70. *Green Fees:* information not available. *Eating facilities:* clubhouse and bar. *Visitors:* always welcome. Tee booking system in operation from May 25th, phone 01946 591144. Professional: Craig Hamilton.
e-mail: whitehavengolf@freeuk.com
website: www.whitehavengolf.freeuk.com

WINDERMERE. **Windermere Golf Club,** Cleabarrow, Windermere LA23 3NB (015394 43123). *Location:* one mile from Bowness-on-Windermere on Crook road, B5284. Idyllic National Park setting. 18 holes, 5122 yards, S.S.S. 65. Practice ground. *Green Fees:* Monday to Friday £25.00 per round, £30.00 per day; weekends and Bank Holidays £30.00 per round, £35.00 per day. *Eating facilities:* restaurant. *Visitors:* welcome with bona fide handicaps and if members of recognised golf clubs. *Society Meetings:* catered for by prior arrangement with Secretary, numbers from twelve to 50, corporate days by arrangement. Professional: W.S.M. Rooke (015394 43550). Secretary: K.R. Moffat (015394 43123). website: www.windermere-golf-club.org.uk

WORKINGTON. **Workington Golf Club Ltd,** Branthwaite Road, Workington CA14 4SS (01900 603460). *Location:* on A596, two miles east of town. Meadowland. 18 holes, 6252 yards. S.S.S. 70. *Green Fees:* weekdays £22.00; weekends and Bank Holidays £27.00. *Eating facilities:* available seven days a week. *Visitors:* welcome without reservation; must have own insurance and must be members of recognised golf club. Buggies only by prior arrangement with Pro. *Society Meetings:* welcome by prior arrangement. Professional: A. Drabble (01900 67828). Secretary: T.F. Stout (01900 603460).

See also Colour Advertisement on page 45

Derbyshire

ALFRETON. **Alfreton Golf Club,** Wingfield Road, Alfreton DE55 7LH (01773 832070). *Location:* B6024 (Matlock Road) one mile from Alfreton. Parkland course. 11holes, 5121 yards. S.S.S. 66. *Green Fees:* £18.00 per round, £25.00 per day. *Eating facilities:* bar snacks except Mondays. *Visitors:* welcome Monday to Friday with reservation. *Society Meetings:* catered for. Professional: (01773 831901). Secretary: E. Brown.

ASHBOURNE. **Ashbourne Golf Club Ltd,** Off Wyaston Road, Ashbourne DE6 1NB (01335 342078; Fax 01335 347937). *Location:* Wyaston Road, Ashbourne, one and a half miles out of Ashbourne. Undulating parkland. 18 holes, 6402 yards. S.S.S. 71. Practice area. *Green Fees:* information on request. *Eating facilities:* available every day; parties must make prior arrangement. *Visitors:* welcome by arrangement with Professional. *Society Meetings:* welcome weekdays. Professional: Andrew Smith (01335 347960). Secretary: J.N. Hammond. (01335 342078).

BAKEWELL. **Bakewell Golf Club,** Station Road, Bakewell DE45 1GB (01629 812307). *Location:* Sheffield Road out of Bakewell, turn right over River Bridge. Parkland, scenic hillside course. 9 holes, 5240 yards. S.S.S. 68. *Green Fees:* weekdays £15.00; weekends £20.00 by arrangement only. *Eating facilities:* bar meals, formal catering except Mondays. *Visitors:* welcome weekdays, occasional weekends by prior arrangement. *Society Meetings:* welcome by arrangement. Secretary: F.I. Parker.

BRAILSFORD. **Brailsford Golf Club,** Pools Head Lane, Brailsford, Near Ashbourne DE6 3BU (01335 360096). *Location:* on the main A52 Derby to Ashbourne road, Derby 6 miles, Ashbourne 5 miles. Parkland course. 9 holes, 6219 yards (18 holes), S.S.S. 70. Practice facilities and driving range. *Green Fees:* weekdays 9 holes £10.00, 18 holes £13.50; weekends 9 holes £12.00, 18 holes £16.50. Special rates for juniors, Senior Citizens (weekdays only). *Eating facilities:* available. *Visitors:* welcome at any time except Sunday mornings. Tuition available - two teaching Professionals. *Society Meetings:* welcome except Sunday mornings. Special rates available. Professional: David McCarthy (01335 360096). Secretary: Mr K. Wilson (01332 553703).

BURTON-ON-TRENT. **Burton-on-Trent Golf Club,** 43 Ashby Road East, Burton-on-Trent DE15 0PS *Location:* three miles east of Burton-on-Trent on the A511 towards Ashby de la Zouch. Undulating parkland course with many trees, exciting finishing hole. 18 holes, 6579 yards. S.S.S. 71. Practice ground. *Green Fees:* weekdays £28.00 per round, £38.00 per day; weekends and Bank Holidays £32.00 per round, £40.00 per day. Special rates by arrangement. *Eating facilities:* dining room, lounge bar. *Visitors:* welcome weekdays, restrictions at weekends and Bank Holidays. *Society Meetings:* welcome, apply in writing for terms. Professional: Gary Stafford (01283 562240). Secretary: D. Hartley (Tel & Fax: 01283 544551).
e-mail: burtongolfclub@btinternet.com
website: www.burtongolfclub.co.uk

BUXTON. **Buxton and High Peak Golf Club,** Town End, Waterswallows Road, Buxton SK17 7EN (01298 23453; Fax: 01298 26333; Office: 01298 26263). *Location:* A6 one mile north of Buxton. Parkland, good positional play required. 18 holes, 5966 yards. S.S.S. 69. Practice facilities. *Green Fees:* weekdays £24.00 per round, £30.00 per day; weekends £30.00 per round, £36.00 per day. *Eating facilities:* full catering facilities. *Visitors:* welcome without reservation, ring at weekends. *Society Meetings:* welcome. Professional: Mr Gary Brown (01298 23112). Secretary: Helen Smith.
e-mail: sec@bhpgc.fsnet.co.uk
website: www.buxtonandhighpeakgolfclub.co.uk

BUXTON. **The Cavendish Golf Club Ltd,** Gadley Lane, Buxton SK17 6XD (01298 23494). *Location:* three quarters of a mile from town centre, on Leek Road A53, signposted. Parkland/moorland course, designed by Dr Alastair McKenzie who designed Augusta. Parkland/moorland course. 18 holes, 5833 yards. S.S.S. 68. Practice ground. *Green Fees:* £26.00 per round weekdays; £35.00 per round weekends. Juniors half price and visitors £15.00 if playing with a member. Visiting parties £26.00. *Eating facilities:* restaurant, usual bar hours, snacks, meals available at all times. *Visitors:* apply to Professional. Snooker. *Society Meetings:* catered for weekdays only except Thursdays, apply to the Professional for booking arrangements. Professional: Paul Hunstone (01298 25052). Secretary: J.D. Rushton (Tel & Fax: 01298 79708).

CHAPEL-EN-LE-FRITH. **Chapel-en-le-Frith Golf Club,** The Cockyard, Manchester Road, Chapel-en-le-Frith SK23 9UH (01298 812118). *Location:* midway between Sheffield and Manchester, 25 miles from each on the B5470. Parkland, scenic. 18 holes, 6434 yards. S.S.S. 71. Practice ground. *Green Fees:* weekdays £24.00 per round, £35.00 per day; weekends £35.00 per round, £50.00 per day. *Eating facilities:* all meals daily. *Visitors:* welcome, small numbers without reservation. *Society Meetings:* catered for by arrangement. Professional: D. Cullen (01298 812118). Secretary: J. Hilton (01298 813943; Fax: 01298 814990).

CHESTERFIELD. **Birch Hall Golf Club,** Sheffield Road, Unstone, Near Chesterfield S18 5DH (01246 291979). *Location:* off A61 between Sheffield and Chesterfield. Moorland course with outstanding views. 18 holes, 6409 yards, 5860 metres. S.S.S. 71. Practice area. *Green Fees:* information not available. *Eating facilities:* bar with meals available. *Visitors:* welcome but prior booking essential. *Society Meetings:* welcome but prior booking essential. Hon. Gen. Secretary: E. Gallagher.

CHESTERFIELD. **Chesterfield Golf Club Ltd,** Matlock Road, Walton, Chesterfield S42 7LA (01246 279256; Fax: 01246 276622). *Location:* two miles from Chesterfield town centre on Matlock road (A632); Junction 29 M1. Parkland with natural hazards. 18 holes, 6281 yards. S.S.S. 70. Practice ground, putting green. *Green Fees:* weekdays £28.00 per round, £35.00 per day; Sundays £30.00 per round after 1.30pm. Subject to review. *Eating facilities:* full catering (dining room), two bars. *Visitors:* welcome weekdays, and Sundays after 1.30pm; other times at weekend as members' guests only. Trolleys. Snooker. *Society Meetings:* catered for on application. Professional: Michael McLean (01246 276297). Secretary: Brian Broughton.

CHESTERFIELD. **Grassmoor Golf Centre,** North Wingfield Road, Grassmoor, Chesterfield S42 5EA (01246 856044; Fax: 01246 853486). *Location:* 4 miles M1 Junction 29 or A61 near Chesterfield. Heathland course incorporating water hazards, testing greens, testing par 3's for distance. 18 holes, 5723 yards, S.S.S. 68. 25 bay covered, floodlit range. 9 hole practice putting area and a practice area. *Green Fees:* weekdays £10.00, weekends £14.00. County Cards reduction. *Eating facilities:* Excellent bar and restaurant facilities available 8am to 10pm. *Visitors:* welcome, weekends included, 6 day's advance booking system by phone. *Society Meetings:* group bookings and societies welcome, including at weekends. Lessons available with Senior PGA Professional. Open daily 8am to 10 pm, everyone welcome. Professional: Gary Hagues. Club Manager: Helen Hagues (01246 856044). website: www.grassmoorgolf.co.uk

CHESTERFIELD. **Stanedge Golf Club,** Walton Hay Farm, Chesterfield S45 0LW (01246 566156). *Location:* five miles south-west of Chesterfield, off

B5057 near "Red Lion" public house. Course 1000ft above sea level, views of four counties. 9 holes, 5786 yards. S.S.S. 68. *Green Fees:* weekdays £15.00, £10.00 with member; Saturdays and Bank Holidays £15.00, must be playing with member. *Visitors:* welcome by prior arrangement. Must book in by 2pm Monday to Fridays. No visitors on Sundays until 4pm and they must be with member. *Society Meetings:* catered for by prior arrangement. Secretary: W.C. Tyzack (01246 276568).

CHESTERFIELD. **Tapton Park Golf & Leisure Centre,** Crow Lane, Chesterfield S41 0EQ (01246 239500; Fax: 01246 555140). *Location:* behind railway station. Wooded parkland course. 18 hole course, 9 hole course and pitch and putt course. 18 hole course - 6025 yards. S.S.S. 69; 9 hole course - 2595 yards, Par 34. Putting and pitching greens. *Green Fees:* information not available. *Eating facilities:* bar and restaurant open to the public. *Visitors:* welcome at all times, booking for 18 hole course taken six days in advance. Club/Trolley/Locker hire. *Society Meetings:* welcome on written application. Professional: Andrew Carnall. Secretary: (01246 273887; Fax: 01246 558024). *

CODNOR. **Ormonde Fields Golf Club,** Nottingham Road, Codnor, Ripley DE5 9RG (01773 744157). *Location:* five miles M1 Junction 26 towards Ripley on A610. Parkland. 18 holes, 6504 yards. S.S.S. 72. Practice area, putting green. *Green Fees:* £20.00 weekdays, £25.00 weekends and Bank Holidays. *Eating facilities:* full restaurant available. *Visitors:* unrestricted. *Society Meetings:* catered for; book through Secretary. Professional: M. Myford (01773 742987). Secretary: Mr K. Constable (01773 570043).

DERBY. **Allestree Park Golf Club,** Allestree Hall, Duffield Road, Allestree, Derby DE22 2EU (01332 552971). Location: 3 miles north of city centre on A6. Municipal course - hilly parkland with outstanding views. 18 holes, 5774 yards. S.S.S. 68. Practice ground. *Green Fees:* information not available. *Eating facilities:* full bar, catering arranged with Steward. *Visitors:* welcome anytime except Sundays morning (club competitions). *Society Meetings:* welcome, details on request. Professional: Steve Lamb (01332 550616; Fax: 01332 541195). Secretary: Mr A.R. Maguire (01283 703702).*

See also Colour Advertisement on page 36

DERBY. **Derby Golf Club,** Shakespeare Street, Sinfin, Derby DE24 9HD (01332 766323). *Location:* two miles city centre, access via Wilmore Road. Parkland. 18 holes, 6144 yards, 5618 metres. S.S.S. 69. Practice area. *Green Fees:* on request. *Eating facilities:* bar and catering available. *Visitors:* welcome weekdays. *Society Meetings:* welcome weekdays. Professional: Steve Astle (01332 766462; Fax: 01332 769004). Secretary: Peter Davidson (01332 766323).

DERBY. **Marriott Breadsall Priory Hotel and Country Club,** Moor Road, Morley DE7 6DL (01332 832235; Fax: 01332 833509). *Location:* turn off the A61 towards Breadsall, proceed on Croft Lane, turn left into Rectory Lane, then bear right onto Moor Road, continue past the Church for approximately one mile. Two courses - Priory is a parkland course and Moorland is a contrast of open moorland. Priory - 18 holes, 5871 yards. S.S.S. 68 off yellow tees; Moorland - 18 holes, 5820 yards. S.S.S. 68 off yellow tees. Practice area and putting green; floodlit driving range. *Green Fees:* from £20.00 to £42.00. Golf days tailor made to customer requirements. *Eating facilities:* Hotel - Priory Restaurant and cocktail bar; leisure club - Longweekends bar, Longweekend restaurant. *Visitors:* welcome any time subject to availability. *Society Meetings:* welcome at any time subject to availability. Hotel has 112 bedrooms, leisure club and conference facilities. Buggies. Professional: Darren Steels (01332 834425). Golf Operations Manager: J. Winterbottom (01332 832235).

DUFFIELD. **Chevin Golf Club,** Golf Lane, Duffield DE56 4EE (01332 841864). *Location:* five miles north of Derby on A6 at Duffield village. Hilly course, part parkland, part moorland with superb views. 18 holes, 6057 yards, 5451 metres. S.S.S. 69. Two practice areas. *Green Fees:* information not available. *Eating facilities:* bar snacks and diningroom. *Visitors:* welcome weekdays, Handicap Certificates required. Snooker. *Society Meetings:* welcome weekdays, but never weekends. Professional: W. Bird (01332 841112). Secretary: J.A. Milner (Tel: 01332 841864; Fax: 01332 844028).

GLOSSOP. **Glossop and District Golf Club,** Sheffield Road, Glossop SK13 9PU (01457 865247). *Location:* off A57, one mile from town centre. Moorland course. 11 holes, 5800 yards. S.S.S. 68. *Green Fees:* information on request. *Eating facilities:* full catering facilities available. *Visitors:* welcome with reservation through Professional, except Saturdays during playing season. *Society Meetings:* welcome, same restrictions as visitors. Professional: Daniel Marsh (01457 853117). Secretary: R. Hargreaves (01457 861977).

HORSLEY. **Horsley Lodge Golf Club**, Smalley Mill Road, Horsley DE21 5BL (01332 780838; Fax: 01332 781118). *Location:* north of Derby on A61, past Little Eaton, right turn to Horsley - signposted. Meadowland. 18 holes, 6381 yards. S.S.S. 70. Par 71. Driving range. *Green Fees:* £40.00; £17.50 as members' guests, weekends by arrangement. *Eating facilities:* two bars, bar meals, à la carte restaurant; function room seats 140. *Visitors:* welcome weekdays and some weekends but not on competition days. Four-star accommodation available. *Society Meetings:* by appointment. Professional: Graham Lyall (01332 780838; Fax: 01332 781118). Company Secretary: Richard Salt. Hon. Secretary (club): George Johnson (01332 880599).

ILKESTON. **Erewash Valley Golf Club Ltd,** Stanton-by-Dale, Near Ilkeston DE7 4QR (0115 932 3258). *Location:* Junction 25 of the M1, Stanton-by-Dale village. Parkland with two holes in an old quarry. 18 holes, 6557 yards, 5996 metres. S.S.S. 71. Driving, pitching and putting practice area. *Green Fees:* weekdays £30.50 per round, £40.50 per day; weekends and Bank Holidays £40.50 per round. DUGC Card reduced rate. *Eating facilities:* bar snacks available at all times, diningroom service on request. *Visitors:* welcome at all times subject to club events and society bookings. *Society Meetings:* welcome Monday, Wednesday and Friday only. Professional: Mike Ronan (0115 932 4667). Secretary: J.A. Beckett (0115 932 2984).

ILKESTON. **Ilkeston Borough Golf Club,** Peewit Municipal Golf Course, West End Drive, Ilkeston DE7 5GH (01602 304550). *Location:* one mile west of Ilkeston market place. Slightly hilly meadowland. 9 holes, 4116 yards. S.S.S. 60. *Green Fees:* information not available. *Eating facilities:* not available. *Visitors:* welcome, no restrictions. Secretary: B. Smith (01602 302114).*

For full details of clubs and courses, plus convenient accommodation, visit the FHG golf website on www.uk-golfguide.com

ILKESTON. **Morley Hayes Golf Club**, Main Road, Morley, Ilkeston (01332 782000). *Location:* just north of Junction 25 of M1, on A608 between Derby and Heanor. Parkland with water features and established trees, surrounded by mature woodland and deer park. Manor course, 18 holes, 6726 yards. Par 72. Tower course, 9 holes, 1614 yards, Par 30. 17 bay driving range. Pay and Play course. *Green Fees:* weekdays: £17.50 18 holes Manor course; £8.50 9 holes Tower course. Weekend: £24.00 18 holes Manor course; £10.50 9 holes Tower course. *Eating facilities:* two bars, bar meals, à la carte restaurant, function suites. *Society Meetings:* company and society days welcome seven days a week. Professional: Mark Marriott. Golf Manager: Patricia Straw (01332 782000).

MATLOCK. **Matlock Golf Club**, Chesterfield Road, Matlock Moor, Matlock DE4 5LZ (01629 582191). *Location:* Matlock-Chesterfield road, A632, one mile out of Matlock, left hand side main road. Moorland with extensive views. 18 holes, yellow tees, 5808 yards. S.S.S. 68. *Green Fees:* information not available. *Eating facilities:* snacks available, luncheons and evening meals by arrangement (except on Mondays). *Visitors:* welcome weekdays. *Society Meetings:* catered for Tuesday to Friday. Professional: M.A. Whithorn (01629 584934). Secretary: J. Odell. *

MICKLEOVER. **Mickleover Golf Club**, Uttoxeter Road, Mickleover, Derby DE3 9AD (Tel & Fax: 01332 516011). *Location:* three miles west of Derby on the A516/B5020 to Uttoxeter. Undulating course. 18 holes, 5702 yards, 5222 metres. S.S.S. 68. *Green Fees:* weekdays £25.00 per day, weekends and Bank Holidays £30.00 per day. Societies £25.00 (no restriction on holes to be played). Eating facilities: full restaurant facilities. *Visitors:* welcome, no restrictions; telephone Professional before arrival. *Society Meetings:* Tuesdays and Thursdays. Company days Fridays. Professional: Tim Coxon (01332 518662). Secretary: Graham Finney (Tel & Fax: 01332 516011).

MICKLEOVER. **Pastures Golf Club**, Social Centre, Pastures Hospital, Mickleover DE3 0DQ (01332 516700). *Location:* four miles west of Derby, A516, half a mile past Mickleover Court Hotel. Undulating meadowland. 9 holes, 5014 yards. S.S.S. 64. Practice area, putting area. *Green Fees:* on application. *Eating facilities:* snacks; bar/lounge bar. *Visitors:* welcome, DUGC Card holders welcome. *Society Meetings:* welcome any weekday by arrangement, catering available. Secretary: S. McWilliams (01332 516700).*

QUARNDON. **Kedleston Park Golf Club**, Kedleston, Quarndon, Derby DE22 5JD (Tel & Fax: 01332 840035). *Location:* Derby, follow signs to Kedleston Hall. Parkland with lakes. 18 holes, 6675 yards. S.S.S. 72. *Green Fees:* weekdays £35.00 per round, £45.00 per day. *Eating facilities:* full catering, bars. *Visitors:* welcome Monday and Friday; weekends with member. Carts available. *Society Meetings:* welcome Monday and Friday. Professional: Paul Wesselingh. Secretary: G. Duckmanton (01332 840035).

RISLEY. **Maywood Golf Club**, Off Rushy Lane, Risley, Draycott DE72 3SW (0115 939 2306). *Location:* between Derby and Nottingham at Risley, two minutes from Junction 25 M1. Parkland course. 18 holes, 6424 yards. S.S.S. 71. Practice area. *Green Fees:* infomation not available. *Eating facilities:* licensed bar and bar meals. *Visitors:* welcome, please phone to check availability. *Society Meetings:* rates on request. Professional: Simon Purcell-Jackson (0115 949 0043). Manager: Miss Tory Moon. Proprietors: P. and B. Moon.

SHEFFIELD. **Renishaw Park Golf Club**, Golf House, Station Road, Renishaw, Sheffield S21 3UZ (01246 432044). *Location:* A6135 Barlborough (Junction 30 M1) to Sheffield. Parkland/meadowland. 18 holes, 6262 yards. S.S.S. 70. Practice area. *Green Fees:* weekdays £28.00 per round, £37.50 per day; weekends £42.00 per round/day. *Eating facilities:* bar meals, full restaurant. *Visitors:* welcome without reservation (advisable to ring Pro prior to arrival). *Society Meetings:* by prior arrangement. Full day package available. Professional: J. Oates (01246 435484). Secretary: T.J. Childs (01246 432044).

SHEFFIELD. **Sickleholme Golf Club,** Bamford, Hope Valley S33 0BN (01433 651306). *Location:* 3A625 west of Sheffield, right at Marquis of Granby, Bamford. Scenic wooded course in the Peak District. 18 holes, 6064 yards. S.S.S. 69. Practice ground, putting green. *Green Fees:* weekdays £29.00 per day; weekends £34.00 per day. *Eating facilities:* bar snacks and restaurants. *Visitors:* no visitors Wednesday mornings; must be members of a recognised Golf Club; advance booking required. *Society Meetings:* welcome by prior arrangement. Professional/ Secretary: P. H. Taylor (01433 651316).

SHIRLAND. **Shirland Golf Club,** Lower Delves, Shirland, Alfreton DE55 6AU (01773 834969). *Location:* one mile north of Alfreton off A61, three miles from M1 Junction 28 via A38. Tree-lined rolling parkland, 18 holes, 6072 yards. S.S.S. 69. Par 71. Two practice grounds. *Green Fees:* £19.00 per round, £30.00 per day weekdays; £26.00 per round, £40.00 per day weekends. *Eating facilities:* bar meals. Conference and banquet rooms. *Visitors:* unrestricted weekdays, but must book through Professional at weekends. *Society Meetings:* welcome. Professional: Neville Hallam (01773 834935). Secretary: Mrs C.S. Fincham (01773 832515).

SINFIN. **Derby Sinfin Public Course,** Wilmore Road, Sinfin, Derby DE24 9HD (01332 766462). *Location:* 1 mile south of Derby on A5111, off A52. 18 holes, 6163 yards. S.S.S. 69. *Green fees:* £12.00. Visitors: unrestricted. *Society Meetings:* welcome by prior arrangement. Professional: S. Astle (01332 766462). Secretary: P. Davidson (01332 766323).

STOCKPORT. **The New Mills Golf Club,** Shaw Marsh, New Mills, High Peak SK22 4QE (01663 743485). *Location:* signposted off the B6101 from Marple to New Mills, between Buxton and Stockport. Relatively flat upland course, magnificent views, excellent greens. 18 holes, 5604 yards. S.S.S. 69. Large practice area and driving range. New members accepted. *Green Fees:* information not available. *Eating facilities:* full catering, very good value; wide range of food. *Visitors:* welcome any day but not competition days, contact the Professional for these dates. *Society Meetings:* welcome. Professional: Carl Cross (01663 746161). Secretary: Philip Jenkinson (01663 744305).

Devon

AXMOUTH. **Axe Cliff Golf Club,** Squires Lane, Axmouth, Seaton EX12 4AB (Tel & Fax: 01297 24371). *Location:* A35 from Sidmouth to Lyme Regis, turn right on to B3172 at junction with A358 Seaton. Clifftop course. 18 holes, 5969 yards, 5460 metres. S.S.S. 70. *Green Fees:* weekdays £18.00 per day, weekends £22.00 per day. *Eating facilities:* bar and small restaurant. *Visitors:* welcome without reservation, course closed until 11am on Sundays, Wednesdays till 10.30am and Fridays till 9.30am. Handicap Certificate preferred. *Society Meetings:* welcome at special rates for large bookings. Secretary: John Davies (01297 24371).

BARNSTAPLE. **Portmore Golf Park,** Landkey Road, Barnstaple EX32 9LB (01271 378378). *Location:* A361 just east of Barnstaple, turn right to Landkey 200 yards, turn right Newport, turn right again after a mile. Two parkland 9-hole courses. The Landkey, Par 3. The Barum, Par 70. 24 bay floodlit golf range, chipping green, bunker, putting green. *Green Fees:* Landkey £7.50 9 holes, £12.00 18 holes; Barum £12.50 for 9 holes, £18.00 18 holes. *Eating facilities:* full catering available. *Visitors:* welcome at all times, must telephone for tee times. Full dress code applies for Barum course. Tuition available. *Society Meetings:* welcome with prior booking, group rates available. Professionals: Steve Gould, Darren Everet. e-mail: colin@portmoregolfpark.freeserve.co.uk website: www.portmoregolf.co.uk

BIDEFORD near. **Hartland Forest Golf Club,** Near Clovelly, Bideford EX39 5RA (01237 431442; Fax: 01237 431734). *Location:* between Bideford and Bude A39, signposted from main A39 road. Parkland with water hazards. 18 holes, 5870 yards. S.S.S. 68. Par 70. *Green Fees:* from £20.00 all day, from £15.00 for 18 holes, from £10.00 for 9 holes. *Visitors:* welcome at all times. Buggies for hire. Luxury accommodation, indoor pool, spa, sauna, tennis and fishing. *Society Meetings:* welcome. Secretary: Kevin Murphy (01271 343160). e-mail: hartlandgolfsec@hotmail.com

BIGBURY. **Bigbury Golf Club Ltd**, Bigbury, Kingsbridge TQ7 4BB. *Location:* off main Plymouth to Kingsbridge road, turn right at Harraton Cross. Undulating cliff top course. 18 holes, 5896 yards. S.S.S. 68. *Green Fees:* information not available. *Eating facilities:* catering facilities available every day. *Visitors:* welcome, Handicap Certificate required. *Society Meetings:* catered for by prior arrangement. Professional: Simon Lloyd (01548 810412). Secretary: Martin Lowry (01548 810557). website: www.Bigburygolfclub.com

BRIXHAM. **Churston Golf Club Ltd**, Dartmouth Road, Churston, Near Brixham TQ5 0LA (01803 842751; Fax: 01803 845738). *Location:* A379 from Torquay to Brixham. At Windy Corner take A3022 to Brixham. Club situated half-a-mile on. Downland/parkland course stretching westward along the cliffs towards Brixham. 18 holes, 6219 yards. S.S.S. 70. *Green Fees:* information not available. *Eating facilities:* restaurant, bar and separate function room. *Visitors:* welcome, must be members of recognised club. Conference facilities available. Handicap Certificate required. *Society Meetings:* catered for by arrangement. Mondays, Thursdays and Fridays only. Professional: Neil Holman (01803 843442; Fax: 01803 845738). Manager: S.R. Bawden (01803 842751; Fax: 01803 845738).*

BUDLEIGH SALTERTON. **East Devon Golf Club,** Links Road, Budleigh Salterton EX9 6DG (01395 445195). *Location:* exit M5 Junction 30; follow A376 and B3179 for Exmouth/Budleigh Salterton. Cliff top and heathland; special features: Superb greens, spectacular views over English Channel. 18 holes, 6239 yards. S.S.S. 70. *Green Fees:* 18 holes £30.00, 27 or 36 holes £40.00, weekly ticket £140.00. *Eating facilities:* full bar and restaurant. *Visitors:* anytime by prior arrangement. Handicap Certificate required. Ladies' Day Tuesdays. *Society Meetings:* catered for Thursdays only by arrangement. Professional: T. Underwood (01395 445195). Secretary: Robert Burley (01395 443370).

CHITTLEHAMHOLT. **Highbullen Hotel Golf & Country Club**, Chittlehamholt, Umberleigh EX37 9HD (01769 540561; Fax: 01769 540492). *Location:* M5 Tiverton Exit 27, A361 to South Molton, B3226 five miles. Right uphill following tourist signs through Chittlehamholt. Undulating parkland setting amongst mature specimen trees and water hazards, spectacular views to Exmoor and Dartmoor. 18 holes, 5562 yards. S.S.S. 67. Practice ground, golf simulator, indoor putting green. *Green Fees:* weekdays £20.00; weekends £24.00. *Eating facilities:* restaurant, brasserie and bars. *Visitors:* welcome, check availability. Accommodation on site at Highbullen Hotel. New leisure complex and healthspa with full shower and changing facilities. *Society Meetings:* golf societies welcome subject to availablilty. Professional: Paul Weston (01769 540530). Secretary: Julian Reynolds (01769 540664).

CHULMLEIGH. **Chulmleigh Golf Course,** Leigh Road, Chulmleigh EX18 7BL (Tel & Fax: 01769 580519). *Location:* approximately midway between Barnstaple and Crediton on A377. North Devon's only tailor-made short game course. Undulating parkland course. 18 holes, 1450 yards Summer, 2353 yards Winter for 18 holes. S.S.S. 54. *Green Fees:* from £7.50. *Eating facilities:* licensed bar, bar snacks. *Visitors:* welcome. No Handicap Certificate required. Suitable for experienced golfers to improve short game, ideal for beginners, Juniors and retired golfers. Teaching available for beginners, juniors and adults by arrangement. Holiday cottage available. *Society Meetings:* welcome by prior arrangement. Secretary: Roy Dow. Proprietors: Mr and Mrs R.W Dow. e-mail: chulmleighgolf@aol.com website: www.chulmleighgolf.co.uk

CREDITON. **Downes Crediton Golf Club,** Hookway, Crediton EX17 3PT (01363 773025; Fax: 01363 775060). *Location:* off Crediton-Exeter road. Part flat, part hilly course featuring woods and water. 18 holes, 5951 yards. S.S.S. 69. *Green Fees:* £24.00 per day weekdays; £27.00 per day weekends. Special rates on application. *Eating facilities:* available from 11.30am to one hour before bar closes. *Visitors:* welcome, advisable to phone first and must produce Handicap Certificate. *Society Meetings:* by arrangement. Professional: Scott Macaskill (01363 774464). Managing Secretary: Philip Lee (01363 773025; Fax: 01363 775060).

CREDITON near. **Waterbridge Golf Course,** Down St Mary, Near Crediton EX17 5LG (01363 85111). *Location:* on the A377 north of Crediton (one mile north of Copplestone). Attractive, gentle parkland course in a beautiful setting. 9 holes (18 tees), 3910 yards, S.S.S. 64. *Green Fees:* weekdays £7.00 9 holes, £11.50 18 holes; weekends £8.00 9 holes, £13.50 18 holes. 10% discount on parties of 10 and over. *Eating facilities:* licensed bar, lunches. *Visitors:* welcome. Club and trolley hire available. *Society Meetings:* welcome. Professional: David Ridyard. Secretary: Mrs A. Wren.
website: www.waterbridge.fsbusiness.co.uk

CULLOMPTON. **Padbrook Park Golf Club,** Padbrook Park, Cullompton EX15 1JQ (01884 38286; Fax: 01884 34359). *Location:* Junction 28 of M5, one mile away. Parkland. 9 holes (18 tees), 6108 yards. S.S.S. 70. Nets. *Green Fees:* weekdays £10.00 9 holes, £15.00 18 holes; weekends £12.00 9 holes, £18.00 18 holes. Juniors half price. *Eating facilities:* two bars and restaurant. *Visitors:* always welcome. Indoor bowls, fishing; full conference and meeting facilities. New Health and Fitness studio. *Society Meetings:* welcome by prior arrangement.

Professional: Robert Thorpe. General Manager: Richard Chard.
e-mail: padbrookpark@fsmail.net
website: www.padbrookpark.co.uk

DARTMOUTH. **Dartmouth Golf and Country Club,** Blackawton, Near Dartmouth TQ9 7DE (01803 712686; Fax: 01803 712628). *Location:* five miles from Dartmouth on the A3122. Undulating inland course with lakes, rock faces and multiple tees. Dartmouth Course: 9 holes, 2583 yards. S.S.S. 33. Championship Course: 18 holes, 7191 yards. S.S.S. 74. 15-bay driving range. *Green Fees:* £30.00 weekdays, £40.00 weekends. *Eating facilities:* full restaurant and lounge bar. *Visitors:* welcome daily, Handicap Certificate not essential. 3 Star hotel accommodation in 35 en suite bedrooms; 3 stone self-catering cottages. Leisure suite with pool, gym and beauty therapy etc. Buggies available £25.00 per round. *Society Meetings:* welcome daily. Professional: Steve Dougan (01803 712650). Secretary: Bob Clark (01803 712016).
e-mail: info@dgcc.co.uk   website: www.dgcc.co.uk

DAWLISH. **Warren Golf Club,** Dawlish Warren EX7 0NF (01626 862255; Fax: 01626 888005). *Location:* 12 miles south of Exeter off A379. Links golf course lying on a spit of land between the sea and Exe Estuary. A challenging course situated in an internationally renowned conservation area. 18 holes, 5912 yards. S.S.S. 68. *Green Fees:* weekdays £25.00, weekends and Bank Holidays £28.00 (half price with a member). *Eating facilities:* bar and full catering available. *Visitors:* members of other bona fide golf clubs welcome. *Society Meetings:* welcome by arrangement, Special Packages available. Professional: D. Prowse (01626 864002). Club Secretary: Tim Aggett (01626 862255).

EXETER. **Exeter Golf and Country Club,** Countess Wear, Exeter EX2 7AE (Tel & Fax: 01392 874139; Course Information: 01392 876413). *Location:* near M5, exit Junction 30, take main Plymouth/Torquay Road. Turn left Topsham, 300 yards left. Flat parkland course, many trees. 18 holes, 6000 yards. S.S.S. 69. Large practice ground. *Green Fees:* on application. *Eating facilities:* sports bar, lounge bar, diningroom. *Visitors:* welcome except Tuesdays (Ladies' Day) and Saturdays very busy course, booking sheet in operation, Bookings taken one week prior subject to availability. Booking number 01392 876303. Function suite. *Society Meetings:* catered for Thursdays only. Professional: Mike Rowett (01392 875028; Fax: 01392 874914). Secretary: Keith Ham (01392 874639; Fax: 01392 874139).

EXETER near. **Fingle Glen Hotel, Golf and Country Club,** Tedburn St. Mary, Near Exeter EX6 6AF (01647 61817; Fax: 01647 61135). *Location:* A30 five miles from Exeter on the Okehampton Road. Parkland with streams and lakes. 9 holes, 2475 yards. S.S.S. 63 (18 holes). Golf academy, 12 bay floodlit driving range. *Green Fees:* information not available. *Eating facilities:* restaurant, bar snacks, sun terrace. *Visitors:* welcome at all times. En suite accommodation available. *Society Meetings:* welcome at all times. Pro Shop: Mervyn Kemp. Teaching Professional: Stephen Gould. Secretary: Peter Miliffe. Manager: A. Bridgeman. *

EXETER near. **Teign Valley Golf Club,** Christow, Near Exeter EX6 7PA. (01647 253026). *Location:* Four miles off the A38 Devon Expressway between Exeter and Plymouth. Varied and interesting course set in beautiful valleys in the Dartmoor National Park. Probably the best value golf in Devon,18 holes, 6000 yards. *Green Fees:* Monday £16.00, Tuesday to Friday £18.50, weekends and Bank Holidays £23.00. *Eating facilities:* a welcoming spirit in the friendly clubhouse offering tasty bar snacks and a choice of real ales. *Visitors:* welcome. *Society Meetings:* welcome. Conference facilities for 40 available.

EXETER near. **Woodbury Park Golf and Country Club,** Woodbury Castle, Woodbury, Near Exeter EX5 1JJ (01395 233382; Fax: 01395 233384). *Location:* six miles east of Exeter between Sidmouth and Exmouth. Parkland with many water hazards. 18 hole championship course and 9 hole course. 18 holes, 6905 yards. S.S.S. 73. 18 bay driving range, practice green. *Green Fees:* weekdays £32.00; weekends £40.00. *Eating facilities:* two restaurants, two bars. *Visitors:* welcome at all times. Buggies for hire. Leisure Centre and conference facilities. Five chalet-style luxury lodges ideal for four/six golfers in each. 55 bedroomed hotel. *Society Meetings:* welcome, please ring; Golf Packages available. Bookings (01395 233500). Professional: Alan Perry. Golf Manager: Alan Richards.

HOLSWORTHY. **Holsworthy Golf Club,** Kilatree, Holsworthy EX22 6LP (Tel & Fax: 01409 253177). *Location:* leave Holsworthy on Bude road, A3072; one and a half miles on left. Parkland - gentle undulating hills. 18 holes, 6062 yards. S.S.S. 69. Practice area. *Green Fees:* £25.00. Twilight after 6 pm £10.00. *Eating facilities:* bar, dining room. *Visitors:* welcome anytime. *Society Meetings:* welcome, special reductions for parties of 12 or more. Professional: Graham Webb (01409 254771; Fax: 01409 253177). Secretary: Barry Megson (Tel & Fax: 01409 253177).
e-mail: hgcsecretary@aol.com
website: www.holsworthygolfclub.co.uk

HONITON. **Honiton Golf Club**, Middlehills, Honiton EX14 9TR (01404 44422). *Location*: one mile south of town proceed from A35 at Tower Cross to Farway. Flat parkland. 18 holes, 5902 yards. S.S.S. 68. Small practice ground. *Green Fees:* weekdays £24.00 per day, weekends and Bank Holidays £30.00. *Eating facilities:* bar and restaurant. *Visitors:* bona fide members of other clubs welcome, with restrictions on Wednesdays (Ladies' day) and weekends (club competitions). Facilities for 10 touring caravans during summer months with electrics. *Society Meetings:* bookable on Thursdays only. Professional: Adrian Cave (01404 42943). Secretary: Brian Young (01404 44422; Fax: 01404 46383).

HONITON. **Otter Valley Golf Centre**, Upottery, Honiton EX14 9QP (Tel & Fax: 01404 861266). *Location*: Take the A303 from Honiton, continue one and a half miles, turn off left at Upottery and Rawridge. Rolling parkland course. 9 holes, 1500 yards. Par 29. Four indoor practice bays, large putting green, eight tees on the driving range, chipping green. *Green Fees*: information not available. *Eating facilities*: snacks and refreshments, hot and cold drinks. Lounge with TV. *Visitors*: welcome, no restrictions. Holiday cottages, video analysis, lessons. *Society Meetings*: Societies and Company Days very welcome. Please phone for information. Professional: Andrew Thompson. Secretary: Mike Arscott.*
e-mail: andrewthompson@otter-golf.co.uk
website: www.otter-golf.co.uk

ILFRACOMBE. **Ilfracombe Golf Club, Hele Bay, Ilfracombe EX34 9RT. *Location*: on main coastal road between Ilfracombe and Combe Martin. Undulating parkland with spectacular views of sea and moors from every tee and green. 18 holes, 5893 yards. S.S.S. 68. 9 hole practice area and driving range. *Green Fees*: weekdays £22.00; weekends £27.00. *Eating facilities*: catering available all day. *Visitors*: welcome (Handicap/ membership Certificate preferred). Members only before 10am weekends. *Society Meetings*: welcome, but book in advance. Bookings: (01271 863328). Catering: (01271 862675). Professional: Mark Davies (01271 863328). Club Secretary: J.E. Hoskings (01271 862176; Fax: 01271 867731).**

ILFRACOMBE. **Ilfracombe and Woolacombe Golf Range**, Woolacombe Road, Ilfracombe EX34 7HF (01271 866222; Fax: 01271 342939). *Location*: on main road between Ilfracombe and Woolacombe. Flat course. 9 holes, 695 yards. 300 yard driving range with covered bays, 18 hole putting course, golf shop. *Green Fees*: information not available. *Eating facilities*: pre-packed snacks and drinks available. *Visitors*: everyone is welcome. Tennis court. Lessons and custom built clubs provided. Professional: Jimmy McGhee. Secretary: David Crocker-White.

IVYBRIDGE. **McCaulay's Fitness and Golf,** Dinnaton Golf Club, Ivybridge PL21 9HU (01752 892512; Fax: 01752 698334). *Location*: from the Ivybridge turnoff on A38, we are just two minutes drive, please follow the brown tourist signs. 9 holes, 2028 yards. Par 32. *Green Fees:* 9 holes £7.50, 18 holes £11.00. *Eating facilities*: coffee bar. *Visitors*: always welcome. No Handicap Certificate required. Other facilities offered include gym, 25m heated swimming pool, aerobics studio, tennis, squash, sauna, solarium and steam room. Contact: Jamie Phillips.

MORETONHAMPSTEAD. **Bovey Castle**, Moretonhampstead TQ13 8RE (01647 445000; Fax: 01647 440961). *Location:* Junction 31 from M5, B3212 for two miles. Parkland with rivers and narrow fairways. 18 holes, 6252 yards, 5450 metres. S.S.S. 70. Practice ground, Par 3 course. *Green Fees:* On application. *Eating facilities:* brunch service, cream teas, bar. *Visitors:* welcome. Please book in advance, golf shoes must be worn. Accommodation in 5 star Hotel, tennis courts; buggies and carts available. *Society Meetings:* by prior arrangement. Professional/Secretary: Richard Lewis (01647 440998; Fax: 01647 440961).

MORTEHOE. **Mortehoe and Woolacombe Golf Club,** Easewell, Mortehoe EX34 7EH (01271 870225). *Location:* just outside Mortehoe village. Parkland course with superb sea views. 9 holes (18 tees), 4690 yards, S.S.S. 63. Practice nets. *Green Fees:* information not available. *Eating facilities:* clubhouse; restaurant and bar snacks. *Visitors:* welcome at all times. Cafeteria and golf shop with extensive range of equipment. Touring campsite facilities. Indoor bowls, short mat bowls, table tennis, indoor heated pool; trolleys available. *Society Meetings:* welcome by prior booking. Secretary: Malcolm Wilkinson (01271 870745).*

NEWTON ABBOT. **Dainton Park Golf Club,** Totnes Road, Ipplepen, Newton Abbot TQ12 5TN (01803 815000). *Location:* on A381 between Newton Abbot and Totnes. Undulating parkland course. 18 holes, 6300 yards. S.S.S. 70. Driving range and practice area. *Green Fees:* weekdays £18.00; weekends £20.00. *Eating facilities:* full catering and licensed bar. *Visitors:* unrestricted. *Society Meetings:* welcome by arrangement. Professional: Martin Tyson. Secretary: Mike Penlington.
website: www.daintonparkgolf.co.uk

NEWTON ABBOT. **Hele Park Golf Club,** Ashburton Road, Newton Abbot TQ12 6JN (01626 336060; Fax: 01626 332661). *Location:* A383 on Newton Abbot to Ashburton road, one and a half miles from Newton Abbot town centre. Parkland course. 9 holes, 5168 yards. S.S.S. 65 (for 18 holes). Floodlit driving range. *Green Fees:* from £9.50 for 9 holes and £16.00 for 18 holes. *Eating facilities:* bar and restaurant. *Visitors:* welcome. Booking advised. Normal dress rules apply. Pay as you play and members' club. *Society Meetings:* welcome, special rates on application. Professionals: James Langmead and Jon Langmead. Secretary: A.J. Taylor. Manager: W. Stanbury.
e-mail: info@heleparkgolf.co.uk
website: www.heleparkgolf.co.uk

NEWTON ABBOT. **Newton Abbot (Stover) Golf Club,** Bovey Road, Newton Abbot TQ12 6QQ (01626 352460; Fax: 01626 330210). *Location:* A382 three miles north of Newton Abbot. Tight wooded parkland course with river in play on 8 holes. 18 holes, 5764 yards, 5271 metres. S.S.S. 68. *Green Fees:* £32.00 per day; half price with a member. *Eating facilities:* full catering daily from 10am. *Visitors:* welcome on production of Handicap Certificate or membership card of county affiliated golf club. Must telephone in advance. *Society Meetings:* catered for on Thursdays. Professional: Malcolm Craig (01626 362078). Secretary: G.W. Rees (01626 352460).

OKEHAMPTON. **Okehampton Golf Club,** Off Tors Road, Okehampton EX20 1EF (01837 52113). *Location:* from A30 take turning from centre of Okehampton then follow the signposts. Parkland. 18 holes, 5286 yards. S.S.S. 65. *Green Fees:* weekdays £20.00; Saturdays £25.00; Sundays £20.00. *Eating facilities:* bar and dining room. *Visitors:* welcome; contact by telephone or letter. *Society Meetings:* welcome by prior arrangement. Professional: Ashley Moon (01837 53541). Administrator: Clive Yeo
e-mail: okehamptongc@btconnect.com

OKEHAMPTON near. **Ashbury Hotel,** Higher Maddaford, Ashbury, Near Okehampton EX20 4NL (01837 55453; Fax: 01837 55468). *Location:* signposted "Ashbury" off the B3079, three miles west of Okehampton. Hilly, wooded courses. Ashbury, three courses: Pines 18 holes, 5628 yards, Par 69; Beeches 18 holes, 5351 yards, Par 68; Willows 18 holes, Par 3. Oakwood Course 18 holes, 5374 yards, Par 68. Practice area, putting green and 8-bay covered driving range. *Green Fees:* information not available. *Eating facilities:* fully licensed bar, bar snacks 12 noon to 5pm. *Visitors:* welcome, after midday, please telephone to arrange a tee time. Buggies, clubs and trolleys for hire. Coaching available. Accommodation in 2 star hotel, tennis, bowls, swimming (01837 53053). Professional: Reg Cade. Secretary: Paul Rattenbury.

PLYMOUTH. **Elfordleigh Hotel, Golf and Leisure Club,** Colebrook, Plympton, Plymouth PL7 5EB (01752 336182; Fax: 01752 344581). *Location:* one mile from Plympton. Woodland course in picturesque countryside. 18 holes, S.S.S. 67. Practice area. *Green Fees:* weekdays £25.00; weekends £30.00. *Eating facilities:* Churchill Restaurant; bar meals available from Country Bar. *Visitors:* welcome. Hotel accommodation available. *Society Meetings:* catered for, contact Golf Manager. Professional/Director of Golf: Dominik Naughton (01752 348425).
website: www.elfordleigh.co.uk

PLYMOUTH. **Sparkwell Golf Club,** Sparkwell, Plympton, Plymouth PL7 5DF (Tel & Fax: 01752 837219). *Location:* Sparkwell village centre. Parkland course. 9 holes, 5772 yards, S.S.S. 68. Practice area, pitch and putt. *Green Fees:* information not available. *Eating facilities:* restaurant and bar. *Visitors:* all welcome – pay-as-you-play course. *Society Meetings:* all welcome. Secretary: J. M. Sandiford.

PLYMOUTH. **Staddon Heights Golf Club,** Staddon Heights, Plymstock, Plymouth PL9 9SP (01752 402475). *Location:* from city centre follow signs to Kingsbridge, then Turnchapel then Bouvisand. Cliff tops course overlooking Plymouth Sound. 18 holes, 5845 yards. S.S.S. 70. Practice area. *Green Fees:* information not available. *Eating facilities:* full bar and restaurant facilities. *Visitors:* welcome except Wednesday. *Society Meetings:* welcome. Professional: Ian Marshall (Tel & Fax: 01752 492630). Secretary: Mr K. Bravant (01752 402475).*

FREE GOLF ALL YEAR ROUND

INDOOR SPORT - Bowls, Tennis, Badminton, Squash, Table Tennis, 10-Pin, Snooker - FREE

OUTDOOR SPORT - Tennis, Bowls, Pitch & Putt, Guided Walks, Crazy Golf - FREE

LEISURE - Pools, Spas, Saunas, Solarium, Steam Room - FREE

CRAFT CENTRE - Pottery + 9 Tutored Crafts, including Picture Framing, Glass Engraving, Candle Making & Enamelling- prices at cost

Buggy Prices £6 – £12

Mid March	3 nts	£153/£163	4 nts	£180/£192
Mid May	3 nts	£180/£187	4 nts	£228/£236
June–mid July	3 nts	£178/£185	4 nts	£226/£234
August	3 nts	£199/£221	4 nts	£269/£295
September	3 nts	£194/£206	4 nts	£246/£263

Price per Person–*Full Board*

All rooms en suite, TV/Video, Safe (F.O.C.) and telephone.

Party Discounts ~ Bargain Breaks

Manor House & Ashbury Hotels, Okehampton, Devon EX20 4NA

AA ★★ www.manorhousehotel.co.uk   Freephone 0800 197 7556 **AA** ★★

www.ashburygolfhotel.co.uk   Bookings 01837 53053

See also Colour Advertisement on page 15

ELFORDLEIGH
HOTEL : GOLF : LEISURE

Elfordleigh offers peace, calm and tranquillity in acres of glorious parkland, minutes from the heart of Plymouth.
Our 18 hole golf course offers residential golfing breaks, society packages, practice facilities and expert tuition from **PGA Golf Professional Scott Macaskill.**

Our Oasis Leisure facilities include:

SQUASH COURT • 2 SPAS • SAUNA • STEAM ROOM
• SWIMMING POOL • SEPARATE CHILDREN'S POOL • FULLY EQUIPPED GYMNASIUM • SUN TERRACE • DANCE STUDIO
• 3 TENNIS COURTS • SOLARIUM • BEAUTY THERAPY
• HAIRDRESSER • JOGGING TRACK

Churchills Restaurant offers fine wine and cuisine and excellent service-(need we say more!). Elfordleigh has 2 function suites, ideal for civil weddings or wedding receptions.

ELFORDLEIGH HOTEL
COLEBROOK, PLYMPTON, PLYMOUTH, DEVON PL7 5EB
Tel: 01752 336428 Fax: 01752 344581
E-mail:elfordleigh@btinternet.com
Website:www.elfordleigh.co.uk

See also Colour Advertisement on page 14

SAUNTON. **Saunton Golf Club,** Saunton, Braunton EX33 1LG (01271 812436; Fax: 01271 814241). *Location:* eight miles west of Barnstaple. Two traditional links courses. East course 18 holes, 6729 yards. S.S.S. 72. West course 18 holes, 6403 yards. S.S.S. 71. Practice ground and covered practice range. *Green Fees:* £50.00 per 18 holes, £70.00 per day. All green fees inclusive of meal voucher. *Eating facilities:* full catering available. *Visitors:* welcome, no play before 9.30am, Handicap Certificate required. Prior booking recommended. *Society Meetings:* welcome with prior booking. Professional: A.T. MacKenzie (01271 812013; Fax: 01271 812126). Secretary: T.C. Reynolds (01271 812436; Fax: 01271 814241).
e-mail: info@sauntongolf.co.uk
website: www.sauntongolf.co.uk

SIDMOUTH. **Sidmouth Golf Club,** Cotmaton Road, Peak Hill, Sidmouth EX10 8SX (01395 513451; Fax: 01395 514661). *Location:* half a mile from town centre, 12 miles south east of M5 Junction 30. Parkland with breathtaking views over Sid Valley and Lyme Bay. 18 holes, 5068 yards. S.S.S. 65. *Green Fees:* weekdays £22.00 per round, £26.00 per day; weekends £27.00 per round. Summer and winter packages from £17.00. Society packages from £24.00. *Eating facilities:* catering every day. *Visitors:* welcome anytime depending on tee reservations. *Society Meetings:* by arrangement with Professional: (01395 516407). Secretary: Ian M. Smith (01395 513451 Fax: 01395 514661).
e-mail: terry-carter@tiscali.co.uk

SOUTH BRENT. **Wrangaton Golf Club,** Golf Links Road, Wrangaton, South Brent TQ10 9HJ (01364 73001). *Location:* A38 from Exeter (Wrangaton Cross turn off), from Plymouth A38 Ivybridge turn off via Bittaford. Parkland course, first 9 holes on Dartmoor. 18 holes, 6063 yards. S.S.S 69. Practice ground, putting green and net. *Green Fees:* weekdays £20.00; weekends and Bank Holidays £25.00. *Eating facilities:* full catering and bar facilities available. *Visitors:* welcome at all times but telephone first in case of club competition. *Society Meetings:* all welcome, written notice required. Professional: Glenn Richards (01364 72161). Secretary: Graham Williams (Tel & Fax: 01364 73229).

TAVISTOCK. **Hurdwick Golf Club,** Tavistock Hamlets, Tavistock PL19 0LL (01822 612746). *Location:* one mile north of Tavistock on the Brentor Road. Parkland. 18 holes. S.S.S. 67. *Green Fees:* £15.00 all day. *Eating facilities:* fresh sandwiches, licensed bar. *Visitors:* welcome anytime. *Society Meetings:* (10 or more) 36 holes and buffet for £18 a head. Professional: available. Secretary: Roger Cullen and R. Hurle.

TAVISTOCK. **Tavistock Golf Club,** Down Road, Tavistock PL19 9AQ (Tel & Fax: 01822 612344). *Location:* Whitchurch Down one mile from Tavistock. Moorland course with spectacular views. 18 holes, 6495 yards. S.S.S. 71. Practice ground. *Green Fees:* weekdays £26.00 per day, weekends and Bank Holidays £32.00 per day. *Eating facilities:* all day catering and bar. *Visitors:* welcome, telephone first. *Society Meetings:* by prior arrangement, fees negotiable. Professional: D. Rehaag (01822 612316). Secretary: M.J. O'Dowd (Tel & Fax: 01822 612344).

TEIGNMOUTH. **Teignmouth Golf Club,** Haldon Moor, Teignmouth TQ14 9NY (01626 777070). *Location:* two miles north of Teignmouth on the Exeter Road - B3192. Level heathland course, designed by Dr Mackenzie (also designed Augusta National USA), with panoramic views. 18 holes, 6090 yards. S.S.S. 70. *Green Fees:* On application. *Eating facilities:* catering from 9 am to 6 pm. *Visitors:* welcome with reservation if members of another club with Handicap Certificate. *Society Meetings:* catered for Thursdays. Professional: Robert Selley (01626 772894). Club Manager: Will Hendry (01626 777070; Fax: 01626 777304).

THURLESTONE. **Thurlestone Golf Club,** Thurlestone, Kingsbridge TQ7 3NZ (01548 560405). *Location:* turn off A379 near Kingsbridge. Undulating beside sandy beaches and over cliff tops, with superb coastal views. 18 holes, 6340 yards. S.S.S. 70. Practice area. *Green Fees:* £32.00 per day. Weekly and fortnightly tickets available. *Eating facilities:* catering available from 10.00am until 5.30pm daily. *Visitors:* must produce Handicap Certificate, please telephone in advance. *Society Meetings:* not catered for. Professional: Peter Laugher (Tel & Fax: 01548 560715). Secretary: J.R. Scott (01548 560405; Fax: 01548 562149).

TIVERTON. **Tiverton Golf Club,** Post Hill, Tiverton EX16 4NE (01884 252187; Fax: 01884 251607). *Location:* three miles east of Tiverton, Junction 27 of M5, proceed through Sampford Peverell and Halberton. Parkland, tree-lined fairways. 18 holes, 6236 yards. S.S.S. 71. *Green Fees:* on application. *Eating facilities:* snacks, lunches, teas and evening meals. *Visitors:* welcome, must ring Pro Shop in advance. Handicap Certificate or introduction required. *Society Meetings:* by arrangement with Secretary/ Manager. Professional: Mike Hawton (01884 254836). Secretary/Manager: Richard Jessop (01884 252187).

TORQUAY. **Torquay Golf Club,** 30 Petitor Road, St Marychurch, Torquay TQ1 4QF (01803 327471; Fax: 01803 316116). *Location:* north east of Torquay at St. Marychurch. Parkland. 18 holes, 6192 yards. S.S.S. 70. *Green Fees:* information not available. *Eating facilities:* lunches, teas and evening meals available. *Visitors:* welcome if members of a golf club with Handicap Certificate. *Society Meetings:* ring for rates. Professional: M. Ruth (01803 329113). Secretary: B.G. Long (01803 314591).*

TORRINGTON. **Great Torrington Golf Club,** Weare Trees, Torrington EX38 7EZ (01805 622229; Fax: 01805 623878). *Location:* one mile north of Torrington on Weare Giffard road. Heathland course with excellent views. 9 holes, 4419 yards. S.S.S. 62. Small practice area. *Green Fees:* information not available. *Eating facilities:* full meals and bar snacks available during bar hours. *Visitors:* welcome except on Tuesdays, Wednesdays, Saturdays and Sundays before noon and during club and open competitions. *Society Meetings:* catered for by arrangement. Secretary: Mrs J.M. Cudmore (01271 375927).

UMBERLEIGH. **Libbaton Golf Club Ltd.**, High Bickington, Umberleigh EX37 9BS (01769 560269; Fax: 01769 560342). *Location:* A377 Exeter to Barnstaple, turn off on B3227 to Torrington, at Atherington, turn off B3217 to High Bickington. Parkland with many lakes. 18 holes, 6494 yards. S.S.S. 71. Driving range, teaching centre. *Green Fees:* weekdays £20.00; weekends £24.00. *Eating facilities:* bar, bar meals and first class restaurant. *Visitors:* always welcome, seven days a week. Dress code must be observed. *Society Meetings:* welcome by prior arrangement. Special Society Packages. Fully stocked golf shop with custom club maker. Lessons available by pre-booking. Secretary: Anne Fenge (01769 560269; Fax: 01769 560342).

WESTWARD HO!. **Royal North Devon Golf Club,** Golf Links Road, Westward Ho!, Bideford EX39 1HD (01237 473817). *Location:* two miles North Bideford. Oldest links course in England. 18 holes, 6653 yards. S.S.S. 72. Practice area. *Green Fees:* £32.00 per round weekdays; £38.00 per round weekends. Society discounts and winter rates available. *Eating facilities:* full catering available. *Visitors:* welcome with Handicap Certificate. Tee reservations should be made in advance. *Society Meetings:* catered for. Professional: Richard Herring (01237 477598; Fax: 01237 475347). Secretary: Bob Fowler (Tel: 01237 473817; Fax: 01237 423456).

YELVERTON. **Yelverton Golf Club,** Golf Links Road, Yelverton PL20 6BN (01822 852824). *Location*: eight miles north of Plymouth on A386 road. Testing moorland course with views across Dartmoor. 18 holes, 6363 yards. S.S.S. 71. Practice ground. *Green Fees:* weekdays £30.00 per day or part day; weekends and Bank Holidays £40.00 per day or part day. *Eating facilities:* full catering and bar facilities available. *Visitors:* welcome if member of a recognised golf club or golf society. Handicap Certificate required. Snooker. *Society Meetings:* catered for, welcome by arrangement with Secretary. Professional: T. McSherry (01822 853593). Secretary: S. M. J. Barnes (Tel & Fax: 01822 852824).

THE APPEARANCE OF AN ASTERISK * AT THE END OF A CLUB OR COURSE ENTRY INDICATES THAT UP-TO-DATE INFORMATION HAS NOT BEEN SUPPLIED

Dorset

BLANDFORD. **Ashley Wood Golf Club,** Wimborne Road, Blandford Forum, Dorset DT11 9HN (01258 452253). *Location:* half a mile south of Blandford on B3082. Downland with magnificent views over Tarrant and Stour valleys. 18 holes, 6276 yards. S.S.S. 70. Practice ground, putting green. *Green Fees:* weekdays £25.00; weekends £30.00 after 1pm. *Eating facilities:* hot and cold snacks all day. *Visitors:* welcome during week; after 12 noon Saturday and Sundays with Handicap Certificate or with member only. Ladies only Tuesday mornings. *Society Meetings:* welcome by arrangement with Secretary. Professional: Jon Shimmons (01258 480379). Manager: Paul Bodle (01258 452253).

BOURNEMOUTH. **Knighton Heath Golf Club,** Francis Avenue, Bournemouth BH11 8NX (01202 572633; Fax: 01202 590774). *Location:* A348 and A3049 roundabout exit Francis Avenue. Undulating heathland, 18 holes, 6094 yards. S.S.S. 69. *Green*

Fees: weekdays £25.00 per round, £30.00 per day. *Eating facilities:* meals and bar snacks available daily. *Visitors:* welcome with reservation, after 9.30am weekdays. Restrictions on competition days. Not at weekends unless with a member. Handicap Certificate required. *Society Meetings:* catered for if arranged in advance. Professional: Paul Brown (01202 578275). Secretary: R.C. Bestwick (01202 572633; Fax: 01202 590774). e-mail: khgc@btinternet.com

BOURNEMOUTH. **Meyrick Park Golf Club**, Central Drive, Bournemouth BH2 6LH (01202 786040). *Location:* one mile from Bournemouth town centre. Beautiful and challenging woodland course. 18 holes, 5802 yards. S.S.S. 68. Practice area. *Green Fees:* from £15.00. *Eating facilities:* Pulse Cafe Bar and Summer Terrace. *Visitors:* welcome. Lodge on site offering 17 en suite bedrooms – golf breaks available. *Society Meetings:* welcome by prior arrangement. Professional: David Miles (01202 786040).

The Grosvenor Bournemouth

AA ★★★

Recently awarded
2 RAC
Dining Awards 2003

We welcome you as guests and bid farewell as friends

GOLF PRE-ARRANGED

'A hotel of style and charm'

... is the way guests who have discovered the unique hotel regard the 3 ★ Grosvenor in Bournemouth. Ideally situated in the very heart of the town, just a short stroll from golden beaches, the cosmopolitan town centre and within easy driving distance from many quaint villages, 35 golf courses and The Purbeck Hills, recently designated a world heritage site.

With 40 comfortable, delightfully decorated bedrooms, renowned award winning cuisine, airy sun lounge, comfortable bar and state of the art leisure suite, it is the perfect choice for those of discerning taste.

Tel: 01202 558858

enquiries@grosvenor-bournemouth.co.uk

See also Inside Back Cover

BOURNEMOUTH. **Queens Park (Bournemouth) Golf Club**, Queens Park West Drive, Bournemouth BH8 9BY (01202 396198). *Location*: off Wessex Way. Parkland course in centre of Bournemouth. 18 holes, 6305 yards. S.S.S. 70. Small practice area. *Green Fees*: information on application. *Eating facilities*: restaurant and bar. *Visitors*: welcome anytime, last tee off times Sundays 12 noon. *Society Meetings*: welcome by prior arrangement. Professional: R. Hill (01202 396817). Secretary: Mrs D. J. Gibb (Tel & Fax: 01202 302611).

BOURNEMOUTH. **Solent Meads Golf Club,** Rolls Drive, Hengistbury Head, Bournemouth (01202 420795). *Location:* south of Christchurch. Seaside course. 18 holes, 2182 yards. S.S.S. 54. Driving range, 9 hole pitch and putt. *Green Fees:* £7.20 for 18 holes, concessions available. *Eating facilities:* cafe. *Visitors:* no restrictions. Professional: R. Watkins (01202 420795).
e-mail: golfforallltd@aol.com

BOURTON. **Bullpits Golf Club,** Bourton, Near Gillingham SP8 5AX (01747 840700; Fax: 01747 840229). *Location:* off the A303 at Bourton and follow signs in village. Wooded parkland with lake and River Stour. 9 holes, 18 tees, 3362 yards. S.S.S. 57. Putting green. *Green Fees:* £9.00; reductions for students and juniors; 2 fore 1 welcome. *Eating facilities:* light refreshments and bar facilities. *Visitors:* welcome at all times except Sunday mornings. Five holiday cottages around the course. *Society Meetings:* welcome by appointment. Owner: Simon Bull. Contact: Rupert Ross Hirst.

BRIDPORT. **Bridport and West Dorset Golf Club**, Burton Road, Bridport DT6 4PS (01308 421095). *Location*: one-and-a-half miles east of Bridport on B3157. Clifftop links course. 18 holes, 5729 yards. Par 70. Driving range, 9 hole pitch and putt course, 18 hole putting green (May to September). *Green Fees*: £22.00, £16.00 after 12pm weekdays, (2pm weekends), £10.00 after 5pm. *Eating facilities*: lounge and dining room, spikes bar. *Visitors*: welcome, but not before 9.30am Mondays, Wednesdays, Fridays and Saturdays, and after 12.30pm Tuesdays, Thursdays and Sundays. Members only 8am - 9.30am daily and 12pm -2pm weekends. Please check with professional in advance. *Society Meetings*: catered for by prior arrangement. Clubhouse: (01308 422597). Professional: David Parsons (01308 421491). Secretary: Peter Ridler (Tel & Fax: 01308 421095).

BROADSTONE. **Broadstone (Dorset) Golf Club,** Wentworth Drive, Broadstone BH18 8DQ (01202 692595). *Location:* off A349 to B3072 to Broadstone. Heathland. 18 holes, 6315 yards. S.S.S. 70. Practice area. *Green Fees:* weekdays £40.00 per round, £55.00 per day. Weekend/Bank Holidays one round £45.00 (very limited). *Eating facilities:* full catering service. *Visitors:* welcome weekdays, weekends by prior arrangement, current Handicap Certificate required. *Society Meetings:* welcome by arrangement except weekends. Professional: Nigel Tokely (Tel & Fax: 01202 692835). Secretary: Colin Robinson (Tel & Fax: 01202 692595).
e-mail: admin@broadstonegolfclub.com
website: www.broadstonegolfclub.com

CHRISTCHURCH. **Dudmoor Farm Golf Course,** Dudmoor Farm Road, Christchurch, Dorset BH23 6AQ. *Location:* off Fairmile road, near Christchurch Hospital. Wooded course. 9 holes. Longest hole 280 yards. *Green Fees:* £7.00 for 18 holes. *Eating facilities:* tea, coffee, crisps, chocolate, ice cream. *Visitors:* welcome, no need to book. Riding instruction and trekking available. (01202 473826; Fax: 01202 480207).

CHRISTCHURCH. **Highcliffe Castle Golf Club,** 107 Lymington Road, Highcliffe BH23 4LA (01425 272953). *Location:* on the coastal road linking Lymington and Christchurch. Flat, wooded course. 18 holes, 4776 yards, 4347 metres. S.S.S. 63. Two practice nets. *Green Fees:* weekdays £25.50; weekends £35.50. Reductions during winter months and after 4pm in summer. Must be in possession of Handicap Certificate. *Eating facilities:* full bar/catering facilities. *Visitors:* welcome after 9.30am if member of recognised golf club. Please phone to check tee reservations. *Society Meetings:* catered for by prior arrangement. Secretary: Mr Graham Fisher (01425 272210).

CHRISTCHURCH. **Parley Court Golf Club**, Parley Green Lane, Hurn, Christchurch BH23 6BB (01202 591600). *Location*: opposite Bournemouth International Airport. Flat course. 9 holes, 2469 yards. S.S.S. 64, Par 68. Putting and chipping areas. *Green Fees*: weekdays £9.00 18 holes, £6.50 9 holes; weekends (no booking required) £10.00 18 holes, £7.50 9 holes. *Eating facilities:* licensed bar. *Visitors:* welcome. Membership available. *Society Meetings:* welcome. Secretary: S.D. Mitchell (01202 591600).

DORCHESTER. **Came Down Golf Club,** Came Down, Dorchester DT2 8NR (01305 812531). *Location:* two miles south of Dorchester. Downland course on chalk downs with excellent drainage and magnificent views, Birthplace of the Ryder Cup. Designed by Harry S. Colt. 18 holes, 6224 yards, 5914 metres. S.S.S. 71. Practice area and nets. *Green Fees:* weekdays £24.00; weekends £28.00. *Eating facilities:* full catering facilities. *Visitors:* welcome without reservation except Sunday mornings - phone in advance. All visitors must have Handicap Certificate. Established in 1896. *Society Meetings:* Wednesdays only. Package (around £30) includes golf (36 holes), morning coffee, lunch and evening meal. Professional: Nick Rodgers (01305 812670). Manager: (Tel & Fax: 01305 813494). e-mail: manager@camedowngolfclub.co.uk website: www.camedowngolfclub.co.uk

DORCHESTER. **Charminster Golf Club,** Wolfedale Golf Course, Dorchester DT2 7SG (01305 260186; Fax: 01305 257074). *Location:* Dorchester. Parkland course. 18 holes, 5467 yards. S.S.S. 67. 6 hole practice area. *Green Fees:* information not available. *Eating facilities:* Caddy Shack bar and restaurant. *Visitors:* welcome anytime. Sundays mainly competition days. *Society Meetings:* welcome. Professional: Tim Lovegrove (01305 260186; Fax: 01305 257074). Secretary: Ray Walker (01305 833668).

DORCHESTER. **Lyons Gate Golf Club,** Lyons Gate, Dorchester DT2 7AZ (01300 345239). *Location:* on A352 going north from Dorchester about 11 miles, or south from Sherborne about seven miles. Parkland with spectacular views, probably England's most challenging 9 hole course, famous for its wild flowers. 9 holes, 18 tees, 3834 yards. S.S.S. 60. Practice net. *Green Fees:* weekdays £6.00 for 9 holes, £10.00 for 18 holes; weekends £7.00 for 9 holes, £11.00 for 18 holes. Children under 18 years half price. *Eating facilities:* snacks and refreshments at fully licensed bar. *Visitors:* welcome, no restrictions, dogs on leads. *Society Meetings:* by arrangement. Secretary: Mr N.W. Pires (01300 345239).

FERNDOWN. **Dudsbury Golf Club,** Christchurch Road, Ferndown BH22 8ST (01202 593499; Fax: 01202 594555). *Location:* Ferndown town centre. Follow signs for Poole on A348, turn left at first mini roundabout, turn left to Hurn Airport, 200 yards. Club on right hand side. Parkland course designed by Donald Steel, featuring six lakes in beautiful Dorset countryside rolling gently down to the River Stour. 18 holes, 6904 yards. S.S.S 73. 6 hole academy course, driving range. *Green Fees:* weekdays £34.00; weekends and Bank Holidays £39.00. *Eating facilities:* two bars, spike bar, food served all day. *Visitors:* welcome at all times. Buggies and trolleys available. *Society Meetings:* welcome, phone Secretary for details. Professional: Kevin Spurgeon (01202 594488). Secretary: Giles Legg.

FERNDOWN. **Ferndown Forest Golf Club,** Forest Links Road, Ferndown BH22 9QE (01202 876096; Fax: 01202 894095). *Location:* off main A31 trunk road. Flat, wooded parkland. 18 holes, 5200 yards, Par 68. Covered, floodlit driving range; large practice putting green. *Green Fees:* information not available. *Eating facilities:* licensed bar and patio serving breakfast, lunch, dinner. *Visitors:* all welcome. *Society Meetings:* welcome. Professional/ Secretary: Mike Dodd (07989 137662).*

FERNDOWN. **Ferndown Golf Club,** 119 Golf Links Road, Ferndown BH22 8BU (01202 872022). *Location:* off A31. Wooded heathland. 18 holes, 6452 yards. S.S.S. 71. 9 holes, 5604 yards. S.S.S. 68. Practice ground. *Green Fees:* Old Course: £45.00 weekdays, £50.00 weekends. President's Course: £20.00 weekdays, £25.00 weekends. Societies £65.00 for the day. *Eating facilities:* available. *Visitors:* welcome but prior permission recommended. Handicap Certificate required from a recognised golf club. Professional: Iain Parker (01202 873825). Secretary: M.C. Davies (01202 874602; Fax: 01202 873926).

LYME REGIS. **Lyme Regis Golf Club,** Timber Hill, Lyme Regis DT7 3HQ (01297 442043). *Location:* between Lyme Regis and Charmouth (A35). Cliff top course (not hilly) with fine coastal views. 18 holes, 6283 yards. S.S.S. 70. Practice ground, chipping area and bunker. *Green Fees:* information not available. *Eating facilities:* bars (normal hours) and catering every day. *Visitors:* welcome, but not before 9.30am weekdays and Saturdays, Thursdays after 2.15pm and Sundays after 12 noon. Best to check with Professional. Handicap Certificate or proof of membership of a golf club required. *Society Meetings:* minimum for Tee Booking 12. Professional: Duncan Driver (01297 443822). Secretary: Stephen Wright (01297 442963).

OKEFORD FITZPAINE. **Dorset Heights Golf Club**, Okeford Fitzpaine, Near Blandford DT11 0EG (01258 861386; Fax: 01258 860900). *Location:* A357 Sturminster Newton, Bulbarrow Hill. Parkland/wooded course. 18 holes, 6138 yards. S.S.S. 70. Large practice ground, putting green. *Green Fees:* information not available. *Eating facilities:* bars and restaurant. *Visitors:* welcome all week. *Society Meetings:* welcome by appointment only. Professional: Andy Stuart (01258 861386). Secretary: Jayne Burton (01258 861386; Fax: 01258 860900). *

POOLE. **Parkstone Golf Club,** 49a Links Road, Parkstone, Poole BH14 9QS (01202 707138). *Location:* off A35 Bournemouth to Poole. Wooded heathland. 18 holes, 6250 yards. S.S.S. 70. *Green Fees:* £40.00 per round, £60.00 per day weekdays; £50.00 per round, £70.00 per day weekends and Bank Holidays (subject to review). *Eating facilities:* comprehensive. *Visitors:* welcome with booking and Handicap Certificate. *Society Meetings:* catered for as above. Professional: Martyn Thompson (01202 708092). General Manager: Christine Radford (01202 707138; Fax: 01202 706027).

POOLE near. **Bulbury Woods Golf Club,** Bulbury Lane, Lytchett Matravers, Poole BH16 6EP (01929 459574; Fax: 01929 459000). *Location:* just off A35 , one mile after the Bakers Arms roundabout, three miles from Poole centre. Excellent woodland course, superbly manicured, panoramic views across Poole harbour and the Purbeck Hills. 18 holes, 6000 yards, par 71. Practice ground. *Green Fees:* weekdays £15.00, weekends £20.00. *Eating facilities:* fully licensed bar and restaurant. *Visitors:* welcome anytime subject to availability. *Society Meetings:* societies and corporate days by prior arrangement.

SHERBORNE. **Sherborne Golf Club,** Higher Clatcombe, Sherborne DT9 4RN (01935 814431; Fax: 01935 814218). *Location:* one mile north of Sherborne off the B3145 to Wincanton. Parkland with extensive views. 18 holes, 6414 yards. S.S.S. 71. Practice ground. *Green Fees:* £25.00 weekdays, £36.00 weekends. *Eating facilities:* snacks, lunches, suppers, teas; dinners to order. *Visitors:* as commitment allows, telephone in advance. Handicap Certificates required. Thursday is Ladies' Day. *Society Meetings:* catered for Tuesdays and Wednesdays. Professional: Alistair Tressider (Tel & Fax: 01935 812274). Secretary/ Manager: Phil Gamble (01935 814431; Fax: 01935 814218).

SOUTH PERROTT. **Chedington Court Golf Club,** South Perrott DT8 3HU (01935 891413). *Location:* three miles south east of Crewekerne on A356. Parkland course surrounded by woods, very

picturesque, several ponds. 18 holes, 5924 yards, S.S.S. 70. 5-acre practice area. *Green Fees:* information not available. *Eating facilities:* restaurant and bar open all day. *Visitors:* all welcome, bookings taken. Dress restrictions. Trolleys, buggies and clubs for hire. *Society Meetings:* all welcome, special rates available. General Manager: Ray Gudge.

STUDLAND. **Isle of Purbeck Golf Club,** Studland, Swanage BH19 3AB (01929 450361). *Location:* A351 towards Swanage, at Corfe Castle turn onto B3351 to Studland. Heathland courses with wonderful views. Purbeck - 18 holes, 6295 yards. S.S.S. 70. Dene - 9 holes, 2022 yards. S.S.S. 30. *Green Fees:* Weekdays £35.00 per round, £45.00 per day, weekends £40.00 per round, £47.50 per day. *Eating facilities:* bar and restaurant. *Visitors:* welcome. Buggies available. *Society Meetings:* catered for by arrangement, minimum 8. Professional: Ian Brake (01929 450354). Secretary: Mrs J. Robinson (01929 450361; Fax: 01929 450501).
e-mail: bookings@purbeckgolf.co.uk
website: www.purbeckgolf.co.uk

VERWOOD. **Crane Valley Golf Club,** The Clubhouse, Verwood BH31 7LE (01202 814088; Fax: 01202 813407). *Location:* on B3081 Verwood to Cranborne Road. Parkland featuring lakes and River Crane. 18 holes, 6400 yards. S.S.S. 71. 9 hole woodland course, 2100 yards. Covered driving range. *Green Fees:* 18 hole course weekdays £25.00, weekends £35.00; 9 hole course weekdays £5.50; weekends £6.50. *Eating facilities:* restaurant and spikes bar. *Visitors:* welcome at all times. Accommodation adjoining course at West Farm. *Society Meetings*: by appointment. Secretary/ Manager: Darrel Ranson.

WAREHAM. **The Dorset Golf & Country Club,** Bere Regis, Near Poole BH20 7NT (01929 472244; Fax: 01929 471294). *Location:* take A352 off Wareham by-pass, enter Puddletown Road, Worgret Heath or the Wool road from Bere Regis. After 4 miles, the Club is clearly signposted. Two courses: Lakeland Course 18 holes, 7027 yards. S.S.S. 74, Par 72. Woodland Course 2x9 holes, 4887 yards. S.S.S. 64, Par 66. Driving range and Pro Shop. *Green Fees:* weekdays £30.00; weekends £35.00. *Eating facilities*: excellent bar and restaurant. *Visitors:* welcome anytime with prior tee reservation. *Society Meetings:* welcome by advance booking. The Dorset Golf Hotel overlooks course – 16 en suite bedrooms available for short breaks, etc. Professional: Derwynne Honan (01929 472244). Secretary: Graham Packer (01929 472244; Fax: 01929 471294).
e-mail: admin@dorsetgolfresort.com
website: www.dorsetgolfresort.com

WAREHAM. **Wareham Golf Club,** Sandford Road, Wareham BH20 4DH (01929 554156; Fax: 01929 557993). *Location*: adjoining A351 north of Wareham. Partly wooded course with splendid views over Purbeck Hills and Poole Harbour. 18 holes, 5753 yards, S.S.S. 68. Practice ground, putting green. *Green Fees*: £22.00 per round, £28.00 per day weekdays after 9.30am; weekends after 1pm £25.00 per round. *Eating facilities*: excellent bar and restaurant. *Visitors*: welcome, after 9.30am weekdays and after 1pm weekends. Handicap Certificate preferred. *Society Meetings*: very welcome, special packages available.

WEYMOUTH. **Wessex Golf Centre,** Radipole Lane, Weymouth DT4 9HX (01305 784737). *Location:* Wessex roundabout off Weymouth by pass, behind football stadium. Flat public course. 9 holes, 1432 yards. Par 3. Large driving range, putting green, practice bunker. *Green Fees*: £4.50. *Visitors:* welcome; public course. Shop. Professional: Jon Bevan.

WEYMOUTH. **Weymouth Golf Club Ltd,** Links Road, Weymouth DT4 0PF (01305 784994; Fax: 01305 788029). *Location:* A354 from Dorchester, take last exit at Manor roundabout then second left at Chafeys roundabout. Undulating parkland. 18 holes, 5981 yards. S.S.S. 69. Practice area. *Green Fees:* weekdays £24.00 per day, weekends and Bank Holidays £30.00. £15.00 after 4pm. Half price playing with a member. Juniors half price. Green fees are subject to review. *Eating facilities:* full restaurant and bar. *Visitors:* welcome, but only with EGU or Club Handicap Certificate. *Society Meetings:* welcome by prior arrangement except weekends. Special rates for Society, Company/ Corporate Days. Conference facilities and local transport arranged. Professional: Des Lochrie (01305 773997). Secretary/Manager: Brian Chatham (01305 773981; Fax: 01305 788029). e-mail: weymouthgolfclub@aol.com
website: www.weymouthgc.co.uk

WIMBORNE. **Canford Magna Golf Club,** Knighton Lane, Wimborne BH21 3AS (01202 592552; Fax: 01202 592550). *Location*: off A341, near Bear Cross roundabout on the main A348 Ringwood Road. Three courses: Parkland – 18 holes, 6495 yards; Riverside – 18 holes, 6231 yards; Knighton – 9 holes, 2754 yards, Par 3. 6-hole academy course and driving range, practice area. *Green Fees*: Riverside – weekdays £10.00 for 9 holes, £17.00 for 18 holes, weekends £13.00 for 9 holes, £20.00 for 18 holes; Knighton – weekdays £7.00 for 9 holes, £14.00 for 18 holes, weekends £9.00 for 9 holes, £17.00 for 18 holes. Parkland – weekdays £12.00 for 9 holes, £21.00 for 18 holes, weekends £15.00 for 9 holes, £25.00 for 18 holes. Under 18s £10.00. *Eating facilities*: two bars, meals served throughout day; restaurant. *Visitors*: welcome. Prior booking advisable (one week in advance). Club hire and lessons; Pro Shop. Handicap Certificate not required. Conference facilities. Professionals: 6 full-time professionals headed by PGA Pro Martin Cummins. General Manager: Trevor Smith.
e-mail: admin@canfordmagnagc.co.uk
website: www.canfordmagnagc.co.uk

WIMBORNE. **Canford School Golf Club**, Canford School. Wimborne BH21 3AD (01202 841254; Fax: 01202 881009). *Location*: Close to Wimborne, Poole and Bournemouth. Flat Parkland course. 9 (x2) holes, 5934 yards, S.S.S. 69. *Green Fees*: information not available. *Society Meetings*: Contact Secretary. Secretary: Mark Burley (01202 841254; Fax: 01202 881009).*

WIMBORNE. **Sturminster Marshall Golf Club,** Moor Lane, Sturminster Marshall, Wimborne BH21 4AH (01258 858444; Fax: 01258 858262). *Location:* Poole to Blandford Forum road, A350 signposted at village. Flat parkland course, suits golfers of all abilities. 9/18 holes, 5028 yards. S.S.S. 65. Practice net. *Green Fees:* information not available. *Eating facilities:* fully licensed snack bar. *Visitors:* welcome, no restrictions. *Society Meetings:* welcome. Professional: Graham Howell. Secretary: D.R. Holdsworth.*

Durham

BARNARD CASTLE. **Barnard Castle Golf Club,** Harmire Road, Barnard Castle DL12 8QN (01833 638355 or 637237). *Location:* one mile north of Barnard Castle Town Centre on the B6278. Open parkland with a number of streams to be crossed and with maturing copses. 18 holes, 6406 yards. S.S.S. 71. Practice area. *Green Fees:* weekdays £20.00 per round, £24.00 per 27 holes; weekends and Bank Holidays £30.00 per round, £35.00 27 holes. Reduced rates playing with member. *Eating facilities:* full catering. *Visitors:* welcome, but formal booking system applies at weekends and Bank Holidays. *Society Meetings:* catered for by prior arrangement. Professional: Darren Pearce (01833 631980). Secretary: J. Kilgarriff (01833 638355).

BEAMISH. **Beamish Park Golf Club,** Beamish, Stanley DH9 0RH (0191-370 1382; Fax: 0191-370 2937). *Location:* follow directions to Beamish Museum. Parkland, 18 holes, 6205 yards. S.S.S. 70. Two practice areas. *Green Fees:* information not available. *Eating facilities:* bar and à la carte menu. *Visitors:* welcome weekdays. Carts for hire. *Society Meetings:* welcome. Professional: Chris Cole (0191-370 1984). Hon. Secretary: Ged Cushlow.

BILLINGHAM. **Billingham Golf Club,** Sandy Lane, Billingham TS22 5NA (01642 554494). *Location:* off A19 trunk road, one mile west of Billingham town centre. Undulating parkland. 18 holes, 6333 yards. S.S.S. 70. Practice area including pitching green and putting greens. *Green Fees:* weekdays £25.00, £15.00 with member; weekends £40.00, £20.00 with member. *Eating facilities:* full catering. Caterer D. Bittlestone. *Visitors:* welcome weekdays, prior booking advised. *Society Meetings:* catered for by prior arrangement with Secretary. Caterer (01642 554494). Professional: M. Ure (01642 557060). Secretary: P.B. Hodgson (Tel & Fax: 01642 533816). e-mail: billinghamgc@onetel.net.uk

BISHOP AUCKLAND. **Bishop Auckland Golf Club,** High Plains, Durham Road, Bishop Auckland DL14 8DL (01388 602198). *Location:* leave Bishop Auckland Market Place on route to Spennymoor/Durham, half a mile on left. Parkland, 18 holes, 6379 yards. S.S.S. 70 (Par 72). Practice fairways. *Green Fees:* weekdays £24.00 per round, £30.00 per day; weekends £30.00 per round. *Eating facilities:* bar, full catering facilities. *Visitors:* welcome mid-week only. Ladies' Day Tuesday. Two snooker tables. *Society Meetings:* catered for on application, not weekends and Christmas period, and official Handicap required. Special package £31.00 for parties of 4 or more, includes catering. Professional: D. Skiffington (01388 661618). Secretary: A. Milne (01388 663648). e-mail: enquiries@bagc.co.uk website: www.bagc.co.uk

BRANCEPETH. **Brancepeth Castle Golf Club,** The Clubhouse, Brancepeth DH7 8EA (0191-378 0075; Fax: 0191-378 3835). *Location:* A690 Durham to Crook, turn left at crossroads in Brancepeth village, take immediate left at the castle gates, 200 yards down lane. Parkland course undulating in parts. 18 holes, 6285 yards, S.S.S. 70. Practice field, putting green. *Green Fees:* information not available. *Eating facilities:* full bar and restaurant facilities. *Visitors:* parties welcome weekdays, individuals only at weekends. Changing rooms and showers, lessons by arrangement. *Society Meetings:* welcome weekdays, good rates available. Tee available 9.30am and 1.30pm. Professional: D. Howdon (0191-378 0183). Secretary: Mr B. Cullen (0191-378 0075; Fax: 0191-378 3835).

CHESTER-LE-STREET. **Chester-le-Street Golf Club,** Lumley Park, Chester-le-Street DH3 4NS (0191 3883218; Fax: 0191 3881220). *Location:* half a mile east of Chester-le-Street adjacent to Lumley Castle. Fairly flat parkland. 18 holes, 6457 yards, 5535 metres. S.S.S. 71. Practice area. *Green Fees:* information not available. *Eating facilities:* snacks, lunches, dinners. *Visitors:* welcome 9.30am to 12 noon, 1.30pm to 4.30pm weekdays; 10.30am to 12 noon, 2pm onwards weekends. Must be members of a golf club and have a Handicap. Hotel adjacent. *Society Meetings:* welcome except weekends and Public Holidays. Professional: D. Fletcher (0191 3890157; Fax: 0191 3881220). Secretary: B. Forster (0191 3883218; Fax: 0191 3881220).

CHESTER-LE-STREET. **Roseberry Grange Golf Club,** Grange Villa, Chester-le-Street DH2 3NF (0191-370 0670). *Location:* three miles west of Chester-le-Street on A693. Parkland course. 18 holes, 5809 yards. S.S.S. 68. Driving range. *Green Fees:* mid week £13.00; weekend £17.00; visiting party packages. *Eating facilities:* bar meals 12 noon to 2pm and 7pm to 9.30pm. *Visitors:* welcome, no restrictions weekdays, Saturdays 7am to 10.30am, Sundays 7am to 11.30am. Professional: C. Jones (0191-370 0660). Secretary: Raymond McDermott (0191-370 2047).

CONSETT. **Consett and District Golf Club Ltd,** Elmfield Road, Consett DH8 5NN (01207 502186; Fax: 01207 502186). *Location:* 14 miles north of Durham on A691 (hidden turning on steep hill). 18 holes, 6023 yards. S.S.S. 69. Parkland, undulating, excellent views over Derwent Valley. *Green Fees:* weekdays £18.00; weekends £26.00, half fees with member. *Eating facilities:* full catering available (limited on Mondays). *Visitors:* welcome most times, phone Secretary or Professional. *Society Meetings:* catered for by arrangement, enquiries welcomed through Secretary. Professional: S. Ord (01207 580210). Secretary: I.B. Murray (01207 505060 Fax/Answer machine)

CROOK. **Crook Golf Club,** Low Jobs Hill, Crook DL15 9AA (01388 762429). *Location:* eleven miles west of Durham City on A690. Scenic views; excellently conditioned course. 18 holes, 6102 yards, 5902 metres. S.S.S. 69. Practice area. *Green Fees:* Monday to Saturday (incl) £18.00 per day, £14.00 per round; reductions when playing with member. *Eating facilities:* available, limited Mondays. *Visitors:* welcome but limited times at weekends. *Society Meetings:* welcome by arrangement with Secretary. Special packages available. Hon Secretary: Les Shaw (01388 762429).

DARLINGTON. **Blackwell Grange Golf Club,** Briar Close, Blackwell, Darlington DL3 8QX (01325 464464). *Location:* one mile south of Darlington on A66 turn into Blackwell. Signposts to Club. Parkland course. 18 holes, 5621 yards. S.S.S. 68. *Green Fees:* weekdays £20.00 per round, £25.00 per day; weekends and Bank Holidays £30.00 per round. *Eating facilities:* full menu except Sundays and Mondays. *Visitors:* welcome without reservation except weekends. *Society Meetings:* catered for except Wednesdays and weekends. Professional: Joanne Furby (01325 462088). Secretary: Peter Burkill (Tel & Fax: 01325 464458).

DARLINGTON. **The Darlington Golf Club (Members) Ltd,** Haughton Grange, Darlington DL1 3JD (01325 355324; Fax: 01325 480668). *Location:* northern outskirts of town, A1150 off A167, easy access from A1(M) or A19. Flat wooded parkland course designed by Dr. Alister Mackenzie. 18 holes, 6181 yards. S.S.S. 69. 10 acre practice ground, chipping area and net. *Green Fees:* weekdays £25.00 per round, £30.00 per day (£10.00 with Member). *Eating facilities:* dining room, lounge and bar. *Visitors:* welcome weekdays and selected weekends with reservation. Must be members of recognised golf club. Buggies available for hire. *Society Meetings:* package deals by arrangement weekdays, 18, 28 or 36 holes, inclusive of all food

and golf - Bronze package £31.00, Silver package £33.00, Gold package £35.00. Professional: Craig Dilley (01325 484198). Secretary: George W. Storey (01325 355324 Ext. 1 or 2).
e-mail: darlington.golfclub@virgin.net
website: www.darlington-gc.co.uk

DARLINGTON. **Dinsdale Spa Golf Club,** Neasham Road, Middleton-St-George, Darlington DL2 1DW (01325 332222). *Location:* near Teesside Airport. Parkland. 18 holes, 6090 yards. S.S.S. 69. Large practice ground. *Green Fees:* £25.00 per day. Playing with a member £12.50 weekdays, £15.00 weekends. *Eating facilities:* bar, catering. *Visitors:* welcome weekdays, weekends with a member only. *Society Meetings:* catered for Monday, Wednesday, Thursday and Friday by advance booking. Professional: Neil Metcalfe (Tel & Fax: 01325 332515). Secretary: P. Davison (01325 332297).

DARLINGTON. **Hall Garth Golf and Country Club Hotel,** Coatham, Mundeville, Darlington DL1 3LU (01325 300400; Fax: 01325 310083). *Location:* A1 J59, follow the A167 toward Darlington, after 300 yards turn left at Brafferton, entrance after 200 yards on right. Parkland course. 9 holes, 6621 yards. S.S.S. 72. *Green Fees:* information not available. *Eating facilities:* Stables Country Pub. *Visitors:* always welcome. *Society Meetings:* welcome; prices on request.*

DARLINGTON. **Stressholme Golf Club,** Snipe Lane, Darlington DL2 2SA (01325 461002; Fax: 01325 461002). *Location:* signposted off the A66 Teesside to Scotch Corner outside of Darlington. Parkland course with water features. 18 holes, 6431 yards. S.S.S. 71. 25 bay driving range with nets, chipping greens, distance markers, etc. *Green Fees:* information not available. *Eating facilities:* bar in clubhouse with extensive catering facilities. *Visitors:* welcome all week. Professional /Secretary: Ralph Givens (01325 461002; Fax: 01325 461002).*

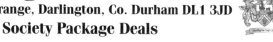

DURHAM. **Durham City Golf Club,** Littleburn, Langley Moor, Durham DH7 8HL (0191-378 0806). *Location:* from Durham City take A690 to Crook - course signposted in Langley Moor. Parkland, bordered by the River Browney. 18 holes, 6326 yards. S.S.S. 70. Large practice area. *Green Fees:* weekdays £24.00, weekends £30.00. Half fees if playing with a member. Substantial discounts for parties of 20 or more. *Eating facilities:* no catering Mondays or Thursday evenings. *Visitors:* welcome at all times, only restrictions when club competitions are being held - ring Professional for details. *Society Meetings:* welcome, but restricted to weekdays. Professional: S. Corbally (0191-378 0029). Assistant Secretary: Ian Wilson (0191-386 4434).

DURHAM. **Mount Oswald Manor and Golf Course,** South Road, Durham DH1 3TQ (0191-386 7527; Fax: 0191-386 0975; *Location:* A1(M) Junction marked Bowburn, A177 Durham City follow signs for Darlington. Parkland, partially wooded. 18 holes, 6101 yards. S.S.S. 69. *Green Fees:* weekdays £12.50; weekends £15.00; winter rates available. *Eating facilities:* bar meals, Sunday lunches, set meals, etc. *Visitors:* welcome except Sunday mornings before 10am (members only). Bookings only at weekends and Bank Holidays. *Society Meetings:* welcome, same restrictions as visitors. Must order food. General Manager: Mr N. P. Galvin (0191-386 7527). e-mail: information@mountoswald.co.uk website: www.mountoswald.co.uk

DURHAM. **Ramside Hall Hotel and Golf Club,** Carrville DH1 1TD (0191-386 9514; Fax: 0191- 386 9519). *Location:* two miles north-east of Durham on A690. A1 (M) Junction 62. 27 holes, 6217/6851 yards. S.S.S. 70/73. Driving range and golf academy. *Green Fees:* please telephone for information. *Eating facilities:* choice of three eating areas. *Visitors:* welcome. Professional: R. Lister (0191-386 9514). Secretary: T. Flowers.*

EAGLESCLIFFE. **Eaglescliffe Golf Club Ltd,** Yarm Road, Eaglescliffe, Stockton-on-Tees TS16 0DQ (01642 780098; Office: 01642 780238). *Location:* on A135 one mile north of Yarm and three miles south of Stockton. Hilly parkland course, sloping to River Tees. 18 holes, 6245 yards. S.S.S. 70. Practice area and putting green. *Green Fees:* weekdays £27.00 per round, £37.00 per day.; weekends and Bank Holidays £36.00 per round, £50.00 per day. *Eating facilities:* two bars, meals available, separate diningroom. *Visitors:* welcome weekdays, restriction on Tuesdays and Fridays. *Society Meetings:* societies and visiting parties catered for weekdays, some restrictions Tuesdays and Fridays. Professional: Graeme Bell (01642 790122). Secretary: M.R. Sample (01642 780238).

HARTLEPOOL. **Castle Eden Golf Club,** Castle Eden, Hartlepool TS27 4SS (01429 836220). *Location:* two miles south of Peterlee, use exits from A19. Picturesque parkland course. 18 holes, 6262 yards. S.S.S. 70. Practice ground. *Green Fees:* weekdays £25.00; weekends and Bank Holidays £35.00. *Eating facilities:* restaurant, lounge and bar and snooker room. *Visitors:* welcome weekdays 9.30am–11.30am, 1.45pm– 3.30pm. Tuesday Ladies' day. No visiting parties weekends or Bank Holidays. *Society Meetings:* weekdays only with reservation. Professional: Peter Jackson (01429 836689). Secretary: Derek Livingston (01429 836510).

HARTLEPOOL. **Hartlepool Golf Club Ltd,** Hart Warren, Hartlepool TS24 9QF (01429 274398; Fax: 01429 274129). *Location:* turn right off A1086 at Hart Station – north of town, signposted. Seaside links course. 18 holes, 6125 yards. S.S.S. 70. *Green Fees:* information not available. *Eating facilities:* full catering available except Mondays. *Visitors:* welcome (excluding Sunday) without reservation. Caddy carts. *Society Meetings:* catered for by prior arrangement. Professional: G. Laidlaw (01429 267473). Hon. Secretary: L.G. Gordon (01429 261723). website: www.hartlepoolgolfclub.co.uk

HARTLEPOOL. **High Throston Golf Club,** Hart Lane, Hartlepool TS26 0UG (01429 275325). *Location:* two miles from A19. Course designed by Jonathan Gaunt (USGA specification) with natural banks, rolling countryside with sea views - 7000 trees planted. 18 holes, 6247 yards, S.S.S. 71. Practice nets, putting green. *Green Fees:* information not available. *Eating facilities:* only light refreshments available at present. *Visitors:* welcome usually at all times. Secretary: Mrs J. Sturrock (01429 268071). *

HARTLEPOOL. **Seaton Carew Golf Club,** Tees Road, Seaton Carew, Hartlepool TS25 1DE (01429 266249). *Location:* two miles south of Hartlepool on A178. Championship seaside links. 22 holes. Old Course: 6658 yards. S.S.S. 72. Brabazon Course: 6900 yards. S.S.S. 73. Micklem Course: 6574 yards. S.S.S. 71. *Green Fees:* Iinformation not available. *Eating facilities:* bar snacks, full catering to order. *Visitors:* welcome midweek and some weekends. Advance booking recommended. Buggies for hire. *Society Meetings:* catered for by arrangement. Professional: Mark Rogers (01429 890660). Secretary: J. Hall (Tel & Fax: 01429 261040)

visit the FHG golf website on
www.uk-golfguide.com

MIDDLESBROUGH. **Middlesbrough Municipal Golf Centre**, Ladgate Lane, Middlesbrough TS5 7YZ (01642 315533; Fax: 01642 300726). *Location*: three miles south of Middlesbrough on A174. Parkland course with featured streams. 18 holes, 6333 yards. S.S.S. 71. Floodlit driving range, practice area and putting green. *Green Fees:* information not available. *Eating facilities:* lunches available seven days, snacks at all other times. *Visitors:* welcome anytime, but starting times must be booked in advance. *Society Meetings:* by prior arrangement, special golf packages available. Professional: Alan Hope (01642 300720). Manager: Mr M. Gormley (01642 315533). Secretary: J. C. Taylor (01642 590910).*

NEWTON AYCLIFFE. **Oak Leaf Golf Complex**, School Aycliffe Lane, Newton Aycliffe DL5 6QZ (01325 310820). Location: three miles from A1(M) and A68 on the outskirts of Newton Aycliffe. Rolling parkland. 18 holes, 5818 yards. S.S.S. 68. Driving range (floodlit), chipping and bunker practice. *Green Fees:* information not available. *Eating facilities:* bar and catering available at Oakleaf Golf Complex. Contact (01325 300600). *Visitors:* public course. Visiting parties by appointment. Showers/toilets/ changing facilities. Squash/Indoor Bowls at Oakleaf Golf Complex. *Society Meetings:* all welcome by prior arrangement. Professional: Ernie Wilson (01325 310820) Secretary: Mr R. Mitchie (Club) (01325 316040).

NEWTON AYCLIFFE. **Woodham Golf and Country Club**, Burnhill Way, Newton Aycliffe DL5 4PN (01325 320574; Fax: 01325 315254). *Location:* A167, one mile north of Newton Aycliffe on the Shildon road. Parkland, wooded with lakes. 18 holes, 6771 yards. S.S.S. 72. Practice grounds, putting green. *Green Fees:* information not available. *Eating facilities:* bar/restaurant. *Visitors:* welcome Monday Friday between 10.30am and 12 noon, and from 2pm to 3pm. Weekends 11.30am to 12.30pm & 2pm to 3pm. Buggies, trolleys available. *Society Meetings:* all welcome. Professional: Peter Kelly (01325 315257; Fax: 01325 315254). Secretary: John D. Jenkinson. Steward: (01325 301551).

SALTBURN BY THE SEA. **Saltburn by the Sea Golf Club Ltd,** Hob Hill, Saltburn by the Sea TS12 1NJ (01287 622812). *Location*: from Saltburn take Guisborough Road, one mile out of town on left. 18 holes, 5846 yards. S.S.S. 68. *Green Fees:* information not available. *Eating facilities:* available except Mondays. *Visitors:* welcome, limited Sundays and Thursdays and no visitors Saturdays. *Society Meetings:* catered for by arrangement. Professional: Mike Nutter (01287 624653). Secretary: Mike Murtha (01287 622812).

SEAHAM. **Seaham Golf Club,** Shrewsbury Street, Seaham SR7 7RD (0191-581 2354). *Location:* Dawdon, two miles north east of A19 leave for Seaham. Heathland. 18 holes, 6017 yards. S.S.S. 69. Practice area. *Green Fees:* weekdays £20.00 (£12.00 playing with a member); weekends and Bank Holidays £25.00 (£14.00 playing with a member). *Eating facilities:* snacks available, meals on request. *Visitors:* welcome, unrestricted weekdays, booking for weekends. *Society Meetings:* welcome on application. Professional: Glyn Jones (0191-513 0837). Secretary: V. Smith (0191-581 1268).

STANLEY. **South Moor Golf Club,** The Middles, Craghead, Stanley DH9 6AG (01207 232848; Fax: 01207 284616). *Location:* eight miles north-west of Durham, seven miles west of A1 (M) from Chester-le-Street. Parkland and moorland. 18 holes, 6307 yards. S.S.S. 70. *Green Fees:* weekdays £15.00 per round, £22.00 per day; with a member £10 per round, £15.00 per day; weekends and Bank Holidays £26.00 per day; with a member £12.00 per round, £18.00 per day. *Eating facilities:* available. *Visitors:* members only between 10am and 11.30am and 2pm to 3.30pm. No casual visitors weekends or Bank Holidays unless with member. *Society Meetings:* catered for except Sundays. Professional: Shaun Cowell (01207 283525). Secretary: B. Davison (01207 232848).

STOCKTON-ON-TEES. **Knotty Hill Golf Centre,** Sedgefield, Stockton-on-Tees TS21 2BB (01740 620320; Fax: 01740 622227). *Location:* A1 (M) Junction 60, one mile north of Sedgefield A177. Princes Course set in rolling parkland with many holes routed through shallow valleys. Bishops Course, a developing course with varied water features laid out within attractive rolling terrain. Princes Course – 18 holes, 6577 yards, 6323 metres, S.S.S. 71, par 72; Bishops Course – 18 holes, 5915 yards, 5406 metres, par 70. Indoor Golf Academy, video and tuition range, high quality floodlit driving range, open grass tee area, chipping and putting greens, practice bunker. *Green Fees:* 9 holes £8.00, 18 holes £13.00. *Eating facilities:* restaurant, coffee shop. *Visitors:* welcome at all times. Buggy and cart hire. *Society Meetings*: welcome, information on request. Secretary: Mrs J. Reynolds (01740 620320).

STOCKTON-ON-TEES. **Norton Golf Course,** Junction Road, Norton, Stockton-on-Tees TS20 2SU (01642 676385; Fax: 01642 608467). *Location:* turn into Junction Road to Norton from A177 at Horse and Jockey, two miles north of Stockton roundabout. Slightly hilly course with five lakes. 18 holes, 5393 yards. S.S.S. 70. *Green Fees:* weekdays £10.00 for 18 holes, weekends and Bank Holidays £12.00. Subject to review. E*ating facilities:* catering and bar available (Bar 01642 612452). *Visitors:* must have golf shoes and own clubs; no jeans. Parties welcome weekdays. *Society Meetings:* rates on application. Secretary: Mrs Dianne Harper (01642 674636).

STOCKTON-ON-TEES. **Teesside Golf Club**, Acklam Road, Thornaby, Stockton-on-Tees TS17 7JS (01642 676249; Fax: 01642 676252). *Location*: A19 - A1130 to Thornaby, 0.7 miles on right hand side. Flat parkland, partly tree-lined. 18 holes, 6535 yards. S.S.S. 71. Practice ground, putting green. *Green Fees:* weekdays £26.00, weekends £30.00. *Eating facilities:* catering except Mondays, bar 11am to 11pm. *Visitors:* welcome mid-week up to 4.30pm, weekends after 11am by arrangement. *Society Meetings:* catered for midweek only. Special rates and conditions for parties and guests. Professional: K.W. Hall (01642 673822). Secretary: M. Fleming (01642 616516).
e-mail: teessidegolfclub@btconnect.com
website: www.teessidegolfclub.com

184 Essex / ENGLAND

THE GOLF GUIDE 2004

Essex

BASILDON. **Basildon Golf Club,** Clay Hill Lane, Basildon SS16 5JP (01268 533297). *Location:* off A13 or A127 on A176 – Kingswood Roundabout. Undulating woodland. 18 holes, 6236 yards. S.S.S. 70. Practice area. *Green Fees:* £9.50 weekdays; £16.00 weekends; Senior Citizens weekdays £6.30. *Eating facilities:* snacks, full meals, bar. *Visitors:* welcome anytime, booking system at weekends and Bank Holidays. *Society Meetings:* welcome, booking through Professional. Professional: Mike Oliver (01268 533532). Secretary: A.M. Burch (Tel & Fax: 01268 533849).

BILLERICAY. **Stock Brook Golf & Country Club,** Queens Park Avenue, Stock, Near Billericay CM12 0SP (01277 653616; Fax: 01277 633063). *Location:* nearest main roads A12 and A127, Billericay. Parkland - gently undulating with featured lakes. 18 hole championship course, 6905 yards. S.S.S. 73. Manor - 9 holes, 2997 yards. Driving range, putting green and three par 3 practice holes. *Green Fees:* information not available. *Eating facilities:* bar meals available. *Visitors:* welcome. Handicap Certificate required. Extensive conference and banqueting facilities. Country club, swimming pool, tennis courts, gym. *Society Meetings:* welcome. Professional: Craig Laurence (01277 653616). Membership, Corporate and Society enquiries: Caron Morton.

BRAINTREE. **Braintree Golf Club,** Kings Lane, Stisted, Braintree CM77 8DD (01376 346079; Fax: 01376 348677). *Location:* A120 to Colchester, 300 yards east of Braintree by-pass, signposted Stisted and Golf Club. Parkland, with slopes down to the river, many specimen trees. 18 holes, 6228 yards, S.S.S. 70. Practice ground, pitching area. *Green Fees:* weekdays £32.00 per day, £25.00 per round; £42.00 Saturdays only. *Eating facilities:* available. *Visitors:* welcome Monday to Fridays (weekends must have Handicap Certificate). *Society Meetings:* catered for Mondays, Wednesdays and Thursdays. Professional: A.K. Parcell (01376 343465). Secretary: Mrs N. Wells (01376 346079; Fax: 01376 348677).

BRAINTREE. **Towerlands Golf Club,** Panfield Road, Braintree CM7 5BJ (01376 326802; Fax: 01376 552487). *Location:* off A120 into Braintree, then B1053. Undulating course. 9 holes, 2749 yards. S.S.S. 66. Practice area. *Green Fees:* information not available. *Eating facilities:* bars and restaurants. *Visitors:* welcome. We have equestrian facilities, squash courts, full sports hall and indoor bowls, no accommodation. *Society Meetings:* by arrangement. Secretary: Mr B. Clark (01376 326802; Fax: 01376 552487).

BRENTWOOD. **Bentley Golf Club,** Ongar Road, Brentwood CM15 9SS (01277 373179). *Location:* situated on A128 approximately five miles from Junction 28 of M25. Flat parkland course. 18 holes, 6709 yards, 6136 metres. S.S.S. 72. Practice field. *Green Fees:* information not available. *Eating facilities:* food and bar available all day. *Visitors:* welcome weekdays; Bank Holidays after 11am. *Society Meetings:* welcome by prior arrangement. Professional: Nick Garrett (01277 372933). Secretary: J.A. Vivers (01277 373179).

BRENTWOOD. **Hartswood Golf Club,** (Play on Brentwood Municipal), King George's Playing Fields, Ingrave Road, Brentwood CM15 8AY (01277 218850). *Location:* one mile south of Brentwood on A128. Parkland, 18 holes, 6238 yards. S.S.S. 70. *Green Fees:* information not available. *Eating facilities:* full catering available. *Visitors:* welcome without reservation. Tee Reservation – 01277 214830. *Society Meetings:* unlimited weekdays. Professional: Stephen Cole (01277 218714). Secretary: D. Mancey (01277 218850).*

BRENTWOOD. **South Essex Golf and Country Club,** Brentwood Road, Herongate, Brentwood CM13 3LW (01277 811006; Fax: 01277 811304). *Location:* Halfway House Exit from A127 (Junction 29 - M25). Gently rolling countryside incorporating established woodland. 27 holes, 10174 yards. S.S.S. 73. Covered 14 bay driving range. *Green Fees:* Monday to Thursday £18.00, Fridays £20.00; weekends £24.00. Twilight ticket available. *Eating facilities:* restaurant/bar. *Visitors:* welcome, no restrictions. Buggies, carts available. *Society Meetings:* welcome, including weekends. General Manager, Robert Brewer (01277 811289; Fax: 01277 811304).

BRENTWOOD. **Thorndon Park Golf Club Ltd,** Thorndon Park, Ingrave, Brentwood CM13 3RH (01277 811666). *Location:* three miles south of Brentwood on A128. 18 holes, 6492 yards. S.S.S. 71. *Green Fees:* £60.00 per day, £45.00 per round weekdays, £50.00 per round after 1pm Sundays. Saturday and Sunday morning with members only. Subject to review. *Eating facilities:* lunches served at club. *Visitors:* welcome with reservation, weekdays subject to prior permission. *Society Meetings:* catered for. Professional: Brian White (01277 810736). Secretary: Lt Col R.M. Estcourt (01277 810345). website: www.thorndonparkgolfclub.com

BRENTWOOD. **The Warley Park Golf Club,** Magpie Lane, Little Warley, Brentwood CM13 3DX (01277 224891). *Location:* leave M25 at Intersection 29. A127 towards Southend. Turn left three-quarters-of-a-mile Little Warley, Hall Lane. Turn left into Magpie Lane. Parkland, 3 Courses, (27 holes). S.S.S. 70-70-69. Large practice area, putting greens. *Green Fees:* weekdays £30.00 per round, £40.00 per day. *Eating facilities:* lounge bar and restaurant/spike bar. *Visitors:* welcome Monday to Friday, must produce club Handicap Certificate. *Society Meetings:* catered for. Professional: K. Smith (01277 200441). Secretary: K. Regan (01277 224891).

BRENTWOOD. **Weald Park Golf Club,** Coxtie Green Road, South Weald, Brentwood CM14 5RJ (01277 375101). *Location:* M25 and A12 junction (map available). Parkland course surrounded by countryside. 18 holes, 6612 yards. S.S.S. 72/70. *Green Fees:* information not available. *Eating facilities:* bar and restaurant. *Visitors:* welcome. *Society Meetings:* welcome Monday to Friday. Professional: Dean Vickerman (01277 375101; Fax: 01277 374888). General Manager: Darcy Tallon (01277 375101; Fax: 01277 374888).*

BULPHAN. **The Langdon Hills Golf & Country Club,** Lower Dunton Road, Bulphan RM14 3TY (01268 548444; Fax: 01268 490084). *Location:* eight miles from M25, Dartford River crossing, Basildon three miles between A127 and A13. Gently undulating parkland. Three loops of 9 holes – 27 holes, 6504, 6426, 6186 yards, S.S.S. 71, 71, 70. 22 bay floodlit driving range, 3 hole academy course, practice area and two putting greens. *Green Fees:* information not available. *Eating facilities:* brasserie restaurant, spike bar, Function Suite available. *Visitors:* welcome at all times subject to availablity. Hotel accommodaton and function suite available. *Society Meetings:* welcome. Professional: Terry Moncur (01268 544300; Fax: 01268 490084). Secretary: Brian Hardie (01268 548444; Fax: 01268 490084). Manager: Colin Phillips.

BURNHAM-ON-CROUCH. **Burnham-on-Crouch Golf Club Ltd,** Ferry Road, Creaksea CM0 8PQ (01621 785508). *Location:* Burnham-on-Crouch, one and a half miles before Burnham town. Undulating meadowland rolling alongside River Crouch. 18 holes, 6056 yards. S.S.S. 69. Par 70. Practice ground. *Green Fees:* weekdays £26.00, £14.00 with a member. *Eating facilities:* bar, full catering. *Visitors:* welcome weekdays with Handicap Certificate. *Society Meetings:* welcome Mondays, Tuesdays, Wednesdays and Fridays only. Secretary: (01621 782282). Private members club.

CANVEY ISLAND. **Castle Point Golf Club,** Somnes Avenue, Canvey Island SS8 9FG (01268 696298). *Location:* A13 towards Southend, A130 to Canvey Island, opposite sports centre. Links course, with views of Hadleigh Downs and Castle. 18 holes, 6176 yards. S.S.S. 69. Floodlit driving range. *Green Fees:* information not available. *Eating facilities:* clubhouse open to public – full catering. *Visitors:* welcome anytime, booking required at weekends. Changing room and showers; buggies available. Pro Shop (01268 510830). *Society Meetings:* welcome. Professional: Michael Utteridge (01268 510830). Secretary: David Thomas (01268 692899).*

CHELMSFORD. **Channels Golf Club,** Belsteads Farm Lane, Little Waltham, Chelmsford CM3 3PT (01245 440005). *Location:* three miles north east of Chelmsford on A130. Reclaimed gravel workings, many lakes, hazards and an abundance of wild life. Two courses – Channels 6402 yards, S.S.S. 71; Belsteads 4779 yards, S.S.S. 63. *Green Fees:* Channels Course (weekdays only) £32.00 per round, £45.00 per day; Belsteads Course £14.00 9 holes, £20.00 18 holes, unrestricted play weekends. *Eating facilities:* excellent restaurant in 13th century clubhouse. *Visitors:* welcome. *Society Meetings:* catered for weekdays. Professional: I.B. Sinclair (01245 441056). Secretary: Mr A.M. Squire (01245 440005; Fax: 01245 442032). e-mail: info@channelsgolf.co.uk website: www.channelsgolf.co.uk

CHELMSFORD. **Chelmsford Golf Club,** Widford Road, Chelmsford CM2 9AP (Tel & Fax: 01245 256483). *Location:* A12–A414 to Chelmsford, first roundabout turn right. Parkland course. 18 holes, 5981 yards. S.S.S. 69. *Green Fees:* weekdays £37.00. *Eating facilities:* dining room and bar. *Visitors:* welcome Monday to Friday with reservation. *Society Meetings:* welcome, discounts available. Professional: Mark Welch (01245 257079). Secretary: G. Winckless. e-mail: office@chelmsfordgc.co.uk website: www.chelmsfordgc.co.uk

CHELMSFORD. **The Regiment Way Golf Centre,** Pratts Farm Lane, Little Waltham, Chelmsford CM3 3PR (01245 361100). *Location:* three miles north east of Chelmsford off A130. Flat parkland, ideal novice course. 9 holes, 2500 yards. S.S.S. 64. 22 bay floodlit driving range. *Green Fees:* weekdays £10.00 9 holes, £14.00 18 holes; weekends £11.00 9 holes, £16.00 18 holes. Student and Senior discount £2.00 9 holes, £3.00 18 holes. *Visitors:* pay as you play. *Society Meetings:* welcome. Professionals: David March and Wendy Dicks. Secretary: Roger Pamphilon.

CHELMSFORD. **Three Rivers Golf and Country Club,** Stow Road, Cold Norton, Purleigh, Near Chelmsford CM3 6RR (01621 828631; Fax: 01621 828060). *Location:* four miles from South Woodham Ferrers, six miles from Maldon. Parkland with lakes and wooded copses; spectacular views. Two courses: 36 holes, 6296 yards Kings Course, 4600 Jubilee Course. S.S.S. Kings 70/Jubilee 64. *Green Fees:* information not available. *Eating facilities:* all day menu and à la carte menu always available, carvery available Saturday night and Sunday lunchtime, bar meals all day. *Visitors:* welcome. Computer club fitting service and swing analysis centre; six en suite bedroomed hotel Other function suites available. Buggies available. *Society Meetings:* very welcome. Specialists in looking after companies and groups. Own suites available weekdays. Professionals: Pat O'Connor/Scott Clark (01621 828631).*

CHIGWELL. **Chigwell Golf Club,** The Clubhouse, High Road, Chigwell IG7 5BH (020 8500 2059; Fax: 020 8501 3410). *Location:* on A113, 14 miles from London, seven miles from Exit 26 on the M25. Testing undulating parkland course. 18 holes, 6279 yards. S.S.S. 70. Practice bays and ground. *Green Fees:* weekdays £35.00 per round (£25.00 after 2.30pm), £45.00 per day; weekends with introduction by member only. *Eating facilities:* restaurant and bars available. *Visitors:* weekdays by prior arrangement, Handicap Certificate required and membership of authorised Golf Club. *Society Meetings:* weekdays by arrangement. Professional: R. Beard (020 8500 2384). Secretary: Richard Danzey (020 8500 2059; Fax: 020 8501 3410). e-mail: info@chigwellgolfclub.co.uk website: www.chigwellgolfclub.co.uk

CHIGWELL. **Hainault Forest Golf Club,** Romford Road, Chigwell IG7 4QW (020 8500 2097). *Location:* off A12 towards Chigwell-Hainault. Undulating wooded course with several lakes. 18 holes, 6600 yards. S.S.S. 71. 18 holes, 5754 yards. S.S.S. 67. Practice field and putting green. *Green Fees:* information not available. *Eating facilities:* course restaurant; bars in private club. *Visitors:* public course. *Society Meetings:* weekdays by arrangement with Secretary. Professional: S. Cranfield (020 8500 2131).*

CHIGWELL. **Woolston Manor Golf Club,** Woolston Manor, Abridge Road, Chigwell IG7 6BX (020 8500 2549; Fax: 020 8501 5452). Private exclusive members' club - for membership enquiries call membership secretary on 020 8500 2549. *Location:* Junction 5, M11 one mile. Parkland, Neil Coles Championship design, 18 holes, 6435 yards. S.S.S. 71. Top golf driving range. *Green Fees:* weekdays £25.00; weekends £35.00. *Eating facilities:* full catering available. *Visitors:* welcome weekdays after 10.30am and after 11.30am weekends. Handicap Certificate required. *Society Meetings:* welcome weekdays only. Professional: Paul Eady (020 8559 8272; Fax: 020 8501 5452). Secretary: Peter Spargo.

CLACTON-ON-SEA. **Clacton-on-Sea Golf Club,** West Road, Clacton-on-Sea CO15 1AJ (01255 421919). *Location:* A12 then A120 to Clacton-on-Sea, follow signs for promenade/pier then turn right along promenade to sharp right hand bend. 250 metres on left. Seaside course. 18 holes, 6532 yards. S.S.S. 71. *Green Fees:* weekdays £20.00 per round, £30.00 per day; weekends £25.00 per round, £40.00 per day. *Eating facilities:* full bar and catering facilities available. *Visitors:* welcome with reservation and current Handicap Certificate. Weekends and Bank Holidays not before 11am. *Society Meetings:* Monday to Friday catered for by arrangement. Professional: S.J. Levermore. Secretary: J.H. Wiggam.

COLCHESTER. **Birch Grove Golf Club,** Layer Road, Colchester CO2 0HS (01206 734276). *Location:* on B1026, two miles south of town. Parkland - small but challenging. 9 holes, 4500 yards. Par 66. *Green Fees:* £10.00 per 9 holes, £13.00 per 18 holes. *Eating facilities:* hot meals and snacks are available during opening hours. *Visitors:* welcome without reservation Monday to Saturday and after 1pm Sundays. *Society Meetings:* catered for weekdays. Secretary: Mrs M. Marston.

COLCHESTER. **Colchester Golf Club,** Braiswick, Colchester CO4 5AU (01206 853396). *Location:* one mile north-west of Colchester North Station, on B1508. Parkland course with wooded areas. 18 holes, 6301 yards. S.S.S. 70. *Green Fees:* information not available. *Eating facilities:* catering available all day. *Visitors:* welcome except Saturday and Sunday mornings, must have Handicap Certificates. *Society Meetings:* catered for by prior arrangement. Professional: Mark Angel (01206 853920). Secretary: Mr W. Beckett (01206 853396; Fax: 01206 852698). e-mail: colchester.golf@btinternet.com

COLCHESTER. **Colne Valley Golf Club,** Station Road, Earls Colne, Colchester CO6 2LT (01787 224343; Fax: 01787 224126). *Location:* off the A1124, 10 miles from Colchester. Parkland course in the Valley of the River Colne. 18 holes, 6286 yards. S.S.S. 70. Practice ground. *Green Fees:* weekdays £25.00 per round; weekends £30.00 per round. *Eating facilities:* two bars and restaurant facilities open all day. *Visitors:* welcome anytime but weekends only after 11am and please phone in advance to confirm. Carts for rental. *Society Meetings:* midweek anytime, weekends after 11am, packages available. Head Professional: Peter Garlick.

COLCHESTER. **Lexden Wood Golf Club,** Colchester and Lexden Golf Centre, Bakers Lane, Colchester CO3 4AU (01206 843333; Fax: 01206 854775). *Location:* one mile north west of Colchester, two minutes on the A12 northbound on A133. Undulating parkland with many water features. 27 holes –18 hole and 9 hole short course. 5300 yards. S.S.S. 67. *Green Fees:* information not available. *Eating facilities:* home cooked food always available during opening hours. *Visitors:* always welcome, please phone to book tee time. Floodlit covered driving range/putting green. *Society Meetings:* always welcome by prior arrangement. Professional: Phil Grice (01206 843333; Fax: 01206 854775). *

COLCHESTER. **The Essex Golf and Country Club,** Earls Colne, Colchester CO6 2NS (01787 224466; Fax: 01787 224410). *Location:* B1024 off the A120 opposite Coggeshall. Flat parkland 18 hole/9 hole courses. 18 holes, 6900 yards. S.S.S. 73. Floodlit driving range. *Green Fees:* information not available. *Eating facilities:* Poolside Grill, sports brasserie, restaurant. *Visitors:* all welcome, no restrictions. Buggies and trolleys available. Full leisure facilities, indoor pool, sauna, steam room, gym, tennis courts. Full day nursery facilities available, conference and entertainment facilities. On site 42 bedroom hotel including two suites. *Society Meetings:* welcome. Professional: Lee Cocker. Secretary: David Clark.* website: www.clubhaus.com

ELSENHAM. **Elsenham Golf Centre,** Hall Road, Elsenham CM22 6DH (01279 812865; Fax: 01279 816970). *Location:* A120 Takley, turn towards Elsenham. Just past the "Jam Factory". Parkland, part wooded course. 9 holes, 3000 yards. S.S.S. 68. 18 bay driving range, 3 hole Academy Course. *Green Fees:* information not available. *Eating facilities:* bar, food. Open to non members, children welcome. *Visitors:* always welcome. Changing facilities. Pro Shop. Teaching facility. *Society Meetings:* all welcome. Professional: Owen McKenna (01279 812865; Fax: 01279 816970). *

EPPING. **North Weald Golf Club,** Rayley Lane, North Weald, Epping CM16 6AR (01992 522118; Fax: 01992 522881). *Location:* from M11 Junction 7 take A414 to Chelmsford, two miles to first roundabout, turn right. Club is 200 yards on left. Parkland and lakes. 18 holes, 6377 yards. S.S.S. 70. Driving range, putting green, chipping green and practice bunker. *Green Fees:* weekdays £17.50;

weekends £25.00. *Eating facilities:* available. *Visitors:* welcome most days by arrangement. *Society Meetings:* welcome by arrangement. Professional: David Rawlings (01992 524725). Secretary: P. H. Newson (01992 522118; Fax: 01992 522881).

EPPING. **Theydon Bois Golf Club**, Theydon Road, Epping CM16 4EH. *Location:* M25 Waltham Abbey/Epping A121 London to Cambridge, turn right at Bell Motel. Wooded course. 18 holes, 5480 yards. S.S.S. 68. Practice area. *Green Fees:* £26.00 per round, £18.00 after 5pm weekdays. *Eating facilities:* restaurant and bar. *Visitors:* welcome except Wednesday and Thursday morning. *Society Meetings:* Monday, Tuesday and Friday. Professional: R. Hall (01992 812460). Manager: M.C. Slatter (01992 813054).

FRINTON-ON-SEA. **Frinton Golf Club**, 1 The Esplanade, Frinton-on-Sea CO13 9EP. *Location*: 17 miles east of Colchester, A12 - A133, B1033. Flat seaside links course, strength of wind always a feature. 18 holes, 6265 yards. S.S.S. 70. Short Course 2508 yards, no Handicap Certificate required. Practice facilities. *Green Fees:* weekdays £32.00 per round. Short course, 18, 27 or 36 holes £10.00. Weekends £35.00 per round. Cheaper green fees during winter period. *Eating facilities:* snack and restaurant facilities. *Visitors:* welcome, check with Secretary. Handicap Certificate required. *Society Meetings:* catered for by arrangement. Professional: Peter Taggart (Tel & Fax: 01255 671618). Secretary: Lt Col R.W. Attrill (01255 674618).
e-mail: frintongolf@lineone.net
website: www.frintongolfclub.com

HALSTEAD. **Gosfield Lake Golf Club,**The Manor House, Gosfield, Halstead CO9 1SE. *Location:* off the A1017 four miles north of Braintree. Gently undulating parkland course with lakes and woods; designed by Sir Henry Cotton. Two courses: Lakes Course 18 holes, 6615 yards. S.S.S. 72; Meadows Course 9 holes (doubled teed to 18), 4180 yards S.S.S. 61. Practice facilities including putting, chipping, bunkers. *Green Fees:* information not available. *Eating facilities:* bar and catering facilities from 12 noon; bar menu. *Visitors:* welcome. Weekdays booking advisable,weekends from 12 noon (booking necessary). Handicap Certificate required for Lakes Course, Meadows Course ideal for beginners/ improvers.Trolley hire. Buggy hire (summer only). *Society Meetings:* welcome by prior arrangement. Professional: Richard Wheeler (01787 474488) Secretary: J.A. O'Shea (01787 474747; Fax: 01787 476044).*
e-mail: gosfieldlakegc@btconnect.com.
website: www.gosfield-lake-golf-club.co.uk

HARLOW. **Canons Brook Golf Club**, Elizabeth Way, Harlow CM19 5BE (01279 425142). *Location*: Turn onto Elizabeth Way at Harlow Town Station on A414 from M11. Parkland course. 18 holes, 6745 yards. S.S.S. 73. *Green Fees*: information not available. *Eating facilities*: available, open all day. *Visitors*: welcome weekdays, weekends with a member. *Society Meetings*: catered for Mondays, Wednesdays and Fridays. Professional: Alan McGinn (01279 418357). Secretary: Mrs S. Langton (01279 421482; Fax: 01279 626393).

HARWICH. **Harwich and Dovercourt Golf Club,** Station Road, Parkeston, Harwich CO12 4NZ (01255 503616; Fax: 01255 503323). *Location*: A120 then to Parkeston Quay, course marked on left hand side of Station Road. Flat course. 9 holes, 5742 yards. S.S.S. 68. *Green Fees*: weekdays £20.00. *Eating facilities*: licensed clubhouse, catering available to order (not Thursdays). *Visitors*: welcome with Handicap Certificates. No visitors Saturdays, Sundays and Bank Holidays unless with a member. *Society Meetings*: small groups welcome by arrangement. Hon. Secretary: Mr A. Boddy (01255 503616).

ILFORD. **Fairlop Waters,** Forest Road, Barkingside, Ilford IG6 3JA (020 8500 9911). *Location:* two miles north of Ilford, half a mile from A12, one and a half miles from southern end of M11. Covered, floodlit range, 36 bays. 18 hole golf course, 9 hole Par 3 course. Individual or group tuition available. *Green Fees:* information not available. Opening hours: 9am to 10pm. *Eating facilities:* bars and diner. Banqueting facilities and conferences. 38 acre sailing lake, 25 acre country park, children's play area. Professional: Paul Davies (020 8501 1881). General Manager: Mr F. Taylor.

ILFORD. **Ilford Golf Club,** 291 Wanstead Park Road, Ilford IG1 3TR (020 8554 2930). *Location:* at end of M11, off A406. Parkland with winding river. 18 holes, 5299 yards. S.S.S. 66. *Green Fees:* weekdays £15.00 plus special offers, weekends £20.00. *Eating facilities:* restaurant and bar. *Visitors:* welcome weekdays, restricted times at weekends. *Society Meetings:* welcome. Professional: S. Dowsett (020 8554 0094). Secretary: G.H. Smith (020 8554 2930; Fax: 020 8554 0822).

INGATESTONE. **Hylands Golf Complex**, Main Road, Margaretting, Ingatestone CM4 0ET (01277 356016; Fax: 01277 356056). *Location*: off A12. Parkland course. 9 holes 2445 yards, 18 holes 6604 yards. Driving range, practice bunker. *Green Fees:* information not available. *Eating facilities:* coffee and soft drinks available. *Visitors:* all welcome. New complex, pay and play only; no membership. Accommodation at Ivy Hill Hotel, Margaretting. Professional: Lee Porter (01277 356016; Fax: 01277 356056).*

Please mention 'The Golf Guide' when enquiring about clubs or accommodation.

LEIGH-ON-SEA. **Belfairs Golf Club,** Eastwood Road North, Leigh-on-Sea SS9 4LR (01702 526911). Park front 9, heavy woodland back 9; easy walking but challenging golf. Play over Belfairs Municipal course, 18 holes, 5857 yards. S.S.S. 68. *Green Fees:* information not available. *Visitors:* unrestricted on the course but no clubhouse facilities available. Bookings required. Professional: Martin Foreman (01702 520202). Secretary: R.N. Mace (01702 520322). *

LITTLE BURSTEAD. **The Burstead Golf Club,** Tye Common Road, Little Burstead CM12 9ST (01277 631171; Fax: 01277 632766). Parkland course. 18 holes, 6275 yards, S.S.S. 70. Practice field, chipping area, putting green. *Green Fees:* information not available. *Eating facilities:* restaurant, bar and spike bar. *Visitors:* welcome Monday to Friday except Bank Holidays, weekends after 1pm. Tuition available. *Society Meetings:* welcome Monday to Friday, except Bank Holidays. Professional: Keith Bridges. Secretary: Lee Mence. *

LOUGHTON. **Loughton Golf Club**, Clay's Lane, Debden Green, Loughton IG10 2RZ (020 8502 2923). *Location:* just north of Loughton, on edge of Epping Forest. Parkland, wooded. 9 holes, 4700 yards. S.S.S. 63. Practice range. *Green Fees:* weekdays £7.50 9 holes, £12.00 18 holes; weekends £8.50 for 9 holes, £14.00 for 18 holes. *Eating facilities:* bar, snacks available. *Visitors:* welcome, telephone to book. *Society Meetings:* welcome. Manager: Alan Day.

MALDON. **Bunsay Downs Golf Club,** Little Baddow Road, Woodham Walter, Maldon CM9 6RW (01245 222648; Fax: 01245 223989). *Location:* 7 miles east of Chelmsford off A414 at Woodham Walter, left onto Little Baddow Road. Undulating landscaped partly wooded course. 9 holes, 2932 yards. S.S.S. 68. Par 3 course. *Green Fees:* information not available. *Eating facilities:* bar/grill restaurant. *Visitors:* welcome at all times. Gift shop. *Society Meetings:* small societies welcome. Professional: Mickey Walker. Secretary: Mr M. Durham (01245 223258).*

MALDON. **Five Lakes Resort**, Colchester Road, Tolleshunt Knights, Maldon CM9 8HX (01621 868888; Fax: 01621 869696). *Location*: seven miles from A12 on B1026 north of Maldon and south of Colchester. Parkland. Two courses: Links Course - 18 holes, 6181 yards, S.S.S. 70; Lakes Course - 18 holes, 6751 yards, S.S.S. 72. Driving range, three putting greens. *Green Fees:* Links - weekdays £22.00, weekends £29.00; Lakes - weekdays £29.00, weekends £38.00. *Eating facilities:* three restaurants and two bars. *Visitors:* welcome at most times except before 10am weekend mornings. 194 en suite bedrooms, conference and banqueting facilities, indoor pool, air conditioned gym, health club, sauna, steam room and spa bath, tennis, squash and badminton. *Society Meetings:* catered for by appointment. Professional: Gary Carter (01621 862326; Fax: 01621 862320). Golf Consultant: James Taylor (01621 862307; Fax: 01621 862320).

MALDON. **Forrester Park Golf and Tennis Club,** Beckingham Road, Great Totham, Near Maldon CM9 8EA (Tel & Fax: 01621 891406). *Location:* three miles off A12 Rivenhall turn-off, on B1022 in Great Totham, near Maldon between Compasses and Bull. Parkland course. 18 holes, 6073 yards. S.S.S. 69. Practice ground. *Green Fees:* weekdays £19.00 per round, £25.00 per day; weekends £21.00 after 12 noon only. *Eating facilities:* full catering and bar facilities. *Visitors:* welcome subject to prior booking, but not before 12 noon Tuesdays, Wednesdays and weekends. Trolley hire. Buggy hire (summer only). *Society Meetings:* welcome subject to prior booking. Professional: Gary Pike (01621 893456). Manager: Tim Forrester-Muir (Tel & Fax: 01621 891406).

MALDON. **Maldon Golf Club,** Beeleigh, Langford, Maldon CM9 6LL (01621 853212). *Location:* B1019 two miles northwest of Maldon, turn off by the Museum of Power. Flat parkland. 9 holes, 6253 yards, 5718 metres. S.S.S. 70. *Green Fees:* 18 holes £15.00, all day £20.00 weekdays; weekends 18 holes £12.00, all day £17.00 with a member only. *Eating facilities:* full catering service, bar. *Visitors:* welcome weekdays, club or society Handicap Certificates required. *Society Meetings:* catered for by arrangement. Secretary: G.R. Bezant.

MALDON. **Warren Golf Club,** Woodham Walter, Maldon CM9 6RW (01245 223198/223258; Fax: 01245 223989). *Location:* close to Chelmsford. A414 turn off to Maldon. Undulating wooded course. 18 holes, 6211 yards. S.S.S. 70. Large practice area. *Green Fees:* information not available. *Eating facilities:* restaurant, bar, bar snack menu. *Visitors:* welcome with reservation weekdays except Wednesday mornings. Handicap Certificate required. Golf Academy. *Society Meetings:* catered for weekdays - up to 40 players. Professional: Mickey Walker (01245 224662). Managing Director: M.F.L. Durham.*

NAZEING. **Nazeing Golf Club,** Middle Street, Nazeing EN9 2LW (01992 893915; Fax: 01992 893882). *Location:* from Waltham Abbey Town Centre - signposted. Parkland course, American design (sand boxed greens and tees). 18 holes, 6617 yards. S.S.S. 72. Continental style driving range. *Green Fees:* information not available. *Eating facilities:* available. *Visitors:* welcome anytime except weekend mornings, must ring and book through Pro shop. Buggies, trolleys available. *Society Meetings:* welcome. Professional: Robert Green (01992 893798; Fax: 01992 893882).*

OCKENDON. **Belhus Park Golf Club,** Belhus Park, Aveley By-Pass, South Ockendon RM15 4QR (01708 852248 complex, 01708 854748 office). *Location:* on A13 London - Southend Road, approximately one mile from Dartford Tunnel. Parkland. 18 holes, 5350 yards. S.S.S. 69. Driving range. *Green Fees:* information not available. *Eating facilities:* cafe and bar. *Visitors:* welcome anytime (municipal course), but booking essential weekends and Bank Holidays. Swimming pool. *Society Meetings:* by arrangement, telephone complex. Professional: Gary Lunn (01708 854260). Secretary: J. Cleary (01708 865645). *

ONGAR. **Toot Hill Golf Club,** School Road, Toot Hill, Near Ongar CM5 9PU (01277 365523; Fax: 01277 364509). *Location:* A128 to Ongar, A414 to Harlow, two miles left at Blakeshall Road. Parkland course, lakes and brook. 18 holes, 6053 yards, 5535 metres. S.S.S. 69. Practice range, putting and chipping green. *Green Fees:* information not available. *Eating facilities:* available, clubhouse and spike bar. *Visitors:* welcome. *Society Meetings:* welcome Tuesdays and Thursdays, various packages. Professional: Mark Bishop (01277 365747). Secretary: Mrs C. Cameron.

ORSETT. **Orsett Golf Club,** Brentwood Road, Orsett RM16 3DS (01375 891352). *Location:* A13 Junction roundabout with A128. South towards Chadwell St Mary on A128. Heathland course. 18 holes, 6693 yards. S.S.S. 72. *Green Fees:* weekdays £30.00 per round, £40.00 per day. *Eating facilities:* full catering available. *Visitors:* welcome on weekdays only by arrangement. Must be members of a club and have Handicap. Proof must be produced. *Society Meetings:* welcome on Mondays, Tuesdays and Wednesday afternoons. Professional: P.L. Joiner (01375 891797). Secretary: Office (01375 891352; Fax: 01375 892471).

RAYLEIGH. **Hanover Golf and Country Club,** Hullbridge Road, Rayleigh SS6 9QS (01702 232377; Fax: 01702 231811). *Location:* A130, A127 Rayleigh. Parkland course, seven lakes. 18 holes, 6669 yards. S.S.S. 72. Par 73. Putting green. *Green Fees:* information not available. *Eating facilities:* two bars, restaurant, bar meals, function rooms. *Visitors:* welcome weekdays, Club Handicap required. *Society Meetings:* welcome weekdays. Professional: A. Blackburn (01702 230033). Secretary: T. Harrold.

ROCHFORD. **Rochford Hundred Golf Club,** Hall Road, Rochford SS4 1NW (01702 544302; Fax: 01702 541343). *Location:* A127 towards Southend on Sea, turning for Rochford. Flat parkland course, ancient clubhouse, course surrounds church. 18 holes, 6176 yards (white boxes). S.S.S. 71. *Green Fees:* information not provided. *Eating facilities:* full restaurant and snack facilities and bars. *Visitors:* welcome, Tuesday mornings ladies only. Handicap Certificate necessary. *Society Meetings:* catered for except Tuesday mornings, Fridays and weekends. Professional: G. Hill (01702 548968). Secretary: A.H. Bondfield.

ROCHFORD near. **Ballards Gore Golf and Country Club,** Gore Road, Canewdon, Near Rochford SS4 2DA (01702 258917). *Location:* Southend Airport three miles, London via A127, club two miles from Rochford. Parkland with lakes. 18 holes, 6845 yards. S.S.S. 73. Practice area. *Green Fees:* information not available. *Eating facilities:* diningroom (100 covers). *Visitors:* welcome weekdays, except Tuesday mornings. *Society Meetings:* catered for by arrangement. Professional: Richard Emery (01702 258924; Fax: 01702 258924 Secretary:Mr A. S. Hall (01702 258917; Fax: 01702 258571).

ROMFORD. **Maylands Golf and Country Club,** Harold Park, Romford RM3 0AZ (01708 342055). *Location:* turn off Junction 28 M25, directly on A12 between Romford and Brentwood. 18 holes, 6182 yards. S.S.S. 70. Practice field and putting green. *Green Fees:* information not available. *Eating facilities:* bar, spike bar, restaurant and bar snacks. *Visitors:* welcome midweek if members of recognised clubs with Handicap Certificates. *Society Meetings:* catered for Mondays, Wednesdays and Fridays. Professional: John Hopkin (01708 346466). Secretary/Proprietor: P. S. Taylor (Tel & Fax: 01708 373080).*

ROMFORD. **Risebridge Golf Centre,** Risebridge Chase, Romford RM1 4DG (01708 741429). Location: off Lower Bedfords Road, between Collier Row and Harold Hill, signposted from Gallows Corner (A12). Mature parkland course with some long tough holes. 18 holes, 6342 yards. S.S.S. 70. 9 hole Par 3 course, driving range, practice green. *Green Fees:* information not available. *Eating facilities:* cafe and spike bar. *Visitors:* welcome at all times except weekend mornings 8am to 10am. *Society Meetings:* all welcome, for details contact the Professional. Professional/Secretary: Mr P. Jennings (Tel & Fax: 01708 741429). *

SAFFRON WALDEN. **Saffron Walden Golf Club,** Windmill Hill, Saffron Walden CB10 1BX (01799 522786). *Location:* end of town on A130 to Cambridge. 18 holes, 6606 yards. S.S.S. 72. *Green Fees:* £35.00 per day or round (weekdays only). *Eating facilities:* snacks, lunches and evening meals (by prior arrangement). *Visitors:* welcome with current Handicap Certificate Monday to Friday. *Society Meetings:* catered for Mondays, Wednesdays and Thursdays. Professional: Philip Davis. General Manager: Chris Charlton.

SOUTH BENFLEET. **Boyce Hill Golf Club Ltd,** **Vicarage Hill, South Benfleet SS7 1PD (01268** **793625).** *Location*: one-and-a-half-miles south of A13/A127. Hilly course, 18 holes, 6003 yards, 5489 metres. S.S.S. 69. *Green Fees:* £30.00 18 holes, £40.00 36 holes. *Eating facilities*: full bar and dining facilities daily. *Visitors*: welcome, except Tuesday mornings and weekends. 24 hours notice of booking and Handicap Certificate required. *Society Meetings*: catered for Thursdays only. Professional: G. Burroughs (01268 752565). Secretary: P.D. Keeble (01268 793625; Fax: 01268 750497).

SOUTHEND-ON-SEA. **Southend-on-Sea Golf Club**, Belfairs Lodge, Belfairs Park, Leigh-on-Sea SS9 4LR (01702 524836). *Location*: A127 London to Southend Road. Parkland/wooded course (Belfairs Municipal course). 18 holes, 5877 yards. S.S.S. 68. *Green Fees:* information not available. *Eating facilities:* restaurant in the park near Starter's Hut. *Visitors:* welcome, unrestricted, but bookings required by phone to Starter's Hut (01702 525345). Professional: Martin Foreman (01702 520202). Secretary: Alan Wood (01702 474737). *

SOUTHEND-ON-SEA. **Thorpe Hall Golf Club,** Thorpe Hall Avenue, Thorpe Bay, Southend-on-Sea SS1 3AT (Tel & Fax: 01702 582205). *Location:* one mile east of Southend-on-Sea. Parkland. 18 holes, 6421 yards. S.S.S. 71. *Green Fees:* £40.00 per round or day. *Eating facilities:* Two restaurants and bars. *Visitors:* welcome weekdays with Handicap Certificate, weekends with members only. Squash, snooker and sauna available. *Society Meetings:* welcome Fridays only. Professional: Bill McColl (01702 588195). Secretary: G.H. Smith (01702 582205; Fax: 01702 584498).

STANFORD LE HOPE. **St. Cleres Hall Golf Club,** St. Cleres Hall, London Road, Stanford le Hope SS17 0LX (Tel & Fax: 01375 361565). *Location:* from M25, A13 Stanford turnoff, Linford exit on roundabout, course half mile on left hand side. Parkland course with Thames Estuary views, sand based, year round play. 18 holes, 6474 yards. S.S.S. 71. 15 bay floodlit driving range, chipping and putting greens. *Green Fees:* information not provided. *Eating facilities:* bar; restaurant. *Visitors:* welcome, enquire about tee closures. *Society Meetings:* welcome anytime weekdays; weekends afternoons only. Please telephone for details. Professional/Secretary: David Wood.*

STAPLEFORD ABBOTTS. **Stapleford Abbotts Golf Club,** Horseman's Side, Tysea Hill, Stapleford Abbotts, Romford RM4 1JU (01708 381108; Fax: 01708 386345). *Location:* three miles from Junctions 28 and 29 of the M25, off main Ongar Road B175 at Stapleford Abbotts. Parkland course with many mature trees, large bunkers and water hazards. 18 holes, 6501 yards, S.S.S. 72. Par 3 9-hole course. Two practice grounds and practice nets. *Green Fees:* information not available. *Eating facilities:* fully licensed bar, extensive menu. *Visitors:* welcome weekdays, weekends after 12 noon; welcome all week on 9-hole course. Correct golfing attire must be worn. *Society Meetings:* welcome, call 01708 381108 for more information. Pro Shop: 01708 381278 .*

STAPLEFORD TAWNEY. **Abridge Golf and Country Club,** Epping Lane, Stapleford Tawney RM4 1ST (01708 688396). *Location:* A113 from London through Chigwell to Abridge, left at The Rodings, right after 300 yards. Two miles on. Parkland. 18 holes, 6690 yards. S.S.S. 72. *Green Fees:* on application. *Eating facilities:* bar lunches, drinks, snacks available all week. *Visitors:* welcome but must be a member of a recognised golf club and produce evidence of current Handicap, weekdays only. Heated swimming pool. *Society Meetings:* catered for on Mondays, Wednesdays and Fridays only by arrangement. Professional: Stuart Layton (01708 688333). Secretary: Mr M Gottlieb (Fax: 01708 688550).
e-mail:info@abridgegolf.com
website: www.abridgegolf.com

STOCK. **Crondon Park Golf Club,** Stock Road, Stock CM4 9DP (01277 841115; Fax: 01277 841356). *Location:* off the A12, on to B1007 towards Billericay. Set in parkland valley with trees, lakes and magnificent greens, longest hole in the country (18th 655yds). 18 holes, 6250 yards (Club). S.S.S. 70. 9-hole Par 3 course. Driving range and putting green. Academy Lessons. *Green Fees:* weekdays £20.00; weekends £30.00. *Eating facilities:* bar, restaurant. *Visitors:* welcome weekdays; weekend afternoons only. Modern changing rooms, showers, etc. *Society Meetings:* welcome weekdays (Monday to Friday). Professional: Paul Barham (Head Pro), Fred Sunderland (01277 841887). Secretary: Paul Cranwell (01277 841115).

STOKE BY NAYLAND. **Stoke by Nayland Golf Club,** Keepers Lane, Leavenheath, Colchester CO6 4PZ (01206 262836; Fax: 01206 263356). *Location:* just off A134 Colchester to Sudbury on B1068 towards Stoke by Nayland. Undulating parkland with water hazards. Two courses - Gainsborough - 18 holes, 6516 yards. S.S.S. 71. (2) Constable - 18 holes, 6544 yards. S.S.S. 71. 20 bay covered range, practice area. *Green Fees:* on request. *Eating facilities:* full catering and bars. *Visitors:* welcome, please ring for availability and tee bookings. *Society Meetings:* welcome weekdays, book well in advance. Seasonal packages offered. Extensive Health and Leisure Facility including gymnasium, pool, sauna, jacuzzi

and spa; modern, spacious, en suite hotel rooms overlooking lake and fairways. Professional: Kevin Lovelock (01206 262769). Golf Secretary: Peter Barfield (01206 265815).
e-mail: info@stokebynaylandclub.co.uk
website: www.stokebynaylandclub.co.uk

UPMINSTER. **Top Meadow Golf Club and Hotel,** Fen Lane, North Ockendon, Upminster RM14 3PR (01708 852239; Fax: 01708 852598) *Location*: M25, A127, B186 towards North Ockendon - Fen Lane. Parkland course with panoramic views of Essex countryside. 18 holes, 6227 yards. S.S.S. 72. Practice range. On site hotel. *Green Fees:* £12.00 Monday to Friday. *Eating facilities:* fully licensed bar and à la carte restaurant. *Visitors:* Visitors and Societies welcome Monday to Friday. Golfing holidays available midweek and weekends. Professional: Roy Porter (01708 859545). Secretary: Daniel Stock (01708 852239).

WITHAM. **Benton Hall Golf Club,** Wickham Hill, Witham CM8 3LH (01376 502454; Fax: 01376 521050). *Location:* one mile from A12 between Chelmsford and Colchester. Wooded course with natural lakes. 18 holes 6495 yards. S.S.S. 72. 9 hole executive par three course. *Green Fees:* information not available. *Eating facilities:* Blackwater Suite function room, Waterside Bar and Restaurant. *Visitors:* welcome, not before 12 noon at weekends. *Society Meetings:* welcome. Director of Golf: Colin Fairweather. General Manager: David Reeves.*

WITHAM. **Braxted Park Golf Club,** Braxted Park, Witham CM8 3EN (01376 572372; Fax: 01621 892840). *Location:* A12 south of Witham; from Chelmsford take Rivenhall turn-off, if travelling towards Colchester take Silver End turn-off. Established 50 years, set in 18th century parkland. 9 holes, 5880 yards. Par 35, S.S.S. 34. Practice ground. *Green Fees:* information not available. *Eating facilities:* clubhouse (licensed), snacks. *Visitors:* welcome. Corporate entertainment available, activity days, wedding receptions. *Society Meetings:* welcome. Professional: John Hudson. *

WOODFORD GREEN. **Woodford Golf Club,** Sunset Avenue, Woodford Green (020 8504 3330). *Location*: near The Harvester (formerly The Castle Public House), Woodford High Road. Forest land. 9 holes, 5867 yards. S.S.S. 68. *Green Fees:* £15.00 per 18 holes. *Eating facilities:* bar. *Visitors:* no green fees Tuesday mornings, Saturdays all day, Sundays before 11.30pm. Red (scarlet) clothing must be worn - trousers or top. *Society Meetings:* welcome. Professional: Richard Layton (020 8504 4254). Hon Secretary: R.S. Crofts (020 8504 3330; Fax: 020 8559 0504).
e-mail: office@woodfordgolfclub.fsnet.co.uk

visit the FHG golf website on
www.uk-golfguide.com

Gloucestershire

BRISTOL. **Bristol and Clifton Golf Club,** Beggar Bush Lane, Failand, Bristol BS8 3TH (01275 393474). *Location:* M5 Junction 19 - A369 towards Clifton, turn right at A.T.S. into Beggar Bush Lane. Parkland course. 18 holes, 6294 yards. S.S.S. 70. Practice ground. *Green Fees:* weekdays £35.00; weekends £40.00. *Eating facilities:* available. *Visitors:* welcome weekdays without reservation, must have current golf club Handicap. *Society Meetings:* most welcome, Thursdays. Professional: Paul Mitchell (Tel & Fax: 01275 393031). Secretary: Charles Vane Percy (01275 393474; Fax: 01275 394611). website: www.bristolgolf.co.uk

BRISTOL. **Chipping Sodbury Golf Club**, Chipping Sodbury, Bristol BS37 6PU (01454 319042). *Location:* 12 miles north of Bristol, nine miles from Junction 14 on M5 and three miles from Junction 18 on M4. Parkland course. 6786 yards. *Green Fees:* 18-hole course weekdays £22.00; weekends £27.00. *Eating facilities:* full catering available. *Visitors:* welcome except Saturday/Sunday morning and Bank Holidays. Must have Handicap Certificate. *Society Meetings:* catered for by prior arrangement weekdays only. Professional: Mike Watts (01454 314087). Secretary: R.D.J. Wilmott.

BRISTOL. **Filton Golf Club,** Golf Course Lane, Filton, Bristol BS34 7QS (0117 9694169; Fax: 0117 9314359). *Location:* Off A38 north of Bristol. Parkland, 18 holes, 6208 yards. S.S.S. 70. Three practice grounds. *Green Fees:* weekdays £22.00 per round, £27.00 per day, £15.00 with member; weekends £15.00 with member only. *Eating facilities:* available. *Visitors:* welcome except at weekends unless with a member. Buggies and carts for hire. *Society Meetings:* all catered for, subject to programme - must book well in advance. Professional: (0117 9696968; Fax: 0117 9236968). Secretary: Mrs E. Mannering (0117 9694169; Fax: 0117 9314359).

BRISTOL **"The Gloucestershire"**, Tracy Park Estate, Bath Road, Wick, Near Bristol BS30 5RN (0117 937 2251; Fax: 0117 937 4288). *Location:* M4 Junction 18, A46 towards Bath, A420 towards Bristol. Turn left at bottom of steep hill for Lansdown/Bath. Wooded parkland, 400-year-old trees with water hazards and magnificent views of surrounding countryside. Two courses: Crown Course - 18 holes, 6252 yards, Par 69; Cromwell Course - 18 holes, 6246 yards, Par 71. 13 bay driving range. *Green Fees:* weekdays £36.00 (Fairway £18.00); weekends £44.00 (Fairway £22.00). *Eating facilities:* full catering available all day. *Visitors:* welcome – telephone ahead. *Society Meetings:* welcome. 18 en suite bedrooms. Professional: David Morgan. Tee reservations (0117 937 2251; Fax: 0117 937 4288). Secretary: David Knipe. e-mail: info@thegloucestershire.com website: www.thegloucestershire.com

BRISTOL. **Henbury Golf Club,** Henbury Road, Westbury-on-Trym, Bristol BS10 7QB (0117 9500044). *Location:* north M5 Junction 17 A4018 to Westbury-on-Trym; right to Blaise Castle, top of hill turn left. Wooded parkland, very pretty; easily accessible from City Centre and M5. 18 holes, 6007 yards. S.S.S. 70. Practice ground. *Green Fees:* £25.00 per round/day. *Eating facilities:* bars and dining room. *Visitors:* welcome weekdays, Handicap required. Clubs and trolleys for hire. *Society Meetings:* Tuesdays and Fridays only, minimum number 20. Professional: Nick Riley (Tel & Fax: 0117 9502121) Secretary: John Keight (0117 9500044; Fax: 0117 9591928). e-mail: thesecretary@henburygolfclub.co.uk

BRISTOL. **The Kendleshire Golf Club,** Henfield Road, Coalpit Heath, Bristol BS36 2UY (0117 956 7007; Fax: 0117 957 3433). *Location:* Henfield Road, off Westerleigh Road from New Avon Ring Road, five minutes from junction 1 M32. Parkland with water features. 27 holes, from 6001 to 6507 yards. S.S.S. 71. Practice range. *Green Fees:* weekdays £28.00, weekends £35.00, after 3pm £25.00. *Eating facilities:* two bars, restaurant, and function room. *Visitors:* welcome but prior booking essential. *Society Meetings:* welcome weekdays, packages available. Professional: Mike Bessel. Secretary: Patrick Murphy.

BRISTOL. **Knowle Bristol Golf Club,** Fairway, West Town Lane, Brislington, Bristol BS4 5DF (0117 977 6341). Location: three miles south of city centre, left off Wells Road. A4 - Bath. Parkland course. 18 holes, 6006 yards. S.S.S. 69. Practice field, putting green. Green Fees: weekdays £22.00 for 18 holes, £27.00 for 27 holes; weekends £27.00 for 18 holes, £32.00 for 27 holes. Eating facilities: bar/dining room, dinners by arrangement with Steward. Visitors: welcome with Handicap Certificate. Society Meetings: Thursdays only. Professional: Mr Rob Hayward (0117 977 9193). Secretary: Mr Mike Harrington (0117 977 0660; Fax: 0117 972 0615). website: www.knowlegolfclub.co.uk

BRISTOL. **Long Ashton Golf Club,** Clarken Coombe, Long Ashton, Bristol BS41 9DW (01275 392229; Fax: 01275 394395). *Location:* three miles south-west of Bristol on the B3128 Clevedon/Bristol Road. Wooded parkland. 18 holes, 6077 yards. S.S.S. 70. Practice ground. *Green Fees:* weekdays £30.00 18 holes, £35.00 36 holes; weekends £35.00 18 holes. *Eating facilities:* full catering daily, bar open Monday to Sunday (11am to 10.30pm). *Visitors:* welcome, must have current Handicap Certificate. *Society Meetings:* by arrangement with Secretary. Professional: Mike Hart (01275 392229). Secretary: R.J. Williams (01275 392229).

BRISTOL. **Shirehampton Park Golf Club,** Park Hill, Shirehampton, Bristol BS11 0UL (0117 982 2083). *Location:* two miles from Junction 18 on M5 on B4054 to Shirehampton. Parkland course with spectacular views across Avon Gorge. 18 holes, 5430 yards. S.S.S. 66. *Green Fees:* weekdays £20.00, weekends £17.00 only with member. *Eating facilities:* lunches, snacks, teas, etc available daily. *Visitors:* welcome. *Society Meetings:* catered for by prior arrangement. Professional: Brent Ellis (0117 982 2488). Secretary: (0117 982 2083).

BRISTOL. **Shortwood Lodge Golf Club,** Carsons Road, Mangotsfield, Bristol BS16 9LW (0117 9565501). *Location:* four miles M32 via Downend, one mile Warmley A420. Parkland, hilly course. 18 holes, 5337 yards, 4877 metres. S.S.S. 66. Small practice area. *Green Fees:* information not available. *Eating facilities:* no restriction on food and drink. *Visitors:* welcome anytime, no restrictions. *Society Meetings:* catered for weekdays only. Professional/Secretary: Craig Trewin.*

BRISTOL. **Thornbury Golf Centre,** Bristol Road, Thornbury, Bristol (01454 281144; Fax: 01454 281177). *Location:* five miles A38 north from Junctions M4/M5 at Almondsbury. Parkland course overlooking River Severn. 18 holes, 6237 yards. S.S.S. 71. Driving range, video bay, Par 3 course. *Green Fees:* £18.00 per round, £27.00 per day weekdays; £22.50 per round £26.00 per day weekends. *Eating facilities:* restaurant and licensed bar. *Visitors:* welcome, no restrictions. Smart casual clothing desirable. Golf Lodge available with 11 bedrooms. *Society Meetings:* welcome. Professional: Simon Hubbard. Secretary/Manager: Ian Gibson.

BRISTOL. **Woodlands Golf and Country Club,** Trench Lane, Almondsbury, Bristol BS32 4JZ (01454 619319). *Location:* Junction 16 M5 - A38 towards Bristol. Left off AZTEC roundabout, first left Woodlands Lane. Attractive parkland course with five lakes and ponds, elevated tees and two drop holes. 18 holes, 6068 yards. S.S.S. 69. Practice area. *Green Fees:* weekdays £14.00 per round, weekends £16.00 per round. *Eating facilities:* bar/lounge, bar snacks. *Visitors:* welcome, no restrictions and hire of clubs available. Trolleys and twelve buggies available £10.00 per round. *Society Meetings:* bookable in advance. Large well stocked Pro shop. Professional: Leigh Riddiford. Secretary: Ian Knipe (Fax: 01454 619397; Shop: 01454 619319). website: www.woodlands-golf.com

BROADWAY. **Broadway Golf Club,** Willersey Hill, Broadway WR12 7LG (01386 853683; Fax: 01386 858643). *Location:* one-and-a-half-miles east Broadway (A44). 18 holes, 6211 yards. S.S.S. 70 *Green Fees:* on application. *Eating facilities:* available daily (except Mondays during Winter). *Visitors:* welcome; reservation advised. Handicap Certificates required. Saturdays (April/September) with member only before 3pm. October/March no restrictions. Affiliated to the "Gloucestershire Golf Union". Society Meetings: by arrangement (Wednesday, Thursday and Friday). Professional: Martyn Freeman (01386 853275). Managing Secretary: B. Carnie (01386 853683).

CHELTENHAM. **Cleeve Cloud Golf Club,** Cleeve Hill, Near Cheltenham GL52 3PW (01242 672025). *Location:* three miles north of Cheltenham on B4632. Hilltop inland links with gorse and natural quarries. Outstanding views from the highest point in the Cotswolds. 18 holes, 6411 yards. S.S.S. 72. *Green Fees:* weekdays £12.00; weekends £15.00. *Eating facilities:* full restaurant and bar facilities. *Visitors:* welcome with prior booking. *Society Meetings:* welcome with prior booking (01242 672025). Professional: Dave Finch (01242 672592). Secretary: Hugh Fitzsimons (01242 521003 evenings only).

CHELTENHAM. **Lilley Brook Golf Club,** Cirencester Road, Charlton Kings, Cheltenham GL53 8EG (01242 526785). *Location:* two miles south-east of Cheltenham on main Cirencester road (A435). Parkland, 18 holes, 6212 yards. S.S.S. 70. Practice field. *Green Fees:* weekdays £25.00 per round, £30.00 per day; weekends £30.00 per round, £35.00 per day. *Eating facilities:* full catering available. *Visitors:* welcome weekdays, weekends subject to availability. Handicap Certificates required. *Society Meetings:* by arrangement. Professional: Karl Hayler (01242 525201). Secretary: M.F. Jordan (01242 526785; Fax: 01242 256880).

CHELTENHAM. **Naunton Downs Golf Club Ltd,** Naunton, Cheltenham GL54 3AE (01451 850092; Fax: 01451 850091). Rolling Cotswold countryside with a valley running through course. 18 holes, 6135 yards. S.S.S. 70. Practice ground. *Green Fees:* information not available. *Eating facilities:* available. *Visitors:* welcome anytime, must book at all times. *Society Meetings:* welcome. Professional: Nick Ellis (01451 850092); Golf Manager: Nick Ellis (01451 850090); Club Steward: Christine Dwyer (01451 850093).

CHELTENHAM. **Ullenwood Manor Golf Course,** National Star College, Ullenwood, Cheltenham GL53 9QU (01242 527631). *Location*: turn off the A436 past junction with A417. Parkland course, 18 holes (using 9 fairways). 2795 yards S.S.S. 54. Designed by Norm Allen, opened in 1975. *Green Fees*: £10.00 all day. *Eating facilities*: catering available at Air Balloon pub half a mile away. *Visitors*: welcome anytime. *Society Meetings*: welcome anytime. Secretary: Richard Greenwell.

CHELTENHAM near. **Cotswold Hills Golf Club Ltd,** Ullenwood, Near Cheltenham GL53 9QT (01242 522421). *Location:* at Ullenwood, off the A436 south of Cheltenham (two miles from town). Undulating Cotswold country course, excellent drainage. 18 holes, 6565 yards. S.S.S. 71. Large practice ground. *Green Fees:* weekdays £34.00 18 holes; weekends £39.00 18 holes. *Eating facilities:* full restaurant and bars. *Visitors:* no restrictions as a rule, but it is wise to telephone. *Society Meetings:* catered for by arrangement with Secretary. Professional: Norman Allen (01242 515263). Secretary: Paul Burroughes (01242 515264).

CHURCHDOWN. **Brickhampton Court Golf Complex,** Cheltenham Road, Churchdown GL2 9QF (01452 859444; Fax: 01452 859333). *Location:* midway between Cheltenham and Gloucester on B4063; close to Junction 11 of M5. Rolling parkland courses featuring lakes, streams, strategic white sand bunkers, tree plantations and no steep hills. Two courses: Spa Course – 18 holes, 6449 yards, 5222 metres. S.S.S. 71; Glevum Course – 9 holes, 1859 yards, 1695 metres. Par 31. 26 bay floodlit covered driving range, golf academy with PGA tuition. *Green Fees:* Spa Course – weekdays £21.00 per round, £30.00 per day; weekends and Bank Holidays £27.50 per round, £35.00 per day. Glevum Course – weekdays £7.50 9 holes, £13.00 18 holes; weekends and Bank Holidays £9.50 9 holes, £15.00 18 holes. *Eating facilities:* spike bar and restaurant offering varied menu and Sunday lunches. *Visitors:* welcome although pre-booking may be advisable and evidence of golfing ability preferred. Buggies and trolleys for hire. Two fully stocked Pro shops. Social functions catered for. *Society Meetings:* fully catered for (generally weekdays only). Information pack available. Professional: Bruce Wilson and Chris Gillick. Operations Director: Rob East. website: www.brickhampton.co.uk

CIRENCESTER. **Cirencester Golf Club,** Cheltenham Road, Bagendon, Cirencester GL7 7BH (01285 653939; Fax: 01285 650665). *Location:* two miles north of Cirencester on A435 Cheltenham road. Scenic and free-draining Cotswold course. 18 holes, 6055 yards. S.S.S. 69. Driving range, par-3 course. *Green Fees:* weekdays £27.00 per round/day; weekends and Bank Holidays £32.00 per round/day. *Eating facilities:* bar and restaurant - snacks always available. *Visitors:* welcome, Handicap Certificate required. Buggies for hire. *Society Meetings:* catered for Tuesday, Wednesday and Friday only. Professional: Peter Garratt (01285 656124). General Manager: Robert Caldecott (01285 652465).

COLEFORD. **Forest Hills Golf Club Ltd.,** Mile End Road, Coleford GL16 7BY (01594 810620; Fax: 01594 810823). *Location:* 10 miles from Severn Bridge, six miles from Monmouth M5, M50. Coleford town centre on Gloucester Road. Parkland with panoramic views to Welsh hills. 18 holes, 6300 yards. Par 72. Practice ground, driving range. *Green Fees:* information not available. *Eating facilities:* bar, restaurant. *Visitors:* welcome, no restrictions. Buggies available. *Society Meetings:* very welcome. Professional: Richard Ballard. Secretary: Colin Revill.*

COLEFORD. **Forest of Dean Golf Club,** Lords Hill, Coleford GL16 8BD (01594 832583; Fax: 01594 832584). *Location:* quarter of a mile from Coleford town centre on B4431 Coleford to Parkend Road, 10 miles from Severn Bridge, M4, M5 and M50. Parkland course in Forest of Dean. 18 holes, 6033 yards. S.S.S. 69. Practice area. *Green Fees:* information not available. *Eating facilities:* food available all day - breakfast, coffee, lunches, teas and dinner. Table d'hôte restaurant, bar open all day. *Visitors:* always welcome, please book teeing-off times with Professional. Own 52 bedroom Hotel, the regions largest golf shop on site, tennis court, bowling green, golf cars available. *Society Meetings:* welcome. Professional: Andy Grey (01594 833689). Secretary: Mrs J. Sandalls (01594 832583).*

DURSLEY. **Stinchcombe Hill Golf Club,** Stinchcombe Hill, Dursley GL11 6AQ (01453 542015; Fax: 01453 549545). *Location:* M5 between Junctions 13 and 14, A38 to Dursley. At traffic lights in centre of Dursley turn right to enter May Lane, continue to top of Hill and turn right onto Golf Course. A gently undulating course situated on a hilltop at the southern edge of the Cotswolds, spectacular views. 18 holes, 5734 yards. S.S.S. 68. Practice and teaching areas. *Green Fees:* £24.00 per round, £30.00 per day weekdays (£12.00 with member); £30.00 per round, £40.00 per day weekends and Bank Holidays (£15.00 with member). *Eating facilities:* full catering and bar service available. *Visitors:* welcome, please call the Professional in advance for availability. *Society Meetings:* Monday, Wednesday and Friday. Professional: Paul Bushell (01453 543878). Secretary: P.H. Jones (01453 542015). e-mail: stinchcombehill@golfers.net

GLOUCESTER. **Ramada Hotel and Resort,** Matson Lane, Gloucester GL4 9EA (01452 411331; Fax: 01452 307212). *Location:* follow signs off B4073. Challenging 18 hole, par 70 course commanding stunning views across the Cotswolds and complemented by a par 3, 9 hole course. Floodlit under cover, 12 bay driving range and practice ground. *Green Fees:* information on request *Eating facilities:* full catering available. *Visitors:* welcome subject to golfing ability and availability. Buggies and trolleys available. 107 bedroom Hotel including five suites. Extensive Leisure Club and Ski Centre. Golfing breaks available. An ideal venue for golfing individuals, clubs, societies and business events. Professionals: Chris Gillick and John Whiddon.*

GLOUCESTER. **Rodway Hill Golf Course,** Highnam, Gloucester GL2 8DN (01452 384222). 18 holes, 6070 yards. S.S.S. 69. Practice area. *Green Fees:* £12.00 weekdays, £14.00 weekends. *Eating facilities:* Cosy bar and restaurant. *Visitors:* all welcome - pay as you play. *Society Meetings:* special rates available. Professional: Tony Grubb.

LYDNEY. **Lydney Golf Club,** The Links, off Lakeside Avenue, Lydney GL15 5QA (01594 842614). *Location:* between by-pass and the town, note - no access off by-pass, enter the town and take Hams Road off the main thoroughfare of Newerne Street. Lakeside Avenue is the 7th road on the left hand side. Flat meadowland with views over the River Severn. 9 holes, 5298 yards. S.S.S. 66. Small practice area. *Green Fees:* £10.00 per day weekdays; weekends £10.00 with a member only. *Eating facilities:* snack meals only. *Visitors:* welcome weekdays, only with a member at weekends/Bank Holidays. *Society Meetings:* welcome by prior arrangement (maximum 36). Hon. Secretary: D.A. Barnard (01594 843940).

MINCHINHAMPTON. **Minchinhampton Golf Club (Old Course),** Minchinhampton, Stroud GL6 9AQ (01453 832642). *Location:* three miles east of Stroud. Easy walking course. 18 holes, 6019 yards. S.S.S. 69. Practice area. *Green Fees:* weekdays £12.00, weekends and Bank Holidays £15.00. *Eating facilities:* bar and restaurant available. *Visitors:* welcome. *Society Meetings:* most welcome by arrangement. Admin Manager: A.P. Dangerfield (01453 832642). Shop: (01453 836382). e-mail: mail@mincholdcourse.co.uk website: www.mincholdcourse.co.uk

MINCHINHAMPTON. **Minchinhampton Golf Club (New Courses),** Minchinhampton, Stroud GL6 9BE (01453 833866; Fax: 01453 837360). *Location:* five miles east of Stroud. Reasonably level, set in typical Cotswold countryside. Avening is cleverly bunkered, Cherington has large undulating greens of superb quality. A members' club with two fine and challenging courses and a fine Cotswold stone clubhouse, all set in lovely countryside. Two courses: both 18 holes, Cherington 6434 yards S.S.S. 71, Avening 6263 yards. S.S.S. 70. Practice area. *Green Fees:* information not available. *Eating facilities:* dining room and bar. *Visitors:* welcome, telephone booking essential on 01453 833840. Handicap Certificate required. *Society Meetings:* welcome weekdays, details on application. Professional: Chris Steele (Tel & Fax: 01453 837351). Secretary: David Calvert (01453 833866; Fax: 01453 837360).*

PAINSWICK. **Painswick Golf Club,** Painswick, Near Stroud GL6 6TL (01452 812180). *Location:* one mile north of Painswick village on A46 turn left. Hilltop, wooded course. 18 holes, 4900 yards. S.S.S. 65. *Green Fees:* information not available. *Eating facilities:* lunches at clubhouse bar anytime, evening meals in restaurant subject to availability of tables. *Visitors:* welcome weekdays and Saturday mornings. Saturday afternoons, Sunday mornings and Public Holidays only with member. *Society Meetings:* welcome weekdays. Secretary: N. Hindmarch.*

TETBURY. **Westonbirt Golf Course,** c/o Bursar, Westonbirt School Ltd, Westonbirt, Near Tetbury GL8 8QG (01666 880 242). *Location:* three miles south from Tetbury on A433 to Bath. Parkland. 9 holes, 4504 yards. S.S.S. 61. Practice area and green. *Green Fees:* information not available. *Eating facilities:* tea and refreshments from seasonal caravan. *Visitors:* welcome without reservation. *Society Meetings:* welcome. Enquiries: Bursar's office, Westonbirt School.

TEWKESBURY. **Hilton Puckrup Hall,** Puckrup, Tewkesbury GL20 6EL (01684 296200; Fax: 01684 850788). *Location:* leave M5 at Junction 8. Take M50 one mile to Junction 1, leave and bear left taking A38 towards Tewkesbury, Puckrup is half a mile along on the right. Undulating parkland with water hazards, spectacular views of the Malverns. 18 holes, 6189 yards. S.S.S. 70. Practice ground. *Green Fees:* weekdays £25.00; weekends £30.00. Day ticket £30.00 weekdays, £35.00 weekends. *Eating facilities:* choice of bars and restaurants. *Visitors:* welcome, subject to golfing ability and course availability. Buggies available. 112 bedroomed hotel with full leisure facilities. Golfing Breaks available. *Society Meetings:* welcome, packages available from £19.50. Golf Operations Manager: Nigel Whitton (01684 271591; Fax: 01684 850788). Secretary: Graham Spring (01452 780358).

TEWKESBURY. **Sherdons Golf Centre,** Tredington, Tewkesbury GL0 7BP (01684 274782; Fax: 01684 275358). *Location:* follow brown sign directions from A38 two miles south of Tewkesbury or A46 two miles east. Countryside course with gentle slopes and new plantations. 9 holes, 5308 yards. S.S.S. 66. 26 bay floodlit driving range. *Green Fees:* weekdays 9 holes £7.00, 18 holes £12.00; weekends 9 holes £8.00, 18 holes £15.00. *Eating facilities:* bar, coffee and light snacks available. *Visitors:* welcome at all times. *Society Meetings:* by arrangement, weekdays only. Professionals: Philip Clark and John Parker (01684 274782). Secretary: Richard Chatham (01684 274782; Fax: 01684 275358).

TEWKESBURY. **Tewkesbury Park Hotel Golf and Country Club,** Lincoln Green Lane, Tewkesbury GL20 7DN (01684 295405; Fax: 01684 292386). *Location:* off Junction 9 of M5 through Tewkesbury on A38 - signposted. Parkland. 18 holes, 6533 yards. S.S.S. 71. Golf range, and pitching and chipping greens. *Green Fees:* weekdays £25.00, with a member £16.00; weekends £35.00, with a member £16.00. *Eating facilities:* full Hotel facilities. *Visitors:* welcome, reservation required. Valid Handicap Certificate required. 80-bedroom hotel plus leisure section. *Society Meetings:* all welcome by prior arrangement. Professional: Charlie Boast (01684 272320; Fax: 01684 292386).

WOTTON-UNDER-EDGE. **Cotswold Edge Golf Club,** Upper Rushmire, Wotton-under-Edge GL12 7PT (01453 844167). *Location:* eight miles from Junction 14 M5, on B4058 Tetbury road. Fairly flat course with magnificent views. 18 holes, White Tees - 6170 yards. S.S.S. 70; Yellow Tees - 5816 yards. S.S.S. 69. *Green Fees:* information not available. *Eating facilities:* good lunch time catering service, usual bar facilities. *Visitors:* welcome weekdays. Telephone call in advance advisable. *Society Meetings:* by arrangement with Secretary. Professional: Rod Hibbitt (01453 844398). Secretary: E. Johnson (01453 844167; Fax: 01453 845120).

N O T E   All the information regarding Golf Clubs in this guide is given in good faith in the belief that it is correct. However, the publishers cannot guarantee the facts given in these pages, neither are they responsible for changes in ownership or facilities, such as green fees, that may take place after the date of going to press. Readers should always satisfy themselves that the facilities they require are available and that the terms, if quoted, still apply.

Hampshire

ALDERSHOT. **Army Golf Club,** Laffan's Road, Aldershot GU11 2HF (01252 336776; Fax: 01252 337562). *Location:* access from Eelmoor Bridge off A323 Aldershot Fleet Road - second oldest course in Hampshire. 18 holes, 6533 yards. S.S.S. 71. *Green Fees:* special rates for servicemen. *Eating facilities:* a range of catering is available. *Visitors:* weekdays only, members' guests anytime. *Society Meetings:* catered for. Professional: G. Cowley (01252 336722; Fax: 01252 336686). Secretary: Maj. (Rtd) J. Douglass (01252 337272; Fax: 01252 337562).

ALRESFORD. **Alresford Golf Club, Cheriton Road, Tichborne Down, Alresford SO24 0PN (01962 733746; Fax: 01962 736040).** *Location*: **on B3046 one mile south of A31, two miles north A272. Rolling downland, wooded. 18 holes, 5905 yards, 5397 metres. S.S.S. 68. Practice area.** *Green Fees:* **weekdays £25.00 per round, £35.00 per day; weekends and Bank Holidays £40.00 per round. Eating facilities: full catering.** *Visitors*: **welcome but not before 12 noon weekdays/Bank Holidays.** *Society Meetings*: **welcome. Professional: Malcolm Scott (Tel & Fax: 01962 733998). Secretary: (01962 733746; Fax: 01962 736040).**

ALTON. **Alton Golf Club**, Old Odiham Road, Alton GU34 4BU (01420 82042). *Location:* off B3349 (turn off at Golden Pot). Undulating meadowland, wooded course. 9 holes, 5744 yards. S.S.S. 68. Practice area, putting green. *Green Fees:* information on request. *Eating facilities:* bar, hot and cold snacks all day. *Visitors:* weekdays welcome without reservation. Weekends and Bank Holidays with Handicap Certificate. Trolleys for hire. *Society Meetings:* welcome weekdays only. Professional/Secretary: Richard Keeling (01420 86518).

ALTON. **Blacknest Golf & Country Club,** Blacknest Road, Blacknest, Alton GU34 4QL (01420 22888). *Location:* Bently exit of A31, between Farnham and Alton. Parkland course with several water features. 18 holes, Par 69. Par 3 course. *Green Fees:* weekdays £20.00 18 holes, weekends £25.00. *Eating facilities:* bar and dining available from 8am to 5pm. *Visitors:* welcome by arrangement. *Society Meetings:* welcome. Professional: Tony Cook.

ALTON. **Worldham Park Golf Club,** Caker Lane, Worldham, Alton GU34 3BF (01420 543151). *Location:* B3004 Alton to Bordon road, one mile from Alton. Parkland course with views of the Wey Valley. 18 holes, 6199 yards. S.S.S. 70. 14 bay driving range. *Green Fees:* weekdays £12.00; weekends £15.00. *Eating facilities:* spike bar with hot and cold food, lounge area. *Visitors:* welcome - pay and play. Booking required at weekends. Professional shop. *Society Meetings:* welcome any day. Professional: Jon Le Roux (01420 543151). Secretary: Neil Harvey (01420 544606).

AMPFIELD. **Ampfield Par Three Golf and Country Club,** Winchester Road, Ampfield, Near Romsey SO51 9BQ (01794 368480). *Location:* A31 Winchester to Romsey road, next door to White Horse Public House. Parkland course designed by Henry Cotton. All holes par 3. 18 holes, 2478 yards. S.S.S. 53. *Green Fees:* information not available. *Eating facilities:* restaurant meals and snacks, bar facilities. *Visitors:* welcome, but best to phone first. Recognised golf shoes must be worn. *Society Meetings:* catered for by prior arrangement. Professional: Richard Benfield (01794 368750). Secretary: Miss J. Johnston. *

ANDOVER. **Andover Golf Club,** 51 Winchester Road, Andover SP10 2EF (01264 323980). *Location:* Stockbridge Exit from A303, left towards Andover, quarter of a mile on right. Gently sloping downland course with views over town and country. 9 holes, 6096 yards. S.S.S. 69. *Green Fees:* weekdays £15.00 per round, £10.00 with a member, £20.00 per day, £15.00 with a member; £20.00 weekends and Bank Holidays, £15.00 with a member. *Eating facilities:* full catering available. *Visitors:* welcome, check tee reservations with Professional. *Society Meetings:* welcome, please phone for availability. Professional: D. Lawrence (01264 324151). Secretary: Martin Bennet (01264 358040). Clubhouse Manager: (01264 323980).

ANDOVER. **The Hampshire Golf Club,** Winchester Road, Goodworth Clatford, Andover SP11 7TB (01264 357555; Fax: 01264 356606). *Location:* one mile south of Andover on A3057 Stockbridge Road. Downland with new trees and lakes. 18 holes, 6338 yards. S.S.S. 70. 10 bay covered driving range. *Green Fees:* weekdays £17.00, weekends £27.00. 9 hole, par 3 course £4.50 weekdays, £6.50 weekends. *Eating facilities:* full catering facilities, bar seven days a week. *Visitors:* always welcome. *Society Meetings:* welcome weekdays only. Professional: Stewart Cronin (01264 357555). Secretary: Iain Powell (01264 356462; Fax: 01264 356606).

BARTON-ON-SEA. **Barton-on-Sea Golf Club,** Milford Road, New Milton BH25 5PP (01425 615308; Fax: 01425 621457). *Location:* one mile from centre of New Milton on B3058 towards Milford-on-Sea. Cliff top links with easy walking; superb views of Isle of Wight and Christchurch. 27 holes. S.S.S. 72 any 18 holes. *Green Fees:* £35.00 per day weekdays; £40.00 weekends and Bank Holidays. Subject to review. *Eating facilities:* lunch, snacks and teas daily, full bar service. *Visitors:* welcome after 8.30am weekdays; weekends and Bank Holidays after 9.30am; evening green fees after 5pm. Handicap Certificate required. Buggies for hire. *Society Meetings:* welcome by arrangement Mondays, Wednesdays and Fridays. Professional: P. Rodgers (01425 615308). Secretary/Manager: Gary Prince. website: www.barton-on-sea-golf.co.uk

BASINGSTOKE. **Basingstoke Golf Club,** Kempshott Park, Basingstoke RG23 7LL (01256 465990; Fax: 01256 331793). *Location:* M3 Junction 7, A30 three miles west of town. Parkland course - easy walking. 18 holes, 6350 yards. S.S.S. 70. Small practice ground. *Green Fees:* information not available. *Eating facilities:* dining room, lounge and back bar. *Visitors:* welcome weekdays. Buggies, trolleys for hire. *Society Meetings:* catered for Wednesdays and Thursdays. Professional: G. Shoesmith (01256 351332). Secretary: W.A. Jefford (01256 465990; Fax: 01256 331793).

BASINGSTOKE. **Bishopswood Golf Club,** Bishopswood Lane, Tadley, Basingstoke RG26 4AT (0118-981 2200; Fax: 0118-940 8606). *Location:* six miles north of Basingstoke off the A340. Parkland/ wooded course. 9 holes, 6474 yards. S.S.S. 71. 12 bay floodlit driving range open seven days a week. *Green Fees:* weekdays only, £12.00 for 9 holes, £18.00 for 18 holes, OAP and Junior rates available. *Eating facilities:* lounge and spike bars - snacks, bar meals and 50 seater restaurant facility. *Visitors:* welcome weekdays only by prior booking. *Society Meetings:* welcome by arrangement. Professional: S. Ward (Tel & Fax: 0118-981 5213; Fax: 0118-940 8602). Manager: D. Goss (0118-981 2200). website: www.bishopswoodgolfcourse.co.uk

BASINGSTOKE. **Sandford Springs Golf Club,** Sandford Springs, Wolverton, Tadley RG26 5RT (01635 296800; Fax: 01635 296801). *Location:* on north side of A339 Basingstoke to Newbury road at Kingsclere. Three scenic loops of 9 holes combines woodland, parkland and lakes quite beautifully. 27 holes. S.S.S. 69/70/69. Driving range and putting green. *Green Fees:* telephone for details. *Eating facilities:* available all day; also conference and banqueting facilities. *Visitors:* welcome every day, subject to availability. *Society Meetings:* welcome, subject to availability. Professionals: G. Edmunds, J Barnes, C. Duffy (01635 296808).

BASINGSTOKE. **Test Valley Golf Club,** Micheldever Road, Overton, Near Basingstoke RG25 3DS (01256 771737; Fax: 01256 771285). *Location:* on the C79, one mile north of A303 signposted Overton. Downland course; easy walking; beautiful countryside views; excellent drainage, playable all year. 18 holes, 6897 yards. S.S.S. 73. Full practice facilities. *Green Fees:* weekdays £20.00, weekends £28.00. *Eating facilities:* spike bar; main bar, full dining facility. *Visitors:* welcome weekdays, or weekends after 10.30am. *Society Meetings:* welcome weekdays. Professional/ Secretary: Alistair Briggs (01256 771737). Venue for Hippo Tour, Hampshire Open and Lombard Top Club Trophy.

BASINGSTOKE. **Tylney Park Golf Club,** Rotherwick, near Hook RG27 9AY (01256 762079; Fax: 01256 763079). *Location:* M3 Junction 5 one-and-a-half miles. Parkland course with mature trees. 18 holes, 6135 yards. S.S.S. 69, Par 70. Good practice ground. *Green Fees:* information not available. *Eating facilities:* catering and bar available. *Visitors:* weekdays unrestricted, weekends with Handicap Certificate or as a guest of a member. *Society Meetings:* welcome Mondays to Thursdays. Secretary: M.R. Alcock.*

BASINGSTOKE. **Weybrook Park Golf Club,** Rooksdown Lane, Basingstoke RG24 9NT (01256 320347; Fax: 01256 812973). *Location:* two miles north west of Basingstoke town centre, A339 Newbury Road, turn at first crossroads on A339. Parkland course with magnificent views, pleasantly undulating and picturesque landscape, excellent chalk drainage ensures continuous play. 18 holes, 6468 yards, 5914 metres. S.S.S. 71. Driving range, practice area. *Green Fees:* information not available. *Eating facilities:* bar with restaurant and spike bar. *Visitors:* welcome, advisable to telephone in case of competitions. All players must have their own clubs, suitable casual/smart attire must be worn. *Society Meetings:* welcome, telephone for booking and costs. Professional: Mr Anthony Dillon (01256 333232; Fax: 01256 334242). Secretary: Mr G.E. Carpenter (01256 320347; Fax: 01256 812973).*

BASINGSTOKE near. **Dummer Golf Club,** Dummer Village, Near Basingstoke RG25 2AR (01256 397888; Fax: 01256 397889). *Location:* at Junction 7 of M3. A downland course designed by Clark/Alliss - easy walking, panoramic views, free draining; genuine all-year-round course. Par 72, 6403 yards.S.S.S. 70. 10 bay driving range plus teaching studios and practice facilities. *Green Fees*: £30.00 weekdays, £34.00 weekends after 1pm. *Eating facilities*: Spike Bar, conservatory and dining room. *Visitors*: welcome midweek and after 1pm at weekends. Handicap preferred. *Society Meetings*: welcome. Professionals: Andrew Fannon, Scott Watson and David Chivers. Secretary: Roger Corkhill. website: www.dummergc.co.uk

BORDON. **Blackmoor Golf Club,** Firgrove Road, Whitehill, Bordon GU35 9EH (01420 472775; Fax: 01420 487666). *Location:* lies midway between Petersfield and Farnham on A325. Parkland, wooded course. 18 holes, 6164 yards. S.S.S. 69. *Green Fees:* weekdays £35.00 per round, £47.00 36 holes. *Eating facilities:* dining room. *Visitors:* welcome weekdays, Handicaps necessary, Sat/Sun no visitors for golf but open for catering. Suitable dress code - no jeans in club or on course. Trolleys available. *Society Meetings:* catered for weekdays: Monday, Wednesday, Thursday and Friday. Morning coffee, lunch, evening meal. Professional: Stephen Clay (01420 472345). Secretary: Mr Tony Harris (01420 472775; Fax: 01420 487666). e-mail: admin@blackmoorgolf.co.uk

BORDON near. **Kingsley Golf Club**, Main Road, Kingsley, Near Bordon GU35 9NG (01420 489478). *Location:* B3004 off A325 Farnham to Petersfield road. Ideal beginners' course. 9 holes. *Green Fees*: information not available. Trolleys available. Professional/Acting Secretary: C. Howard.*

BROCKENHURST. **Brokenhurst Manor Golf Club,** Sway Road, Brockenhurst SO42 7SG (01590 623332; Fax: 01590 624140). *Location:* one mile from Brockenhurst. Beautiful New Forest parkland course. 18 holes, 6222 yards. S.S.S. 70. Practice ground. *Green Fees:* weekdays £48.00 per round, £58.00 per day; weekends and Bank Holidays £58.00 per round, £73.00 per day. Subject to review. *Eating facilities:* restaurant and bar. *Visitors:* welcome by arrangement. Handicap Certificate required. *Society Meetings:* welcome Thursdays by arrangement. Professional: Bruce Parker (01590 623092). Secretary: Paul E. Clifford (01590 623332; Fax: 01590 624140).

CRONDALL. **Oak Park Golfing Complex,** Heath Lane, Crondall, Near Farnham, Surrey GU10 5PB (01252 850880; Fax: 01252 850851). *Location:* one and a half miles off A287 Farnham-Odiham road, five miles from Junctions 4, 4a and 5 of M3 motorway. Gently undulating parkland course. Woodland Course - 18 holes, 6247 yards. S.S.S. 70; Village Course - 9 holes, 3279 yards. Par 36. 16 bay covered driving range, putting green, chipping green and practice bunker. *Green Fees:* information not available. *Eating facilities:* Restaurant: available for private hire and special occasions. Bar snacks available. *Visitors:* welcome; must book through Professional; reserved tee system at all times. *Society Meetings:* by arrangement. Professional: Gary Muton (01252 850066; Fax: 01252 850851). Manager: Mr. D. Maskery (01252 850880).*

DENMEAD. **Furzeley Golf Club,** Furzeley Road, Denmead PO7 6TX (023 9223 1180; Fax 023 9223 0921). *Location:* A3(M) Exit for Waterlooville, follow the B2150 to Denmead. Parkland course. 18 holes, 4363 yards. S.S.S. 61. *Green Fees:* information not available. *Eating facilities:* restaurant. *Visitors:* welcome anytime - Pay and Play and membership available. *Society Meetings:* always welcome. Professional: Derek Brown (023 9223 1180; Fax: 023 9223 0921). Secretary: Terri Brown.

DIBDEN. **Dibden Golf Centre,** Main Road, Dibden, Hythe, Southampton SO45 5TB Bookings: (023 8020 7508). *Location:* half-mile off A326 Totton to Fawley road, on the road to Hythe. Parkland course with views over Southampton Water. 18 holes, 5965 yards, 5455 metres. S.S.S. 69. 9 hole course, 24 bay floodlit driving range. *Green Fees:* information not available. *Eating facilities:* full catering facilities available. *Visitors:* welcome. *Society Meetings:* welcome by prior booking. Catering: Clare Flowers (02380 845060) Professionals: John Slade/ Paul Smith (023 8084 5596). *
website: www.nfdc.gov.uk/golf

EASTLEIGH. **Fleming Park Golf Course,** Magpie Lane, Eastleigh SO50 9NL (023 8061 2797). *Location:* two miles off M27 Eastleigh Airport turning. Parkland. 18 holes, 4376 yards. S.S.S. 61. *Green Fees:* information not available. *Eating facilities:* bar. *Visitors:* welcome, book on day or one week in advance. *Society Meetings:* all welcome. Professional: Mr C. Strickett (023 8061 2797). Secretary: A. Wheavil (023 8061 2797).*

FAREHAM. **Cams Hall Estate Golf Club,** Fareham PO16 8UP (01329 827732; Fax: 01329 827111). *Location:* Junction 11 M27 follow signs to Fareham/Portchester, take A27 to Portchester. 18 hole creek course links, 9 hole parkland course; five lakes, 99 bunkers, Fareham Creek. Creek course 18 holes, 6244 yards. S.S.S. 71; Park Course 9 holes, 3247 yards. S.S.S. 36. Practice ground, putting green, chipping green. *Green Fees:* weekdays £24.00; weekends £32.00. 50% reduction at off-peak times. One free in every four ball. *Eating facilities:* Bar food. *Visitors:* welcome. Luxurious clubhouse, spacious locker rooms, sauna. *Society Meetings:* welcome. Professional: Jason Neve (01329 827732; Fax: 01329 827111). General Manager: Steve Wright (01329 827222; Fax: 01329 827111).
e-mail: camshall@americangolf.uk.com

FAREHAM. **Southwick Park Golf Club,** Pinsley Drive, Southwick, Fareham PO17 6EL (023 9237 0683; Fax: 023 9221 0289). Location: near Southwick village, adjacent to P144, HMS Dryad (B2177). Parkland. 18 holes, 5884 yards. S.S.S. 69. Practice area, pitch and putt. *Green Fees:* weekdays £18.00 per round, weekends after 2pm £20.00. Subject to review. *Eating facilities:* bar and snacks available. *Visitors:* weekdays. *Society Meetings:* book through Manager. Professional: J. Green (023 9238 0442). Manager: N.W. Price (023 9238 0131).

FAREHAM. **Wickham Park Golf Club,** Titchfield Lane, Wickham, Fareham PO17 5PJ (01329 833342; Fax: 01329 834798). *Location:* 2 miles north of Fareham, J10 of M27. Undulating parkland course. 18 holes, 5733 yards. S.S.S. 67. Two practice grounds and net. *Green Fees:* weekdays £14.00, weekends £17.00. Special rates for Juniors and Senior Citizens. *Eating facilities:* full menu. *Visitors:* welcome at all times but must pre-book. *Society Meetings:* welcome Monday to Friday - please telephone to book in advance. Professional: Scott Edwards. Manager: Ian Yates.

FARNBOROUGH. **Southwood Golf Course,** Ively Road, Cove, Farnborough GU14 0LJ (01252 548700). *Location:* approximately half a mile west of A325. Flat parkland. 18 holes, 5738 yards. S.S.S. 68. Putting green. *Green Fees:* £15.90 weekdays, £18.00 weekends. *Eating facilities:* bar and diningroom available. *Visitors:* welcome, bookable at all times. *Society Meetings:* catered for by arrangement. Professional: Matt Robbins. Secretary: Mike Pettifor.

FLEET. **North Hants Golf Club,** Minley Road, Fleet GU13 8RE (01252 616443). *Location:* B3013 off A30, M3 Junction 4a. 400 yards from railway station. Heathland. 18 holes, 6519 yards. S.S.S. 72, Par 71. Practice ground. *Green Fees:* information not available. *Eating facilities:* lunch daily, evening meals by prior arrangement. *Visitors:* welcome weekdays only by prior arrangement, Handicap Certificates required, Thursdays Ladies' Day. *Society Meetings:* Tuesdays and Wednesdays only, maximum 42. Professional: Steve Porter (01252 616655). Secretary: I.R. Goodliffe (01252 616443; Fax: 01252 811627).*

FOURMARKS. **Fourmarks Golf Club**, Headmore Lane, Fourmarks GU34 3ES (01420 587214; Fax: 01420 587313). *Location*: A31 to Fourmarks follow brown signs to golf course. Parkland course. 9 holes, 2300 yards, S.S.S 62. Practice nets. *Green Fees*: weekdays 9 holes £7.95; weekends 9 holes £8.95. *Eating facilities*: bar snacks and drinks available. *Visitors*: welcome at all times. Tuition by Professional available. *Society Meetings*: welcome at any time. Professional: Peter Chapman (01420 587214). Secretary: Wayne Falloon (01420 587313). e-mail: fourmarksgolf@btopenworld.com

GOSPORT. **Fleetlands Golf Club**, DARA Fleetlands, Fareham Road, Gosport PO13 0AW (023 9254 4492). *Location*: two miles south of Fareham on Fareham/Gosport Road. Flat/wooded Course. 9 holes, 4852 yards. S.S.S. 64. *Green Fees*: information not available. *Eating facilities*: bar/clubhouse. *Visitors*: by appointment with member only. *Society Meetings*: by appointment with member only. Secretary: Mr R. Sheehan (023 9254 4903). *

GOSPORT. **Gosport and Stokes Golf Club**, off Fort Road, Haslar, Gosport PO12 2AT (023 9258 1625). *Location*: A32 to Gosport, course is one mile east of Stokes Bay, near Gilkicker Point. Water course, natural hazards. 9 holes, 5957 yards. S.S.S. 70. Nets and putting green. *Green Fees*: information not available. *Eating facilities*: full catering service, fully licensed bar. *Visitors*: welcome all week, restricted Sundays and Thursdays. *Society Meetings*: by arrangement. Secretary/Manager: Mr P. Lucas (Tel & Fax: 023 9252 7941).*

HARTLEY WINTNEY. **Hartley Wintney Golf Club**, London Road, Hartley Wintney, Basingstoke RG27 8PT (01252 844211; Fax: 01252 844211). *Location*: on A30 between Camberley and Basingstoke. Parkland, wooded. 18 holes, 6240 yards. S.S.S. 71. Practice area. *Green Fees*: £25.00 per round, £35.00 per day. *Eating facilities*: full catering facilities available. *Visitors*: restricted Wednesdays (Ladies' Day); weekends and Bank Holidays with member only. *Society Meetings*: catered for Mondays, Tuesdays, Thursdays and Fridays on application. Professional: Martin Smith (01252 843779). Secretary: (Tel & Fax: 01252 844211).

HAVANT. **Rowlands Castle Golf Club**, 31 Links Lane, Rowlands Castle PO9 6AE (023 9241 2216). *Location*: four miles north of Havant or Horndean/ Rowlands Castle Junction from A3M. Flat parkland, wooded course. 18 holes, 6612 yards White Tees, 6386 yards Yellow Tees. S.S.S. 72 (White), 70 (Yellow). *Green Fees*: weekdays £34.00 per round/day; weekends £38.00. Subject to review. *Eating facilities*: full catering and bar facilities. *Visitors*: welcome, except Saturdays unless playing with a member, maximum 12 visitors on a Sunday and Bank Holidays. *Society Meetings*: catered for Tuesdays and Thursdays, bookings through Secretary. Professional: Peter Klepacz (023 9241 2785). Secretary: Mr K.D. Fisher (023 9241 2784).

HAYLING ISLAND. **The Hayling Golf Club**, Links Lane, Hayling Island PO11 0BX (023 9246 4491). *Location:* A3023 five miles south of Havant. Seaside links. 18 holes, 6531 yards, 5965 metres. S.S.S. 71. *Green Fees:* weekdays £40.00 per day, £32.00 per round; weekends £50.00 per day, £40.00 per round. Concessions for Juniors. Subject to review. *Eating facilities:* breakfasts, lunches and afternoon teas available and dinners by arrangement. *Visitors:* welcome with current Handicap Certificate and must be members of recognised clubs. *Society Meetings:* Tuesdays and Wednesdays only by arrangement with the Secretary. Professional: Ray Gadd (023 9246 4491). Secretary: C.J. Cavill (023 9246 4446; Fax: 02392 461119).
e-mail: hgcltd@aol.com
website: www.haylinggolf.co.uk

LEE-ON-THE-SOLENT. **Lee-On-The-Solent Golf Club**, Brune Lane, Lee-on-the-Solent PO13 9PB (023 9255 0207). *Location:* M27 Exit 9 eastbound, Exit 11 westbound, three miles south of Fareham. Flat parkland course. 18 holes, 5962 yards. S.S.S. 69. Practice range. *Green Fees:* weekdays £32.00; weekends £36.00. *Eating facilities:* full catering, extensive bar snack menu, lounge bar. *Visitors:* welcome weekdays, Handicap Certificate required. *Society Meetings:* welcome Thursdays, other days by special arrangement. Professional: Rob Edwards (023 9255 1181). Manager: Michael Topper (023 9255 1170; Fax: 023 9255 4233).

LIPHOOK. **Liphook Golf Club**, Wheatsheaf Enclosure, Liphook GU30 7EH (01428 723271; Fax: 01428 724853). *Location:* one mile south of Liphook on B2070 (old A3). Heathland. 18 holes, 6167 yards. S.S.S. 69. *Green Fees:* information not available. *Eating facilities:* bar and restaurant. *Visitors:* welcome, Handicap Certificate required, check with Secretary. Buggy available for hire. *Society Meetings:* catered for Wednesdays to Fridays. Professional: (01428 723271; Fax: 01428 724853). Secretary: Major J.B. Morgan MBE (01428 723785; Fax: 01428 724853).
e-mail: liphookgolfclub@btconnect.com

LIPHOOK. **Old Thorns Hotel, Golf & Country Club,** Longmoor Road, Liphook GU30 7PE (01428 724555). *Location:* A3 to Griggs Green then 500 yards on right. Parkland, wooded, with natural streams and lakes. 18 holes, 6529 yards. S.S.S. 72. Practice range, putting green, buggies, Pro shop. *Green Fees:* information not available. *Eating facilities:* choice of Sands Brasserie or award-winning Japanese Restaurant. *Visitors:* welcome at all times. *Society Meetings:* a range of golf days available for booking. Range of individual and corporate membership available. Facilities: 32 en suite bedrooms, indoor swimming pool, sauna, solarium, steam room, massage, fitness centre, treatment rooms, two tennis courts, conference and banqueting rooms. General Manager: Ken Flockhart. * website: www.oldthorns.com

LYNDHURST. **Bramshaw Golf Club,** Brook, Lyndhurst SO43 7HE (023 8081 3433). *Location:* M27 (Interchange 1) one mile from M27 (north) at Brook. Two courses: one parkland, one woodland. Both 18 holes. Forest Course 5774 yards. S.S.S. 68. Manor Course 6517 yards. S.S.S. 71. Practice facilities. *Green Fees:* contact club or check website for current rates. *Eating facilities:* clubhouse and restaurant, also Bell Inn close by. *Visitors:* welcome. Accommodation in 22 bedroomed hotel. *Society Meetings:* catered for by arrangement. Professional: Clive Bonner (023 8081 3434). General Manager: Bob Tingey (023 8081 3433). e-mail: golf@bramshaw.co.uk website: www.bramshaw.co.uk

LYNDHURST. **New Forest Golf Club,** Southampton Road, Lyndhurst SO43 7BU (023 8028 2752; Fax: 023 8028 2484). *Location:* on the A35 between Ashurst and Lyndhurst. Forest heathland course. 18 holes, 5772 yards. S.S.S. 69. Practice ground. *Green Fees:* weekdays £12.00 per round, £18.00 per day. Weekends £14.00 per round, £20.00 per day. *Eating facilities:* bar, dining room. *Visitors:* welcome, weekdays after 9am, Saturdays after 10am and Sunday afternoons. *Society Meetings:* advance booking only. Professional: Warren Butcher (07836 643975). Secretary: Mrs Barbara Shaw (Tel & Fax: 023 8028 2484)

PETERSFIELD. **Petersfield Golf Club (New Course)**, Tankerdale Lane, Liss GU33 7QY. *Location:* from the north, first turning left past the Liss exit on the Petersfield by-pass; from the south, leave by-pass at the Liss turn off (B3006), join the Southern dual carriage way then take the first turning left. Members club in Area of Outstanding Natural Beauty, gently undulating and wooded. 18 holes. White, 6450 yards, S.S.S. 71, Par 72. Yellow, 6000 yards, S.S.S. 69, Par 69. Red, 5447 yards, S.S.S. 71, Par 72. Practice ground, nets and putting green. *Green Fees:* weekdays £25.00 per round, weekends £30.00. Booking required at weekends. *Eating facilities:* full bar and catering service. *Visitors:* welcome, Handicap Certificate or proof of club membership required. Booking required for weekends via Professional. *Society Meetings:* welcome, see our website for details of packages. Professional: Greg Hughes (01730 895216). General Manager: Richard Hine (01730 261675; Fax: 01730 894713). website: www.petersfieldgolfclub.co.uk

PETERSFIELD. **Petersfield Golf Club (Pay & Play Course)**, Sussex Road, Petersfield. *Location:* from Petersfield, take the B2146 (Sussex Road), the club is situated on the right hand side, just past the car park for Heath Lake. 9 hole pay & play course (plans to extend to 12 holes during 2004). Level outside course. *Green Fees:* weekdays £7.00 per round, weekends £8.00 per round. *Eating facilities:* limited, tea, coffee and cold drinks available. *Visitors:* welcome, booking advisable, especially at weekends (01730 267732). Equipment hire available. General Manager: Richard Hine (01730 261675; Fax: 01730 894713). website: www.petersfieldgolfclub.co.uk

PORTSMOUTH. **Great Salterns Golf Course**, Burrfields Road, Portsmouth PO3 5JJ (023 9266 8667). *Location:* public golf course and home of Southsea Golf Club. South on A2030 off M27 signposted "Southsea". Flat meadow-land course. 18 holes, 5737 yards. S.S.S. 68. Floodlit driving range. *Green Fees:* information not available. *Eating facilities:* full bar and catering service at Farmhouse Pub next door. *Visitors:* always welcome, tee time booking required one week ahead. Innlodge Hotel overlooks 18th green (73 bedrooms). *Society Meetings:* welcome, administered by Noreen Jefferies. Professional: Terry Healy (023 9266 4549; Fax: 023 9265 0525).

PORTSMOUTH. **Portsmouth Golf Club (1926)**, Crookhorn Lane, Widley, Waterlooville PO7 5QL (023 9237 2210). *Location:* two thirds of a mile from junction of B2177 and A3. Hilly course with views of harbour; outstanding 6th hole. 18 holes, 6139 yards. S.S.S. 70. Practice ground, putting green. *Green Fees:* £14.00. Reduced rates for juniors and over 60s. *Eating facilities:* full restaurant and bar. *Visitors:* welcome, tee bookings required. *Society Meetings:* welcome by prior arrangement with Pro Shop. Professional: Jason Banting (023 9237 2210; Fax: 023 9220 0766). Secretary: D. Houlihan (023 9220 1827).

PORTSMOUTH. **Waterlooville Golf Club**, Cherry Tree Avenue, Cowplain, Waterlooville PO8 8AP (023 9226 3388; Fax: 023 9234 7513). *Location:* off A3 or A3 (M), 10 miles north of Portsmouth. Parkland course. 18 holes, 6602 yards. S.S.S. 72. *Green Fees:* £30.00 per round, £35.00 per day, weekdays only. *Eating facilities:* full catering service available, bar facilities. *Visitors:* welcome weekdays, weekends as members' guests only. *Society Meetings:* Thursdays only by prior arrangement. Professional: John Hay (Tel & Fax: 023 9225 6911). Secretary: David Nairne.

RINGWOOD. **Burley Golf Club**, Cott Lane, Burley, Ringwood BH24 4BB (01425 402431/403737; Fax: 01425 404168). *Location:* A31 from Ringwood and turn right at Picket Post and on through Burley Street. Open heathland course in the New Forest. 9 holes, 6149 yards. S.S.S. 69, Par 71. *Green Fees:* weekdays £16.00 per round (£10.00 with member), £20.00 per day; weekends and Bank Holidays £20.00 per round (£15.00 with member), £25.00 per day. Under 18s £8.00 per round weekdays, £9.00 per round weekends. Weekly ticket £75.00. *Eating facilities:* bar open, food available lunchtimes most days. *Visitors:* welcome, but not before 4pm Saturdays, 8am Sundays, and 1.45pm Wednesdays. Handicap Certificates preferred. *Society Meetings:* limited to 14 players Tuesdays or Fridays. Secretary: Mr G.J. Stride (01425 402431; Fax: 01425 404168). e-mail: secretary@burleygolfclub.fsnet.co.uk

RINGWOOD. **Moors Valley Golf Course**, Horton Road, Ashley Heath, Ringwood BH24 2ET (01425 479776). *Location:* signposted from A338/A31 roundabout. Parkland course set in the valley of the Moors River. 18 holes, 6337 yards. S.S.S. 72. 4 hole Par 3 course, full size pitching green and practice nets. *Green Fees:* Monday to Thursday off-peak £15.00 (excluding Bank Holidays); Friday, Saturday, Sunday and Bank Holidays £19.00. *Eating facilities:* snack bar and bar. *Visitors:* welcome. *Society Meetings:* welcome by arrangement. Professional: James Daniels (Tel & Fax: 01425 479776). Secretary: Desmond Meharg (Tel: 01425 479776).

ROMSEY. **Dunwood Manor Golf Club**, Danes Road, Awbridge, Near Romsey SO51 0GF (01794 340549; Fax: 01794 341215). *Location:* four miles from Romsey off A27. Undulating parkland - five new holes now in play. 18 holes, 5767 yards. S.S.S. 68. Practice area. *Green Fees:* £25.00 per round, £37.00 per day weekdays; £30.00 per round weekends after 11am. Society rates from £29.00. *Eating facilities:* full catering, all day bar. *Visitors:* welcome by prior arrangement. Self-catering accommodation for up to 32 people available. *Society Meetings:* welcome by prior arrangement. Professional: Heath Teschner (01794 340663; Fax: 01794 341215). Secretary: Roger Basford (01794 340549; Fax: 01794 341215).

ROMSEY. **Paultons Golf Centre,** Old Salisbury Road, Ower, Near Romsey SO51 6AN (023 8081 3345; Fax: 023 8081 3993). *Location:* off M27 at Junction 2, A36 towards Salisbury, at first roundabout take first exit, then first right at the Vine Public House. Parkland/woodland laid out within the original grounds of Paulton House, landscaped by Capability Brown. 18 holes, 6200 yards, 5670 metres. S.S.S. 71. 9-hole academy course. 24-bay floodlit driving range. *Green Fees:* information not available. *Visitors:* welcome anytime. *Society Meetings:* welcome anytime with prior booking. Professional/ Secretary: R. Park.*

ROMSEY. **Wellow Golf Club,** Ryedown Lane, East Wellow, Romsey SO51 6BD (01794 322872; Fax: 01794 323832). *Location:* M27 Junction 2 - A36 Salisbury, one mile right to East Wellow, one mile right Ryedown Lane. Parkland. 27 holes (three loops of 9 holes). S.S.S. 69, 70, 68. Large practice ground. *Green Fees:* weekdays £17.00; weekends £21.00. *Eating facilities:* full catering and bar facilities available all day. *Visitors:* welcome - advise phone to confirm availability. Correct dress code must be observed. *Society Meetings:* all welcome. Professional: Mr Neil Bratley (01794 323833). Secretary: Mrs C. Gurd.

SHEDFIELD. **Marriott Meon Valley Hotel and Country Club Resort,** Sandy Lane, Shedfield, Southampton SO32 2HQ (01329 833455; Fax: 01329 834411). *Location:* leave M27 at Exit 7, take A334 to Botley then towards Wickham. Sandy Lane is 2 miles on the left. Wooded course. 18 holes, 6520 yards. S.S.S. 71. 9 holes, 2714 yards. S.S.S. 34. Covered practice area. *Green Fees:* weekdays £44.00; weekends £48.00. *Eating facilities:* Treetops Restaurant, The Long Weekend Restaurant and three bars. *Visitors:* welcome, no restrictions. Handicap Certificates required to play. 113 bedroomed 4 Star Hotel. *Society Meetings:* welcome, arranged in advance. Professional: Rod Cameron (01329 832184; Fax: 01329 834411). Director of Golf: George McMenemy (01329 833455; Fax: 01329 834411).

SOUTHAMPTON. **Botley Park Golf Club,** Winchester Road, Botley, Southampton SO3 2UA (01489 780888; Fax: 01489 789242). *Location:* approximately two miles from Junction 7 on M27. Parkland. 18 holes, 6341 yards. S.S.S. 70. Driving range. *Green Fees:* information not available. *Eating facilities:* two bars, main restaurant and club lounge. *Visitors:* welcome by prior booking by phone. Handicap Certificate required. 100 bedroomed hotel on site; tennis, squash, swimming, sauna, solarium, steam room, fitness suite, beauty spa, snooker. Dance studio. *Society Meetings:* weekdays only. Professional: Kevin Caplehorn (01489 789771; Fax: 01489 789242). Secretary/Golf Manager: Justine Hopper (01489 796000).

SOUTHAMPTON. **Chilworth Golf Club**, Main Road, Chilworth, Southampton SO16 7JP (02380 740544; Fax: 02380 733166). *Location*: situated off the A27. Parkland course. 18 holes, 5837 yards, S.S.S. 68. Covered driving range. *Green Fees*: weekdays 18 holes £12.00, 9 holes £6.00; weekends 18 holes £15.00, 9 holes £7.50. *Eating facilities*: bar. *Visitors*: welcome, must follow dress code, please telephone for details. Pro shop. Tuition available. Professional: Darren Newing. Secretary: Fred Bendal.

SOUTHAMPTON. **Corhampton Golf Club**, Corhampton, Southampton SO32 3LP (01489 877279; Fax: 01489 877680). *Location:* one mile from Corhampton on the Bishops Waltham - Corhampton road (B3135). Free draining downland course. 18 holes, 6444 yards. S.S.S. 71. Large practice ground. *Green Fees:* weekdays £30.00 per round, £40.00 per day; weekends £15.00 with a member only. *Eating facilities:* full catering. *Visitors:* welcome Monday to Friday; weekends and Bank Holidays with a member. Buggies and trolleys for hire. *Society Meetings:* Mondays and Thursdays. Professional: Ian Roper (01489 877638; Fax: 01489 877680).

SOUTHAMPTON. **Romsey Golf Club Ltd**, Nursling, Southampton SO16 0XW (023 8073 4637; Fax: 023 8074 1036). *Location:* two miles south east of Romsey on A3057, M27/M271 Junction 3. Well wooded, undulating course with extremely good views. 18 holes, 5856 yards. S.S.S. 68. *Green Fees:* weekdays £27.50 per round, £33.00 per day; weekends with a member only. *Eating facilities:* bar and restaurant. *Visitors:* welcome weekdays only. *Society Meetings:* welcome Mondays, Tuesdays or Thursdays only. Professional: Mark Desmond (023 8073 6673). Secretary: Michael Batty.

SOUTHAMPTON. **Southampton Golf Club** (Play over the Municipal Golf Course), Golf Course Road, Bassett, Southampton (023 8076 7942). *Location:* off Bassett Avenue. Parkland course. 18 holes, 6218 yards, S.S.S. 70. 9 hole Par 32. Practice area and putting greens. *Green Fees:* information not provided. *Eating facilities:* bar and full catering (023 8076 7996). *Visitors:* welcome but must book at weekends - three and four ball play only at weekends, book through manager. Professional: L. Booth (023 8076 8407). Secretary: D. J. Campbell. (023 8076 8407). Bookings: (023 8076 0546).

SOUTHAMPTON. **Stoneham Golf Club,** Monks Wood Close, Bassett, Southampton SO16 3TT (023 8076 9272). *Location:* A33/M27 north of Southampton find Chilworth roundabout, take road to Airport (A27), half mile on left. Undulating parkland course, used for Brabazon Trophy 1993, English County Finals 1998 and English Ladies' Championship 2001. 18 holes, 6387 yards. S.S.S. 70. *Green Fees:* weekdays £35.00 per round, £40.00 per day; weekends £45.00 per round, £57.00 per day. *Eating facilities:* full catering, bar open all day. *Visitors:* welcome, except competition days. *Society Meetings:* catered for Monday, Thursday and Friday by arrangement. Professional: Ian Young (023 8076 8397). Manager: Richard Penley-Martin (023 8076 9272; Fax: 023 8076 6320).

WINCHESTER. **Hockley Golf Club,** Twyford, Near Winchester SO21 1PL (01962 713165; Fax: 01962 713612). *Location:* 100 yards Junction 11 M3 motorway. Downland with excellent views of Winchester and surrounding areas. James Braid designed course, long vistas. 18 holes, 6336 yards. S.S.S. 71. Large practice ground. *Green Fees:* April to September £35.00 per 18 holes, £45.00 per day; October to March £45.00 per 18 holes, £48.00 per 36 holes. *Eating facilities:* full catering and bar facilities. *Visitors:* welcome. Handicap Certificate required. *Society Meetings:* welcome by prior arrangement. Professional: (01962 713678). Secretary: Mrs Lyn Dyer. e-mail: secretary@hockleygolfclub.com website: www.hockleygolfclub.org.uk

WINCHESTER. **Otterbourne Golf Centre**, Poles Lane, Otterbourne, Winchester SO21 1DZ (Tel & Fax: 01962 775225). Parkland course. 9 holes, 1939 yards, S.S.S. 30. 10 bay uncovered driving range. *Green Fees:* information not available. *Visitors:* welcome, pay as you play. Tuition available. *Society Meetings:* open to discussion. Professional: Garry Stubbington.*

WINCHESTER. **The Park Golf Course,** Avington, Winchester SO21 1DA (01962 779945; Fax: 01962 779530). *Location:* 5 miles east of Winchester. Mature parkland course. 9 holes, 1907 yards, S.S.S. 58. *Green Fees:* information not available. *Visitors:* always welcome, please telephone to book. *

WINCHESTER. **Royal Winchester Golf Club,** Sarum Road, Winchester SO22 5QE (01962 852462). *Location:* from Junction 11 M3 follow signs to Oliver's Battery. At Pitt roundabout follow signs to Winchester then left into Kilham Lane. At end turn right into Sarum Road. Traditional downland course. 18 holes, 6216yards, 5685 metres. S.S.S. 70. *Green Fees:* weekdays 18 holes £46.00; weekends with member only. *Eating facilities:* full catering and bar facilities available. *Visitors:* welcome weekdays, Handicap Certificate required. *Society Meetings:* by prior arrangement. Professional: Steven Hunter (01962 862473). Secretary: Andrew Buck (01962 852462; Fax: 01962 865048). e-mail: manager@royalwinchestergolfclub.com website: www.royalwinchestergolfclub.com

WINCHESTER. **South Winchester Golf Club**, Romsey Road, Pitt, Winchester SO22 5QX (01962 877800; Fax: 01962 877900). *Location:* situated between Winchester and Hursley in the village of Pitt. Championship links-style course - home of the Hampshire PGA. 18 holes, 7086 yards. S.S.S. 74. Driving range. Chipping green, practice bunker and practice green. *Green Fees:* call Pro-shop for details (01962 840469). *Eating facilities:* two bars, one dining room, one conservatory/dining room, food available all day. *Visitors:* visiting golfers welcome. Golf days for non members by arrangement with the Professional. Professional: Richard Adams (01962 840469). General Manager: Laurence Ross website: www.crown-golf.co.uk

Herefordshire

BELMONT. **Belmont Lodge and Golf,** Belmont, Hereford HR2 9SA (01432 352666; Fax: 01432 358090). *Location:* one and a half miles south of Hereford, off A465 to Abergavenny. Parkland running alongside the River Wye offering tremendous views. 18 holes, 6511 yards. S.S.S. 72. *Green Fees:* weekdays from £12.00; weekends from £15.00. Twilight ticket after 3pm. *Eating facilities:* restaurant meals and bar snacks. *Visitors:* welcome at all times, advisable to check availability first. Other facilities available include a 30 bedroomed hotel, bowls, tennis, fishing and walking; buggies and trolleys for hire. *Society Meetings:* catered for, special packages available. Professional: Mike Welsh (01432 352717). Reception/Reservaions: (01432 352666; Fax: 01432 358090).
e-mail: info@belmont-hereford.co.uk
website: www.belmont-hereford.co.uk

HAY-ON-WYE. **Summerhill Golf Course,** Clifford, Near Hay-on-Wye HR3 5EW (01497 820451). *Location:* half a mile out of Hay on B4350 for Clifford and Whitney Toll Bridge and Hereford Road A438. Parkland. 9 holes 2929 yards (18 holes, 5858 off white tees). S.S.S. 68. 3 Hole par 3 course opening 2002. *Green Fees:* weekdays £12.00, weekends £15.00. *Eating facilities:* restaurant, two bars and large function room. *Visitors:* welcome, not on Thursday evening or Sunday mornings. *Society Meetings:* welcome Monday, Wednesday and Friday, £10.00 for society bookings of over eight in number. Professional: Mr Andy Gealy. Secretary: Mr Mike Tom.

HEREFORD. **Burghill Valley Golf Club,** Tillington Road, Burghill, Hereford HR4 7RW (01432 760456; Fax: 01432 761654). *Location:* three miles north-west of Hereford. From Worcester and North (avoiding Hereford city), take A4103 for two miles, first right after traffic lights. From south (via Hereford city) take A4110, turn left at traffic lights after Three Elms Inn and then first right. Follow signs to club. Pleasantly undulating parkland including two lakes, and easy walking with some interesting holes through mature cider orchards. 18 holes, 6239 yards. S.S.S. 70.

Large practice area. *Green Fees:* weekdays £20.00; weekends £27.00. *Eating facilities:* bar and dining room with full catering available every day. *Visitors:* welcome at any time, must book tee time with Professional. *Society Meetings:* by prior arrangement with the Manager. Special rates available, please enquire. Professional: Nigel Clarke PGA (01432 760808; Fax: 01432 761654). General Manager: Keith Smith.
e-mail: golf@bvgc.co.uk
website: www.bvgc.co.uk

HEREFORD. **The Herefordshire Golf Club**, Ravens Causeway, Wormsley, Hereford HR4 8LY (01432 830219). *Location:* six miles north-west of Hereford on a B road to Weobley. Undulating parkland course. 18 holes, 6031 yards. S.S.S. 69. *Green Fees:* information available on request. *Eating facilities:* catering available at all times. *Visitors:* welcome. *Society Meetings:* welcome, packages arranged through Secretary. Professional: (01432 830465). Secretary: (01432 830219).

HEREFORD. **Hereford Municipal Golf Course,** Hereford Leisure Centre, Holmer Road, Hereford HR4 9UD (01432 344376; Fax: 01432 266281). *Location:* follow A49 Leominster to Hereford road; north of city centre next to Leisure Centre. Flat parkland course with excellent greens all year round. 9 holes, 3060 yards. S.S.S. 69 for 18 holes. Large practice area, bunker and practice green. *Green Fees:* please ring for details. *Eating facilities:* full catering and bar in Leisure Centre. *Visitors:* welcome at all times. *Society Meetings:* welcome, prices on application. Professional: Gary Morgan (01432 344376; Fax: 01432 266281).

KINGTON. **Kington Golf Club,** Bradnor Hill, Kington HR5 3RE (01544 230340). *Location*: one mile out of Kington, on B4355 to Presteigne. Easy walking hill course with superb greens and views over seven counties. Highest 18 hole course in England. 18 holes, 5820 yards. S.S.S. 68. *Green Fees:* weekdays £16.00 per round, £22.00 per day; weekends and Bank Holidays £21.00 per round, £27.00 per day. *Eating facilities:* full catering and bar facilities. *Visitors:* welcome. Please contact Professional to ensure course is available. *Society Meetings:* by arrangement with the Professional. Professional: Andy Gealy (01544 231320). Secretary: Glyn R. Wictome (Tel & Fax: 01544 340270).

LEOMINSTER. **Grove Golf Centre,** Fordbridge, Leominster HR6 0LE (01568 610602). *Location:* three miles south of Leominster on A49. Challenging wooded course with many water features, U.S.G.A. spec greens. 9 holes, 1780 yards. S.S.S. 60. New 9 holes opening 2004, S.S.S.72. Floodlit, covered driving range. Golf shop. *Green Fees:* information not available. *Eating facilities:* full catering and bar. *Visitors:* welcome anytime. Professional: Phil Brookes (01568 615333).

LEOMINSTER. **Leominster Golf Club,** Ford Bridge, Leominster HR6 0LE (01568 610055). *Location:* three miles south of Leominster on A49 bypass, clearly signed. Undulating parkland with some holes alongside River Lugg and extensive views over Herefordshire countryside. 18 holes, 6025 yards. S.S.S. 69. Driving range adjacent to course. *Green Fees:* weekdays £15.50 per round, £19.00 per day; Mondays and Fridays £8.00 after 9.30am; weekends £22.00 per round, £25.00 per day. *Eating facilities:* bar open daily, full catering daily except Mondays when bar snacks only available. *Visitors:* welcome every day; please telephone to check availability. Trolley and buggy hire available. *Society Meetings:* most welcome. Full weekday £29.00, weekends £34.00 golf and catering. Professional: Andrew Ferriday (01568 611402). Secretary: Les Green (Tel & Fax: 01568 610055). Manager: Jessica Kingswood.

ROSS-ON-WYE. **The Ross-on-Wye Golf Club,** Gorsley, Ross-on-Wye HR9 7UT (01989 720267; Fax: 01989 720212). *Location:* adjacent Junction 3 M50, five miles east of Ross-on-Wye. Tree lined, undulating parkland course. 18 holes, 6491 yards. S.S.S. 71. Driving range, practice area. *Green Fees:* £38.00 per round. £48.00 per day. Societies: £32.00 for 18 holes, £38.00 for 27 holes. *Eating facilities:* full restaurant catering, excluding Mondays. *Visitors:* welcome any day if prior arrangement made with Professional or Secretary. Snooker tables (2). *Society Meetings:* welcome, minimum 16. Tee reservations Wednesdays to Fridays. Professional: Nick Catchpole (01989 720439). Secretary: P.H. Plumb (01989 720267; Fax: 01989 720212). e-mail: secretary@therossonwyegolfclub.co.uk website: www.therossonwyegolfclub.co.uk

ROSS-ON-WYE. **South Herefordshire Golf Club,** Twin Lakes, Upton Bishop, Ross-on-Wye HR9 7UA (01989 780535; Fax: 01989 740611). *Location:* end roundabout of M50 at Ross take B4221 to Upton Bishop, in Upton Bishop turn right, club half a mile. Good test of golf for all standards with variety of holes. Superb views. No temporary greens in Winter. 18 holes S.S.S. 72. 16 bay covered, floodlit driving range. *Green Fees:* weekdays £15.00; weekends £20.00. *Eating facilities:* fully licensed bar serving snacks and full meals. *Visitors:* always welcome, no restrictions. Ring to reserve tee time. Buggies and trolleys available. *Society Meetings:* always welcome; weekend prices from £19.00 for day's golf. Manager: Edward Litchfield. e-mail: shgc.golf@clara.co.uk

Hertfordshire

BARKWAY. **Barkway Park Golf Club,** Nuthampstead Road, Barkway SG8 8EN (01763 849070). *Location:* A10 north from M25 for 15 miles, B1368 to Barkway 8 miles. Inland links. 18 holes, 6997 yards. S.S.S. 74. Practice areas. *Green Fees:* information not available. *Eating facilities:* bar, restaurant. *Visitors:* welcome at all times. *Society Meetings:* always welcome. Professional: Jamie Bates. Secretary: Val Sadler. *

BARNET. **Arkley Golf Club**, Rowley Green Road, Barnet EN5 3HL (Fax: 020 8440 5214). *Location:* follow A411 from A1 Stirling Corner towards Barnet, left into Rowley Lane. Wooded parkland.9 holes, 6117 yards. S.S.S. 69. Practice ground. *Green Fees:* weekdays £25.00 per round/day; weekends with a member only £12.00. *Eating facilities:* available, no catering Mondays. *Visitors:* welcome weekdays, please phone Professional. *Society Meetings:* catered for Wednesdays, Thursdays and Fridays; special rates available. Professional: Martin Porter (020 8440 8473). Secretary: Mr Campbell (020 8449 0394).

BARNET. **Hadley Wood Golf Club**, Beech Hill, Near Barnet EN4 0JJ (020 8449 4328). *Location:* off the exit from M25 at Junction 24 on to A111 Cockfosters. Down hill, third turning on the right. Very attractive undulating parkland with lakes. 18 holes, 6506 yards. S.S.S. 71. Practice range open to members and green fees only. Chipping and putting areas. *Green Fees:* on application. *Eating facilities:* available weekdays. *Visitors:* welcome weekdays, (not Tuesday a.m.), with club Handicap Certificate or letter of introduction. *Society Meetings:* corporate and society days catered for weekdays except Tuesday mornings and Wednesdays. Professional: Peter Jones (020 8449 3285). General Manager: Chris S. Silcox (020 8449 4328; Fax: 020 8364 8633).
e-mail: gen.mgr@hadleywoodgc.com
website: www.hadleywoodgc.com

BERKHAMSTED. **Ashridge Golf Club,** Little Gaddesden, Berkhamsted HP4 1LY (01442 842379). *Location:* on B450, five miles north west of Berkhamsted. Parkland. 18 holes, 6580 yards. Par 72. Practice area, putting green. *Green Fees:* on application. *Eating facilities:* dining room and spike bar, 2 lounges. *Visitors:* welcome with reservation weekdays only. *Society Meetings:* welcome. Professional: Andrew Ainsworth (01442 842307). Secretary: Martin S. Silver (01442 842244; Fax: 01442 843770).
e-mail: info@ashridgegolfclub.ltd.uk
website: www.ashridgegolfclub.ltd.uk

BERKHAMSTED. **Berkhamsted Golf Club**, The Common, Berkhamsted HP4 2QB (01442 865832; Fax: 01442 863730). *Location:* A41 to Berkhamsted, up past the castle to the common. Heathland, wooded, grass bunkers. 18 holes, 6605 yards. S.S.S. 72. Two practice grounds. *Green Fees:* weekdays £37.00 per round, £50.00 per day; weekends £45.00 per round after 11.30am. (2003 prices subject to review). *Eating facilities:* bar and restaurant. *Visitors:* welcome, best to phone first. Handicap Certificate required. *Society Meetings:* catered for Mondays, Wednesdays and Fridays. Professional: John Clarke (01442 865851). Secretary: Barry Hill (01442 865832).

BISHOP'S STORTFORD. Bishop's Stortford Golf Club, Dunmow Road, Bishop's Stortford CM23 5HP (01279 654027). *Location*: M11 Junction 8, follow signs for Bishop's Stortford, entrance quarter of a mile on left. Undulating parkland, fairly flat: well-established course and a true test of golf. 18 holes, 6404 yards. S.S.S. 71. *Green Fees*: weekdays £30.00 per round, £39.00 per day, 27 holes £35.00; weekends as guest of member. *Eating facilities*: restaurant and bar service. *Visitors*: welcome weekdays including Public Holidays; weekends with member only. Valid Handicap Certificate required. *Society Meetings*: catered for weekdays except Tuesdays (minimum 12). Special rates available. Professional: Stephen M. Bryan (01279 651324). Secretary: Barry Collins (01279 654715; Fax: 01279 655215). e-mail: office@bsgc.co.uk
website: www.bsgc.co.uk

BISHOP'S STORTFORD. **Great Hadham Golf and Country Club,** Great Hadham Road, Much Hadham, Near Bishop's Stortford SG10 6JE (01279 843558; Fax: 01279 842122). *Location:* two miles west of Bishop's Stortford on the B1004, four miles west of Junction 8 M11 motorway. Rolling meadowland course. 18 holes, 6854 yards. S.S.S. 73. Three Par 3 practice holes, practice bunker, 18 bay driving range. *Green Fees:* information not available. *Eating facilities:* well stocked bar, comfortable lounge and dining room/spike bar. *Visitors:* welcome weekdays (Ladies' Day Wednesday mornings), weekends after 12 noon. Health Club with fitness centre facilities. *Society Meetings:* welcome weekdays. Professional: Kevin Lunt. Secretary: Ian Bailey.

BROXBOURNE. **The Hertfordshire Golf & Country Club,** Broxbournebury Mansion EN10 7PY (01992 466666; Fax: 01992 470326). *Location:* 10 minutes north on A10 from Junction 25 of M25 take Broxbourne exit, third left Bell Lane, over A10 right hand side. 18 hole "Nicklaus" design set around a Grade II Listed clubhouse, full USGA Specifications - irrigated and drained. 18 holes, 6388 yards. S.S.S. 70. 30 bay floodlit driving range. *Green Fees*: information not available. *Eating facilities:* Spike Bar, Cocktail Bar. Health club, golf academy, indoor and outdoor tennis courts, indoor swimming pool. *Visitors:* welcome weekdays, weekends restricted. *Society Meetings:* welcome. Head Teaching Professional: David Smith. Head Professional: Russell Hind. Pro Shop: (01992 441268). General Manager: James Hetherington.*

BUNTINGFORD. **East Herts Golf Club Ltd,** Hamels Park, Buntingford SG9 9NA (01920 821923). *Location:* one mile north of Puckeridge on A10. 18 holes, 6456 yards. S.S.S. 71. *Green Fees:* details on application. *Eating facilities:* separate restaurant. *Visitors:* welcome, with members only at weekends. *Society Meetings:* catered for weekdays. Professional: G. Culmer (01920 821922). Secretary:Colin Day (01920 821978; Fax: 01920 823700). e-mail: secretary@ehgc.fsnet.co.uk

BUSHEY. **Bushey Country Club,** High Street, Bushey WD23 1TT (020 8950 2215). *Location:* Junction 5 of M1 onto A41, south to second roundabout, turn right to Bushey Heath; take A411 towards Watford, entrance down hill on left. 9 holes. Par 70. Driving range. *Green Fees:* information not available. *Eating facilities:* bar and dining facilities open from 8am to 11pm. *Visitors:* welcome. *Society Meetings:* welcome. Professional: G. Atkinson.

BUSHEY. **Bushey Hall Golf Club,** Bushey Hall Drive, Bushey WD23 2EP (01923 222253; Fax: 01923 229759). *Location:* one mile from M1 Junction 5, off Aldenham Road roundabout. Undulating parkland. 18 holes, 6099 yards, 6670 metres. S.S.S. 69. Practice nets, putting green. *Green Fees:* weekdays £25.00, weekends £32.00. *Eating facilities:* full catering available, two bars. *Visitors:* welcome, no restrictions. *Society Meetings:* catered for weekdays. Professional: Ken Wickham (01923 225802). Secretary/Manager: Roy Penman (01923 222253). e-mail: info@golfclubuk.co.uk website: www.golfclubuk.co.uk

BUSHEY HEATH. **Hartsbourne Golf and Country Club,** Hartsbourne Avenue, Bushey Heath WD2 1JW (020 8950 1133; Fax: 020 8950 5357). *Location:* five miles south east of Watford. Parkland. 18 holes,

6385 yards. S.S.S. 70. 9 holes, 5773 yards. S.S.S. 68. *Green Fees:* information not available. *Eating facilities:* restaurant and snack bar available. *Visitors:* guests of members only. *Society Meetings:* catered for Mondays and Fridays. Professional: Alistair Cardwell (020 8950 2836). General Manager: Shaughn Whyte (020 8950 1133 or 4346; Fax: 020 8950 5357). *

CHORLEYWOOD. **Chorleywood Golf Club Ltd.,** Common Road, Chorleywood WD3 5LN (01923 282009; Fax: 01923 286739). *Location:* half a mile from Junction 18 of M25 via A404, three miles from Rickmansworth. A challenging mix of heath and woodland with natural hazards. 9 holes, 5686 yards. S.S.S. 67. *Green Fees:* £20.00 weekdays, £25.00 weekends. *Eating facilities:* meals available at most times. *Visitors:* welcome weekdays except Tuesday mornings, restricted at weekends. *Society Meetings:* contact Secretary for details. Secretary: Rod Botham (01923 282009; Fax: 01923 286739). e-mail: chorleywood.gc@btclick.com

DAGNALL. **Whipsnade Park Golf Club,** Studham Lane, Dagnall HP4 1RH (0144-284 2330/2331; Fax: 0144-284 2090). *Location:* between Dagnall and Studham. Junction 11 M1 (from north), Junction 9 (from south). Parkland. 18 holes, 6800 yards. S.S.S. 72. Large practice area. *Green Fees:* £28.00 per round, £38.00 per day weekdays, weekends with member only. *Eating facilities:* restaurant open daily, two bars. *Visitors:* welcome weekdays with reservation. *Society Meetings:* welcome with reservation. Professional: Daren Turner (0144-284 2310). Secretary: Andrea King (0144-284 2330). e-mail: whipsnadepark@talk21.com website: www.whipsnadeparkgc.co.uk

ELSTREE. **Elstree Golf and Country Club**, Watling Street, Elstree WD6 3AA (020 8953 6115; Fax: 020 8207 6390). *Location:* between Radlett and Elstree. Watling Street is also known as A5 (A5183) road. Close to M1, M25, A41, A1 (map available on request). Parkland course - undulating with ponds and ditches. 18 holes, 6556 yards. S.S.S. 72. 60 bay driving range. *Green Fees*: weekdays £27.50, weekends £33.00, subject to change. Please check for special offers. *Eating facilities:* bar, restaurant, conservatory available all day. *Visitors:* welcome weekdays anytime, weekends after 10.30am. Buggy and trolley hire, lockers/showers; large car park. Conference and function facilities. *Society Meetings*: welcome, information pack sent on request. Professionals: Marc Warwick, Mark Wood. Managing Director: Dean Cottrell. Secretary: Kathy Roberts (020 8238 6942). e-mail: admin@elstree-golf.co.uk website: www.elstree-golfclub.co.uk

HARPENDEN. **Aldwickbury Park Golf Club,** Piggottshill Lane, Harpenden AL5 1AB (01582 760112; Fax: 01582 760113). *Location:* east of Harpenden on the Wheathampstead Road, Luton and St. Albans 10 minutes' drive. Rolling parkland with mature woodland. Two courses. Park Course – 18 holes, 6350 yards. S.S.S. 70. Manor Course – 9 holes, 1000 yards. Par 3. Practice area. *Green Fees:* weekdays £26.00; weekends £30.00 afternoons only. Twilight ticket £12.00. *Eating facilities:* licensed bar/restaurant and all day snack menu available. *Visitors:* welcome, call first; no weekend mornings play. PGA tuition, buggies and trolleys for hire. *Society Meetings:* welcome weekdays, please call for further details/prices. Professional: Paul Toyer (01582 760112; Fax: 01582 760113). Secretary: Allan Knott (01582 765112; Fax: 01582 760113). website: www.aldwickburyparkgolfclub.com

HARPENDEN. **Harpenden Common Golf Club,** East Common, Harpenden AL5 1BL (01582 711320). *Location:* on A1081 between Harpenden and St. Albans. Flat heathland. 18 holes, 6214 yards. S.S.S. 70. *Green Fees:* weekdays £25.00 per round, £30.00 per day; weekends £30.00 per round. *Eating facilities:* bar and restaurant daily. *Visitors:* welcome weekdays (not Tuesdays) and weekends. *Society Meetings:* Thursday and Friday only. Professional: D. Fitzsimmons (01582 460655). Manager: Peter Clarke (01582 711320; Fax: 01582 711321) e-mail: admin@hcgc.co.uk

HARPENDEN. **Harpenden Golf Club,** Hammonds End, Redbourn Lane, Harpenden AL5 2AX (01582 712580; Fax: 01582 712725). *Location:* turn off A1081, four miles after St. Albans on B487. Parkland course. 18 holes, 6381 yards. S.S.S. 70. *Green Fees:* weekdays £26.00 per round, £36.00 per day; weekends £30.00 per round. *Eating facilities:* snacks and lunches, order in advance. *Visitors:* welcome weekdays and weekends strictly by arrangement. *Society Meetings:* by arrangement only. Professional: Peter Cherry (01582 767124; Fax: 01582 712725). General Manager: Frank Clapp.

HATFIELD. **Brookmans Park Golf Club,** Golf Club Road, Brookmans Park, Hatfield AL9 7AT (01707 652459; Fax: 01707 661851). *Location:* A1000, just north of Potters Bar; M25 Junction 24. Parkland, two lakes. 18 holes, 6249 yards. S.S.S. 71. Practice ground and putting green. *Green Fees:* weekdays £32.00 per round, £42.00 per day; weekends with a member only. Handicap Certificate required. *Eating facilities:* bar snacks and lunches weekdays. *Visitors:* welcome weekdays; weekends with member only. *Society Meetings:* catered for Wednesdays and Thursdays. Professional: Ian Jelley (01707 652468). Secretary: Peter A. Gill (01707 652487; Fax: 01707 661851).

HATFIELD. **Hatfield London Country Club,** Bedwell Park, Essendon, Hatfield AL9 6HN (01707 260360; Fax: 01707 278475). *Location:* four miles south of Junction 4 A1(M), five miles north east of Junction 24 M25 Potters Bar. 9 holes Pitch and Putt. 36 holes (Old Course, 18 holes, 6808 yards, Par 72; New Course, 18 holes, 6938 yards, Par 72). Practice ground. *Green Fees:* information not provided. *Eating facilities:* bar and restaurant with full catering available. *Visitors:* welcome, advance bookings only. *Society Meetings:* always welcome.

HEMEL HEMPSTEAD. **Boxmoor Golf Club,** 18 Box Lane, Boxmoor, Hemel Hempstead HP3 0DJ (01442 242434). *Location:* two miles from Hemel Hempstead, three-quarters of a mile from Hemel Hempstead Station on A41. Hilly/moorland course, 9 holes, 4112 yards. S.S.S. 62. *Green Fees:* information not available. *Eating facilities:* ring Steward. *Visitors:* welcome without reservation, except on Sundays. *Society Meetings:* catered for on application. Secretary: G. Newark. *

HEMEL HEMPSTEAD. **Little Hay Golf Complex,** Box Lane, Hemel Hempstead HP3 0DQ (01442 833798). *Location:* just off A41, along Chesham Road from Hemel Hempstead. Parkland. 18 holes, 6678 yards. S.S.S. 72. 9 hole pitch & putt course, short game practrice area, floodlit driving range. *Green Fees:* information not provided. *Eating facilities:* available, open all day. *Visitors:* welcome. *Society Meetings:* welcome by arrangement. Professionals: Nick Allen and Michael Perry (01442 833798). Complex Manager: Chris Gordon (01442 833798).

HEMEL HEMPSTEAD. **Shendish Manor Golf Club,** London Road, Apsley, Hemel Hempstead HP3 0AA (01442 251806; Fax: 01442 230683). *Location:* Two miles from J20 M25 on the west side of A4251 London Road (ex A41) between Kings Langley and Hemel Hempstead. Mature parkland course. 18 holes, 5660 yards. S.S.S. 67 (Par 70). 9 hole pitch and putt course. *Green Fees:* information not available. *Eating facilities:* Sportsman's bar and Brasserie. *Visitors:* no restrictions, please telephone to ensure tee time. Conference and full banqueting facilities, health club and putting green. *Society Meetings:* welcome seven days a week. Professional: Murray White (01442 251806). Secretary: Ralph Thornberry.*

HERTFORD. **Brickendon Grange Golf Club,** Brickendon, Near Hertford SG13 8PD (01992 511258; Fax: 01992 511411). *Location:* three miles south of Hertford, one mile from Bayford Railway Station. Undulating parkland with specimen trees. 18 holes, 6315 yards. S.S.S. 70. Excellent practice area. *Green Fees:* £30.00 per round, £40.00 per day. *Eating facilities:* bar and restaurant, snack meals available lunchtimes. *Visitors:* welcome weekdays only, Handicap Certificate required. *Society Meetings:* catered for by arrangement. Professional: G. Tippett (01992 511218). General Manager: Martin Bennet (01992 511258; Fax: 01992 511411). e-mail: play@brickendongrangegc.co.uk website: www.brickendongrangegc.co.uk

HITCHIN. **Chesfield Downs Golf Club,** Jack's Hill, Graveley, Near Hitchin SG4 7EQ (01462 482929). *Location*: just off Junction 8 of the A1(M), approximately two miles along the B197. Parkland. Two Courses: Chesfield Downs–18 holes, 6646 yards. S.S.S. 72. Par 71. Lannock Links–Par 3. 9 holes, 975 yards. S.S.S. 27. 27 bay floodlit driving range/practice bunker, putting green. *Green Fees*: information not available. *Eating facilities*: "Chesfields Restaurant and Bar". *Visitors*: welcome, advance booking system available to reserve tee-off times. Geoff Budds Golf Emporium, Learn Golf Academy, changing facilities. Part of the Leisure Links International Group. *Society Meetings*: catered for by arrangement. Head Professional: Keith Bond. General Manager: Paul Barnfather.

KNEBWORTH. **Knebworth Golf Club,** Deards End Lane, Knebworth SG3 6NL (01438 812752). *Location:* one mile south of Stevenage, off B197 (A1(M)) turnoff no. 7. Undulating parkland. 18 holes, 6492 yards. S.S.S. 71. *Green Fees:* weekdays £35.00. *Eating facilities:* full facilities available. *Visitors:* welcome weekdays, with members only at weekends. *Society Meetings:* welcome Mondays, Tuesdays and Thursdays only. Professional: G. Parker (01438 812757). Secretary: M. Parsons MBE (01438 812752).

LETCHWORTH. **Letchworth Golf Club,** Letchworth Lane, Letchworth SG6 3NQ. *Location:* two miles from A1 (M) near village of Willian, adjacent to Letchworth Hall Hotel. Parkland course. 18 holes, recently extended to 6420 yards. S.S.S. 71. Large practice ground with 9 hole pitch and putt course. *Green Fees:*

weekdays (except Mondays) £30.00 per round, £35.00 for 27 holes, £41.00 per day; Mondays £17.00 per round, £27.00 per day; weekend accompanied only. *Eating facilities:* bars and restaurant (limited menu Monday lunchtime only). *Visitors:* Handicap Certificate required. *Society Meetings:* catered for Wednesdays, Thursdays and Fridays. Professional: Karl Teshner (01462 682713). Secretary: Clive Allen (01462 683203; Fax: 01462 484567).

POTTERS BAR. **Potters Bar Golf Club,** Darkes Lane, Potters Bar EN6 1DE (01707 652020; Fax: 01707 655051). *Location:* one mile north of M25 exit 24 signposted Potters Bar, turn right at third traffic lights, club on left at end of shopping centre. Parkland course, well wooded, undulating with streams. 18 holes, 6279 yards. S.S.S. 70. Small practice ground. *Green Fees:* weekdays £25.00 per round, £35.00 per day; weekends with member only. *Eating facilities:* luncheons and bar available from 11.30am. *Visitors:* weekdays only, must produce valid Handicap Certificate. *Society Meetings:* welcome weekdays, Wednesday afternoons only. Professional: Gary A'ris (01707 652987; Fax: 01707 655051). Secretary: Peter Watson (01707 652020; Fax: 01707 655051). e-mail: info@pottersbargolfclub.com

RADLETT. **Porters Park Golf Club**, Shenley Hill, Radlett WD7 7AZ (01923 854127; Fax: 01923 855475). *Location*: approximately 3 miles south west of Junction 22 (M25), three miles north-east Junction 5 (M1), half a mile north of Radlett Station on Shenley Hill. Undulating parkland with fine trees and a brook. 18 holes, 6313 yards. S.S.S. 70. Open and Regional qualifying course. Three practice areas, putting. *Green Fees:* information not available. *Visitors:* welcome Monday to Friday. Handicap Certificate required. *Society Meetings:* catered for Wednesday and Thursday. Professional: David Gleeson (01923 854366). Managing Secretary: P.A. Marshall (01923 854127; Fax: 01923 855475).*
e-mail: info@porterspark.fsnet.co.uk

REDBOURN. **Redbourn Golf Club**, Kinsbourne, Green Lane, Redbourn AL3 7QA (01582 793493; Fax: 01582 794362). *Location*: one mile east of M1 Junction 9, four miles north of St. Albans, four miles south of Luton. Parkland course on which water comes into play on several holes. Two courses - Ver 18 holes. 6506 yards. S.S.S. 71. Kinsbourne Course - challenging Par 3, 9 holes, 1361 yards. S.S.S. 27. Driving range. *Green Fees:* information not available. *Eating facilities:* licensed bar, restaurant, snacks and hot meals readily available. *Visitors:* welcome weekdays, weekends and Bank Holidays after 12 noon. *Society Meetings:* welcome weekdays only. Professional: Stephen Hunter. Golf Secretary: Stuart Hatch (01582 794888).
email:golfclubsecretary@redbourngolfclub.com
website: www.redbourngolfclub.com

RICKMANSWORTH. **Batchworth Park Golf Club**, London Road, Rickmansworth WD3 1JS (01923 711400; Fax: 01923 710200). *Location*: situated five miles from Junction 17 M25 on the A404. Undulating parkland course. 18 holes, 6723 yards. S.S.S. 72. Practice range, putting green and chipping area. *Green Fees:* information not supplied. *Eating facilities:* bar, dining room - food served all day. *Visitors:* guests of members only. Professional: Stephen Proudfoot (01923 714922).

THE APPEARANCE OF AN ASTERISK * AT THE END OF A CLUB OR COURSE ENTRY INDICATES THAT UP-TO-DATE INFORMATION HAS NOT BEEN SUPPLIED

RICKMANSWORTH. **Moor Park Golf Club**, Moor Park, Rickmansworth WD3 1QN (01923 773146; Fax: 01923 777109). *Location*: Junction 18 of M25 and follow signs to Moor Park Golf Club. Parkland course with rolling fairways. High Course: 18 holes, 6713 yards (white), 6370 (yellow). S.S.S. 72 (white), 70 (yellow). West Course: 18 holes, 5815 yards (white), 5516 yards (yellow). S.S.S. 68 (white), 67 (yellow). Practice ground. *Green Fees:* weekdays High Course £72.50, West Course £47.50. *Eating facilities:* full catering available. *Visitors:* welcome on weekdays only by prior arrangement. *Society Meetings:* welcome weekdays only. Professional: L. Farmer (Tel & Fax: 01923 774113). Secretary: J. Moore.
e-mail: enquiries@moorparkgc.co.uk
website: www.moorparkgc.co.uk

RICKMANSWORTH. **Rickmansworth Public Golf Course**, Moor Lane, Rickmansworth WD3 1QL (01923 775278). *Location*: from town centre along A404 to Waterworks, left along B4504, then first right. Testing, undulating parkland course. 18 holes, 4557 yards, Par 65. *Green Fees:* weekdays £12.50, weekends £17.50. Seniors £7.00. *Eating facilities:* bars, restaurant. *Visitors:* welcome. *Society Meetings:* catered for, contact Professional. Professional: Alan Dobbins (01923 775278). Secretary: Andre de Bruin (01895 270453).

ROYSTON. **Heydon Grange Golf and Country Club**, Heydon, Royston SG8 7NS (01763 208988; Fax: 01763 208926). *Location*: A505 10 minutes drive east of Royston and minutes from M11 Duxford. Parkland course, gently rolling countryide. 27 holes, 6512 yards. S.S.S. 71. Practice ground. *Green Fees:* information not provided. *Eating facilities:* bar menu including Pakistani; bar, patio. *Visitors:* welcome all times. Buggies available. *Society Meetings:* welcome. Professional: J. O'Leary.

ROYSTON. **Malton Golf**, Meldreth, Royston SG8 6PE (01763 262200; Fax: 01763 262209). *Location*: Junction 12 of M11, A603 West to Orwell, through village, right to Malton. 230 acres beautiful landscaped countryside, lightly wooded with River Cam running through the course. 18 holes, 6708 yards, 6134 metres. S.S.S. 72. Driving range. *Green Fees:* weekdays £10.00; weekends £16.00. Twilight (from 4pm over Summer) £7.00/£10.00. Membership available £40.00 per year. *Eating facilities:* clubhouse(seats 50 diners) providing bar, snacks and hot meals. *Visitors:* all welcome, no restrictions. *Society Meetings:* all welcome, (handicap not required) Packages from £12.00 (18 holes, including food). Secretary: A.R. Boyce (01638 751222; Fax: 01638 751821).
website: www.maltongolf.co.uk

ROYSTON. **Royston Golf Club (Founded 1892),** Baldock Road, Royston SG8 5BG (01763 242696). *Location:* alongside the A505 on right hand side when approaching from Baldock, clubhouse at top of hill before entering town. Links - undulating heathland. 18 holes, 6086 yards. S.S.S. 69 yellow, 70 white. Practice fairway. *Green Fees:* weekdays £25.00 per round, £30.00 per day; weekends with a member only. *Eating facilities:* lounge bar - 19th hole bar, diningroom and bar meals. *Visitors:* welcome weekdays; weekends only with member. *Society Meetings:* weekdays only, book through Secretary. Professional: S. Clark (01763 243476). Secretary: J Beech (Tel & Fax: 01763 242696).

ST ALBANS. **Batchwood Golf and Tennis Centre,** Batchwood Drive, St Albans AL3 5XA (01727 844250; Fax: 01727 858506). *Location:* near City Hospital, close to St Albans town centre. Flat, parkland, wooded course. 18 holes, 6463 yards. S.S.S. 71. *Green Fees:* information not available. *Eating facilities:* bar and restaurant. *Visitors:* welcome. *Society Meetings:* welcome with reservation. Bookings: (01727 844250) PGA Professional: Mark Flitton (07797 386003). Secretary: Bernard Hudson (01582 833530).*

ST ALBANS. **Mid-Herts Golf Club,** Gustard Wood, Lamer Lane, Wheathampstead, Near St Albans AL4 8RS (01582 832242). *Location:* B651, six miles north of St Albans. Flat heathland, short and tight course. 18 holes, 6060 yards. S.S.S. 69. Course record 63. *Green Fees:* weekdays £25.00 per round; weekends and Bank Holidays with member only. *Eating facilities:* by arrangement. *Visitors:* welcome weekdays with reservation; Handicap Certificate required. *Society Meetings:* catered for by arrangement. Professional: Barney Puttick (01582 832788). Secretary: R.J.H. Jourdan (01582 832242; Fax: 01582 834834).
e-mail: secretary@mid-hertsgolfclub.co.uk

ST ALBANS. **Verulam Golf Club,** 226 London Road, St Albans AL1 1JG (01727 839016). *Location:* M25 Junction 22a or 22 to A1081 to St. Albans, course is off London Road (A1081) near railway bridge. Easy walking parkland course designed by James Braid. 18 holes, 6457 yards. S.S.S. 71. Practice ground, nets, putting and chipping green, bunker and driving tee. *Green Fees:* information not available. *Eating facilities:* bar snacks from 7.30am to close, other dining by prior arrangement. *Visitors:* welcome weekdays except Wednesday mornings. *Society Meetings:* welcome by prior arrangement with Secretary - deposit required. Professional: Nick Burch (01727 861401). General Manager: Mr Bob Kelly (01727 853327; Fax: 01727 812201).
e-mail: genman@verulamgolf.co.uk
website: www.verulamgolf.co.uk

SAWBRIDGEWORTH. **Manor of Groves,** High Wych, Sawbridgeworth CM21 0JU (01279 600777; Fax: 01279 600374). *Location:* Junction 7 off M11 follow A414 to High Wych. Parkland/woodland course with water features. 18 holes, 6228 yards. S.S.S. 71. Practice ground.Soft spikes only. *Green Fees:* weekdays £23.00. Saturday and Sunday after 12 noon £27.00. *Eating facilities:* restaurant, bar. *Visitors:* welcome anytime weekdays, advise phoning; weekends after 12 noon only. Accommodation available in our 80 bedroomed Hotel. Leisure facilities including pool, gym, aerobics studio, Clarins beauty salon. *Society Meetings:* most welcome. General Manager: James Jude.

STEVENAGE. **Stevenage Golf Centre,** Aston Lane, Stevenage SG2 7EL (01438 880322). *Location:* turn off A1(M) at Stevenage South Junction onto A602 to Hertford, course signposted at Van Hagues Garden Centre. Water hazards on course. 18 holes, 6451 yards. S.S.S. 71. Par 72. 20 bay driving range. *Green Fees:* information not available. *Eating facilities:* restaurant and bar. *Visitors:* welcome. Municipal course, advance booking system available to reserve tee-off times. Shower facilities. *Society Meetings:* catered for by arrangement. Professional: Steve Barker (01438 880322). Secretary: Mrs S. Elwin (01438 880322).

TRING near. **Stocks,** Stocks Road, Aldbury, Near Tring HP23 5RX (01442 851341; Fax: 01442 851253). *Location:* M1 Junction 11 or 9, A41 (Tring) follow signs to Tring B.R. Parkland course, feature lake second and 10th holes, a test of length and accuracy. 18 holes, 7016 yards. S.S.S. 74. Practice range, practice green, chipping green. *Green Fees:* weekdays £35.00 per round; weekends £45.00. Residential golfing breaks and society packages available. *Eating facilities:* Cedars Restaurant, club house bar snack menu, private rooms available. *Visitors:* welcome, after 12pm weekends. Accommodation available in 15 individual bedrooms; leisure facilities. *Society Meetings:* welcome weekdays only. Director of Golf: Peter Lane (01442 852511). Golf Manager: Robin Darling (01442 852504).
e-mail: plane@stocksgolf.co.uk
　　　　rdarling@stocksgolf.co.uk
website: www.stocksgolf.co.uk

WALTHAM CROSS. **The Cheshunt Golf Club,** The Clubhouse, Park Lane, Cheshunt EN7 6QD (01992 629777). *Location:* M25 Junction 25 to Hertford, A10 left at second set of traffic lights, turn right at mini roundabout then approximately quarter of a mile. Flat parkland course. 18 holes, 6608 yards. S.S.S. 71. Practice area. *Green Fees:* information not available. *Eating facilities:* public cafe. *Visitors:* welcome anytime. For tee-off times phone Pro Shop (01992 624009). Professional: D. Banks (01992 624009). Secretary: B. Furne (01992 629777).*

 For full details of clubs and courses, plus convenient accommodation, visit the FHG golf website

www.uk-golfguide.com

WARE. **Briggens House Golf Club**, Briggens Park, Stanstead Road, Stanstead Abbotts, Ware SG12 8LD (01279 793742; Fax: 01279 793685). *Location:* A414 near Harlow, Essex. Parkland course. 9 holes, 5582 yards. S.S.S. 69. Practice area. *Green Fees:* weekdays £15.00 for 18 holes, £10.00 for 9 holes; weekends £17.00 for 18 holes. *Eating facilities:* hotel restaurant and coffee shop with snacks, both with bars. *Visitors:* welcome anytime except Sunday mornings. *Society Meetings:* very welcome. Professional: Alan McGinn. Secretary: Alan Battle.

WARE. **Chadwell Springs Golf Club**, Hertford Road, Ware SG12 9LE (01920 461447). *Location:* just off A10 Hertford to Ware. Heathland. 9 holes, 6418 yards, S.S.S. 71. Practice ground. *Green Fees:* information not available. *Eating facilities:* bar, bar meals; function room. *Visitors:* welcome weekdays except Tuesday and Thursday mornings; weekends with member only. Carts available. *Society Meetings:* welcome weekdays by arrangement. Professional: Mark Wall. Secretary: D. Evans (01920 461447). *

WARE. **Hanbury Manor Golf and Country Club**, Ware SG12 0SD (01920 487722; Fax: 01920 487692). *Location:* leave the M25 at Junction 25 and take the A10 towards Hertford, continue for 12 miles and Hanbury Manor is located on the left. Parkland and Championship course designed by Jack Nicklaus II. 18 holes, 7052 yards. S.S.S. 74 (blue tees). Putting green, practice ground. *Green Fees:* information not available. *Eating facilities:* two award-winning restaurants in five star Marriott Hotel which overlooks course. *Visitors:* golf available only to Club members or hotel guests. Club and buggy hire, golf shop. Host to 1997, 1998 and 1999 English Open. *Society Meetings:* Corporate Golf Days are available. Director of Golf: Iain McInally.

WARE. **Whitehill Golf Club**, Whitehill Golf Centre, Dane End, Ware SG12 0JS (01920 438495; Fax: 01920 438891). *Location:* turn off A10 at Happy Eater, High Cross. Undulating course. 18 holes, 6618 yards. S.S.S 72. 25 bay floodlit driving range. *Green Fees:* information not available. *Eating facilities:* bar, restaurants and function room. *Visitors:* welcome. Snooker room. *Society Meetings:* welcome, groups of 12 or more. Professional: Matt Belsham. Secretary: Andrew Smith. *
e-mail: whitehillgolfcentre@btinternet.com

WATFORD. **Aldenham Golf and Country Club,** Church Lane, Aldenham, Watford WD25 8NN (01923 853929; Fax: 01923 858472). *Location:* three minutes from M1 Junction 5, off B462 to Radlett. Flat parkland course. 18 holes, 6500 yards. S.S.S. 71. 9 holes, 2350 yards. Practice area. *Green Fees:* weekdays £28.00 and £10.00, weekends £36.00 and £12.00. *Eating facilities:* full catering and bar facilities. *Visitors:* welcome, weekends after 12 noon. Buggy cars for hire. *Society Meetings:* welcome by prior arrangement. Professional: Tim Dunstan (01923 857889. Secretary: (01923 853929).
e-mail: aldenhamgolf@ukonline.co.uk

WATFORD. **West Herts Golf Club**, Cassiobury Park, Watford WD3 3GG (01923 236484). *Location:* off Rousebarn Lane from Links Way, A412 at Croxley Green. Parkland. 18 holes, 6488 yards. S.S.S. 71. *Green Fees:* weekdays £35.00 per round; weekends £45.00. *Eating facilities:* catering (including breakfast) available seven days a week. *Visitors:* welcome. *Society Meetings:* catered for. Professional: Charles Gough (01923 220352). General Manager: Clive Dodman (01923 236484; Fax: 01923 222300).

WELWYN GARDEN CITY. **Brocket Hall Golf Club**, Welwyn Garden City AL8 7XG (01707 368808; Fax: 01707 390052). *Location:* A1(M) two minutes from Junction 4. Parkland course and woodland course. 36 holes, 6600 yards and 7050 yards, S.S.S. 72 and 73 respectively. Par 3 course, Nick Faldo Academy. *Green Fees:* information not available. *Eating facilities:* available all day. *Visitors:* must be a member's guest. *Society Meetings:* winter packages; corporate days welcome. Professional: Keith Wood. Secretary: Paul Densham.*
e-mail: paulden@brocket-hall.co.uk
website: www.brocket-hall.co.uk

WELWYN GARDEN CITY. **Mill Green Golf Club,** Gypsy Lane, Welwyn Garden City AL7 4TY (01707 276900; Fax: 01707 276898). *Location:* from A1 North exit 4 (Hatfield) A414 to Hertford, take first slip road on left to A1000, left at lights, second right Ascots Lane, mini roundabout turn right into Gypsy Lane. Parkland course. Peter Alliss and Clive Clarke designed. 18 holes, 6615 yards. S.S.S. 72. Two contrasting loops of 9 holes. Front 9 open and elevated, back 9 long narrow fairways through woodland. Par 3 course, driving range, putting green. *Green Fees:* weekdays £25.00, weekends £30.00. *Eating facilities:* Full bar menu available along with extensive conference and banqueting facilities. *Visitors:* Monday to Friday all day, after midday at weekends. *Society Meetings:* welcome Monday to Friday. Professional: Ian Parker. General Manager: Tim Hudson
e-mail: millgreen@americangolf.uk.com

WELWYN GARDEN CITY. **Panshanger Golf Complex**, Old Herns Lane, Panshanger, Welwyn Garden City AL7 2ED (01707 333312; Fax: 01707 390010). *Location*: just off Junction 6 A1(M), 10 minutes from M25. Parkland set in the Mimram Valley. 18 holes, 6347 yards. S.S.S. 70. Practice ground, 9 hole pitch and putt. *Green Fees:* information not available. *Eating facilities:* Fairway Tavern and cafe. *Visitors:* municipal course, pay as you play, all welcome, dress conditions. *Society Meetings:* welcome weekdays. Professionals: Bryan Lewis and Michael Corlass (01707 333350; Fax: 01707 339507). Secretary: Sheila Ryan (01707 332837). General Manager: Ruth Preece.

WELWYN GARDEN CITY. **Welwyn Garden City Golf Club Ltd.,** Mannicotts, High Oaks Road, Welwyn Garden City AL8 7BP (01707 325243). *Location*: from north Junction 5 on A1M and take B197 to Valley Road. From south Junction 4 on A1M to Lemsford Lane and Valley Road. Undulating parkland. 18 holes, 6200 yards. S.S.S. 69. Practice ground. *Green Fees:* £25.00 weekdays. *Eating facilities:* by order for lunches; sandwiches available. *Visitors:* welcome weekdays with Handicap Certificate; weekends with member only. *Society Meetings:* Mondays, Wednesdays and Thursdays only (£60.00 per person per day). Professional: R. May (01707 325525). General Manager: (01707 325243; Fax: 01707 393213).

WHEATHAMPSTEAD. **Lamerwood Country Club,** Codicote Road, Wheathampstead AL4 8GB (01582 833013; Fax: 01582 832604). *Location:* from London take A1(M) exit at Junction 4. After Hatfield Tunnel take B653 towards Wheathampstead. Set in 240 acres of mature wood and parkland. 18 holes, 6953 yards. S.S.S. 73. 9 hole short course and practice facilities available. *Green Fees:* information not available. *Eating facilities:* full bar and restaurant, private function rooms. *Visitors:* always welcome. *Society Meetings:* always welcome. Accommodation available at Sopwellhouse Hotel and Country Club, St. Albans (01727 864477; Fax: 01727 844741). Professional: Matthew Masters (01582 833013). Director: Mr. S. Takabatake. *

Isle of Wight

COWES. **Cowes Golf Club,** Crossfield Avenue, Cowes, Isle of Wight PO31 8HN (Tel & Fax: 01983 292303). *Location:* entrance adjacent Cowes High School. Parkland with sea views. 9 holes, 5934 yards. S.S.S. 68. *Green Fees:* weekdays £15.00; weekends £18.00. *Eating facilities:* snack meals available in bar in summer. Bar open 11am to 2pm summer months. *Visitors:* welcome except Sunday before 1pm and Thursday, Ladies' Day (11.30am to 3pm). *Society Meetings:* welcome Mondays to Wednesdays by arrangement with Secretary. Society rates by arrangement. Secretary: D.C. Weaver (01983 292303).

EAST COWES. **Osborne Golf Club,** Osborne House Estate, East Cowes PO32 6JX (01983 295421). *Location:* off A3021 south-east of East Cowes. One mile from Southampton/East Cowes ferry terminal; 4 miles from Portsmouth/Fishbourne ferry terminal. Parkland. 9 holes, 6372 yards. S.S.S. 70. Practice area. *Green Fees:* weekdays £20.00; weekends and Bank Holidays £22.00. Subject to review. *Eating facilities:* catering available each day, bar facilities. *Visitors:* welcome except Tuesday, Saturday and Sunday before noon. Telephone for tee availability. *Society Meetings:* catered for (24 maximum). Secretary: Roy Jones (01983 295421).

FRESHWATER. **Freshwater Bay Golf Club,** Afton Down, Freshwater (Tel & Fax: 01983 752955). *Location*: western end of Island, approximately half-a-mile east of Freshwater Bay on coast road to Ventnor. Links type course on chalk uplands. 18 holes, 5725 yards. S.S.S. 68. *Green Fees:* £22.00 weekday, £26.00 weekends. *Eating facilities:* licensed bar, catering. *Visitors:* welcome. *Society Meetings:* welcome by arrangement. Secretary: Terry Riddett. e-mail: tr.fbgc@btopenworld.com

NEWPORT. **Newport (Isle of Wight) Golf Club,** St Georges Down, Near Shide, Newport PO30 2JB (01983 526711). *Location*: one mile south east of Newport, taking Sandown road. Testing downland course. 9 holes, 5704 yards. S.S.S. 68. *Green Fees*: information not available. *Eating facilities*: full catering available- breakfast, lunches, evening dinners. *Visitors*: welcome anytime except Wednesday 12pm-3pm, Saturday before 3pm and Sunday before noon. *Society Meetings*: groups of 12 plus welcome by arrangement weekdays except Wednesdays and not before 3pm on Saturdays or noon on Sundays. Secretary: Robert Buchanan (01983 525076). *

RYDE. **Ryde Golf Club,** Binstead Road, Ryde, Isle of Wight PO33 3NF. *Location:* on A3054 Ryde to Newport Road, just outside Ryde. Parkland course. 9 holes, extended June 2002 to 5772 yards. Par 70. S.S.S. 68. *Green Fees:* weekdays £18.00; weekends and Bank Holidays £20.00. *Eating facilities:* Bar and catering available all day April to September; lunchtime only October to March. *Visitors:* welcome, restrictions Wednesdays and Sundays. *Society Meetings:* catered for. Limited Pro Shop on site. Secretary: Richard Dean (01983 614809; Fax: 01983 567418).
e-mail: secretary@rydegolfclub.freeserve.co.uk
website: www.rydegolf.co.uk

SANDOWN. **Shanklin and Sandown Golf Club,** The Fairway, Lake, Sandown PO36 9PR (01983 404424/403217). *Location:* from Sandown travel towards Shanklin. Soon after Heights Leisure Centre turn right into The Fairway. One mile to Club. A traditional, beautiful heathland County Championship course. The 13th hole is one of the best in Southern England. 18 holes, 6062 yards. S.S.S. 69. Practice ground. *Green Fees:* £27.50 weekdays; £33.00 weekends. Three day ticket weekdays £66.00. *Eating facilities:* full catering and bar facilities. *Visitors:* welcome. Handicap Certificate preferred. *Society Meetings:* welcome by arrangement. Professional: Peter Hammond (01983 404424). Secretary: A. Creed (01983 403217).

UPPER VENTNOR. **Ventnor Golf Club,** Steephill Down Road, Upper Ventnor PO38 1BP (01983 853326). *Location:* northwest boundary of Ventnor. Downland undulating with side slopes overlooking the sea. 12 holes, 5767 yards. S.S.S. 68. *Green Fees:* information not available. *Eating facilities:* bar snacks only. *Visitors:* welcome, Sundays after 1pm, Ladies' Day Monday tee closed 11am till 1pm. Secretary: Stewart Blackmore. *

PLEASE MENTION THIS GUIDE WHEN YOU
WRITE OR PHONE TO ENQUIRE ABOUT
CLUBS OR ACCOMMODATION.

Sandpipers Hotel

& FAT CAT ON THE BAY RESTAURANT

Escape to Sandpipers – all the facilities of an excellent English hotel, then we add our own special 'touch of magic'.

This spacious Victorian building nestles in an acre of garden in a sheltered spot just yards from the water's edge. A short walk or two minute drive away is Freshwater's 18-hole golf course, with spectacular views of the cliffs and sea. Special discounts for Sandpiper guests. Return to relax in the lounge or the Fat Cat Bar, or enjoy a meal in the renowned Fat Cat on the Bay Restaurant which offers table d'hôte and à la carte menus.

SANDPIPERS HOTEL, FRESHWATER BAY, ISLE OF WIGHT PO40 9QX
Tel: **01983 758500** • Fax: **01983 754364** • **www.sandpipershotel.com**

See also Colour Advertisement on page 23

Located on the south side of the Island, **Channel View** is well situated for all the Island courses. The hotel has an excellent reputation for hospitality, good food and accommodation. It also has an indoor heated pool, sauna, solarium, licensed bar, aromatherapy and reflexology. *Car ferry inclusive packages always available. A perfect choice for that short break away.*

Hope Road, Shanklin, Isle of Wight PO37 6EH
Tel: 01983 862309 • Fax: 01983 868400

enquiries@channelviewhotel.co.uk • www.channelviewhotel.co.uk

See also Colour Advertisement on page 24

Culver Lodge Hotel

A comfortable licensed hotel offering traditional English hospitality. Set in delightful suntrap gardens with swimming pool and close to all Sandown's leisure facilities.

• Relax in our bright and cheerful lounge or lounge bar
• All rooms en suite with colour TV, radio, hairdryers and tea/coffee facilities • Ample parking
• Wide range of entertainment available locally
• Few minutes' walk from beach, town and bus stops
• Games room • Snacks and drinks served in bar

Albert Road, Sandown PO36 8AW • Tel: 01983 403819

See also Colour Advertisement on page 23

NOTE

All the information regarding Golf Clubs in this guide is given in good faith in the belief that it is correct. However, the publishers cannot guarantee the facts given in these pages, neither are they responsible for changes in ownership or facilities, such as green fees, that may take place after the date of going to press. Readers should always satisfy themselves that the facilities they require are available and that the terms, if quoted, still apply.

Kent

ASH. **The London Golf Club,** South Ash Manor Estate, Ash TN15 7EN (01474 879899; Fax: 01474 879912). *Location:* Turn off A20 towards Brands Hatch. Parkland course and Inland Links course. The Heritage course - 18 holes, 7208 yards, 6333 metres. S.S.S. 70. The International course - 18 holes, 7005 yards, 6128 metres. S.S.S. 69. Practice range (350 yards), bunker and chipping facilities, two putting greens. *Green Fees:* weekdays £75.00, weekends £80.00 The International course only. *Eating facilities:* restaurant, terrace bar and spike bar. *Visitors:* by prior arrangement or with a member. *Society Meetings:* welcome by prior arrangement. General Manager: Mr D. Loh. Professional: Mr Bill Longmuir.

ASH. **Redlibbets Golf Club,** Manor Lane, West Yoke, Ash TN15 7HT (01474 879190). Undulating woodland 18 hole course. Practice range, practice short game area, putting green and indoor net room. *Green Fees:* information not available. *Eating facilities:* Bar and restaurant. Secretary: J. Potter.*

ASHFORD. **Ashford Great Chart Golf & Leisure,** Great Chart, Ashford (01233 645858). *Location:* signposted from Great Chart, Ashford. 9 hole, Par 3 course. 26 bay floodlit covered driving range. *Green Fees:* 9 holes weekday £8.50; weekend £11.50. *Eating facilities:* bar, cafe. *Visitors:* welcome, juniors and families welcome. Tuition, video tuition, shop, practice bunkers. Professional: Cameron Cowie. Secretary: Grant Kay/ John Kay.

ASHFORD. **Ashford (Kent) Golf Club,** Sandyhurst Lane, Ashford TN25 4NT (01233 620180). *Location:* just off A20, one and a half miles west of Ashford. Parkland - stream cutting through course. 18 holes, 6261 yards. S.S.S. 70. *Green Fees:* weekdays £28.00 per round, £38.00 per day; weekends and Bank Holidays £35.00 (November to February reduced green fees). *Eating facilities:* available every day. *Visitors:* welcome. Handicap Certificate required. *Society Meetings:* catered for Tuesdays and Thursdays by arrangement. Professional: Hugh Sherman (01233 629644). Secretary: A.H. Story (Tel & Fax: 01233 622655).

ASHFORD. **Chart Hills Golf Club,** Weeks Lane, Biddenden, Ashford TN27 8JX (01580 292222; Fax: 01580 292233). *Location:* M25, M20 Leeds Castle turn off (B2163), A274 to Tenterden. Parkland course designed by Nick Faldo. 18 holes, 7119 yards. S.S.S. 74. Short game area, golf academy. *Green Fees:* weekdays £60.00 per round, weekends £70.00 per round. Phone for further details on seasonal promotions and special offers. *Eating facilities:* restaurant, bar snacks, bar, conference facilities. *Visitors:* welcome, limited at weekends, members only on Mondays and Wednesdays. Gymnasium, fitness centre. *Society Meetings:* mid-week only, contact events co-ordinator.
e-mail: info@charthills.co.uk
website: www.charthills.co.uk

ASHFORD. **The Homelands Bettergolf Centre,** Ashford Road, Kingsnorth, Ashford TN26 1NJ (01233 661620; Fax: 01233 720553). *Location:* take exit 10 off M20, follow A2070 course signposted from second roundabout to Kingsnorth. 9 hole parkland course. 2250 yards, S.S.S. 62. *Green Fees:* information not available. *Visitors:* welcome at all times. Buggies, trolleys and clubs available for hire. *Society Meetings:* welcome with prior notice. Short breaks organised. Professional: Tony Bowers. Secretary: Ian S. Johnson. *

BECKENHAM. **Beckenham Place Park Golf Club,** Beckenham Hill Road, Beckenham. *Location:* on A222 north of Bromley. Parkland. 18 holes, 5722 yards. S.S.S. 68. Practice ground, nets, putting green. *Green Fees:* information not available. *Eating facilities:* bar and cafeteria. *Visitors:* welcome but must book in advance. *Society Meetings:* catered for. Other facilities include tennis courts and putting green. Professional: H. Davies-Thomas (020 8650-2292). Secretary: T. A. Moorcroft (Mobile: 0468 448792).*

BECKENHAM. **Braeside Golf Club,** Beckenham Place Park, Beckenham Hill, Beckenham (020 8650 2292). Parkland course. 18 holes, 5722 yards, 5230 metres. S.S.S. 69. Practice area, putting green and nets. *Green Fees:* information not available. *Eating facilities:* cafe and bar. *Visitors:* welcome, will need to book weekends. Secretary: Mr Nicholas Wilkins.*

BECKENHAM. **Langley Park Golf Club,** Barnfield Wood Road, Beckenham BR3 6SZ (020 8658 6849). *Location:* one mile from Bromley South station. Flat wooded parkland. 18 holes, 6469 yards, 5916 metres, S.S.S. 71. Practice areas and nets. *Green Fees:* £30.00 per round, £40 per day. *Eating facilities:* bar snacks, restaurant/dining room. *Visitors:* welcome weekdays by arrangement with Pro Shop. Handicap Certificate required. *Society Meetings:* Wednesdays and Thursdays by arrangement with the Club Manager. Other days considered. Professional: Colin Staff (020 8650 1663). Club Manager: Rodger Pollard (020 8658 6849).

BEXLEYHEATH. **Bexley Heath Golf Club,** Mount Road, Bexley Heath DA6 8JS (020 8303 6951). *Location:* adjacent to A2. Hilly parkland. 9 holes, 5239 yards, 4788 metres. S.S.S. 66. *Green Fees:* £20 (approximately). Weekends with member only. *Eating facilities:* catering available. *Visitors:* weekdays only. Professional: To be appointed. Secretary: S.E. Squires.

BIGGIN HILL. **Cherry Lodge Golf Club,** Jail Lane, Biggin Hill TN16 3AX (01959 572250; Fax: 01959 540672). *Location:* A233 to M25 Junction 5, Bromley, eight miles. Undulating Parkland 600 ft. above sea level with panoramic views of surrounding countryside. 18 holes, 6652 yards, 6084 metres.

S.S.S. 73. Extensive practice ground. *Green Fees:* £20.00 to £35.00. *Eating facilities:* bar snacks all day, Sunday lunches. *Visitors:* welcome weekdays except Bank Holidays. *Society Meetings:* welcome weekdays (except Bank Holidays) by arrangement. Professional: Nigel Child (01959 572989; Fax: 01959 540672). Secretary: W. Tombling (01959 572250; Fax: 01959 540672).
e-mail: info@cherrylodgegc.co.uk
website: www.cherrylodgegc.co.uk

BRENCHLEY. Moatlands Golf Club, Waterman's Lane, Brenchley TN12 6ND (01892 724400; Fax: 01892 723300). *Location:* from A21 take the B2160 to Matfield/Paddock Wood. Drive through Matfield and continue downhill through double bends until road flattens, turn right at post box into Chantlers Hill and then right again into Watermans Lane. Take the train from Charing Cross Station (London) to Paddock Wood (approximately 45 minutes). Parkland course built on the slopes of the Kentish High Wealds, full advantage has been taken of the individual contours and environmental features found on the Moatland Estate. Developed to the highest standards and specifications, Moatlands is an all year round championship course. 18 holes, 7060 yards (Blue tees), 6693 (white tees), 6230 (yellow tees), 5471 (black tees), 5413 (red tees). S.S.S. 72. Full practice facilities. *Green Fees:* information not available. *Eating facilities:* bars, à la carte restaurant, private room. *Visitors:* welcome, but subject to availability of tee times (01892 724252). *Society Meetings:* welcome by arrangement (01892 724400; Fax: 01892 723300).
e-mail: info@moatlands.com
website: www.moatlands.com

BROADSTAIRS. North Foreland Golf Club, The Clubhouse, Convent Road, Broadstairs CT10 3PU (01843 862140). *Location:* Broadstairs Station, A2, M2, A299, A253, A256, B2052. Cliff top, chalk based, free draining. 18 holes, 6382 yards. S.S.S. 71. Short Course: 18 holes, 1752 yards. Par 3. *Green Fees:* main course: weekdays £35.00 per round, £50.00 per day; weekends £50.00 per round. Par 3 course: weekdays £7.00 per day; weekends £8.00 per day. *Eating facilities:* bar, dining room and "Halfway House". *Visitors:* welcome weekdays and weekend afternoons with current Handicap Certificate. Tennis. *Society Meetings:* Wednesdays and Fridays by prior arrangement with Secretary. Professional: Darren Parris (01843 604471; Fax: 01843 862663). Secretary: Tony Adams (01843 862140).
website: www.northforeland.co.uk

BROMLEY. Magpie Hall Lane Municipal Golf Club, Magpie Hall Lane, Bromley. *Location:* off Bromley Common on A21. 9 holes, 5490 yards, 5014 metres. S.S.S. 67. *Green Fees:* weekdays £6.10, weekends £8.00, concessions (weekdays only) £3.10. *Eating facilities:* bar/bar food. *Visitors:* welcome anytime without reservation. *Society Meetings:* phone the Professional for details. Professional: Alan Hodgson (020 8462 7014).

BROMLEY. Shortlands Golf Club, Meadow Road, Shortlands, Bromley BR2 0DX (020 8460 2471; Fax: 020 8460 8828). *Location:* car park and entrance in Ravensbourne Avenue, off the main Beckenham to Bromley Road, adjacent Shortlands B.R. Station. 9 holes, 5261 yards. S.S.S. 66. *Green Fees:* £15.00 for 18 holes, £10.00 for 9 holes. *Eating facilities:* available. *Visitors:* restricted to playing with a member. *Society Meetings:* only when member involved. Professional: (020 8464 6182). Manager: P.S. May (020 8460 8828).

BROMLEY. Sundridge Park Golf Club, Garden Road, off Plaistow Lane, Bromley BR1 3NE (020 8460 0278). *Location:* five minutes' walk from Sundridge Park station. Wooded parkland. 36 holes. East 6538 yards. West 6016 yards. S.S.S. 71 and 69. Two practice grounds. *Green Fees:* £55.00 per day weekdays. *Eating facilities:* restaurant, spike bar, lounge bar, members' bar and snack bar. *Visitors:* welcome weekdays only, with Handicap Certificate. *Society Meetings:* catered for by arrangement. Professional: Stuart Dowsett (020 8460 5540). General Manager: Charles Winning (020 8460 0278; Fax: 020 8289 3050).

CANTERBURY. Broome Park Golf Club, Broome Park Estate, Barham, Near Canterbury CT4 6QX (01227 830728; Fax: 01227 832591). *Location:* off the A2 at the A260 in the direction of Folkestone, half a mile on right. Undulating parkland, lake in front of 18th green. 18 holes, 6580 yards, S.S.S. 71. Driving range and practice ground. *Green Fees:* weekdays £30.00; weekends £35.00. *Eating facilities:* available all week. *Visitors:* welcome. Handicap Certificate required. *Society Meetings:* welcome weekdays by arrangement. Professional: Tienie Britz (01227 831126). Golf Manager: Graeme Robins (01227 830728; Fax: 01227 832591).
e-mail: broomepark@o2.co.uk
website: www.broomepark.co.uk

CANTERBURY. Canterbury Golf Club, Scotland Hills, Littlebourne Road, Canterbury CT1 1TW (01227 453532; Fax: 01227 784277). *Location:* one mile from centre of Canterbury on the A257 road to Sandwich. Parkland and wooded course. 18 holes, 6249 yards. S.S.S. 70. Practice ground. *Green Fees:* weekdays £30.00 per round, £36.00 per day; weekends £40.00 per round (after 11.30am only). *Eating facilities:* full bar and catering service (snacks, sandwiches, lunches, dinners). *Visitors:* welcome without reservation but Handicap Certificate necessary (or evidence that visitor is bona fide playing member of another club). *Society Meetings:* catered for Tuesday, Thursday and Friday. Professional: Paul Everard (01227 462865). Secretary: John Morgan (01227 453532).

CHISLEHURST. **Chislehurst Golf Club,** Camden Park Road, Chislehurst BR7 5HJ (020 8467 3055). *Location:* between Bromley and junction of A222 and Sidcup bypass. Parkland. 18 holes, 5128 yards. S.S.S. 65. *Green Fees:* £30.00 per day weekdays; £15.00 per day if introduced by a member, £7.50 Juniors. A Kent County Card member pays £15.00. Weekends with member only. *Eating facilities:* catering available. Large parties by prior arrangement. *Visitors:* welcome but restricted to weekdays (except Wednesday mornings) and only with a member at weekends. *Society Meetings:* catered for by arrangement. Professional: Jonathan Bird (020 8467 6798). Secretary: Peter Foord (020 8467 2782; Fax: 020 8295 0874). Caterers: Mr & Mrs L. de Bruyn.

CHISLEHURST. **World of Golf**, A20 Sidcup Bypass, Chislehurst BR7 6RP (020 8309 0181; Fax: 020 8308 1691). *Location:* six miles from Junction 3 on M25 heading towards London on A20. Parkland. Short game practice area, 54-bay driving range, adventure putting. *Eating facilities:* licensed cafe/bar. *Visitors:* welcome, no restrictions. Tennis courts. *Society Meetings:* welcome. Head Golf Professional: David Young. Centre Manager: Colin Payne.

CRANBROOK. **Hemsted Forest Golf Club,** Golford Road, Cranbrook TN17 4AL (01580 712833; Fax: 01580 714274). *Location:* two miles south of Sissinghurst. Parkland, a beautiful tree lined course in superb condition. 18 holes, 6305 yards. S.S.S. 71. *Green Fees:* weekdays £28.00 per round, weekends £36.00 per round. *Eating facilities:* open all day, special menus catered for. *Visitors:* welcome weekdays after 8.30am and weekends after 11am. *Society Meetings:* available weekdays. Professional: Karl Steptoe (01580 712833; Fax: 01580 714274). Secretary: Karl Stevenson (01580 712833; Fax: 01580 714274).

DARTFORD. **Birchwood Park Golf Centre**, Birchwood Road, Wilmington, Dartford DA2 7HJ (01322 662038; Fax: 01322 667283). *Location:* from Junction 3 of M25, B2173 towards Sidcup. Turn right into Birchwood Road at Vauxhall Garage. Attractive undulating course surrounded by ancient woodland. Two courses - Main Course: 18 holes, 6364 yards, S.S.S. 70; Orchard Course: 9 holes, 1274 yards. 41 bay floodlit driving range. *Green Fees:* information not available. *Eating facilities:* snacks and bar food always available, dining/function room. *Visitors:* very welcome but advised to book tee times in advance. London Golf Centre Superstore, health and fitness facilities. *Society Meetings:* welcome, a variety of packages available. Teaching Professionals: Cranfield Golf Academy (Fax: 01322 667283). Manager: Julie Carter (01322 660554; Fax: 01322 667283).*

DARTFORD. **Dartford Golf Club Ltd.,** The Clubhouse, Heath Lane (Upper), Dartford DA1 2TN (01322 223616). *Location:* backing on to A2, one mile from Dartford Tunnel and M25. Flat parkland. 18 holes, 5914 yards. S.S.S. 69. *Green Fees:* weekdays £22.50 per round, £31.50 per day; weekends (accompanied by member): one round £14.00, Two rounds £20.00. *Eating facilities:* catering available.

Visitors: welcome on weekdays with reservation, must be member of another golf club. *Society Meetings:* welcome on Mondays and Fridays by prior arrangement with Secretary. Professional: John Gregory (01322 226409). Secretary: Ken Rawlins (Tel & Fax: 01322 226455).
e-mail: dartfordgolf@hotmail.com

DARTFORD. **Fawkham Valley Golf Club,** Fawkham Valley Road, Fawkham, Longfield DA3 8LY (01474 707144). *Location:* off the A2 East of Dartford/off A20 North of Brands Hatch. Wooded course (tree lined), special feature being lakes in front of the 3rd and 6th greens. 9 holes, 6547 yards. S.S.S. 72. Practice area and putting green. *Green Fees:* information not available. *Eating facilities:* members' bar. *Visitors:* welcome weekends and Bank Holidays. *Society Meetings:* welcome Mondays, Wednesdays and Fridays. Professional: Nigel Willis. Secretary: Jo Marchant.
e-mail: fvgc@cjb.co.uk
website: www.fawkhamvalley.co.uk.

DEAL. **Royal Cinque Ports Golf Club,** Golf Road, Deal CT14 6RF (01304 374007; Fax: 01304 379530). *Location:* A258 from Sandwich. In Upper Deal leave for Middle Deal Road, left turn into Albert Road, Western Road, on to Golf Road (or from Dover, A258 via Sea front and Godwin Road). Championship 18 hole links course. 18 holes, 6899 yards. S.S.S. 73. Par 72. Large practice area. *Green Fees:* weekdays £75.00 per round, £85.00 per day. *Eating facilities:* hot and cold comprehensive bar snack menu. *Visitors:* welcome, 4 ball rounds may be played on Tuesdays and Thurdays. Special packages available. Handicap Certificate required (max 22); times must be pre-booked. Buggies; cart and caddies by arrangement. *Society Meetings:* by arrangement. Professional: Andrew Reynolds (01304 374170; Fax: 01304 379530). Secretary: Ian Symington (01304 374007; Fax: 01304 379530).
e-mail: rcpgcsec@aol.com
website: www.royalcinqueports.com

DEAL. **Walmer and Kingsdown Golf Club,** The Leas, Kingsdown, Deal CT14 8EP (01304 373256). *Location:* take A258 from Dover (A2) to Deal, Kingsdown club signposted at village of Ringwould. Downland course on the White Cliffs of Dover overlooking the English Channel. 18 holes, 6444 yards. S.S.S. 71. Practice ground. *Green Fees:* information not available. *Eating facilities:* full catering and bar service. *Visitors:* welcome after 9.30am weekdays and 12 noon at weekends. *Society Meetings:* catered for by arrangement. Professional: Matthew Paget (01304 363017). Secretary: Reg Harrison (01304 373256; Fax: 01304 382336).
e-mail: Kingsdown.golf@gtwiz.co.uk

DEANGATE. **Deangate Ridge Golf Club,** Duxcourt Road, Hoo, Rochester ME3 8RZ (01634 250537). *Location:* three miles from Rochester off A228 towards Isle of Grain. Municipal course – wooded. 18 holes, 6300 yards. S.S.S. 70. 18 hole Pitch and Putt; 11-bay driving range. *Green Fees:* information not available. Special rates for Senior Citizens. *Eating* *facilities:* available. *Visitors:* welcome without reservation, bookings required for weekends. *Society Meetings:* catered for, book through Professional. Professional: Richard Fox (01634 251180). Secretary: C.J. Williams (01634 251950).

EDENBRIDGE. **Edenbridge Golf Club and Country Club,** Crouch House Road, Edenbridge TN8 5LQ (01732 867381; Fax: 01732 868060). *Location:* from M25 take A25, at Limpsfield take B2026 to Edenbridge. Parkland. Old Course 18 holes, 6577 yards. S.S.S. 70. Jubilee Course 18 holes, 5695 yards. S.S.S. 72. 20 bay floodlit driving range, state of the art teaching facilities and club fitting centre. *Green Fees:* Old Course - weekdays £25.00 per round, weekends and Bank Holidays £35.00 per round; Jubilee Course - weekdays £15.00, weekends £20.00. *Eating facilities:* bar and restaurant. *Visitors:* welcome, call for start time. Buggies and carts available. Health and fitness club. *Society Meetings:* societies welcome weekdays and weekends. Conference facility - seats up to 65. Director of Golf: Mark Chatfield (01732 867381; Fax: 01732 868060).

EDENBRIDGE. **Sweetwoods Park Golf Club,** Cowden, Edenbridge TN8 7JN (01342 850729; Fax: 01342 850866). *Location:* directly off the A264 at Holtye, 5 miles east of East Grinstead. Wooded, parkland course with many water features. 18 holes, 5285-6610 yards, S.S.S., 69-73 Par 72. Practice ground, driving range and carts available. *Green Fees:* information not available. *Visitors:* welcome anytime, no restrictions, can book up to 6 days in advance. *Society Meetings:* welcome Monday to Friday and Saturday pm. Professional: Paul Lyons (01342 850729). Secretary: Daniel Howe (01342 850942).* website: www.sweetwoodspark.com

ETCHINGHILL. **Etchinghill Golf Club,** Canterbury Road, Etchinghill CT18 8FA (01303 863863; Fax: 01303 863210). *Location:* one mile north of M20 Junction 12 on B2065. 27 holes, 6121 yards. S.S.S. 69. 9 hole Par 3 course. Covered and floodlit driving range. *Green Fees:* please phone for details. *Eating facilities:* full range of catering facilities available. *Visitors:* welcome. Professional: C. Hodgson (01303 863966).

EYNSFORD. **Austin Lodge Golf Club,** Upper Austin Lodge Road, Eynsford DA4 0HU (01322 863000; Fax: 01322 862406). *Location:* Enysford - 10 minutes' drive from Junction 3 of M25, M20, A20. Secluded rolling countryside with lakes. 18 holes, 6575 yards Yellow Tees, 7118 yards White Tees. S.S.S. 73. Practice ground. *Green Fees:* weekdays £22.00, weekends £30.00. *Eating facilities:* bar, restaurant with light meals all day. *Visitors:* welcome weekdays, and after 12noon weekends. Buggies available. *Society Meetings:* welcome, telephone booking only. Professional/Manager: Greg Haenan.

FARNBOROUGH. **High Elms Golf Club,** High Elms Road, Downe BR6 7SL (01689 853232). *Location:* two miles from Farnborough Hospital on A21, turn right at Shire Lane, second on left. Beautiful parkland. 18 holes, 6210 metres. S.S.S. 70. *Green Fees:* weekdays £12.30; weekends £16.10. *Eating facilities:* food available every day. *Visitors:* welcome, no restriction but should phone in advance. *Society Meetings:* apply to Catering Manageress - Mrs Griggs. Professional: Peter Remy (01689 858175). Secretary: Mrs P. O'Keeffe.

FAVERSHAM. **Boughton Golf Club,** Brickfield Lane, Boughton, Faversham ME13 9AJ (01227 752277; Fax: 01227 7523610. *Location:* north-east of Boughton, near M2/A2 interchange; six miles west of Canterbury 18 holes, 6452 yards. S.S.S. 71. Driving range. *Green Fees:* information not available. *Eating facilities:* available. *Visitors:* welcome. Professional: T. Dungate.

FAVERSHAM. **Faversham Golf Club Ltd.,** Belmont Park, Faversham ME13 0HB (01795 890561). *Location:* M2 Faversham Exit (A251) to A2 junction, left to Brogdale Road, left to Belmont. Long established (1902) very attractive parkland course in rural surroundings. 18 holes, 6021 yards. S.S.S. 69. *Green Fees:* £30.00 per round, £35.00 per day. *Eating facilities:* full catering. *Visitors:* welcome weekdays (Handicap Certificate required); weekends with member only. *Society Meetings:* catered for Mondays, Wednesdays and Fridays only. Professional: S. Rokes (01795 890275). Secretary: J. Edgington (01795 890561; Fax: 01795 890760).

FOLKESTONE. **Sene Valley Golf Club,** Sene, Folkestone CT18 8BL (01303 268513; Fax: 01303 237513). *Location:* M20 Junction 12, take A20 to Ashford turn left at first roundabout. Downland course with magnificent views over English Channel. 18 holes, 6196 yards. S.S.S. 70. Practice area. *Green Fees:* weekdays £25.00; weekends £30.00. *Eating facilities:* snacks, meals on request. *Visitors:* welcome, Handicap Certificate required. Preferable to book in advance. Snooker. *Society Meetings:* welcome by prior arrangements. Professional: Nick Watson (Tel & Fax: 01303 268514). Manager: Gordon Sykes.
e-mail: svgc@svgc.freeserve.co.uk
website: www.sceneatsene.co.uk

GILLINGHAM. **Gillingham Golf Club Ltd.,** Woodlands Road, Gillingham ME7 2AP (01634 850999). *Location:* on old A2 Gillingham. Flat parkland. 18 holes, 5557 yards, 5077 metres. S.S.S. 69. Practice nets. *Green Fees:* weekdays £28.00 per day; weekends £16.00 with a member only. Special rates on application. *Eating facilities:* available. *Visitors:* welcome at all times except weekends. Must have proof of Handicap or membership of another club. *Society Meetings:* welcome, maximum 30/36 players. Professional: Steven Green (01634 855862).General Manager: C. Cooper (01634 853017; Fax: 01634 574749).

GRAVESEND. **Mid-Kent Golf Club,** Singlewell Road, Gravesend DA11 7RB (01474 352387). *Location:* A227 off A2. Parkland. 18 holes, 6218 yards. S.S.S. 70. *Green Fees:* weekdays £25.00 per round, £35.00 per day; weekends with member only. *Eating facilities:* breakfast, dinner by arrangement, lunch every day, bar 11am to 11pm. *Visitors:* welcome weekdays except competition days with Handicap Certificate. *Society Meetings:* catered for Tuesdays only. Professional: Mark Foreman (01474 332810). Secretary: P. Gleeson (01474 568035; Fax: 01474 564218).

GRAVESEND. **Southern Valley Golf Course,** Thong Lane, Shorne, Gravesend DA12 4LF (01474 568568; Fax: 01474 360346). *Location:* take J4 off A2 (not M2), signposted "Inn on the Lake/Thong", at top of slip road turn left into Thong Lane at T-junction. Golf course is approx. one mile along on right-hand side. Undulating greens and rolling fairways. 18 holes, 6100 yards. Par 69. Practice area, putting green. *Green Fees:* Monday to Thursday £16.50, weekends £19.00. *Eating facilities:* fully licensed bar and restaurant. *Visitors:* all welcome. No jeans or tracksuits; golf shoes must be worn. Tuition available; golf shop; buggies for hire April to October. *Society Meetings:* welcome, telephone in advance. Professional: Larry Batchelor. Club Administrator: Mrs Anne Green (01474 740026).

HALSTEAD. **Broke Hill Golf Club, Sevenoaks Road, Halstead, Kent TN14 7HR (01959 533225; Fax: 01959 532680).** *Location:* **four minutes from M25 Junction 4, A21, four miles from Bromley and two miles from Orpington. Parkland course, with strategically placed bunkers and 5 holes where water comes into play. 18 holes, 6415 yards. S.S.S. 71.Two practice**

grounds. *Green Fees:* available on request. *Eating facilities:* lounge bar, restaurant and banqueting facilities. *Visitors:* welcome weekdays only, strict dress code applies. Soft spikes or dimple shoes preferred. Golf buggies and carts available. *Society Meetings:* weekdays only. Professional: Cameron McKillop (01959 533810; Fax: 01959 532680). General Manager: Bill Thompson (01959 533225; Fax: 01959 532680).

HAWKHURST. **Hawkhurst Golf Club**, High Street, Hawkhurst TN18 4JS (01580 754074/752396; Fax: 01580 754074). *Location:* on A268 from Flimwell to Hawkhurst. Undulating parkland. 9 holes, 5751 yards. S.S.S. 68. Practice ground. *Green Fees:* £20.00 per round weekdays; £24.00 weekends with member only. *Eating facilities:* bar, spike bar, dining room. *Visitors:* welcome weekdays, weekends with member only. Handicap Certificate recommended. Squash courts. Clubs, trolleys and buggies are available for hire. *Society Meetings:* welcome Wednesdays and Fridays. Professional: Tony Collins (Tel & Fax: 01580 753600). Secretary: Brian Morrison (Tel & Fax: 01580 754074).

HEADCORN. **Weald of Kent Golf Course,** Maidstone Road, Headcorn TN27 9PT (01622 891671; Fax: 01622 891793). *Location:* Junction 8 M20, five miles south of Maidstone on A274. Scenic undulating parkland course with many ditches, ponds and lakes. 18 holes, 6169 yards. S.S.S. 70. *Green Fees:* information not available. *Eating facilities:* 65 cover restaurant and an extensive bar menu available from 7.30am to 10pm. Banqueting and conference facilities also available (30 to 200 delegates). *Visitors:* welcome anytime, bookings available three days in advance (01622 890866). *Society Meetings:* welcome seven days a week with advance booking required, minimum 12. Manager: Philip Bryant.*

HERNE BAY. **Herne Bay Golf Club,** Eddington, Herne Bay CT6 7PG (01227 373964). *Location:* off the New Thanet Way. Parkland/links course. 18 holes, 5567 yards. S.S.S. 68. Practice ground. *Green Fees:* information not available. Twilight fee after 3pm. *Eating facilities:* bar meals, restaurant by arrangement. *Visitors:* welcome weekdays unrestricted, weekends and Bank Holidays after 12 noon only. Handicap Certificate required. *Society Meetings:* welcome by prior arrangement. Professional: D. Ledingham (01227 374727).

HEVER. **Hever Castle Golf Club,** Hever, Edenbridge TN8 7NP (01732 700771; Fax: 01732 700775). *Location:* at Junction 6 take A22 turning to Godstone, then turn left onto the A25 to Sevenoaks, after three and a half miles take the Edenbridge road. Adjacent to Hever Castle. Go past the entrance to castle and the club is one mile further on the right. Parkland, wooded. 27 holes. Kings and Queens course: 18 holes, 7002 yards. S.S.S. 74. Princes course: 9 holes, 2784 yards. S.S.S. 67 (for 18 holes). Large practice range, chipping and pitching areas, practice bunker, putting green. *Green Fees:* weekdays £35.00 18 holes, £50.00 per day; weekends £55.00 18 holes, £75.00 per day. *Eating* *facilities:* restaurant and bars. *Visitors:* welcome by appointment, or with a member; limited weekends. *Society Meetings:* welcome by prior arrangement; competitive rates available. Head PGA Professional: Peter Parks. General Manager: Mark Hickson.

HYTHE. **Hythe Imperial Golf Club,** Princes Parade, Hythe CT21 6AE (01303 267441). *Location:* come off M20 Junction 11, directions for Hythe A261. Flat seaside course. 9 holes, 5533 yards. S.S.S. 67. Practice ground. *Green Fees:* information not available. *Eating facilities:* available at the hotel. *Visitors:* welcome weekdays, no green fees weekends up to 1pm. *Society Meetings:* welcome weekdays only. Professional: Gordon Ritchie (01303 267441). Professional Shop: (01303 233745) Secretary: Mr R. Duncan (Tel & Fax: 01303 267554).

LYDD. **Lydd Golf Club and Driving Range,** Romney Road, Lydd, Romney Marsh TN29 9LS (01797 320808; Fax: 01797 321482). *Location:* B2075 within half a mile of Lydd Airport. Traditional links course with added water hazards. 18 holes, 6517 yards. S.S.S. 71. 24 bay floodlit driving range. *Green Fees:* weekdays £17.00 per round; weekends £25.00 per round. *Eating facilities:* bar and restaurant. *Visitors:* no restrictions. Pull trollies, electric trollies and golf carts. *Society Meetings:* welcome, discount rates available. Professional: Stuart Smith (01797 321201). Secretary: Brian Evans (01797 320808; Fax: 01797 321482).

MAIDSTONE. **Bearsted Golf Club,** Ware Street, Bearsted ME14 4PQ (01622 738389). *Location:* Junction 7 off M20, turn right to Bearsted and follow signs. Undulating parkland course with view of North Downs. 18 holes, 6320 yards, 5739 metres. S.S.S. 70. Practice area, putting green, net. *Green Fees:* £32.00/£42.00 weekdays; weekends with a member. *Eating facilities:* bar/restaurant, open all day. *Visitors:* welcome weekdays, weekends must be with members. Current Handicap Certificates required. *Society Meetings:* catered for Tuesdays to Fridays by prior arrangement. Professional: Tim Simpson (01622 738024). Secretary: Mrs L.M. Siems (01622 738198; Fax: 01622 735608).

MAIDSTONE. **Cobtree Manor Park Golf Club,** Chatham Road, Sandling, Maidstone ME14 3AZ (01662 753276). *Location:* M20, A229 Chatham (not Maidstone). Undulating course with trees, and interesting 12th hole over lake. 18 holes, 5611 yards. S.S.S. 69. Tuition, practice, putting. *Green Fees:* information on request. *Eating facilities:* restaurant and bar. *Visitors:* welcome, book four days in advance through Professional. *Society Meetings:* welcome phone (01622 751881). Professional: Paul Foston (01622 753276).

MAIDSTONE. **Leeds Castle Golf Course**, Leeds Castle, Near Maidstone ME17 1PL (01622 767828). *Location:* M20 Junction 8, A20 near Maidstone. Situated in the grounds of Leeds Castle, parkland. 9 holes, 2681 yards. S.S.S. 33. Putting green and practice nets. *Green Fees:* weekdays £11.00 9 holes, £18.50 18 holes; Juniors / Senior Citizens £8.00 / £15.50; weekends and Bank Holidays £13.00 9 holes,

£26.00 18 holes. *Eating facilities:* Leeds Castle Restaurant on Leeds Castle Estate. *Visitors:* welcome anytime, bookings taken from six days in advance. Correct dress must be worn - no denim jeans allowed, golf shoes preferred. *Society Meetings:* welcome weekdays. Professional: Steve Purves. Secretary: Ann Bishop.

MAIDSTONE. **Marriott Tudor Park Hotel and Country Club,** Ashford Road, Bearsted, Maidstone ME14 4NQ (01622 734334). *Location:* east of Maidstone, on A20 at Bearsted. Off Junction 8 of M20. Parkland. 18 holes, 6085 yards. S.S.S. 69. Practice area. *Green Fees:* weekdays £35.00; weekends £40.00. *Eating facilities:* restaurants and bars. *Visitors:* Hotel with 120 bedrooms, leisure and conference facilities. *Society Meetings:* Societies and Company Days catered for. Professional: Nick McNally (01622 739412). Secretary: John Ladbrooke (01622 737119). Golf Operations Manager: Jason King.

MAIDSTONE. **The Ridge Golf Club,** Chartway Street, East Sutton, Maidstone ME17 3DL (01622 844243; Fax: 01622 844168). *Location:* Junction 8 M20, past Leeds Castle on Sutton Valence Road to A274 turn left and first turning on left. 18 holes, 6254 yards. S.S.S. 71. Driving range. *Green Fees:* information not available. *Eating facilities:* two bars, bar snack menu and full menu. *Visitors:* welcome. *Society Meetings:* welcome Monday to Sunday. (01622 844243).

MAIDSTONE. **West Malling Golf Club**, London Road, Addington, West Malling ME19 5AR (01732 844785; Fax: 01732 844795). *Location:* M20, A228 turn off. Parkland/wooded course. Spitfire Course - 18 holes, 6142 yards. S.S.S. 70. Hurricane Course - 18 holes, 6300 yards. S.S.S 70. Practice ground. *Green Fees:* weekdays £25.00 per round, £40.00 per day; weekends £30.00 per round after 12 noon. *Eating facilities:* restaurant available. *Visitors:* welcome weekdays anytime, weekends after 12 noon. Conference/function facilities available. Buggies available. *Society Meetings:* catered for by prior arragement. Professional: Duncan Lambert (01732 844022). Secretary: Mike Ellis (01732 844785; Fax: 01732 844795).

NEW ROMNEY. **Littlestone Golf Club,** St Andrews Road, Littlestone, New Romney TN28 8RB (01797 362231; Fax: 01797 362740). *Location:* M20 Junction 10 (Ashford), B2070 to Brenzett - New Romney, one mile from New Romney. Seaside Championship links course. 18 holes, Blue tees 6676 yards, S.S.S. 73, White tees 6486 yards, S.S.S 72. Driving range, practice ground, chipping and putting greens. *Green Fees:* £60.00 per day weekdays; £70.00 per day weekends. *Eating facilities:* full dining room and bar. *Visitors:* Handicap Certificate required. Visitors restricted at weekends in Winter, in Summer only after 3pm, singles and foursomes only. Caddie cars available. *Society Meetings:* welcome. Professional: Andrew Jones (01797 362231). Secretary: Col. Charles Moorhouse (01797 363355; Fax: 01797 362740).
e-mail: secretary@littlestonegolfclub.org.uk
website: www.littlestonegolfclub.org.uk

St Augustine's Golf Club

Cottington Road, Cliffsend, Ramsgate, Kent CT12 5JN

SOCIETY PACKAGES AVAILABLE
18 HOLE COURSE

GREEN FEES:
Weekdays £25 full day
£18 per round

Weekends £30 full day
£19.50 per round

Full catering facilities available
Licensed bar

See also Colour Advertisement on page 24

Secretary: 01843 590333
Professional: 01843 590222
Fax: 01843 590444
e-mail: sagc.@ic24.net

NEW ROMNEY. **Romney Warren Golf Club,** St. Andrews Road, Littlestone, New Romney TN28 8RB (01797 362231; Fax: 01797 362740). *Location:* one mile from New Romney off A259, down B2070; 20 minutes from J10 on M20. Undulating seaside links crisscrossed with dykes. 18 holes, 5126 yards. S.S.S. 67. Practice range. *Green Fees:* weekdays £17.00 per round, £29.00 per day; weekends £22.00 per round, £38.00 per day. *Eating facilities:* bar and restaurant. *Visitors:* welcome. *Society Meetings:* welcome by arrangement. Professional: Andrew Jones . Hon. Secretary: Mr J. Purkiss (01797 362768). website: www.romneywarrengolfclub.org

ORPINGTON. **Chelsfield Lakes Golf Centre,** Court Road, Orpington BR6 9BX (01689 896266; Fax: 01689 824577). *Location:* M25 Junction 4, A224 Court Road. Gently undulating course with hazards and sandtraps; played through some orchards. 18 holes, 6077 yards. S.S.S. 69. 9 holes, 1188 yards. Par 3. 40 bay floodlit driving range, practice area. *Green Fees:* information not available. *Eating facilities:* bar and restaurant. *Visitors:* welcome, pay as you play facility, non members can book 7 days in advance. Pro shop. *Society Meetings:* welcome. Professionals: Nigel Lee, Bill Hodkin.*

visit the FHG golf website on
www.uk-golfguide.com

ORPINGTON. **Cray Valley Golf Club,** Sandy Lane, St. Paul's Cray, Orpington BR5 3HY. *Location:* Ruxley roundabout A20; turn off into Sandy Lane, half a mile on left. Parkland. 18 holes, 5624 yards. S.S.S. 67. Also 9 hole course. *Green Fees:* information not available. *Eating facilities:* hot meals available lunchtimes, also bar. *Visitors:* welcome all week. *Society Meetings:* welcome. Professional: Gary Stewart (01689 837909). General Manager: Tom Ashman (01689 839677). *

ORPINGTON. **Lullingstone Park Golf Club,** Park Gate Road, Chelsfield, Near Orpington, Kent BR6 7PX (01959 533794). *Location:* two miles from Junction 4 off M25, fifth exit on left (signposted). Undulating parkland. 18 holes, 6779 yards. S.S.S. 72. 9 holes, 2432 yards. Par 33. 22 bay driving range, pitch and putt course, putting green. *Green Fees:* information not available. *Eating facilities:* cafeteria and bar. *Visitors:* bookings welcome. *Society Meetings:* very welcome, telephone Professional for package details. Professional: Mark Watt (01959 533793; Fax: 01959 534129). Secretary: Chris Pocock.

ORPINGTON. **Ruxley Park Golf Centre,** Sandy Lane, St. Pauls Cray, Orpington BR5 3HY (01689 871490; Fax: 01689 891428). *Location:* off old A20 at Ruxley Corner. 18 holes, Par 71. 9 hole Academy course. 24 bays, covered, floodlit, grassed. *Green Fees:* information not available. *Eating facilities:* breakfast, lunch available, bar open all day. *Society Meetings:* welcome all week. Head Professional: Mike Worley. General Manager: Tom Ashman.*

ORPINGTON. **West Kent Golf Club,** West Hill, Downe, Near Orpington BR6 7JJ (01689 851323). *Location:* from Downe village south along Luxted Lane, 600 yards turn right into West Hill. 18 holes, 6399 yards. S.S.S. 70. *Green Fees:* £35.00 per round, £50.00 per day. *Eating facilities:* meals by arrangement. *Visitors:* welcome weekdays only with recognised handicap. Casual golfers should phone at least 24 hours in advance. *Society Meetings:* catered for. Professionals: R.S. Fidler and K. Smithson (Tel & Fax: 01689 856863). Secretary: Tony Barclay (01689 851323).

RAMSGATE. **St. Augustine's Golf Club,** Cottington Road, Cliffsend, Ramsgate CT12 5JN (01843 590333; Fax: 01843 590444). *Location:* two miles south-west of Ramsgate – approaching from A253 or A256 follow signs to St. Augustine's Cross. Entrance 75 yards beyond Cross by railway bridge. Mainly parkland, flat - tight and challenging course. 18 holes, 4999 yards, 4572 metres. S.S.S. 64. *Green Fees:* weekdays £18.00, £25.00 per day; weekends and Bank Holidays £19.50, £30.00 per day. Weekly £65.00, monthly £195.00. *Eating facilities:* full catering except Mondays when sandwiches and beverages only, usual bar facilities. *Visitors:* welcome, proof of Handicap required, advisable to ring Professional the day before to check periods booked for competitions, societies, etc. *Society Meetings:* catered for, book through Secretary. Professional: D. Scott (01843 590222). Secretary: L.P Dyke (01843 590333). e-mail: sagc@ic24.net

RAMSGATE. **Stonelees Golf Centre,** Ebbsfleet Lane, Near Ramsgate CT12 5DJ (01843 823133; Fax: 01843 850569). *Location:* near junction of A256 and the B2048 (Ebbsfleet Lane). Undulating seaside/ parkland courses. Excutive course - 9 holes, 1510 yards, 1393 metres. S.S.S. 29; Par 3 course - 9 holes, 1159 yards, 1069 metres. S.S.S. 27. Full length 9 hole course under construction. *Green Fees:* Executive - weekdays £6.00 9 holes, £9.30 18 holes; weekends £6.60 9 holes, £10.00 18 holes. Par 3 - weekdays £4.50 9 holes, £7.70 18 holes; weekends £5.30 9 holes, £8.80 18 holes. Prices subject to review. Junior rates available, membership discounts. Full length 9-hole course (3400 yards) under construction; 6 holes in play as academy course. Day ticket £7.00 weekdays, £10.00 weekends. *Eating facilities:* licensed bar, restaurant. *Visitors:* always welcome, no restrictions. Excellent teaching facilities, 20 bay driving range, Smart Golf simulator, practice putting green, chipping area, miniature putting course.*Society Meetings:* small societies/groups welcome. Professional: David Bonthron. Manager: Dr Peter Nicholson.

ROCHESTER. **Rochester and Cobham Park Golf Club,** Park Pale, by Rochester ME2 3UL (01474 823411; Fax: 01474 824446). *Location:* on A2, two miles east of Gravesend East turn-off. Undulating parkland. 18 holes, 6597 yards. S.S.S. 72. Driving range, practice ground. *Green Fees:* weekdays £35.00 per round, £45.00 per day. *Eating facilities:* morning coffee, lunch, tea, dinner available, two bars. *Visitors:* welcome midweek only with Handicap Certificate. *Society Meetings:* welcome Tuesdays and Thursdays, must be pre-booked. Professional: I. Higgins (01474 823658). Manager: D.W. Smith (01474 823411; Fax: 01474 824446).

SANDWICH. **Royal St. Georges Golf Club,** Sandwich CT13 9PB (01304 613090; Fax: 01304 611245). *Location:* one mile from Sandwich on the road to Sandwich Bay. From Canterbury A257, from Dover A258. Links. 18 holes, Championship 7102 yards, Medal 6607 yards. S.S.S. Championship 74, Medal 72. Practice ground. *Green Fees:* £90.00 for one round, £125.00 for two rounds weekdays. Subject to review. *Eating facilities:* snack bar and dining room. *Visitors:* welcome weekdays only, must

be pre-booked. No visitors at weekends or on Public Holidays. Must have Handicap Certificate (under 18) and be member of club affiliated to E.G.U. Caddies to be booked in advance, trolleys available. *Society Meetings:* catered for by arrangement. All players must meet requirements for visitors. Professional: A. Brooks (01304 615236). Secretary: H.C.G. Gabbey (01304 613090; Fax: 01304 611245). Caddiemaster: (01304 617380).

SANDWICH BAY. **Prince's Golf Club,** Prince's Drive, Sandwich Bay, Sandwich (01304 611118; Fax: 01304 612000). *Location:* four miles from Sandwich through the Sandwich Bay Estate. Seaside links. 27 holes arranged as 3 loops of 9 holes named "Dunes", "Himalayas", "Shore". D & H 6262 - 6776 yds, Par 71, S.S.S. 70-73. H & S 6238 - 6813 yds, Par 71, S.S.S. 70-73. S & D 6466-6947 yds, Par 72, S.S.S. 71-73. Championship 7181 yards. Driving range, full practice facilities. *Green Fees:* £40.00 to £70.00 depending on season. Packages available. *Eating facilities:* breakfast, lunch, dinner available every day (pre-booking advisable); bar; light snacks throughout the day. *Visitors & Societies:* welcome without restriction, Company days and private parties catered for. Brochure available on request. Professional: Derek Barbour (01304 613797). Information & Bookings: Ali McGuirk (01304 611118). General Manager: W.M. Howie (01304 613388; Fax: 01304 612000).
e-mail: golf@princes-leisure.co.uk
website: www.princes-leisure.co.uk

SEVENOAKS. **Darenth Valley Golf Course Ltd,** Station Road, Shoreham, Near Sevenoaks TN14 7SA (01959 522944; Fax: 01959 525089). *Location:* A225 between Otford and Eynsford, approximately four miles north of Sevenoaks. Pay and play parkland course. 18 holes, 6258 yards. S.S.S. 72. Practice area, putting green. *Green Fees:* weekdays £17.50, weekends £23.00 (subject to review). *Eating facilities*: bar snacks and meals; diningroom, functions up to 150 covers. *Visitors:* welcome with reservation through Pro shop. *Society Meetings:* welcome by arrangement. Professional: David Copsey (01959 522922). General Manager: Jonathan Cooper (01959 522944; Fax: 01959 525089).

SEVENOAKS. **Knole Park Golf Club**, Seal Hollow Road, Sevenoaks TN15 0HJ (01732 452150; Fax: 01732 463159). *Location:* one mile north-east of Sevenoaks town centre. Deer Park; beautiful, natural course. Second to none in the South East. 18 holes, 6246 yards. S.S.S. 70. Practice ground and nets. *Green Fees:* weekdays only, £35.00 per round, £46.00 per day. Subject to review. *Eating facilities:* full bar and catering. *Visitors:* welcome by appointment, Handicap Certificate required. Squash courts. Society Meetings: catered for by arrangement only. Professional: (01732 451740). Secretary: Peter Mitchell (01732 452150; Fax: 01732 463159). website: www.knoleparkgolfclub.co.uk

SEVENOAKS. **Wildernesse Club**, Park Lane, Seal, Sevenoaks TN15 0JE (01732 761526). Location: A25 between Sevenoaks and Borough Green. Park and woodland. 18 holes, 6440 yards. S.S.S. 71. Large practice ground. *Green Fees:* information not available. *Eating facilities:* by arrangement. *Visitors:* welcome weekdays only by prior arrangement; Handicap Certificate required. *Society Meetings:* catered for Mondays, Thursdays and Fridays. Professional: Craig Walker (01732 761527). Secretary: R.A. Foster (01732 761199). *

SEVENOAKS. **Woodlands Manor Golf Club**, Tinkerpot Lane, Woodlands, Near Otford, Sevenoaks TN15 6AB (01959 523805). *Location:* Junction 3, M25 take "Brands Hatch" sign on A20, seven miles. Parkland, designated Area of Outstanding Natural Beauty. 18 holes, 6100 yards. S.S.S. 69. Six acre practice ground. *Green Fees:* on application. *Eating facilities:* bar daily. *Visitors:* welcome weekdays, Handicap Certificate required at weekends after 1pm. Buggies for hire. *Society Meetings:* welcome by arrangement Monday to Friday. Professional: Philip Womack (01959 524161). Secretary: C.G. Robins (01959 523806).

SEVENOAKS. **Wrotham Heath Golf Club,** Seven Mile Lane, Comp, Sevenoaks TN15 8QZ (01732 884800). *Location:* on B2016 half-a-mile south of junction with A20. Woodland/heathland. 18 holes, 5954 yards. S.S.S. 69. *Green Fees:* information not available. *Eating facilities:* bar and snacks, meals by arrangement, except Mondays. *Visitors:* welcome on weekdays with Handicap Certificate, but not Bank Holidays. *Society Meetings:* catered for Thursdays and Fridays only, no more than 30 people. Professional: H. Dearden (01732 883854). Secretary: L.J. Byrne (01732 884800).

SHEERNESS. **Sheerness Golf Club,** Power Station Road, Sheerness ME12 3AE (01795 662585). *Location:* follow A249 then A250 towards Sheerness. Flat marshland/meadowland; numerous water hazards. 18 holes, 6460 yards. S.S.S. 71. Practice area. *Green Fees:* weekdays £20.00 per round, £28.00 per day; weekends £25.00 per round (by appointment only). *Eating facilities:* available. *Visitors:* weekdays only except with member. *Society Meetings:* catered for weekdays, except Mondays, by previous arrangement. Secretary: A. Jones.

SIDCUP. **Sidcup Golf Club (1926) Ltd,** 7 Hurst Road, Sidcup DA15 9AE (020 8300 2150). Location: three minutes' walk from Sidcup Station. Parkland. 9 holes, 5571 yards. S.S.S. 68. Practice area. *Green Fees:* weekdays £18.00. *Eating facilities:* restaurant and bar. *Visitors:* welcome weekdays except Bank Holidays. *Society Meetings:* (up to 30 members) catered for by arrangement. Secretary: John Aughterlony (020 8300 2150).

SITTINGBOURNE. **The Oast Golf Centre Ltd**, Church Road, Tonge, Sittingbourne ME9 9AR (01795 473527). *Location:* one mile north A2 between Faversham and Sittingbourne, take the turning to Tonge at Bapchild, signposted from A2. 9 hole, 800 yards, Par 3. Pay and play. *Green Fees:* information not available. *Eating facilities:* sandwiches, rolls available. *Visitors:* welcome. Tuition available, golf shop. Two short mat bowls facility. Function rooms available for business or social purpose. *Society Meetings:* welcome. Professional: David Chambers. Secretary: Sally Chambers. e-mail: mail@oastgolf.co.uk

SITTINGBOURNE. **Sittingbourne and Milton Regis**, Wormdale, Newington, Sittingbourne ME9 7PX (01795 842261; Fax: 01795 844117). *Location:* Junction 5 M2, follow signs to Danaway Chestnut Street, three quarters of a mile, first left over Bridge to Wormdale. Undulating course with trees. 18 holes, 6291 yards, 5771 metres. S.S.S. 70. *Green Fees:* 18 holes £28.00, 36 holes £35.00. No visitors weekends. *Eating facilities:* available. *Visitors:* welcome weekdays, Handicap Certificate or letter of introduction required. *Society Meetings:* catered for Tuesdays and Thursdays by arrangement. Professional: J. Hearn (01795 842775). Manager: H.D.G. Wylie.

SITTINGBOURNE near. **Upchurch River Valley Golf Courses**, Oak Lane, Upchurch, near Sittingbourne ME9 7AY (01634 360626; Fax: 01634 387784). *Location:* M2, Junction 4 (A278) or Junction 5 (A249) onto A2 between Rainham and Newington, Oak Lane (opposite Little Chef). Undulating parkland with ponds and panoramic views. 18 holes, 6237 yards, 5701 metres. S.S.S. 70. 9 holes, 1596 yards, Par 30. Driving range. *Green Fees:* information not available. *Eating facilities:* 120 seater à la carte restaurant, all day food and drinks lounge. *Visitors:* unrestricted. Swimming pool. *Society Meetings:* welcome weekdays. Professional: Roger Cornwell (01634 379592). Secretary: (Members only) D. Candy (01634 260594). Course Controller: URVGC Ltd. *

SNODLAND. **Oastpark Golf Course,** Malling Road, Snodland ME6 5LG (01634 242661). *Location:* half a mile from M20, two miles from M2; five miles from Maidstone. Easy walking, good test of golf, lots of water/sand/trees. 9 holes, 3150 yards. S.S.S. 70. Extensive practice facilities. Floodlit driving range. *Green Fees:* information not available. *Eating facilities:* full bar and catering service. *Visitors:* welcome, no restrictions. No jeans, tracksuits; golf shoes must be worn. *Society Meetings:* all welcome weekdays, and weekends after 11am. Professional: David Porthouse (01634 242661). Secretary: Mrs Lesley Murrock (01634 242818; Fax: 01634 240744).

SWANLEY. **Pedham Place Golf Centre**, London Road, Swanley BR8 8PP (01322 867000; Fax: 01322 861646). *Location:* 300 yards east of Junction 3 M25, on A20 towards Brands Hatch. Two elevated links-style courses. 18 holes, 6444 yards. S.S.S. 71, Par 72; 9 holes, 1165 yards, Par 3. 40-bay floodlit driving range, putting green, practice facilities. *Green Fees:* information not available. *Eating facilities:* bar snacks to full meals; licensed bar. Modern marquee for larger groups. *Visitors:* all welcome. Thursday morning Ladies' day, Wednesday morning Veterans. Appropriate clothing/footwear must be worn. Buggy hire available. *Societies:* welcome, special rates available. Secretary: Laurence Goodwin. Professionals: Fred Hanlon, Ron Mitchell.*
e-mail: golf@ppgc.co.uk
website: www.ppgc.co.uk

TATSFIELD. **Park Wood Golf Club**, Chestnut Avenue, Tatsfield, Near Westerham TN16 2EG (01959 577744). *Location:* on B2024 Croydon road which becomes Clarks Lane. At Church Hill junction join Chestnut Avenue. In an area of natural beauty, flanked by an ancient woodland, with superb views across Kent and Surrey. Undulating course, tree-lined and with some interesting water features. Playable in all weather. 18 holes, 6835 yards. Par 72. S.S.S. 72. Course record 66. *Green Fees:* on application. *Visitors:* telephone in advance. May not play on Bank Holidays. *Societies:* apply in writing/telephone. Professional: Nick Terry. Assistant Professional: Robert Parkhouse.

TENTERDEN. **Tenterden Golf Club,** Woodchurch Road, Tenterden TN30 7DR (Tel & Fax: 01580 763987). *Location*: 30 minutes from Channel Tunnel and west of Ashford International Station, on B2067 Woodchurch Road, Tenterden. Parkland course set in beautiful undulating Wealden countryside. 18 holes, 6152 yards. S.S.S. 70. Practice ground. *Green Fees:* weekdays £23.00; weekends/Bank Holidays with a member only. *Eating facilities:* available, breakfast on request, lunch, snacks and dinner, all day bar. *Society Meetings:* dedicated society days by prior arrangement. Professional: (01580 762409). Secretary: Norman Taylor (01580 763987).
website: www.tenterdengolfclub.co.uk

TONBRIDGE. **Hilden Golf Centre**, Hilden Park, Rings Hill, Hildenborough, Tonbridge TN11 8LX (01732 833607; Fax: 01732 834484). *Location*: take exit off A21 for Tonbridge North/Hildenborough; take second turning right (Watts Cross Road), follow road past station to bottom of the hill, golf centre is on the left. 36 bay covered, floodlit and grassed driving range. *Fees:* £2.00 for 40 balls. *Green Fees:* 9 holes weekdays £6.50; weekends £8.50. *Eating facilities:* fully licensed cafe bar open 8am to 10pm.

all year round. Opening hours: weekdays 8am to 10pm, weekends 7.30am to 8pm. Three PGA professionals (tuition available), large golf shop, 9 hole golf course and putting green. Leisure centre and creche. Teaching academy and large golf discount store stocking all the top brands at discount prices. Professionals: Nicky Way, Rupert Hunter and Matt Jarvis. Secretary: Vicki Brett (01732 834404; Fax: 01732 834484).

TONBRIDGE. **Nizels Golf Club**, Nizels Lane, Hildenborough, Near Tonbridge TN11 8NU (01732 833833; Fax: 01732 833492). *Location:* M25 B245 off A21. Take signs to Tonbridge North, Club 1 mile, Nizels Lane. Undulating parkland, several holes where water comes into play, many mature trees. 18 holes, 6297 yards off white tees. S.S.S. 71. Par 72. Limited practice area. *Green Fees:* information not available. *Eating facilities:* bar snacks and fine dining available. *Visitors:* welcome Monday - Friday after 9.30am, Saturday - Sunday after 12.30pm. *Society Meetings:* weekdays only after 9.30am. Professional: Neil Thirkell (01732 838926).

TONBRIDGE. **Poult Wood Public Golf Centre,** Higham Lane, Tonbridge TN11 9QR (01732 364039). *Location:* signposted from the A26 between Hadlow and Tonbridge. Parkland, very wooded. 18 holes, 5569 yards. S.S.S. 67. 9 hole course, practice ground. *Green Fees:* information not available. *Eating facilities:* restaurant, bar, snack bar. *Visitors:* welcome every day. *Society Meetings:* welcome by booking only (01732 366180). Squash court. Professional: Chris Miller (01732 364039). *

TUNBRIDGE WELLS. **Lamberhurst Golf Club**, Church Road, Lamberhurst TN3 8DT (01892 890241; Fax: 01892 891140). *Location:* A21 from Tunbridge Wells to Hastings, turn left prior to descending hill to Lamberhurst then first right. Attractive parkland course. 18 holes, 6364 yards. S.S.S. 70. Small practice ground. *Green Fees:* information not available. *Eating facilities:* full catering by arrangement. *Visitors:* welcome after 8am weekdays, 12 noon weekends and Bank Holidays. Handicap Certificate required. *Society Meetings:* catered for Tuesdays, Wednesdays and Thursdays by arrangement. Professional: Brain Impett (01892 890552). Secretary: R.J. Walden (01892 890591; Fax: 01892 891140). *

TUNBRIDGE WELLS. **Nevill Golf Club,** Benhall Mill Road, Tunbridge Wells TN2 5JW (01892 527820; Fax: 01892 517861). *Location:* off Forest Road, south of Tunbridge Wells. Parkland course with trees. 18 holes, 6349 yards. S.S.S. 70. Practice ground. *Green Fees:* weekdays £25.00 per round, £33.00 two rounds; weekends and Bank Holidays £46.00. *Eating facilities:* lunches at club by prior arrangement. *Visitors:* welcome with 48 hours notice. Handicap Certificate required. Trolley hire. *Society Meetings:* welcome with previous booking. Professional: Paul Huggett (01892 532941). Secretary: Mr T.J. Fenson (01892 525818; Fax: 01892 517861). website: www.nevillgolfclub.co.uk

TUNBRIDGE WELLS. **Tunbridge Wells Golf Club,** Langton Road, Tunbridge Wells TN4 8XH (01892 523034). *Location:* adjoining Spa Hotel on A264. Parkland. 9 holes, 4725 yards. S.S.S. 62. *Green Fees:* weekdays £14.00 per round, £20.00 per day; weekends £20.00 per 18 holes. *Eating facilities:* menu choices available daily but best to check requirements in advance. *Visitors:* welcome anytime subject to availability. *Society Meetings:* welcome, contact the Secretary for details. Professional: M. Barton (01892 541386). Secretary: R.F. Mealing (01892 536918).

WESTERHAM. **Westerham Golf Club,** Valence Park, Brasted Road, Westerham TN16 1LJ (01959 567100; Fax: 01959 567101). *Location*: midway between Westerham and Brasted on the A25. Mainly wooded with some parkland. 18 holes, 6272 yards. S.S.S. 70. Driving range. **Green Fees**: Monday to Thursday £29.00 per round, £45.00 per day; Friday £32.00 per round, £50.00 per day; weekends and Bank Holidays £36.00 after 12 noon. **Eating facilities**: bar and catering facilities available. **Visitors**: welcome weekdays and weekends (at restricted times). Buggies and carts available for hire. **Society Meetings**: welcome weekdays only. Professional: James Marshall. General Manager: Rob Sturgeon. e-mail: terri.willison@westerhamgc.co.uk website: www. westerhamgc.co.uk

WESTGATE ON SEA. **Westgate and Birchington Golf Club,** 176 Canterbury Road, Westgate on Sea CT8 8LT. *Location:* seaside course between Westgate on Sea and Birchington (A28). Seaside links course. 18 holes, 4926 yards, 4547 metres. S.S.S. 64. *Green Fees:* weekdays £17.00, weekends and Bank Holidays £20.00 (includes £1.00 compulsory insurance). *Eating facilities:* available by prior arrangement with Steward. *Visitors:* welcome after 10am. *Society Meetings:* by arrangement with Secretary. Professional: R. Game (01843 831115). Secretary: T.J. Sharp (01843 831115).

WEST MALLING. **King's Hill Golf Club**, Discovery Drive, King's Hill, West Malling ME19 4AG (01732 875040; Fax: 01732 875019). *Location*: Junction 4 of M20. Heathland course. 18 holes, 6622 yards. S.S.S. 72. *Green Fees*: information not available. *Eating facilities*: restaurant and bar open all day. *Visitors*: welcome Monday to Friday. Tuition available. *Society Meetings*: welcome Monday to Friday. Professional: David Hudspith (01732 842121). Secretary: Margaret Gilbert (01732 875040; Fax: 01732 875019). e-mail: khatkhgolf@aol.com website: www.kingshillgolf.co.uk

WHITSTABLE. **Chestfield (Whitstable) Golf Club,** 103 Chestfield Road, Chestfield, Whitstable CT5 3LU (01227 794411). *Location:* half a mile south of Old Thanet Way (A2990). Parkland with sea views. 18 holes, 6208 yards. S.S.S. 70. *Green Fees:* £25.00 weekdays, £28.00 weekends. *Eating facilities:* lunchtime snacks, bar 11am to 11 pm. *Visitors:* welcome. *Society Meetings:* welcome and catered for weekdays. Professional: John Brotherton (01227 793563). e-mail: secretary@chestfield-golfclub.co.uk website: www.chestfield-golfclub.co.uk

WHITSTABLE. **Whitstable and Seasalter Golf Club,** Collingwood Road, Whitstable CT5 1EB (01227 272020). *Location:* course adjoins town centre, take Nelson Road turning off main street. Flat seaside links. 9 holes, 5357 yards. S.S.S. 63. Practice net. *Green Fees:* £20.00, green fees are accepted at weekends by prior arrangement. *Eating facilities:* bar snacks. Secretary: M.D. Moore.

Lancashire

ACCRINGTON. **Accrington and District Golf Club,** New Barn Farm, West End, Oswaldtwistle, Accrington (01254 381614; Fax: 01254 233273). *Location*: on A679, 2 miles from Blackburn. 18 holes, 6060 yards. S.S.S. 69. *Green Fees*: Monday to Thursday £24.00, Friday to Sunday £30.00. *Eating facilities*: lunches and evening meals. *Visitors*: welcome by prior arrangement. *Society Meetings*: prior bookings catered for. Professional: Bill Harling (01254 231091). Hon Secretary: G. Dixon (01254 381614).

ACCRINGTON. **Green Haworth Golf Club,** Green Haworth, Accrington BB5 3SL (01254 237580). *Location*: off A679, one mile Town Centre, via Willows Lane, turn left 300 yards beyond Red Lion Inn. Moorland. 9 holes, 5557 yards. S.S.S. 67. *Green Fees*: information not available. *Eating facilities*: full catering and bar facilities. *Visitors*: welcome, no visitors on Saturdays or Sundays March to October. *Society Meetings*: catered for weekdays only. Packages available. Secretary: Paul Phillips (01254 382510; Fax: 01254 396176). *

BACUP. **Bacup Golf Club,** Bankside Lane, Bacup OL13 1HY (01706 873170; Fax: 01706 87726). *Location*: one mile from Bacup centre. Moorland. 9 holes, 6018 yards. S.S.S. 69. *Green Fees*: telephone for details. *Eating facilities*: by arrangement except Mondays. *Visitors*: welcome without reservation except Mondays and Saturdays. Secretary: T. Leyland (01706 879644).*

BAXENDEN. **Baxenden and District Golf Club,** Wooley Lane, Baxenden BB5 2EA **(01254 234555).** *Location*: towards Accrington from M65, past Hollands Pies right, signposted. Hilly golf course with fantastic views as far as the Fylde Coast and Ingleborough. 9 holes, 5702 yards. S.S.S. 68. *Green Fees*: weekdays only £15.00, with member £9.00. Society package £28.00 includes 27 holes of golf and meals. Details on request. *Eating facilities*: available. *Visitors*: welcome weekdays only. *Society Meetings*: welcome by arrangement with Secretary. Secretary: N. Turner (01254 234555). e-mail: baxgolf@hotmail.com website: www.baxendengolf.co.uk

BLACKBURN. **Blackburn Golf Club,** Beardwood Brow, Blackburn BB2 7AX (01254 51122; Fax: 01254 665578). *Location*: off A677 within easy reach of M6 (Junction 31), M61 and M65; west end of Blackburn. Parkland with superb views of Lancashire coast and Pennine Hills. 18 holes, 6144 yards. S.S.S. 70. Par 71. Practice area. *Green Fees*: weekdays £26.00 (£10.00 with a member); weekends and Bank Holidays £30.00 (£10.00 with a member). *Eating facilities*: full catering and bar facilities (restricted Mondays). *Visitors*: welcome without reservation except on competition days. *Society Meetings*: catered for by arrangement. Professional: Alan Rodwell (01254 55942). Secretary: K. Taylor (01254 51122; Fax: 01254 665578).

BLACKBURN. **Great Harwood Golf Club,** Harwood Bar, Great Harwood, Blackburn BB6 7TE (01254 884391). Flat wooded course. 9 holes, 6411 yards, 5862 metres. S.S.S. 71. Practice area. *Green Fees*: weekdays £16.00, weekends and Public Holidays £22.00. *Eating facilities*: all meals catered for, bar hours 12-2pm, 4-11pm. *Visitors*: welcome Wednesday - Friday. *Society Meetings*: catered for by advance bookings. Secretary: J. Spibey (01254 884391).

BLACKBURN. **Mytton Fold Hotel & Golf Complex,** Whalley Road, Langho, Blackburn BB6 8AB (01254 245392/240662). *Location*: from Junction 31 of M6, follow A59 towards Whalley/Clitheroe for 10 miles. At second roundabout follow Whalley sign, entrance 500 yards on right. Undulating parkland with panoramic views over the Ribble Valley. 18 holes. Par 70. *Green Fees*: information not available. *Eating facilities*: bar open all day, food till 9.30pm. *Visitors*: prior booking essential. Buggies available. Professional: Gary Coope. * e-mail: mytton_fold.hotel@virgin.net

BLACKBURN. **Pleasington Golf Club,** Pleasington, Near Blackburn (01254 202177). *Location*: M6 north to Junction 31. Blackburn eight miles. Undulating woodland. 18 holes, 6445 yards. S.S.S. 71. *Green Fees*: weekdays £38.00 for 18 holes, £44 per day, weekends and Bank Holidays £44.00. *Eating facilities*: full catering available. *Visitors*: welcome by prior arrangement. *Society Meetings*: Mondays, Wednesdays, Fridays by arrangement. Professional: G.J. Furey (01254 201630). Secretary: M. Trickett (01254 202177). Caterer: D. Whittam (01254 207346). e-mail: secretary-manager@pleasington-golf.co.uk

BLACKBURN. **Rishton Golf Club,** Eachill Links, Rishton BB1 4HG (01254 884442; Fax: 01254 887701). *Location*: between Junctions 6 and 7 M65 signposted from Rishton village centre. Moorland course. 9 holes, 6094 yards. S.S.S. 69. *Green Fees*: £17.00 without member, £10.00 with member; weekends and Bank Holidays £12.00 with member only. *Eating facilities*: full catering by prior arrangement. *Visitors*: welcome on weekdays and with a member at weekends and on Bank Holidays. *Society Meetings*: visiting parties welcome by prior arrangement, special rates can be obtained. Secretary: T. Charnock (01254 57727).

BLACKBURN. **Wilpshire Golf Club Ltd,** 72 Whalley Road, Wilpshire, Blackburn BB1 9LF (Tel: 01254 248260; Fax: 01254 246745). *Location*: A666 three miles north of Blackburn on Blackburn to Whalley road. Parkland/moorland. 18 holes, 5961 yards. S.S.S. 69. Practice ground. *Green Fees*: information not available. *Eating facilities*: lunch, high tea, dinner except Mondays. *Visitors*: welcome, no restrictions except competition days. Clubs and trolley hire. *Society Meetings*: catered for by prior booking through the Secretary. Professional: Walter Slaven (01254 249558; Fax: 01254 246745). Secretary: S.P. Gallagher.*

BLACKPOOL. **Blackpool North Shore Golf Club,** Devonshire Road, Blackpool FY2 0RD (01253 351017; Fax: 01253 591240). *Location:* north Blackpool on A587 behind North Prom. Undulating parkland. 18 holes, 6431 yards. S.S.S. 71. *Green Fees:* weekdays £32.00 day; weekends £38.00 day. Society Package £40.00, *Eating facilities:* full catering and bar facilities. *Visitors:* welcome except Thursdays and Saturdays. Professional: Brendan Ward (01253 354640). Secretary: John Morris (01253 352054).

BLACKPOOL. **Blackpool Park Golf Club,** North Park Drive, Blackpool FY3 8LS (Tel & Fax: 01253 397916). *Location:* one mile east of Tower. Parkland course. 18 holes, 6089 yards. S.S.S. 69. *Green Fees:* information not available. *Eating facilities:* full restaurant facilities. *Visitors:* welcome (bookings for tee reservations must be made to Blackpool Borough Council). *Society Meetings:* Apply to Blackpool Borough Council in writing. Professional: B. Purdie (01253 391004). Secretary: Mr David Stones (Tel & Fax: 01253 397916).*

BLACKPOOL. **De Vere Herons' Reach Golf Club,** East Park Drive, Blackpool FY3 8LL (01253 766156; Fax: 01253 798800). *Location:* leave M55 at Junction 4, follow signs for Stanley Park and Victoria Hospital. Designed by Peter Alliss & Clive Clark. Testing championship course with 10 man-made lakes- all year round play course. Herons Reach Course -18 holes, 6461 yards, S.S.S. 72. 18 bay floodlit driving range, putting and chipping green. *Green Fees*: information not available. *Eating facilities*: Nineteen Bar serving from 7am daily, leisure bar and Brasserie open seven days. *Visitors:* welcome. 164 bedroomed hotel with extensive conference and banqueting facilities for up to 600 plus leisure complex. *Society Meetings*: welcome. Golf Services Manager; (01253 766156; Fax: 01253 798800).

BLACKPOOL. **Knott End Golf Club Ltd,** Wyre Side, Knott End-on-Sea, Poulton-le-Fylde FY6 0AA (01253 810576). *Location:* M55 Exit 3, A585 Fleetwood Road then A588 to Knott End. Scenic riverside course, slight undulations. 18 holes, 5843 yards. S.S.S. 68. Practice ground. *Green Fees:* £25.00 per day weekdays, weekends £30.00. *Eating facilities:* full catering and bar. *Visitors:* welcome, time sheet in use, contact Professional with 24 hours notice. *Society Meetings:* by arrangement weekdays only. Professional: Paul Walker (01253 811365). Secretary: Anthony Crossley (01253 810576; Fax: 01253 813446). Manager: Louise Freeman.

BLACKPOOL. **Poulton-le-Fylde Golf Club,** Myrtle Farm, Breck Road, Poulton-le-Fylde, Blackpool FY6 7HJ (01253 893150; Fax: 01253 892444). *Location:* from M55 follow Poulton/Thornton/Cleveleys, roundabout with River Wyre pub on left, turn left and follow signs. Parkland/wooded course. 9 holes, 3260 yards. Par 36. Practice and putting facilities. *Green Fees:* weekdays £8.50 for 9 holes (£7.00 Seniors/Juniors), £13.00 day ticket, weekends 9 holes for £10.00, £15.00 day ticket. *Eating facilities:* breakfast and lunch served, all day bar in summer.

Visitors: welcome anytime, bookings taken up to one week in advance (01253 892444). Snooker. *Society Meetings:* welcome by prior booking. Professional: John Greenwood (Tel & Fax: 01253 892444). Secretary: Victoria Taylor (01253 893150; Fax: 01253 892444).

BOLTON. **Bolton Municipal Golf Course,** Links Road, off Chorley New Road, Bolton BL2 9XX (01204 844170). *Location:* midway between Horwich and Bolton, A673. Fairly flat parkland. 18 holes, 6336 yards, 5570 metres. S.S.S. 69. 2 practice areas and putting green. *Green Fees:* information not available. *Eating facilities:* snack and meal facilities available and bar. *Visitors:* welcome at any time. *Society Meetings:* advance booking. Mid-week Society package available. Tee reservations: (01204 495421).*

BOLTON. **Bolton Open Golf Course,** Longsight Park, Longsight Lane, Harwood, Bolton (01204 597659). *Location:* one and a half miles from Bolton town centre. Parkland, mature wooded, superb layout. 18 holes, 6000 yards. S.S.S. 68. 20 bay floodlit driving range. *Green Fees:* weekdays £10.00; weekends and Bank Holidays £12.00. *Eating facilities:* one bar, all day catering. *Visitors:* no restrictions, everyone welcome at all times. *Society Meetings:* welcome anytime, discounts available.

BOLTON. **Douglas Valley Golf Club**, A6 Blackrod By-Pass, Blackrod, Bolton BL6 5HX. *Location:* M61 Junction 6, off A6. Parkland greens. 9 holes, 2190 yards, 2004 metres. 22 bay floodlit driving range. *Green Fees:* information not available. *Visitors:* welcome, anytime bookings two days in advance. Dress code at all times, collared shirt, tailored trousers. Hamshaws Discount Golf Store and A-Star Teaching Academy. *Society Meetings:* welcome at all times. Teaching Professionals: Mark Saunders, Andrew Green (01257 474844). Manager: Julie Downes (01257 474844).*

BURNLEY. **Burnley Golf Club,** Glen View, Burnley BB11 3RW (01282 421045). *Location:* 300 yards from junction of A56 and A646. Moorland. 18 holes, 5939 yards, 5430 metres. S.S.S. 69. *Green Fees:* weekdays £20.00; weekends and Bank Holidays £25.00. *Eating facilities:* available except Mondays and Tuesdays. *Visitors:* welcome except Saturdays. *Society Meetings:* catered for. Professional: Paul McEvoy (01282 455266; Fax: 01282 455020). Secretary: R.D.M. Wills (Tel & Fax: 01282 451281).

BURNLEY. **Towneley Golf Club,** Towneley Park, Todmorden Road, Burnley BB11 3ED (01282 415636). *Location:* Todmorden Road, Burnley, Top Gates to Towneley Park. Guarded greens (ie. bunkered) and internal O.B.B. 18 holes, 5811 yards. S.S.S. 68. Practice ground. *Green Fees:* information not available. *Eating facilities:* full licensed bar and catering (full meals). *Visitors:* welcome but make tee reservations in advance. *Society Meetings:* welcome, apply to course booking shop. Secretary: Nigel Clark (01282 414555). *

CARNFORTH. **Silverdale Golf Club,** Redbridge Lane, Silverdale, Carnforth LA5 0SP (01524 701300). *Location:* M6 to Carnforth, then two miles west, adjacent to railway station. Testing heathland course with rock outcrops and excellent views. 18 holes, 5535 yards. S.S.S. 68. *Green Fees:* weekdays from £20.00, weekends and Bank Holidays from £25.00. *Eating facilities:* full catering and bar facilities. *Visitors:* welcome except Sundays in the summer unless with a member. *Society Meetings:* welcome by arrangement with Secretary. Secretary: K. Smith (Tel & Fax: 01524 702074).

CHORLEY. **Charnock Richard Golf Club,** Preston Road, Charnock Richard, Chorley PR7 5LE (01257 470707). *Location:* on A49 between M6 turn-offs for Standish and Leyland, five minutes from Camelot Theme Park. Parkland with water features. 18 holes. Par 71. Buggy hire. *Green Fees:* information not available. *Eating facilities:* restaurant. Professional: L. Taylor.*

CHORLEY. **Chorley Golf Club,** Hall o' the Hill, Heath Charnock, Chorley PR6 9HX (01257 480263; Fax: 01257 480722). *Location:* south of Chorley, just off the A673 at the junction with the A6. Scenic course with some of the finest views in Lancashire. 18 holes, 6269 yards. S.S.S. 70. *Green Fees:* weekdays £30.00. *Eating facilities:* restaurant and lounge bar. *Visitors:* welcome by prior arrangement except Mondays, Bank Holidays or weekends. Two buggies and carts for hire. *Society Meetings:* catered for by arrangement. Professional: M.N. Bradley (01257 481245). Secretary: Mrs A. Allen (01257 480263). Catering: (01257 474664).

CHORLEY. **Duxbury Park Golf Club (Municipal),** Duxbury Hall Road, Duxbury Park, Chorley PR7 4AS (01257 265380, 01257 241634). *Location:* one mile south of town centre off A6. Wooded parkland with water hazards on several holes. 18 holes, 6390 yards, 5843 metres. S.S.S. 70. Practice area. *Green Fees:* weekdays £8.25; weekends £10.75. *Eating facilities:* Golf Cafe open 7 days a week, very reasonable prices. For details contact Paul (01257 277049). *Visitors:* welcome, book seven days in advance. *Society Meetings:* book in advance. Professional: (01257 265380). Secretary: F. Holding (01257 262209). Membership available, contact Secretary.

CHORLEY. **Euxton Park Golf Centre,** Euxton Lane, Chorley PR7 6DL (01257 261601; Fax: 01257 261601). *Location:* Euxton Lane, between A6 and A49, next to Royal Ordnance factory. A short, yet challenging Par 3 course, ideal for beginners. 9 holes, Par 3. 40 bay driving range, practice bunkers. *Green Fees:* £3.50 (9 holes); Juniors £2.50 9 holes. 12 month contract unlimited golf £60.00. *Eating facilities:* fully licensed bar. *Visitors:* welcome every day, no need to book, pay and play course. *Society Meetings:* welcome, professionally catered for. Virtual golf indoor simulator. Professional: Jon Haines (01257 233500). Secretary: T.R. Evans (Tel & Fax: 01257 261601).

CHORLEY. **Shaw Hill Hotel Golf and Country Club,** Preston Road, Whittle-le-Woods, Chorley PR6 7PP (01257 269221; Fax: 01257 261223). *Location:* A6 between Chorley and Preston. (Near M6 J28 & M61 J8) Parkland course with many water hazards. 18 holes, 6109 yards. S.S.S. 69 yellow. Practice area. *Green Fees:* information not available. *Eating facilities:* spike bar and formal bar, à la carte restaurant. *Visitors:* welcome weekdays only, must hold current Handicap Certificate. Hotel with 30 bedrooms available. Golf trolleys and buggies also available. *Society Meetings:* catered for midweek only. Professional: D. Clarke (01257 279222). General Manager: Mr G. Tyrer. Secretary: L. Bateson.

CLITHEROE. **Clitheroe Golf Club,** Whalley Road, Pendleton, Clitheroe BB7 1PP (Tel & Fax: 01200 422292). *Location:* A59, junction A671 (south of Clitheroe); 300m turn left (signposted Barrow) clubhouse 100m on right. Parkland with extensive countryside views. 18 holes, 6326 yards, 5785 metres. S.S.S. 71. Practice ground and range. *Green Fees:* weekdays from £30.00; weekends and Bank Holidays £40.00. With a member £12.00. Subject to review. *Eating facilities:* full service available. *Visitors:* welcome but restricted to times available. No jeans, trainers, track/shell suits. *Society Meetings:* catered for, maximum 48 Monday, Tuesday, Wednesday, Friday; maximum 24 Thursday. No parties Saturdays. Professional: John E. Twissell (01200 424242). Secretary: Trevor Ashton (Tel & Fax: 01200 422292).
e-mail: secretary@clitheroegolfclub.com
website: www.clitheroegolfclub.com

CLITHEROE. **Whalley Golf Club**, Clerk Hill Rd, Whalley, Clitheroe BB7 9DR (01254 822236). *Location:* seven miles east of Blackburn on A59. Parkland. 9 holes, 6258 yards, 5727 metres. S.S.S. 71. *Green Fees:* information not available. *Eating facilities:* full catering and bar facilities. *Visitors:* welcome except Thursday afternoons and Saturdays April to September. *Society Meetings:* welcome by appointment. Professional: Jamie Hunt (01254 822236).*

COLNE. **Colne Golf Club,** Law Farm, Skipton Old Road, Colne BB8 7EB (01282 863391). *Location:* come off eastern end of M65. Carry on one mile to next roundabout and take first exit on left, Goup Hill. Flat scenic moorland course with trees. 9 holes, 6053 yards, 5535 metres. S.S.S. 69. Full practice facilities. *Green Fees:* £20.00 weekdays, £25.00 weekends and Bank Holidays (subject to review). Parties of 12 or more £19.00 per person (not weekends, Thursdays or competition days). *Eating facilities:* available daily except Mondays. *Visitors:* welcome except on competition days; two-balls only on Thursdays. *Society Meetings:* welcome except weekends, Thursdays and competition days. Secretary: A. Turpin.

DARWEN. **Darwen Golf Club**, Winter Hill, Darwen BB3 0LB (01254 704367). *Location*: one-and-a-half miles from Darwen centre. Moorland. 18 holes, 6354 yards. S.S.S. 71. Large practice area. *Green Fees*: information not available. *Eating facilities*: full catering. *Visitors*: welcome, not Tuesdays (Ladies' day) or Saturdays. *Society Meetings*: welcome, except Saturdays. Professional: W. Lennon (01254 776370). Secretary: J.R. Lawson (01254 704367).

FLEETWOOD. **Fleetwood Golf Club Ltd.,** The Golf House, Princes Way, Fleetwood FY7 8AF (01253 873114; Fax: 01253 773573). *Location:* on Fylde Coast, eight miles from Blackpool, Coast Road Blackpool to Fleetwood, two miles west of Fleetwood Centre. Seaside, true links. White course 18 holes, 6557 yards, S.S.S. 71; Yellow course 18 holes, 6308 yards, S.S.S. 70. *Green Fees:* weekdays £30.00; weekends £40.00. Special rates available on request. *Eating facilities:* full catering and bar service. *Visitors:* welcome weekdays, certain Saturdays and Sundays. *Society Meetings:* welcome by arrangement. Professional: S. McLaughlin (01253 873661). Secretary/Manager: N. Robinson (01253 773573).

HEYSHAM. **Heysham Golf Club,** Trumacar Park, Middleton Road, Heysham LA3 3JH (01524 851011; Fax: 01524 853030). *Location:* five miles from M6 via Lancaster and Morecambe. Parkland, flat, part-wooded. 18 holes, 6338 yards. S.S.S. 70. Two practice grounds, driving range and chipping green. *Green Fees:* weekdays £25.00 per round, £30.00 per day; weekends and Bank Holidays £40.00. Subject to review. Special rates for parties on application. *Eating facilities:* full catering seven days, closed Mondays October to March. Visitors: welcome with Handicap Certificates. Tee reserved for members 1pm to 1.45pm. *Society Meetings:* catered for by arrangement with Secretary. Professional: R. Done (01524 852000). Secretary: F.A. Bland (01524 851011).

LANCASTER. **Lancaster Golf Club Ltd,** Ashton Hall, Ashton-with-Stodday, Lancaster LA2 0AJ (01524 752090). *Location:* three miles south of Lancaster on A588. Parkland. 18 holes, 6282 yards. S.S.S. 71. *Green Fees:* information not available. *Eating facilities:* available (Caterer: 01524 751105). *Visitors:* welcome weekdays only unless staying in the Dormy House. Club has a Dormy House (part of Ashton Hall), single and double rooms with en suite facilities, 2 nights minimum stay. *Society Meetings:* catered for weekdays only. Professional: David Sutcliffe (01524 751802). Secretary: P.J. Irvine (01524 751247; Fax: 01524 752742). e-mail: secretary@lancastergc.co.uk

LANCASTER. **Lansil Golf Club,** Caton Road, Lancaster LA1 3PE (01524 39269/61233). *Location:* A683, towards Lancaster from Junction 34 M6. Parkland. 9 holes, 5608 yards. S.S.S. 67. *Green Fees:* information not available. *Eating facilities:* bar meals available - contact Steward. Visitors: welcome weekdays, not before 1pm Sundays. *Society Meetings:* groups of 12 plus welcome weekdays by prior arrangement. Steward: 01524 39269. *

LEYLAND. **Leyland Golf Club Ltd.,** Wigan Road, Leyland, Preston PR5 2UD (01772 421359). *Location*: leave M6 at Exit 28, turn right to traffic lights, (200 yards) turn right onto the A49, course located one mile on left. Flat parkland. 18 holes, 6298 yards. S.S.S. 70. *Green Fees:* £25.00 weekdays. *Eating facilities:* full catering except Mondays. *Visitors:* welcome weekdays; weekends only with a member.

Society Meetings: welcome by arrangement with Secretary. Professional: C. Burgess (01772 423425). General Manager: J. Ross (01772 436457). e-mail: manager@leylandgolfclub.com website: www.leylandgolfclub.com

LYTHAM ST ANNES. **Fairhaven Golf Club Ltd.,** Lytham Hall Park, Ansdell, Lytham St Annes FY8 4JU (01253 736741). *Location:* on B5261, two miles from Lytham, eight miles from Blackpool. 18 holes, 6880 yards. S.S.S. 73. *Green Fees:* information not available. *Eating facilities:* full catering. *Visitors:* welcome with reservation. Handicap Certificate required.*Society Meetings:* catered for by arrangement Mondays, Tuesdays, Wednesdays and Fridays. Professional: B. Plucknett (01253 736976). Secretary: Stephen Last (01253 736741; Fax: 01253 731461).

LYTHAM ST ANNES. **Lytham Green Drive Golf Club**, Ballam Road, Lytham St Annes FY8 4LE (01253 737390; Fax: 01253 731350). *Location:* one mile from town centre. Flat parkland course. 18 holes, 6163 yards. *Green Fees:* £32.00 per round, £40.00 per day weekdays; £35.00 per round weekends. Guests of member £12.00. *Eating facilities:* catering available daily. *Visitors:* welcome weekdays only. *Society Meetings:* welcome by prior arrangement. Professional: A. Lancaster (01253 737379). Secretary: S. Higham (01253 737390; Fax: 01253 731350).

LYTHAM ST ANNES. **Royal Lytham and St Annes Golf Club**, Links Gate, Lytham St Annes FY8 3LQ (01253 724206; Fax: 01253 780946). *Location:* within one mile of the centre of St Annes on Sea. Seaside Championship links course. 18 holes, 6334 yards. S.S.S. 71. Practice ground. *Green Fees:* Mondays and Thursdays £105.00, limited availability on Sundays £155.00. 2003 rates, subject to review. *Eating facilities:* restaurant and bar. *Visitors:* welcome, times by arrangement. Dormy House accommodation available. *Society Meetings:* by arrangement. Professional: Eddie Birchenough (01253 720094). Secretary: R.J.G Cochrane.

LYTHAM ST. ANNES. **St. Annes Old Links Golf Club,** Highbury Road, Lytham St. Annes FY8 2LD (01253 723597). *Location:* M55 via Blackpool South Shore, following airport signs. Past airport down to coast road, turn left and first left at next real traffic lights. The only true links course in Lancashire. 18 holes, 6616 yards. S.S.S. 72. Practice ground, putting and chipping greens. *Green Fees:* weekdays £45.00 per day, £30.00 for 18 holes after 1.30pm; weekends £50.00. *Eating facilities:* restaurant and snack facilities, bar. Visitors: welcome, not Saturdays, restricted Sundays. Tuesday is ladies' day. *Society Meetings:* restricted to those with Handicaps and membership of other clubs. Professional: D. Webster (01253 722432). Secretary: R.V. Beach (01253 723597; Fax: 01253 781506). e-mail: secretary@coastalgolf.co.uk website: www.coastalgolf.co.uk

MORECAMBE. **Morecambe Golf Club Ltd.,** The Club House, Bare, Morecambe LA4 6AJ (01524 418050). *Location:* on A589 leaving Morecambe towards Carnforth. Parkland course affected by sea breezes and offering superb views. 18 holes, 5770 yards. S.S.S. 69. *Green Fees:* weekdays £24.00 per round, £29.00 per day; weekends and Bank Holidays £29.00 per round, £34.00 per day. Subject to review. Special rates for visiting parties, package deals. *Eating facilities:* diningroom and bar snacks. *Visitors:* welcome at all times, tee reserved for members up to 9.30am and from 12 noon to 1.30pm. *Society Meetings:* welcome at all times. Professional: Simon Fletcher (Tel & Fax: 01524 415596). Secretary: Mrs Judith Atkinson (Tel & Fax: 01524 412841; Fax: 01524 400088).

NELSON. **Marsden Park Golf Club**, Nelson Municipal Golf Course, Walton Lane, Nelson BB9 8DG (01282 661912; Fax: 01282 661221). *Location:* off Junction 13 of M65 towards Nelson. Hilly parkland. 18 holes, 5813 yards. S.S.S. 68. *Green Fees:* information not available. *Eating facilities:* bar, meals available in bar lounge. *Visitors:* welcome without restriction, booking advised. *Society Meetings:* welcome with prior arrangement except Saturdays. Bookings: (01282 661912). Secretary: N. Standage (01282 661915).

NELSON. **Nelson Golf Club,** King's Causeway, Brierfield, Nelson BB9 0EU (01282 614583). *Location:* leave M65 at Junction 12, take A682 for Brierfield, turn left at Brierfield centre traffic lights, course on the right at top of the hill. Wooded moorland, good views of the surrounding Pendle Area. 18 holes, 6007 yards. S.S.S. 69. Large practice area. *Green Fees:* weekdays £25.00; weekends £30.00. *Eating facilities:* lunches, dinners by arrangement except Mondays. *Visitors:* weekdays except Thursdays (Ladies Day), or Saturdays during Competition season. Formal dress (jacket, collar and tie) weekend evenings. Carts. *Society Meetings:* daily except Monday, Thursday and Saturday. Professional: Neil Reeves (01282 617000). Secretary: B.R. Thomason (01282 611834).

ORMSKIRK. **Mossock Hall Golf Club**, Liverpool Road, Bickerstaffe, Ormskirk L39 0EE (01695 424969). *Location:* one mile from Junction 3 of M58 or two miles from Junction 1 of M57, between Kirby and Ormskirk. Parkland course; USGA greens with water in play on four holes. 18 holes. Par 71. *Green Fees:* £30 weekdays, £35 weekends. *Eating facilities:* available from 11am. Professional: Phil Atkiss.

ORMSKIRK. **Ormskirk Golf Club**, Cranes Lane, Lathom L40 5UJ (01695 572112). *Location:* two miles east of Ormskirk. Parkland course. 18 holes, 6358 yards. S.S.S. 70. *Green Fees:* weekdays (not Wednesday) £40.00 per round, £50.00 per day, weekends and Wednesdays £45.00 per round, £55.00 per day. *Eating facilities:* available except Monday. *Visitors:* welcome, Handicap Certificates required, notice advised with reservation. *Society Meetings:* catered for, book in advance. Professional: J. Hammond (01695 572074). Secretary: R.D.J. Lawrence (01695 572227).

PRESTON. **Ashton and Lea Golf Club Ltd,** Tudor Avenue, off Blackpool Road, Lea, Preston PR4 0XA (01772 726480; Fax: 01772 735762). *Location:* on A5085, three miles west of Preston, turn opposite Toby Carvery. Parkland with water features. 18 holes, 6334 yards. S.S.S. 70. Small practice ground. *Green Fees:* weekdays £26.00; weekends and Bank Holidays £30.00. Reduced rates if playing with member. *Eating facilities:* full catering every day. *Visitors:* welcome but please telephone the Professional to reserve tee time. Conference and function facilities available. *Society Meetings:* catered for weekdays only, contact the Secretary. Professional: Mike Greenough (01772 720374). Secretary: Ian Hulley (01772 735282). e-mail: ashtonleagolf@supanet.com website: www.ukgolfer.org

PRESTON. **Fishwick Hall Golf Club,** Glenluce Drive, Farringdon Park, Preston PR1 5TD (01772 798300). *Location:* two minutes from Junction 31 M6, off A59 Blackburn to Preston Road. Parkland, part wooded, bounded by river. 18 holes, 6045 yards. S.S.S. 69. Small practice area. *Green Fees:* weekdays £26.00; weekends and Public Holidays £31.00. Reductions if playing with members. *Eating facilities:* bar, full catering available except Mondays. *Visitors:* welcome unless club competition on. *Society Meetings:* welcome weekdays, including Mondays. Professional: M. Watson (01772 795870). Secretary: J.P. Davis (01772 798300; Fax: 01772 704600).

PRESTON. **Ingol Golf Club,** Tanterton Hall Road, Ingol, Preston PR2 7BY (01772 734556; Fax: 01772 729815). *Location:* two miles from Junction 32 M6 (joins M55). Parkland. 18 holes, 6294 yards, Par 72.. Chipping and putting practice areas. *Green Fees:* Winter (Oct - mid April) 18 holes mid week £18.00, 18 holes weekend £22.00; Summer 2004 (Apr-Oct) 18 holes mid week £25.00, £18 holes weekend £30.00. *Eating facilities:* bar/restaurant. *Visitors:* welcome anytime, please telephone to check tee reservations. Buggies and trolleys available. Squash courts. Meeting room available. Stay and play packages. *Society Meetings:* welcome by arrangement. Professional: Ryan Grimshaw (01772 769646). Manager: Alan Read (01772 734556; Fax: 01772 729815).

PRESTON. **Longridge Golf Club,** Fell Barn, Jeffrey Hill, Longridge, Preston PR3 2TU (01772 783291; Fax: 01772 783022). *Location:* eight miles north-east of Preston off B6243. Moorland with extensive spectacular views. One of the oldest clubs in England (Est. 1877). 18 holes, 5975 yards. S.S.S. 69. *Green Fees:* weekdays £25.00 per day, £16.50 per round;

weekends £25.00. *Eating facilities:* full catering and bars. *Visitors:* welcome. *Society Meetings:* welcome by prior arrangement. Professional: Stephen Taylor. Secretary: David Simpson. e-mail: secretary@longridgegolfclub.fsnet.co.uk website: www.longridgegolfclub.com

PRESTON. **Penwortham Golf Club Ltd.,** Blundell Lane, Penwortham, Preston PR1 0AX (01772 743207; Fax: 01772 744630). *Location:* one mile west of Preston on main Southport to Liverpool road. Parkland. 18 holes, 6056 yards. S.S.S. 69. *Green Fees:* £25.00 weekdays; £33.00 weekends. *Eating facilities:* lunches and dinners served at Club. Visitors: welcome. *Society Meetings:* by arrangement Monday, Wednesday, Thursday, Friday only. Professional: Darren Hopwood (01772 742345). Secretary: Neil Annandale (01772 744630; Fax: 01772 740172).

PRESTON. **Preston Golf Club,** Fulwood Hall Lane, Fulwood, Preston PR2 8DD (01772 700011; Fax: 01772 794234). *Location:* exit 32 on M6 marked Preston & Garstang, partway to Preston turning at Watling Street Road. Parkland course. 18 holes, 6312 yards. S.S.S. 71. *Green Fees:* weekdays £40.00 per day. *Eating facilities:* first class dining room, bars. *Visitors:* welcome weekdays, weekends or Bank Holidays must be accompanied by a member. *Society Meetings:* welcome except Tuesdays, weekends or Bank Holidays. Handicap Certificate required. Professional: Andrew Greenbank (01772 700022). Secretary: S.H. Newland (01772 700011).

ROCHDALE. **Tunshill Golf Club Ltd,** Kiln Lane, Milnrow, Rochdale OL16 3TS (01706 342095). *Location:* two miles east of Rochdale, M62 J21. Hillside course adjacent to M62 motorway. 9 holes/18 tees, 5743 yards. S.S.S. 68. *Green Fees:* £16.00. *Visitors:* welcome during the week. *Society Meetings:* welcome.

ROSSENDALE. **Rossendale Golf Club Ltd.,** Ewood Lane Head, Haslingden, Rossendale BB4 6LH (01706 831686). *Location:* 14 miles north of Manchester, easy access from M66 and A56. 18 holes, 6293 yards. S.S.S. 71. *Green Fees:* weekdays £25.50; Sundays and Bank Holidays £30.50. *Eating facilities:* full catering; bar. *Visitors:* welcome except Saturdays during season. *Society Meetings:* welcome. Professional: S.J. Nicholls (01706 213616). Hon. Secretary: A.V. Townsend (01706 831339; Fax: 01706 228669). e-mail: rgc@golfers.net info@rossendalegolfclub.net website: www.rossendalegolfclub.net

Tanterton Hall Road, Ingol, Preston PR2 7BY
Tel: 01772 734556 • Fax: 01772 729815
• Visitors welcome anytime, please telephone Pro Shop 01772 769646 for tee times. Buggies and trolleys available.
• Bar/restaurant • Society Meetings welcome by arrangement.
www.ingolgolfclub.co.uk • 18 holes, 6294 yards, Par 72. • Chipping and putting practice areas.

ST HELENS. **Houghwood,** Billinge Hill, Crank Road, Crank, St Helens WA11 8RL (Tel & Fax: 01744 894754). *Location*: ten minutes from M6 - two minutes from Billinge Hospital. Parkland. 18 holes, 6268 yards. S.S.S. 69. Practice ground. Snooker table. *Green Fees*: weekdays £25.00, weekends £35.00. Special rates - 4 ball £75.00 Mon/Tue/Thur or £99.50 with bar meal. *Eating facilities*: spike bar open 11am to 11pm every day. First floor public restaurant with quality food, reasonable prices and superb views, soft spikes required by all. *Visitors*: always welcome. *Society Meetings*: welcome Mondays, Tuesdays and Thursdays. Professional: Paul Dickenson (01744 894444; Fax: 01744 894754). Secretary: Julie Melling (Tel & Fax: 01744 894754).

SCARISBRICK. **Hurlston Hall Golf Club,** Hurlston Lane, Scarisbrick L40 8JD (01704 840400; Fax: 01704 841404). *Location:* six miles from Southport and two miles from Ormskirk along A570 trunk road; eight miles from M58. Parkland with several lakes and streams. 18 holes, 6746 yards. S.S.S. 72. Golf centre with 18-bay driving range, putting green, large shop. Flood-lit driving range. *Green Fees:* weekdays £35.00, weekends £40.00. For winter fees please telephone Golf Shop (01704 841120). *Eating facilities:* three bars; à la carte restaurant. *Visitors:* welcome, must book in advance. Handicap Certificate or letter of introduction preferred. *Society Meetings:* by arrangement, registered Golf Societies only. Professional: Jon Esclapez (01704 841149/ 841120; Fax: 01704 841404). General Manager: Malcolm Atherton (01704 840400; Fax: 01704 841404). e-mail: hurlston_hall@btinternet.com website: www.HurlstonHall.co.uk

UPHOLLAND. **Beacon Park Golf Course,** Beacon Lane, Dalton WN8 7RU (01695 625551; Fax: 01695 622700). *Location:* ten minutes from J26 of M6. Follow signs for A577 Upholland. Undulating parkland course. 18 holes, 5996 yards. S.S.S. 69. Driving range, practice ground. *Green Fees:* information not available. *Eating facilities:* fully licensed restaurant as part of the complex. *Visitors:* welcome, no restrictions, a six day advance booking system applies. Tuition available. *Society Meetings:* welcome, special deals on offer that include food and golf. Professional: Gary Nelson (Tel & Fax: 01695 622700). Secretary: Tommy Harris.*

UPHOLLAND. **Dean Wood Golf Club,** Lafford Lane, Upholland, Skelmersdale WN8 0QZ (01695 622219). *Location:* Exit 26 from M6 signposted for Wigan. Follow A577 to Upholland, first right after church. Wooded parkland course. 18 holes, 6137 yards. S.S.S. 70. *Green Fees:* weekdays £30.00; weekends £33.00. *Eating facilities:* daily catering available, bar. *Visitors:* welcome with reservation, not before 10.30am weekends and Bank Holidays. *Society Meetings:* catered for by prior arrangement. Professional: Stuart Danchin. Secretary: A.S. McGregor (01695 622219).

WIGAN. **Standish Court Golf Club,** Rectory Lane, Standish, Wigan WN6 0XD (01257 425777; Fax: 01257 425888). *Location:* one mile off M6 Junction 27, on A5209 through Standish. Undulating parkland, back nine holes through picturesque woodland. 18 holes, 4860 yards, S.S.S. 68. Large chipping and putting green. *Green Fees:* Monday and Tuesday £7.50, Wednesday through Friday £10.00, weekends and Bank Holidays £15.00. *Eating facilities:* food available all day in bistro; spike bar. *Visitors:* welcome all week, phone in advance to reserve tee times. *Society Meetings:* welcome all week by prior arrangement. Professional/General Manager: Blake Toone. e-mail: info@standishgolf.co.uk website: www.standishgolf.co.uk

WIGAN. **Wigan Golf Club,** Arley Hall Haigh, Wigan WN1 2UH (01257 421360). *Location*: M6 Exit 27, two miles on B5329, east of Standish. Parkland. 18 holes, 6026 yards. Par 70. *Green Fees*: information not available. *Eating facilities*: meals and bar snacks available. Visitors: welcome anytime except Tuesdays and Saturdays. *Society Meetings*: catered for on Wednesdays, Thursdays and Fridays. Secretary: E. Walmsley (01942 244429).*

> **THE APPEARANCE OF AN ASTERISK (*) AT THE END OF A CLUB OR COURSE ENTRY INDICATES THAT UP-TO-DATE INFORMATION HAS NOT BEEN SUPPLIED**

Visitors and Societies welcome 7 days a week. Packages from £8.00pp. A picturesque course with panoramic views of the West Pennines.

Summer greens all year round. Find us 2 miles from Junction 27 M6 or 6 miles from Junction 6 M61.

STANDISH COURT GOLF CLUB

Tel: 01257 425777 • www.standishgolf.co.uk • info@standishgolf.co.uk

See also Colour Advertisement on page 48

Leicestershire

ASHBY DE LA ZOUCH. **Willesley Park Golf Club,** Measham Road, Ashby de la Zouch LE65 2PF (01530 411532). *Location:* on B5006 towards Tamworth, one mile from centre of Ashby. Wooded parkland, semi-heathland. 18 holes, 6304 yards. S.S.S. 70. *Green Fees:* weekdays £28.00 per round, £40.00 per day, weekends £35.00 per round, £50.00 per day. *Eating facilities:* dining room and bar, no catering Mondays. *Visitors:* welcome with reservation. *Society Meetings:* catered for Wednesday, Thursday and Friday, £30.00 per day. Professional: B.J. Hill (01530 414820). Secretary: R.E. Brown (01530 414596).

BIRSTALL. **Birstall Golf Club, Station Road, Birstall LE4 3BB (0116 267 4322).** *Location*: **adjacent to Great Central Steam Railway. Parkland. 18 holes, 6213 yards. S.S.S. 70. Practice ground.** *Green Fees*: **£25.00 per round; £30.00 per day (weekdays).** *Eating facilities*: **bar, diningroom.** *Visitors*: **welcome Mondays, Wednesdays and Fridays.** *Society Meetings*: **minimum 12, catered for by prior arrangement from £22.00 per person.** Professional: D. Clark (0116 267 5245). Secretary: Mrs S.E. Chilton (0116 267 4322).

BLABY. **Blaby Golf Centre,** Lutterworth Road, Blaby, Leicester LE8 4DP (0116 278 4804). *Location*: situated just off the Blaby by-pass. Flat parkland course. 9 holes, 2466 yards, S.S.S. 66. 27 bay floodlit covered range, putting green. *Green Fees:* information not available. *Eating facilities*: outside catering. *Visitors*: welcome. Lessons available 6 days a week. Professional: Matt Fisher (0116 278 4804).* website: www.blabygolfcourse.com

BOTCHESTON. **Forest Hill Golf Club,** Markfield Lane, Near Botcheston LE9 9FJ (01455 824800; Fax: 01455 828522). *Location*: M1 Junction 22, take Leicester exit on A50, at first roundabout turn right towards Desford, golf course 3 miles on left. Parkland course with trees, easy walking. 18 holes, 6126 yards. S.S.S. 69, Par 71. Floodlit driving range. *Green Fees*: please telephone for details. *Eating facilities*: available. *Visitors*: welcome Monday to Thursday. Professional tuition available. Conference facilities available. *Society Meetings*: welcome by prior arrangement Monday to Thursday. Professional: Glyn Quilter (01455 824800). Secretary: Gerry Hyde (01455 824800). e-mail: gerry@hyde14.fsnet.co.uk

COSBY. **Cosby Golf Club,** Chapel Lane, off Broughton Road, Cosby, Leicester (0116 2864759; Fax: 0116 2864484). *Location:* eight miles south of Leicester, four miles from Junction 21 M1. Undulating parkland. 18 holes, 6410 yards. S.S.S. 71. *Green Fees:* £25.00 per round, £35.00 per day. Special rates for societies over 20 in number. *Eating facilities:* bar and food available, wide range of meals by arrangement. *Visitors:* most welcome before 4pm weekdays. Handicap Certificates may be required for all visitors. *Society Meetings:* welcome, prior booking essential. Professional: Martin Wing (0116 2848275). Secretary: D. Jones (0116 2864759; Fax: 0116 864484). e-mail: secretary@cosby-golf-club.co.uk website: www.cosby-golf-club.co.uk

EAST GOSCOTE. **Beedles Lake Golf Centre,** 170 Broome Lane, East Goscote LE7 3WQ (0116 2607086). *Location:* off A46 just north of Leicester, through village of Ratcliffe on the Wreake. Fairly flat course in river valley, adjoining lake. 18 holes, 6732 yards, 6156 metres. S.S.S. 72. 17 bay floodlit driving range. *Green Fees:* weekdays £12.00, weekends £16.00. Twilight fees £10.00. *Eating facilities:* restaurant and bar available. *Visitors:* always very welcome. *Society Meetings:* welcome but with restricted tee-times at weekends. Steward: (0116 260 7086). Professional: Sean Byrne (0116 260 6759). General Manager: Les Emery (0116 260 4414).

ENDERBY. **Enderby Golf Course,** Mill Lane, Enderby (0116 2849388) *Location:* two miles from M1/M69 junction 21 roundabout. Gently undulating course with lakes and ditches. 9 holes. 2856/5712 yards. S.S.S. 61. Par 36/72. *Green Fees:* weekdays £5.75/£6.95; weekend £6.95/£9.25. *Eating facilities:* two bars, restaurants, open 9.30am to 10.30pm. *Visitors:* welcome at all times, no booking required. Leisure centre, bowls, squash, badminton, sauna, solarium, fitness suite, etc. Professional/Secretary: Chris d'Araujo.

HINCKLEY. **Hinckley Golf Club,** Leicester Road, Hinckley LE10 3DR (01455 615124; Fax: 01455 890841). *Location:* situated one mile from Hinckley, just off Hinckley's A47 perimeter road. Parkland with lakeside features. 18 holes, 6517 yards, 5959 metres. S.S.S. 71. Practice area for members. *Green Fees:* weekdays £30.00 per round, £35.00 per day; weekends with a member only. *Eating facilities:* bar meals daily except Sundays. *Visitors:* welcome except Tuesdays and weekends. *Society Meetings:* Mondays and Wednesdays by appointment. Professional: R. Jones (01455 615014). Finance and Administration Manager: L. Jackson (01455 615124).

KIRBY MUXLOE. **Kirby Muxloe Golf Club,** Station Road, Kirby Muxloe LE9 2EP (0116 2393457). *Location:* Junction 21a M1, just off A47 heading to Hinckley, towards Kirby Muxloe village. Parkland, fourth tee is set outside the course. 18 holes, 6351 yards. S.S.S. 71. Driving range, practice area and tuition from Professional. *Green Fees:* information not available. *Eating facilities:* full restaurant and bar. *Visitors:* welcome weekdays except Tuesdays and Thursday 12 noon to 2pm. Advisable to phone in advance. Snooker room. *Society Meetings:* by arrangement with Manager. Professional: Mr B. Whipham (Tel & Fax: 0116 2392813). Club Manager: Mr B. Woodcock (Tel & Fax: 0116 2393457).*

LEICESTER. **Humberstone Heights Golf Club**, Gipsy Lane, Leicester LE5 0TB (0116 276 1905). *Location:* A563 ring road, Uppingham side of Leicester. Parkland. 18 holes, 6343 yards. S.S.S. 70. 30 bay driving range, 9 hole pitch and putt course. *Green Fees:* weekdays £9.99 per round; weekends £12.50. 9 holes £6.99, Twilight £9.50, Senior Citizens and Juniors £4.99. Subject to review. *Eating facilities:* bar, snacks; clubhouse closed Mondays. *Visitors:* welcome (Municipal Golf Course). Green Fee ticket gains entry to Clubhouse. *Society Meetings:* welcome. Professional: P. Highfield (0116 229 5570). Secretary: Brian Tuttle (0116 276 3680).

LEICESTER. **Kibworth Golf Club,** Weir Road, Kibworth Beauchamp, Leicester LE8 0LP (0116 2796172). *Location:* A6, four miles Market Harborough, 12 miles Leicester. Flat wooded course. 18 holes, 6354 yards. S.S.S. 71. 8 bay golf range. *Green Fees:* Monday to Friday £25.00; Saturday and Sunday with member only. *Eating facilities:* Contact Catering (0116 2796560). *Visitors:* welcome, Handicap Certificate required or introduction from club member. *Society Meetings:* welcome, prior booking essential; reductions for large societies. Professional: Bob Larratt (0116 2792283). Secretary: J. Noble (Tel: 0116 2792301; Fax: 0116 2796434). e-mail: secretary@kibworthgolfclub.freeserve.co.uk

LEICESTER. **The Leicestershire Golf Club,** Evington Lane, Leicester LE5 6DJ (Tel & Fax: 0116 2738825). *Location:* Evington Village, two miles from city centre off A6 road. Parkland. 18 holes, 6329 yards. S.S.S. 71. Practice area. *Green Fees:* information not available. *Eating facilities:* available. *Visitors:* welcome but not normally weekends or Tuesdays. Handicap Certificate required. *Society Meetings:* welcome. Professional: D. Jones (Tel & Fax: 0116 2736730) Secretary: C.R. Chapman (0116 2738825; Fax: 0116 2731900).* e-mail: secretary@thelgc.co.uk

LEICESTER. **Scraptoft Golf Club,** Beeby Road, Scraptoft, Leicester LE7 9SJ (0116 241 9000). *Location:* off A47 Scraptoft. Undulating. 18 holes, 6235 yards. S.S.S. 70. *Green Fees:* £29.00 per day weekdays, £29.00 per round weekends. Sunday mornings with club member only. *Eating facilities:* full restaurant service seven days a week from April to October. *Visitors:* welcome, proof of Handicap required. *Society Meetings:* catered for on application weekdays only (contact Secretary). Professional: Simon Wood (0116 2419138).

LEICESTER. **Western Park Golf Club,** Scudamore Road, Braunstone Frith, Leicester LE3 1UQ. *Location:* four miles west of Junction 21 (M1) and M69. Flat, wooded course. 18 holes, 6518 yards. S.S.S. 71. Practice area. *Green Fees:* information not available. *Eating facilities:* full catering facilities. *Visitors:* welcome, book weekends - Tuesdays at 8am for Saturdays and Wednesdays at 8am for Sundays. Indoor school; carts for hire. *Society Meetings:* all welcome, contact Professional. Professional: Mr Dave Butler (Tel: 01162 995566; Fax: 01162 995567). Secretary: Ian Nicolson (0116 287 6158).*

LEICESTER. **Whetstone Golf Club and Driving Range,** Cambridge Road, Cosby LE9 5SH (Tel & Fax: 0116 286 1424). *Location:* 10 minutes off Junction 21 M1, between Cosby and Whetstone. Flat parkland. 18 holes, 5795 yards. S.S.S. 68. Driving range, putting green. *Green Fees:* information not available. *Eating facilities:* bar/lounge serving full range of meals. Smart casual dress please. *Visitors:* Handicap not required. Welcome by prior arrangement. Dress code to be observed. *Society Meetings:* welcome by prior arrangement. Professional: D. Raitt. Secretary: J. Fisher.*

LOUGHBOROUGH. **Charnwood Forest Golf Club,** Breakback Road, Woodhouse Eaves, Near Loughborough LE12 8TA (01509 890259; Fax: 01509 890925). *Location:* A6 to B591 or M1 Junction 23 - A512 - Snells Nook Lane. Heather, gorse and bracken - no bunkers. Oldest golf club in Leicestershire played around volcanic rocks. 9 holes, 5960 yards. S.S.S. 69. *Green Fees:* weekdays £20.00 per 18 holes, £30.00 per day; weekends £25.00 per 18 holes. Winter green fees; 9 holes £12.50; 18 holes £20.00; 27 holes £25.00. *Eating facilities:* full catering. *Visitors:* welcome Wednesdays and Thursdays, Mondays and Fridays by special arrangement, not Tuesdays (Ladies' Day). *Society Meetings:* welcome by prior arrangement on Wednesdays, Thursdays and Fridays only, no more than 40 in party. Secretary: Mr A. Flamson (01509 890259).

LOUGHBOROUGH. **Longcliffe Golf Club,** Snell's Nook Lane, Nanpantan, Loughborough LE11 3YA (01509 239129; Fax: 01509 216321). *Location:* M1 Junction 23 – A512 Loughborough, first right, Snells Nook Lane. Wooded heathland, EGU Championship course. 18 holes, 6672 yards. S.S.S. 73. Practice ground. *Green Fees:* weekdays £30.00 per round, £40.00 per day. *Eating facilities:* bar and restaurant. *Visitors:* welcome Monday, Wednesday, Thursday and Friday; must be introduced and playing with member at weekends and Bank Holidays. Handicap Certificate required. *Society Meetings:* welcome by arrangement only on Mondays, Wednesdays, Thursdays and Fridays. Professional: D.C. Mee (01509 231450). Secretary: P. Keeling (01509 239129; Fax: 01509 216321).
website: www.longcliffegolf.co.uk

LOUGHBOROUGH. **Park Hill Golf Club,** Park Hill, Seagrave, Loughborough LE12 7NG (01509 815454; Fax: 01509 816062). *Location:* 5 miles from J21a of M1 northbound. Just off the A46 northbound. Undulating parkland course with rolling tree-lined fairways and excellent views – the closing hole is a challenging par 5 with water protecting both sides of the green. Excellent playing conditions all year round! 18 holes, 7219 yards. S.S.S. 74. Large practice area and putting green. 20 bay covered driving range, including grass bays. *Green Fees:* weekdays £22.00, with a member £11.00; weekends and Bank Holidays £26.00, with a member £13.00. Seniors (55 years and over); £10.00 (Monday to Thursday). *Eating facilities:* lunch/dinner/bar snacks, fully licensed bar. *Visitors:* welcome at all times Monday

to Friday, after 9am at weekends. Conference room for up to 120 people (function room). *Society Meetings:* all welcome by prior arrangement. Special rates for societies over 12 people. Professional: Matt Ulyett (01509 815775; Fax: 01509 816062). Secretary: Jonathan Hutson (01509 815454; Fax: 01509 816062).
e-mail: mail@parkhillgolf.co.uk
website: www.parkhillgolf.co.uk

LUTTERWORTH. **Lutterworth Golf Club,** Rugby Road, Lutterworth LE17 4HN. *Location:* Junction 20 M1; Junction 1 M6. Parkland course. 18 holes, 6226 yards. S.S.S. 70. Practice area, computerised indoor teaching academy. *Green Fees:* £22.00 per round, £30.00 per day. *Eating facilities:* catering available and bar facilities. *Visitors:* welcome all day Monday to Thursday, and Friday till noon. *Society Meetings:* welcome Monday to Thursday all day, and Friday mornings. Secretary: John Faulks (01455 552532). Professional: Roland Tisdall (01455 557199). Bar/Catering (01455 557141).

LUTTERWORTH near. **Ullesthorpe Court Golf Club,** Frolesworth Road, Ullesthorpe, Near Lutterworth LE17 5BZ. *Location:* 10 minutes M1, M6, M69, A5; near Lutterworth between Leicester and Coventry. Open parkland course, with interesting greens, a fair test for all abilities; lakes on three holes. 18 holes, 6662 yards. S.S.S. 72. *Green Fees:* £22.00 per round. *Eating facilities:* à la carte restaurant, bar meals, club bar. *Visitors:* welcome weekdays, except Bank Holidays, and must book in advance. Hotel with 38 en suite bedrooms and full leisure centre. *Society Meetings:* five packages available, bookable in advance. Tel: Golf Office 01455 209023. Professional: David Bowring (01455 209150; Fax: 01455 202537). e-mail: bookings@ullesthorpecourt.co.uk

MARKET HARBOROUGH. **Market Harborough Golf Club,** Great Oxendon Road, Market Harborough LE16 9HB (01858 463684). *Location:* one mile south of Market Harborough on A508. Parkland. An excellent testing course, lovely views and lakes a feature of the course. 18 holes, 6070 yards. S.S.S. 69. Practice ground. *Green Fees:* information not available. *Eating facilities:* bar snacks and full meals available. *Visitors:* welcome weekdays; weekends only with a member. *Society Meetings:* welcome on application. Professional: F. Baxter. Secretary: Mr A.P. Price-Jones (01858 525688).*

MELTON MOWBRAY. **Melton Mowbray Golf Club,** Waltham Road, Thorpe Arnold, Melton Mowbray LE14 4SD (01664 562118). *Location:* A607 road two miles north-east of Melton Mowbray. Undulating parkland, course established in 1925. A private members club. 18 holes, 6222 yards, S.S.S. 70. Practice ground. *Green Fees:* weekdays £25.00; weekends £30.00. *Eating facilities:* full catering and bar facilities. *Visitors:* welcome before 3pm. *Society Meetings:* by prior arrangement weekdays only. Professional: Neil Curtis (01664 569629). Office: (01664 562118).

MELTON MOWBRAY. **Six Hills Golf Club,** Six Hills, Melton Mowbray LE14 3PR (01509 881225). *Location*: On B676, half way between Melton Mowbray and Loughborough. Flat course. 18 holes, 5758 yards, S.S.S. 69. Practice green and ground. Driving range. *Green Fees*: £12.00 weekdays, £15.00 weekends. *Eating facilities:* Cafe style; new restaurant and bar. *Visitors*: No restrictions. Professional: Matt Alls. Secretary: Mrs J. Showler.

NORTH KILWORTH. **Kilworth Springs Golf Club,** South Kilworth Road, North Kilworth LE17 6HJ (01858 575082; Fax: 01858 575078). *Location*: six miles from Junction 20, four miles M6 - A14 Junction. Links type, parkland course. 18 holes, 6718 yards. S.S.S. 72. Driving range. *Green Fees*: weekdays £12.00 9 holes, £20.00 18 holes; weekends £13.50 9 holes, £22.00 18 holes. Day rate £32.00. Special society rates for 12 people or over. *Eating facilities*: restaurant, bar, bar snacks. *Visitors*: welcome at all times subject to tee times being available. Buggies available. *Society Meetings*: welcome. Professional: Anders Mankert (01858 575974; Fax: 01858 575078). Secretary: Ann Vicary.

OADBY. **Glen Gorse Golf Club,** Glen Road, Oadby LE2 4RF (0116 271 4159). *Location:* on A6, four and a half miles south of Leicester between Oadby and Great Glen. Fairly flat parkland course, some ridge and furrow. 18 holes, 6648 yards, 6079 metres. S.S.S. 72. *Green Fees:* weekdays £25.00 per round, £30.00 per day (£10.50 with member); weekends £10.50 with member only. *Eating facilities:* bar and meals/snacks. *Visitors:* welcome weekdays, weekends with members only. Snooker room. *Society Meetings:* welcome Monday to Friday by prior arrangement. Professional: Dominic Fitzpatrick (0116 271 3748). Secretary: Mrs. J. James (Tel & Fax: 0116 271 4159).

OADBY. **Oadby Golf Course,** Leicester Road, Oadby, Leicester LE2 4AB (0116 270 0215). *Location:* on A6 south of Leicester, one mile from City boundary, at Leicester Racecourse. Parkland. 18 holes, 6376 yards, 5827 metres. S.S.S. 70. Practice ground, coaching. *Green Fees:* information not available. *Eating facilities:* snacks always available, bar with meals on prior notice. *Visitors:* welcome, booking is advised at weekends and Bank Holidays. Please contact Professional. *Society Meetings:* welcome, bookings taken through Golf Shop (0116 270 9052).Caterers (0116 270 0215).*

ROTHLEY. **Rothley Park Golf Club,** Westfield Lane, Rothley, Leicester LE7 7LH (0116 2302019). *Location:* off A6, north of Leicester. Parkland. 18 holes, 6481 yards. S.S.S. 71. *Green Fees:* £25.00 per round, £30.00 per day (mid-week). *Eating facilities:* available daily. *Visitors:* welcome except Tuesdays, weekends and Bank Holidays, must be members of recognised golf club with Handicap. *Society Meetings:* As visitors' restrictions and by prior arrangement only. Professional: Danny Spillane (Tel & Fax: 0116 2303023). Secretary: S.G. Winterton (Tel & Fax: 0116 2302809). e-mail: secretary@rothleypark.co.uk website: www.rothleypark.com

RUTLAND. **Greetham Valley Golf Club,** Wood Lane, Greetham, Near Oakham, Rutland LE15 7NP (01780 460004; Fax: 01780 460623). *Location:* one mile off A1 between Stamford and Grantham on the B668. Four miles from Rutland Water. Parkland, gently undulating with many water features. Many holes playing over natural valley. 36 holes. "The Lakes" 6736 yards, S.S.S 72; "The Valley" 5595 yards, S.S.S. 68; Academy Course 9 holes, 1263 yards, S.S.S. 27. 21 bay floodlit driving range. *Green Fees:* weekdays £32.00; weekends £36.00. *Eating facilities:* excellent clubhouse, lounge, bar and restaurant. *Visitors:* welcome any time, please phone first. Bowls green, meeting room, conference facilities, pool table. Buggies and electric trolleys for hire. *Society Meetings:* welcome except weekends and Bank Holidays. Professional: John Pengelly (01780 460666; Fax: 01780 460623). Secretary: Maggie Davidson (01780 460004; Fax: 01780 460623). e-mail: gvgc@rutnet.co.uk website: www.greethamvalleygolf.co.uk

WOODHOUSE EAVES. **Lingdale Golf Club,** Joe Moore's Lane, Woodhouse Eaves, Near Loughborough LE12 8TF (01509 890035). *Location:* on B5300, Anstey – Shepshed road, three miles from Exit 23 on M1. Woodland and parkland – set in Charnwood Forest. 18 holes, 6545 yards. S.S.S. 71. Practice ground. *Green Fees:* weekdays £23.00 per round, £30.00 per day; weekends £28.00 per round, £40.00 per day. Societies £20.00 per 18 holes, £25.00 per 27/36 holes. *Eating facilities:* full catering available. *Visitors:* welcome, but please telephone first. *Society Meetings:* catered for Mondays to Fridays and pm on Sundays. (one month's notice required). Professional: P. Sellears (01509 890684). Secretary: M. Green (01509 890703).

FHG PUBLICATIONS

publish a large range of well-known accommodation guides. We will be happy to send you details or you can use the order form at the back of this book.

Lincolnshire

ALFORD. **Woodthorpe Hall Golf Club,** Woodthorpe, Alford LN13 0DD (01507 450294). *Location:* on the B1373, 3 miles north of Alford, 8 miles SE of Louth. Undulating parkland. 18 holes, 5140 yards. S.S.S. 65. *Green Fees:* £10.00 per round, £15.00 per day. *Eating facilities:* at Woodthorpe Country Inn on site; conference rooms also available (01507 450079). *Visitors:* welcome, unrestricted. *Society Meetings:* by prior arrangement with the Secretary. Secretary: Mrs J. Smith. (Tel & Fax: 01507 450000).

BOSTON. **Boston Golf Club**, Cowbridge, Horncastle Road, Boston PE22 7EL (01205 350589; Fax: 01205 367526). *Location:* two miles north of Boston on B1183. Look for sign to right if travelling north. Parkland with featured water. 18 holes, 6490 yards, 5930 metres. S.S.S. 71. *Green Fees:* weekdays £22.50 per round, £30.00 per day; weekends and Bank Holidays £27.50 per round, £30.00 per day. *Eating facilities:* daily by arrangement with resident Steward (01205 352533). *Visitors:* welcome without reservation. *Society Meetings:* small groups catered for midweek. Professional: N. Hiom (01205 362306). Secretary: S.P. Shaw (Tel & Fax: 01205 350589).

BOSTON. **Boston West Golf Club,** Hubberts Bridge, Boston PE20 3QX (01205 290670; Fax: 01205 290725). *Location:* Junction of A1121 and B1392, one-and-a-half miles west of Boston. Parkland course with 25,000 trees and scrubs planted, with water in play on five holes. 18 holes, 6299 yards. S.S.S. 70. 6 hole short course, putting greens, practice bunker. 20 bay floodlit driving range. *Green Fees:* weekdays £16.00; weekends £18.00. *Eating facilities:* catering available all day in newly extended Clubhouse, with restaurant overlooking the course. *Visitors:* no restrictions but must book in advance. Lessons available from Austin Curtis. VI Digital Coaching System available. *Society Meetings:* welcome at all times, including weekends. Special rates on request. Secretary: Mike Couture (01205 290670). e-mail: info@bostonwestgolfclub.co.uk website: www.bostonwestgolfclub.co.uk

BOSTON. **Kirton Holme Golf Club**, Holme Road, Kirton Holme, Boston PE20 1SY (01205 290669). *Location:* four miles west of Boston, signposted off A52. Flat parkland. 9 holes, 2884 yards. S.S.S. 34. Small practice area includes net. *Green Fees:* weekdays £5.50 per 9 holes, £9.00 per day; weekends and Bank Holidays £6.50 per 9 holes, £10.00 per day. *Eating facilities:* bar open 11am to dusk, snack meals available. *Visitors:* always welcome - smart dress required. *Society Meetings:* by arrangement. Secretary: T. Welberry (01205 290669).

BOURNE. **The Toft Hotel Golf Club,** Toft, Near Bourne PE10 0JT (01778 590614; Fax: 01778 590264). *Location:* in Toft village on A6121 Stamford to Bourne road. Undulating course with natural lake. 18 holes, 6486 yards. S.S.S. 71. Practice area. *Green Fees:* weekdays £20.00 per round, £25.00 per day; weekends £25.00 per round, £35.00 per day. *Eating facilities:* bar open all day; bar snacks and restaurant. *Visitors:* welcome at all times, prior booking essential. Hotel has 22 bedrooms. *Society Meetings:* welcome, prior booking essential. Professional: Mark Jackson (01778 590616). Secretary: Robin Morris (01778 590616). website: www.thetofthotelgolfclub.com

BRIGG. **Elsham Golf Club,** Barton Road, Elsham, Brigg DN20 0LS (01652 680291; Fax: 01652 680308). *Location:* off M180 at J5 or A15 through Brigg to Barton. Wooded parkland course. 18 holes, 6428 yards. S.S.S. 71. Outdoor practice ground. *Green Fees:* weekdays only £24.00 for 18 holes, £30.00 for 36 holes. £12.00 with a member both during the week and at weekends. Special rates for societies of 12 or more. *Eating facilities:* full catering. *Visitors:* welcome weekdays. *Society Meetings:* catered for on weekdays. Steward (01652 688382). Professional: Stuart Brewer (01652 680432). Secretary: T. Hartley (01652 680291).

BRIGG. **Forest Pines Golf Club,** The Forest Pines Hotel, Ermine Street, Broughton, Near Brigg DN20 0AQ (01652 650770; Fax: 01652 650495). *Location:* 200 yards from Junction 4 M180 towards Scunthorpe. Three 9 hole courses – Forest, Pines, Beeches. Forest/Pines Championship Course: 6882 yards, S.S.S. 73. Pines/Beeches: 6693 yards, S.S.S. 72. Forest/Beeches: 6393 yards, S.S.S. 70. Practice range, practice green, bunkers. *Green Fees:* £36.00 per round, £48.00 per day. *Eating facilities:* clubhouse. *Visitors:* welcome; telephone in advance. Compulsory 'soft spikes' or dimples, no steel spikes. All facilities of The Forest Pines Hotel, golf course and spa available - 114 bedrooms. Buggies, carts, caddies for hire; residential golf schools, leisure club (swimming, gym, sauna and jacuzzi). *Society Meetings:* welcome. Various packages available from £49.95, residential Golfing Breaks available. Professional/Director of Golf: David M. Edwards (01652 650756; Fax: 01652 650495).

CLEETHORPES. **Cleethorpes Golf Club Ltd.,** Golf House, Kings Road, Cleethorpes DN35 0PN (01472 816110). *Location:* approximately one mile south of Cleethorpes Leisure Centre. Mature coastal course, slight undulations give variation but local topography makes for easy walking. Presented to the highest standards the course provides a challenge to all level of players. 18 holes, 6349 yards. S.S.S. 70. Large and small practice areas. *Green Fees:* weekdays £20.00, £10.00 with member, weekends £25.00, £15.00 with member). Handicap Certificate required. *Eating facilities:* bar lunches, evening meals by arrangement. *Visitors:* welcome anytime except Wednesdays, but must be member of another golf club. *Society Meetings:* only by arrangement with the Secretary. Attractive packages available Monday, Thursday, Friday and Sunday. Professional: P. Davies (01472 814060). Secretary: John Ashton (01472 816110).

GAINSBOROUGH. **Gainsborough Golf Club**, Thonock, Gainsborough DN21 1PZ (01427 613088; Fax: 01427 810172). *Location:* signposted from A631 Gainsborough to Grimsby Road. Thonock Park Course is a parkland course with many deciduous trees, Karsten Lakes Course is a Championship Course designed by Neil Coles (opened 1.4.97). Thonock Park Course - 18 holes, 6620 yards. Par 70, S.S.S. 70. Karsten Lakes Course - 18 holes, 6724 yards. Par 72, S.S.S. 72. 20 bay floodlit driving range. *Green Fees:* Thonock Park Course - weekdays £25.00 per round, £40.00 per day, weekends with a member only; Karsten Lakes Course - £30.00 per round, £40.00 per day. *Eating facilities:* restaurant and coffee shop, two bars. *Visitors:* welcome, seven days on both courses (tee time bookings available). *Society Meetings:* welcome (booking in advance necessary). Professional: Stephen Cooper. Secretary: J.D. Bowers.

GRANTHAM. **Belton Park Golf Club,** Belton Lane, Londonthorpe Road, Grantham NG31 9SH (01476 567399; Fax: 01476 592078). *Location:* two miles from Grantham. 250 acre Deer Park adjacent to the historical Belton House. Three loops of 9 holes each beginning and ending at the clubhouse: Brownlow Course 6472 yards (Championship). S.S.S. 71. Ancaster Course 6325 yards. S.S.S. 70. Belmont Course 6075 yards. S.S.S. 69. Two large practice areas. *Green Fees:* weekdays £30.00 per round, £36.00 per day; weekends and Bank Holidays £36.00 per round, £42.00 per day. Special winter rates November to March. *Eating facilities:* full restaurant facilities every day except Mondays. *Visitors:* welcome without reservation. *Society Meetings:* catered for by arrangement weekdays only (except Tuesday). Special day package. Professional: B. McKee (01476 563911). Secretary: T. Ireland. e-mail: greatgolf@beltonpark.co.uk

GRANTHAM. **Stoke Rochford Golf Club,** Stoke Rochford, Near Grantham NG33 5EW (01476 530275). *Location:* five miles south of Grantham on A1. Entrance at "MacDonalds" service area. Parkland. 18 holes, 6313 yards. S.S.S. 70. Small practice ground. *Green Fees:* information not available. *Eating facilities:* meals available daily, to be booked before playing. *Visitors:* cannot commence play before 10.30am at weekends or on Public Holidays. No visitors on Sundays November, December and January. Buggies and numerous trolleys for hire. Snooker room. *Society Meetings:* by prior arrangement. Professional: A.E. Dow (01476 530218). Secretary: J.Martindale (01572 756305).

GRANTHAM. **Sudbrook Moor Golf Club,** Charity Street, Carlton Scroop, Grantham (01400 250796). *Location:* A607 Lincoln to Grantham, six miles north-east of Grantham. Private course in picturesque valley; easy walking parkland/meadowland. 9 holes, 4827 yards. S.S.S. 63/64/64. Practice ground and net. *Green Fees:* winter weekdays £5.00, winter weekend £7.00; summer weekdays £7.00, summer weekend £9.00. *Eating facilities:* Spike Bar and dining room (alcohol-free). *Visitors:* welcome by appointment. Professionals: Tim Hutton/Ben Hutton. Club Secretary: Judith M. Hutton (01400 250796). Catering: (01400 250876).

GRANTHAM near. **De Vere Belton Woods Hotel and Country Club,** Belton, Near Grantham NG32 2LN (01476 593200; Fax: 01476 574547). *Location:* three miles from Grantham, two miles from the A1. Parkland course. Belton Woods Hotel, the golfers' paradise, offers not only one but three challenges, two 18 hole courses: the Championship Course, the Lakes, 6774 yards and the Championship length the Woodside; 6834 yards and the Red Arrows a 9 hole par 3 course, 1184 yards. 20 bay floodlit driving range. *Green Fees:* information not available. *Eating facilities:* Spikes Bar, food all day choice of two restaurants and three bars in hotel. *Visitors:* welcome at all times, check in advance for availability. Accommodation in Hotel – 136 luxurious bedrooms and suites, with extensive leisure and conference facilities. Golfing Breaks and society meetings a speciality. *Society Meetings:* welcome, ring for society offers/golf breaks. Golf and Leisure Manager: Andrew Cameron. Golf Professional: Steve Sayers. Golf Sales: Rina Ozolins (01476 514308).*

GRIMSBY. **Grimsby Golf Club Ltd**, Littlecoates Road, Grimsby DN34 4LU (01472 342823). *Location:* two miles west of town centre, one mile from A180 and A46. Undulating parkland course. 18 holes, 6098 yards. S.S.S. 69. Practice ground, chipping area. *Green Fees:* information not available. *Eating facilities:* quality food available at all times and bar facilities. *Visitors:* welcome weekdays, must be members of golf clubs. *Society Meetings:* catered for Mondays and Fridays by arrangement with Secretary (Club Ladies' Day Tuesday, club ladies have priority in the afternoons). Professional: Richard Smith (01472 356981). Secretary: Mr V. McAfee (Tel & Fax: 01472 342630).*

GRIMSBY. **Manor Golf Club,** Laceby Manor, Laceby, Grimsby DN37 7EA (01472 873468; Fax: 01472 276706). *Location:* A18 to Louth, half a mile on left hand side from Oaklands Hotel, situated at Laceby roundabout. Parkland - tree lined fairways, many water features including green surrounded by water. 18 holes, 6354 yards. S.S.S. 70. Netted driving area, putting green, chipping area. *Green Fees:* £18.00. Twilight £12.00 (not feasible to complete 18 holes at this time). Subject to review. *Eating facilities:* bar, lounge bar, dining area. *Visitors:* welcome any day. Booked tee system operated all days, non members may book up to six days in advance. *Society Meetings:* welcome by prior arrangement. Professional: (01472 873468). Secretary: Judith MacKay.

GRIMSBY. **Waltham Windmill Golf Club,** Cheapside, Waltham, Grimsby DN37 0HT (01472 824109). *Location:* off A16 main Louth to Grimsby road. Parkland course incorporating seven lakes. 18 holes, 6442 yards. S.S.S. 71. Practice ground. *Green Fees:* weekdays £20.00, with member £13.00; weekends £27.00, with member £20.00. Reductions for societies; minimum 12. *Eating facilities:* bar and restaurant. *Visitors:* welcome, telephone booking. *Society Meetings:* welcome, contact the Secretary. Professional: Nigel Burkitt (01472 823963). Secretary: George W. Fielding (01472 824109; Fax: 01472 828391).

HORNCASTLE near. **Horncastle Golf Club**, West Ashby, Near Horncastle LN9 5PP (01507 526800). *Location:* just off A158 between Horncastle and Baumber. Parkland course - water features on 14 holes. 18 holes, 5800 yards. S.S.S. 70. *Green Fees:* information not available. *Eating facilities:* bars, restaurant. *Visitors:* welcome anytime but helpful to phone. Special package available golf range, golf course, food and drink. Ballroom and conference facilities. Accommodation available, caravan site. Carts. Fishing lakes. *Society Meetings:* please phone in advance. Professional: E.C. Wright. Secretary: Derek Hendry.*

IMMINGHAM. **Immingham Golf Club,** St Andrew's Lane, Church Lane, Immingham DN40 2EU (01469 575298; Fax: 01469 577636). *Location:* two miles off A180, behind St Andrew's Church, Immingham. Undulating parkland with water hazards. Drainage dyke comes into play for over half the holes. Excellent greens. 18 holes, 6215 yards, 5682 metres. S.S.S. 70. Small practice area. *Green Fees:* weekdays £15.00

per round, £10 with member; weekends £20.00 per round; £12.00 with member. *Eating facilities:* snacks; full catering (book in advance). *Visitors:* welcome anytime except Thursday pm, Saturday pm and Sunday am. Handicap Certificate preferred. *Society Meetings:* welcome midweek during the day, limited availability at weekends. Professional: Nick Harding (01469 575493). Manager: D. McCully (01469 575298). e-mail: admin@immgc.com website: www.immgc.com

LINCOLN. **Blankney Golf Club,** Blankney, near Metheringham, Lincoln LN4 3AZ (01526 320263; Fax: 01526 322521). *Location:* near Metheringham on B1188 Lincoln to Sleaford Road. Parkland, slightly undulating. 18 holes, 6638 yards. S.S.S. 73. Practice area, putting green and snooker. *Green Fees:* weekdays £25.00; weekends £35.00. Special rates available Tuesday/Thursday. *Eating facilities:* dining room and bar meals. *Visitors:* welcome except Wednesday mornings, limited numbers at weekends. Accommodation for six persons. Trolley hire. *Society Meetings:* welcome with prior booking. Professional: G. Bradley (01526 320202). General Manager: D.A. Priest (01526 320263; Fax: 01526 322521). website: www.blankneygolf.co.uk

LINCOLN. **Canwick Park Golf Club,** Canwick Park, Washingborough Road, Lincoln LN4 1EF (01522 522166). *Location:* two miles east of Lincoln on B1190. Parkland, wooded course - two testing Par 3's (5th & 13th). 18 holes, 6160 yards, 5600 metres, S.S.S. 69. Practice ground. *Green Fees:* £17.00 weekdays, £21.00 weekends. *Eating facilities:* bar snacks and meals to order. *Visitors:* welcome weekdays; weekends after 3pm without a member. Locker rooms. *Society Meetings:* welcome by prior arrangement. Professional: S.J. Williamson (Tel & Fax: 01522 536870). Manager: P. Roberts (01522 542912; Fax: 01522 526997). e-mail: manager@canwickpark.co.uk website: www.canwickpark.co.uk

LINCOLN. **Carholme Golf Club,** Carholme Road, Lincoln LN1 1SE (01522 523725). *Location:* one mile from city centre on A57 to Worksop. Flat parkland. 18 holes, 6215 yards. S.S.S. 70. *Green Fees:* £18.00 per round, £22.00 per day. *Eating facilities:* full service. *Visitors:* welcome most days subject to restrictions regarding starting times, information available on request. *Society Meetings:* by prior arrangement only. Professional: Martin Ross (01522 536811). Secretary: J. Lammin (01522 523725).

LINCOLN. **Lincoln Golf Club,** Torksey, Lincoln (Tel & Fax: 01427 718721). *Location:* A156 approximately 6 miles south of Gainsborough. Mature, testing championship standard course built on sandy subsoil. 18 holes, 6438 yards. S.S.S. 71. *Green Fees:* £28.00 per round, £35.00 per day. Subject to review. Winter packages available. *Eating facilities:* full facilities available. *Visitors:* welcome anytime except Tuesday mornings (Ladies' Day). *Society Meetings:* welcome by prior arrangement (not weekends). Professional: Ashley Carter (Tel & Fax: 01427 718273). Secretary: Derek B. Linton (Tel & Fax: 01427 718721). e-mail: info@lincolngc.co.uk website: www.lincolngc.co.uk

LINCOLN. **Pottergate Golf Club**, Moor Lane, Branston, Lincoln (01522 794867). *Location:* south of Lincoln on B1188 to Branston. Turn left at Moor Lodge Hotel into Moor Lane. Parkland course. 9 holes. Par 34. Indoor golf simulator with 17 golf courses and driving range. Putting green. *Green Fees:* weekdays £8.00, weekends £9.50 (reductions for senior citizens/students/juniors, please phone for prices).. *Eating facilities:* bar and food from 11am to 10pm(light snacks available). Food by prior arrangement. *Society Meetings:* welcome. Professional: Lee Tasker. Proprietor: Robert Mawer.

LINCOLN. **RAF Coningsby Golf Club**, Coningsby, Lincoln LN4 4JT (01526 342581). *Location*: on the B1192 halfway between Tattershall Thorpe and Woodhall Spa, signposted RAF Woodhall. Parkland course. 9 holes (18 tees), 5354 yards, S.S.S. 66. *Green Fees*: £8.00, with member £6.00, juniors £4.00. Day ticket £10.00, Juniors £4.00. *Visitors*: welcome weekdays except Monday am (Ladies). *Society Meetings*: welcome weekdays by appointment. Secretary: Shaun Ellis (01526 347640; Fax: 01526 347413).

LINCOLN. **Welton Manor Golf Centre**, Hackthorn Road, Welton, Lincoln LN2 3PD (01673 862827). *Location:* six miles north of Lincoln. Off A46 to Welton village, through Welton, turn left at mini roundabout signposted Spridlington, entrance half-a-mile on left. Undulating parkland with streams, ponds and tree-lined fairways. 18 holes, Par 70/71. *Green Fees:* information not available. *Eating facilities:* bar and dining from 8am to 11pm. Professional: Gary Leslie*

LOUTH. **Louth Golf Club,** 59 Crowtree Lane, Louth LN11 9LJ (01507 603681; Fax: 01507 608501). *Location:* western outskirts of Louth. Undulating parkland course in an Area of Outstanding Natural Beauty. 18 holes, 6430yards. S.S.S. 71. Practice ground, putting green. *Green Fees:* £20.00 per round, £26.00 per day weekdays; £30.00 per round, £35.00 per day weekends and Bank Holidays. Discounts for large parties may be available. *Eating facilities:* full catering 11am to 9pm (earlier to order). *Visitors:* welcome without reservation other than notification and dress rules. Squash court. *Society Meetings:* catered for. Professional: A.J. Blundell (01507 604648). Secretary: Mr Robert Perkins (01507 603681; Fax: 01507 608501). website: louthgolfclub.com

See also Colour Advertisement on page 37

LOUTH. **Kenwick Park Golf Club,** Kenwick Park, Louth LN11 8NY (01507 605134; Fax: 01507 606556). *Location:* one mile south of Louth. Undulating parkland, wooded course. 18 holes, 6815 yards. S.S.S. 73. Driving range, teaching facilities. *Green Fees:* information not available. *Eating facilities:* contact 01507 608210. *Visitors:* welcome but please telephone in advance. Buggies available. Hotel (01507 608806). *Society Meetings:* welcome, contact Secretary. Professional: Eric Sharp (Tel & Fax: 01507 607161). Secretary: Paddy Shillington (01507 605134; Fax: 01507 606556).
e-mail: golfatkenwick@nascr.net
website: www.louthnet.co.uk

MABLETHORPE. **Sandilands Golf Club**, Roman Bank, Sandilands, Sutton-on-Sea LN12 2RJ (01507 441432). *Location:* A52 one mile south of Sutton-on-Sea. Seaside links adjacent to sea and sand. 18 holes, 6173 yards. S.S.S. 69. 40 acre practice area. *Green Fees:* information not available. *Eating facilities:* bar and restaurant. *Visitors:* welcome. *Society Meetings:* welcome with reductions for numbers, catered for weekdays. Manageress: Michelle Ives. Secretary: Chris Carpenter (01507 441432).*

MARKET RASEN. **Market Rasen and District Golf Club**, Legsby Road, Market Rasen LN8 3DZ (01673 842319). *Location:* A46 to Market Rasen - one mile east of town. Wooded heathland course. 18 holes, 6209 yards. S.S.S. 70. Practice ground. *Green Fees:* weekdays £29.00 per day, £20.00 per round; weekends only with member. *Eating facilities:* available all day, Mondays up to 3pm only. *Visitors:* welcome with reservation, not Wednesday between 11.00 and 1.30pm. Must be member of bona fide golf club. Weekends with members only. *Society Meetings:* catered for Tuesdays and Fridays. Professional: A.M. Chester (01673 842416). Secretary: J.A. Brown (01673 842319).

MARKET RASEN. **Market Rasen Racecourse 9-Hole Pay and Play Course,** Legsby Road, Market Rasen LN8 3EA (01673 843434; Fax: 01673 844532). *Location:* on A631 Market Rasen to Louth road, midway between Lincoln and Grimsby. Course is in centre of picturesque National Hunt racecourse. 9 holes, 2532 yards. S.S.S. 33. *Green Fees:* information

not available. *Eating facilities:* hot and cold drinks and sweet shop available April to October. *Visitors:* no restrictions. Golf course is closed on race days. *Society Meetings:* welcome on application to Secretary. Secretary: Pip Adams*

METHERINGHAM. **Martin Moor Golf Club**, Martin Road, Blankney LN4 3BE (01526 378243). *Location:* B1188 between Martin and Metheringham. Flat wooded course. 9 holes (yellow Tees), 18 tees including three Par 5's, 6132 yards. S.S.S. 69. Large practice area. *Green Fees:* 9 holes £6.50, 18 holes £9.00. *Eating facilities:* bar and snacks. *Visitors:* welcome. Lessons by arrangement. *Society Meetings:* welcome. Rates negotiable. Catering on request. Secretary: M. J. Lovett (01526 378243).

SCUNTHORPE. **Ashby Decoy Golf Club**, Burringham Road, Scunthorpe, North Lincolnshire DN17 2AB (01724 866561; Fax: 01724 271708). *Location:* leave M181 Scunthorpe South, turn right, right again, third right by ASDA Superstore. Flat wooded, parkland course. 18 holes, 6281 yards. S.S.S. 70. Large practice area. *Green Fees:* information not available. *Eating facilities:* full catering and bar available. *Visitors:* welcome weekdays only, not Tuesdays. *Society Meetings:* by arrangement weekdays, except Tuesdays. Professional: Andrew Miller (01724 868972). Secretary: Mrs J.A. Harrison (01724 866561; Fax: 01724 271708).*
e-mail: jane@ashbydecoy.co.uk
website: www.ashbydecoy.co.uk

SCUNTHORPE. **Grange Park Golf Club,** Butterwick Road, Messingham, Scunthorpe DN17 3PP (01724 762945). *Location:* five miles south of Scunthorpe between Messingham and East Butterwick, four miles south of Junction 3 of M180. New parkland course with interesting water features. 18 holes (opening May 2003 - exact yardage and S.S.S. to be confirmed). Second 9 hole course – flat parkland course, 1300 yards. S.S.S 27. Floodlit driving range. New cluhouse also opening. *Green Fees:* weekdays £10.50, weekends £12.50, Juniors £6.00. Memberships available. *Eating facilities:* full catering facilities available. *Visitors:* welcome at all times. Pro shop. *Society Meetings:* welcome. Golf Professional: Jonathan Drury. Manager: Ian Cannon.

SCUNTHORPE. **The Lincolnshire Golf Course,** Crowle, Scunthorpe DN17 4BU (01724 711619). *Location:* M180 Junction 2, A161 to Crowle Goole, course 800 yards on left. Flat parkland. 18 holes, 6430 yards. S.S.S.70. Practice green. *Green Fees:* information not available. *Eating facilities:* bar and restaurant. *Visitors:* welcome, no restrictions. *Society Meetings:* welcome, no restrictions. Proprietor: A. York. Secretary: J. Middlehurst.

SCUNTHORPE. **Holme Hall Golf Club,** Holme Lane, Bottesford, Scunthorpe DN16 3RF (Tel & Fax: 01724 862078). *Location:* M180 Exit 4 (Scunthorpe East). Heathland with sandy subsoil. 18 holes, 6404 yards. S.S.S. 71. Full size practice ground. *Green Fees:* £25.00 per round, £35.00 per day. *Eating facilities:* full catering available all week. *Visitors:* welcome Monday to Friday. *Society Meetings:* daily packages available by arrangement with the Secretary. Professional: R. McKiernan (01724 851816). Secretary: Miss T.L. Curtis. e-mail: tracey.curtis@btconnect.com

SCUNTHORPE. **Normanby Hall Golf Club,** Normanby Park, Near Scunthorpe DN15 9HU (01724 720226). *Location:* five miles north of Scunthorpe on B1130. Follow signs for Normanby Hall Country Park. Parkland. 18 holes, 6561 yards. S.S.S. 71. Practice area. *Green Fees:* £9.50 per round, £19.00 per day; weekends £10.00. Twilight ticket weekdays £6.75, weekends £7.35. *Eating facilities:* fully licensed Clubhouse, restaurant; meals most times. *Visitors:* welcome, check times in advance with Professional. *Society Meetings:* bookings taken for weekdays. Professional: Chris Mann (01724 720226). Manager: Susan Hopkinson (01724 720588).

SKEGNESS. **North Shore Hotel and Golf Club,** North Shore Road, Skegness PE25 1DN (01754 763298; Fax: 01754 761902). *Location:* north of town one mile. Part links, part parkland, challenging course situated overlooking the sea. 18 holes, 6134 yards. S.S.S. 71. Putting green. *Green Fees:* information not available. *Eating facilities:* formal restaurant, spike bar serving home cooked bar food 10am to 9 pm. Hotel accommodation on course 36 en suite bedroomed hotel. Special winter deals available. *Visitors:* welcome, prior notice required. Golf schools and instruction provided by professional; juniors welcome. *Society Meetings:* welcome, catering from between 4 and 200. Professional: John Cornelius (01754 764822). General Manager: N. Wardle e-mail: golf@north-shore.co.uk

SKEGNESS. **Seacroft Golf Club,** Drummond Road, Seacroft, Skegness PE25 3AU (Tel & Fax: 01754 763020). *Location:* towards Gibraltar Nature Reserve. Seaside links course. 18 holes, 6490 yards. S.S.S. 71. *Green Fees:* weekdays £32.50 per round, £42.50 per day; weekends and Bank Holidays £37.50 per round, £47.50 per day. *Eating facilities:* available all day/evenings. *Visitors:* welcome after 9.30am if members of recognised club or society, Handicap Certificate required. *Society Meetings:* societies/ company golf days and groups catered for. Professional: R. Lawie (01754 769624). Secretary: Richard England (Tel & Fax: 01754 763020). e-mail: richard@seacroft-golfclub.co.uk website: www.seacroft-golfclub.co.uk

SKEGNESS. **Southview Golf Club,** Southview Leisure Park, Burgh Road, Skegness PE25 2LA (01754 760589; Fax: 01754 768455). *Location:* half a mile from Skegness towards Burgh Le Marsh A158. Flat parkland. 9/18 holes, 4358 yards. S.S.S. 61. *Green Fees:* £8.00. *Eating facilities:* full bar and meals service. *Visitors:* welcome. *Society Meetings:* welcome weekdays. Golf Manager: P. Cole.

SLEAFORD. **Sleaford Golf Club,** Willoughby Road, South Rauceby, Sleaford NG34 8PL (01529 488273). *Location:* off A153, two miles west of Sleaford. Inland links-type course, fairly flat and lightly wooded. 18 holes, 6503 yards. S.S.S. 71. Practice field, 6 hole pitch and putt. *Green Fees:* weekdays £22.00 per round, £30.00 per day, £12.00 with a member, juniors £5.00 per round or day, with or without a member; weekends £36.00 per round or day, £16.00 per round or day with member, juniors as per adults. Subject to review. *Eating facilities:* full catering except Mondays. Bar open seven days. *Visitors:* welcome without reservation, except winter weekends. Handicap Certificate required and must be members of a recognised club. *Society Meetings:* catered for weekdays only by prior arrangement. Professional: J.N. Wilson (01529 488644). Secretary: T.E. Gibbons (01529 488273; Fax: 01529 488326).

SOUTH KYME. **South Kyme Golf Club,** Skinners Lane, South Kyme LN4 4AT (01526 861113; Fax: 01526 861080)). *Location:* approximately four miles off A153 road from Sleaford to Horncastle, turn right before North Kyme. Four miles off A17 from Sleaford to Boston, turn left before East Heckington. An interesting "inland links" with excellent greens all year round. 18 holes, 6597 yards White, 6222 yards Yellow, Red. S.S.S. White 71, Yellow 70, Red 70. 6 hole Par 3 course, practice ground. *Green Fees:* weekdays £15.00 per round, £20.00 per day; weekends £18.00 per round, £20.00 per day. Subject to review. Society discount for 8 players or more. Expert golf instruction available, send for brochure. *Eating facilities:* bar and restaurant. Snacks available all day. Lunch menu available. *Visitors:* no restrictions at present but advisable to check at weekends in case of competitions. *Society Meetings:* welcome with prior booking. PGA Director of Golf/Secretary: Peter Chamberlain. e-mail: southkymegc@hotmail.com website: www.skgc.co.uk

SPALDING. **The Spalding Golf Club,** Surfleet, Spalding PE11 4EA (01775 680234). *Location:* four miles from Spalding on A16 to Boston. Parkland course, water features on many of the holes with the drive on the second over the River Glen. 18 holes, 6478 yards. S.S.S. 71. Large practice area. *Green Fees:* weekdays £25.00 per round, £30.00 per day, £12.00 with a member; weekends £30.00, £15.00 with a member. *Eating facilities:* full catering and bar facilities except Tuesdays when there is a bar and filled rolls only. *Visitors:* welcome, advisable to telephone in advance. Handicap Certificates required. *Society Meetings:* catered for on Thursday all day and Tuesday afternoons only April to October. Professional: John Spencer (01775 680474). Secretary: Barrie Walker (Tel & Fax: 01775 680988).

SPALDING. **Sutton Bridge Golf Club,** New Road, Sutton Bridge, Spalding PE12 9RQ (01406 350323). *Location:* off A17 between Long Sutton and King's Lynn, New Road leads off Sutton Bridge main street (Bridge Road), almost opposite church. Parkland course built around former Victorian dock basin. 9 holes. Small practice ground, new driving range from June 2002. *Green Fees:* April to September £20.00; October to March £15.00. £10.00 with a member. *Eating facilities:* bar - open 7 days, catering Tuesday to Sunday. *Visitors:* welcome weekdays except Tuesday after 3pm, and Wednesday mornings. *Society Meetings:* welcome weekdays by arrangement; some restrictions, contact club for details. Special concessions for groups of 8 or more; package available. Professional: Simon Dicksee (01406 351422). Secretary: N. E. Davis (01945 582447).

SPALDING near. **Gedney Hill Golf Course**, West Drove, Gedney Hill, Near Spalding PE12 0NT (01406 330183). *Location:* six miles from Radar Tower near Crowland, off B1073 follow signs or follow 1066 off A47. Testing interesting course, Guiness Book of Records for longest hole in Britain (671 yards). 18 holes, 5357 yards. S.S.S. 66. 10 bay driving range, practice/putting area. *Green Fees:* £7.00 midweek, £11.50 weekends. *Eating facilities:* two bars (one casual spike bar), restaurant (80 seater). *Visitors:* welcome, no restrictions. Full snooker room/snookerette table, new restaurant conservatory. *Society Meetings:* all very welcome. Golf shop: Olly Tyler (01406 330922). Secretary: M. Page.

STAMFORD. **Burghley Park (Stamford) Golf Club,** St. Martins Without, Stamford PE9 3JX (Tel & Fax: 01780 753789). *Location:* leave A1 at roundabout on B1081 south of Stamford, club one mile on right. Flat parkland. 18 holes, 6236 yards. S.S.S. 70. *Green Fees:* weekdays £25.00, weekends as members' guests only. Half price after 5pm May to September. *Eating facilities:* restaurant and bar. *Visitors:* welcome weekdays. Handicap Certificates required. Visit Burghley House, the greatest of Elizabethan mansions. *Society Meetings:* Wednesdays and Thursdays only. Professional: Glenn Davies (Tel & Fax: 01780 762100). Secretary: Howard Mulligan (Tel & Fax: 01780 753789). e-mail: burghley.golf@lineone.net

STAMFORD. **Luffenham Heath Golf Club,** Ketton, Stamford PE9 3UU (01780 720205). *Location:* one-and-a-half miles south-west of Ketton on A6121. Undulating heathland, in conservation area for flora and fauna. 18 holes, 6315 yards. S.S.S. 70. Practice ground. *Green Fees:* £40.00 per round, £50.00 per day. *Eating facilities:* snacks available daily, full meals by arrangement. *Visitors:* welcome, advisable to contact Secretary first. Handicap Certificate required. *Society Meetings:* by arrangement through the Secretary. Professional: Ian Burnett (Tel & Fax: 01780 720298). Secretary: John R. Ingleby (01780 720205; Fax: 01780 722146). e-mail: jringleby@theluffenhamheathgc.co.uk website: www.luffenhamheath.co.uk

STAMFORD. **Rutland County Golf Club**, Great Casterton, Stamford PE9 4AQ (Tel & Fax: 01780 460330). *Location:* head north on A1 from Stamford roundabout, take Pickworth turn, follow golf signs. Inland links, easy walking. 18 holes, 6401 yards. S.S.S. 71. 9 holes short course. 20 bay driving range, practice bunker, chipping green, putting green. *Green Fees:* weekdays £25.00 to £30.00 per day; weekends £30.00 to £35.00 per day. *Eating facilities:* bar meals, lounge bar, dining room. *Visitors:* welcome. *Society Meetings:* welcome on application. Professional: Fred Fearn (01780 460239). Secretary: Steve Lowe.

WOODHALL SPA. **The National Golf Centre,** Woodhall Spa LN10 6PU (01526 352511; Fax: 01526 351817). *Location:* 19 miles from Lincoln, Boston, Sleaford; 33 miles from Skegness; 50 miles from Nottingham. Hotchkin is a flat heathland course and Bracken is a flat parkland course. Hotchkin Course: 18 holes, 7080 yards. S.S.S. 75; Bracken Course:18 holes, 6735 yards S.S.S. 74. Driving range, practice and pitch and putt course. *Green Fees:* Hotchkin – £60.00 per round, £100.00 per day; Bracken – £40.00 per round, £65.00 per day. Reduced rates for Juniors and EGU members. *Eating facilities:* clubroom with bar, dining room with all facilities. *Visitors:* welcome at all times by prior arrangement. Handicap Certificates required. *Society Meetings:* catered for if booked in advance. Director of Golf: R.A. Latham.

Greater Manchester

ALTRINCHAM. **Altrincham Golf Club**, Stockport Road, Timperley, Altrincham, Cheshire WA15 7LP (0161-928 0761). *Location:* one mile east of Altrincham on A560. Parkland. 18 holes, 6190 yards, 5659 metres. S.S.S. 69. Driving range. *Green Fees:* information not available. *Eating facilities:* Old Hall Hotel attached to course. *Visitors:* welcome any time, book one week in advance. Public course. Professional: Scott Parkington. Secretary: Peter Yates.*

ALTRINCHAM. **Dunham Forest Golf and Country Club,** Oldfield Lane, Altrincham WA14 4TY (0161-928 2605; Fax: 0161-929 8975). *Location:* approximately 9 miles south of Manchester off A56. Wooded parkland. 18 holes, 6772 yards. S.S.S. 72. *Green Fees:* weekdays £40.00; weekends and Bank Holidays £45.00. *Eating facilities:* clubhouse restaurant and bar open daily. *Visitors:* welcome, but should telephone to check availability. *Society Meetings:* welcome by prior arrangement. Professional: I. Wrigley (0161-928 2727). Secretary: Mrs S. Klaus (0161-928 2605).

ALTRINCHAM. **Hale Golf Club**, Rappax Road, Hale, Altrincham WA15 0NU (0161-980 4225). *Location:* off Bankhall Lane near Altrincham Priory Hospital. Undulating parkland with River Bollin featuring on 3 holes. 9 holes (2 rounds), 5780 yards, S.S.S. 68. Practice ground. *Green Fees:* information not available. *Eating facilities:* by arrangement with Steward; snack lunches available, dinner; two bars. *Visitors:* welcome weekdays (except Thursday), weekends with a member only. Meetings: by arrangement with Hon. Secretary. Professional: Alec Bickerdike (0161-904 0835). Hon. Secretary: John Goodman (0161-980 4225).

ALTRINCHAM. **The Ringway Golf Club Ltd,** Hale Road, Hale Barns, Altrincham WA15 8SW (0161-904 9609). *Location:* Junction 6, M56 then A538 signposted Hale and Altrincham, one mile. Parkland. 18 holes, 6482 yards. S.S.S. 71. Putting green, short game area and practice ground. *Green Fees:* weekdays £35.00, weekends and Bank Holidays £45.00. Subject to review. *Eating facilities:* full service except Mondays (snacks only). *Visitors:* generally not on Tuesdays, Fridays or Saturdays. *Society Meetings:* catered for by arrangement. Professional: Nick Ryan (0161-980 8432). Secretary: A. Scully (0161-980 2630; Fax: 0161-980 4414).

ASHTON-IN-MAKERFIELD. **Ashton-in-Makerfield Golf Club Ltd,** Garswood Park, Liverpool Road, Ashton-in-Makerfield, Wigan WN4 0YT (01942 727267). *Location:* M6, Junction 23 from south, Junction 24 from north. Parkland course. 18 holes,

6205 yards. S.S.S. 70. *Green Fees:* £28.00 per round, £30.00 per day. *Eating facilities:* available. *Visitors:* welcome mid-week (except Wednesday) with reservation but not before 9.45am. *Society Meetings:* catered for Mondays, Tuesdays, Thursdays and Fridays by prior appointment. Professional: P. Allan (01942 724229). Secretary: J.W. Ball (01942 719330).

ASHTON-UNDER-LYNE. **Ashton-under-Lyne Golf Club**, Gorsey Way, Ashton-under-Lyne OL6 9HT (0161-330 1537; Fax: 0161-330 6673). *Location:* three miles from town centre, Mossley Road, left at Queens Road, right at Nook Lane, Clubhouse top of St. Christopher's Road. Wooded course. 18 holes, 6209 yards. S.S.S. 70. Practice ground. *Green Fees:* £25.00; weekends £25.00 with member only. *Eating facilities:* full catering except Mondays. *Visitors:* welcome weekdays except Wednesdays; members of recognised golf clubs welcome without reservation. *Society Meetings:* catered for on application: special daily rates. Professional: Mr Colin Boyle (0161-308 2095). Secretary: Mr A.H. Jackson.*

BOLTON. **Bolton Golf Club Ltd,** Lostock Park, Chorley New Road, Bolton BL6 4AJ (01204 843067). *Location:* off main road half-way between Bolton and Horwich. 18 holes, 6237 yards. S.S.S. 70. *Green Fees:* weekdays £32.00 per round, £38.00 per day; weekends, Bank Holidays £35.00 per round, £42.00 per day. *Eating facilities:* luncheons and evening meals. *Visitors:* welcome with reservation. *Society Meetings:* catered for weekdays except Tuesdays. Professional: R. Longworth (01204 843073). Secretary: Mrs H.M. Stuart (Tel & Fax: 01204 843067).

BOLTON. **Bolton Old Links Golf Club Ltd,** Chorley Old Road, Montserrat, Bolton BL1 5SU (01204 840050). *Location:* on B6226, 400 yards north of roundabout on ring road. Championship course, moorland. 18 holes, 6469 yards. S.S.S. 71. Practice facilities, Indoor net. *Green Fees:* weekdays £30.00, weekends £40.00. Special rates for groups over 20. *Eating facilities:* available. *Visitors:* welcome except weekends. *Society Meetings:* catered for weekdays. Professional: P. Horridge (01204 843089). Secretary: Mrs J. Boardman (01204 842307).

BOLTON. **Breightmet Golf Club**, Red Bridge, Ainsworth, Bolton BL2 5PA (01204 27381). *Location:* leave Bolton on main road to Bury, turn left two miles on Milnthorpe road for the bridge. 9 holes, 6418 yards. S.S.S. 71. *Green Fees:* information not available. *Eating facilities:* lunches and light refreshments. *Visitors:* welcome, preliminary phone call advisable. *Society Meetings:* catered for on application. Secretary: S.P. Griffiths *

For full details of clubs and courses, plus convenient accommodation, visit the FHG golf website on **www.uk-golfguide.com**

BOLTON. **Deane Golf Club,** Broadford Road, Deane, Bolton (01204 61944). *Location:* one mile east of Junction 5 of M61 towards Bolton Centre. Rolling parkland with number of small ravines to cross. 18 holes, 5652 yards, 5168 metres. S.S.S. 67. *Green Fees:* weekdays £24.00; weekends £28.00. *Eating facilities:* lunches and evening meals by arrangement. *Visitors:* welcome. *Society Meetings:* Tuesdays, Thursdays and Fridays only. Professional: David Martindale. Secretary: P. Parry (01204 651808; Fax: 01204 652047).

BOLTON. **Dunscar Golf Club Ltd,** Longworth Lane, Bromley Cross, Bolton BL7 9QY (01204 598228). *Location:* one and a half miles north of Bolton on A666. Parkland, moorland course. 18 holes, 6085 yards. S.S.S. 69. Practice ground available. *Green Fees:* not yet finalised. *Eating facilities:* available. *Visitors:* welcome except weekends. Carts available. *Society Meetings:* catered for by arrangement with the Secretary. Professional: Gary Treadgold (01204 592992). Secretary: John William Jennings (01204 303321).

BOLTON. **Great Lever and Farnworth Golf Club Ltd,** Plodder Lane, Farnworth, Bolton BL4 0LQ (01204 656650; Fax: 01204 656137). *Location:* A666 or M61 (Junction 4), two miles from Bolton town centre. Parkland. 18 holes, 5833 yards. S.S.S. 68. Practice ground. *Green Fees:* weekdays £20.00; weekends £27.00. *Eating facilities:* restaurant and bar every day except Monday. *Visitors:* welcome, preferably by appointment. *Society Meetings:* welcome weekdays. Professional: Tony Howarth (01204 656650). Secretary: Mrs J. Ivill (Tel & Fax: 01204 656137).

BOLTON. **Harwood Golf Club,** Springfield, Roading Brook Road, Harwood, Bolton BL2 4JD (01204 522878). *Location:* situated just off the B6196 three miles east of Bolton – A58 from Bury, turn right through Ainsworth village. Parkland/meadowland course. 18 holes, 5783 yards. S.S.S. 68. Par 70. Large practice area. *Green Fees:* with a member £12.00 weekdays and weekends, without a member £20.00 weekdays only. *Eating facilities:* catering available Tuesday to Sunday (Monday by arrangement). *Visitors:* welcome weekdays only, weekends only with a member. Should be members of recognised golf club or society. Carts allowed. *Society Meetings:* welcome Monday, Tuesday, Thursday and Friday by arrangement with the Secretary. Society packages available from £23.00 per person. Professional: Paul Slater (01204 362834). Secretary: Ian W. Lund (01204 524233). e-mail: secretary@harwoodgolfclub.co.uk website: www.harwoodgolfclub.co.uk

BOLTON. **Regent Park Golf Club Ltd,** Links Road, off Chorley New Road, Lostock, Bolton BL2 9XX (01204 844170). *Location:* midway between Bolton and Horwich - look for municipal golf course. Nearest motorway M61 Junction 5 or 6. Parkland, stream and ditches cross five fairways, tough finish with three Par 3s on last four holes. 18 holes, 6217 yards. S.S.S. 69. Two practice areas. *Green Fees:* information not available. *Eating facilities:* meals/bar available. Visitors: welcome seven days, telephone Professional to book time slot. Buggies and club hire. *Society Meetings:* welcome midweek, book in advance. Professional: Bob Longworth (01204 842336/495421). Secretary: D.W. Bunting (01942 238561).*

BOLTON. **Turton Golf Club**, Wood End Farm, Chapeltown Road, Bromley Cross, Bolton BL7 9QH (01204 852235). *Location:* three miles north of Bolton off the A666; near Last Drop Hotel, Hospital Road, Bromley Cross, Bolton. Moorland course with extensive views. 18 holes, 6124 yards. S.S.S. 69. Practice area. *Green Fees:* weekdays £20.00 per day; weekends £25.00 per day. *Eating facilities:* to order except Mondays. *Visitors:* welcome weekdays; Sundays by arrangement, restrictions Wednesdays (Ladies' Day) 10.30am to 3.00pm. *Society Meetings:* welcome on Tuesdays to Fridays by arrangement. Secretary: M.J. McNeill (01204 852235).

BURY. **Bury Golf Club**, Unsworth Hall, Blackford Bridge, Bury BL9 9TJ (0161-766 4897; Fax: 0161-766 3480). Location: A56 between Whitefield and Bury. Semi-moorland course, tight fairways, good greens. 18 holes, 5927 yards. S.S.S. 69. Small practice area. *Green Fees:* weekdays £28.00, with a member £12.00; weekends £32.00, with a member £15.00. *Eating facilities:* restaurant and bar. *Visitors:* welcome, Tuesday is Ladies Day. Handicap Certificate will be required prior to play. *Society Meetings:* welcome except weekends (£38.00 per person including meal). Professional: Mr D. Procter (0161-766 2213; Fax: 0161-766 3495). Secretary: Mr R. Adams.

BURY. **Greenmount Golf Club,** Greenhalgh Fold Farm, Greenmount, Bury BL8 4EH (01204 883712). *Location:* three miles north of Bury. Undulating parkland. 9 holes, 6214 yards. S.S.S. 70. *Green Fees:* £15.00, £10.00 with member. *Eating facilities:* available, clubhouse closed all day Monday. *Visitors:* welcome, weekends with members only, Tuesday – Ladies' Day. *Society Meetings:* welcome, £15.00 per player. Professional: Kevin Duffy (01204 888616). Secretary: Martin Barron (Tel & Fax: 01204 888629).

TURTON GOLF CLUB   TEL: 01204 852235

Wood End Farm, Chapeltown Road, Bromley Cross, Bolton BL7 9QH

18 holes, 6124 yards. S.S.S. 69. Practice area. Green Fees: weekdays £20.00 per day; weekends £25.00 per day. Visitors: welcome weekdays, restrictions Wednesday (Ladies' Day) 10.30am to 3.00pm. Society Meetings: welcome on Tuesdays to Fridays and Sundays, by arrangement. Secretary: M.J. McNeill (01204 852235).

BURY. **Lowes Park Golf Club Ltd,** Hill Top, Lowes Road, Bury BL9 6SU (0161-764 1231). *Location:* take A56 north from Bury, turn right at Sundial Inn into Lowes Road. Moorland course, exposed, easy walking. 9 holes, 6009 yards. S.S.S. 69. Small practice area. *Green Fees:* £15.00, £10.00 with member. *Eating facilities:* full catering except Mondays. *Visitors:* welcome weekdays except Wednesdays (Ladies' Day); weekends, Sunday by appointment. *Society Meetings:* catered for by appointment with Secretary. Secretary: John Entwistle (Tel & Fax: 0161-763 9503).
e-mail: lowes@parkgc.fsnet.co.uk

BURY. **Pike Fold Golf Club,** Hills Lane, Unsworth, Bury BL9 8QP (0161-766 3561). *Location:* just off the Whitfield turn off on the M60. New course with an abundance of water and USA specification greens. 9 holes, 6312 yards. S.S.S. 72. *Green Fees:* weekdays £20 per round; weekends £25 per round. *Eating facilities:* restaurant and bar facilities avaialble at all times. *Visitors:* welcome weekdays without reservation. *Society Meetings:* catered for Monday to Saturday. Professional: Andrew Cory.

BURY. **Walmersley Golf Club,** Garretts Close, Walmersley, Bury BL9 6TE (0161-764 1429). *Location:* leave A56 approximately two miles north of Bury at Walmersley Post Office into Old Road, right at Masons Arms Inn. Moorland course. 18 holes, 5341 yards, 4872 metres. S.S.S. 67. *Green Fees:* weekdays £20.00 per day, £10.00 with member; weekends £10.00 with a member only. *Eating facilities:* lunches and evening meals served except Mondays. *Visitors:* welcome weekdays except Tuesdays 1pm to 4.30pm. *Society Meetings:* catered for weekdays. Professional: P. Thorpe (0161-763 9050). Secretary: R.O. Goldstein (0161-764 7770).

DAVYHULME. **Davyhulme Park Golf Club,** Gleneagles Road, Davyhulme, Urmston M41 8SA (0161-748 2260). *Location:* one mile from M60/M62. Wooded parkland, flat course. 18 holes, 6237 yards. S.S.S. 70. *Green Fees:* weekdays: 18 holes £24.00, 27 holes £30.00. *Eating facilities:* lunches and dinners. *Visitors:* welcome Tuesdays and Thursdays. *Society Meetings:* catered for Tuesdays and Thursdays. Professional: Dean Butler (0161-748 3931). Secretary: Mr L.B. Wright (0161-748 2260).

DENTON. **Denton Golf Club,** Manchester Road, Denton M34 2GG (0161-336 3218; Fax: 0161-336 4751). *Location:* M60 Junction 24 to Manchester (A57), after quarter of a mile turn right at traffic lights. Parkland. 18 holes, 6528 yards, 5876 metres. S.S.S. 71.Large practice area and putting green. *Green Fees:* weekdays £25.00; weekends and Bank Holidays £30.00. £12.00 with a member. *Eating facilities:* catering by arrangement except Mondays. *Visitors:* welcome with Club Handicap. *Society Meetings:* catered for on Wednesday to Friday. Professional: Michael Hollingworth (0161-336 2070; Fax: 0161-336 4751). Secretary: E.W. Tewson (0161-336 3218; Fax: 0161-336 4751).

DUKINFIELD. **Dukinfield Golf Club**, Lyne Edge, Yew Tree Lane, Dukinfield SK16 5DB (0161-338 2340). Location: six miles east of Manchester via Ashton-under-Lyne. Parkland. 18 holes, 5303 yards. S.S.S. 66.

Green Fees: information not available. *Eating facilities:* full catering and bar facilities. *Visitors:* welcome except Wednesdays noon to 2pm and 4pm to 6pm and weekends. Times may be booked in advance by phoning Pro's Shop. *Society Meetings:* catered for by prior arrangement; special package rates available. Professional: Andrew Jarrett. Secretary: Ken Marsh (0161-368 6457).

ECCLES. **Worsley Golf Club,** Stableford Avenue, Monton, Eccles M30 8AP (0161-789 4202). *Location:* A580 East Lancs Road, one mile from Junction 13 M62. Parkland. 18 holes, 6200 yards. S.S.S. 70. *Green Fees:* information not available. *Eating facilities:* snacks, lunches and evening meals. *Visitors:* welcome, if past or present members of recognised golf clubs. *Society Meetings:* catered for Mondays, Wednesdays and Thursdays. Professional: Ceri Cousins. Hon. Secretary: A. Henshaw.

FLIXTON. **Acre Gate Golf Club,** Pennybridge Lane, Flixton, Manchester M41 3DN (0161-748 1226). *Location:* off Flixton Road near Bird in the Hand public house. Flat parkland course. 18 holes, 4395 yards. S.S.S. 60. Chipping area, putting green, practice net and bunker. *Green Fees:* information not available. *Eating facilities:* by arrangement; deposit required. *Visitors:* course is Municipal (William Wroe Municipal Course) therefore no restrictions. *Society Meetings:* catered for but must apply in writing giving plenty of notice. Professional: S. Partington. Secretary: W.S. Milton (0161-748 1226).

HORWICH. **Horwich Golf Club,** Victoria Road, Horwich, Bolton BL6 5PH (01204 696980). *Location:* Junction 6 M61 - Chorley New Road - Victoria Road, Horwich. Tight tricky course, hilly with fast greens. 9 holes, 5286 yards, 4832 metres. S.S.S. 66. *Green Fees:* information not available. *Eating facilities:* dining and bar. *Visitors:* Wednesday Ladies' Day but tee times still available. Snooker room. *Society Meetings:* by arrangement. Professional: B. Sharrock. Secretary: C. Sherborne.

HYDE. **Werneth Low Golf Club Ltd**, Werneth Low Road, Hyde, Cheshire SK14 3AF (0161-368 2503). *Location:* M67 to Hyde, through town to Gee Cross turn left to NLQC. Scenic, hilly course with excellent views, postage stamp greens, terrific test of golf. 18 holes,(7,4,7) 6550 yards. S.S.S. 70. *Green Fees:* information not available. *Eating facilities:* bar snacks daily, à la carte by arrangement. *Visitors:* welcome any time except Sunday before 4pm and Tuesday mornings and after 4pm. *Society Meetings:* catered for by prior arrangement. Professional: Tony Bacchus (0161-367 9376). Secretary: M. Gregg (0161-336 9496; Fax: 0161-320 0053).*
e-mail: mel.gregg@btinternet.com

LEIGH. **Pennington Golf Club (Municipal)**, Pennington Golf Course, Pennington Country Park, off St Helens Road, Leigh WN7 3PA. *Location:* Junction 23 on M6 follow A580 towards Manchester, then follow signs for Pennington Flash. Flat parkland with water coursing through. 9 holes, 5516 yards. S.S.S. 68. *Green Fees:* information not available. *Eating facilities:* snack facilities. *Visitors:* welcome, no restrictions. Professional: Mr T. Kershaw (01942 607278). Secretary: B. Lythgoe (01942 741873).*

LITTLEBOROUGH. **Whittaker Golf Club,** Whittaker Lane, Littleborough OL15 0LH (01706 378310). *Location:* one mile from town centre along Blackstone Edge Old Road. Moorland course. 9 holes, 5632 yards. S.S.S. 67. *Green Fees:* information not available. *Eating facilities:* bar only. *Visitors:* welcome without reservation, except Tuesday afternoons and Sundays. *Society Meetings:* weekdays and Saturdays only by prior arrangement with Secretary. Secretary: Mr S. Noblett (01706 842541).

MANCHESTER. **Blackley Golf Club,** Victoria Avenue East, Blackley, Manchester M9 7HW (0161-643 2980). *Location:* five miles north from City Centre. Parkland. 18 holes, 6217 yards, 5708 metres. S.S.S. 70. *Green Fees:* information not available. *Eating facilities:* diningroom/bar. *Visitors:* welcome, Thursdays and weekends with member only. *Society Meetings:* catered for. Professional: Craig Gould (0161-643 3912). Secretary: Steve Mainwaring (0161-654 7770; Fax: 0161 653 8300).

MANCHESTER. **Brookdale Golf Club Ltd,** Medlock Road, Woodhouses, Failsworth, Manchester M35 9WQ (Tel & Fax: 0161-681 4534). *Location:* five miles north of Manchester. Parkland course, hilly with river running through. 18 holes, 5874 yards. S.S.S. 68. Small practice ground. *Green Fees:* weekdays £26.00; weekends and Bank Holidays as member's guest only. *Eating facilities:* bar snacks available; evening meal by prior arrangement. *Visitors:* welcome, only with a member weekends. *Society Meetings:* welcome except Tuesdays (Ladies' Day). Package Deal £35.00 by arrangement. Professional: Tony Cuppello (0161-681 2655). Secretary: M.J. Chadwick (Tel & Fax: 0161-681 4534). website: www.brookdalegolfclub.co.uk

MANCHESTER. **Chorlton-cum-Hardy Golf Club,** Barlow Hall Road, Chorlton-cum-Hardy M21 7JJ (0161-881 3139; Fax: 0161-881 4532). *Location:* near junction of A5145 and A5103 (M60) Barlow Moor Road, South Cemetery. Meadowland. 18 holes, 5980 yards. S.S.S. 69. *Green Fees:* weekdays £25.00; weekends and Bank Holidays £30.00. *Eating facilities:* catering provided 7 days a week. *Visitors:* welcome without reservation, except on Competition days, must provide proof of recognised Handicap. *Society Meetings:* catered for Thursdays and Fridays by arrangement with Secretary. Professional: D.R. Valentine (0161-881 9911). Secretary: Mr I.R. Booth (0161-881-5830).

MANCHESTER. **Didsbury Golf Club Ltd,** Ford Lane, Northenden, Manchester M22 4NQ (0161-998 2743). *Location:* Junction 5 on M60 to Palatine Road, to Church Road, to Ford Lane. Riverside parkland. 18 holes, 6276 yards. S.S.S. 70. Good practice facilities. *Green Fees:* information not available. *Eating facilities:* fully equipped bar and restaurant. *Visitors:* welcome 10am to 12 noon and 1.30pm to 4pm except competition times and match days. *Society Meetings:* catered for Thursdays and Fridays. Professional: P. Barber (Tel & Fax: 0161-998 2811). Manager: A.L. Watson (0161-998 9278; Fax: 0161-902 3060). e-mail: golf@didsburygolfclub.com website: www.didsburygolfclub.com

MANCHESTER. **Ellesmere Golf Club,** Old Clough Lane, Worsley, Manchester M28 7HZ (0161-790 2122). *Location:* off A580 East Lancs Road, adjacent to M60 (clockwise) northbound, (eastbound) access. Wooded parkland. 18 holes, 6247 yards. S.S.S. 70. *Green Fees:* weekdays £22.00 per round, £28.00 per day; weekends £28.00 per day. *Eating facilities:* bar; catering available, with or without reservation. *Visitors:* members of recognised golf clubs welcome, but not during club competitions or Bank Holidays, contact Professional for restrictions. *Society Meetings:* catered for by appointment. Professional: Terry Morley (0161-790 8591). Secretary: A. Chapman (0161-799 0554).

MANCHESTER. **Fairfield Golf and Sailing Club,** "Boothdale", Booth Road, Audenshaw, Manchester M34 5GA (0161-370 1641). *Location:* off A635, five miles east of Manchester. Parkland bounded in part by reservoir. 18 holes, 4956 yards. S.S.S. 68. *Green Fees:* information not provided. *Eating facilities:* available. *Visitors:* welcome, restrictions Wednesdays, Thursdays and weekends. *Society Meetings:* catered for by prior arrangement mid-week. Professional: Steven Pownell (0161-370 2292). Manager: H. Jagger (0161-301 4528; Fax: 0161 301 4254). e-mail: manager@fairfieldgolf.co.uk

MANCHESTER. **Flixton Golf Club,** Church Road, Flixton, Urmston M41 6EP (Tel & Fax: 0161-748 2116). *Location:* five miles from Manchester on B5213. Parkland. 9 holes, 6410 yards. S.S.S. 71. *Green Fees:* £8.00 weekdays, Bank Holidays and Christmas and New Year holiday period - playing with a member. £16.00 weekdays without a member. *Eating facilities:* daily. *Visitors:* welcome, please contact professional. Hand pulled golf carts for hire from Professional. *Society Meetings:* catered for by arrangement. Professional: G. Coope (Tel & Fax: 0161-746 7160). Hon. Secretary: P.Gollagles (Tel & Fax: 0161-748 2116). Catering: (0161-749 8834).

MANCHESTER. **Heaton Park Golf Centre,** Middleton Road, Prestwich, Manchester M25 2SW (0161-654 9899; Fax: 0161-653 2003). *Location:* Junction 19 M60. Undulating mature parkland, J.H. Taylor designed. 18 holes, 5755 yards. S.S.S. 70. 18-hole Par 3 course. *Green Fees:* weekdays £10.00, weekends £13.00, half price for Seniors and Juniors. *Eating facilities:* two bars; range of meals and bar snacks. *Visitors:* welcome at all times. PlayGolf Teaching Academy, practice range, Pro Shop. *Society Meetings:* catered for; society teaching and clinics. Professional: Gary Dermott. Manager: John Mort.

MANCHESTER. **Houldsworth Golf Club Ltd,** Houldsworth Street, Reddish, Stockport SK5 6BN (0161-442 1712). *Location:* off A6 between Manchester and Stockport, adjacent to M63. Flat parkland with water hazards. 18 holes, 6209 yards. S.S.S. 70, Par 71. Practice area. *Green Fees:* weekdays £24.00 per day; weekends £30.00 per day. Half price with member. *Eating facilities:* bar snacks, or full restaurant service. *Visitors:* must be pre-arranged with Professional or Hon. Secretary. *Society Meetings:* Monday, Thursday and Friday, catered for on application (0161-442 1712). Professional: David Naylor (0161-442 1714). Secretary: D. Robertson (0161-442 1712).

MANCHESTER. **Manchester Golf Club,** Hopwood Cottage, Rochdale Road, Middleton, Manchester M24 6QP (0161-643 3202; Fax: 0161-643 9174). *Location:* M62 Junction 20 to Middleton. Moorland/parkland. 18 holes, 6454 yards, 5895 metres. S.S.S. 72. Large practice ground. Driving range. *Green Fees:* weekdays £20.00 per round, £30.00 per day; weekends £35.00 per round. *Eating facilities:* two bars; restaurant booking by arrangement. *Visitors:* welcome weekdays. *Society Meetings:* parties up to 120 catered for by arrangement. Professional: B. Connor (0161-643 2638). Secretary: K.G. Flett (0161-643 3202; Fax: 0161-643 9174).

MANCHESTER. **New North Manchester Golf Club Ltd,** Rhodes House, Manchester Old Road, Middleton, Manchester M24 4PE (0161-643 2941). *Location:* A576, less than one mile from Junction 19 on M60. Rolling parkland including lakes. 18 holes, 6527 yards, 5987 metres. S.S.S. 72. Large practice area. *Green Fees:* £25.00 per round, £28.00 per day. Weekends £30.00. *Eating facilities:* catering every day except Tuesdays. *Visitors:* welcome most days, please telephone for course availability. *Society Meetings:* welcome, contact Professional for details. Reductions available for societies over 15. Professional: J. Peel (0161-643 7094). Secretary: D. Parkinson (0161-643 9033; Fax: 0161-643 7775). e-mail: secretary@nmgc.co.uk

MANCHESTER. **Northenden Golf Club,** Palatine Road, Northenden, Manchester M22 4FR (0161-998 4738; Fax: 0161-945 5592). *Location:* half a mile off Junction 9 M56, half a mile off Junction 5 M60. Parkland with plenty of trees, first six tees on bank of river. 18 holes, 6432 yards. S.S.S. 71. Practice net. *Green Fees:* information not available. *Eating facilities:* available (0161-998 4079). *Visitors:* welcome most days, preferably with reservation. Restrictions 12 noon to 1.30pm Tuesdays and Fridays. Carts available. *Society Meetings:* catered for Tuesdays and Fridays only. Professional: James Curtis (0161-945 3386; Fax: 0161-945 5592). Manager: F.L. Woodworth (0161-998 4738; Fax: 0161-945 5592). Steward: L. Smith (0161-998 4079).*

MANCHESTER. **Prestwich Golf Club,** Hilton Lane, Prestwich, Manchester M25 9XB (0161-773 2544). *Location:* 1 mile from Junction 17 of the M60 on the A6044. Parkland. 18 holes, 4757 yards. S.S.S. 64. *Green Fees:* information not available. *Eating facilities:* by arrangement. *Visitors:* welcome weekdays. *Society Meetings:* catered for weekdays, special rates for parties of 16 and over. Professional: Simon Wakefield (Tel & Fax: 0161-773 1404). Secretary: J. Liwosz (0161-773 2544).*

MANCHESTER. **Stand Golf Club,** The Dales, Ashbourne Grove, Whitefield, Bury, Manchester M25 7NL (0161-766 2388). *Location:* M62 Exit 17, A56/A665 one mile. Undulating parkland with sandy subsoil, playable all year round. 18 holes, 6426 yards. S.S.S. 71. *Green Fees:* weekdays £30.00; weekends £35.00. Various Society packages; information on request. *Eating facilities:* meals served daily and bar except Mondays, order in advance. *Visitors:* welcome Monday to Friday; weekends by prior arrangement. *Society Meetings:* welcome Wednesday/Friday by prior arrangement. Professional: Mark Dance (0161-766 2214). Hon. Secretary: Trevor E. Thacker (0161-766 3197; Fax: 0161-796 3234).

MANCHESTER. **Swinton Park Golf Club,** East Lancashire Road, Swinton, Manchester M27 5LX (0161-794 1785). *Location:* on the A580 Manchester to Liverpool Road, five miles from Manchester centre. Parkland course. 18 holes. White tees 6726 yards – Yellow tees 6519 yards. Practice area. *Green Fees:* on application. *Eating facilities:* available. *Visitors:* welcome Mondays, Tuesdays, Wednesdays and Fridays, tee reservations 10am-noon, 2pm-4pm. *Society Meetings:* catered for by prior arrangement. Extensive function room for seminars available. Professional: J. Wilson (0161-793 8077). General Manager: T. H. Glover (0161-794 0861; Fax: 0161-281 0698).

THE APPEARANCE OF AN ASTERISK (*) AT THE END OF A CLUB OR COURSE ENTRY INDICATES THAT UP-TO-DATE INFORMATION HAS NOT BEEN SUPPLIED

Heaton Park Golf Centre

Middleton Road, Prestwich, Manchester M25 2SW

Tel: 0161 654 9899 • Fax: 0161 653 2003

Picturesque 18-hole Championship Course situated in the scenic grounds of Manchester's Heaton Park.

• Par 70, 5755 yards. • Ideal for golf societies or groups.

Summer specials: Full breakfast, 18 holes of golf, and meal from only £20. Golf only from £10 for groups of 8 or more.

• Clubhouse with bar, restaurant, changing rooms, showers and golf shop, plus club and trolley hire.

• Function room available for hire – free to all group bookings.

Located just off Junction 19 of the M60

MANCHESTER. **Withington Golf Club,** 243 Palatine Road, West Didsbury, Manchester M20 2UE (0161-445 3912). *Location:* three miles from Manchester city centre, adjacent M56 and M63. Flat parkland. 18 holes, 6410 yards. S.S.S. 70. *Green Fees:* weekdays only (except Thursdays) £28.00 per round, £32.00 per day; weekends by prior arrangement only (£30.00 per round, £35.00 per day). *Eating facilities:* lunches and evening meals to order. Snacks available at all times except Mondays. *Visitors:* welcome except Thursdays, and weekends which are by prior arrangement. Ring Professional for times. *Society Meetings:* catered for by arrangement with the Secretary. Professional: R.J. Ling (0161-445 4861). Secretary/Manager: B. Grundy (0161-445 9544).

MARPLE. **Marple Golf Club,** Barnsfold Road, Marple, Stockport SK6 7EL (0161-427 2311). *Location:* off A6 at Hawk Green sign. Parkland. 18 holes, 5565 yards. S.S.S. 67. Practice area. *Green Fees:* information not available. *Eating facilities:* full meals available except Mondays when bar snacks only. *Visitors:* welcome, not competition days or Thursday between 11am and 3.30pm. *Society Meetings:* all welcome by arrangement with Professional. Professional: D. Myers (0161-427 1195). Secretary: W.M. Buchanan (Tel & Fax: 0161-427 1125).*
e-mail: marple.golf.club@ukgateway.net

OLDHAM. **Crompton and Royton Golf Club Ltd,** High Barn, Royton, Oldham OL2 6RW (0161-624 0986; Fax: 0161-652 4711). *Location:* near Junction 20 follow signs to Oldham/Royton. Heathland. 18 holes, 6186 yards. S.S.S. 70. Nets. *Green Fees:* £25.00 weekdays, £35.00 weekends. *Eating facilities:* lunches and meals served, except Mondays. *Visitors:* welcome without reservation, not at weekends. *Society Meetings:* catered for by arrangement with Steward. Professional: D.A. Melling (0161-624 2154). Hon. Secretary (0161-624 0986). Steward: (0161-624 9867).

OLDHAM. **Oldham Golf Club,** Lees New Road, Oldham OL4 5PN (0161-624 4986). *Location:* B6194 between Ashton-under-Lyne and Oldham. Moorland course. 18 holes, 5122 yards. S.S.S. 65. *Green Fees:* information not available. *Eating facilities:* full catering. *Visitors:* welcome, telephone to check for competitions, especially weekends. *Society Meetings:* catered for by prior arrangement with Secretary. Professional: R. Heginbotham (0161-626 8346). Secretary: J. Brooks (0161-624 4986).

OLDHAM. **Saddleworth Golf Club,** Mountain Ash, Ladcastle Road, Uppermill, Near Oldham OL3 6LT (01457 873653). *Location:* five miles from Oldham – M62. A moorland course with superb views of the Pennines. 18 holes, 6118 yards. S.S.S. 69. Practice

area. *Green Fees:* weekdays £23.00 (£9.00 per day with member), weekends and Bank Holidays £30.00 (£12.00 per day with member). *Eating facilities:* snacks and meals available. *Visitors:* welcome weekdays. Ladies' Day Thursdays. Buggies available. *Society Meetings:* groups of 12 or more catered for except weekends. Professional: R.I. Johnson (01457 810412; Fax: 01457 820647). Secretary: A.E. Gleave (01457 873653).

OLDHAM. **Werneth Golf Club,** 124 Green Lane, Garden Suburb, Oldham OL8 3AZ (0161-624 1190). Semi moorland. 18 holes, 5363 yards. S.S.S. 66. Practice ground. *Green Fees:* £16.00 weekdays only. *Eating facilities:* full catering service available. *Visitors:* welcome, ring for details. *Society Meetings:* catered for, ring for details. Professional: Roy Penney (Tel & Fax: 0161-628 7136). Secretary: John Barlow.

ROCHDALE. **Castle Hawk Golf Club,** Chadwick Lane, Castleton, Rochdale OL11 3BY (01706 640841; Fax: 01706 860587). *Location:* five minutes from exit 20 M62. Parkland course. 18 holes, 2699 yards. S.S.S. 55. 9 holes, 5398 yards, S.S.S. 66. Driving range. *Green Fees:* information not available. *Eating facilities:* fully licensed bar and restaurant. *Visitors:* welcome. Trolley and equipment hire. Tuition available, fully stocked Pro's shop. *Society Meetings:* welcome. Professional: Andy Duncan. Secretary: Louise Entwistle.*
e-mail: teeoff@castlehawk.co.uk
website: www.castlehawk.co.uk

ROCHDALE. **Lobden Golf Club,** Whitworth, Near Rochdale OL12 8XJ (Tel & Fax: 01706 343228). *Location:* take A671 from Rochdale, turn right at Dog and Partridge Pub in Whitworth. Moorland. 9 holes, 5697 yards, 5212 metres. S.S.S. 68. *Green Fees:* weekdays £12.00; weekends £15.00, £10.00 at all times with a member. Subject to review. *Eating facilities:* by prior arrangement with Secretary. *Visitors:* welcome all week except Saturday. *Society Meetings:* catered for by arrangement. Secretary: John A. Keate (01706 345598).

ROCHDALE. **Rochdale Golf Club,** The Clubhouse, Edenfield Road, Rochdale OL11 5YR (01706 646024; Fax: 01706 861113). *Location:* three miles from M62, Junction 20, on A680. Parkland. 18 holes, 6034 yards. S.S.S. 69. Practice ground, putting green. *Green Fees:* per round or day – weekdays £20.00, £13.00 with a member; weekends £25.00, £15.00 with a member. *Eating facilities:* meals and bar snacks available. *Visitors:* welcome, please check for tee closures. *Society Meetings:* catered for by prior arrangement Mondays, and Wednesdays. Professional: A. Laverty (01706 522104). Secretary: P. Chappell (01706 643818).

ROCHDALE. **Springfield Park Golf Club,** Springfield Park, Bolton Road, Marland, Rochdale OL11 4RE (01706 56401 weekends only). *Location:* A58 out of Rochdale, along Bolton Road on right. Parkland. 18 holes, 5237 yards. S.S.S. 66. *Green Fees:* information not available. *Visitors:* welcome, no restrictions weekdays, booking in advance weekends. Professional: Mr D. Wills (01706 49801). Secretary: Mr J. Wallis (01706 623570).*

SALE. **Ashton-on-Mersey Golf Club,** Church Lane, Ashton-on-Mersey, Sale M33 5QQ (0161-973 3220). *Location:* M60 Junction 7; 1½ miles, off Glebelands Road. Parkland course. 9 holes, 6242 yards. S.S.S. 69. *Green Fees:* £20.50 weekdays, £8.00 with a member. *Eating facilities:* available weekdays except Mondays. *Visitors:* welcome on weekdays. Saturdays, Sundays and Bank Holidays only with member. *Society Meetings:* Thursdays. Professional: M.J. Williams (0161-962 3727). Secretary: C.W. Hill (0161-976 4390).

SALE. **Sale Golf Club,** Sale Lodge, Golf Road, Sale M33 2XU (0161-973 1638; Fax: 0161-962 4217). *Location:* M60 Junction 6, A6144. Flat parkland course. 18 holes, 6368 yards. S.S.S. 70. Practice ground. *Green Fees:* information not available. *Eating facilities:* catering and bar facilities 7 days. *Visitors:* welcome Mondays, Tuesdays, Wednesdays and Sundays. Carts available for hire. *Society Meetings:* welcome by arrangement with Professional. Professional: Mike Stewart (0161-973 1730). Hon. Secretary: M.G. Stanistreet (0161-973 1638; Fax: 0161-962 4217).

SALFORD. **Brackley Golf Club,** Bullows Road Little Hulton, Worsley M38 9TR (0161-790 6076). Location: Off Captain Fold Lane. M61 to Junction 4 onto A6, left at roundabout onto A6 (Walkden), half a mile turn left at White Lion pub. Flat parkland course. 9 holes, 3003 yards, 2747 metres. S.S.S. 69. *Green Fees:* information not available. *Visitors:* welcome anytime. *Society Meetings:* welcome. Secretary: Gary Jones (0161-790 6076). *

STOCKPORT. **Bramall Park Golf Club,** 20 Manor Road, Bramhall, Stockport SK7 3LY (0161-485 3119). *Location:* 10 miles south of Manchester, 3 miles from Cheadle Hulme. Parkland. 18 holes, 6214 yards. S.S.S. 70. *Green Fees:* weekdays £30.00; weekends and Bank Holidays £40.00. *Eating facilities:* full eating facilities except Mondays. *Visitors:* welcome, apply to Professional. *Society Meetings:* catered for Tuesdays and Thursday afternoons. Professional: M. Proffitt (0161-485 2205). Secretary:C.J. Shallcross (Tel & Fax: 0161-485 7101).

STOCKPORT. **Bramhall Golf Club,** The Clubhouse, Ladythorn Road, Bramhall, Stockport SK7 2EY (0161-439 6092). *Location:* half-a-mile from Bramhall Railway Station off Bramhall Lane South. Parkland with views of Pennines and Lyme Park. 18 holes, 6340 yards, 5799 metres. S.S.S 70. Practice ground. *Green Fees*: information available on request. *Eating facilities:* full bar and dining facilities and bar snacks. *Visitors*: welcome except Thursdays and Competition Days. *Society Meetings*: catered for Wednesdays, minimum 24; Fridays maximum 24. Professional: R. Green (0161-439 1171; Fax: 0161-439 0789). Secretary: (0161-439 6092).

STOCKPORT. **Hazel Grove Golf Club,** Buxton Road, Hazel Grove, Stockport SK7 6LU (0161-483 3217 clubhouse). *Location*: A6 to Buxton out of Hazel Grove, three miles south of Stockport. Parkland with tree-lined fairways. 18 holes, 6310 yards. S.S.S. 71. *Green Fees*: weekdays £25.50; weekends and Public Holidays £30.50. Subject to review. Society booking £38.00 for parties of 12 or more. *Eating facilities*: available daily. *Visitors*: welcome, ring Professional for booking of tee times. *Society Meetings*: catered for on Mondays, Thursdays and Fridays. Professional: James Hopley (0161-483 7272). Secretary: David J. Billington (0161-483 3978).

STOCKPORT. **Heaton Moor Golf Club,** Mauldeth Road, Heaton Mersey, Stockport SK4 3NX (0161-432 2134). *Location*: M56 to A34 or M60 Junction 1; near Glass Pyramid – Didsbury Road. Flat parkland course, tree lined fairways. 18 holes, 5968 yards. S.S.S. 69. Practice ground. *Green Fees*: weekdays £23.00; weekends £31.00; winter green fees: £18.00 weekdays, £26.00 weekends. *Eating facilities*: lunches and evening meals available; bar. *Visitors*: welcome all times. Trolley hire. *Society Meetings*: catered for by arrangement. Professional: Simon Marsh (0161-432 0846). Secretary: John R. Smith (0161-432 2134).

STOCKPORT. **Mellor and Townscliffe Golf Club Ltd,** Gibb Lane, Mellor, Tarden, Stockport SK6 5NA (0161-427 9700 – Clubhouse/Steward). *Location:* seven miles south-east of Stockport off A626. Parkland with trees/moorland. 18 holes, 5925 yards. S.S.S. 69. *Green Fees:* weekdays £22.00 per day, £9.00 with a member; weekends and Bank Holidays £31.00, with a member £11.00. *Eating facilities:* available daily except Tuesdays. *Visitors:* welcome weekdays, no casual visitors weekends. *Society Meetings:* catered for by prior arrangement. Professional: Gary R. Broadley (0161-427 5759). Secretary: G. Lee (0161-427 2208). website: www.mellorgolf.co.uk

PLEASE MENTION THIS GUIDE WHEN YOU WRITE OR PHONE TO ENQUIRE ABOUT CLUBS OR ACCOMMODATION.

STOCKPORT. **Reddish Vale Golf Club,** Southcliffe Road, Reddish, Stockport SK5 7EE (0161-480 2359). *Location:* one mile north east of Stockport. Varied undulating heathland course, designed by Dr Alister MacKenzie. 18 holes, 6086 yards. S.S.S. 69. *Green Fees:* weekdays £25.00; weekends with member. *Eating facilities:* bar and catering. *Visitors:* welcome on weekdays (not 12.30-1.30pm). *Society Meetings:* catered for by arrangement, groups of eight or more. Professional: Bob Freeman (0161-480 3824). Secretary: B.J.D. Rendell J.P. (0161-480 2359).

STOCKPORT. **Romiley Golf Club Ltd,** Goosehouse Green, Romiley, Stockport SK6 4LJ (0161-430 2392). *Location:* B6104 off A560, signposted from Romiley village. Parkland. 18 holes, 6454 yards. S.S.S. 71. *Green Fees:* weekdays £30.00 per round, £40.00 per day; weekends and Bank Holidays £40.00 per round, £50.00 per day. Reduced rates for visitors by arrangement. *Eating facilities:* full catering by arrangement. *Visitors:* welcome all week except Saturdays. *Society Meetings:* catered for by prior arrangement with Secretary. Professional: Lee Paul Sulliivan (0161-430 7122). Secretary: P.R. Trafford (0161-430 2392).

STOCKPORT. **Stockport Golf Club Ltd,** Offerton Road, Offerton, Stockport, Cheshire SK2 5HL (0161-427 2001). *Location:* one mile from lights at Hazel Grove, along Torkington Road. Parkland. 18 holes, 6326 yards. S.S.S. 71. *Green Fees*: weekdays £40.00 per round, weekends £50.00 per round. *Eating facilities*: available, excellent. *Visitors:* welcome weekdays, contact Professional at weekends. *Society Meetings:* catered for. Professional: M. Peel (0161-427 2421). Secretary: Mr D.R.G. Mitchell (0161-427 8369; Fax: 0161-449 8293).

TRAFFORD. **William Wroe Municipal Golf Course,** Pennybridge Lane, off Flixton Road, Flixton, Trafford M41 5DC (0161-748 8680). Course and shop managed by Trafford Borough Council, Acre Gate Golf Club play over the course. *Location:* from M60 follow Urmston, Flixton Road to Bird i'th Hand pub. Flat parkland course. 18 holes, 4395 yards. S.S.S. 61. Driving range two miles from course. *Green Fees:* weekdays information not available. *Eating facilities:* at Bird i'th Hand Public House. *Visitors:* public course - book seven days in advance, weekend mornings some restrictions. *Society Meetings:* booking accepted in writing. Professional: Mr Scott Partington (0161-928 0761).*

WESTHOUGHTON. **Westhoughton Golf Club,** Long Island, School Street, Westhoughton, Bolton BL5 2BR (01942 511085). *Location:* four miles south west of Bolton on A58. Parkland. 9 holes, 5702 yards. S.S.S. 68. *Green Fees:* £18.00 per day; with a member £10.00. *Eating facilities:* bar meals and home cooking. *Visitors:* welcome weekdays except Tuesdays – Ladies' Day. Snooker room. *Society Meetings:* welcome weekdays except Tuesdays, maximum 32. Professional: Kevin Duffy (01942 840545). Secretary: F. Donohue (01942 608958).

WHITEFIELD. **Whitefield Golf Club,** Higher Lane, Whitefield, Manchester (0161-351 2700; Fax: 0161-351 2712). *Location*: Exit 17, off M60 then take road to Radcliffe for half a mile. 18 holes, 6063 yards. S.S.S. 69. **Green Fees**: on application. **Eating facilities**: restaurant facilities every day. **Visitors**: welcome. **Society Meetings**: catered for. Professional: P. Reeves (0161-351 2709). Secretary: Mrs A. Schofield (0161-351 2700; Fax: 0161-351 2712).
e-mail: enquiries@whitefieldgolfclub.com

WIGAN. **Gathurst Golf Club,** Miles Lane, Shevington, Wigan WN6 8EW (01257 252861). *Location:* one mile south of Junction 27 M6. Parkland course. 18 holes, 6016 yards (from men's tee). S.S.S.69. *Green Fees:* £26.00; weekends with a member only. *Eating facilities:* available bar hours, daily except Monday. *Visitors:* welcome Monday, Tuesday, Thursday and Friday with reservation. *Society Meetings:* catered for by appointment with Secretary. Professional: David Clarke (01257 255882). Secretary: Mrs. I. Fyffe (01257 255235).

WIGAN. **Haigh Hall Golf Club,** Haigh Country Park, Aspull, Near Wigan WN2 1PE (01942 831107). *Location:* well signposted from M6, Junction 27 and M61, Junction 5. Balcarres 18 hole course, 6358 yards. Par 70. Crawford course 9 holes, 1446 yards. Par 28. 18 hole Himalayan putting green and golf academy practice facilities. All U.S.G.A specification greens and tees. Brand new golf complex in the superb surroundings of Haigh Country Park. *Green Fees:* information not available. *Eating facilities:* full catering available, bar facilities and function rooms in The Stables Golf & Visitor Centre. *Visitors:* welcome at all times. *Society Meetings:* welcome at all times - packages available. Professional: Ian Lee (01942 831107). Members' Secretary: William Fleetwood (01942 833337).
e-mail: hhgen@wiganmbc.gov.uk
website: www.Haighhall.net

WIGAN. **Hindley Hall Golf Club,** Hall Lane, Hindley, Wigan WN2 2SQ (01942 525020). *Location:* two miles east of Wigan, Junction 6 M61, or A58 to Ladies Lane/Hall Lane. 18 holes, 5913 yards. S.S.S. 68. *Green Fees:* £20.00 weekdays; £27.00 weekends and Bank Holidays. *Eating facilities:* book before playing. *Visitors:* welcome without reservation if members of a recognised golf club. *Society Meetings:* catered for by arrangement with the Secretary. Professional: D. Clarke (01942 255991). Secretary: L. Hedley (01942 255131).

WORSLEY. **Marriott Worsley Park Hotel & Country Club**, Worsley Park, Worsley, Manchester (0161 975 2043). *Location:* Junction 13 off M60, follow A575 to Worsley. Challenging new parkland course. 18 holes. Par 71. *Green Fees:* information not available. *Eating facilities:* bar and dining facilities 8am to 10pm. *Visitors:* welcome. Handicap Certificate is required. *Society Meetings:* details of golf and leisure breaks on request. Conference and banqueting facilities available. Superbly equipped country club, including 20-metre pool, spa bath, sauna, steam room and health and beauty salons. Professional: David Screeton.
website: www.marriott.com/marriot/mangs

See also Colour Advertisement on page 50

Merseyside

BIDSTON. **Bidston Golf Club Ltd**, Bidston Link Road, Wallasey, Wirral CH44 2HR (0151-638 3412). *Location:* M53 Junction 1 (from Chester direction) turn right at roundabout, course entrance 200 yards on dual carriageway. Mixture of links and parkland. 18 holes, 6140 yards. S.S.S. 69. Practice ground and nets. *Green Fees:* information not available. *Eating facilities:* restaurant, snacks, lounge bar. *Visitors:* welcomed weekdays and weekends. *Society Meetings:* welcome weekdays and weekends. Professional: Mark Eagles (0151-638 3412). Secretary:J. Whitton.*

BIRKENHEAD. **Arrowe Park Golf Course**, Arrowe Park, Birkenhead CH49 5LW. *Location:* Mersey Tunnel into Brough Road, then Woodchurch Road, head for Arrowe Park roundabout, bear left approximately 400 yards, turn right into Arrowe Park. Flat tree-lined parkland. 18 holes, 6396 yards, 5885 metres. S.S.S. 71. 9 hole pitch and putt, putting green. *Green Fees:* £8.50. *Eating facilities:* restaurant/cafe - bar. *Visitors:* welcome except weekends before noon. *Society Meetings:* by arrangement through Professional. Professional: Colin Disbury (0151-677 1527). Secretary: P. Hickey (0151-678 3296).

BIRKENHEAD. **Prenton Golf Club,** Golf Links Road, Prenton, Birkenhead CH42 8LW (0151-608 1053). *Location:* M53 Junction 3, off A552 towards Birkenhead. Parkland course. 18 holes, 6411 yards. S.S.S. 71. *Green Fees:* £30.00 weekdays; £40.00 weekends. *Eating facilities:* full catering facilities available. *Visitors:* welcome, reservation advisable. *Society Meetings:* catered for Mondays, Wednesdays and Fridays. Professional: Robin Thompson (0151-608 1636). Secretary: N. Brown.

BIRKENHEAD. **The Wirral Ladies' Golf Club Ltd,** 93 Bidston Road, Oxton, Birkenhead CH43 6TS (0151-652 5797). *Location:* off the M53 Junction 1 or 3. Acid heath/gorse and heather course. 18 holes, 4948 yards (Ladies), 5182 yards (Men). S.S.S. 69 (Ladies), S.S.S. 65 (Men). Practice ground. *Green Fees:* £25.50 per round, £35.00 per day. *Eating facilities:* dining room, meals during day to order. *Visitors:* welcome weekdays; weekends after 11am Club Competitions permitting. Trolleys. *Society Meetings:* welcome weekdays only. Professional: Angus Law (0151-652 2468). Secretary: S.A. Headford (0151-652 1255; Fax: 0151-653 4323).

BLUNDELLSANDS. **West Lancashire Golf Club,** Hall Road West, Blundellsands, Merseyside L23 8SZ (0151-924 1076; Fax: 0151-931 4448). *Location:* A565 Liverpool - Southport to Crosby, follow signs to West Lanc Golf Club from Crosby. Links Course. 18 holes, 6767 yards. S.S.S. 73. Substantial practice ground. *Green Fees:* weekdays £60.00 per round, £75.00 per day; weekends £80.00 per round. *Eating facilities:* full bar and catering available. *Visitors:* welcome on weekdays except Tuesdays. All subject to availability. *Society Meetings:* booking in advance with Secretary. Professional: Gary Edge (0151-924 5662). Secretary: Stewart King (0151-924 1076; Fax: 0151-931 4448).
e-mail: golf@westlancashiregolf.co.uk
website: www.westlancashiregolf.co.uk

BOOTLE. **Bootle Golf Club,** 3 Dunnings Bridge Road, Bootle L30 2PP (0151-928 6196). *Location:* five miles north of Liverpool, one mile from M57 and M58. Links course. 18 holes, 6362 yards. S.S.S. 70. *Green Fees:* information not available. *Eating facilities:* full catering as required by arrangement. *Visitors:* welcome weekdays and by arrangement at weekends. *Society Meetings:* by arrangement. Professional: Alan Bradshaw (0151-928 1371). Secretary: John Morgan (07966 208972).

BROMBOROUGH. **Bromborough Golf Club,** Raby Hall Road, Bromborough, Wirral, Merseyside CH63 0NW(0151-334 2155). *Location:* Exit 4 Wirral Motorway M53. Parkland. 18 holes, 6547 yards. S.S.S. 72. *Green Fees:* £35.00. *Eating facilities:* bar and full catering facilities. *Visitors:* welcome weekdays, but essential to ring in advance for weekends and Bank Holidays. *Society Meetings:* catered for by prior arrangement. Professional: G. Berry (0151-334 4499). Secretary: J.T. Barraclough (0151-334 2155; Fax: 0151-334 7300).

CALDY. **The Caldy Golf Club Ltd,** Links Hey Road, Caldy, Wirral CH48 1NB. *Location:* one mile south of West Kirby on the River Dee, 10 miles from Chester. Undulating heathland with cliff top, links, open aspect with views across the Dee to the North Wales hills. 18 holes, 6601 yards, 6036 metres. S.S.S. 72. Practice ground and putting green. *Green Fees:* weekdays £37.00 per round, £42.00 per day; weekends with member only. *Eating facilities:* bars and restaurant throughout the day. *Visitors:* welcome weekdays with advance booking and Handicap Certificate. Restrictions Tuesdays and Wednesdays. Jeans not allowed on course or in Clubhouse. *Society Meetings:* Thursdays by prior arrangement. Professional: Kevin Jones (Tel & Fax: 0151-625 1818). Secretary/Manager: G.M. Copple (0151-625 5660; Fax: 0151-625 7394).
e-mail: GAIL@caldygolfclub.fsnet.co.uk
website: www.caldygolfclub.co.uk

EASTHAM. **Eastham Lodge Golf Club,** 117 Ferry Road, Eastham, Wirral, Merseyside CH62 0AP (0151-327 3003). *Location:* exit Junction 5 M53 into Eastham village from A41, follow signs for Eastham Country Park. Flat pleasant parkland course with many trees. 18 holes, 5706 yards. S.S.S. 68. *Green Fees:* weekdays £23.50; weekends with a member only £12.50. *Eating facilities:* bar snacks, full restaurant (book in advance). *Visitors:* welcome weekdays, with member weekends. *Society Meetings:* welcome mainly Tuesdays, some Mondays/Fridays by special arrangement; £22.00 per day, £18.00 per round. Professional: Nick Sargent (0151-327 3008). Secretary: C.S. Camden (0151-327 3003).

FORMBY. **Formby Golf Centre,** Moss Side, Formby L37 0AF (01704 875952). *Location:* off Formby bypass A565 (Liverpool to Southport road). 20 bay driving range, 9 hole pitch and putt. *Green Fees:* £4.00 for 18 holes (twice round). *Eating facilities:* small cafe. *Visitors:* welcome anytime. Golf shop. Professional: Michael Mawdsley. Proprietors: Mike and Caroline Mawdsley.

FORMBY. **Formby Golf Club,** Golf Road, Formby, Liverpool L37 1LQ (01704 872164). *Location:* one mile west of A565 by Freshfield Station. Seaside links, wooded. 18 holes, 6701 yards. S.S.S. 73. *Green Fees:* £85.00 per day. *Eating facilities:* available. *Visitors:* welcome by arrangement with the Secretary, except before 10am Wednesdays, weekends or Bank Holidays. Handicap Certificate/ introduction required. "Dormy" accommodation available. *Society Meetings:* catered for Tuesdays, Thursdays and Fridays. Professional: G.H Butler (01704 873090). Secretary: (01704 872164; Fax: 01704 833028).
e-mail: info@formbygolfclub.co.uk

FORMBY. **Formby Ladies' Golf Club,** Golf Road, Formby, Liverpool L37 1YH (01704 873493). *Location:* A565 (Southport Bypass) to Formby. Seaside links. 18 holes, 5374 yards, 4914 metres. S.S.S. 71. Practice area. *Green Fees:* weekdays £35.00; weekends £40.00; Ladies Package - £30.00 includes sandwich and cake. *Eating facilities:* light lunches, afternoon teas. *Visitors:* by prior reservation. *Society Meetings:* catered for with prior reservation. Professional: Mr Gary Butler (01704 873090). Secretary: Mrs J Houghton (Tel & Fax: 01704 873493).

HESWALL. **Heswall Golf Club,** Cottage Lane, Gayton, Wirral CH60 8PB (0151-342 1237). *Location:* off A540, eight miles north-west of Chester. Parkland on the banks of River Dee estuary overlooking Welsh coast and hills. 18 holes, 6472 yards, 5909 metres. S.S.S. 72. Large practice area. *Green Fees:* information not provided. *Eating facilities:* bar snacks, full meals by arrangement. *Visitors:* welcome anytime subject to availability. Must have accredited Handicaps. *Society Meetings:* catered for fully on Wednesdays and Fridays only. Winter packages available October/March. Professional: Alan Thompson (0151-342 7431). Secretary: (0151-342 1237).
e-mail: dawn@heswallgolfclub.com

For full details of clubs and courses, plus convenient accommodation, visit the FHG golf website on **www.uk-golfguide.com**

HOYLAKE. **Royal Liverpool Golf Club**, Meols Drive, Hoylake, Wirral, Merseyside CH47 4AL (0151-632 3101 *Location:* 10 miles southwest of Liverpool on Wirral Peninsula. Approach from M6, M56 and M53 Junction 2. Championship links. 18 holes, 6847 yards. S.S.S. 74. Large practice area. *Green Fees:* weekdays £95.00 per round, £120.00 per round, weekends £120.00 per round, after 2pm only. Subject to review. *Eating facilities:* buffet lunch included in green fee. *Visitors:* welcome weekdays except Thursday mornings (Ladies' Day) and very limited at weekends. Proof of handicap required. Caddies available. *Society Meetings:* catered for Wednesdays and Fridays. Professional: John Heggarty (0151-632 5868). Secretary: Group Captain C.T. Moore CB (0151-632 3101).
e-mail: sec@royal-liverpool-golf.com
website: www.royal-liverpool-golf.com

HUYTON. **Bowring Municipal**, Bowring Park, Roby Road, Knowsley L36 4HD (0151-489 1901). *Location:* Junction 5, M62 signposted. 200 metres. Parkland. 18 holes, S.S.S. 73. *Green Fees:* information not available. *Eating facilities:* limited. Private club facilities on site, bar. *Visitors:* no restrictions. *Society Meetings:* bookings required.*

HUYTON. **Huyton and Prescot Golf Club Ltd**, Hurst Park, Huyton Lane, Huyton, Liverpool L36 1UA (0151-489 1138). *Location:* from M57 Junction 2 follow B5199 signposted Huyton. Parkland. 18 holes, 5779 yards. S.S.S. 68 white, 67 yellow. *Green Fees:* information not available. *Eating facilities:* bar snacks and restaurant area 9am to 5pm; normal bar hours. *Visitors:* welcome, midweek days 9.30am to 12.00pm, 2pm to 4pm, except Tuesdays. Snooker table. *Society Meetings:* catered for Mondays, Wednesdays, Thursdays and Fridays. Summer and Winter packages available. Professional: John Fisher (0151-489 2022). Secretary: David Hughes (0151-489 3948; Fax: 0151-489 0797).*

LIVERPOOL. **Allerton Park Golf Club**, Allerton Municipal Golf Course, Allerton Road, Liverpool L18 3JT (0151-428 8510). *Location:* end of M62, two miles to Allerton Road, one and a half miles along Allerton Road. Undulating parkland course. 18 holes, 5494 yards, 5023 metres. S.S.S. 67. 9 hole course 1685 metres. S.S.S. 34. *Green Fees:* information not available. *Eating facilities:* in clubhouse, (bar snacks only), licensed bar. *Visitors:* welcome anytime, booking system for all games. *Society Meetings:* welcome by prior arrangement with the Professional. Professional: Barry Large (0151-428 7490). Secretary: H. O'Neill.*

LIVERPOOL. **The Childwall Golf Club Ltd.**, Naylors Road, Gateacre, Liverpool L27 2YB (0151-487 9982). *Location:* Exit 6 M62 to Liverpool, follow Huyton A5080 to second set of traffic lights, turn left into Wheathill Road. Parkland, flat, designed by James Braid. 18 holes, 6425 yards. S.S.S. 72. Practice area. *Green Fees:* weekdays £35.00. Subject to review. *Eating facilities:* bar, snacks and restaurant. *Visitors:* no visitors weekends and Tuesdays. *Society Meetings:* catered for on weekdays, contact the Manager. Professional: Mr N.M. Parr (0151-487 9871). Manager: (0151-487 0654; Fax: 0151-487 0882).

LIVERPOOL. **Dudley Golf Club**, Allerton Municipal Golf Course, Menlove Avenue, Allerton, Liverpool L18 3EE (0151-428 8510). *Location:* end of M62, then two miles on Allerton road, five miles from city centre. Wooded parkland. Two courses. (1) 18 holes, 5459 metres. S.S.S. 67. (2) 9 holes, 1685 metres. S.S.S. 34. *Green Fees:* information not available. *Eating facilities:* licensed bar, bar snacks. *Visitors:* welcome at any time, please book in advance. *Society Meetings:* welcome by advance booking. Professional: Barry Large (0151-428 1046). Secretary: Brian L. Harris (01244 661511). *

LIVERPOOL. **Lee Park Golf Club**, Childwall Valley Road, Liverpool L27 3YA (0151-487 9861). *Location:* Childwall Valley Road. Parkland. 18 holes, 6074 yards. Medal tees: 5569 yards. Front tees: S.S.S. 68. Ladies' tee: 5650 yards. S.S.S. 72. *Green Fees:* information not available. *Eating facilities:* restaurant and bar snacks daily. *Visitors:* welcome anytime except between 12.15pm and 2.15pm daily (reserved for members). *Society Meetings:* catered for. Secretary: Angela Fagan (0151-487 3882).*

LIVERPOOL. **West Derby Golf Club**, Yew Tree Lane, West Derby, Liverpool L12 9HQ (0151-228 1540). Flat parkland course. 18 holes, 6277 yards. S.S.S. 70. *Green Fees:* weekdays £28.50 per round; weekends £37.00 after 2pm. *Eating facilities:* soup and sandwiches, light meals available at lunch. Evening meals by prior arrangement. *Visitors:* welcome if members of a recognised golf club. *Society Meetings:* catered for only by arrangement with Secretary. Professional: Andrew Witherup (0151-220 5478). Secretary: A.P. Milne (0151-254 1034; Fax: 0151-259 0505).

LIVERPOOL. **Woolton Golf Club,** Doe Park, Speke Road, Woolton, Liverpool L25 7TZ (0151-486 1601). *Location:* South Liverpool, one mile from Woolton Village. Parkland, rolling terrain, excellent springy fairways affording inviting lies. 18 holes, 5717 yards. S.S.S. 68. *Green Fees:* weekdays £24.00, weekends £35.00. *Eating facilities:* bar snacks daily, evening dining by arrangement. *Visitors:* welcome; very few restrictions. *Society Meetings:* catered for by arrangement with the Secretary; various packages - information pack on request. Professional: D. Thompson (0151-486 1298). Secretary: K. Hamilton (0151-486 2298; Fax: 0151-486 1664).

MORETON. **Leasowe Golf Club,** Leasowe Road, Moreton, Wirral, Merseyside CH46 3RD (0151-677 5852; Fax: 0151 604 1448). *Location:* Exit 1 from M53, one mile towards Hoylake. Flat seaside links. 18 holes, 6263 yards, S.S.S. 71. Practice area. *Green Fees:* £27.50 weekdays; £32.50 weekends. *Eating facilities:* dining room and bar snacks. *Visitors:* welcome anytime except Saturdays and Sunday mornings. Phone first. *Society Meetings:* available at discount, catered for except Saturdays , must book in advance. Professional: Andrew Ayre (0151-678 5460). Secretary/Manager: L. Jukes (0151-677 5852).

NEWTON-LE-WILLOWS. **Haydock Park Golf Club,** Newton Lane, Newton-le-Willows WA12 0HX (01925 224389). *Location:* off East Lancs Road (A580) and M6, three quarters of a mile from Newton-le-Willows High Street. Flat, wooded parkland course in beautiful setting. 18 holes, 6058 yards. S.S.S. 69. Large practice ground. *Green Fees:* weekdays £30.00; weekends £10.00 with member only. *Eating facilities:* restaurant and two bars. *Visitors:* welcome weekdays except Tuesdays, identification (club membership card) or letter of introduction required. *Society Meetings:* catered for by arrangement. Professional: P. Kenwright (01925 226944). Secretary: Mrs V. Wiseman (01925 228525).

RAINHILL. **Blundells Hill Golf Club,** Blundells Lane, Rainhill L35 6NA (0151-426 9040; Fax: 0151-426 5256). *Location:* three minutes from Junction 7 of M62, course lies adjacent to eastbound M62. Built on a gently sloping hill, created from some 120 acres of parkland surroundings with wide fairways, big bunkers and large undulating greens, several ponds, ditches and a beautifully landscaped lake. 18 holes, 6256 yards. S.S.S. 71. Practice ground, putting green. *Green Fees:* weekdays £27.50 per round, £40.00 per day; weekends £35.00 per round, £45.00 per day. Guest of member £15.00 per round weekdays, £20.00 per day; £18.00 per round weekends and Bank Holidays, £22.50 per day. *Eating facilities:* licensed bar, restaurant, snooker room, function room, Sky TV. *Visitors:* all welcome, call 0151-430 0100 to pre-book tee times. No jeans, tracksuits, tee shirts, trainers, short socks, etc. Expert tuition. *Society Meetings:* welcome, packages available; call 0151-430 9551 for brochure. Professional: Richard Burbidge (0151-430 0100). Hon. Secretary: Andy Roberts (0151-430 9551; Fax: 0151-426 5256).

RAINHILL. **Eccleston Park Golf Club,** Rainhill Road, Rainhill, Prescot L35 4PG (0151 493 0033). *Location:* Junction 7 of M62, follow A57 towards Prescot; at traffic lights after humpback bridge, turn right into Rainhill. Gently undulating open parkland layout. 18 holes. Par 70. *Green Fees:* information not available. *Eating facilities:* bar and dining from 8am to 11pm (9am to 6pm during winter). *Visitors:* Handicap Certificate required at weekends. e-mail: eccleston-sales@crown-golf.co.uk

ST HELENS. **Grange Park Golf Club,** Prescot Road, St. Helens WA10 3AD (Tel & Fax: 01744 26318). *Location:* one and a half miles south west of St. Helens on A58. Wooded parkland. 18 holes, 6422 yards. S.S.S. 71. Practice area. *Green Fees:* weekdays £26.00; weekends £33.00. *Eating facilities:* full catering and bar facilities. *Visitors:* welcome anytime except Tuesdays and times are often not available at weekends/Bank Holidays; reservation through Professional recommended. *Society Meetings:* welcome except Tuesdays, Bank Holidays and weekends. Professional: Paul Roberts (01744 28785; Fax: 01744 26318). Secretary: Ian Fisher (Tel & Fax: 01744 26318). e-mail: gpgc@ic24.net

ST HELENS. **Sherdley Park Municipal Golf Course and Driving Range,** Off Elton Road, Sutton, St Helens WA9 5DE (01744 813149). *Location:* Exit 7 off M62, follow St Helens Linkway to second island, turn right for 300 yards, course on left hand side. Undulating parkland course. 18 holes, 5974 yards. S.S.S. 71. Driving range. *Green Fees:* for information and bookings phone (01744 813149). *Eating facilities:* Licensed bar and Hot Putt Cafe open most times, phone Karen on (01744 815518) for more information. *Visitors/Society Meetings:* welcome mid-week and weekends (book early). Booking system operates up to six days in advance. Golf Professional: Danny Jones. Manager: Jeff Barston (01744 817967). *

For full details of clubs and courses, plus convenient accommodation, visit the FHG golf website on

www.uk-golfguide.com

SOUTHPORT. **Hesketh Golf Club,** Cockle Dicks Lane, Cambridge Road, Southport PR9 9QQ (01704 536897). *Location:* one mile north of town centre. Seaside links Championship course. 18 holes, 6572 yards. S.S.S. 72. Practice ground. *Green Fees:* weekdays £40.00 per round, £50.00 per day; weekends and Bank Holidays £50.00 per round. *Eating facilities:* bar snacks and dining room; three bars. *Visitors:* welcome by prior arrangement with Secretary. *Society Meetings:* catered for by arrangement with Secretary; special rates for parties over 12 in number. Professional: John Donoghue (01704 530050). Secretary: Martyn G. Senior (01704 536897; Fax: 01704 539250).
e-mail: hesketh@ukgolfer.orgk
website: www.ukgolfer.org/clubs/hesketh

SOUTHPORT. **Hillside Golf Club,** Hastings Road, Hillside, Southport PR8 2LU (01704 567169; Fax: 01704 563192). *Location:* three miles south of town centre on A565, Hillside station one mile. Championship links course. 18 holes, 6850 yards.

S.S.S. 74. Practice ground. *Green Fees:* Monday to Friday £55.00 per round, £70.00 per day; Sunday £70.00 per round (2003). *Eating facilities:* bar and restaurant. *Visitors:* welcome, book through Office. Tuesday up to 2pm Ladies' Day; no visitors Saturdays, limited Sundays. Buggies and carts for hire. *Society Meetings:* welcome with prior reservations. Professional: B. Seddon (01704 568360). Secretary: John G. Graham (01704 567169; Fax: 01704 563192).

SOUTHPORT. **Royal Birkdale Golf Club,** Waterloo Road, Birkdale, Southport PR8 2LX (01704 567920; Fax: 01704 562327). *Location:* one mile south of Southport town centre. Classic Links on the Open Championship rota. 18 holes, 6703 yards. S.S.S. 73. *Green Fees:* contact the Secretary. *Visitors:* welcome but it is essential to make prior arrangements with the Secretary's office, official golf Handicap required. *Society Meetings:* catered for, dining room facilities. Professional: Brian Hodgkinson (01704 568857). Secretary: M.C. Gilyeat (01704 567920).

Southport
England's Golfing Capital

For the discerning golfer, the finest Links courses in England

Centrally situated on the North West coast of England, the vibrant resort of Southport, and the surrounding area, offers a truly exceptional choice of courses set in some of the finest sand dunes in the world.

The mouth-watering collection includes:
■ ROYAL BIRKDALE ■ HILLSIDE
■ SOUTHPORT & AINSDALE ■ HESKETH

Just a few miles along the coast you will find 2 further jewels:
■ FORMBY ■ FORMBY HALL

Travel a little further along the coast and you will find the testing:-
■ WEST LANCASHIRE GOLF CLUB

Within a short drive there are also 2 more Open Championship venues: -
■ ROYAL LYTHAM ST ANNES ■ ROYAL LIVERPOOL

There are 160 courses within an hour's drive of Southport, and when you've finished the round, this elegant resort offers a stunning variety of restaurants, lively nightlife and superb shopping.

There's a wide range of accommodation on offer too - from four star hotels to top quality self-catering accommodation - offering a warm welcome to golfers. For a FREE copy of our Golf Guide call our

hotline on **01704 533333** and please quote **TGG04** or visit our website at **www.golf-england.co.uk**

See also Colour Advertisement on page 47

SOUTHPORT. **Southport and Ainsdale Golf Club,** Bradshaw's Lane, Off Liverpool Road, Ainsdale, Southport PR8 3LG (01704 578000; Fax: 01704 570896). *Location:* south of Southport on A565. Links course. 18 holes, 6687 yards. S.S.S. 73. *Green Fees:* weekdays £55.00 per round, £75.00 per day; weekends £75.00 per round. *Eating facilities:* full catering available. *Visitors:* welcome at all times; by arrangement at weekends. *Society Meetings:* catered for by arrangement. Professional: J. Payne (01704 577316). Secretary: Mrs C.A. Birrell (01704 578000; Fax: 01704 570896). e-mail: secretary@sandagolfclub.co.uk website: www.sandagolfclub.co.uk

SOUTHPORT. **Southport Municipal Golf Club,** Park Road West, Southport PR9 0JR (01704 55130). *Location:* Park Road West, north end of Promenade, near Marine Lake, Southport. Flat seaside links. 18 holes, 6139 yards. S.S.S. 70. *Green Fees:* information not available. *Eating facilities:* licensed cafe. *Visitors:* booking system operates up to seven days in advance (visitors unrestricted). *Society Meetings:* welcome, book in advance. Professional: William Fletcher (01704 35286)*

SOUTHPORT. **Southport Old Links Golf Club,** Moss Lane, Churchtown, Southport PR9 7QS (01704 228207). *Location:* end of Roe Lane, Churchtown, at the rear of Meols Hall. Tree lined links course. 9 holes, (x2), 6371 yards. S.S.S. 71. *Green Fees:* weekdays £22.00; weekends £30.00. *Eating facilities:* available daily except Mondays. *Visitors:* welcome except Wednesdays, Sundays and Bank Holidays. *Society Meetings:* catered for by arrangement, letter of application required. Secretary: B. Kenyon (01704 228207; Fax: 01704 505353).

WALLASEY. **Wallasey Golf Club,** Bayswater Road, Wallasey CH45 8LA (0151-691 1024; Fax: 0151-638 8988). *Location:* via M53 through Wirral or 15 minutes from Liverpool centre via Wallasey Tunnel. Championship seaside links. 18 holes, 6503 yards. S.S.S. 72. *Green Fees:* weekdays £50.00 per round, £60.00 per day; weekends and Bank Holidays £65.00 per round, £75.00 per day. *Eating facilities:* snacks and full catering facilities. *Visitors:* welcome with reservation. *Society Meetings:* catered for by arrangement. Professional: Mike Adams (0151-638 3888). Secretary: Alan M. O'Callaghan (0151-691 1024).

WALLASEY. **Warren Golf Club,** The Grange, Grove Road, Wallasey CH45 0JA (0151-639 8323). *Location:* 300 yards Grove Road Station. Seaside links course, wonderful view over Mersey. 9 holes, 5914 yards. S.S.S. 68. *Green Fees:* information not available. *Visitors:* welcome Mondays to Saturdays. *Society Meetings:* welcome. Professional: Steve Konrad (0151-639 5730). Secretary: David Farrington (0151-630 7086). *
e-mail: golfer@warrengc.freeserve.co.uk

WIRRAL. **Brackenwood Golf Club,** Bracken Lane, Bebington, Wirral L63 2LY (0151-608 5394). *Location:* M53 Clatterbridge roundabout Junction 4. Flat parkland. 18 holes, 5745 yards. S.S.S. 70. *Green Fees:* information not available. *Eating facilities:* bar facilities on certain days, but being reviewed. *Visitors:* welcome, weekends must be booked through Professional one week in advance. *Society Meetings:* welcome, book through Professional. Professional: Ken Lamb (0151-608 3093). Secretary: G.W. Brogan (0151-339 9817).

WIRRAL. **Hoylake Golf Club,** Carr Lane, Hoylake, Wirral CH47 4BG (0151-632 2956). *Location:* turn at roundabout Hoylake town centre, over railway. Part flat semi links. 18 holes, 6313 yards, 5780 metres. S.S.S. 70. *Green Fees:* £8.50 weekdays/ weekends; Senior Citizens and Juniors £4.25. *Eating facilities:* cafe and bar. Phone in advance (0151-632 4883). *Visitors:* welcome, booking fee required in advance. *Society Meetings:* society bookings weekdays and after 1.30pm Saturday ; after 12 mid-day Sunday. Professional: S.N. Hooton (0151-632 2956). Secretary: M.E. Down (0151-632 6823).

Norfolk

CROMER. **Links Country Park Hotel and Golf Club,** Sandy Lane, West Runton, Cromer NR27 9QH (01263 838383). *Location:* midway between Cromer and Sheringham on the A149, turn left opposite the village inn. Undulating parkland with narrow fairways and tricky greens. 9 holes, 4814 yards, S.S.S. 64. *Green Fees:* information not available. *Eating facilities:* grill room, snacks, hotel restaurant table d'hôte and à la carte. *Visitors:* welcome weekdays, restrictions weekends. Adjoining Hotel offers free golf to residents; gym, sauna, solarium, swimming pool etc. *Society Meetings:* welcome. Professional: James Tuck (01263 838215; Fax: 01263 838264). Hon. Secretary: Carl Abbott (01263 838383; Fax: 01263 838264).

CROMER. **Royal Cromer Golf Club,** 145 Overstrand Road, Cromer NR27 0JH (01263 512884; Fax: 01263 512430). *Location:* one mile east of Cromer on B1159 Coast Road. Undulating cliff top course. 18 holes, 6280 yards. S.S.S. 72. Large practice ground. *Green Fees:* £37.00 weekdays, £50.00 weekends; weekly tickets available, also joint tickets with Sheringham. *Eating facilities:* full catering and bar snacks. *Visitors:* welcome, booking essential from 1st April to 31st October, Handicap Certificates required. *Society Meetings:* welcome. Professsional: Lee Patterson (Tel & Fax: 01263 512267). General Manager: R. Fields (Tel & Fax: 01263 512884).

DEREHAM. **Dereham Golf Club**, Quebec Road, Dereham NR19 2DS (01362 695900; Fax: 01362 695904). *Location:* three-quarters of a mile from town centre on B1110. Wooded parkland. 9 holes (double tees), 6225 yards. S.S.S. 70. Practice nets, practice ground. *Green Fees:* £17.50 per round, £22.50 per day. *Eating facilities:* full restaurant (except Mondays). *Visitors:* welcome with prior notice. Handicap Certificates required. *Society Meetings:* catered for with advance booking. Professional: Neil Allsebrook (01362 695631). Secretary: S. Kaye (01362 695900; Fax: 01362 695904).

DISS. **Diss Golf Club,** Stuston Common, Diss IP21 4AA (01379 641025). *Location:* B1077 off A140, half-a-mile from Diss railway station, one mile from town centre. The course complete with its natural hazards provides a good test of golf. 18 holes, 6206 yards. S.S.S. 69. Par 70. New 15 bay driving range one mile from clubhouse adjacent to 15th hole. *Green Fees:* £25.00, £12.50 if playing with a member. *Eating facilities:* are excellent. *Visitors:* welcome but weekends only with a member. *Society Meetings:* Golf Societies are welcome. There is a well stocked shop and lessons are available from the professional. Well supported club with membership available. Contact Secretary/Manager for details; easy payment terms optional. Professional: Nigel Taylor (01379 644399). Secretary: Mr Chris Wellstead (01379 641025; Fax: 01379 644586). Steward: J.W. Mackrell (01379 642847).
e-mail: sec.dissgolf@virgin.net
www.club-noticeboard.co.uk/diss

DOWNHAM MARKET. **Ryston Park Golf Club,** Ely Road, Denver, Downham Market PE38 0HH (01366 382133; Fax: 01366 383834). *Location:* one mile south Downham Market on A10. 36 miles north Cambridge. Parkland with mature trees and water on three holes. 9 holes, 6310 yards, 5774 metres. S.S.S. 70. Practice ground, practice putting green, practice bunker. *Green Fees:* weekdays £20.00, weekends restricted – contact Club. *Eating facilities:* restaurant and bar. *Visitors:* welcome weekdays, weekends by prior arrangement. *Society Meetings:* welcome (up to 50 members). Secretary: Joe Flogdell (01366 382133).

FAKENHAM. **Fakenham Golf Club,** Gallow Sports Centre, Hempton Road, Fakenham NR21 7LA (01328 862867). *Location:* half-a-mile town centre on Swaffham Road. Parkland. 9 holes, 6245 yards. S.S.S. 70. Large practice area. *Green Fees:* information not available. *Eating facilities:* available in Sports Centre. *Visitors:* welcome by appointment. *Society Meetings:* welcome, reduced rates. Professional: Martin Clarke (01328 863534). Secretary: G.G. Cocker (01328 855665). *

GREAT YARMOUTH. **Caldecott Hall Golf Club and Hotel,** Beccles Road, Fritton, Great Yarmouth NR31 9EY (01493 488488; Fax: 01493 488561). *Location:* on the A143 just north of the village of Fritton. Parkland. 18 holes, 6685 yards, S.S.S. 72. 9-hole short course, 1400 metres, S.S.S. 27. Floodlit driving range, 9-hole pitch and putt, putting and pitching practice area. *Green Fees:* weekdays £20.00 per day, weekends £26.00. Short course £6.00. Eating facilities: bar, restaurant. *Visitors:* welcome at all times, starting sheets weekends and Bank Holidays. Luxury en suite rooms. Packages available. *Society Meetings:* welcome by arrangement. Professional: Syer Shulver PGA (01493 488488: Fax: 01493 488561). Secretary: Roger Beales.

GREAT YARMOUTH. **Gorleston Golf Club,** Warren Road, Gorleston, Great Yarmouth NR31 6JT (01493 661082). *Location:* A12 Lowestoft to Great Yarmouth. Seaside links, seventh green is the most easterly green in the British Isles. 18 holes, 6400 yards. S.S.S. 71. *Green Fees:* weekdays £25.00; weekends and Public Holidays £30.00, £18.00 after 5pm. Weekly £90.00. Reductions if playing with member. *Eating facilities:* restaurant/bars open seven days. *Visitors:* welcome, advisable to check in advance for details of restrictions. *Society Meetings:* catered for by prior arrangement (membership of recognised club required). Professional: Nick Brown (01493 662103). Secretary: J.E. Woodhouse (01493 661911).

THE APPEARANCE OF AN ASTERISK (*) AT THE END OF A CLUB OR COURSE ENTRY INDICATES THAT UP-TO-DATE INFORMATION HAS NOT BEEN SUPPLIED

GREAT YARMOUTH. **Great Yarmouth and Caister Golf Club,** Beach House, Caister-on-Sea, Great Yarmouth NR30 5TD (01493 728699). *Location:* A149 coast road, two miles north of Great Yarmouth. Links. 18 holes, 6330 yards. S.S.S. 70. Practice ground. *Green Fees:* £30.00, £18.00 after 2.30pm weekdays; £35.00, £22.00 after 2.30pm weekends. Members' guests 50%. *Eating facilities:* full range of catering; bar. *Visitors:* welcome, not before 10.30am Saturdays and not before 11.30am Sundays. *Society Meetings:* catered for. Clubhouse Catering (01493 720214). Professional: Martyn Clarke (01493 720421). Secretary: R. Peck.
e-mail: office@caistergolf.co.uk
website: caistergolf.co.uk

HUNSTANTON. **Hunstanton Golf Club**, Golf Course Road, Old Hunstanton PE36 6JQ (01485 532811; Fax: 01485 532319). *Location:* off A149. Adjoins Old Hunstanton village, approximately half a mile north east of Hunstanton. Championship links course with excellent fast greens. 18 holes, 6735 yards. S.S.S. 72. Practice ground. *Green Fees:* weekdays £60.00 per day; weekends £70.00 per day. Special rates in winter, also after 4pm all year. Subject to review. *Eating facilities:* catering and bar facilities. *Visitors:* welcome but limited times available at weekends. Prior booking advisable. Visitors must be member of recognised golf club and hold a current Handicap. Play in two-ball format only. *Society Meetings:* welcome. Professional: Jim Dodds (01485 532751). Secretary: Derek Thomson (01485 532811).

HUNSTANTON. **Searles Resort Golf Course,** Searles Leisure Resort, South Beach Road, Hunstanton PE36 5BB (01485 534211; Fax: 01485 533815). *Location:* A149 from King's Lynn to Hunstanton; at roundabout on hill at Hunstanton take 2nd left down Oasis Way; at mini-roundabout straight over and immediate left into Leisure Resort; follow signs. Seaside links-style course. 9 holes, 2850 yards. S.S.S. 34. 10-bay covered driving range. Putting. *Green Fees:* £8.00 adults, £6.50 under-18s (add £1.00 for weekends). *Eating facilities:* new clubhouse with bar, restaurant, shop, changing facilities etc. *Visitors:* welcome at all times. Lodges and cabin on site available for hire. Club hire. Fishing lake and bowling green. *Society Meetings:* all welcome. Secretary/Manager: Paul Searle.
e-mail: golf@searles.co.uk

KING'S LYNN. **Eagles Golf Club,** 39 School Road, Tilney All Saints, King's Lynn PE34 4RS (01553 827147). *Location:* off A47 between King's Lynn and Wisbech. Parkland. 9 holes, 4284 yards. S.S.S. 61. Par 3 course, driving range, practice bunkers and putting green. *Green Fees:* weekdays £7.95 9 holes, £11.75 18 holes; weekends and Bank Holidays £8.95 9 holes, £14.75 18 holes. Weekday special Seniors/Juniors £5.50 9 holes, £9.00 18 holes. *Eating facilities:* bar/restaurant. *Visitors:* welcome, restrictions at weekends; no visitors before 10am. Dress code must be adhered to at all times. *Society Meetings:* apply to Secretary. Professional: Nigel Pickerell. Secretary: R. K. Shipman (Tel & Fax: 01553 829777).

KING'S LYNN. **King's Lynn Golf Club,** Castle Rising, King's Lynn PE31 6BD (01553 631654; Fax: 01553 631036). *Location:* four miles north-east of King's Lynn. Undulating wooded course. 18 holes, 6646 yards. S.S.S. 73. Practice areas. *Green Fees:* on request. *Eating facilities:* snacks, lunches, teas available; dinners by arrangement; two bars. *Visitors:* welcome on production of Handicap Certificate. *Society Meetings:* catered for by prior arrangement. Professional: J. Reynolds (01553 631655). General Manager: M.P. Sackree.

KING'S LYNN. **Middleton Hall Golf Club,** Middleton, King's Lynn PE32 1RH (Tel & Fax: 01553 841800). *Location:* on A47 King's Lynn to Norwich, 3 miles from King's Lynn. Undulating parkland. 18 holes, 6004 yards. S.S.S. 69. Floodlit driving range, practice greens. *Green Fees:* weekdays £25.00, weekends £30.00. *Eating facilities:* full restaurant services. *Visitors:* welcome. *Society Meetings:* welcome, special rates available. Professional: Steve White (01553 841801). Secretary: J. Holland (Tel & Fax: 01553 841800).

KING'S LYNN. **Royal West Norfolk Golf Club,** Brancaster, Near King's Lynn PE31 8AX (01485 210223). *Location:* one mile off A149, Beach Road junction, seven miles east of Hunstanton. Seaside links. 18 holes, 6428 yards. S.S.S. 71. *Green Fees:* weekdays £65.00 per day; weekends £75.00 per day. *Eating facilities:* available. *Visitors:* all visitors must be members of a recognised Golf Club, hold an official Handicap and must make prior arrangements with the Secretary to play. No visitors prior to 10am Sundays and no visitors in August. Maximum numbers in party 24. Professional: S. Rayner (01485 210616). Secretary: Major N.A. Carrington Smith (Tel & Fax: 01485 210087).

MATTISHALL. **Mattishall Golf Club,** South Green, Mattishall, Dereham NR20 3JZ (01362 850111). *Location:* Signposted from Mattishall Church. 9 hole (18 tees), flat course, 6170 yards, SSS 69. *Green Fees:* £8.00 for 9 holes. *Eating facilities:* small bar only. *Visitors:* welcome seven days, no restrictions. Secretary: Mrs Bridgette Hall.

NORWICH. **Barnham Broom Hotel & Country Club,** Barnham Broom, Norwich NR9 4DD (01603 759393 (Hotel); 01603 759552 (Golf Shop); Fax: 01603 758224). *Location:* situated 10 miles west of Norwich off A47 and A11 trunk routes; follow brown tourist signs. Two 18 hole courses in 250 acres of the beautiful River Yare Valley. The Valley Course: 6483 yards, S.S.S. 71; The Hill Course: 6495 yards, S.S.S. 71. Exceptional practice facilities including 5 acre practice ground and three full length academy holes. Group and individual tuition by the Peter Ballingall Golf School. *Green Fees:* information not available. *Eating facilities:* Flints Restaurant, Sports Bar and Cafe (serving light meals and drinks throughout the day).Conference and private dining for up to 200 people. *Visitors:* welcome anytime. Hotel with 52 en suite bedrooms. Leisure Club. *Society Meetings:* welcome all year; corporate Golf Events. Professionals: Peter Ballingall (Golf Director) (01603 757504) / Adrian Rudge (Head Professional) (01603 757504).
website: www.barnham-broom.co.uk
website: www.pbgolfschool.com

NORWICH. **Bawburgh Golf Club,** Glen Lodge, Marlingford Road, Bawburgh, Norwich NR9 3LU (01603 740404; Fax: 01603 740403). *Location*: directly off Norwich Southern Bypass – exit follow Royal Norfolk Showground/Bawburgh. Rolling landscape mixture of heath and parkland. 18 holes, 6231 yards. S.S.S. 70. Driving range covered and floodlit, group tuition. *Green Fees*: weekdays £25.00; weekends £28.00 on application. *Eating facilities*: restaurant and bar, snacks. *Visitors*: welcome, advisable to ring in advance. *Society Meetings*: welcome on application, Corporate Days arranged. Professional: Chris Potter (01603 742323). Director of Golf: Ian Ladbrooke.
e-mail: info@bawburgh.com
website: www.bawburgh.com

NORWICH. **Costessey Park Golf Course,** Old Costessey, Norwich NR8 5AL (01603 746333). *Location*: off the A47 Norwich to King's Lynn road, in the village of Old Costessey (adjacent to Norwich). Set in river valley with some parkland. 18 holes, 5820 yards. S.S.S. 69. Par 71. Practice area. *Green Fees*: £30.00 per day. *Eating facilities*: bar and bar snacks; set meals available. *Visitors*: welcome anytime except weekends when visitors allowed only after 11am. Handicap Certificates required weekends only. Golf carts available for hire. *Society Meetings*: catered for by arrangement. Professional: Andrew Young (01603 747085).

NORWICH. **De Vere Dunston Hall**, Ipswich Road, Norwich NR14 8PQ (Hotel: 01508 470444; Fax: 01508 470689; Shop: 01508 470178). *Location*: on A140 Ipswich Road. Parkland, wooded, with many water features. USGA spec. greens. 18 holes, 6319 yards. Par 71. 22 bay covered driving range, putting green. *Green Fees*: information not available. E*ating facilities*: three restaurants, two bars. *Visitors*: pay and play course, all welcome at any time. Golfing weekends; accommodation available in 130-bedroom Hotel; tennis courts; leisure centre with indoor pool, sauna, steam room and jacuzzi. *Society Meetings*: special packages available. Professional: Peter Briggs.*

NORWICH. **Eaton (Norwich) Golf Club,** Newmarket Road, Norwich NR4 6SF (Tel & Fax: 01603 451686). *Location*: off A11, one and a half miles from city centre. Parkland course – "the hidden gem". 18 holes, 6114 yards. S.S.S. 70. Practice areas available. *Green Fees*: information not available. *Eating facilities*: full bar, snacks, lunches, dinners by arrangement. *Visitors*: welcome; only after 11.30am weekends. Handicap Certificate required. *Society Meetings*: welcome, fees by arrangement. Professional: Mark Allen (01603 452478). Secretary: Mrs L. Bovill (Tel & Fax: 01603 451686).
e-mail: administrator@eatongc.co.uk
website: www.eatongc.co.uk

NORWICH. **Marriot Sprowston Manor Hotel and Country Club,** Wroxham Road, Norwich NR7 8RP (0870 400 7229; Fax: 0870 400 7329). *Location*: off A1151 Norwich to Wroxham. £1.6 million Championship Standard course set in mature parkland. Host to Sky Televised PGA Europro Tour 2004. Full USGA specification greens and tees. Designed by Ross McMurray (European Golf Design), who has also designed the Marquess at Woburn and improvements at Celtic Manor for 2010 Ryder Cup. 18 holes, 6547 yards. S.S.S. 71. Putting green, chipping and bunker practice area. 27 bay floodlit driving range, PGA tuition including Explanar and GASP video analysis. *Green Fees*: weekdays £30.00 per round; weekends £38.00 per round. *Eating facilities*: Full clubhouse facilities and four star hotel on site. *Visitors*: always welcome. Bookings 10 days in advance. *Society Meetings*: special packages available - must be pre-booked. Preferential green fee rates and group packages available for residents. Professional: Guy Ireson (01603 254290). Secretary: Mr J. O'Malley (01603 254290).
website: www.marriott.co.uk

NORWICH. **Mundesley Golf Club,** Links Road, Mundesley, Norwich NR11 8ES (Tel & Fax: 01263 720279). *Location*: one mile from village centre. Undulating, fairly exposed parkland course with fine panoramic views. 9 holes, 5377 yards. S.S.S. 66. Covered driving range, small practice area. *Green Fees*: information not available. *Eating facilities*: full catering facilities. *Visitors*: welcome, but course reserved for members until 11.30am at weekends and Bank Holidays and 11.00am to 3.30pm Wednesdays. *Society Meetings*: catered for, restrictions as for visitors. Professional: T.G. Symmons (0831 455461). Secretary: Jim Woodhouse (01263 720095; Fax: 01263 720279). *

NORWICH. **Royal Norwich Golf Club,** Drayton High Road, Hellesdon, Norwich NR6 5AH (01603 429928; Fax: 01603 417945). *Location*: centre of city and thence by A1067 Fakenham or via Ring Road, then 500 yards along A1067. Mature parkland. 18 holes, 6506 yards. S.S.S. 72. Large practice ground. *Green Fees*: weekdays £40.00 per day; weekends and Bank Holidays £50.00 per day. Reduction if playing with a member, special winter rates available on request. *Eating facilities*: two bars, restaurant plus bar menu. Prior booking required for evening meals. *Visitors*: welcome weekdays after 9am, weekends by prior booking only. Handicap Certificate required. *Society Meetings*: welcome weekdays except Wednesday by prior arrangement. Professional: Dean Futter (01603 408459). General Manager: John Meggy.
e-mail: mail@royalnorwichgolf.co.uk
website: www.royalnorwichgolf.co.uk

NORWICH. **Wensum Valley Hotel, Golf and Country Club,** Beech Avenue, Taverham, Norwich NR8 6HP (01603 261012; Fax: 01603 261664). *Location*: five miles out of Norwich on the A1067 to Fakenham. Two courses. Parkland and very picturesque set in the valley. Wensum Course: 18 holes, 6037 yards S.S.S. 69. Valley Course: 18 holes, 6223 yards. S.S.S. 70. Covered, floodlit driving range. *Green Fees*: information not available. *Eating facilities*: full catering and bar facilities. *Visitors*: always welcome. Hotel on site with en suite twin bedrooms. Special golf, fishing and leisure breaks available. *Society Meetings*: all welcome; package available. Professional: Peter Whittle. Secretary: Bridgette Hall (01603 261012).
e-mail: enqs@wensumvalley.freeserve.co.uk
website: www.wensumvalley.freeserve.co.uk

NORWICH. **Weston Park Golf Club,** Weston Longville, Norwich (01603 872998; Fax: 01603 873040). *Location:* nine miles north west of Norwich off the A1067 Norwich to Fakenham road. Parkland, wooded course. 18 holes, 6606 yards. S.S.S. 72. Practice ground and net. *Green Fees:* weekdays £32.00; weekends £40.00 (subject to review). *Eating facilities:* available. *Visitors:* welcome. Must book teeing off times. Handicap Certificate required. Two tennis courts and croquet lawn. *Society Meetings:* welcome. Professional: Michael Few (01603 872998). Secretary R.R. Wright (01603 872363).

REYMERSTON. **The Norfolk Golf and Country Club,** Hingham Road, Reymerston NR9 4QQ (01362 850297; Fax: 01362 850614). *Location:* Dereham B1135 five miles, Wymondham 10 miles. Parkland course. 18 holes, 6609 yards. S.S.S. 72. *Green Fees:* weekdays £22.00; weekends £27.00. *Eating facilities:* clubhouse, bar, function room. *Visitors:* welcome subject to availability. Advisable to check in advance. Full Leisure facilities in Leisure Centre; swimming pool, sauna, gym, spa bath. *Society Meetings:* society and conference packages available. Professional: Tony Varney (01362 850297; Fax: 01362 850614). Secretary: Mike de Boltz.
e-mail: suzy@the-norfolk.co.uk
website: www.the-norfolk.co.uk

SHERINGHAM. **Sheringham Golf Club,** Weybourne Road, Sheringham NR26 8HG (01263 822038). *Location:* one mile west of town on Weybourne Road (A149). Clifftop course. 18 holes, 6456 yards. S.S.S. 71. Large practice area. *Green Fees:* weekdays £40.00; weekends and Bank Holidays £50.00. *Eating facilities:* full catering to order. *Visitors:* welcome, telephone first, with reservation for members of other clubs, Handicap Certificate required. *Society Meetings:* catered for by prior arrangement with Secretary except weekends from 1st April to 31st October. Professional: M.W. Jubb (01263 822980). Secretary: P.J. Mounfield (01263 823488).

SWAFFHAM. **Dunham Golf Club,** Canister Hall, Little Dunham near Swaffham PE32 2DF (Tel. & Fax: 01328 701906). *Location:* off A47 four miles from Swaffham at Necton Q8 garage. Follow Tourist Board golf flags. Parkland with lakes. 9 holes, 4986 yards. S.S.S. 64. *Green Fees:* weekdays information not available. *Eating facilities:* restaurant and bar. *Visitors:* welcome with dress restrictions. Accommodation and swimming pool. *Society Meetings:* welcome,

telephone for details. Professional: Gary Potter (01328 701906). Secretary: F. Reid (01328 701718).*

SWAFFHAM. **Swaffham Golf Club,** Cley Road, Swaffham PE37 8AE (01760 721611/721621). *Location:* two miles south-west of Swaffham Market Place (signposted) on Cley Road. Heathland course. 18 holes, 6533 yards. S.S.S. 71. Practice ground. *Green Fees:* £25.00 per round, £35.00 per day weekdays. *Eating facilities:* full catering now available every day. *Visitors:* welcome without reservation weekdays, weekends only if playing with member. *Society Meetings:* catered for subject to prior notice being given. Professional: Peter Field. Secretary: M. Rust.

THETFORD. **Feltwell Golf Club,** Thor Avenue, off Wilton Road, Feltwell, Thetford IP26 4AY (01842 827644). *Location:* take the B1386 off the A10 at Southery (five miles south of Downham Market). Inland links – can be windy! 9 holes, 6488 yards, 6197 metres. S.S.S. 71. Practice range and nets. *Green Fees:* weekdays £16.00 per day, £10.00 with a member; weekends £25.00, per day, £16.00 with a member. *Eating facilities:* bar, hot and cold food available Tuesday through Sunday from noon. *Visitors:* welcome at all times but check with Secretary. *Society Meetings:* welcome, packages available. Professional: Christian Puttock (01842 829089). Secretary: Linda Ball (01842 827644).

THETFORD. **Richmond Park Golf Club,** Saham Road, Watton, Thetford IP25 6EA (01953 881803; Fax: 01953 881817). **Location:** half a mile north west of Watton town centre. Parkland. 18 holes, 6289 yards. S.S.S. 70. Driving range. **Green Fees:** weekdays £22.00 per round, £30.00 per day; weekends £30.00. £15.00 with a member. **Eating facilities:** bar, bar food, restaurant. **Visitors:** always welcome. Accommodation available on site. **Society Meetings:** welcome, excellent facilities available. Professional/ Secretary: Alan Hemsley.

THETFORD. **Thetford Golf Club,** Brandon Road, Thetford IP24 3NE (01842 752258). *Location:* one mile west of Thetford on B1107 Brandon Road. Wooded breckland course. 18 holes, 6849 yards. S.S.S. 73. Practice ground. *Green Fees:* £38.00 weekdays. *Eating facilities:* catering and bar service. *Visitors:* welcome weekdays. *Society Meetings:* catered for Wednesdays, Thursdays and Fridays – Handicap Certificate needed. Professional: Gary Kitley (01842 752662). Secretary: Mrs S.A. Redpath (01842 752169; Fax: 01842 766212).

Northamptonshire

CORBY near. **Priors Hall Golf Club**, Stamford Road, Weldon, Near Corby NN17 3JH (01536 260756). *Location:* on the A43, four miles from Corby on the Stamford Road. Parkland course. 18 holes, 6631 yards, 6063 metres. S.S.S. 72. Practice nets and ground. *Green Fees:* weekdays £13.00; weekends £16.50. Certain concessions apply to local residents. *Eating facilities:* bar meals. *Visitors:* welcome at all times pre-booking advisable starting sheet in operation. *Society Meetings:* welcome by prior arrangement. Professional: Jeff Bradbrook. Secretary: Terry Arnold.

DAVENTRY. **Daventry and District Golf Club**, Norton Road, Daventry NN11 5ZS(01327 702829). *Location:* on Borough Hill, site of Iron Age Fort and Roman Camp. 9 holes, 5812 yards. S.S.S. 68. *Green Fees:* weekdays £12.00; weekends and Bank Holidays £20.00. *Visitors:* welcome weekdays and weekends except Sunday before 11.30am. *Society Meetings:* welcome with prior booking. Secretary: E. G. Smith.

DAVENTRY. **Staverton Park Golf Club**, Daventry Road, Staverton, Near Daventry NN11 6JT (01327 302000; Fax: 01327 311428). *Location:* one mile from Daventry on A425 to Leamington Spa. Easy access from M1 Junctions 16 or 18. Undulating parkland. 18 holes, 6002 yards. S.S.S. 73. Championship Venue. Practice range, two putting greens. *Green Fees:* information not available. *Eating facilities:* full catering available at all times. *Visitors:* always welcome. Handicap Certificate required at weekends. Advance Tee Time (visitors) booking (01327 705506). 225 bedroomed hotel with leisure and conference facilities. Residential golf packages available. Buggies, trolleys and clubs for hire. *Society Meetings:* welcome, please enquire about our Society Package. Professional: Richard Mudge (Tel & Fax: 01327 311119). Secretary: Mrs Anne Radford (Tel & Fax: 01327 704978).*

HELLIDON. **Hellidon Lakes Golf Club**, Hellidon Lakes Hotel, Hellidon, Daventry NN11 6GG (01327 262550; Fax: 01327 262559). *Location:* one and a half miles from A361, six miles from Daventry, 12 miles from Banbury. Parkland. 27 hole championship course, putting green. *Green Fees;* information not available. *Eating facilities:* themed 100 seater casual bar and restaurant. AA rosette restaurant, top-class restaurant. *Visitors:* always welcome, Handicap Certificate required at weekends. 51 en suite bedrooms, leisure centre, tennis, health and beauty centre with salon, gym, sunbed, steam room, whirlpool bath and heated indoor swimming pool. Indoor golf simulator, 4-lane tenpin bowling. *Society Meetings:* all welcome. Professional: Gary Wills (01327 262551). Secretary: Mrs J.A. Nicoll (01327 262550; Fax: 01327 262559). *
e-mail: stay@hellidon.demon.co.uk
website: www.hellidon.demon.co.uk

KETTERING. **Kettering Golf Club**, Headlands, Kettering NN15 6XA (01536 511104). *Location:* off A14 (Junction 8) A43 to Kettering, right at 1st roundabout and follow signs for golf club. Flat parkland. 18 holes, 6035 yards, 5515 metres. S.S.S. 69. *Green Fees:* information not provided. *Eating facilities:* by prior arrangement. *Visitors:* welcome weekdays only. *Society Meetings:* catered for Wednesdays and Fridays only by arrangement. Professional: K. Theobald (01536 481014). Secretary: N. Sandell (Tel & Fax: 01536 511104).

MARKET HARBOROUGH near. **Stoke Albany Golf Club,** Ashley Road, Stoke Albany, Market Harborough LE16 8PL (01858 535208; Fax: 01858 535505). *Location:* A427, A14 five minutes away, Market Harborough 10 minutes. Undulating parkland. 18 holes, 6132 yards. S.S.S. 69. Practice area, putting green. *Green Fees:* weekdays £17.00; weekends £21.00 per round. *Eating facilities:* restaurant, bar and spike bar. *Visitors:* welcome, no restrictions. *Society Meetings:* all welcome, but booking is essential. Professional: Adrian Clifford. Secretary: R. Want.

NORTHAMPTON. Brampton Heath Golf Centre, Sandy Lane, Church Brampton, Northampton NN6 8AX (01604 843939; Fax: 01604 843885). *Location:* **signposted off A5099 five miles north of Northampton town centre. Undulating heathland course, very dry winter conditions. 18 holes, 6533 yards. S.S.S 71, par 72. 18 bay covered, floodlit driving range, PGA Short Course British Championships par 3 course.** *Green Fees:* **weekdays £16.00; weekends £20.00.** *Eating facilities:* **full facilities available from 7.30am.** *Visitors:* **welcome, no restrictions, advisable to book. Buggies and carts available all year round. Short course available - ideal for beginners. Golf superstore.** *Society Meetings:* **welcome seven days. Professional: Richard Hudson. Manager: David Coulson.**
website: www.bhgc.co.uk

NORTHAMPTON. **Cold Ashby Golf Club**, Stanford Road, Cold Ashby, Northampton NN6 6EP (Tel & Fax: 01604 740548). *Location:* midway between Rugby, Leicester and Northampton, close to Junction 1 A14 and Junction 18 M1. Undulating parkland. 27 holes, 6308 yards. S.S.S. 70. Good practice area. Driving range. *Green Fees:* midweek £16.00 per round, £25.00 per day; weekends £18.50 per round, £28.50 per day. *Eating facilities:* meals and bar snacks available daily. *Visitors:* welcome midweek anytime, weekends must reserve a starting time. *Society Meetings:* catered for weekdays and some weekends. Professional: Shane Rose (01604 740099; Fax: 01604 740548). Secretary: David Croxton. e-mail: coldashby.golfclub@virgin.net
website: www.coldashbygolfclub.com

NORTHAMPTON. **Collingtree Park Golf Course,** Windingbrook Lane, Northampton NN4 0XN (01604 700000; Fax: 01604 702600). *Location:* take Junction 15 off M1-A508 Northampton. 18 holes, 6692 yards. S.S.S. 72. 18th hole is an island green, set in parkland. Floodlit, covered 16 bay driving range, academy practice holes. *Green Fees:* information not available. *Eating facilities:* bar and restaurant. *Visitors:* welcome - advised to book in advance, members only before 12 noon at weekends. Handicap Certificates required. *Society Meetings:* welcome, advisable to book in advance; corporate golf packages available. Golf Academy which includes two par 4 and one par 3 practice holes, as well as 16 driving range bays. Hi-tech indoor teaching rooms also. The finest teaching facility for golf, special teaching programmes available. Professionals: Geoff Pook and Henry Bareham (01604 701202/ 700000). General Manager: Jamie Hammond (01604 700000). *

NORTHAMPTON. **Delapre Park Golf Club,** Eagle Drive, Nene Valley Way, Northampton NN4 7DU (01604 764036; Fax: 01604 706378). *Location:* two miles from Junction 15 (M1), A45 to Wellingborough (exit at Swallow Hotel). Parkland. Two courses - Main Course 18 holes, 6269 yards. S.S.S. 70. Hardingstone Course 9 holes, 2109 yards. S.S.S. 32. 40 bay driving range, two practice putting greens, pitch and putt course. *Green Fees:* weekdays 18 holes £12.50; weekends 18 holes £17.50. Par 3 weekdays £5.50; weekend £6.00. *Eating facilities:* public restaurant open 9am to 9.30pm daily, public bar open 11am onwards Monday to Saturday, Sundays 12 noon onwards. *Visitors:* welcome, advisable to book in advance for main 18 holes and Hardingstone 9 courses, Par 3 and Pitch and Putt no booking required. Club and trolley hire. *Society Meetings:* catered for - advance payment required. Professional/Secretary: John Corby (01604 763957 or 01604 764036; Fax: 01604 706378).

NORTHAMPTON. **Kingsthorpe Golf Club,** Kingsley Road, Northampton NN2 7BU (01604 711173). *Location:* off M1 and A43. Undulating parkland. 18 holes, 5918 yards. S.S.S. 69. *Green Fees:* (provisional) weekdays £25.00 per round/day; weekends £12.00 per round/day (must play with member). *Eating facilities:* full catering. *Visitors:* welcome weekdays, but must have a Certificate of Handicap. Weekends must be guest of member. *Society Meetings:* catered for by arrangement normally Thursdays and Fridays only; brochure available. Professional: Paul Armstrong (01604 719602). Secretary: John Harris (Tel & Fax: 01604 710610).
e-mail: secretary@kingsthorpe-golf.co.uk
website: www.kingsthorpe-golf.co.uk

NORTHAMPTON. **Northampton Golf Club,** Harlestone, Northampton NN7 4EF (01604 845102; Fax: 01604 820262). *Location:* on A428 north-west of Northampton in the village of Harlestone. Parkland with a lake coming into play 16th and 18th holes. 18 holes, 6615 yards. S.S.S. 72. Practice ground. *Green Fees:* £40.00 weekdays, weekends must play with a member. *Eating facilities:* restaurant and bar snacks.

Visitors: welcome weekdays but must have a Certificate of Handicap. *Society Meetings:* weekdays except Wednesdays. Inclusive packages available. Professional: Barry Randall (01604 845167). Secretary/Manager: Mr Sean Malherbe (01604 845155; Fax: 01604 820262).
e-mail: golf@northamptongolfclub.co.uk
website: www.northamptongolfclub.co.uk

NORTHAMPTON. **Northamptonshire County Golf Club,** Sandy Lane, Church Brampton, Northampton NN6 8AZ (01604 842951). *Location:* four miles north west of Northampton between A50 and A428. Heathland with woods, gorse and stream. 18 holes, 6505 yards, 5948 metres. S.S.S. 72. Practice ground, indoor net. *Green Fees:* information not available. *Eating facilities:* restaurant and bar. *Visitors:* by prior arrangement, must have Club Handicap. *Society Meetings:* catered for Wednesdays, small groups on Thursdays. Professional: T. Rouse (Tel & Fax: 01604 842226). Secretary: (01604 843025; Fax: 01604 843463).*

NORTHAMPTON. **Overstone Park Golf and Country Club,** Billing Lane, Northampton NN6 0AP (01604 647666; Fax: 01604 642635). *Location:* seven miles from Junction 15 M1 A508 merges with A45. Follow signs for Overstone from Billing turn off Undulating parkland with some water features. 18 holes, 6602 yards. S.S.S. 72. Practice ground. *Green Fees:* telephone for up to date prices. *Eating facilities:* bar, brasserie/restaurant and spike bar. *Visitors:* welcome seven days - must pre book at weekends. *Society Meetings:* welcome Monday to Friday, special packages available. Accommodation consisting 30 en suite rooms. Leisure Club. Professional: Brian Mudge (01604 643555). General Manager: Allan McLundie.

OUNDLE. **Oundle Golf Club,** Benefield Road, Oundle, Peterborough PE8 4EZ (01832 273267). *Location:* one mile from Oundle on Corby Road A447. Parkland course. Home of "The Oundle Putter".18 holes, 6265 yards. Par 72 S.S.S. 70. *Green Fees:* weekdays £18.50 per round, £25.50 per day; weekends £35.50 per round/day. *Eating facilities:* bar meals/restaurant. *Visitors:* welcome, check with Professional. *Society Meetings:* welcome by arrangement. Professional: R. Keys (01832 272273). Secretary: D Foley (Tel & Fax: 01832 273267).
e-mail: oundlegc@btopenworld.com
website: www.oundlegolfclub.com

RUSHDEN. **Rushden Golf Club,** Kimbolton Road, Chelveston, Wellingborough NN9 6AN (01933 418511). *Location:* on B645 two miles east of Higham Ferrers. Undulating meadowland. 10 holes, 6249 yards. S.S.S. 70. Small practice area. *Green Fees:* weekdays £18.00, weekends restricted. *Eating facilities:* bar and dining area - no catering Mondays. *Visitors:* welcome except Wednesday afternoons, weekends must play with member. *Society Meetings:* small societies catered for weekdays. Secretary: D.L. Waite (01933 418511).

TOWCESTER near. **Farthingstone Golf Club and Hotel**, Farthingstone, Near Towcester NN12 8NA (01327 361291; Fax: 01327 361645). *Location:* just a few minutes from Junction 16 of the M1, close to A5 and A45. Major towns within easy reach include Milton Keynes, Banbury, Oxford, Rugby and Northampton. Undulating wooded countryside. 18 holes, 6299 yards. S.S.S. 70 (Par). Practice area. *Green Fees:* information not available. *Eating facilities:* bar snacks and restaurant. *Visitors:* welcome, advance bookings available. Rental of golf buggies. Hotel, squash court. *Society Meetings:* bookings welcome. Professional: Luke Brockway (01327 361533). Secretary: Christian Donaldson.

WELLINGBOROUGH. **Wellingborough Golf Club**, Harrowden Hall, Great Harrowden, Wellingborough NN9 5AD (01933 678833; Fax: 01933 676134). *Location:* one mile out of Wellingborough on A509, turn right at crossroads by Great Harrowden Church. Undulating parkland. 18 holes, 6617 yards, 6039 metres. S.S.S. 72. Practice ground. *Green Fees:* £30.00 per round, £40.00 per day weekdays; weekends as member's guest only £20.00. *Eating facilities:* bar with casual lunch or dinner menu, restaurant. *Visitors:* weekdays only. Buggies available. *Society Meetings:* welcome by appointment. Conference facilities available. Professional: David Clifford (01933 678752). Secretary: Roy Tomlin (01933 677234; Fax: 01933 679379).

TOWCESTER near. **Whittlebury Park Golf and Country Club**, Whittlebury, Near Towcester NN12 8WP (01327 858092; Fax: 01327 858009). *Location:* 15 minutes from M1 and M40, from A43 on to A413 to Whittlebury. 4 championship 9 hole courses, each with its own distinctive character. Mature oak parkland with freshwater lakes and ancient copses. Large practice ground with 32 bay driving range. *Green Fees:* weekdays £20.00 per round, weekends and Bank Holidays £30.00 per round. Twilight rounds can be arranged with staff in the Pro Shop (01327 858588) for £10.00. *Eating facilities:* bar/bistro within clubhouse plus special function suites. *Visitors:* individual golfers, societies and corporate guests welcome seven days. Other sports and activities offered. *Society Meetings:* welcome seven days, by arrangement. Bookings: please contact Events Management team on (01327 858092).

Whittlebury Park Golf & Country Club

*36 Hole
Championship
Course
set in
Historic Parkland*

Towcester. **Whittlebury Park Golf & Country Club**: Whittlebury, Near Towcester NN12 8WP
Tel: 01327 858092   Fax: 01327 858009
Website: www.whittlebury.com   E-Mail: enquiries@whittlebury.com
Location: 15 minutes from M1 & M40 - From A43 on to A413 to Whittlebury

4 Championship 9 Hole Courses each with its own distinctive character, set in mature oak parkland
with freshwater lakes and ancient copses. Large practice ground with 32 Bay Driving Range.
Green fees: Weekends & Bank Holidays £30.00 per round. Weekdays £20.00 per round.
Twilight rounds at £10.00 can be arranged with the staff in the Pro-shop on 01327 858588
Eating facilities: Bar/Bistro within clubhouse plus special function suites.
Visitors: Individual golfers, Societies or Corporate guests welcome seven days.
Other sports and activities offered. Meeting facilities arranged.

Bookings & Membership enquiries: call 01327 858092

WELLINGBOROUGH
GOLF  CLUB

**Harrowden Hall, Great Harrowden
Wellingborough, Northamptonshire NN9 5AD**

TELEPHONE 01933 677234
FACSIMILE 01933 679379

*The house rebuilt in 1719, has been in recent years restored and is now home to Wellingborough
Golf Club, a private members club and one of the best in the country. Wellingborough Golf Club,
situated at Harrowden Hall in the heart of the English countryside, presents a magnificent golf
course with facilities for conferences, business meetings and private functions.
We cater for numbers from 4 to 80 at competitive inclusive rates.*

★ **All facilities within a short distance of the main motorway network.**
★ **Telephone and fax available.** ★ **Easy parking available.**
★ **Coffee on arrival.** ★ **Snack available throughout the day.** ★ **Full lunch and dinner menus daily.**

*Situated 2 miles from Wellingborough on the A509,
68 miles from London and 3 miles from A1/M1 link.*

– For further details contact: The Secretary/Manager on 01933 677234 –

See also Colour Advertisement on page 38

Northumberland

ALNMOUTH. **Alnmouth Golf Club Ltd**, Foxton Hall, Lesbury, Alnwick NE66 3BE (01665 830231). *Location:* four miles east of Alnwick. 18 holes, 6414 yards, 5855 metres. S.S.S. 71. *Green Fees:* £32.00 per person per day, Juniors £12.00 *Eating facilities:* diningroom and bars. *Visitors:* welcome Monday to Thursday and Sundays. Packages available. Handicap Certificate required. Dormy House accommodation available. *Society Meetings:* welcome Monday to Thursday and Sundays. Secretary: Peter Simpson (01665 830231; Fax: 01665 830922).

ALNMOUTH. **Alnmouth Village Golf Club**, Marine Road, Alnmouth (01665 830370; Fax: 01665 602096). *Location:* leave A1 from Alnwick to Alnmouth. Seaside links course. 9 holes, 6090 yards, 5572 metres. Par 71. S.S.S. 70. *Green Fees:* weekdays £15.00 per 18 holes; weekends and Bank Holidays £20.00 per 18 holes, weekly ticket £50.00. *Eating facilities:* available. *Visitors:* welcome, restrictions on club competition days. *Society Meetings:* must book in advance and only with official Golf Club Handicaps. Secretary: W. MacLean (01665 602096). e-mail: bill@billmaclean.fsnet.co.uk

ALNWICK. **Alnwick Golf Club,** Swansfield Park, Alnwick NE66 2AB (01665 602632). *Location:* signposted from the south A1 slip road. A friendly welcome awaits you at Alnwick Golf Club. Established in 1907, extended to 18 holes in 1995. Superb layout set in mature parkland, open grassland and gorse with panoramic views out to sea. 18 holes, 6250 yards. S.S.S. 70. *Green Fees:* information not available. *Eating facilities*: catering and bar facilities available most times. *Visitors:* welcome most times, part restrictions during competitions. Buggies available. Packages available, minimum four players. *Society Meetings:* welcome by prior arrangement with the Secretary. Secretary: Lawrie E. Stewart (01665 602499). * e-mail: mail@alnwickgolfclub.co.uk website: www.alnwickgolfclub.co.uk

BAMBURGH. **Bamburgh Castle Golf Club**, The Club House, Bamburgh NE69 7DE (01668 214378). *Location:* midway between Alnwick and Berwick upon Tweed on A1, take B1341 or B1342 to Bamburgh village. Seaside course with outstanding views of Farne Island, Holy Island and magnificent coastal area. 18 holes, 5621 yards, 5132 metres. S.S.S. 67. Practice area. *Green Fees:* weekdays £30.00 per round, £40.00 per day; weekends and Bank Holidays £35.00 per round, £45.00 per day. Five-day weekday ticket £95.00. Juniors £20.00. Restricted play at weekends. *Eating facilities:* bar snacks, lunch, high tea, beverages, etc. *Visitors:* welcome except on competitions days and Bank Holidays. Buggy hire. *Society Meetings:* welcome, by written application. Secretary: R.A. Patterson (01668 214321).

BEDLINGTON. **Bedlingtonshire Golf Club,** Acorn Bank, Bedlington NE22 6AA (01670 822457). *Location:* one mile south west of Bedlington on A1068. Parkland. 18 holes, 6813 yards, 6230 metres. S.S.S. 73. Practice ground and putting green. *Green Fees:* £18.00 per round midweek; £26.00 per round weekends and Bank Holidays. *Eating facilities:* catering, bar services, open all day. *Visitors:* welcome, but not before 9.00am weekdays and 10.00am weekends. *Society Meetings:* welcome, contact the Secretary. Professional: Marcus Webb (01670 822457). Secretary: (01670 822457).

BELFORD. **Belford Golf Club**, South Road, Belford NE70 7HY (01668 213433; Fax: 01668 213919). *Location:* turn off A1 at sign for Belford, first turning on right. Parkland. 9 holes, 6304 yards, 5768 metres. S.S.S. 70. Floodlit driving range. *Green Fees:* weekdays £15.00 per round, £18.00 per day; weekends and Bank Holidays £18.00 per round, £23.00 per day. *Eating facilities:* meals and bar seven days a week. *Visitors:* welcome anytime. Buggy hire available. *Society Meetings:* welcome. Secretary: A.M. Gilhome (01668 213433).

BELLINGHAM. **Bellingham Golf Club**, Boggle Hole, Bellingham, Hexham NE48 2DT (01434 220152). *Location:* 15 miles north of Hexham on B6320. Situated in the picturesque North Tyne Valley between Hadrian's Wall and the Scottish Border. Rolling parkland course with an abundance of natural hazards. 18 holes, 6077 yards, 5557 metres. S.S.S. 70. Driving range. *Green Fees:* weekdays £20.00; weekends and Bank Holidays £25.00. *Eating facilities:* full bar and catering available throughout the golf season. *Visitors:* welcome at all times, daily starting sheet, casual visitors advised to book in advance. Buggies for hire. *Society Meetings:* welcome by advance booking. Secretary: Peter Cordiner (01434 220152; Fax: 01434 220160).

BERWICK-UPON-TWEED. **Berwick-upon-Tweed (Goswick) Golf Club**, Goswick, Berwick-upon-Tweed TD15 2RW (01289 387256; Fax: 01289 387334). *Location:* signposted off A1, five miles south of Berwick-upon-Tweed. Seaside links, undulating fairways, elevated tees. 18 holes, 6686 yards. S.S.S. 72. Driving range, practice ground. *Green Fees:* weekdays £28.00 per round, £33.00 per day; weekends £33.00 per round, £43.00 per day. *Eating facilities:* full catering available. *Visitors:* welcome at all times, must book at weekends. Buggies and carts for hire. *Society Meetings:* welcome midweek and weekends. Professional: Paul Terras (01289 387380). Secretary: M.D. Rowell (01289 387256; Fax: 01289 387334). e-mail: goswickgc@btconnect.com website: www.goswicklinksgc.co.uk

NOTE

All the information regarding Golf Clubs in this guide is given in good faith in the belief that it is correct. However, the publishers cannot guarantee the facts given in these pages, neither are they responsible for changes in ownership or facilities, such as green fees, that may take place after the date of going to press. Readers should always satisfy themselves that the facilities they require are available and that the terms, if quoted, still apply.

BERWICK-UPON-TWEED. **Magdalene Fields Golf Club,** Magdalene Fields, Berwick-upon-Tweed TD15 1NE (01289 306384). *Location:* five minutes' walk from town centre and railway station. Seaside, parkland course with stunning scenic views. 18 holes, 6407 yards. S.S.S. 71. Practice area and putting area. *Green Fees:* weekdays £20.00 per round; weekends £22.00 per round. Reductions for Senior Citizens, Ladies, Juniors, parties. Fees subject to review. *Eating facilities:* bar and dining area - first class meals. *Visitors:* welcome Monday to Saturday, restrictions on Sundays. Member of Passport to Scenic Northumberland. *Society Meetings:* all welcome. Club Manager: M. Lynch (01289 306130). Secretary: M.J. Lynch (01289 306130). website: www.magdalene-fields.co.uk

BLYTH. **Blyth Golf Club Ltd,** New Delaval, Blyth NE24 9DB. *Location:* 12 miles north of Newcastle near the coast. Flat parkland, water hazards. 18 holes, 6430 yards. S.S.S. 71. Large practice area. *Green Fees:* £21.00 per round, £26.00 per day (with a member £11.00) weekdays; weekends £25.00 per round. Juniors £11.00 at all times. *Eating facilities:* bar and full catering. *Visitors:* welcome weekdays between 10am and 4pm. *Society Meetings:* welcome, packages available. Professional: Mr Andrew Brown (01670 356514). Manager: Mr Jim Wright (01670 540110).

CARLISLE. **Haltwhistle Golf Course**, Banktop, Greenhead, Via Carlisle CA6 7HN (016977 47367). *Location*: off the A69 at the village of Greenhead on Gilsland Road, two and a half miles west of Haltwhistle. Undulating parkland course with wooded areas. 18 holes, 5532 yards. S.S.S. 67. Practice area. *Green Fees*: information not available. *Eating facilties*: clubhouse bar, catering by prior arrangement. *Visitors*: welcome, no restrictions except Sundays 8am to 11am competition days. *Society Meetings*: welcome by prior arrangement. Secretary: Mr K.L. Dickinson (01434 320708).

EMBLETON. **Dunstanburgh Castle Golf Club,** Embleton NE66 3XQ (01665 576562). *Location:* seven miles off A1, to the north-east of Alnwick. Seaside links course in area of outstanding natural beauty. Designed by James Braid. 18 holes, 6298 yards. S.S.S. 70. *Green Fees:* weekdays £20.00 per day; weekends £24.00 per round, £29.00 per day. *Eating facilities:* snacks, lunches, high teas; bar. *Visitors:* welcome without reservation. Clubs for hire. *Society Meetings:* catered for. Secretary: P F. C. Gilbert.

HEXHAM. **Allendale Golf Club**, High Studdon, Allenheads Road, Allendale, Hexham NE47 9DH (01434 683926). *Location:* B6295 Allendale to Allenheads Road, 10 miles south of Hexham. Parkland course, hilly but not too severe. 9 holes, 16 tees. 4501 yards. S.S.S. 64. Driving net and putting green. *Green Fees:* £12.00. £2.00 reduction if playing with a member. Special rates after 5pm weekdays, and for visiting parties. *Eating facilities:* new clubhouse with licensed bar, catering by arrangement. *Visitors:* welcome anytime other than August Bank Holiday Monday before 3pm. *Society Meetings:* welcome, contact Secretary. Secretary: Dr T.S. Norton (01434 685051)

HEXHAM. **Hexham Golf Club**, Spital Park, Hexham NE46 3RZ (01434 603072; Fax: 01434 601865). *Location:* 20 miles west of Newcastle upon Tyne, one mile west of Hexham town centre. An undulating parkland course, one of the driest in the area, with superb views of the north and south Tyne valleys. 18 holes, 6000 yards. S.S.S. 68. *Green Fees:* weekdays £30.00 per round, £40.00 per day; weekends and Bank Holidays £40.00 per round only. Special packages available. *Eating facilities:* lunches and evening meals. *Visitors:* welcome without reservation. Preliminary booking advisable. *Society Meetings:* catered for Monday to Friday by arrangement. Professional: M.W. Forster (01434 604904). Secretary: Dawn Wylie (01434 603072; Fax: 01434 601865).

HEXHAM. **Tynedale Golf Club,** Tynegreen, Hexham NE46 3HQ (01434 608154). *Location:* off A69 towards Hexham over Tyne Bridge, first roundabout turn right - golf course at the end of road. Flat, parkland course along the banks of the river. 9 holes, 5403 yards. S.S.S. 67. *Green Fees:* 18 holes £12.00; 9 holes £8.00. *Eating facilities:* full catering available. *Visitors:* welcome, restricted Sunday mornings 11.30am members only. *Society Meetings:* welcome, discounts for parties over 10 people. Secretary: Trevor Hodge.

MATFEN. **Matfen Hall Golf Club**, Matfen, Newcastle-upon-Tyne NE20 0RH (01661 886400; Fax: 01661 886055). *Location:* 15 miles west of Newcastle, five miles north of Corbridge, off B6318 (Military Road). Lovely parkland setting directly in front of Matfen Hall, with natural and added water hazards. 18 holes, 6516 yards. S.S.S. 71. 9 hole, Par 3 course. Range-type practice ground. *Green Fees:* weekdays £30.00 per round, £40.00 per day; weekends £40.00 per round, £50.00 per day. *Eating facilities:* bar, dining room. *Visitors:* very welcome any day; after 11am weekends. Good locker room facilities. 'Stay and Play' packages available at Matfen Hall Country House Hotel. *Society Meetings:* very welcome. Professional: John Harrison; Golf Manager: David Burton.

MORPETH. **Burgham Park Golf and Leisure Club,** Near Felton, Morpeth NE65 8QP (01670 787898; Fax: 01670 787164). *Location:* seven miles north of Morpeth, one mile west of A1 on Longhorsley Road. 18 holes, 6751 yards, 6173 metres. S.S.S. 72. Practice area. *Green Fees:* on application. *Eating facilities:* catering and bar available daily. *Visitors:* welcome; special rates for parties by arrangement. Professional: Alan Hartley. Secretary: Jim Carr.

MORPETH. **Linden Hall**, Longhorsley, Morpeth NE65 8XF (01670 500011; Fax: 01670 500001). *Location:* A697 from A1, half a mile from Longhorsley. Mature woodland parkland and rolling countryside with many water features. 18 holes, 6846 yards. S.S.S. 73. Driving range, pitching green, putting green. *Green Fees:* weekdays £25.00, weekends £30.00. Handicap Certificate required. *Eating facilities:* Linden Tree (traditional country pub), Dobson Restaurant, function suites. *Visitors:* welcome, prior booking essential, packages available. *Society Meetings:* welcome, telephone for enquiries. Professional/Golf Manager: David Curry.

MORPETH. **Longhirst Hall Golf Course**, Longhirst, Morpeth NE61 3LL (Reservationa: 01670 791505; Fax: 01670 818309). *Location:* on A1 3 miles north from Morpeth take B1337 Hebron road. Parkland with water featuring on many holes. Two 18 hole courses from June 2003. Greens built to U.S.G.A. specifications. Astro Turf driving range. *Green Fees:* £20.00, twilight rate £10.00. Subject to change. *Eating facilities:* bar and restaurant. *Visitors:* welcome. *Society Meetings:* welcome. 75 bedroom hotel on site with sports village. Bar Manager: (01670 791505). Bookings Administrator: Ian Brodie.
e-mail: enquiries@longhirstgolf.co.uk
website: www.longhirstgolf.co.uk

MORPETH. **The Morpeth Golf Club Ltd.**, The Clubhouse, Morpeth NE61 2BT (01670 515675). *Location:* turn off A1 for Morpeth, A167 south side of town. Easy walking parkland. 18 holes, 6206 yards. S.S.S. 69. Practice area. *Green Fees:* weekdays £25.00 per round, £30.00 per day; weekends £30.00 per round, £40.00 per day. *Eating facilities:* restaurant/bar meals/snacks etc. *Visitors:* welcome, weekdays after 9.30am, Handicap Certificates may be asked for. Venue for 1997 County Strokeplay and 2000 County Matchplay Championships. *Society Meetings:* catered for weekdays by prior arrangement; discounts available for large parties. Professional: M.R. Jackson (01670 515675). Secretary: K.D. Cazaly (01670 504942; Fax: 01670 504918).

MORPETH. **Swarland Hall Golf Club**, Coast View, Swarland, Morpeth NE65 9JG (01670 787940). *Location:* approximately one mile west of A1 trunk road, eight miles south of Alnwick. Undulating parkland course within mature woodland. 18 holes, 6628 yards, 6060 metres. S.S.S. 72. *Green Fees:* information not available. *Eating facilities:* full dining facilities, bar meals, licensed bar. *Visitors:* welcome any day, but suggest telephoning to avoid club competitions on Sundays. *Society Meetings:* welcome. Golf Shop: (01670 787010). Secretary: Keith Rutter (01670 787010). *

See also Colour Advertisement on page 49

NEWBIGGIN-BY-THE-SEA. **Newbiggin-by-the-Sea Golf Club**, Clubhouse, Prospect Place, Newbiggin-by-the-Sea NE64 6DW (01670 817344; Fax: 01670 520236). *Location:* take signpost for Newbiggin off A189 (spine road from Tyne Tunnel). Clubhouse at most easterly point of village, adjacent to Church Point Caravan Park. Links course. 18 holes, 6452 yards, 5900 metres. S.S.S. 71. Practice area. *Green Fees:* information not available. *Eating facilities:* restaurant, bar and lounge. *Visitors:* welcome, not before 10am or on competition days. *Society Meetings:* catered for by prior arrangement with Secretary. Secretary: George Beattie (01670 817344).*

NEWCASTLE UPON TYNE. **Arcot Hall Golf Club Ltd,** Arcot Hall, Dudley, Cramlington NE23 7QP (0191-236 2794; 0191-217 0370). *Location:* seven miles north of Newcastle. Turn off A1 for Cramlington and then signposted. Flat, parkland – mostly tree lined. 18 holes, 6389 yards, 5840 metres. S.S.S. 70. Practice ground, chipping area, putting green. *Green Fees:* weekdays £26.00 (£21.00); weekends £30.00. *Eating facilities:* good restaurant, bar. *Visitors:* welcome, booking is essential due to popularity of the course. *Society Meetings:* catered for on application to Secretary. Professional: (0191-236 2794). Secretary: Frank Elliott (0191-236 2794).

NEWCASTLE UPON TYNE. **De Vere Slaley Hall Hotel, Golf Resort and Spa,** Hexham NE47 0BY (01434 673350; Fax: 01434 673152). *Location*: 20 miles west of Newcastle upon Tyne, seven miles south of Corbridge, signposted off A68. Set in parkland and moorland with an abundance of lakes and streams, woodland and heather. PGA European Tour Venue 2000. Hunting Course:- Championship Standard, home of the Compaq European Grand Prix: 18 holes, 7088 yards (5903 yards - ladies). S.S.S. 74, 72. Priestman Course: Championship Standard, 18 holes, 6951 yards (5755 yards - ladies). S.S.S 72, 73. Golf academy and driving Range. *Green Fees:* information not available. *Eating facilities:* clubhouse bar and restaurant; hotel bar and restaurant. *Visitors:* welcome, prior booking essential. 4 star hotel. Buggy hire. *Society Meetings:* welcome anytime, book through Golf Co-ordinator. Pro Shop (01434 673154) Manager: Mark Stancer (01434 673350; Fax: 01434 673152). *
e-mail: slaley@dircon.co.uk

NEWCASTLE UPON TYNE. **Ponteland Golf Club**, Bell Villas, Ponteland, Newcastle upon Tyne NE20 9BD (01661 822689). *Location:* A696, one and a half miles north of Newcastle Airport. Parkland. 18 holes, 6524 yards. S.S.S. 71. Large practice area. *Green Fees:* £25.00 per day or round (inclusive VAT). *Eating facilities:* full menu in restaurant and bar. *Visitors:* welcome Monday to Thursday, must be member's guest Friday, weekends and Bank Holidays. Handicap Certificate required. *Society Meetings:* Tuesdays or Thursdays, catered for with pre-booking agreed by Secretary/Manager. Professional: Alan Crosby (01661 822689). Secretary: J.N. Dobson (01661 822689). e-mail: secretary@thepontelandgolfclub.co.uk website: www.thepontelandgolfclub.co.uk

PRUDHOE. **Prudhoe Golf Club**, Eastwood Park, Prudhoe NE42 5DX (01661 832466; Fax: 01661 830710). *Location:* 10 miles west of Newcastle upon Tyne, off A695 to Hexham. Wooded parkland with scenic views of the Tyne Valley. 18 holes, 5839 yards. S.S.S. 69. Practice area. *Green Fees:* £20.00 weekdays; £25.00 weekends. £11.00 with a member, parties £18.00. *Eating facilities:* bar facilities and bar meals available. *Visitors:* welcome midweek and after 4pm weekends. *Society Meetings:* welcome. Professional: John Crawford (01661 836188). Secretary: I. Pauw (01661 835168).

ROTHBURY. **Rothbury Golf Club**, Old Race Course, Thopton Road, Rothbury, Morpeth NE65 7TR (01669 621271). *Location:* 15 miles north of Morpeth, take A697 turn off at Weldon Bridge for Rothbury. Flat course on Haugh alongside river. 9 holes, 5779 yards. S.S.S. 67. *Green Fees:* £13.00 per day weekdays, £18.00 per day weekends. *Eating facilities*: catering and bar facilities available (April to November). *Visitors:* welcome weekdays except Wednesday mornings and weekends by arrangement. *Society Meetings:* welcome by arrangement; discounts available. Secretary: D. Woolley (01669 630378).

SEAHOUSES. **Seahouses Golf Club**, Beadnell Road, Seahouses NE68 7XT (01665 720794; Fax: 01665 721994). *Location:* 15 miles north of Alnwick, turn off A1 for B1340. Flat seaside links with water hazards. 18 holes, 5542 yards. S.S.S. 67. Practice ground. *Green Fees:* weekdays £18.00 per round, £25.00 per day; weekends £25.00 per round, £30.00 per day. Juniors under 16 half rates. *Eating facilities:* full catering and bar. *Visitors:* welcome with no restrictions, please telephone clubhouse. *Society Meetings:* by arrangement. Secretary: John A. Gray (01665 720794/720056; Fax: 01665 721994). e-mail: secretary@seahousesgolf.co.uk website: www.seahousesgolf.co.uk

STOCKSFIELD. **Stocksfield Golf Club**, New Ridley, Stocksfield NE43 7RE (01661 843041; Fax: 01661 843046). *Location:* 15 miles west of Newcastle on A69, and three miles east of A68. Half woodland, half parkland, slight hillside. 18 holes, 5945 yards. S.S.S. 69. Small practice areas. *Green Fees:* weekdays £30.00 per round, £35.00 per day; weekends and Bank Holidays £35.00 per round. Reduced rates for parties of over 10 and 20. *Eating facilities:* available, also bar. 2-for-1 tickets accepted. *Visitors:* welcome except Wednesday mornings and not until 4.30pm Saturdays. Full size snooker table, Sky TV. Buggies, trolleys and clubs for hire. *Society Meetings:* catered for by prior arrangement. Professional: (01661 843041; Fax: 01661 843046). Secretary: B. Slade (01661 843041; Fax: 01661 843046).

TYNEMOUTH. **Tynemouth Golf Club Ltd**, Spital Dene, Tynemouth NE30 2ER (0191 257 4578). *Location:* on A695. 18 holes, 6359 yards. S.S.S. 70. *Green Fees:* £22.50 per round, £25.50 per day. *Eating facilities:* lunches and high teas served at club. *Visitors:* welcome Monday to Friday after 9.30am. Tuesday is Ladies Day. *Society Meetings:* welcome weekdays by prior arrangement. Professional: John McKenna. Secretary: T.J. Scott.

WARKWORTH. **Warkworth Golf Club,** The Links, Warkworth, Morpeth NE65 0SW (01665 711596). *Location:* off A1068 at Warkworth. Seaside links orginally designed by "Old Tom Morris" in 1891. 9 holes, 5986 yards, S.S.S. 69. Practice area. *Green Fees:* weekdays £12.00 per day, weekends £20.00 per day. Eating facilities: bar open 11.30am to 2.30pm and from 7.30pm to 11pm during season. *Visitors:* welcome except Tuesdays and Saturdays. *Society Meetings:* welcome by arrangement. Secretary: M. Rowe (01665 711596).

WOOLER. **Wooler Golf Club**, Dod Law, Doddington, Wooler NE71 6EA. *Location:* situated on the high ground named Dod Law to the east of the B6525 Wooler–Berwick road. The route is signposted from Doddington village. Hillside course with exceptional panoramic views. 9 holes (18 tees), 6411 yards. S.S.S. 71. Limited practice area. *Green Fees:* weekdays £15.00 per day, weekends and Bank Holidays £20.00 per day. *Eating facilities:* bar open evenings (operated voluntarily). *Visitors:* always welcome except during all day competitions, check with Secretary. Buggies available. *Society Meetings:* welcome by arrangement with Secretary. Secretary: S. Lowrey (01668 281631).

Nottinghamshire

BRAMCOTE. **Bramcote Hills Golf Course,** Thoresby Road, off Derby Road, Bramcote NG9 3EP (0115 928 1880). *Location:* A52 Nottingham to Derby road, close to Bramcote Leisure Centre, turn off A52 at Bramcote into Thoresby Road, half a mile on left hand side. Mainly flat parkland but some slightly hilly areas. 18 holes, 1500 yards. Par 3. *Green Fees:* weekdays £6.50 per round; weekends £7.00; £5.50 Senior Citizens, students and Juniors. *Eating facilities:* refreshments available. *Visitors:* always welcome anytime, pay and play course. *Society Meetings:* welcome.
website: www.bramcotehillsgolf.com

BULWELL. **Bulwell Forest Golf Club,** Hucknall Road, Bulwell NG6 9LQ (0115 977 0576) *Location:* A610 north of Nottingham, M1 Junction 26, three miles from course. Heathland or links type course, very tight. 18 holes, 5616 yards. S.S.S. 67. *Green Fees:* £12.50 per round weekdays; £15.50 per round weekends. Visitors 4 ball £44.00. *Eating facilities:* bar snacks available, societies or parties catered to order. *Visitors:* welcome weekdays except Tuesdays mornings (Ladies' Day) and limited times weekends. Flat green bowls, hard tennis court and children's play ground all on site. *Society Meetings:* catered for, but book well in advance. Professional: Roy Truman (Tel & Fax: 0115 976 3172). Secretary: D. Waddilove (home: 0115 960 8435).

CALVERTON. **Ramsdale Park Golf Centre,** The Clubhouse, Oxton Road, Calverton NG14 6NU (0115 9655600; Fax: 0115 9654105). *Location:* course alongside B6386 between Calverton and Oxton north east of Nottingham. Flat first 9 holes then undulating back 9. Two courses: High Course: 18 holes, 6546 yards, 5985 metres, S.S.S. 71. Low Course: 18 holes, 2844 yards, S.S.S. 54. 25 bay floodlit driving range, new video teaching bay. *Green Fees:* weekdays High Course £17.50, Low Course £8.90; weekends

High Course £22.00, Low Course £9.50. *Eating facilities:* bar food always available, also large dining room. *Visitors:* welcome, pay as you play; small membership. No Handicap required. Advance booking for High Course. Extensive golf shop specialising in ladieswear. *Society Meetings:* welcome. Professional: Robert Macey. Secretary: Nick Birch.

CALVERTON. **Springwater Golf Club,** Moor Lane, Calverton, Nottingham NG14 6FZ (0115 965 4946). *Location:* A614 Calverton turn off, head for village, golf club is located at the other end of village. Hillside course set in an orchard with new and mature trees, four ponds, well drained. 9 holes, 6406 yards. S.S.S. 71. Extended to 18 holes, opened Spring 1998. Floodlit driving range. *Green Fees:* information not provided. *Eating facilities:* fully licensed, bar food, and function rooms available every day. *Visitors:* welcome, weekdays and weekends off peak, five day booking in advance for non-members. Dress code in operation. *Society Meetings:* weekdays and off peak weekends. Professional: Mr Paul Drew (0115 965 2129). Secretary: Bill Turner (0115 965 2565). *

EAST LEAKE. **Rushcliffe Golf Club,** Stocking Lane, East Leake, Near Loughborough LE12 5RL (01509 852209). *Location:* on A60 signposted eight miles south of Nottingham. Wooded hills on edge of the Wolds. 18 holes, 6013 yards, 5800 metres. S.S.S. 70. Practice ground. *Green Fees:* weekdays £25.00; weekends £30.00. *Eating facilities:* full catering except Mondays when bar snacks only. *Visitors:* welcome with reservation, weekends without a member between 9.30am to 11am and 3pm to 4.30pm. *Society Meetings:* catered for Mondays, Wednesdays, Thursdays and Fridays strictly by prior booking. Professional: Chris Hall (01509 852701). Secretary: K.W. Hodkinson (01509 852959).

Ramsdale Park Golf Centre

Oxton Road, Calverton Nottingham NG14 6NU

A 'BURHILL GOLF CENTRES Ltd' course.
6500yd High Course. A fairly flat front nine is followed by an undulating back nine that has the reputation of being one of the best nine holes in the area.
2800yd Low Course. An outstanding par 3 course designed to sharpen and improve a player's short game. Enables societies the opportunity to play two courses in one day.
Covered 23 bay floodlit driving range with video bay. Modern clubhouse includes well stocked shop. Society and company days a speciality.
Tel: 0115 965 5600   Fax: 0115 965 4105   View the course on: www.ramsdaleparkgc.co.uk

EDWALTON. **Edwalton Municipal Golf and Social Club**, Wellin Lane, Edwalton NG12 4AH (0115 923 4775). *Location:* follow Nottingham ring road, course signposted from island on ring road. Gently sloping parkland. 9 holes, 3342 yards. S.S.S. 72. Also 9 hole par 3 course. Large practice ground. *Green Fees:* prices on application. *Eating facilities:* first class catering, bar open all day. *Visitors:* welcome anytime except club competitions (contact Professional for dates). Professional: J.A. Staples (0115 923 4775). Secretary: Mrs D.J. Parkes (0115 914 8978).*

HUCKNALL. **Leen Valley Golf Centre**, Wigwam Lane, Hucknall, Nottingham NG15 7TA (0115 9642037; Fax: 0115 9642724). *Location:* 300 yards from Hucknall Railway Station (signposted). Parkland course. 18 holes, 6521 yards. S.S.S. 70. 9 hole, Par 3 course and putting green. *Green Fees:* weekdays £10.00, weekends £15.00. *Eating facilities:* "Swan" bar and restaurant. *Visitors:* always welcome. Handicap certificates not required. *Society Meetings:* always welcome. Professional: John Lines. Manager: Bernard Goodman.

KIRKBY-IN-ASHFIELD. **Notts. Golf Club Ltd,** Hollinwell, Kirkby-in-Ashfield, Nottingham NG17 7QR (01623 753225; Fax: 01623 753655). *Location:* three miles from Exit 27 on M1, turn off M1 then left on A611. Testing heathland championship course. 18 holes, 7098 yards. S.S.S. 75. *Green Fees:* on application. *Visitors:* welcome on production of Handicap Certificate (weekends and Bank Holidays on application only). Advisable to book beforehand. *Society Meetings:* welcome weekdays. Professional: Alasdair Thomas. Secretary: Brian Noble.

LENTON LANE. **Riverside Golf Centre**, Trentside, Lenton Lane NG7 2SA. *Location:* A52 Nottingham to Grantham, two miles from Nottingham city centre, near Clifton Bridge. Flat course, easy to walk. 9 holes, 2000 yards. S.S.S. 31. New Par 3, 9 hole course opening in Spring 2003. *Green Fees:* information not available. *Eating facilities:* licensed restaurant/bar. Excellent facilities. *Visitors:* welcome all week. Pay and play course, booking required. *Society Meetings:* very welcome. Professionals: Neil Thacker, Russell Meek (0115 9862179; Fax: 01159 865989). Secretary: G. Meek (0115 9862220; Fax: 01159 865989).*

LONG EATON. **Trent Lock Golf Centre**, Lock Lane, Sawley, Long Eaton, Nottingham NG10 2FY (0115 9464398; Fax: 0115 9461183). *Location:* Sawley/Long Eaton, two miles from M1 Junctions 24 and 25. Set in rural countryside with six lakes and River Trent. 18 holes, 6000 yards, Par 69. 9 hole Pay and Play, 2990 yards, Par 36. 23 bay floodlit driving range.

Green Fees: weekdays £15.00; weekends £17.50. 9 hole course £6.00 per round midweek, £7.50 weekends. *Eating facilities:* à la carte restaurant (0115 9461184), bar food, 200 seater function room. *Visitors:* welcome anytime. *Society Meetings:* all welcome. Professional: Mark Taylor. Director of Golf: E.W. McCausland (0115 9464398).

MANSFIELD. **Coxmoor Golf Club,** Coxmoor Road, Sutton in Ashfield, Mansfield NG17 5LF (01623 559878). *Location:* exit Junction 27 M1, A611 for three miles. Testing heathland championship course. 18 holes, 6589 yards. S.S.S. 72. Practice area and nets. *Green Fees:* weekdays £40.00 per round, £50.00 per day. Golf/food packages available. *Eating facilities:* restaurant and bars. *Visitors:* welcome except weekends and Bank Holidays, pre-book through Professional. (Tuesday Ladies' Day). *Society Meetings:* catered for by prior application to Secretary. Professional: David Ridley (01623 559906). Secretary: P. Snow (01623 557359).
e-mail: coxmoor@freeuk.com
website: www.coxmoor.freeuk.com

MANSFIELD. **Mansfield Woodhouse Golf Club,** Leeming Lane North, Mansfield Woodhouse NG19 9EU (01623 23521). *Location:* Junction 27 of M1, A60 Mansfield – Warsop. Flat parkland. 9 holes, 2446 yards. S.S.S. 64. *Green Fees:* information not available. *Eating facilities:* bar snacks. *Visitors:* welcome, unrestricted – pay and play. Professional: L. Highfield Jnr. (01623 23521). Manager/Secretary: S.L. Highfield (01623 623521). *

MANSFIELD. **Sherwood Forest Golf Club,** Eakring Road, Mansfield NG18 3EW (01623 623327). *Location:* leave M1 at Exit 27, take signs for Mansfield, proceed via Southwell Road and Oak Tree Lane - course is located one mile east on Eakring Road. Traditional heathland course with an abundance of heather, pines and silver birch. 18 holes, 6849 yards. S.S.S. 74. Two practice grounds. *Green Fees:* on application. *Eating facilities:* gent's bar with snooker table, mixed lounge and dining room; full catering service every day. *Visitors:* welcome by arrangement and must be member of a recognised golf club with a Handicap. *Society Meetings:* catered for by arrangement. Professional/ Golf Manager: K. Hall (01623 627403; Fax: 01623 420412).
e-mail: sherwood@forest43.freeserve.co.uk

Please mention
'THE GOLF GUIDE'
when enquiring about
clubs or accommodation.

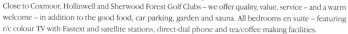

MAPPERLEY. **Mapperley Golf Club,** Central Avenue, Plains Road, Mapperley NG3 5RH (0115 9556672). *Location:* B684, four miles north east of centre of Nottingham. Hilly picturesque course. 18 holes, 6303 yards. S.S.S. 70. Practice ground. *Green Fees:* weekdays £17.00 per round, £22.00 per day; weekends £22.00 per round, £28.00 per day. Weekdays only 4 ball £60.00, 3 ball £45.00 per round. *Eating facilities:* bar and food all day. *Visitors:* welcome except Saturdays and Ladies' Day (Tuesdays). *Society Meetings:* catered for, please ring professional for price. Professional: Jasen Barker (0115 9556673). Secretary: Alan Newton (0115 9556672).

NEWARK. **Newark Golf Club,** Coddington, Newark NG24 2QX (01636 626241; Fax: 01636 626497). *Location:* off the A17 Sleaford road four miles east of Newark. Parkland, wooded course. 18 holes, 6444 yards. S.S.S. 71. Practice ground. *Green Fees:* £24.00 weekdays; weekends £30.00. *Eating facilities:* full catering, bar all day. *Visitors:* welcome with reservation. Handicap Certificates will be required. Restriction at peak times Saturday and Sunday, Ladies' Day Tuesday. Snooker. Professional tuition and computer/video analysis. *Society Meetings:* welcome except Tuesdays, weekends. Professional: P. Lockley (01636 626492). Secretary: D.A. Collingwood (01636 626282).

NOTTINGHAM. **Beeston Fields Golf Club,** Old Drive, Wollaton Road, Beeston NG9 3DD (0115 925 7062). *Location:* Wollaton road off A52 Derby road, M1, Exit 25. Parkland. 18 holes, 6414 yards. S.S.S. 71. Practice ground and net available. *Green Fees:* weekdays £28.00, weekends £35.00. Eating facilities: available daily. *Visitors:* welcome with reservation, Tuesday not until 2.30pm. *Society Meetings:* catered for Mondays and Wednesdays. Professional: Alun Wardle (0115 925 7062). Secretary: J. Lewis (0115 925 7062).

NOTTINGHAM. **Chilwell Manor Golf Club**, Meadow Lane, Chilwell, Nottingham NG9 5AE (0115 925 8958; Fax: 0115 922 0575). *Location:* four miles from Nottingham on main Nottingham to Birmingham road. Flat parkland course. 18 holes, 6379 yards. S.S.S. 70. *Green Fees:* weekdays £20.00; weekends £20.00. *Eating facilities:* available. *Visitors:* welcome weekdays with reservation, restricted at certain busy times. *Society Meetings:* societies catered for by appointment (minimum 16). Professional: P. Wilson. Hon. Secretary: R.A. Westcott.
e-mail: chilwellmanorgolfclub@barbox.net

NOTTINGHAM. **Cotgrave Place Golf and Country Club**, Stragglethorpe, Nottingham NG12 3HB (0115 9333344; Fax: 0115 9334567). *Location:* two minutes east of Nottingham on the A52 towards Radcliffe-on-Trent, 20 miles from M1. Lakeside and parkland course. Two courses: Open Course 18 holes, 6290 yards; Master Course 18 holes, 5933 yards. 10 bay floodlit driving range, practice net, short game area, putting green. *Green Fees:* weekdays £22.00/£21.00; weekends £25.00. *Eating facilities:* restaurant and snack bar. *Visitors:* welcome

at all times, subject to reservation. Conference facilities for up to 200 people. *Society Meetings:* welcome, please telephone for packages. Professional: Robert Smith. Secretary: Mike Evans. e-mail: cotgrave@americangolf.com

NOTTINGHAM. **Nottingham City Golf Club,** Lawton Drive, Bulwell, Nottingham NG6 8BL (0115 927 8021). *Location:* exit 26 M1, at first roundabout follow signs for Bulwell. Parkland. 18 holes, 6218 yards. S.S.S. 70. Practice area. *Green Fees:* £10.00. *Eating facilities:* available. *Visitors:* welcome anytime except Saturdays. *Society Meetings:* welcome by prior arrangement. Professional: C. Jepson (0115 927 2767). Secretary: David Buxton (Tel & Fax: 0115 927 6916).

NOTTINGHAM. **Oakmere Park Golf Club,** Oaks Lane, Oxton, Near Southwell NG25 0RH (0115 965 3545; Fax: 0115 965 5628). *Location:* eight miles north east of Nottingham on A614. Parkland course. Admirals Course: 18 holes, 6612 yards, S.S.S. 72. Commanders Course: 9 holes, 6573 yards. S.S.S. 72. 20 bay floodlit driving range. *Green Fees:* Admirals Course: weekdays £20.00; weekends £26.00. Special rates for High Season (April - September) and reduced rates for twilight. Commanders Course: weekdays 9 holes £6.00; 18 holes £10.00; weekends 9 holes £8.00, 18 holes £14.00. *Eating facilities:* clubhouse bar, spike bar, restaurant and resident chef. *Visitors:* welcome at all times, phone to book. *Society Meetings:* welcome, weekends after 2.00pm require maximum notice possible. Professional/ Director of Golf: Daryl St. John Jones.

NOTTINGHAM. **Ruddington Grange Golf Club**, Wilford Road, Ruddington, Nottingham NG11 6NB (0115 9214139). *Location:* M1 Junction 24 Nottingham road, A52 to Nottingham Knight island, right to Ruddington, half a mile outside Ruddington. Parkland. 18 holes, 6543 yards, 5984 metres. S.S.S. 72. *Green Fees:* information not available. *Eating facilities:* full restaurant. *Visitors:* welcome all the time but at weekends members have priority. Tee times must be booked, *Society Meetings:* welcome Monday to Friday. Professional: R. Simpson (0115 9211951). Secretary: A. Johnson.* e-mail: info@ruddingtongrange.com website: www.ruddingtongrange.com

NOTTINGHAM. **Wollaton Park Golf Club,** Lime Tree Avenue, Wollaton Park, Nottingham NG8 1BT (0115 978 7574; Fax: 0115 970 0736). *Location:* entrance off slip road from A52 Derby Road at junction A614 Nottingham Ringroad. Traditional parkland course with many mature trees; two deer herds roam the course. 18 holes, 6445 yards. S.S.S. 71. Two practice areas and pitch and putt course. *Green Fees:* weekdays £30.00/£42.00; weekends £35.00/£48.00. Special rates on application for visiting societies. *Eating facilities:* full restaurant and snack bar. *Visitors:* welcome at all times except Wednesday which is Ladies' Day. *Society Meetings:* catered for Tuesdays and Fridays. Professional: John Lower (0115 978 4834). Secretary: Michael Harvey (0115 978 7574). e-mail: wollatonparkgc@aol.com

RADCLIFFE-ON-TRENT. **Radcliffe-on-Trent Golf Club,** Dewberry Lane, Cropwell Road, Radcliffe-on-Trent NG12 2JH (0115 9333000). *Location:* A52 from Nottingham turn right at traffic lights on Cropwell Road; 400 yards along on left hand side. Flat, wooded parkland. 18 holes, 6423 yards. S.S.S. 71. Two large practice areas. *Green Fees:* weekdays £24.00 per day, weekends £30.00 per day (reductions for members' guests). *Eating facilities:* snacks, meals and bar. *Visitors:* welcome, confirm course availability with Professional or Secretary. *Society Meetings:* catered for on Wednesdays. Professional: Craig George (Telephone & Fax: 0115 9332396). Secretary: Les Wake (0115 9333000; Fax: 0115 9116991).
e-mail: les.rotgc@talk21.com
website: www.radcliffeontrentgc.com

RETFORD. **Retford Golf Club Ltd,** Brecks Road, Ordsall, Retford DN22 7UA (01777 711188). *Location:* one mile south off A620 midway between Worksop and Gainsborough. Wooded parkland. 18 holes, 6409 yards. S.S.S. 72, Par 72. Practice ground. *Green Fees:* information not provided. *Eating facilities:* meals available and licensed bar. *Visitors:* welcome, except Tuesday mornings. *Society Meetings:* welcome by prior arrangement. Professional: C. Morris (01777 703733). Secretary/Manager: Mrs Linda Colclough (01777 711188; Fax: 01777 710412).
e-mail: retfordgolfclub@lineone.net

RUFFORD. **Rufford Park Golf & Country Club,** Rufford Lane, Rufford, Newark NG18 4SY (01623 825253; Fax: 01623 825254). *Location:* 400 yards off A614, two miles south of Ollerton roundabout. Map available on request. Scenic parkland course. 18 holes, 6173 yards. S.S.S. 69. 16-bay floodlit driving range, practice facilities. *Green Fees:* weekdays £16.00 winter, £18.00 summer; weekends £20.00. Day ticket £20.00. *Eating facilities:* clubhouse and restaurant with spectacular views. Large function suite and meeting rooms for up to 200 people. *Visitors:* always welcome; buggies for hire. *Society Meetings:* corporate hospitality and society days catered for. *Professionals:* James Thompson and John Vaughan. Secretary: Kay Whitehead.
website: www.ruffordpark.co.uk

SOUTHWELL. **Norwood Park Golf Course Ltd,** Norwood Park, Southwell NG25 0PF (01636 816626). *Location:* half-a-mile west of Southwell, off the road to Kirklington. American style layout in beautiful grounds of stately home. Natural water features and large undulating greens. 18-acre practice ground. 18 holes, 6805 yards from the back tees. Par 72. *Green Fees:* £17.00 weekdays, £24.00 weekends and Bank Holidays. Prices subject to change. *Eating facilities:* available. *Visitors:* welcome. *Society Meetings:* welcome. Professional: Paul Thornton. Secretary: Ron Beckett.
e-mail: norwoodgolf@mail.com

SOUTHWELL. **Southwell Golf Club**, Southwell Racecourse, Rolleston, Newark NG25 0TS (01636 816501/813706). Flat parkland course with water features. 18 holes, 5770 yards, S.S.S. 68. Driving nets, pitching, putting green, practice area. *Green Fees*: weekdays £15.00, with member £10.00; weekends £18.00, with member £10.00. *Eating facilities*: full service all day. *Visitors*: welcome, please book in advance. 12 bedroomed Motel on site. Professional: Stephen Meade (01636 813706). Secretary: Mike Harness (01636 821651). e-mail: misylharness@btinternet.com

STANTON-ON-THE-WOLDS. **Stanton-on-the-Wolds Golf Club**, Golf Road, Stanton-on-the-Wolds NG12 5BH (0115 937 4885). *Location:* seven miles south of Nottingham, one mile west of main Nottingham - Melton road. Meadow land. 18 holes, 6437 yards, 5886 metres. S.S.S. 71. Practice ground. *Green Fees:* information not available. *Eating facilities:* restaurant and bar. *Visitors:* welcome by prior arrangement with Secretary, weekends with member only. *Society Meetings:* catered for by arrangement with Secretary. Professional: Nick Hernon (0115 937 2390). Secretary: A.R. Evans (0115 937 4885).*

WORKSOP. **Bondhay Golf Club**, Bondhay Lane, Whitwell, Worksop S80 3EH (01909 723608 Fax: 01909 720226. *Location:* from Junction 30 M1, A619 signposted after three-and-a-half miles. Turn left onto Bondhay lane. Flat with bordering woodland. 18 holes, 6839 yards. S.S.S.72. Par 3 family course, floodlit driving range, putting green, buggies for hire. *Green Fees:* information not provided. *Eating facilities:* full catering service available. *Visitors:* welcome. *Society Meetings:* welcome, phone for brochure. Assistant Professional: M. Ramsden. Director: Helen Hardisty.

WORKSOP. **College Pines Golf Club**, Worksop College Drive, Worksop S80 3AP (Clubhouse 01909 488785; Pro Shop: 01909 501431; Fax: 01909 481227). *Location:* situated on outskirts of town on B6034, Edwinstowe road adjacent to Worksop College. Heathland course surrounded by woodland; very well drained, with Winter play a speciality. 18 holes, 6801 yards. S.S.S. 73. Driving range and short game practice area. *Green Fees:* weekdays £13.00 per round, £8.00 with a member; weekends £18.00, £11.00 with a member. Discounts for parties of 20 plus. Subject to review. *Eating facilities:* full facilities. *Visitors:* welcome by appointment; phone for starting times. *Society Meetings:* welcome by appointment. Golf Director/ Professional: Charles Snell (01909 501431).

WORKSOP. **Kilton Forest Golf Club**, Blyth Road, Worksop S81 0TL (01909 479199). *Location:* main Worksop to Blyth road, right hand side. Undulating parkland. 18 holes, 6424 yards. S.S.S. 71, Par 72. Practice and putting areas. *Green Fees:* weekdays £9.50; weekends £12.50. Reduction with Bassetlaw District Council leisure pass. *Eating facilities:* bar meals and restaurant area. *Visitors:* welcome, club competitions most Sundays – check with Professional. *Society Meetings:* by arrangement with Professional. Professional: Stuart Betteridge (01909 486563). Secretary: Alan Mansbridge (01909 486269).

WORKSOP. **Lindrick Golf Club**, Lindrick Common, Worksop S81 8BH (01909 485802). *Location:* on A57 four miles west of Worksop. M1 Junction 31 on to A57 Worksop. Heathland. 18 holes, 6612 yards, 6046 metres. S.S.S. 71. Two practice areas. *Green Fees:* £50.00 per round, £55.00 per day; winter (1 Dec–31 Mar) £35.00 per day. *Eating facilities:* dining room. *Visitors:* welcome weekdays, except Tuesday mornings. Prior booking required. *Society Meetings:* catered for weekdays. Professional: John King (01909 475820). Secretary: John Armitage (01909 475282; Fax: 01909 488685). website: www.lindrickgolf.com

WORKSOP. **Worksop Golf Club**, Windmill Lane, Worksop S80 2SQ (01909 477731; Fax: 01909 477732). *Location:* just off Worksop bypass (A57), take B6034 Edwinstowe immediately left; clubhouse 400 yards. Heathland with gorse, broom, birch and oak; easy walking. 18 holes, 6660 yards. S.S.S. 73. Practice ground. *Green Fees:* weekdays £32.00, per day £40.00; weekends £40.00 (18 holes only). *Eating facilities:* dining room and bar. *Visitors:* welcome, except weekends November to March without member. Advise preliminary phone call to Professional. Snooker table. *Society Meetings:* weekdays only by arrangement with Professional. Not Bank Holidays. Professional: C. Weatherhead (01909 477732). Secretary: D.A. Dufall 01909 477731; Fax: 01909 477732).

Please mention
'THE GOLF GUIDE'
when enquiring about
clubs or accommodation.

Oxfordshire

ABINGDON. **Frilford Heath Golf Club**, Abingdon OX13 5NW (01865 390864; Fax: 01865 390823). *Location:* on A338 Oxford/Wantage Road seven miles south-west of Oxford, four miles west of Abingdon. Flat, wooded heathland. Red course: 18 holes, 6617 yards yellow tees, 6884 white tees. S.S.S. 71/73; Green course: 18 holes, 5763 yards yellow tees, 6006 white tees. S.S.S. 69; Blue course: 18 holes, 6379 yards yellow tees, 6728 white tees. S.S.S 71/72. Three practice areas. *Green Fees:* weekdays £50.00; weekends and Bank Holidays £65.00; after 5pm £30.00 all week. *Eating facilities:* first class restaurant and bars. *Visitors:* welcome weekdays with Handicap Certificate, phone ahead for weekends and Bank Holidays. *Society Meetings:* welcome weekdays, enquire at office. Professional: D.C. Craik (01865 390887). Secretary/Manager: S. Styles (01865 390864).
e-mail: reservations@frilfordheath.co.uk

BANBURY. **Banbury Golf Centre**, Aynho Road, Adderbury, Banbury OX17 3NT (01295 810419; Fax: 01295 810056). *Location*: 6 miles south of Banbury on B4100. M40 junction 10 or 11. Undulating wooded course with water features. Three 9 hole courses, can be played in various combinations. Red & Yellow Course, 18 holes, 6553 yards, S.S.S. 71. Yellow & Blue Course, 6599 yards, S.S.S. 71. Red & Blue course, 6706 yards, S.S.S. 72. *Green Fees:* approximately £17.00 midweek, £23.00 weekends and Bank Holidays. *Eating facilities:* bar menu and 3 course meals available. *Visitors:* welcome at all times. Tuition available. *Society Meetings:* welcome at all times. Professional: Stuart Kier (01295 812880; Fax: 01295 810056). Secretary: M.A. Reed.
e-mail: office@banburygolfcentre.co.uk
website: www.banburygolfcentre.co.uk

BANBURY. **Cherwell Edge Golf Club,** c/o Cherwell Edge Course, Chacombe, Banbury OX17 2EN (01295 711591). *Location:* half-a-mile off M40 at Banbury. Parkland. 18 holes, 5947 yards. S.S.S. 68 men, 69 ladies. Practice area. *Green Fees:* information not available. *Eating facilities:* restaurant and bar. *Visitors:* welcome, some time restrictions. *Society Meetings:* welcome, some time restrictions. Professional: Jason Newman (01295 711591). Secretary: Mr R.A. Beare (01295 275679 home).*

BANBURY. **Rye Hill Golf Course**, Milcombe, Banbury OX15 4RU (01295 721818; Fax: 01295 720089). *Location:* six miles from Junction 11 M40 at Banbury, turn off A361 and follow signs through to Milcombe. Naturally free draining course. 18 holes, 6919 yards. S.S.S 73. Practice ground, three teaching academy holes. *Green Fees:* weekdays £17.00, weekends £22.00. 9-hole rates. *Eating facilities:* spike bar and restaurant. *Visitors:* welcome, no restrictions. Booking advisable at weekends. Trolleys can always be used. *Society Meetings:* welcome; various packages available. Professional: T. Pennock.

BANBURY. **Tadmarton Heath Golf Club**, Wigginton, Banbury OX15 5HL (01608 737278; Fax: 01608 730548). *Location:* off M40 Junction 11, off A41, off B4035, five miles west of Banbury. Flat lying; heathland. 18 holes, 5917 yards. S.S.S. 69. Practice area. *Green Fees:* weekdays Winter £30.00, Summer £40.00; weekends £25.00 with a member only. *Eating facilities:* full catering and bars. *Visitors:* welcome weekdays (restrictions Thursdays); weekends with member only. Must be member of another golf club with Handicap Certificate. Hand carts available. *Society Meetings:* welcome weekdays by prior arrangement. Professional: Tom Jones (01608 730047). Secretary: J. R. Cox (01608 737278; Fax: 01608 730548).

BICESTER. **Bicester Golf & Country Club**, Chesterton, Near Bicester OX6 8TE (01869 241204). *Location:* five minutes from Junction 9 M40, one mile off A421, Bicester/Oxford. Two miles south-west of Bicester. Flat parkland course. 18 holes, 6013 yards. S.S.S. 70. Practice ground and putting green. *Green Fees:* Monday to Friday 18 holes £20.00, weekends 18 holes £27.50 before 1pm, £22.50 after 1pm. *Eating facilities:* restaurant and bar meals available daily. *Visitors:* welcome at all times, telephone bookings up to four days ahead. *Society Meetings:* welcome by prior arrangement. Professional: Julian Goodman (01869 242023). Manager: Paul Fox(01869 241204).

BURFORD. **Burford Golf Club**, Burford OX18 4JG (01993 822149). *Location:* A40 - Burford roundabout. Flat parkland with superb greens. 18 holes, 6432 yards. S.S.S. 71. *Green Fees:* £36.00 per day weekdays. *Eating facilities:* full catering. *Visitors:* welcome weekdays by arrangement with the Secretary. *Society Meetings:* catered for on application. Professional: Michael Ridge (01993 822344). Secretary: Robinn Thompson (01993 822583; Fax: 01993 822801).

CHIPPING NORTON. **Chipping Norton Golf Club**, Southcombe, Chipping Norton OX7 5QH (01608 642383; Fax: 01608 645422). *Location:* Junction of A3400 and A44, 18 miles from Oxford, 20 miles from Stratford-on-Avon. Downland with lakes and trees and four Par 3's. 18 holes, 6280 yards, 5743 metres. S.S.S. 70. Practice ground and putting green. *Green Fees:* £32.00 per day. *Eating facilities:* diningroom and bars – new clubhouse. *Visitors:* welcome Monday to Friday but not Bank Holidays. *Society Meetings:* welcome Mondays to Fridays by arrangement. Professional: Neil Rowlands (01608 643356; Fax: 01608 645422). Secretary: Simon Chislett (01608 642383; Fax: 01608 645422).

visit the FHG golf website on
www.uk-golfguide.com

CHIPPING NORTON. **The Wychwood Golf Club,** Lyneham, Chipping Norton OX7 6QQ (01993 831841; Fax: 01993 831775). *Location:* six miles from Burford off the A361 Burford to Chipping Norton Road. Parkland, several interesting water holes. 18 holes, 6669 yards, 6099 metres. S.S.S. 72. Practice range (15 bays). *Green Fees:* weekdays £23.00 per round, £30.00 per day; weekends £28.00 per round, £37.00 per day. *Eating facilities:* bar, dining room, lounge. *Visitors:* always welcome, can book start time three days in advance. *Society Meetings:* welcome, special rates available, assistance available for starting, score cards, notice board, etc. Professional: James Fincher. Secretary: Cyril Howkins.

DIDCOT. **Hadden Hill Golf Club,** Wallingford Road, Didcot OX11 9BJ (01235 510410). *Location*: on A4130, half-a-mile east of Didcot on the Wallingford road. Well drained parkland with superb greens - never closed for rain! 18 holes, 6563 yards. S.S.S. 71. 20-bay floodlit driving range. *Green Fees:* 18 holes - weekdays £17.00, weekends £22.00. *Eating facilities*: good food all day, every day. *Visitors*: telephone bookings for tee times. *Society Meetings*: very welcome weekdays only. Professional: Ian Mitchell (01235 510410). Secretary: Michael Morley (01235 510410; Fax: 01235 511260). website: www.haddenhillgolf.co.uk

DRAYTON. **Drayton Park Golf Course,** Steventon Road, Drayton, near Abingdon OX14 4LA (01235 528989; Fax: 01235 525731). *Location:* A34 Didcot turn off, through Steventon to Drayton (south of Oxford). 18 hole Par 67 golf course, 9 hole Par 3 course. Driving range. Tuition from PGA qualified professionals. *Green Fees:* weekdays £17.75 18 holes, £24.75 27 holes, £29.50 36 holes; weekends £19.75 18 holes, £29.75 27 holes, £34.75 36 holes. *Eating facilities:* full catering and bar facilities. Clubhouse open to visitors. *Visitors:* welcome. Clubhouse available for conferences and weddings; large function room. *Society Meetings:* welcome. Professional: M. Morbey (01235 550607). Secretary: G. Masey (01235 528989). e-mail: draytonpark@btclick.com

FARINGDON. **Carswell Golf and Country Club**, Carswell Home Farm, Carswell, Faringdon SN7 8PU (01367 870422; Fax: 01367 870592). *Location*: just off A420 between Oxford and Swindon, near Faringdon. Parkland course with many trees and water hazards. 18 holes, 6200 yards. S.S.S. 72. 19-bay floodlit driving range, practice area with putting green. *Green Fees:* weekdays £18.00, weekends £25.00. Twilight fees available, telephone for more details and prices. *Eating facilities:* clubhouse bar serving varied menu. *Visitors:* welcome, soft spikes preferred. Golf shop; club, cart and buggy hire. Clubhouse accommodation - four en suite rooms. *Society Meetings:* all welcome

weekdays, please telephone for information on packages. Health Club on site, call for details. Professional: Mr Steve Parker (01367 870422). Secretary: Sarah Booth (01367 870422).

HENLEY-ON-THAMES. **Aspect Park Golf Club**, Remenham Hill, Henley-on-Thames RG9 3EH (Tel & Fax: 01491 578306). *Location:* M40 Junction 4 Exit or M4 Junction 8 Exit to Maidenhead, A4130 to Henley. Listed parkland course. 18 holes, 6595 yards, S.S.S. 72. Range, putting, pitch and putt. *Green Fees:* information not available. *Eating facilities:* bar, restaurant and function room. *Visitors:* welcome anytime except Saturday morning during medal play. Golf attire on course. Manager/Professional: Terry Notley (01491 577562).

HENLEY-ON-THAMES. **Badgemore Park Golf Club**, Badgemore, Henley-on-Thames RG9 4NR (01491 572206). *Location:* one mile from Henley town centre on road to Rotherfield Greys. Mature parkland course. 18 holes, 6129 yards. S.S.S. 69. Chipping green, two putting greens, practice net, bunker practice. *Visitors:* always welcome, weekends during summer after 12 noon, winter after 11am. Professional lessons available. Large car park. Accommodation on site. *Society Meetings:* welcome Wednesdays, Thursdays, Fridays. Professional: Jonathan Dunn (01491 574175). Secretary: Mr J. Connell (01491 572206; Fax: 01491 576899).

HENLEY-ON-THAMES. **Henley Golf Club,** Harpsden, Henley-on-Thames RG9 4HG (01491 575781). *Location:* from centre of Henley-Reading, one mile from Harpsden Way to clubhouse. Parkland with many trees. 18 holes, 6329 yards. S.S.S. 70. *Green Fees:* weekdays £42.00; weekends with member only £18.50. *Eating facilities:* bar snacks at all times, meals by arrangement. *Visitors:* welcome weekdays, weekends and Bank Holidays with a member only. Handicap Certificate required. *Society Meetings:* catered for Wednesdays and Thursdays. Professional: Mark Howell (01491 575710). Secretary: Andrew Chaundy (01491 575742; Fax: 01491 412179).

HENLEY-ON-THAMES. **Huntercombe Golf Club,** Nuffield, Henley-on-Thames RG9 5SL (01491 641207). *Location:* A4130, six miles west of Henley-on-Thames. Downland wooded course. 18 holes, 6301 yards. S.S.S. 70. Practice ground. *Green Fees:* information not available. *Eating facilities:* catering and bar facilities. *Visitors:* welcome by prior arrangement only. *Society Meetings:* Tuesdays and Thursdays by arrangement. Professional: David Reffin (01491 641241). Secretary: Ken McCrea (Fax: 01491 642060).

HORTON-CUM-STUDLEY. **Studley Wood Golf Club**, The Straight Mile, Horton cum Studley, Oxford OX33 1BF (01865 351144; Fax: 01865 351166). *Location*: 4 miles east of Oxford. Gently undulating mature woodland course. 18 holes, 6722 yards, S.S.S. 72. 15 bay covered driving range, Callaway Custom Fit Centre, short game academy. *Green Fees*: please phone pro Shop for details. *Eating facilities*: function room, Bistro restaurant and bar. *Visitors*: welcome at all times weekdays, afternoons only at weekends, must play to Handicap standard. Tee time bookings taken four days in advance. Buggies available. *Society Meetings*: welcome any time Mondays to Thursdays, and Friday mornings. Packages from £30.00. per person. Professional: Tony Williams (01865 351122). Secretary: Richard Booth.
e-mail: admin@swgc.co.uk
website: www.studleywoodgolf.co.uk

KIRTLINGTON. **Kirtlington Golf Club**, Lince Lane, Kirtlington OX5 3JY (01869 351133; Fax: 01869 351143). *Location*: A4095, Witney/Bicester, half a mile outside Kirtlington. Undulating, dry, open parkland course with well contoured greens. 18 holes, 6107 yards. S.S.S. 69. Driving range, pitching/putting. *Green Fees*: weekdays £20.00; weekends £25.00. Special rates on application. *Eating facilities*: available. *Visitors*: very welcome. *Society Meetings*: welcome. Secretary: Pamela Smith.
e-mail: info@kirtlingtongolfclub.co.uk
website: www.kirtlingtongolfclub.co.uk

MAPLEDURHAM. **Mapledurham Golf & Health Club**, Chazey Heath, Mapledurham, Reading RG4 7UD (01189 463353; Fax: 01189 463363). *Location*: leave Reading on A4074 towards Mapledurham, Woodcote and Wallingford, club is on the right immediately after leaving built up area. Parkland. 18 holes, 5635 yards. S.S.S. 67. Practice ground. *Green Fees*: weekdays £20.00, weekends £25.00. *Eating facilities*: bar/lounge, food available. *Visitors*: welcome, no restrictions. Facilities include fully equipped gym, sauna, steam room, spa. *Society Meetings*: welcome. Professional: Dan Peck. Manager: David Reeves.

OXFORD. **Hinksey Heights Golf Course**, South Hinksey OX1 5AB (01865 327775; Fax: 01865 736930). *Location*: Exit A34 north towards Oxford, past Abingdon exit then turn left at sign for garden centre. From M40, A34 towards Oxford, past Botley then take exit for South Hinksey. Undulating course. 18 holes, 6936 yards, 6342 metres. S.S.S. 73; driving range; indoor and outdoor practice areas. 9 hole par 3 course. *Green Fees*: weekdays £16.50 per round, £27.50 per day; weekends £20.00 per round, £33.00 per day. *Eating facilities*: Spike Bar, bar and restaurant. *Visitors*: welcome including weekends. Contact General Manager or Professional. *Society Meetings and Company Days*: welcome including weekends with forward booking. Contact General Manager or Professional. Professional: David Bolton. General Manager: John Lidstone.
e-mail: play@oxford-golf.co.uk
website: www.oxford-golf.co.uk

OXFORD. **North Oxford Golf Club**, Banbury Road, Oxford OX2 8EZ (01865 554415; Fax: 01865 515921). *Location*: just north of Oxford on the Banbury Road to Kidlington. Flat parkland course with tree-lined fairways - six Par 3 holes. 18 holes, 5736 yards, S.S.S. 67. Indoor driving bay in Pro shop. *Green Fees*: £25.00 per day, £18.00 per round, twilight £14.00 after 5.00pm excluding Thursday and Friday. *Eating facilities*: dining room, lounge and stud bar. *Visitors*: welcome weekdays and after 4pm weekends and Bank Holidays. *Society Meetings*: welcome, details on request. Professional: R.J. Harris (01865 553977). Secretary: G.W. Pullin (01865 554924; Fax: 01865 515921).
e-mail: secretary@nogc.co.uk
website: www.nogc.co.uk

OXFORD. **Southfield Golf Club**, (home of Oxford City Golf Club, Oxford Ladies Golf Club, Oxford University Golf Club), Hill Top Road, Oxford OX4 1PF. *Location*: one mile from Rover Works, along Cowley Road, turn right into Southfield Road, then right at end of road. Hilly parkland. 18 holes, 6328 yards. S.S.S. 70. Practice ground available. *Green Fees*: £25.00 per day weekdays. *Eating facilities*: restaurant facilities available, bar open seven days. *Visitors*: welcome except weekends and Public Holidays. *Society Meetings*: welcome by arrangement (not weekends or Bank Holidays). Professional: Tony Rees (01865 244258). Admin. Secretary: Charles Maxted (01865 242158).

OXFORD. **Waterstock Golf Club & Driving Range**, Thame Road, Waterstock, Oxford OX33 1HT (01844 338093; Fax: 01844 338036). *Location*: on Junction 8 and 8A, M40, at the Wheatley Service Station, five minutes from Thame and Oxford, 30 minutes from London and Birmingham. Rolling parkland with 15,500 young trees. 18 holes, 6535 yards, S.S.S. 73. Practice bunkers and putting facilities, 22 bay driving range. *Green Fees*: information not provided. *Eating facilities*: full bar and restaurant. *Visitors*: no restrictions, welcome at all times. Changing rooms. *Society Meetings*: fully catered for, packages available on request. Head Professional: Paul Bryant. Secretary: Andrew Wyatt.
e-mail: wgc_oxfordgolf@btinternet.com
website: www.waterstockgolf.co.uk

OXON/BUCKINGHAMSHIRE. **Magnolia Park Golf & Country Club**, Arncott Road, Boarstall, Buckinghamshire HP18 9XX (01844 239700). *Location*: B4011 south from Bicester or north from Thame; two miles north of Oakley turn to Boarstall. Parkland and landscaped terrain with seven lakes. 18 holes. Par 72. *Green Fees*: weekdays £35.00, weekends £50.00. *Eating facilities*: Bar and dining 8am to 8pm (to 6pm during winter), function room available. *Society Meetings*: societies and corporate days welcome. Professional: Jeremy Dale.

For full details of clubs and courses, plus convenient accommodation, visit the FHG golf website on

www.uk-golfguide.com

THAME. **The Oxfordshire Golf Club**, Rycote Lane, Milton Common, Thame OX9 2PU (01844 278300; Fax: 01844 278003). *Location:* from south Junction 7 M40, A329 to Thame. From north Junction 8 M40, A418 to Thame then A329. A combination of mounded fairways and lakes offers American-style target golf. 18 holes, 6856 yards. S.S.S. 74. Practice driving range. *Green Fees:* on application. *Eating facilities:* spike bar, lounge bar and restaurant (private rooms available). *Visitors:* accepted upon written application (01844 278500). Electric trolleys, pull trolleys and caddies (reserved in advance) available. *Society Meetings:* on application. Professional: (01844 278505).

WALLINGFORD. **The Springs Hotel and Golf Club,** Wallingford Road, North Stoke, Wallingford OX10 6BE (01491 836687; Fax: 01491 836877). *Location:* two miles south-west of Wallingford on the B4009. M40 Junction 6. 18 holes, 6470 yards. par 72. *Green Fees:* weekdays £29.00, weekends £35.00. *Eating facilities:* restaurant and clubhouse. *Visitors:* by arrangement. Professional: P. Ivil (01491 827310; Fax: 01491 827312).
e-mail: info@thespringshotel.com
      golfclub@thespringshotel.com
website: www.thespringshotel.com

WITNEY. **Witney Lakes Golf Club,** Witney Lakes Resort, Downs Road, Witney OX8 5SY (01993 893011; Fax: 01993 778866). *Location*: two miles west of Witney town centre, turn into Downs Road. From B4095. Parkland with five large lakes. 18 holes, 6500 yards. S.S.S. 71. 22-bay floodlit covered driving range, practice area. *Green Fees:* £18.00 midweek, £25.00 weekends. *Eating facilities:* Greens Sports Bar and Greens Restaurant. *Visitors:* no restrictions. Function/ conference room; health and fitness club includes swimming pool, gymnasium and sauna. Large well-stocked golf shop, three teaching Professionals. *Society Meetings:* all welcome. Professional: Adam Souter (01993 893011; Fax: 01993 778866). Secretary (01993 893005; Fax: 01993 778866).
e-mail: golf@witney-lakes.co.uk
website:www.witney-lakes.co.uk

Shropshire

BRIDGNORTH. **Bridgnorth Golf Club**, Stanley Lane, Bridgnorth WV16 4SF (01746 763315; Fax: 01746 761381). *Location:* one mile from town centre on Broseley road. Parkland, alongside River Severn. 18 holes, 6582 yards. S.S.S. 73. Practice ground. *Green Fees:* weekdays £24.00, weekends £30.00. Two for one offers available. *Eating facilities:* full catering available except Mondays. *Visitors:* welcome weekdays except Wednesday. Handicap Certificate or bona fide club membership required. *Society Meetings:* catered for Monday, Tuesday, Thursday, Friday only. Professional: Paul Hinton (01746 762045). Secretary: G.C. Kelsall.

BRIDGNORTH. **Chesterton Valley Golf Club**, Chesterton, Near Worfield, Bridgnorth WV15 5NX (01746 783682). *Location:* B4176 Dudley/Telford road. 18 holes, Par 69. *Green Fees:* £14.00. Visitors; no restrictions but can book 24 hours in advance. Professional/Secretary: Philip Hinton.

BRIDGNORTH. **Severn Meadows Golf Club**, Highley, Bridgnorth (01746 862212; Fax: 01746 861098). *Location:* seven miles from Bridgnorth on B4555. Eight miles from Bewdley on B4194. Signposted from village. Undulating woodland course. Severn Valley Steam Railway runs through the middle of the course, on the banks of the River Severn. 18 holes, 6388 yards. S.S.S. 70. *Green Fees:* information not available. *Eating facilities:* by arrangement. *Visitors:* welcome anytime weekdays but must book tee times at weekends. *Society Meetings:* by arrangement only. Secretary: Colin Harrison (01746 861296). *

CHURCH STRETTON. **Church Stretton Golf Club**, Trevor Hill, Church Stretton SY6 6JH (01694 722281). *Location:* one mile west of A49, adjacent to Carding Mill Valley. Set on the lower slopes of the Longmynd Hills, with wonderful springy turf and panoramic views of the surrounding country. No winter greens. 18 holes, 5020 yards. S.S.S. 65. *Green Fees:* £18.00 weekdays, £26.00 weekends and Bank Holidays. Reductions in winter. No pre booking necessary. *Eating facilities:* meals and snacks available daily, full bar facilities. *Visitors:* welcome, Saturdays not between 9am and 10.30am and 1pm to 2.30pm (Winter 12noon to 1.30pm), Sundays not before 10.30am or between 1pm and 2.30pm (Winter 12noon to 1.30pm). *Society Meetings:* welcome. Contact Hon. Secretary or Professional to pre-book. Professional: James Townsend (01694 722281; mobile: 07973 762510). Hon. Secretary John Povall (01743 860679; mobile: 07817 538080).
e-mail: secretary@churchstrettongolfclub.co.uk
website: www.churchstrettongolfclub.co.uk

CLEOBURY MORTIMER. **Cleobury Mortimer Golf Club,** Wyre Common, Cleobury Mortimer, Near Kidderminster DY14 8HQ (01299 271112). *Location:* two miles out of Cleobury on B4201. 27 hole course comprising three loops of nine holes. Badgers Sett 3271 yards, Foxes Run 2960 yards, Deer Park 3167 yards, giving three 18 hole courses with S.S.S. 71, 70, 69. *Green Fees:* weekdays £20.00 per round (£10.00 with member), £30.00 per day; weekends £24.00 per round (£14.00 with member), £36.00 per day. *Eating facilities:* restaurant and Spike Bar. *Visitors:* welcome midweek; weekends by arrangement. Snooker room. Golf Buggies for hire - £15 per round, trolleys £2.00 per round bookable in advance. Golf packages with nearby Hammond House Hotel available. *Society Meetings:* welcome by prior arrangement, ring for details. PGA Professional: Martin Payne (01299 271112; Fax: 01299 271628). Director of Golf: Jon Jones. Secretary/Manager: Graham Pain (01299 271112; Fax: 01299 271468).
e-mail: enquiries@cleoburygolfclub.com
website: www.cleoburygolfclub.com

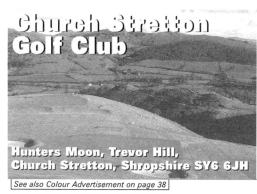

LUDLOW. **Ludlow Golf Club**, Bromfield, Ludlow SY8 2BT (01584 856285; Fax: 01584 856366). *Location:* A49 one mile north of Ludlow bypass, turn right onto the Bridgnorth road. Well signposted. Heathland course based on sandy soil providing springy fairways and superb greens. 18 holes, 6277 yards. S.S.S. 70. Practice ground. *Green Fees:* weekdays £22.00; weekends £25.00 (reductions with member). *Eating facilities:* full catering and bar service during normal hours. *Visitors:* welcome weekdays and weekends with prior booking. *Society Meetings:* catered for weekdays only; packages start from £27.50. Professional: R. Price (Tel & Fax: 01584 856366). Administrator: Roger Heath (01584 856285; Fax: 01584 856366).

MARKET DRAYTON. **Market Drayton Golf Club**, Sutton, Market Drayton TF9 2HX (01630 652266). *Location:* A41 south towards Newport, turn left at crossroads just past Tern Hill Barracks. Parkland with exceptional views. 18 holes, 6214 yards, 5702 metres. S.S.S. 70. *Green Fees:* information not provided. *Eating facilities:* bar and high class catering open all day. *Visitors:* welcome weekdays only; first tee closed daily until 9.30am and from 12.30pm to 1.30pm. Tuesday Ladies' Day. Bungalow (sleeps 6) available for letting. *Society Meetings:* catered for weekdays by prior arrangement. Professional: Russell Clewes (01630 656237). Secretary: David Palmer (01630 652266). Steward: Michael Clancy (01630 658083).
e-mail: marketdraytongc@btinternet.com

NEWPORT. **Aqualate Golf**, Stafford Road, Newport TF10 9DB (01952 811699). *Location:* two miles east of Newport town centre; 400 yards from the junction with A41. Parkland course with gentle gradients and water hazards. 18 holes, 5659 yards. S.S.S. 67. 20 bay floodlit driving range, practice putting green. *Green Fees:* weekdays £10.00 per round (£6.00 for Juniors); weekends £13.00 per round (£9.00 for Juniors). *Eating facilities:* coffee bar. *Visitors:* welcome at all times (pay and play), but advance booking advisable. No handicap restrictions. *Society Meetings:* welcome by prior arrangement. Hire clubs and trolleys available. Professional: Kevin Short (01952 811699). Director: H. Brian Dawes (01952 811699).

NEWPORT. **Lilleshall Hall Golf Club**, Lilleshall, Near Newport TF10 9AS (01952 603840 or Tel & Fax: 01952 604776). *Location:* at Lillyhurst turn north off Abbey Road, which joins Wellington Road near Lilleshall and the B4379 near Sheriffhales. Wooded parkland. 18 holes, 5813 yards. S.S.S. 68. Practice ground. *Green Fees:* information not available. *Eating facilities:* meals served 9am to 5pm, order in advance. *Visitors:* welcome on weekdays, check with Professional for tee restrictions. *Society Meetings:* catered for by prior arrangement with Secretary. Professional: S. McKane (01952 604104). Secretary: B.C. Stephens (Tel & Fax: 01952 604776).*

OSWESTRY. **Llanymynech Golf Club**, Pant, Near Oswestry SY10 8LB (01691 830542). *Location:* six miles south of Oswestry on A483, turn at Cross Guns Inn, Pant. Undulating hilltop course with extensive views, 15 holes in Wales, three in England. 18 holes, 6047 yards. S.S.S. 69. Practice area and putting green. *Green Fees:* weekdays £20.00 per round, £25.00 per day; weekends £25.00 per round, subject to review. Half price with member. Reductions for Juniors. *Eating facilities:* restaurant and bar. *Visitors:* welcome weekdays; some weekends by prior arrangement; prior enquiry advisable. *Society Meetings:* weekdays by arrangement with Secretary. Professional: A.P. Griffiths (01691 830879). Secretary: D.R. Thomas (01691 830983).

OSWESTRY. **Mile End Golf Club**, Mile End, Oswestry SY11 4JE (01691 671246 (bookings); Fax: 01691 670580). *Location:* signposted off A5, one mile south-east of Oswestry. Gently undulating course with water features. 18 holes, 6194 yards. S.S.S. 69. Driving range. *Green Fees:* weekdays £16.00 per round, £24.00 per day; weekends £22.00 per round, £30.00 per day. *Eating facilities:* full bar/catering available. *Visitors:* welcome at all times subject to course availability. Extensively stocked quality golf shop with all top name brands. *Society Meetings:* welcome weekdays by prior arrangement. Professional: Scott Carpenter (01691 671246). Secretary: Richard Thompson (Tel & Fax: 01691 670580)
e-mail: mileendgc@aol.com
website: www.mileendgolfclub.co.uk

OSWESTRY. **Oswestry Golf Club**, Aston Park, Oswestry SY11 4JJ. *Location:* a friendly members' club four miles south-east of Oswestry on A5. Mature parkland course with many feature trees, laid out by James Braid in rolling Shropshire countryside. Well drained soils ensure excellent year-round play. 18 holes, 6038 yards. S.S.S. 69. Practice ground. *Green Fees:* £26.00. *Eating facilities:* dining room and bar. *Visitors:* welcome; must be member of another club with a recognised Handicap Certificate or playing with a member. Snooker table. *Society Meetings:* societies of 16 plus welcomed Wednesdays and Fridays by arrangement with the Secretary. Smaller groups catered for by arrangement with the Professional. Professional: David Skelton (01691 610448). Secretary: Peter Turner (Tel & Fax: 01691 610535).
e-mail: secretary@oswestrygolfclub.co.uk
website: www.oswestrygolfclub.co.uk

SHIFNAL. **Shifnal Golf Club**, Decker Hill, Shifnal TF11 8QL (01952 460330; Fax: 01952 461127). *Location:* one mile north east of Shifnal, one mile from A5, Junction 4 M54. Parkland course. 18 holes, 6504 yards. S.S.S. 71. *Green Fees:* £25.00 per round, £30.00 per day; weekends with member only. *Eating facilities:* full catering service. *Visitors:* welcome, phone first, not weekends or Bank Holidays. *Society Meetings:* catered for by arrangement with Secretary. Professional: J. Flanagan (01952 460457). Secretary: M.J. Vanner (01952 460330; Fax: 01952 461127).
e-mail: secretary@shifnalgolfclub.co.uk
website: www.shifnalgolfclub.co.uk

SHREWSBURY. **Arscott Golf Club**, Arscott, Pontesbury, Shrewsbury SY5 0XP (Tel & Fax: 01743 860114). *Location:* 10 minutes from Shrewsbury off the A488 Bishops Castle road. Set in mature parkland with stunning views of South Shropshire and Welsh Borders. 18 holes, 6158 yards. S.S.S. 69. Practice area, putting green and driving net. *Green Fees:* £17.00 weekdays; £22.00 weekends. *Eating facilities:* food and beverages available from 11am daily. *Visitors:* welcome at all times. Please telephone Shop to book tees. *Society Meetings:* by arrangement, please telephone. Secretary: Brian Harper (01743 860114 or 01743 860881).

SHREWSBURY. **Hawkstone Park**, Weston-under-Redcastle, Shrewsbury SY4 5UY (01939 200611; Fax: 01939 200311). *Location*: 14 miles north of Shrewsbury off A49. Hawkstone Course – parkland, 18 holes, 6491 yards (white). S.S.S. 71; Windmill Course – parkland (designed by Brian Huggett), 18 holes, 6476 yards (white). S.S.S. 71; Academy Par 3 Course – 6 holes, 741 yards. Par 18, S.S.S. 18. Target practice ground, putting green and short game area. Open all year. **Green Fees**: weekdays £34.00; weekends £44.00; please call for winter rates. **Eating facilities**: Terrace Room, all day bar and restaurant. **Visitors**: welcome. 66 room Hotel and Historic park. **Society Meetings**: welcome. Reservations for bookings: 01939 200611. Professional: Stuart Leech (01939 200611).
e-mail: bookings@hawkstone.co.uk
website: www.hawkstone.co.uk

SHREWSBURY. **Shrewsbury Golf Club,** Condover, Shrewsbury SY5 7BL (01743 872976; Fax: 01743 874647). *Location:* A49 two miles south west of Shrewsbury. Parkland first 9 holes, undulating back 9 holes with fine views of Longmynd. 18 holes, 6207 yards. S.S.S. 70. Large practice ground. *Green Fees:* £22.00 per round, £25.00 per day weekdays; £26.00 per round, £30.00 per day weekends and Bank Holidays. Weekly ticket (Monday-Friday) £87.00. *Eating facilities:* full facilities available seven days. *Visitors:* welcome at all times except Wednesday mornings and weekends before 10am. *Society Meetings:* welcome by arrangement. Professional: Peter Seal (01743 874581). Secretary: Mrs S.M. Kenny (01743 872977).

TELFORD. **Telford Golf and Country Club**, Great Hay Drive, Sutton Heights, Telford TF7 4DT (01952 429977; Fax: 01952 586602). *Location:* turn off A442 between Bridgnorth and Telford, two miles to M54 Junction 4. Rolling wooded parkland with water features, suspended water table greens as at Augusta. 18 holes, 6761 yards. S.S.S. 72. All-weather driving range, putting green. *Green Fees:* information not available. *Eating facilities:* clubroom, coffee bar and restaurant, lounge, Sky TV, also private rooms for Societies. *Visitors:* welcome anytime but advance booking essential. Handicap Certificates or membership of bona fide golf club essential. Leisure Centre with swimming pool, gym, etc. *Society Meetings:* by arrangement. Professional: Dan Bateman (01952 586052). Secretary: Ian Lucas (01952 429977).*

TELFORD. **The Shropshire**, Muxton, Telford TF2 8PQ (01952 677800; Fax: 01952 677622). *Location:* off Junction 4 of M54, follow signs for Muxton (signposted). Parkland course featuring several lakes. Three courses (Blue, Silver, Gold): 27 holes, 3286 yards, 3303 yards, 3334 yards, S.S.S. 71, 72, 72. 30 bay floodlit driving range, 12 hole short course, 18 hole putting green. *Green Fees:* information not available. *Eating facilities:* Greenkeeper Bar and Monkey Puzzle Brasserie, seven function rooms. *Visitors:* welcome, no restrictions. Pay as you Play. 15 buggies, golf school. *Society Meetings:* very welcome, packages available. Professional: Andrew Heath (0789 0078490). *

TELFORD. **Wrekin Golf Club**, Ercall Woods, Golf Links Lane, Wellington, Telford TF6 5BX (01952 244032; Fax: 01952 252906). *Location:* from M54 Junction 7 to Wellington, turn back along Holyhead road towards Wellington for three-quarters-of-a-mile. Golf Links Lane on right hand side. Undulating parkland. 18 holes, 5570 yards. S.S.S. 67. Small practice ground. *Green Fees:* weekdays £22.00, weekends and Bank Holidays £30.00 (numbers limited). Contact Secretary for available discounts. *Eating facilities:* restaurant and bar facilities by arrangement with Stewardess. *Visitors:* welcome except weekends and Bank Holidays when limited. *Society Meetings:* by arrangement with the Secretary. Professional: K. Housden (01952 223101). Secretary: D. Briscoe (01952 244032; Fax: 01952 252906).

WHITCHURCH. **Hill Valley Golf and Country Club**, Terrick Road, Whitchurch SY13 4JZ (01948 663584; Fax: 01948 665927). *Location:* signposted from Whitchurch Bypass. Magnificent Alliss/Thomas Emerald Championship Course. 18 holes, 6628 yards. Par 73. Sapphire Course 4801 yards, Par 66. *Green Fees:* information not available. *Eating facilities:* full restaurant/bars, snacks available. *Visitors:* welcome without reservation. Hotel (28 en suite bedrooms); Leisure facilities also available. *Society Meetings:* please contact for details. Professional: Clive Burgess (01948 663032). Secretary: John Pickering (01948 860425).* e-mail: info@hill-valley.co.uk website: www.hill-valley.co.uk

WOLVERHAMPTON. **Patshull Park Hotel, Golf and Country Club**, Patshull Park, Pattingham, Near Wolverhampton WV6 7HR (01902 700100; Fax: 01902 700874). *Location:* take Junction 3 off M54, turn left on A41 back towards Wolverhampton and fork right into Albrighton. From main crossroads turn right along Cross Road, taking T-junction with A464 Wolverhampton/Shifnal Road and turning right towards Shifnal. Signposted Patshull Park Golf Course. Glorious parkland course set in landscapes by Capability Brown; John Jacobs designed course. 18 holes, 6345 yards. S.S.S. 69. Large practice area. *Green Fees:* £40.00 per 18 holes, £60.00 per 36 holes. Please pre-book. Handicap Certificates required. *Eating facilities:* Lakeside Restaurant and two bars. Earl's Bar. *Visitors:* welcome on application. 49 bedroomed hotel, country club and swimming pool, fishing lakes (80 acres). Residential Breaks. Buggies available. *Society Meetings:* corporate and society meetings welcome; special group rates and facilities. Professional: Richard Bissell (01902 700342).

WORFIELD. **Worfield Golf Club**, Roughton, Worfield, Near Bridgnorth WV15 5HE (01746 716541; Fax:01746 716302). *Location:* A454 Wolverhampton to Bridgnorth Road, three miles from Bridgnorth. Parkland course set on rolling countryside. 18 holes, 6440 yards. S.S.S. 71. Chipping area, practice area, putting greens. *Green Fees:* weekdays £20.00. weekends after 1pm £25.00. *Eating facilities:* restaurant and bar meals all day. *Visitors:* welcome. Buggies available. *Society meetings:* all welcome. Professional: Stephen Russell (01746 716541). Secretary: William Weaver (01746 716372; Fax: 01746 716302).

N
O
T
E

All the information regarding Golf Clubs in this guide is given in good faith in the belief that it is correct. However, the publishers cannot guarantee the facts given in these pages, neither are they responsible for changes in ownership or facilities, such as green fees, that may take place after the date of going to press. Readers should always satisfy themselves that the facilities they require are available and that the terms, if quoted, still apply.

Somerset

BATH. **Bath Golf Club**, Sham Castle, North Road, Bath BA2 6JG (01225 425182). *Location:* off A36, one mile south-east of Bath City Centre. Hilltop, undulating downland course with views of Bath and the surrounding countryside. 18 holes, 6442 yards, 5891 metres. S.S.S. 71. *Green Fees:* weekdays £28.00; weekends and Bank Holidays £34.00. *Eating facilities:* catering every day. *Visitors:* with bona fide Handicap welcome. *Society Meetings:* catered for Wednesday and Friday. Professional: Peter Hancox (Tel & Fax: 01225 466953). Managing Secretary: S.P. Watkins (01225 463834; Fax: 01225 331027).

BATH. **Entry Hill Golf Club**, Entry Hill, Bath BA2 5NA (01225 834248). *Location:* one mile south of city centre, off A367 road to Wells. Hilly parkland course with many young trees. 9 holes, 2103 yards, 1922 metres. S.S.S. 61 (18 holes). Practice net. *Green Fees:* information not available. *Visitors:* no restrictions but pre-booking up to one week in advance essential. Well equipped Pro Shop. *Society Meetings:* reduced green fees for pre-booked groups of 10 or more. Professional: T. Tapley (01225 834248). Secretary: J. Sercombe (01225 834248).*

BATH. **Fosseway Golf Club and Centurion Hotel**, Charlton Lane, Midsomer Norton, Bath BA3 4BD (01761 412214; Fax: 01761 418357). *Location:* off A367 Bath to Wells/Shepton Mallet. Flat parkland course on the edge of the Mendips. 9 holes, 2304 yards. S.S.S. 65. *Green Fees:* information not available. *Eating facilities:* full à la carte restaurant, five bars with bar meals. *Visitors:* welcome except Sunday mornings and Wednesday evenings. Accommodation available, gym, sauna, steam, Jacuzzi, swimming and bowls (outdoor). *Society Meetings:* welcome. Secretary: P.J. Jordan (01761 417711).
e-mail: centurion@centurionhotel.co.uk
website: www.centurionhotel.com

BATH. **Lansdown Golf Club**, Lansdown, Bath BA1 9BT. *Location:* M4 Junction 18, A46 towards Bath, follow signs for Lansdown Park and Ride, adjacent Bath Racecourse. Flat parkland, 800ft above sea-level, panoramic views. 18 holes, 6316 yards, 5773

metres. S.S.S. 70. Practice ground. *Green Fees:* weekdays £22.00, weekends £28.00. *Eating facilities:* dining room for 100, snacks, lunch or dinner. *Visitors:* welcome, must have Handicap Certificate. Trolleys for hire. *Society Meetings:* welcome weekdays. Professional: Terry Mercer (01225 420242; Fax: 01225 483597). Secretary: Erica Bacon (01225 422138; Fax: 01225 339252).
e-mail: admin@lansdowngolfclub.co.uk
website: www.lansdowngolfclub.co.uk

BATH/BRISTOL. **Farrington Golf and Country Club**, Marsh Lane, Farrington Gurney, Near Bristol BS39 6TS (01761 451596; Fax: 01761 451021). *Location:* 12 miles south of Bristol, 10 miles east of Bath (through Midsomer Norton) at the junction of the A37 and A362 roads. Wooded, undulating 27 hole complex, 6 lakes, USGA-spec greens (no temporaries), tees up to 800 square yards, irrigated. Championship Course - 18 holes, (Blue tees) 6716 yards, S.S.S. 72; (White tees) 6335 yards, S.S.S. 71; (Yellow tees) 5943 yards, S.S.S. 68; (Ladies' Red tees), 5595 yards, S.S.S 73 . Executive Course - 9 holes, 3002 yards, par 54, S.S.S. 53. Floodlit, covered driving range, 300 yard practice ground, two extensive putting greens, chipping green, three practice bunkers, video professional teaching, winter coaching base for Somerset county juniors. *Green Fees:* Championship Course £18.00 weekdays, £25.00 weekends and holidays. Special twilight offers. Executive Course (9 holes): £7.00 weekdays, £9.00 weekends. *Eating facilities:* Large clubhouse of character, full meals service, Sunday lunches, bars, dining room, patio and courtyard. Horizon Banqueting and Function Suite and King Charles Hall both licensed for civil weddings. *Visitors:* most welcome, 2 for 1 vouchers accepted, booking essential weekends. *Society Meetings:* special midweek packages available. PGA Professional: Jonathan Cowgill (01761 451046). Secretary: Stephen Cook. Owner: Paul Harwood. General Manager (for society and membership enquiries): Debbie Cole (01761 451596).
e-mail: info@farringtongolfclub.net
website: www.farringtongolfclub.net

BRIDGWATER. **Enmore Park Golf Club**, Enmore, Bridgwater TA5 2AN (01278 671481). *Location:* M5 Exit 23/24, left at lights in town to Spaxton, course signposted two miles on right. Wooded parkland course on Quantock foothills. 18 holes, 6406 yards, 5910 metres. S.S.S. 71. Large practice ground. *Green Fees:* £25.00 per round, £35.00 per day weekdays; £35.00 per round weekends. *Eating facilities:* lunch and evening meal available. *Visitors:* welcome weekdays, weekends if no competitions. Buggy available. *Society Meetings:* welcome by arrangement. Professional: Nigel Wixon (01278 671519; Fax: 01278 671740). Secretary: David Weston (01278 671481; Fax: 01278 671740).

BRIDGWATER. **Cannington Golf Course**, Cannington College, Cannington, Bridgwater TA5 2LS (01278 652394; Fax: 01278 652479). *Location:* M5 Junction 24, off A39 Bridgwater to Minehead road. Flat, with slight undulations, on parkland turf; exposed to sea breezes. 9 holes (18 tees to 9 greens), 6072 yards. S.S.S. 70. Small practice area. 10 bay floodlit driving range. *Green Fees:* information not available. *Eating facilities:* College restaurant. *Visitors:* pay and play course. *Society Meetings:* by arrangement with Professional/Course Manager. Professional/Course Manager: Ron Macrow (01278 655050; Fax: 01278 655055).*

BRISTOL. **Mendip Spring Golf Club**, Honeyhall Lane, Congresbury, Bristol BS49 5JT (01934 852322; Fax: 01934 853021). *Location:* between Congresbury and Churchill off B3133 (A370 and A38). Fairly flat courses with a lot of water hazards. Brinsea Course: 18 holes, 6352 yards. S.S.S. 70 men, 76 ladies; Lakeside Course: 9 holes, 2260 yards, S.S.S. 65 men and ladies. 15 bay floodlit driving range, putting green. *Green Fees:* Brinsea: weekdays £25.00 – £34.00 per day, weekends £35.00. Lakeside: £8.50 for 9 holes, £17.00 per day. *Eating facilities:* full restaurant and bar facilities. *Visitors:* welcome at any time. Tuition available. Buggies available April to September. *Society Meetings:* welcome, corporate days available by arrangement. Professionals: John Blackburn and Robert Moss. Secretary: A. Melhuish.

BRISTOL. **Stockwood Vale Golf Club**, Stockwood Lane, Keynsham, Bristol BS18 2ER (0117 9866505). *Location:* one mile from Hicks Gate - Bristol Ring Road. Testing parkland course set in beautiful surroundings. 18 holes, 6031 yards. S.S.S. 69. Driving range, practice green/bunker. *Green Fees:* weekdays £15.50 per round; weekends £18.00 per round. *Eating facilities:* licensed bar and restaurant. *Visitors:* welcome at all times, must reserve start times. *Society Meetings:* welcome weekdays, prior booking essential; packages available. Professional: Mr John Richards (0117 9866505). Secretary: Mr M. Edenborough (0117 9860509; Fax: 0117 9868974).

BRISTOL. **Tall Pines Golf Club**, Cooks Bridle Path, Downside, Backwell, Bristol BS48 3DJ (01275 472076). *Location:* between A370 and A38 to Bristol Airport. Parkland. 18 holes, 6049 yards, 5420 metres. S.S.S. 70. Practice ground, putting green. *Green Fees:* £18.00. *Eating facilities:* fully licensed bar and restaurant. *Visitors:* welcome at all times, bookings at weekends. *Society Meetings:* welcome, weekends after 1.00pm. Professional: Alex Murray. Secretary: T. Murray (01275 472076; Fax: 01275 474869).

BURNHAM-ON-SEA. **Brean Golf Club at Brean Leisure Park**, Coast Road, Brean, TA8 2QY (Tel & Fax: 01278 752111). *Location:* leave M5 at Junction 22, follow signs to Brean Leisure Park (five miles). Flat moorland, easy access to five mile sandy beach (400 yards via path). 18 holes, 5565 yards. S.S.S. 67 (Par 69). Practice area, green and bunker. *Green Fees*: weekdays from £18.00 per round; weekends from £20.00 per round. Reduced rates with a member. *Eating facilities:* snacks at bar, meals in main restaurant. *Visitors:* welcome weekdays and after 11am weekends and Bank Holidays. Prior booking advised to Pro Shop (01278 752111). Buggy and trolleys for hire. *Society Meetings:* welcome by prior booking. Professional: David Haines.

BURNHAM-ON-SEA. **Burnham and Berrow Golf Club**, St. Christopher's Way, Burnham-on-Sea TA8 2PE (01278 783137; Fax: 01278 795440). *Location:* one mile north of Burnham-on-Sea. Leave M5 at Exit 22. Seaside links. 18 holes, 6393 yards. S.S.S. 71; 9 holes, 6332 yards. S.S.S. 70. *Green Fees:* £45.00 weekdays, £60.00 weekends and Bank Holidays; 9 hole course £15.00. *Eating facilities:* catering available daily 11am to 6pm (other meals by arrangement). *Visitors:* welcome with reservation if members of a recognised golf club and with Handicap Certificate. *Society Meetings:* catered for. Professional: M. Crowther-Smith (01278 784545). Managing Secretary: Mr P.E. Ware (01278 785760).

CHARD. **Windwhistle Golf Club Ltd**, Cricket St. Thomas, Near Chard, Somerset TA20 4DG (01460 30231; Fax: 01460 30055) Established 1932. *Location:* on A30 between Chard and Crewkerne, opposite Cricket St. Thomas Wildlife Park and Warner's Hotel. Parkland course with breathtaking views. 18 holes, 6510 yards Par 73, S.S.S. 71. Driving range. Golf Shop. *Green Fees:* information not provided. *Eating facilities:* bar service, snacks and cooked meals daily. *Visitors:* welcome - starting time system in operation, bookings accepted up to seven days in advance. *Society Meetings:* Golfing and non-golfing, separate suite for 40 available. Squash courts available. Professional: Paul Deeprose. Secretary: Sue Davidge.
website: www.windwhistlegolf.co.uk

CLEVEDON. **Clevedon Golf Club**, Castle Road, Walton, Clevedon BS21 7AA (01275 874057; Fax: 01275 341228). *Location:* M5 Junction 20, follow signs "Portishead", turn left into Holly Lane. Spectacular scenic parkland course overlooking Bristol Channel. 18 holes, 6557 yards. S.S.S. 72. Practice area. *Green Fees:* weekdays £28.00 per round/day; weekends and Bank Holidays £40.00 per round/day. *Eating facilities:* full catering every day. *Visitors:* welcome, please telephone Professional beforehand. Handicap Certificate essential. *Society Meetings:* welcome by prior arrangement. Professional: Robert Scanlan (01275 874704).

FROME. **Orchardleigh Golf Club**, Frome BA11 2PH (01373 454200; Fax: 01373 454202) *Location*: A362 Frome - Radstock. Parkland. 18 holes, 6800 yards. S.S.S. 73. Three practice greens, driving range. *Green Fees*: weekdays £30.00, weekends £40.00; member's guest £15.00 and £20.00. *Eating facilities:* bar menu. Society and groups menu. *Visitors*: welcome anytime except before 11.00am Saturday and Sundays. *Society Meetings:* all very welcome, competitive rates. Professional: Ian Ridsdale (01373 454206; Fax: 01373 454202) Secretary: Trevor Atkinson.

HALSTOCK. **Halstock Golf Club**, Common Lane, Halstock BA22 9SF (01935 891689; Fax: 01935 891839). *Location:* six miles south of Yeovil near Sutton Bingham Reservoir, signposted in village. Flat parkland course, short, tight but challenging. 18 holes, 4481 yards. S.S.S. 63. 12 bay driving range. *Green Fees:* weekdays £12.00; weekends £13.00. *Eating facilities:* light refreshments available, bar, restaurant (01935 891747). *Visitors:* welcome at all times. Please telephone for booking. Secretary: Les R. Church.

LANGPORT near. **Long Sutton Golf Club**, Long Sutton, Near Langport TA10 9JU (01458 241017; Fax: 01458 241022). *Location:* from Podimore roundabout on A303 towards Langport turn left for Long Sutton. Gently undulating course. 18 holes, 6368 yards. S.S.S. 70. Floodlit driving range. *Green Fees:* weekdays £18.00; weekends £22.00. *Eating facilities:* bar and food. *Visitors:* welcome at all times, phone for tee reservations at weekends. Golfing breaks available. *Society Meetings:* welcome. Professional: Andrew Hayes.

MINEHEAD. **Minehead and West Somerset Golf Club**, The Warren, Minehead TA24 5SJ (01643 702057). *Location:* beside the beach at eastern end of the town, three-quarters of a mile from town centre. Flat seaside links. 18 holes, 6228 yards. S.S.S. 70. *Green Fees:* weekdays £26.00; weekends and Bank Holidays £30.00. *Eating facilities:* available at clubhouse, bar open every day. *Visitors:* welcome with tee reservation at Pro's shop. *Society Meetings:* welcome with tee reservations. Society groups numbering 12 or more qualify for 10 per cent discount. Wide wheel trolleys only. Professional: Ian Read (01643 704378). Secretary: Bob Rayner (01643 702057; Fax: 01643 705095).
e-mail: secretary@mineheadgolf.co.uk
website: www.mineheadgolf.co.uk

SALTFORD. **Saltford Golf Club**, Golf Club Lane, Saltford, Bristol BS31 3AA (01225 873220; Fax: 01225 873525). *Location:* A4 between Bristol and Bath. Wooded parkland course. 18 holes, 6081 yards. S.S.S. 69. Practice area, chipping green. *Green Fees:* information not available. *Eating facilities:* restaurant, bar service. *Visitors:* welcome, restricted to one round of golf per day weekends and during Summer. *Society Meetings:* accepted by arrangement Mondays and Thursdays. Professional: Dudley Millensted (01225 872043). Secretary: Valerie Radnedge (01225 873513).

SHEPTON MALLET. **The Mendip Golf Club Ltd.,** Gurney Slade, Radstock, Shepton Mallett BA3 4UT (01749 840570; Fax: 01749 841439). *Location:* three miles north of Shepton Mallet (A37). Downland, undulating course. 18 holes, 6383 yards. S.S.S. 71. Practice ground. *Green Fees:* weekdays £21.00 per round, £26.00 per day (with a member £12.50); weekends and Bank Holidays £31.00 per day (with a member £12.50). *Eating facilities:* bar and restaurant open seven days a week. *Visitors:* welcome every day, telephone Professional to check availability. *Society Meetings:* catered for Mondays to Fridays by arrangement. Professional: Adrian Marsh (01749 840793). Secretary: Jim Scott (01749 840570; Fax: 01749 841439).
e-mail: mendipgolfclub@lineone.net
website: www.mendipgolfclub.co.uk

SOMERTON. **Wheathill Golf Club,** Wheathill, Somerton TA11 7HQ (01963 240667; Fax: 01963 240230). *Location:* On B3153 three miles west of Castle Cary. Flat parkland. 18 holes, 5351 yards. S.S.S. 66. Large practice ground and 4 hole academy course. *Green Fees:* information not available. *Eating facilities:* bar and restaurant. *Visitors:* welcome. *Society Meetings:* welcome. Professional: Andrew England. Secretary: John Goymer.*

STREET. **Kingweston Golf Club,** (Millfield School), Street TA11 6PP (01458 444320). *Location:* one mile south of Butleigh Village, near Street, Somerset. Flat course - trees. 9 holes, 2307 yards. S.S.S. 61. Practice area. *Green Fees:* information not available. *Eating facilities:* pub half a mile. *Visitors:* welcome only with a member. Secretary: G.L. Frisby (01458 832068).*

TAUNTON. **Oake Manor Golf Club,** Oake, Taunton TA4 1BA (01823 461993; Fax: 01823 461995). *Location:* seven minutes' drive from Junction 26 of the M5 - take A38 towards Taunton and follow signs to Oake. Enjoyable and challenging parkland course with water features on 10 of the 18 holes. Magnificent setting with views of the Blackdown and Quantock Hills. 18 holes, 6109 yards. S.S.S 69. Driving range, practice holes. *Green Fees:* 18 holes weekdays £22.00; weekends £25.00. Afternoon special £13.00. Phone (01823 461993) for Golf Reservations. *Eating facilities:* bar, restaurant, lounge. *Visitors:* welcome any day but booking tee time essential. Function rooms (seat up to 300). *Society Meetings:* by arrangement, contact Golf Manager. Golf Manager & Professional: Russell Gardner (01823 461993).
e-mail: russell@oakemanor.com
website: www.oakemanor.com

TAUNTON. **Taunton and Pickeridge Golf Club,** Corfe, Taunton TA3 7BY (01823 421240). *Location:* four miles south of Taunton on the B3170. Undulating parkland. 18 holes, 5926 yards. S.S.S. 68. Practice ground, indoor shed. *Green Fees:* £24.00/£28.00 weekdays, £35.00 weekends. *Eating facilities:* restaurant and bar. *Visitors:* welcome. *Society Meetings:* by arrangement with the Secretary. Professional: G.J. Milne (01823 421790). Secretary: M.P.D. Walls (01823 421537; Fax: 01823 421742).
e-mail: sec@taunt-pickgolfclub.sagehost.co.uk

TAUNTON. **Taunton Vale Golf Club,** Creech Heathfield, Taunton TA3 5EY (01823 412220; Fax: 01823 413583). *Location:* just off A361 at Junction with A38 between Junctions 24 and 25 of M5; easily accessible. Parkland. Two courses. 18 holes, 6167 yards. S.S.S. 69. 9 holes, 1943 yards. S.S.S. 31. 10 bay floodlit driving range. *Green Fees:* weekdays £20.00 for 18 holes, £10.00 for 9 holes; weekends £25.00 for 18 holes, £12.00 for 9 holes. Special daily rates and Society rates available, please enquire. *Eating facilities:* two bars with dining facilities. *Visitors:* welcome, telephone for bookings essential. *Society Meetings:* welcome by arrangement. For all the latest information see our website. Professional: Martin Keitch (01823 412880). Secretary: Joanne Wyatt (01823 412220; Fax: 01823 413583).
e-mail: tvgc@easynet.co.uk
website: www.tauntonvalegolf.co.uk

TAUNTON. **Vivary Golf Course,** Vivary Park, Taunton TA1 3JW (01823 289274). *Location:* turn into Wilton Road at side of police station. Turn left at Vivary Arms Inn. Flat parkland course with ponds and ducks. 18 holes, 4620 yards. S.S.S. 63. Practice area, tennis courts. *Green Fees:* information not provided. *Eating facilities:* licensed bar and restaurant. Available for private functions. *Visitors:* always welcome. Professional: Dave Hawker (01823 333875). Secretary: Dave Pike (01823 289274).

TICKENHAM. **Tickenham Golf Club,** Clevedon Road, Tickenham BS21 6RY (01275 856626). *Location:* M5 Junction 20, signposted Nailsea on left after Tickenham. Challenging championship style contoured greens. 9 holes, 2000 yards. S.S.S. 58, Par 60. 24 bay floodlit driving range, power tees, putting green, bunkers. *Green Fees:* weekday £7.00 9 holes, £11.00 18 holes; weekends £9.00 9 holes, £14.00 18 holes. *Eating facilities:* 19th hole licensed bar, hot and cold food. *Visitors:* welcome. *Society Meetings:* welcome, telephone for rates. Professionals: A. Sutcliffe, S. Jarrett, A. Smith.

WEDMORE. **Isle of Wedmore Golf Club,** Lineage, Wedmore BS28 4QT (01934 713649; Fax: 01934 713696). *Location:* from A38 Bristol/Bridgwater Road, take Wedmore Road from Lower Weare. Parkland, gently undulating fairways with magnificent views. Practice area. 18 holes, 6057 yards. S.S.S. 69. Small practice area, putting green. *Green Fees:* weekdays £20.00 per round, £30.00 per day; weekends £20.00 per round, £30.00 per day; reduced rates with member. *Eating facilities:* full bar and restaurant, upstairs function/society room. *Visitors:* always welcome. Soft spikes only. *Society Meetings:* welcome. Professional: Graham Coombe (01934 712452; Fax: 01934 713554). Secretary: Andrew Edwards (01934 713649; Fax: 01934 713696).

WELLS. **Wells (Somerset) Golf Club Ltd**, East Horrington Road, Wells BA5 3DS (01749 675005). *Location:* one mile east of city centre off B3139. Parkland, wooded. 18 holes, 6018 yards. S.S.S. 69. Practice area. 12 bay floodlit driving range open to the public. *Green Fees:* weekdays £24.00; weekends and Bank Holidays £30.00. *Eating facilities:* restaurant and bar. *Visitors:* welcome, no play before 9.30am weekends and Public Holidays. *Society Meetings:* full packages available at all times. Professional: Adrian Bishop (01749 679059). Secretary: Christine Searle (Tel & Fax: 01749 683171). e-mail: secretary@wellsgolfclub99.freeserve.co.uk

WESTON-SUPER-MARE. **Weston-Super-Mare Golf Club**, The Clubhouse, Uphill Road North, Weston-Super-Mare BS23 4NQ (01934 626968). *Location:* M5 Junction 21 - on the sea front. Flat links course with excellent greens. 18 holes, 6251 yards. S.S.S. 70. Practice area plus nets. *Green Fees:* information not available. *Eating facilities:* full bar and catering facilities. *Visitors:* welcome weekdays and weekends. Handicap Certificate required. *Society Meetings:* catered for weekdays. Professional: Mike LaBand (Tel & Fax: 01934 633360). Secretary: (01934 626968; Fax: 01934 621360).* e-mail: karen@wsmgolfclub.fsnet.co.uk

---

WESTON-SUPER-MARE. **Worlebury Golf Club,** Monks Hill, Worlebury, Weston-Super-Mare BS22 9SX (01934 623214). *Location:* from M5 (Junction 21) then A370 and first exit left onto old Bristol Road to town for two miles. Turn right into Baytree Road and continue to top of Milton Hill. Hill top with extensive views of the Severn Estuary and Wales. 18 holes, 5936 yards. S.S.S. 69. Practice ground and putting green. *Green Fees:* weekdays £20.00 per day, £12.00 with a member; weekends and Bank Holidays £30.00 per day, £17.00 with a member. *Eating facilities:* bar and restaurant. *Visitors:* welcome without reservation. *Society Meetings:* catered for by arrangement. Professional: Gary Marks (01934 418473). Secretary: Mike W. Wake (01934 625789; Fax: 01934 621935).

WINCANTON. **Wincanton Golf Club**, The Racecourse, Wincanton BA9 8BJ (01963 34606; Fax: 01963 34668). *Location:* in the middle of the racecourse, half a mile from the town centre. Very flat course, testing layout; large bunkers protecting very well maintained greens. 18 holes, 6182 yards. Par 70, S.S.S. 69. Good practice facilities. Teaching/coaching on individual or group basis; hire of clubs/trolley/buggy. *Green Fees:* information not available. *Eating facilities:* coffee shop. *Visitors:* welcome at all times. *Society Meetings:* can be catered for if booked in advance. Professionals: Andrew England and Tony Isaacs.

YEOVIL. **Yeovil Golf Club,** Sherborne Road, Yeovil BA21 5BW (01935 422965). *Location:* on A30, one mile from town centre towards Sherborne on right before Babylon Hill. Parkland. 18 holes, 6150 yards. S.S.S. 70. 9 holes, 4891 yards. S.S.S. 65. Practice ground and putting green. 20-bay floodlit range. *Green Fees:* Old course £25.00 per round weekdays, £30.00 per round weekends and Bank Holidays; 9 hole course £18.00 weekdays, £20.00 weekends and Bank Holidays. *Eating facilities:* bars and dining room with full menu every day. *Visitors:* welcome, Handicap Certificates required for 18 hole course, telephone Pro shop to check times. *Society Meetings:* welcome weekdays except Tuesdays. Professional: G. Kite (01935 473763; Fax: 01935 478605). Secretary/ Manager: G. Dodd (01935 422965; Fax: 01935 411283).

THE APPEARANCE OF AN
ASTERISK (*)
AT THE END OF A CLUB OR
COURSE ENTRY INDICATES
THAT UP-TO-DATE
INFORMATION
HAS NOT BEEN SUPPLIED

Staffordshire

BARLASTON. **Barlaston Golf Club,** Meaford Road, Stone ST15 8UX (Tel & Fax: 01782 372795). *Location:* one mile south of Barlaston off A34; between Stoke and Stone. 18 holes, 5801 yards. S.S.S. 68. *Green Fees:* information not provided. *Eating facilities:* dining room and bar snacks with lounge bar. *Visitors:* welcome anytime. *Society Meetings:* welcome weekdays. Professional: Ian Rogers. Secretary: H Thompson (Tel & Fax: 01782 372867).
e-mail: barlaston.gc@virgin.net
website: www.bgc.evelplay.net

BURTON UPON TRENT. **The Branston Golf and Country Club,** Burton Road, Branston, Burton upon Trent DE14 3DP (01283 512211; Fax: 01283 566984). *Location:* A38 Junction A5121. Flat parkland adjacent to the River Trent, spectacular 18th hole, water on 13 holes (flowing). 18 holes, 6697 yards. S.S.S. 72. 9 holes 1856 yards, S.S.S. 58. *Green Fees:* weekdays £30.00; weekends £40.00. *Eating facilities:* restaurant, bar, spikes bar, private rooms. *Visitors:* welcome, two week advance booking system in operation, restrictions weekends. Buggy hire, trolleys available. Country Club has extensive leisure facilities. *Society Meetings:* welcome midweek, special rates. Professional: Richard Odell (01283 512211; Fax: 01283 566984). Golf and Estates Manager: Graham Pyle (01283 512211; Fax: 01283 566984).

BURTON UPON TRENT. **The Craythorne,** Craythorne Road, Stretton, Burton upon Trent DE13 0AZ (01283 564329; Fax: 01283 511908). *Location:* A38 first turning to Burton from Derby, A5121 signposted Stretton. Parkland. 18 holes, 5556 yards. S.S.S. 68. Floodlit driving range, pitch and putt course. *Green Fees:* weekdays £30.00 per round; weekends and Bank Holidays £36.00 per round, £40.00 all day. Evening rate available during summer, winter rates available. *Eating facilities:* bars and restaurant open daily; function room. *Visitors:* welcome at all times, booking required at weekends. Special society and golfing packages. *Society Meetings:* welcome, special rates for parties over 16. Professional: Steve Hadfield (01283 533745). Managing Director: Tony Wright.
e-mail: admin@craythorne.co.uk
website: www.craythorne.co.uk

CANNOCK. **Beau Desert Golf Club,** Rugeley Road, Hazel Slade, Cannock WS12 5PJ (01543 422626; Fax: 01543 451137). *Location:* A460 Hednesford, signposted. Heathland course. 18 holes, 6310 yards. S.S.S. 71. Driving Range. Practice ground. *Green Fees:* £40.00 weekdays; £50.00 weekends. *Eating facilities:* full catering and bar. *Visitors:* welcome anytime subject to availability. *Society Meetings:* catered for Monday to Thursday. Professional: Barrie Stevens (01543 422492). Secretary: J.N. Bradbury.

CANNOCK. **Cannock Park Golf Club,** Stafford Road, Cannock WS11 2AL (01543 578850). *Location:* on the A34 Stafford Road, quarter of a mile from

Cannock town centre. Parkland course, playing alongside Cannock Chase. 18 holes, 5149 yards. S.S.S. 65. *Green Fees:* £9.00 weekdays, £11.00 weekends. Phone bookings up to two weeks in advance. Reductions for Juniors. *Eating facilities:* available. *Visitors:* welcome every day. Golf shop, inside leisure centre. *Society Meetings:* welcome weekdays. Professional: David Dunk (Tel & Fax: 01543 578850). Secretary: Chris Milne (01543 571091).

CHEADLE near. **Whiston Hall Golf Club and Mansion Court Hotel,** Whiston, Near Cheadle ST10 2HZ (01538 266260). *Location:* A52 Stoke to Ashbourne road, three miles from Alton Towers. Scenic course set in beautiful countryside. 18 holes, 5784 yards. S.S.S. 69. *Green Fees:* information not available. *Eating facilities:* extensive Clubhouse Bar Menu available from 8.00am onwards. *Visitors:* welcome at any time. Golfing theme rooms for all types of golfing breaks. Snooker, fly fishing. *Society Meetings:* all welcome 7 days a week. 27 hole package and lunch, three course evening meal (choice of menu). Golf breaks also available. Secretary: Mr R. Cliff.*

LEEK. **Leek Golf Club,** Cheddleton Road, Birchall, Leek ST13 5RE. (01538 385889). *Location:* one mile south of Leek on A520. Undulating parkland. 18 holes, 6218 yards. S.S.S. 70. *Green Fees:* weekdays £26.00; weekends and Bank Holidays £32.00. *Eating facilities:* full catering facilities 11.30am-11pm. Light refreshments from 10am. *Visitors:* welcome most times by prior arrangement. *Society Meetings:* catered for by arrangement Wednesdays only. Catering (01538 381983). PGA Professional: Ian Benson (01538 384767). Secretary: J.B. Cooper. (01538 384779; Fax: 01538 384535).

LEEK. **Leek Westwood Golf Club,** Newcastle Road, Leek ST13 7AA (01538 398385). *Location:* A53 one and a half miles south of Leek. Moorland/parkland. 18 holes, 6207 yards. S.S.S. 70. Practice area, nets, chipping green. *Green Fees:* weekdays £20.00, weekends £20.00 - phone first. *Eating facilities:* full facilities. *Visitors:* welcome weekdays. *Society Meetings:* weekdays by arrangement. Professional: Darren Squire (01538 398897). Secretary:Craig Reid (Tel & Fax: 01538 398385; Fax: 01538 382485). Club Administrator: Carol Povey.

LICHFIELD. **The Seedy Mill Golf Club,** Elmhurst, Near Lichfield WS13 8HE (01543 417333; Fax: 01543 418098). *Location:* just off A51 north of Lichfield. Parkland with lakes, ponds and streams. The Mill: 18 holes, 6305 yards. S.S.S. 70; The Spires: 9 holes, Par 3. 26 bay floodlit driving range. *Green Fees:* weekdays £24.00; weekends £29.00. Society and corporate packages. *Eating facilities:* full clubhouse facilities open 7.30am to 11pm. *Visitors:* welcome at all times. *Society Meetings:* welcome weekdays and weekends. Professional: Chris Stanley. Secretary: Kevin Denver. General Manager: Richard Lee.

LICHFIELD. **Whittington Heath Golf Club,** Tamworth Road, Lichfield WS14 9PW (01543 432317). *Location:* on A51 Tamworth-Lichfield Road. Wooded heathland. 18 holes, 6490 yards. S.S.S. 71. Practice ground. *Green Fees:* weekdays £35.00 per round, £50.00 36 holes. *Eating facilities:* meals available at all times. *Visitors:* welcome weekdays only. Handicap Certificate, EGU Card or letter of introduction required. *Society Meetings:* catered for Wednesdays and Thursdays by arrangement. Professional: Adrian Sadler (01543 432261). Secretary: Mrs J.A. Burton (01543 432317; Fax: 01543 433962). Steward: 01543 432212. e-mail: info@whgcgolf.freeserve.co.uk

NEWCASTLE-UNDER-LYME. **Jack Barkers Keele Golf Centre,** Keele Road, Newcastle-under-Lyme ST5 5AB (01782 627596). *Location:* A525 Newcastle to Whitchurch, opposite University of Keele. Undulating parkland. 18 holes, 6396 yards, 5822 metres, S.S.S. 70. Driving range. *Green Fees:* weekdays £9.50 weekends £13.50. Juniors £5.50 weekdays, £10.50 weekends. *Eating facilities:* available. *Visitors:* welcome at all times. Hire: Buggies £10.00 per round; Clubs £6.00 per round; Trolleys £2.50 per round. *Society Meetings:* welcome by arrangement. Manager: Mr N. Worrall.

NEWCASTLE-UNDER-LYME. **Newcastle-under-Lyme Golf Club,** Whitmore Road, Newcastle-under-Lyme ST5 5AB (01782 616583). *Location:* M6 Junction 15, one mile from Newcastle-under-Lyme. Parkland. 18 holes, 6317 yards white, 6201 yards yellow. S.S.S. 71 white, 70 yellow. *Green Fees:* information not available. *Eating facilities:* restaurant and bar meals. *Visitors:* welcome. Restrictions at weekends. *Society Meetings:* Wednesdays, Thursdays and a limited number of Fridays. Contact Secretary/Manager for details. Professional: P. Symonds (01782 618526). Secretary/ Manager: K.P. Geddes (01782 617006).*

PENKRIDGE. **The Chase Golf Club,** Pottal Pool Road, Penkridge ST19 5RN (01785 712191). *Location:* M6 Junction 13, take the A449 to Wolverhampton, then left onto B5012 towards Cannock then onto Rugeley Road. Flat parkland with Links characteristics. 18 holes, 6613 yards. S.S.S. 71. 20 bay floodlit driving range and teaching academy. Putting green, bunker, and chip and run facility. *Green Fees:* weekdays incl. Fridays £20.00, weekends £25.00. *Eating facilities:* excellent clubhouse facilities. *Visitors:* please ring to book, members have priority. Fully stocked pro shop. *Society Meetings:* welcome at reduced rates. Professional: James Green. General Manager: Mark Clarke.

RUGELEY. **Lakeside Golf Club,** Rugeley Power Station, Armitage Road, Rugeley WS15 1PR (01889 575667). *Location:* nearest town Rugeley (between Lichfield and Stafford), course over power station grounds. Flat parkland adjacent River Trent. 18 holes, 5765 yards. S.S.S. 68. *Green Fees:* £10.00 with member. *Eating facilities:* bar, lunchtime weekends and every evening. *Visitors:* must be accompanied by member. *Society Meetings:* welcome if arranged in advance. Secretary: T. D. Moore (01889 575667).

RUGELEY near. **St Thomas's Priory,** Armitage Lane, Armitage, Near Rugeley (01543 491116; Fax: 01543 492244). *Location:* one mile south-east of Rugeley on A513, opposite Ash Tree Inn. Undulating parkland. 18 holes, 5969 yards. S.S.S. 70. Practice area available. *Green Fees:* information not available. *Eating facilities:* full restaurant and bar facilities. *Visitors:* welcome weekdays, weekends, Handicap Certificates required. *Society Meetings:* by arrangement. Professional: Richard O'Hanlon (Tel & Fax: 01543 492096).

STAFFORD. **Brocton Hall Golf Club,** Brocton, Stafford ST17 0TH (01785 661901; Fax: 01785 661591). *Location:* off A34 Stafford to Cannock four miles south east of Stafford. Undulating parkland. 18 holes, 6095 yards. S.S.S. 69. *Green Fees:* weekdays £33.00; weekends and Bank Holidays £40.00. *Visitors:* by arrangement. *Society Meetings:* by arrangement Tuesdays and Thursdays. Professional: Nevil Bland (01785 661485). Secretary: Graham Nicholls (01785 661901).

STAFFORD. **Ingestre Park Golf Club,** Ingestre, Near Stafford ST18 0RE (01889 270845; Fax: 01889 271434). *Location:* six miles east of Stafford, between Tixall and Great Haywood. Parkland. 18 holes, 6352 yards. S.S.S. 70. Extensive practice ground. *Green Fees:* 18 holes £25.00, £30.00 more than 18 holes weekdays. *Eating facilities:* lunch and dinner menu. *Visitors:* welcome weekdays before 3.30pm. Handicap Certificate required. Buggies available. *Society Meetings:* welcome with reservation except Wednesday. £42.00 all inclusive 27 holes package for Societies. Special winter rates on application. Professional: Danny Scullion (01889 270304). Manager: C.J. Radmore (01889 270845).

STAFFORD. **Stafford Castle Golf Club,** Newport Road, Stafford ST16 1BP (01785 223821). *Location:* M6 Junction 13 or 14, two miles from club. Parkland course. 9 holes, (18 tees). 6383 yards. S.S.S. 70, Par 71. **Green Fees:** weekdays £16.00 per day; weekends £20.00 per day. Subject to review. Special winter rates on application. *Eating facilities:* snacks and full catering available except Mondays. **Visitors:** welcome except Sunday mornings. Handicap Certificate required. **Society Meetings:** catered for by arrangement. Administrator: S. Calvert.

STOKE-ON-TRENT. **Burslem Golf Club Ltd,** Wood Farm, High Lane, Tunstall, Stoke-on-Trent ST6 7JT (01782 837006). *Location:* leave Burslem centre by Hamil Road, turn left at High Lane junction, one mile on right. Parkland. 9 holes, 5360 yards. S.S.S. 66. *Green Fees:* weekdays £16.00 per day. *Eating facilities:* meals and refreshments by arrangement except Wednesday and Sunday. *Visitors:* welcome weekdays with reservation. Bona fide golf club members only. *Society Meetings:* catered for.

STOKE-ON-TRENT. **Goldenhill Golf Course,** Mobberley Road, Goldenhill, Stoke-on-Trent ST6 5SS (01782 784715). *Location:* on A34 between Tunstall and Kidsgrove, north of Stoke city centre. Rolling parkland course, panoramic views of Mow Cop and Newchapple. 18 holes, 5957 yards, 5447 metres. S.S.S. 69. *Green Fees:* information not available. *Eating facilities:* fully licensed bar and cafeteria. *Visitors:* municipal course with small membership, visitors and societies always welcome.*

STOKE-ON-TRENT. **Jack Barker's Greenway Hall,** Stanley Road, Stockton Brook, Stoke-on-Trent ST9 9LJ (01782 503158). *Location:* M6 (Junction15) - A500 - A53 to Leek, right at crossroads in Stockton Brook. Countryside course with wooded areas and some beautiful scenic views. 18 holes, 5681 yards, 5194 metres. S.S.S. 67. *Green Fees:* start from just £6.00. *Eating facilities:* meals available from 10am to 11pm. *Visitors:* welcome. *Society Meetings:* welcome, packages available on request. Manager: Mark Armitage.

STOKE-ON-TRENT. **Parkhall Golf Course,** Hulme Road, Weston Coyney, Stoke-on-Trent ST3 5BH (01782 599584). *Location:* one mile east of Longton. Tight unforgiving heathland course, great character and ideal for new golfers looking to improve their game. 18 holes, 2335 yards, 2136 metres. S.S.S. 54. Par 3. *Green Fees:* information not available. *Eating facilities:* chocolate, crisps, pop, tea and coffee. *Visitors:* all welcome. Golf clubs and trolley hire available. Seven days advance booking required for weekends and Bank Holidays. *Society Meetings:* welcome.

STOKE-ON-TRENT. **Trentham Golf Club,** 14 Barlaston Old Road, Trentham, Stoke-on-Trent ST4 8HB (01782 642347). *Location:* off A34 travelling south of Newcastle (Staffs.). Left at Trentham Gardens onto Longton Road; right at National Westminster Bank. Open Chamionship Regional Qualifying course. 18 holes, 6619 yards. S.S.S. 72. Practice ground. *Green Fees:* weekdays £40.00, weekends £50.00 (Sundays after 12 noon). Playing with member first guest £10.00, second guest £15.00. *Eating facilities:* lunches and dinners available. *Visitors:* welcome, weekends from 12 noon onwards. Handicap Certificate required. *Society Meetings:* welcome by prior arrangement. Professional: S. Wilson (01782 657309). Secretary: R.N. Portas (01782 658109).

STOKE-ON-TRENT. **Trentham Park Golf Club,** Trentham Park, Trentham, Stoke-on-Trent ST4 8AE (Tel & Fax: 01782 658800). *Location:* off A34 adjoining Trentham Gardens near Junction 15 on M6. 18 holes, 6425 yards. S.S.S. 71. *Green Fees:* information not available. Visitors: welcome weekdays with reservation. *Society Meetings:* catered for Wednesdays and Fridays only. Professional: Brian Rimmer (01782 642125; Fax: 01782 658800). Secretary: Trevor Berrisford (Tel & Fax: 01782 658800).*

STONE. **Izaak Walton Golf Club,** Eccleshall Road, Cold Norton, Stone ST15 0NS (01785 760900). *Location:* on the B5026 linking Stone and Eccleshall. Testing course with many water features. 18 holes, 6298 yards. S.S.S. 72. Driving range. *Green Fees:* weekdays £15.00, weekends £20.00. *Eating facilities:* available. *Visitors:* welcome with some restrictions. *Society Meetings:* welcome with some restrictions. Contact the Secretary Mr T. T. Tyler for information. Professional: Julie Brown.

STONE. **Stone Golf Club,** The Fillybrooks, Stone ST15 0NB (01785 813103). *Location:* one mile north west of Stone on the A34 adjacent to the Walton Inn. Parkland. 9 holes, 6299 yards. S.S.S. 70. *Green Fees:* weekdays £20.00. *Eating facilities:* full meals to order, snacks always available, bar. *Visitors:* welcome weekdays only, not Bank Holidays. Snooker table. *Society Meetings:* catered for by arrangement. Secretary: P.R. Farley (01785 284875).

STOURBRIDGE. **Enville Golf Club Ltd,** Highgate Common, Enville, Stourbridge DY7 5BN (01384 872074). *Location:* leave A449 at Stewpony Hotel taking Bridgnorth Road A458, fork right after Fox Inn following signs for Halfpenny Green Airport. Two flat wooded heathland courses. Highgate Course: 18 holes, 6556 yards. S.S.S 72; Lodge Course: 18 holes, 6217 yards. S.S.S. 70. *Green Fees:* weekdays £30.00 18 holes, £40.00 36 holes. *Eating facilities:* meals available. *Visitors:* welcome weekdays with Handicap Certificate, advisable to phone prior to visit. Ladies' Day Thursday; weekends with members only. *Society Meetings:* welcome except Thursdays and weekends. Party of 30 or more receives a 10% discount. Professional: S. Power (01384 872585). Secretary/Manager: J.J. Bishop (01384 872074; Fax: 01384 873996).

STREETLY. **Little Aston Golf Club,** Streetly, Sutton Coldfield B74 3AN (0121-353 2066). *Location:* off A454. Parkland course. 18 holes, 6670 yards. S.S.S. 73. *Green Fees:* £50.00 weekdays. *Eating facilities:* dining room and bars, lunch and dinner. *Visitors:* welcome on weekdays by prior arrangement, weekends with a member. *Society Meetings:* welcome Tuesday, Wednesday and Friday. Professional: Brian Rimmer (0121-353 0330). Manager: (0121-353 2942; Fax: 0121-580 8387). website: littleastongolf.co.uk

TAMWORTH. **Drayton Park Golf Club**, Centenary Drive, Drayton Park, Tamworth B78 3TN (01827 251139; Fax: 01827 284035). *Location:* follow signs for Drayton Pleasure Park, adjacent drive at the top. Parkland with well defined wooded holes. 18 holes, 6473 yards. S.S.S. 71. Practice ground. *Green Fees:* weekdays £36.00 per round/day. Weekends £40 per round. Special rates for Societies over 12 - £30.00. *Eating facilities:* full catering facilities. *Visitors:* welcome weekdays except Wednesday mornings. *Society Meetings:* catered for Tuesdays and Thursdays, booked through Secretary. Professional: M.W. Passmore (01827 251478). Secretary: D.O. Winter (01827 251139; Fax: 01827 284035). website: www.draytonparkgc.co.uk

TAMWORTH. **Tamworth Golf Club**, Eagle Drive, Amington, Tamworth B77 4EG (01827 709303; Fax: 01827 709304). *Location:* Junction 10 M42 Tamworth, A5, towards Amington. Parkland course used by NAPGC for Juniors' and Ladies' Championships. 18 holes, 6488 yards. Par 73 S.S.S. 72. Practice driving ground, putting green. *Green Fees:* information not available. *Eating facilities:* lounge bar with catering. *Visitors:* welcome. *Society Meetings:* contact pro shop for information. Professional: Wayne Alcock (01827 709303). Secretary: Mrs J.P. Cornall.*

UTTOXETER. **Manor Golf Club**, Leese Hill, Kingstone, Uttoxeter ST14 8QT (01889 563234). *Location*: A518, Uttoxeter to Stafford road, 3 miles from Uttoxeter. Grassland course. 18 holes, 6008 yards. S.S.S. 69. Practice range and putting green. *Green Fees*: weekdays £15.00; weekends £25.00. *Eating facilities*: bar meals available Monday to Friday from 12pm till 4pm, Saturday and Sunday from 11am to 4pm. *Visitors*: welcome every day, please book in advance for Saturdays and Sundays. Tuition available. *Society Meetings*: welcome Monday to Friday, please call for rates. Course Manager: Ant Foulds. e-mail: ant-foulds@bigfoot.com

UTTOXETER. **Uttoxeter Golf Club**, Wood Lane, Uttoxeter ST14 8JR (01889 566552; Fax: 01889 567501). *Location:* approximately half a mile past the main entrance to the racecourse. Undulating parkland, very picturesque scenery. 18 holes, 5801 yards. S.S.S. 69. Practice area and putting green. *Green Fees:* weekdays £24.00 per day, weekends and Bank Holidays £30.00 per day. *Eating facilities:* bar, clubhouse dining room. *Visitors:* welcome except on days of "major" competitions. A starting sheet operates at weekends. Buggies and trolleys available for hire. *Society Meetings:* welcome by arrangement (maximum 60). but not at weekends or on Bank Holidays. Professional: Mr Adam McCandless (01889 564884; Fax: 01889 567501). Secretary: Alastair Griffiths (01889 566552; Fax: 01889 567501).

WOLSTANTON. **Wolstanton Golf Club,** Dimsdale Old Hall, Hassam Parade, Wolstanton, Newcastle ST5 9DR (01782 622413; Fax: 01782 622718). *Location:* one mile north of Newcastle, turn right off A34 (Dimsdale Parade), first right (Hassam Parade) then right again 75 yards. Flat parkland. 18 holes, 5807 yards. S.S.S. 68. *Green Fees:* weekdays £25.00, £10.00 as member's guest; weekends as member's guest only, £25.00. *Eating facilities:* full catering service and bar. *Visitors:* welcome weekdays; weekends only as member's guest. Trolleys available. *Society Meetings:* catered for by arrangement. Professional: Simon Arnold (Tel & Fax: 01782 622718). Secretary: Valerie Keenan (01782 622413; Fax: 01782 622718).

Please mention
'THE GOLF GUIDE'
when enquiring about clubs or accommodation.

THE APPEARANCE OF AN ASTERISK * AT THE END OF A CLUB OR COURSE ENTRY INDICATES THAT UP-TO-DATE INFORMATION HAS NOT BEEN SUPPLIED

Suffolk

ALDEBURGH. **Aldeburgh Golf Club,** Saxmundham Road, Aldeburgh IP15 5PE (01728 452890). *Location:* A12 north from Ipswich; turn right on A1094 to Aldeburgh. Heathland course, abundance of dense gorse, many challenging Par 4s, no Par 5s. 18 holes, 6349 yards. S.S.S. 71; also 9 holes, 2114 yards. S.S.S. 32. *Green Fees:* weekdays £50.00 per day, £40.00 after 12 noon; weekends £60.00 per day, £40.00 after 12 noon. *Eating facilities:* lunches by arrangement. *Visitors:* welcome by arrangement, to play on 18-hole course must have club Handicap Certificate. No three or four balls allowed. *Society Meetings:* by arrangement. Professional: K.R. Preston (01728 453309). Secretary: 01728 452890; Fax: 01728 452937).

BECCLES. **Beccles Golf Club,** The Common, Beccles NR34 9BX (01502 712244). *Location:* A146 Beccles by-pass, to town centre at Safeway roundabout. left over level crossing past Jet filling station. Flat commonland. 9 holes, 5558 yards, 5084 metres. S.S.S. 67. *Green Fees:* weekdays £8.00 (with member £5.00); weekends and Bank Holidays £10.00 (with member £5.00). Twilight fee (after 4pm) £5.00. *Eating facilities:* two bars, snacks available. Meals to order. *Visitors:* welcome anytime. *Society Meetings:* catered for by prior arrangement. Secretary: D.W. Trunks (01502 712244).

BUNGAY. **Bungay and Waveney Valley Golf Club,** Outney Common, Bungay NR35 1DS (01986 892337; Fax: 01986 892222). *Location:* a quarter mile from town centre and alongside A143. Flat, heath-type course. 18 holes, 6044 yards. S.S.S. 69. *Green Fees:* £24.00 18 holes, £30.00 day, £15.00 county card. Subject to alteration for 2004. *Eating facilities:* available except Mondays. *Visitors:* welcome weekdays, weekends with member only. Must telephone (01986 892337) prior to a visit to book a tee time. *Society Meetings:* by arrangement with Secretary. Professional: N. Whyte (01986 892337; Fax: 01986 892222). Secretary: R.W. Stacey (01986 892337; Fax: 01986 892222).

BURY ST EDMUNDS. **Bury St Edmunds Golf Club,** Tut Hill, Bury St Edmunds IP28 6LG. *Location:* B1106 just off A14. Flat parkland. 18 holes, 6675 yards. S.S.S. 72; 9 holes, 2217 yards. S.S.S. 31. Practice facilities. *Green Fees:* weekdays £30.00 on 18-hole course; two rounds on 9 hole course £13.00 weekdays, £15.50 weekends. *Eating facilities:* available. *Visitors:* welcome Monday to Friday on both courses; weekends on 9 hole course only. *Society Meetings:* catered for. Professional: Mark Jillings (01284 755978). Secretary: John Taylor (01284 755979; Fax: 01284 763288). e-mail: info@burygolf.co.uk

BURY ST EDMUNDS. **Flempton Golf Club**, Flempton, Bury St Edmunds IP28 6EQ (01284 728291). *Location:* follow A1101 from Bury St Edmunds towards Mildenhall for about four miles, course on right. 9 holes, 6240 yards. S.S.S. 70. *Green Fees:* £30.00 per day. *Eating facilities:* by arrangement. *Visitors:* welcome, except Bank Holidays. Must produce Handicap Certificate. Professional: Chris Aldred (01284 728291). Secretary: M.S. Clark.

BURY ST EDMUNDS. **The Suffolk Golf and Country Club**, Fornham St Genevieve, Bury St Edmunds IP28 6JQ (01284 706777; Fax: 01284 706721). *Location:* Exit A14 at Bury St Edmunds West and travel north on B1106 for approx. 2 miles. Mature parkland, testing water hazards. Putting green and practice ground. 18 hole Genevieve course 6350 yards. S.S.S. 71. *Green Fees:* information not provided. *Eating facilities:* Bars and restaurant; residential packages available. *Visitors:* welcome, booking advised. Club, buggy and trolley hire. Indoor pool, with spa sauna and steam room. 41 bedroom en suite hotel. Conference facilities. *Society Meetings:* society packages available. Professional: Stephen Hall. Secretary: Mervyn Aho. e-mail: thelodge@the-suffolk.co.uk website: www.the-suffolk.co.uk

DISS. **Diss Golf Club**, Stuston Common, Diss IP21 4AA (01379 641025). *Location:* B1077 off A140, half-a-mile from Diss railway station, one mile from town centre. The course complete with its natural hazards provides a good test of golf. 18 holes, 6206 yards. S.S.S. 69. Par 70. *Green Fees:* £25.00, £12.50 if playing with a member. New 15 bay driving range one mile from Clubhouse adjacent to the 15th hole. *Eating facilities:* are excellent. *Visitors:* welcome but weekends only with a member. *Society Meetings:* Golf Societies are welcome. There is a well stocked shop and lessons are available from the professional. Well supported club with membership available. Contact Secretary/Manager for details; easy payment terms optional. Professional: Nigel Taylor (01379 644399). Secretary: Mr Chris Wellstead (01379 641025; Fax: 01379 644586). Steward: J.W. Mackrell (01379 642847). e-mail: sec.dissgolf@virgin.net website: www.club-noticeboard.co.uk/diss

FELIXSTOWE. **Felixstowe Ferry Golf Club**, Ferry Road, Felixstowe IP11 9RY (01394 283060). *Location*: one mile from town centre, follow signs to Golf Club. Seaside links course. 18 holes, 6308 yards. S.S.S. 70. Also a 9 hole course. Practice area. *Green Fees*: weekdays £30.00 per day; £20.00 after 1pm. *Eating facilities*: diningroom and bar. *Visitors*: welcome weekdays, but advisable to check first; weekends must play with member. Handicap Certificates required. Two self catering flats available, free golf included in charges. *Society Meetings*: catered for Tuesdays, Wednesdays and Fridays. Professional: Ian MacPherson (01394 283975). Secretary: Richard Tibbs (01394 286834).

FRAMLINGHAM. **Cretingham Golf Club**, Swans Lane, Cretingham, Woodbridge IP13 7BA (01728 685275). *Location:* off A1120, signposted to Cretingham, 10 miles north of Ipswich. Wooded inland course, challenging water holes. 18 holes, 4966 yards. Par 68. Practice 9 hole course. *Green Fees:* weekdays 9 holes £10.00, 18 holes £14.00; weekends and Bank Holidays 9 holes £10.00, 18 holes £16.00. *Eating facilities:* restaurant and fully licensed bar. *Visitors:* always welcome, no restrictions. Please book in advance. Tennis available. Caravans and log cabin available to let. *Society Meetings:* welcome. Professional: Neil Jackson (01728 685275). Secretary: Kate Jackson.

HAVERHILL. **Haverhill Golf Club Ltd,** Coupals Road, Haverhill CB9 7UW (Tel & Fax: 01440 761951). *Location:* Sturmer Road turn into Chalkestone Way, right into Coupals Road. Club is one mile on right. Undulating parkland with river and ravine. 18 holes, 5929 yards. S.S.S. 69. Practice ground. *Green Fees:* weekdays £28.00 per day, weekends and Bank Holidays £35.00. Half price if playing with a member. *Eating facilities:* clubhouse, snacks, hot meals, bar. *Visitors:* welcome at all times except when first tee booked for matches and societies. *Society Meetings:* welcome. Professional: Nick Duc (01440 712628; Fax: 01440 712628). Secretary: Jill Edwards (Tel & Fax: 01440 761951).

IPSWICH. **Fynn Valley Golf Club,** Witnesham, Ipswich IP6 9JA (01473 785267; Fax: 01473 785632). *Location:* two miles north of Ipswich on B1077. Attractive, undulating parkland along the Fynn Valley. 18 holes, 6361 yards. S.S.S. 71. 9 hole Par 3 course, 23 bay floodlit golf range (10 undercover), practice bunker and putting green. *Green Fees:* £22.00 per round weekdays; £25.00 per round weekends (twilight discounts). *Eating facilities:* bar, terrace, gourmet restaurant. *Visitors:* welcome, members only Sunday mornings, Ladies priority Wednesday mornings. Special rates for parties of 12 or more. Two golf shops. Teaching facilities, golf buggies and caravan site. *Society Meetings:* welcome. Professionals: Kelvin Vince, Paul Wilby, Alex Lucas, Simon Dainty. (Tel & Fax: 01473 785463). Secretary: A.R. Tyrrell (01473 785267; Fax: 01473 785632). e-mail: enquiries@fynn-valley.co.uk website: www.fynn-valley.co.uk

> THE APPEARANCE OF AN ASTERISK (*)
> AT THE END OF A CLUB OR COURSE
> ENTRY INDICATES THAT
> UP-TO-DATE INFORMATION
> HAS NOT BEEN SUPPLIED

IPSWICH. **Hintlesham Hall Golf Club,** Hintlesham, Ipswich IP8 3NS (01473 652761; Fax: 01473 652750). *Location:* four miles west of Ipswich on the A1071 to Sudbury. Parkland, championship standard - Architect: Martin Hawtree. 18 holes, 6638 yards. S.S.S. 72. Full practice facilities. *Green Fees:* information not available. *Eating facilities:* full catering facilities. *Visitors:* please telephone for tee off times. Accommodation available at Hintlesham Hall Hotel. *Society Meetings:* telephone enquiries welcome. We have a growing national reputation for the organisation of golf days. Professional: Alastair Spink.*

IPSWICH. **Ipswich Golf Club,** Purdis Heath, Bucklesham Road, Ipswich IP3 8UQ. *Location:* three miles east of Ipswich on Bucklesham Road. Heathland. 18 holes, 6435 yards. S.S.S. 71. 9 holes, 1930 yards. S.S.S. 59. *Green Fees:* weekdays £30.00 per round, £40.00 per day, 9 holes £10.00 per day; weekends and Bank Holidays 18 holes with a member only, 9 holes £12.50 per day. *Eating facilities:* full catering facilities available for visitors to 18 hole course only. *Visitors:* by prior arrangement for 18 hole course, and must produce Handicap Certificate or letter of introduction. No restriction for 9 hole course. *Society Meetings:* by special reservation only and on Society terms. Professional: S.J. Whymark (01473 724017). Secretary: N.M. Ellice (01473 728941).

IPSWICH. **Rushmere Golf Club,** Rushmere Heath, Woodbridge Road, Ipswich IP4 5QQ (01473 727109). *Location:* off A1214 north from Ipswich, 300 yards signposted. Heathland course. 18 holes, 6262 yards. S.S.S. 70. Practice facilities. *Green Fees:* £30.00. *Eating facilities:* full catering available. *Visitors:* welcome except 4.30-5.30pm, weekends after 2.30pm. Handicap Certificate required. *Society Meetings:* welcome. Professional: N.T.J. McNeill (01473 728076). Secretary:R.W.G. Tawell (01473 725648).
e-mail: rushmeregolfclub@talk21.com
website: www.club-noticeboard.co.uk/rushmere

IPSWICH/WOODBRIDGE. **Best Western Ufford Park Hotel, Golf and Leisure**, Yarmouth Road, Ufford, Woodbridge, Near Ipswich IP12 1QW (01394 383555; Fax: 01394 383582). *Location:* A12 northwards to A1152 to Melton. In Melton turn left at traffic lights, one mile on the right hand side. Challenging 120-acre parkland course. A "Top 40 British Winter Course" for the last 3 years. 18 holes, 6485 yards. S.S.S. 71. Practice ground. *Green Fees:* weekdays £25.00; weekends £30.00. Special Golf Breaks available. *Eating facilities:* bar snacks, carvery and à la carte restaurant. *Visitors:* welcome anytime, need to book tee time in advance. 50 en-suite bedroomed hotel including a 6 bedroomed golfers' lodge. Ideal for groups, and full leisure centre including pool, gym, sauna, steam room, jacuzzi etc..Beauty and hair salons. Buggies for hire, tuition breaks available. *Society Meetings*: welcome, competitive rates, details on request. PGA Head Professional. Stuart Robertson (01394 383480 (Golf Academy)). Secretary: Bob Tidy. (01394 382836; Fax: 01394 383582).
website: www.uffordpark.co.uk
website: www.golfacademy.co.uk

LOWESTOFT. **Rookery Park Golf Club,** Beccles Road, Carlton Colville, Lowestoft NR33 8HJ (Tel & Fax: 01502 509190). *Location:* A146 Beccles to Lowestoft road. Parkland. 18 holes, 6729 yards. S.S.S. 72. 9 hole Par 3 course. Practice ground. *Green Fees:* weekdays £25.00, with a member £15.00; weekends £30.00, with a member £17.50. *Eating facilities:* bar, restaurant. *Visitors:* welcome weekdays (Saturdays and Bank Holidays after 11am). Handicap Cards must be produced. *Society Meetings:* welcome. Professional: M. Elsworthy (01502 515103). Secretary/Manager: A. Atkinson (01502 509190; Fax: 01502 509191).

MILDENHALL. **Royal Worlington and Newmarket Golf Club,** Golf Links Road, Worlington, Bury St. Edmunds IP28 8SD (01638 712216; Fax: 01638 717787). *Location:* seven miles north east of Newmarket, signposted off A11 just south of Barton Mills roundabout. Inland links type course. 9 holes, 3105 yards. S.S.S. 70 (18 holes). Practice ground. *Green Fees:* weekdays £55.00 per day, £40.00 if after 2pm (12 noon in winter). *Eating facilities:* lunch and tea available with prior notice; no evening meals. *Visitors:* welcome weekdays only, Handicap Certificate or letter of introduction from home club required. Trolleys for hire. Professional: Malcolm Hawkins (01638 715224). Secretary: Squadron Leader K.J. Weston (Tel & Fax: 01638 717787).

NEWMARKET. **Links Golf Club,** Cambridge Road, Newmarket CB8 0TG (01638 663000; Fax: 01638 661476). *Location:* one mile south-west of Newmarket, opposite racecourse. Relatively flat parkland. 18 holes, 6582 yards. S.S.S. 72. Two practice grounds. *Green Fees:* midweek £24.00 per round, £32.00 per day; weekends and Bank Holidays £28.00 per round, £36.00 per day. *Eating facilities:* restaurant and bar. *Visitors:* welcome, not before 11.30am Sundays. Handicap Certificate required. *Society Meetings:* by arrangement. Professional: Mr John Sharkey (01638 662395). Secretary: M.L. Hartley (01638 663000; Fax: 01638 661476). website: www.club-noticeboard.co.uk/newmarket

RAYDON. **Brett Vale Golf Club,** Noakes Road, Raydon, Ipswich IP7 5LR (01473 310718). *Location:* midway between Colchester and Ipswich, just off A12 on B1070 to Hadleigh, head for Raydon Water Tower. Undulating countryside parkland course within Dedham Vale in natural valley setting. 18 holes, 6000 yards. S.S.S. 69. 5 bay outdoor Golf Academy, practice ground, putting green. *Green Fees:* weekdays £22.50, day ticket £40.00; weekends £28.00. *Eating facilities:* clubroom bar and restaurant; society/function room and bar. *Visitors:* welcome anytime. Pro shop; buggies and power trolley hire. *Society Meetings:* welcome anytime, various packages available. Professional: Robert Taylor (01473 310718). Secretary: John Reid (01473 310718).

SOUTHWOLD. **Southwold Golf Club,** The Common, Southwold IP18 6TB (01502 723234). *Location:* from A12 Blythburgh turn off on A1095 to Southwold. Flat common land with sea views. 9 holes, 6052 yards. S.S.S. 69. *Green Fees:* weekdays £26.00 per round, weekends £28.00 per round. Weekly tickets £75.00. Daily ticket £35.00. *Visitors:* welcome, phone for availability. *Society Meetings:* welcome, Fridays only. Professional: B.G. Allen (01502 723790). Hon. Secretary: P. Obern (01502 723248).

STOKE-BY-NAYLAND. **Stoke by Nayland Golf Club,** Keepers Lane, Leavenheath, Colchester CO6 4PZ (01206 262836; Fax: 01206 263356). *Location:* just off A134 Colchester to Sudbury on B1068 towards Stoke by Nayland. Undulating parkland with water hazards. Two courses (1) Gainsborough - 18 holes, 6516 yards. S.S.S. 71. (2) Constable - 18 holes, 6544 yards. S.S.S. 71. 20 bay covered range, practice area. *Green Fees:* on request. *Eating facilities:* full catering and bars. *Visitors:* welcome, please ring for availability and tee bookings. *Society Meetings:* welcome weekdays, book well in advance. Seasonal packages offered. Extensive Health and Leisure Facility including gymnasium, pool, sauna, jacuzzi and spa; modern, spacious, en suite hotel rooms overlooking lake and fairways. Professional: Kevin Lovelock (01206 262769). Secretary: Peter Barfield (01206 265815).
e-mail: info@stokebynaylandclub.co.uk
website: www.stokebynaylandclub.co.uk

STOWMARKET. **Stowmarket Golf Club Ltd,** Lower Road, Onehouse, Stowmarket IP14 3DA (01449 736473; Fax: 01449 736826). *Location:* on B1508 from Stowmarket to Onehouse. Parkland. 18 holes, 6101 yards. S.S.S. 69. Driving range. *Green Fees:* weekdays £31.00 per round, £37.00 per day; weekends £34.00 per round, £46.00 per day. *Eating facilities:* lunches, snacks all week. *Visitors:* welcome, avoid Wednesdays. Handicap Certificate required. *Society Meetings:* catered for Thursdays and Fridays only. Professional: D. Burl (01449 736392). Secretary: G.R. West (01449 736473).

SUDBURY. **Newton Green Golf Club**, Newton Green, Sudbury CO10 0QN. *Location:* on A134 three miles east of Sudbury. Flat course. 18 holes, 5947 yards. Par 69. Practice ground. *Green Fees:* day ticket £30.00, 18 holes £22.00. *Eating facilities:* fully licensed bar, full catering facilities, separate dining room available. *Visitors:* welcome (except Sundays and Tuesdays before 12.30pm); trolleys for hire. *Society Meetings:* welcome by arrangement. PGA Professional: Tim Cooper (01787 313215). Secretary/Manager: Ray Baines (01787 377217). e-mail: info@newtongreengolfclub.co.uk website: www.newtongreengolfclub.co.uk

THORPENESS. **Thorpeness Golf Club and Hotel,** Thorpeness, Leiston IP16 4NH (01728 452176; Fax: 01728 453868). *Location:* leave A12 at Aldeburgh turnoff. Heathland coastal course. 18 holes, 6271 yards. S.S.S. 71. *Green Fees:* weekdays £33.00 per day; weekends £38.00 per day. *Eating facilities:* bar, restaurant, terrace and garden. *Visitors:* welcome on application, telephone Pro shop for times. Handicap Cetificate required. Accommodation available – 30 bedrooms. Snooker room, seven tennis courts. *Society Meetings:* welcome. Professional: Frank Hill (01728 454926). Golf Manager: Charlie Langlands (01728 452176).

WOODBRIDGE. **Seckford Golf Club,** Seckford Hall Road, Great Bealings, Near Woodbridge IP13 6NT (01394 388000; Fax: 01394 382818). *Location:* between Martlesham and Woodbridge just off A12. Undulating parkland course maintained in excellent condition. 18 holes, 4936 yards. Par 67. Full length driving range and putting green. *Green Fees:* information not available. *Eating facilities:* fully licensed bar, restaurant. *Visitors:* always welcome, telephone to book your place. Golf shoes must be worn and no jeans. *Society Meetings:* Groups and societies welcome, please book in advance. All enquiries (01394 388000; Fax: 01394 382818).

WOODBRIDGE. **Waldringfield Golf Club,** Newbourne Road, Waldringfield, Woodbridge IP12 4PT (01473 736768). *Location:* five miles north of Ipswich, off the old A12. Easy walking, picturesque heathland course with attractive water features. 18 holes, 6079 yards. S.S.S. 69. Limited practice area available. *Green Fees:* weekdays £22.00 per round, £30.00 per day; weekends £26.00 per round, £36.00 per day. Special rates available for societies by arrangement. *Eating facilities:* full service. *Visitors:* welcome weekdays and weekends. *Society Meetings:* welcome weekdays and weekends by arrangement. Course Administrator: (01473 736417). Manager: Pat Whitham (01473 736768. Fax: 01473 736793)

WOODBRIDGE. **Woodbridge Golf Club,** Bromeswell Heath, Woodbridge IP12 2PF (01394 382038; Fax: 01394 382392). *Location:* leave A12 at Melton Roundabout. After traffic lights, follow A1152 over level crossing, fork left at roundabout. Club is 400 yards on right. Heathland. 18 holes, 6299 yards. S.S.S. 70. 9 holes, 3191 yards. S.S.S. 70. Large practice ground. *Green Fees:* information not available. *Eating facilities:* main bar, casual bar and restaurant. *Visitors:* not before 9.30am, not at weekends. Handicap Certificates mandatory on 18 hole course, no restriction on 9 hole course. Telephone call advisable. *Society Meetings:* by prior arrangement, maximum number 36. Professional: C. Elliot (01394 383213). Secretary: A. Theunissen (01394 382038; 01394 382392).* .

Surrey

BAGSHOT. **Pennyhill Park Hotel and Country Club**, London Road, Bagshot GU19 5EU (01276 471774; Fax: 01276 473217). *Location:* just off A30 at Bagshot. Wooded, hilly course. 9 holes, 2000 yards. S.S.S. 64. *Green Fees:* information not available. *Eating facilities:* Ascot Bar, St James Brasserie restaurant, Latymer à la carte restaurant, five star hotel with 123 luxury bedrooms; tennis court, outdoor heated swimming pool, clay pigeon shooting, gym etc. *Visitors:* prior booking must be made in advance. *Society Meetings:* welcome anytime. Country Club Manager: Claire Williams.*

BAGSHOT. **Windlesham Golf Club**, Grove End, Bagshot GU19 5HY. *Location:* A30 west from Sunningdale at Junction of A30 and A332 or Junction 3 from M3 and take the A322 to Bracknell then junction of A30/A332. Challenging parkland course designed by Tommy Horton - USPGA, greens and tees of highest specification. 18 holes, 6650 yards. S.S.S. 72. Practice range with three covered bays, practice hole. *Green Fees:* information not available. *Visitors:* welcome, please ring first on weekdays, weekends after 12 noon: no visitors on Bank Holidays. Teaching Academy School; carts available. Professional Lee Mucklow (01276 472323). Secretary: R. Park (01276 452220; Fax: 01276 452290).

BANSTEAD. **Cuddington (Banstead) Golf Club Ltd**, Banstead Road, Banstead SM7 1RD (020 8393 0952; Fax: 020 8786 7025). *Location:* 200 yards from Banstead Railway Station. 18 holes, 6614 yards. S.S.S. 71. *Green Fees:* on application. *Visitors:* welcome with reservation. *Society Meetings:* catered for on Thursdays and some Tuesdays pm. Professional: M. Warner. Secretary: D. M. Scott. e-mail: ds@cuddingtongc.co.uk website: www.cuddingtongc.co.uk

BLETCHINGLEY. **Bletchingley Golf Club,** Church Lane, Bletchingley RH1 4LP (01883 744666; Fax: 01883 744284). *Location:* off A25, three miles west from Junction 6 M25. Parkland course, sand based. 18 holes, 6531 yards. S.S.S. 71. Practice ground. *Green Fees:* weekdays £25.00, weekends £30.00. *Eating facilities:* lounge/dining room, large function room, bar. *Visitors:* welcome. Carts available. *Society Meetings:* welcome. Professional: A. Dyer (01883 744848; Fax; 01883 744284). Manager: R. Borer (01883 744666; Fax: 01883 744284).

CAMBERLEY. **Camberley Heath Golf Club,** Golf Drive, Portsmouth Road, Camberley GU15 1JG (01276 23258; Fax: 01276 692505). *Location:* adjacent to Ravenswood roundabout on the A325. Heathland and pine, designed by Harry Colt - his best, established 1913. 18 holes, 6337 yards, 5794 metres. S.S.S. 70. Practice ground. *Green Fees:* £52.00. *Eating facilities:* restaurants and Teppan Yaki (Japanese Steak Bar). *Visitors:* welcome weekdays only by prior arrangement. *Society Meetings:* welcome by prior arrangement weekdays only; various packages available. Professional: Glenn Ralph (01276 27905). Secretary/General Manager: M.C.G. Harris (01276 23258).

CARSHALTON. **Oaks Sports Centre Ltd**, Woodmansterne Road, Carshalton SM5 4AN (020 8643 8363; Fax: 020 8770 7303). *Location:* on the B2032 past Carshalton Beeches Station, Oaks Sports Centre signposted north of A2022, half way between A217 and A237. Open 6am, 7 days, 364 days per year. Meadowland course. 18 holes, 6023 yards. S.S.S 69. 9 holes, 1590 yards. S.S.S 28. 18 bay golf range. *Green Fees:* information not provided. *Eating facilities:* bar lounge and cafeteria. *Visitors:* public course, everyone welcome. Five squash courts, changing rooms. Conference facilities. *Society Meetings:* by arrangement. Professional: Mr G.D. Horley. Secretary: Mr D.J. Capper. e-mail: golf@oaks.sagehost.co.uk website: www.oakssportscentre.co.uk

CATERHAM. **Surrey National Golf Club,** Rook Lane, Chaldon, Caterham CR3 5AA (01883 344555). *Location:* M25, Junction 7 (M23) towards Croydon. After two miles turn right into Dean Lane and then left into Rook Lane, entrance on the left. Mature landscape with stunning views of South Downs. 18 holes. 6850 yards. Par 72. Green Fees: Monday to Friday £25.00 per round, £40.00 per day; weekends and Bank Holidays £28.00 after 11am. *Eating facilities:* bar and catering facilities available. *Visitors:* welcome weekdays and weekends at restricted times. Buggies and carts available for hire. *Society Meetings:* welcome weekdays and weekends at restricted times. Professional: David Kent. General Manager: Simon Hodsdon. e-mail: caroline@surreynational.co.uk website: www.surreynational.co.uk

CATERHAM near. **The Woldingham Golf Club,** Halliloo Valley Road, Woldingham, near Caterham CR3 7HA (01883 653501; Fax: 01883 653502). *Location:* Caterham, Junction 6 M25, 3 miles. Downland course. 18 holes. 6393 yards. S.S.S. 71. Putting greens, practice ground. *Green Fees:* information not available. *Eating facilities:* Balcony bar, Spike bar, Brasserie restaurant. *Visitors:* welcome, not before 12 noon at weekends. *Society Meetings:* welcome Monday to Friday. "ASTAR" video studio on site. Professional: Nick Carter (01883 653541). Secretary: Greg Lewis.* website: www.woldinghamgc.co.uk

CHERTSEY. **Barrow Hills Golf Club**, Longcross, Chertsey KT16 0DS (01344 635770). *Location:* four miles west of Chertsey, adjacent to M3 at Longcross. 18 holes, 3090 yards. S.S.S. 53. *Green Fees:* information not available. *Visitors:* only with a member. Secretary: Mr R. Hammond (01483 234807 home).

CHERTSEY. **Laleham Golf Club,** Laleham Reach, Mixnams Lane, Chertsey KT16 8RP (01932 562188; Fax: 01932 564448). *Location:* M25 to Junction 11, follow directions to Thorpe Park, entrance opposite roundabout. Flat but interesting parkland course with water features. 18 holes, 6211 yards. S.S.S. 70. *Green Fees:* weekdays £30.00 per day, £25.00 per round; weekends with member only. *Eating facilities:* full restaurant and bar facilities. *Visitors:* welcome weekdays only, please phone to ensure no tee reservations. *Society Meetings:* catered for Mondays to Wednesdays at competitive rates. Professional: Hogan Stott (01932 562877). Secretary: Mrs Pauline Kennett (01932 564211; Fax: 01932 564448). e-mail: sec@laleham-golf.co.uk

CHESSINGTON. **Chessington Golf Club,** Garrison Lane, Chessington KT9 2LW (020 8391 0948). *Location:* off A243, 500 yards from Chessington World of Adventure. Opposite Chessington South Station, Junction 9 M25. Parkland course. 9 holes, 1679 yards. S.S.S. 28. Covered floodlit driving range. *Green Fees:* weekdays £8.50; weekends and Bank Holidays £10.00 (for 9 holes). Reductions for Juniors and Senior Citizens. *Eating facilities:* bar, coffee, catering available. *Visitors:* welcome. Facilities open to public 8.00am until 10.00pm (9.00 pm Saturday and Sunday). *Society Meetings:* welcome. Professional: Mark Janes (020 8391 0948; Fax: 020 8397 2068). Secretary: Martin Bedford (020 8391 0948; Fax: 020 8397 2068).

CHESSINGTON. **Surbiton Golf Club,** Woodstock Lane, Chessington KT9 1UG (020 8398 3101; Fax: 020 8339 0992). *Location:* two miles east of Esher, off A3 at Ace of Spades roundabout. Undulating parkland. 18 holes, 6055 yards. S.S.S. 69, Par 70. Practice area. *Green Fees:* information not provided. *Eating facilities:* snacks and lunches to order by reservation weekdays. *Visitors:* at weekends play with member only. *Society Meetings:* catered for Monday and Friday only. Professional: Paul Milton (020 8398 6619). Secretary: Chris Cornish (020 8398 3101). e-mail: surbitongolfclub@hotmail.com

CHIDDINGFOLD. **Chiddingfold Golf Club**, Petworth Road, Chiddingfold GU8 4SL (01428 685888). *Location:* Exit 10 off M25, A3 towards Portsmouth, take A283 turn off, golf course quarter-of-a-mile past Chiddingfold village. Parkland. 18 holes, 5500 yards. Par 70 S.S.S. 67. *Green Fees:* All days of the week and weekends, including Bank Holidays. *Visitors:* welcome. *Society Meetings:* welcome seven days, including Bank Holidays. Professionals: Malcolm Churchill, Reece McRae. Manager/Secretary: Adrian Hewat. e-mail: chiddingfoldgolf@btconnect.com website: www.chiddingfoldgc.co.uk

CHIDDINGFOLD. **Shillinglee Park Golf Club,** Chiddingfold, Godalming GU8 4TA (01428 708158; Fax: 01428 644391). *Location:* off A283 near Chiddingfold. Parkland. 9 holes, 5300 yards. S.S.S. 64. 6 hole pitch and putt course, ideal for learners. Well equipped Pro Shop. *Green Fees:* information not available. *Eating facilities:* excellent menu from snacks to à la carte. *Visitors:* welcome all week apart from Saturday and Thursday mornings. Advisable to book. Instruction available. *Society Meetings:* always welcome. Professional: Mark Dowdell (01428 653237). Secretary: Nikki Taylor. *

CHIPSTEAD. **Chipstead Golf Club Ltd,** How Lane, Coulsdon CR5 3LN (01737 555881; Fax: 01737 555404). *Location:* by Chipstead Station (Chipstead Valley Road). Parkland. 18 holes, 5504 yards, 5332 metres. S.S.S. 67. *Green Fees:* weekdays £30.00 per round, £40.00 per day, twilight £20.00; weekends only with a member. *Eating facilities:* full catering seven days a week, bar. *Visitors:* welcome weekdays except Tuesday mornings. *Society Meetings:* welcome full or half days. Director of Golf: Gary Torbett (01737 554939).

COBHAM. **Silvermere Golf and Leisure Complex,** Redhill Road, Cobham KT11 1EF (01932 584300). *Location:* half a mile from Junction 10 of M25 at A3. Wooded, parkland course with water on two holes. 34 bay driving range. *Green Fees:* £22.00; weekends £35.00 Twilight tickets available at reduced rates. *Eating facilities:* £½million new lakeside clubhouse serving food all day from 7am to 9pm, bar meals, snacks and lunches. *Visitors:* welcome every day but not early weekend mornings. *Society Meetings:* welcome, contact Secretary for details. Professional: Doug McClelland PGA (01932 584348). Secretary: Pauline Devereux (01932 584306; Fax: 01932 584301).

COULSDON. **Coulsdon Manor Hotel and Golf Centre,** Coulsdon Court Road, Coulsdon CR5 2LL (020 8668 0414; Fax: 020 8668 0342). *Location:* off J7 of M25 through Coulsdon towards Caterham B2030 turning left via Stoneyfield Road and left in Coulsdon Court Road. Parkland. 18 holes, 6037 yards. Par 70. S.S.S. 68. *Green Fees:* information not available. *Eating facilities:* Terrace bar/Orangery and Manor House Restaurant. *Visitors:* welcome, subject to availability. *Society Meetings:* welcome Mondays, Tuesdays, Thursdays and Fridays. Extensive banquet and conference facilities, 35 luxurious bedrooms, all en-suite. Professionals: Gordon Ritchie and James Leaver (020 8660 6083; Fax: 020 8668 3118). General Manager: Philip Thomas. *

COULSDON. **Woodcote Park Golf Club Ltd,** Meadow Hill, Bridle Way, Coulsdon CR5 2QQ. *Location:* south of Croydon, off A237. Parkland course. 18 holes, 6680 yards. S.S.S. 72. *Green Fees:* weekdays £35.00 per round, or per day. *Eating facilities:* meals at all times. *Visitors:* welcome with reservation. Handicap Certificate required. *Society Meetings:* up to 90 catered for, by arrangement. Professional: Wraith Grant (020 8668 1843). Secretary: A. Dawson (020 8668 2788; Fax: 020 8660 0918). e-mail: info@woodcotepgc.com website: www.woodcotepgc.com

CRANLEIGH. **Cranleigh Golf and Country Club**, Barhatch Lane, Cranleigh GU6 7NG (01483 268855; Fax: 01483 267251). *Location:* Guildford A281 Horsham take Cranleigh turn-off. Interesting parkland course. 18 holes, 5648 yards. S.S.S. 67. Covered driving range, practice ground. *Green Fees:* information not available. *Eating facilities:* bar, bar snacks, banqueting facilities available. *Visitors:* welcome weekdays after 10am; Thursdays and weekends afternoons only subject to availability. *Society Meetings:* welcome weekdays. Professional: Trevor Longmuir (01483 277188). Secretary: Mike Hale (01483 268855; Fax: 01483 267251). *

CRANLEIGH. **Wildwood Country Club**, Horsham Road, Alfold, Cranleigh GU6 8JE (01403 753255; Fax: 01403 752005). *Location:* 10 miles from Guildford on the A281 to Horsham, near Cranleigh. Only 40 minutes from London on the A3. Championship course set in wood and parkland, with mature woodland and many water hazards. An exhilarating challenge to all golfers. 27 holes, 6655 yards. S.S.S. 72. All weather practice range and 9 hole course. *Green Fees:* weekdays 18 holes £35.00, weekends 18 holes £50.00. *Eating facilities:* full bar/restaurant. *Visitors:* after 12 noon weekends. *Society Meetings:* after 12 noon weekends. Accommodation available locally. Professional: Mark Dowdell.

CRONDALL. **Bowenhurst Golf Centre Ltd,** Mill Lane, Crondall, Near Farnham GU10 5RP (01252 851695). *Location:* public golf course, south of M3, 5 miles from exit 5 Farnham side on A287 (behind garage). Parkland course with mature trees and lakes. 3658 yards S.S.S. 60. 20 bay floodlit driving range, two practice putting greens, practice bunker. *Green Fees:* weekdays £8.00, weekend £9.50 for 9 holes, £14.00 for 18 holes. Reduced rates weekdays seniors and juniors. *Visitors:* welcome at any time. Pro shop. *Society Meetings:* welcome, rates on application. Professional:Adam Hart (01252 851344). Secretary: Geoffrey Corbey.

CROYDON. **Addington Court Golf Ltd,** Featherbed Lane, Addington, Croydon CR0 9AA (020 8657 0281; Fax: 020 8651 0282). *Location:* two miles east of Croydon. Leave B281 at Addington Village. Dry, well-drained, wooded parkland course. Four

courses: Championship 5755 yards, S.S.S. 67. Falconwood 5513 yards, S.S.S. 67. Lower 9 hole course S.S.S 62. 18 hole, Par 3 course. 32-bay floodlit driving range. *Green Fees:* information not available. *Eating facilities:* restaurant, bar. *Visitors:* welcome anytime, no restrictions, public courses. *Society Meetings:* welcome. Professional: Tony Healy (020 8657 0281). *

CROYDON. **The Addington Golf Club,** 205 Shirley Church Road, Croydon CR0 5AB (020 8777 1055; Fax: 028 777 1701). *Location:* Wickam Road, Shirley. 30 minutes from centre of London. Heath and woodland as set out by the famous J.F. Abercromby with the world renowned 13th Par 3. 18 holes, 6338 yards. S.S.S. 71. *Green Fees:* £50.00. *Eating facilities:* bar and restaurant with full snack menu. *Visitors:* welcome weekdays. *Society Meetings:* by prior arrangement. Secretary: Bob Hill (020 8777 1055). e-mail: theaddgc@dialstart.net

CROYDON. **Addington Palace Golf Club,** Gravel Hill, Addington, Croydon CR0 5BB (020 8654 3061). *Location:* two miles east of Croydon Station. Undulating parkland course. 18 holes, 6339 yards. S.S.S. 71. *Green Fees:* information not available. *Eating facilities:* bar all day, catering 10am to 6.30pm. *Visitors:* welcome weekdays, weekends and Bank Holidays must be accompanied by a member. *Society Meetings:* welcome on Tuesdays, Wednesdays and Fridays. Professional: Roger Williams (020 8654 1786). Secretary: Mr David Monk (020 8654 3061).

CROYDON. **Le Meridien Selsdon Park & Golf Course**, Sanderstead, South Croydon CR2 8YA (020 8657 8811; Fax: 020 8651 6171). *Location:* three miles south of Croydon on A2022 Purley-West Wickham road. Parkland course, designed by J.H. Taylor. 18 holes, 6473 yards, 5919 metres. S.S.S. 71. Practice ground. *Green Fees:* please call for details. *Eating facilities:* hotel bars, restaurant and grill. *Visitors:* welcome all week with pre-bookable tee-off times, some times reserved for hotel guests. Buggies. *Society Meetings:* welcome by prior arrangement. P.G.A. Professional: Malcolm Churchill (020 8657 4129). Golf Reservations: (020 8657 8811). *

CROYDON. **Croham Hurst Golf Club,** Croham Road, South Croydon CR2 7HJ (020 8657 2075; Fax: 020 8657 3229). *Location:* midway between Croydon and Selsdon. Parkland. 18 holes, 6290 yards. S.S.S. 70. *Green Fees:* weekdays £40.00; weekends £50.00. *Eating facilities:* lunches, teas, snacks. *Visitors:* welcome with reservation on weekdays. *Society Meetings:* catered for booked one year ahead. Professional: (020 8657 7705). Secretary: David Free (020 8657 5581).
e-mail: secretary@chgc.co.uk
website: www.chgc.co.uk

CROYDON. **Shirley Park Golf Club Ltd,** 194 Addiscombe Road, Croydon CR0 7LB (020 8654 1143; Fax: 020 8654 6733). *Location:* on A232 one and a half miles from East Croydon Station. Parkland. 18 holes, 6210 yards. S.S.S. 70. Practice area. *Green Fees:* £35.00 weekdays; Saturday with a member only. Winter rate £28.00. Subject to review. *Eating facilities:* seven day catering, two bars. *Visitors:* welcome weekdays and Sunday afternoons. Trolleys and caddies if booked in advance. Reduced accommodation charges available from Croydon Park Hotel if booked through the Secretary. *Society Meetings:* welcome Mondays, Tuesdays, Thursdays and Fridays. Professional: Michael Taylor (020 8654 8767; Fax: 020 8654 6733). Secretary: David Roy (020 8654 1143; Fax: 020 8654 6733).
e-mail: secretary@shirleyparkgolfclub.co.uk
website: www.shirleyparkgolfclub.co.uk

DORKING. **Betchworth Park Golf Club (Dorking) Ltd,** Reigate Road, Dorking RH4 1NZ (01306 882052). *Location:* on A25 half-a-mile east of Dorking on Reigate Road. Parkland course. 18 holes, 6266 yards, 5730 metres. S.S.S 70. *Green Fees:* information not available. *Eating facilities:* lunches available daily. *Visitors:* welcome, not permitted Tuesday and Sunday mornings. Handicap Certificate required Fridays. *Society Meetings:* welcome Mondays and Thursdays. Professional: A Tocher (01306 884334). Manager: John Holton (01306 882052; Fax: 01306 877462).

DORKING. **Dorking Golf Club,** Chart Park, Dorking RH5 4BX (01306 886917). *Location:* on A24 half-a-mile south of junction with A25. Parkland/downland. 9 holes, alternative tees second 9, 5106 yards. S.S.S. 65. *Green Fees:* weekdays £15.00, £10.00 after 4pm. *Eating facilities:* full catering. *Visitors:* weekdays only without reservation. *Society Meetings:* catered for up to 24, over this number by arrangement. Professional/ Manager: A. Smeal.

DORKING. **Gatton Manor Hotel, Golf and Country Club,** Standon Lane, Ockley, Near Dorking RH5 5PQ (01306 627555; Fax: 01306 627713). *Location:* to the west of the village of Ockley on the A29 between Dorking and Horsham, easy access from M25 Junction 9. 18 hole championship length course in parkland, makes good use of the many rivers and lakes to make it a picturesque but challenging course. 18 holes, 6653 yards. S.S.S. 72.

Green Fees: information not available. *Eating facilities:* full à la carte restaurants and bars with bar meals. *Visitors:* welcome anytime except Sunday mornings. Hotel with 18 bedrooms all en suite, conference suites, gym and health club. Fishing and tennis available. *Society Meetings:* welcome weekdays only. Professional: Rae Sargent (01306 627557). Secretary: Linda Heath (01306 627555; Fax: 01306 627713.*
e-mail: gattonmanor@enterprise.net

EAST HORSLEY. **Drift Golf Club,** The Drift, East Horsley KT24 5HD (01483 284641). *Location:* the club is located just off the Drift Road which runs between Ockham Road (B2039) and Forest Road, East Horsley. Picturesque woodland course set in the heart of Surrey countryside. 18 holes, 6425 yards, 5877 metres. S.S.S. 72. Driving range and putting green. *Green Fees:* information not provided. *Eating facilities:* full bar, lounge, restaurant and bar snacks. *Visitors:* welcome Monday to Friday, must book in advance up to seven days. *Society Meetings:* catered for weekdays. General Manager: Liam Greasley (01483 284641).

EFFINGHAM. **Effingham Golf Club,** Guildford Road, Effingham KT24 5PZ (01372 452203; Fax: 01372 459959). *Location:* A246 between Guildford and Leatherhead. Downland course with magnificent views towards London. 18 holes, 6542 yards. S.S.S. 71. Large practice ground. *Green Fees:* weekdays £50.00 full day, £40.00 for 18 holes; weekends with a member only. *Eating facilities:* full bar and catering facilities. *Visitors:* welcome Monday-Friday. Handicap Certificate required. *Society Meetings:* welcome Wednesdays, Thursdays, Fridays. Professional: Steve Hoatson (01372 452606). Secretary: Simon Sheppard (01372 452203).

EPSOM. **Epsom Golf Club,** Longdown Lane South, Epsom KT17 4JR (01372 721666; Fax: 01372 817183). *Location:* off A240 into B288, 200 yards south of Epsom Downs Station. Downland, links-type course with fast, undulating greens. 18 holes, 5658 yards. S.S.S. 68. Par 69. Practice nets and putting green. *Green Fees:* £29.00/£32.00 per round weekday /weekend. *Eating facilities:* bar snacks available from two bars; dining room. *Visitors:* welcome anytime except am on Tuesday, Saturday and Sunday. *Society Meetings:* always welcome with similar exceptions to visitors. Professional and Tee Reservations: R. Goudie (01372 741867).
e-mail: secretary@epsomgolfclub.co.uk
website: www.epsomgolfclub.co.uk

EPSOM. **Horton Park Golf & Country Club,** Hook Road, Epsom KT19 8QG (020 8393 8400; Fax: 020 8394 1369). *Location:* Junction 9 of M25 four miles. Epsom Town and station five minutes car or taxi. Attractive parkland course situated within a picturesque country park with water hazards and lakes. *Eating facilities:* bar food, restaurant and function room. *Visitors:* welcome. *Society Meetings:* welcome weekdays and weekend afternoons. Pro shop (020 8394 2626). Professional: Martyn Hirst. General Manager: Anthony Picariello.

ESHER. **Moore Place Golf Club,** Portsmouth Road, Esher KT10 9LN (01372 463533). *Location:* half a mile from Esher town centre on Portsmouth Road. Undulating parkland course with featured trees - recently lengthened. 9 holes, 2148 yards. S.S.S. 60. *Green Fees:* weekdays £6.30; weekends £8.00. *Eating facilities:* bar and restaurant. *Visitors:* welcome, unrestricted. Smart casual dress; golf shoes required, hire available. *Society Meetings:* welcome anytime, 10% reduction for groups of 10 or more. Professional: Nick Gadd (01372 463533). Hon. Secretary: J. Darby (01932 880186). website: www.moore-place.co.uk

ESHER. **Sandown Golf Centre,** More Lane, Esher KT10 8AN. *Location:* signposted from A3, centre of Sandown Park Racecourse. Three golf courses; floodlit 33-bay driving range, plus grassed area. Cranfield Golf Academy. *Green Fees:* on application. *Eating facilities:* bar and restaurant. *Visitors:* welcome. *Society Meetings:* welcome. General Manager: David Parr (01372 461234; Fax: 01372 461203).

ESHER. **Thames Ditton and Esher Golf Club,** Portsmouth Road, Esher KT10 9AL (020 8398 1551). *Location:* "Scilly Isles" roundabout(s), Junction Kingston by-pass, A3. Wooded commonland. 9 holes played twice from different tees, 5149 yards. S.S.S. 65. Practice nets. *Green Fees:* information not available. *Eating facilities:* bar snacks, meals by arrangement. *Visitors:* welcome except Sunday mornings. Trolleys. *Society Meetings:* always welcome, phone the Professional. Professional: Rob Jones. Secretary: Allan Barry. *

FARNHAM. **Farnham Golf Club Ltd,** The Sands, Farnham GU10 1PX (01252 782109; Fax: 01252 781185). *Location:* off A31 at Seale or Runfold slip roads. Follow signs to The Sands club situated at junction of Sands Road and Blighton Lane. Mixture of wooded parkland and heathland. 18 holes, 6447 yards. S.S.S. 71. Large practice ground. *Green Fees:* weekdays £40.00 round, £45.00 day; weekends with a member £16.50 per day. May to August twilight rate £25.00 inclusive, after 5.30pm. *Eating facilities:* two bars and diningroom, full high standard catering.

Visitors: welcome weekdays with Handicap Certificate. *Society Meetings:* welcome Wednesday to Friday by prior booking. Professional: Grahame Cowlishaw (01252 782198; Fax: 01252 781185). Secretary: Mrs J. Elliott (01252 782109; Fax: 01252 781185).

FARNHAM. **Hankley Common Golf Club,** Tilford Road, Tilford, Farnham GU10 2DD (01252 792493; Fax: 01252 795699). *Location:* off A3, right at lights at Hindhead. Off A31 (Farnham by-pass) left at lights, three miles beyond level crossing. Heathland, dry and sandy links-type course. 18 holes, 6438 yards. S.S.S. 71. Practice ground. *Green Fees:* weekdays £50.00 per round, £65.00 per day; weekends £65.00 per round after 2pm. *Eating facilities:* full range available, restaurant and two bars. *Visitors:* welcome by appointment with Secretary. Handicap Certificate required. *Society Meetings:* catered for on Tuesdays and Wednesdays. Professional: Peter Stow (01252 793761). Secretary: J.S.W. Scott (01252 792493).

GODALMING near. **Hurtmore Golf Club,** Hurtmore Road, Near Godalming GU7 2RN (01483 426492; Fax: 01483 426121). *Location:* A3 Guildford, M25 (15 minutes) A3 exit Guildford to Portsmouth. Undulating parkland with seven large lakes. 18 holes, 5530yards. S.S.S. 67 men, 68 ladies. Practice nets and putting green. *Green Fees:* weekdays £13.00; weekends £18.00. Twilight fees: weekdays £8.00, weekends £10.00. *Eating facilities:* bar, restaurant. *Visitors:* welcome at all times, pay and play course with 200 members. Bookings taken by telephone. *Society Meetings:* welcome by prior booking. Professional and General Manager: Maxine Burton.

GODALMING. **West Surrey Golf Club,** Enton Green, Godalming GU8 5AF (01483 421275). *Location*: off the A3 south of Guildford, half mile past Milford Station/crossing. Wooded parkland. 18 holes, 6479 yards, 5944 metres. S.S.S. 71. Practice ground. *Green Fees*: weekdays £35.00; weekends £45.00. *Eating facilities*: bar, diningroom. *Visitors*: welcome, must be member of recognised golf club and have current Handicap Certificate. *Society Meetings*: catered for by prior arrangement. Professional: A. Tawse (01483 417278). Secretary: R.T. Crabb (01483 421275).

GUILDFORD. **Bramley Golf Club,** Bramley, Near Guildford GU5 0AL (01483 892696; Fax: 01483 894673). *Location:* three miles south of Guildford on the Horsham road, A281. Parkland. 18 holes, 5882 yards. S.S.S. 69. Practice area, driving range. *Green Fees:* weekdays £35.00 per round, £40.00 per day; weekends with member only. *Eating facilities:* catering from 7:30am to 9pm, bar from 11am to 10pm. *Visitors:* welcome Monday to Friday. *Society Meetings:* by prior arrangement with the Club . Professional Shop: 01483 893685. General Manager / Director of Golf: Gary Peddie (01483 892696).

GUILDFORD. **Guildford Golf Club,** High Path Road, Merrow, Guildford GU1 2HL (01483 563941). Steward: (01483 5631842). *Location:* from Guildford take Epsom Road (A246) turn right at the third set of traffic lights. Downland course. 18 holes, 6090 yards. S.S.S. 70. Practice area. *Green Fees:* £35.00 per round, £45.00 per day weekdays; weekends with a member only. Subject to review. *Eating facilities:* snacks and restaurant service. *Visitors:* welcome weekdays, with member weekends. *Society Meetings:* catered for Tuesday to Friday. Professional: P. G. Hollington (01483 566765). Secretary: B.J. Green (01483 563941; Fax: 01483 453228).

GUILDFORD. **Merrist Wood Golf Club,** Coombe Lane, Worplesdon, Guildford GU3 3PE (01483 238890; Fax: 01483 238896). *Location:* three miles from Guildford, off A323 to Aldershot. 18 holes, 6909 yards. S.S.S. 73. *Green Fees:* £30.00 per round, or £100 for fourball. *Visitors:* welcome; after 11am at weekends. Please call for up to date specials. *Society Meetings:* welcome. Professional: Chris Connell (01483 238894). Manager: Rob Gumbrell.

GUILDFORD. **Puttenham Golf Club,** Heath Road, Puttenham, Guildford GU3 1AL (01483 810498; Fax: 01483 810988). *Location:* Farnham and Guildford, signposted off Hog's Back (A31). Wooded/heathland course. 18 holes, 6211 yards. S.S.S. 70. Practice ground. *Green Fees:* on application. *Eating facilities:* dining room, bar and 19th. *Visitors:* welcome weekdays only by prior arrangement. (Weekends playing with a member). *Society Meetings:* catered for Wednesdays and Thursdays. Secretary and Professional: Gary Simmons. e-mail: enquiries@puttenhamgolfclub.co.uk website: www.puttenhamgolfclub.co.uk

GUILDFORD. **Roker Park Golf Club,** Fairlands Farm, Aldershot Road, Guildford GU3 3PB (01483 236677 Fax: 01483 232324). *Location:* from A3 Guildford take A323 to Aldershot, course two miles on right. Flat parkland course. 9 holes, 3037 yards. S.S.S.72. *Green Fees:* weekdays £8.50, Juniors and Senior Citizens £6.00, weekends £10.00, unlimited golf £12.50 Monday - Friday. *Eating facilities:* restaurant and bar. *Visitors:* welcome, pay and play course. *Society Meetings:* welcome weekdays only, reductions for parties over 12. Driving range, £2.70 for bucket of 60 balls, or £1.50 for 30 balls. Professional: Adrian Carter. Secretary: Mrs. C.A. Tegg (Tel & Fax: 01438 232324).

GUILDFORD near. **Sutton Green Golf Club,** New Lane, Sutton Green, Near Guildford GU4 7QF (01483 766849). *Location:* midway between Guildford and Woking, just off A3. Easy walking parkland course, co-designed by Laura Davies, water features on nine holes. 18 holes, 6300 yards. S.S.S. 70. Practice ground. *Green Fees:* weekdays £40.00; weekends £50.00. *Eating facilities:* fully air conditioned bar and restaurant. *Visitors:* welcome midweek, weekends after 2pm. Golf buggies and carts available; changing room. *Society Meetings:* welcome midweek. Professional: Paul Tedder (01483 766849; Fax: 01483 750289). Secretary: John Buchanan (01483 747898; Fax: 01483 750289).

HINDHEAD. **The Hindhead Golf Club,** Churt Road, Hindhead GU26 6HX (01428 604614; Fax: 01428 608508). *Location:* one and a half miles north of Hindhead on A287 to Farnham. The course is played over heathland and wooded valleys. Open Championship regional qualifying venue. 18 holes, White Tees 6356 yards, S.S.S. 70; Yellow Tees 6106 yards, S.S.S. 69. *Green Fees:* £50.00 per day weekdays; £60.00 weekends. *Eating facilities:* restaurant, snack bar, summer bar and members' bar. *Visitors:* welcome with Handicap Certificate, weekends by appointment. *Society Meetings:* Wednesdays and Thursdays only. Professional: Neil Ogilvy (01428 604458). Secretary: John A. Davies.

KINGSTON-UPON-THAMES. **Coombe Hill Golf Club,** Golf Club Drive, off Coombe Lane West, Kingston KT2 7DF (020 8336 7600; Fax: 020 8336 7601). *Location:* from A3 take A238 to Kingston. Hilly and tree lined. 18 holes, 6293 yards. S.S.S. 71. *Green Fees:* information not available. *Eating facilities:* diningroom 8am to 3.30pm weekdays, bar (varying hours). *Visitors:* weekdays only, with a member weekends. *Society Meetings:* please contact Secretary. Director of Golf/Professional: Craig Defoy (020 8949 3713). Secretary: Mrs Christina Defoy.*

KINGSTON-UPON-THAMES. **Coombe Wood Golf Club,** George Road, Kingston Hill KT2 7NS (020-8942 0388). *Location:* from A3 take A308(east) or A238(west). Wooded course. 18 holes, 5300 yards. S.S.S. 66. *Green Fees:* weekdays £25.00, £16.00 after 6pm; weekends £35.00, afternoons only. *Eating facilities:* catering all week. *Visitors:* welcome; weekends afternoons only. *Society Meetings:* by arrangement Wednesday to Friday. Professional: P. Wright (020-8942 6764). Secretary: M.T. Newey (020-8942 0388; Fax: 020 8942 5665). website: www.coombewoodgolf.com

KINGSWOOD. **Kingswood Golf and Country Club Ltd,** Sandy Lane, Kingswood, Tadworth KT20 6NE (01737 833316; Fax: 01737 833920). *Location:* five miles south of Sutton just off A217/Junction 8 M25. 18 holes, 6904 yards. S.S.S. 73. Large practice area. *Green Fees:* weekdays £40.00 per round; weekends £55.00 per round. *Eating facilities:* table d'hôte Monday to Friday (reservations only) and bar snacks. *Visitors:* welcome anytime, restricted times at weekends. Squash courts, snooker tables. *Society Meetings:* Corporate Golf Days catered for. Professional: Terry Sims (01737 832334). Administration: Lisa Andrews/Elaine Labbett (01737 832188).

LEATHERHEAD. **Leatherhead Golf Club,** Kingston Road, Leatherhead KT22 0EE (01372 843966; Fax: 01372 842241). *Location:* off Junction 9 of M25, onto A243 to Kingston. Parkland, many mature trees. 18 holes, 6203 yards. S.S.S. 70. Practice ground, putting green. *Green Fees:* weekdays £37.50 18 holes, £55.00 36 holes; weekends £37.50 one round afternoons only. *Eating facilities:* à la carte restaurant, cafe/ brasserie and lounge bar. *Visitors:* welcome, no visitors Saturday or Sunday mornings. *Society Meetings:* welcome, from 16 to 100 by reservation. Professional: Dene Mara (01372 843956). Director of Golf: Simon Norman (01372 843966).
e-mail: secretary@lgc-golf.co.uk
website: www.lgc-golf.co.uk

LEATHERHEAD. **Pachesham Park Golf Centre,** Oaklawn Road, Leatherhead KT22 0BT (01372 843453; Fax: 01372 844076). *Location:* half a mile outside Leatherhead just off A244, quarter of a mile off Junction 9 M25. Undulating parkland course. 9 holes, 2806 yards. S.S.S. 67. 33 bay floodlit driving range, putting green, chipping area. *Green Fees:* weekdays £9.00 9 holes; weekends £10.50 9 holes. *Eating facilities:* fully licensed bar, restaurant. *Visitors:* welcome, bookings taken two days in advance. Must wear golf shoes. *Society Meetings:* welcome. Professional/Secretary: Phil Taylor.

LEATHERHEAD. **Tyrrells Wood Golf Club Ltd,** Leatherhead KT22 8QP (01372 376025). *Location:* south-east on A24 Leatherhead by-pass, half a mile left to Headley, then 200 yards right. Hillside, wooded course with glorious views. 18 holes, 6234 yards. S.S.S. 70. Small practice ground. *Green Fees:* information not available. *Eating facilities:* catering by arrangement with Manager. *Visitors:* no visitors Saturday or Sunday mornings. *Society Meetings:* catered for by arrangement with Manager. Professional: Simon Defoy (01372 375200). Secretary: C.G.R. Kydd (01372 376025).

LINGFIELD. **Lingfield Park Golf Club,** Racecourse Road, Lingfield Park, Lingfield RH7 6PQ (01342 834602; Fax: 01342 836077). *Location:* A22 turn off at Blindley Heath, six miles from M25 Junction 6. Parkland/wooded course with streams. 18 holes, 6472 yards. S.S.S. 72. Driving range and practice ground. *Green Fees:* weekdays £42.00 per round, weekends £58.00; weekends after 1.00pm four for £160.00. *Eating facilities:* lounge, dining room, spike bar. *Visitors:* welcome midweek only by arrangement. Changing rooms. *Society Meetings:* catered for weekdays only. Professional/Secretary: C.K. Morley (01342 834602; Fax: 01342 836077).

MILFORD. **Milford Golf Club**, Station Lane, Milford, Near Godalming GU8 5HS (01483 419200; Fax: 01483 419199). *Location:* five minutes from Guildford on the A3, follow signs to Milford train station, just this side of it. Parkland course which plays like a links in the wind, mixture of attractive water holes. 18 holes, 5960 yards. S.S.S. 68. Excellent practice facilities. *Green Fees:* information not available. *Eating facilities:* restaurant and pleasant bar area. *Visitors:* welcome at most times, must phone for reservations. *Society Meetings:* all welcome, packages available, please phone Sales Manager. Professional: Paul Creamer (01483 416291). Secretary: Richard Griffiths *

MITCHAM. **Mitcham Golf Club,** Carshalton Road, Mitcham Junction CR4 4HN (020 8648 1508; Fax: 020 8648 4197). *Location:* Carshalton Road, aim for Mitcham Junction Station. Flat course. 18 holes, 5935 yards. S.S.S. 68. *Green Fees:* Monday to Friday £18.00, Senior £11.00; weekends and Bank Holidays £20.00, £12.00 Junior only. *Eating facilities:* meals and snacks available. *Visitors:* welcome, book times via Professional. *Society Meetings:* catered for, book through Secretary. Professional: J.A. Godfrey (020 8640 4280). Secretary: W.J. Dutch (Tel & Fax: 020 8648 4197).

NEWDIGATE. **Rusper Golf Club,** Rusper Road, Newdigate RH5 5BX (Tel & Fax: 01293 871456). *Location:* Dorking-Horsham A24. Beare Green roundabout left to Newdigate, through Newdigate, right to Rusper, course on right. Parkland course with mature woodland and natural water features.18 holes, 6621 yards. S.S.S. 72. Driving range. *Green Fees:* weekdays £10.00 per 9 holes, £15.00 per 18 holes; weekends £13.50 per 9 holes, £18.50 per 18 holes. Prices subject to change. *Eating facilities:* bar menu and full bar. *Visitors:* welcome every day, times bookable in advance. No Handicaps required. Golf Shop (01293 871871). *Society Meetings:* welcome, groups up to 50, various packages. Professional: Janice Arnold. Secretary: Mrs Jill Thornhill.

NEW MALDEN. **Malden Golf Club**, Traps Lane, New Malden KT3 4RS (020 8942 0654; Fax: 020 8336 2219). *Location:* half a mile from Malden Station - near A3, between Wimbledon and Kingston. Fairly flat parkland. 18 holes, 6295 yards. S.S.S. 70. *Green Fees:* information not available. *Eating facilities:* restaurant and bar. *Visitors:* welcome weekdays, restricted weekends and Bank Holidays. Advisable to telephone Professional. Buggies and trolleys for hire. *Society Meetings:* catered for Wednesday, Thursday and Friday. Professional: Robert Hunter (020 8942 6009). Secretary: Mrs Angela Besant (020 8942 0654; Fax: 020 8336 2219).

OTTERSHAW. **Foxhills,** Stonehill Road, Ottershaw KT16 0EL (01932 872050; Fax: 01932 874762). *Location:* Exit 11 M25, follow signs to Woking, right at roundabout, left at next roundabout, left at junction into Stonehill Road. Parkland course (Bernard Hunt) 18 holes, 6734 yards, S.S.S. 72. Wooded course (Longcross) 18 holes, 6417 yards, S.S.S. 71. Par 3 course (9 holes). *Green Fees:* information not available. *Eating facilities:* clubhouse bar open from 7am till 8pm. Manor Restaurant: breakfast, lunch and dinner daily. *Visitors:* welcome from 7.30am weekdays and after 12 noon at weekends. 38 rooms; tennis, squash, gym, swimming pools. *Society Meetings:* bookings for weekdays only. Head Professional: Alasdair Good; Professionals: Bernard Hunt MBE, Richard Summerscales (01932 704065). Golf Manager: Ashley Laking. *

OXTED. **Limpsfield Chart Golf Club,** Westerham Road, Limpsfield, Oxted RH8 0SL (01883 722106). *Location:* on A25 between Westerham and Oxted. Heathland, now well wooded plus heather, gorse. Second/eleventh is played over an old gravel pit, a carry of 140 yards. 9 holes – alternate tees for 18 holes, 5718 yards. S.S.S. 68. Small practice area, practice net, putting green. *Green Fees:* weekdays £18.00, evenings £10.00; weekends £20.00 with a member only. *Eating facilities:* snacks always available 11.30am to 8pm; breakfast, lunch, dinner by prior arrangement. *Visitors:* welcome weekdays, Thursdays after 3pm, weekends by appointment. *Society Meetings:* catered for by prior arrangement. Secretary: Mr M.A. Baker (01883 723405).

OXTED. **Tandridge Golf Club,** Oxted RH8 9NQ (01883 712274; Fax: 01883 730537). *Location:* from M25 Junction 6 take A22 south to A25 east, two miles. Parkland with flat first nine and undulating second nine. 18 holes, 6250 yards. S.S.S. 70. *Green Fees:* £52.00 (Summer). *Eating facilities:* full catering facilities. *Visitors:* welcome Monday, Wednesday and Thursday only. *Society Meetings:* catered for Mondays, Wednesdays and Thursdays. Professional: Chris Evans (01883 713701). Secretary: Lt. Cdr. S.E. Kennard.

PIRBRIGHT. **Goal Farm Golf Course,** Gole Road, Pirbright, Woking GU24 0PZ (01483 473183). *Location:* between Woking and Guildford, off A322. Challenging, picturesque course. 9 holes, 1273 yards. S.S.S. 48. Practice net, putting green, bunker. *Green Fees:* weekdays £4.75 9 holes; weekends and Bank Holidays £5.00. *Eating facilities:* bar, light refreshments. *Visitors:* welcome, restrictions Saturday and Thursday mornings (Club Competitions). Secretary: Graham Williams (01483 473182).

PURLEY. **Purley Downs Golf Club**, 106 Purley Downs Road, South Croydon CR2 0RB (020 8657 1231). *Location:* three miles south of Croydon, one mile east of A235. Undulating downland course. 18 holes, 6296 yards, 5724 metres. S.S.S. 70. Practice area, nets. *Green Fees:* weekdays £40.00 per day, £30.00 per round; weekends with member £16.00. *Eating facilities:* dining room, bar snacks, two bars. *Visitors:* welcome weekdays. *Society Meetings:* catered for all days except Tuesday mornings and Fridays. Professional: G. Wilson (020 8651 0819). Secretary/Manager: Mrs S.J. Burr (020 8657 8347; Fax: 020 8651 5044).

REDHILL. **Redhill Golf Centre,** Canada Avenue, Redhill RH1 5BF (01737 770204). *Location:* in the grounds of East Surrey Hospital. Parkland. 9 holes, 1632 yards. S.S.S. 58 (18 holes); 29 (9 holes). 37 bay floodlit driving range. *Green Fees:* 9 holes £5.50 weekdays, £6.50 weekends. *Eating facilities:* available at Causeway Pub. Open 8am to 10pm; weekends 9pm. *Visitors:* welcome no restrictions. Sponsored by Golf Foundation to give free junior coaching. *Society Meetings:* welcome. Professional: James Edgar. Secretary: Steven Furlonger.

REDHILL. **Redhill and Reigate Golf Club,** Clarence Lodge, Pendleton Road, Redhill RH1 6LB (01737 244626; Fax: 01737 242117). *Location:* one mile south of Reigate between A23 and A25 – Junction 8 M25. Flat well wooded parkland course. 18 holes, 5272 yards, 4978 metres. S.S.S. 68. Small practice area. *Green Fees:* weekdays £20.00, weekends £30.00. *Eating facilities:* available seven days a week. *Visitors:* welcome weekdays, Saturdays with booking 11am to 12.30pm, Sundays please telephone. *Society Meetings:* catered for by arrangement with Manager. Professional: Warren Pike (01737 244433). Manager: Carol Gadsden (01737 240777; Fax: 01737 242117).

REIGATE. **Reigate Heath Golf Club,** The Clubhouse, Reigate Heath, Reigate RH2 8QR (01737 242610). *Location:* south of A25 on western boundary of Reigate. Heathland. 9 holes, 5658 yards. S.S.S. 67. *Green Fees:* on application. *Eating facilities:* lunches and snacks available. *Visitors:* welcome weekdays, advisable to telephone before coming. *Society Meetings:* catered for on Thursdays. Secretary: R.J. Perkins (01737 226793; Fax: 01737 249226). e-mail: reigateheath@surreygolf.co.uk

REIGATE. **Reigate Hill Golf Club**, Gatton Bottom, Reigate RH2 0TU (01737 645577; Fax: 01737 642650). *Location:* J8, M25 (two minutes). Parkland. 18 holes, 6148 yards. S.S.S. 70. Practice range, practice bunker and putting green. *Green Fees:* information not available. *Eating facilities:* Extensive bar menu, spike bar, lounge bar. *Visitors:* Monday - Friday no restrictions, weekends and Bank Holidays after 12.00 pm. *Society Meetings:* welcome. Professional: Chris Forsyth (01737 646070). Manager: Michael Lang.

RICHMOND. **Richmond Golf Club,** Sudbrook Park, Petersham, Richmond TW10 7AS (020 8940 1463; Fax: 020 8332 7914). *Location:* off A307 two miles south of Richmond, end of Sudbrook Lane. Parkland. 18 holes, 6100 yards. S.S.S. 70. Practice driving range. *Green Fees:* weekdays £40.00; weekends £45.00 after 3.30 pm. *Eating facilities:* lunches available Monday to Friday. *Visitors:* welcome weekdays without reservation. *Society Meetings:* welcome Mondays, Tuesdays, Thursdays and Fridays by arrangement with General Manager. Professional: Nicholas Job (020 8940 7792; Fax: 020 8332 6694). General Manager: D. Cromie (020 8940 4351; Fax: 020 8332 7914).

RICHMOND. **Royal Mid-Surrey Golf Club,** Old Deer Park, Richmond TW9 2SB (020 8940 1894; Fax: 020 8332 2957). *Location:* entrance on A316, five minutes from Richmond station. Flat parkland, wooded course. Two 18 hole courses, Inner: 5544 yards, S.S.S. 67 men, 71 ladies; Outer: 6385 yards, S.S.S. 70. Practice ground, putting green, pitching green. *Green Fees:* weekdays £68.00 (£45.00 after 1.00pm and in winter). Playing as member's guest: £18.50 weekdays, £23.50 weekends. *Eating facilities:* bar and dining area. *Visitors:* welcome weekdays only. *Society Meetings:* corporate and society golf days welcome. Professional: Philip Talbot (020 8940 0459; Fax: 020 8332 6066).

SUNNINGDALE. **Sunningdale Golf Club,** Ridgemount Road, Sunningdale, Ascot SL5 9RR (01344 621681; Fax: 01344 624154). *Location:* 350 yards west of station, off A30, 25 miles from London. Heathland, 36 holes, 2 courses. *Green Fees:* £125.00 Old Course, £95.00 New Course, £165.00 both courses. *Eating facilities:* Diningroom and three bars. *Visitors:* require introduction from Secretary of own club plus Handicap Certificate on weekdays. Fridays and weekends with member only. *Society Meetings:* accepted Tuesdays, Wednesdays and Thursdays only, by arrangement. Professional: Keith Maxwell (01344 620128). Secretary: Stewart Zuill. Caddiemaster for bookings (01344 626064).

SUTTON. **Banstead Downs Golf Club,** Burdon Lane, Belmont, Sutton SM2 7DD (020 8642 2284; Fax: 020 8642 5252). *Location:* A217 (10 minutes from Belmont Station). 18 holes, 6194 yards. S.S.S. 69. *Green Fees:* weekdays £35.00 mornings, £25.00 afternoons (October to March £40.00 mornings, £30.00 afternoons). *Eating facilities:* lunches served at Club every day. *Visitors:* welcome on weekdays with letter of introduction, at weekends with member. *Society Meetings:* catered for all day Thursdays. Professional: Ian Golding (020 8642 6884). Secretary/Manager: Gary Oatham.

TADWORTH. **Walton Heath Golf Club,** Deans Lane, Walton-on-the-Hill, Tadworth KT20 7TP (01737 812060). *Location:* Junction 8 M25, A217 towards London, B2032 towards Dorking, turning right hand side Deans Lane. Two 18 hole heathland courses. Old: 6817 yards, S.S.S. 73. New: 6613 yards, S.S.S. 72. Large putting green; indoor nets and small outdoor practice facilities. *Green Fees:* £80.00 weekdays, after 11.30am £70.00. Special rates November-mid March. *Eating facilities:* restaurant and two bars. *Visitors:* welcome by previous arrangement, Handicap Certificate or letter of introduction required; limited play weekends. *Society Meetings:* catered for by arrangement. A variety of packages available for both summer and winter. Professional: Ken MacPherson (01737 812152). Secretary: Mike Bawden.

VIRGINIA WATER. **Wentworth Club Ltd,** Wentworth Drive, Virginia Water GU25 4LS (01344 842201; Fax: 01344 842804). *Location:* 21 miles south-west of London, just off the A30 at junction with A329 to Ascot. M25 and M3 three miles. Wooded heathland. West course - 18 holes, 7047 yards, S.S.S. 74; East course - 18 holes, 6201 yards, S.S.S. 70; Edinburgh course - 18 holes, 7004 yards, S.S.S. 74; Executive course - 9 holes. Driving range. *Green Fees:* on request. *Eating facilities:* dining room, ballroom, private rooms, bar. *Visitors:* welcome weekdays only by appointment. Handicap Certificates required: Ladies 32, Men 24. Accommodation available. *Society Meetings:* welcome by prior arrangement. Professional: David Rennie (01344 846306). Managing Director: Julian Small (01344 842201). Deputy General Manager: Stuart Christie (01344 846313).

WALTON-ON-THAMES. **Burhill Golf Club,** Burwood Road, Walton-on-Thames KT12 4BL. *Location:* M25 Junction 10, take A3 London turn off, A245 Weybridge, right into Seven Hills Road and again into Burwood Road. Two 18 hole parkland courses both differing in character, Old Course 6479 yards. S.S.S. 71, New Course 6940 yards, S.S.S. 72 - opened May 2001. Full irrigation on both courses. Practice area, driving range, putting green and short game practice area. *Green Fees:* weekdays £65.00 per round, £90.00 per day. Special rates November to March. *Eating facilities:* Orangery Restaurant, Captains Bar, Honours Bar, Iveagh Lounge, Barnes Wallis suite for private dining, and the exclusive Hospitality Suite for special occasions. *Visitors:* welcome Monday to Friday. *Society Meetings:* catered for Monday to Friday. Golf Days organised to suit your particular requirements. Professional: Lee Johnson (01932 221729; Fax: 01932 252533). General Manager: David Cook (01932 227345; Fax: 01932 267159). Sales Manager: Sally Owen (01932 227345; Fax: 01932 267159). e-mail: info@burhillgolf-club.co.uk

WARLINGHAM near. **Farleigh Court Golf Club,** Old Farleigh Road, Farleigh CR6 9PX (01883 627711; Fax: 01883 627722). *Location:* south of Croydon. Exciting course utilising two landscaped valleys with many natural features. 27 holes (18 holes members, 9 hole pay and play). 9155 yards, 8368 metres. Practice bunker, chipping green, putting green and 285 yard practice range. *Green Fees:* information not available. *Eating facilities:* full catering facilities available (seven days). *Visitors:* welcome anytime after 10am weekdays or weekends on members course and anytime on 9 hole pay and play. *Society Meetings:* welcome anytime. Professional/Secretary: Scott Graham.

WEST BYFLEET. **West Byfleet Golf Club,** Sheerwater Road, West Byfleet KT14 6AA (01932 343433). *Location:* Junction 10 M25 onto A245 – half a mile west of West Byfleet. Easy walking, woodland course. 18 holes, 6211 yards. S.S.S. 70. *Green Fees:* weekdays £50.00 per round, £75.00 per day. *Eating facilities:* lunches, bar snacks, teas and evening meals available. Catering: (01932 353525). Bar: (01932 345230). *Visitors:* welcome weekdays with reservation, weekends with member only. *Society Meetings:* catered for, advance bookings, minimum group size 20. Professional: David Regan (01932 346584). Secretary: D. Lee (01932 343433).

WEST CLANDON. **Clandon Regis Golf Club Ltd,** Epsom Road, West Clandon GU4 7TT (01483 224888; Fax: 01483 211781)*.Location:* between Guildford and Leatherhead on A246. Parkland setting, fairly mature for new course, four areas of water. Course designed by David Williams. 18 holes, 6419 yards. S.S.S. 71/69. Indoor practice nets, full length driving area, putting green, chipping area. *Green Fees:* weekdays £30.00; weekends £40.00 (limited). *Eating facilities:* bar meals, restaurant available for booking. *Visitors:* welcome weekdays, weekends depending on club bookings. *Society Meetings:* welcome weekdays only. Professional: Steve Lloyd (01483 223922). Secretary: Mrs Wendy Savage.

WEYBRIDGE. **New Zealand Golf Club,** Woodham Lane, Woodham, Addlestone KT15 3QD (01932 345049). *Location:* junction Woodham Lane and Sheerwater Road on A245. A traditional club with secluded heathland course in heather and woodland setting. 18 holes, 6075 yards. S.S.S. 69. *Green Fees:* information on request. *Eating facilities:* lunch available Tuesdays to Fridays. *Visitors:* welcome by prior arrangement. *Society Meetings:* catered for Tuesday, Wednesday, Thursday and Friday. Professional: V.R. Elvidge. Secretary: R.A. Marrett Esq.*

WEYBRIDGE. **St. George's Hill Golf Club,** Golf Club Road, St. George's Hill, Weybridge KT13 0NL (01932 847758; Fax: 01932 821564). *Location:* M25, Junction 10 take A3 towards London, turn off towards Byfleet (A245) then B374 Brooklands Road, entrance to St. George's Hill estate one mile on right. Hilly, Surrey heathland - well wooded with plentiful heather and rhododendron. 27 holes, 6513 yards. S.S.S. 71. *Green Fees:* weekdays £80.00 per round, £105.00 per day. Subject to review for 2004. No credit cards accepted. *Eating facilities:* dining room, two bars. *Visitors:* welcome Wednesdays, Thursdays. Fridays only by prior arrangement with Secretary's

office. *Society Meetings:* catered for on Wednesdays, Thursdays and Fridays by prior arrangement. Professional: A.C. Rattue (01932 843523). Secretary: J. Robinson (01932 847758).

WOKING. **Chobham Golf Club,** Chobham Road, Knaphill, Woking GU21 2TZ (01276 855584; Fax: 01276 855663). *Location:* on A3046 one mile outside Chobham village, ten minutes from M3 Junction 3. Wooded parkland course. 18 holes, 5959 yards, S.S.S. 69. Practice area, putting green. *Green Fees:* information not available. *Eating facilities:* bar snacks and restaurant. *Visitors:* welcome, with prior agreement with General Manager. *Society Meetings:* welcome. Professional: Tim Coombes (01276 855748). Secretary: Terry Pond.
website: www.chobhamgolfclub.co.uk
e-mail: info@chobhamgolfclub.co.uk

WOKING. **Hoebridge Golf Centre,** Old Woking Road, Old Woking GU22 8JH (01483 722611; Fax: 01483 740369). *Location*: Undulating parkland on well-draining sand, well established wooded location. Three courses: Hoebridge Course - 18 holes, Back Tees 6536 yards, Par 72, Yellow Tees 6178 yards, Par 71, Ladies 5842 yards, Par 73; Maybury Course – 18 holes, 2230 yards, Par 54; Shey Copse – 9 holes, 2294 yards, Par 33. 36 bay covered, floodlit driving range. *Green Fees:* weekdays Hoebridge Course £18.75, Maybury Course £8.00, Shey Copse £10.00; weekends Hoebridge Course £24.75, Maybury Course £9.00, Shey Copse £11.00. Reductions for Senior Citizens, Juniors and at twilight times. *Eating facilities*: full catering and bar facilities open all day. *Visitors*: welcome. Pay-and-Play facility. Clubs for hire. *Society Meetings*: welcome weekdays by prior arrangement, various packages available. Professional: Tim Powell. Secretary: P. Dawson. **website: www.hoebridge.co.uk**

WOKING. **West Hill Golf Club,** Bagshot Road, Brookwood GU24 0BH (01483 472110). *Location:* M3, Junction 3, A322 entrance adjacent railway bridge Brookwood. Heathland, wooded course. Golf World "Top 100 courses in UK" listed. 18 holes, 6368 yards. S.S.S. 70. Practice range and net. *Green Fees:* weekdays £50.00 per round, £75.00 per day. *Eating facilities:* bar snacks available, meals including dinner by prior arrangement. *Visitors:* members' guests only at weekends. Buggies, caddies by arrangement. *Society Meetings:* catered for by arrangement through the Secretary. Professional: J.C. Clements (01483 473172). Secretary: I.M. McColl (01483 474365; Fax: 01483 474252).
e-mail: secretary@westhill-golfclub.co.uk
website: www.westhill-golfclub.co.uk

WOKING. **Windlemere Golf Club,** Windlesham Road, West End, Near Woking GU24 9QL (01276 858727). *Location:* off A322. Well designed parkland course. 9 holes, 2673 yards. S.S.S. 33. Floodlit 12-bay driving range. *Green Fees:* information not available. *Eating facilities:* bar with light menu, normal clubhouse facilities. *Visitors:* always welcome, may book up to one week in advance. Snooker, pool facilities. *Society Meetings:* welcome to book. Professional: Dave Thomas. Secretary: M. Walsh (01276 858727).*

WOKING. **Traditions Golf Course 1999**, Pyrford Road, Pyrford, Woking GU22 8UE (01932 350355; Fax: 01932 350234). *Location:* into West Byfleet and turn at traffic lights into Pyrford Road. Peter Alliss design with tree-lined holes, lakes and many streams. 18 holes. Par 71. *Green Fees:* information not available. *Eating facilities:* from 7am to 10pm (to 6pm in winter). Professional: Nick Stoner.*

WOKING. **Woking Golf Club,** Pond Road, Hook Heath, Woking GU22 0JZ (01483 760053; Fax: 01483 772441). *Location:* via Hollybank Road and Golf Club Road or Hook Heath Road and Pond Road. Traditional heathland course. 18 holes, 6340 yards. S.S.S. 70. Practice ground. *Green Fees:* information not provided. *Eating facilities:* lunches and snacks available. *Visitors:* welcome but only by prior arrangement, Handicap Certificate required. *Society Meetings:* welcome by prior arrangement. Professional: C.I. Bianco (01483 769582). Secretary: G.T. Ritchie.

WOKING. **Worplesdon Golf Club,** Heath House Road, Woking. *Location:* off A322, six miles from Guildford and six miles from Junction 3 (M3). Wooded heathland course. 18 holes, 6440 yards. S.S.S. 71. *Green Fees:* £55.00 per round, £75.00 per day. *Eating facilities:* lunches served at club. *Visitors:* weekdays only. *Society meetings:* by arrangement. Professional: Jim Christine (01483 473287). Secretary: J.T. Christine (01483 472277; Fax: 01483 473303).

WOKING near. **Pyrford Golf Club 1993**, Warren Lane, Pyrford, Near Woking, GU22 8XR (01483 723555; Fax: 01483 729777). *Location:* A3 - Ripley turn off, turn next to Mitsubishi garage, continue for approximately two miles, on the right Warren Lane. Inland water links, 23 acres of water. 18 holes, 6230 yards. Par 72. Practice range, putting green. *Green Fees:* weekdays £40.00, weekends £45.00. *Eating facilities:* bar snack menu available all day. *Visitors:* welcome anytime Monday to Friday and after 12 noon at weekends, tee times MUST be booked. *Society Meetings:* welcome weekdays only. Professional: Darren Brewer (01483 751070). Secretary: Ian Bartlett.
e-mail: pyrford@americangolf.uk.com

WOLDINGHAM. **North Downs Golf Club,** Northdown Road, Woldingham, Caterham CR3 7AA (01883 652057). *Location:* Eastbourne Road roundabout at Caterham. Two miles Woldingham road. 18 holes, 5857 yards, S.S.S. 68. *Green Fees:* £30.00 per round, £40.00 per day. *Eating facilities:* full restaurant facilities. *Visitors:* welcome with Handicap Certificate Monday to Friday (Thursdays after 12 noon only). *Society Meetings:* catered for. Professional: M. Homewood (01883 653004). Secretary/Manager: D. Sinden (01883 652057).

YATELEY. **Blackwater Valley Golf Course**, Chandlers Lane, Yateley GU46 7SZ (01252 874725). *Location:* Junction 4 of M3. Into Yateley to White Lion pub roundabout, into Vicarage Road, then Vicarage Lane. Parkland course with lakes and mature trees. 9 holes. Par 34. Driving range. *Green Fees:* £9.00. *Eating facilities:* From 11am to 10pm (to 8pm during winter). Professional: James Rodger.

East Sussex

BATTLE. **Battle Golf Club**, Netherfield Hill, Battle TN33 0LH (Tel & Fax: 01424 777497). *Location*: A2100, just 1½ miles outside historic town of Battle. Parkland, woodland course. Panoramic views, gently undulating. 9 holes, 18 tees, 5941 yards. S.S.S 68. Practice ground. *Green Fees*: weekdays 9 holes £11.00, 18 holes £18.00; weekends 9 holes £12.00, 18 holes £18.00. Senior Citizens and Juniors welcome, special rates. *Eating facilities:* large bars, 3-course meals and bar snacks available. *Visitors:* welcome daily from 7am. Strict dress code. Tuition available for individuals and groups. *Society Meetings*: welcome, special rates, please telephone for details. Secretary: Clare Lyons (01424 777497).

BEXHILL-ON-SEA. **Cooden Beach Golf Club,** Cooden Sea Road, Bexhill-on-sea TN39 4TR (Tel & Fax: 01424 842040). *Location:* A259 Eastbourne to Hastings road, follow `Cooden Beach' sign at Little Common roundabout (one mile). Seaside course, slightly undulating. 18 holes, 6500 yards. S.S.S. 72. Practice facilities. *Green Fees:* weekdays £32.00; weekends and Bank Holidays £35.00. *Eating facilities:* catering and bar every day. *Visitors:* welcome, preferably by prior arrangement. Buggies for hire. *Society Meetings:* prior booking necessary. Professional: Jeffrey Sim (01424 843938; Fax: 01424 842040). Secretary: Keith Wiley (Tel & Fax: 01424 842040). Caterers: (01424 843936).

BEXHILL-ON-SEA. **Highwoods Golf Club**, Ellerslie Lane, Bexhill-on-sea TN39 4LJ (01424 212625). *Location:* off A259 north west of town. Parkland, wooded course. 18 holes, 6218 yards. S.S.S. 70. *Green Fees:* £30.00 all day, £18.00 with member. *Eating facilities:* snacks, lunches and teas always available. *Visitors:* welcome Monday to Saturday. Sunday mornings with member only. *Society Meetings:* welcome Thursdays by arrangement. Professional: M. Andrews (01424 212770). Secretary: Lawrence Dennis-Smither (01424 212625; Fax: 01424 216866).

BRIGHTON. **Brighton and Hove Golf Club,** Devil's Dyke Road, Brighton BN1 8YJ (01273 507861). *Location:* A27 Brighton bypass exit for Devil's Dyke, club one and a half miles north of A27. Downland course with sea views. 9 holes, 5704 yards. S.S.S. 68. Practice area. *Green Fees:* (18 holes) weekdays £18.00; weekends and Bank Holidays £25.00. *Eating facilities:* bar and restaurant daily, limited on Mondays. *Visitors:* welcome, phone call advisable Wednesday after 12 noon, Friday after 11am, Saturday and Sunday after 12 noon. *Society Meetings:* catered for – up to 30, eating 60. Professional: Phil Bonsall (01273 540560). Secretary: (01273 556482).

BRIGHTON. **The Dyke Golf Club,** Devil's Dyke, Devil's Dyke Road, Brighton BN1 8YJ (01273 857296; Fax: 01273 857078). *Location:* A23 onto A27 (New Brighton By-pass) heading west to Worthing, turn off for Devil's Dyke and follow signs for same. Brighton's premier downland course. 18 holes, 6627 yards. S.S.S. 72. Practice fairway and putting green. *Green Fees:* weekdays £28.00 per round, £38.00 per day; weekends £35.00 per round. Twilight round £15.00 weekdays, £25.00 weekends. *Eating facilities:* full restaurant and bar available. *Visitors:* welcome with reservation, not before 12 noon Sundays. *Society Meetings:* catered for by appointment, £53.00 for full day inclusive of snack lunch and evening meal. Professional: Richard Arnold (01273 857260; Fax: 01273 857564). Secretary: (01273 857296; Fax: 01273 857078).

BRIGHTON. **East Brighton Golf Club,** Roedean Road, Brighton BN2 5RA (01273 604838). *Location:* one and a half miles east of Palace Pier, just off A259, behind the Marina. Undulating downland course offering superb views over the Channel. 18 holes, 6346 yards. S.S.S. 70. Putting green. *Green Fees:* weekdays £27.50 per round, £37.50 per day; weekends and Bank Holidays £32.50 per round. *Eating facilities:* restaurant, diningroom, bars. *Visitors:* welcome from 9am weekdays, after 11am weekends and Bank Holidays. Handicap Certificate required. Buggy hire available. *Society Meetings:* welcome, full days golf and catering from £39.00 per person. Manager of Golf Operations: Mark Stuart-William (01273 603989). Office Manager: Max Page (01273 604838; Fax: 01273 680277).

BRIGHTON. **Hollingbury Park Golf Club**, Ditchling Road, Brighton BN1 7HS (01273 552010). *Location:* between A23 and A27. 18 holes, 6502 yards. S.S.S. 71. *Green Fees*: weekdays £13.00 per round, £20.00 per day; weekends £18.00 per round. *Visitors*: welcome. All bookings through Professional. *Society Meetings*: catered for weekdays only. Professional: Graeme Crompton (01273 500086). Secretary: (Tel & Fax: 01273 552010).

BRIGHTON. **Pyecombe Golf Club,** Clayton Hill, Pyecombe, Brighton BN45 7FF (01273 845372; Fax: 01273 843338). *Location:* four miles north of Brighton on A273 Burgess Hill Road. Downland with magnificent views. 18 holes, 6278 yards, 5790 metres. S.S.S. 70. Two practice areas. *Green Fees:* weekdays £25.00; weekends and Bank Holidays £30.00. *Eating facilities:* catering/bars from 11am daily. *Visitors:* welcome, after 9.15am weekdays (11am on Tuesdays). *Society Meetings:* welcome Mondays, Wednesdays and Thursdays by prior arrangement. Professional: C. White (01273 845398; Fax: 01273 843338). Secretary: I. Bradbery (01273 845372; Fax: 01273 843338).

BRIGHTON. **Waterhall Golf Club,** Saddlescombe Road, Brighton BN1 8YN (01273 508658). *Location:* off A27 Brighton bypass, take Devil's Dyke turn off, course on the right. Downland course. 18 holes, 5773 yards, 5328 metres. S.S.S. 68. Practice area. *Green Fees:* information not available. *Visitors:* welcome except weekends. *Society Meetings:* catered for except weekends or Bank Holidays by prior arrangement with Secretary. Professional: Graeme Crompton (01273 555529). Secretary: L.B. Allen.

CROWBOROUGH. **Crowborough Beacon Golf Club,** Beacon Road, Crowborough (01892 654016). *Location:* nine miles south of Tunbridge Wells on the A26. Heathland, superb views to the sea and South Downs (on clear days). 18 holes, 6273 yards. S.S.S. 70. *Green Fees:* £32.00 per round, £44.00 per day weekdays. *Eating facilities:* restaurant available. *Visitors:* welcome weekdays, Handicap Certificate or letter of introduction essential. Please contact either the Professional or Secretary. *Society Meetings:* bookings welcome through the Secretary's office. Professional: D.C Newnham (01892 653877). Secretary: Mrs V. Harwood (01892 661511; Fax: 01892 667339).
e-mail: cbgc@eastsx.fsnet.co.uk

DITCHLING. **Mid-Sussex Golf Club,** Spatham Lane, Ditchling BN6 8XJ (01273 846567; Fax: 01273 845767). *Location:* five minutes from A23, one mile east of Ditchling. Mature parkland course with superbly contoured greens and strategic bunkers. 18 holes, 6431 yards. S.S.S. 71. Practice ground, driving range and short game areas. *Green Fees:* weekdays £28.00, over 55's £15.00; weekends £30.00. Early and twilight rates available. *Eating facilities:* full bar/restaurant facilities. *Visitors:* welcome weekdays, weekends restricted. Buggies available. *Society Meetings:* welcome weekdays only. Professional: Neil Plimmer. Director of Golf: Andy McNiven.

EASTBOURNE. **Eastbourne Downs Golf Club,** East Dean Road, Eastbourne BN20 8ES (01323 720827; Fax: 01323 412506). *Location:* half a mile west of Eastbourne on A259. Downland course with spectacular views to the South Downs and over the sea. 18 holes, 6601 yards. S.S.S. 72. Practice area. *Green Fees:* weekdays £18.00 per round, £23.00 per day; weekends £25.00 per round, £30.00 per day. *Eating facilities:* two bars; restaurant open seven

days a week 7.30am to 8.30pm. *Visitors:* welcome unrestricted after 9am weekdays and 11.15am weekends. Trolleys for hire. *Society Meetings:* welcome – full day with coffee, lunch and four-course dinner. Professional: Terry Marshall (01323 732264). Secretary: Tony Reeves (01323 720827; Fax: 01323 412506).

EASTBOURNE. **Eastbourne Golfing Park,** Lottbridge Drove, Eastbourne BN23 6QJ (Tel & Fax: 01323 520400). *Location:* end of A22; half a mile south of Hampden Park and one mile north of the sea. Pleasant easy walk, a fairly short flat course but with water on seven of the nine holes it tests the accuracy of any golfer. 9 holes, 5046 yards. S.S.S. 66. 21-bay floodlit driving range. *Green Fees:* 9 holes £9.00, Senior Citizens and Juniors £8.00, 18 holes £15.00, Senior Citizens and Juniors £12.00. Weekends 9 holes £10.00, 18 holes £16.00. All day golf £18.00, Senior Citizens and Juniors £15.00, after 6pm £8.00 unlimited golf. *Eating facilities:* full bar and restaurant open to all. *Visitors:* welcome at all times. Equipment hire available. *Society Meetings:* all welcome, please ring to book. Professionals: Barrie Finch and Jim Whitbread. Secretary: Jenny Plumley (Tel & Fax: 01323 520400).

EASTBOURNE. **Royal Eastbourne Golf Club,** Paradise Drive, Eastbourne BN20 8BP (01323 729738). *Location:* one mile from town centre via Meads Road and Compton Place Road. Undulating downland and parkland. Devonshire course:18 holes, 6074 yards. S.S.S. 69. Hartington course: 9 holes, 2147 yards. S.S.S. 61. *Green Fees:* Devonshire course – weekdays £25.00 per round, £40.00 per day; weekends and Bank Holidays £30.00 per round, £50.00 per day. Hartington course £15.00. *Eating facilities:* full catering. *Visitors:* welcome. Handicap Certificate required Long Course only. Cottage accommodation for four people. *Society Meetings:* catered for. Professional: Alan Harrison (Tel & Fax: 01323 736986). Secretary: (01323 729738).

EASTBOURNE. **Willingdon Golf Club,** Southdown Road, Willingdon, Eastbourne BN20 9AA (01323 410983). *Location:* north of Eastbourne, one mile from station, just off A22 at traffic lights (signposted). Downland course of particular beauty. 18 holes, 6113 yards, 5589 metres. S.S.S. 69. Practice ground

CROWBOROUGH BEACON
GOLF CLUB

This well established 18 hole heathland course, founded in 1895, stands some 800 feet above sea level and with views on clear days of the Downs, Eastbourne and the sea, it must have arguably one of the finest panoramas in Sussex. Pine and fir trees are scattered around the course and there is plenty of heather and gorse. This course will test your accuracy rather than length off the tee!

Crowborough Beacon Golf Club, Beacon Road, Crowborough, East Sussex TN6 1UJ
Tel: 01892 661511   Fax: 01892 667339
e-mail: cbgc@eastsx.fsnet.co.uk
www.crowboroughbeacongolfclub.co.uk

See also Colour Advertisement on page 27

and nets. *Green Fees:* weekdays £18.00 Winter, £20.00 Summer; weekends £20.00 Winter, £22.00 Summer. *Eating facilities:* diningroom, lounge and casual bar. *Visitors:* welcome weekdays with Handicap after 9am. Buggies and trolleys available. *Society Meetings:* welcome, book well in advance. Professional: Troy Moore (01323 410984; Fax: 01323 411510). Secretary: Mrs Jacqueline Packham (01323 410981; Fax: 01323 411510).

FOREST ROW. **Royal Ashdown Forest Golf Club (Old Course)** Chapel Lane, Forest Row, Near East Grinstead RH18 5LR (01342 822018; Fax: 01342 825211). *Location:* three miles south of East Grinstead to Forest Row. Take B2110 to Tunbridge Wells in the middle of village (left at second mini-roundabout) then take fourth turning on right into Chapel Lane, turn sharp left at top of Chapel Lane then bear right through golf course to Clubhouse. Undulating heathland. 18 holes, 6477 yards. S.S.S. 71. Selected to host regional qualifier for 2004 Open Championship. *Green Fees:* weekdays £45.00 per round, £60.00 per day; weekends £60.00 per round. *Eating facilities:* lunch and tea, bar snacks. *Visitors:* welcome by prior arrangement. *Society Meetings:* welcome on Wednesday, Thursday and Friday; prior reservation essential. Steward: (01342 823014). Professional: M. Landsborough (01342 822247) Secretary: D. Neave (01342 822018; Fax: 01342 825211). e-mail: office@royalashdown.co.uk website: www.royalashdown.co.uk

FOREST ROW. **Royal Ashdown Forest Golf Club (West Course)** Chapel Lane, Forest Row, Near East Grinstead RH18 5LR (01342 824866; Fax: 01342 825211). *Location:* three miles south of East Grinstead to Forest Row. Take B2110 to Tunbridge Wells in the middle of village (left at second mini-roundabout) then take fourth turning on right into Chapel Lane, turn sharp left at top of Chapel Lane then bear right through golf course to Clubhouse. 5606 yards, S.S.S. 67, a shorter, but not easier, version of the Old Course with, according to the late Henry Longhurst, "one of the finest par fours in the South of England" as its closing hole. *Green Fees:* weekdays £22.00 per round, £32.00 per day; weekends £26.00 per round, £38.00 per day. *Eating facilities:* excellent snacks all day. *Visitors and Societies:* welcome by prior arrangement. Professional: M. Landsborough (01342 822247).

HAILSHAM near. **Wellshurst Golf and Country Club,** North Street, Hellingly, Near Hailsham BN27 4EE (01435 813636; Fax: 01435 812444). *Location:* two miles from the A22 roundabout at Hailsham on the A267. Parkland course. 18 holes, 5771 yards, S.S.S. 68. 16 bay driving range with two bunker bays. *Green Fees:* information not available. *Eating facilities:* bar and restaurant open seven days a week. *Visitors:* no restrictions, pay as you play course; advisable to book at weekends. Leisure club, conference/wedding suite. *Society Meetings:* all welcome at any time, good rates. Professional: Mr Mark Jarvis (01435 813456). Secretary: Mr M. Adams.

HASTINGS. **Ten 66 Golf Club Ltd**, Beauport Park, Battle Road, St. Leonards-on-Sea TN37 7RP (01424 854245; Clubhouse functions 01424 851165). *Location:* A2100 between Hastings and Battle, in the heart of 1066 Country in an Area of Outstanding Natural Beauty. Scenic, tree-lined undulating parkland course said to be among the best in Southern England and a very good test for all handicaps. 18 holes, 6180 yards. S.S.S. 70, 9 hole par 3 short course, 14 bay driving range. *Green Fees:* information not available. *Eating facilities:* clubhouse; hotel, restaurant and bar. *Visitors:* unrestricted. Professional coaching; indoor teaching facilities; Golf Educational Packages. Riding Stables and other activities available at adjacent Beauport Park Country House. *Society Meetings:* welcome; special rates available on request for societies/Corporate Days and for group or family membership. Managing Director: Deborah Mahon. e-mail: info@ten66golfclub.com. website: www.ten66golfclub.com

HEATHFIELD. **Horam Park Golf Course**, Chiddingly Road, Horam, near Heathfield TN21 0JJ (01435 813477, Fax: 01435 813677). *Location*: 13 miles north of Eastbourne, seven miles east of Uckfield. Follow signs to Heathfield and turn right onto the Eastbourne Road A267, go through Horam village, club on right hand side. A delightful parkland course with wooded areas and several lakes and ponds. 9 holes (18 tees), 6128 yards, S.S.S. 70. Floodlit driving range, practice ground, Par 3 5 hole course. *Green Fees*: weekdays £11.00 9 holes, £16.50 18 holes; weekends £11.50 9 holes, £18.00 18 holes. *Eating facilities*: restaurant and bar facilities open all day seven days a week, also spike bar. *Visitors*: all facilities at Horam Park are open to the general public with no restrictions, everybody welcome. Golf tuition available from PGA Pros seven days a week. *Society Meetings*: welcome seven days a week, special cheap rates from January/March every year. Professional: Giles Velvick (01435 813477). Secretary: Angie Briggs.

HOVE. **West Hove Golf Club Ltd**, Church Farm, Hangleton, Hove BN3 8AN (01273 419738; Fax: 01273 439988). *Location*: A27 adjacent to Brighton bypass, take Hangleton Interchange exit. Downland course overlooking the sea. 18 holes, 6216 yards. S.S.S. 70. Practice range, driving range, putting green. *Green Fees*: weekdays £25.00; weekends £30.00. *Eating facilities*: bar and catering all day. *Visitors*: welcome. Phone Professional for tee times. *Society Meetings*: welcome, phone for prices. Professional: D. Cook (01273 413494). Secretary: Megan Bibby (01273 419738; Fax: 01273 439988). e-mail: info@westhovegolf.co.uk website: www.westhovegolfclub.info

LEWES. **Lewes Golf Club**, Chapel Hill, Lewes BN7 2BB (01273 473245). *Location*: east of town centre from A27 and A26. Downland course with spectacular views of Sussex countryside. 18 holes, 6220 yards. S.S.S. 70. Practice ground, practice putting green. *Green Fees*: £28.00 per round, £40.00 per day weekdays; £36.00 weekends. *Eating facilities*: hot and cold food available from 10am seven days a week, bar open from 11am. *Visitors*: welcome, no green fees after 2pm Tuesdays (Summer months) or before 2pm (11am Winter) at weekends. *Society Meetings*: welcome, special rates available. Professional: Paul Dobson (01273 483823). Secretary: Joan Raffety (Tel & Fax: 01273 483474).

NEWHAVEN. **Peacehaven Golf Club**, The Clubhouse, Brighton Road, Newhaven BN9 9UH (01273 514049). *Location*: one mile from Newhaven on the right hand side of A259 towards Brighton. Downland course, short but challenging. 9 holes, 5488 yards. S.S.S. 67. *Green Fees*: weekdays £15.00 18 holes, £10.00 9 holes; weekends £20.00 18 holes, £14.00 9 holes. *Eating facilities*: snacks, meals, full bar. *Visitors*: welcome but not before 11am weekends. *Society Meetings*: welcome except weekends, from £22.00 including lunch. Professional: Ian Pearson (01273 512602). Manager: Dawn Corke (01273 512571).

ROTHERFIELD. **Dewlands Manor Golf Course**, Dewlands Manor, Rotherfield TN6 3JN (01892 852266; Fax: 01892 853015). *Location*: three quarters of a mile south of village of Rotherfield, just off

B2101. Challenging undulating course on second highest point of Sussex. Very high quality greens with fine bents and fescue. No mats or temporary greens used. 9 holes, 3186 yards (18 - 6372 yards). Par 72. Practice hole. *Green Fees*: information not available. *Eating facilities*: bar lunches/snacks on request. *Visitors*: welcome at all times by telephone booking. Tee times set at 15 minute intervals. Handicap not required. Dress and etiquette a prerequisite. Indoor teaching with computer analysis. Buggies, trolleys for hire. *Society Meetings*: welcome, maximum 28. Professional: Nick Godin. Course Director: Trevor Robins (01892 852266).

RYE. **Rye Golf Club,** Camber, Rye TN31 7QS (01797 225241/225460). *Location*: A259 from Rye, take Camber road to coast. Seaside links. Old Course: 18 holes, 6308 yards. S.S.S. 71. Jubilee Course: 9 holes, 6118 yards. S.S.S. 71. *Green Fees*: information not available. *Eating facilities*: lunch and tea only. Bars. *Visitors*: welcome, only on introduction by a member. Dormy house accommodation available – contact I. Rayson (01797 227882). *Society Meetings*: very limited. Professional: Michael Lee (01797 225218). Secretary: J.A.L. Smith (01797 225241; Fax: 01797 225460). *

SEAFORD. **Seaford Golf Club,** East Blatchington, Seaford BN25 2JD (01323 892442; Fax: 01323 894113). *Location*: turn inland at War Memorial in Seaford, follow the road for one and a quarter miles. Downland course with magnificent views over Seaford Head and The Channel. 18 holes, 6233 yards, 5700 metres. S.S.S. 70. Practice ground. *Green Fees*: information not available. *Eating facilities*: bar and dining room open all day. Dormy House, 10 twin bedded rooms with en suite facilities. *Visitors*: welcome weekdays other than Tuesdays. Telephone first. *Society Meetings*: catered for Wednesdays and Thursdays. Professional: David Mills (01323 894160). Secretary: Philip Court (01323 892442; Fax: 01323 894113). website: www.seafordgolfclub.co.uk

SEAFORD. **Seaford Head Golf Club**, Southdown Road, Seaford BN25 4HR (01323 894843). *Location*: midway between Eastbourne and Brighton on A259, signposted on entering Seaford. Downland course along cliff edge with view of "Seven Sisters". 18 holes, 5848 yards. S.S.S. 68. *Green Fees*: information not available. *Eating facilities*: bar snacks and catering for Society Meetings. *Visitors*: welcome without reservation. *Society Meetings*: welcome, bookings with Professional. Professional: A. J. Lowles (01323 890139). Secretary: I. Perkins (01323 894843).*

SEDLESCOMBE. **Sedlescombe Golf Club**, Kent Street, Near Battle, TN33 0SD (01424 871700). Home of The James Andrews School of Golf. *Location*: 1066 Country, five miles north of Hastings on the A21, three miles from Battle. Gently undulating parkland course, 18 holes, 6269 yards. S.S.S. 70. 24 bay floodlit driving range, four practice putting greens, academy hole and bunkers. Residential golf school with 2,3 and 5 day intensive courses for all ages and abilities. Five PGA Professionals. Facilities include indoor video and computer analysis centre, on-site hotel, golf shop and tennis courts. *Green Fees*: weekdays £16.00, weekends £20.00. *Eating facilities:* bar and restaurant open seven days. *Visitors:* Course open to public. *Society Meetings:* welcome. Head Professional: James Andrews (01424 871700). Club Secretary (01424 871700). Golf School (01424 871717) website: www.golfschool.co.uk

UCKFIELD. **East Sussex National Golf Club**, Little Horsted, Uckfield TN22 5ES (01825 880088; Fax: 01825 880066). *Location:* off the A22 Eastbourne road following the Uckfield by-pass, 30 minutes from Gatwick. American style, wooded, bent grasses. Two Championship courses; 1: 18 holes, 6760 yards. S.S.S. 72; 2: 18 holes, 6638 yards. S.S.S. 72. 3 hole teaching academy, driving range. *Green Fees:* summer weekdays £45.00 per round; summer weekends £55.00 per round. Please telephone for further prices. *Eating facilities:* full restaurant facilities. *Visitors:* welcome anytime. Luxury country house hotel accommodation at Horsted Place situated on the West Course. *Society Meetings:* booking allowed six months in advance. General Manager: Derek Howe, M.Inst.GCM..
e-mail: golf@eastsussexnational.co.uk
website: www.eastsussexnational.co.uk

UCKFIELD. **Piltdown Golf Club,** Piltdown, Uckfield TN22 3XB (01825 722033; Fax: 01825 724192). *Location:* one mile west of Maresfield off A272, signposted. Undulating gorse and heather. 18 holes, 6070 yards. S.S.S. 69. Practice ground, putting green. *Green Fees:* £35.00 per round, £45.00 per day.

Reductions after 1.30pm and 4pm. County cards £25.00 per round. *Eating facilities:* bar, full catering – please telephone to book. *Visitors:* welcome but must bring Handicap Certificate or letter of introduction from own club Secretary. Some time restrictions. No visitors before 9.30am. Jacket and tie obligatory in lounge and diningroom. Smart dress on course. *Society Meetings:* catered for by prior arrangement. Professional: Jason Partridge (01825 722389). Hon. Secretary: P.A. de Pinna (01825 722033).
e-mail: piltdowngolf@lineone.net

WADHURST. **Dale Hill Golf Club**, Ticehurst, Wadhurst TN5 7DQ (01580 201090 Fax: 01580 201249). *Location:* on B2087, one mile off A21 to west of Flimwell, 50 miles south of London, 16 miles north of Hastings. Open front nine and wooded back nine. 18 holes, 5856 yards. S.S.S. 68. Ian Woosnam Course (buggy only), 18 holes, 6512 yards. S.S.S. 71. Designed by Ian Woosnam to championship standards. Practice area and green, driving range. *Green Fees:* midweek £25.00 18 holes, £40.00 per day; weekends £35.00 18 holes. Twilight round mid-week £15.00, weekends £20.00. Ian Woosnam Course £55.00 weekdays; £65.00 weekends. *Eating facilities:* bar and brasserie. *Visitors:* welcome after 7.30am. 35 room luxury hotel, gym and swimming pool. Conference facilities. Buggies, trolleys. *Society Meetings:* catered for by prior arrangement. Secretary: (01580 201800).
e-mail: info@dalehill.co.uk
website: www.dalehill.co.uk

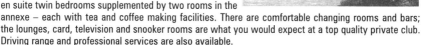

West Sussex

ALBOURNE. **Singing Hills Golf Course Ltd.**, Albourne BN6 9EB (01273 835353; Fax: 01273 835444). *Location:* on the B2117 just off the A23. Gently undulating parkland course with spectacular views of the South Downs. 3 x 9 hole courses. S.S.S. 70. 15 bay driving range, putting green. *Green Fees:* weekdays £23.00 18 holes, £33.00 all day; weekends £31.00 18 holes, £41.00 all day. Students and County Cards £19.50; Senior Citizens £16.00 weekdays only. *Eating facilities:* Pavilion Restaurant, large bar. *Visitors:* welcome, no restrictions. *Society Meetings:* welcome, variety of golf and food packages for minimum 12 players. Professional: Wallace Street. Secretary: Donald Weston.

ANGMERING. **Ham Manor Golf Club Ltd**, Angmering BN16 4JE (01903 775653). *Location:* on A259 between Worthing and Littlehampton. Flat parkland course. 18 holes, 6216 yards. S.S.S. 70. *Green Fees:* information not available. *Eating facilities:* lunches served at club except on Mondays. *Visitors:* welcome with reservation. Handicap Certificate required. *Society Meetings:* catered for weekdays only. Professional: Simon Buckley (01903 783732). Secretary: Major Vic Chaszczewski (01903 783288).*

BILLINGSHURST. **Foxbridge Golf Club**, Foxbridge Lane, Plaistow Road, Kirdford, Billingshurst RH14 0LB (Tel & Fax: 01403 753303). *Location:* B2133, A281 Guildford to Horsham Road. Parkland course with eight lakes. 9 holes, 6236 yards. S.S.S. 70. Practice ground. *Green Fees:* weekdays 9 holes £12.00 and 18 holes £18.00; weekends 9 holes £14.00 and 18 holes £25.00. *Eating facilities:* restaurant and bar. *Visitors:* welcome, must pre-book tee times at least one day in advance. Strict dress code. Buggies and carts available. *Society Meetings:* welcome Mondays, Tuesdays and Wednesdays only. Professional: S. Hall. Secretary: Paul Clark (Tel & Fax: 01403 753303).

BOGNOR REGIS. **Bognor Regis Golf Club**, Downview Road, Felpham, Bognor Regis PO22 8JD (01243 865867; Fax: 01243 860719). *Location:* turn north at traffic lights on A259 at Felpham village. Flat parkland, many dogleg holes and water hazards. 18 holes, 6238 yards. S.S.S. 70. Practice area. *Green Fees:* £25.00 weekdays, £30.00 weekends and Bank Holidays. *Eating facilities:* bar open every day; hot and cold snacks available weekdays, light snacks available weekends. *Visitors:* welcome weekdays (Ladies' Day Tuesday), weekends only with a member. Handicap Certificate required. *Society Meetings:* welcome by arrangement (minimum 16). Professional: Stephen Bassil (01243 865209). Secretary: (01243 821929; Fax: 01243 860719). website: www.bognorgolfclub.co.uk

BURGESS HILL. **The Burgess Hill Golf Academy**, Cuckfield Road, Burgess Hill RH15 8RE (01444 258585; Fax: 01444 247318). *Location:* on the B2036 north of Burgess Hill, on the Burgess Hill to Cuckfield road. An excellent short course in undulating wooded, parkland setting. 9 holes, 1250 yards. Par 3. 28 bay floodlit driving range, practice area, PGA teaching academy, Pro shop. *Green Fees:* information not available. *Eating facilities:* bar and restaurant. *Visitors:* welcome, open from 8am to 9pm. Professional/Secretary: Mark Collins (01444 258585; Fax: 01444 247318).

CHICHESTER. **Chichester Golf Club**, Hunston Village, Chichester PO20 1AX (01243 533833). *Location:* take B2145 south of Chichester, on left hand side after Hunston Village. 45 hole golf complex. Cathedral course 18 holes "Florida style", 6442 yards, Par 72; Tower course 18 holes "Parkland style", 6109 yards, Par 69. Separate family golf centre: Par 3, 829 yards short course, American style 12 hole mini golf, Mizuno golf school and 27 bay floodlit driving range including new automated power tee system. *Green Fees:* weekdays Tower £16.00, Cathedral £22.00; weekends Tower £18.50, Cathedral £30.00. *Eating facilities:* fully licensed clubhouse, bar and farmhouse cooking. *Visitors:* welcome anytime. *Society Meetings:* welcome, catered for by prior arrangement. Well stocked golf shops. Teaching Professional: Emma Fields (01243 528999). Proprietor: Richard Haygarth (01243 536666; Fax: 01243 539922). e-mail: enquiries@chichestergolf.com website: www.chichestergolf.com

CHICHESTER. **Goodwood Golf Club**, Kennel Hill, Goodwood, Chichester PO18 0PN. *Location:* one mile north of Chichester at east end of Chichester Bypass (A27). Undulating downland. 18 holes, 6401 yards. S.S.S. 71. Practice ground, nets, putting greens. *Green Fees:* telephone the Secretary. *Eating facilities:* full catering and bar. *Visitors:* welcome, must show Handicap Certificate. *Society Meetings:* all welcome on Wednesdays and Thursdays only. Professional: Damon Allard (01243 755135). Secretary: (01243 755130; Fax: 01243 755135). e-mail: golf@goodwood.co.uk

CHICHESTER. **Marriott Goodwood Park Hotel & Country Club**, Goodwood, Chichester PO18 0QB (0870 400 7225; Fax: 0870 400 7325). *Location:* set amidst the 12,000 acre Goodwood Estate, ancestral home of the Dukes of Richmond, yet only three miles from Chichester. Parkland course designed by Donald Steel and built in 1988. 6650-yards, Par 72. Tuition programmes available; fourteen bay golf range (eight covered); short game practice area; putting green; pro shop; trolleys, buggies and clubs for hire. *Green Fees:* £35.00 per round, 7 days. *Eating facilities:* full facilities available. *Visitors:* welcome, no restrictions. *Society Meetings:* welcome. Professional: Adrian Wratting.

CHICHESTER. **Selsey Golf Club,** Golf Links Lane, Selsey, Chichester PO20 8HX (01243 602203). *Location:* B2145, seven miles south of Chichester. Flat course. 9 holes playing 18, 5532 yards. S.S.S. 68. Green Fees: information not provided. Eating facilities: lunches and snacks served in club. Visitors: welcome with bona fide Handicap Certificate or playing with a member. Society Meetings: small societies catered for weekdays only. Professional: P. Grindley (01243 602203). Secretary: P. Carter (Tel & Fax: 01243 602203).

COWDRAY PARK **Cowdray Park Golf Club**, Midhurst GU29 0BB (01730 813599; Fax: 01730 815900). *Location:* one mile east of Midhurst on A272 between Midhurst and Petworth. A testing parkland course with scenic views of the Downs and polo fields and Cowdray ruins. 18 holes, 6212 yards. S.S.S. 70. Driving range and Par 3 Academy. *Green Fees:* from £40.00 weekdays and weekends. *Eating facilities:* restaurant and bar snacks. *Visitors:* welcome. Dormy house. *Society Meetings:* catered for. Professional: Richard J. Gough. Secretary: Paul Fairminer.
e-mail: cowdray-golf@lineone.net

CRAWLEY. **Cottesmore Golf and Country Club**, Buchan Hill, Pease Pottage, Crawley RH11 9AT (01293 528256; Fax: 01293 522819). *Location:* one mile west of Junction 11 off M23 on road to Pease Pottage and Horsham. Two mature golf courses set in 247 acres of rolling Sussex countryside. The fairways are lined with rhododendrons, silver birch, oak and chestnut trees. Four holes over lakes. Griffin Course 18 holes, 6248 yards. S.S.S. 70, par 71. Phoenix Course 18 holes, 5514 yards. S.S.S. 67, par 69. Practice ground, putting greens. *Green Fees:* information not available. *Eating facilities:* restaurant, coffee shop, two bars. *Visitors:* welcome. Handicap Certificate required for Griffin course. Health Club including indoor heated pool, tennis courts and gymnasium; en suite accommodation (12 rooms) also available. Trolleys and buggies available. *Society Meetings:* welcome, advance bookings required. Professional: Calum Callan (01293 535399; Fax: 01293 522819). General Manager: Brodie Pearmaine (01293 528256).*

CRAWLEY. **Copthorne Golf Club**, Borers Arms Road, Copthorne, Crawley RH10 3LL (01342 712033). *Location:* off Exit 10 M23, one mile on A264 towards East Grinstead. Flat wooded course. 18 holes, 6505 yards. S.S.S. 71. Practice area. *Green Fees:* weekdays £32.00 per round, £40.00 per day; weekends £34.00 after 1pm. Half fees if playing with member. *Eating facilities:* catering all day, bar. *Visitors:* welcome weekdays without reservation, after 1pm weekends. *Society Meetings:* welcome with advance bookings. Professional: Joe Burrell (01342 712405). Secretary: J. Pyne (01342 712508; Fax: 01342 717682).

CRAWLEY. **Ifield Golf and Country Club,** Rusper Road, Ifield, Crawley RH11 0LN (01293 520222). *Location:* outskirts of Crawley near A23 to Gossops Green. Undulating parkland. 18 holes, 6314 yards. S.S.S. 70. Practice ground. *Green Fees:* £26.00 per round, £36.00 per day weekdays; weekends with a member only. *Eating facilities:* fully licensed bar, à la carte restaurant. *Visitors:* welcome, please telephone. Trolley and Buggies for hire. *Society Meetings:* welcome. Professional: Jon Earl (01293 523088; Fax: 01293 612973). Secretary: D. Knight (01293 520222; Fax: 01293 612973).

CRAWLEY. **Pease Pottage Golf Course and Driving Range**, Horsham Road, Pease Pottage, Crawley (01293 521706; Fax: 01293 521706). *Location:* M23 Junction 11, Pease Pottage, James King Pub. Wooded areas surrounding golf course. 9 holes, 1864 yards. S.S.S. 60, Par 4/3. *Green Fees:* weekdays £8.50; weekends £11.00 for 18 holes. Senior Citizens £5.00. *Eating facilities:* restaurant, coffee shop. *Visitors:* welcome, no restrictions. Two PGA Professionals available for tuition. New Golf Superstore. Full on site repair service. *Society Meetings:* welcome. Professional: David Blair (01293 521706). Secretary: Natalie Leszczar.

See also Colour Advertisement on page 28

CRAWLEY. **Tilgate Forest Golf Centre,** Titmus Drive, Tilgate, Crawley RH10 5EU (01293 530103). *Location:* Crawley, five minutes from Junction 11 M23. Wooded parkland. 18 holes, 6167 yards, 5643 metres. Par 72. 35 bay floodlit driving range. Par 3 course. *Green Fees:* information not available. *Eating facilities:* restaurant and bar. *Visitors:* welcome at all times but there is a booking system in operation. *Society Meetings:* welcome Mondays to Thursdays. Professional: Sean Trussell (01293 530103; Fax: 01293 523478). *

CUCKFIELD. **Cuckfield Golf Centre,** Staplefield Road, Cuckfield RH17 5HY (01444 459999). *Location:* one mile north west of Cuckfield village. Undulating open parkland course with outstanding views in an Area of Outstanding Natural Beauty. 9 holes, 2860 yards. S.S.S. 36. Putting green. *Green Fees:* weekdays £8.00; weekends £9.00; £1.00 discount juniors and Senior Citizens. *Eating facilities:* snacks and licensed bar available. *Visitors:* always welcome. Pay and play - no Handicap Certificate required. Hire clubs and trolleys, golf cars £10.00 9 holes, £18.00 18 holes, please phone for availability. *Society Meetings*: always welcome. Professional: Robert Dickman. Secretary: Mrs L. Dickman.
e-mail: lucy@cuckfieldgolf.co.uk
website: www.cuckfieldgolf.co.uk

EAST GRINSTEAD. **Chartham Park,** Felcourt Road, Felcourt, East Grinstead RH19 2JT (01342 870340; Fax: 01342 870719). *Location:* Felcourt Road off A22 on north side of East Grinstead. Parkland. 18 holes, 6680 yards. S.S.S. 72. Driving range, putting green. *Green Fees:* information not available. *Eating facilities:* restaurant, light snacks and bar all day. *Visitors:* pre-booking required. Golf carts and trolleys can be hired. *Society Meetings:* by prior arrangement. Professional: David Hobbs. General Manager: Patrick Ferguson.

EAST GRINSTEAD. **Holtye Golf Club,** Holtye Common, Cowden, Near Edenbridge TN8 7ED (01342 850635). *Location:* four miles east of East Grinstead on A264, seven miles west of Tunbridge Wells. Undulating forest course; alternate tees. 9 holes, 5325 yards. S.S.S. 66. Large practice ground. *Green Fees:* weekdays £16.00; weekends £18.00. *Eating facilities:* available every lunchtime, some evenings in summer season. *Visitors:* welcome, restrictions Wednesday, Thursday and weekend mornings. *Society Meetings:* catered for. Professional: Kevin Hinton (01342 850635). Secretary: J.P. Holmes (01342 850576).

EFFINGHAM. **Effingham Park Golf Club**, West Park Road, Copthorne RH10 8AL (01342 716528). *Location:* Junction 10 M23, two miles east on A264. Parkland (wooded), large lake in play over four holes. 9 holes, 1815 yards. S.S.S. 57 (18 holes). *Green Fees:* information not available. *Eating facilities:* club bar and restaurant. *Visitors:* welcome, restricted Tuesday evenings, Wednesday and Thursday mornings. Five star Hotel on site and leisure club. *Society Meetings:* catered for anytime weekdays, weekends after 12 noon. Club Professional: Mark Root. Secretary: Ian McRobbie. *

HASSOCKS. **Hassocks Golf Club**, London Road, Hassocks BN6 9NA . *Location:* on the A273 between Burgess Hill and Hassocks. Gently undulating pay and play course. 18 holes, 5698 yards, 5210 metres. S.S.S. 68. Practice ground. *Green Fees:* weekdays £15.00; weekends £19.95, early morning/twilight rates available on application. *Eating facilities:* restaurant, bar, stud bar. *Visitors:* welcome anytime. Buggy for hire, £20.00. *Society Meetings:* welcome. Professional: Charles Ledger (01273 846990). Manager: Jaki Brown (01273 846630; Fax: 01273 846670).
e-mail: hgc@hassocksgolfclub.co.uk
website: www.hassocksgolfclub.co.uk

HAYWARDS HEATH. **Haywards Heath Golf Club**, High Beech Lane, Haywards Heath RH16 1SL (01444 414457). *Location:* two miles north of Haywards Heath. Parkland. 18 holes, 6216 yards. S.S.S. 70. Practice area. *Green Fees:* weekdays £26.00 per round, £36.00 for 36 holes; weekends and Bank Holidays £35.00 per round, £40.00 for 36 holes. Packages for societies. *Eating facilities:* bar and catering both available. *Visitors:* welcome, by arrangement, phone Professional; Handicap Certificate required. *Society Meetings:* catered for Wednesdays and Thursdays by arrangement with the Secretary. Professional: M.P. Henning (01444 414866).

HORSHAM. **Horsham Golf and Fitness,** Worthing Road, Horsham RH13 7AX (01403 271525; Fax: 01403 274528). *Location:* A24 Horsham bypass (southwest roundabout), 200 yards towards Horsham. Parkland with several water features. 9 holes, 4122 yards. S.S.S. 60. Driving range. *Green Fees*: £7.00 weekdays; £8.00 weekends. *Eating facilities:* restaurant/bar open all day. *Visitors:* welcome at all times. Large well stocked shop, new fitness suite now on site. *Society Meetings*: welcome with booking. Professional: Alex Paterson. Secretary: Elaine Purton.

HORSHAM. **Mannings Heath Golf Club,** "Fullers", Hammerpond Road, Mannings Heath, Near Horsham RH13 6PG (01403 210228; Fax: 01403 270974). *Location:* off Junction 11 M23, three miles south of Horsham off A281. Undulating wooded course with featured streams. Waterfall - 18 holes, 6378 yards (White tees). S.S.S. 70; Kingfisher Course - 18 holes, 6217 yards. S.S.S. 70. Driving range, two practice putting greens, chipping green. *Green Fees*: information not available. *Eating facilities*: luxurious clubhouse "Fullers", full bar, restaurant and spike bar facilities. *Visitors:* welcome, may book 14 days in advance (by phone). Tennis court, conference/ meeting facilities. *Society Meetings*: welcome at all times, full or half day. Professional: Clive Tucker. General Manager: Steven Kershaw.
e-mail: s.kershaw@manningsheath.com
website: www.manningsheath.com

HORSHAM near. **Slinfold Park Golf and Country Club,** Stane Street (A29), Slinfold, Near Horsham RG13 7RE (01403 791154; Fax: 01403 791465). *Location:* situated on the A29, four miles west of Horsham with good road links to the M23 and East/West on the A272. A gently undulating parkland course with many interesting water features and mature trees. 18 Hole Championship Course, 6418 yards. 9 Hole course. S.S.S. 71. 19 bay floodlit driving range. *Green Fees:* information not available. *Eating facilities:* purpose built clubhouse with restaurant and bar. *Visitors:* welcome subject to tee time availability. Reservations can be made up to seven days in advance. No handicap required. *Society Meetings:* welcome weekdays, minimum group size 10; call for society pack. Professional: Tony Clingan (01403 791555). Secretary: Stephen Blake (01403 791154).*

LINDFIELD. **Paxhill Park,** East Mascalls Lane, Lindfield RH16 2QN (01444 484467; Fax: 01444 482709). *Location:* take Lewes Road out of Lindfield village one mile then left. Parkland with water and River Ouse. 18 holes, 6200 yards. S.S.S. 70. Practice ground, putting green. *Green Fees:* weekdays £17.00; weekends £22.00. *Eating facilities:* restaurant and bar. *Visitors:* welcome daily; after 12 noon weekends and Bank Holidays. Trolleys. *Society Meetings:* all welcome. Professional: Marcus Green (01444 484000). Secretary: J.D. Bowen.

LITTLEHAMPTON. **Littlehampton Golf Club**, 170 Rope Walk, Riverside West, Littlehampton BN17 5DL (01903 717170; Fax: 01903 726629). *Location:* leave A259 one mile west of Littlehampton at sign. Seaside links. 18 holes, 6244 yards. S.S.S. 70. *Green Fees:* information not available. *Eating facilities:* restaurant and two bars. *Visitors:* welcome weekdays, weekends after midday, but phone prior to arrival. *Society Meetings:* societies only, minimum number 12. Professional: Guy McQuitty (01903 716369). Secretary: Steven Graham.
e-mail: lgc@talk21.com
website: www.littlehamptongolf.co.uk

PETWORTH. **Petworth Golf Course,** "Osiers Farm", London Road, Petworth GU28 9LX (01798 344097; Fax: 01798 342528; Mobile: 07932 163941). Open all year round. *Location:* 2 miles north of Petworth on A283, heading northbound towards Guildford. Undulating natural farmland course, plenty of hedges and ditches. 18 holes, 6191 yards, S.S.S. 71. Nets and course practice holes. *Green Fees:* £11.00 weekdays and weekends. *Eating Facilities:* clubhouse catering for up to 80 people. *Visitors:* welcome anytime, B&B on site. Tuition available. *Society Meetings:* welcome, rates from £14.00 to £40.00. Professional: Andy Long (01798 344097; Fax: 01798 342528). Secretary: Dennis Windows (01730 817707).

PULBOROUGH. **West Sussex Golf Club,** Golf Club Lane, Wiggonholt, Pulborough RH20 2EN (01798 872563). *Location:* between Storrington and Pulborough on the A283. Heathland. 18 holes, 6223 yards. S.S.S. 70. *Green Fees:* £60.00 for 18 holes, £75.00 for 36 holes. Subject to review. Driving range. *Eating facilities:* lunch and tea daily, bars. *Visitors:* welcome by prior arrangement (not Fridays and weekends). No three or four balls. *Society Meetings:* catered for Wednesdays and Thursdays. Professional: T. Packham (01798 872426). Secretary: C.P. Simpson (01798 872563; Fax: 01798 872033).
e-mail: secretary@westsussexgolf.co.uk
website: www.westsussexgolf.co.uk

RUSTINGTON. **Rustington Golf Centre,** Golfers Lane, Angmering BN16 4NB (01903 850790; Fax: 01903 850982). *Location:* on A259 at Rustington, near Littlehampton. 18 holes, 5735 yards, S.S.S. 70. 9 hole Par 3 course, three hole academy course, putting green, 30 bay floodlit driving range (11 automated). *Green Fees:* information not provided. *Eating facilities:* coffee shop and licensed bar. *Visitors:* welcome at all times. Scott Cranfield Golf Academy available for tuition of all standards. *Society Meetings:* societies and corporate days welcome by appointment. Centre Manager/Secretary: Gary Salt (01903 850790; Fax: 01903 850982)

Mannings Heath Golf Club
'Fullers', Hammerpond Road, Mannings Heath, Near Horsham, W. Sussex RH13 6PG
Tel: 01403 210228 ❖ Fax: 01403 270974 ❖ www.manningsheath.com
- ❖ Situated off Junction 11 of the M23, three miles south of Horsham off A281.
- ❖ Undulating wooded course with featured streams.
  Waterfall Course – 18 holes, 6378 yards. S.S.S. 70.
  Kingfisher Course – 18 holes, 6217 yards. S.S.S. 70.
- ❖ Driving range, two practice putting greens, chipping green.
- ❖ Other amenities include a tennis court and a fully stocked 14-acre fishing lake.
- ❖ Stylish and luxurious clubhouse with our award-winning AA Rosette 'Goldings' Restaurant.

See also Colour Advertisement on page 28

WEST CHILTINGTON. **West Chiltington Golf Club,** Broadford Bridge Road, West Chiltington RH20 2YA (01798 813574; Fax: 01798 812631). *Location:* A29 Bognor from London Road, left at Adversane village B2132 then signposted. Gently undulating parkland with spectacular views of South Downs. 18 holes, 6389 yards. S.S.S. 69. 9 holes, 1360 yard short course ideal for beginners. 13 bay driving range. *Green Fees:* weekdays £19.00, weekends £23.50. Saturdays, Sundays and Bank Holidays £80.00 per fourball after 10am. Twilight rounds £11.00 weekdays, £13.00 weekends. *Eating facilities:* bar and restaurant open all day every day. *Visitors:* always welcome, smart dress. Tee times may be booked through Pro Shop (01798 812115). *Society Meetings:* welcome, apply to Secretary. Secretary: Debbie Haines. General Manager: George McKay. website: www.westchiltgolf.co.uk

WORTHING. **Hill Barn Golf Course**, Hill Barn Lane, Worthing BN14 9QE (01903 233918). *Location:* signposted on the roundabout at the top of Broadwater, Worthing on the A27. Downland course with a few trees but generally fairly open. 18 holes, 6229 yards. S.S.S. 70. Small practice area (balls not provided) and putting green. *Green Fees:* information not available. *Eating facilities:* clubhouse and bar. *Visitors:* welcome, no restrictions or Handicap required (municipal course). *Society Meetings:* welcome. Professional/Manager: Simon Blanshard (01903 237301; Fax: 01903 217613).

WORTHING. **Worthing Golf Club,** Links Road, Worthing BN14 9QZ (01903 260801; Fax: 01903 694664). *Location:* on A27 250 yards east of junction with A24 (Offington Roundabout). Two downland courses. Lower course: 18 holes, 6530 yards. S.S.S. 72. Upper course: 5243 yards. S.S.S. 66. *Green Fees:* weekdays £38.00 per day; weekends and Bank Holidays £40.00 per round. *Eating facilities:* dining room, lounge and bar. *Visitors:* welcome, check in advance with Secretary. No visitors at weekends (for golf) during G.M.T. *Society Meetings:* catered for by arrangement. Professional: Stephen Rolley (01903 260718; Fax: 01903 694613). Secretary: Ian Evans (01903 260801; Fax: 01903 694664).

Centrally located between Horsham and Worthing, with stunning views of the South Downs, West Chiltington has so much more to offer than the average golf club.

- 27 holes, large putting green, covered driving range.
- Green fees weekdays £19, weekends £23.50.
- Modern, attractive clubhouse; bar and restaurant.
- Friendly and co-operative staff
- Society packages available

We shall be delighted to tailor a day for you. Ring for more details or visit our website.

West Chiltington Golf Club

Broadford Bridge Road, West Chiltington, West Sussex RH20 2YA
Tel: 01798 813574 • Fax: 01798 812631
www.westchiltgolf.co.uk

See also Colour Advertisement on page 28

Tyne & Wear

BIRTLEY. **Birtley Golf Club**, Birtley Lane, Birtley DH3 2LR(0191-410-2207). *Location:* just off old Durham road and main A1. Parkland. 9 holes, 5660 yards. S.S.S. 67. *Green Fees:* visitors welcome weekdays £14.00, £7.00 with member; weekends with member only £10.00. *Eating facilities:* bar open only after 7.30pm, snacks available. *Visitors:* welcome weekdays; weekends and Bank Holidays with a member only. *Society Meetings:* welcome, must be pre-booked. Secretary: T. Hardy (0191 410 2207).

CHOPWELL. **Garesfield Golf Club**, Chopwell NE17 7AP (Tel & Fax: 01207 561309; Bar/Catering 01207 561278). *Location:* leave A694 at Rowlands Gill, follow signposts for Chopwell, approximately three miles. Undulating wooded parkland 18 holes, 6403 yards. par 72. Practice ground, nets and putting green. *Green Fees:* weekdays £25.00 per day, £19.00 per round; weekends: details on request. *Eating facilities:* full catering except Mondays. *Visitors:* welcome weekdays; weekends and Bank Holidays after 4.30pm. Buggies available £15.00 per round. *Society Meetings:* welcome. Group rates (min. 12, max. 24 on Sundays): £29.00 per round. Professional: D. Race (01207 563082). Secretary: Mrs J. Barclay. (Tel & Fax: 01207 561309).

EAST BOLDON. **Boldon Golf Club Ltd**, Dipe Lane, East Boldon NE36 0PQ (0191-536 4182). *Location:* near Sunderland, approximately one mile from roundabout at junction of A19 and A184 highways. Fairly flat parkland. 18 holes, 6348 yards. S.S.S. 70. *Green Fees:* weekdays £20.00, with a member £14.00; weekends £24.00, with a member £16.00. *Eating facilities:* bar snacks and restaurant. *Visitors:* welcome, not between 9am and 10am, 12.30pm and 1.30pm or 4.30pm and 6pm. Not before 3.30pm at weekends. *Society Meetings:* catered for. Professional: Phipps Golf (0191-536 5835; Fax: 0191-537 2270). Secretary: R.W. Benton (0191-536 5360; Fax: 0191-537 2270). e-mail: info@boldongolfclub.co.uk

GATESHEAD. **Heworth Golf Club**, Gingling Gate, Heworth, Gateshead. *Location:* A1 (M) south east boundary of Gateshead. Flat wooded course. 18 holes, 6422 yards. S.S.S. 71. Practice area. *Green Fees:* £18.00 per day. *Eating facilities:* diningroom, two bars. *Visitors:* weekdays up to 4pm, no visitors Saturdays; but after 10am on Sundays. *Society Meetings:* welcome mid-week only up to 4pm. Professional: A. Marshall (0191-438 4223). Secretary: G. Holbrow (0191-469 4424).

GATESHEAD. **Ravensworth Golf Club Ltd**, 'Angel View', Longbank, Gateshead NE9 7NE (0191-487 6014). *Location:* two miles south of Gateshead town centre, near A1 (Angel of the North). Parkland course. 18 holes, 5931 yards. S.S.S. 69. *Green Fees:* 1st April to 30th September: Monday to Friday £18.00 (£12.00 with a member), weekends and Bank Holidays £25.00 (£18.00 with a member). 1st October to 31st March: Monday to Friday £13.00 (£9.00 with a member), weekends and Bank Holidays £20.00 (£13.00 with a member). Subject to review. *Eating facilities:* meals served with reasonable notice (not Mondays). *Visitors:* welcome, weekends very restricted. *Society Meetings:* catered for. Secretary: Bob Hill (0191-442 1042).

HEDDON ON THE WALL. **Close House Golf Club**, Heddon on the Wall, Newcastle upon Tyne NE15 0HT (01661 852953). *Location:* 10 miles west of Newcastle off A69 to Wylam. A picturesque parkland/part wooded course set in the Tyne Valley. 18 holes, 5571 yards. S.S.S. 67. Golf packages available for visiting parties. *Green Fees:* provided on request. *Eating facilities:* catering available with golf packages. *Visitors:* welcome at restricted times, preliminary phone call advisable. *Society Meetings:* welcome on weekdays only by prior arrangement with the Secretary. Secretary: M.E. Pearse (Tel & Fax: 0191 4886515).

HETTON-LE-HOLE. **Elemore Golf Course**, Elemore Lane, Hetton-Le-Hole (0191-517 3057; Fax: 0191 517 3054). *Location:* follow signs to Easington Lane, located off A1068, following signs to Elemore/ Pittington. Flat meadowland Public Pay & Play golf course. 18 holes, 5947 yards. S.S.S. 69. Practice area. *Green Fees:* weekdays £10.00 adults, £6.00 senior citizens (over 60) and ladies; day tickets £13.00. Weekends £14.00 adults, £8.00 senior citizens (over 60) and ladies. *Eating facilities:* clubhouse with bar/lounge serving snacks and meals. *Visitors:* welcome, no restrictions. Buggy Hire £12.00 per round. *Society Meetings:* welcome throughout the year. Contact Course Manager for advance bookings (14 days' notice required). Professional: To be arranged. Course Manager: Barbara Blenkinsop.

HOUGHTON-LE-SPRING. **Houghton-le-Spring Golf Club**, Copt Hill, Houghton-le-Spring (0191 5841198). *Location:* off A690 Durham Road, take Houghton to Seaham road, course is situated at the top of Copt Hill bank. Testing hillside course. 18 holes, 6416 yards, 5867 metres. S.S.S. 71. *Green Fees:* information not provided. *Eating facilities:* available most days, bar open every day. *Visitors:* welcome most days but not on competition days (Sundays). *Society Meetings:* catered for by arrangement. Professional: K. Gow (0191 5847421). Secretary: N. Wales (0191 5841198).

NEWCASTLE UPON TYNE. **City of Newcastle Golf Club**, Three Mile Bridge, Gosforth, Newcastle upon Tyne NE3 2DR (0191-285 1775; Fax: 0191-284 0700). *Location:* B1318 three miles north of city. Flat parkland. 18 holes, 6528 yards. S.S.S. 71. *Green Fees:* weekdays £25.00, £32.00 per day; weekends and Bank Holidays £30.00. Discount for parties over 12. *Eating facilities:* bar, meals. *Visitors:* welcome without reservation, restricted times Fridays. *Society Meetings:* very welcome. Professional: S. McKenna (0191-285 5481; Fax: 0191-284 0700). Club Manager: A.J. Matthew (0191-285 1775; Fax: 0191-284 0700). e-mail: info@cityofnewcastlegolfclub.com website: www.cityofnewcastlegolfclub.com

NEWCASTLE UPON TYNE. **Gosforth Golf Club**, Broadway East, Gosforth, Newcastle upon Tyne NE3 5ER (0191-285 6710). *Location:* three miles north of Newcastle near Great North Road, B1318. Parkland with stream. 18 holes, 6024 yards. S.S.S. 69. *Green Fees:* £25.00 per round, £30.00 per day including weekends. *Visitors:* welcome weekdays. *Society Meetings:* catered for by arrangement with the Secretary, including some weekends and Bank Holidays. Professional: G. Garland (0191-285 0553). Secretary: Brian Pluse (0191-285 3495; Fax: 0191-284 6274).

NEWCASTLE UPON TYNE. **Hobson Golf Club**, Hobson, Burnopfield, Newcastle upon Tyne NE16 6BZ (01207 271605). *Location:* on main Newcastle to Consett road. Fairly flat, well designed course. 18 holes, 6403 yards, 5854 metres. S.S.S. 71. Practice area. *Green Fees:* information not available. *Eating facilities:* bar, lounge and restaurant. *Visitors:* no restrictions; booking system at weekends. *Society Meetings:* by prior arrangement with Professional (all bookings). Professional: J.W. Ord (01207 271605). Secretary: R.J. Handrick (01207 570189).*

NEWCASTLE UPON TYNE. **Newcastle United Golf Club**, 60 Ponteland Road, Cowgate, Newcastle upon Tyne NE3 3JW (0191-286 9998). *Location:* two miles west of city centre in direction of airport. Moorland. 18 holes, 6617 yards, 6048 metres. S.S.S. 72. Practice area. *Green Fees:* weekdays £22.00 per day; weekends, £25.00 per day (if there is no competition on). £14 00 with a member. *Eating facilities:* bar meals available. *Visitors:* no restrictions midweek, welcome weekends if no competitions. Book through the golf shop or see our website. *Society Meetings:* welcome, book through Secretary. Golf Shop: (0191-286 9998). Secretary: S. Darbyshire. website: www.nugc.co.uk

NEWCASTLE UPON TYNE. **Parklands Golf Club**, High Gosforth Park, Newcastle upon Tyne NE3 5HQ (0191-236 4867). *Location:* three miles north of centre of Newcastle, off the A1 follow signs for Gosforth Park. Parkland. 18 holes, 6013 yards, 5742 metres. S.S.S. 69. 9 holes pitch and putt, 45 bay floodlit driving range. *Green Fees:* weekdays £15.00; weekends £18.00. *Eating facilities:* restaurant and bar. *Visitors:* welcome, no restrictions. *Society Meetings:* catered for. General Manager: Brian Rumney (0191-236 4480). Secretary: Brian Woof (0191-236 4480).

NEWCASTLE UPON TYNE. **The Northumberland Golf Club Ltd**, High Gosforth Park, Newcastle upon Tyne NE3 5HT (0191-236 2498). *Location:* off A1. 18 holes, 6629 yards. S.S.S. 72. *Green Fees:* £40.00 per round weekdays only. *Visitors:* welcome with prior reservation or introduction. *Society Meetings:* catered for except on Mondays and weekends. Secretary: J.M. Forteath (0191-236 2498).

NEWCASTLE UPON TYNE. **Tyneside Golf Club Ltd**, Westfield Lane, Ryton NE40 3QE (0191-413 2177; Fax: 0191-413 2742). *Location:* seven miles west of Newcastle upon Tyne, off B6317 in Ryton Village. Parkland, hilly with water hazards. Large practice area. 18 holes, 6009 yards, 5477 metres. S.S.S. 69. Practice field. *Green Fees:* weekdays £22.00; weekends negotiable. *Eating facilities:* full catering. *Visitors:* bona fide golfers welcome by arrangement with the Secretary. *Society Meetings:* weekdays by arrangement with Secretary; possibly Sunday afternoons. Professional: M. Gunn (0191-413 1600). Secretary: Ed Stephenson (0191-413 2742).

NEWCASTLE UPON TYNE. **Westerhope Golf Club**, Whorlton Grange, Westerhope, Newcastle-upon-Tyne NE5 1PP (0191-286 9125). *Location:* Stamfordham Road, Westerhope, near Jingling Gate Public House. Parkland/wooded. 18 holes, 6444 yards. S.S.S. 71. Two practice areas. *Green Fees:* £20.00 per round. *Eating facilities:* lunches and high teas. *Visitors:* welcome weekdays, weekends and Bank Holidays with a member only. *Society Meetings:* welcome weekdays. Professional: N. Brown (0191-286 0594). Secretary: B. Bell (0191-286 7636).

NEWCASTLE UPON TYNE. **Whickham Golf Club Ltd**, Hollinside Park, Fellside Road, Whickham, Newcastle upon Tyne NE16 5BA (0191-488 7309). *Location:* five miles south-west of Newcastle upon Tyne, turn off A1 at sign for Whickham. In Whickham take road signposted to Burnopfield (ie Fellside Road) and proceed to golf club. Parkland course - undulating with attractive panoramic views. 18 holes, 6500 yards. Par 71. Practice grounds and putting green. *Green Fees:* weekdays £20.00; weekends £25.00. *Eating facilities:* lunches, teas, evening meals available by prior order, bar snacks all day. *Visitors:* welcome except Saturdays and Sundays without reservation. Smart casual wear on course and in clubhouse. *Society Meetings:* welcome by arrangement. Professional: Andrew Hall (0191-488 8591). Hon. Secretary: Mrs J. Miller (0191-488 1576; Fax: 0191-488 1577).

RYTON. **Ryton Golf Club**, Dr. Stanners, Clara Vale, Ryton NE40 3TD (0191-413 3737). *Location:* off A695 eight miles west of Newcastle at Crawcrook to Clara Vale. Flat parkland, wooded, running alongside River Tyne. 18 holes, 6042 yards, 5499 metres. S.S.S. 69. Practice area. *Green Fees:* weekdays £15.00 per round, £20.00 per day; weekends £20.00 per round by arrangement, £10.00 per round with member. *Eating facilities:* available by arrangement with Steward. *Visitors:* welcome weekdays, weekends with member or by prior arrangement. *Society Meetings:* catered for by arrangement with Secretary. Secretary: S. Dix (0191-413 3253; Fax: 0191-413 1642).

SHIREMOOR. **Backworth Golf Club**, The Hall, Backworth, Shiremoor NE27 0AH (Course Information Service: 0191-268 9131; Club Steward: 0191-268 1048). *Location:* A191 Newcastle to Whitley Bay; at Shiremoor crossroads turn left one mile. Flat parkland, part wooded. 9 holes, 5930 yards. S.S.S. 69. Putting/chipping area. *Green Fees:* iformation not available. *Eating facilities:* dinner booked in advance; bar meals/snacks. *Visitors:* welcome by arrangement but not Tuesday (Ladies' Day), not Saturday until 5.30pm (Summer), not Sunday mornings. *Society Meetings:* welcome by prior arrangement only. Secretary: G.M. Sales (0191-280 8107).*

SOUTH SHIELDS. **South Shields Golf Club Ltd**, Cleadon Hills, South Shields NE34 8EG (0191-456 0475). *Location:* near A19 and A1 M, Cleadon Chimney prominent landmark. 18 holes, 6174 yards, 5729 metres. S.S.S. 70. Excellent greens, heathland/links, practice area. *Green Fees:* weekdays £22.00, weekends and Bank Holidays £27.00. *Eating facilities:* meals available at all times, bar. *Visitors:* welcome at all times without reservation. *Society Meetings:* catered for by arrangement. Professional: M. Ellis. (0191-456 0110). Secretary: R. Stanness (0191-456 8942).

SOUTH SHIELDS. **Whitburn Golf Club Ltd**, Lizard Lane, South Shields NE34 7AF (0191-529 2144). *Location:* between Sunderland and South Shields adjoining Coast Road. Parkland. 18 holes, 5944 yards, S.S.S. 68. *Green Fees:* weekdays £22.00, with a member £12.00; weekends and Bank Holidays £27.00, with a member £17.00. *Eating facilities:* available. *Visitors:* welcome except on Sunday when competitions being held and restricted Tuesdays (Ladies' Day). *Society Meetings:* catered for on weekdays by prior reservations. Professional: D. Stephenson (0191-529 4210). Secretary: Mr A. Atkinson (0191-529 4944).

SUNDERLAND. **Wearside Golf Club**, Cox Green, Sunderland SR4 9JT (0191-534 2518). *Location:* on south bank of River Wear, one mile west of A19. From A19 exit for A183, direction Chester-le-Street, at 100 yards turn right, signposted Offerton/Cox Green, then left at T junction, down hill over humped bridge. Parkland, bordered on north by River Wear,

deep wooded gully traverses course. 18 holes, 6323 yards. S.S.S. 70. 4 holes Par 3 field and separate practice field. *Green Fees:* weekdays £18.00 per round, £20.00 per day; weekends and Bank Holidays £26.00. Society rates available. *Eating facilities:* full catering and bar service (sandwiches only on Mondays). *Visitors:* welcome most times, telephone Professional for information. *Society Meetings:* by advance application. Professional: Doug Brolls (0191-534 4269). Secretary: M. Gowland (0191-534 2518).

WALLSEND. **Wallsend Golf Club**, Bigges Main, Wallsend NE28 8SU. *Location:* western boundary. Parkland. 18 holes, 6571 yards, 6043 metres. S.S.S. 71. Driving range. *Green Fees:* weekdays £15.50; weekends £18.50. *Eating facilities:* meals available on request. *Visitors:* restricted weekends - not before 12.30pm April to October. *Society Meetings:* weekdays only. Professional: K. Phillips (0191-262 4231). Secretary: D. Souter (0191-262 1973).

WASHINGTON. **George Washington Golf and Country Club,** Stone Cellar Road, Washington NE37 1PH (0191-402 9988). *Location:* Washington New Town, one mile from A1M Junction A194. Parkland course with many tree-lined fairways. 18 holes, 6604 yards, 6038 metres. S.S.S. 72. 21 bay floodlit driving range, 9 hole Par 3 course. *Green Fees:* Monday to Thursday £20.00; Friday to Sunday £25.00. *Eating facilities:* fully licensed hotel on site. *Visitors:* welcome by arrangement. Special rates for visiting parties of over 10 midweek. Hotel with 103 bedrooms. *Society Meetings:* society/corporate golf days catered for. Professional: David Patterson (0191 417 8346). Golf Manager: Graeme Robinson.

WHITLEY BAY. **Whitley Bay Golf Club**, Claremont Road, Whitley Bay NE26 3UF (0191-252 0180). *Location:* north side of town. Simulated links. 18 holes, 6529 yards. S.S.S. 71. *Green Fees:* weekdays £24.00 per round, £33.00 per day; weekends £35.00. Reductions for visiting societies. *Eating facilities:* full catering every day. *Visitors:* welcome with reservation weekdays, weekends only with member. *Society Meetings:* catered for by arrangement with Secretary. Professional: G. Shipley (0191-252 5688). Secretary: Mr Harry Hanover (0191-252 0180).

Warwickshire

ATHERSTONE. **Atherstone Golf Club**, The Outwoods, Coleshill Road, Atherstone CV9 2RL (01827 713110). *Location:* off Coleshill Road, Atherstone, five miles north of Nuneaton and seven miles south of Tamworth. Undulating parkland. 18 holes, 6006 yards. S.S.S. 71. *Green Fees:* £25.00 per day/round Tuesday to Friday, £12.00 with a member; Saturdays with member only. *Eating facilities:* bar and dining room. *Visitors:* welcome weekdays without reservation, Saturdays with member only, not Sundays. Ladies' Day Wednesday. *Society Meetings:* 12 and above by prior arrangement with Secretary. Secretary: V.A. Walton (01827 892568).

BERKSWELL. **Nailcote Hall Golf Club**, Nailcote Lane, Berkswell CV7 7DE (02476 466174; Fax: 02476 470720). Parkland setting. Cromwell Course - 9 holes, 1037 yards. *Green Fees:* information not available. *Eating facilities:* two restaurants and two bars. *Visitors:* welcome. Host venue to the "British Professional Short Course Championship". Accommodation in hotel and leisure club facilities. Professional: Sid Mouland.*

BIDFORD. **Bidford Grange Golf Club**, Stratford Road, Bidford B50 4LY (01789 490319; Fax: 01789 490998). *Location:* 6 miles west of Stratford-upon-Avon on the B439. American links course with a variety of water holes. 18 holes, 7233 yards. S.S.S. 74. Driving range and putting green. *Green Fees:* information not available. *Eating facilities:* Spikes Bar and restaurant. *Visitors:* welcome any day, after 9am. On-site Hotel. *Society Meetings:* please call for details or view website. Secretary: Daniel Broadhurst.*
e-mail: enquiries@bidfordgrange.com
website: www.bidfordgrange.com

BRAILES. **Brailes Golf Club Ltd**, Sutton Lane, Lower Brailes, Banbury OX15 5BB (01608 685633; Fax: 01608 685205). *Location:* M40 Exit 11 Banbury, 10 miles west on B4035; A3400 Shipston on Stour, four miles east on B4035. Parkland/meadowland course. 18 holes, 6311 yards. S.S.S. 70. Practice ground. *Green Fees:* weekdays £25.00 per round, £35.00 per day, twilight (times vary) £12.00 per round; weekends £35.00 per round, twilight (times vary) £18.00 per round. *Eating facilities:* modern clubhouse; bar (10.30am to 11pm) and restaurant (8am to 4pm then 6pm to 11pm) facilities. *Visitors:* welcome subject to availability. Tuition; buggies and trolleys for hire. *Society Meetings:* welcome subject to availability; from £22.00 per head. Professional: Alistair Brown (01608 685633). Secretary: R.A.S. Malir (01608 685336).
e-mail: office@brailes-golf-club.co.uk
website: www.brailes-golf-club.co.uk

COVENTRY. **City of Coventry Brandon Wood Golf Course**, Brandon Lane, Wolston, Near Coventry CV8 3GQ (024 7654 3141). *Location:* six miles south of Coventry off southbound carriageway

A45. Parkland on banks of River Avon. 18 holes, 6521 yards. S.S.S. 71. Floodlit driving range. *Green Fees:* £11.35 weekdays; £15.10 weekends and Bank Holidays. *Eating facilities:* bar and restaurant. *Visitors:* welcome anytime, unrestricted, bookings available up to seven days in advance, telephone Pro shop. *Society Meetings:* phone Pro shop for details. Professional/Secretary: Chris Gledhill (024 7654 3141). Stewardess Mrs Jean Brown (024 7654 3133).

HENLEY-IN-ARDEN. **Henley Golf and Country Club**, Birmingham Road, Henley-in-Arden B95 5QA (01564 793715; Fax: 01564 795754). *Location*: two miles from M40 Junction 16; 20 minutes from Birmingham, Solihull, Stratford-upon-Avon and Warwick. Parkland, with lovely countryside views. 18 holes, 6933 yards. S.S.S. 73. Practice range. *Green Fees*: weekdays £25.00; weekends £30.00. *Eating facilities*: bar lounge menu, Brasserie. *Visitors*: no restrictions, but must book in advance. Smart casual dress required, no denim. *Society Meetings*: very welcome. Professional: Neale Hyde.

KENILWORTH. **Kenilworth Golf Club Ltd**, Crewe Lane, Kenilworth CV8 2EA (01926 854296; Fax: 01926 864453). *Location:* A429 Coventry to Kenilworth adjacent to A46 Coventry to Warwick Road. Parkland and wooded course. 18 holes, 6400 yards. S.S.S. 71. Practice ground and 6 hole Par 3 course. *Green Fees:* £35.00 weekdays; £45.00 weekends and Bank Holidays. *Eating facilities:* diningroom, bar snacks, bar. *Visitors:* must be members of another club with official Handicap Certificate. *Society Meetings:* groups (under 20 in number) weekdays, Societies (over 20) Wednesday only. Professional: S. Yates (01926 512732). Secretary: J.H. McTavish (01926 858517; Fax: 01926 864453).

LEAMINGTON SPA. **Leamington and County Golf Club**, Golf Lane, Whitnash, Leamington Spa (01926 420298). *Location:* three and a half miles from M40 south of town centre of Royal Leamington Spa. 18 holes, 6430 yards, 5878 metres. S.S.S. 71. *Green Fees:* weekdays £35.00 per round, £45.00 per day; weekends £40.00 per round. *Eating facilities:* luncheons, teas, evening meals and snacks. *Visitors:* welcome without reservation. *Society Meetings:* catered for. Professional: J. Mellor (01926 428014). Secretary: David M. Beck (01926 425961).

LEAMINGTON SPA. **Newbold Comyn Golf Club**, Newbold Terrace East, Leamington Spa CV32 4EW (01926 421157). *Location:* signposted off Willes Road. Parkland, front 9 hilly, back 9 flat. 18 holes, 6315 yards. S.S.S. 70. Practice area. *Green Fees:* weekdays £8.60 per 18 holes; weekends £12.70 per 18 holes. *Eating facilities:* Newbold Arms on site. *Visitors:* welcome, unrestricted, but please book. Leisure centre on site. *Society Meetings:* catered for, book through Professional. Professional: Ricky Carvell (01926 421157). Secretary: C.V. Baker (01926 887220).

MERIDEN. **Stonebridge Golf Centre,** Somers Road, Meriden CV7 7PL (01676 522442; Fax: 01676 522447). *Location:* two minutes from N.E.C., M42 Junction 6, just off the A45. Parkland. 18 holes, 6240 yards. S.S.S. 70. 21 bay floodlit driving range. *Green Fees:* information not available. *Eating facilities:* Spike Bar 8am to 8pm, restaurant Wednesday to Saturday evenings, Sunday lunch. *Visitors:* welcome, nine day advance booking facility for tee-times. Coarse and trout fisheries on site. Conference and private function suite available. *Society Meetings:* welcome weekdays, packages available. Professional and Director of Golf: Robert Grier (01676 522442; Fax: 01676 522447).*

NORTH WARWICKSHIRE. **Purley Chase Golf Club,** Ridge Lane, Near Nuneaton CV10 0RB (024 7639 3118; Fax: 024 7639 8015). *Location:* three miles off A5 between Atherstone and Nuneaton. Slightly undulating parkland. 18 holes, 6772 yards. S.S.S. 72. Conference and corporate. *Green Fees:* information not available. *Eating facilities:* restaurant. *Visitors:* welcome. *Society Meetings:* welcome, weekdays only. Special rates. Professional: Gary Carver (024 7639 5348). Secretary: Linda Jackson (024 7639 3118; Fax: 024 7639 8015).

NUNEATON. **Bramcote Waters Golf Course,** Bazzard Road, Bramcote, Nuneaton CV11 6QJ (01455 220807). *Location:* approximately five miles from Nuneaton, off B4114. Undulating parkland. 9 holes, 2491 yards. S.S.S. 64. *Green Fees:* weekdays £7.00 9 holes, £12.00 18 holes; weekends £8.00 9 holes, £13.00 18 holes. Reductions for Juniors. *Visitors:* always welcome, pay and play or book up to one week in advance. *Society Meetings:* welcome. Professional: Nic Gilks. Secretary: K. Knight.

NUNEATON. **Nuneaton Golf Club,** Golf Drive, Whitestone, Nuneaton CV11 6QF (024 7638 3281). *Location:* Nuneaton Road, B4112 cross with two small roundabouts, Lutterworth Road. Wooded course. 18 holes, 6429 yards. S.S.S. 71. Practice ground. *Green Fees:* £29.00 per round, £35.00 per day. *Eating facilities:* catering available except Mondays; bar open usual hours. *Visitors:* welcome weekdays. *Society Meetings:* welcome - special days Wednesdays. Professional: Mr John Salter (024 7634 0201). Secretary: Mr P. Smith (024 7634 7810; Fax: 024 7632 7563).

NUNEATON. **Oakridge Golf Club,** Arley Lane, Ansley Village, Nuneaton CV10 9PH (01676 541389; Fax: 01676 542709). *Location:* on outskirts of Nuneaton, approximately 15 minutes from town centre, 20 minutes from Coventry and 25 minutes from Tamworth. Woodland; undulating fairways with many water hazards. 18 holes, 6242 yards. S.S.S. 70. Practice area, Pro shop, putting green. *Green Fees:* weekdays £16.00 for 18 holes, £25.00 for 36 holes. *Eating facilities:* à la carte restaurant, bar meals, lounge bar. *Visitors:* welcome. Snooker room. *Society Meetings:* welcome weekdays (Monday - Friday). Golf Shop: Tony Harper Golf (01676 540542). Secretary (Admin. and Society Bookings): Mrs S. Lovric; Mr K. Clegg (Golf Section Secretary)

RUGBY. **Rugby Golf Club,** Clifton Road, Rugby CV21 3RD (01788 544637). *Location:* one mile from Rugby town centre on the Clifton road. Parkland course. 18 holes, 5457 yards. S.S.S. 67. Practice ground. *Green Fees:* information not available. *Eating facilities:* bar and dining facilities daily except Tuesdays. *Visitors:* welcome weekdays; weekends and Bank Holidays only with a member. Ladies' Day Wednesday. Snooker room. Carts for hire. *Society Meetings:* welcome if pre-booked. Professional: Nat Summers (01788 575134). Secretary: Norman Towler (Tel & Fax: 01788 542306).

RUGBY near. **Whitefields Hotel Golf and Country Club,** Coventry Road, Thurlaston, Near Rugby CV23 9JR (01788 815555; Fax: 01788 817777). *Location:* A45 near Rugby where it meets the M45. Undulating Parkland course, with water feature. Not hilly. Backdrops onto Draycote Water to the south. 18 holes, 6223 yards. S.S.S. 70, Par 71. 16 bay floodlit driving range. *Green Fees:* information not available. *Eating facilities:* restaurant, spike bar, 19th hole. *Visitors:* welcome. Accommodation available in 50 en suite bedrooms all with SkyTV. Five conference rooms available. Golf Shop (01788 815555; Fax: 01788 817777). *Society Meetings:* welcome. Special rates and packages available. Secretary: Brian Coleman (01788 815555; Fax: 01788 817777). *

STONELEIGH. **Stoneleigh Deer Park Golf Club,** The Old Deer Park, Coventry Road, Stoneleigh CV8 3DR (024 7663 9991; Fax: 024 7651 1533). *Location:* A46 Stoneleigh Village, close to N.A.C. Stoneleigh. Parkland. 18 holes, 6056 yards. S.S.S. 69. 9 hole par 3 course; putting green and practice area. *Green Fees:* Monday to Thursday £20.00, Friday £22.00, weekends and Bank Holidays £30.00. *Eating facilities:* bar and restaurant with full catering. *Visitors:* welcome midweek, restrictions at weekends. *Society Meetings:* welcome midweek, restrictions at weekend. Professional: Matt McGuire (024 7663 9912). Secretary: Cherry Reay.

STRATFORD-UPON-AVON. **Ingon Manor Hotel &
Golf Club,** Ingon Lane, Snitterfield, Stratford-upon-
Avon CV37 0QE (01789 731938). *Location:* Junction
15 of M40, A46 to Stratford, then signposted 'Ingon
Manor'. Undulating greens with stunning views
across Welcombe Hills. 18 holes, 6554 yards. Par 72.
Large practice area, putting green, driving range.
Green Fees: information not available. *Eating
facilities:* available daily. Professional: Paul Taylor. *
e-mail: info@ingonmanor.co.uk
website: www.ingonmanor.co.uk

STRATFORD-UPON-AVON. **Stratford-on-Avon
Golf Club,** Tiddington Road, Stratford-upon-Avon
CV37 7BA (01789 205749). *Location:* half a mile
from town on B4086. Flat parkland. 18 holes, 6374
yards. S.S.S. 71. *Green Fees:* £37.00 weekdays,
£40.00 weekends. *Eating facilities:* full catering/bar
service. *Visitors:* welcome any time subject to
domestic commitments. *Society Meetings:* catered
for Tuesdays and Thursdays. Professional: D.
Sutherland (01789 205677). Secretary: N.S. Dodd
(01789 205749).

STRATFORD-UPON-AVON. **Welcombe Hotel and
Golf Course,** Warwick Road, Stratford-upon-Avon
CV37 0NR (01789 295252; Fax: 01789 414666).
Location: exit M40 at Junction 15, follow signs to
Stratford. Club is on A439 after five miles. Or take
A439 out of town and club is on left after one mile.
Undulating parkland with mature trees, lakes and
waterfall. 18 holes, 6288 yards. S.S.S. 70. Practice
area and putting green. *Green Fees:* information not
available. *Eating facilities:* clubhouse with Atrium
Brasserie and private function suites *Visitors:*
welcome, please telephone for starting times. Hotel
on site, four star facilities. *Society Meetings:*
welcome. Please contact Corporate Golf Office. Jane
Plevey (01789 295252; Fax: 01789 266336) *

WARWICK. **Warwick Golf Club,** Warwick Golf
Centre, Racecourse, Warwick CV34 6HW (01925
494316). *Location:* off M40, from A41/A46 junction,
travel half a mile towards Warwick, turn right into
racecourse. Flat parkland course. 9 holes, 2682
yards. Driving range (floodlit). *Green Fees:*
weekdays £5.00 per 9 holes; weekends £5.50 per 9
holes. *Eating facilities:* bar open 7 to 10.30pm
weekdays, no catering. *Visitors:* welcome any time
except Sunday mornings. *Society Meetings:*
accepted, must book in advance. Professional: P.
Sharp (01926 491284). Secretary: R. Dunkley.

WARWICK. **The Warwickshire,** Leek Wootton, Near
Warwick CV35 7QT (01926 409409; Fax: 01926
497911). *Location:* on B4115, just off A46, five
minutes from M40 Junction 15. Parkland and
woodland courses with many attractive holes over
water. North/West Course: 18 holes, 7407 yards.
S.S.S. 74. South/East Course: 18 holes, 7157 yards.
S.S.S. 74. 9-hole Par 3 course, driving range, practice
and putting greens. *Green Fees:* information not
available. *Eating facilities:* bar and restaurant.
Visitors: welcome at all times. Conference facilities
available. *Society Meetings:* Golf Days arranged for
groups from 12 to 300. Professional: D. Peck (01926
409409). General Manager: Mark Warne (Tel & Fax:
01926 409409). *

*Ingon Lane, Snitterfield,
Stratford-upon-Avon CV37 0QE*
**TEL: 01789 731857
FAX: 01789 731657**

INGON MANOR GOLF
& COUNTRY CLUB

Country house hotel, set within 171 glorious acres of the Welcombe Hills.
• **18 hole, Par 72, 6554 Yard Championship Golf Course** •
Large practice area. Putting green/Driving range.
PGA professional available. Shop offers full range of golfing equipment.
*Attached to the clubhouse are 9 bedrooms all beautifully decorated
with en suite bathrooms.
Private functions and Hospitality suites also available to hire for
business or pleasure including parties, weddings and conferences.*

See also Colour Advertisement on page 40

Visit the FHG website
www.holidayguides.com
for details of the wide choice of accommodation
featured in the full range of FHG titles

West Midlands

BIRMINGHAM. **Brandhall Golf Club**, Heron Road, Oldbury, Warley B68 8AQ (0121-552 2195). *Location:* Wolverhampton Road A4123 off Junction 2 M5; right at Hen and Chickens Junction. Wooded course, elevated tees. 18 holes, 5833 yards. S.S.S. 68. *Green Fees:* information not available. Senior Citizens cards. *Visitors:* welcome, ring course for details. Tuition available, buggies (summer only) for hire. *Society Meetings:* welcome by prior arrangement. Professional: Carl Yates.*

BIRMINGHAM. **Cocks Moors Woods Golf Club**, Alcester Road South, Kings Heath, Birmingham B14 4ER (0121-464 3584; Fax: 0121 441 1305). *Location:* A435 Alcester Road, three and a half miles from M42 Junction 3. Undulating woodland course, many meandering streams. 18 holes, 5769 yards, Par 69. S.S.S. 68. *Green Fees:* information not available. *Eating facilities:* adjacent to leisure centre offering excellent bar and catering facilities. *Visitors:* welcome at all times. Full range of leisure facilities within complex. *Society Meetings:* welcome during quiet times, please telephone. Professional: Steve Ellis.

BIRMINGHAM. **Edgbaston Golf Club Ltd**, Church Road, Edgbaston, Birmingham B15 3TB (0121-454 1736; Fax: 0121-454 2395). *Location*: from Birmingham City Centre take A38 (Bristol Road). After one mile and at third set of traffic lights turn right into Priory Road, at end of which turn into Church Road; the club entrance is 80m on the left. **Undulating parkland course set in the grounds of historic Edgbaston Hall, which is now the club house. Course designed by H.S. Colt in 1935. Ancient trees, sloping fairways and a large lake contribute to the challenge and enjoyment of the course which is also a conservation area. 18 holes, 6106 yards. S.S.S. 69, Par 69. Practice area. Green Fees: weekdays £40.00, weekends £50.00 (summer); weekdays £25.00 (winter). Eating facilities: fully licensed, lunches, teas daily and bar meals daily; other meals by prior arrangement. Visitors: welcome subject to some restrictions on starting times, and the production of Handicap Certificate. Facilities for business meetings/seminars; snooker rooms; fully stocked shop, offering tuition, organisation of competitions, prizes, clinics. Society Meetings: welcome by arrangement with Secretary. Professional: Jamie Cundy (0121-454 3226; Fax: 0121-454 2395). Secretary: Peter Heath (0121-454 1736).** e-mail: secretary@edgbastongc.co.uk website: www.edgbastongc.co.uk

BIRMINGHAM. **Fulford Heath Golf Club Ltd**, Tanners Green Lane, Wythall, Birmingham B47 6BH (01564 822806). *Location:* one mile from Alcester Road, via Tanners Green Lane. Parkland with two lakes and River Cole. 18 holes, 6179 yards. S.S.S. 70. Practice ground. *Green Fees:* weekdays £35.00

(Societies £30.00). Subject to review. *Eating facilities:* available. *Visitors:* welcome weekdays, not at weekends and Bank Holidays. Buggies for hire. *Society Meetings:* catered for on application. Professional: R. Dunbar (01564 822930). Secretary: Mrs M. Tuckett (01564 824758; Fax: 01564 822629).

BIRMINGHAM. **Gay Hill Golf Club**, Hollywood Lane, Hollywood, Birmingham B47 5PP (0121-430 8544; Fax: 0121 436 7796). *Location:* M42 Junction 3, three miles. Flat course. 18 holes, 6406 yards. S.S.S. 72. Practice area. *Green Fees:* information not provided. *Eating facilities:* available. *Visitors:* welcome all week. *Society Meetings:* catered for by arrangement Thursdays. Professional: Andrew Potter (0121-474 6001). Secretary: Mrs Julie Morris (0121-430 8544).

BIRMINGHAM. **Great Barr Golf Club**, Chapel Lane, Great Barr, Birmingham B43 7BA (0121-357 1232). *Location:* six miles north-west of Birmingham M6 Junction 7. Parkland. 18 holes, 6523 yards. S.S.S. 72. *Green Fees:* information not available. *Eating facilities:* meals served, order in advance. *Visitors:* welcome weekdays, restricted at weekends. Weekends maximum handicap 18. Handicap Certificate required. *Society Meetings:* small groups catered for. Professional: R. Spragg (0121-357 5270). Secretary: D. Smith (0121-358 4376).

BIRMINGHAM. **Handsworth Golf Club**, 11 Sunningdale Close, Handsworth Wood, Birmingham B20 1NP (0121-554 0599). *Location:* M5 Junction 1. A41 left at first lights, left at next set of lights, second left, second left/M6 Junction 7. A34 Birmingham Road, Old Walsall Road, Vernon Avenue, Westover Road, Craythorne Avenue. Parkland course. 18 holes, 6272 yards, 5733 metres. S.S.S. 70. Large practice area and putting green. *Green Fees*: information not available. *Eating facilities*: bar snacks to à la carte menu in restaurant. *Visitors*: welcome weekdays with Handicap Certificate. *Society Meetings*: catered for by arrangement with Secretary. Special packages available. Professional: Mr L. Bashford (0121-523 3594). Secretary: P.S. Hodnett (0121-554 3387).

BIRMINGHAM. **Harborne Golf Club**, 40 Tennal Road, Harborne, Birmingham B32 2JE (0121-427 1728). *Location:* A4123, A456, B4124 three miles west Birmingham city centre. Undulating parkland/moorland. 18 holes, 6210 yards. S.S.S. 70. *Green Fees:* weekdays £30.00. *Eating facilities:* bar and dining area daily. *Visitors:* welcome except weekends and Bank Holidays. Trolleys for hire. *Society Meetings:* welcome with pre-booking. Special rates for parties comprising over 20 players. Professional: Paul Johnson (0121-427 3512). Secretary: Garry Tozer (0121-427 3058).

BIRMINGHAM. **Harborne (Church Farm) Golf Club**, Vicarage Road, Harborne, Birmingham B17 0SN (0121-427 1204; Fax: 0121-428 3126). *Location:* signposted from Harborne Centre. Parkland, brooks a special feature on five holes. 9 holes, 2441 yards. S.S.S. 64. *Green Fees:* weekdays 9 holes £6.00, 18 holes £9.00; weekends 9 holes £7.00, 18 holes £10.50. Phone for details of "Link Card", Senior Citizens and Juniors reduced green fees. *Eating facilities:* canteen serves hot and cold snacks. *Visitors:* welcome anytime - phone call required as a booking system is in operation. *Society Meetings:* by arrangement with the Professional. Professional: Paul Johnson. Secretary: William Flanagan (0121-427 1204; Fax: 0121-428 3126).

BIRMINGHAM. **Hatchford Brook Golf Club**, Coventry Road, Sheldon, Birmingham B26 3PY (0121-743 9821; Fax: 0121 743 3420). *Location:* on A45 three miles from Junction 6 of M42, next to Birmingham International Airport. Parkland course with wide fairways and large greens. 18 holes, 6137 yards. S.S.S. 69. Large practice area. *Green Fees:* weekdays £9.50; weekends £11.00; special rates for Senior Citizens, unemployed and Link Card holders. *Eating facilities:* restaurant and bar in clubhouse. *Visitors:* welcome with some restrictions. *Society Meetings:* contact Professional. Professional: Mark Hampton (0121 743 9821). Secretary: Ian Thomson (0121 742 6643).

BIRMINGHAM. **Hilltop Golf Course**, Park Lane, Handsworth, Birmingham B21 8LJ (0121-554 4463; Fax: 0121-515 2842). *Location:* Two miles from M5 J1, turn into Park Lane opposite West Bromwich Albion football ground. Wide fairways. 18 holes, 6254 yards. S.S.S. 70. *Green Fees:* information not available. *Eating facilities:* cafe serving drinks and hot meals. *Visitors:* welcome anytime, Municipal course. *Society Meetings:* bookings available through Professional. Professional: Kevin Highfield.*

BIRMINGHAM. **Kings Norton Golf Club Ltd.**, Brockhill Lane, Weatheroak, Alvechurch, Birmingham B48 7ED (01564 826706; Fax: 01564 826955). *Location:* M42 Junction 3, A435 to Birmingham, sign on left to Weatheroak, follow for one mile, over first crossroads. Club on right hand side. Parkland course. 27 holes, 7000 yards. S.S.S. 72, plus 12 hole par 3 course and 22 acre practice field. *Green Fees:* £32.00 per round; £40.00 all day. *Eating facilities:* excellent restaurant and bar snacks available. *Visitors:* welcome weekdays only, weekends with member. *Society Meetings:* catered for weekdays only; minimum number 20. Buggies available. Professional: Mr Kevin Hayward (01564 822635). Manager: Mr Terry Webb (01564 826789). e-mail: info@kingsnortongolfclub.co.uk website: www.kingsnortongolfclub.co.uk

BIRMINGHAM. **Maxstoke Park Golf Club**, Castle Lane, Coleshill, Birmingham B46 2RD (01675 462158). *Location:* three miles north east of Coleshill on B4114, turn right for Maxstoke. Parkland with trees and lake. Water-filled moat surrounding Maxstoke Castle. 18 holes, 6442 yards, S.S.S. 71. Two practice areas. *Green Fees:* £27.50 per round, £38.00 per day. *Eating facilities:* restaurant and bar. *Visitors:* welcome weekdays only, weekends with member. Handicap Certificate required. *Society Meetings:* catered for Tuesdays/Thursdays. Professional: N. McEwan (01675 464915). Secretary: G. Crawford (01675 466743; Fax: 01675 466185).

BIRMINGHAM. **Moseley Golf Club**, Springfield Road, Kings Heath, Birmingham B14 7DX (0121-444 2115). *Location:* from M42 take A435 north to Kings Heath, turn right into Wheelers Lane (A4040), left into Barn Lane crossing Addison Road into Springfield Road where the club is on the right hand side. Rolling parkland course with major water feature. 18 holes, 6300 yards. S.S.S. 70. Practice area. *Green Fees:* £37.00. *Eating facilities:* dining room and bar. *Visitors:* welcome midweek only by prior arrangement. Handicap Certificates required. *Society Meetings:* welcome Wednesdays and Fridays, minimum of 12 players. Professional: Martin Griffin (0121-444 2063). Secretary: Tony Sanders (0121-444 4957; Fax: 0121-441 4662).

BIRMINGHAM. **North Worcestershire Golf Club**, Frankley Beeches Road, Northfield, Birmingham B31 5LP (0121-475 1026). *Location:* A38 from Birmingham City Centre. Parkland, established inland course. 18 holes, 5959 yards. S.S.S. 68. *Green Fees:* information not provided. *Eating facilities:* catering facilities on request, normal bar opening hours. *Visitors:* welcome weekdays. *Society Meetings:* catered for Tuesdays and Thursdays. Professional: I.F. Clark (0121-475 5721). Secretary: D. Wilson (0121-475 1047; Fax: 0121-476 8681).

BIRMINGHAM near. **Rose Hill Golf Club,** Rose Hill, Rednal, Near Birmingham B45 8RR (0121-453 9156; Fax: 0121-447 7311). *Location:* Lickey Hills Country Park, Junction 1 M42, Junction 4 M5. Established 1921, parkland, semi flat course. 18 holes, 5890 yards. S.S.S. 68. *Green Fees:* information not available. *Eating facilities:* no bars, restaurant all day. *Visitors:* welcome with prior bookings only via Professional. Old Rose and Crown Hotel on course. *Society Meetings:* welcome with prior booking via Professional. Professional: Mark Toombs (0121-453 3159). Secretary: A Cushing (07976 793698; Fax: 0121-447 7311).*

COVENTRY. **Ansty Golf Centre**, Brinklow Road, Ansty, Coventry CV7 9JH (024 7662 1341; Fax: 024 7660 2671). *Location:* half a mile from Junction 2 M6 and parallel to the M69 is the B4065 signposted to Ansty. Parkland. 18 holes, 6150 yards. S.S.S. 69, Par 71. 9 hole par 3 course. Driving range. *Green Fees:* weekdays £10.00, weekends £15.00. Golf day package £37.50 weekdays, £46.00 weekends. *Eating facilities:* fully licensed restaurant with family room. *Visitors:* always welcome. Golf Shop, teaching academy, open 7 days regardless of weather, driving range, putting green, practice area. *Society Meetings:* welcome. Individual parties, corporate golf days and society golf days tailored to individual requirements. Professional: Simon Firkin (024 7662 1341; Fax: 024 7660 2568). Secretary: K. Smith (Tel & Fax: 024 7660 2671).

COVENTRY. **Coventry Golf Club**, St. Martins Road, Finham Park, Coventry CV3 6RJ (024 7641 4152; Fax: 024 7669 0131). *Location:* south Coventry off A45, one mile along B4113. Gently undulating parkland course designed by Vardon/Hawtree, an exciting challenge to all golfers. 18 holes, 6601 yards. S.S.S. 73. Practice ground. *Green Fees:* information not provided. *Eating facilities:* full catering in lounge bar, restaurant (maximum 120). *Visitors:* welcome weekdays. Fully stocked shop. *Society Meetings:* welcome Wednesdays and Thursdays by prior arrangement with Secretary's Office. Handicap Certificates required. Group bookings accepted two years in advance. Professional: P. Weaver (024 7641 1298). Secretary: Anne Smith (024 7641 4152).

COVENTRY. **Coventry Hearsall Golf Club**, Beechwood Avenue, Coventry CV5 6DF (024 7671 3470; Fax: 024 7669 1534). *Location:* off A45 south of Coventry, one mile south of city centre. Flat parkland, easy walking. 18 holes, 6005 yards. S.S.S. 69, Par 70. *Green Fees:* Mondays to Fridays £30.00, weekends only as guest of a member. *Eating facilities:* restaurant open six days a week; closed Mondays but snack meals offered. *Visitors:* welcome weekdays, as a member's guest only at weekends. Electric trolleys and pull carts for hire. *Society Meetings:* welcome, must book in advance with Secretary. Professional: Michael Tarn (024 7671 3156). Secretary: Mrs Marie Hudson (024 7671 3470; Fax: 024 7669 1534).

COVENTRY. **Marconi Golf Club**, Copsewood, Coventry (024 7656 3339). *Location:* three miles from centre of Coventry on A427/A428 road to Rugby, Lutterworth. 9 holes, 6048 yards. S.S.S. 71. *Green Fees:* information not provided. *Visitors:* welcome except Saturdays, weekday evenings or Sunday mornings. Secretary: R.E.C. Jones (024 7645 2793).

COVENTRY. **Marriott Forest of Arden Hotel & Country Club**, Maxstoke Lane, Meriden, Coventry CV7 7HR (0870 400 7272; Fax: 0870 400 7372). *Location:* take Junction 6 from M42, follow A45 to Coventry. After one mile turn left into Shepherds Lane, hotel is one and a half miles on left. Parkland and greenside water hazards. Home to the British Masters 2003. Two courses. The Arden - 7213 yards. S.S.S. 73; The Aylesford - 5801 yards. S.S.S. 68. Floodlit golf academy. *Green Fees:* information not provided *Eating facilities:* bars and restaurants available. *Visitors:* welcome seven days subject to tee-time availability. 214-bedroom four star hotel with extensive conference and luxurious leisure facilities. *Society Meetings:* enquiries welcome. Professional: Philip Hoye (0958 632170). Director of Golf: Stephen Follett.

COVENTRY. **North Warwickshire Golf Club Ltd**, Hampton Lane, Meriden, Warwickshire CV7 7LL (01676 522915; Fax: 01676 523004). *Location:* on B4102, one mile from Stonebridge on A45, approximately midway between Birmingham and Coventry. Parkland. 9 holes, 6352 yards. S.S.S. 71. Small practice ground. *Green Fees:* £20.00 weekdays; weekends £10.00 with member only. *Eating facilities:* snack lunch, meals by prior arrangement. *Visitors:* welcome weekdays without reservation except Thursdays, weekends by invitation. *Society Meetings:* catered for by prior arrangement, limited numbers. Professional: Andrew Bownes (01676 522259). Secretary: Mrs A. Dicks (01676 522915; Fax: 01676 523004).

Please mention
'The Golf Guide' when
enquiring about clubs
or accommodation.

COVENTRY. **Windmill Village Hotel and Golf Club,** Birmingham Road, Allesley, Coventry CV5 9AL (024 7640 4041; Fax: 024 7640 4042). *Location:* A45 westbound, west of Coventry. Rolling parkland with water features. 18 holes, 5213 yards. S.S.S. 66. Course record 63 Pro, 66 Amateur. *Green Fees:* Monday to Thursday £14.50, Friday to Sunday £17.95. Seasonal twilight price - call for details. *Eating facilities:* food and drinks available all day. *Visitors:* welcome with booking. 100 bedroomed hotel with leisure centre; conferences, weddings catered for. *Society Meetings:* welcome, special rates available. Professional: Robert Hunter. Managers: Marci Hartland and Brian Brodie.

DUDLEY. **Dudley Golf Club Ltd**, Turners Hill, Rowley Regis, Warley (01384 253719). *Location:* one mile south of Dudley town centre on Blackheath Road. 18 holes, 5654 yards. S.S.S. 68. *Green Fees:* weekdays £25.00 per day. Weekends only with member. *Eating facilities:* full catering facilities available. *Visitors:* welcome but only with a member at weekends. *Society Meetings:* by prior arrangement. Professional: Guy Dean (01384 254020). Secretary: R.P. Fortune (01384 233877). e-mail: info@dudleygc.fsnet.co.uk

DUDLEY. **Himley Hall Golf Centre**, Log Cabin, Himley Park, Himley Road, Dudley DY3 4DF (01902 895207). *Location:* just off A449 at Himley near Dudley. Parkland. 9 holes, 3145 yards. S.S.S. 35 for 9 holes. Practice ground, pitch and putt. *Green Fees:* £7.50 for 9 holes, £11.00 for 18 holes. Juniors and Senior Citizens reduced rate. *Eating facilities:* snacks - hot and cold. *Visitors:* welcome weekdays, weekends with booking. *Society Meetings:* mid-week only. Professional: J. Nicholls (01902 895207). Secretary: M. Harris (01384 831932).

DUDLEY. **Sedgley Golf Centre**, Sandyfields Road, Sedgley, Dudley DY3 3DL (01902 880503). *Location:* half a mile from Sedgley town centre near Cotwall End Valley Nature Reserve, just off the A463. Undulating contours and mature trees with extensive views over surrounding countryside. 9 holes, 3147 yards. S.S.S. 71 (18 holes). Covered and floodlit golf range. *Green Fees:* £7.00 9 holes, £9.50 18 holes. Reductions weekdays for Juniors and Senior Citizens. *Eating facilities:* hot and cold snacks

available on request. *Visitors:* pay and play course throughout the week, booking advisable at weekends. *Society Meetings:* weekdays preferred by prior arrangement. Professional: Garry Mercer (01902 880503). Secretary: J.A. Cox (01902 672452).

DUDLEY. **Swindon Ridge Driving Range, Shop and Golf Club,** Bridgnorth Road, Swindon, Dudley DY3 4PU (01902 896765). *Location:* B4176 Bridgnorth/Dudley Road, three miles from Himley A449. Wooded. 18 holes, 6026 yards. S.S.S. 69. 27 bays *Green Fees:* information not available. *Eating facilities:* restaurant/bar. *Visitors:* welcome at all times. *Society Meetings:* welcome. Professional: Phil Lester (01902 896191). Shop Manager: Russel Powers. Secretary: Rosemary Pope (01902 897031).*

DUDLEY near. **Swindon Golf Club**, Bridgnorth Road, Swindon, Near Dudley DY3 4PU (01902 897031). *Location:* B4176 Dudley/Bridgnorth Road, three miles from A449 at Himley. Woodland and parkland course with exceptional views. 27 holes; 9 holes- 1135 yards, 18 holes - 6121 yards. S.S.S. (18) 70, 9 Par 3. *Green Fees:* £20.00 per round, £30.00 per day weekdays; £30.00 per round, £40.00 per day weekends and Bank Holidays. *Eating facilities:* fully licensed bar and restaurant. *Visitors:* always welcome, booking not required. Buggies available. Fishing. *Society Meetings:* by arrangement weekdays only. Secretary: E.G.J. Greenway (01902 897031; Fax: 01902 326219).

HALESOWEN. **Halesowen Golf Club**, The Leasowes, Leasowes Lane, Halesowen B62 8QF (Tel & Fax: 0121-501 3606). *Location:* exit Junction 3 M5, A456 (Kidderminster) two miles, Halesowen town centre one mile. Parkland course in the Midlands with a Grade 1 Listed clubhouse and park. 18 holes, 5754 yards. S.S.S. 69. *Green Fees:* weekdays £26.00 per round, £31.00 per day; weekends by special arrangement. *Eating facilities:* available every day. *Visitors:* welcome weekdays. *Society Meetings:* by arrangement with Secretary. Professional: Jon Nicholas (Tel & Fax: 0121-503 0593). Secretary: Peter Crumpton (Tel & Fax: 0121-501 3606).

REDNAL. **Lickey Hills Golf Club**, Rose Hill, Rednal, Birmingham B45 8RR (0121-453 3159; 0121-457 8779). *Location:* Three miles from M42 J1 or M5 J4 at the bottom of Rose Hill on Lickey Hills Country Park. Picturesque course with dramatic slopes and banks of pine trees. 18 holes, 5866 yards. S.S.S. 68. *Green Fees:* information not available. *Eating facilities:* cafe at clubhouse. *Visitors:* welcome. Professional: Mark Toombs.*

SOLIHULL. **Copt Heath Golf Club**, 1220 Warwick Road, Knowle, Solihull B93 9LN (01564 772650). *Location:* on A4141 half-a-mile south of Junction 5 with M42. Flat parkland. 18 holes, 6517 yards. S.S.S. 71. Full practice facilities available. *Green Fees:* weekdays £40.00. Weekends and Public Holidays must be introduced by a member. *Eating facilities:* lunch and evening meal available except Mondays. *Visitors:* no restrictions weekdays. *Society Meetings:* by arrangement with Secretary. Professional: Brian Barton. Secretary: Clive Hadley.
e-mail: golf@copt-heath.co.uk
website: www.coptheathgolf.co.uk

SOLIHULL. **Ladbrook Park Golf Club Ltd**, Poolhead Lane, Tanworth-in-Arden, Solihull B94 5ED (01564 742220). *Location:* south from Junction 3 M42. Parkland, gently undulating. 18 holes, 6427 yards. S.S.S. 71. Practice ground. *Green Fees:* weekdays £28.00 18 holes, £43.00 36 holes; weekends with a member only. *Eating facilities:* excellent dining. *Visitors:* welcome weekdays, prior telephone call suggested. Weekends with member only. *Society Meetings:* catered for by prior arrangement with the Secretary. Professional: Richard Mountford (01564 742581). Seccretary: Mrs S.E. Burrows (01564 742264; Fax: 01564 742909).

SOLIHULL. **Olton Golf Club Ltd**, Mirfield Road, Solihull B91 1JH (0121-705 1083; Fax: 0121-711 2010). *Location:* approximately two miles off Junction 5 (M42), A41 - Birmingham. Parkland. 18 holes, 6229 yards, 5694 metres. S.S.S. 71. *Green Fees:* from £25.00 weekdays. Discounts for large groups. *Eating facilities:* by arrangement. *Visitors:* welcome weekdays only except Wednesdays. *Society Meetings:* catered for by arrangement. Professional: C. Haynes (0121-705 7296). Hon. Secretary: Rob Weatherley (0121-704 1936; Fax: 0121-711 2010).

THE APPEARANCE OF AN ASTERISK (*) AT THE END OF A CLUB OR COURSE ENTRY INDICATES THAT UP-TO-DATE INFORMATION HAS NOT BEEN SUPPLIED

SOLIHULL. **Robin Hood Golf Club**, St. Bernards Road, Solihull B92 7DJ (0121-706 0159). *Location:* eight miles south of Birmingham, off A41 Birmingham to Warwick road. Flat parkland. 18 holes, 6635 yards, 6067 metres. S.S.S. 72. *Green Fees:* £30.00 per round, £35.00 per day weekdays. *Eating facilities:* by prior arrangement with Steward (0121-706 0159). *Visitors:* welcome weekdays only subject to limitations. Arrange with Secretary or Professional. *Society Meetings:* catered for by prior booking. Professional: A.R. Harvey (0121-706 0806). Secretary: Miss J.S. Evans (Tel & Fax: 0121-706 0061).

SOLIHULL. **Shirley Golf Club**, Stratford Road, Monkspath, Solihull B90 4EW (0121-744 6001; Fax: Fax: 0121-746 5645). *Location:* (A3400), Junction 4 M42, towards Birmingham. Parkland. 18 holes, 6507 yards. S.S.S. 71. Practice ground, putting area. *Green Fees:* £25.00 per round, £35.00 per day. *Eating facilities:* bar and restaurant. *Visitors:* welcome weekdays without reservation, must have Handicap. Trolleys available. *Society Meetings:* welcome by arrangement. Professional: Stuart Bottrill (Tel & Fax: 0121-746 5646). Secretary: R. Maclean (0121-744 6001; Fax: 0121-746 5645)
e-mail: shirleygolfclub@btclick.com

SOLIHULL. **Tidbury Green Golf Club,** Tilehouse Lane, Shirley, Solihull B90 1HP (01564 824460). *Location:* two miles from Shirley and three miles off the M42. To play over numerous ponds, lakes and the River Coal. 18 holes, 4792 yards, 4382 metres. S.S.S. 64. 15 bay driving range. *Green Fees:* information not available. *Eating facilities:* excellent bar and restaurant facilities. *Visitors:* welcome, no restrictions. Facilities for fishing, crazy golf. *Society Meetings:* catered for. Professional: Ray Thompson. Secretary: L.M. Broadhurst. *

SOLIHULL. **Widney Manor Golf Club,** Saintbury Drive (off Widney Lane), Widney Manor, Solihull B91 3SZ (0121-704 0704; Fax: 0121-704 7999). *Location:* exit M42 Junction 4 and follow signs for Shirley, then Monkspath. A challenging course for golfers of all abilities, set in parkland with mature oaks and water hazards. 18 holes, 5500 yards. 14-bay covered driving range. *Green Fees:* weekdays £10.95, weekends £15.95 (am), £10.95 (pm). *Eating facilities:* normal bar hours, catering facilities available all day. *Visitors:* welcome at all times with advance booking available. Casual but smart dress code. *Society Meetings:* welcome any day. Tailor-made to suit the customer. Professional Tim Atkinson. Secretary: Ron Guthrie.
e-mail: wmgc.co.uk

Halesowen Golf Club, The Leasowes, Halesowen B62 8QF

The Club, which has been established for over 90 years, has an 18 hole course set in the only Grade 1 Listed Park in the Midlands, with excellent panoramic views of Worcestershire, and is always in excellent condition. Visitors fees £26 per round, £31 daily. Food available all day, except Mondays. Well stocked shop. Playing membership of over 500 but visitors and new members are always welcome. Places available.

Arrangements with the Secretary on 0121 501 3606, or Professional 0121 503 0593

SOLIHULL. **West Midlands Golf Club,** Marsh House Farm Lane, Barston, Solihull B92 0LB (0121 704 0704). *Location:* located between Birmingham and Coventry, five minutes from National Exhibition Centre, Junction 4 of M6, Junction 6 of M42. Take A452 towards Leamington and Warwick (Balsall Common) turn right to Barston and right again into Marsh House Farm Lane. USGA Golf Course over rolling parkland with island green. Putting green, open driving range, practice green. 18 holes, 6250 yards. S.S.S. 70. *Green Fees:* weekdays £19.95; weekends £24.95. *Eating facilities:* spike bar serving light meals and à la carte restaurant. *Visitors:* welcome, except before 10am at weekends. *Society Meetings:* please call for information, we will tailor a package to suit your needs. Professional: Mr Tim Atkinson. Secretary: Mr Ron Guthrie. e-mail: westmidlandsgc@aol.com website: www.wmgc.co.uk

STOURBRIDGE. **Stourbridge Golf Club,** Worcester Lane, Pedmore, Stourbridge DY8 2RB (01384 395566). *Location:* situated between Hagley and Stourbridge on Worcester road. Parkland. 18 holes, 6231 yards. S.S.S. 70. Small practice ground. *Green Fees:* weekdays £30.00; weekends with a member only £14.00. *Eating facilities:* bar meals available, lunch, dinner. *Visitors:* welcome weekdays, weekends with member. *Society Meetings:* catered for. Professional: Mark Male (01384 393129). Secretary: Mrs M.A. Betts (01384 395566; Fax: 01384 444660). e-mail: secretary@stourbridge-golf-club.co.uk website: www.stourbridge-golf-club.co.uk

SUTTON COLDFIELD. **Aston Wood Golf Club,** Blake Street, Little Aston, Sutton Coldfield B74 4EU (0121-580 7800; Fax: 0121-353 0354). *Location:* situated on Blake Street off A5127 Lichfield to Sutton Coldfield Road. Gently rolling Allis-Clark designed course with many water hazards.18 holes, 6480 yards. S.S.S. 71. Practice area, bunker and green. *Green Fees:* information not provided. *Eating facilities:* superb restaurant and bars open daily 7.30am 11pm. *Visitors:* weekdays only. Buggies. *Society Meetings:* corporate and societies welcome. Excellent packages available. Superb functions and conference facilities. Professional: Mr Simon Smith (0121-580 7800). General Manager: Ken Heathcote (0121-580 7803).

SUTTON COLDFIELD. **Boldmere Golf Club,** Monmouth Drive, Sutton Coldfield B73 6JL (0121-354 3379; Fax: 0121-355 4534). *Location:* off A452 (Chester road North), next to Sutton Park on Monmouth Drive. Flat parkland, wooded. 18 holes, 4463 yards. S.S.S. 62. Practice net and putting area. Shorter, lush course ideal for those who prefer a less exhaustive round of golf. *Green Fees:* weekdays £9.50; weekends £11.00. 50% discount for seniors and unemployed only with a 'Passport to Leisure'. *Eating facilities:* cafe in clubhouse. *Visitors:* welcome, Link Card system in operation. *Society Meetings:* welcome at quiet times, to be arranged with the Professional. Professional: Trevor Short (0121-354 3379; Fax: 0121-354 4534). Secretary: Roy Leeson (0121-354 3379; Fax: 0121-354 4534). e-mail: boldmeregolfclub@hotmail.com

SUTTON COLDFIELD. **Moor Hall Golf Club Ltd,** Moor Hall Drive, Sutton Coldfield B75 6LN (0121-308 0103). *Location:* one mile east of Sutton Coldfield, A446. Parkland. 18 holes, 6249 yards. S.S.S. 70. Practice area. *Green Fees:* £33.00 per round, £44.00 day ticket. *Eating facilities:* available weekdays except for Mondays. *Visitors:* welcome weekdays only (not Thursday mornings). 4-star Moor Hall Hotel on golf estate (independently owned). *Society Meetings:* catered for. Professional: Alan Partridge (0121-308 5106). Secretary: D.J. Etheridge (0121-308 6130).

SUTTON COLDFIELD. **Pype Hayes Golf Club,** Eachelhurst Road, Walmley, Sutton Coldfield B76 8EP (0121-351 1014). *Location:* off the A38 Kingsbury Road, one and a half miles from Junction 9 M42. Flat wooded course with small greens, four demanding Par 3's. 18 holes, 5996 yards. S.S.S. 69. *Green Fees:* information not available. *Eating facilities:* cafeteria. *Visitors:* welcome but must book via telephone. *Society Meetings:* welcome but must book via telephone. Professional: Joe Kelly. Secretary: L. Brogan (0121-773 2958).*

SUTTON COLDFIELD. **Sutton Coldfield Golf Club,** Thornhill Road, Streetly, Sutton Coldfield B74 3ER (0121-353 9633; Fax: 0121-353 5503). *Location:* situated in Sutton Park, one mile off A452, seven miles from centre of Birmingham. Natural heathland. 18 holes, 6549 yards. S.S.S. 71. *Green Fees:* weekdays £30.00 per round, £40.00 all day; weekends £40.00 per round. *Eating facilities:* by arrangement with Chef

West Midlands Golf Club
Marsh House Farm Lane, Barston, Solihull, West Midlands B92 0LB

Located just 5 minutes from the NEC, between Meriden and Balsall Common, this superb new course (6600 yards, par 72) has been built to the highest specification with USGA tees and greens. Several holes demand tee shots and approach shots over water, including the signature 18th hole, par 3 with an island green.

www.wmgc.co.uk   01675 444890

See also Colour Advertisement on page 39

(0121-353 2014). *Visitors:* welcome without reservation but please ring Professional to check availability of tees. Handicap Certificate required. *Society Meetings:* Special arrangements for societies by arrangement with Secretary. Professional: J.K. Hayes (0121-580 7878). Secretary: R.G. Mitchell (0121-353 9633; Fax: 0121-353 5503).

SUTTON COLDFIELD. **Walmley Golf Club**, Brooks Road, Wylde Green, Sutton Coldfield B72 1HR (0121-373 0029; Fax: 0121-377 7272). *Location:* Birmingham/ Sutton Coldfield main road, turn right at Green Hill Road. Flat parkland. 18 holes, 6585 yards. S.S.S. 72. Practice ground. *Green Fees:* weekdays £30.00, £10.00 with a member. 10% reductions for 30 or more players. *Eating facilities:* lunch and evening meals available. *Visitors:* welcome weekdays only. *Society Meetings:* catered for Wednesdays, Thursdays and some Fridays only. Professional: Chris Wicketts (0121-373 0029 Ext.1). Secretary: Mrs Ann Clibbery (Tel & Fax: 0121-377 7272).
e-mail: walmleygolfclub@aol.com

WALSALL. **Bloxwich Golf Club (1988) Ltd**, 136 Stafford Road, Bloxwich, Walsall WS3 3PQ (01922 476593; Fax: 01922 493449). *Location:* off main Walsall-Cannock road (A34). Semi parkland. 18 holes, 6257 yards. S.S.S. 71. *Green Fees:* weekdays £30.00 per round, £35.00 per day. *Eating facilities:* available. *Visitors:* welcome with or without reservation except weekends and Bank Holidays. *Society Meetings:* catered for midweek, reduced rates for 20 or more. Professional: R.J. Dance (01922 476889; Fax: 01922 493449). Secretary/Manager: D.A. Frost (01922 476593; Fax: 01922 493449).

WALSALL. **Calderfields Golf Club Ltd**, Aldridge Road, Walsall WS4 2JS (01922 632243; Fax: 01922 640540). *Location:* A454 between Aldridge and Walsall, Junction 10 M6. Parkland, water hazards. 18 holes, 6509 yards, S.S.S. 71. 27 bay floodlit driving range, practice bunkers, putting green. *Green Fees:* £12.00 per round, £20.00 per day. *Eating facilities:* clubhouse - restaurant and bar. *Visitors:* welcome at all times. Discount warehouse. *Society Meetings:* welcome at all times. Booking Tee Time (01922 632243). Professional: David Williams (01922 613675). Secretary: K. Williams (Tel & Fax: 01922 640540). website: www.calderfieldsgolf.com

WALSALL. **Druids Heath Golf Club**, Stonnall Road, Aldridge, Walsall WS9 8JZ (01922 455595; Fax: 01922 452887). *Location:* off A452 near Little Aston – Aldridge. Testing undulating heathland course. 18 holes, 6661 yards. S.S.S. 73. Practice ground and net. *Green Fees:* £30.00 weekdays; £38.00 weekends after 2pm. *Eating facilities:* dining room and bar snacks. *Visitors:* welcome by prior arrangement. *Society Meetings:* catered for by prior arrangement. Professional: Glenn Williams (01922 459523). Secretary: K.I Taylor.

WALSALL. **Walsall Golf Club,** The Broadway, Walsall WS1 3EY (01922 613512; Fax: 01922 616460). *Location:* one and a half miles from M6/M5 junction. Wooded course. 18 holes, 6259 yards. S.S.S. 71. *Green Fees:* on application. *Eating facilities:* all facilities available. *Visitors:* welcome weekdays only. *Society Meetings:* catered for. Professional: R. Lambert (01922 626766). Secretary: J.K. Harding (01922 613512).

WARLEY. **Warley Woods Golf Club**, The Pavillion, Lightwoods Hill, Smethwick B67 5EO (0121-429 2440; Fax: 0121-434 4430). *Location:* Hagley Road. Adjacent to Warley Woods. Warley water tower at top of course. Parkland course. 9 holes, 2686 yards. S.S.S. 66. *Green Fees:* information not provided. *Eating facilities:* cafe. *Visitors:* welcome, advised to book in advance as this is a very busy club. *Society Meetings:* welcome during quiet times, telephone Professional for details. Professional: David Ashington (0121-429 2440; Fax: 0121-434 4430). Secretary: Alan Woolridge (0121-686 2619; Fax: 0121-241 3451).

WEST BROMWICH. **Dartmouth Golf Club**, Vale Street, West Bromwich B71 4DW (0121-588 2131). *Location:* one mile from West Bromwich town centre. All Saints Way A4031, turn right at McDonalds and follow signposts. Part flat, part undulating course, a good test for all categories. 9 holes, 6036 yards. S.S.S. 70. Practice area, putting green. *Green Fees:* 18 holes £25.00, 9 holes £10.00; with a member 18 holes £12.00, 9 holes £8.00. *Eating facilities:* bar snacks always available, meals by prior arrangement. *Visitors:* welcome weekdays, weekends with a member only. *Society Meetings:* welcome by prior arrangement. Secretary: Mr C.F. Wade (0121-532 4070).

WEST BROMWICH. **Sandwell Park Golf Club Ltd,** Birmingham Road, West Bromwich B71 4JJ (0121-553 4637; Fax: 0121-525 1651). *Location:* on A41 to Birmingham 200 yards from Junction 1 M5, turn left under footbridge. Wooded, heathland course. 18 holes, 6468 yards. S.S.S. 73. Two practice areas, chipping green. *Green Fees:* £36.00 18 holes, £42.00 36 holes. Special rates for parties over 11. *Eating facilities:* full restaurant facilities and two bars. *Visitors:* welcome weekdays, weekend and Bank Holidays with a member only. Handicap Certificate required. *Society Meetings:* by prior arrangement with the Secretary. Professional: Nigel Wylie (0121-553 4384). Secretary: D.A. Paterson (0121-553 4637).

WISHAW. **The De Vere Belfry**, Wishaw B76 9PR (01675 470301; Fax: 01675 470178). *Location:* leave M42 at Junction 9 and follow signs for Lichfield, The Belfry is on A446. Parkland courses. The Brabazon at The Belfry - 18 holes, 7118 yards. S.S.S. 74. PGA National - 18 holes, 7053 yards. S.S.S. 72. The Derby - 18 holes, 6009 yards. S.S.S. 69. Driving range, putting green. *Green Fees:* The Brabazon at The Belfry £130.00 summer, £70.00 winter; PGA National £70.00 summer, £40.00 winter; The Derby £35.00 summer, £20.00 winter. Subject to review. Reduced residents' rates available on request. *Eating facilities:* use of hotel facilities including five restaurants and eight bars. *Visitors:* welcome. 324 bedroomed four-star hotel, 21 conference rooms, leisure club, indoor heated pool, sauna, solarium, hairdressing salon, beauty rooms, Aqua Spa, gymnasium. two squash courts, snooker room, pool tables, outdoor tennis courts and jogging trail. Bel Air Night Club situated within hotel grounds. Buggies, carts and caddies available. *Society Meetings:* always welcome subject to availablity. Professional: Peter McGovern (01675 470301). e-mail: enquiries@thebelfry.com website: www.thebelfry.com

WOLVERHAMPTON. **Oxley Park Golf Club Ltd**, Stafford Road, Bushbury, Wolverhampton WV10 6DE. *Location:* one and a half miles M54/A449 junction. One and a half miles Wolverhampton town centre. Undulating parkland. 18 holes, 6226 yards. S.S.S. 71. *Green Fees:* £25.00 per round, £29.00 per day. *Eating facilities:* available daily except Monday. *Visitors:* welcome weekdays, weekends by arrangement with Professional. *Society Meetings:* preferred day Wednesday; for alternatives please contact Secretary. Professional: Leslie Burlison (01902 425445). Secretary: R.J. Wormstone (01902 425892; Fax: 01902 773981).

WOLVERHAMPTON. **Penn Golf Club Ltd**, Penn Common, Penn, Wolverhampton WV4 5JN (01902 341142). *Location:* two miles south west of Wolverhampton, off A449. Heathland. 18 holes, 6462 yards. S.S.S. 71. *Green Fees:* £23.00 per round, £28.00 per day. *Eating facilities:* full catering and bar facilities. *Visitors:* welcome weekdays, advance booking preferred. *Society Meetings:* catered for. Professional: B. Burlison (01902 330472). Secretary: M.H. Jones (01902 341142).

WOLVERHAMPTON. **Perton Park Golf Club,** Wrottesley Park Road, Perton, Wolverhampton WV6 7HL (01902 380103). *Location:* just off the A454 Bridgnorth Road or A41 Wolverhampton to Newport road. Flat meadowland. 18 holes, 6520 yards, S.S.S. 71. Driving range, putting green. *Green Fees:* information not available. *Eating facilities:* available, also bar. *Visitors:* always welcome, booking times available. Buggies and trolleys for hire. *Society Meetings:* catered for. Secretary: E.G.J. Greenway (01902 380073; Fax: 01902 326219).*

WOLVERHAMPTON. **The South Staffordshire Golf Club**, Danescourt Road, Tettenhall, Wolverhampton WV6 9BQ (01902 751065). *Location:* A41 out of Wolverhampton (approximately three miles). Parkland. 18 holes, 6513 yards. S.S.S. 71. Practice area (approximately 10 acres). *Green Fees:* £38.00 weekdays; £53.00 weekends. *Eating facilities:* excellent catering facilities - Steward: Hugh Campbell (01902 756401). *Visitors:* welcome weekdays except Tuesdays. No mobile phones in clubhouse and surrounds, or on the course. *Society Meetings:* by arrangement with the Secretary weekdays except Tuesdays. Professional: M. Sparrow (01902 754816). Club Manager: W.R. Benton (Fax: 01902 741753).

WOLVERHAMPTON. **Wergs Golf Club**, Keepers Lane, Tettenhall, Wolverhampton WV6 8UA (01902 742225; Fax: 01902 744748). *Location:* from centre of Wolverhampton, take A41 (to Newport), after two and a half miles turn right, half a mile on right. Open parkland. 18 holes, 6949 yards. S.S.S. 73. 20 acre practice area. *Green Fees:* weekdays £15.00; weekends and Bank Holidays £20.00. Senior Citizens and Juniors £12.50 weekdays, £17.00 weekends and Bank Holidays. *Eating facilities:* full catering and bar facilities. *Visitors:* always welcome. Membership available. *Society Meetings:* welcome anytime during week, after 10am at weekends. Secretary: Mrs G. Parsons.

Wiltshire

BRADFORD-ON-AVON. **Cumberwell Park Golf Club**, Bradford-on-Avon BA15 2PQ (01225 863322; Fax: 01225 868160). *Location*: on A363 between Bath and Bradford-on-Avon, close to J17 and 18 of M4. The natural contours of the landscape shape the design, encompassing 315 acres of parkland, enhanced by nine lakes, 34 acres of forest and streams. 27 holes (3 x 9), 6723 yards (18 holes), S.S.S. 72. Practice greens, 10 acre driving range. *Green Fees*: weekdays £25.00 per round, weekends and Bank Holidays £30.00 per round. *Eating facilities*: private dining rooms and spikes bar. *Visitors*: always welcome. accommodation can be arranged nearby. *Society Meetings*: packages including catering available from £23.00 winter, from £34.00 summer. Golf days tailored to individual requirements. Professional: John Jacobs. e-mail: enquiries@cumberwellpark.com website: www.cumberwellpark.com

CALNE. **Bowood Golf and Country Club**, Derry Hill, Calne SN11 9PQ (01249 822228; Fax: 01249 822218). *Location:* A4 between Marlborough and Chippenham, signposted off M4 Junction 17. Grade I listed, Capability Brown landscaped, parkland. 18 holes, 7317, 6890, 6566: 6027 yards. S.S.S. 74, 73, 71: 75. Ladies 6015 yards, S.S.S. 75. Three academy holes, floodlit driving range, two putting greens. *Green Fees*: weekdays £38.00 per round, weekends £40.00 per round. Special rates available in winter and summer evenings. *Eating facilities:* public restaurant, private dining for up to 200. *Visitors:* welcome at all times except before 12 noon at weekends, bookings required. Four (double/twin) bedroomed house in centre of course, large clubhouse extension for banqueting, conferences, weddings, etc. Buggies, trolleys and clubs for hire; fully stocked Pro shop. *Society Meetings:* welcome, special packages available. Head Golf Professional: Max Taylor. Proprietor: The Marquis of Lansdowne.

CASTLE COMBE. **The Manor House Golf Club at Castle Combe**, Castle Combe SN14 7JW (01249 782982; Fax: 01249 782992). *Location:* on the B4039 midway between M4 Junction 17 and 18. Parkland course situated in a series of wooded valleys in an Area of Outstanding Natural Beauty. 18 holes, 6286 yards. S.S.S. 71. Practice range. *Green Fees:* Mondays to Thursdays £55.00; Fridays to Sundays £70.00. *Eating facilities:* full restaurant and bar facilities. *Visitors:* welcome by prior arrangement provided they have a club Handicap Certificate. The luxurious Manor House Hotel (four red stars) adjoins the course offering exceptional accommodation and an award-winning restaurant. *Society Meetings:* welcome by prior arrangement. Professional: Peter Green (01249 782982; Fax: 01249 782992. General Manager: Paul Hinton (01249 782982; Fax: 01249 782992).

CHIPPENHAM. **Chippenham Golf Club**, Malmesbury Road, Chippenham SN15 5LT (01249 652040). *Location:* A350 one mile from Chippenham,

two miles from M4 (Junction 17). Parkland. 18 holes, 5570 yards. S.S.S. 67. *Green Fees:* weekdays £22.00, weekends £27.00. *Eating facilities:* snacks and evening à la carte (not Mondays). *Visitors:* welcome, prior arrangement necessary. *Society Meetings:* catered for Tuesdays, Thursdays and Fridays only. Professional: Bill Creamer (01249 655519). Secretary: B. Cook (01249 652040).

CHIPPENHAM. **Monkton Park Golf Club**, Monkton Park, Chippenham SN15 3PE (Tel & Fax: 01249 653928). *Location:* centre of Chippenham, two miles from M4 Junction 17. Parkland Par 3 course. Probably the best Par 3 course in the south west of England. 9 holes, 1000 yards. S.S.S. 27. Crazy golf. *Green Fees:* information not provided. *Eating facilities:* coffee bar. *Visitors:* always welcome 364 days of the year! Golf clubs available. American pool. *Society Meetings:* welcome. Professional: Mr M. Dawson. Secretary: Mrs B. Dawson. website: www.pitchandputtgolf.com

CORSHAM. **Kingsdown Golf Club**, Corsham SN13 8BS (01225 742530). *Location:* five miles east of Bath. Heathland. 18 holes, 6445 yards, 5891 metres. S.S.S. 71. *Green Fees:* weekdays £26.00. *Eating facilities:* lounge bar and diningroom. *Visitors:* welcome except at weekends and Bank Holidays and must have current Handicap Certificate. *Society Meetings:* catered for by arrangement. Professional: Andrew Butler (01225 742634). Secretary: Jim Elliott (01225 743472).

CRICKLADE. **Cricklade Hotel & Country Club**, Common Hill, Cricklade SN6 6HA (01793 750751; Fax: 01793 751767). *Location:* A419 3 miles north of Swindon, B4040 out of Cricklade town by 1/2 mile. Undulating course set around hotel. 9 holes, 1830 yards. S.S.S. 58 (18 holes). *Green Fees:* weekdays 18 holes £16.00, £25.00 per day, members and hotel guests £10.00. *Eating facilities:* full à la carte restaurant and bar with snacks available. *Visitors:* guests of hotel welcome at all times, tee times must be booked at weekends. Weekends members and hotel guests only. 46-room hotel on site. *Society Meetings:* on application. Professional: Ian Bolt. Secretary: Colin Withers. e-mail: june@cric-kladehotel.fsnet.co.uk website: www.crickladehotel.co.uk

DEVIZES. **Erlestoke Sands Golf Club**, Erlestoke, Near Devizes SN10 5UB (Tel & Fax: 01380 831284). *Location:* six miles east of Westbury on B3098. Downland course, on two levels, spectacular 7th hole, 170 yards Par 3, with green 100ft below, one of the finest short holes in the West Country. 18 holes, 6406 yards. S.S.S. 71, Par 73. Large practice ground. *Green Fees:* weekdays £24.00; weekends £28.00. *Eating facilities:* full catering service, lounge, bar and diningroom. *Visitors:* welcome, booking advisable (01380 830300). *Society Meetings:* catered for by prior arrangement (01380 831069). Professional: Michael Walters (01380 831027). Office: M. Pugsley (01380 831069).

DEVIZES. **North Wilts Golf Club**, Bishop's Cannings, Devizes SN10 2LP (01380 860257). *Location:* one and a half miles from A4 east of Calne. Four miles from Devizes. Downland, undulating course with spectacular views. 18 holes, 6414 yards. S.S.S. 71. Practice ground. *Green Fees:* weekdays £30.00 per day; weekends £35.00 per round. *Eating facilities:* full catering service. *Visitors:* welcome, except on medal days. *Society Meetings:* catered for by prior arrangement. Professional: Graham Laing (01380 860330; Fax: 01380 860061). Secretary: Mrs Trish Stephenson (01380 860627; Fax: 01380 860877).

HIGHWORTH. **Highworth Community Golf Centre**, Swindon Road, Highworth SN6 7SJ. *Location:* on A361 just south of the town. Undulating parkland. 9 holes, 3120 yards, 2851 metres. Par 35. 9 hole pitch and putt, 4 hole practice course. *Green Fees:* information not provided. *Eating facilities:* vending machines. *Visitors:* municipal course, no restrictions. *Society Meetings:* welcome any day. Professional: Barry Sandry (01793 766014). Secretary: Steve Kearley.

HIGHWORTH. **Wrag Barn Golf and Country Club**, Shrivenham Road, Highworth, Swindon SN6 7QQ (01793 861327; Fax: 01793 861325). *Location:* just six miles off the M4. Undulating, set in beautiful Wiltshire countryside, three lakes and moat around 17th green. 18 holes, 6633 yards. S.S.S. 71. 12 bay driving range, practice area. *Green Fees:* weekdays £30.00; weekends £35.00. *Eating facilities:* spike bar, restaurant, function rooms. *Visitors:* welcome weekdays and after 2.00pm weekends. Buggies and trolleys for hire. *Society Meetings:* welcome any weekday. Professional: Barry Loughrey (01793 766027: Fax: 01793 861325). Secretary: M. Betteridge (01793 861327; Fax: 01793 861325).

MARLBOROUGH. **Marlborough Golf Club**, The Common, Marlborough SN8 1DU (01672 512147; Fax: 01672 513164). *Location:* about one mile north of Marlborough town centre on A346 towards Swindon. Seven miles south of J15 of the M4. Downland with panoramic views into the Og Valley and over the Marlborough Downs. 18 holes, 6514 yards, 5952 metres. S.S.S. 71, Par 72. Large practice ground and putting green. *Green Fees:* weekdays £27.00 per round, £36.00 per day; weekends £33.00

per round (after 4.00pm £17.00), £45.00 per day. *Eating facilities:* full restaurant facility, plus bar snacks open all day. *Visitors:* welcome generally, but it is best to telephone in advance; some restrictions at weeekends. *Society Meetings:* discounted rates and packages available. Essential to book in advance. Professional: Simon Amor (01672 512493; Fax: 01672 513164). General Manager: J.A.D. Sullivan (01672 512147; Fax: 01672 513164). e-mail: contactus@marlboroughgolfclub.co.uk

SALISBURY. **Hamptworth Golf and Country Club**, Hamptworth Road, Hamptworth, Near Landford SP5 2DU (01794 390155; Fax: 01794 390022). *Location:* off A36 Salisbury to Southampton Road, turning off B3079. Parkland, wooded course with river running through. 18 holes, 6516 yards, 5957 metres. S.S.S. 71. Practice area. *Green Fees:* Mondays and Tuesdays £25.00; weekdays April to October £30.00, weekends (pm only) £35.00. Weekdays September to March £20.00, weekends (pm only) £25.00. *Eating facilities:* new clubhouse with full catering and bar. *Visitors:* welcome, must have tee reservation and Handicap Certificate. Buggies. *Society Meetings:* welcome. Professional: M. White.

SALISBURY. **High Post Golf Club Ltd**, Great Durnford, Salisbury SP4 6AT (01722 782356; Fax: 01722 782674). *Location:* midway between Salisbury and Amesbury on A345. Downland and blackthorn. 18 holes, 6305 yards. S.S.S. 70. Large practice ground. *Green Fees:* £30.00 per round, £40.00 per day midweek; £40.00 per round, £50.00 per day weekends. *Eating facilities:* full catering and bars available. *Visitors:* welcome weekdays no restrictions, weekends and Bank Holidays require Handicap Certificate. *Society Meetings:* catered for weekdays only, from £45.00 to £60.00. Professional: Tony Isaacs (01722 782219). Manager: Peter Grimes.

SALISBURY. **Rushmore Golf Club**, Tollard Royal, Salisbury SP5 5QB (01725 516326). *Location:* off the B3081 between Tollard Royal and Sixpenny Handley. Parkland and wooded course. 18 holes, 6131 yards. S.S.S. 70. Covered driving range and large practice area. *Green Fees:* from £20.00. *Eating facilities:* Spike Bar plus new restaurant, home cooked food seven days a week. *Visitors:* welcome any time. *Society Meetings:* welcome by prior arrangement. Professional: Sean McDonagh.

SALISBURY. **Salisbury and South Wilts Golf Club**, Netherhampton, Salisbury SP2 8PR (01722 742131). *Location:* on A3094, two miles from Salisbury, Wilton, opposite Netherhampton village. Parkland. 27 holes, 6528 yards. S.S.S. 71. Practice ground; 3-hole academy course. *Green Fees:* weekdays £25.00 per round, weekends and Bank Holidays £40.00 per round. *Eating facilities:* full catering service and bar. *Visitors:* welcome without reservation at all times, but preliminary phone call advised. *Society Meetings:* catered for by prior arrangement. Professionals: John Cave, Geraldine Teschner (Tel & Fax: 01722 742929). General Manager: Pat Clash (Tel & Fax: 01722 742645). e-mail: mail@salisburygolf.co.uk
website: www.salisburygolf.co.uk

SHRIVENHAM. **Shrivenham Park Golf Course**, Penny Hooks Lane, Near Swindon SN6 8EX (01793 783853/4). *Location:* M4 Exit 15. Follow signs to Shrivenham, go through village, golf club on right. A delightful parkland course in excellent condition. 18 holes, 5713 yards. S.S.S 69. Practice area. *Green Fees:* Monday to Thursday £14.00, Friday to Sunday £18.00. *Eating facilities:* restaurant and bar open seven days a week, families welcome. *Visitors:* open to all, Handicaps not required. *Society Meetings:* packages available. Professional: Tony Pocock. Director of Golf: Stuart Ash (01793 783853).

SWINDON. **Broome Manor Golf Complex**, Pipers Way, Swindon SN3 1RG (01793 495761; Fax: 01793 433255 (Manager)). *Location:* two miles from Junction 15, M4 (follow signs to Swindon Town Centre then follow signs for "Golf Complex"). Wooded parkland. Two courses, 18 holes, 6283 yards, Par 71, S.S.S. 70. 9 holes, 5380 yards, Par 66, S.S.S. 66. 34 bay floodlit covered driving range. *Green Fees:* £11.60 for 9 holes, £19.10 for 18 holes

- 2003 rates, subject to review. *Eating facilities:* spike bar, conference facilities, restaurant. *Visitors:* welcome, no restrictions, booking essential for 18 hole course. *Society Meetings:* catered for weekdays. Professional: Barry Sandry (01793 491911; Fax 01793 433255). Manager: Steve Lewis (01793 495761; Fax: 01793 433255).

SWINDON. **Ogbourne Downs Golf Club**, Ogbourne St. George, Marlborough SN8 1TB (01672 841287). *Location:* A346, four miles south of Junction 15 (M4), three miles north of Marlborough. Downland course with extensive views. 18 holes, 6363 yards. S.S.S. 70. Practice area, baskets of practice balls for hire. *Green Fees:* weekdays £20.00; weekends £35.00. *Eating facilities:* full catering and bar service. *Visitors:* welcome weekdays, phone Professional at weekends for starting times. Buggy hire. *Society Meetings:* welcome, packages available. Professional: Andrew Kirk (01672 841287). Office: (01672 841327).

SWINDON. **The Wiltshire Golf and Country Club**, Wootton Bassett, Swindon SN4 7PB (01793 849999). *Location:* through Wootton Bassett, head for Calne A3102, one mile on left hand side out of town. Parkland course with water features designed by Peter Alliss and Clive Clark. 18 holes, 6666 yards. S.S.S. 72. Practice area, putting green. *Green Fees:* £25.00 per round weekdays, £35.00 per round weekends. *Eating facilities:* bars and restaurant. *Visitors:* welcome, booking advised. Club, buggy and trolley hire. Indoor pool with spa, sauna and steam room. Hotel with 52 en suite bedrooms. *Society Meetings:* conference and residential packages available. Professional: Kevin Pickett. e-mail: tracey@the-wiltshire.co.uk
website: www.the-wiltshire.co.uk

TIDWORTH. **Tidworth Garrison Golf Club**, Bulford Road, Tidworth SP9 7AF (Tel & Fax: 01980 842301). *Location:* A338 Salisbury to Marlborough Road, golf course off Bulford Road. Undulating downland course. 18 holes, 6320 yards. S.S.S. 70. Practice driving area, chipping and putting greens. *Green Fees:* £32.00 per round/day, reductions when playing with member. *Eating facilities:* full bar and catering facilities except for Mondays (sandwiches only). *Visitors:* welcome at all times, except Friday mornings and normally after 2pm at weekends and Bank Holidays. *Society Meetings:* catered for Tuesdays and Thursdays. Professional: Terry Gosden (Tel & Fax: 01980 842393). Secretary: Tim Harris (Tel & Fax: 01980 842301). e-mail: tidworth@garrison-golfclub.fsnet.co.uk website: www.tidworthgolfclub.co.uk

TROWBRIDGE. **Bradford-on-Avon Golf Course Ltd**, Avon Close, Trowbridge Road, Bradford-on-Avon, Trowbridge BA15 1JJ (Tel & Fax: 01225 752180). *Location*: M4, exit at Bath then take road to Bradford-on-Avon into centre, turn right on Trowbridge Road for half a mile, signpost for golf course on left. Parkland river bank course, mature trees, lakes. 9 holes Pay & Play course. *Green Fees*: information not available. *Visitors*: welcome. *Society Meetings*: welcome, please telephone for arrangements. Professional/Secretary: Richard Hussey (Tel & Fax: 01225 752180). *

UPAVON. **Upavon Golf Club,** Douglas Avenue, Upavon SN9 6BQ (01980 630787; Fax: 01980 635419). *Location:* off A342 Upavon to Andover Road, one-and-a-half miles out of Upavon. Undulating chalk downland course. 18 holes, 6402 yards. S.S.S. 71. Two practice areas. *Green Fees:* weekdays £25.00 per day, £80.00 four ball; weekends £30.00 per round, reductions when playing with a member. *Eating facilities:* bar and catering every day (restricted hours in winter). *Visitors:* visitors and societies welcome at Wiltshire's friendliest club. All County Cards and 2-fore-1 accepted. Professional: Richard Blake (Tel: 01980 630281). Secretary: Les Mitchell (Tel & Fax: 01980 630787). e-mail: play@upavongolfclub.co.uk

WARMINSTER. **West Wilts Golf Club**, Elm Hill, Warminster BA12 0AU (01985 213133; Fax: 01985 219809). *Location:* one mile off the A350 north of Warminster sign posted to the town centre. Chalk downland course 200 metres above sea level. 18 holes, 5754 yards. S.S.S. 68. Practice ground. *Green Fees:* weekdays £25.00 per round, £30.00 per day; weekends £30.00 per round, £40.00 per day. *Eating facilities:* full catering service. *Visitors:* welcome, except Saturdays, must produce a Handicap Certificate. *Society Meetings:* Wednesdays only, package details available on request. Professional: Simon Swales (Tel & Fax: 01985 212110). Secretary: Geoff Morgan (01985 213133; Fax: 01985 219809). House Manager: Sandra Frankle (01985 212702).

WESTBURY near. **Thoulstone Park Golf Club**, Chapmanslade, Near Westbury BA13 4AQ (01373 832825; Fax: 01373 832821). *Location:* A36 between Warminster and Westbury. Parkland course with trees and two lakes. 18 holes, 6300 yards. S.S.S. 70. Driving range, practice putting green. *Green Fees:* information not available. *Eating facilities:* Spikes Bar, function rooms. *Visitors:* welcome weekdays, weekends after 11.30am. *Society Meetings:* welcome weekdays, very attractive packages available. Professional: Tony Isaac (01373 832808; Fax: 01373 832821). Secretary: Mrs Jean Pearce. *

Worcestershire

BEWDLEY. **Little Lakes Golf Club**, Lye Head, Bewdley, Worcester DY12 2UZ (01299 266385; Fax: 01299 266398). *Location:* take Lye Head turn - off A456, three miles west of Bewdley. Parkland course with superb views, wonderful walks, undulating. 18 holes, 6278 yards. S.S.S. 70. Practice ground. *Green Fees:* weekdays £17.00; weekends £22.00. *Eating facilities:* bars, restaurant, cafe. *Visitors:* welcome most days by prior arrangement. Buggies available £15 per round. *Society Meetings:* welcome by prior arrangement. All-day package £37.50 includes breakfast, lunch, three-course carvery plus two rounds of golf. Professional: Mark Laing. Secretary: Mrs J. Dean (01562 741704).

BEWDLEY. **Wharton Park Golf Club**, Longbank, Bewdley DY12 2QW (01299 405222; Fax: 01299 405121). *Location:* A456 from Kidderminster, top of Bewdley by-pass. Championship course with woods and parkland. 18 holes, 6603 yards. S.S.S. 71, Par 72. Practice range. *Green Fees:* weekdays £25.00 for 18 holes, £37.50 per day; weekends £30.00 for 18 holes. *Eating facilities:* full facilities available including "Franco's" Restaurant open Wednesday, Thursday, Friday and Saturday evenings, plus Sunday lunchtimes. *Visitors:* welcome weekdays, after 2pm weekends. Functions/Conferences catered for. *Society Meetings:* welcome weekdays, limited at weekends. Ring for details. Professional: Angus Hoare (01299 405163). Secretary: (01299 405222).

BLACKWELL. **Blackwell Golf Club,** Blackwell, Near Bromsgrove B60 1PY (0121-445 1994). *Location:* approximately 10 miles south of Birmingham and three miles east of Bromsgrove. Parkland. 18 holes, 6230 yards. S.S.S. 71. *Green Fees:* weekdays only £55.00 per round, £65.00 per day. *Eating facilities:* bar snacks at all times, meals by arrangement. *Visitors:* welcome by arrangement. *Society Meetings:* catered for by arrangement through Secretary. Professional: Nigel Blake (0121-445 3113). Secretary: J.T. Mead (0121-445 1994; Fax: 0121-445 4911).

BLAKEDOWN. **Churchill and Blakedown Golf Club,** Churchill Lane, Blakedown, Near Kidderminster DY10 3NB (01562 700200). *Location:* off A456 Birmingham/Kidderminster road at Blakedown. Undulating parkland, partially wooded course. 9 holes, 6488 yards. S.S.S. 71. *Green Fees:* £25.00, £10.00 with a member. *Eating facilities:* snacks and full meals except Monday. *Visitors:* welcome weekdays, weekends with member only. Handicap Certificate required. *Society Meetings:* weekdays only by arrangement through the Secretary. Golf Shop: (01562 700454). Secretary: P. Bailey (01562 700018).

BRANSFORD. **Bransford Golf Club**, Bank House Hotel, Golf and Country Club, Bransford, Worcester WR6 5JD (Tel & Fax: 01886 833545). *Location:* From Junction 7 M5 follow signs to Malvern, Ross then pick up signs to Hereford A4103, Hotel is approx. 2 miles on left of small traffic island. 'Florida' style golf course, flat, 14 lakes, island greens, dog legs, etc. 18 holes, 6204 yards. S.S.S. 71. 20 bay driving range and short game practice area. *Green Fees:* weekdays £20.00; weekends £28.00. Members only up to 9.30am, tees bookable. *Eating facilities:* hotel and clubhouse bars. *Visitors:* welcome, not before 9.30am. Smart golf attire. Accommodation in 70 bedroomed hotel, golf breaks available. *Society Meetings:* welcome, special packages available. Professional: Scott Fordyce (01886 833621). Golf Manager: Margaret Robert (Tel & Fax: 01886 833545). e-mail: info@bransfordgolfclub.co.uk website: www.thebankhousehotel.com

BROMSGROVE. **Bromsgrove Golf Centre**, Stratford Road, Bromsgrove B60 1LD (01527 575886; Course Reception 01527 570505; Conference and Restaurant 01527 579179). *Location:* easily located on the junction of the A38 and A448, one mile from Bromsgrove town centre. Just five minutes' drive from juctions 4 and 5 of the M5 and Junction 1 of the M42 (exit west bound only). Gently undulating parkland course, large contoured greens with superb views over Worcestershire. 18 holes, 5969 yards. S.S.S. 68. 35 bay floodlit driving range, large multilevel putting green. *Green Fees:* weekdays £17.70; weekends and Bank Holidays £23.50. Special rates: Associate Scheme (£3.00 to join, one-off fee) weekdays £15.50, weekends and Bank Holidays £20.50. *Eating facilities:* friendly clubhouse with full bar and restaurant facilities available to non members. *Visitors:* most welcome. Tee times bookable up to seven days in advance. Golf shoes or similar, with socks, collared shirts, tailored trousers/shorts. Wide range of tuition available with resident PGA Professionals (Tuition Fees list available). New "Teaching Studio" complete with state of the art computerised video systems. *Society Meetings:* welcome by prior arrangement, packages available on request. Head Professional: Graeme Long . Assistant Professional: Danny Wall. Secretary: David Went. e-mail: enquiries@bromsgrovegolf.f9.co.uk website: www.bromsgrovegolfcentre.co.uk

BROMYARD. **Sapey Golf Club**, Upper Sapey, Worcester WR6 6XT (01886 853288). *Location:* situated six miles north of Bromyard on B4203. Parkland course with water features, outstanding views over Malvern Hills. The Rowan: 18 holes, 5935 yards. S.S.S. 68. The Oaks: 9-holes, 1203 yards. Practice, putting green. *Green Fees:* The Rowan – weekdays £20.00; weekends £25.00. The Oaks – weekdays £5.00. weekends £6.00. *Eating facilities:* bar and restaurant meals available seven days a week. *Visitors:* always welcome. Buggies, power trolleys, trolleys for hire. Fully stocked Pro Shop with PGA tuition available for all, including Junior coaching under the Golf Foundation Scheme. *Society Meetings:* always welcome. Professional: Chris Knowles (01886 853288). Secretary: Lynn Stevenson (01886 853506; Fax: 01886 853485). e-mail: anybody@sapeygolf.co.uk website: www.sapeygolf.co.uk

DROITWICH. **Droitwich Golf and Country Club Ltd**, Westford House, Ford Lane, Droitwich WR9 0BQ. *Location*: between Junction 5 of M5 and Droitwich just off A38. Parkland, undulating, wooded. 18 holes, 5976 yards. S.S.S. 69. Practice area. *Green Fees*: £26.00 weekdays, with a member £10.00; £12.00 weekends playing with a member only. *Eating facilities*: full catering and bar facilities available. *Visitors*: welcome without reservation Mondays to Fridays (Ladies Day Tuesday, tee closed to 12 noon), weekends with member only. *Society Meetings*: catered for Wednesdays or Fridays, £26.00 per player. Professional: Mr C.S. Thompson (01905 770207). Secretary: Mike Ashton (01905 774344; Fax: 01905 797290).

DROITWICH near. **Ombersley Golf Club**, Bishops Wood Road, Lineholt, Ombersley, Near Droitwich WR9 0LE (01905 620747; Fax: 01905 620047). *Location:* from A449, two and a half miles north of Ombersley, take A4025 then first left. High, though gently undulating course enjoying panoramic views over Severn Valley. 18 holes, 6139 yards. S.S.S. 69. Covered driving range, chipping green and bunker, putting green. *Green Fees:* 18 holes weekdays £18.00, weekends £26.50. 9 holes £11.40 weekdays, £15.90 weekends. Discounts for Senior Citizens and Juniors. *Eating facilities:* bar facilities, snacks and meals available. *Visitors:* all visitors welcome, bookable seven days in advance. Eight buggies, cart rental available. *Society Meetings:* welcome by arrangement – we specialise in corporate golf. Professional/General Manager: Mr Graham Glenister.

DROITWICH SPA. **Gaudet Luce Golf Club**, Middle Lane, Hadzor, Droitwich Spa WR9 7DP (Tel: 01905 796375; Fax: 01905 797245). *Location:* Junction 5 or 6 off M5, Droitwich Spa, A38 onto B4090 follow signposts to golf club, located just off Tagwell Road. Undulating parkland course with a mixture of long and short holes offering a demanding challenge for all golfers. 18 holes, 5887 yards. S.S.S. 69. Sister club to Little Lakes Golf Club, Bewdley. *Green Fees:* information not available. *Eating facilities:* full clubhouse facilities including restaurant, lounge and bar. *Visitors:* welcome most days (essential to phone the Pro Shop before visit). Fully stocked Pro Shop

with PGA tuition available for all, including Junior coaching under the Golf Foundation scheme. *Society Meetings:* welcome most weekdays by prior arrangement with Pro Shop. Professional: Philip Cundy. Secretary: Mrs J. Purcell.*
e-mail: info@gaudet-luce.co.uk
website: www.gaudet-luce.co.uk

EVESHAM. **Evesham Golf Club**, Craycombe Links, Fladbury Cross, Pershore WR10 2QS (01386 860395). *Location:* M5 at Junction 6, A4538 and A44 to Evesham approximately 10 miles then towards Worcester for about three miles. Meadowland, tree-lined fairways. 9 holes (18 tees), 6415 yards, 5866 metres. S.S.S. 71. Practice area. *Green Fees:* £20.00. *Eating facilities:* diningroom and bar. *Visitors:* must be members of a recognised club and have a certified handicap. Tuesday Ladies' Day, play is not possible in summer until after 3.15pm approx. *Society Meetings:* catered for by prior arrangement. Professional: Dan Cummins (01386 861144). Secretary: Lin Tattersall.

HAGLEY. **Hagley Golf and Country Club,** Wassell Grove, Hagley, Stourbridge DY9 9JW (01562 883701; Fax: 01562 887518). *Location:* A456 Birmingham to Kidderminster Road. Wooded undulating course with many testing holes. 18 holes, 6553 yards. S.S.S. 72. Practice ground. *Green Fees:* £26.00 per round, £31.00 per day weekdays; weekends with a member. *Eating facilities:* full à la carte restaurant and bars. *Visitors:* welcome to play Monday to Friday, weekends with a member only. Buggies available. *Society Meetings:* welcome weekdays by prior arrangement. Professional: Iain Clark (01562 883852). Secretary: Graham F. Yardley.

KIDDERMINSTER. **Habberley Golf Club**, Habberley, Kidderminster DY11 5RF. *Location:* north west side of Kidderminster. Hilly parkland course. 9 holes, 5481 yards. S.S.S. 68. *Green Fees:* weekdays £12.00. *Eating facilities:* food and bar available. *Visitors:* welcome weekdays, without reservation; weekends with member only. *Society Meetings:* welcome, on application. Group rate £10.00 per person. Secretary: B. Blakeway (01562 745756).

KIDDERMINSTER. **Kidderminster Golf Club**, Russell Road, Kidderminster DY10 3HT (01562 822303; Fax: 01562 827866). *Location:* signposted off A449 Worcester-Wolverhampton Road. Wooded parkland course. 18 holes, 6422 yards. S.S.S. 71. Practice ground. *Green Fees:* £30.00 per round, £35.00 per day weekdays. *Eating facilities:* bar and restaurant available. *Visitors:* welcome weekdays only if bona fide member of another club, weekends if guest of member. Snooker room with bar. *Society Meetings:* catered for weekdays only. Professional: N.P. Underwood (01562 740090). Secretary: Alan Biggs (01562 822303; Fax: 01562 827866). e-mail: info@kiddigolf.com

KIDDERMINSTER. **Wyre Forest Golf Club**, Zortech Avenue, Kidderminster DY11 7EX (01299 822682; Fax: 01299 879433). *Location:* from Kidderminster to Stourport-on-Severn on the A451. Flat inland links type course. Full practice facilities. 18 holes, 57901 yards. S.S.S. 68. *Green Fees:* weekdays £12.50, weekends £17.00. *Eating facilities:* clubhouse bar open until 2.30pm daily. *Visitors:* can book 6 days in advance. Must book at weekends. *Society Meetings:* catered for. Packages start from £18.50 including golf and two-course meal. Professional/General Manager: Simon Price. e-mail: SimonPrice@wyreforestgolf.com

MALVERN WELLS. **The Worcestershire Golf Club,** Wood Farm, Malvern Wells WR14 4PP (01684 575992; Fax: 01684 893334). *Location:* two miles south of Great Malvern, near junction of A449 and B4209. Exceptionally scenic - Malvern Hills and Vale of Evesham. 18 holes, 6500 yards. S.S.S. 72. *Green Fees:* weekdays £30.00 per day; weekends £40.00 per day. *Eating facilities:* available. *Visitors:* visitors unaccompanied by a member must provide a current Handicap Certificate. Weekends after 10am. *Society Meetings:* catered for Mondays, Thursdays and Fridays only on application. Professional: R. Lewis (Tel & Fax: 01684 564428). Secretary/Manager: Mrs J.P. Howe (01684 575992; Fax: 01684 893334). e-mail: secretary@theworcestershiregolfclub.co.uk

PERSHORE. **The Vale Golf Club**, Hill Furze Road, Bishampton, Near Pershore WR10 2LZ (01386 462781; Fax: 01386 462597). *Location:* off the A44 road, between Evesham and Pershore at Fladbury crossroads. Feature lakes and wooded surrounds. Two courses: The Lenches, 9 holes, 2628 to 2918 yards. S.S.S 66 to 68; The International Championship Course, 18 holes, 6663 to 7174 yards. S.S.S. 72/74. Driving range. *Green Fees:* weekdays £25.00 International, £10.00 Lenches; weekends £35.00 International, £11.00 Lenches. *Eating facilities:* Vale restaurant, spike bar, Sir William Lyons Suite. *Visitors:* welcome. *Society Meetings:* corporate and society days welcome. Professional: Caroline Griffiths (01386 462520; Fax: 01386 462660). General Manager: Rob Griffiths. e-mail: tvgcc@crown-golf.co.uk

REDDITCH. **Pitcheroak Golf Course**, Plymouth Road, Redditch B97 4PB (01527 541043). Location: 500 yards from bus/train stations. Hilly parkland course very tricky, lots of trees and bunker. 9 holes (18 tees), 4561 yards. S.S.S. 62. Practice grounds, nets, putting green. *Green Fees:* information not available. *Eating facilities:* bar and cafeteria facilities open all day. *Visitors:* welcome any time, municipal course. Changing rooms (ladies and gents). *Society Meetings:* welcome. Professional: D. Stewart (01527 541054). Secretary: Ray Barnett (01386 743370). *

REDDITCH. **Redditch Golf Club**, Lower Grinsty, Green Lane, Callow Hill, Redditch B97 5PJ (01527 543079; Fax: 01527 547413). *Location:* three miles west of Redditch town centre, off Redditch to Bromsgrove road (A448), or Astwood Bank to Redditch (A441), take Windmill Drive, look for Callow Hill signs. First 9 holes parkland, second 9 holes wooded. White - 18 holes, 6671 yards. S.S.S. 72; Yellow - 18 holes, 6285 yards. S.S.S. 70. Two practice areas. *Green Fees:* 18 holes £35.00, 27 holes £40.00, 36 holes £45.00;£5.00pp discount for parties of 20+. Weekends £10.00 with member only. *Eating facilities:* restaurant and bar with bar snacks except Mondays. *Visitors:* welcome, weekends with member. *Society Meetings:* catered for by arrangement. Professional: David Down (01527 546372). Secretary: T.J. Sheldon (01527 543079; Fax 01527 547413).

REDDITCH. **Redditch Kingfisher Golf Club**, Pitcheroak Golf Course, Plymouth Road, Redditch B97 4PB (01527 541043). *Location:* just up from the station. Hilly parkland course. 9 holes, 4561 yards. S.S.S. 62. Practice, nets, putting green. *Green Fees:* information not available. *Eating facilities:* full catering and bar facilities. *Visitors:* welcome at all times. Showers/changing rooms. *Society Meetings:* welcome at all times. Professional: Mr David Stewart (01527 541054). Secretary: Ray Barnett.*

TENBURY WELLS. **Cadmore Lodge Golf and Country Club**, Berrington Green, Tenbury Wells WR15 8TQ (01584 810044). *Location:* two miles south of Tenbury Wells, just off A4112 to Leominster. Parkland with lake and streams in constant play. *Green Fees:* information not provided. *Eating facilities:* hotel bar and restaurant. *Visitors:* welcome, no restrictions. Hotel with AA Rosette restaurant and 14 en suite bedrooms. *Society Meetings:* welcome. Secretary: R.V. Farr (01584 810306 home).

WORCESTER. **Perdiswell Park Golf Club**, Bilford Road, Worcester WR3 8DX (01905 754668). Location: 600 yards from A38, north of the city centre. A testing 18 hole parkland course with many natural features. *Green Fees:* information not available. *Eating facilities:* food available. *Visitors:* welcome at any time, but advised to phone first. *Society Meetings:* welcome. PGA Professional: Mark Woodward (01905 754668). Secretary: Richard Gardner (01905 452399; Fax: 01905 453133). *

WORCESTER. **Ravenmeadow Golf Club**, Hindlip Lane, Claines, Worcester WR3 8SA (01905 757525; Fax: 01905 458876). *Location:* Junction 6 (M5 motorway) A449, leave at Blackpole exit; at main road turn right then first left into Hindlip Lane, entrance is half-mile on the left. Gently undulating course, with greens and tees to USGA standards; Barbourne Brook meanders through the course. 10 holes (18 tees). 5352 yards, S.S.S. 66. Excellent practice facilities: driving range, 9 hole pitch and putt, adults and children's practice greens, chipping green. *Green Fees:* weekdays 9 holes £8.00, 18 holes £12.00; weekends 9 holes £10.00, 18 holes £15.00. Monday - Over 50s 9 holes £5.00, 18 holes £7.00. Wednesday Ladies' Day 9 holes £5.00, 18 holes £7.00. *Eating facilities:* Bar open 7 days, food available from 11am. *Visitors*: always welcome, telephone to reserve tee times. *Society Meetings:* welcome every day. Telephone (01905 458876) for special rates. Professional: Mark Slater (PGA) (01905 756665). Manager: Tony Senter (01905 458876; Fax: 01905 458876).

WORCESTER. **Tolladine Golf Club**, The Fairway, Tolladine Road, Worcester WR4 9BA (01905 21074). *Location:* M5, Exit 6. Warndon turn-off, one mile. Tolladine Road, opposite Virgin Tavern. Hilly course. 9 holes, 5630 yards (for 18 holes). S.S.S. 67. *Green Fees:* information not available. *Eating facilities:* bar (limited opening). *Visitors:* welcome. *Society Meetings:* welcome. Secretary: Mr D. Turner (01905 354039).*

WORCESTER. **Worcester Golf and Country Club**, Boughton Park, Worcester WR2 4EZ (01905 421132). *Location*: one-and-a-quarter miles west of city on A4103 (to Hereford). Parkland with lakes and specimen trees. 18 holes, 6251 yards. S.S.S. 70. Practice areas. *Green Fees:* information not available. *Eating facilities:* full catering available. *Visitors:* welcome weekdays, telephone Professional. Handicap Certificate required. *Society Meetings:* welcome, telephone Secretary. Professional: Colin Colenso (01905 422044). Secretary: (01905 422555). Caterer: Mr J. Owen (01905 421132). Steward: Ms M.P. Jewell (01905 421132).

For full details of clubs and courses, plus convenient accommodation, visit the **FHG** golf website

www.uk-golfguide.com

East Yorkshire

BEVERLEY. **Beverley and East Riding Golf Club,** Westwood, Beverley HU17 8RG (01482 867190). *Location:* one mile west of Beverley on Walkington Road. Common pastureland, undulating course with 18 distinctively different holes. 18 holes, 6127 yards. S.S.S. 69. *Green Fees:* £15.00 weekdays, £20.00 weekends and Bank Holidays. *Eating facilities:* bar snacks available 11.30am until 2.00pm, evening meals by arrangement. *Visitors:* welcome any time. Cart and club hire. *Society Meetings:* welcome weekdays by prior arrangement. Professional: Alex Ashby (01482 869519). Secretary: Mike Drew (Tel & Fax: 01482 868757).

BEVERLEY. **Cherry Burton Golf Club**, Leconfield Lane, Cherry Burton, Beverley HU17 7RB (Tel & Fax: 01964 550924). *Location*: off the B1248 3 miles north of Beverley. Parkland course with lakes. 9 holes, 6480 yards, S.S.S 72. Driving range, putting green. *Green Fees*: information not available. *Eating facilities*: licensed bar, snacks, sandwiches. *Visitors*: welcome. Pro shop, tuition, golf academy. *Society Meetings*: welcome, please telephone. Professional: James Calam (07979 596134; Fax: 01964 550924). Secretary: James Walmsley (Tel & Fax: 01964 550924).
website: www.cherryburtongolfclub.co.uk

BRIDLINGTON. **Bridlington Golf Club,** Belvedere Road, Bridlington YO15 3NA (01262 672092). *Location:* A165 main Hull to Bridlington Road. Flat parkland course with sea views, excellent greens with ponds, ditches, bunkers and trees. 18 holes, 6638 yards. S.S.S. 72. Practice area. *Green Fees:* weekdays £20.00 per round, £30.00 per day; weekends and Bank Holidays £35.00 per round or per day. Subject to review. Parties over 12 in number 10% discount per player. *Eating facilities:* food available, bar meals and full menu/usual bar hours. *Visitors:* welcome most days but limited on Wednesdays/ Sundays. Advisable to book in advance. *Society Meetings:* catered for. Professional: A.R.A. Howarth (01262 674721). Secretary: C.B. Rhodes (01262 606367).
e-mail: enquiries@bridlingtongolfclub.co.uk
website: www.bridlingtongolfclub.co.uk

BRIDLINGTON. **The Bridlington Links**, Flamborough Road, Marton, Bridlington YO15 1DW (01262 401584; Fax: 01262 401702). *Location:* on the B1255 between Bridlington and Flamborough. Links course on clifftop with spectacular views over Bridlington Bay. 18 holes, 6719 yards. S.S.S. 72. 9-hole course (7 par 3's and 2 par 4's). Driving range and Golf Academy. Golf schools weekly during Summer. *Green Fees:* information not available. *Eating facilities:* bar, function suite, and restaurant. *Visitors:* welcome at all times, no restrictions. *Society Meetings:* very welcome anytime, society packages available. Professional: Steve Raybould. *
website: www.bridlington-links.co.uk

BRIDLINGTON. **Flamborough Head Golf Club,** Lighthouse Road, Flamborough, Bridlington (01262 850333/417; Fax: 01262 850279). *Location:* situated five miles north-east of Bridlington on the Flamborough headland. Links type course. 18 holes, 6189 yards. S.S.S. 69, Par 71. *Green Fees:* £20.00 per day weekdays, £25.00 per day weekends and Bank Holidays. *Eating facilities:* available; seafood a speciality in season. *Visitors:* welcome, limited Sunday and Wednesday mornings. *Society Meetings:* catered for, apply to Secretary. Secretary: G.S. Thornton (01262 850333).

BROUGH. **Brough Golf Club,** Cave Road, Brough HU15 1HB (01482 667291; Fax: 01482 669873). *Location:* 10 miles west of Hull off A63. Parkland. 18 holes, 6075 yards. S.S.S. 69 (white tees). Practice facilities. *Green Fees:* on application. *Eating facilities:* full restaurant and bar snack menu available on request. *Visitors:* welcome Mondays, Tuesdays, Thursdays and Fridays after 9.30am. *Society Meetings:* on application. Director of Golf: G. Townhill (01482 667291).
gt@brough-golfclub.co.uk
www.brough-golfclub.co.uk

BROUGH. **Cave Castle Golf Club**, South Cave, Brough HU15 2EU (01430 421286; Fax: 01430 421118). *Location:* minutes from M62/A63. Undulating parkland course in 150 acres. 18 holes, 6524 yards. S.S.S. 71. *Green Fees:* £14.00 per round, £20.00 per day weekdays; £20.00 per round, £27.00 per day weekends. *Eating facilities:* licensed clubhouse. *Visitors:* welcome anytime weekdays, after 11am weekends. Must have valid Handicap Certificate. Idyllic setting, superb hotel with 53 en suite bedrooms, restaurant, lounge bar. Golf break packages include double bed and breakfast plus use of the leisure complex. *Society Meetings:* welcome. Professional: Stephen MacKinder (01430 421286).

CONISTON. **Ganstead Park Golf Club,** Longdales Lane, Coniston, Near Hull HU11 4LB (Tel & Fax: 01482 817754). *Location:* A165 to Bridlington, five miles from Hull City Centre. Easy walking parkland course with lakes. 18 holes, 6801 yards. S.S.S. 71 yellow, 73 white, 73 red. Nets, chipping area, putting green. *Green Fees:* weekdays £18.00 per round, £24.00 per day; weekends £26.00. With member £12.00 weekdays, £13.00 weekends. Special rates for parties. *Eating facilities:* full facilities. *Visitors:* welcome, restrictions Wednesday and Sunday mornings. *Society Meetings:* welcome; apply to Secretary or Professional. Professional: Mike Smee (01482 811121). Secretary: Geoff Drewery (Tel & Fax: 01482 817754).
e-mail: secretary@gansteadpark.co.uk
website: www.gansteadpark.co.uk

COTTINGHAM. **Hessle Golf Club,** Westfield Road, Raywell, Cottingham HU16 5YL (01482 659187). *Location:* three miles south west of Cottingham. Parkland. 18 holes, 6291 yards, S.S.S. 70. Two practice areas. *Green Fees:* weekdays £25.00 per round, £32.00 per day; weekends £32.00 per round. *Eating facilities:* snack lunches Tuesday to Sunday, set lunches by arrangement. *Visitors:* mid-week unrestricted except Tuesdays 9am - 1pm. Weekend visitors may play after 11.30am at Professional's discretion. *Society Meetings:* catered for weekdays only by arrangement. Professional: G. Fieldsend (01482 650190). Secretary: Derrick Pettit (01482 650171; Fax: 01482 652679).

DRIFFIELD. **Driffield Golf Club,** Sunderlandwick, Beverley Road, Driffield YO25 9AD (01377 253116; Fax: 01377 240599). *Location:* from Driffield A164 to Beverley 300 yards from main roundabout on right. Mature parkland course within the attractive Sunderlandwick Estate. 18 holes, 6215 yards. S.S.S. 70. Two practice areas, practice green and two practice putting greens. *Green Fees:* Summer (1st April to 31st October): weekdays £20.00 per round, £25.00 per day; weekends £30.00 per round, £40.00 per day. Winter: weekdays £15.00 per round, £20.00 per day; weekends £20.00 per round, £25.00 per day. *Eating facilities:* full catering and bar service. *Visitors:* welcome by arrangement with Secretary. Limit of 24 players weekends and Bank Holidays. 18 holes only tee 10/11am. *Society Meetings:* welcome by prior arrangement. Professional: Kenton Wright (01377 241224). Secretary: John R. Nicholson.

HORNSEA. **Hainsworth Park Golf Club,** Brandesburton, Near Driffield YO25 8RT (01964 542362). *Location:* eight miles north east of Beverley, just off A165 road to Bridlington, at the Brandesburton roundabout. Easy going, well drained parkland course with mature trees. 18 holes, 6362 yards. S.S.S. 71, Par 71. Practice area. *Green Fees:* weekdays £20.00 - £24.00; weekends £24.00 - £29.00, subject to confirmation. *Eating facilities:* bar and full catering. *Visitors:* welcome anytime, please phone. Hotel accommodation. *Society Meetings:* welcome. Professional: P. Binnington (Tel & Fax: 01964 542362). Secretary: R. Hounsfield (Tel & Fax: 01964 542362). e-mail: hainsworth@hemscott.net

HORNSEA. **Hornsea Golf Club,** Rolston Road, Hornsea HU18 1XG (Tel & Fax: 01964 532020). *Location:* follow signs for Hornsea Freeport - Golf Course 200 yards past Pottery. Flat parkland. 18 holes, 6661 yards. S.S.S. 72. Practice area. *Green Fees:* weekdays £26.00 per round, £34.00 per day; Saturday after 3pm £34.00 per round, Sundays after 2pm £26.00 per round. *Eating facilities:* available every day. *Visitors:* welcome, please ring Professional for a time. Ladies' Day Tuesdays. Snooker room. *Society Meetings:* welcome by prior arrangement with the Secretary. Professional: S. Wright (01964 534989). Secretary: Mr David Crossley (Tel & Fax: 01964 532020).

HOWDEN. **Boothferry Golf Club,** Spaldington Lane, Howden, Near Goole DN14 7NG (01430 430364). *Location:* two and a half miles from Junction 37 of the M62 on the B1228 road between Howden and Bubwith. Flat meadowland, with natural dykes and ponds. 18 holes, 6651 yards. S.S.S. 72. Large practice area. *Green Fees:* weekdays £10.00 per round, weekends £15.00 per round. *Eating facilities:* restaurant and bar facilities available. *Visitors:* welcome at all times. No jeans, trainers or collarless shirts. *Society Meetings:* all Golf Societies and individual parties welcome with prior booking through the Professional. Professional: James Major (01430 430364; Fax: 01430 430567).

HULL. **Cottingham Parks Golf & Country Club,** Woodhill Way, Cottingham HU16 5RZ (01482 846030; Fax: 01482 845932). *Location:* from the Humber Bridge to Beverley road, take the B1233 turnoff at the Skidby roundabout to Cottingham Golf Club turnoff. Mature parkland with several water hazards. 18 holes, 6459 yards. S.S.S. 71. Two tier driving range. *Green Fees:* weekdays £16.00, weekends £24.00. *Eating facilities:* bar snacks and full dining room menu available. *Visitors:* welcome. *Society Meetings:* welcome with restrictions at weekends. Special packages available. Conference and social functions catered for; full leisure facilities including gym, 20 metre pool, steam room and jacuzzi. Professional: Chris Gray (01482 842394). Administrative Office: 01482 846030; Fax: 01482 845932.

HULL. **Hull Golf Club (1921) Ltd.,** The Hall, 27 Packman Lane, Kirk Ella, Hull HU10 7TJ. *Location:* five miles west of Hull. Parkland and wooded. 18 holes, 6242 yards. S.S.S. 70. *Green Fees:* on application. *Eating facilities:* available. *Visitors:* welcome weekdays except Wednesday. *Society Meetings:* by prior arrangement. Professional: David Jagger (01482 653074). Office Manager: Mrs C. Toffolo (Tel & Fax: 01482 658919).

HULL. **Springhead Park Golf Club**, Willerby Road, Hull HU5 5JE (01482 614968 - TICKET OFFICE). *Location:* off the M62/M18 onto the A63. Parkland surrounded by many trees, some undulating fairways, three ponds and many ditches around course. 18 holes, 6102 yards, 5680 metres. S.S.S. 71. Two practice areas. *Green Fees:* information not available. *Eating facilities:* mobile sandwich bar on course, restaurant meals for club members and societies. *Visitors:* welcome by booking only, some restrictions. Tuition and club hire available. *Society Meetings:* welcome. Secretary: Mrs J. Garforth (01482 656958 - Home, or phone clubhouse number 01482 656309). *

HULL. **Sutton Park Golf Club**, Saltshouse Road, Hull HU8 9HF (01482 374242). *Location:* A63, north ring road, Sutton Road, Leads Road, Robson Way. Flat parkland course. 18 holes, 6251 yards. S.S.S. 70. Practice area and nearby driving range. *Green Fees:* information not available. *Eating facilities:* restaurant/bar. *Visitors:* welcome, no restrictions. *Society Meetings:* welcome, bookings via Secretary. Professional: To be appointed. Secretary: C. Alsop (Tel & Fax: 01482 701428).*

KILNWICK PERCY. **Kilnwick Percy Golf Club**, Kilnwick Percy, Pocklington YO42 1UF (01759 303090). *Location:* one mile east of Pocklington off B1246. Scenic, undulating parkland course on the edge of the wolds above Pocklington. 18 individually designed holes, 6214 yards. S.S.S. 70. *Green Fees:* weekdays £15.00 per round, £21.00 per day; weekends and Bank Holidays £18.00 per round, £25.00 per day. *Eating facilities:* bar snacks available all day; evening meals by prior arrangement for 10 or more golfers. *Visitors:* welcome. Buggy, trolley and club hire; professional tuition available. Accommodation locally at discounted rates for golf club visitors. *Society Meetings:* special packages, tailored to your requirements. Secretary/Manager: Mrs Anne Clayton (01759 303090).

WITHERNSEA. **Withernsea Golf Club**, Chestnut Avenue, Withernsea HU19 2PG (01964 612078 or 612258). *Location:* 25 miles north-east of Hull on main road into Withernsea (signposted). Flat course. 9 holes, 6207 yards. S.S.S. 70. *Green Fees:* weekdays £12.00, with a member £10.00; weekends £12.00. *Eating facilities:* bar and meals available (except Monday). *Visitors:* welcome weekdays, weekends after 1.00pm Sunday. *Society Meetings:* by arrangement. Special rates available. Administrator: John Boasman (01964 612078)

North Yorkshire

ALDWARK. **Aldwark Manor Golf Club,** Aldwark, Alne, York YO61 1UF (01347 838353; Fax: 01347 833991). *Location:* in village of Aldwark, five miles south-east of Boroughbridge off A1 and12 miles north-west of York off A19. Easy walking parkland with water hazards. 18 holes, 6187 yards. S.S.S. 70. Practice ground, putting green, practice bunker. *Green Fees:* weekdays £25.00 per round, £35.00 per day; weekends and Bank Holidays £30.00 per round, £40.00 per day. *Eating facilities:* two restaurants and two bars. *Visitors:* always welcome weekdays, restricted weekends. 60 bedroomed hotel on the course. *Society Meetings:* societies and corporate meetings always welcome, restricted weekends. Manager: Geoff Platt (01347 838353; Fax: 01347 833991).

BARNOLDSWICK. **Ghyll Golf Club**, Ghyll Brow, Barnoldswick, Colne, Lancs BB8 6JH (01282 842466). *Location:* M65 to Colne. Parkland course. 9 holes, 5706 yards, 5213 metres. S.S.S. 68. *Green Fees:* weekdays £15.00 per day (£7.50 with a member), weekends £18.00 per day (£10 with a member). *Eating facilities:* bar, evening only. *Visitors:* welcome except Sundays and some Saturdays. *Society Meetings:* catered for by arrangement. Secretary: John L. Gill (01524 412958).

BEDALE. **Bedale Golf Club**, Leyburn Road, Bedale DL8 1EZ. *Location*: from A1 take A684 at Leeming Bar to Bedale; club is situated 400 yards out of town on the Leyburn Road. Undulating parkland with tree-lined fairways and water hazards. 18 holes, 6610 yards. S.S.S. 72. Practice facilities, fully stocked golf shop, lessons available. *Green Fees*: £23.00 per day weekdays; £34.00 per day weekends. Subject to review. *Eating facilities*: bar and catering always available. *Visitors*: welcome weekdays and weekends. *Society Meetings*: catered for weekdays by prior arrangement, limited availability on some Saturday afternoons; tailor-made packages and discounts available. Professional: Tony Johnson (01677 422443). Secretary Mrs Glenys Brown (01677 422451; Fax: 01677 427143). e-mail: bedalegolfclub@aol.com website: www.bedalegolfclub.com

BENTHAM. **Bentham Golf Club,** Robin Lane, Bentham, Near Lancaster LA2 7AG (01524 262455). *Location:* B6480 north-east of Lancaster towards Settle. Parkland with magnificent views. 18 holes, 5914 yards. *Green Fees:* £25.00 weekdays and weekends. *Eating facilities:* hot and cold snacks and meals available. *Visitors:* welcome all week. *Society Meetings:* welcome–contact Secretary. Secretary: John Mann (01524 262455).

BROTTON. **Hunley Hall Golf Club & Hotel,** Brotton, Saltburn TS12 2QQ (01287 676216; Fax: 01287 678250). *Location:* off A174 at St. Margarets Way in Brotton. Signposted through housing estate, approximately half-a-mile to club. Picturesque 27 hole coastal courses adjacent to Heritage Coast. Morgan's Course 18 holes, 6918 yards, 6320 metres. S.S.S. 73. Millennium Course, 18 holes, 6510 yards, S.S.S. 68. Floodlit driving range, large practice and chipping area. *Green Fees:* weekdays £25.00, weekends and Bank Holidays £35.00. Discounts for parties and guests staying at the hotel. *Eating facilities:* excellent facilities including two restaurants, lounge bar, spike bar, golfers' bar; quality food served daily 8am to 9.30pm. *Visitors:* always welcome. Two Star Hotel offering en suite rooms, etc. Club hire, buggy hire and tuition available. *Society Meetings:* welcome Monday to Saturday, packages available. Golfing Holidays and golf schools available. Professional: Andrew Brook (Tel & Fax: 01287 677444). Secretary: Liz Lillie (01287 676216; Fax: 01287 678250). e-mail: enquiries@hunleyhall.co.uk website: www.hunleyhall.co.uk

CATTERICK. **Catterick Golf Club,** Leyburn Road, Catterick Garrison, Catterick DL9 3QE (01748 833401). *Location:* six miles south-west Scotch Corner, A1 turn off to Catterick Garrison. Undulating parkland/moorland with spectacular views. 18 holes, 6329 yards, S.S.S. 71. Practice ground. *Green Fees:* weekdays £24.00; weekends and Bank Holidays £33.00. *Eating facilities:* bar and restaurant. *Visitors:*

See also Colour Advertisement on page 49

welcome without reservation. *Society Meetings:* catered for by appointment only. Professional: Andy Marshall (01748 833671). Secretary: Mr Grant McDonnell (Tel & Fax: 01748 833268).

EASINGWOLD. **Easingwold Golf Club,** Stillington Road, Easingwold, York YO61 3ET (01347 821486; Fax: 01347 822474). *Location:* 12 miles north of York, course one mile along Stillington Road. Flat, wooded parkland established 1930. 18 holes, 6717 yards, 6142 metres, S.S.S. 73. Practice ground. *Green Fees:* weekdays £28.00 per round, £35.00 per day; weekends and Bank Holidays £35.00. £15.00 playing with a member, £15.00 1st November to 31st March. *Eating facilities:* available. *Visitors:* welcome weekdays only, prior booking essential, contact Secretary. *Society Meetings:* weekdays only, prior booking essential, contact Secretary. Professional: John Hughes (01347 821964). Secretary: D.B. Stockley (Tel & Fax: 01347 822474).
e-mail: brian@easingwold-golf-club.fsnet.co.uk
website: www.easingwold-golf-club.co.uk

FILEY. **Filey Golf Club,** The Clubhouse, West Avenue, Filey YO14 9BQ (01723 513293; Fax: 01723 514952). *Location:* one mile south of town centre. Links, parkland course. 18 holes, 6112 yards. S.S.S. 69. 9 holes, 1513 yards. Par 30. Two practice grounds. *Green Fees:* information on request. *Eating facilities:* full dining and bar facilities. *Visitors:* welcome, no restrictions. *Society Meetings:* welcome by arrangement with the Secretary. Professional: Gary Hutchinson (01723 513134). Secretary: Davina Willis (01723 513293; Fax: 01723 514952).

HARROGATE. **Crimple Valley Golf Club,** Hookstone Wood Road, Harrogate HG2 8PN (01423 883485; Fax: 01423 881018). *Location:* one mile south from town centre. Turn off A61 at Nidd Vale Garage on to Hookstone Road, signposted to right. Gently sloping fairways in rural setting. 9 holes, 2500 yards. S.S.S. 33. *Green Fees:* weekdays 9 holes £7.00, 18 holes £11.00, £15.00 per day; weekends 9 holes £8.00, 18 holes £12.00. *Eating facilities:* licensed bar, lunches available except Sunday. *Visitors:* welcome at all times. *Society Meetings:* special rates available. Club Proprietor: Pauline Lumb.

HARROGATE. **Harrogate Golf Club Ltd,** Forest Lane Head, Harrogate HG2 7TF (01423 863158). *Location:* two miles from Harrogate on the A59 Harrogate/Knaresborough road. Parkland, wooded. 18 holes, 6241 yards, 5706 metres. S.S.S. 70. Large practice ground, covered net. *Green Fees:* weekdays £36.00 per round/per day, weekends £40.00 per round/per day. *Eating facilities:* chef catering and bar menu, lounge and casual spike bars. *Visitors:* welcome subject to club events. Society Meetings: catered for weekdays except Tuesdays. Parties of 12 or more welcome. Professional: P. Johnson (01423 862547). Secretary: Mr Peter Banks (01423 862999). Caterer: (01423 860278).
e-mail: Hon.secretary@harrogate-gc.co.uk
website: www.harrogate-gc.co.uk

HARROGATE. **Oakdale Golf Club,** Oakdale Glen, Harrogate HG1 2LN (01423 502806). *Location:* five minutes from Harrogate town centre, off Ripon road into Kent Road, follow signs. Parkland, with featured stream. 18 holes, 6456 yards. S.S.S. 71. Practice ground. *Green Fees:* weekdays £33.00 per round, £40.00 per day; weekends £45.00 per round. *Eating facilities:* first class restaurant, bar. *Visitors:* welcome at all times, Tuesday Ladies' Day. *Society Meetings:* welcome weekdays by arrangement. Professional: Clive Dell (01423 560510). Secretary: (01423 567162; Fax: 01423 536030).

HARROGATE. **Pannal Golf Club**, Follifoot Road, Pannal, Harrogate HG3 1ES (01423 872628; Fax: 01423 870043). *Location:* two miles south of Harrogate A61 (Leeds Road). 18 holes, 6622 yards. S.S.S. 72. Large practice ground with driving range facility. *Green Fees*: weekdays £41.00 per round, £51.00 per day; weekends and Bank Holidays £51.00 per round. *Eating facilities*: lunch available daily, dinner by arrangement. *Visitors:* welcome Monday to Friday, enquiry advised. *Society Meetings*: catered for Monday, Tuesday (pm only), Wednesday, Thursday and Friday. Professional: Mr D. Padgett (01423 872620). Secretary: R.V. Braddon (01423 872628; Fax: 01423 870043).
e-mail: secretary@pannalgc.co.uk
website: www.pannalgc.co.uk

HARROGATE. **Rudding Park Golf,** Harrogate HG3 1JH (01423 872100; Fax: 01423 873011). *Location*: lies just off the A658 linking the A61 from Leeds to the A59 York Road. Parkland course designed to USGA specifications. 18 holes, 6883 yards, Par 72. 18 bay floodlit driving range with four Professionals. *Green Fees*: Winter (November 1st '03 until March 31st '04: Mondays to Thursdays £16.00, Fridays to Sundays £20.00. Summer (April 1st '04 until October 31st '04): Mondays to Thursdays £27.50, Fridays to Sundays £33.00. *Eating facilities*: clubhouse bar open all day, every day; spike bar. *Visitors*: welcome at all times, must have a Handicap Certificate. Shop and buggies available all year round, with all-year-weather buggy tracks; caddies on request. *Society Meetings*: society and corporate days welcome. Professional: Mark Moore (01423 873400).
e-mail: golf.admin@ruddingpark.com
website: www.ruddingpark.com

KIRKBYMOORSIDE. **Kirkbymoorside Golf Club,** Manor Vale, Kirkbymoorside, York YO62 6EG (01751 431525). *Location*: on A170 through Kirkbymoorside. Undulating parkland. 18 holes, 6112 yards, 5491 metres. S.S.S. 69. Practice area, putting green. *Green Fees*: weekdays £22.00 per round, £28.00 per day; weekends and Bank Holidays £32.00 . Reduced fees in winter. *Eating facilities*: available every day. *Visitors*: welcome after 9am, not during weekend Medal competitions. *Society Meetings*: catered for by arrangement with Rose Rivis, Club Administrator. Professional: J. Hinchliffe (01751 430402). Secretary: R.J. Butler (Fax: 01751 433190).

KNARESBOROUGH. **Knaresborough Golf Club,** Boroughbridge Road, Knaresborough HG5 0QQ (01423 863219). *Location*: one-and-a-half miles from town centre, direction A1 Boroughbridge. Wooded parkland. 18 holes, 6354 yards. S.S.S.70. Large practice area. *Green Fees*: £30.00 per round, £40.00 per day. Package rates for parties of 12 and more. Please contact Manager for further details. *Eating facilities*: full catering. *Visitors*: welcome but not before 9.30am weekdays and 2pm weekends and Bank Holidays. *Society Meetings*: welcome by prior arrangement. Professional: Gary J. Vickers (01423 864865). Manager: J.L Hall. (01423 862690).

MALTON. **Malton and Norton Golf Club,** Welham Park, Malton YO17 9QE (01653 692959). *Location:* off A64 to Malton between York and Scarborough. One mile south on Welham road turn right at Norton level crossing. 27 holes - Longest 18: 6456 yards. S.S.S. 71. Medal Course: 6141 yards. S.S.S. 69 (Club). Practice ground. *Green Fees:* weekdays £25.00; weekends and Bank Holidays £30.00. *Eating facilities:* full bar and catering available. *Visitors:* welcome without reservation except club match

days, and weekends from 1st November to 31st March unless with member. *Society Meetings:* catered for by arrangement with Secretary. Professional: S. Robinson (01653 693882). Secretary: E. Harrison (01653 697912).

MIDDLESBROUGH. **Middlesbrough Golf Club,** Brass Castle Lane, Marton, Middlesbrough TS8 9EE (01642 311515; Fax: 01642 319607). *Location:* five miles south of Middlesbrough west of the A172. Parkland course. 18 holes, 6255 yards. S.S.S./Par 70. Practice facilities available. *Green Fees:* weekdays £15.00/ £35.00 per day; weekends £20.00/£40.00 per day. *Eating facilities:* lunches, teas and dinners. *Visitors:* welcome when tee not booked. Venue of the North of England Open Amateur Youth Golf Championship. Conference facilities. *Society Meetings:* welcome Mondays, Wednesdays, Thursdays and Fridays. Professional: Don Jones (01642 311766). Secretary: P.M. Jackson (01642 311515).

NORTHALLERTON. **Romanby Golf Course,** Yafforth Road, Northallerton DL7 0PE. *Location:* west of Northallerton on the B6271 Richmond Road. Parkland course with formidable "Great Lake Complex" on the 2nd, 11th and 12th. 18 holes, 6663 yards. 12 bay floodlit driving range. *Green Fees:* on application. *Visitors:* always welcome, best to telephone for tee times. *Society Meetings:* golf parties a speciality. Bookings telephone (01609 778855; Fax: 01609 779084).
e-mail: mark@romanby.com
website: www.romanbygolf.com

REDCAR. **Cleveland Golf Club,** Majuba Road, Redcar TS10 5BJ. *Location:* on entering town via A1042 or A1085 follow signs to Esplanade, course runs adjacent to beach on north side of town. Flat seaside links course, easy walking. Championship course: 18 holes, 6696 yards. S.S.S. 72. Oldest golf course in Yorkshire, founded 1887. *Green Fees:* on application. *Eating facilities:* full catering at all times. *Visitors:* welcome anytime subject to availability. *Society Meetings:* welcome by prior arrangement, special rates available. Professional: Craig Donaldson (01642 483462). Secretary: J.A. Moran (Tel & Fax: 01642 471798)
e-mail: secretary@clevelandgolfclub.co.uk
website: www.clevelandgolfclub.co.uk

REDCAR. **Wilton Golf Club**, Wilton, Redcar TS10 4QY (01642 465265). *Location:* eight miles east of Middlesbrough (A174), four miles west of Redcar. Parkland course, partly wooded. 18 holes, 6126 yards. S.S.S. 69. Small practice area. *Green Fees:* weekdays £22.00 per day; Sundays and Bank Holidays £26.00 per day. *Eating facilities:* lunches, including Sundays; evening meals by arrangement, lounge bar and 19th bar. *Visitors:* welcome except Saturdays; weekdays and Sundays not before 10am. Tuesdays ladies playing in competitions have priority. *Society Meetings:* by arrangement on Mondays, Wednesdays, Thursdays, Fridays and Sundays. Please contact the Club Secretary. Special rates for parties over 20. Professional: Miss P.D. Smillie (01642 452730). Secretary: Ray Douglas (01642 465265). e-mail: secretary@wiltongolfclub.co.uk

RICHMOND. **Richmond (Yorkshire) Golf Club,** Bend Hagg, Richmond DL10 5EX (01748 825319). *Location:* Scotch Corner (A1). Wooded, parkland, some hills. 18 holes, 5704 yards. S.S.S. 68. *Green Fees:* information not available. *Eating facilities:* bar and catering. *Visitors:* welcome but not before 3.30pm Sundays. Pro Shop. *Society Meetings:* catered for, book with Professional. Professional: Paul Jackson (01748 822457). Secretary: B.D. Aston (01748 823231).*

RIPON. **Masham Golf Club**, Burnholme, Swinton Road, Masham, Ripon HG4 4HT (01765 689379). *Location:* nine miles north of Ripon just off A6108. Parkland, River Burn flows through course and is featured in several holes. 9 holes, 6068 yards. S.S.S. 69. *Green Fees:* information not available. *Eating facilities:* mainly mid-day catering, bar all day. *Visitors:* welcome Mon-Fri, not weekends or Bank Holidays. *Society Meetings:* by arrangement with Secretary. Secretary: J McGee (Office: 01765 689148).*

RIPON. **Ripon City Golf Club,** Palace Road, Ripon HG4 3HH (01765 603640). *Location:* one mile north of Ripon on A6108 (Masham). Undulating parkland with magnificent views over Ure Valley, city of Ripon, Hambleton Hills. 18 holes, 6084 yards. S.S.S. White 69, Yellow 68. Nearby golf range. *Green Fees:* information not available. *Eating facilities:* available every day. *Visitors:* welcome (not Saturdays). *Society Meetings:* welcome. Professional: S.T. Davis (01765 600411). Secretary: C.J. Webb (01765 603640). *

SCARBOROUGH. **Ganton Golf Club Ltd,** Ganton, Near Scarborough YO12 4PA (01944 710329; Fax: 01944 710922). *Location*: on A64, nine miles west of Scarborough. Heathland/links course. 18 holes, 6734 yards. S.S.S. 73. *Green Fees*: weekdays £60.00 per round or day; weekends and Bank Holidays £70.00 per round or day. *Eating facilities*: available. *Visitors*: welcome by prior arrangement. *Society Meetings*: catered for with reservation. Professional: Gary Brown. Secretary: Major R.G. Woolsey (01944 710329). e-mail: secretary@gantongolfclub.com website: www.gantongolfclub.com

SCARBOROUGH. **Scarborough North Cliff Golf Club,** North Cliff Avenue, Scarborough YO12 6PP (01723 360786; Fax: 01723 362134). *Location:* two miles north of Scarborough on coastal road to Whitby. Mainly parkland course with a cliff top start and finish; views of North Bay and Castle. 18 holes, 6425 yards. S.S.S. 71. Practice ground, chipping green, putting green. *Green Fees:* weekdays £26.00 per round, £32.00 per day; weekends and Bank Holidays £30.00 per round, £36.00 per day. Subject to review. *Eating facilities:* available. *Visitors:* welcome (restrictions on competition days, not allowed Sundays before 10.30am.). Must be members of golf club. Electric trolleys, carts available. *Society Meetings:* catered for, parties from 8 to 40. Prior booking through Secretary. Professional: S.N. Deller (01723 365920). Secretary: Mrs J H Lloyd (01723 360786).

SCARBOROUGH. **Scarborough South Cliff Golf Club Ltd**, Deepdale Avenue, Scarborough YO11 2UE (01723 360522). *Location:* one mile south of Scarborough off Filey road. Parkland and clifftop with panoramic sea views. 18 holes, 6405 yards. S.S.S. 71 (white tees), 69 (yellow tees). Practice ground. *Green Fees:* information not available. *Eating facilities:* dining room, bar; full catering facilities. *Visitors:* welcome when course available. *Society Meetings:* catered for by prior arrangement. Professional: T. Skingle (01723 365150). Secretary: David Roberts (Tel & Fax: 01723 374737).

SELBY. **Selby Golf Club,** Mill Lane, Brayton Barff, Selby YO8 9LD (01757 228622). *Location:* three miles south of Selby off A19 Selby/Doncaster road. Links-type course, very well drained. 18 holes, 6374 yards. S.S.S. 71. Practice ground. *Green Fees:* information not available. *Eating facilities:* restaurant and bar. *Visitors:* welcome weekdays. Snooker tables. *Society Meetings:* welcome Wednesday to Friday. Professional: Andrew Smith (01757 228785). Secretary: Neil Proctor. *

SETTLE. **Settle Golf Club,** Buck Haw Brow, Giggleswick, Settle BD24 0DH (Tel & Fax: 01729 825288). *Location:* one mile north of Settle on B6480. Moorland. 9 holes, 6200 yards. S.S.S. 72. *Green Fees:* £15.00. *Eating facilities:* bar only on Sundays. *Visitors:* welcome, restrictions Sundays. *Society Meetings:* welcome with prior notice. Secretary: J. Ketchell (01729 823727).

SKIPTON. **Skipton Golf Club Ltd,** Short Tee Lane, Skipton BD23 3LF (01756 793922). *Location:* one and a half miles northwest of Skipton town centre on A65. Undulating, with panoramic views, some water hazards. 18 holes, 6049 yards. S.S.S. 69. Practice ground. *Green Fees:* weekdays £24.00; weekends £26.00. *Eating facilities:* full bar and catering daily. *Visitors:* welcome at all times, some restrictions weekends and Tuesdays. *Society Meetings:* welcome by prior arrangement. Special package rates. Professional: P. Robinson (01756 793257). Business Manager: T.H. Newman (01756 795657; Fax: 01756 796665).

STOCKTON-ON-TEES. **Teesside Golf Club,** Acklam Road, Thornaby, Stockton-on-Tees TS17 7JS (01642 676249; Fax: 01642 676252). *Location*: A19 - A1130 to Thornaby, 0.7 miles on right hand side. Flat parkland, partly tree-lined. 18 holes, 6535 yards. S.S.S. 71. Practice ground, putting green. *Green Fees:* weekdays £26.00, weekends £30.00. *Eating facilities:* catering except Mondays, bar 11am to 11pm. *Visitors:* welcome mid-week up to 4.30pm, weekends after 11am by arrangement. *Society Meetings:* catered for midweek only. Special rates and conditions for parties and guests. Professional: K.W. Hall (01642 673822). Secretary: M. Fleming (01642 616516).
e-mail: teessidegolfclub@btconnect.com
website: www.teessidegolfclub.com

STUTTON. **Cocksford Golf Club,** Stutton, Tadcaster LS24 9NG (Tel & Fax: 01937 834253). *Location:* from A64 at Tadcaster to Stutton. Meadowland course in picturesque valley with Cock Beck running through. 18 holes, 5501 yards. S.S.S. 70. Practice facilities. *Green Fees:* information not available. *Eating facilities:* Cocksford Bar. *Visitors:* no restrictions apart from competitions - telephone prior to visit. *Society Meetings:* welcome by prior arrangement. Professional: Graham Thompson. Secretary: Sarah Watkinson.

TADCASTER. **Scarthingwell Golf Course,** Scarthingwell. Tadcaster LS24 9PF (01937 557878; Fax: 01937 557909). *Location*: 4 miles south of Tadcaster on the A162 Tadcaster/Ferrybridge Road approximately 3 miles from A1. Parkland Course. 18 holes, 6771 yards. *S.S.S.*72. *Green Fees*: information not available. *Eating facilities*: licenced clubhouse facilities and snooker table, restaurant. *Visitors*: welcome every day except before 2pm on Saturdays. *Society Meetings*: welcome, packages and special rates available. Professional: Steve Footman (01937 557864). Secretary: Kathryn Pick (01937 557878).

THIRSK. **Thirsk and Northallerton Golf Club,** Thornton-le-Street, Thirsk YO7 4AB (01845 522170). *Location:* on Northallerton Road (A168), two miles from Thirsk. Flat parkland with excellent views of Hambleton Hills. 18 holes, 6530 yards. S.S.S. 71. Practice ground. *Green Fees:* on application. *Eating facilities:* catering and bar. *Visitors:* welcome, phone before arrival. Trolleys, buggies for hire. *Society Meetings:* welcome. Handicaps required. Professional: Robert Garner (01845 526216). Secretary: S.P. Gaskell (01845 525115).

WHITBY. **Whitby Golf Club,** Sandsend Road, Low Straggleton, Whitby YO21 3SR (01947 602768). *Location:* on the A174, one mile from Whitby. Picturesque coastal course on cliff tops, three holes over ravines. 18 holes, 5963 yards. S.S.S. 70. *Green Fees:* £28.00 weekends, £22.00 midweek. *Eating facilities:* dining room and bar. *Visitors:* welcome, parties over 12 by prior reservation, all must be bona fide golfers. *Society Meetings:* catered for by prior arrangement. Professional: Tony Mason (Tel & Fax: 01947 602719). Secretary: (Tel & Fax: 01947 600660).

YORK. **Forest Park Golf Club,** Stockton on Forest, York YO32 9UW (01904 400425). *Location:* one and a half miles from east end of York bypass, follow signs for Stockton on Forest. Flat parkland type course with trees and stream running through. 18 holes, 6600 yards. S.S.S. 71; 9 holes, 3186 yards. S.S.S. 70 (twice round). Open air driving range and 8 bay driving range, practice area. *Green Fees:* weekdays £8.00 for 9 holes, £18.00 per round, £24.00 per day; weekends £10.00 for 9 holes, £23.00 per round, £30.00 per day. Subject to review for 2004. Special party and package rates; quotation on request. *Eating facilities:* full bar and golf club catering facilities. *Visitors:* welcome mid week, limited availability weekends. *Society Meetings:* welcome by prior arrangement. Secretary: Nicola Crossley (01904 400688).

YORK. **Forest of Galtres Golf Club,** Moorlands Road, Skelton, York YO32 2RF (Tel & Fax: 01904 766198). *Location:* two miles from the northern section of the ring road around the historic city of York. Parkland course, designed by Simon Gidman. 18 holes, 6412 yards. S.S.S. 70. Open air driving range and practice ground. *Green Fees:* weekdays £20.00 per round, £25.00 all day; weekends and Bank Holidays £27.00 per round, £32.00 all day. Midweek Specials starting from £27.00 including food. *Eating facilities:* full facilities available. *Visitors:* welcome any day. *Society Meetings:* welcome but must be pre-booked with Secretary, No Societies on Saturdays. Professional: Phil Bradley P.G.A. (Tel & Fax: 01904 766198). Secretary: Mrs Sue Procter (Tel & Fax: 01904 769400).
website: www.forestofgaltres.co.uk

YORK. **Fulford (York) Golf Club Ltd,** Heslington Lane, York YO10 5DY (01904 413212). *Location:* A19 (Selby) from city, turn left to Heslington (signposted to University). Heathland. 18 holes, 6775 yards. S.S.S. 72. Practice ground. *Green Fees:* weekdays £40.00 per round, £48.00 per day; weekends £48.00. *Eating facilities:* lounge, diningroom and bar. *Visitors:* welcome Monday to Friday, prior reservation recommended. Snooker table. *Society Meetings:* Monday to Friday by arrangement with Manager. Professional: Martin Brown (01904 412882). General Manager: Ian Mackland (01904 413579; Fax: 01904 416918).
e-mail: info@fulfordgolfclub.co.uk

YORK. **Heworth Golf Club,** Muncaster House, Muncastergate, York YO31 9JY (01904 426156). *Location:* one and a half miles east of City Centre on A1036 Malton/Scarborough road. Parkland, easy walking. 12 holes, 6141 yards, 5613 metres. S.S.S. 69. Practice ground. *Green Fees:* weekdays £15.00 per round, £20.00 per day; weekends and Bank Holidays £20.00 per round, £25.00 per day. All-in rates for parties (coffee, 9 holes, soup and sandwiches, 18 holes, evening meal) £27.50. *Eating facilities:* bar (snacks), dining room. *Visitors:* generally welcome, advisable to telephone Professional in advance. Carts for hire. *Society Meetings:* by written arrangement with Professional. Professional: Stephen Burdett (Tel & Fax: 01904 422389). Secretary: Richard Hunt (Tel & Fax: 01904 426156).

YORK. **Pike Hills Golf Club,** Tadcaster Road, Askham Bryan, York YO23 3UW (01904 706566). *Location:* four miles from York on Tadcaster Road (A64), left hand side going east. Flat parkland surrounding wildlife reserve. 18 holes, 6146 yards. S.S.S. 70. *Green Fees:* £22.00 per round, £26.00 per day. *Eating facilities:* restaurant and bar facilities. *Visitors:* welcome except weekends or Bank Holidays. *Society Meetings:* welcome by arrangement. Professional: Ian Gradwell (01904 708756). Secretary: L. Hargrave (Tel & Fax: 01904 700797).

YORK. **The Oaks Golf Club,** Aughton Common, Aughton, York YO42 4PW (01757 288577; Fax: 01757 288232). *Location:* on the B1228 one mile north of Bubwith village. Wooded course with seven lakes that come into play. 18 holes, 6743 yards, 6035 metres. S.S.S. 72. Practice ground. *Green Fees:* £25.00 per round, £35.00 per day. *Eating facilities:* lounge bar, normal meals, à la carte restaurant. *Visitors:* welcome weekdays. Accommodation available, for details telephone (01757 288577). *Society Meetings:* on application. Professional: Joe Townhill. Secretary: Sheila Nutt.
e-mail: oaksgolfclub@hotmail.com
website: www.theoaksgolfclub.co.uk

YORK. **The York Golf Club,** Lords Moor Lane, Strensall, York YO32 5XF (01904 490304). *Location:* two miles north of York ring road (A1237). Wooded heathland. 18 holes, 6301 yards. S.S.S. 70. Practice ground; Professional shop. *Green Fees:* weekdays £33.00 per round, £37.00 for 27 holes, £41.00 per day; parties Sundays £47.00 for 27 holes. *Eating facilities:* full catering. *Visitors:* welcome weekdays, but advisable to ring before visiting. *Society Meetings:* catered for weekdays and Sundays. Professional: A.P. Hoyles (01904 490304). Secretary: Steve G. Watson (01904 491840; Fax: 01904 491852).

THE APPEARANCE OF AN ASTERISK (*) AT THE END OF A CLUB OR COURSE ENTRY INDICATES THAT UP-TO-DATE INFORMATION HAS NOT BEEN SUPPLIED

See also Colour Advertisement on page 50

South Yorkshire

BARNSLEY. **Barnsley Golf Club,** Wakefield Road, Staincross, Barnsley S75 6JZ (01226 382856). *Location:* A61 three miles north of Barnsley, five miles south of Wakefield. Parkland course. 18 holes, 6048 yards, 5529 metres. S.S.S. 69. *Green Fees:* information not available. *Eating facilities:* full catering and licensing facilities all day every day. *Visitors:* welcome, no restrictions; booking through Professional. Professional: S. Wyke (01226 380358). Secretary: Melvyn Gillott (01226 382856).*

BARNSLEY. **Sandhill Golf Club,** Middlecliffe Lane, Little Houghton, Barnsley S72 0HW (Tel & Fax: 01226 753444). *Location:* 6 miles east of Barnsley, off A635. 18 holes, 6250 yards. S.S.S. 70. *Green Fees:* on request. *Eating facilities:* licensed bar providing tea, coffee, biscuits and meals at various prices. *Visitors:* welcome. Buggies available. *Society Meetings:* welcome with various packages on request. Winter Society Specials available. Secretary: Mrs V. Wistow.

BARNSLEY. **Silkstone Golf Club**, Field Head, Elmhirst Lane, Silkstone, Barnsley S75 4LD (01226 790328). *Location:* one mile from Junction 37 (M1) along A628 (the road to Manchester). Parkland/downland course. 18 holes, 6069 yards. S.S.S. 70. Practice ground. *Green Fees:* weekdays £30.00 per day, £24.00 per round; weekends with a member only. Packages available - full day golf and food £40.00, one round and meal £33.00. *Eating facilities:* full catering facilities and bar. *Visitors:* welcome weekdays, Ladies Day Tuesdays, with a member only at weekends and Bank Holidays. Caddie cart and buggy hire. *Society Meetings:* by arrangement Wednesdays, Thursdays and Fridays. Professional: Kevin Guy (01226 790128). Acting Secretary: Mr A Butcher (01226 790328).

**Please mention
'The Golf Guide' when
enquiring about clubs
or accommodation.**

DONCASTER. **Austerfield Golf Club,** Cross Lane, Austerfield, Doncaster DN10 6RF (Tel & Fax: 01302 710841). *Location:* two miles from Bawtry on the A614. Parkland. 18 holes, 6900 yards. S.S.S. 73. 10 bay floodlit golf range, practice ground, family Par 3 (18 hole) course. *Green Fees:* information not available. *Eating facilities:* bar snacks and full restaurant. *Visitors:* welcome without reservation. Flat bowling green; trolley and cart hire; buggies. *Society Meetings:* welcome, special package rates. Professional: Fax: 01302 710841). Secretary: Robin Whalley (Tel & Fax: 01302 710841). *

DONCASTER. **Crookhill Park (Municipal) Golf Club,** Carr Lane, Conisborough, Doncaster DN12 2AH (01709 862979). *Location:* off A630 Doncaster–Rotherham Road turn on A6094 (opposite castle) then one mile. 18 holes, 5846 yards. Parkland, special hole 11 (index 1) – approach to green over small wall to elevated green. S.S.S. 68. Practice area. *Green Fees:* weekdays £9.95, weekends £11.30 (per round). *Eating facilities:* buffet lunches at club. *Visitors:* welcome pre-book with Professional if specific time is required. Professional: Richard Swaine (01709 862979). Hon. Secretary: T.A. Cusack (01709 862974).

DONCASTER. **Doncaster Golf Club,** Bawtry Road, Doncaster DN4 7PD (01302 868316). *Location:* four miles south of Doncaster town centre on the A638. Wooded, heathland course. 18 holes, 6220 yards. S.S.S. 70. Practice area, putting green. *Green Fees:* £30.00 per round, £36.00 per day. *Eating facilities:* all day catering Monday to Saturday, up to 4pm Sundays. *Visitors:* welcome weekdays, Wednesday Ladies' Day; restricted tee times at weekends and Bank Holidays. *Society Meetings:* by arrangement, contact Secretary. Professional: G. Bailey (01302 868404). Secretary: G.J. Needham (01302 865632; Fax: 01302 865994).
e-mail: doncastergolf@aol.com
website: www.doncastergolfclub.org.uk

DONCASTER. **Doncaster Town Moor Golf Club**, Bawtry Road, Belle Vue, Doncaster DN4 5HU (01302 533167). *Location:* clubhouse approximately 300 yards from racecourse roundabout travelling south towards Bawtry, same entrance as Doncaster Rovers Football Club. Flat parkland/lowland heath, centre of Doncaster racecourse. 18 holes, 5650 yards, S.S.S. 69. *Green Fees:* weekdays £19.00, with a member £11.00; weekends £21.00, with a member £13.00. Special rates for societies. *Eating facilities:* restaurant and bar meals. *Visitors:* welcome by arrangement. *Society Meetings:* catered for by arrangement with Professional. Discount package available. Professional: Steve Shaw (01302 535286). Secretary: Mrs J. Stoddart (01302 533778).

DONCASTER. **Hickleton Golf Club,** Lidgett Lane, Hickleton, Near Doncaster DN5 7BE (01709 896081; Fax: 01709 896083). *Location:* from Junction 37 A1(M) six miles on A635 to Barnsley, in Hickleton village turn right to Thurnscoe, 500 yards on right. Undulating parkland. 18 holes, 6434 yards. S.S.S. 71. Practice ground. *Green Fees:* weekdays £20.00; weekends and Bank Holidays £27.00. Winter and Summer packages available. *Eating facilities:* available seven days a week. *Visitors:* welcome by arrangement, restricted times at weekends. Buggies by arrangement with Professional. *Society Meetings:* welcome by arrangement. Professional: Paul Audsley (Tel & Fax: 01709 888436). Secretary: J. Mills (01709 896081; Fax: 01709 896083). e-mail: hickleton@hickletongolfclub.freeserve.co.uk website: www.hickletongc.co.uk

DONCASTER. **Robin Hood Golf Club**, Owston Hall, Owston, Askern, Doncaster DN6 9JF (01302 722231; Fax: 01302 728885). *Location:* 5 miles north of Doncaster on the A19 from Doncaster to Askern, take the B1220 and turn right through the stone gates. Host to the 2002 PGA Euro Pro Tour. Parkland with mature trees. 18 holes, 6937 yards. S.S.S. 72. Putting Green, practice net. *Green Fees:* weekdays £16.00; weekends £22.00. *Eating facilities:* bar lunches and full evening menu. *Visitors:* welcome, booking at weekends recommended. Function and conference rooms. Hotel with 42 de luxe bedrooms; gym. *Society Meetings:* packages available - please phone for brochure. Dress code applies - locker changing and shower facilities. Lessons available. Professional: Jason Laszkowicz (01302 722231; Fax: 01302 728885). Secretary: Colin Tanswell (01302 722800). e-mail: reservations@owstonhall.com website: www.robinhoodgolfclub.com

DONCASTER. **Serlby Park Golf Club**, Serlby, Doncaster DN10 6BA (01777 818268). *Location:* between Bawtry and Blyth. Parkland, wooded course. 9 holes, 5300 yards. S.S.S. 66. *Green Fees:* information not available. *Eating facilities:* catering and bar. *Visitors:* welcome only if playing with member. *Society Meetings:* some visiting parties allowed, please contact the Secretary prior to 1st January for bookings the following year. Secretary: Mr K.J. Crook (01302 742280). *

DONCASTER. **Thorne Golf Club**, Kirton Lane, Thorne, Near Doncaster DN8 5RJ (01405 812084; Fax: 01405 741899). *Location:* M18 Junction 5, onto M180, take first junction onto A614 Thorne, follow signposts. Flat parkland with three ponds. 18 holes, 5366 yards. S.S.S. 66. Practice ground and putting green. *Green Fees:* weekdays £9.50 18 holes; weekends and Bank Holidays £10.50 18 holes; twilight £6.50 18 holes. Subject to review. *Eating facilities:* snacks and meals available. *Visitors:* welcome, no restrictions. *Society Meetings:* welcome, please book in advance. Secretary/Professional: Edward Highfield. Proprietor: Richard Highfield.

DONCASTER. **Thornhurst Park Golf Course,** Holme Lane, Owston, Doncaster DN5 0LR (01302 337799). *Location:* 10 minutes from centre of Doncaster through Bentley on A19 to Selby. Flat, parkland course with excellent countryside views. 18 holes, 6490 yards. S.S.S. 71. Practice area, putting green. *Green Fees:* weekdays 18 holes £11.00; weekends 18 holes £13.00. 9 holes: weekdays £6.50, weekends £7.50. *Eating facilities:* restaurant, lounge bar, function room. *Visitors:* welcome every day, members have priority between 8am and 9am. *Society Meetings:* welcome any day. Professional: Kevin M. Pearce. Secretary: Dave Trent (01226 792825).

DONCASTER. **Wheatley Golf Club**, Armthorpe Road, Doncaster DN2 5QB (01302 831655). *Location:* follow East Coast route alongside Racecourse boundary to water tower at first crossroads. Flat parkland, water hazards between 10th and 18th holes. 18 holes, 6209 yards, S.S.S. 70 (yellow markers); 6405 yards, S.S.S. 71 (white markers). Practice area and putting green. *Green Fees:* weekdays £27.00 per round, £33.00 per day; weekends £38.00 per round. *Eating facilities:* restaurant and bars. *Visitors:* welcome if member of another club. *Society Meetings:* catered for weekdays only on written application. Professional: S. Fox (01302 834085). Secretary: Mr R.T.J. Bruno (01302 831655).

ROTHERHAM. **Grange Park Golf Club,** Upper Wortley Road, Kimberworth Park, Rotherham S61 2SJ (01709 558884). Municipal golf course, private clubhouse. *Location:* A629 from Rotherham, easy access from M1. Parkland. 18 holes, 6353 yards. S.S.S. 71. Practice ground, driving range. *Green Fees:* information not available. *Eating facilities:* licensed bar and full catering. *Visitors:* welcome without restriction. *Society Meetings:* contact Professional in first instance. Professional: Eric Clark (01709 559497). Secretary: Roy Charity (01709 583400 home, 01709 558884 club). *

ROTHERHAM. **Phoenix Golf Club,** Phoenix Sports and Social Club, Pavilion Lane, Brinsworth, Rotherham S60 5PA (Tel & Fax: 01709 363788). *Location:* M1 (J34) Tinsley roundabout, Bawtry Road, Pavilion Lane one mile on left. 18 holes, 6181 yards. S.S.S. 70. Practice area, 20 bay driving range. *Green Fees:* weekdays £18.00 per round, £24.00 per day; £10.00 with a member; weekends £24 per round, £32.00 per day, £13.00 with a member. Special rates for parties. *Eating facilities:* snacks or full meals. *Visitors:* welcome anytime. *Society Meetings:* welcome weekdays only. Professional: M. Roberts (01709 382624). Secretary: A. Webb (Tel & Fax: 01709 363788).

ROTHERHAM. **Rotherham Golf Club Ltd,** **Thrybergh Park, Doncaster Road, Thrybergh, Rotherham S65 4NU (01709 850466).** *Location*: three and a half miles east of Rotherham on A630. Wooded parkland. 18 holes, 6234 yards, 5701 metres. S.S.S. 70. Practice ground. *Green Fees*: weekdays £33.00 per round, £38.00 per day; weekends £40.00. Reductions for societies over 16. *Eating facilities*: full catering, bar and restaurant. *Visitors*: welcome all day with limitations. *Society Meetings*: catered for weekdays only except Wednesdays. Professional: Simon Thornhill (01709 850480). Manager: Mrs C. Davison (01709 859500; Fax: 01709 859517).

ROTHERHAM. **Roundwood Golf Club,** Green Lane, Rawmarsh, Rotherham S62 6LA (01709 826134). *Location:* half a mile from the A633. Flat course, easy walking. 18 holes, 5568 yards, S.S.S. 67. *Green Fees:* weekdays £15.00 per day, weekends and Bank Holidays £20.00 per day. *Eating facilities:* bar open seven days a week, food available Fridays and Saturdays. *Visitors:* welcome midweek and Sunday afternoons. *Society Meetings:* welcome weekdays and Sunday afternoons. Secretary: G. Billups (01709 525208).

ROTHERHAM. **Sitwell Park Golf Club,** Shrogswood Road, Rotherham S62 7AP (01709 700799; Fax: 01709 703637). *Location:* A631 off M18, Bramley turn off to Rotherham thence to Sheffield, Exit 33 off M1, follow A631 to Bawtry. Undulating parkland. 18 holes, 6229 yards. Par 71. Practice ground. *Green Fees:* weekdays £25.00 per round, £30.00 per day; Sundays and Bank Holidays £30.00 per round, £35.00 per day. Parties of 30 or more players 10% discount. *Eating facilities:* restaurant and bar. *Visitors:* welcome with reservation, Saturdays only with member, Sundays after 11.30am. Carts available. *Society Meetings:* catered for if pre-arranged with Secretary. Not Saturdays; Sundays after 11.30am only. Professional: N. Taylor (01709 540961). Secretary: G. Simmonite (01709 541046; Fax: 01709 703637).

ROTHERHAM. **Wath Golf Club,** Abdy, Rawmarsh, Rotherham S62 7SJ (01709 872149). *Location:* A633 from Rotherham, through Rawmarsh, taking B6090 towards Wentworth, right along B6089 taking signed road to Clubhouse 300 yards on right. Flat parkland course with small greens, dykes and two ponds. 18 holes, 6123 yards. S.S.S. 70. Limited practice area. *Green Fees:* £24.00 per round, £29.00 per day. Golf/meal package £33.00/£38.00. *Eating facilities:* lounge bar and dining area with seating for up to 150 people. *Visitors:* weekdays only. *Society Meetings:* welcome weekdays only by prior arrangement. Professional: Chris Bassett (01709 878677). Secretary: M. Godfrey (Tel & Fax: 01709 878609).

SHEFFIELD. **Abbeydale Golf Club,** Twentywell Lane, Dore, Sheffield S17 4QA (0114 2360763; Fax: 0114 2360762). *Location*: A621 five miles south of Sheffield. Parkland. 18 holes, 6261 yards. S.S.S. 71. Practice ground. *Green Fees*: weekdays £30.00; weekends and Bank Holidays £40.00. *Eating facilities:* restaurant and bar meals. *Visitors:* welcome by arrangement. Starting time restrictions April-October. *Society Meetings*: catered for by arrangement. Professional: N. Perry (0114 2365633). Secretary: Mr G.L. Lord (0114 2360763; Fax: 0114 2360762).

SHEFFIELD. **Beauchief Golf Club,** Abbey Lane, Beauchief, Sheffield S8 0DB (0114 236 7274). *Location:* near the junction with A621 Abbeydale Road 5 miles SW of Sheffield. Access from J33 or J29 via outer ring road. 'Pay and Play' parkland course with some hilly holes. 18 holes, 5452 yards,. S.S.S. 66. Practice area. *Green Fees:* information not provided. *Eating facilities:* cafe/bar, open daily from 11am to dusk. *Visitors:* welcome weekdays and after 10am at weekend. *Society Meetings:* welcome weekdays and after 10am weekend, contact Mr. A. Carnel, Sheffield International Venues (01142 797451) Professional: M. Trippett (01142 367274). Secretary: Mrs B. Fryer (0114 236 5628).

SHEFFIELD. **Birley Wood Golf Club,** Birley Lane, Sheffield S12 3BP (0114 264 7262). *Location:* Junction 30 M1 then A616 to Sheffield. Undulating meadowland course with good views. 18 holes, 5647 yards. S.S.S. 67. Short Birley Course 18 holes, 4906 yards. Par 66. S.S.S. 65. Practice field near course. Membership available. *Green Fees:* infromation not available. *Eating facilities:* restaurant and bar meals at adjacent Fairway Inn. *Visitors:* welcome anytime. *Society Meetings:* contact A. Carnall (0114 279 7451). Secretary: P. Renshaw (0114 265 3784).*

SHEFFIELD. **Concord Park Municipal Golf Course,** Shiregreen Lane, Shiregreen, Sheffield S5 6AE (0114 2577378). *Location:* M1 Junctions 34/35, one and a half miles north of junctions. Parkland, hilly, good views. 18 holes, 4872 yards, S.S.S. 64, Par 67. Driving range; buggies available. *Green Fees:* £8.00 per round. Leisure Card rates available. *Eating facilities:* available in new clubhouse. *Visitors:* welcome any time; busy Saturday and Sunday mornings. *Society Meetings:* welcome. Professional: W. Allcroft (0114 2577378). Secretary: P.J. Wilson (0114 2347792).

SHEFFIELD. **Dore and Totley Golf Club,** The Clubhouse, Bradway Road, Bradway, Sheffield S17 4QR (0114 236 0492; Fax: 0114 235 3436). *Location:* leave M1 at Junction 33. Flat, easy walking parkland course. 18 holes, 6256 yards. S.S.S. 70. *Green Fees:* information not available. *Eating facilities:* bar catering facilities available except Mondays. *Visitors:* welcome. After 10am Tuesdays and Thursday; afternoons only Wednesdays and Sundays. No visitors on Saturdays. Handicap Certificates may be requested. *Society Meetings:* welcome by arrangement. Special all day price; catering by arrangement with Stewardess. Professional: Gregg Roberts (Tel & Fax: 0114 236 6844). Secretary: J. Johnson (0114 2369872). *

SHEFFIELD. **Hallamshire Golf Club Ltd,** Sandygate, Sheffield S10 4LA (0114 230 1007; Fax: 0114 230 2153). *Location:* A57 out of Sheffield, four miles out of city then fork left for Lodge Moor. Undulating moorland course, not suitable for beginners. 18 holes, 6359 yards, 5815 metres. S.S.S. 71. *Green Fees:* £41.00 weekdays; £44.00 weekends. Large party rates available through the Secretary. *Eating facilities:* dining room/verandah, two bars. *Visitors:* welcome weekdays by arrangement, some weekends. Dress code. Snooker table. *Society Meetings:* catered for by arrangement with Secretary. Professional: Geoffrey Tickell (0114 230 5222). Secretary: Mrs K.E. Renshaw (Tel & Fax: 0114 230 2153).

SHEFFIELD. **Hallowes Golf Club,** Hallowes Lane, Dronfield, Near Sheffield S18 1UA (Tel & Fax: 01246 411196). *Location:* six miles south of Sheffield on old A61 (not bypass to Chesterfield). Moorland/parkland. 18 holes, 6342 yards. S.S.S. 71. Large practice area and short game facility. *Green Fees:* information not available. *Eating facilities:* bars, dining room. *Visitors:* weekdays only, no visitors at weekends and Bank Holidays except with members. *Society Meetings:* EGU registered societies welcome. special reduced packages available. Professional: Philip Dunn (01246 411196). Secretary: T. Marshall (01246 413734).

SHEFFIELD. **Hillsborough Golf Club Ltd,** Worrall Road, Sheffield S6 4BE (0114 234 9151 – Office; 0114 234 4103 – Steward). *Location:* three miles from city centre. Worrall Road via Middlewood Road, Dykes Hall Road. Undulating wooded parkland and heath. 18 holes, 6035 yards. S.S.S. 70. Practice field. *Green Fees:* weekdays £30.00, weekends and Bank Holidays £35.00. *Eating facilities:* snacks available; lunches, teas, evening meals by arrangement (not Fridays). *Visitors:* welcome weekdays, weekends with a member only. *Society Meetings:* catered for by arrangement with Professional. Professional: Lewis Horsman (0114 233 4100). Secretary: T.C. Pigott (0114 234 9151).

SHEFFIELD. **Lees Hall Golf Club Ltd,** Hemsworth Road, Norton, Sheffield S8 8LL (0114 255 4402). *Location:* three miles south of Sheffield, between A61 and A6102 ring road. Undulating parkland with extensive views over Sheffield. 18 holes, 6171 yards. S.S.S. 70. *Green Fees:* information not available. *Eating facilities:* available daily. *Visitors:* welcome, except Saturday and Sunday before 10.30am. *Society Meetings:* by arrangement only. Professional: Simon Berry (0114-250 7868). Secretary: J.W. Poulson (0114 255 2900). *

SHEFFIELD. **Rother Valley Golf Centre,** Mansfield Road, Wales Bar, Sheffield S26 5PQ (0114 2473000; Fax: 0114 2476000). *Location:* centrally situated between Sheffield, Rotherham, and Chesterfield. Two miles from Junction 31 of M1, signposted. Parkland with water features. Island green at 7th hole and monster par 5 18th hole. Floodlit driving range and 9 hole pitch and putt course. Jack Barker golf school. 18 holes, 6602 yards. S.S.S. 72. *Green Fees:* weekdays £12.00, weekends £17.50. *Eating facilities:* Bar open 9am to 10.30pm. *Visitors:* welcome. *Society Meetings:* welcome including weekends. Phone for special offers. General Manager: Maureen Goodman.

SHEFFIELD. **Stocksbridge and District Golf Club Ltd,** 30 Royd Lane, Deepcar, Sheffield S36 2RZ (0114 2882003). *Location:* 10 miles from Sheffield on A616 heading towards Manchester. Moorland course. 18 holes, 5200 yards. S.S.S. 65. Practice ground. *Green Fees:* weekdays £17.00 per round (unaccompanied), £21.00 per day; weekends £30.00. Visiting parties £25.00 – 18 holes, soup and sandwiches, 18 holes, dinner. *Eating facilities:* dining room and bars available. *Visitors:* welcome weekdays, restrictions weekends. *Society Meetings:* catered for during the week. Professional: Roger Broad (0114 2882779). Secretary: Roy Milnes (0114 2882003).

SHEFFIELD. **Tankersley Park Golf Club Ltd,** High Green, Sheffield S30 4LG (0114 2468247; Fax: 0114 2457818). *Location:* M1 north to Junction 35a, A616, golf club on right. M1 south Junction 36, A61 Sheffield, left on A616, golf club on left. Parkland/wooded. 18 holes, 6212 yards. S.S.S. 70. Practice area and practice green. *Green Fees:* £27.00 per round, £36.00 per day. 10% discount for parties of 20 or more players. *Eating facilities:* sandwiches, bar and evening meals. *Visitors:* welcome on weekdays without reservation but not before 3pm weekends. *Society Meetings:* catered for by prior arrangement with Secretary. Professional: Mr I. Kirk (Tel & Fax: 0114 2455583). Secretary: A. Brownhill (0114 2468247).

SHEFFIELD. **Tinsley Park Golf Club (Municipal),** High Hazels Park, Darnall, Sheffield S9 4PE (0114 2037435). *Location:* three miles from Junction 33 M1, exit – A6102. Wooded course. 18 holes, 6096 yards. S.S.S. 69. Practice facilities. *Green Fees:* information not available. *Eating facilities:* cafe (closed Tuesday); meals if ordered from Stewardess. Time must be booked on arrival. *Visitors:* welcome without restriction, no booking facilities. *Society Meetings:* book through Sheffield International Venues. Professional: Mr A.P. Highfield (0114 203 7435). Secretary: Mr M. Shillito (01709 368539).*
e-mail: tinsleyparkgc@hotmail.com

SHEFFIELD. **Wortley Golf Club,** Hermit Hill Lane, Wortley, Near Sheffield S35 7DF (0114 2888469; Fax: 0114 2888488). *Location:* leave M1 Junction 36 or 35A - A616 or A61 to A629 leading to Wortley Village. Parkland. 18 holes, 6035 yards, 5520 metres. S.S.S. 69. Practice ground. *Green Fees:* information not available. *Eating facilities:* order in advance, not Mondays. *Visitors:* welcome, no restrictions. Golf trolleys and club hire available. *Society Meetings:* welcome, must pre-book. Professional: Ian Kirk (0114 2886490). Secretary: Dr. F.A. Wilson (Tel & Fax: 0114 2888469).*
e-mail: wortley.golfclub@virgin.net

WORKSOP. **Lindrick Golf Club,** Lindrick Common, Worksop S81 8BH (01909 485802). *Location:* on A57 four miles west of Worksop. M1 Junction 31 on to A57 Worksop. Heathland. 18 holes, 6612 yards, 6046 metres. S.S.S. 71. Two practice areas. *Green Fees:* information not available. *Eating facilities:* dining room. *Visitors:* welcome weekdays, except Tuesday mornings. Prior booking required. *Society Meetings:* catered for weekdays. Professional: John R. King (01909 475820). Secretary: John Armitage (01909 475282; Fax: 01909 488685).*
website: www.lindrickgolf.com

West Yorkshire

BINGLEY. **Bingley (St Ives) Golf Club,** The Golf Clubhouse, Harden, Bingley BD16 1AT (01274 562436; Fax: 01274 511788). *Location:* A650 Keighley/Bradford Road. Parkland/moorland. 18 holes, 6480 yards. S.S.S. 71. Practice ground. *Green Fees:* weekdays £25.00; weekends and Bank Holidays £30.00. *Eating facilities:* daily. *Visitors:* welcome weekdays, limited availability weekends. *Society Meetings:* welcome, book through Professional. Professional: R.K. Firth (01274 562506). Manager: Mary Welch (01274 562436; Tel & Fax: 01274 511788).

BRADFORD. **Baildon Golf Club,** Moorgate, Baildon, Shipley BD17 5PP (01274 584266; Fax: 01274 530551). *Location:* five miles north-west of Bradford via Shipley. Hilly, moorland course. 18 holes, 6225 yards. S.S.S. 70. *Green Fees:* information not provided. *Eating facilities:* catering except Mondays. Bar and separate dining room. *Visitors:* welcome, restricted at weekends and Tuesdays. *Society Meetings:* welcome weekdays only, by written application. Professional: R. Masters (01274 595162). Secretary: John Cooley.

BRADFORD. **Bradford Moor Golf Club**, Scarr Hall, Pollard Lane, Bradford BD2 4RW (01274 771716). *Location:* A658 two miles from top of M606. Moorland, undulating course. 9 holes, 5854 yards. S.S.S. 68. *Green Fees:* weekdays £10.00 (with a member £6.00); weekends with a member only (£8.00). *Eating facilities:* available by appointment only. *Visitors:* welcome weekdays. *Society Meetings:* welcome weekdays. Secretary: Chris Bedford (01274 771693).

BRADFORD. **Clayton Golf Club**, Thornton View Road, Clayton, Bradford BD14 6JX (01274 880047). *Location:* two miles south west of Bradford, via Thornton Road, then Listerhills Road. Parkland course. 9 holes, 5488 yards. S.S.S. 67. *Green Fees:* information not available. *Eating facilities:* diningroom – meals and snacks daily; evening meals by arrangement; two bars. *Visitors:* welcome at all times except before 4.00pm on Sundays. Snooker room. *Society Meetings:* catered for by arrangement. Secretary: D.A. Smith (01274 572311). *

BRADFORD. **East Bierley Golf Club**, South View Road, East Bierley, Bradford BD4 6PP (01274 683666). *Location*: situated about three miles east of Bradford on the Wakefield/Heckmondwike Road. Turn off at Bierley Bar and down South View Road. Parkland course. 9 holes, 4308 metres. S.S.S. 63. *Green Fees*: information not available. *Eating facilities*: lunchtime and evening catering (except Tuesdays). *Visitors*: welcome, not Sundays or Mondays after 4pm. Secretary: Mr R.J. Welch (01274 683666). Hon. Secretary: R.J. Welch. Steward: (01274 680450).*

BRADFORD. **Headley Golf Club**, Headley Lane, Thornton, Bradford BD13 3LX (01274 833481). *Location:* five miles west of Bradford. Undulating parkland, excellent views. 9 holes, 4914 yards. S.S.S. 65. *Green Fees:* information not available. *Eating facilities:* dining room and bar. *Visitors:* weekdays only. *Society Meetings:* welcome weekdays, special packages available. Hon. Secretary: D. Greenwood (01274 833481).

BRADFORD. **Northcliffe Golf Club,** High Bank Lane, Shipley BD18 4LJ (01274 584085). *Location:* three miles west of Bradford on A650; turn left at roundabout Junction of A650/A657. Undulating woodland parkland with feature holes. 18 holes, 6104 yards. S.S.S. 70. *Green Fees:* weekdays £25.00; weekends and Bank Holidays £30.00. *Eating facilities:* bars 11am to 11pm, food 11.30am to 11pm Summer months. No catering or bar facilities Mondays, except Bank Holidays. *Visitors:* Monday to Friday, Saturday after 4.30pm, Sunday all day. Wide wheel/electric trolleys for hire. *Society Meetings:* welcome, packages available. Professional: M. Hillas (01274 587193). Hon. Secretary:I. Collins (Tel & Fax: 01274 596731).

BRADFORD. **Queensbury Golf Club,** Brighouse Road, Queensbury, Bradford BD13 1QF (01274 882155). *Location:* M62 Junction 25, A644 to Brighouse, Hipperholme and Queensbury. Wooded course. 9 holes, 5024 yards. S.S.S. 65. *Green Fees:* information not provided. *Eating facilities:* lunches, teas except Monday. Bar available. *Visitors:* welcome any day, must have Handicap. No parties at weekends. *Society Meetings:* by arrangement. Professional: D. Delaney (01274 816864). Secretary: B. Cox (01422 346603).

Bingley St. Ives Golf Club, The Clubhouse, Harden, Bingley BD16 1AT
Superb course and facilities with magnificent views of the Aire valley.
Visitors welcome, special package rates all year round.
Contact Pro: 01274 562506 • Manager: 01274 562436 for details
e-mail: bingleyst-ives@harden.freeserve.co.uk

BRADFORD. **Shipley Golf Club**, Beckfoot Lane, Cottingley Bridge, Bingley BD16 1LX (01274 563212; Fax: 01274 567739). *Location:* off A650 at Cottingley Bridge, Bradford six miles, Bingley one mile. Flat parkland. 18 holes, 6235 yards. S.S.S. 70. Practice area and net putting green. *Green Fees:* weekdays £35.00 per day; weekends and Bank Holidays £40.00 per day. Winter rates by arrangement. *Eating facilities:* available. *Visitors:* welcome by arrangement with Golf Manager; not Tuesdays or Saturdays. *Society Meetings:* catered for by arrangement with Golf Manager. Packages available. Professional/Golf Manager: R. Parry (01274 563674; Fax: 01274 568652). Secretary: Mrs M.J. Bryan (01274 568652; Fax: 01274 567739).

BRADFORD. **South Bradford Golf Club,** Pearson Road, Odsal, Bradford BD6 1BH (01274 679195 Club; 01274 690643 Office). *Location:* follow signs for Odsal Stadium, roundabout at Stadium turn left and first left again, road leads down to clubhouse. Parkland type course with some hilly sections. 9 holes, 6004 yards. S.S.S. 69. Practice ground. *Green Fees:* information not available. *Eating facilities:* bar meals available except Mondays. *Visitors:* welcome; not before 3.30pm on weekends and Bank Holidays. Must provide Handicap Certificate. *Society Meetings:* welcome – must apply in writing. Professional: Mr Paul Cooke (01274 673346). Secretary: Mr B. Broadbent (01274 679195).

BRADFORD. **The Manor Golf Club,** Bradford Road, Drighlington, Bradford BD11 1AB (0113 2852644). *Location:* between Leeds and Bradford, just off M62 Junction 27. Undulating parkland/meadowland, features six lakes. 18 holes, 6506 yards, 5947 metres. S.S.S 71, Par 72. 20 bay floodlit driving range, 6 hole Par 3 course. *Green Fees:* on application. *Eating facilities:* clubhouse. *Visitors:* welcome at all times but prior enquiry advised. *Society Meetings:* welcome with reservation. Professional: Jim Crompton. Secretary: J. Crompton.*

BRADFORD. **West Bowling Golf Club Ltd**, Newall Hall, Rooley Lane, Bradford BD5 8LB (01274 393207; Fax: 01274 393207). *Location:* junction of M606 (off M62) and Bradford ring road (east). Parkland. 18 holes, 5779 yards. S.S.S. 68. Practice facilities. *Green Fees:* weekdays £20.00; weekends £30.00 (restricted). *Eating facilities:* full dining except Mondays. *Visitors:* welcome Wednesday, Thursday and Friday, contact Professional or Secretary. Carts for hire. Snooker. *Society Meetings:* by arrangement as above. Steward: (01274 724449). Professional: Ian A. Marshall (01274 728036). Secretary: (Tel & Fax: 01274 393207).

BRADFORD. **West Bradford Golf Club Ltd,** Chellow Grange Road, Haworth Road, Bradford BD9 6NP. *Location:* three miles west of city centre off B6144 Haworth Road. Easy walking, undulating, wooded parkland course. 18 holes, 5723 yards. S.S.S. 68, Par 69. *Green Fees:* £20.00. Package deals for parties and societies from £15.00 (unlimited golf). Happy hour weekends after 4pm – reduced green

fee. *Eating facilities:* available every day except Monday. *Visitors:* welcome, except Saturdays before 4pm. *Society Meetings:* welcome by arrangement. Professional: Nigel M. Barber (01274 542102). Secretary: I.P. Milnes (01274 542767; Fax: 01274 482079).

BRIGHOUSE. **Castlefields Golf Club,** Rastrick Common, Rastrick, Brighouse HD6 3HL. *Location:* one mile out of Brighouse on A643. Parkland course, founded 1903. 6 holes, 2406 yards. S.S.S. 50, Par 54. *Green Fees:* information not available. *Eating facilities:* Globe Inn 200 yards away. *Visitors:* welcome at all times but must be accompanied by a member. *Society Meetings:* contact Secretary for details. Secretary: F.C. Tolley (01484 713276). *

BRIGHOUSE. **Crow Nest Park Golf Club,** Coach Road, Hove Edge, Brighouse HD6 2LN (01484 401121). *Location:* Bradford Road out of Brighouse, left at Ritz Ballroom, right after one mile. Gently undulating parkland. 9 holes, 6020 yards. S.S.S. 69. Floodlit driving range with power tees. *Green Fees:* 9 holes £12.00, 18 holes £24.00. *Eating facilities:* food available from 11.30am till 2.30pm and then from 5.30pm till 9.30pm, bar open from 11am until 11pm. *Visitors:* welcome but tees must be booked in advance with Professional. *Society Meetings:* welcome by prior arrangement. Professional: Paul Everitt. Secretary: (01484 401121). Clubhouse: Jean Metcalfe (01484 401152).
e-mail: crownest@btconnect.com
website: www.crownestgolf.co.uk

BRIGHOUSE. **Willow Valley Golf and Country Club,** Highmoor Lane, off Walton Lane, Clifton, Brighouse HD6 4JB (01274 878624). *Location:* Junction 25 off M62 to Brighouse A644, right at roundabout A643, two miles on right. American-style island greens, undulating fairway, water. 18 holes, 7025 yards. S.S.S. 72. 9 hole course. 18 bay covered range. *Green Fees:* Monday to Friday £23.00; Saturday and Sunday £28.00. 9-hole course £7.00. *Eating facilities:* fully licensed bar and catering. *Visitors:* always welcome. *Society meetings:* welcome, please contact the Manager/Professional. Manager/ Professional: Julian Haworth.
website: www.wvgc.co.uk

CLECKHEATON. **Cleckheaton and District Golf Club Ltd,** Bradford Road, Cleckheaton BD19 6BU (01274 874118; Fax: 01274 871382). *Location:* four miles south of Bradford on A638, 200 yards from Junction 26 M62. Parkland course. 18 holes, 5860 yards. S.S.S. 68. Practice area. *Green Fees:* information not available. *Eating facilities:* available except Mondays. *Visitors:* welcome except Saturdays, suggest prior enquiry. *Society Meetings:* catered for by prior arrangement with Secretary except Saturdays. Professional: Mike Ingham (01274 851267). Secretary: R.J. Anderson (01274 851266; Fax: 01274 871382). Assistant Secretary: Mrs R. Newsholme.*
e-mail: info@cleckheatongolf.fsnet.co.uk

DEWSBURY. **Hanging Heaton Golf Club**, White Cross Road, Dewsbury WF12 7DT (01924 461606; Fax; 01924 430100). *Location:* one mile from town centre on main A653 Dewsbury to Leeds road. 9 holes, 5836 yards (for 18 holes). S.S.S. 68. *Green Fees:* weekdays £16.00 (£11.00 with member); weekends with member £15.00. Green fees not taken weekends or Bank Holidays without member's introduction. *Eating facilities:* available. *Visitors:* welcome without reservation, except weekends. *Society Meetings:* catered for by arrangement with Secretary. Professional: G. Moore (01924 467077). Secretary: Ken Wood (01924 430100).

ELLAND. **Elland Golf Club**, Hammerstone Leach Lane, Elland HX5 0TA (01422 372505). *Location:* M62 Junction 24 exit off roundabout for Blackley, one mile. Parkland. 9 holes, 5498 yards. S.S.S. 67. *Green Fees:* weekdays £15.00; weekends £25.00. *Eating facilities:* meals/bar snacks except Mondays. *Visitors:* welcome weekdays except Thursdays. *Society Meetings:* by arrangement. Professional: N. Krzywicki (01422 374886). Secretary: A.D. Blackburn (01422 372014).

GUISELEY. **Bradford Golf Club,** Hawksworth Lane, Guiseley, Leeds LS20 8NP (01943 875570). *Location:* Shipley to Ilkley road, left at top of Hollins Hill, one mile up Hawksworth Lane. Moorland/parkland. 18 holes, 6259 yards. S.S.S. 71. *Green Fees:* £30 per round, £35 per day. Discounts available for parties over 20.. *Eating facilities:* every day, preferably by prior arrangement. *Visitors:* welcome, phone professional for availability, not on weekends without prior arrangement. *Society Meetings:* catered for on weekdays (except Tuesdays) by prior arrangement. Professional: Sydney Weldon (01943 873719). Secretary: Mr T. Eagle (01943 875570).

HALIFAX. **Halifax Bradley Hall Golf Club,** Holywell Green, Halifax HX4 9AN (01422 374108). *Location:* three miles south of Halifax on B6112. Undulating moorland. 18 holes, 6138 yards. S.S.S. 70. Practice ground. *Green Fees:* weekdays £25.00 per round, weekends £30.00 per round; limitede tee times available at '4 to play 3 to pay'. Reservations only (01422 370231). *Eating facilities:* full catering by arrangement except Mondays, seven day bar. *Visitors:* welcome. Snooker. *Society Meetings:* welcome with prior reservation weekdays. Handicap Certificate. Professional: P. Wood (01422 370231). Secretary: M. Dredge (01422 374108).

HALIFAX. **The Halifax Golf Club Ltd,** Union Lane, Ogden, Halifax HX2 8XR (01422 244171; Fax: 01422 241459). *Location:* four miles out of Halifax, A629 towards Keighley. Moorland. 18 holes, 6037 yards. S.S.S. 70. *Green Fees:* weekdays £20.00 per round, £25.00 per day; weekends £25.00 per round, £35.00 per day. *Eating facilities:* luncheons and dinners served. Good restaurant facilities. *Visitors:* welcome most days by arrangement (not Saturdays). *Society Meetings:* catered for by arrangement: £24.00 - £40.00. Professional: Michael Allison (01422 240047)

HALIFAX. **Lightcliffe Golf Club**, Knowle Top Road, Lightcliffe, Halifax HX3 8RG (01422 202459). *Location:* three miles east of Halifax on A58 (main Halifax to Leeds road). Parkland. 9 holes, 5388 metres. S.S.S. 68. *Green Fees:* information not provided. *Eating facilities:* bar snacks and meals (except Mondays). *Visitors:* welcome without reservation but must confirm with Professional. Not Wednesdays. *Society Meetings:* catered for. Professional: Robert Kershaw (01422 202459). Secretary: Chris Balaam (01422 202054).

HALIFAX. **Ryburn Golf Club,** The Shaw, Norland, Sowerby Bridge, Near Halifax HX6 3QP (01422 831355). *Location:* Station Road Halifax to Sowerby Bridge, turn right up hill, right towards Hobbit Inn (signposted), left after cottages. Demanding, hilly, windy course. 9 holes, 5127 yards. S.S.S. 68. *Green Fees:* information not available. *Eating facilities:* good catering facilities and bar. *Visitors:* welcome weekdays, weekends by prior arrangement. *Society Meetings:* welcome by prior arrangement. Secretary: Jack Hoyle (01422 843070 home).

.HALIFAX. **West End Golf Club (Halifax) Ltd,** Paddock Lane, Highroad Well, Halifax HX2 0NT (01422 344627). *Location:* two miles west of town centre. Parkland. 18 holes, 5937 yards. S.S.S. 68 (White markers). *Green Fees:* weekdays £25.00 per round, £30.00 per day; weekends and Bank Holidays £30.00 per round, £35.00 per day. Subject to review. *Eating facilities:* full bar and catering except Mondays. *Visitors:* welcome except Saturdays - please check with Professional. No visiting parties on Saturdays. *Society Meetings:* catered for by arrangement with Secretary. Professional: David Rishworth (01422 363293). Secretary: G. Gower (Tel & Fax: 01422 341878).
e-mail: info@westendgc.co.uk

HEBDEN BRIDGE. **Hebden Bridge Golf Club,** Wadsworth, Hebden Bridge HX7 8PH (01422 842896). *Location:* one mile upwards past Birchcliffe Centre. Moorland with superb Pennine views. 9 holes, 5242 yards. S.S.S. 67. *Green Fees:* weekdays £12.00; weekends £15.00. 50% reduction for Juniors or if playing with member. Subject to review. *Eating facilities:* bar and dining room facilities. *Visitors:* welcome, please check first at weekends. *Society Meetings:* welcome midweek only except by special arrangement. Secretary: Mrs J. Walker (01422 843453).

HUDDERSFIELD. **Bradley Park Municipal Golf Course,** Off Bradley Road, Huddersfield HD2 1PZ (01484 223772). *Location:* M62 Junction 25, follow Huddersfield signs then A6107. Parkland course, rolling hills with panoramic views. 18 holes, 6220 yards. S.S.S. 70. Floodlit driving range, 9 hole Par 3 course. *Green Fees:* information not available. *Eating facilities:* full catering. *Visitors:* welcome, no restrictions. No block bookings for parties at weekends, only telephone bookings to the Professional for individuals. *Society Meetings:* all welcome, book through Professional. Professional: P.E. Reilly. Secretary: K Blackwell (01484 223772; Fax: 01484 451613).*

HUDDERSFIELD. **Crosland Heath Golf Club Ltd,** Felk Stile Road, Crosland Hill, Huddersfield HD4 7AF (01484 653216). *Location:* three miles from town centre off A62 Oldham road. Flat heathland with extensive views. 18 holes, 6004 yards. S.S.S. 69. Practice facilities. *Green Fees:* on application. *Eating facilities:* full catering except Mondays. *Visitors:* welcome, suggest prior enquiry. *Society Meetings:* catered for by arrangement. Professional: (01484 653877). Secretary: D. Walker (01484 653216 mornings; 01484 653262 home).

HUDDERSFIELD. **Huddersfield Golf Club,** Fixby Hall, Lightridge Road, Fixby, Huddersfield HD2 2EP (01484 426203; Fax: 01484 424623). *Location:* M62 Junction 24; A643 from Cedar Court Hotel; turn right first traffic lights by Sun Inn. Parkland course. 18 holes, 6432 yards. S.S.S. 71. Practice ground. *Green Fees:* weekdays £37.00 for 18 holes, £47.00 for 27/36 holes; weekends and Public Holidays £45.00 for 18 holes, £55.00 for 27/36 holes. £13.00 playing with a member. *Eating facilities:* available. *Visitors:* always welcome, reservation advised but not essential. Tuesday is Ladies' Day and no visitors Saturdays. Snooker. *Society and Company Days:* catered for except weekends, well appointed private rooms. Catering to suit all occasions. Professional: P. Carman (01484 426463). Office Manager: Mrs D. Lockett (01484 426203). General Manager: Mrs S. Dennis (01484 426203). e-mail: secretary@huddersfield-golf.co.uk website: www.huddersfield-golf.co.uk

HUDDERSFIELD. **Longley Park Golf Club,** Maple Street (off Somerset Road), Aspley, Huddersfield HD5 9AX (01484 426932). *Location:* one mile town centre, Wakefield side. 9 holes, 5212 yards. S.S.S. 66. *Green Fees:* information not available. *Eating facilities:* available. *Visitors:* welcome Mondays, Tuesdays and Fridays, other times by previous arrangement only. *Society Meetings:* welcome by previous arrangement with Secretary. Professional: Nick Leeming (01484 422304). Secretary: E. Bradshaw. *

HUDDERSFIELD. **Marsden Golf Club,** Hemplow, Marsden, Huddersfield HD7 6NN (01484 844253). *Location:* eight miles west of Huddersfield off A62 from Huddersfield to Manchester. Moorland. 9 holes, 5702 yards. S.S.S. 68. *Green Fees:* weekdays £10.00 per round; with member £5.00 *Eating facilities:* lunches and snacks available except Tuesdays. *Visitors:* welcome weekdays, with a member only weekends. *Society Meetings:* catered for by arrangement. Society package from £16.50 for day golf and evening meal. Professional: Rob Johnson (01484 843300). Secretary: S. J. Boustead (01457 874158).

HUDDERSFIELD. **Meltham Golf Club,** Thick Hollins Hall, Meltham, Huddersfield HD9 4DQ (01484 850227; Fax: 01484 859051). *Location:* half mile east of Meltham, six miles south west of Huddersfield (B6107). Gently sloping course in wooded valley. 18 holes, 6390 yards, 5832 metres. S.S.S. 70. Restricted practice area. *Green Fees:* weekdays £25.00 per round, £30.00 per day; weekends and Bank Holidays £30.00 per round, £35.00 per day. Subject to review. *Eating facilities:* lunches, dinners (with reservation), bar meals available. *Visitors:* welcome weekdays and Sundays without reservation, not Saturdays. *Society Meetings:* catered for by arrangement. Professional: P. Davies (01484 851521). Secretary: C.J. Naylor. website: www.meltham-golf.co.uk

HUDDERSFIELD. **Woodsome Hall Golf Club,** Woodsome Hall, Fenay Bridge, Huddersfield HD8 0LQ (01484 602739). *Location:* A629 five miles from Huddersfield. Parkland and wooded course. 18 holes, 6096 yards. S.S.S. 69. Practice ground. *Green Fees:* information not available. *Eating facilities:* bar snacks and dining available; new casual bar open. *Visitors:* welcome Mondays, Wednesdays, Thursdays and Fridays, limited on Sundays by application. *Society Meetings:* welcome by arrangement, jacket and tie in public rooms. Professional: M. Higginbottom (01484 602034). Hon Secretary: R.B. Shaw (01484 602739; Fax: 01484 608260). Managing Secretary: Mrs T.J. Mee (01484 602739).

ILKLEY. **Ben Rhydding Golf Club,** High Wood, Ben Rhydding, Ilkley LS29 8SB (01943 608759). *Location:* one mile south-east of Ilkley town centre via Ben Rhydding Road or Wheatley Lane. Turn up Wheatley Grove and keep going up and left.Moorside parkland course with fine panoramic views over Wharfedale and surrounding moors. 9 holes, 4611 yards (18 holes). S.S.S. 63. *Green Fees:* weekdays £12.00 per round/day; Bank Holidays £17.00. *Visitors:* welcome weekdays and Bank Holidays; as members' guests only at weekends. *Society Meetings:* by prior arrangement. Secretary: Steve Brown (01943 816067).

ILKLEY. **Bracken Ghyll Golf Club,** Skipton Road, Addingham, Ilkley LS29 0SL (01943 831207; Fax: 01943 839453). *Location:* situated between Ilkley and Skipton on the A65, signposted just after roundabout indicating Silsden and Keighley. Parkland course in rolling dales countryside. 18 holes, 5310 yards, S.S.S. 66. Indoor nets, practice fairway and putting green. *Green Fees:* weekdays £18.00, weekends £20.00. *Eating facilities:* fully licensed bar, lunches served seven days a week in season. *Visitors:* welcome at all times outside competitions weekends and Tuesday and Thursday mornings. Telephone bookings accepted. *Society Meetings:* welcome, brochure on application. Secretary: John Williams.
e-mail: office@brackenghyll.co.uk
website: www.brackenghyll.co.uk

ILKLEY. **Ilkley Golf Club,** Nesfield Road, Ilkley LS29 0BE (01943 607277). *Location:* 15 miles north of Bradford. Flat course. 18 holes, 6262 yards. S.S.S. 70. *Green Fees:* weekdays £40.00; weekends £47.00. Subject to review. *Eating facilities:* by arrangement. *Visitors:* welcome by arrangement. *Society Meetings:* catered for by arrangement. Professional: J.L. Hammond (01943 607463). Secretary: Peter G. Richardson(01943 600214; Fax: 01943 816130).
e-mail: honsec@ilkleygolfclub.co.uk
website: www.ilkleygolfclub.co.uk

KEIGHLEY. **Branshaw Golf Club,** Branshaw Moor, Oakworth, Keighley BD22 7ES (01535 643235). *Location:* on B6143, two miles from town centre. Moorland with extensive views. 18 holes, 5858 yards. S.S.S. 69. *Green Fees:* weekdays £20.00 per day; weekends £30.00. Reduced rates after 3pm. Winter rates applicable. *Eating facilities:* full catering except Mondays. *Visitors:* welcome anytime by prior arrangement. *Society Meetings:* catered for weekdays only. Professional: (01535 647441). Secretary: Mr T. O'Hara (01535 643235).

KEIGHLEY. **Keighley Golf Club,** Howden Park, Utley, Keighley BD20 6DH (01535 604778). *Location:* one mile west of Keighley towards Utley on A629. Parkland. 18 holes, 6141 yards. S.S.S. 70. Practice ground and green. *Green Fees:* weekdays 18 holes £33.00, 27 holes £41.00; weekends and Bank Holidays 18 holes £37.00, 27 holes £45.00 per day. Full package for 16 or over £40.00. Subject to review. *Eating facilities:* full catering and bar facilities available. *Visitors:* welcome by prior arrangement. Tuesday Ladies' Day. *Society Meetings:* catered for by arrangement. Professional: Mike Bradley (01535 665370). Secretary: Cameron Dawson (01535 604778; Fax: 01535 604833).

KEIGHLEY. **Riddlesden Golf Club,** Howden Rough, Riddlesden, Keighley BD20 5QN (01535 602148). *Location:* A650 Keighley-Bradford road, left into Bar Lane, left on Scott Lane, which leads on to Scott Lane West and Elam Wood Road, approximately two miles. Moorland, with spectacular par 3s. 18 holes, 4295 yards. S.S.S. 61. *Green Fees:* information not available. *Eating facilities:* catering available during bar hours. *Visitors:* welcome except between 10am–2pm Saturdays and before 2pm Sundays. *Society Meetings:* catered for by prior arrangement. Secretary: Mr M. Nield (01535 271714).*

KEIGHLEY. **Silsden Golf Club,** Brunthwaite Lane, Brunthwaite, Silsden, Near Keighley BD20 0ND (01535 652998). *Location:* five miles north of Keighley. Undulating downland with extensive views. 18 holes, 5062 yards. S.S.S. 64. Practice area and putting green. *Green Fees:* weekdays £20.00 (£10.00 with a member), weekends £25.00 (£10.00 with a member). *Eating facilities:* licensed bar, full catering available except Mondays. *Visitors & Society Meetings:* Welcome anytime by prior arrangement with the office (01535 652998).

KNOTTINGLEY. **Ferrybridge Golf Club,** PO Box 39, Stranglands Lane, Knottingley WF11 8SQ. *Location:* off the A1 at Ferrybridge and quarter of a mile towards Castleford on the B6136. Undulating land. 9 holes, 6047/6076 yards. S.S.S. 69. Architect: George Barton. Practice ground. *Green Fees:* £10.00 per day. *Visitors:* welcome by prior booking. *Society Meetings:* by prior arrangement with Secretary. Secretary: Mr T.D. Ellis (01977 674188).

LEEDS. **Alwoodley Golf Club,** Wigton Lane, Alwoodley, Leeds LS17 8SA (0113 2681680). *Location:* five miles north of Leeds on A61 (Leeds to Harrogate). 18 holes, 6666 yards. S.S.S. 72. *Green Fees:* £60.00 weekdays; £75.00 weekends. *Eating facilities:* available. *Visitors:* welcome by arrangement. *Society Meetings:* catered for by arrangement. Professional: J.R. Green (0113 2689603). Secretary: C.D. Wilcher (Fax: 0113 2939458).
website: www.alwoodley.co.uk

LEEDS. Calverley Golf Club, Woodhall Lane, Pudsey, Leeds LS28 5QY (0113 256 9244; Fax: 0113 256 4362). *Location:* off Leeds outer ring road, signposted Pudsey. Take Bradford turn off, turn right at next roundabout onto Woodhall Lane. Parkland course. 18 holes, 5590 yards. S.S.S. 67. (9 hole course closed for redevelopment). Practice ground, putting green. *Green Fees:* weekdays £13.00, with a member £9.00; weekends £16.00, with a member £12.00. Juniors £7.00. *Eating facilities:* full bar and catering facilities available. *Visitors:* very welcome, booking advisable. Members only weekends till 1pm. Buggies. Tuition available. *Society Meetings:* welcome by prior arrangement. Professional: Neil Wendel-Jones (0113 256 9244; Fax: 0113 256 4362). Hon. Secretary: Mr Phil Dyson (0113 256 9244; Fax: 0113 256 4362).

LEEDS. **Cookridge Hall Golf Club,** Cookridge Lane, Leeds LS16 7NL (0113 2300641; Fax: 0113 2030198). *Location:* five miles to north of Leeds, two miles from Leeds and Bradford Airport on Cookridge Lane. Heavily mounded American parkland course. Designed by Karl Litten who designed The Emirates Golf Course in Dubai and The Warwickshire in the West Midlands. 18 holes, 6779 yards, 6000 metres. S.S.S. 72. 20 bay driving range with floodlights. *Green Fees:* weekdays from £19.00; weekends from £24.00. *Eating facilities:* clubhouse with full bar and restaurant. *Visitors:* very welcome, weekends after 2pm tee times can be reserved 7 days in advance, subject to availability. Academy and lessons. *Society Meetings:* all welcome with appropriate advance booking. For information please contact General Manager or Sales Manager.

LEEDS. **Garforth Golf Club Ltd,** Long Lane, Garforth, Leeds LS25 2DS (0113 286 2021). *Location:* six miles east of Leeds on A63, then turn left on to A642. Flat parkland. 18 holes, 6306 yards. S.S.S. 70. Practice area. *Green Fees:* weekdays £36.00 per round, £42.00 per day. *Eating facilities:* available. *Visitors:* welcome, but not before 9.30am or between 12 noon and 2pm (1.30pm Tuesdays and Thursdays). Weekend as member's guest only. *Society Meetings:* catered for. Professional: K. Findlater (0113 286 2063). Managing Secretary: Neil Douglas (Tel & Fax: 0113 286 3308).

LEEDS. **Gotts Park Municipal Golf Club**, Gotts House, Gotts Park, Armley Ridge Road, Leeds LS12 2QX (0113 231 0492). *Location:*two miles west of city centre off A647 Stanningley Road. Undulating parkland. 18 holes, 4319 yards. S.S.S. 64. Putting green and practice area. *Green Fees:* information not available. *Eating facilities:* cafe, bar facilities evenings/weekends only. *Visitors:* welcome, tee reserved Sundays 7am to 10am for members. Professional: J. Marlow (0113 231 1896). Secretary: Maurice Gill (0113 256 2994). *

LEEDS. **Headingley Golf Club,** Back Church Lane, Adel, Leeds LS16 8DW (0113 2673052). *Location:* leave Leeds/Otley road (A660) at Church Lane, Adel about five miles from city centre. 18 holes, 6298 yards. S.S.S. 70. *Green Fees:* £30.00 per round, £35.00 per day weekdays; £40.00 per round or day weekends and Bank Holidays. *Eating facilities:* full catering and bar facilities. *Visitors:* members of other golf clubs welcome, preferably with prior reservation. Two snooker tables. *Society Meetings:* catered for by arrangement. Professional: N.M. Harvey (0113 2675100). Secretary: (0113 2679573; Fax: 0113 2817334). Manager: J.R. Burns (0113 2679573).

LEEDS. **Horsforth Golf Club Ltd,** Layton Rise, Horsforth, Leeds LS18 5EX (0113 258 6819; Fax: 0113 258 9336). *Location:* approximately midway between Leeds and Bradford, close to the Leeds and Bradford Airport. Easily accessible from the Leeds outer ring road and the main Bradford to Harrogate road. Set in open countryside. White tees 6219 yards, Yellow tees 5879, Ladies tees 5435 yards. Par 71. *Green Fees:* weekdays £26.00 per round, £32.00 per day; weekends (limited) £36.00 per day. *Eating facilities:* Bar sevice available from 11.30am to 11pm. Catering ranges from coffees, breakfast, light or full lunches and both buffet and formal evening meals. *Visitors:* welcome, must comply with dress code. *Society Meetings:* welcome. Professionals: Dean Stokes & Simon Booth (0113 258 5200) Steward: Mr C. Taylor (0113 258 1703). Secretary: Mrs L. Harrison (0113 258 6819).
e-mail: secretary@horsforthgolfclubltd.co.uk
website: www.horsforthgolfclubltd.co.uk

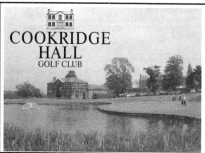

LEEDS. **Howley Hall Golf Club,** Scotchman Lane, Morley, Leeds LS27 0NX (01924 350107; Fax: 01924 350104). *Location:* turn off the A650 Bradford/Wakefield road at the Halfway House Public House, take the B6123 towards Batley – the course is on the left. Parkland. 18 holes, 6346 yards, S.S.S. 71. Practice ground. *Green Fees:* weekdays £30.00 per round, £36.00 per day; weekends £40.00. *Eating facilities:* dining room and bar snacks available. *Visitors:* welcome. *Society Meetings:* welcome by reservation. Professional: Gary Watkinson (01924 350102). Secretary/Manager: David Jones (01924 350100; Fax: 01924 350104).
e-mail: office@howleyhall.co.uk

LEEDS. **Leeds Golf Club,** Cobble Hall, Elmete Lane, Leeds LS8 2LJ (0113 2658775). *Location:* Leeds ring road to A58, turn left if from east, right if from west, fork right at dual carriageway, turn right after 250 yards. 18 holes, 6078 yards. S.S.S. 69. *Green Fees:* £35.00 per day, £30.00 per round weekdays only; weekends with only with a member. Subject to review. Golf packages available with restrictions. *Eating facilities:* full catering, all day bar. *Visitors:* welcome. *Society Meetings:* very welcome. Some limited society days available on Sundays. Professional: Simon Longster (0113 2658786). Secretary: Stephen Clarkson (0113 2659203; Fax: 0113 2323369).

LEEDS. **Middleton Park (Municipal) Golf Club,** Ring Road, Beeston, Middleton, Leeds LS10 3TN (0113 270 0449). *Location:* ring road to Middleton off A653 (Water Tower). Parkland, wooded course. 18 holes, 5036 yards. S.S.S. 66. Practice ground. *Green Fees:* information not provided. *Visitors:* welcome weekdays, contact the Professional for bookings. *Society Meetings:* contact the Professional. Professional: J. Pape (0113 270 9506). Secretary: Mrs Lynn Ratcliffe (0113 277 7715).
e-mail: lynn@ratcliffel.fsnet.co.uk

LEEDS. **Moor Allerton Golf Club,** Coal Road, Wike, Leeds LS17 9NH (0113 2661154; Fax: 0113 2371124). *Location:* A61 from Leeds city centre, north to Alwoodley then Scarcroft. Undulating parkland, championship course designed by Robert Trent Jones. 27 holes - three loops of 9 holes. Any combination playable. 6 bay driving range, practice ground. *Green Fees:* information not available. *Eating facilities:* full restaurant facilities plus snack bar. *Visitors:* welcome but must pre-book via Professional Shop. No visitors Sundays. Crown bowling green and sauna. Banqueting facilities for 160 people; conference/room hire for groups of all sizes. *Society Meetings:* welcome by prior arrangement via club office. Professional: Richard Lane (0113 2665209) Secretary/Manager: Mr N.C. Lomas (0113 2661154; Fax: 0113 2371124).*
e-mail: moorallerton.demon.co.uk

LEEDS. **Moortown Golf Club**, Harrogate Road, Alwoodley, Leeds LS17 7DB (0113 2686521; Fax: 0113 2680986). *Location:* five miles north of Leeds centre, A61 Leeds to Harrogate road. 18 holes, 6453 yards. S.S.S. 72. Large practice field. *Green Fees:* weekdays £60.00 per round/day, weekends and Bank Holidays £70.00 per round/day. *Eating facilities:* lunches every day, evening meals Tuesday to Saturday. *Visitors:* welcome weekdays, some tee-off time restrictions. *Society Meetings:* catered for. Professional:M. Heggie (0113 2683636). Secretary: K.C. Bradley (0113 2686521).

LEEDS. **Oulton Park**, Rothwell Lane, Rothwell, Leeds LS26 8EX (0113 282 3152; Fax: 0113 282 6290). *Location:* M62 - Rothwell turn off, Junction 30; left at second roundabout. Parkland course built by Dave Thomas, many bunkers. 27 holes, 22 bay driving range, putting green. *Green Fees:* information not available. *Eating facilities:* restaurant and bar. *Visitors:* welcome, no restrictions; advance booking (five days) available. Dress code on course. *Society Meetings:* welcome except weekends. Professional: Steve Gromett. Manager: Allan Cooper.*

LEEDS. **Rawdon Golf and Lawn Tennis Club,** Buckstone Drive, Micklefield Lane, Rawdon, Leeds LS19 6BD (0113-250 6040). *Location:* eight miles north of Leeds on A65, left at Rawdon traffic lights on to Micklefield Lane. Undulating parkland, with trees a special feature. 9 holes (18 tees), 5964 yards. S.S.S. 69. *Green Fees:* information not available. *Eating facilities:* meals and bar snacks except Mondays. *Visitors:* welcome. Facilities for tennis, visitors welcome. *Society Meetings:* catered for on application to Secretary. Secretary: Ray Adams (0113-250 6064).*

LEEDS. **Roundhay Golf Club,** Park Lane, Leeds LS8 2EJ (0113 2662695). *Location:* four miles north of Leeds city centre, leave A58 to Wetherby at Oakwood. Wooded parkland. 9 holes, 5322 yards. S.S.S. 65. Practice ground. *Green Fees:* on application. *Eating facilities:* bar for members and guests, restaurant in evenings. *Visitors:* welcome without reservation. *Society Meetings:* arrangements to be made with Leeds City Council. Professional: J. Pape (0113 2661686). Hon. Secretary: R.H. McLauchlan (0113 2664225).

LEEDS. **Sand Moor Golf Club**, Alwoodley Lane, Leeds LS17 7DJ (0113 2681685). *Location:* five miles north of Leeds off A61. Moorland, overlooking picturesque Wharfedale. 18 holes, 6414 yards, 5862 metres. S.S.S. 71. *Green Fees:* information on request. *Eating facilities:* lunches daily, evening meals by arrangement. *Visitors:* welcome most weekdays and Sundays by arrangement. *Society Meetings:* catered for by arrangement. Professional: Peter Tupling (0113 2683925). Secretary: Ian Kerr (0113 2685180; Fax: 0113 2661105).

LEEDS. **Scarcroft Golf Club,** Syke Lane, Leeds LS14 3BQ (0113 289 2263). *Location:* A58 Wetherby road; turn left at Bracken Fox Public House, Scarcroft village seven miles north of Leeds. Undulating parkland. 18 holes, 6426 yards. S.S.S. 71. Practice ground. *Green Fees:* information not available. *Eating facilities:* bar and restaurant except Mondays. *Visitors:* casuals after 9.30am. *Society Meetings:* accepted Mondays to Fridays April to October. Must have official Handicaps. Party rates for groups of 20 or more. Professional: Darren Tear (0113 289 2780). General Manager: Darren Tear (0113 289 2311).*

LEEDS. **South Leeds Golf Club,** Parkside Links, Gipsy Lane, Leeds LS11 5TU (0113 270 0479). *Location:* M62 and M1 within five minutes' drive, Leeds City Centre 5 minutes' drive. Parkland course with undulating fairways. 18 holes, 5769 yards. S.S.S. 69. Practice ground and net. *Green Fees:* £18.00 weekdays; £32.00 weekends and Bank Holidays (rates may change). *Eating facilities:* full catering except Mondays; bar. *Visitors:* welcome weekdays. *Society Meetings:* catered for by prior arrangement. Professional: Mike Lewis (0113 270 2598). Secretary: John Neal (0113 277 1676).

LEEDS. **Temple Newsam Golf Club,** Temple Newsam, Leeds LS15 0NL (0113 264 5624). *Location:* easily reached by public transport from City (to Temple Newsam or Halton). Two 18 hole courses. No. 1 Course 6448 yards. S.S.S. 71. No. 2 Course 5731 yards. S.S.S. 70. *Green Fees:* as decided by City Council. *Eating facilities:* cafe open six days a week 7.30am till 4.00pm weekends, 10.00am till 4.00pm midweek. *Visitors:* welcome without reservation, except that parties must book in advance. *Society Meetings:* catered for. Professional: A. Swain (0113 264 1464). Secretary: G. Gower. *

MIRFIELD. **Dewsbury District Golf Club**, The Pinnacle, Sands Lane, Mirfield WF14 8HJ (01924 491928). *Location:* turn off A644 opposite Swan Inn, two miles west of Dewsbury. Undulating moorland/parkland with panoramic views over surrounding countryside. 18 holes, 6360 yards. S.S.S. 71. Practice field, putting green. *Green Fees:* weekdays £18.00 per round, £24.00 per day; weekends £15.00 after 3pm. Subject to review. *Eating facilities:* bar and restaurant (catering every day). *Visitors:* welcome without reservation weekdays, weekends with member only before 4pm. *Society Meetings:* welcome by prior arrangement. Parties over 12 - day £20.50 per person. Professional: N.P. Hirst (01924 496030). General Manager: Ray Dando (01924 492399).
e-mail: dewsbury.golf@btopenworld.com

OTLEY. **Otley Golf Club,** West Busk Lane, Otley LS21 3NG (01943 465329). *Location:* off main Bradford to Otley road. Parkland with magnificent views across Wharfedale. 18 holes, 6256 yards. S.S.S. 70. Large practice ground. *Green Fees:* weekdays £29.00 for 18 or 27 holes, £36.00 for two rounds; weekends £36.00 for 18 or 27 holes, £42.00 for two rounds. *Eating facilities:* large dining rooms. *Visitors:* welcome without reservation except Tuesday mornings and Saturdays. Trolleys and clubs for hire. *Society Meetings:* catered for by arrangement; special facilities for company days. Professional: Steven Tomkinson (01943 465329 ext. 203; Fax: 01943 463403). Secretary/Manager: Peter J. Clarke (01943 465329 ext 202; Fax: 01943 850387).

OUTLANE. **Outlane Golf Club,** Slack Lane, off New Hey Road, Outlane, Near Huddersfield HD3 3YL (01422 374762; Fax: 01422 311789). *Location:* from Huddersfield (A640) through Outlane Village, entrance on left just after bus terminus. Semi-moorland course, part wooded. Offers panoramic views and is challenge to the amateur. 18 holes, 6100 yards. S.S.S. 69. Practice areas and nets available. *Green Fees:* £19.00 mid week; £29.00 weekends and Bank Holidays. Reduced rates playing with member and after 1pm Sundays. *Eating facilities:* full catering available except Mondays. *Visitors:* welcome except Saturdays; Sundays by arrangement. Carts available. *Society Meetings:* welcome with reservation. Professional: D.M. Chapman (01422 374762; Fax: 01422 311789). Secretary: P. Jackson (Tel & Fax: 01422 311789). Stewardess: Mrs C.E. Hirst.

PONTEFRACT near. **Mid-Yorkshire Golf Club,** Havercroft Lane, Darrington, Near Pontefract (01977 704522; Fax: 01977 600823). *Location:* 300 yards from A1 at Darrington half-mile south of A1/M62 interchange. Undulating with established woodland and lakes. 18 holes, 6424 yards. Par 72. 23 bay floodlit driving range, tee to green irrigation, 18 greens played all year round. *Green Fees:* information not provided. *Eating facilities:* two bars with private functions catered for. *Visitors:* welcome weekdays, afternoons only at weekends. Buggies available. *Society Meetings:* welcome weekdays. Professional: Mike Hessay (01977 600844). Secretary: Linda Darwood.
website: www.midyorkshiregolfclub.com

See also Colour Advertisement on page 49

PONTEFRACT. **Pontefract and District Golf Club,** Park Lane, Pontefract WF8 4QS (01977 792241). *Location:* M62 Exit 32, one mile from Pontefract on B6134. Parkland. 18 holes, 6227 yards. S.S.S. 70. Practice ground. *Green Fees:* weekdays £22.00 per round, £28.00 per day; weekends £32.00. *Eating facilities:* available all week. *Visitors:* welcome. *Society Meetings:* catered for Mondays, Tuesdays, Thursdays and Fridays by arrangement. Professional: Nick J. Newman (01977 706806). Manager: (01977 792241).
e-mail: manager@pdgc.co.uk
website: www.pdgc.co.uk

PUDSEY. **Fulneck Golf Club Ltd,** Fulneck, Pudsey LS28 8NT (0113 2565191). *Location:* between Leeds and Bradford. Undulating wooded parkland course. 9 holes, 5456 yards. S.S.S. 67. *Green Fees:* £15.00 (£8.00 with member) weekdays, weekends with a member only. *Society Meetings:* catered for by arrangement. Secretary: Mrs P.A. Warburton (0113 2562606).

PUDSEY. **Woodhall Hills Golf Club Ltd,** Woodhall Road, Calverley, Pudsey, Leeds LS28 5UN (0113 256 4771). *Location:* signposted Calverley from A647 Leeds to Bradford Road, quarter of a mile beyond Calverley Golf Club. Parkland course. 18 holes, 6184 yards. S.S.S. 70. *Green Fees:* information not available. *Eating facilities:* available daily except Mondays. *Visitors:* welcome without reservation. *Society Meetings:* catered for by previous arrangement. Golf Manager/Professional: W. Lockett (0113 256 2857). Club Office: (0113 255 4594).*

SHIPLEY. **Marriott Hollins Hall Hotel & Country Club**, Hollins Hill, Baildon, Shipley BD17 7QW (01274 534212). Home to the PGA European Professional Tour. *Location:* North/South Leeds Ring Road, take A65 Skipton Road, then A6038 (towards Shipley), entrance on right. Superb championship heathland course in the beautiful Yorkshire Dales. 18 holes. Par 71. *Green Fees:* information not available. *Eating facilities:* available all day. *Visitors:* welcome. Trolley, buggy and shoe hire. *

TODMORDEN. **Todmorden Golf Club**, Rive Rocks, Cross Stone Road, Todmorden OL14 8RD (01706 812986). *Location:* A646 Halifax Road, half a mile left Cross Stone Road, half a mile, bear left at top. Moorland. 9 holes, 5902 yards. S.S.S. 68. *Green Fees:* weekdays £15.00; weekends and Bank Holidays £20.00. Packages (18 or 27 holes from £25.00) available Monday, Tuesday, Wednesday and Sunday, includes coffee and biscuits on arrival, soup and sandwiches, evening meal. *Eating facilities:* available, order in advance. *Visitors:* welcome without reservation, but advisable to phone beforehand. Thursday is Ladies' Day. *Society Meetings:* welcome, please phone for course availability.

WAKEFIELD. **City of Wakefield Golf Club,** Lupset Park, Horbury Road, Wakefield WF2 8QS (01924 360282). *Location:* one mile from city centre, two miles from M1 Junctions 39/40. Undulating partially wooded parkland. 18 holes, 6319 yards, 5760 metres. S.S.S. 70. *Green Fees:* on application. *Eating facilities:* full or snack catering, bar available. *Visitors:* weekdays ball chute operates, weekends booked times only. *Society Meetings:* only by arrangement with Stewardess (01924 367242). Professional: Roger Holland (01924 360282). Secretary: Mrs P. Ambler (01924 367442).

WAKEFIELD. **Lofthouse Hill Golf Club,** Wakefield Road, Wakefield WF3 3LR (Tel & Fax: 01924 823703). *Location*: A61 between Leeds and Wakefield. New parkland course. 18 holes, 5933 yards, S.S.S. 68. Driving Range. *Green Fees:* £10.00. *Eating facilities*: food available all day in bar. *Visitors:* welcome, please telephone. Teaching professional. *Society Meetings*: welcome, see website. Professional: Derek Johnson (Tel & Fax: 01924 823703). Secretary: David Nicklin.
website: www. lofthousehillgolfclub.co.uk

WAKEFIELD. **Low Laithes Golf Club Ltd,** Parkmill Lane, Flushdyke, Ossett, Wakefield WF5 9AP (01924 273275). *Location:* one mile from Junction 40 M1, or along A638 Dewsbury to Wakefield road. Parkland, undulating. 18 holes, 6456 yards. S.S.S. 71. Practice area. *Green Fees:* information not available. *Eating facilities:* bar and catering. *Visitors:* welcome weekdays after 9.30am to 12 noon and after 1.30pm weekends and Bank Holidays. *Society Meetings:* by arrangement, not weekends or Bank Holidays - 27 holes and catering. Professional: Paul Browning (01924 274667). Secretary: Paul Browning (Tel & Fax: 01924 266067). *

WAKEFIELD. **Normanton Golf Club,** Hatfeild Hall. Aberford Road, Stanley WF3 4JP (01924 377943; Fax: 01924 200777). *Location:* M62 Junction 30, A642 toward Wakefield. Parkland course. Practice area. 18 holes, 6191 yards, 5662 metres. S.S.S. 70. *Green Fees:* information not available. *Visitors:* welcome weekdays. Saturday limited access. Sundays after 3.30 pm. *Society Meetings:* welcome during the week. Restricted at weekend. Professional: F. Houlgate (01924 200900). General Manager (01924 377943).

THE APPEARANCE OF AN ASTERISK * AT THE END OF A CLUB OR COURSE ENTRY INDICATES THAT UP-TO-DATE INFORMATION HAS NOT BEEN SUPPLIED

WAKEFIELD. **Painthorpe House Golf and Country Club,** Painthorpe Lane, Crigglestone, Wakefield WF4 5AZ (01924 255083; Fax: 01924 252022). *Location:* half a mile from Junction 39 M1. Undulating parkland. 9 holes, 4548 yards. S.S.S. 62. *Green Fees:* weekdays £6.00, weekends £7.00. *Eating facilities:* four bars, extensive catering for private functions. Two ballrooms (one holding 450, the other 60), Saturday dinner dances. *Visitors:* welcome, by appointment if parties, after 1.30pm on a Sunday. Bowling green. *Society Meetings:* by arrangement. Secretary: H. Kershaw (01924 274527; Fax: 01924 252022).

WAKEFIELD. **Wakefield Golf Club,** Woodthorpe Lane, Sandal, Wakefield WF2 6JH (01924 258778; Fax: 01924 242752). *Location:* leave M1 at Junction 39, golf club off Barnsley Road. Parkland. 18 holes, 6653 yards. S.S.S. 72. *Green Fees:* weekdays £30.00 per round, £35.00 per day, with a member £12.00 per day; weekends and Bank Holidays £40.00, with a member £20.00. *Eating facilities:* full catering available. *Visitors:* visiting parties by arrangement Wednesdays, Thursdays and Fridays. *Society Meetings:* welcome, catered for by arrangement. Professional: I.M. Wright (01924 255380). Secretary: A..J. McVicar (01924 258778).

WAKEFIELD. **Woolley Park Golf Club,** 2 Home Farm, Woolley, Wakefield WF4 2JS (01226 380144; Fax: 01226 390295; 01226 382209 (Office)). *Location:* half a mile from A61 half way between Barnsley and Wakefield. Parkland course. 18 holes, 6606 yards (white tees), S.S.S. 72. Practice area, putting green. *Green Fees:* weekdays £16.00; weekends £24.00. *Eating facilities:* food available all day every day, bar. *Visitors:* welcome all week, weekend bookings from Thursday only. Tuition available. *Society Meetings:* welcome, please telephone for details. Professional: Jon Baldwin (01226 380144; Fax: 01226 390295). Secretary: David Rowbottom (01226 382209; Fax: 01226 390295).
website: www.woolleypark.co.uk.

WETHERBY. **Wetherby Golf Club,** Linton Lane, Linton, Wetherby LS22 4JF (01937 582527; Fax: 01937 581915). *Location:* three quarters of a mile west from A1 roundabout. Parkland course adjoining River Wharfe. 18 holes, 6213 yards. S.S.S. 70. Practice ground. *Green Fees:* weekdays £28.00 per round, £35.00 per day; weekends £40.00 per round/day. *Eating facilities:* available seven days a week. *Visitors:* welcome, advisable to phone first. *Society Meetings:* catered for weekdays except Tuesday mornings. Professional: Mark Daubney (01937 583375). Golf Club Manager: Barry Groves (01937 580089).

N O T E

All the information regarding Golf Clubs in this guide is given in good faith in the belief that it is correct. However, the publishers cannot guarantee the facts given in these pages, neither are they responsible for changes in ownership or facilities, such as green fees, that may take place after the date of going to press. Readers should always satisfy themselves that the facilities they require are available and that the terms, if quoted, still apply.

Golf in Scotland

WHERE TO PLAY •
WHERE TO STAY

The scenery and hospitality alone are reasons enough to plan a visit to Scotland but when you add the quality and variety of courses available, what more could you ask for? With more than its fair share of championship courses, Scotland has always had the claim to fame of being the 'home' of golf. With most of the top courses such as St Andrews, Turnberry, Gleneagles, Royal Dornoch etc. all willing to allow access to visitors, golfers might be forgiven for trying to pick only the 'known' courses, but remember there is a huge variety available, each with its own unique challenge and often a 'hidden gem' can be found where the course is less busy but the golf is just as good. Try an 'Augusta Style' par 3 at Letham Grange, or enjoy a walk on a footbridge over the river Tay at Aberfeldy or try not to be distracted by the scenery at Callander or Boat of Garten, the list is endless.

A book which readers of *The Golf Guide* may find to be of interest is '*The Wee Yellow Book*'.

This publication, produced by Les Starkings as a hobby over 15 years ago, contains details of Open Competitions throughout Scotland, giving golfers a chance to plan their season and visit new courses, playing in tournaments ranging from Scratch Opens, Senior Opens, Mixed Foursomes, Ladies and Junior Opens etc.

Making use of *The Golf Guide* to give you information on the course, including contact details etc., you can decide which courses you would like to visit and check the 'Wee Yellow Book' to see when a suitable tournament is being run.

'*The Wee Yellow Book*' is available from most clubs or in case of difficulty contact:

The Star-King Press, 31 Curriehill Castle Drive, Balerno, Edinburgh EH14 5TA Tel & Fax: 0131 451 5782 e-mait lstarkings@btinternet.com or les@weeyellowbook.com.

In recent years the Scottish Wee Yellow Book has been joined by Wee Blue Books for English regions and a Wee Red Book for Wales.

HISTORIC HOTELS
with great golf on your doorstep

If you're looking for great golf in superb surroundings, head for Macdonald Hotels in Scotland's magnificent North East corner, home to some of the country's best courses.

Ardoe House, Blairs, Aberdeen

Four of our finest hotels blend history and character with every modern luxury and offer superb facilities including award-winning restaurants and exclusive health and leisure spas.

Choose from Ardoe House on the banks of the River Dee upstream from Balmoral Castle, or 17th century Pittodrie House set in 2,000 glorious acres. Head for the rural hideaway of Thainstone House in private parkland, or the more modern comforts of Waterside Inn on the banks of the River Ugie a few miles from Peterhead.

Pittodrie House, Inverurie

Thainstone House, Inverurie

Whatever your choice, the warmest hospitality is guaranteed with unrivalled golf on your doorstep. Welcome to golf at Macdonald Hotels.

For information and reservations call
Ardoe House - 01224 860 600
Pittodrie House - 01467 681 444
Thainstone House - 01467 621 643
Waterside Inn - 01779 471 121

MACDONALD
HOTELS

See also Colour Advertisement on page 64

Waterside Inn, near Peterhead

Aberdeenshire, Banff & Moray

ABERDEEN. **Auchmill Golf Club**, Bonnyview Road, West Heatheryfold, Aberdeen AB2 7FQ (01224 715214). *Location:* approximately four miles from city centre, beside Bucksburn area. Parkland, wooded course. 18 holes. S.S.S. 70. Practice drive and putting. *Green Fees:* £11.25. *Eating facilities:* private club, municipal course, pre-arrange any meals. *Visitors:* welcome anytime. Secretary: S. Marr (01224 692570).

ABERDEEN. **Balnagask Golf Course**, City of Aberdeen District Council, Arts and Recreation Division, St. Nicholas House, Broad Street, Aberdeen AB9 1XJ (01224 276276). *Location:* on coast beside Girdleness Lighthouse between Aberdeen Harbour and Nigg Bay, south side of city. Seaside links. 18 holes, 5472 metres. *Green Fees:* information not available. *Visitors:* welcome. Starter: (01224 876407).*

ABERDEEN. **Bon Accord Municipal Golf Club**, 19 Golf Road, Aberdeen AB24 5QB (01224 633464). *Location:* next to Pittodrie Stadium at Aberdeen beach. Seaside links. 18 holes, 6300 yards. S.S.S. 69. *Green Fees:* information not available. *Eating facilities:* meals on request. *Visitors:* welcome; please call starters box (01224 632269) for information regarding booking of tee times and green fees. *Society Meetings:* bookings in advance. Secretary: Frank N. Shand.

Visitor's Package
5 days unlimited golf
• Auchmill Golf Course
• Balnagask Golf Courses
• Hazlehead Golf Courses
• Kings Links Golf Courses

Aberdeen City Golf

Visitor's Package only £50 when you quote "Golf Guide"

Special Offer

01224 647647
for further info

ABERDEEN CITY COUNCIL

See also Colour Advertisement on page 71

ABERDEEN. **Caledonian Golf Club**, 20 Golf Road, Aberdeen AB24 5QB (01224 632443). *Location:* 50 yards to right of Richard Donald Stand/Pittodrie Football Club. Seaside links. 18 holes, 6437 yards. S.S.S. 69. 6 hole course; driving range nearby. *Green Fees:* information not available. *Eating facilities:* clubhouse snacks and meals. *Visitors:* welcome. Entertainment is provided in clubrooms on Fridays and Saturdays for members and their guests. Secretary: D. Esson.*

ABERDEEN. **Deeside Golf Club**, Golf Road, Bieldside, Aberdeen AB15 9DL (01224 867697). *Location:* A93 from Aberdeen to Braemar. Wooded parkland. 18 holes, 6264 yards. S.S.S. 70. Also 9 hole course, 3316 yards. S.S.S. 36. Practice ground. *Green Fees:* information not available. *Eating facilities:* full catering and bar facilities. *Visitors:* welcome weekdays up to 4pm, weekends after 4pm. *Society Meetings:* by arrangement, Thursday afternoons only. Professional: F.J. Coutts (01224 861041). Managing Secretary: J.W. Keepe (Tel & Fax: 01224 869457).
e-mail: dgc@bieldside28.freeserve.co.uk
website: www.deesidegolfclub.com

ABERDEEN. **Hazlehead Golf Course**, City of Aberdeen District Council, Arts and Recreation Division, St. Nicholas House, Broad Street, Aberdeen AB9 1XJ (01224 276276). *Location:* situated on west edge of city, four miles from city centre. From A944 into Aberdeen turn off into Groats Road. Two courses - 18 holes, 5673 metres; 18 holes, 5303 metres. 9 hole course, 2531 metres. *Green Fees:* information not available. *Eating facilities:* restaurant adjoining park. *Visitors:* welcome. Professional: Mr I. Smith (01224 317336). Starter: (01224 321830).*

ABERDEEN. **Murcar Golf Club,** Bridge of Don, Aberdeen AB23 8BD (01224 704354). *Location:* A90 Aberdeen - Fraserburgh Road, 5 miles north of Aberdeen city centre. Championship seaside links. 18 holes, 6314 yards. S.S.S. 72; Strabathie 9-hole course, 5369 yards. S.S.S 66. Practice ground. *Green Fees:* Murcar, weekdays £50.00 per round, £70.00 per day; weekends £60.00 per round, £80.00 per day after 11am Sundays. Strabathie, weekdays £10.00 per 9 holes, £25.00 per day; weekends £15.00 per 9 holes, £35.00 per day. *Eating facilities:* dining room/bars. *Visitors:* welcome by advance booking. Hand trolleys for hire. *Society Meetings:* catered for by advance booking. Professional: Gary Forbes (Tel & Fax: 01224 704370). Secretary/Manager: Barbara Rogerson (Tel & Fax: 01224 704354).
e-mail: golf@murcar.co.uk
website: www.murcar.co.uk.

visit the FHG golf website on
www.uk-golfguide.com

ABERDEEN. **Nigg Bay Golf Club,** St. Fitticks Road, Torry, Aberdeen AB1 3QT (01224 871286; Fax: 01224 873418). *Location:* junction of Victoria Road and St. Fitticks Road. Seaside links, hills and hidden holes. 18 holes, 5986 yards, 5472 metres. S.S.S. 69. 9 hole pitch and putt. *Green Fees:* on request, municipal course. *Eating facilities:* full catering facilities. *Visitors:* welcome anytime (Municipal course); golfers welcome in clubhouse after playing. Secretary: Alan Fraser.

ABERDEEN. **Northern Golf Club** 22 Golf Road, Aberdeen AB24 5QB (01224 636440; Fax: 01224 622679). *Location:* Golf Road, opposite Pittodrie Stadium. 18 holes, 5731 metres. S.S.S. 70. 6 hole course, 1251 metres; driving range next door. *Green Fees:* information not available. *Visitors:* welcome, book in person on the day of play. Public bookings restricted on Saturdays for club matches. *Society Meetings:* all welcome by writing to Aberdeen District Council (14 days notice). Professional: Mr B. Davidson (01224 641577). Secretary: Alfred Garner (Tel & Fax: 01224 622679). Steward: (01224 636440).*

ABERDEEN. **Royal Aberdeen Golf Club,** Links Road, Balgownie, Bridge of Don AB23 8AT (01224 702571; Fax: 01224 826591). *Location:* on A92 Aberdeen/Fraserburgh Road, cross Bridge of Don, second right. Seaside links. Two Courses - Championship (Balgownie): 18 holes, 6372 yards, 5828 metres. S.S.S. 72; Silverburn: 18 holes, 4021 yards, 3717 metres. S.S.S. 61. Practice putting green. *Green Fees:* information not available. *Eating facilities:* Old Bar, main lounge and dining room - jacket and tie. *Visitors:* welcome weekdays 10am to 11.30am and 2pm to 3.30pm, weekends after 3.30pm. Letter of introduction or Handicap Certificate required. Hire carts. *Society Meetings:* welcome. Professional/ Director of Golf: Ronnie MacAskill (01224 702221; Fax: 01224 826591). Exe. Secretary: Sandra Nicholson.*

ABERDEEN. **Tarland Golf Club,** Aberdeen Road, Tarland, Aboyne AB34 4TB (Tel & Fax: 013398 81000). *Location:* six miles north of Aboyne on A93, 30 miles west of Aberdeen on B9119. Difficult upland course in picturesque scenery. 9 holes, 5816 yards for 18 holes, S.S.S. 68. Small practice area. *Green Fees:* weekdays £15.00 per day; weekends £20.00. Weekly tickets £75.00, fortnightly tickets £120.00. *Eating facilities:* catering available, bar 11am to midnight. *Visitors:* welcome without reservation but phone call advisable due to club competitions at weekends. *Society Meetings:* catered for with prior reservation at all times. Secretary: Mrs V. Ward (013398 81967).

ABOYNE. **Aboyne Golf Club,** Formaston Park, Aboyne AB34 5HP (013398 86328). *Location:* A93, 30 miles west of Aberdeen. Part parkland, part hilly with lovely views. 18 holes, 5944 yards. S.S.S. 69. Practice ground. *Green Fees:* weekdays £20.00 per round, £25.00 per day; weekends £25.00 per round, £30.00 per day. *Eating facilities:* full restaurant and bar facilities. *Visitors:* welcome without reservation. *Society Meetings:* by arrangement with Secretary. Professional: Steven Moir. (013398 86328). Secretary: (013398 87078; Fax: 013398 87592). e-mail: aboynegolf@btinternet.com website: www.aboynegolf.com

ALFORD. **Alford Golf Club,** Montgarrie Road, Alford AB33 8AE (Tel & Fax: 019755 62178; Fax: 019755 64910). *Location:* A944, 26 miles west of Aberdeen. Flat, parkland course. 18 holes, 5483 yards. S.S.S. 66. Practice area. *Green Fees:* £13.00 per round, £19.00 per day weekdays; £20.00 per round, £26.00 per day weekends. Subject to review. *Eating facilities:* catering and bar services available. *Visitors:* always welcome; call club to book tee, weekends very busy. Changing rooms and showers. Buggy Hire available. *Society Meetings:* welcome by prior arrangement. Catering available. Secretary: Irene Currie. e-mail: info@alford-golf-club.co.uk website: www.golf.alford.co.uk

AUCHENBLAE. **Auchenblae Golf Course,** Auchenblae Parks Committee, Linwood, Auchenblae AB30 1WQ. *Location:* five miles north of Laurencekirk, off A90, two miles west of Fordoun. Parkland. 9 holes, 4434 yards SSS 61. *Green Fees:* £12.00 (concessions). *Eating facilities:* shop open April to October. *Visitors:* welcome. Telephone Pavilion (01561 320002) for details of club nights and current information. Trolleys for hire. *Society Meetings:* welcome. Treasurer: J.M. Thomson (01561 320245).

BALLATER. **Ballater Golf Club,** Victoria Road, Ballater AB35 5QX (013397 55567; Fax: 013397 55057). *Location*: A93, 42 miles west of Aberdeen and 62 miles from Perth. Flat picturesque parkland course close to Balmoral Castle. 18 holes, 5638 yards. S.S.S. 67. Practice ground, putting. *Green Fees:* information not available. *Eating facilities*: full catering and refreshments April to October. *Visitors:* all welcome, booking well in advance is advisable. Tennis, bowling. *Society Meetings:* all welcome, book well in advance. Professional: Bill Yule (013397 55658). Secretary: Mr A.E. Barclay (013397 55567; Fax: 013397 55057).* e-mail: sec@ballatergolfclub.co.uk website: www.ballatergolfclub.co.uk

BALMEDIE. **East Aberdeenshire Golf Centre,** Millden, Balmedie AB23 8YY (01358 742111; Fax: 01358 742123). *Location*: 3 miles from the Aberdeen Exhibition Centre, on left side of road before you reach Balmedie, on the Peterhead/Fraserburgh road. Parkland course. 18 holes, 6276 yards, S.S.S. 71. 16 bay floodlit driving range, practice chipping green, 5 hole Par 3 course. *Green Fees*: information not available. *Eating facilities*: bar, restaurant, function room, all with public house licence. *Visitors*: welcome any time, no jeans on course please. *Society Meetings*: welcome, midweek rate includes tea/coffee, bacon roll, 18 holes, two-course meal plus five free buggies. Professional: Ian Bratton (01358 742111). Secretary: Kevin Forrest (01358 742111).* e-mail: info@eagolf.com AND kevin@eagolf.com website: www.eagolf.com

Inchmarlo Royal Deeside

Inchmarlo Royal Deeside, Banchory, is a relatively new golf attraction to the North East of Scotland.

Inchmarlo Royal Deeside

Ponds, meandering burns and even dry stone walls, combine with the more traditional bunkers to test the skill of even the most accomplished player, at the same time rewarding the accuracy of the short game expert. The Laird's Course opened for play in July 2001 and at 6218 yards, this championship standard par 71 course is set to be one of Scotland's most sought after golfing venues, complementing the existing nine hole course and the Centre's other facilities, including tuition from a team of PGA Professionals.

View from 2nd Tee

Catering for all age groups, the recently refurbished Golf Professional's shop is stocked with all the latest in golf fashion.

Golf Professional's Shop

Cuisine of the highest standard is available in our various bars and restaurant, and a warm and friendly welcome is assured.

Classic Golf Course design, stunning scenery, excellent facilities....
The Laird's at Inchmarlo is ready for the challenge - are you?

For further details contact Hector Emslie
Tel: 01330 826424
e-mail: info@inchmarlo.com • website: www.inchmarlo.com

See also Colour Advertisement on page 66

BANCHORY. **Banchory Golf Club**, Kinneskie Road, Banchory AB31 5TA (01330 822365; Fax: 01330 822491). *Location:* 100 yards off the A93 Aberdeen to Braemar Road. Flat parkland course, several holes on the banks of the River Dee. 18 holes, 5781 yards. S.S.S. 68. Practice ground and putting green. *Green Fees:* weekdays £20.00 per round, £28.00 per day; weekends £23.00 per round. Weekly ticket available £80.00, 7 month season ticket £260.00, 12 monthly season ticket £300.00. *Eating facilities:* attractive lounge and dining room. *Visitors:* welcome any time, restrictions on Tuesdays and weekends. *Society Meetings:* welcome except Tuesdays and weekends. Professional: David Naylor (Tel & Fax: 01330 822447). Secretary: William Crighton (01330 822377; Fax: 01330 822491).
e-mail: info@banchorygolfclub.co.uk
website: www.banchorygolfclub.co.uk

BANCHORY. **Inchmarlo Golf Centre**, Glassel Road, Inchmarlo AB31 4BQ (Tel & Fax: 01330 826424). *Location:* half a mile from A93 Aberdeen-Braemar road, 25 minutes from Aberdeen city centre. 9-hole course: beautiful but tricky parkland course, 4300 yards, S.S.S. 62, Par 64. 18 hole championship Laird's Course, 6394 yards, Par 71, S.S.S. 71. 30-bay floodlit driving range. *Green Fees:* Laird's Course: £25.00 weekdays, £30.00 weekends. 9 hole course £10.00 for 9 holes, £15.00 for 18 holes weekdays; £11.00 for 9 holes, £17.00 for 18 holes weekends. *Eating facilities:* restaurant, function/conference room, choice of bars. *Visitors:* very welcome any time, advisable to book in advance. *Society Meetings:* welcome all year by prior arrangement. Secretary: Andrew Shinie.
e-mail: info@inchmarlo.com
website: www.inchmarlo.com

BANCHORY. **Lumphanan Golf Club**, Main Road, Lumphanan, Banchory AB31 4PW (01339 883480). *Location:* situated on the road between Torphins and Lumphanan about 10 miles from Banchory. Hilly, quiet, village course. 9 holes, 3718 yards, S.S.S 62. Course re-designed in 2000. *Green Fees:* £8.00 per round, £12.00 per day; weekends £10.00 per round, £15.00 per day. *Eating facilities:* clubhouse/bar open weekends and some evenings; food available weekends only. *Visitors:* welcome - no need to book. *Society Meetings:* outings welcome by arrangement with Secretary. Secretary: Pamela Thorn (01339 883589).
e-mail: lumphanan.golf.club@lineone.net
website: www.lineone.net/~lumphanan.golf.club

BANFF. **Duff House Royal Golf Club,** The Barnyards, Banff AB45 3SX (01261 812062; Fax: 01261 812224). *Location:* two minutes from town centre, A97, A98. Level parkland. 18 holes, 6161 yards. S.S.S. 70. Practice putting area. *Green Fees:* information not provided. *Eating facilities:* lounge bar and full catering service. *Visitors:* welcome weekdays after 9.30am, restrictions at weekends but times available. Pro shop. *Society Meetings:* catered for by prior arrangement. Professional: R.S. Strachan (01261 812075). Secretary: H. Liebnitz (01261 812062).
e-mail: duff_house_royal@btinternet.com

BRAEMAR. **Braemar Golf Club**, Cluniebank Road, Braemar AB35 5XX (013397 41618). *Location:* about one mile from centre of the village, signposted opposite Fife Arms Hotel. Flat parkland, highest 18 hole course in Scotland, course split in two by River Clunie. 18 holes, 5030 yards. S.S.S. 64. *Green Fees:* weekdays £20.00 per round, £25.00 per day; weekends £23.00 per round, £28.00 per day. Weekly ticket £80.00. Special rates for parties of more than 12. *Eating facilities:* full bar and catering facilities. *Visitors:* No restrictions on visitors but advisable to 'phone in advance' for weekends. *Society Meetings:* welcome - book through Secretary. Secretary: Colin McIntosh (013397 41595).

BUCKIE. **Buckpool Golf Club (Buckie)**, Barhill Road, Buckie AB56 1DU (Tel & Fax: 01542 832236). *Location:* turn off A98 signposted Buckpool. Links course with superlative view over Moray Firth. 18 holes, 6257 yards. S.S.S. 70. Putting green and net area. *Green Fees:* weekdays £15.00 per round, £20.00 per day, Senior Citizens £13.00 per round; weekends £20.00 per round, £25.00 per day. Reductions during winter months and for Juniors, discounts for parties. *Eating facilities:* full catering daily, normal bar hours. *Visitors:* no restrictions except when there are scheduled competitions and visiting parties; advisable to telephone first. Two changing rooms with showers, etc; snooker, pool and squash. *Society Meetings:* welcome by prior arrangement. Secretary: Miss Myra Coull (Tel & Fax: 01542 832236).

BUCKIE. **Strathlene Golf Club**, Portessie, Buckie AB56 2DJ (01542 831798). *Location:* equidistant between Aberdeen and Inverness. Raised links course which follows the natural contours of the land. 18 holes, 5996 yards. S.S.S 69. Practice facilities. *Green Fees:* information not available. *Eating facilities:* summer catering and all-day bar. *Visitors:* prior booking advised; avoid Saturday and Sunday mornings. Locker room. *Society Meetings:* booking required. Secretary: George Jappy (01542 831798). *

BUCKSBURN. **Craibstone Golf Centre**, Craibstone Estate, Bucksburn AB21 9YA (01224 716777; Fax: 01224 711298). *Location:* on A96 5 miles north of Aberdeen turn left at Craibstone Roundabout (private access) through Estate to T-junction, left then first right. Parkland course. 18 holes S.S.S. 67. *Green Fees:* information not available. *Eating facilities:* available, also bar. *Visitors:* welcome. Accommodation on site. *Society Meetings:* welcome - please telephone for details. Secretary: Susan May (01224 711195). *

CAWDOR CASTLE. **Cawdor Castle Golf Course**, Cawdor Castle, Nairn IV12 5RD (01667 404401; Fax: 01667 404674). *Location:* situated between Inverness and Nairn on the B9090 off A96. Parkland. 9 holes, 1429 yards. S.S.S. 32. *Green Fees:* £6.00. Subject to review. *Eating facilities:* licensed restaurant in Castle, snack bar in grounds. *Visitors:* welcome every day from 1st May to second Sunday in October, 10am to 5pm.
e-mail: info@cawdorcastle.com
website: www.cawdorcastle.com

The Burnett Arms Hotel 25 High Street, Banchory, Aberdeenshire AB31 5TD

With over 20 golf courses within 45 minutes by car, the hotel is ideally situated for golf outings wishing to play on more than one course. The hotel has 16 en suite rooms, 2 bars cater for all tastes, serving bar lunches and suppers. High teas and dinners available in the restaurant. *Special rates for golfers available on request*

STB ★★★, AA/RAC ★★   Tel: 01330 824944 • Fax: 01330 825553

See also Colour Advertisement on page 70

DUFF HOUSE ROYAL
GOLF CLUB
THE BARNYARDS, BANFF AB45 3SX
OFFICE: 01261 812062 PRO SHOP: 01261 812075
e-mail: duff_house_royal@btinternet.com

* 18-HOLE PARKLAND COURSE * PRACTICE PUTTING AREA
* GOLF SHOP * PGA PROFESSIONAL * PUTTING GREEN
* LOUNGE BAR * CATERING FACILITIES
* OPEN DAYS * CHANGING FACILITIES

VISITORS AND SOCIETIES CATERED FOR ALL YEAR ROUND

See also Colour Advertisement on page 71

BANFF SPRINGS HOTEL

Golden Knowes Road, Banff AB45 2JE
Tel: 01261 812881 Fax: 01261 815546
STB ★★★ HOTEL AA ★★★
www.banffspringshotel.co.uk

A truly special Family-Run hotel offering a warm welcome and service with a smile from the excellent staff

★ 31 en suite bedrooms, all with TV, many overlook the golden sands of the Moray Firth to the mountains of Sutherland and Wester Ross ★ Superb food – bar and restaurant menus ★ Club storage and drying facilities ★ Special offers every season and Group Discounts ★ Close proximity to area's attractions

Banff is a beautiful and unexploited part of Scotland with great facilities for golf, fishing and relaxing. Reasonable green fees on most local courses.

Dinner, Bed & Breakfast from £48.25(min stay 2 nights)   *Come, Relax and Enjoy!*

See also Colour Advertisement on page 69

Recommended   **FHG**

Country Inns & Pubs of Britain

Where to enjoy the best of traditional British hospitality – a large selection of pubs, inns and small hotels, with separate supplements for pet-friendly and family-friendly establishments.

Available from bookshops and larger newsagents for £6.99

FHG PUBLICATIONS LTD
Abbey Mill Business Centre, Seedhill, Paisley PAI 1TJ
www.holidayguides.com

FHG For full details of clubs and courses, plus convenient accommodation, visit the FHG golf website
www.uk-golfguide.com

CULLEN. **Cullen Golf Club**, The Links, Cullen AB56 4WB (01542 840685). *Location:* off A98 midway between Aberdeen and Inverness, on Moray Firth coast. Seaside links with elevated section, natural rock landscaping and sandy beach coming into play at several holes. 18 holes, 4597 yards. S.S.S. 62. Putting green and net area. *Green Fees:* weekdays £15.00 per round, £22.00 per day; weekends £20.00 per round, £26.00 per day. Winter Greens weekdays £8.00 per round, £10.00 per day; weekends £12.00 per round, £14.00 per day. Junior rates, weekly and fortnightly rates available with prices on request. All prices subject to review. *Eating facilities:* catering and bar facilities. *Visitors:* welcome, may be restrictions Wednesdays and Saturdays (club competitions). *Society Meetings:* catered for. e-mail: cullengolfclub@btinternet.com

DUFFTOWN. **Dufftown Golf Club**, Tomintoul Road, Dufftown AB55 4BS (Tel & Fax: 01340 820325). *Location:* on B9009 Dufftown to Tomintoul Road, one mile from Dufftown. Moorland/ Parkland course, partially hilly. 18 holes, 5308 yards. S.S.S. 67. Practice and putting facilities. *Green Fees:* £12.00 per round. Weekly (five day) ticket £50.00. Reductions for parties of 12 or more. Juniors half price. *Eating facilities:* available by arrangement. *Visitors:* welcome at all times. Tee reserved at some times Tuesdays, Wednesdays and Sundays . Please phone for details. Trolleys and clubs for hire, advance notice. *Society Meetings:* welcome by arrangement. Administrator: Marion Swann. (Tel & Fax 01340 820325).

ELGIN. **Elgin Golf Club**, Hardhillock, Birnie Road, Elgin IV30 8SX (01343 542338; Fax: 01343 542341). *Location:* half a mile south of Elgin town centre just off A941 Rothes Road; on Birnie Road. Undulating parkland on sandy subsoil, many tree-lined fairways. 18 holes, 6411 yards. S.S.S. 71. Driving range, practice ground and net. *Green Fees:* £28.00 per round, £38.00 per day (seven days). *Eating facilities:* bar and catering every day. *Visitors:* welcome, arrangement through Secretary is advisable. *Society Meetings:* by arrangement with Secretary. Professional: Kevin Stables (Tel & Fax: 01343 542884). Secretary: David F. Black (01343 542338). website: www.elgingolfclub.com

ELGIN. **Hopeman Golf Club**, Hopeman, Elgin IV30 5YA (01343 830578). *Location:* 7 miles north-east of Elgin on B9012. Seaside links, with spectacular 12th hole. 18 holes, 5590 yards. S.S.S. 67. *Green Fees:* weekdays £16.00 per round, £21.00 per day; weekends £21.00 per round, £26.00 per day. Juniors half price. Senior Citizens: weekdays £14.00 per round, £16.00 per day; weekends £16.00 per round, £21.00 per day. Generous discounts for parties of ten or more *Eating facilities:* bar, catering. *Visitors:* welcome, some restrictions on tee times at weekends. Trolleys and golf buggy for hire. *Society Meetings:* welcome by arrangement. Secretary: Jim Fraser (01343 830578; Fax: 01343 830152). e-mail: hopemangc@aol.com website: www.hopeman-golf-club.co.uk

ELLON. **McDonald-Ellon Golf Club**, Hospital Road, Ellon AB41 9AW (01358 720576). *Location:* A90 from Aberdeen to Ellon. One mile down A948, on left. Flat parkland with trees and stream. 18 holes, 5986 yards. S.S.S. 70. Putting green and practice nets. *Green Fees:* on application. *Eating facilities:* full catering and bar facilities all week. *Visitors:* welcome at all times weekdays, after 10am and booking advisable at weekends. *Society Meetings:* must book in advance. Professional: Ronnie Urquhart (01358 722891). Secretary: Iain Shaw (01358 720576). e-mail: mcdonald.golf@virgin.net

FOCHABERS. **Garmouth & Kingston Golf Club**, Spey Street, Garmouth, Fochabers IV32 7NJ (Tel & Fax: 01343 870388). *Location:* three miles north from A96 at Mosstodloch crossroads. Flat parkland/part links. 18 holes, 5935 yards. S.S.S. 69. Practice net. *Green Fees:* weekdays £18.00 per round, £25.00 per day, half price for Senior Citizens; weekends £25.00 per round or day. Reductions for parties over 10. *Eating facilities:* catering available on request. *Visitors:* very welcome except 4pm to 7pm Tuesdays (Ladies) and during club competitions (evenings). *Society Meetings:* welcome by arrangement with Admin. Assistant (I. Fraser). Secretary: A. Robertson (01343 870231).

FORRES. **Forres Golf Club,** Muiryshade, Forres IV36 2RD (Tel & Fax: 01309 672250). *Location:* one mile south from clock tower in town centre; 26 miles east of Inverness on A96. Parkland - feature hole 16th. 18 holes, 6236 yards. S.S.S. 70. Practice ground and putting green. *Green Fees:* £24.00 per round, £30.00 per day. *Eating facilities:* bar and catering all day every day. *Visitors:* welcome - booking system in operation by Professional. Buggies/Trolleys for hire. *Society Meetings:* welcome. Professional: S. Aird (Tel & Fax: 01309 672250). Secretary: (01309 672949; Fax: 01309 672261).

FORRES. **Kinloss Country Golf Course**, Kinloss, Forres IV36 2UB (01343 850585). *Location*: 4 miles east of Forres on B9089. Parkland courses. Two 9 hole courses, Course 1 - 2535 yards, Course 2 - 2939 yards. Putting green, driving net. *Green Fees*: weekdays £12.00 9 holes, £19.00 18 holes; weekends £12.00 9 holes, £21.00 18 holes. *Eating facilities*: hot and cold drinks, ice cream, confectionery available. *Visitors*: welcome everyday, pay-as-you-play. Trolleys, clubs and buggies for hire. *Society Meetings*: discounts for large parties. Corporate outings catered for. Secretary: Sylvia Verner (01343 850242 or 01343 850585).

FRASERBURGH. **Fraserburgh Golf Club**, Philorth, Fraserburgh AB43 8TL (01346 518287). *Location:* turn right at roundabout on entry to town from Aberdeen then first right. Splendid true seaside links. 18 holes, 6308 yards. S.S.S. 71. Additional 9 hole Rosehill Family Course 2400 yards. Practice area. *Green Fees:* to be arranged, single round, day tickets, weekly and monthly tickets available. *Eating facilities:* full bar and catering facilities. *Visitors:* welcome, some restrictions weekends. Pro Shop. *Society Meetings:* welcome, book in advance. Secretary/Manager: James Mollison (01346 516616).

GRANTOWN-ON-SPEY. **Craggan Golf Club**, Grantown-on-Spey PH26 3NT (01479 873283; Fax: 01479 872325). *Location*: situated beside the A95, one mile south of Grantown-on-Spey. Parkland course. 18 holes, 2005 yards. *Green Fees*: £10.00. 10% discount for groups of ten or more. *Eating facilities*: snacks and soft drinks available. *Visitors*: welcome at all times. Secretary: Fergus Laing (01479 873283).
website: www.cragganforleisure.co.uk

GRANTOWN-ON-SPEY. **Grantown-on-Spey Golf Club,** The Clubhouse, Golf Course Road, Grantown-on-Spey PH26 3HY (01479 872079; Fax: 01479 873725). *Location:* turn off main road opposite police station. Parkland and woodland. 18 holes, 5710 yards, S.S.S. 68, Par 70. Practice ground and putting green. *Green Fees:* weekdays £20.00 per day; weekends £25.00 per round, £30.00 per day. Evening round £10.00. 50% reduction for under 18s. *Eating facilities:* full bar and catering facilities. *Visitors:* welcome, members have priority before 10am weekends. Shop. *Society Meetings:* welcome except before 10am weekends.   Secretary: James Macpherson (01479 872079/ 873154; Fax: 01479 873725).
e-mail: secretary@grantownonspeygolfclub.co.uk
website: www.grantownonspeygolfclub.co.uk

HUNTLY. **Huntly Golf Club**, Cooper Park, Huntly AB54 4SH (01466 792643). *Location:* north side of Huntly, 38 miles from Aberdeen on A96. Open parkland course between The Rivers Deveron and Bogie. 18 holes, 5399 yards. S.S.S. 66. Practice area. *Green Fees:* information not available. *Eating facilities:* full catering by arrangement, lounge bar. *Visitors:* welcome, no restriction except Wednesday and Thursday evenings. Carts for hire. *Society Meetings:* by arrangement with Secretary, maximum of 40. Special package deal Mon - Fri. Secretary: Eddie Stott (01466 792360).

INSCH. **Insch Golf Club**, Golf Terrace, Insch AB52 6JY (Tel & Fax: 01464 820363). *Location:* A96 27 miles from Aberdeen. Parkland - trees, water hazards. 18 holes, 5350 yards. S.S.S. 67. *Green Fees:* £16.00 per round/day, all week (Monday to Friday). *Eating facilities:* bar and catering available. *Visitors:* welcome except Mondays from 4.30pm, Tuesdays from 5pm and Wednesdays from 3.30pm. *Society Meetings:* welcome. Secretary: Ean Johnston.

INVERALLOCHY. **Inverallochy Golf Club**, Whitelink, Inverallochy, Fraserburgh AB43 8XY (01346 582000). *Location:* three miles south of Fraserburgh. Seaside links course. 18 holes, 5431 yards. S.S.S. 66. *Green Fees:* information not available. *Eating facilities:* full catering/ fully licensed, advance booking required. *Visitors:* welcome, apply in writing. *Society Meetings:* welcome, apply in writing. Secretary: George Young. *

INVERURIE. **Inverurie Golf Club**, Blackhall Road, Inverurie AB51 5JB (01467 624080; Fax: 01467 621051). *Location*: off third roundabout from Kintore on A96. Parkland with three tree-lined (wood holes). 18 holes, 5483 yards. S.S.S. 67. Practice ground. *Green Fees*: weekdays £16.00 per round, £20.00 per day; weekends £20.00 per round, £26.00 per day. *Eating facilities*: full catering, bar and lounge area. *Visitors*: welcome, phone 01467 620193 for times. Saturdays could be difficult. Wide wheeled carts only. *Society Meetings*: catered for. Professional: John Logue (01467 620193). Secretary: Arthur Angus (01467 624080; Fax: 01467 621051).

INVERURIE. **Kintore Golf Club**, Balbithan Road, Kintore, Inverurie AB51 0UR (01467 632631). *Location:* off A96 12 miles north of Aberdeen. Undulating moorland course. 18 holes, 5323 yards. S.S.S. 66. *Green Fees:* weekdays £15.00 per round, £20.00 per day; weekends £20.00 per round, £25.00 per day. Weekly tickets available. *Eating facilities:* available all day during the season, by arrangement at other times. *Visitors:* welcome daily except Mondays, Wednesdays and Fridays between 4pm and 7pm. Trolleys and buggies for hire during season. *Society Meetings:* welcome by appointment. Secretary: James Black.

KEITH. **Keith Golf Club**, Mar Court, Fife Keith, Keith AB55 5DF (01542 882469; Fax: 01542 888176). *Location:* leave A96 on B9014 take first right. Parkland, open, panoramic views. 18 holes, 5800 yards, 5300 metres. S.S.S. 68. Small practice area and putting green. *Green Fees:* weekdays £13.00 per round, £15.00 per day; weekends £15.00 per round, £20.00 per day. *Eating facilities:* catering available by arrangement, normal bar hours. *Visitors:* welcome anytime, advisable to telephone in advance during playing season. *Society Meetings:* all welcome, applications to Outings Convener J. Rutherford. e-mail: Secretary@keithgolfclub.org.uk website: www.keithgolfclub.org.uk

KEMNAY. **Kemnay Golf Club**, Monymusk Road, Kemnay AB51 5RA (01467 642225). *Location:* from A96 main Aberdeen/Inverness road. Take B994 signposted Kemnay and pass through village of Kemnay to find golf course on left hand side on leaving village. Flat wooded parkland. 18 holes, 6342 yards, 5398 metres. S.S.S. 71. *Green Fees:* weekdays £20.00 per round, £26.00 per day; weekends £24.00 per round, £30.00 per day. *Eating facilities:* bar and full catering. *Visitors:* welcome at all times except during club competitions/matches; phone club shop to book tee time. *Society Meetings:* welcome by arrangement. Professional: R. McDonald (01467 642225). Secretary: Y. Moir (Tel & Fax: 01467 643746). Club Shop: (01467 642225). Administrator: (Tel & Fax: 01467 643746).

LOSSIEMOUTH. **Moray Golf Club**, Stotfield Road, Lossiemouth IV31 6QS (01343 812018; Fax: 01343 815102). *Location*: five miles from Elgin on A941, 40 miles from Inverness A96 Links course. Old Course 18 holes, 6617 yards. S.S.S. 71. New Course 18 holes, 6004 yards. S.S.S. 69. Practice ground, putting green. *Green Fees*: Old Course per round - £40.00 weekdays, £50.00 weekends; New Course per round - £30.00 weekdays, £35.00 weekends. Rates for playing a round on both courses £50.00 weekdays, £60.00 weekends. Discounts through local hotel and for parties of 12 or more. *Eating facilities*: bar plus full catering. *Visitors*: welcome every day. Secretary will advise on availability. Carts, caddies. *Society Meetings*: welcome by arrangement with Secretary. Professional: Alastair Thomson (01343 813330). Secretary: S. Crane (01343 812018; Fax: 01343 815102). e-mail: secretary@moraygolf.co.uk website: www.moraygolf.co.uk

MACDUFF. **Royal Tarlair Golf Club,** Buchan Street, Macduff AB44 1TA (01261 832897). *Location:* A98 Fraserburgh to Inverness road. Seaside cliff top course, beautiful seascapes, 13th feature hole. 18 holes, 5866 yards, 5373 metres. S.S.S. 68. *Green Fees:* £15.00 per round; £20 per two rounds (seven days). 10% reduction for parties over 15. *Eating facilities:* full catering and bar available. *Visitors:* very welcome. *Society Meetings:* welcome, bookings through Secretary. Secretary: Caroline Davidson.

◆

Please mention
'THE GOLF GUIDE'
when enquiring about
clubs or accommodation.

◆

NAIRN. **The Nairn Golf Club,** Seabank Road, Nairn IV12 4HB (01667 453208; Fax: 01667 456328). *Location:* Nairn West Shore, on the southern shore of the Moray Firth, 16 miles east of Inverness on A96. Hosted "Amateur" Championship in 1994. Traditional Scottish links championship course, hosted 37th Walker Cup in 1999. Championship Course - 18 holes, 6705 yards. S.S.S. 74 (blue tees); Medal Course 18 holes, 6430 yards. S.S.S 73 (white tees); 9 holes (Newton Course), 1918 yards. Practice area. *Green Fees:* information not available. *Eating facilities:* full catering facilities and two bars available. *Visitors:* welcome subject to availability, restrictions at weekends - 8am to 11.00am and from 12 noon to 2.30pm for members only. Full size snooker table. *Society Meetings:* welcome subject to availability. Professional: Mr Robin P. Fyfe (01667 452787). Secretary: Mr David Corstorphine (01667 453208; Fax: 01667 456328). Catering Manager: (01667 452103). e-mail: bookings@nairngolfclub.prestel.co.uk website: www.nairngolfclub.co.uk

NEWBURGH. **Newburgh-on-Ythan Golf Club,** Beach Road, Newburgh (01358 789058). *Location:* 12 miles north of Aberdeen off A92. Seaside links course. 18 holes, 6162 yards. S.S.S. 71. Practice area. Driving bays. *Green Fees:* weekdays £20.00 per round, £25.00 per day; weekends £25.00, per round, £30.00 per day, subject to review. Special rates for parties. *Eating facilities:* full catering available; bar. *Visitors:* very welcome by prior arrangement, except Saturday mornings. *Society Meetings:* by arrangement. Manager: Roger Bruce (01358 789084; Fax: 01358 788104). e-mail: secretary@newburgh-on-ythan.co.uk website: www.newburgh-on-ythan.co.uk

NEWMACHAR. **Newmachar Golf Club,** Swailend, Newmachar AB21 7UU (01651 863002). *Location:* two and a half miles north of Dyce on A947. Two courses: Hawkshill – Championship standard wooded parkland course with ponds being main feature. 18 holes, 6659 yards. S.S.S. 74; Swailend: undulating parkland course. 18 holes, 6388 yards. S.S.S. 71. 12 bay driving range, practice bunker and putting green. *Green Fees:* information not available. *Eating facilities:* fully licensed clubhouse with restaurant. *Visitors:* welcome weekdays by prior arrangement. Handicap Certificate required. *Society Meetings:*

welcome weekdays by prior arrangement. Director of Golf: Gordon Simpson (01651 863222). Secretary: Sam Wade (01651 863002; Fax: 01651 863055). *

OLDMELDRUM. **Oldmeldrum Golf Club,** Kirk Brae, Oldmeldrum, Inverurie AB51 0DJ (01651 872648). *Location:* 17 miles north-west of Aberdeen on A947 to Banff. First on right entering from Aberdeen direction. Undulating parkland with tree-lined fairways and water features. 18 holes, 5988 yards, 5479 metres. S.S.S. 69. Practice area. *Green Fees:* weekdays £18.00 per round/ day, weekends £24.00 per round, £26.00 per day. *Eating facilities:* fully licensed bar, full catering. *Visitors:* welcome, advisable to phone first. Professional's Shop: (01651 873555) for tee reservations. *Society Meetings:* catered for by arrangement. Professional: Hamish Love (01651 873555). Secretary: John Page.

PETERCULTER. **Peterculter Golf Club,** Oldtown, Burnside Road, Peterculter, Aberdeen AB14 0LN (01224 735245; Fax: 01224 735580). *Location:* from North Deeside Road (A93) at west end of Peterculter travel southwards, following signs for club. Scenic, undulating course, bounded by River Dee, excellent views of hills to west. 18 holes, Medal 5924 yards, Forward Tees 5601 yards, S.S.S. Medal 69, Forward Tees 68. Small practice/teaching area. *Green Fees:* call for prices. *Eating facilities:* dining room, lounge bar. *Visitors:* welcome except weekdays 4pm to 6pm. *Society Meetings:* welcome Tuesdays to Fridays. Not Public/local holidays. Professional: Dean Vannet (01224 734994). Secretary: Robert Burnett. e-mail: info@petercultergolfclub.co.uk website: www.petercultergolfclub.co.uk

PETERHEAD. **Cruden Bay Golf Club,** Aulton Road, Cruden Bay, Peterhead AB42 0NN (01779 812285). *Location:* seven miles south of Peterhead, 23 miles north east of Aberdeen, just off A92. Traditional seaside links with magnificent views near Bay of Cruden. 18 holes, 6395 yards. S.S.S. 72; 9 holes, 2553 yards. S.S.S. 65. Covered driving range. *Green Fees:* information not available. *Eating facilities:* full bar and catering facilities. *Visitors:* welcome but restricted at weekends, telephone for details. *Society Meetings:* welcome weekdays only. Professional: Mr Robbie Stewart (Tel & Fax: 01779 812414). Secretary: Mrs Rosemary Pittendrigh (01779 812285; Fax: 01779 812945).

Newmachar Golf Club ~ Swailend Course

Excellent for outings the Swailend course (6388 yard, SSS 71), *designed by Dave Thomas,* offers a reasonable challenge with its well-positioned bunkers and testing greens. Packages (for 8 to 100) can be tailored to suit any budget.

Other facilities at Newmachar include Hawkshill 18-hole championship course, a floodlit driving range, two putting greens, bunkers and a pitching green. A team of PGA Professionals offer a full range of teaching packages. On an elevated site the Clubhouse enjoys spectacular views, and golfers can celebrate sinking that final putt in the lounge bar or dining room.

Newmachar Golf Club, Swailend, Newmachar, Aberdeenshire AB21 7UU • Tel: 01651 863002
Fax: 01651 863055 • www.newmachargolfclub.co.uk • e-mail: info@newmachargolfclub.co.uk

See also Colour Advertisement on page 71

PETERHEAD. **Longside Golf Club**, West End, Longside, Peterhead AB42 7XJ (01779 821558; Fax: 01779 821564). *Location*: take A950 west from Peterhead towards Mintlaw. Wooded course with river. 18 holes, 5225 yards, S.S.S 66. *Green Fees*: weekdays £10.00 per round, £14.00 per day; Sundays £15.00 per round, £20.00 per day. Members' guests and juniors half price. *Eating facilities*: full bar and catering facilities. *Visitors*: always welcome - no visitors before 10.30am on Sunday. *Society Meetings*: welcome, £24.00 Monday to Saturday, £26 Sunday, booking forms available from club. Secretary: Mrs Kathleen Allan (01771 622424).

PETERHEAD. **Peterhead Golf Club,** Riverside Drive, Peterhead AB42 1LT (01779 472149; Fax: 01779 480725). *Location:* north end of town off Blackhouse Terrace at mouth of River Ugie. Seaside links - can be affected by variable wind conditions. Old Course - 18 holes, 6173 yards. S.S.S. 71; New Course - 9 holes, 2228 yards. Par 62 for 4456 yards. Practice area. *Green Fees:* weekdays £22.00 per round, day ticket weekdays £30.00, 9 hole £10.00; weekends £28.00 per round, £36.00 per day. *Eating facilities:* snacks, meals, full bar facilities. *Visitors:* welcome anytime except some restrictions on a Saturday. Phone call advised. *Society Meetings:* welcome by arrangement. Handicap Certificate may be asked for. Secretary: D.G. Wood (Tel & Fax: 01779 480725).

PORTLETHEN. **Portlethen Golf Club**, Badentoy Road, Portlethen, Aberdeen AB12 4YA (01224 781090). *Location:* five miles south of Aberdeen on main Stonehaven Road. Rolling parkland. 18 holes, 6670 yards. S.S.S. 72. Large practice area. *Green Fees:* weekdays £15.00 per round, £22.00 per day; weekends £22.00 per round. Subject to review. *Eating facilities:* bar and restaurant. *Visitors:* welcome, no visitors Saturdays, Sundays also difficult in summer. Golf buggies for hire. Snooker. *Society Meetings:* welcome weekdays by arrangement. Professional: Muriel Thomson (01224 782571). Bar/catering: 01224 782575.

ROSEHEARTY. **Rosehearty Golf Club**, C/o Masons Arms Hotel, 1 Castle Street, Rosehearty, Fraserburgh AB43 4JP (01346 571250). *Location:* east of Rosehearty on Fraserburgh Road. Seaside links. 9 holes, 2197 yards. S.S.S. 62. Driving range and golf shop. *Green Fees:* day ticket £10.00, weekend ticket £12.00. *Eating facilities:* Masons Arms Hotel adjacent to course. *Visitors:* always welcome. *Society Meetings:* welcome by prior arrangement. Lessons available. Teaching facilities across road from Masons Arms Hotel. Professional: Scott Hornal. Secretary: Alan Watt (01346 571250).

ROTHES. **Rothes Golf Club**, Blackhall, Rothes, Aberlour AB38 7BJ (01340 831443). *Location:* south west of Rothes, off A941 Elgin to Craigellachie road. A hilly course with fine views over the River Spey. 9 holes (18 tees), 2486 yards (4972 yards), 2273 metres (4546 metres). S.S.S. 64. Practice net. *Green Fees:* information not available. *Eating facilities:* licensed bar open summer evenings and weekends, catering for parties by arrangement. *Visitors:* always welcome, tee reserved for Ladies 5pm to 7.30pm Tuesdays, and 5pm to 6.30pm Mondays for Juniors. *Society Meetings:* welcome, contact Secretary. Secretary: J.A. Eddie (01340 831617).*

SPEY BAY. **Golf Spey Bay**, Spey Bay Hotel, Spey Bay, Fochabers IV32 7PJ (01343 820424 all enquiries). *Location:* halfway between Inverness and Aberdeen, at the mouth of River Spey. Traditional 18-hole championship links. Special characteristics being small greens and tight, gorse-lined fairways with superb scenic views over the Moray Firth. 6230 yards. S.S.S. 70. Driving range, practice area and putting green. *Green Fees:* winter from £13.00, summer from £20.00, daily and weekly passes available. Buggy and trolley hire available. *Eating facilities:* The on-site three star hotel offers Bed and Breakfast, snacks, lunch and dinner. *Visitors:* all visitors welcome all year round. *Society Meetings:* catered for by prior arrangement. Special golf breaks tailor-made to suit individual requirements. All enquiries contact The Spey Bay Hotel. e-mail: info@speybay.com website: www.speybay.com

STONEHAVEN. **Stonehaven Golf Club**, Cowie, Stonehaven AB39 3RH (01569 762124; Fax: 01569 765973). *Location:* A92, one mile north of town signposted at mini roundabout at Comodore Hotel. Parkland course on cliffs overlooking North Sea with some challenging holes over natural gullies. 18 holes, 5128 yards. S.S.S. 65. Limited practice area. *Green Fees:* weekdays:£15.00 per round, £20.00 per day; weekends: £22.00 per round, £25.00 per day. *Eating facilities:* full catering including bar lunches. *Visitors:* welcome, but advised to reserve tee time in advance, restricted Saturdays after 4pm. *Society Meetings:* catered for except for Saturday. Secretary/Manager: W.A. Donald. e-mail: stonehaven.golfclub@virgin.net

TORPHINS. **Torphins Golf Club**, Bog Road, Torphins, Banchory AB31 4JU (013398 82115). *Location:* through village towards Lumphanan, club signposted to right. Parkland with lovely views to Highlands. 9 holes, 4738 yards (18 holes). S.S.S. 64. *Green Fees:* £13.00 weekdays; £14.00 weekends. £7.00 for 9 holes. Juniors half price, after 6.30pm £6.00. *Eating facilities:* light refreshments at weekends, unlicensed. *Visitors:* welcome at weekends; on medal days by arrangement. *Society Meetings:* welcome; at weekends by arrangement. Secretary: Stuart MacGregor (013398 82402).

TURRIFF. **Turriff Golf Club**, Rosehall, Turriff AB53 4HD (01888 562982; Fax: 01888 568050). *Location:* A947 signposted on south side of Turriff. Wooded parkland course. 18 holes, 6095 yards. S.S.S. 69. Practice area, putting green. *Green Fees:* weekdays £20.00 per round, £24.00 per day; weekends £24.00 per round, £30.00 per day. *Eating facilities:* bar and restaurant. *Visitors:* no visitors before 10am weekends, selected times on Medal days. Tee reservation by contacting Professional – during the week up to four days in advance, weekends up to two days in advance. *Society Meetings:* by arrangement with Secretary. Professional: John R. Black (Tel & Fax: 01888 563025). Secretary: W Steve Duguid (01888 562982; Fax: 01888 568050). Administrator: Grace Stephen e-mail: grace@turriffgolf.sol.co.uk website: www.turriffgolfclub.com

WESTHILL. **Westhill Golf Club**, Westhill Heights, Westhill, Aberdeenshire AB32 6RY (01224 742567; Fax: 01224 749124). *Location:* six miles from Aberdeen on A944. Parkland course. 18 holes, 5849 yards. S.S.S. 69. Practice ground. *Green Fees:* weekdays £14.00 per round, £20.00 per day; Sundays and Public Holidays £20.00 per round, £25.00 per day. Special packages available on request . *Eating facilities:* lounge bar and dining area. *Visitors:* welcome except Saturdays. *Society Meetings:* welcome per visitors' times by arrangement. Professional: George Bruce (01224 740159).

THE APPEARANCE OF AN ASTERISK * AT THE END OF A CLUB OR COURSE ENTRY INDICATES THAT UP-TO-DATE INFORMATION HAS NOT BEEN SUPPLIED

Argyll & Bute

CAMPBELTOWN. **Machrihanish Golf Club**, Machrihanish, by Campbeltown PA28 6PT (01586 810213). *Location:* five miles west of Campbeltown on B843 road. Championship standard natural links course. 18 holes, 6225 yards. S.S.S. 71. Also 9 holes, 2395 yards. Practice area. *Green Fees:* Sunday to Fridays £30.00 per round, £50.00 per day; Saturdays £40.00 per round, £60.00 per day. Advance booking necessary. Subject to review. *Eating facilities:* full catering and bar facilities. *Visitors:* welcome, some restrictions on competition days. Open competitions in summer. Special Flight/Golf packages available through Loganair, Glasgow Airport, Paisley. *Society Meetings:* as visitors. Professional: Ken Campbell (01586 810277; Fax: 01586 810221). Secretary: Mrs Anna Anderson (01586 810213).

CARRADALE. **Carradale Golf Club,** Carradale, By Campbeltown PA28 6RY. *Location:* 15 miles north of Campbeltown on B842. Seaside course, short but demanding, unbelievable views. 9 holes. Medal Tees – 2358 yards out, 2336 yards in; Yellow Tees – 1999 yards. S.S.S. 64 (18 holes). Practice green. *Green Fees:* £10.00 per day; £50.00 per week. Country Membership £79.50 per annum (may take part in competitions). *Eating facilities:* Carradale Hotel at first tee, Ashbank Hotel 100 yards. Dunvalanree close by. Network centre 1 mile (open Easter to October for midday meals and snacks). *Visitors:* all welcome, no restrictions. *Society Meetings:* welcome, would be advisable to book tee-off times. Secretary: Dr R.J. Abernethy (01583 431321).

DALMALLY. **Dalmally Golf Club,** C/o Orchy Bank, Dalmally PA33 1AS (01838 200370; Fax: 01838 200264). *Location:* alongside the A85, two miles west of Dalmally. Flat parkland course bounded by the River Orchy and surrounded by mountains. 9 holes, 2264 yards. S.S.S. 63. *Green Fees:* £10.00. *Eating facilities:* bar and snacks by arrangement. *Visitors:* welcome at all times. Clubs and carts by arrangement. *Society Meetings:* all welcome by arrangement. Secretary: A.J. Burke (01838 200370).

DUNOON. **Blairmore and Strone Golf Club**, High Road, Strone, by Dunoon PA23 8TH (01369 840676). *Location:* take A880, five miles north of Dunoon and first left after leaving Kilmun. A Braid designed course set above the Clyde with spectacular views, mixture of hill and flatter parkland. 9 holes, 2112 yards, 1933 metres. S.S.S. 62. *Green Fees:* weekdays and weekends, £10.00. *Eating facilities:* bar facilities Saturdays and lunchtimes in Summer. *Visitors:* welcome but some restrictions on competition days. *Society Meetings:* welcome, apply through Secretary. Secretary: Mrs J.C. Fleming (01369 860307).

DUNOON. **Cowal Golf Club,** Ardenslate Road, Kirn, Dunoon PA23 8LT (01369 702216). *Location:* quarter mile off A815 at Kirn (north-east boundary of Dunoon). Rising wooded parkland with superb views over Firth of Clyde. 18 holes, 6063 yards. S.S.S. 70. Practice area. *Green Fees:* weekdays £22.00 per round, £34.00 per day; weekends £34.00 per round, £54.00 per day; weekly ticket £100.00 (prices may be subject to increase). *Eating facilities:* full service available. *Visitors:* welcome weekdays, possible restrictions weekends. Separate visitor changing/shower facilities. Local hotels offer golf holidays – apply to Secretary for details. *Society Meetings:* welcome, special rates available. Professional: R.D. Weir (01369 702395). Secretary: Alan Douglas (Tel & Fax: 01369 705673). website: www.cowalgolfclub.co.uk

DUNOON. **Innellan Golf Club**, Innellan, By Dunoon PA23 (01369 830242). *Location:* south of Dunoon to Innellan Pierhead, then follow signposts. Parkland course in elevated position overlooking Firth of Clyde. 9 holes, 2343 yards. S.S.S. 64. *Green Fees:* £12.00 per round, £9.00 for 9 holes. 25% discount for parties. *Eating facilities:* snack/bar; food by arrangement. *Visitors:* welcome, except Monday evenings, Ladies welcome Thursday evenings. *Society Meetings:* welcome by arrangement. Secretary: Andrew Wilson (01369 702573).

INVERARAY. **Inveraray Golf Club**, c/o The Secretary, Inveraray. *Location:* on the A83 Campbeltown road, one mile west of Inveraray, signposted. Testing course, wooded with natural trees, oak, birch, etc. Flat, some water hazards. 9 holes, 2814 yards. S.S.S. 68. *Green Fees:* weekdays and weekends £15.00 per day/round; Juniors £5.00, Seniors £10.00. *Eating facilities:* none at course but good choice locally. *Visitors:* very few restrictions weekdays, occasionally at weekends. *Society Meetings:* welcome by prior arrangement through Calum Morrison (01499 302079).

ISLE OF BUTE. **Bute Golf Club**, c/o St. Ninians, 32 Marine Place, Ardbeg, Rothesay PA20 0LF (01700 502158). *Location:* six miles from Rothesay on the A845, situated on shores of Stravanan Bay. Flat seaside links in beautiful setting. 9 holes, 2497 yards, 2284 metres. S.S.S. 64 (18 holes). *Green Fees:* £8.00 adults, £4.00 Juniors. *Visitors:* welcome any day, Saturdays after 11.30am. *Society Meetings:* catered for by arrangement. Secretary: Frazer Robinson (01700 502158).
e-mail: secretary@butegolfclub.com
website: www.butegolfclub.com

LOCHGILPHEAD. **Lochgilphead Golf Club**, Blarbuie Road, Lochgilphead PA31 8LE (01546 602340). *Location:* close to Argyll and Bute Hospital, Lochgilphead. Signposted from town centre. Parkland. 9 holes, 4518 yards. S.S.S. 63. *Green Fees:* £15.00. *Eating facilities:* limited snacks available at weekends. *Visitors:* welcome but some restriction on competition days. *Society Meetings:* welcome by arrangement. Secretary: Mr R. Foyle (01546 510383).

OBAN. **Glencruitten Golf Club**, Glencruitten Road, Oban PA34 4PU (01631 562868). *Location:* one mile from town centre. Hilly parkland. 18 holes, 4452 yards. S.S.S. 63. Practice area. Putting green. *Green Fees:* weekdays £17.00, weekends £20.00. *Eating facilities:* full catering and bar facilities. *Visitors:* welcome, restrictions on Saturdays and Thursdays during competition times. *Society Meetings:* welcome. Shop: (01631 564115). Secretary: A.G. Brown (01631 564604).

OBAN. **Isle of Seil Golf Club**, Balvicar, Isle of Seil. *Location:* turn off the A816 Oban - Lochgilphead Road at Kilninver onto the B844, follow B844, cross the Atlantic Bridge onto Seil, then on to Balvicar. Partly on shore of Balvicar Bay, partly on reclaimed quarry land. 9 holes, 2335 yards, Par 32. *Green Fees:* £8.00 per day. *Visitors:* welcome all day, every day. *Society Meetings:* by arrangement. Secretary: Mr B.R. Mitchell (01852 300348).

ROTHESAY. **Port Bannatyne Golf Club**, Bannatyne Mains Road, Port Bannatyne (01700 504544). *Location:* two miles north of Rothesay (ferry terminal). Hill course overlooking bays and sea lochs. 13 holes, 5085 yards, S.S.S. 65. *Green Fees:* weekdays £11.00 per round, £15.00 per day; weekends £16.00 per round, £20.00 per day. *Eating facilities:* can be arranged in new clubhouse. *Visitors:* welcome – almost unrestricted. *Society Meetings:* very welcome. Secretary: Mrs B.K. Burnett (01700 505142).

 For full details of clubs and courses, plus convenient accommodation, visit the FHG golf website
www.uk-golfguide.com

ROTHESAY. **Rothesay Golf Club,** Canada Hill, Rothesay PA20 9HN. *Location:* Beautiful island in the Firth of Clyde, frequent ferries from Wemyss Bay, 35 miles south-west of Glasgow and from Colintraive in mainland Argyll. One of Scotland's most scenic island courses, designed by James Braid and Ben Sayers. 18 holes, 5419 yards. S.S.S. 67. Practice area. *Green Fees:* on request. *Eating facilities:* full catering and bar facilities. *Visitors:* welcome, but prior booking at weekends through Professional. *Society Meetings:* welcome by arrangement. PGA Professional: James M. Dougal (Tel & Fax: 01700 503554). Hon Secretary: D.W.W. Craig website: www.rothesaygolfclub.com

SOUTHEND. **Dunaverty Golf Club,** Southend, Campbeltown PA28 6RN (Tel & Fax: 01586 830677). *Location:* about 10 miles south of Campbeltown on B842. Scenic seaside course with great views to Ireland and Mull of Kintyre. 18 holes, 4799 yards. S.S.S. 63. Small practice ground. *Green Fees:* information not available. *Eating facilities:* snacks, teas/coffees, meals by arrangement; no bar. *Visitors:* welcome, phone if visiting at weekends. Limited equipment hire. *Society Meetings:* welcome, phone or write to N. Hind for bookings. Hon Secretary: B. Brannigan (01586 830329). Steward: N. Hind.*

TARBERT. **Tarbert Golf Club,** Kilberry Road, Tarbert PA29 6XX (01880 820565). *Location:* approximately one mile south of Tarbert on B8024. Hilly wooded parkland. 9 holes, 4460 yards. S.S.S. 63. *Green Fees:*

£10.00 per day. *Eating facilities:* licensed clubhouse, open weekends. *Visitors:* welcome at all times. *Society Meetings:* by arrangement. Secretary: Peter Cupples (01546 606896).

TAYNUILT. **Taynuilt Golf Club,** Taynuilt PA35 1JE (01866 822429). *Location:* 12 miles from Oban on A85, quarter of a mile, through the village, from the main road. Situated in a scenic and majestic location, surrounded by mountains and overlooking picturesque Loch Etive. Dominated by Ben Cruachan at 3695 feet, the challenging 9 hole course of undulating parkland was founded in 1987 and officially opened by Michael Bonallack of the R&A in 1991. 9 Holes, 4510 yards. S.S.S.63. Gents, 67 Ladies. *Green Fees:* not available - two hotels and a tearoom nearby. *Visitors:* welcome most days, some restrictions Tuesdays and Sundays. Toilet facilities available. *Society Meetings:* welcome. Secretary: Mike J.P. Urwin (01866 833341). e-mail: michael.urwin@which.net

TIGHNABRUAICH. **Kyles Of Bute Golf Club,** Kames, Tighnabruaich PA21 2BA. *Location:* access from Dunoon and Strachur. Clubhouse by Kames Farm, turn south off B8000 Kames to Millhouse road. Hillside course with magnificent views. 9 holes, 4778 yards. S.S.S. 64. *Green Fees:* weekdays £10.00 per day; weekends £10.00. *Eating facilities:* no bar, but snacks and soft drinks occasionally available. *Visitors:* welcome, except Sunday mornings. *Society Meetings:* by special arrangement. Secretary: Dr Jeremy Thomson (01700 811603).

Ayrshire & The Island of Arran

AYR. **Belleisle Golf Course**, Doonfoot Road, Ayr KA7 4DU (01292 441258). *Location:* follow main road south through Ayr. Gently sloping parkland course with fine mature trees. 18 holes, 6477 yards. S.S.S. 72. Practice area. *Green Fees:* please telephone for information. *Eating facilities:* hotel and bars with catering. *Visitors:* no restrictions but booking in advance advisable. Juniors under 17 must have handicap of 15 or under. *Society Meetings:* catered for, groups up to 40; groups over 40 by special application. Professional: David Gemmell (Tel & Fax: 01292 441314). Starter: (01292 441258; Fax: 01292 442632).

AYR. **Dalmilling Golf Course,** Westwood Avenue, Ayr KA8 0QY (01292 263893; Fax: 01292 610543). *Location:* A77, on north-east boundary, one mile from town centre. Parkland. 18 holes, 5724 yards. S.S.S. 68. Practice area. *Green Fees:* weekdays £13.00 per round, £21.00 per day; weekends £16.50 per round, £29.00 per day. *Eating facilities:* snacks/lunches/high teas, table licence. *Visitors:* welcome, not before 9.30am weekends, telephone to ensure availability. *Society Meetings:* welcome by arrangement. Professional: Philip Cheyney. Secretary: Stewart Graham (01292 262468).

AYR. **Seafield Golf Course**, Doonfoot Road, Ayr KA7 4DU (01292 441258). *Location:* follow main road south through Ayr. Parkland and links, gently sloping. 18 holes, 5498 yards. S.S.S. 66. *Green Fees:* information not available. *Eating facilities:* hotel and bars with catering. *Visitors:* welcome, no restrictions but booking in advance advisable. *Society Meetings:* catered for, groups up to 40; groups over 40 by special application. Professional: David Gemmell (Tel & Fax: 01292 441314). Starter: (01292 441258; Fax: 01292 442632). *

BEITH. **Beith Golf Club**, Threepwood Road, Beith KA15 2JR (01505 503166). *Location:* first left off Beith bypass road travelling south. Hilly parkland

course with trees and gorse. 18 holes, 5616 yards. S.S.S. 68. *Green Fees:* available on request. *Eating facilities:* snacks and meals available, bar open 9am to 11pm. *Visitors:* welcome. Restrictions as follows; Tuesday 4.30pm to 6.30pm. Saturday 7am to 2pm. Sunday 1pm to 2.30pm. *Society Meetings:* welcome by prior arrangement. Secretary: Margaret Murphy (Tel & Fax: 01505 506814).

DAILLY. **Brunston Castle Golf Course**, Dailly, Girvan KA26 9GD (01465 811471). *Location:* five miles north of Girvan on B471. 18 hole championship course in most scenic part of Ayrshire. *Green Fees:* weekdays £28.00 per round, £45.00 per day; weekends £32.00 per round, £50.00 per day. *Eating facilities:* full bar and restaurant facilities. Visitors: welcome. Driving Range. Full PGA tuition by Professional. Full practice facilities. Professional: Allan Reid.
website: www.brunstoncastle.co.uk

GALSTON. **Loudoun Gowf Club**, Galston KA4 8PA (01563 820551). *Location:* five miles east of Kilmarnock on A71. Fairly flat parkland. 18 holes, 6016 yards. S.S.S. 69. *Green Fees:* £21.00 per round, £31.00 per day weekdays. Subject to review. *Eating facilities:* full catering and bar. *Visitors:* welcome weekdays only. Trolleys and buggies available for hire. *Society Meetings:* welcome by arrangement. Secretary: (01563 821993; Fax: 01563 820011).

GIRVAN. **Girvan Golf Course**, 40 Golf Course Road, Girvan, KA26 9HW (01465 714346). *Location:* A77 from Glasgow, through Ayr, on coast road to Stranraer, off A77 north of Harbour. 8 holes seaside, 10 holes parkland. 18 holes, 5064 yards. S.S.S. 64. Practice area. *Green Fees:* information not available. *Eating facilities:* full catering available in clubhouse. *Visitors:* welcome, no restrictions except when course closed for local competitions (approximately 4 per year). *Society Meetings:* welcome, book through Starter. Secretary: W.B. Tait.*

See also Colour Advertisement on page 73

IRVINE. **Glasgow Golf Club,** Gailes, Irvine KA11 5AE (01294 311258; Fax: 01294 279366). *Location:* eight miles from Kilmarnock, two miles south of Irvine, four miles north of Troon. Championship links course with heather lined fairways. 18 holes, 6539 yards. S.S.S. 72, Par 71. Practice ground. *Green Fees:* weekdays £45.00 per round, £60.00 per day; Saturday and Sunday afternoons £58.00. Subject to review. *Eating facilities:* full catering and bar facilities. *Visitors:* welcome weekdays 9.30am to 4.30pm, weekend afternoons. Prior booking recommended through the Secretary. Caddy cars for hire, caddies by arrangement. *Society Meetings:* by application to Club Secretary. Professional: Jack Steven (01294 311561). Secretary: D.W. Deas (0141-942 2011; Fax: 0141-942 0770). e-mail: secretary@glasgow-golf.com

IRVINE. **The Irvine Golf Club,** Bogside, Irvine KA12 8SN (01294 275979). *Location:* through Irvine going towards Kilwinning, turn left at Ravenspark Academy. Flat links course. 18 holes, 6408 yards. S.S.S. 72. Practice ground. *Green Fees:* information not available *Eating facilities:* dining room and bars. *Visitors:* welcome, after 3pm weekends. *Society Meetings:* welcome. Professional: J. McKinnon (01294 275626). Secretary: W.J. McMahon (01294 275979).

IRVINE. **Irvine Ravenspark Golf Club**, 13 Kidsneuk Lane, Irvine KA12 8SR (01294 271293). *Location:* on A78 between Irvine and Kilwinning at Irvine Royal Academy. Flat parkland course. 18 holes, 6453 yards. S.S.S. 71. *Green Fees:* see website for latest. *Eating facilities:* diningroom, bar. *Visitors:* welcome, except on Saturdays before 2.30pm March to October. No jeans or training shoes allowed in the clubhouse. *Society Meetings:* welcome, by arrangement weekends. Professional: P. Bond (01294 276467). Secretary: S. Howie (01294 553904). Steward: J. McVay (01294 271293). e-mail: secretary@irgc.co.uk website: www.irgc.co.uk

IRVINE. **Western Gailes Golf Club**, Gailes, By Irvine KA11 5AE (01294 311649; Fax: 01294 312312). *Location:* three miles north of Troon. Seaside links. 18 holes, 6639 yards, 6179 (yellow tees). S.S.S. 74. Par 71. Limited practice facilities. *Green Fees:* weekdays £90.00 per round, £125.00 per day, both include lunch; Sunday after 2.30pm £90.00 per round (lunch not included). *Eating facilities:* full bar and catering facilities. *Visitors:* welcome Mondays,

Wednesdays and Fridays and Sunday afternoons, advance booking required, telephone Club Manager. Handicap Certificate required. Caddies and caddy cars available for hire. *Society Meetings:* welcome by arrangement with Secretary. Secretary: Andrew M. McBean C.A.

KILBIRNIE. **Kilbirnie Place Golf Club,** Largs Road, Kilbirnie KA25 7AT (01505 683398). *Location:* on main Kilbirnie to Largs Road, left hand side just outside town boundary. Parkland. 18 holes, 5116 yards. S.S.S. 67. *Green Fees:* information not available. *Eating facilities:* catering and bar. *Visitors:* welcome weekdays and Sundays only, no visiting parties Saturdays. Secretary: C. McGurk (01505 684444/683398).

KILMARNOCK. **Annanhill Golf Club,** Irvine Road, Kilmarnock KA1 2RT (01563 521644). *Location:* between Kilmarnock and Crosshouse on road to Irvine. Parkland course with excellent views and tree-lined fairways. 18 holes, 6285 yards. S.S.S. 70. Practice area. *Green Fees:* prices on request to Starter on (01563 521512). *Eating facilities:* full catering available on application. *Visitors:* no parties Saturdays, but welcome Sundays and weekdays by reservation. *Society Meetings:* catered for. Secretary: Thomas C. Denham (01563 521644).

KILMARNOCK. **Caprington Golf Club,** Ayr Road, Kilmarnock (01563 523702). Parkland/wooded course. 18 holes, 5810 yards. S.S.S. 68. *Green Fees:* information not available. *Eating facilities:* available. *Visitors:* welcome except Saturdays. *Society Meetings:* all welcome. Secretary: Gordon Bray (01563 520566).

LARGS. **Largs Golf Club,** Irvine Road, Largs KA30 8EU (01475 674681). *Location:* A78, south end of Largs town (opposite Marina). Parkland/woodland with scenic views over Cumbraes and Isle of Arran. 18 holes, 6115 yards. S.S.S. 71. *Green Fees:* £30.00 per round, £40.00 per day. *Eating facilities:* full catering and bar. *Visitors:* welcome, tee can be reserved one day ahead of play. Carts, caddies by arrangement. *Society Meetings:* catered for Tuesdays and Thursdays only by prior arrangement. Professional: Kenneth Docherty PGA (01475 686192). Secretary: Jim Callaghan (Tel & Fax: 01475 673594). e-mail: secretary@largsgolfclub.co.uk website: www.largsgolfclub.co.uk

See also Colour Advertisement on page 74

LARGS. **Routenburn Golf Club,** Routenburn, Largs KA30 9AH (01475 673230). Hilly moorland course. 18 holes, 5765 yards. S.S.S. 67. *Green Fees:* information not provided. *Eating facilities:* lunches at club except Thursdays, order in advance. *Visitors:* welcome with reservation. *Society Meetings:* catered for on application to club. Professional: Greig McQueen (01475 687240). Secretary: Mr R.B. Connal.

LARGS. **sportscotland National Centre: Inverclyde, Golf Training Facility,** Burnside Road, Largs KA30 8RW (01475 674666). *Location:* 40 minutes from Glasgow and Prestwick airports. Parkland, links, training bunkers. 6 hole practice area plus driving bays. *Green Fees:* local membership basis, pre-booking facility available. *Eating facilities:* cafeteria, dining room, accommodation and bar. *Visitors:* one and two day ladies' and mixed beginners' courses, booking essential. Professionals: David Scott, Kenny Docherty, Grant Gilmour. Assistant Pro: Derek Watters. Admin. Co-ordinator: Sandra Samuel. Manager: Angela Liddel.

MAUCHLINE. **Ballochmyle Golf Club,** Mauchline KA5 6LE (Tel & Fax: 01290 550469). *Location:* on B705 off A76, one mile south of Mauchline. Wooded parkland course. 18 holes, 5990 yards. S.S.S. 69. *Green Fees:* £30.00 per day weekdays; £35.00 per day weekends. *Eating facilities:* all day bar opening from 1st April until 30th September, snacks and meals available during bar hours. *Visitors:* welcome every day except Saturdays. Dress regulations both on and off the course must be adhered to. Two full size snooker tables. *Society Meetings:* all welcome to a total of 30 per party. Secretary: R. Leslie Crawford (01290 550469).

MAYBOLE. **Maybole Golf Course,** Memorial Park, Kirkoswald Road, Maybole KA19 7DX (01292 612000). *Location:* A77 from Glasgow. By-pass Ayr to Girvan road, on main Girvan road at Maybole. Hilly parkland. 9 holes, 2635 yards. S.S.S. 33. *Green Fees:* information not available. *Visitors:* welcome. *Society Meetings:* welcome. Secretary: A. Ferguson. Starter (01655 889770).*

MUIRKIRK. **Muirkirk Golf Club,** "Southside", Furnace Road, Muirkirk KA18 3RE. *Location:* 10 miles off A74 on A70 to Ayr. Picturesque country scenery, the course nestles amongst heather clad hills. 9 holes, 5380 yards. S.S.S. 67. *Green Fees:* information not available. *Eating facilities:* can be accommodated. Secretary: Mr Robert Bradford (01290 660184).*

NEW CUMNOCK. **New Cumnock Golf Club,** Lochhill, New Cumnock KA18 4BQ (01290 338848). *Location:* A76, one mile west of New Cumnock. Parkland, protected area for wildlife birds, next to loch. 9 holes, 5176 yards (18). S.S.S. 66. *Green Fees:* information not available. *Eating facilities:* Lochside House Hotel sits on the edge of the course. *Visitors:* welcome at all times except Sunday up to 4pm for competitions. Clubhouse. *Society Meetings:* welcome. Secretary: John McGinn (01290 338041).*

PATNA. **Doon Valley Golf Club,** Hillside, Patna KA6 7JT (01292 531607). *Location:* 10 miles south of Ayr on the A713 Ayr to Castle Douglas road. Undulating hillside parkland course. 9 holes, 5859 yards, 5402 metres. S.S.S. 70. *Green Fees:* £10.00 per round, £15.00 per day. *Eating facilities:* bar open weekdays 7pm to 11pm, weekends 12 noon to 12 midnight. *Visitors:* welcome anytime weekdays, weekends by arrangement. *Society Meetings:* welcome, groups of more than six must apply for tee off times. Secretary: Hugh Johnstone MBE (01292 550411).

PRESTWICK. **Prestwick Golf Club,** Links Road, Prestwick KA9 1QG (01292 477404). *Location:* one mile from Prestwick airport, 40 minutes by car from Turnberry Hotel, 10 minutes from Troon, 15 minutes from Ayr. 18 holes, 6544 yards. (No LGU tees). S.S.S. 73. *Green Fees:* weekdays £90.00 per round, £130.00 per day. *Eating facilities:* dining room (male only: prior booking required) open from 12.30pm to 2.30pm. Cardinal Room (light lunches) open to ladies and gentlemen from 10.00am until 3.30pm. *Visitors:* welcome with reservation. *Society Meetings:* catered for. Professional: F. Rennie. Secretary: I.T. Bunch (01292 477404; Fax: 01292 477255). e-mail: secretary@prestwickgc.co.uk website: www.prestwickgc.co.uk

PRESTWICK. **Prestwick St Cuthbert Golf Club,** East Road, Prestwick KA9 2SX (01292 477101; Fax: 01292 671730). *Location:* south-east area of Prestwick near A77 Whitletts roundabout, follow signs for Heathfield and Prestwick Airport. Flat, some trees; semi-parkland. 18 holes, 6470 yards, 6063 metres. S.S.S. 71. Limited practice area. *Green Fees:* £38.00 per day, £29.00 per round, weekdays only. *Eating facilities:* bar and restaurant. *Visitors:* welcome except weekends unless introduced by and playing with member. *Society Meetings:* catered for. Secretary: J.C. Rutherford (01292 477101).

PRESTWICK. **Prestwick St Nicholas Golf Club,** Grangemuir Road, Prestwick KA9 1SN (01292 477608; Fax: 01292 473900). *Location:* Grangemuir Road is half a mile from town centre on Prestwick to Ayr Road. Traditional links course enjoying wonderful panoramic views across Firth of Clyde to island of Arran. 18 holes, 5952 yards, 5441 metres. S.S.S. 69. *Green Fees:* weekdays £36.00 per round, £56.00 per day; weekends £41.00 per round. Discounted rates November to March. *Eating facilities:* full service. *Visitors:* welcome most weekdays and Sunday afternoons. *Society Meetings:* welcome by arrangement. Secretary: T.D.M. Hepburn (01292 477608; Fax: 01292 473900). e-mail: secretary@prestwickstnicholas.com website: www.prestwickstnicholas.com

SKELMORLIE. **Skelmorlie Golf Club**, Beithglass Road, Skelmorlie PA17 5ES (01475 520152). *Location:* two/three miles from Wemyss Bay Pier. Hillside, moorland course. 18 holes, 5013 yards. S.S.S. 65. *Green Fees:* weekdays £20.00 per round/day; weekends £25.00 per round/day. Discounts to local hotel residents. *Eating facilities:* bar 11am to 11 pm, some catering. *Visitors:* welcome except Saturdays before 4pm. *Society Meetings:* welcome by arrangement. Parties at discounted "all-in" rate. Secretary: Mrs A. Fahey (01475 520774).

STEVENSTON. **Ardeer Golf Club**, Greenhead, Stevenston KA20 4JX (01294 464542). *Location:* north of Ayr, six miles from Irvine New Town, off A78. Parkland course lined with trees incorporating water on several holes. 18 holes, 6409 yards. S.S.S. 71. *Green Fees:* weekdays £22.00 per round, £35.00 per day; weekends £30.00 per round, £45.00 per day. Special all-in packages weekdays £35.00, Sundays £50.00 for two rounds and full catering for parties over 12. *Eating facilities:* restaurant and bars. *Visitors:* welcome except Saturdays. *Society Meetings:* all parties holding Handicap Certificates welcome except Saturdays. Starter: R. Summerfield (01294 601327). Secretary: Peter Watson (Tel & Fax: 01294 465316).

STEVENSTON. **Moorpark Golf Club,** Auchenharvie Golf Complex, Moorpark Road West, Stevenston KA20 3HU. *Location:* on the A738 Stevenston/Saltcoats; five miles from Irvine, 20 miles from Glasgow. Flat parkland course with water feature incorporated into two holes. 18 holes, 5203 yards. S.S.S. 66. 18 bay floodlit driving range. *Green Fees:* information not available. *Eating facilities:* privately owned lounge bar within complex open to public, bar meals, functions, snacks available (01294 469051). *Visitors:* welcome, restrictions when there are club competitions. *Society Meetings:* all welcome. The course is situated right next door to Sandylands Caravan Park and there are plenty of other golf courses to play all within easy reach. Professional: Robert Rodgers (01294 603103). Secretary: G. Bruce (01294 467731). *

TROON. **Kilmarnock (Barassie) Golf Club**, 29 Hillhouse Road, Barassie, Troon KA10 6SY (01292 313920; Fax: 01292 318300). *Location:* two miles north of Troon. Links course. 27 holes: Barassie Links 18 holes, 6484 yards. S.S.S. 74; Hillhouse 9 holes, 2888 yards, par 34. Practice ground. *Green Fees:* £58.00 per day Monday to Friday, £60.00 per round Saturday and Sunday. *Eating facilities:* coffee, lunches, snacks, high teas. *Visitors:* welcome Mondays, Tuesdays, Thursdays and Friday afternoons; limited visitors Wednesdays; Saturdays after 3pm, Sundays after 2pm. All visitors must adhere to club dress code — no denim, trainers, etc. *Society Meetings:* catered for Tuesdays and Thursdays. Professional: Gregor Howie (Tel & Fax: 01292 311322). Secretary: Donald D. Wilson (01292 313920/311077). e-mail: barassiegc@lineone.net website: www.kbgc.co.uk

TROON. **Troon Municipal Golf Courses**, Harling Drive, Troon (01292 312464). *Location:* adjacent to railway station, one mile off the Ayr-Glasgow road. Three 18 hole courses. Lochgreen 6820 yards. S.S.S. 73. Darley 6360 yards. S.S.S. 72. Fullarton 4870 yards. S.S.S. 63. *Green Fees:* information not available. *Eating facilities:* hot snacks, 8am - 6pm. Bar snacks and lunches, evening meals bookings only. *Visitors:* catered for. Broad wheeled trolleys only. *Society Meetings:* catered for. Caterer: John Darge. Professional: Gordon McKinley. Advance booking should be made in writing to Starter's Office, Troon Municipal Golf Courses, Harling Drive, Troon, Ayrshire (Fax: 01292 312578). Special short breaks and day tickets available, for details telephone 01292 616270.

TROON. **Royal Troon Golf Club,** Craigend Road, Troon KA10 6EP (01292 311555; Fax: 01292 318204). *Location:* three miles from A77 (Glasgow/Ayr trunk road). Old Course (Championship) 18 holes, 6493 metres, 7101 yards. S.S.S. 74. Portland Course 18 holes, 5751 metres, 6289 yards. S.S.S. 71. *Green Fees:* on request. *Eating facilities:* full restaurant service available, including bar snacks. *Visitors:* Mondays, Tuesdays and Thursdays between 9.30 and 11.00am and 14.30 and 16.00pm. Letter of introduction from own club and Handicap Certificate required (maximum: male 20; Ladies 30). Golfers under 18 years play on the Portland Course. *Society Meetings:* parties in excess of 24 not accepted. Professional: Brian Anderson (01292 313281). Secretary/Manager: J.W. Chandler (01292 311555; Fax: 01292 318204). e-mail: bookings@royaltroon.com website: www.royaltroon.com

modern luxury

play the legend

TURNBERRY. **Turnberry Hotel, Golf Courses and Spa**, Maidens Road, Turnberry KA26 9LT (01655 331000; Fax: 01655 331069). *Location:* on main A77 between Maybole and Girvan. Two Championship Links Courses, Ailsa (host to British Open) 18 holes, 6976 yards. S.S.S. 72; The Kintyre (open Summer 2001) 6827 yards. S.S.S. 72. The Colin Montgomerie Links Golf Academy, putting greens. *Green Fees:* on application. *Eating facilities:* clubhouse, restaurant and bar. *Visitors:* written requests only. Accommodation at Turnberry Hotel. *Society Meetings:* written requests only. Director of Golf: Paul Burley (01655 334000; Fax: 01655 331069). Golf Sales Manager: E.C. Bowman (01655 331000 extension 4501).

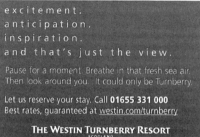
See also Colour Advertisement on page 75

WEST KILBRIDE. **The West Kilbride Golf Club,** 33-35 Fullerton Drive, Seamill, West Kilbride KA23 9HT (01294 823911; Fax: 01294 829573). *Location:* midway between Largs (to north) and Ardrossan (south) on A78. Seaside links course with magnificent views to Isle of Arran and Cumbraes across Firth of Clyde. 18 holes, 6452 yards, 5898 metres. S.S.S. 71. Practice area, putting greens. *Green Fees:* £39.00 per day, £29.00 per round. *Eating facilities:* bar, lounge, dining room. *Visitors:* welcome weekdays only. Caddy cars for hire. *Society Meetings:* catered for Tuesdays and Thursdays. Handicap Certificates required. Professional: Graham Ross (01294 823042). Secretary: Hamish Armour (01294 823911).

THE ISLAND OF ARRAN

BLACKWATERFOOT. **Shiskine Golf and Tennis Club,** Blackwaterfoot, Shiskine KA27 8HA (Tel: 01770 860226. Fax: 01770 860205). *Location:* off B880 at Blackwaterfoot. Seaside links with outstanding views. 12 holes, 2990 yards. S.S.S. 41. Putting green, nets. *Green Fees:* weekdays £15.00 per round, £25.00 per day; weekends £19.00 per round, £30.00 per day. Special rates: Week £90.00, Fortnight £130.00. Subject to review. Maximum of two rounds per day. *Eating facilities:* tearoom, lunches, high teas, dinner. *Visitors:* welcome, preferably with Club Handicap. July and August are very busy so prefer visitors September to June. Tennis and bowls. Shop open Easter–October. *Society Meetings:* only if pre-booked with Match Secretary. Proof of Handicap required. Club Manager: Fiona M. Crawford. e-mail: info@shiskinegolf.com website: www.shiskinegolf.com

BRODICK. **Brodick Golf Club,** Brodick KA27 8DL (Tel & Fax: 01770 302349). *Location:* one mile north of pier. Flat seaside course. 18 holes, 4736 yards. S.S.S. 64. Practice area. *Green Fees:* information not available. *Eating facilities:* bar snacks available. *Visitors:* welcome without restriction. *Society Meetings:* welcome with reservation by letter. Professional: P.S. McCalla (01770 302513). Secretary: H.M. Macrae (Tel & Fax: 01770 302349).*

CORRIE. **Corrie Golf Club**, Sannox, Corrie KA27 8JD (01770 810223). *Location:* seven miles north of Brodick. Short 9 hole course, full of character and very picturesque with some magnificent views. 9 holes, 1948 yards. S.S.S. 61. *Green Fees:* £12.00 per day ticket; twilight ticket £6.00. *Eating facilities:* meals available 8am to 8pm April to October. *Visitors:* welcome, course closed Saturday afternoons, Ladies medal first Thursday of every month. *Society Meetings:* catered for by arrangement (maximum number 12). Secretary: George E. Welford (01770 600403).

LAMLASH. **Lamlash Golf Club,** Lamlash KA27 8JU (Tel & Fax: 01770 600296). *Location:* A841, three

miles south of Brodick Pier ferry terminal. Undulating heathland course. 18 holes, 4640 yards. S.S.S. 64. *Green Fees:* weekdays £18.00 per day; weekends £22.00. After 4pm any day £14.00 per round. Reductions for Senior Citizens. Rates subject to review. *Eating facilities:* catering, lounge bar. *Visitors:* welcome, no restrictions. Pro shop: (01770 600196). Carts/buggies for hire. *Society Meetings:* welcome, book in advance by letter. Secretary: J. Henderson (01770 600272). Starter: (01779 600196). website: www.arrangolf.co.uk

LOCHRANZA. **Lochranza Golf,** Isle of Arran KA27 8HL (01770 830273; Fax: 01770 830600). *Location:* in Lochranza village. A special golf course, possibly unique, certainly interesting, always challenging. 18 holes from 18 tees to 12 greens (six single six double) designed to be different, 5470 yards, 5033 metres. S.S.S. 70. *Green Fees:* information not available. *Visitors:* welcome daily mid April to October. Annual Club Memberships available. Proprietor. I.M. Robertson.* e-mail: golf@lochgolf.demon.co.uk website: www.lochgolf.co.uk

MACHRIE. **Machrie Bay Golf Course,** Machrie, Near Brodick KA27 8DZ (01770 850232). *Location:* on A841, 3½ miles north from Blackwaterfoot. Flat seaside course. 9 holes, 2200 yards. S.S.S. 32. Putting green and small practice area. *Green Fees:* £12.00 per day. Weekly £45.00, two weeks £60.00. *Eating facilities:* tea room, snacks/meals; no licence. *Visitors:* welcome anytime. *Society Meetings:* by arrangement. Secretary: R. Waine (01770 860380).

WHITING BAY. **Whiting Bay Golf Club,** Golf Course Road, Whiting Bay, Brodick KA27 8QT (01770 700487/700775). *Location:* eight miles south of Brodick. Undulating parkland. 18 holes, 4405 yards. S.S.S. 63. Practice net. *Green Fees:* £16.00. *Eating facilities:* catering and bar. *Visitors:* welcome anytime. Clubhouse, shower, snooker and pool rooms; buggies and caddy cars for hire. *Society Meetings:* by prior booking. Secretary: Margaret Auld (01770 820208).

Borders

ASHKIRK. **Woll Golf Course,** New Woll Estate, Ashkirk, Selkirk TD7 4PE (01750 32711). *Location:* just through the village of Ashkirk off the A7. Challenging course in natural parkland setting of outstanding beauty incorporating the Woll Burn; flat. 9 holes, 6504 yards. S.S.S. 71. 18 holes from June 2004. *Green Fees:* £18.00 (subject to review). *Eating facilities:* full clubhouse facilities available spring 2004, bar and restaurant. *Visitors:* welcome. Luxury self-catering accommodation available on the course. Enquiries to Course Manager.
e-mail: wollgolf@btinternet.com
website: www.wollgolf.co.uk

COLDSTREAM. **Hirsel Golf Club**, Kelso Road, Coldstream TD12 4NJ (01890 882678; Fax: 01890 882233). **Location**: A697 west end of Coldstream. Parkland. 18 holes, 6111 yards, 5570 metres. S.S.S. 70. Practice ground. **Green Fees**: weekdays £24.00; weekends £30.00. **Eating facilities**: full catering all year. Snack catering November to mid-March. **Visitors**: welcome, no restrictions; groups of over 10 players must book in advance. Two person golf carts for hire (6). **Society Meetings**: catered for by arrangement.

DUNS. **Duns Golf Club,** Hardens Road, Duns TD11 3NR (01361 882194). *Location:* about one mile west of Duns just off A6105, signposted Longformacus. Upland, undulating course with view south to Cheviot Hills. A burn runs through the course and is the main hazard. 18 holes, 6209 yards. S.S.S. 70. Practice ground. New driving range 2 miles from golf course. *Green Fees:* weekdays £20.00 per round, £24.00 per day; weekends £23.00 per round, £29.00 per day. Children £5.00 per round. Reductions 1st November to 15th March. *Eating facilities:* lounge bar open weekdays and weekends, light snacks and full catering available. *Visitors:* welcome at all times except during club competitions, visitors must tee off before 4pm Mondays, Tuesdays and Wednesdays. *Society Meetings:* welcome, booking through Clubhouse (01361 882194). Secretary: Alex Preston (01361 883599).

EYEMOUTH. **Eyemouth Golf Club**, Gunsgreenhill, Eyemouth TD14 5SF (018907 50004). *Location:* eight miles north of Berwick-on-Tweed, one mile off the A1 towards the coast. Superb cliff-top course with spectacular sea views. 18 holes, 6520 yards, Par 72. Practice area. *Green Fees:* weekdays £22.00 per round, £30.00 per day; weekends £27.00 per round, £35.00 per day. Winter £15.00 per round or day, 7 days. *Eating facilities:* full catering and bar; meals and High Teas available daily. *Visitors:* very welcome, phone Professional for booking. Games room, lounge area, TV; changing rooms, showers. *Society Meetings:* welcome, special discount packages for parties of 8 or more. Professional: Paul Terras (018907 50004). Secretary: Mrs M. Gibson (018907 50551).

GALASHIELS. **Galashiels Golf Club**, Ladhope Recreation Ground, Galashiels TD1 2NJ (01896 753724). *Location*: north end of town, quarter of a

DUNS GOLF CLUB

TEL: 01361 882194

The course is 6,209 yards from the medal tees, SSS 70. Visitors play from the yellow tees 5,763 yards, ladies from the red tees 5,405 yards. The Wellrig burn runs through the course and comes into play on several of the holes. There are two or three short climbs but otherwise the course has gentle slopes and gives lovely views of the countryside around Duns and towards the Cheviot Hills to the south. Full bar and catering facilities. Parties and visitors very welcome.

HARDEN ROAD, DUNS, BERWICKSHIRE TD11 3NR

See also Colour Advertisement on page 75

mile off A7 on Ladhope Drive. Parkland with hill connecting two halves. 18 holes, 5185 yards. Par 67. Practice area. *Green Fees*: weekdays £20.00 per round, £25.00 per day; weekends £25.00 per round, £30.00 per day. Subject to review. Package deals available for parties on application to the Visitors Contact. *Eating facilities*: catering midweek by arrangement only. *Visitors*: welcome anytime, booking essential for weekends. Ladies' night Tuesday 5pm to 7.30pm. Society Meetings: catered for. Contact: Miller Young (01896 753724).

GALASHIELS. **Torwoodlee Golf Club,** Edinburgh Road, Galashiels TD1 2NE (01896 752260). *Location:* leave Galashiels on A7 for Edinburgh. Entrance to course one mile on left. Parkland with wooded greens alongside river and splendid par 5. Designed by Willie Park/John Garner. 18 holes, 6087 yards. S.S.S. 70. *Green Fees:* weekdays £26.00 per round, £36.00 per day; weekends £32.00 per round, £42.00 per day. Weekly rate £100.00. *Eating facilities:* bar, dining room. *Visitors:* welcome except 8.30 to 9.30, 12.30 to 13.30, weekdays or 07.30 to 10.15, 12.15 to 15.00 and 16.15 to 17.00 Saturdays. Showers available. *Society Meetings:* bookings required in advance, packages available. Secretary: A. Owenson (01896 752260).
website: www.torwoodleegolfclub.org.uk

HAWICK. **Hawick Golf Club,** Vertish Hill, Hawick TD9 9JY (01450 372293). *Location:* north along A7 from Carlisle or south on A7 from Edinburgh. Course situated half a mile south-west of town. Hill course with spectacular views. 18 holes, 5929 yards, 5422 metres. S.S.S. 69. Restricted practice area. *Green Fees:* £24.00 per round, £30.00 per day. Reductions for Senior Citizens and Juniors. Packages on request. Contact Tourist Board re Freedom of Fairways promotions. *Eating facilities:* full bar and catering daily. *Visitors:* welcome Saturdays and after 10am Sundays. *Society Meetings:* catered for, advisable to book in advance. Secretary: J. Reilly (01450 375594).

HAWICK. **Minto Golf Club,** Denholm, Hawick TD9 8SH (01450 870220). *Location:* five miles north-east of Hawick leaving A698 at Denholm village. Parkland, trees. Course alterations for year 2000. 18 holes, 5542 yards, 4992 metres. S.S.S. 67. Practice area. *Green Fees:* information not available. *Eating facilities:* full facilities, except Thursday. *Visitors:* welcome, with prior booking. *Society Meetings:* accepted with Handicap Certificate (weekends difficult). Secretary: Peter Brown (01450 375841).

INNERLEITHEN. **Innerleithen Golf Club,** Leithen Water, Leithen Road, Innerleithen EH44 6NL (01896 830951). *Location:* 25 miles south of Edinburgh, six miles south of Peebles, off A72 less than one mile from main street. Attractive 9 hole course set in valley with lovely views of surrounding hills, easy walking but challenging. 9 holes, 3033 yards, 2773 metres. S.S.S. 69. Practice ground. *Green Fees:* information not available. *Eating facilities:* by prior arrangement. *Visitors:* welcome without reservation, though parties should book. *Society Meetings:* catered for by arrangement, limit 40. Secretary: Norman Smith (01896 830050). *

JEDBURGH. **Jedburgh Golf Club,** Dunion Road, Jedburgh TD8 6TA (01835 863587). *Location:* one mile south of Jedburgh on Dunion Road to Hawick. Undulating course with trees. 9 holes, 5555 yards. S.S.S. 67. *Green Fees:* information not available. *Eating facilities:* bar open 7.30pm Monday – Thursday; 2.30pm Friday; 11am weekends. Catering available Friday/Saturday/ Sunday. Bar and catering for parties on request. *Visitors:* welcome. *Society Meetings:* group discount on application. Secretary: George B. McEwen (01835 862360).*

KELSO. **Kelso Golf Club,** Berrymoss, Kelso TD5 7SL (01573 223009). *Location:* one mile north-east of town within Kelso Racecourse. Flat parkland within racecourse. 18 holes, 6066 yards. S.S.S. 69. Practice ground. *Green Fees:* information not available. *Eating facilities:* light catering Mondays and Tuesdays, full catering other days. *Visitors:* welcome without reservation. *Society Meetings:* welcome with reservation. Secretary: Donald R. Jack (01573 223009; 01573 223175 after 7pm).*

KELSO. **The Roxburghe Golf Club,** The Roxburghe Hotel, Heiton, by Kelso TD5 8JZ (01573 450333; Fax: 01573 450611). *Location:* eight miles east of Jedburgh on the A698, three miles south of Kelso. Parkland, woodland course with water set in 200 acres alongside the River Teviot; designed by Dave Thomas to USPGA specifications. The Championship Course is home to the Scottish Seniors Open. 18 holes, 7111 yards. Chipping area, putting green, practice ground. *Green Fees:* £60.00, day ticket £80.00 subject to review. It is advisable to pre-book tee times. *Eating facilities:* spike bar, fine dining. *Visitors:* welcome at all times, Handicap Certificate required. *Society Meetings:* welcome by prior arrangement. Accommodation available; tuition, clay pigeon shooting. The course is owned by the Duke and Duchess of Roxburghe. Professional: Craig Montgomerie. General Manager: William Kirby. e-mail: hotel@roxburghe.net website: www.roxburghe.net

FHG

For full details of clubs and courses, plus convenient accommodation,

visit the FHG golf website on

www.uk-golfguide.com

LAUDER. **Lauder Golf Club,** Galashiels Road, Lauder TD2 6PA (01578 722526). *Location*: off A68, 28 miles south of Edinburgh. Undulating course, originally designed by W. Park of Musselburgh, on Lauder Hill. 9 holes, 6049 yards. S.S.S. 69. Practice ground. *Green Fees:* £10.00 anyday. *Eating facilities*: none - good Hotels in Lauder. *Visitors*: welcome except Wednesdays between 5pm and 7pm and Sundays before 12 noon. Secretary: D. Dickson (01578 722526).

MELROSE. **Melrose Golf Club**, Dingleton Road, Melrose (01896 822855). *Location:* 4 miles west of Galashiels, less than one hour from Edinburgh. Tree-lined parkland course situated beneath Eildon Hills. 9 holes, 5562 yards, 5075 metres. S.S.S. 68. *Green Fees:* £20.00 per round/day. Juniors £10.00. *Eating facilities:* bar open at given times, catering on request for larger parties. *Visitors:* welcome anytime when no competitions taking place, Ladies have priority on Tuesdays; Juniors have priority on Wednesday mornings during school holidays. Locker room, shower. *Society Meetings:* welcome by arrangement. Secretary: James Orrett (01896 822788).

NEWCASTLETON. **Newcastleton Golf Club,** Holm Hill, Newcastleton TD9 0QD. *Location:* midway between Carlisle 25 miles and Hawick 21 miles; off A7 at Canonbie. Hilly course with picturesque views, first three holes uphill. 9 holes, 5483 yards. S.S.S. 70. *Green Fees:* weekdays £10.00; weekends £10.00. Weekly ticket £35.00. *Eating facilities:* can be arranged. *Visitors:* welcome, no restrictions except competition days. *Society Meetings:* welcome. Secretary: G.A. Wilson (013873 75608).

PEEBLES. **Macdonald Cardrona Hotel, Golf and Country Club,** Cardrona, Peebles EH45 6LZ (01896 831971; Fax: 01896 831166). *Location:* from Edinburgh take 'Bridges' road to Cameron Toll; turn right at roundabout; heading to Penicuik take A703 to Peebles, turn left to Innerleithen. Club situated 3 miles out of Peebles. Flat parkland/woodland championship standard course. 18 holes, 6856 yards. S.S.S. 72. Putting/practice area. *Green Fees:* information not available. *Eating facilities:* Spikes Bar. *Visitors:* welcome at any time. *Society Meetings:* welcome at any time, special rates on request. 100-bedroom de luxe hotel on site. Secretary: David Mackinnon (01896 831144; Fax: 01896 831166).* e-mail: cardrona@macdonald-hotels.co.uk website: www.macdonald-hotels.co.uk

PEEBLES. **Peebles Golf Club,** Kirkland Street, Peebles EH45 8EU (01721 720197). *Location:* 51 miles from Glasgow, off A72 at west side of town, 23 miles from Edinburgh. Undulating parkland with panoramic views. 18 holes, 6137 yards. S.S.S. 70. *Green Fees:* weekdays £32.00 per round, £45.00 per day; weekends £39.00 per round, £53.00 per day. Generous discounts for society bookings. *Eating facilities:* full catering daily. *Visitors:* welcome subject to tee availability. Golf buggy hire April to September. *Society Meetings:* catered for subject to prior booking, groups of up to 40 persons catered for. Secretary: Hugh Gilmore.

ST BOSWELLS. **St Boswells Golf Club,** Braeheads, St Boswells, Melrose TD6 0DE (01835 823527). *Location:* quarter of a mile off trunk route A68 at St. Boswells Green. Flat attractive scenery along the banks of the River Tweed. 9 holes, 5250 yards. S.S.S. 66. *Green Fees:* weekdays £18.00, weekends £20.00 (subject to review). *Visitors:* no visitors after 4pm on a weekday and when competitions are being held. Secretary: J.G. Phillips (01835 823527).

SELKIRK. **Selkirk Golf Club,** The Hill, Selkirk TD7 4NW (01750 20621). *Location:* one mile south of Selkirk on A7 road. Heather covered hill course, superb views of Border valleys. 9 holes, 5620 yards. S.S.S. 68. *Green Fees:* £20.00 per day. *Eating facilities:* bar/meals by arrangement during day, open evenings. *Visitors:* welcome morning and afternoon weekdays, weekends booking needed. *Society Meetings:* welcome. Secretary: A.M Wilson (01750 20621).

WEST LINTON. **Rutherford Castle Golf Club**, West Linton EH46 7AS (Tel & Fax: 01968 661233). *Location:* A702 ten miles south of Edinburgh City Bypass. Undulating parkland course at the foot of the Pentland Hills. 18 holes, 6525 yards, 5872 metres. S.S.S. 71. *Green Fees:* information not available. *Eating facilities:* limited facilities but can be expanded for societies by advance notice. *Visitors:* no restrictions. *Society Meetings:* all welcome, booking form available on application in writing, package available for ten or more. Buggy and trolley hire. Contact: (01968 661233).* e-mail: info@ruth-castlegc.co.uk website: www.ruth-castlegc.co.uk

WEST LINTON. **West Linton Golf Club,** West Linton EH46 7HN (01968 660463). *Location:* A702 road 17 miles south west of Edinburgh. Scenic moorland course. 18 holes, 6132 yards, 5607 metres. S.S.S. 70. Two practice areas. *Green Fees:* weekdays £25.00 per round, £40.00 per day; weekends £40.00 per round (group discounts available). Weekly ticket (Mon-Fri) £85.00. Season ticket (10 rounds) £125.00. Fees subject to review. *Eating facilities:* lunches, bar snacks, high teas, morning coffee, bar. *Visitors:* welcome at all times except on Medal days and weekends before 1pm. Buggy and carts for hire. *Society Meetings:* catered for weekdays. Professional: I. Wright (01968 660256). Secretary: J.S. Macnab (01968 660970).

Dumfries & Galloway

ANNAN. **Powfoot Golf Club**, Cummertrees, Annan DG12 5QE (Tel & Fax: 01461 700276). *Location*: three miles from Annan on the B724, turnoff in the village of Cummertrees. Semi-links course on Solway shore with outstanding views. 18 holes, 6266 yards, 5745 metres. S.S.S. 71. Two practice grounds. *Green Fees*: information not available. *Eating facilities*: morning coffee, lunches and teas in clubhouse - ordering in advance essential for large parties. Steward (01461 700227). *Visitors*: welcome weekdays 9am till 11am, 1pm till 4pm. Saturday members only; Sunday visitors welcome after 1pm. All bookings through the office. *Society Meetings*: as per visitors. Professional: Stuart Smith. Office Manager: Claire McDairmant (Tel & Fax: 01461 700276).
e-mail: bsutherland@powfootgolfclub.fsnet.co.uk

CASTLE DOUGLAS. **Castle Douglas Golf Club**, Abercromby Road, Castle Douglas (01556 502801). *Location:* half a mile from town centre on A713 Castle Douglas to Ayr Road. Parkland. 9 holes, 5408 yards. S.S.S. 66. *Green Fees:* information not available. *Eating facilities:* catering during summer season. *Visitors:* welcome without reservation, except Tuesdays or Thursdays after 4pm and competition days. *Society Meetings:* by arrangement. Secretary: R. Stewart (01556 502877).*

DALBEATTIE. **Colvend Golf Club**, Sandyhills, Colvend, By Dalbeattie DG5 4PY (01556 630398). *Location:* six miles from Dalbeattie on the A710, Solway Coast road, between Dalbeattie and Dumfries. Picturesque course on the Solway Coast with superb views over Galloway Hills and the Solway Firth. 18 holes visitors' tees, 4929 yards, 4519 metres. S.S.S. 66; medal tees 5250 yards 4813 metres. S.S.S. 67. *Green Fees:* £22.00. Juniors £10.00. *Eating facilities:* modern clubhouse with full changing, catering and bar facilities. *Visitors:* all welcome. Buggies available. *Society Meetings:* welcome by booking through the club. Secretary: (01556 630398).

DALBEATTIE. **Craigieknowes Golf Club**, Barnbarroch Farm, Kippford, Dalbeattie (01556 620244). *Location:* half a mile from Kippford on side road from A710, three miles from Dalbeattie. Parkland course with lots of rocks. 9 holes, Par 3, 1391 yards. S.S.S. 54. Putting green. *Green Fees:* adult £6.00 9 holes, £10.00 per day, Junior £4.00 9 holes, £6.00 per day. Weekly ticket adults £30.00, Juniors £15.00. *Eating facilities:* tearoom. *Visitors:* welcome, no restrictions on times of play. Car park, club hire. *Society Meetings:* welcome by arrangement. Secretary: Mr S. Roan.

DALBEATTIE. **Dalbeattie Golf Club**, c/o The Secretary, 60 Maxwell Park, Dalbeattie DG5 4LS (Tel & Fax: 01556 610311; mobile: 07733 221850). Clubhouse (01556 611421 – not always manned). *Location*: signed off the B794 Haugh of Urr Road on the outskirts of Dalbeattie. Slightly undulating parkland course. 9 holes, 5710 yards (18 holes). S.S.S. 68. *Green Fees*: information not available. *Eating facilities*: bar and food available. *Visitors*: very welcome anytime and should club competitions be in progress, every effort will be made to accommodate them. *Society Meetings*: all welcome. Contact Secretary for further information regarding tee times, accommodation, restaurants, etc. Secretary: Arthur Howatson (Tel & Fax: 01556 610311; mobile: 07733 221850).*
e-mail: ArthurHowatson@aol.com

DUMFRIES. **Crichton Golf Club**, Bankend Road, Dumfries DG1 4TH (01387 247894). *Location:* directly opposite Dumfries and Galloway Royal Infirmary, one mile outside Dumfries on Bankend Road. Wooded parkland. 9 holes, 5952 yards. S.S.S. 69. *Green Fees:* £15.00 for 18 holes, £28.00 for 36 holes, £50.00 for a weekly ticket Monday to Friday. *Visitors:* welcome, restrictions depending on club competitions, Thursdays last tee off time 1pm. *Society Meetings:* on application to the Administrator. Match Secretary: Alan Cathro.

See also Colour Advertisement on page 652

DUMFRIES. **Dumfries and County Golf Club,** Nunfield, Edinburgh Road, Dumfries DG1 1JX (01387 253585). *Location:* one mile north-east town centre on A701. 18 holes, 5918 yards. S.S.S. 69. *Green Fees:* £27.00 per round, £33.00 per day. *Eating facilities:* restaurant and bar snacks. *Visitors:* welcome except on competition days. *Society Meetings:* by arrangement with Club Professional. Professional: S.J. Syme (Tel & Fax: 01387 268918). Secretary: B.R.M. Duguid (Tel & Fax: 01387 253585). e-mail: dumfriesc@aol.com
website: www.dumfriesandcounty-gc.fsnet.co.uk

DUMFRIES. **Dumfries and Galloway Golf Club**, 2 Laurieston Avenue, Dumfries DG2 7NY (01387 253582). *Location:* one mile from Dumfries on Castle Douglas/Stranraer road, A780. Parkland course. 18 holes, 6325 yards. S.S.S. 71 (under revision). Practice area. Putting green. *Green Fees:* weekdays £27.00 per day/round; weekends £33.00 per day/round. *Eating facilities:* full catering during bar hours. *Visitors:* welcome, except on competition days. Ladies' Day Tuesday. *Society Meetings:* catered for weekdays, except Tuesdays or Saturdays. Professional: Joe Fergusson (01387 256902; Fax: 01387 276297). Secretary: Tom Ross (Tel & Fax: 01387 263848). e-mail: info@dggc.co.uk
website: www.dggc.co.uk

DUMFRIES. **Southerness Golf Club,** Southerness, Kirkbean, Dumfries DG2 8AZ (01387 880677; Fax: 01387 880644). *Location:* 16 miles south west of Dumfries on A710 (Solway Coast Road). Natural challenging Championship links, designed by MacKenzie Ross, with panoramic views of Solway Firth and Galloway hills. Hosted British Ladies' Amateur 1989 and British Youths' 1990. Scottish Amateur 1995. Scottish Amateur Stroke-play 2002. 18 holes, 6566 yards. S.S.S. 73. Practice ground. *Green Fees:* weekdays £38.00 per day; weekends £48.00 per day. Weekly (Monday to Friday) ticket £150.00. *Eating facilities:* full bar and catering facilities. *Visitors:* welcome every day other than 9 days when there are Open Competitions, other golf club members only with Handicap Certificates. Trolley hire. *Society Meetings:* welcome by prior arrangement. Secretary: I.A. Robin.

DUMFRIES. **The Pines Golf Centre**, Lockerbie Road, Dumfries DG1 3PF (Tel & Fax: 01387 247444). *Location:* beside A75 Dumfries bypass off Lockerbie Road roundabout. Mixed park and heathland with mature trees and water features. 18 holes, 5940 yards. S.S.S.70. 20 bay driving range with video teaching facility. Short game practice area and large undulating putting green. *Green Fees:* £14.00 per round (with member £7.00). *Eating facilities:* bar with meals. *Visitors:* welcome. *Society Meetings:* welcome. Professionals: Brian Gemmell and Bruce Gray.

GATEHOUSE OF FLEET. **Cally Palace Hotel,** Gatehouse of Fleet DG7 2DL. (01557 814341; Fax: 01557 814522). *Location*: one and a half hours drive from M6 and A74, nearest large town - Dumfries. Parkland. 18 holes, 6062 yards. Par 70. Course is restricted to hotel residents and those of sister hotels - North West Castle Hotel, Stranraer & Kirroughtree Country House Hotel in Newton Stewart. *Visitors/Society Meetings*: course open only to hotel residents and those of sister hotels, North West Castle, Stranraer, and Kirroughtree Country House, Newton Stewart. *Eating facilities*: conservatory bar for snacks and dining room lunch.

GATEHOUSE OF FLEET. **Gatehouse of Fleet Golf Club,** Laurieston Road, Gatehouse of Fleet, Castle Douglas (01557 814766). *Location:* quarter of a mile north of Gatehouse – Laurieston road. Sloping and wooded course with magnificent views of hills and over Fleet Bay. Very well drained; rarely closed. 9 holes, 2521 yards. S.S.S. 66. Practice net. *Green Fees:* £12.00 per day (£6.00 for Juniors) all year round. *Visitors:* welcome at all times except Sunday mornings before 11.30am. *Society Meetings:* all welcome. Administrator: Keith Cooper (01644 450260).

GRETNA. **Gretna Golf Club,** "Kirtle View", Gretna DG16 5HD (01461 338464). *Location:* south side of A75, one mile from A74. Scenic parkland course. 9 holes, 3215 yards, S.S.S. 72. *Green Fees:* information not available. *Visitors:* welcome, no restrictions. *Society Meetings:* welcome on application.*

KIRKCUDBRIGHT. **Brighouse Bay Golf Club and Driving Range,** Borgue, Kirkcudbright DG6 4TS (Tel & Fax: 01557 870357). *Location:* 6 miles south-west of Kirkcudbright off the B727. Beautifully situated, free-draining coastal course with glorious clifftop views. With four tees on each hole it combines natural coastal undulations with several water hazards making an exceptional test of golf, whatever your ability, playable all year. 18 holes, 6602 yards. S.S.S.73. Carts, club and trolley hire, driving range, short game area, changing and shower facilities. New 9 hole course now open. *Green Fees:* £20.00 per day ticket (reduced winter fees). *Eating facilities:* full range of bar and catering facilities in bistro, lounge bar and function suite. *Visitors:* welcome at all times by prior arrangement, sensible dress at all times. Award-winning holiday park adjacent with accommodation and leisure facilities available all year. *Society Meetings:* welcome, inclusive golf packages now available, book in advance. website: www.brighousebay-golfclub.co.uk

KIRKCUDBRIGHT. **Kirkcudbright Golf Club,** Stirling Crescent, Kirkcudbright DG6 4EZ (01557 330314). *Location:* signposted near centre of town. Hilly parkland. 18 holes, 5896 yards. S.S.S. 69. Carts available. *Green Fees:* £20.00 per round. *Eating facilities:* coffee, lunch, evening meal, usual bar hours. *Visitors:* welcome most days with phone call for availability; Tuesday Ladies' Day, Wednesday Men's. *Society Meetings:* welcome, advance bookings. Secretary: Dave MacKenzie. website: www.kirkcudbrightgolf.co.uk

LANGHOLM. **Langholm Golf Club,** Whitaside, Langholm DG13 0JS (013873 81247). *Location:* on A7 Carlisle-Edinburgh road. Turn off at market place in centre of town. Hillside course with stunning views over the town and down towards the "Lakes". 9 holes, 6180 yards. S.S.S. 70. Practice ground. *Green Fees:* £10.00; £5.00 playing with a member. *Eating facilities:* on request, bar open weekends. *Visitors:* welcome without reservation; restrictions Saturday 9am to 9.45am, 1pm to 2pm and 4pm to 5pm, Sunday 9am to 10am (Competition times). *Society Meetings:* apply in writing to Secretary. Secretary: W. Goodfellow (013873 81408/81247).

LOCHMABEN. **Lochmaben Golf Club,** Castlehillgate, Lochmaben, Lockerbie DG11 1QF (01387 810552). *Location:* Lockerbie four miles, Dumfries eight miles on A709 road. Attractive parkland course surrounding the Kirk Loch, excellent views on this well-maintained course. 18 holes, 5357 yards, 4863 metres. S.S.S. 67. Practice area. *Green Fees:* weekdays £20.00 per round, £25.00 per day; weekends £25.00 per round, £30.00 per day. *Eating facilities:* full catering and bar. *Visitors:* welcome, bookings advisable (01387 810552). Caddy car and buggy hire. *Society Meetings:* welcome. Secretary: J.M. Dickie (01387 810552 or 810713 evenings). website: www.lochmabengolf.co.uk

LOCKERBIE. **Hoddom Castle Golf Course**, Hoddom, Lockerbie DG11 1BE (01576 300251). *Location:* A74, Junction 19 Ecclefechan. Follow signs to Hoddon Castle or A75 Annan, B723 and follow signs to Hoddon Castle. Parkland, partially wooded, bounded on two sides by River Annan. 9 holes, 2274 metres. S.S.S. 33. *Green Fees:* weekdays £8.00 per day; weekends £10.00 per day. *Eating facilities:* bar. *Visitors:* welcome anytime.

LOCKERBIE. **Lockerbie Golf Club,** Corrie Road, Lockerbie DG11 2ND (Tel & Fax: 01576 203363). *Location:* leave M74, proceed to town centre and follow signs. Parkland featuring pond which is in play on three holes – fair test of golf for all standards of golfers. 18 holes, 5614 yards. S.S.S. 67. Small practice area. *Green Fees:* weekdays £18.00 per round, weekends £20.00 per round, Juniors £4.00. *Eating facilities:* catering available 8am - 8pm, bar 11am - 11pm. *Visitors:* welcome, restricted on Sundays. Caddy cars and buggies available. *Society Meetings:* welcome by arrangement. Secretary: Jim Thomson (Tel & Fax: 01576 203363).

MOFFAT. **The Moffat Golf Club,** Coatshill, Moffat DG10 9SB (01683 220020). *Location:* leave M74 at Beattock. Take A701 for Moffat, club signposted one mile on left. Scenic moorland course with tree plantations. 18 holes, 5259 yards. S.S.S. 67. Putting green and practice net. *Green Fees:* weekdays £19.50 per round, £24.00 per day; weekends £27.00 per round, £33.00 per day. Subject to review. Special Packages include: £26.50 to £32.00 weekdays; £35.00 to £42.50 weekends for parties of eight and over– two rounds of golf, coffee/biscuits on arrival, soup and rolls lunchtime, and evening meal. *Eating facilities:* bar meals served all day, bar open 11am to 11pm; dining room. *Visitors:* welcome without reservation, except Wednesday after 3pm. Games room (two full-size snooker tables, pool table, darts, TV area). Trolleys and clubs for hire. *Society Meetings:* welcome, make reservations with Clubmaster. Secretary: Jim Mein (01683 220020). Clubmaster: Toby Downer.

NEW GALLOWAY. **New Galloway Golf Club,** New Galloway, Castle Douglas DG7 3RN (Tel & Fax: 01644 450685). *Location:* one mile off A713 Castle Douglas to Ayr road. Scenic with fine turf. 9 holes, 5006 yards. S.S.S. 67. *Green Fees:* £15 per day, subject to review. *Eating facilities:* bar. *Visitors:* very welcome without reservation. Accommodation and meals available in village. *Society Meetings:* by arrangement with Secretary. Secretary: N.E. White (Tel & Fax: 01644 450685).

NEWTON STEWART. **Newton Stewart Golf Club,** Kirroughtree Avenue, Newton Stewart DG8 6PF (01671 402172). *Location:* outskirts of Newton Stewart off the A75, Euroroute to Ireland. Parkland course set amidst Galloway Hills with pine forest backdrop, views from most tees have to be seen to be believed. 18 holes, 5903 yards. S.S.S. 70. Practice area. *Green Fees:* weekdays £22.00 per round, £25.00 per day; weekends and Bank Holidays £25.00 per round, £29.00 per day; weekly £110.00. Discounts for groups. *Eating facilities:* bar meals, lunches and high teas. *Visitors:* welcome all year round after 9.45am. Phone call in advance advisable. Caddy cars and buggies available. *Society Meetings:* all welcome, booking required.

NEWTON STEWART. **Wigtownshire County Golf Club,** Mains of Park, Glenluce, Newton Stewart DG8 0NN (Tel & Fax: 01581 300420). *Location:* A75 two miles west Glenluce, eight miles east Stranraer. Seaside links. 18 holes, 5847 yards, 5347 metres. S.S.S. 68. Four and a half acre practice area. *Green Fees:* weekdays £21.00 per round, £27.00 per day; weekends £23.00 per round, £29.00 per day. Half price for under 18s. Discounts for parties of 10 and over. *Eating facilities:* available all year round. *Visitors:* unrestricted except Wednesday evenings and competitions. Hand trolleys. *Society Meetings:* catered for but should pre-book. Secretary: Mr R. McKnight (01581 300532). e-mail: enquiries@wigtownshirecountygolfclub.com website: www.wigtownshirecountygolfclub.com

LOCKERBIE GOLF CLUB
founded 1889
A74 to Lockerbie • take Corrie Road • 500 yards on right.
Tel/Fax: 01576 203363

Parkland featuring the only pond hole in the area which is in play on 3 holes. 18 holes • 5614 yards • SSS 67 • Practice area, putting green.
Green Fees: per round – weekdays £18, weekends £20. Juniors £4.
Eating Facilities: catering 8am-8pm • Bar 11am-11pm.
Visitors: welcome, restricted on Sundays.
Society Meetings: welcome by arrangement. **Secretary:** Mr Thomson

BUCCLEUCH ARMS HOTEL
High Street, Moffat, Dumfriesshire DG10 9ET Telephone 01683 220003 Fax: 01683 221291
2 Single • 14 Double/Twin • 2 Family • (14 En suite, 2 Private facilities)
• B&B per person • Single £40.00 • Double/Twin £35.00
• Room only £35.00 • Children and Pets welcome.
Within easy reach of many golf courses.

The Friendly Place to Play

If you love golf, you'll love it here

See also Colour Advertisement on page 76

Nestling in the heart of the Galloway Hills, Newton Stewart offers spectacular scenery to complement the challenging mature parkland course. Each hole is unique, with excellent greens with subtle borrows; water comes into play over two of the holes. Renowned for its hospitality, visitors are welcome all year round. The clubhouse is fully licensed and offers excellent catering facilities in a friendly environment.

NEWTON STEWART GOLF CLUB
KIRROUGHTREE AVE, MINNIGAFF, NEWTON STEWART DG8 6PF
TEL & FAX: **01671 402172**
NO HANDICAP CERTIFICATE REQUIRED

PORTPATRICK. **Lagganmore Golf Club & Hotel**, Lagganmore, Portpatrick DG9 9AB (Tel & Fax: 01776 810499). Two miles outside Portpatrick, six miles from Stranraer. 18 holes parkland heath course, 5698 yards. S.S.S. 68. Par 69. *Green Fees:* weekdays £15.00; weekends £17.00. *Eating facilities:* bar food and beverages served all day. *Visitors:* welcome, packages available for parties, to include dinner, bed and breakfast and unlimited golf, from £40.00 per person per night. Hotel on site, all rooms en suite. Buggie hire available. *Society Meetings:* welcome, telephone (01776 810499).
website: www.lagganmorehotel.co.uk

PORTPATRICK. **Portpatrick Golf Club,** Clubhouse, Golf Course Road, Portpatrick DG9 8TB (01776 810273; Fax: 01776 810811). *Location:* A77 to Stranraer, follow signs to Portpatrick; A75 fork left one and a half miles after Glenluce bypass, follow signs to Portpatrick. Enter village, fork right at war memorial, then 300 yards on right. Cliff top links-type course. "Dunskey" 18 holes, 5908 yards. S.S.S. 69; "Dinvin" 9 holes, 1504 yards. S.S.S. 27. Practice ground. *Green*

Fees: weekdays £25.00 per round, £35.00 per day; weekends £30.00 per round, £40.00 per day. *Eating facilities:* available all year round except Mondays November to mid-March. *Visitors:* advisable to book in advance (members times). Handicap Certificate required for Dunskey Course. *Society Meetings:* catered for by prior arrangement. Secretary: J. McPhail (01776 810273; Fax: 01776 810811).
e-mail: enquiries@portpatrickgolfclub.com
website: www.portpatrickgolfclub.com

PORT WILLIAM. **St Medan Golf Club**, Monreith, Port William, Newton Stewart DG8 8NJ (01988 700358). *Location:* on A747, three miles south of Port William. Seaside links course with panoramic views of Mull of Galloway and Isle of Man - Scotland's most southerly course. 9 holes, 4552 yards. S.S.S. 63. Practice driving net and green. *Green Fees:* 9 holes £10.00, 18 holes £15.00, day £20.00; weekly £45.00. *Eating facilities:* available (also bar), summer only. *Visitors:* welcome without reservation. Telephone clubhouse for further information.

SANQUHAR. **Sanquhar Golf Club,** Euchan Course, Barr Road, Sanquhar (01659 50577). *Location*: situated quarter-of-a-mile from A76 Dumfries-Kilmarnock trunk road. Undulating parkland with views across the town. Practice areas/net. 9 holes, 5144 metres. S.S.S. 68. *Green Fees*: weekdays £10.00 per day; weekends £12.00 per day. Subject to review. *Eating facilities*: bar available if requested in advance. Visitors: welcome without reservation. Licensed clubhouse with full-size snooker table. *Society Meetings*: Golf package including catering for parties of 12 and over £19.95 per person.

STRANRAER. **Stranraer Golf Club,** Creachmore, Leswalt, Stranraer DG9 0LF (01776 870245; Fax: 01776 870445). *Location:* three miles from Stranraer on the Kirkcolm Road (A718). Parkland, seaside – the last course James Braid designed. 18 holes, 6308 yards. S.S.S. 72. Practice area and putting green. *Green Fees:* weekdays £25.00 per round, £35.00 per day; weekends £29.00 per round, £40.00 per day. 27 holes: weekdays £31.00; weekends £36.00. Fees subject to review. *Eating facilities:* full catering all day, lounge bar overlooks course. *Visitors:* weekdays 9.15am to 12.30pm then 1.30 to 5pm; weekends 9.30am to 11.45am then 1.45pm to 5pm. Pull trolleys and golf carts available for hire. *Society Meetings:* all welcome with prior arrangement. Secretary: Bryce C. Kelly (01776 870245; Fax: 01776 870445).

THORNHILL. **Thornhill Golf Club**, Blacknest, Thornhill DG3 5DW (01848 330546) *Location:* 14 miles north of Dumfries on A76, 1 mile east of village. Parkland/open moorland. 18 holes, 6085 yards. S.S.S. 70. Practice ground (two areas). *Green Fees:* on application. *Eating facilities:* catering available, bar facility. *Visitors:* welcome without reservation, but please contact Alex Hillier to ensure tee times are available. *Society Meetings:* welcome, contact Alex Hillier (01848 331779). e-mail: coordinatorthornhillgc@btinternet.com

WIGTOWN. **Wigtown and Bladnoch Golf Club**, Lightlands Terrace, Wigtown, Newton Stewart DG8 9DY (01988 403354). *Location:* 200 yards from square in Wigtown. Parkland course. 9 holes, 5400 yards. S.S.S. 67. Practice bays. *Green Fees:* £15.00 for 18 holes, £10.00 for 9 holes; Senior Citizens £10.00 (9 or 18 holes), £20.00 per day; Juniors £6.00 (9 or 18 holes). Five day ticket £50.00. *Visitors:* welcome most days, tee reserved for open competitions occasional weekends. No prior booking necessary. *Society Meetings:* welcome by arrangement.

Friendly

There is always an atmosphere of friendliness and welcome at the North West Castle. The large dining room is a hub of activity and conversation.

Curling

Throughout the winter months, from October until March, North West Castle runs sponsored mixed curling weekend competitions. Competitors return year after year, with people meeting up with friends old and new!

Golfing

During the summer, excellent inclusive golf packages are available. You can play golf daily on a choice of four local courses including the exclusive Cally Course at Gatehouse of Fleet.

Relaxing

The hotel has a swimming pool, sauna, Jacuzzi and a games room with full-size snooker table. From October to March, dance the night away after dinner with our Scottish Band playing for residents only.

Stranraer DG9 8EH • Tel: 01776 704413

www.northwestcastle.co.uk

See also Colour Advertisement on page 63

Dunbartonshire

ALEXANDRIA. **Vale of Leven Golf Club**, Northfield Road, Bonhill, Alexandria G83 9ET (01389 752351). *Location:* A82 to Dumbarton, follow signs at roundabout at Dumbarton for Bonhill then club signs. Parkland with splendid views of Loch Lomond. 18 holes, 5165 yards. S.S.S. 66. *Green Fees:* weekdays £16.00 per round, £24.00 per day; weekends £20.00 per round, £30.00 per day. Weekly ticket (Monday to Friday) £70.00. (under review). *Eating facilities:* catering and bar available. *Visitors:* welcome except Saturdays between March and October. Full changing and locker facilities. Shop - Mr Barry Campbell. *Society Meetings:* on application. Club Administrator: Richard Barclay (01389 752351). e-mail: richardbarclay@valeoflevengolfclub.org.uk website: www.valeoflevengolfclub.org.uk

CARDROSS. **Cardross Golf Club**, Main Road, Cardross G82 5LB (01389 841213). *Location:* on A814 west of Dumbarton. Championship parkland course. 18 holes, 6469 yards. S.S.S. 72. Practice ground. *Green Fees:* weekdays £30.00 per round, £45.00 day ticket. *Eating facilities:* lunches/bar snacks available during bar hours. *Visitors:* weekdays only (by phoning Professional to book time). *Society Meetings:* catered for weekdays by arrangement. Professional: Robert Farrell (01389 841350). Secretary: Iain T. Waugh (01389 841754; Fax: 01389 842162). e-mail: golf@cardross.com website: www.cardross.com

CLYDEBANK. **Clydebank and District Golf Club**, Glasgow Road, Hardgate, Clydebank G81 5QY (01389 873289). *Location:* Hardgate village. Off A82 10 miles west of Glasgow (off Great Western Road). 18 holes, 5832 yards, 5325 metres. S.S.S. 68. *Green Fees:* weekdays £16.00 per round. *Eating facilities:* catering as required. *Visitors:* welcome weekdays only. Professional: Paul Jamieson (01389 383835). Secretary: Mrs K. Stoddart (01389 383831; Fax: 01389 383831 by request).

CLYDEBANK. **Clydebank Municipal Golf Course**, Overtoun Road, Clydebank G81 3RE (0141-952 6372). *Location:* one mile west of Clydebank centre off Duntocher Road. Parkland course - one of the best Par 3's in Scotland. 18 holes, 5349 yards. S.S.S. 66. *Green Fees:* on application to Secretary. *Eating facilities:* tearoom. *Visitors:* municipal course, tee closed Saturdays 7.30am till 10.00am and 11.00am to 3.00pm. *Society Meetings:* contact District Council. Secretary: District Council (01389 738762).*

DUMBARTON. **Dumbarton Golf Club,** Broadmeadow, Dumbarton G82 2BQ (01389 732830; Fax: 01389 765995). *Location:* off A82, one mile from town centre. Flat parkland. 18 holes, 6017 yards. S.S.S. 69. Practice area. *Green Fees:* £25.00 weekdays. *Eating facilities:* bar available, meals by previous arrangement with Caterer. *Visitors:* welcome weekdays not Saturday, Sunday or Bank Holidays. No jeans or shellsuits on course or in clubhouse. *Society Meetings:* all welcome with prior bookings through Secretary. Secretary: D.M. Mitchell.

HELENSBURGH. **Helensburgh Golf Club**, 25 East Abercromby Street, Helensburgh G84 9HZ (01436 674173; Fax: 01436 671170). *Location*: A82 from Dumbarton. Moorland course with panoramic views across Loch Lomond and The Clyde Estuary. 18 holes, 6104 yards. S.S.S. 69 Practice area and putting green. *Green Fees*: £25.00 per round, £35.00 per day weekdays. Winter conditions £15.00 per day. *Eating facilities*: full catering and bar. *Visitors*: welcome weekdays only, dress in recognised golfing attire, no denims or trainers. Clubs and golf carts for hire. *Society Meetings*: welcome by arrangement. Professional: David Fotheringham (Tel & Fax: 01436 675505). Secretary: Kim Print (01436 674173; Fax: 01436 671170).

KIRKINTILLOCH. **Kirkintilloch Golf Club,** Campsie Road, Kirkintilloch G66 1RN (0141-776 1256). *Location:* from Glasgow to Bishopbriggs, then straight on to Kirkintilloch. Undulating, parkland course. 18 holes, 5860 yards. S.S.S. 69. Par 70. Putting green and practice areas. *Green Fees:* on application. *Eating facilities:* dining room and bar. *Visitors:* must be introduced by a member. *Society Meetings:* catered for Monday to Friday, information from Secretary including catering. Secretary: I.M. Gray (0141-775 2387).

LENZIE. **Lenzie Golf Club,** 19 Crosshill Road, Lenzie, Glasgow G66 5DA (0141-776 1535; Fax: 0141-777 7748). *Location:* two miles from A90 Junction to Kirkintilloch. Parkland. 18 holes, 5982 yards. S.S.S. 69. Practice ground. *Green Fees:* weekdays £24.00 per round, £30.00 per day. *Eating facilities:* bar and catering facilities available. *Visitors:* welcome any day except weekends. Carts for hire. Private room available for meetings or dinners. *Society Meetings:* welcome. Professional: James McCallum (Tel & Fax: 0141-777 7748). Secretary: Scott M. Davidson (Tel & Fax: 0141-812 3018). website: www.lenziegolfclub.com

FHG PUBLICATIONS

publish a large range of well-known accommodation guides. We will be happy to send you details or you can use the order form at the back of this book.

Dundee & Angus

ARBROATH. **Arbroath Golf Course**, Elliot, By Arbroath DD11 2PE (Tel & Fax: 01241 875837). *Location*: off Dundee Road. Seaside links course. 18 holes, 6185 yards. S.S.S 70. Practice area, new putting green. *Green Fees*: weekdays £18.00 per round, £24.00 per day; weekends £24.00 per round, £32.00 per day. *Eating facilities*: full catering and bar facility. *Visitors*: welcome. *Society Meetings:* all welcome. Professional: L. Ewart (Tel & Fax: 01241 875837). Secretary: Scott Milne (01382 229111).

ARBROATH near. **Letham Grange Golf Course,** Colliston, By Arbroath DD11 4RL (01241 890377; Fax: 01241 890725). *Location:* follow brown Scottish Tourist Board signs for Letham Grange from Arbroath. Two courses – Old Course is a blend of tree-lined parkland and open rolling fairways; water plays a major role which makes the course both scenic and dramatic. Glens Course is slightly shorter and without water hazards, offers golfers a more relaxed and less arduous round; however, it could be deceptive! 36 holes, Old 6968 yards, Glen's 5528 yards. S.S.S Old 73, Glen's 68. Very large practice area, practice putting green, practice chipping green. *Green Fees:* information not provided. *Eating facilities:* golfers' bar and restaurant. *Visitors:* welcome, except reserved members' tee off times. Four star Hotel on site. Trolley, club and buggy hire, PGA Professional group tuition available. *Society Meetings:* all most welcome. Golf shop (01241 890377 or 01241 890373).

BARRY. **Panmure Golf Club,** Burnside Road, Barry, By Carnoustie DD7 7RT (01241 853120). *Location:* two miles west of Carnoustie on A930, signposted from centre of Barry village. Championship links. 18 holes, 6317 yards. S.S.S. 71. Driving range, practice area. *Green Fees:* information not available. Subject to review. *Eating facilities:* full catering seven days a week. *Visitors:* welcome daily except Tuesday and Saturdays mornings. Buggy hire. *Society Meetings:* restricted but welcome. Professional: Neil Mackintosh (01241 852460). Secretary: Major (Rtd) Graeme Paton (01241 855120; Fax: 01241 859737). Bookings 01241 855120.*
e-mail: secretary@panmuregolfclub.co.uk

BRECHIN. **Brechin Golf and Squash Club,** Trinity, By Brechin DD9 7PD (01356 622383). *Location*: Trinity Village, one mile north of Brechin just off A90. Rolling parkland course with glorious views of Grampian Mountains. 18 holes, 6096 yards. S.S.S. 70. Practice ground. *Green Fees*: weekdays £20.00 per round, £28.00 per day; weekends £25.00 per round, £33.00 per day. Mid week package for parties of eight or more £30.00. for two rounds of golf and all catering. *Eating facilities*: excellent catering available at all times; large bar. *Visitors*: welcome, except weekends 7.30am to 10am and noon to 2.30pm. Buggies, carts, club hire. Two squash courts. *Society Meetings*: catered for, reservations in advance. Professional: Stephen Rennie (01356 625270).

CARNOUSTIE. **Carnoustie Golf Links**, Links Parade, Carnoustie DD7 7JE (01241 853789; Fax: 01241 852720). *Location:* 12 miles east of Dundee. Three 18-hole courses. Championship Course 6941 yards. S.S.S. 75; Burnside Course 6020 yards. S.S.S. 69; Buddon Links 5420 yards. S.S.S. 66. Golf trolleys permitted from May to October only. *Green Fees:* Championship Course £82.00 per round; Burnside Course £30.00 per round; Buddon Links Course £25.00 per round. Subject to review. Juvenile rates available. *Eating facilities:* catering facilities can be arranged with the local golf clubs. *Visitors:* welcome, times must be booked. Handicap Certificates required for play on Championship Course. *Society Meetings:* catered for by arrangement. Professional: Colin Sinclair. Course Manager: John Philp. General Manager: G.Duncan. Golf Services Manager: Colin McLeod.

THE APPEARANCE OF AN ASTERISK (*) AT THE END OF A CLUB OR COURSE ENTRY INDICATES THAT UP-TO-DATE INFORMATION HAS NOT BEEN SUPPLIED

PANMURE GOLF CLUB
Great Golf at Carnoustie
Tel: 01241 855120
www.panmuregolfclub.co.uk

A traditional links of great character - Carnoustie's other Championship Course
Located 10 miles east of Dundee, midway between the Championship courses of Carnoustie and Monifieth, and signposted from the A930 which runs through the village of Barry. Though not exceptionally long by today's standards, Panmure requires accurate driving and iron play.
• Driving range • Full catering service • Locker room •
Visitors most welcome apart from Saturday and Tuesday mornings, which are reserved for members and their guests.
Panmure Golf Club, Barry, Carnoustie DD7 7RT

See also Colour Advertisement on page 76

DUNDEE. **Ballumbie Castle Golf Club,** 3 Old Quarry Road, Off Ballumbie Road, Dundee DD4 0SY (01382 730026; Fax: 01382 730008). *Location*: one and a half miles north of Claypotts Junction, less than 2 miles from Dundee city centre. Parkland/heathland course. 18 holes, 6127 yards, S.S.S. 70. 22 bay driving range, putting green, chipping green. *Green Fees*: information not available. *Eating facilities*: clubhouse facilities with menu and full bar. Public house licence. *Visitors*: welcome. Tuition available at driving range. *Society Meetings*: welcome, please telephone for details. Professional: Lee Sutherland (01382 770028).*
e-mail: ballumbie2000@yahoo.com
website: www.ballumbie.golf.com

DUNDEE. **Caird Park Golf Club,** Mains Loan, Dundee DD4 9BX (01382 453606). *Location:* northern edge of city, off Kingsway. Wooded parkland. 18 holes, 6273 yards, 5740 metres. S.S.S. 70. Practice range on course. *Green Fees:* information available from Starter 01382 438871. *Eating facilities:* at clubhouse. *Visitors:* welcome, must book in advance to ensure game. *Society Meetings:* see Dundee District Council, Parks Department. Professional: Jackie Black (01382 459438). Secretary: Greg Martin (01382 864029).

DUNDEE. **Camperdown Golf Club,** Camperdown House, Camperdown Park, Dundee DD2 4TF (01382 623398). *Location:* two miles north-west of city, enter at Kingsway/Coupar Angus road junction. Wooded parkland. 18 holes, 6561 yards. S.S.S. 72, Par 71. *Green Fees:* day ticket £25.00, single round £15.00. *Eating facilities:* must be booked in advance. *Visitors:* welcome, bookable all week, contact Art and Recreation Division, Leisure Centre, Dundee. *Society Meetings:* by arrangement, catered for once booked by Parks Dept. for date and times. Professional: Roddy Brown (01382 623398). Secretary: Isobel Finegan (01382 623398).

DUNDEE. **Downfield Golf Club,** Turnberry Avenue, Dundee DD2 3QP (01382 825595; Fax: 01382 813111). *Location:* follow tourist signs from the main A90 Kingsway for Downfield Golf Course. Wooded, parkland course. 18 holes, 6802 yards, 6266 metres. S.S.S. 73. Large practice area. *Green Fees:* weekdays £45.00 per day, £34.00 per round; weekends £36.00 per round (2003). *Eating facilities:* full catering and bar seven days. *Visitors:* welcome weekdays 9.30am to 11.15am and 2.15pm to 3.30pm, Sunday after 2pm only, pre-booking essential. Carts for hire. Professional: Kenny Hutton (01382 889246). Secretary: Margaret Stewart (01382 825595; Fax: 01382 813111).

DUNDEE. **Piperdam Golf and Leisure Resort,** Foulis, Dundee DD2 5LP (01382 581374; Fax: 01382 581102). *Location:* off A923 Coupar Angus road. Parkland course, 18 holes, 6500 yards. S.S.S. 72.12 bay driving range. *Green Fees:* information not available. *Eating facilities:* restaurant and bar. *Visitors:* welcome. No restrictions. Leisure Centre and Spa. Two and three bedroom lodges. *Society Meetings:* welcome. Packages available. Director: Murdie Smith.*
e-mail: piper.dam@virgin.net
website: www.piperdam.com

EDZELL. **Edzell Golf Club,** High Street, Edzell DD9 7TF (01356 647283; Fax: 01356 648094). *Location:* travelling north from Dundee on A90, take B966 north of Brechin by-pass, continue 3.5 miles to village of Edzell. Parkland course with tree-lined fairways at the entrance to the Angus Glens and in the foothills of the Grampians. "Golfers who are visiting the Angus area cannot afford to miss what is one of Scotland's true hidden gems" Golf Monthly, 1999. 18 holes, 6367 yards. S.S.S. 71. 9-hole West Water Course 4114 yards, S.S.S. 61. 300 yard driving range, chipping area and putting green. *Green Fees:* weekdays £25.00 per round, £35.00 per day; weekends £31.00 per round, £45.00 per day. West Water Course; Monday to Sunday £10.00 per 9 holes, £15.00 per 18 holes. *Eating facilities:* dining room, lounge and bar. *Visitors:* welcome, apply to Secretary. *Society Meetings:* welcome apply to Secretary. Professional: Alistair J. Webster (01356 648462). Secretary: Ian G. Farquhar (01356 647283). Caterer: Mr Peter Wilkie (01356 648235).
e-mail: alastair.webster@virgin.net
      secretary@edzellgolfclub.net
website: www.edzellgolfclub.net

FORFAR. **Forfar Golf Club,** Cunninghill, Arbroath Road, Forfar DD8 2RL (01307 462120). *Location:* one mile from Forfar on A932 to Arbroath. Undulating wooded heathland course. 18 holes, 6066 yards. S.S.S. 70. *Green Fees:* weekdays £24.00 per round, £30.00 per day; weekends £28.00 per round, £35.00 per day (2003 prices). *Eating facilities:* available. *Visitors:* welcome. *Society Meetings:* catered for. Professional: Peter McNiven (01307 465683). Secretary: William Baird (01307 463773; Fax: 01307 468495).

KIRRIEMUIR. **Kirriemuir Golf Club Ltd,** Northmuir, Kirriemuir DD8 4LN (01575 573317; Fax: 01575 574608). *Location:* 20 miles north-west of Carnoustie and six miles north-west of Forfar on A926 and A928, just on edge of Kirriemuir, north of town centre. Parkland and heathland course with stunning views of Angus Glens. 18 holes, 5510 yards, 5038 metres. S.S.S. 67. Putting green, practice ground. *Green Fees:* weekdays £21.00 per round, £28.00 per day; weekends £28.00 per round, £37.00 per day. *Eating facilities:* full catering and bar facilities. *Visitors:* welcome weekdays; at weekends by arrangement. *Society Meetings:* by prior arrangement. Special golf/catering packages available. Professional: Karyn Dallas (01575 573317; Fax: 01575 574608).

MONIFIETH. **Broughty Golf Club,** 6 Princes Street, Monifieth, Dundee DD5 4AW (01382 532147). Starter (01382 532767). *Location:* eight miles east of Dundee, in village of Monifieth. Seaside links, some fairways fringed with trees. Medal Course: 18 holes, 6655 yards. S.S.S. 72. Ashludie Course: 18 holes, 5123 yards. S.S.S. 65. Practice area. *Green Fees:* on request. *Eating facilities:* full catering; no catering Tuesdays or Thursdays. *Visitors:* no visitors before 2pm on Saturdays or before 10am Sundays. All tee times must be booked through Starter's Box. *Society Meetings:* by arrangement. Professional: Mr I. McLeod. Secretary: Peter Flynn.

Kirriemuir is a pleasant mixture of heathland and parkland, situated within some beautiful Angus countryside and is renowned for its superb panoramic views across the Glens. The course was the work of the famous James Braid who was also the inspiration behind Gleneagles.

At 5510 yards, this Par 68 makes for some low scoring. Heathers and whins wind their way strategically along the fairways, making direction, not length, the priority, with fast rolling greens demanding accurate approach play.

We guarantee an enjoyable day at Kirriemuir, with full bar and catering facilities available.

KIRRIEMUIR GOLF CLUB NORTHMUIR, KIRRIEMUIR, ANGUS TEL: 01575 573317

See also Colour Advertisement on page 77

MONIFIETH. **Monifieth Golf Links,** Princes Street, Monifieth, Angus DD5 4AW (01382 532767). *Location:* seven miles east of Dundee, Monifieth High Street. Seaside links. Medal Course 18 holes, 6657 yards. S.S.S. 72; Ashludie Course 18 holes, 5123 yards. S.S.S. 64. Practice facilities. *Green Fees:* Medal Course £38.00 per round; Ashludie Course £20.00 per round - Mondays to Fridays; Medal Course £45.00 per round, Saturdays/Sundays. Ashludie Course £18.00 Monday to Friday, £22.00 per round Saturdays/Sundays. Golf Package - one round on each course plus catering £55.00, available Monday to Friday only. Reduced rates for Panmure Hotel residents. *Eating facilities:* clubs and Hotel. *Visitors:* welcome after 9.30am Monday to Friday; Saturdays after 2pm; Sundays after 10am. *Society Meetings:* parties over 12, must provide club Handicap Certificates. Professional: Ian McLeod (01382 532945). Managing Secretary: S. Fyffe (01382 535553; Fax: 01382 535816).
e-mail: monifiethgolf@freeuk.com
website: www.monifiethgolf.co.

EDZELL GOLF CLUB

Midway between Dundee and Aberdeen.

"Golfers who are visiting the Angus area cannot afford to miss what is one of Scotland's true hidden gems" – *Golf Monthly, June 1999.*

Secretary: 01356 647283; Professional: 01356 648462
website: www.edzellgolfclub.net

Panmure Arms Hotel 52 High Street, Edzell, Angus DD9 7TA

Ideally situated in the picturesque village of Edzell, minutes from the local 18 hole golf course. The large level of varied clubs in close proximity makes the Panmure Arms Hotel the perfect destination for your golfing holiday. Refurbished to the Scottish Tourist Board three star level, with family rooms, twin rooms, double rooms and singles, all en suite. Here the emphasis is on quality and service. The Panmure Arms Hotel provides quality meals at competitive prices, warm and clean surroundings, pleasant and attentive staff and, of course, a plentiful selection of wines, beers and spirits.

For rates and availability telephone David on 01356 648950 • Fax: 01356 648000
e-mail: david@panmurearmshotel.co.uk • website: www.panmurearmshotel.co.uk

See also Colour Advertisement on page 77

AA★★★ The Glenesk Hotel Edzell, Angus DD6 7TF   RAC★★★

This splendid family-run hotel is situated in its own grounds ADJOINING THE 18 HOLE GOLF COURSE. 25 comfortable bedrooms all with modern facilities. Recommended by both golf parties and families who enjoy the friendly atmosphere and Scottish hospitality given by resident directors.

ENJOY OUR LEISURE COMPLEX
Indoor Pool, Sauna, Jacuzzi, and Solarium.
Special Breaks always available.

See our colour advertisement on page 78

Telephone: (01356) 648319 • Fax: (01356) 647333   STB ★★★ Hotel

---

Located four miles from Carnoustie and ½ hour from St Andrews. Two courses offer golf for all levels with the Medal being used as an Open Championship Qualifier. These beautiful links courses also feature tree-lined fairways in many places.

Medal Course £35, Ashludie Course £17; a package includes a round of golf on each course, coffee, bacon roll, soup and sandwiches, and high tea at the day's end. All for £55!

For bookings call the Links Secretary on
01382 532767
The Starter's Box, Monifieth Links,
Princess Street, Monifieth DD5 4AN
monifiethgolf@freeuk.com

The hidden gem in Angus
Monifieth Golf Links

See also Colour Advertisement on page 77

PLEASE MENTION THE GOLF GUIDE WHEN YOU WRITE OR PHONE TO ENQUIRE ABOUT CLUBS OR ACCOMMODATION.

MONTROSE. **Montrose Links Trust**, Traill Drive, Montrose DD10 8SW (01674 672932). *Location*: A92 runs from Dundee to Aberdeen, through Montrose. Links Medal Course 6544 yards. Par 71. S.S.S. 72. Broomfield Course 4830 yards. Par 66. S.S.S. 63. *Green Fees*: Medal: weekdays £36.00 per round, £46.00 per day, Juniors £15.00, UB40 £18.00 per round; weekends £40.00 per round, £54.00 per day, Juniors £17.00, UB40 £20.00 per round. Broomfield: Monday to Friday £18.00 per round, Juniors £6.00 per round, UB40 £9.00; weekends £20.00 per round, juniors £6.00, UB40 £10.00. Composite day fees and special rates on request. Green fees subject to review. *Eating facilities*: catering facilities available by arrangement in golf clubs. *Visitors*: very welcome, no visitors prior to 2.45pm on Medal Course on Saturdays and before 10am on Sundays. *Society Meetings*: welcome by arrangement. Temporary membership available at the following clubs: Caledonia Golf Club (01674 672313); Mercantile Golf Club (01674 672408); Royal Montrose (01674 672376). Professional: Jason J. Boyd. Secretary: Mrs Margaret Stewart (01674 672932; Fax: 01674 671800). e-mail: secretary@montroselinks.co.uk website: www.montroselinks.co.uk

MONTROSE. **Royal Montrose Golf Club,** Dorward Road, Montrose DD10 8SW (01674 672376). *Location:* A92 north from Dundee. Private club playing over the Montrose courses. 18 holes, 6533 yards. S.S.S. 72. *Green Fees:* information not provided. *Eating facilities:* available. *Visitors:* apply Montrose Links Trust. *Society Meetings:* apply Montrose Links Trust. Professional: Jason Boyd. Secretary: J.D. Sykes (01674 672376)

Edinburgh & Lothians

ABERLADY. **Craigielaw Golf Club,** Aberlady EH32 0PY (01875 870800; Fax: 01875 870620). *Location:* half mile west of Aberlady on A198. Links course. 18 holes, 6601 yards, S.S.S. 71, Par 71. Golf Academy and short course. *Green Fees:* information not available. *Eating facilities:* full catering all day; restaurant open to public. *Visitors:* welcome anytime except competition days; advisable to book in advance. Club and buggy hire. *Society Meetings:* society and group bookings welcome. website: www.carigielawgolfclub.com

ABERLADY. **Kilspindie Golf Club**, The Clubhouse, Aberlady, East Lothian EH32 0QD (Tel & Fax: 01875 870358). *Location:* A198 North Berwick Road (off A1 East of Edinburgh) sign posted at east end of Aberlady, overlooking nature reserve and Aberlady Bay. Traditional Scottish links course. 18 holes, 5480 yards, S.S.S. 66, Par 69. *Green Fees:* weekdays £27.50 per round, £44.00 per day; Saturdays and Sundays £33.00 per round, £55.00 per day. *Eating facilities:* dining room with full catering and licensed bars with snack menu. *Visitors:* welcome booking advisable. *Society Meetings:* welcome, prior booking essential. Professional: Graham Sked (Tel & Fax: 01875 870695). General Manager: P.B. Casely (Tel & Fax: 01875 870358). e-mail: kilspindie@btconnect.com

ABERLADY. **Luffness New Golf Club**, Aberlady EH32 0QA (01620 843336; Fax: 01620 842933). *Location:* A198 - 17 miles east of Edinburgh. One mile from Gullane. Links course, 18 holes, 6122 yards. S.S.S. 70. *Green Fees:* provided on application. *Eating facilities:* dining room except Mondays. *Visitors:* weekdays only (require introduction). *Society Meetings:* by prior arrangement. Secretary: Group Captain A.G. Yeates (01620 843336; Fax: 01620 842933).

BATHGATE. **Bathgate Golf Club,** Edinburgh Road, Bathgate EH48 1BA (01506 652232; Fax: 01506 636775). *Location:* three miles from M8, 400 yards east of George Square, the town centre and railway station. Flat course. 18 holes, 6328 yards. S.S.S. 70. Practice area. *Green Fees:* weekdays £20.00 per round, £25.00 per day; weekends £25.00 per round, £35.00 per day. *Eating facilities:* dining rooms open all week. *Visitors:* welcome without reservation except on Competition days at weekends. Handicap Certificates preferred. Electric buggies available. *Society Meetings:* welcome, numbers limited at weekends. Professional: Sandy Strachan (01506 630553). Secretary: W. Allan Osborne (01506 630505; Fax: 01506 636775).

BO'NESS. **West Lothian Golf Club,** Airngath Hill, By Linlithgow EH49 7RH (01506 826030; Fax: 01506 826462). *Location:* situated midway between Linlithgow and Bo'ness. Undulating parkland course with panoramic views over River Forth beyond Stirling to below the Bridges. 18 holes, 6249 yards. S.S.S. 71. Practice ground. *Green Fees:* Round/day £20.00/£25.00 weekdays; £30.00 weekends. *Eating facilities:* bar and catering service. *Visitors:* welcome, advisable to phone weekends. Trolleys. *Society Meetings:* welcome by arrangement. Professional: Ian Taylor (01506 825060). Secretary: Ian Osborough.

BONNYRIGG. **Broomieknowe Golf Club Ltd,** 36 Golf Course Road, Bonnyrigg EH19 2HZ (0131-663 9317; Fax: 0131-663 2152). *Location:* south of Edinburgh, A6094 from Dalkeith. Flat parkland course. 18 holes, 6150 yards. S.S.S. 70. Practice ground. *Green Fees:* weekdays £19.00 per round, £28.00 per day; £20.00 per round at weekends. *Eating facilities:* meals and snacks. *Visitors:* welcome Monday to Friday 9.30am to 4pm, weekends by prior arrangement. *Society Meetings:* welcome weekdays by arrangement. Professional: Mark Patchett (0131-660 2035). Secretary: John D. Fisher (0131-663 9317; Fax: 0131-663 2152). e-mail: administrator@broomieknowe.com website: www.broomieknowe.com

See also Colour Advertisement on page 78

DALKEITH. **Newbattle Golf Club Ltd,** Abbey Road, Dalkeith EH22 3AD (0131-663 2123). *Location:* approximately seven miles south-east of Edinburgh A7 to Eskbank Toll (Newbattle exit). Parkland, wooded course. 18 holes, 6012 yards, 5498 metres. S.S.S. 70. Small practice area. *Green Fees:* £20.00 per round, £30.00 per day. Package deals available. *Eating facilities:* full catering available on request. *Visitors:* weekdays only. No jeans/trainers on course or in clubhouse. *Society Meetings:* welcome. Professional: S. McDonald (0131-660 1631). Secretary: H.G. Stanners (0131-663 1819).

DUNBAR. **Dunbar Golf Club,** East Links, Dunbar EH42 1LL (01368 862317; Fax: 01368 865202). *Location:* coast half a mile east of Dunbar. Seaside links, used for final qualifying 1992 and 2002 Open Championship. 18 holes, 6404 yards, 5855 metres. S.S.S. 71. *Green Fees:* weekdays £37.00 per round, £50.00 per day; weekends £45.00 per round, £60.00 per day. Subject to review. *Eating facilities:* full catering facilities. *Visitors:* no visitors on Thursdays or before 9.30am and between 12.30pm and 2pm weekdays; or before 10am and between 12 noon and 2pm weekends. *Society Meetings:* welcome. Professional: Jacky Montgomery (01368 862086). Secretary: Liz Thom (01368 862317; Fax: 01368 865202). e-mail: secretry@dunbargolfclub.sol.co.uk website: www.dunbar-golfclub.co.uk

DUNBAR. **Winterfield Golf Club**, St. Margarets, North Road, Dunbar EH42 1AU (01368 862280). Seaside course. 18 holes, 4686 metres. S.S.S. 64. *Green Fees:* weekdays £15.50 per round, £22.00 day ticket; weekends £18.00 per round, £27.00 day ticket. *Eating facilities:* Full catering and bar facilities. *Visitors:* welcome without reservation or restriction. Secure changing facilities. *Society Meetings:* welcome without reservation. The Pro Shop: (01368 863562). Professional: Kevin Phillips (01368 863562) Vice Captain: A. Coull; Captain: G. Davidson (01368 862280).

EDINBURGH. **Baberton Golf Club,** 50 Baberton Avenue, Juniper Green, Edinburgh EH14 5DU (0131-453 4911). *Location:* five miles west of Edinburgh on the A70. 18 holes, 6123 yards. S.S.S. 70. *Green Fees:* weekdays £25.00 per round, £35.00 per day; weekends £28.00 per round. *Eating facilities:* by arrangement (phone Angela McKeown (0131-453 4911). *Visitors:* welcome by arrangement with Secretary. *Society Meetings:* catered for. Professional: K. Kelly (Tel & Fax: 0131-453 3555). Club Manager: B.M. Flockhart (0131-453 4911; Fax: 0131-453 4678).

EDINBURGH. **Braid Hills Golf Course,** Braid Hills Approach, Morningside, Edinburgh EH10 6JY *Location:* Braid Hills on south side of Edinburgh. Two 18 hole courses. No. 1 – 5880 yards. S.S.S. 68. No. 2 – 4495 yards. S.S.S. 64. *Green Fees:* information not available. *Visitors:* welcome. Public courses, clubs on hire. Braids United Golf Club, Edinburgh Thistle Golf Club, Edinburgh Western Golf Club and Harrison Golf Club all have clubhouses at Braid Hills and welcome visitors. No Sunday golf on No.1 Course. Sunday catering available on request. Managed by Edinburgh Leisure.*

EDINBURGH. **Bruntsfield Links Golfing Society Ltd,** The Clubhouse, 32 Barnton Avenue, Edinburgh EH4 6JH (0131-336 2006). *Location:* off A90 at Davidson's Mains. Mature parkland course with magnificent views to north over Firth of Forth and to the west. 18 holes, 6407 yards. S.S.S. 71. Excellent practice facilities. *Green Fees:* weekdays £45.00 per round, £65.00 per day; weekends £50.00 per round, £70.00 per day. *Eating facilities:* morning coffee, lunches, dinner by arrangement. *Visitors:* welcome - telephone Professional to arrange times. *Society Meetings:* catered for by arrangement. Professional: Brian MacKenzie (0131-336 4050). Secretary: Cdr D.M. Sandford (0131-336 1479; Fax: 0131-336 5538).

EDINBURGH. **Carrick Knowe Golf Course**. *Location:* situated on the west side of the city on Glendevon Park. Undulating parkland course which has recently undergone a major remodelling. 18 holes, 6150 yards. S.S.S. 69. *Green Fees:* information not available. *Visitors:* welcome. Managed by Edinburgh Leisure. *

EDINBURGH. **City of Edinburgh Golf Club,** Edinburgh Leisure, 54 Nicolson Street, Edinburgh EH8 9DT. *Location:* Club plays over the following municipal courses - Carrick Knowe: 18 holes, 6150 yards. S.S.S. 69; Braids No.1: 18 holes, 5692 yards. S.S.S. 67; Princes Course: 9 holes, 3800 yards. Par 60; Portobello: 9 holes, 4816 yards. S.S.S. 64; Silverknowes: 18 holes, 6198 yards. S.S.S. 69; Craigentinny: 18 holes, 5413 yards. S.S.S. 66. *Green Fees:* from £7.20, membership from £15.00. *Visitors:* welcome all year round. Secretary: Alasdair Dunlop (0131-650 1001). website: www.edinburghleisure.co.uk/webpages/golf.php

EDINBURGH. **Craigentinny Golf Course**. *Location:* Situated on the east side of the city on Fillyside Road. Undulating parkland course. 18 holes, 5413 yards. S.S.S. 66. *Green Fees:* information not available. *Visitors:* welcome. Managed by Edinburgh Leisure.*

EDINBURGH. **Craigmillar Park Golf Club**, 1 Observatory Road, Edinburgh EH9 3HG (0131-667 2837). *Location:* A702 from City Centre on Mayfield Road, right at King's Buildings. Parkland. 18 holes, 5851 yards, 5350 metres. S.S.S. 69. *Green Fees:* £20.00 per round, £30.00 per day. *Eating facilities:* lunches, snacks, high teas and dinners. *Visitors:* welcome weekdays only before 4pm and on Sunday after 2.30pm. *Society Meetings:* catered for by previous arrangement. Professional: B. McGhee (0131-667 2850). Secretary: B. Knowles (0131-667 0047).

EDINBURGH. **Duddingston Golf Club Ltd,** Duddingston Road West, Edinburgh EH15 3QD (0131-661 1005). *Location:* adjacent to A1 Willowbrae Road, turn right at Duddingston crossroads then one mile on Duddingston Road West. Undulating parkland with stream. 18 holes, 6473 yards. S.S.S. 72. *Green Fees:* weekdays only £35.00 per round, £45.00 per day. *Eating facilities:* full catering and bar facilities. *Visitors:* welcome weekdays only. *Society Meetings:* by arrangement (rates on request). Professional: Alistair McLean (0131-661 4301). General Manager: Ian F. Sproule (0131-661 7688).

EDINBURGH. **Kingsknowe Golf Club,** 326 Lanark Road, Edinburgh EH14 2JD (0131-441 1144). *Location:* on the western boundary of Edinburgh with easy access from the City Bypass (Calder Junction). The Clubhouse is located on the A70 Lanark Road. Parkland course. 18 holes, 5979 yards, 5466 metres. S.S.S. 69. Practice area. *Green Fees:* weekdays £22.00 per round, £30.00 per day; weekends £22.00 per round (after 3pm). *Eating facilities:* lounge bar, snacks and meals available. *Visitors:* welcome Monday to Friday, also weekends subject to availability. *Society Meetings:* catered for. Professional: Chris Morris (0131-441 4030). Secretary/Manager: L.I. Fairlie (0131-441 1145).

EDINBURGH. **Liberton Golf Club,** 297 Gilmerton Road, Edinburgh EH16 5UJ (0131-664 3009; Fax: 0131-666 0853). *Location:* Corporation transport to Lodge Gate, buses 3 and 8 from Edinburgh. By car on A7 (Visitors' car park). Parkland, rolling. 18 holes, 5170 yards, 4730 metres. S.S.S. 65. *Green Fees:* information not available. *Eating facilities:* full catering and bar service. *Visitors:* not before 1.30pm weekends. *Society Meetings:* catered for by arrangememt except weekends. Professional: I. Seath (0131-664 1056). Secretary: A. McMillan (0131-664 3009).

EDINBURGH. **Lothianburn Golf Club**, 106a Biggar Road, Edinburgh EH10 7DU (0131-445 2206). *Location:* south on the A702 approximately four miles from city centre or easily reached from Edinburgh bypass road coming off at Lothianburn junction. Hill course close to Pentland Hills. 18 holes, 5662 yards. S.S.S. 68. Practice ground. *Green Fees:* weekdays £16.50 per round, £22.50 per day; weekends £22.50 per round, £27.50 per day. *Eating facilities*: normal bar hours, no hot food on Wednesdays. *Visitors*: welcome mid-week, weekends restricted. *Society Meetings*: catered for by prior arrangement with the Secretary. Professional: Kurt Mungall (0131-445 2288). Secretary: W.F.A. Jardine (0131-445 5067). website: www.lothianburngolfclub.com

EDINBURGH. **Melville Golf Centre, Golf Course, Range and Shop**, Lasswade, Near Edinburgh EH18 1AN (0131-663 8038; Fax: 0131-654 0814). *Location:* three minutes from Edinburgh City Bypass (signposted), on A7. Short but challenging parkland course with large tees and greens, lying in the Esk Valley with panoramic views. 9 holes, 2265 yards, 2070 metres. Par 66. S.S.S. 62. Built to USPGA standard. Floodlit range, 9-hole pay and play course, 4-hole practice/short game area, bunker and putting green. *Green Fees:* weekdays 9 holes £9.00, 18 holes £16.00; weekends 9 holes £11.00, 18 holes £20.00. Concessions available. *Eating facilities:* vended hot and cold drinks and rolls available. *Visitors:* welcome at all times. 24 hour bookings available, full club equipment and shoe hire, PGA tuition. Golf shop; fully stocked ladies, gents, and juniors on-line catalogue (www.shopecosse.com). Tuition available. A Junior Golf Foundation Starter Centre. *Society Meetings:* welcome, advance bookings arranged. Professional : Gary Carter. Contact Mr & Mrs MacFarlane (0131-663 8038 course; Fax: 0131-654 0814).
e-mail: golf@melvillegolf.co.uk
website: www.melvillegolf.co.uk

EDINBURGH. **Merchants Of Edinburgh Golf Club,** 10 Craighill Gardens, Edinburgh EH10 5PY (0131-447 1219; Fax: 0131-446 9833). *Location:* car park Glenlockhart Road, Edinburgh EH10. Hilly, parkland. 18 holes, 4889 yards. S.S.S. 64. *Green Fees:* £16.00 per round, £24.00 per day. *Eating facilities:* full catering available daily. *Visitors:* welcome weekdays, weekends by arrangement. *Society Meetings:* catered for except weekends. Professional: N.E.M. Colquhoun (0131-447 8709). Administrator: John Elvin.
e-mail: admin@merchantsgolf.com
website: www.merchantsgolf.com

EDINBURGH. **Mortonhall Golf Club**, 231 Braid Road, Edinburgh EH10 6PB. *Location:* take A702 south from City to Morningside traffic lights, up Braid Road one mile, course on left. Moorland course with scenic views. 18 holes, 6502 yards. S.S.S. 72. *Green Fees:* £30.00 per round, £40.00 per day. *Eating facilities:* lunch and bar snacks available. *Visitors:* welcome with introduction. *Society Meetings:* catered for (not at weekends). Professional: Malcolm Leighton. Club Manager: Bernadette M. Giefer (0131-447 6974).

EDINBURGH. **Murrayfield Golf Club Ltd,** 43 Murrayfield Road, Edinburgh EH12 6EU (0131-337 3478; Fax: 0131-313 0721). *Location:* Corstorphine Road, two miles west of city centre. Parkland on east side of Corstorphine Hill. 18 holes, 5794 yards. S.S.S. 69. Practice area, net and putting green. *Green Fees:* weekdays £32.00 per round, £37.00 per day. *Eating facilities:* lunch each day except Mondays, snacks in casual bar, also full bar facilities. *Visitors:* welcome playing with member or by prior arrangement only. No visitors weekends. *Society Meetings:* catered for by prior arrangement. Professional: K. Stevenson (Tel & Fax: 0131-337 3479). Club Manager: Mrs M.K. Thomson (0131-337 3478; Fax: 0131-313 0721).

EDINBURGH. **Portobello Golf Course**, Stanley Street, Portobello, Edinburgh EH15 1JJ (0131-669 4361). *Location:* on A1 at Milton Road East. Parkland course. 9 holes, 2400 yards, 2167 metres. S.S.S. 32. *Green Fees:* £5.00 per round (9 holes) weekdays; £6.00 per round (9 holes) weekends. Reductions for Juniors and Senior Citizens. *Visitors:* welcome. *Society Meetings:* not catered for. Managed by Edinburgh Leisure.

EDINBURGH. **Prestonfield Golf Club**, 16 Priestfield Road North, Edinburgh EH16 5HS (0131-667 1273; Fax: 0131-667 9665). *Location:* off Dalkeith Road, near Royal Commonwealth Pool on A7. Parkland. 18 holes, 6214 yards. S.S.S. 70. Practice area. *Green Fees:* weekdays £22.00 per round, £33.00 per day. *Eating facilities:* full catering. *Visitors:* welcome weekdays. Petrol buggies available. *Society Meetings:* welcome weekdays. Professional: J. Macfarlane (0131-667 8597). Secretary: A.S. Robertson (0131-667 9665).
e-mail: prestonfield@btclick.com
website: www.prestonfieldgolfclub.co.uk

EDINBURGH. **Ratho Park Golf Club Ltd,** Ratho, Edinburgh EH28 8NX (0131-335 0069). *Location:* west side of Edinburgh near Airport, access from A71 or A8. Flat parkland course of outstanding natural beauty. 18 holes, 5960 yards. S.S.S. 68. *Green Fees:* weekdays £25.00 per round, £35.00 per day; weekends £35.00 per round. *Eating facilities:* full catering available (not Mondays). *Visitors:* very welcome, please telephone Professional in advance. *Society Meetings:* welcome on Tuesdays, Wednesdays and Thursdays. Professional: Alan Pate (0131-333 1406). Secretary/Manager: Craig R Innes (0131-335 0068).
e-mail: secretary.rpgc@btconnect.com
website: www.rathoparkgolfclub.com

EDINBURGH. **Ravelston Golf Club Ltd**, 24 Ravelston Dykes Road, Blackhall, Edinburgh EH4 3NZ (Tel & Fax: 0131-315 2486). *Location:* A90 Queensferry Road (leading to Forth Road Bridge). Left at traffic lights by Kwik-Fit garage to Strachan Road, cross Craigcrook Road, clubhouse on right. Parkland course. 9 holes, 2600 yards, 2377 metres. S.S.S. 66. *Green Fees:* £15.00 weekdays. Subject to review. Eating facilities; tea, coffee, soft drinks and light snacks. *Visitors:* welcome during quiet periods weekdays only. *Society Meetings:* permitted by special application only. Secretary: Jim Lowrie.

EDINBURGH. **Royal Burgess Golfing Society of Edinburgh,** 181 Whitehouse Road, Barnton, Edinburgh EH4 6BU. *Location:* A90 to Forth Road Bridge, behind Barnton Hotel. Parkland. 18 holes, 6494 yards. S.S.S. 71. *Green Fees:* on request. *Eating facilities:* snacks and lunches available. *Visitors:* welcome weekdays. *Society Meetings:* catered for Tuesdays, Thursdays and Fridays. Professional: Steven Brian (0131-339 6474). Secretary: Graeme Seeley (0131-339 2075; Fax: 0131-339 3712). e-mail: secretary@royalburgess.co.uk website: www.royalburgess.co.uk

EDINBURGH: **Silverknowes Golf Course**, Silverknowes, Parkway, Edinburgh EH4 5ET (0131-336 5359). *Location:* nearest main road Queensferry Road; signs Davidson Mains, Silverknowes. Parkland, flat. 18 holes, 6216 yards. S.S.S. 71. *Green Fees:* information not available. *Eating facilities:* catering available on request. Managed by Edinburgh Leisure.*

EDINBURGH. **Swanston Golf Club**, 111 Swanston Road, Edinburgh EH10 7DS (0131-445 2239). *Location:* five miles from centre of Edinburgh, west of Biggar Road (A702) on the lower slopes of the Pentland Hills. Parkland course. 18 holes, 5024 yards. S.S.S. 66. *Green Fees:* weekdays £15.00 per round, £20.00 day ticket; weekends £17.50 per round, £25.00 day ticket. *Eating facilities:* full catering facilities. *Visitors:* welcome without reservation weekdays, weekends restricted. *Society Meetings:* catered for. Professional: Stu Pardoe (0131-445 4002). Golf carts available. Secretary: John Allan (0131-445 2239).

EDINBURGH. **Torphin Hill Golf Club**, Torphin Road, Edinburgh EH13 0PG (0131-441 4061). *Location:* south west of Colinton Village at terminus of No. 10 bus. Holes 5 to 15 on plateau with outstanding views of Edinburgh. 18 holes, 5091 yards. Par 67. Practice area. *Green Fees:* weekdays £14.00 per round; weekends £20.00 per round. *Eating facilities:* dining room and bar snacks. *Visitors:* welcome without reservation except on Competition Days. No visiting parties at weekends. *Society Meetings:* catered for weekdays only. Reduced rates for parties over 20. Professional: Jamie Browne (0131-441 4061). Secretary: Andrew Hepburn (0131-441 1100).

EDINBURGH. **Turnhouse Golf Club,** Lennie Park, 154 Turnhouse Road, Edinburgh EH12 0AD (0131-339 1014). *Location:* to Glasgow first right at Maybury roundabout. Old established course. 18 holes, 6153 yards. S.S.S. 70. Par 69. *Green Fees:* weekdays £20.00 per round, £30.00 per day; weekends £30.00 per round. *Eating facilities:* full service. *Visitors:* welcome, contact Professional. *Society Meetings:* welcome by prior arrangement with Professional. Professional: John Murray (0131-339 7701). Secretary: A.B. Hay (0131-539 5937). e-mail: secretary@turnhousegc.com website: www.turnhousegc.com

FAULDHOUSE. **Greenburn Golf Club,** 6 Greenburn Road, Fauldhouse EH47 9AY (01501 770292). *Location:* four miles south of Junctions 4 and 5 of M8 motorway. Undulating course, a mixture of moorland and parkland settings. 18 holes, 6055 yards. S.S.S. 70. Practice area. *Green Fees:* information not available. *Eating facilities:* catering available all week. *Visitors:* welcome. *Society Meetings:* welcome by arrangement with Administrator. Professional: Scott Catlin (01501 771187). Club Administrator: Alan Harris.

GULLANE. **Gullane Golf Club,** West Links Road, Gullane EH31 2BB (01620 842255; Fax: 01620 842327). *Location:* 18 miles east of Edinburgh on A198 Edinburgh to North Berwick Road. Links. Three 18 hole courses. No. 1 - (Medal) 6466 yards, 5913 metres. S.S.S. 72; (FWD) 6077 yards, 5557 metres. S.S.S. No. 2 - 6244 yards, 5710 metres. S.S.S. 70. No. 3 - 5252 yards, 4775 metres. S.S.S. 66. Practice, driving range. *Green Fees:* weekdays: No. 1 course £70.00 per round, £95.00 per day; No. 2 course £29.00 per round, £41.00 per day; No. 3 course £17.00 per round, £25.00 per day; weekends No. 1 £85.00 per round, No. 2 £35.00 per round, £50.00 per day, No. 3 £24.00 per round, £33.00 per day. Weekly and combination rates available. Subject to review. *Visitors:* welcome. *Society Meetings:* catered for. Professional: Alasdair Good (01620 843111; Fax: 01620 843090). Club Manager: Stan Owram (01620 842255; Fax: 01620 842327). Starters: (01620 843115). e-mail: manager@gullanegolfclub.com website: www.gullanegolfclub.com

GULLANE. **The Honourable Company Of Edinburgh Golfers,** Muirfield, Gullane EH31 2EG (01620 842123; Fax: 01620 842977). *Location:* 20 miles from Edinburgh along the coast road to North Berwick. Championship links course. 18 holes, 6601 yards. S.S.S. 73. *Green Fees:* information not available. *Eating facilities:* morning coffee, lunches and afternoon teas if ordered in advance. *Visitors:* welcome Tuesdays and Thursdays, maximum Handicap 18 for men, 24 for ladies. Secretary: Group Captain J.A. Prideaux. e-mail: hceg@btinternet.com

HADDINGTON. **Castle Park Golf Club,** Gifford EH41 4PL (01620 810733; Fax: 01620 810723). *Location:* B6369 from Haddington to Gifford, Castle Park is 2 miles south of Gifford, well signposted. Originally 9 holes, now extended to 18 (opened in 2002) combines a unique test of golf with stunning views. 6121 yards (white), 5848 yards (yellow), S.S.S. 70. 8 bay driving range, 6 hole putting green and practice bunker. *Green Fees:* weekdays £20.00 per 18 holes, weekends £25.00 per 18 holes. *Eating facilities:* bar with full catering available. *Visitors:* welcome with some restrictions. Buggies with GPS system available for hire. *Society Meetings:* welcome. Professional: Derek Small (01368 862872; mobile: 07968 209167). Secretary: Stuart Fortune.

HADDINGTON. **Haddington Golf Club,** Amisfield Park, Haddington, East Lothian EH41 4PT (01620 822727). *Location*: three-quarters of a mile from A1, 17 miles east of Edinburgh. Wooded parkland, slightly undulating. 18 holes, 6335 yards. S.S.S. 70. Practice area. **Green Fees**: weekdays from £20.00 per round, £30.00 per day; weekends £30.00 per round, £40.00 per day. **Eating facilities**: two bars and dining room. **Visitors**: welcome, midweek no restrictions, weekends permitted 10am-12 noon, 2-4pm. **Society Meetings**: catered for. Professional: J. Sandilands (01620 822727). Club Manager: (01620 823627; Fax: 01620 826580).
e-mail: hadd.golf1@tesco.net
website: www.haddingtongolf.co.uk

HADDINGTON near. **Gifford Golf Club**, Edinburgh Road, Gifford, Near Haddington EH41 4JE (0162-810 591). *Location:* quarter of a mile west of village. Undulating parkland with burn crossing the course. 9 holes, 6050 yards. S.S.S. 69. *Green Fees:* £15.00 per round, day ticket £25.00 (weekdays only); 9 holes £10.00; Juniors (under 18s) £5.00, weekends £15.00. *Visitors:* closed all day first Sunday in the month. Secretary: G. MacColl (01620 810267). Starter (01620 810 591).

KIRKNEWTON. **Marriott Dalmahoy Hotel and Country Club,** Kirknewton, Midlothian EH27 8EB (Hotel 0131-333 1845; Fax: 0131-335 3203). *Location:* seven miles west of Edinburgh on A71. Parkland courses. East Course: (Championship) host to many major tournaments, 18 holes, 6684 yards. S.S.S. 72. West Course:with a finish around the Gogar Burn that will test your nerve. 18 holes, 5185 yards. S.S.S. 66. Driving range, extensive practice area. *Green Fees:* East Course: Monday to Thursday £55.00 per round, Friday to Sunday £65.00; West Course: Monday to Thursday £35.00 per round, Friday to Sunday £40.00. Winter rates available November to March. *Eating facilities:* The Long Weekend Restaurant and Club Bar in Country Club, restaurant and bars in Hotel also. *Visitors:* welcome 7 days. Hotel accommodation. Golf buggies, trolleys and clubs for hire. Country Club facilities include swimming pool, two outdoor tennis courts, sauna, steam room, spa, gymnasium, fitness and aerobics studio. *Society Meetings:* welcome weekdays only. Director of Golf: Iain Burns (0131-335 8010). Secretary: Mrs Jennifer Bryans (0131-335 8010).

LASSWADE. **Kings Acre Golf Course and Academy,** Lasswade, EH18 1AU (0131 663 3456; Fax: 0131 663 7076). *Location:* A720 Edinburgh City Bypass. Lasswade is two minutes from City Bypass. Parkland course with matured woodland and large contoured greens, set in picturesque countryside close to Edinburgh City Bypass.18 holes (pay and play), 5935 yards. S.S.S. 68. State of the art practice facility. *Green Fees:* weekdays £19.00; weekends £26.00. *Eating facilities:* spike bar, fully licensed restaurant. *Visitors:* all visitors welcome all year (no restrictions), accomodation available on site. PGA tuition, buggy and club hire. *Society Meetings:* all welcome. Director of Golf: Alan Murdoch. Secretary: Lizzie King.
e-mail: info@kings-acregolf.com
website: www.kings-acregolf.com

LINLITHGOW. **Bridgend & District Golf Club**, Willowdean, Bridgend, Linlithgow EH49 6NW (01506 834140; Fax: 01506 834706). *Location:* between Winchburgh and Linlithgow, signposted on main road. 9 holes, 5480 yards, S.S.S. 67. *Green Fees:* £12.00 midweek; £15.00 weekends. *Eating facilities:* catering every day, bar facilities all week. *Visitors:* welcome any time. Secretary: Rich Bertram.

LINLITHGOW. **Linlithgow Golf Club,** Braehead, Linlithgow EH49 6QF (01506 844356; Fax: 01506 842764). *Location:* M8, M9, 20 miles west of Edinburgh, west end of Linlithgow - fork left. Parkland and wooded course with panoramic views. 18 holes, 5729 yards, 5239 metres. S.S.S. 68. Practice area. *Green Fees:* weekdays £20.00 per round, £25.00 per day; Sunday £25.00 per round, £30.00 per day. *Eating facilities:* full catering available, bar open every day. *Visitors:* welcome except Saturdays. *Society Meetings:* welcome by arrangement with Secretary. Professional: Steven Rosie (01506 844356). Secretary: W.S. Christie (01506 842585).

LIVINGSTON. **Deer Park Golf & Country Club**, Golf Course Road, Carmondeans, Livingston EH54 8AB (01506 446699; Fax: 01506 435608). *Location:* off M8 Junction 3 onto Deer Park roundabout. Parkland course, first 9 holes flat, back 9 holes hilly. 18 holes, 6688 yards. S.S.S. 72. *Green Fees:* 18 holes from £28.00. 27 hole package from £42.00. *Eating facilities:* four bars, catering seven days. *Visitors:* welcome. Snooker, ten pin bowling. *Society Meetings:* catered for. Professional: Brian Dunbar.

LIVINGSTON. **Pumpherston Golf Club,** Drumshoreland Road, Pumpherston, Livingston EH53 0LQ (01506 432869). *Location:* one mile east of Livingston, one and a half miles south of M8. Challenging parkland course, recently redeveloped. 18 holes, 6006 yards, 5492 metres. Par 70, S.S.S. 69. Practice area with pitching and bunker facilities, putting green, designed particularly for juniors. *Green Fees:* on application. *Eating facilities:* new clubhouse with bar, dining room and entertainment facilities; junior lounge. *Visitors:* welcome. *Society Meetings:* Mondays to Thursdays, maximum number 30. Professional: R. Fyvie (01506 433337). Secretary: I. McArthur (01506 854584).

LONGNIDDRY. **Longniddry Golf Club Ltd**, Links Road, Longniddry EH32 0NL (01875 852141; Fax: 01875 853371). *Location:* at the foot of Links Road in Longniddry village. Mainly parkland course with links features. Superb views over the Firth to Edinburgh and Fife. 18 holes, 6260 yards, 5690 metres. S.S.S. 70. Practice area, putting green, nets. *Green Fees:* weekdays £35.00 per round, £50.00 per day; weekends £45.00 per round. Subject to review. *Eating facilities:* Catering available seven days, two bars and dining room. *Visitors:* welcome daily, though limited availability at weekends; advance booking recommended. *Society Meetings:* welcome Monday to Friday with Handicap Certificates. Professional: John Gray (01875 852228). Secretary: Neil Robertson (01875 852141).
e-mail: secretary@longniddrygolfclub.co.uk
website: www.longniddrygolfclub.co.uk

MUSSELBURGH. **Musselburgh Golf Club,** Monktonhall, Musselburgh EH21 6SA (0131-665 2005). *Location:* from the A1 end of the Edinburgh City bypass, on the B6415 to Musselburgh. Wooded parkland, rivers. 18 holes, 6725 yards. S.S.S. 73. *Green Fees:* on application. *Eating facilities:* catering available. *Visitors:* welcome with reservation. *Society Meetings:* catered for. Professional: F. Mann (0131-665 7055).

MUSSELBURGH. **Musselburgh Old Course Golf Club**, 10 Balcarres Road, Musselburgh EH21 7SD (0131-665 6981). *Location*: A199 road at Musselburgh racecourse one-and-a-half miles east of town centre. Seaside links course. 9 holes, 2887 yards. S.S.S. 69. Large practice area. *Green Fees*: £8.50 9 holes. *Eating facilities*: available. *Visitors*: welcome. Starter (0131-665 5438). Secretary: L. Freedman (0131 665 4861).
e-mail: mocgc@breathemail.net
website: www.musselburgholdlinks.co.uk

NORTH BERWICK. **Glen Golf Club**, East Links, Tantallon Terrace, North Berwick EH39 4LE (01620 892726; Fax: 01620 895447). *Location:* one mile east of town centre, off A198. Seaside links with magnificent panoramic views. 18 holes, 6243 yards. S.S.S. 70. Practice ground, putting green. *Green Fees:* weekdays £25.00 per round, £36.00 per day; weekends £35.00 per round, £45.00 per day. Reductions for Senior Citizens and Juniors weekdays. *Eating facilities:* full facilities available. *Visitors:* welcome anytime, no restrictions. Pro Shop (01620 894596). Trolleys and caddies available. *Society Meetings:* welcome, advance booking required. Secretary: Mr Kevin Fish (01620 892726; Fax: 01620 895447). Starter: (01620 892726). website: www.glengolfclub.co.uk

NORTH BERWICK. **The North Berwick Golf Club**, New Clubhouse, Beach Road, North Berwick EH39 4BB (01620 895040; Fax: 01620 893274). Location: 24 miles east of Edinburgh, A1 to Meadowmill roundabout then A198 to North Berwick. Seaside links. 18 holes, 6420 yards. S.S.S. 71. Practice ground. *Green Fees:* weekdays £45.00 per round, £70.00 per day; weekends and Public Holidays £70.00 per round, £85.00 per day. *Eating facilities:* diningroom and bar. *Visitors:* welcome from 10am, book ahead Saturdays - restricted when there are club fixtures. Lounge and changing rooms available. *Society Meetings:* catered for by arrangement. Professional: D. Huish (01620 893233). Secretary: N.A. Wilson (01620 895040). Advance Bookings: (01620 892135).

PENICUIK. **Glencorse Golf Club,** Milton Bridge, Penicuik EH26 0RD (01968 677177). *Location:* A701 nine miles south of Edinburgh on Peebles Road. Parkland course with stream affecting 10 holes. 18 holes, 5217 yards. S.S.S. 66. *Green Fees:* weekdays £25.00 per round, £32.00 per day; weekends £32.00 per round. Package deals available. *Eating facilities:* all day catering and bar. *Visitors:* welcome at all times subject to Club Competitions. *Society Meetings:* catered for Mondays to Thursdays and Sunday afternoons. Professional: Cliffe Jones (01968 676481). Secretary: Bill Oliver (01968 677189; Fax: 01968 674399).

PRESTONPANS. **Royal Musselburgh Golf Club**, Prestongrange House, Prestonpans EH32 9RP (Tel & Fax: 01875 810276). *Location:* B1361 North Berwick Road, Prestonpans. Fairly flat parkland, wooded course. 18 holes, 6237 yards. S.S.S. 70. *Green Fees:* weekdays £25.00 per round, £35.00 per day; weekends £35.00 per round. *Eating facilities:* available seven days a week. *Visitors:* welcome. *Society Meetings:* welcome by arrangement with the Management Secretary. Professional: John Henderson (Tel & Fax: 01875 810139). Management Secretary: Thos. H. Hardie (Tel & Fax: 01875 810276). e-mail: royalmusselburgh@btinternet.com
website: www.royalmusselburgh.co.uk

SOUTH QUEENSFERRY. **Dundas Parks Golf Club,** Dundas Estate, South Queensferry, West Lothian EH30 9SS. *Location:* five miles west of Edinburgh, on South Queensferry to Kirkliston road on right of A8000. Parkland course in open countryside. 9 holes (x 2), 6024 yards, 5510 metres. S.S.S. 70. Small practice area. *Eating facilities:* no bar or food facilities. *Visitors:* welcome with member, or by prior arrangement with Club Administrator. *Society Meetings:* by prior arrangement with Club Administrator. Club Administrator: Christine Wood (0131-319 1347).

UPHALL. **Uphall Golf Club**, Uphall, West Lothian EH52 6JT (01506 856404; Fax: 01506 855358). *Location:* eight miles west of Edinburgh Airport on the A89 Edinburgh to Glasgow road. Established parkland course. 18 holes, S.S.S. 67. *Green Fees:* information not available. *Eating facilities:* hot and cold snacks, lunches, high teas and bars, à la carte available Saturday evenings. *Visitors:* welcome weekdays without reservation. A booking through the Professional is required at weekends. *Society Meetings:* catered for. Professional: Gordon Law (01506 855553). Club Administrator: Mima O'Connor: (01506 856404; Fax: 01506 855358). Secretary: Bill Crighton (01506 856404).*

WEST CALDER. **Harburn Golf Club,** Harburn, West Calder EH55 8RS (01506 871256). *Location:* two miles south of West Calder on B7008. Parkland course. 18 holes, 5921 yards. S.S.S. 69. Practice ground. *Green Fees:* Monday to Thursday £20.00 per round, £27.00 per day; Friday £23.00 per round, £30.00 per day; weekends £25.00 per round, £35.00 per day. *Eating facilities:* full catering and bar service available. *Visitors:* welcome any time – no restrictions. *Society Meetings:* catered for by advance arrangement. Professional: S.J. Mills (01506 871582). Secretary: Mr J. McLinden (01506 871131; Fax: 01506 870286).

THE APPEARANCE OF AN ASTERISK * AT THE END OF A CLUB OR COURSE ENTRY INDICATES THAT UP-TO-DATE INFORMATION HAS NOT BEEN SUPPLIED

WHITBURN. **Polkemmet Golf Course**, Polkemmet Country Park, Whitburn, West Lothian (01501 743905). *Location:* off B7066, one mile west of Whitburn. Inland course set within old private estate, mature varied woodland with belts of rhododendrons. 9 holes, 2969 metres. Par 37. 15 bay floodlit driving range. *Green Fees:* weekdays (summer) £5.10 per round, concessions £3.75; weekends and Public Holidays (summer) £5.95 per round, concessions £4.45. *Eating facilities:* restaurant and bar complex. *Visitors:* welcome. Public course. Facilities include bowling green, picnic areas, etc. Caddy cart hire £1.10. Secretary: West Lothian Council, Countryside Section, Property Services, Development and Environmental Services, Lammermuir House, Livingston.

WHITEKIRK. **Whitekirk Golf & Country Club**, Whitekirk, Near North Berwick EH39 5PR (01620 870300; Fax: 01620 870330). *Location:* East of North Berwick, off the main A1 Edinburgh - Berwick upon Tweed road, on the A198. Heathland, wooded, lakes, commanding views over East Lothian. 18 holes, 6526 yards. S.S.S. 72. *Green Fees:* weekdays £25.00 per round, £35.00 per day; weekends £35.00 per round, £50.00 per day. *Eating facilities:* lunches, dinners, bar snacks. *Visitors:* welcome, no restrictions. Golf academy; buggies and carts available. *Society Meetings:* welcome seven days, special rates available. Professional: Paul Wardell (01620 870300; Fax: 01620 870330) Secretary: David Brodie (01620 870300; Fax: 01620 870330). e-mail: countryclub@whitekirk.com website: www.whitekirk.com

WINCHBURGH. **Niddry Castle Golf Club,** Castle Road, Winchburgh EH52 6RQ (01506 891097). *Location:* 10 miles west of Edinburgh on A803 between Kirkliston and Linlithgow. Wooded, natural parkland. 18 holes, 5514 yards. S.S.S. 69. Practice net. *Green Fees:* information not available. *Eating facilities:* full catering; bar. *Visitors:* welcome weekdays before 4.30pm, weekends on competition days after 3.30pm. *Society Meetings:* by arrangement. Secretary: Mr J. Thomson.

GLENCORSE GOLF CLUB
MILTON BRIDGE, PENICUIK EH26 0RD

An extremely picturesque 18 hole parkland course of 5217 yards with an SSS of 66. Green fees are **£25** per round on weekdays and **£32** at weekends and public holidays. A day ticket is also available for **£32**. Packages available on request. Outings are welcome from Monday to Thursday and Sunday afternoons only.

Please contact: W. Oliver (*Secretary*)
Tel: 01968 677189 Fax: 01968 674399
Professional: Cliff Jones 01968 676481

See also Colour Advertisement on page 80

A warm welcome awaits you

Host to the PGA Europro Tour Event

Visitors are most welcome to this challenging course in a spectacular setting near North Berwick.

Society packages designed to suit every golfers need.
Warm & friendly public bar & restaurant.

Green Fees: Weekday £20 per round, £30 per day
Weekend £30 per round, £45 per day

WHITEKIRK
GOLF & COUNTRY CLUB

Whitekirk Golf & Country Club
North Berwick • East Lothian • EH39 5PR
Tel: 01620 870300 • 01620 870330
Email: countryclub@whitekirk.com
Website: www.whitekirk.com

See also Colour Advertisement on page 79

For full details of clubs and courses, plus convenient accommodation, visit the FHG golf website
www.uk-golfguide.com

Fife

ABERDOUR. **Aberdour Golf Club**, Seaside Place, Aberdour KY3 0TX (01383 860080; Fax:01383 860050 *Location:* take Shore Road from centre of village. Parkland course situated along the shoreline of the River Forth. 18 holes, 5460 yards. S.S.S. 66. *Green Fees:* weekdays £20.00 per round, £30.00 per day; weekends £35.00 per round/day Sundays only. *Eating facilities:* full catering. *Visitors:* welcome. *Society Meetings:* catered for on weekdays and Sundays. On Sundays, maximum size of group 24. Professional: David Gemmell (01383 860256). Secretary. (01383 860080; Fax: 01383 860050).

ANSTRUTHER. **Anstruther Golf Club**, Marsfield, Shore Road, Anstruther KY10 3DZ (01333 310956). *Location:* nine miles south of St Andrews, west side of Anstruther. Seaside links course. 9 holes, 4532 yards. S.S.S. 63. *Green Fees:* 9 holes weekdays £9.00; weekends £10.00. 18 holes: weekdays £14.00, weekends £16.00. *Eating facilities:* lounge bar and dining room. *Visitors:* welcome except during club competitions. *Society Meetings:* welcome except Saturdays and competition days. Secretary: S. Gardner (01333 310956/312283).

BURNTISLAND. **Burntisland Golf House Club,** Dodhead, Burntisland KY3 9LQ (01592 874093). *Location:* Rossend Castle, near Kirkcaldy. Parkland with some hills. 18 holes, 5965 yards. S.S.S. 70. Practice ground and net. *Green Fees:* weekdays £20.00 per round, £30.00 per day; weekends £30.00 per round, £40.00 per day. *Eating facilities:* all day bar and catering. *Visitors*: all parties catered for. Changing room. *Society Meetings*: welcome with advance bookings. Professional: P. Wytrazek (01592 872116). Manager: Wendy Taylor (01592 874093).

CARDENDEN. **Auchterderran Golf Club**, Woodend Road, Cardenden KY5 0NH (01592 721579). *Location:* six miles north of Kirkcaldy. Flat course. 9 holes, 5252 yards. S.S.S. 66. *Green Fees*: weekdays £8.00 per round, weekends £10.00 per round. Concessionary ticket available. *Eating facilities:* clubhouse bar facilities, meals available on request, snacks available most times. *Visitors*: all welcome, Saturdays and some Sundays members' competitions held from 7am to 11am and 1pm to 3pm. *Society Meetings:* welcome. Secretary: Charles Taylor (01592 720080).

COLINSBURGH. **Charleton Golf Club**, Colinsburgh Golf Ltd, Charleton, Colinsburgh KY9 1HG (01333 340505; Fax: 01333 340583). *Location:* B942, Colinsburgh (near Elie). Parkland course. 18 holes, 6216 yards, 5684 metres. S.S.S. 72. Driving range, bunker practice area, putting green. *Green Fees:* weekdays £22.00 per round, £35.00 per day; weekends £25.00 per round, £40.00 per day (2003 prices). *Eating facilities:* fully licensed clubhouse with restaurant. *Visitors:* all welcome, pay as you play, no restrictions, please book. Carts, buggies. *Society Meetings:* all welcome. Professional: George Finlayson. Secretary: Peter Griffiths.

COWDENBEATH. **Cowdenbeath Golf Club**, Seco Place, Cowdenbeath KY4 8PD (01383 511918). *Location:* just off the A92 after Dunfermline. Parkland course. 18 holes, 6201 yards. S.S.S. 70. Practice ground and putting green. *Green Fees:.* information not available. *Eating facilities:* full catering in new clubhouse. *Visitors:* welcome at any time. *Society Meetings:* booking available through Fife Council. Secretary: Graham Inglis.

COWDENBEATH. **Dora Golf Course**, Cowdenbeath KY4 8PD (01382 313723). Parkland course, 18 holes. Par 70. *Green Fees:* information not available. *Eating facilities:* Bar and catering available. *

CRAIL. **Crail Golfing Society**, Balcomie Clubhouse, Fifeness, Crail KY10 3XN (01333 450686; Fax: 01333 450416). Instituted 1786. *Location:* eleven miles south-east of St. Andrews on A917. Traditional links courses. Balcomie Links: 18 holes, 5922 yards. S.S.S. 69. Craighead Links: 18 holes, 6728 yards. S.S.S. 73. Practice ground. *Green Fees:* weekdays £32.00 per round, £45.00 per day; weekends and Public Holidays £40.00 per round, £55.00 per day. *Eating facilities:* quality catering and bar. *Visitors:* welcome. *Society Meetings:* advance booking available for parties. Professional: Graeme Lennie (01333 450960). Secretary: A. Busby (01333 450686; Fax: 01333 450416).

CUPAR. **Cupar Golf Club**, Hilltarvit, Cupar KY15 5JT (01334 653549). *Location:* near cemetery on Ceres Road. Hillside/parkland course. 9 holes, 5074 yards. S.S.S. 65. Practice putting green. *Green Fees:* weekdays £15.00; Sundays £15.00. Weekly £50.00. Family per day £30.00. *Eating facilities:* full catering/bar. *Visitors:* welcome, except Saturdays. *Society Meetings:* by arrangement with Secretary. Secretary: John M. Houston (01334 653549). e-mail: secretary@cupargolfclub.freeserve.co.uk website: www.cupargolfclub.co.uk

CUPAR. **Elmwood,** Stratheden, Near Cupar KY15 5RS (01334 658780; Fax: 01334 658781). *Location:* signposted from both A91 and A914, one mile west of Cupar, nine miles from St Andrews. Gently undulating parkland. 18 holes, 5951 yards. S.S.S 68. *Green Fees:* weekdays £18.00 per round, £27.00 per day; weekends £22.00 per round, £31.00 per day, concessions for Seniors and Juniors. *Eating facilities:* full catering and bar. *Visitors:* welcome anytime. Trolleys and buggies available. *Society Meetings:* welcome, advance bookings and special rates. Golf Administrator: Sharif Sulaiman. e-mail: clubhouse@elmwood.ac.uk website: www.elmwoodgc.co.uk

visit the FHG golf website on
www.uk-golfguide.com

Burntisland Golf House Club

Situated at Dodhead, Burntisland, with wonderful views over the River Forth to the Lothians. Our pleasant 5965 yard par 70, parkland course offers a fair test of golf which, combined with our warm hospitality, ensures the makings of a great day out

WEEKDAYS - ROUND £20, DAY £30
WEEKENDS - ROUND £30; DAY £40.

Manager Tel: 01592 874093
Fax: 01592 873247

Charleton Golf Course
Colinsburgh, Fife KY9 1HG
Tel: 01333 340505
Fax: 01333 340583
e-mail: clubhouse@charleton.co.uk
www.charleton.co.uk

Scotland's Premier Pay-as-you-Play Golf Course
Set in stunning parkland, 15 minutes from St Andrews, with spectacular views of the Firth of Forth.

• 18 holes, Par 72 • 9-hole pitch and putt
• Driving range • Clubhouse with restaurant and bar.

Eden House Hotel

2 Pitscottie Road, Cupar, Fife KY15 4HF

The hotel is a Victorian Town House dating from 1876, enjoying a truly superb elevated position overlooking the Haugh Park in the centre of Cupar, one of the oldest burghs in Scotland.
Personal care, attention and the warmest of welcomes awaits.

Tel: 01334 652510 • Fax: 01334 652277
E-mail: info@edenhousehotel.com
Web: www.glenfarghotel.co.uk

Exclusive for guests at the Glenfarg and Eden House Hotels, our private minibus, capable of seating 8 people, is available 24 hours a day for transport to golf course, airport, city... in fact anywhere in the UK. It can be booked at either reception.

See also Colour Advertisement on page 80

Scotstarvit Farm Cupar KY15 5PA Tel & Fax 01334 653591

Ideally situated in an Area of Outstanding Natural Beauty with breathtaking views, this stone-built cottage is well appointed with colour TV/teletext, microwave, washer/dryer and central heating. Private Parking. Enviably placed for the many golf and leisure activities in the area, Scotstarvit is only 10 minutes' drive from St Andrews and Fife's fishing villages. Edinburgh, Dundee, Perth & Aberdeen are within easy reach. Terms from **£140** to **£395** per week. 2 person discounts. Short breaks. Open all year. Quality farmhouse B&B also from **£16** per night.
STB ★★★ Self-Catering.

e-mail: **chrisp.scotstarvit@ukgateway.net**
website: **www.scotstarvitfarm.co.uk**

PLEASE MENTION `THE GOLF GUIDE` WHEN YOU WRITE
OR PHONE TO ENQUIRE ABOUT CLUBS OR ACCOMMODATION.

DUNFERMLINE. **Canmore Golf Club,** Venture Fair, Dunfermline (01383 724969). *Location:* one mile north of town centre on A823. Parkland, undulating. 18 holes, 5347 yards. S.S.S. 66. *Green Fees:* weekdays £16.00 per round, £22.00 per day; weekends £21.00 per round, £32.00 per day (including golfer's insurance). *Eating facilities:* full catering and bar. *Visitors:* welcome weekdays, limited Sundays. *Society Meetings:* we welcome visiting societies with prior reservation (not on Saturdays). Professional: Gavin Cook (01383 728416). Secretary: Charlie Stuart (01383 513604).

DUNFERMLINE. **Dunfermline Golf Club,** Pitfirrane, Crossford, By Dunfermline KY12 8QW (01383 723534). *Location:* two miles west of Dunfermline on A994 to Kincardine Bridge. Undulating parkland. 18 holes, 6121 yards, 5597 metres. S.S.S. 70. Practice area. *Green Fees:* £25.00 per round, £35.00 per day weekdays; £35.00 per round Sundays. *Eating facilities:* full catering, bar snacks available. *Visitors:* welcome 9.30am to 4pm weekdays and Sunday. Must have official Club Handicap. *Society Meetings:* accepted weekdays and Sunday by prior arrangement. Professional: Chris Nugent (01383 729061). Secretary: Robert De Rose (01383 723534).

DUNFERMLINE. **Forrester Park Resort,** Pitdinnie, Cairneyhill KY12 8RF (01383 880505; Fax: 01383 882505). Parkland course with gentle undulations and lots of water features. 300m driving range, practice bunkers, greens and putting green. *Green Fees:* weekdays £30.00, weekends £45.00. *Eating facilities:* Acanthus 5 star à la carte restaurant and bar/bistro. *Visitors:* welcome, no restrictions. *Society Meetings:* always welcome, groups of over 15 in number £28.00. Tuition, golfshop, showers available. Professional: Jamie Mitchell. Secretary: Robert Forrester. e-mail: forresterpark@aol.com website: www.forresterparkresort.com

DUNFERMLINE. **Pitreavie (Dunfermline) Golf Club,** Queensferry Road, Dunfermline KY11 8PR (Tel & Fax: 01383 722591). *Location:* M90 Edinburgh/ Perth, leave at Junction 2 for Dunfermline. Undulating parkland with views across Firth of Forth. 18 holes, 6008 yards. S.S.S. 69. Practice ground. *Green Fees:* information not available. *Eating facilities:* full catering and bar facilities available. *Visitors:* welcome. Please phone the Professional in advance, must have recognised Golf Union Handicap. Trolleys and carts available. *Society Meetings:* catered for, must be booked through Secretary. Professional: Paul Brookes (01383 723151). Secretary: Eddie Comerford (01383 722591).*

DUNFERMLINE. **Saline Golf Club,** Kinneddar Hill, Saline KY12 9LT (01383 852591). *Location:* turn off M90 at Junction 4, 7 miles along B914 to Dollar. Hillside parkland course. 9 holes, 5302 yards. S.S.S. 66. Practice net, putting green. *Green Fees:* weekdays £10.00; weekends £12.00. Reductions for Juniors and Senior Citizens. *Eating facilities:* bar snacks; meals by prior arrangement. *Visitors:* welcome, except Saturdays and certain Sundays. *Society Meetings:* catered for midweek or Sundays; maximum 24. Secretary: Mr P. Bridson (01383 851040).

ELIE. **Earlsferry Thistle Golf Club,** Melon Park, Elie (01333 330301). *Location:* A917 golf course signs in Elie. Seaside links. 18 holes, 6250 yards. S.S.S. 70. *Green Fees:* set by Elie Golf House Club, on application. *Visitors:* welcome weekdays. The course belongs to Elie Golf House Club, also played by Earlsferry Thistle.

ELIE. **Golf House Club,** Elie KY9 1AS (01333 330301; Fax: 01333 330895). *Location:* 10 miles south of St Andrews on A917. Links course. 18 holes, 6273 yards. S.S.S. 70. *Green Fees:* weekdays £40.00 per round, £55.00 per day; weekends £50.00 per round, £65.00 per day. Subject to review. *Eating facilities:* lunches, teas, etc. *Visitors:* welcome with reservation. Elie Sports Centre nearby with leisure facilities and cafeteria. *Society Meetings:* catered for except at weekends. Professional: Robin Wilson (01333 330955). Secretary: Alexander Sneddon (01333 330301; Fax: 01333 330895).

FALKLAND. **Falkland Golf Club,** The Myre, Falkland KY15 7AA (01337 857404). *Location:* entrance on A912, 12 miles from Kirkcaldy – approximately 20 minutes from St. Andrews. Lies at the foot of East Lomond Hills. Flat meadowland, beautiful views. 9 holes, 2608 yards, 2384 metres. S.S.S. 66 for 18 holes. *Green Fees:* information not available. *Eating facilities:* snacks/meals. *Visitors:* welcome, no problem during weekdays, phone for availability weekends. *Society Meetings:* must book in advance. Secretary: Mrs H.H. Horsburgh.*

GLENROTHES. **Glenrothes Golf Club,** Golf Course Road, Glenrothes KY6 2LA (01592 758686). *Location:* at the western end of town, near airfield. Parkland, wide fairways, with burn crossing four fairways on back nine holes. 18 holes, 6444 yards, 5984 metres. S.S.S. 71. *Green Fees:* information not available. *Eating facilities:* full catering service and bar. Temporary day membership of club available to visitors. *Visitors:* welcome, some restrictions weekends. *Society Meetings:* welcome, advance booking, numbers 12-40. Hon. Secretary: Claire Dawson (01592 754561).*
website: www.glenrothesgolf.org.uk

KINCARDINE. **Tulliallan Golf Club,** Alloa Road, Kincardine on Forth, by Alloa FK10 4BB (01259 730396). *Location:* on A908 five miles east of Alloa, one mile north of Kincardine Bridge. Parkland, slightly wooded, burn winds through the course. 18 holes, 6000 yards. S.S.S. 69. Practice ground. *Green Fees:* weekdays £18.00/£32.00; weekends £23.00/ £40.00. *Eating facilities:* dining room, bar 11am to 11pm. *Society Meetings:* catered for by phoning Pro shop. Professional: Steve Kelly (Tel & Fax: 01259 730798). Secretary: Mr N.C. Raleigh (01259 730396).

KINGHORN. **Kinghorn Municipal Golf Club**, MacDuff Crescent, Kinghorn KY3 9RE (01592 890345). *Location:* bus stop at course, railway station three minutes away. Semi links course with hills. 18 holes, 5166 yards, S.S.S. 66. *Green Fees:* information not available. *Eating facilities:* meals at clubhouse on request, local hotels. *Visitors:* welcome at any time; no large parties on Saturdays. *Society Meetings:* catered for by arrangement. Secretary: Iain Gow (01592 265445). Starter: (01592 890978). *

KIRKCALDY. **Dunnikier Park Golf Club,** Dunnikier Way, Kirkcaldy KY1 3LP (01592 261599 (Clubhouse); 01592 642541 (Secretary)). *Location:* one mile off A92 on the B981 north side of Kirkcaldy. Municipal parkland course, not hilly. 18 holes, 6601 yards, 6036 metres. S.S.S. 72. Practice ground. *Green Fees:* weekdays £11.50 per round, £18.00 per day; weekends £15.50 per round, £22.00 per day. Concessions for over 60s. *Eating facilities:* full bar and catering facilities. *Visitors:* welcome, no restrictions. *Society Meetings:* welcome by arrangement with Secretary (min. 12, max. 30). Professional: Gregor Whyte (01592 642121). Secretary: Raymond Johnston (01592 261599).

KIRKCALDY. **Kirkcaldy Golf Club,** Balwearie Road, Kirkcaldy KY2 5LT (01592 260370). *Location:* west end of town adjacent to Beveridge Park. Challenging parkland layout in rural setting with views across Firth of Forth. 18 holes, 6004 yards. S.S.S. 69. Practice ground. *Green Fees:* weekdays £24.00 per round, £30.00 per day; weekends £30.00 per round, £38.00 per day. *Eating facilities:* bar and full catering facilities. Magnificent clubhouse. *Visitors:* welcome except Saturdays, restricted Tuesdays. Professional's shop. Trolleys for hire. *Society Meetings:* welcome but please phone or write in advance. Professional: Anthony Caira (01592 203258). Secretary: Alistair C. Thomson (01592 205240).

LADYBANK. **Ladybank Golf Club,** Annsmuir, Ladybank KY15 7RA (01337 830320). *Location:* on A92 off A91, 15 miles St. Andrews. Wooded heathland. 18 holes, 6641 yards. S.S.S. 72. Practice

ground. *Green Fees:* weekdays £40.00 per round, £50.00 per day; weekends £45.00 very limited. *Eating facilities:* full catering facilities and bar. *Visitors:* welcome without reservation. Party bookings by arrangement with Secretary. *Society Meetings:* by arrangement. Professional: Martin J. Gray (Tel & Fax: 01337 830725). Secretary: D.R. Allan (01337 830814; Fax: 01337 831505).

LESLIE. **Leslie Golf Club,** Balsillie Laws, Leslie, Glenrothes KY6 3EZ (01592 620040). Parkland with small stream running through some fairways. 9 holes, 4940 yards. S.S.S. 64. *Green Fees:* information not available. *Eating facilities:* bar open all day. *Visitors:* always welcome, some restrictions on competition days. Hon Secretary: Gordon Lewis (01592 612617).

LEUCHARS. **St Michaels Golf Club,** Gallowhill, Leuchars KY16 0DX (01334 839365; Fax: 01334 838666). *Location:* quarter of a mile outside Leuchars on A919 towards Dundee. Undulating parkland course surrounded by plantations. 18 holes, 5802 yards. S.S.S. 68. *Green Fees:* all week £25.00 per round, £32.00 for a day ticket. *Eating facilities:* bar and catering available. *Visitors:* welcome anytime but not before 12 noon Sundays. Changing rooms and showers. Trolley hire. *Society Meetings:* by prior arrangement. A booking fee is payable before confirmation of reservation. Secretary: Mr Spong (Tel & Fax: 01334 838666).

LEVEN. **Leven Golfing Society,** PO Box 14609, Links Road, Leven KY8 4HS (01333 426096; Fax: 01333 424229). *Location:* 14 miles south west of St Andrews. Championship Links course used for national and international events, including open qualifying. 18 holes, 6427 yards. S.S.S. 70. *Green Fees:* weekdays £30.00 round, £40.00 day; weekends £35.00 round, £50.00 day. *Eating facilities:* full catering available. *Visitors:* welcome except Saturdays. *Society Meetings:* by arrangement, please contact the Secretary, Links Joint Committee, Promenade, Leven KY8 4HS (01333 428859). Secretary: Alistair McDonald (Tel & Fax: 01333 424229).

Leven Links, in part one of the oldest pieces of golfing ground in the world, is a true seaside links course. It has hosted many national and international events and is used as a final qualifying course for the Open Championship when it is held at St Andrews. The strength of Leven Links lies in its fine variety of links-type holes combined with large greens; turning into the prevailing west wind at the 13th leaves the golfer with a lot of work to do before reaching one of the finest finishing holes in golf.

Leven Links, The Promenade, Leven, Fife KY8 4HS
Tel/Fax: 01333 428859
e-mail: secretary@leven-links.com
See also Colour Advertisement on page 81

LEVEN. **Leven Thistle Golf Club,** Balfour Street, Leven KY8 4JF (01333 426333; Fax: 01333 439910). *Location:* 10 miles south west of St. Andrews. Top championship links used for national and international events including Open qualifying. 18 holes, 6434 yards. S.S.S. 70. *Green Fees:* weekdays £30.00 per round, £40.00 per day; weekends £35.00 per round, £50.00 per day. *Eating facilities:* full catering available, two bars, function hall. *Visitors:* welcome without reservation, except Saturdays. *Society Meetings:* for group bookings contact Leven Links Joint Committee, Promenade, Leven, Fife KY8 4HS (01333 428859). Secretary: J. Scott. Links Secretary: Mr R. Bissett.

LEVEN. **Scoonie Golf Club,** North Links, Leven KY8 4SP (01333 307007). *Location:* nearest town Leven on coastal road to St Andrews. Flat, typical seaside bunkers. 18 holes, 4979 metres. S.S.S. 65. *Green Fees:* information not available. *Eating facilities:* full catering available, bar open normal hours. *Visitors:* welcome anytime. *Society Meetings:* welcome by bookings except Saturdays. Secretary: S. Kuczerepa (01333 307007; Fax: 01333 307008).*

LOCHGELLY. **Lochgelly Golf Club,** Cartmore Road, Lochgelly (01592 780174). *Location:* take M90 to Junction 4 Halbeath Interchange, follow signs. Parkland. 18 holes, 5491 yards, 5063 metres. S.S.S. 67. *Green Fees:* weekdays £16.00 per round, £25.00 per day; weekends £25.00 per round, £32.00 per day. *Eating facilities:* catering available. *Visitors:* welcome, no restrictions weekdays, weekends parties limited to 24. Professional: Martin Goldie (01592 782589). Secretary: R.F. Stuart (01383 512238).

LUNDIN LINKS. **Lundin Golf Club,** Golf Road, Lundin Links KY8 6BA (01333 320202). *Location:* three miles east of Leven, 14 miles east of Kirkcaldy. Seaside links. 18 holes, 6394 yards. S.S.S. 71. Practice ground. *Green Fees:* £37.00 per round, £47.00 per day weekdays; Saturdays after 2.30pm £47.00 per round. *Eating facilities:* bar and dining room. *Visitors:* welcome Monday/Thursday 9am to 3.30pm; Friday 9am to 3pm; Saturdays no visitors before 2.30pm; limited Sunday golf available. *Society Meetings:* limited numbers. Professional: David K. Webster (01333 320051). Secretary: D.R. Thomson (01333 320202).
e-mail: secretary@lundingolfclub.co.uk
website: www.lundingolfclub.co.uk

LUNDIN LINKS. **Lundin Ladies Golf Club,** Woodielea Road, Lundin Links KY8 6AR (01333 320832). *Location:* at Lundin Links on A915, turn into road opposite Royal Bank of Scotland. Excellent parkland course, with famous standing stones. 9 holes, 2365 yards. S.S.S. 67. Putting green. *Green Fees:* Winter Rates: weekdays £5.00 9 holes, £7.50 18 holes; weekends £6.00 9 holes, £10.00 18 holes. Summer Rates: weekdays £8.00 9 holes, £12.50 18 holes; weekends £10.00 9 holes, £15.00 18 holes. *Eating facilities:* tea making facilities only. *Visitors:* welcome, restricted tee times on Wednesdays during season. Starter (01333 320022). Secretary: Mrs M. Mitchell (01333 320832).

MARKINCH. **Balbirnie Park Golf Club,** The Clubhouse, Balbirnie Park, Markinch, Glenrothes KY7 6NR (01592 612095; Fax: 01592 612383). *Location:* outside Markinch near the A92. Wooded parkland course. 18 holes, 6212 yards. S.S.S. 70. *Green Fees:* information not available. *Eating facilities:* snacks, lunch, high tea and full meals available during clubhouse hours. *Visitors:* no restrictions at present other than maximum number of 24 at weekends and no visitors before 10am weekends. *Society Meetings:* welcome. Professional: Craig Donnelly (Tel & Fax: 01592 752006). Club Administrator: Steve Oliver (01592 612095; Fax: 01592 612383). Starter: (01592 752006).*

ST ANDREWS. **Balgove Course,** St Andrews Links Trust, St Andrews KY16 9SF (01334 466666; Fax: 01334 466664). *Location:* A91 to St Andrews, turning is on the left just before the town. Public 9 hole beginners' course, 1520 yards. S.S.S. 60 (18 holes). *Green Fees:* High Season £10.00, Low Season £7.00. *Eating facilities:* adjacent Eden Clubhouse with full facilities. Children's room. *Visitors:* welcome with or without reservation. Trolleys £3.00 per round. *Society Meetings:* welcome.

ST ANDREWS. **Drumoig Hotel and Golf Resort,** Drumoig, Leuchars, St Andrews KY16 0BE (01382 541800; Fax: 01382 542211). *Location:* on A92 (St Andrews to Dundee), four miles south of Dundee. Natural free draining, rolling countryside over sandy based ground featuring spectacular water holes. Unusual quarry greens and views of St Andrews Bay and Carnoustie. 18 holes, 6835 yards. S.S.S 72. Reduced rates for parties of 10 or more. *Green Fees:* information not available. *Eating facilities:* bar and restaurants. *Visitors:* welcome. 29 bedroom hotel, all en suite (5 executive suites). *Society Meetings:* welcome. Home of Scottish National Golf Centre - Europe's Premier indoor and outdoor practice facility.*

ST ANDREWS. **The Duke's Course,** Craigton, St Andrews KY16 8NS (01334 474371; Fax: 01334 479456). *Location:* 2½ miles from town centre, signposted on A91. Inland championship tree-lined course with undulating fairways and American-style greens. 18 holes, 7271 yards. S.S.S. 75. Grassed driving range, putting and short game area. *Green Fees:* £75.00. *Eating facilities:* restaurant and bar; private dining room. *Visitors:* welcome, no restrictions. Trolley and buggy hire; club and shoe hire. *Society Meetings:* please call for details of packages. Professional: Ron Walker. Secretary: Steve Toon. e-mail: reservations@oldcoursehotel.co.uk
website: www.oldcoursehotel.co.uk

ST ANDREWS. **Eden Course,** St Andrews Links Trust, Pilmour House, St Andrews KY16 9SF (01334 466666; Fax: 01334 466664). *Location:* A91 main road into St Andrews, turning is left just before the town; approximately 50 miles from Edinburgh. Seaside links. 18 holes, 6195 yards. S.S.S. 70. 44 bay driving range. Practice facilities. *Green Fees:* High Season £30.00, Low Season £22.00. *Eating facilities:* Eden Clubhouse, lounge bar, dining room (seats 60) children's room. *Visitors:* welcome with or without reservation. Trolleys £3.00 per round. *Society Meetings:* always welcome.

ST ANDREWS. **Jubilee Course,** St Andrews Links Trust, Pilmour House, St Andrews KY16 9SF (01334 466666; Fax: 01334 466664). *Location:* go into St Andrews on the A91, follow signs to West Sands; approximately 50 miles from Edinburgh. Public links. 18 holes, 6742 yards. S.S.S. 73. 44 bay driving range, practice facilities available. *Green Fees:* High Season £50.00, Low Season £32.00. *Eating facilities:* lounge bar, dining room (seats 60). *Visitors:* always welcome. Trolleys £3.00 per round. *Society Meetings:* welcome.

ST ANDREWS. **New Course,** St Andrews Links Trust, Pilmour House, St Andrews KY16 9SF (01334 466666; Fax: 01334 466664). *Location:* go into St Andrews on the A91, follow signs to West Sands; approximately 50 miles from Edinburgh. Public links course. 18 holes, 6604 yards. S.S.S. 73. 44 bay driving range, practice ground. *Green Fees:* High Season £55.00, Low Season £38.00. *Eating facilities:* clubhouse, large bar, dining room (seats 60). *Visitors:* welcome. Buggies may be hired by senior citizens or for those carrying a medical certificate, trolleys are £3.00 per round. *Society Meetings:* welcome.

ST ANDREWS. **Old Course,** St Andrews KY16 9SF (01334 466666; Fax: 01334 466664). *Location:* go into St Andrews on the A91, follow signs to West Sands. Approximately 50 miles from Edinburgh. Public links. 18 holes, 6566 yards, 6004 metres. S.S.S. 72. 44 bay driving range, practice facilities. *Green Fees:* High Season £110.00, Low Season £75.00. *Eating facilities:* clubhouse with full facilities; there is a buggy shuttle run from the clubhouse to the Old Course. *Visitors:* Handicap Certificate required. Handicap limit 24 or less (Men), 36 or less (Ladies). Trolleys allowed after 12 noon from May to September. *Society Meetings:* welcome.

ST ANDREWS. **Strathtyrum Course,** St Andrews Links Trust, Pilmour House, St Andrews KY16 9SF (01334 466666; Fax: 01334 466664). *Location:* A91 main road into St Andrews, turning is on the left just before the town. Approximately 50 miles from Edinburgh. Public links course, 18 holes, 5094 yards. S.S.S. 65. 44 bay driving range, practice ground. *Green Fees:* High Season £20.00, Low Season £16.00. *Eating facilities:* adjacent Eden clubhouse with full facilities. Children's room. *Visitors:* welcome. Buggies may be hired by senior citizens or by those carrying a medical certificate. Trolleys are £3.00 per round. *Society Meetings:* welcome.

TAYPORT. **Scotscraig Golf Club,** Tayport DD6 9DZ (01382 552515; Fax: 01382 553130). *Location:* ten miles north of St Andrews. Links/parkland. 18 holes, 6550 yards. S.S.S. 72. *Green Fees:* information not provided. *Eating facilities:* lunches and high teas. *Visitors:* welcome on weekdays or weekends by prior arrangement. *Society Meetings:* catered for subject to approval. Company Days available. Professional: S.J. Campbell (01382 552855). Secretary: B.D. Liddle (01382 552515).

THORNTON. **Thornton Golf Club,** Station Road, Thornton KY1 4DW (01592 771111 office, 771173 starter). *Location:* southeast Fife located off A92, midway between Glenrothes and Kirkcaldy. Easily walked parkland course bounded by River Ore. Renowned for condition of greens. 18 holes, 6170 yards, 5695 metres. S.S.S. 69. Practice area, chipping and putting areas. *Green Fees:* weekdays £20.00 per round, £30.00 per day; weekends £30.00 per round, £40.00 per day. Parties of 18 or more get one free place. *Eating facilities:* full catering service and bar. *Visitors:* very welcome, restricted weekends before 10am and between 12 noon and 2.30pm. Recently built clubhouse; trolleys for hire. *Society Meetings:* catered for. Secretary: W.D. Rae.

Glasgow & District

BISHOPBRIGGS. **Bishopbriggs Golf Club,** Brackenbrae Road, Bishopbriggs G64 2DX (0141-772 1810). *Location:* quarter mile from Bishopbriggs Cross off Glasgow-Kirkintilloch road. Fairly flat parkland course. 18 holes, 6041 yards. S.S.S. 69. *Green Fees:* on application. *Eating facilities:* full service always available. *Visitors:* weekends/Public Holidays with member only, other times apply to Secretary. *Society Meetings:* catered for Monday to Friday, application to committee at least one month in advance. Secretary: Andrew Smith (0141-772 8938). *

CUMBERNAULD. **Palacerigg Golf Club,** Palacerigg Country Park, Cumbernauld, Near Glasgow G67 2BY (01236 734969). *Location:* Cumbernauld off A80 between Glasgow and Stirling, Palacerigg Road, three miles south of Cumbernauld. Wooded parkland with good views to Campsie Hills, designed by Henry Cotton. 18 holes, 6444 yards, 5894 metres. S.S.S. 71. Practice area. *Green Fees:* weekdays £8.00; weekends £10.00. Full membership available contact Secretary. *Eating facilities:* full catering facilities. *Visitors:* welcome, advance booking recommended for individual rounds. *Society Meetings:* welcome weekdays, full days golf and catering £25.00. Other packages available contact Secretary or club steward. Starter: John Murphy (Tel & Fax: 01236 721461). Secretary: David S.A. Cooper (01236 734969; Fax: 01236 721461). e-mail: palacerigg-golfclub@lineone.net website: www.palacerigggolfclub.co.uk

CUMBERNAULD. **The Westerwood Hotel, Golf and Country Club,** Westerwood, Cumbernauld G68 0EW (01236 457171; Fax: 01236 860730). *Location:* between Glasgow and Stirling, off A80 towards Dullatur. Parkland, rolling American style; designed by Seve Ballesteros and Dave Thomas. 18 holes, 6616 yards. S.S.S. 72. *Green Fees:* weekdays £27.50, weekends £30.00. *Eating facilities:* full catering facilities. *Visitors:* welcome at all times, no restrictions. Advance booking of tee times recommended. 100 bedroom Hotel, full leisure facilities and indoor pool. *Society Meetings:* welcome by arrangement, packages available, including corporate membership. Professional and Club Manager: Alan Tait (Tel & Fax: 01236 725281). e-mail: alantait@morton-hotels.com

GLASGOW. **Alexandra Golf Club,** Alexandra Park, Alexandra Parade, Glasgow G31 8SE (0141-556 1294). *Location:* M8 off ramp to Alexandra Parade. Wooded Parkland, very hilly. 9 holes, 1965 yards, S.S.S. 35. Practice area. *Green Fees:* available on request. *Visitors:* welcome at all times. Blind Club and Unemployed club use this course. Room available for functions, to book phone 0141-770 0519 (24 hours notice is required). Bowling greens are available from Easter to September. Professional: Paul West (0141-556 1294). Secretary: G. Campbell (0141-556 1294).

GLASGOW. **Balmore Golf Club,** Balmore, Torrance G64 4AW (01360 620240; Fax: 01360 622742). *Location:* A803 then A807 from Glasgow. Parkland. 18 holes, 5530 yards. S.S.S. 67. Practice area. *Green Fees:* weekdays £30.00 per round, £40.00 day ticket. *Eating facilities:* catering and bar facilities. *Visitors:* welcome if introduced by member. *Society Meetings:* welcome Monday to Friday only. Professional: Kevin Craggs (01360 620123). Secretary: S.B. Keir (Tel & Fax: 01360 620284).

GLASGOW. **Bearsden Golf Club,** Thorn Road, Bearsden, Glasgow G61 4BP (0141-942 2351). *Location:* seven miles north-west of Glasgow. Parkland. 9 holes, 6014 yards. S.S.S. 69. *Green Fees:* information not available. *Visitors:* welcome, but must be accompanied by member. Secretary: Iain Inglis (0141 586 5300).

GLASGOW. **Blairbeth Golf Club,** Fernbrae Avenue, Rutherglen, Glasgow G73 4SF (0141-634 3355). *Location:* two miles south of Rutherglen off Burnside Road. Parkland. 18 holes, 5518 yards. S.S.S. 68. *Green Fees:* on application. *Eating Facilities:* available. *Visitors:* welcome weekdays only. *Society Meetings:* on application. Secretary: Ian Whyte (0141-634 3325).

GLASGOW. **Bonnyton Golf Club,** Eaglesham, Glasgow G76 0QA (01355 302645; Fax: 01355 303151). *Location:* B764. Moorland course. 18 holes, 6252 yards. S.S.S. 71. *Green Fees:* £40.00 per day. *Eating facilities:* full diningroom and snack facilities. *Visitors:* welcome except weekends. Professional: Kendal McWade (01355 302256). Secretary: A. Hughes (01355 302781).

GLASGOW. **Bothwell Castle Golf Club,** Blantyre Road, Bothwell G71 8PJ (01698 853177; Fax: 01698 854052). *Location:* adjacent to M74, three miles north of Hamilton. Flat parkland course. 18 holes, 6230 yards. S.S.S. 70. Golf clubs and caddy cars for hire. Practice ground. *Green Fees:* £24.00 per round, £32.00 per day. (Playing times must be booked with Professional). *Eating facilities:* full catering and bar. *Visitors:* welcome weekdays 9.30am to 10.30am and 2pm to 3pm only. *Society Meetings:* catered for, courtesy granted by application on Tuesdays only. Professional: A. McCloskey (01698 852052). Secretary: David McNaught (Tel & Fax: 01698 854052).

GLASGOW. **Buchanan Castle Golf Club,** Buchanan Estate, Drymen, Glasgow G63 0HY (01360 660307). *Location:* A811, one mile beyond Croftamie village. Flat parkland course. 18 holes, 6052 yards. S.S.S. 69. 9 hole putting area. *Green Fees:* £34.00 per round, £44.00 per day. *Eating facilities:* full catering and bar available. *Visitors:* welcome except Tuesday and Saturday mornings. *Society Meetings:* welcome Thursdays and Fridays only. Professional: Keith Baxter (01360 660330). Secretary: Richard Kinsella (01360 660307; Fax: 01360 870382).

GLASGOW. **Cambuslang Golf Club,** 30 Westburn Drive, Cambuslang (0141-641 3130). *Location:* half a mile north of Cambuslang main street. Parkland. 9 holes, 6146 yards. S.S.S. 69. *Green Fees:* information not available. *Eating facilities:* bar snacks, lunches, evening meals. *Visitors:* welcome if introduced by a member. *Society Meetings:* by arrangement. Secretary: R.M. Dunlop.

GLASGOW. **Cathcart Castle Golf Club,** Mearns Road, Clarkston, Glasgow G76 7YL (0141-638 0082). *Location:* one and a half miles from Clarkston Toll. Undulating parkland course. 18 holes, 5832 yards. S.S.S. 69. *Green Fees:* £30.00 per round, £45.00 per day. *Eating facilities:* full catering available, lounge bar. *Visitors:* welcome weekdays by prior arrangement. *Society Meetings:* weekdays by application. Professional: Stephen Duncan (0141-638 3436). Secretary: I.G. Sutherland (0141-638 9449).

GLASGOW. **Cathkin Braes Golf Club,** Cathkin Road, Rutherglen, Glasgow G73 4SE (0141-634 6605). Moorland course. 18 holes, 6208 yards. S.S.S. 71. Practice ground. *Green Fees:* £25.00 per round, £35.00 per day. *Eating facilities:* available. *Visitors:* welcome Monday to Friday by prior arrangement. *Society Meetings:* catered for. Professional: Stephen Bree (0141-634 0650). Secretary/Treasurer: Hugh Millar (Fax: 0141-630 9186).
e-mail: golf@cathkinbraes.freesave.co.uk
website: www.cathkinbraesgolfclub.co.uk

GLASGOW. **Cawder Golf Club,** Cadder Road, Bishopbriggs, Glasgow G64 3QD (0141-761 1280; Fax: 0141-761 1285). *Location:* A803 north of city. Parkland. Cawder: 18 holes, 6305 yards, 5737 metres. S.S.S. 71. Keir: 18 holes, 5891 yards, 5373 metres. S.S.S. 68. Practice area. *Green Fees:* £30.00 per round, £40.00 per day. *Eating facilities:* lunches, high teas, dinners available. *Visitors:* welcome when playing with member. *Society Meetings:* catered for mid-week. Professional: Ken Stevely (0141-772 7102). Secretary: (0141-761 1281).
e-mail: secretary@cawdergolfclub.org.uk
website: www.cawdergolfclub.org.uk

GLASGOW. **Clober Golf Club,** Craigton Road, Milngavie G62 7HP (0141-956 1685). *Location:* five minutes from Milngavie centre, seven miles from Glasgow city centre. Very hilly parkland course. 18 holes, 4963 yards. S.S.S. 65. *Green Fees:* weekdays £16.00 per round. *Eating facilities:* morning coffee, lunches, high teas. *Visitors:* welcome Monday to Thursday before 4pm, some Fridays also before 4pm; not at weekends unless introduced by a member. *Society Meetings:* catered for. Professional: C. Elliott (0141-956 6963; Fax: 0141-955 1416). Secretary: Brian Davidson (0141-956 1685).
e-mail: secretary@clober.co.uk
website: www.clober.co.uk

GLASGOW. **Cowglen Golf Club,** 301 Barrhead Road, Glasgow G43 1AU (0141-632 0556). *Location*: south-west Glasgow, follow M77 from Glasgow taking Pollok turnoff, turn left at traffic lights. Course half mile on right. Undulating parkland course. 18 holes, 6079 yards, 5559 metres. S.S.S. 69. Extensive practice facilities available. *Green Fees*: weekdays £25.50 per round, £35.00 per day. *Eating facilities*: full catering facilities available. *Visitors*: welcome if arranged beforehand with Secretary. Lockers and showers available. *Society Meetings*: restricted numbers, apply to Secretary. Professional: Simon Payne (0141-649 9401). Secretary: Ronald J.G. Jamieson, C.A. (Tel & Fax: 01505 503000).
e-mail: r.jamiesonaccountants@fsmail.net

GLASGOW. **Crow Wood Golf Club,** Garnkirk House, Cumbernauld Road, Muirhead G69 9JF (0141-779 2011). *Location:* on A80 on Stirling Road, six miles north east of Glasgow. Wooded parkland. 18 holes, 6160 yards. S.S.S. 70. Practice area. *Green Fees:* weekdays £23.00 per round, £34.00 per day (incl. third-party insurance). *Eating facilities:* fully licensed, snacks or full meals served all day. *Visitors:* welcome Monday to Friday except Bank Holidays and only by arrangement with Secretary. *Society Meetings:* catered for as visitors. Professional: Brian Moffat (0141-779 1943). Secretary: F.M. Davidson (0141-779 4954).

GLASGOW. **Douglas Park Golf Club,** Hillfoot, Bearsden, Glasgow G61 2TJ (0141-942 2220). *Location:* adjacent to railway station, Hillfoot, Bearsden, off Milngavie Road. Undulating parkland course. 18 holes, 5962 yards. S.S.S. 69. *Green Fees:* £23.00 per round, £31.00 per day. *Eating facilities:* full service available, usual licensing hours. *Visitors:* must be introduced and play with member. *Society Meetings:* Wednesdays and Thursdays on application to Secretary. Professional: David B. Scott (0141-942 1482). Secretary: J.G. Fergusson (Tel & Fax: 0141-942 0985).

GLASGOW. **Dullatur Golf Club,** 1A Glen Douglas Drive, Cumbernauld G68 0DW (01236 723230; Fax: 01236 727271). *Location:* 12 miles east of Glasgow - leave A80 for Dullatur then off third roundabout (Craigmarloch). Moorland, rolling courses. Two courses Antonine, 5205 yards and Carrickstone, 5673 yards. 36 holes, S.S.S. 70. *Green Fees:* weekdays £30.00 per day, £20.00 per round; weekends £25.00 per round, £35.00 per day. *Eating facilities:* full catering facilities. *Visitors:* welcome. Smart casual dress required in clubhouse. Full leisure centre. *Society Meetings:* welcome, book through Secretary. Professional: Duncan Sinclair (01236 723230; Fax: 01236 727271). Secretary: Carol Millar.

GLASGOW. **East Kilbride Golf Club,** Chapelside Road, Nerston, East Kilbride G74 4PH (013552 20913). *Location:* Glasgow Road exit from East Kilbride. Parkland course with variable topography. 18 holes, 6419 yards. S.S.S. 71. *Green Fees:* weekdays £25.00 per round, £35.00 per day. *Eating facilities:* full bar and catering facilities seven days per week. *Visitors:* welcome weekdays only. *Society Meetings:* catered for weekdays only. Professional: Paul McKay (01355 222192). Secretary: W.G. Gray (01355 247728).

GLASGOW. **Eastwood Golf Club,** Muirshield, Loganswell, Newton Mearns, Glasgow G77 6RX (01355 500261). *Location:* on main A77 road to Kilmarnock two miles south of Newton Mearns. Moorland course. 18 holes, 5864 yards. S.S.S. 68. Practice area. *Green Fees:* weekdays £24.00 per round, £30.00 per day. *Eating facilities:* snacks or full meals available. *Visitors:* welcome weekdays on application to Secretary. *Visiting parties:* welcomed on prior application. Professional: I.J. Darroch (01355 500285). Secretary: V.E. Jones (01355 500280).

GLASGOW. **Esporta (Dougalston Golf Club)**, Strathblane Road, Milngavie, Glasgow G62 8HA (0141-955 2404; Fax: 0141-955 2406). *Location:* A81 half a mile from Milngavie. Parkland course set in woodland estate. 18 holes, 6040 yards. S.S.S. 70, par 71. Practice ground, putting green, practice nets. *Green Fees:* weekdays £28.00, weekends £35.00. *Eating facilities:* restaurant, sports bar and leisure facilities. *Visitors:* welcome weekdays 8am to 4.30pm. *Society Meetings:* welcome weekdays. Weekends subject to availability. Other facilities include 25 metre swimming pool, along with a health suite, aerobic studios, air-conditioning fitness area, gymnasium, indoor - outdoor tennis, Sports Bar and banqueting facilities. Professional: Craig Everett (0141-955 2404; Fax: 0141-955 2406). Secretary: Hilda Everett (0141-955 2434; Fax: 0141-955 2406).

GLASGOW. **Glasgow Golf Club,** Killermont, Bearsden, Glasgow G61 2TW (0141-942 1713). *Location:* taking Maryhill Road out of Glasgow turn right at Killermont Avenue, half a mile before Canniesburn Toll and then turn immediately right again. Tree-lined parkland. 18 holes, 5977 yards. S.S.S. 69, Par 70. *Green Fees:* on application. *Eating facilities:* bar and dining room. *Visitors:* only if introduced by member; no visitors at weekends. *Society Meetings:* by application to Club Secretary. Professional: Jack Steven (0141-942 8507). Secretary: D.W. Deas (0141-942 2011; Fax: 0141-942 0770). e-mail: secretary@glasgow-golf.com

GLASGOW: **Haggs Castle Golf Club**, Dumbreck Road, Dumbreck, Glasgow G41 4SN (0141-427 0480). *Location:* off Junction 1 of M77 from Glasgow.

Flat, tree-lined course. 18 holes, 6426 yards. S.S.S. 71. Practice area and putting green. *Green Fees:* weekdays £40.00 per round, £50.00 per day. Weekends, members only. *Eating facilities:* full catering available. *Visitors:* welcome except weekends; must book through Professional. Handicap Certificate required. Golf shoes must be worn. *Society Meetings:* by arrangement through Secretary. Professional: C. Elliott (0141-427 3355). Secretary/ Manager: Alan Williams (Tel & Fax: 0141-427 1157).

GLASGOW. **Hayston Golf Club,** Campsie Road, Kirkintilloch, Glasgow G66 1RN (0141-776 1244). *Location:* 10 miles north-east of Glasgow and one mile north of Kirkintilloch. Parkland course with tree-lined fairways. 18 holes, 6042 yards. S.S.S. 70. Practice area. *Green Fees:* £27.00 for 18 holes, £37.00 for 36 holes. *Eating facilities:* lunches, dinners, bar snacks. *Society Meetings:* Tuesdays, Wednesdays and Thursdays on application to Secretary. Professional: Steve Barnett (0141-775 0882). Secretary: J.V. Carmichael (0141-775 0723).

GLASGOW. **Hilton Park Golf Club,** Stockiemuir Road, Milngavie, Glasgow G62 7HB (0141-956 5124). *Location:* on A809. Moorland courses. Allander course: 18 holes, 5487 yards. S.S.S. 67. Hilton course: 18 holes, 6054 yards. S.S.S. 70. Practice area. *Green Fees:* £25.00 per round, £35.00 per day. *Eating facilities:* full catering and bar. *Visitors:* on application to the Secretary (not at weekends). *Society Meetings:* as visitors. Professional: W. McCondichie (0141-956 5125). Secretary: Mrs J.A. Dawson (0141-956 4657/5124).

GLASGOW. **Kirkhill Golf Club,** Greenlees Road, Cambuslang, Glasgow G72 8YN (0141-641 3083). *Location:* between Rutherglen and East Kilbride adjacent to A749, three miles from East Kilbride. Slightly hilly parkland course. 18 holes, 6030 yards. S.S.S. 70. Practice area. *Green Fees:* information not Available. *Eating facilities:* dining room and bar. *Visitors:* welcome weekdays only. *Society Meetings:* welcome weekdays only. Hon. Professional: D. Williamson (0141-641 7972). Hon. Secretary: Carol Downes (Tel & Fax: 0141-641 8499).

GLASGOW. **Knightswood Golf Club,** Lincoln Avenue, Glasgow G13 3DN (0141-959 6358). *Location:* west along Great Western Road, turn left into Lincoln Avenue. Flat parkland course. 9 holes, 2792 yards. S.S.S. 67. *Green Fees:* £3.60 for 9 holes. Passport to Recreation holders £1.80 weekdays until 3.30pm. Subject to review. *Visitors:* tee reserved for Club Wednesdays and Fridays 7.30am to 8.30am and 9.30am to 10.30am, otherwise no restrictions. 24 hours' notice required. Ladies' and gents' changing areas. *Society Meetings:* welcome, as for visitors. Secretary: Mr Douglas Gardner (0141-959 8158).

GLASGOW. **Lethamhill Golf Course**, 1240 Cumbernauld Road, Glasgow G33 1AH (0141-770 6220; Fax: 0141-770 0520). *Location:* 100 yards off M8 Junction 12. Parkland, many holes with views of Hogganfield Loch. 18 holes, 5836 yards. S.S.S. 68. 18 holes pitch and putt course. *Green Fees:* information not available. *Visitors:* welcome at all times - this is a public course, 24 hour in advance booking system. Ladies and gents changing. *Society Meetings:* contact Golf Development Officer on 0141-770 0519; Fax: 0141-770 0520.

GLASGOW. **Linn Park Golf Club**, Simshill Road, Glasgow G44 5EP (0141-633 0377). *Location:* five miles south of city centre near Carmunock Road, near Croftfoot roundabout. Parkland. 18 holes, 5005 yards. S.S.S. 66. *Green Fees:* information not available. *Visitors:* welcome, 24 hours notice required. *Society Meetings:* all welcome. Secretary: T. Dunn (0141-633 0377).*

GLASGOW. **Littlehill Golf Club,** Auchinairn Road, Bishopbriggs, Glasgow G64 1UT. *Location:* from Glasgow on A803, turn off for Stobhill Hospital. Flat, parkland. 18 holes, 6364 yards. S.S.S. 70. Small practice area. *Green Fees:* information not available. *Eating facilities:* canteen open five days weekly in season, three outwith. *Visitors:* welcome without reservation - pay and play. *Society Meetings:* no restrictions. Professional: Kevin Hughes (0141-762 3998). Secretary: W. Burke. *

GLASGOW. **Milngavie Golf Club**, Laighpark, Milngavie, Glasgow G62 8EP (0141-956 1619; Fax: 0141-956 4252). *Location:* situated off Glasgow to Drymen road approximately one mile past Stockiemuir Service Station, turn right at signpost. Moorland course. 18 holes, 5818 yards. S.S.S. 68. *Green Fees:* on application. *Eating facilities:* catering available. *Visitors:* welcome when introduced by member or by prior arrangement with the Secretary. *Society Meetings:* catered for. Secretary: S. Woods.

GLASGOW. **Pollok Golf Club,** 90 Barrhead Road, Glasgow G43 1BG (0141-649 0885; Fax: 0141-649 1398). *Location:* Junction 2 M77. Wooded parkland. 18 holes, 6358 yards. S.S.S. 70. *Green Fees:* £35.00 per round, £45.00 per day. *Eating facilities:* dining room and bar. *Visitors:* welcome with reservation by letter or telephone to Secretary. No visitors Saturday or Sunday. *Society Meetings:* catered for by letter. Secretary: Ian Cumming (0141-632 4351; Fax: 0141-649 1398).

GLASGOW. **Rouken Glen Golf Centre**, Stewarton Road, Thornliebank, Glasgow G46 7UZ (0141-638 7044 or 0141-620 0826). *Location:* on Stewarton Road at Rouken Glen Park, only 250 yards from the A726. Parkland with wooded features, designed by James Braid. 18 holes, 4800 yards. S.S.S. 63 (Par 64). 15-bay floodlit driving range. *Green Fees:* information not available. *Eating facilities:* catering and bar facilities available. *Visitors:* welcome all week. Shop, club hire, etc. *Society Meetings:* bookings taken. Professional: (0141-638 7044). Secretary: Christine Cosh (0141-632 6816).*

GLASGOW. **Sandyhills Golf Club**, 223 Sandyhills Road, Glasgow G32 9NA (0141-778 1179). *Location:* three miles east from centre of Glasgow. Parkland. 18 holes, 6253 yards. S.S.S. 71. *Green Fees:* information not provided. *Eating facilities:* full catering facilities available. *Visitors:* welcome when introduced by a member. *Society Meetings:* welcome by prior arrangement. Secretary: C.J. Wilson C.A. (01698 282062; Fax: 01698 425840).

GLASGOW. **Whitecraigs Golf Club**, 72 Ayr Road, Giffnock, Glasgow G46 6SW (0141-639 4530; Fax: 0141-616 3648). *Location:* on A77 south of city, two miles from Eastwoodmains roundabout. Parkland course. 18 holes, 6013 yards. S.S.S. 70. *Green Fees:* £40.00 per round, £50.00 per day (includes food). *Eating facilities:* restaurant and lounge bar. *Visitors:* welcome mid week, letter of introduction required. *Society Meetings:* catered for Wednesday only. Professional: Alastair Forrow (0141-639 2140). Secretary: Alan Keith (0141-639 4530).

THE APPEARANCE OF AN ASTERISK (*) AT THE END OF A CLUB OR COURSE ENTRY INDICATES THAT UP-TO-DATE INFORMATION HAS NOT BEEN SUPPLIED

GLASGOW. **Williamwood Golf Club,** Clarkston Road, Glasgow G44 3YR (0141-637 1783; Fax: 0141-637 6688). *Location:* behind service station on Clarkston Road. Attractive parkland course designed by James Braid. 18 holes, 5878 yards. S.S.S. 69. Practice area and putting. *Green Fees:* weekdays £27.00 per round, £37.00 per day. *Eating facilities:* meals must be ordered. *Visitors:* welcome by arrangement with Secretary or Professional. *Society Meetings:* weekdays only by arrangement. Professional: Stewart G. Marshall (0141-637 2715; Fax: 0141-637 2600). Secretary: R.J. Templeton (0141-637 1783).

GLASGOW. **Windyhill Golf Club,** Baljaffray Road, Bearsden, Glasgow G61 4QQ (0141-942 2349; Fax: 0141-942 5874). *Location:* one mile north from Bearsden Cross. Undulating parkland course. 18 holes, 6254 yards. S.S.S. 70. Practice area. *Green Fees:* £30.00; weekends £6.00 with member only. *Eating facilities:* full catering and bar. *Visitors:* welcome weekdays only. *Society Meetings:* welcome weekdays by arrangement. Professional: Christopher Duffy (0141-942 7157; Fax: 0141-942 5874). Secretary: Walter Proven (0141-942 2349; Fax: 0141-942 5874).

KILSYTH. **Kilsyth Lennox Golf Club,** Tak-Ma-Doon Road, Kilsyth, Glasgow G65 0RS (01236 824115). *Location:* 12 miles from Glasgow on A80. Parkland/moorland, undulating ground with superb views across central Scotland. 18 holes, 5912 yards. S.S.S. 70. *Green Fees:* information not available. *Eating facilities:* new clubhouse. *Visitors:* welcome weekdays up to 5.00pm, Saturdays after 5.00pm, not Sundays. *Society Meetings:* welcome, details on application. Professional: R. Abercrombie. Secretary: A.G. Stevenson (01236 823213).*

NEWTON MEARNS. **The East Renfrewshire Golf Club,** Pilmuir, Newton Mearns, Glasgow G77 6RT (01355 500256). *Location:* on A77, one and a half miles south of Newton Mearns. Moorland course with plantations of evergreen trees. 18 holes, 6097 yards, 5577 metres. S.S.S. 70. *Green Fees:* weekdays £40.00 per round, £50.00 per day. *Eating facilities:* by prior arrangement with club manager. *Visitors:* welcome except Saturdays but always by prior arrangement with Professional. *Society Meetings:* welcome Tuesdays and Thursdays. Professional: Stewart Russell (01355 500206). Manager: D.S. McKenzie (01355 500256; Fax: 01355 500323).
e-mail: david@eastrengolfclub.demon.co.uk

PLEASE MENTION THIS GUIDE WHEN YOU WRITE OR PHONE TO ENQUIRE ABOUT CLUBS OR ACCOMMODATION.

Highlands (North)

BONAR BRIDGE. **Bonar Bridge-Ardgay Golf Club,** Market Stance, Migdale Road, Bonar Bridge IV24 3EJ (01863 766199). *Location:* off the A9, driving north cross Bonar Bridge, straight up hill for half a mile. Wooded heathland. 9 holes, 5284 yards. S.S.S. 66. *Green Fees:* £14.00 per day (2003). Subject to review. *Eating facilities:* limited catering available May to September. *Visitors:* always welcome. *Society Meetings:* limited to weekdays. Joint Secretary: John Reid (01863 766750).
e-mail: bonarardgaygolf@aol.com

BRORA. **Brora Golf Club,** 43 Golf Road, Brora KW9 6QS (+44 (0)1408 621417; Fax: +44 (0)1408 622157). *Location:* 52 miles north of Inverness on A9 trunk road. Traditional links course designed by James Braid. 18 holes, 6110 yards. S.S.S. 69. Practice ground available. *Green Fees:* weekdays £27.00 per round, £35.00 per day; weekends £32.00 per round, £40.00 per day. *Eating facilities:* full catering, bar facilities April to October. *Visitors:* welcome anytime except on tournament days, advisable to book tee times in season. Welcome to participate in open events (Certificate of Handicap required). Carts, caddies, etc available. *Society Meetings:* by arrangement with Secretary. Secretary: James Fraser (01408 621417; Fax: 01408 622157).
e-mail: secretary@broragolf.co.uk

DORNOCH. **The Carnegie Golf Club at Skibo Castle,** Skibo Castle, Dornoch (01862 894600; Fax: 01862 894601). *Location:* off A9 between Tain and Dornoch. Links course, built on peninsula, naturally contoured; Donald Steel designed. 18 holes, 6671 yards. S.S.S. 72. Practice facilities. *Green Fees:* information not available. *Eating facilities:* bar, luncheon table. *Visitors:* by prior arrangement, write or telephone only. Private members club, daily golf membership available, must be booked in advance. *Society Meetings:* welcome. Accommodation available, charges on request. Golf Secretary: Sharon Stewart. Professional: David Thomson (01862 881260).
e-mail: sharon.stewart@carnegieclubs.com

DORNOCH. **Royal Dornoch Golf Club,** Golf Road, Dornoch IV25 3LW (01862 810219; Fax: 01862 810792). *Location:* one mile from A9 to Wick. Seaside links. Championship Course and Struie Course. Championship: 18 holes, 6514 yards, 5958 metres. S.S.S. 73; Struie: 18 holes, 6276 yards, 5793 metres. S.S.S. TBC. Practice area. *Green Fees:* Championship Course: weekdays £45.00/£66.00 per round, weekends £50.00/£76.00 per round. Struie Course: £9.00/£20.00 per round, £12.00/£30.00 day ticket. All green fees are subject to alteration. *Eating facilities:* available. *Visitors:* welcome, no major restrictions other than competitions – bookings can be heavy. Saturdays members only until late afternoon. Handicap Certificates – Men 24, Ladies 39. *Society Meetings:* must be arranged through the Secretary. Professional: A. Skinner (01862 810902; Fax; 01862 811095). Secretary: J.S. Duncan (01862 810219; Fax: 01862 810792).
e-mail: bookings@royaldornoch.com
website: www.royaldornoch.com

DURNESS. **Durness Golf Club**, Balnakiel, Durness. *Location:* 57 miles northwest of Lairg on A838. Links course with final hole played over deep gully. 9 greens, 18 tees, 5555 yards. S.S.S 69. *Green Fees:* £15.00 per day. Weekly ticket £50.00. *Eating facilities:* snacks available 12-5pm June to September. *Visitors:* welcome without reservation, only restriction on Sunday mornings. *Society Meetings:* by arrangement. Secretary: Lucy MacKay (01971 511364).

GOLSPIE. **Golspie Golf Club,** Ferry Road, Golspie KW10 6ST (01408 633266; Fax: 01408 633393). *Location:* 53 miles on A9 north of Inverness. Fairly flat course, seaside links and wooded. 18 holes, 5836 yards. S.S.S. 68. Practice area available. *Green Fees:* information not available. *Eating facilities:* bar and catering service, available all day during season. *Visitors:* welcome, no restrictions except on competition days. Carts, caddies must be booked in advance. *Society Meetings:* welcome by prior arrangement, packages available. Golf Shop.*

THE APPEARANCE OF AN ASTERISK * AT THE END OF A CLUB OR COURSE ENTRY INDICATES THAT UP-TO-DATE INFORMATION HAS NOT BEEN SUPPLIED

Royal Marine & Links Hotels

Golf Road, Brora, Sutherland KW9 6QS
Telephone: (01408) 621252 • Fax: (01408) 621181
e-mail: info@highlandescape.com
website: www.highlandescapehotels.com

Traditional Edwardian hotels with modern facilities, adjacent to James Braid's 18 hole links course and offering magnificent views. Recently refurbished and serving the finest local cuisine. Provides an ideal base for touring the Northern Highlands. Fishing available from hotel boat. Choice of four championship links golf courses including Royal Dornoch, and use of leisure complex, indoor pool, spa, sauna, steam, gym, solarium and curling rink.

★★★

See also Colour Advertisement on page 83

The Royal Dornoch Golf Club *welcomes you*

The Championship Course, 15th amongst the world's top courses, is a classic links challenging the golfer's skills in the traditional manner.
The Struie Links, extended from 18th May 2003 by 5 new holes is, with its own character, suitable for all abilities.
Handicap Certificates (Max: Gentlemen 24, Ladies 39) are required for the Championship Course.

Reservations – Tel: 01862 810219 • Fax: 01862 810792
e-mail: **bookings@royaldornoch.com** • website: **www.royaldornoch.com**
GOLF ROAD, DORNOCH, SUTHERLAND IV25 3LW

See also Colour Advertisement on page 82

Beautifully refurbished to a high standard with 23 en suite bedrooms and new conservatory Garden Restaurant opening out on to the lovely walled gardens, 15th century Dornoch Castle sits proudly in the centre of the historic Highland village of Dornoch.
The Castle is within easy walking distance of the famous Royal Dornoch golf course and within easy driving distance of many other interesting courses.

• *Superb cuisine featuring local produce* • *Excellent wines and malts* • *Roaring log fires* • *Off-season breaks*

Dornoch Castle Hotel, Dornoch, Sutherland IV25 3SD
Tel: +44 (0) 1862 810216 • Fax: +44 (0) 1862 810981
e-mail: enquiries@dornochcastlehotel.com • website: www.dornochcastlehotel.com

See also Colour Advertisement on page 83

THE Golf Links HOTEL

CHURCH STREET, GOLSPIE, SUTHERLAND KW10 6TT　TEL: 01408 633408
e-mail: **golflinkshotel@btconnect.com**　web: **golflinkshotel.co.uk**

An ideal base for exploring the north or for playing the three outstanding courses of Royal Dornoch, Golspie and Brora.
This friendly, family-run hotel has two bars, residents' lounge and dining room and meals are served all day. Sea-front position with distant views. Nine en suite bedrooms with colour TV, electric blankets and tea/coffee making facilities.　　　　　　　　**STB ★★★**

PLEASE MENTION THE GOLF GUIDE WHEN YOU WRITE OR PHONE TO ENQUIRE ABOUT CLUBS OR ACCOMMODATION.

GRANTOWN-ON-SPEY. **Grantown-on-Spey Golf Club,** The Clubhouse, Golf Course Road, Grantown-on-Spey PH26 3HY (01479 872079; Fax: 01479 873725). *Location:* turn off main road opposite police station. Parkland and woodland. 18 holes, 5710 yards, S.S.S. 68, Par 70. Practice ground and putting green. *Green Fees:* weekdays £20.00 per day; weekends £25.00 per round, £30.00 per day. Evening round £10.00. 50% reduction for under 18s. *Eating facilities:* full bar and catering facilities. *Visitors:* welcome, members have priority before 10am weekends. Shop. *Society Meetings:* welcome except before 10am weekends. Secretary: James Macpherson (01479 872079/ 873154; Fax: 01479 873725).
e-mail: secretary@grantownonspeygolfclub.co.uk
website: www.grantownonspeygolfclub.co.uk

HELMSDALE. **Helmsdale Golf Club,** Golf Road, Helmsdale KW8 6JA. *Location:* on A9, 28 miles north of Dornoch, follow signs for Melvich. undulating parkland/moorland course. 9 holes, 3720 yards. S.S.S. 61 (2 x 9 holes). *Green Fees:* payable at house next to clubhouse. Life membership now available, contact Secretary. *Visitors:* welcome at all times. *Society Meetings:* welcome by appointment. Secretary: Ronald Sutherland (01431 821063).

LYBSTER. **Lybster Golf Club,** Main Street, Lybster. *Location:* 14 miles south from Wick on A9, half-way down village street. One of smallest courses in Scotland, heathland/parkland. 9 holes, 1929 yards. S.S.S. 61. *Green Fees:* £10.00 per round/day (adults); £5.00 per round/day (juniors). *Eating facilities:* at nearby hotels in village. *Visitors:* welcome anytime. *Society Meetings:* welcome anytime. Full membership available. Secretary: Alex Calder.

REAY. **Reay Golf Club,** Clubhouse, Reay, By Thurso KW14 7RE (01847 811288). *Location:* 12 miles west of nearest main town of Thurso. Most northerly 18 hole seaside links. 18 holes, 5831 yards. S.S.S. 69. *Green Fees:* £20.00 per day, £60.00 per week. Rates available for fortnight – information from Secretary. *Eating facilities:* restricted: bar open 12-3pm, 8-11pm daily July/August. *Visitors:* welcome anytime, restricted during competitions. *Society Meetings:* welcome, advance bookings via Secretary. Captain: Graeme Dunnett. Secretary: Bill McIntosh (01847 894189).
e-mail: info@reaygolfclub.co.uk
website: www.reaygolfclub.co.uk

THURSO. **Thurso Golf Club,** Newlands of Geise, By Thurso, KW14 7XF (01847 893807). *Location:* two miles from Railway Station, on road to Reay via Westfield. Flat parkland with newly planted trees. 18 holes, 5828 yards, 5290 metres. S.S.S. 69. *Green Fees:* April to September £20.00 per day, £60.00 per week; October to March £10.00 per day. *Eating facilities:* snacks available in the bar during the day June to August. *Visitors:* welcome, no restrictions. *Society Meetings:* welcome, notice required. Secretary: R.M. Black (01847 892575).

WICK. **Wick Golf Club,** Reiss, By Wick KW1 4RW (01955 602726). *Location:* three miles north of Wick on A9. Seaside links course. 18 holes, 6123 yards. S.S.S. 71. Practice area. *Green Fees:* £20.00 per day. *Eating facilities:* licensed; snacks available. *Visitors:* welcome. *Society Meetings:* catered for. Secretary: D.D. Slearer (01955 602935).

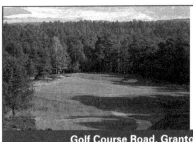

Highlands (Mid)

ALNESS. **Alness Golf Club**, Ardross Road, Alness IV17 0QA (01349 883877). *Location:* 20 miles from Inverness; turn into Alness from A9 (north). Beautiful surroundings with views over Cromarty Firth and Alness River. 18 holes, 4886 yards. S.S.S. 64. Practice. *Green Fees:* information not available. *Eating facilities:* licensed bar and bar snacks. *Visitors:* welcome all week. Please check for competitions. Changing rooms, showers; clubs and trolleys for hire. *Society Meetings:* welcome with advance notice. Secretary: Marie Rogers (01349 883877).*

FORTROSE. **Fortrose and Rosemarkie Golf Club**, Ness Road East, Fortrose IV10 8SE (01381 620529; Fax: 01381 621328). *Location:* on the Black Isle. A9 north from Inverness, across Kessock Bridge, through Munlochy, follow signs to Fortrose. Good links course, sea both sides. 18 holes, 5875 yards. S.S.S. 69. Practice area available Summer. *Green Fees:* information not provided. *Eating facilities:* catering available. *Visitors:* welcome without reservation. *Society Meetings:* catered for.
e-mail: enquiries@fortrosegolfclub.co.uk
website: www.fortrosegolfclub.co.uk

GAIRLOCH. **Gairloch Golf Club**, Gairloch IV21 2BE (01445 712407). *Location:* 75 miles west of Inverness on the A832. Seaside links with superb views. 9 holes, 4093 yards. S.S.S. 62 over 18 holes. Practice net. *Green Fees:* £15.00. Weekly £49.00. Juniors £10.00 per day. Subject to review. *Eating facilities:* licensed bar and light refreshments available. *Visitors:* welcome anytime but must be regular golfers. Tee times must be booked during the summer season - call the clubhouse for details). *Society Meetings:* welcome, no restrictions. Secretary: A. Shinkins (01445 781346).
e-mail: secretary@gairlochgc.fsnet
website: www.gairlochgolfclub.co.uk

INVERGORDON. **Invergordon Golf Club**, King George Street, Invergordon IV18 0BD (01349 852715). *Location:* A9 (B817), two miles, west side of town. Relatively flat, parkland. 18 holes, over 6020 yards. S.S.S. 69. Practice area. *Green Fees:* £20.00 per round, £25.00 per day ticket. *Eating facilities:* bar, bar snacks - normal licensing hours. *Visitors:* welcome without restrictions other than club competition times. Locker rooms with showers. Club/caddy carts for hire. *Society Meetings:* welcome by prior arrangement. Clubhouse Manager: J. Ross (01349 852715).

LOCHCARRON. **Lochcarron Golf Club**, Lochcarron, Ross-shire IV54 8YU. *Location:* one mile east of Lochcarron village by A896. Seaside course, combined parkland and shore. Interesting opening hole. A short course but great accuracy required. 9 holes with some alternative tees for second nine. 3575 yards (18 holes). S.S.S. 60. *Green Fees:* £10.00 per day; £40.00 per week. Juniors (under 16 years old) half price. *Eating facilities:* three hotels within two miles of course. *Visitors:* welcome anytime except Saturdays between 2pm and 5pm. Bookings not required. Clubs for hire. *Society Meetings:* welcome. Secretary: Alastair Beattie (01520 766211).

MUIR OF ORD. **The Muir of Ord Golf Club**, Great North Road, Muir of Ord IV6 7SX (01463 870825; Fax: 01463 871867). *Location:* 15 miles north of Inverness beside A862, 12 miles north of Inverness on A832. Heathland, moorland course, excellent greens. 18 holes, 5559 yards. S.S.S. 68. Practice area. *Green Fees:* weekdays £16.00 per round, £20.00 per day; weekends £20.00 per round, £25.00 per day. Discounts of £1.00 per player if more than 14 players in party; weekends by appointment. *Eating facilities:* lounge bar (snacks all day), meals weekends or by appointment. *Visitors:* welcome weekdays outwith competition times, weekends by appointment. Trolleys available; buggy hire. *Society Meetings:* welcome. Shop (01463 871311). Secretary/Administrator: Mrs J. Gibson (01463 870825).

PORTMAHOMACK. **Tarbat Golf Club**, Tarbatness Road, Portmahomack, Tain IV20 1YB. *Location:* 10 miles east of Tain. B9165 off A9. Seaside links course with scenic views. 9 holes, 5082 yards. S.S.S. 65. Practice area. *Green Fees:* £15.00 per day. £50.00 per week. *Eating facilities:* club room manned from June to August, light snacks; local hotels. *Visitors:* welcome, some restrictions Saturdays. *Society Meetings:* welcome, please telephone Secretary. Secretary: Christina Ince (01862 871486).

STRATHPEFFER. **Strathpeffer Spa Golf Club**, Strathpeffer IV14 9AS (01997 421219 or 01997 421011). *Location:* 20 minutes north of Inverness by A9, 5 miles west of Dingwall, quarter of a mile north of Strathpeffer Square (signposted). Upland course, panoramic views of moorland and mountain; water hazards at 3rd, 10th and 11th. 18 holes, 4792 yards. S.S.S. 64. Small practice area and putting green. *Green Fees:* £18.00 per round, £23.00 per day Juniors £9.00 per round, £11.00 per day. Discounts for groups of over 10. *Eating facilities:* bar and catering available seven days a week. *Visitors:* welcome without reservation, but check weekends and competition days. Club, buggy and trolley hire. *Society Meetings:* catered for by arrangement. Secretary: Gayle Anderson (01997 421011). Club Shop (Bookings) 01997 421011.
e-mail: mail@strathpeffergolf.co.uk
website: www.strathpeffergolf.co.uk

TAIN. **Tain Golf Club**, Chapel Road, Tain IV19 1JE (01862 892314; Fax: 01862 892099). *Location:* off A9, 34 miles north of Inverness. Travelling north, turn right in middle of High Street - Golf Club one mile. Parkland and seaside links. 18 holes, 6404 yards. S.S.S. 71. Practice putting green. *Green Fees:* weekdays £33.00 per round, £40.00 per day ticket; weekends £40.00 per round, £50.00 per day ticket. Discounts of 20% for parties of 12 or more. *Eating facilities:* full catering, licensed. *Visitors:* welcome anytime except when competitions are being held. *Society Meetings:* catered for. Secretary: Mrs Kathleen Ross.
e-mail: info@tain-golfclub.co.uk
website: www.tain-golfclub.co.uk

ULLAPOOL. **Ullapool Golf Club**, North Road, Ullapool IV26 2TH (01854 613323; Fax: 01854 613133). *Location:* situated at the northern outskirts of the village. Parkland seaside course. 18 tees, 9 holes, 5338 yards, S.S.S. 66. 3 hole practice course, bunker, nets. *Green Fees:* £17.00 per day adults, £8.00 per day juniors. *Eating facilities:* catering/bar only available at open competitions and club events. *Visitors:* welcome except during competitions. *Society Meetings:* welcome, group rates by negotiation. Secretary: A. Paterson.
e-mail: info@ullapool-golf.co.uk
website: www.ullapool-golf.co.uk

Strathpeffer Spa Golf Club

Founded in 1888, this is arguably the most scenic course in the North of Scotland, with the drive on the first hole from tee to green featuring the longest drop on any course in the country. Visitors are welcome without reservation (although it is advisable to check in advance). Bar and catering is available daily. Clubs, trolleys and golf buggies are available for hire.

18 holes £18.00 • day ticket £23.00
Special terms for groups • 18 holes, Par 64

Golf Course Road, Strathpeffer, Ross-shire IV14 9AS
01997 421011 or 421219 • www.strathpeffergolf.co.uk
e-mail: mail@strathpeffergolf.co.uk

See also Colour Advertisement on page 84

N O T E — All the information regarding Golf Clubs in this guide is given in good faith in the belief that it is correct. However, the publishers cannot guarantee the facts given in these pages, neither are they responsible for changes in ownership or facilities, such as green fees, that may take place after the date of going to press. Readers should always satisfy themselves that the facilities they require are available and that the terms, if quoted, still apply.

Highlands (South)

ARISAIG. **Traigh Golf Course**, Traigh, Arisaig PH39 4NT (01687 450 337). *Location:* on A830 Fort William to Mallaig Road, 3 miles north of Arisaig. Seaside links, close to sandy beaches on the beautiful Morar coast. 9 holes, 2456 yards. S.S.S 65. Practice green. *Green Fees:* information not available. *Eating facilities:* unlicensed, soft drinks and confectionery only. *Visitors:* welcome at all times. Clubs may be hired. *Society Meetings:* by arrangement. Manager: Bill Henderson (01687 450337/450645).*

BEAULY by. **Aigas Golf Course**, By Beauly IV4 7AD (01463 782942 or 782423). *Location:* A831, five miles from Beauly village. Challenging 9 hole course uniquely set in beautiful Strathglass beside the River Beauly. 9 holes, 2439 yards, S.S.S 63 (2 x 9 holes). *Green Fees:* information not available.*

BOAT OF GARTEN. **Boat of Garten Golf and Tennis Club**, Boat of Garten PH24 3BQ (01479 831282; Fax: 01479 831523). *Location:* A9 six miles north of Aviemore. Wooded course with birch tree-lined fairways, very scenic, overlooking Cairngorm Mountains. 18 holes, 5967 yards, 5456 metres. S.S.S. 69. Practice net. *Green Fees:* weekdays £28.00 per round, £33.00 per day; weekends £33.00 per round, £38.00 per day. Subject to review. *Eating facilities:* catering facilities open 9.30am to 8.00pm, bar open 11am to 11pm daily. *Visitors:* welcome 9.30am to 5.30pm. Two tennis courts. *Society Meetings:* catered for. Professional Shop: J. Ingram (01479 831282; Fax: 01479 831523). Secretary: Paddy Smyth (01479 831282; Fax: 01479 831523). e-mail: boatgolf@enterprise.net website: www.boatgolf.com

CARRBRIDGE. **Carrbridge Golf Club**, Inverness Road, Carrbridge PH23 3AU (01479 841623). *Location:* off A9, 27 miles south of Inverness. Moorland/parkland. 9 holes, 5402 yards. S.S.S 68 Par 71. *Green Fees:* June, July, August, September £15.00 weekdays; £18.00 weekends. Reduced rates Juniors and evenings. Weekly tickets £60.00 adults, £30.00 Juniors. *Eating facilities:* snacks, coffee and light lunches. Clubhouse open April to October only.

Visitors: welcome, course closed Wednesdays after 5pm for members only. *Society Meetings:* welcome. Secretary: (01479 841412). website: www.carrbridgegolf.com

FORT AUGUSTUS. **Fort Augustus Golf Club**, Markethill, Fort Augustus (01320 366660). *Location:* half-a-mile south of village on A82. Moorland course, tree lined to north, heather covered hills to the south. 9 holes (18 tees), 5379 yards. S.S.S. 67. *Green Fees:* £12.00 per round, £15.00 per day. *Eating facilities:* lounge bar. *Visitors:* welcome anytime except Saturday afternoons from 1.30pm to 5pm. Clubs and caddy cars for hire. *Society Meetings:* welcome, please book in advance. Secretary: Alex Barnett (01320 366259).

FORT WILLIAM. **Fort William Golf Club**, Torlundy, Fort William PH33 6SN (01397 704464). *Location:* north from Fort William, approx. 3 miles through town. Parkland course. 18 holes, 6217 yards, S.S.S 71. Practice area. *Green Fees:* £20.00 for 18 holes. *Eating facilities:* snacks available from the bar. *Visitors:* welcome all week except Saturday and Sunday between 8am and 11am. *Society Meetings:* welcome, discount available for parties of more than 15. Secretary: Miss Rosemary MacIntyre.

INVERNESS. **Loch Ness Golf Course**, Castle Heather, Inverness IV2 6AA (01463 713335; Fax: 01463 712695). *Location:* on the outskirts of Inverness, heading west along new Ring Road. Parkland course with panoramic views over Inverness and Moray Firth. Loch Ness Golf Course - 18 holes, 6493 yards (yellow), 6772 yards (white). S.S.S. 70 yellow, 72 white. *Green Fees:* weekdays £25.00 per day; weekends £30.00 per day. *Eating facilities:* lounge bar, members lounge, full catering facilities. *Visitors:* welcome. Buggies, carts and caddies available. *Society Meetings:* most welcome by prior arrangement. Professional: Martin Piggot (01463 713334). Secretary: Neil D. Hampton (01463 713335; Fax: 01463 712695). e-mail: info@golflochness.com website: www.golflochness.com

INVERNESS. **Inverness Golf Club,** The Clubhouse, Culcabock Road, Inverness IV2 3XQ (01463 233422). *Location:* one mile south of town centre. Parkland course. 18 holes, 6256 yards. S.S.S. 70. Two practice grounds. *Green Fees:* £33.00 per round, £42.00 per day. Weekly, fortnightly and monthly tickets by arrangement. *Eating facilities:* sandwiches, lunches, high teas and dinners served at club. *Visitors:* welcome except Saturdays from 25th March to 20th October. *Society Meetings*: catered for, pre-booking essential. Caterer: (01463 233259). Professional: A.P. Thomson (01463 231989). Club Manager: J.S. Thomson (01463 239882).
e-mail: igc@freeuk.com
website: www.invernessgolfclub.co.uk

INVERNESS. **Torvean Golf Club**, Glenurquhart Road, Inverness (Office: 01463 225651). *Location:* A82 towards Fort William, approximately one mile from town centre. Parkland course. 18 holes, 5784 yards, 5288 metres. S.S.S. 68. *Green Fees:* weekdays £15.00 (Adults), £5.00 (Juniors); weekends £18.00 (Adults), £7.50 (Juniors). *Eating facilities:* all day catering provided year round. *Visitors:* booking preferred, especially at weekends (Tel: 01463 711434; Fax 01463 711417 – Starters Office). Clubs and trolleys for hire. *Society Meetings:* discounts for parties over 10. Club Manager: Atholl Menzies.
e-mail: torveangolfclub@btinternet.com

KINGUSSIE. **Kingussie Golf Club**, Gynack Road, Kingussie PH21 1LR (01540 661600). *Location:* half a mile from Kingussie High Street, turning at Duke of Gordon. Hill type course. 18 holes, 5615 yards. S.S.S. 68. *Green Fees:* weekdays £20.00 per round, £25.00 per day; weekends £22.00 per round, £28.00 per day. Juniors £10.00. Weekly (seven days) £60.00. Subject to review. *Eating facilities:* bar and excellent catering. *Visitors:* welcome, certain times reserved for members at weekends. Caravan site. *Society Meetings:* welcome at all times, book in advance. Secretary: Norman MacWilliam (01540 661600).
e-mail: kinggolf@globalnet.co.uk

NAIRN. **Nairn Dunbar Golf Club**, Lochloy Road, Nairn IV12 5AE (01667 452741; Fax: 01667 456897). *Location:* off A96, at east end of town. Championship links. 18 holes, 6765 yards. S.S.S. 74. *Green Fees:* weekdays £39.50 per round, £55.00 per day; weekends £48.00 per round, £65.00 per day. Subject

to review. *Eating facilities:* new spacious clubhouse with full catering and visitors facilities. *Visitors:* welcome, also groups. Secretary: Mr Scott Falconer (01667 452741; Fax: 01667 456897). Professional: David Torrance. (01667 453964)
e-mail: secretary@nairndunbar.com
website: www.nairndunbar.com

NETHYBRIDGE. **Abernethy Golf Club**, Nethybridge PH25 3EB (01479 821305). *Location:* 10 miles from Aviemore lying on the B970 between Boat of Garten and Grantown-on-Spey. Delightful nine hole course close to pine woods and with commanding view of the valley of the River Spey. 9 holes, 5068 yards. S.S.S. 66. *Green Fees:* £14.00 weekdays; £16.00 weekends. *Eating facilities:* clubhouse is unlicensed but there are full catering facilities available. *Visitors:* welcome subject to short restrictions when club competitions being held. *Society Meetings:* by arrangement with the Secretary. Secretary: Bob Robbie (01479 821196).
e-mail: info@abernethygolfclub.com
website: www.abernethygolfclub.com

NEWTONMORE. **Newtonmore Golf Club**, Golf Course Road, Newtonmore PH20 1AT (01540 673878; Fax: 01540 670147). *Location:* turn off A9 at Newtonmore, course in centre of village, 45 miles south of Inverness. Mainly flat course set by River Spey amidst beautiful scenery. 18 holes, 6029 yards. S.S.S. 69. Practice green. *Green Fees:* weekdays £20.00 per round, £22.00 per day; weekends £22.00 per round, £30.00 per day. Subject to review. Special midweek breaks available, apply Secretary. *Eating facilities:* full catering (except Tuesdays) and bar facilities. *Visitors:* welcome by appointment with Secretary. Locker and shower facilities. *Society Meetings:* all welcome. Professional: Robert Henderson (01540 673611). Secretary: C. Bisset (01540 673878; Fax: 01540 670147).

SPEAN BRIDGE. **Spean Bridge Golf Club**, Station Road, Spean Bridge PH34 4EU. *Location:* on main A82, eight miles north of Fort William. Wooded course set on the hillside, full view of Nevis Range ski slopes and Ben Nevis. 9 holes, 2271 yards. S.S.S. 63. *Green Fees:* £12.00 day ticket. *Eating facilities:* Hotel nearby. *Visitors:* welcome, tees reserved Sundays 12 noon to 4pm. *Society Meetings:* all welcome. Secretary: K. Dalziel (01397 703907).

Lanarkshire

ABINGTON. **Abington Golf Club**, Arbory Brae Golf Course, Goldchapel Road, Abington ML12 6RW. *Location*: Junction 13 off M74 at Abington, turn left at Royal Bank of Scotland in Abington Village, follow signs for Hickory Golf for 1000 yards. Undulating parkland course. 9 holes, 1858 yards, S.S.S. 34. *Green Fees*: £24.50, includes Hickory Club hire. *Eating facilities*: light snacks available by arrangement. *Visitors*: welcome any time, sorry no trolleys and no dogs. Historical golfing experience. *Society Meetings*: welcome, rates negotiable, pre booking preferable. Professional: (01864 502882). Secretary: Alfie Ward (07977 385034). e-mail: alfie@fernie55.freeserve.co.uk website: www.hickorygolf.co.uk

AIRDRIE. **Airdrie Golf Club**, Glenmavis Road, Airdrie ML6 0PQ (01236 762195). *Location:* one mile north of Airdrie Cross. 18 holes, 6004 yards. S.S.S. 69. *Green Fees:*information not available. *Eating facilities:* available. *Visitors:* welcome only on application to the Secretary. Professional: G. Monks (01236 754360). Secretary: D.M. Hardie. *

AIRDRIE. **Easter Moffat Golf Club**, Plains, Airdrie ML6 8NP (01236 842878; Fax: 01236 842904). *Location:* three miles east of Airdrie on old Edinburgh Road. 18 holes, 6221 yards. S.S.S. 70. Practice ground. *Green Fees:* £20.00 per round, £30.00 per day. *Eating facilities:* bar and dining room. *Visitors:* welcome except weekends. *Society Meetings:* welcome. Professional: Graham King (01236 843015). Secretary: Gordon Miller (01236 620972). Further information including course planner is available on our website. website: www.emgc.fsnet.co.uk

BELLSHILL. **Bellshill Golf Club**, Community Road, Orbiston, Bellshill ML4 2RZ (01698 745124). *Location:* Bellshill to Motherwell road, turn right. Parkland course. 18 holes, 5852 yards. S.S.S. 69. *Green Fees:* April to October (inclusive) weekdays £16.00 per round, £24.00 per day; weekends £20.00 per round, £30.00 per day. November to March £10.00 per round. Half price rates for juniors and students. Special rates for parties, £35.00 includes two rounds plus meals. *Eating facilities:* by prior arrangement with Clubmaster. *Visitors:* welcome, parties by prior application (not competition days or Sundays). *Society Meetings:* by prior arrangement with Administrator (Alex Smith) or Secretary. Secretary: Tom McLaughlin.

BIGGAR. **Biggar Golf Club**, Broughton Road, Biggar ML12 6HA (01899 220618). *Location:* from Edinburgh A702, from Glasgow A74 or M8, turn off at Newhouse. Flat, scenic parkland course. 18 holes, 5416 yards. S.S.S. 66. *Green Fees:* information not available. *Eating facilities:* all day licence, full catering, snacks only on Tuesdays. *Visitors:* unrestricted, casual dress – no jeans. All weather tennis courts and caravan park. Buggies and carts available. *Society Meetings:* welcome, early reservation essential. Secretary: Tom Rodger. Tee Reservations: (01899 220319). *

CARLUKE. **Carluke Golf Club**, Maudslie Road, Hallcraig, Carluke ML8 5HG (01555 771070). *Location:* Carluke Cross, go west along Clyde Street for two miles. Parkland course. 18 holes, 5800 yards. S.S.S. 68. Practice area. *Green Fees:* information not available. *Eating facilities:* available. *Visitors:* till 4pm weekdays, no visitors weekends. Tuition. *Society Meetings:* by written application to the Secretary, restriction on numbers. Professional: Craig Ronald (01555 751053). Administration: Tom Fraser (01555 770574).

CLEGHORN. **Kames Country Club**, Eastend, Cleghorn ML11 8NR (01555 870015; Fax: 01555 870022). *Location:* situated on the A721 between Carluke and Carnwath. Home of the championship Mouse Valley Golf Course and the delightful Kames 9-hole course. 18 holes, 6600 yards, 5900 metres. S.S.S. 72. *Green Fees:* 18 hole course (Mouse Valley) £15.50 weekdays, £18.50 weekends; 9 hole course (Kames) £8.00. *Eating facilities:* full catering available. *Visitors:* welcome, no restrictions. 30 golf carts for hire. *Society Meetings:* all welcome, weekend bookings taken. Corporate membership available.

COATBRIDGE. **Drumpellier Golf Club**, Drumpellier Avenue, Coatbridge ML5 1RX (01236 424139). *Location:* one mile from town centre. Parkland, wooded. 18 holes, 6227 yards. S.S.S. 70. Practice area. *Green Fees:* £30.00 per round, £40.00 per day weekdays. *Eating facilities:* available seven days. *Visitors:* welcome daily except weekends. *Society Meetings:* catered for by arrangement. Professional: Colin Gillies. Secretary: J.M. Craig (01236 424139; Fax: 01236 428723). website: www.drumpellier.com

DOUGLAS WATER. **Douglas Water Golf Club**, Ayr Road, Rigside, Lanark (01555 880361). *Location:* five miles south of Lanark on A70, Junction 11 from M74. Hilly course, small greens, undulating fairways. 9 holes, 2947 yards, 2694 metres. S.S.S. 69. *Green Fees:* information not available. *Visitors:* welcome any time, except Saturdays because of competitions. *Society Meetings:* contact Secretary. Secretary: D. Hogg (01698 882432).

EAST KILBRIDE. **Torrance House Golf Club**, Calderglen Country Park, Strathaven Road, East Kilbride G75 0QZ (013552 49720). *Location:* East Kilbride boundary on main Strathaven road. Parkland. 18 holes, 6423 yards. S.S.S. 71. Practice area. *Green Fees:* information on request. *Eating facilities:* private clubhouse. *Visitors:* welcome mid-week only. *Society Meetings:* details on request. Secretary: M.D. McKerlie (013552 49720). Booking Office: (01355 248638).

GARTCOSH. **Mount Ellen Golf Club**, Johnstone Road, Gartcosh, Glasgow G69 8EY (01236 872277; Fax: 01236 872249). *Location:* approximately six miles north-east of Glasgow, near old Gartcosh steelworks. Parkland. 18 holes, 5525 yards. S.S.S. 66. *Green Fees:* information not available. *Eating facilities:* bar and full catering service. *Visitors:* welcome weekdays from 9am to 4pm, no weekend visitors. Buggies and carts available for hire. *Society Meetings:* weekdays by arrangement with Secretary. Professional: I. Bilsborough (01236 872632). Secretary: T. Reilly (0141 778 7464).

HAMILTON. **Hamilton Golf Club**, Riccarton, Ferniegair, Hamilton ML3 7UE (01698 282872). *Location:* off M74 Hamilton turn-off, one and a half miles up Larkhall road. Parkland course. 18 holes, 6700 yards. S.S.S. 71. *Green Fees:* information not provided. *Eating facilities:* meals must be ordered. *Visitors:* must be accompanied by a member. *Society Meetings:* by arrangement, contact Secretary. Professional: Derek Wright (01698 282324). Secretary: Graham Chapman (Tel & Fax: 01698 459537).

HAMILTON. **Strathclyde Park Golf Club**, Motehill, Hamilton ML3 6BY (01698 429350). *Location:* Hamilton/Motherwell exit off M74 to roundabout second exit East Kilbride, to new roundabout second exit, to third roundabout third exit straight ahead, to golf course passing ice rink on left hand side. Wooded parkland course surrounded by race course on one side and nature reserve on other. 9 holes, 3128 yards. S.S.S. 70. Large practice area, putting green and driving range (24 bays). *Green Fees:* weekdays £3.50, Juniors/Senior Citizens £1.75; weekends & public holidays £4.10, Juniors/Senior Citizens £2.05. *Eating facilities:* bar within complex. *Visitors:* welcome, same day booking system in operation. Course opens 7am Summer, 8am Winter. *Society Meetings:* welcome by arrangement through management (01698 429350). Professional: W. Walker. Secretary: K. Will (01698 429350).

LANARK. **Carnwath Golf Club**, 1 Main Street, Carnwath ML11 8JX (01555 840251; Fax: 01555 841070). *Location:* on main Ayr/Edinburgh Road. Fairly hilly inland course. 18 holes, 5953 yards. S.S.S. 69. *Green Fees:* weekdays £18.00 per round, £28.00 per two rounds; Sundays £24.00 per round, £34.00 per two rounds. Subject to review. *Eating facilities:* lounge bar and dining room daily. *Visitors:* welcome. Not Saturdays or after 4pm weekdays. Sunday with prior booking. *Society Meetings:* catered for by prior arrangement. Secretary: Mrs L. McPate (01555 840251).

LANARK **Lanark Golf Club**, The Moor, Whitelees Road, Lanark ML11 7RX (01555 663219). *Location:* off A73. Tough moorland course. 18 holes, 6423 yards. S.S.S. 71. Also 9-hole course. Two practice grounds. *Green Fees:* weekdays £30.00 per round, £40.00 per day. 2003 prices, subject to review. *Eating facilities:* full catering and bar. *Visitors:* welcome daily until 4pm, no visitors weekends. *Society Meetings:* groups of 24 and over catered for Mondays to Wednesdays. Professional: Alan White (01555 661456). Secretary: G.H. Cuthill.

LANARK. **Mouse Valley Golf Course**, East End, Cleghorn, Lanark ML11 (01555 870015; Fax: 01555 870022). *Location:* 5 miles from Carluke on A721 Peebles Road. Pay as you play. Links style course, inland undulating terrain. Mouse Water (river) runs through the course. Two courses - Mouse Valley 18 holes, 6376 yards, Par 70 and Kames course - 9 holes, 2538 yards, Par 33 Practice ground. *Green Fees:* information not available. *Eating facilities:* full bar and catering. *Visitors:* welcome, no restrictions. *Society Meetings:* welcome at all times. Company days. Contact: (01555 870015).*

LARKHALL. **Larkhall Golf Club**, Burnhead Road, Larkhall ML9 3AA (01698 889597). *Location:* on A74, close to M74. Parkland. 9 holes, 6432 yards. S.S.S. 70. *Green Fees:* information not available. *Eating facilities:* bar, lunch only on Saturdays. *Visitors:* welcome, but check beforehand; not Saturdays. Secretary: Malcolm Mallinson; Booking Office(01698 881113).*

LEADHILLS. **Leadhills Golf Club**, Leadhills, Biggar ML12 6AR (01659 74356). *Location:* seven miles south of Abington on B797. This short but testing course is the highest in Scotland. 9 holes, 2177 yards. S.S.S. 64. *Green Fees:* information not available. *Eating facilities:* hotel nearby. *Visitors:* welcome any time. *Society Meetings:* welcome. Secretary: Nigel Davies (01659 74356). *

LESMAHAGOW. **Hollandbush Golf Club**, Acretophead, Lesmahagow ML11 0JS (01555 893484). *Location:* off M74 (Junction 9). Golf course is between Lesmahagow and Coalburn. 18 holes, 6246 yards. S.S.S. 70. Practice area. *Green Fees:* information not available. *Eating facilities:* meals at club. *Visitors:* welcome without restriction. *Society Meetings:* catered for. Starter's Office (01555 893646). Secretary: Robert Lynch (01555 893484). *

MOTHERWELL. **Colville Park Golf Club**, Jerviston Estate, Merry Street, Motherwell ML1 4UG (01698 263017; Fax: 01698 230418). *Location:* one mile from town centre and train station (Merry Street, Motherwell). Parkland, wooded first six holes. 18 holes, 6301 yards. S.S.S. 70. *Green Fees:* weekdays £15.00. *Eating facilities:* full facilities. *Visitors:* welcome between 11am and 3pm Mondays to Thursdays only. Advance booking not required. *Society Meetings:* by prior written arrangement, weekdays only. £25.00 day ticket. Professional Shop: (01698 265779). Secretary: Leslie Innes (01698 262808).

MOTHERWELL. **Dalziel Park Golf & Country Club**, 100 Hagen Drive, Motherwell ML1 5RZ (01698 862862; Fax: 01698 862863). *Location:* four miles from Motherwell with good access to M74 and M8 at Junction 6. Midway between Glasgow and Edinburgh. Wooded Parkland. 18 holes, 6300 yards. S.S.S. 70. 15 bay floodlit driving range and extensive dry and outdoor sports facilities. *Green Fees:* £20.00 per round. *Eating facilities:* restaurant, bars and lounges. 10 bedrooms, conference facilities and all functions catered for in Country Club. *Visitors:* all welcome, only restricted on Saturday morning (during Men's medal day). *Society Meetings:* welcome at all times. Secretary: Ian Donnache (01698 862862; Fax: 01698 862863).

SHOTTS. **Shotts Golf Club**, Blairhead, Benhar Road, Shotts ML7 5BJ (01501 822658). *Location:* off M8 at Junction 5, one and a half miles south. Semi-flat moorland/wooded course. 18 holes, 6204 yards. S.S.S. 70. Practice area, professional tuition. *Green Fees:* weekdays £16.00 per round, £26.00 per day; weekends £18.00 per round (Sundays only). *Eating facilities:* full catering and bar service. *Visitors:* welcome anytime except Saturdays, Sundays (prior booking needed) or Public Holidays. *Society Meetings:* weekdays only (not Public Holidays) by arrangement. Professional: John Strachan (01501 822658). Secretary: George Stoddart (01501 825868).

STRATHAVEN. **Strathaven Golf Club**, Overton Avenue, Glasgow Road, Strathaven ML10 6NR. *Location:* on A726 on outskirts of town. 18 holes, 6226 yards. S.S.S. 71. *Green Fees:* please contact Secretary for information. *Eating facilities:* full catering and bar. *Visitors:* welcome weekdays, casual visitors before 4pm; party bookings Tuesdays only by prior arrangement. Professional: Stuart Kerr (01357 521812). Secretary: A.W. Wallace (01357 520421).

UDDINGSTON. **Calderbraes Golf Club**, 57 Roundknowe Road, Uddingston G71 7TS (01698 813425). *Location:* at end of M74, overlooking Calderpark Zoo. 9 holes, 3425 yards. S.S.S. 67. *Green Fees:* information not available. *Eating facilities:* catering available at all times. *Visitors:* welcome weekdays only; must be off course by 5pm. *Society Meetings:* welcome, contact Secretary. Secretary: S. McGuigan.*

WISHAW. **Wishaw Golf Club**, 55 Cleland Road, Wishaw ML2 7PH (01698 372869). *Location:* 400 yards from Wishaw Main Street at West Cross. Tree-lined parkland course. 18 holes, 5999 yards. S.S.S. 69. Practice area. *Green Fees:* weekdays £20.00 per round, Sundays £25.00 per round. Day tickets available. *Eating facilities:* full catering, two bars, and dining room. *Visitors:* welcome before 4pm weekdays, after 10.30am Sundays, no visitors Saturdays. *Society Meetings:* by application. Professional: Stuart Adair (01698 358247). General Manager: James W. Douglas (01698 357480). e-mail: jwdouglas@btconnect.com

Perth & Kinross

ABERFELDY. **Aberfeldy Golf Club**, Taybridge Road, Aberfeldy PH15 2BH (01887 820535). *Location:* A9 from Ballinluig. Scenic riverside course. 18 holes, 5283 yards. S.S.S. 66, Par 68. *Green Fees:* weekdays £18.00 per round; weekends £23.00. *Eating facilities:* high teas, lunches, etc. *Visitors:* welcome anytime. Buggy and trolley hire. *Society Meetings:* catered for. Secretary: Peter Woolley (01887 829422).

ALYTH. **Glenisla Golf Centre,** Pitcrocknie, Alyth PH11 8JJ (01828 632445; Fax: 01828 633749). *Location:* five miles east of Blairgowrie on the B954. Parkland, with undulating, rolling fairways, and featuring over 40 bunkers and 5 water hazards. 'One of Scotland's favourite courses' (Insider Business Magazine Top 500 Survey, March 2001). 18 holes, 6402 yards. S.S.S. 71. *Green Fees:* information not available. *Eating facilities:* superbly appointed, fully licensed clubhouse with panoramic bar and restaurant overlooking the course. *Visitors:* always welcome. Conference and Function facilities and on site B&B and self-catering cottages available. *Society Meetings:* always welcome. Golf Administrator: Ewan Wilson.*
e-mail: info@golf-glenisla.co.uk
website: www.golf-glenisla.co.uk

AUCHTERARDER. **Auchterarder Golf Club**, Orchil Road, Auchterarder PH3 1LS (Tel & Fax: 01764 662804). *Location:* off A9 to southwest of town, next to Gleneagles. Flat parkland, part wooded. 18 holes, 5778 yards. S.S.S. 68. Small practice area. *Green Fees:* weekdays £22.00 per round, £33.00 per day; weekends £27.00 per round, £43.00 per day; weekdays weekly ticket (one round per day) £85.00.

Eating facilities: lounge, dining room, bar. *Visitors:* welcome without reservation except major competition days. *Society Meetings:* welcome, must book 3 months in advance. Professional: Gavin Baxter (Tel & Fax: 01764 663711). Secretary: W.M. Campbell (Tel & Fax: 01764 662804).
e-mail: secretary@auchterardergc.fsnet.co.uk

AUCHTERARDER. **Gleneagles Hotel Golf Courses**, Auchterarder PH3 1NF (Golf Office: 01764 694469; Fax: 01764 694383). *Location:* 20 miles south of Perth, 20 miles north of Stirling. Gleneagles offers two moorland 18 hole courses and a third parkland/moorland course. King's Course: 6125 yards par 68; Queen's Course: 5660 yards par 68; PGA Centenary Course: 18 holes, 6141 yards S.S.S. 72 and a 9 hole course, The Wee Course: 1481 yards par 27. *Green Fees:* on request. *Eating facilities:* at The Dormy Clubhouse (Bar & Restaurant) and The Gleneagles Hotel. *Visitors:* welcome. Professional: Sandy Smith. Hotel General Manager: Patrick Elsmie (01764 62231). Golf Contact: Heather Edment (01764 662231; Fax: 01764 662134).

BLAIR ATHOLL. **Blair Atholl Golf Club**, Blair Atholl, Pitlochry PH18 5TG (01796 481407; Fax: 01796 481751). *Location:* off A9 Perth/Inverness Road, down Invertilt Road. Flat parkland. 9 holes, 5816 yards, 5322 metres. S.S.S. 68. *Green Fees:* weekdays £16.00 per day; weekends £18.00 per day. Weekly £95.00. All rates include insurance. *Eating facilities:* meals/bar. *Visitors:* welcome at all times. Carts and clubs available. *Society Meetings:* by arrangement with Secretary. Secretary: D.A. Boon.

BLAIRGOWRIE. **The Alyth Golf Club**, Pitcrocknie, Alyth, Blairgowrie PH11 8HF (01828 632268; Fax:01828 633491). *Location:* five miles from Blairgowrie on B954. Parkland/heathland course with interesting dog leg Par 4 5th played to a plateau green with out-of-bounds on right. 18 holes, 6205 yards, 5676 metres. S.S.S. 71. Large practice area. *Green Fees:* weekdays £30.00 per round, £35.00 per day; weekends £37.00 per round, £45.00 per day. *Eating facilities:* all day catering and bar. *Visitors:* welcome, phone 01828 632411 six days ahead. *Society Meetings:* welcome, prior booking essential. Professional: Tom Melville (01828 632411). Secretary: Jim Docherty (01828 632268; Fax: 01828 633491). e-mail: enquiries@alythgolfclub.co.uk website: www.alythgolfclub.co.uk

BLAIRGOWRIE. **Blairgowrie Golf Club**, Golf Course Road, Rosemount, Blairgowrie PH10 6LG (01250 872383; Fax: 01250 875451).*Location:* take A923 out of Perth, turn right at "Rosemount" sign. Flat wooded heathland. Rosemount Course: 18 holes, 6588 yards. S.S.S. 72. Lansdowne Course: 18 holes, 6895 yards. S.S.S. 73. Wee Course: 9 holes, 2307 yards. S.S.S. 65. Two practice grounds. *Green Fees:* on application. *Eating facilities:* full catering available. *Visitors:* advance booking Mon/Tues/Thurs/part Fri, 8.30am-4.00pm (through Secretary). Handicap Certificate required. *Society Meetings:* catered for by application to the Secretary. (Maximum 32 without prior permission.) Professional: Charles Dernie (01250 873116). Secretary/Manager: John N. Simpson (01250 872622). e-mail: admin@blairgowrie-golf.co.uk website: www.blairgowrie-golf.co.uk

BLAIRGOWRIE. **Dalmunzie Golf Course**, Spittal O' Glenshee, Blairgowrie PH10 7QG (01250 885226). *Location:* A93 Blairgowrie to Braemar road, left at Spittal O' Glenshee. A small well-kept hill course amid glorious scenery. 9 holes, 2099 yards. *Green Fees:* £12.00 per day. Under 7 free, 7–16 half price (we like young golfers). *Eating facilities:* restaurant facilities at Dalmunzie Hotel. Bar. *Visitors:* welcome without reservation. Self-catering cottages available. *Society Meetings:* catered for. Secretary: Simon Winton.

BLAIRGOWRIE. **Strathmore Golf Centre**, Leroch, Alyth, Blairgowrie (01828 633322; Fax: 01828 633533). *Location:* one mile south of Alyth off A926 Blairgowrie to Kirriemuir road. Rolling parkland course with magnificent views over the valley of Strathmore. Two courses - Rannaleroch Course: 18 holes, 6454 yards, 5901 metres. Par 72. S.S.S. 72; Leitfie Links Course: 9 holes, 1719 yards, 1572 metres. Par 29. S.S.S. 29. Driving range adjacent. *Green Fees:* information not provided. *Eating facilities:* friendly clubhouse with bar and restaurant. *Visitors:* always welcome. *Society Meetings:* always welcome. General Manager: Christopher Spencer. e-mail: enquiries@strathmoregolf.com website: www.strathmoregolf.com

CALLANDER. **Callander Golf Club,** Aveland Road, Callander FK17 8EN (01877 330090; Fax: 01877 330062). *Location:* M9 Stirling, Junction 10 Crianlarich exit to A84 to Callander. Parkland, partly wooded, with panoramic views. 18 holes, 4410 yards (yellow tees). S.S.S. 65. Small practice ground and putting green. *Green Fees:* information not available. *Eating facilities:* bar snacks, lunches, high teas,

dinners by arrangement. *Visitors*: welcome, no restrictions. Handicap Certificate required Wednesdays and Sundays. *Society Meetings*: welcome, book in advance. Professional: A. Martin (01877 330975). Secretary: Mrs Sandra Smart (01877 330090; Fax: 01877 330062).

CRIEFF. **Comrie Golf Club,** Laggan Braes, Comrie PH6 2LR (01764 670055). *Location*: six miles west of Crieff on A85 at east end of village. Parkland, wooded course with two long and tricky Par 3 holes (3rd and 5th) and well guarded Par 5 (6th). 9 holes, 6040 yards. S.S.S. 70. *Green Fees*: weekdays £16.00 per round, £20.00 per day, weekends £20.00 per round, £25.00 per day. Special rates for parties. *Eating facilities*: light refreshments and meals during summer months. *Visitors*: welcome at all times. Club Medals - Monday 1pm and 4.30pm, Ladies Tuesdays 1pm. *Society Meetings*: always welcome. Secretary: Steve Van Der Walt (01764 670055).

CRIEFF. **Crieff Golf Club,** Ferntower, Perth Road, Crieff PH7 3LR (01764 652397; Fax: 01764 655096). *Location*: A85 north-east outskirts of Crieff. Ferntower Course - 18 holes, 6402 yards. S.S.S. 72. Dornock Course - 9 holes, 2386 yards. S.S.S. 63. Two practice areas. *Green Fees*: information not available. *Eating facilities*: full restaurant facilities by arrangement (phone 01764 652397) and bar snacks. *Visitors*: welcome with reservation, prior arrangement advisable by phone. *Society Meetings*: book by phone (01764 652909) and confirm in writing. Professional: David Murchie (01764 652909; Fax: 01764 655096). Managing/ Secretary: J.S. Miller.

CRIEFF. **Foulford Inn Golf Course,** Foulford Inn, by Crieff PH7 3LN (Tel & Fax: 01764 652407). *Location*: 5 miles north of Crieff on the A822 in the direction of Dunkeld. Upland course with water hazards. 9 holes, 916 yards, S.S.S. 27. *Green Fees*: £4.00 per round, £6.00 per day. *Eating facilities*: bar/restaurant. *Visitors*: welcome anytime, accommodation available in Inn. Course free to residents. *Society Meetings*: welcome, on application. Secretary: Mr B.A. Beaumont.
e-mail: foulford@btconnect.com
website: www.foulfordinn.co.uk

CRIEFF. **Muthill Golf Club**, Peat Road, Muthill, Crieff PH5 2DA (01764 681523; Fax: 01764 681557). *Location:* two miles from Crieff at entrance to Muthill. Parkland course with magnificent views. 9 holes, 4700 yards. S.S.S. 63. *Green Fees:* weekdays £15.00 per round; weekends £18.00. Fees subject to review. *Eating facilities:* full meals service available. *Visitors:* no restrictions except after 5pm Wednesday and Thursdays (club competitions). Trolleys available. *Society Meetings:* welcome. Secretary: Jim Elder (01764 681523; Fax: 01764 681557).
e-mail: muthillgolfclub@lineone.net

DUNBLANE. **Dunblane New Golf Club**, Perth Road, Dunblane FK15 0LJ (01786 821521; Fax: 01786 821522). *Location:* two miles off main road M9 at Fourways Roundabout. Parkland/undulating. 18 holes, 5936 yards. S.S.S. 69. *Green Fees:* £25.00 per round, £35.00 per day. *Eating facilities:* available seven days a week. *Visitors:* welcome, 9.30am to 12 noon, 2.30pm to 4pm. *Society Meetings:* catered for weekdays only except Tuesdays. Professional: R.M. Jamieson (01786 821521; Fax: 01786 821522). Secretary: John H. Dunsmore (Tel & Fax: 01786 825281).

DUNKELD. **Dunkeld and Birnam Golf Club**, Fungarth, Dunkeld PH8 0HU (01350 727524; Fax: 01350 728660). *Location:* one mile north of Dunkeld on the A923. Heathland course with panoramic views. 18 holes, 5508 yards. S.S.S. 67. Practice area. *Green Fees:* on application. *Eating facilities:* bar and full catering facilities. *Visitors:* welcome. *Society Meetings:* catered for. Secretary: Richard Barrance (01350 727524: Fax: 01350 728660).

DUNNING. **Dunning Golf Club,** Station Road, Rollo Park, Dunning PH2 0QX (01764 684747). *Location:* 10 miles south-west of Perth, two miles from A9. Parkland, softly undulating. 9 holes, 4885 yards. S.S.S. 63. Small practice area. *Green Fees:* weekdays £14.00 per round, weekends £16.00. *Eating facilities:* tea/ coffee, soft drinks, snacks. Meals can be arranged with the Dunning Hotel at approx £10.50 for a three course meal. *Visitors:* welcome, no restrictions apart from club competitions. *Society Meetings:* welcome weekdays and most Sundays. Secretary: R. Weetman (01764 684897).

DUNNING. **Whitemoss Golf Club**, Whitemoss Road, Dunning PH2 0GX (01738 730300; Fax: 01738 730490). *Location*: 10 miles south-west of Perth, two miles from A9. Parkland course. 18 holes, 5968 yards, S.S.S. 69. Practice range, chipping bunkers, practice net and putting green. *Green Fees*: information not available. *Eating facilities*: New clubhouse with restaurant and bar. *Visitors*: welcome all the time, on medal days after 10am. *Society Meetings*: Welcome, after 10am on medal days. Tuition on request. Shower facilities. Secretary: Victor Westwood (01738 730300). *

KENMORE. **Kenmore Golf Course**, Mains of Taymouth, Kenmore, Aberfeldy PH15 2HN (01887 830226; Fax: 01887 829059). *Location*: west off A9 at Ballinluig on A827, six and a half miles west of Aberfeldy through village of Kenmore on RHS. Testing well kept course on natural undulating terrain, lovely scenery and first class facilities. 9 holes, 6052 yards, 5600 metres. S.S.S. 70. Practice facilities, putting green. *Green Fees*: weekdays 9 holes £9.00 , 18 holes £14.00; weekends 9 holes

£10.00, 18 holes £15.00. Weekly Ticket £45.00. *Eating facilities*: full bar and restaurant facilities in pleasant surroundings. *Visitors*: welcome anytime. Cottages to let (self- catering included). Pro shop; club and trolley hire; changing and shower facilities. *Society Meetings*: all welcome, please book. Secretary: Robin Menzies.
e-mail: golf@taymouth.co.uk
website: www.taymouth.co.uk

KENMORE. **Taymouth Castle Golf Course**, Kenmore, by Aberfeldy PH15 2NT (01887 830228). *Location*: six miles west of Aberfeldy. Parkland set in scenic mountain terrain. 18 holes, 6066 yards. S.S.S. 69. Practice area. *Green Fees*: weekdays £22.00 per round, £34.00 per day; weekends and Bank Holidays £26.00 per round, £40.00 per day. Half price for Juniors (under 14). Subject to review. *Eating facilities*: restaurant and bar. *Visitors*: welcome, tee reservations necessary (phone or letter). Tuition available, motorised buggies. *Society Meetings*: catered for by previous arrangement only. PGA Professional: Gavin Dott (01887 830228).

TAYMOUTH CASTLE
GOLF COURSE
Kenmore, Perthshire
Weekdays:
£22 per round; £34 per day
Weekends:
£26 per round; £40 per day

All Parties welcome

For bookings:
Gavin Dott PGA Professional
Tel & Fax: **01887 830228**

See also Colour Advertisement on page 84

KILLIN. **Killin Golf Club**, Killin FK21 8TX (01567 820312). *Location:* west end of Loch Tay. Hilly parkland amongst beautiful scenery. 9 holes, 2510 yards. S.S.S. 65. Small practice area includes bunker and net. *Green Fees:* £15.00 per round, £20.00 per day. Subject to review. *Eating facilities:* available all day. *Visitors:* welcome. *Society Meetings:* catered for by arrangement. Secretary: Trevor Taylor (01567 820312).

KINNESSWOOD. **Bishopshire Golf Club**, Kinnesswood, By Kinross KY13 9HX. *Location:* take road to Glenrothes from M90, three miles. Course has panoramic views overlooking Loch Leven. 10 holes, 4830 yards, 2268 metres. S.S.S. 64. *Green Fees:* information not available. *Eating facilities:* by arrangement or available at the hotel 400 yards away. *Visitors:* welcome, no restrictions. *Society Meetings:* by arrangement. Secretary: John Proudfoot (01592 780203).*

KINROSS. **Green Hotel Golf Courses**, Green Hotel, The Muirs, Kinross KY13 8AS (01577 863467). *Location:* turn left in Kinross off M90 Junction 6, course 500 yards on right. Parkland. Two courses: Blue 18 holes, 6438 yards, 5888 metres. S.S.S. 71; Red 18 holes, 6256 yards, 5717 metres. S.S.S. 73. Practice ground. *Green Fees:* weekdays £22.00 per round, £35.00 per day; weekends £33.00 per round, £45.00 per day - subject to change. Preferred rates and tee times to Green Hotel residents. *Eating facilities:* in clubhouse. *Visitors:* welcome anytime. Hotel facilities. *Society Meetings:* welcome by arrangement. Professional: Stewart Geraghty (01577 865125). Secretary: Eileen Gray (01577 863407; Fax: 01577 863180).
e-mail: golfing@green-hotel.com

MILNATHORT. **Milnathort Golf Club Ltd,** South Street, Milnathort KY13 9XA (01577 864069). *Location:* one mile north of Kinross, M90 Junction 6 (north) or Junction 7 (south). Undulating inland course with lush fairways and excellent greens, with the addition of extra trees around the margins along with current plantations. Strategically placed copses of trees require acurate tee shots. The course is being made more interesting by the addition of extra tees/greens for some holes. 9 holes, 5973 yards. S.S.S. 69. Practice ground/green. *Green Fees:* weekdays £13.00 per round, £19.00 per day; weekends £15.00 per round, £21.00 per day. 9 hole sundowner ticket £7.00 weekends, £6.00 weekdays (subject to review). *Eating facilities:* full bar available, catering by arrangement. *Visitors:* welcome but suggest you phone. Dress code. *Society Meetings:* must be booked in advance. Secretary: via Club House.

PERTH. **Craigie Hill Golf Club (1982) Ltd**, Cherrybank, Perth PH2 0NE (01738 624377). *Location:* at west end of town, easy access from M90 and A9. Hilly course with panoramic view of Perth and surrounding hills. 18 holes, 5386 yards. S.S.S. 67. Practice ground and putting green. *Green Fees:* weekdays £18.00 per round, £30.00 per day; Sundays £30.00 per day. Visitors with member £7.00, Juniors (weekdays) £3.00 per round. *Eating facilities:* full catering and bar. *Visitors:* welcome Mondays to Fridays; Sundays by arrangement. *Society Meetings:* catered for by written application in first instance. Professional: Ian Muir (01738 622644). Secretary: Andrew Tunnicliffe (Tel & Fax: 01738 620829).

PERTH. **King James VI Golf Club**, Moncreiffe Island, Perth PH2 8NR (01738 625170). *Location:* situated on Island in River Tay, access by Footbridge alongside railway from Tay Street, Perth. Flat parkland course, surrounded by River Tay. 18 holes, 6038 yards. S.S.S. 69. Practice nets. *Green Fees:* weekdays £18.00 per round, £25.00 per day; weekends £20.00 per round, £30.00 per day. April/July/October £15.00 per round, £20.00 per day. *Eating facilities:* full catering. *Visitors:* welcome, phone for reservation, no visitors on Saturdays. Carts available. *Society Meetings:* catered for by prior booking. Fully stocked golf shop. Professional: Andrew Crerar (01738 632460). Secretary: Helen Blair (Tel & Fax: 01738 445132).
e-mail: info@kjvigc.fsnet.co.uk
website: www.kingjamesvi.co.uk

PERTH. **North Inch Golf Course,** c/o C. Glencorse, Environment Services, Perth and Kinross Council, 35 Kinnoull Street, Perth (01738 636481). *Location:* A9 to city centre turnoff, follow Atholl Street to North Inch, course is located at Bell's Sports Centre, Hay Street. Picturesque municipal course alongside River Tay. Putting green. 18 holes, 5442 yards. S.S.S. 66. *Green Fees:* information available by calling Starter (01738 636481). *Eating facilities:* Inch Restaurant, Bell's Sports Centre.

THE APPEARANCE OF AN ASTERISK (*) AT THE END OF A CLUB OR COURSE ENTRY INDICATES THAT UP-TO-DATE INFORMATION HAS NOT BEEN SUPPLIED

PITLOCHRY. **Pitlochry Golf Course**, Pitlochry PH16 5QY (01796 472792). *Location:* half mile from centre of Pitlochry on A9. 18 holes, 5811 yards, S.S.S. 69. *Green Fees:* weekdays £32.00 per day, £22.00 per round; weekends £40.00 per day. £28.00 per round. Subject to review. Restricted course (1st November to 31st March). *Eating facilities:* catering and refreshments available in licensed clubhouse April to end October. *Visitors:* welcome. Caddy cars available for hire. *Society Meetings:* catered for. Phone Professional for all bookings. Professional: Mark Pirie (01796 472792). Secretary: D.C.M. McKenzie (01796 472792; Fax: 01796 473599.

ST FILLANS. **St Fillans Golf Club**, South Loch Earn Road, St Fillans, Loch Earn PH6 2NJ (01764 685312). *Location:* 13 miles west of Crieff on A85; turn off at east end of village, club 300 yards on left. A testing parkland course nestling between magnificent Perthshire mountains with one elevated tee and green. 9 holes length (18 holes), 6054 yards. S.S.S. 69. Practice facilities and putting green. *Green Fees:* weekdays £15.00 per day; weekends and Bank Holidays £20.00 per day. Weekly tickets £50.00. 9 holes £10.00. *Eating facilities:* full meals and snacks available throughout the day. Golf trolleys, powered trolleys, buggy and clubs for hire. *Visitors:* welcome at all times except when matches on. *Society Meetings:* welcome with advance booking. Starter: Gordon Hibbert.

SCONE. **Murrayshall Golf Course**, Murrayshall, Scone, By Perth PH2 7PH (01738 551171). *Location:* three miles north of Perth on A94 Coupar Angus Road. Undulating wooded parkland. 18 holes, 6043 yards. S.S.S. 72. Covered Driving Golf range, a second 18 hole course has been available since July 2000. *Green Fees:* Murrayshall £30.00 weekday, £35.00 weekends. Lynedoch £20.00 weekday, £25.00 weekend. *Eating facilities:* clubhouse open all day. *Visitors:* welcome, no restrictions - advance booking essential. *Society Meetings:* welcome - must pre-book. Professional: Alan Reid (01738 552784). website: www.murrayshall.com

STRATHTAY. **Strathtay Golf Club**, Lyon Cottage, Strathtay, by Pitlochry PH9 OPG. *Location:* on the right, three-quarters of a mile westwards on the minor road to Weem off the A827 Ballinluig to Grandtully. Wooded, mainly hilly course with beautiful panoramic views. 9 holes, 4082 yards. S.S.S. 61. *Green Fees:* £12.00 per day, £15.00 weekends and public holidays. *Visitors:* welcome at any time without restrictions. Changing room, toilets. *Society Meetings:* must be arranged in advance. Secretary: Ian Ramsay. (01887 840211).

Renfrewshire

BARRHEAD. **Fereneze Golf Club**, Fereneze Avenue, Barrhead, Glasgow G78 1HJ (0141-881 1519). *Location:* nine miles south west of Glasgow. Hilly moorland. 18 holes, 5962 yards. S.S.S. 70 *Green Fees:* weekdays £22.00 per round, £25.00 per day. weekends on application. *Eating facilities:* full catering/lounges *Visitors:* welcome by arrangement. *Society Meetings:* welcome, bookings arranged in advance. Professional: Hal Lee (0141-880 7058). Secretary: Graham McCreadie (Tel & Fax: 0141-881 7149).

BISHOPTON. **Erskine Golf Club,** Bishopton PA7 5PH (01505 862302). *Location:* club situated on south bank of the River Clyde. Leave M8 at Junction 30 onto M898 then left onto B815 (before bridge toll barriers), follow sign for Bishopton, Club approximately one mile on right. Parkland course, with breathtaking views over the river to the hills beyond. 18 holes, 6371 yards. S.S.S. 71. Putting green and practice area. *Green Fees:* £31.00 per round, £42.00 per day ticket (2003). *Eating facilities:* restaurant and bar, lunches, teas and dinners served at club. *Visitors:* welcome but must play with a member or be introduced. Professional: Peter Thomson. Secretary: T.A. McKillop.

BRIDGE OF WEIR. **Old Course Ranfurly Golf Club Ltd**, Ranfurly Place, Bridge of Weir PA11 3DE (01505 613612). *Location:* five miles west of Glasgow Airport. Moorland course. 18 holes, 6089 yards. S.S.S. 70. *Green Fees:* weekdays £25.00 per round, £35.00 per day (two rounds); weekends only if introduced by and playing with a member. *Eating facilities:* dining room, lounge. *Visitors:* welcome weekdays, should contact club beforehand. Must be members of recognised golf clubs with Handicap Certificates. *Society Meetings:* on written application only. Secretary: Q.J. McClymont (Tel & Fax: 01505 613214). e-mail: secretary@oldranfurly.com website: www.oldranfurly.com

BRIDGE OF WEIR. **Ranfurly Castle Golf Club Ltd**, Golf Road, Bridge of Weir PA11 3HN (01505 612609). *Location:* M8 from Glasgow exit Junction 29, A240 and A761 to Bridge of Weir. Moorland. 18 holes, 6284 yards. S.S.S. 71. Practice ground. *Green Fees:* weekdays £25.00 per round, £35.00 day ticket. *Eating facilities:* bar snacks all day; lunches, high teas, etc by arrangement. *Visitors:* welcome weekdays, at weekends only if accompanied by member. *Society Meetings:* catered for weekdays only. Professional: Tom Eckford (01505 614795; Fax: 01505 612609). Secretary: J. King (01505 612609)

ELDERSLIE. **Elderslie Golf Club**, 63 Main Road, Elderslie PA5 9AZ (01505 322835). *Location*: off M8 at Linwood turn-off, continue to roundabout, follow Elderslie signs A737. Club on main road. Parkland course. 18 holes, 6175 yards. S.S.S. 70. Practice area. *Green Fees*: £24.50 per round, £32.50 per day weekdays. *Eating facilities*: full meals and bar meals. *Visitors*: welcome weekdays, no visitors weekends. Caddy hire. *Society Meetings*: welcome weekdays, book through Secretary. Professional: Mr R. Bowman (01505 320032). Secretary: Mrs A. Anderson (01505 323956; Fax: 01505 340346). e-mail: aanderson@eldersliegolfclub.freeserve.co.uk website: www.eldersliegolfclub.net

GOUROCK. **Gourock Golf Club**, Cowal View, Gourock PA19 1HD (01475 631001; Fax: 01475 638307). *Location:* two miles west of Gourock Station above Yacht Club. Heathland/parkland with spectacular views. 18 holes, 6512 yards. S.S.S. 72. *Green Fees:* information not available. *Eating facilities:* restaurant, full meals also bar snacks. *Visitors:* welcome Saturdays not before 4 pm. *Society Meetings:* catered for on application. Professional: James Mooney (01475 636834). Secretary: Alan D. Taylor (Tel: 01475 631001).

GREENOCK. **Greenock Golf Club**, Forsyth Street, Greenock PA16 8RE (01475 720793). *Location:* one mile from town centre. Moorland course. 18 holes, 5835 yards. S.S.S. 68. *Green Fees:* information not available. *Eating facilities:* available. *Visitors:* welcome weekdays, not Saturdays. *Society Meetings:* advance booking required. Starter: Jim Duncan (01475 787236). Secretary: Eric J. Black (01475 720793).

GREENOCK. **Greenock Whinhill Golf Club**, Beith Road, Greenock PA16 9LN (01475 724694). *Location:* off Old Largs Road from Drumfrochar Road, Upper Greenock. Municipal course. Situated in hills high above Greenock, panoramic views of River Clyde and the surrounding area. 18 holes, 5504 yards. S.S.S. 68. *Green Fees:* information not available. *Visitors:* welcome except Saturdays. Secretary: David Ellis.*

JOHNSTONE. **Cochrane Castle Golf Club**, Scott Avenue, Craigston, Johnstone PA5 0HF (01505 320146; Fax: 01505 325338). *Location:* turn left off Beith Road at Rannoch Road, second on right to end of Scott Avenue. Parkland course, fairly hilly wth excellent views to north. 18 holes, 6194 yards. S.S.S. 71. Practice area and green. *Green Fees:* weekdays £22.00 per round, £30.00 per day; weekends by introduction only. *Eating facilities:* full catering and bar. *Visitors:* welcome Monday to Friday, limited to 24. Arrangement by letter to Secretary. Trolleys. *Society Meetings:* catered for by arrangement, weekdays only. Professional: Alan J. Logan (01505 328465). Secretary: Mrs P.I.J. Quin (01505 320146).

KILMACOLM. **Kilmacolm Golf Club**, Porterfield Road, Kilmacolm PA13 4PD (01505 872139). *Location:* A761. Moorland course. 18 holes, 5964 yards. S.S.S. 69. Practice area. *Green Fees:* information not available. *Eating facilities:* diningroom and bar. *Visitors:* welcome on weekdays. *Society Meetings:* catered for. Professional: Iain Nicholson (01505 872695). Secretary: D.W. Tinton.*

LANGBANK. **Gleddoch Golf Club,** Langbank PA14 6YE (01475 540304; Fax: 01475 540201). *Location:* M8 west to Greenock/Langbank, exit B789 signposted Langbank/Houston. Parkland/moorland. 18 holes, 6357 yards. S.S.S. 71. Practice area, putting green. *Green Fees:* information not available. *Eating facilities:* bar, lounge and restaurant open all day. *Visitors:* welcome weekdays, restrictions only when competitions. Gleddoch House Hotel, 39 bedrooms plus self catering lodges. *Society Meetings:* welcome weekdays excluding Bank Holidays. Professional: Keith Campbell (01475 540704; Fax: 01475 540201). Secretary: D.W. Tierney (01475 540304; Fax: 01475 540201). *

LOCHWINNOCH. **Lochwinnoch Golf Club**, Burnfoot Road, Lochwinnoch PA12 4AN (01505 842153; Fax: 01505 843668). *Location:* between Johnstone and Beith, off A737 on Largs road A760. Parkland, extremely scenic, set in quiet country village. 18 holes, 6243 yards. S.S.S. 71. Practice area. *Green Fees:* £22.00 per round, £30 per day. *Eating facilities:* licensed bar and catering every day. *Visitors:* welcome weekdays, weekends restricted. *Society Meetings;* welcome weekdays. Professional: Gerry Reilly (01505 843029). Administrator: R.J.G. Jamieson. e-mail: enquiries@lochwinnochgolf.co.uk website: www.lochwinnochgolf.co.uk

PAISLEY. **Barshaw Golf Club**, Barshaw Park, Glasgow Road, Paisley (0141-889 2908). *Location:* one mile from Paisley Cross travelling east towards Glasgow (Glasgow Road). Parkland course, flat/hilly. 18 holes, 5703 yards. S.S.S. 67. Putting green. *Green Fees:* (subject to review) adults £9.00; Senior Citizens, Juniors and Unemployed £4.50 (proof to be shown) valid Monday to Friday from 7.30am to 5pm (Senior Citizens and Juniors Saturday from 7am to 12 noon also). Season tickets available £136.10, Senior Citizens and Juniors £46.40. *Eating facilities:* mobile van rear of clubhouse. *Visitors:* welcome anytime, must have a bag of clubs. *Society Meetings:* apply to Mr Bernard J. Forteath, Director of Environmental Services, Paisley. Secretary: W. Collins (0141-884 2533).

PAISLEY. **Paisley Golf Club**, Braehead, Paisley PA2 8TZ (0141-884 3903). *Location:* up Causeyside Street, Neilston Road, turn right into Glenburn, left at roundabout. Moorland course. 18 holes, 6466 yards. S.S.S. 72. Practice area. *Green Fees:* weekdays £24.00 per round, £35.00 per day. Full day golf package available. *Eating facilities:* bar snacks and full meals. *Visitors:* welcome by prior arrangement with Handicap Certificate, midweek not after 4pm and not at weekends or Public Holidays. *Society Meetings:* by arrangement with Secretary. Professional: Gordon Stewart (0141-884 4114). Club Manager: John Hillis (0141-884 3903).

PAISLEY. **Ralston Golf Club**, Strathmore Avenue, Ralston, Paisley PA1 3DT (0141-882 1349; Fax: 0141 883 9837). *Location:* Glasgow Road, two miles east of Paisley Cross. Parkland course. 18 holes, 6091 yards. S.S.S. 69. *Green Fees:* information not provided. *Eating facilities:* dining room, bar. *Visitors:* welcome subject to course availability. *Society Meetings:* catered for on application subject to course availability. Professional: Colin Munro (0141-810 4925). Secretary: Mr J. Pearson (0141-882 1349; Fax: 0141-883 9837).

PORT GLASGOW. **Port Glasgow Golf Club**, Devol Road, Port Glasgow PA14 5XE (01475 704181). *Location:* M8 to Newark Castle to roundabout, follow signs for Industrial Estate. Heathland with panoramic views of the Clyde and Argyll Hills. 18 holes, 5712 yards, 5224 metres. S.S.S. 68. Practice facilities. *Green Fees:* information not available. *Eating facilities:* full catering service. *Visitors:* welcome, only by prior arrangement. *Society Meetings:* welcome by prior arrangement with Hon. Secretary (36 maximum), full catering available. Golf Shop: 01475 705671. Hon. Secretary: Alex Hughes (01475 704181).*

RENFREW. **Renfrew Golf Club**, Blythswood Estate, Inchinnan Road, Renfrew PA4 9EG (0141-886 6692). *Location:* A8 Renfrew, turn in at Normandy Hotel. Flat parkland, wooded. 18 holes, 6818 yards, 6231 metres. S.S.S. 72. *Green Fees:* £30.00 per round, £40.00 per day. *Eating facilities:* daily restaurant facilities and bar. *Visitors:* welcome on introduction by members. Visiting parties by arrangement. *Society Meetings:* catered for on Mondays, Tuesdays and Thursdays only by written application to Secretary. Professional: Mr David Grant (0141-885 1754). Secretary: Graham Tennant (0141-886 6692; Fax: 0141-886 1808).

UPLAWMOOR. **Caldwell Golf Club Ltd**, Uplawmoor, Glasgow G78 4AU (01505 850329; Fax: 01505 850604). *Location:* five miles south of Barrhead, Glasgow on A736 Irvine Road. Parkland bounded by mature trees and a natural water hazard. 18 holes, 5526 metres. S.S.S. 70. Practice area. *Green Fees:* £25.00 per round, £35.00 per day weekdays. *Eating facilities:* every day bar menu - filled rolls on Thursdays. *Visitors:* welcome weekdays only before 4.30pm, not weekends and Public Holidays (local and national). *Society Meetings:* weekdays only by prior arrangement. Professional: Stephen Forbes (Tel & Fax: 01505 850616). Secretary: H.I.F. Harper (01505 850366; Fax: 01505 850604). e-mail: CaldwellGolfClub@aol.com

Stirling & The Trossachs

ABERFOYLE. **Aberfoyle Golf Club**, Braeval, Aberfoyle, By Stirling FK8 3UY (01877 382493). *Location:* A81 Glasgow–Stirling. Parkland. 18 holes, 5204 yards. S.S.S. 66. *Green Fees:* weekdays £15.00 per round, £20.00 per day; weekends £20.00 per round, £28.00 per day. *Eating facilities:* bar and catering available all day from April to October; restricted service October to March. *Visitors:* welcome anytime but restrictions at weekends. Club Steward: Duncan Brown.

ALLOA. **Alloa Golf Club**, Schawpark Golf Course, Sauchie, Alloa FK10 3AX (01259 722745 Fax: 01259 218796). *Location:* on A908 between Alloa and Tillicoultry. Parkland, tree lined fairways with spectacular views of Ochil Hills and beyond. 18 holes, 6229 yards, 5695 metres. S.S.S. 70. *Green Fees:* weekdays £26.00 per round, £36.00 per day; weekends £30.00 per round, £40.00 per day. *Eating facilities:* recently refurbished restaurant and lounge bar. *Visitors:* welcome. Phone to confirm booking. Guaranteed tee times can be booked. Ladies and gents changing rooms. *Society Meetings:* welcome weekdays only. Package: morning coffee, lunch, high tea, and two rounds of golf £40.00. Professional/ Bookings: Bill Bennett (Tel & Fax: 01259 724476). Secretary: F. Nichols (Tel, & Fax: 01259 218796).

ALLOA. **Braehead Golf Club**, Cambus, By Alloa FK10 2NT (01259 725766). *Location:* one mile west of Alloa on A907. Gently undulating parkland course with scenic views and a variety of challenging holes. 18 holes, 6086 yards. S.S.S. 69. Practice area. *Green Fees:* weekdays £20.00 per round, £30.00 per day; weekends £30.00 per round, £40.00 per day. Green Fees including visitors' insurance. Discounts available for mid-week visiting parties. *Eating facilities:* bar/full catering available all day during Summer months; slightly restricted during Autumn/ Spring. *Visitors:* no restrictions but advisable to telephone in advance. Buggy and cart hire. *Society Meetings:* catered for with prior booking. Professional: Jamie Stevenson. Starter's Shop (01259 722078). Secretary: Mrs Anne Nash.

ALVA. **Alva Golf Club**, Beauclerc Street, Alva FK12 5LH (01259 760431). *Location:* seven miles from Stirling on A91 Stirling to St Andrews Road - course lies at foot of Ochil Hills. Inland wooded hillside course with fast greens. 9 holes, 2423 yards, 2213 metres. S.S.S. 64. *Green Fees:* on application. *Eating facilities:* snacks during bar hours. *Visitors:* welcome at all times. Secretary: Mr R. McMillan (01259 210545).

BALFRON. **Balfron Golf Society**, Kepculloch Road, Balfron, By Glasgow G63 0PZ. *Location:* situated at the north end of the village on the A875, 18 miles from Glasgow and 18 miles from Stirling. Interesting, undulating upland course with splendid views. 18 holes, 5903 yards, S.S.S. 68. *Green Fees:* information not available. *Visitors:* welcome weekdays until 4pm, and at weekends, restrictions during competition days. *Society Meetings:* welcome subject to prior booking. Secretary: Ian Rubython (01360 440915).* website: www.balfrongolfsociety.org.uk

DOLLAR. **Dollar Golf Club,** Brewlands House, Dollar FK14 7EA (01259 742400). *Location:* off A91 in Dollar, signposted. Hillside course without bunkers as designed by Ben Sayers in 1908. 18 holes, 5242 yards, 4796 metres. S.S.S. 66. *Green Fees:* weekdays £13.50 per round, £17.50 per day; weekends £22.00. *Eating facilities:* full catering (except Tuesdays) and bar. *Visitors:* welcome, booking in advance advisable weekends. Snooker table available. Clubs for hire. *Society Meetings:* welcome (maximum 30). Secretary: T. Young.

DOLLAR. **Muckhart Golf Club**, Muckhart, By Dollar FK14 7JH (01259 781423; Fax: 01259 781544). *Location:* off A91 east from Stirling, three miles north of Dollar. Undulating heathland. 18 holes, 6034 yards, 5523 metres. S.S.S. 70; 9 hole course, 3234 yards (medal tees), 3060 yards (casual tees), Par 35. Practice ground. *Green Fees:* information not available. *Eating facilities:* 11 am until 8.45, bar available. *Visitors:* welcome weekdays after 9.30am; weekends not before 10am or between 12 noon and 2.30pm. Trolley hire. *Society Meetings:* catered for. Professional: Keith Salmoni (Tel & Fax: 01259 781493). Secretary: A.B. Robertson. *

DRYMEN. **Strathendrick Golf Club**, Glasgow Road, Drymen, Glasgow G63 0AA (01360 660695). *Location:* one mile south of Drymen on A811. Undulating course, designed by Willie Fernie in 1901. 9 holes, 5116 yards. S.S.S. 64. *Green Fees:* weekdays £14.00 per 18 holes, £16.00 per day. *Visitors:* welcome 8.30am to 2.30pm weekdays only May to September. *Society Meetings:* by arrangement with Secretary. Visitors' Convener: D. McIntyre (01389 753559).

FALKIRK. **Bonnybridge Golf Club**, Larbert Road, Bonnybridge FK4 1NY (01324 812822). *Location:* five miles west of Falkirk. Parkland. 9 holes, 6060 yards. S.S.S. 69. Practice area. *Green Fees:* weekdays £16.00 per round. With a member £6.00. *Eating facilities:* bar open lunchtimes and evenings; all day Saturday and Sunday. *Visitors:* welcome with prior permission, or accompanied by a member. *Society Meetings:* by arrangement with Hon Secretary. Secretary: J. Mullen (01324 812323).

FALKIRK. **Falkirk Golf Club**, 136 Stirling Road, Camelon, Falkirk FK2 7YP (01324 611061; Fax: 01324 639573). *Location:* one and a half miles west of town centre on A9. Parkland with streams. 18 holes, 6282 yards. S.S.S. 70. Large practice area. *Green Fees:* weekdays £20.00 per round, £30.00 per day; Sundays £30.00 per round, £40.00 per day. *Eating facilities:* full catering and bar facilities. *Visitors:* welcome Monday to Friday up to 4.00pm unaccompanied, with member only at weekends. *Society Meetings:* weekdays except Wednesdays, Sundays after 10.30am. Make arrangements with Starter (01324 612219). Professional: Stewart Craig. Secretary: John Elliott (01324 634118). e-mail: carmuirs.fgc@virgin.net

FALKIRK. **Polmont Golf Club**, Manuelrigg, Maddiston, Falkirk FK2 0LS (01324 711277; Fax: 01324 712504). *Location:* first turn to the right past Fire Brigade HQ in Maddiston. Undulating course. 9 holes, 6603 yards. S.S.S. 70. *Green Fees:* information not available. *Eating facilities:* lunches and high teas. *Visitors:* welcome without reservation, no visitors after 5pm weekdays or all day Saturday. *Society Meetings:* catered for. Secretary: Peter Lees (01324 713811). *

LARBERT. **Falkirk Tryst Golf Club**, 86 Burnhead Road, Stenhousemuir, Larbert FK5 4BD (01324 562415). *Location:* three miles from Falkirk (A9/A88), one mile from Larbert Station. Flat/seaside links style surface. 18 holes, 6053 yards, 5533 metres. S.S.S. 69. Practice area. *Green Fees:* weekdays £22.00 per round, £30.00 per day. Golf/Catering Packages available £23.00 to £40.00. *Eating facilities:* full catering - lunches, high teas, bar service. *Visitors:* welcome weekdays only except Bank and local Holidays. *Society Meetings:* catered for weekdays only except Bank and local Holidays. Professional: Mr Steven Dunsmore (01324 562091). Secretary: Mr R.C. Chalmers (01324 562054).

LARBERT. **Glenbervie Golf Club Ltd**, Stirling Road, Larbert FK5 4SJ (01324 562983). *Location:* one mile north of Larbert on A9 Falkirk to Stirling road. Parkland course. 18 holes, 6402 yards. S.S.S. 71. Two practice areas. *Green Fees:* £30.00 per round, £40.00 for two rounds. *Eating facilities:* lunches and high teas, bar snacks. *Visitors:* welcome weekdays until 4pm. Weekends as members' guests only. *Society Meetings:* up to 40 competitors catered for, Tuesdays and Thursdays only. Professional: Mr David Ross (01324 562725). Secretary: Donald McKellar (01324 562605; Fax: 01324 551054).

LENNOXTOWN. **Campsie Golf Club**, Crow Road, Lennoxtown, Glasgow G65 7HX (01360 310244). *Location:* on B822 Lennoxtown to Fintry. Hillside course with panoramic views. 18 holes, 5509 yards. S.S.S. 68. Practice fairway, bunker and putting green. *Green Fees:* £20.00 weekdays, £25.00 weekends. *Eating facilities:* full catering available. *Visitors:* welcome, weekdays unrestricted, weekends by prior arrangement. *Society Meetings:* catered for except weekends. Professional: Mark Brennan (01360 310920). Club Manager: H.B. Weston.

POLMONT. **Grangemouth Golf Club**, Polmonthill, Polmont, Falkirk FK2 0YA (01324 711500). *Location:* quarter of a mile north of Junction 4 M9 motorway. Parkland course. 18 holes, 6314 yards. S.S.S. 70. Practice area. *Green Fees:* information not available. *Eating facilities:* catering and bar facilities available, open all day during season. *Visitors:* welcome, no restrictions. *Society Meetings:* welcome any day except Saturday. Professional: Greg McFarlane (01324 503840). Secretary: Iain Hutton (01324 712585; Fax: 01324 717087. * e-mail: iain@hutton-falkirk.demon.co.uk

STIRLING. **Bridge Of Allan Golf Club**, Sunnylaw, Bridge of Allan FK9 4LY (Tel & Fax: 01786 832332). *Location:* from Stirling, three miles, turn right at Bridge, keep taking the high road. Hilly course. 9 holes, 4932 yards, 4508 metres. S.S.S. 66. *Green Fees:* information not available. *Eating facilities:* by arrangement, licensed bar. *Visitors:* welcome without reservation, Saturdays after 4pm. *Society Meetings:* catered for by arrangement, phone in advance.*

STIRLING. **Brucefields Family Golf Centre**, Pirnhall Road, Bannockburn, Stirling FK7 8EH (01786 818184; Fax: 01786 817770). *Location:* half-a-mile from M9 and M80 interchange on A91. Parkland. 9 holes, 2375 yards. S.S.S. 64. 9 hole par 3 course, driving range. *Green Fees:* weekdays £9.00 for 9 holes, £16.00 for 18 holes; weekends £10.00 for 9 holes, £18.00 for 18 holes; half-price for under-16's. *Eating facilities:* Fairways Cafe Bar and Restaurant. *Visitors:* welcome. *Society Meetings:* welcome. Corporate Membership and packages available. Club Manager: Paul Hamilton. Secretary: Christine Frost.

STIRLING. **Stirling Golf Club**, Queen's Road, Stirling FK8 3AA (01786 464098; Fax: 01786 460090). *Location:* one mile from town centre, rail and bus stations; two miles from Junction 10 M9. Rolling parkland course. 18 holes, 6400 yards. S.S.S. 71. Practice area. *Green Fees:* £28.00 per round; £40.00 per day. *Eating facilities:* full bar and catering. *Visitors:* visiting parties welcome midweek. Casual visitors may reserve tee times only at weekends. *Society Meetings:* welcome. Professional: Ian Collins (01786 471490). Secretary: Alan Rankin (01786 464098; Fax: 01786 460090).

STIRLING. **Tillicoultry Golf Club**, Alva Road, Tillicoultry FK12 6BL (01259 750124). *Location:* on A91, nine miles east of Stirling. Parkland at foot of Ochil Hills. 9 holes, 5358 yards, 4904 metres. S.S.S. 67. *Green Fees:* weekdays £12.00 per round, £13.00 after 4pm; weekends £17.00 per round. *Eating facilities:* clubhouse bar, bar lunches. *Visitors:* welcome at all times outwith competitions. No children under 15 weekends until 4pm. *Society Meetings:* welcome by booking through Club Manager. Club Manager: (01259 750124).

Scottish Islands

COLONSAY

ISLE OF COLONSAY. **Colonsay Golf Club**, Machrins, Isle of Colonsay PA61 7YP. *Location:* two miles from ferry terminal. Traditional links course, reputedly 200 years old, natural, challenging and fun course. The 10th green has one of the best views in golf. 18 holes, 4775 yards. S.S.S. 72. *Green Fees:* information not available. *Eating facilities:* none on course, bar/cafe/shop two miles away. *Visitors:* always welcome. *Society Meetings:* always welcome. Secretary: Hugh McNeill (01951 200364; Fax: 01951 200312). *
e-mail: hughie@calcraig.fsnet.co.uk

CUMBRAE

MILLPORT. **Millport Golf Club**, Golf Road, Millport KA28 0HB (Tel & Fax: 01475 530306). *Location:* Caledonian McBrayne car ferry Largs slip to Cumbrae slip (seven minutes). Millport town four miles. On hill overlooking Firth of Clyde over Bute and Arran to Mull of Kintyre. Heathland with panoramic views. 18 holes, 5828 yards. S.S.S. 69. Large practice area. *Green Fees:* weekdays from £20.00 ; weekends and Bank Holidays from £25.00. *Eating facilities:* full à la carte and bar menu. *Visitors:* welcome without reservation. Tee reservations available for parties. Well stocked Professional's shop. Starter's telephone (01475 530305). *Society Meetings:* catered for. Special open amateur competition, Cumbrae Cup. Professional: (01475 530305). Secretary: Mrs Janette Frazer (Tel & Fax: 01475 530306).
e-mail: secretary@millportgolfclub.co.uk
website: www.millportgolfclub.co.uk

GIGHA

ISLE OF GIGHA. **Isle of Gigha Golf Club**, The Croft, Isle of Gigha PA41 7AA (01583 505287). *Location:* by ferry from Tayinloan to Gigha, course half a mile north from Post Office. Seaside course with scenic views looking over the Sound of Gigha and the Kintyre coast. 9 holes, 5042 yards (18 holes). S.S.S. 65. *Green Fees:* £12.50 per round. Phone for special rates. *Eating facilities:* available at Gigha Hotel. *Visitors:* always welcome. *Society Meetings:* welcome. Secretary: John Bannatyne (01583 505242).

HARRIS

SCARISTA. **Harris Golf Club**, Scarista, Isle of Harris. *Location:* 10 miles south of Tarbert, 50 miles south of Stornoway. Seaside links course on machair land, in an area of outstanding natural beauty. 9 holes, 2432 yards. S.S.S. 64 (18 holes). Practice area. *Green Fees:* £10.00 per day. *Visitors:* welcome, no restrictions. Secretary: John MacLean (01859 550226).

ISLAY

PORT ELLEN. **Islay Golf Club**, 25 Charlotte Street, Port Ellen PA42 7DQ (01496 300094; Fax: 01496 302117). *Location:* five miles north of Port Ellen. Championship course. 18 holes, 6235 yards, 5695 metres. S.S.S. 70. Practice area. *Green Fees:* arranged by Machrie Hotel. *Eating facilities:* full range at adjoining Machrie Hotel. *Visitors:* welcome anytime. Trolleys, caddies by arrangement. *Society Meetings:* all welcome.

PORT ELLEN. **Machrie Golf Club**, The Machrie Hotel and Golf Links, Port Ellen PA42 7AN (01496 302310; Fax: 01496 302404). *Location:* adjacent Airport. Classic links. 18 holes, 6226 yards. S.S.S. 70. *Green Fees:* information not available. *Eating facilities:* full service in hotel. *Visitors:* welcome any day without reservation. *Society Meetings:* any number catered for. Golf packages available. Manager: Ian Brown.
e-mail: machrie@machrie.com
website: www.machrie.com

LEWIS

STORNOWAY. **Stornoway Golf Club**, Lady Lever Park, Stornoway, Isle of Lewis HS2 0XP (01851 70 2240). *Location:* close proximity to town of Stornoway, in grounds of Lews Castle. Hilly parkland course with good views. 18 holes, 5252 yards. S.S.S. 67. *Green Fees:* £15.00 per round, £20.00 per day. Weekly tickets available - no Sunday golf. *Eating facilities:* light bar snacks available. *Visitors:* welcome. Car ferry daily (except Sunday) from Ullapool. Air services daily from Glasgow, Inverness and Edinburgh. *Society Meetings:* welcome, book through Secretary. Secretary: K.W. Galloway (01851 702240).
e-mail: admin@stornowaygolfclub.co.uk
website: www.stornowaygolfclub.co.uk

MULL

CRAIGNURE. **Craignure Golf Club**, Scallastle, Craignure PA65 6AY (01680 300402). *Location:* one mile from Oban/Mull main ferry terminal. Links course - first layout 1895, superb natural setting. 9 holes, 18 tees, 5351 yards. S.S.S. 66. Small practice area. *Green Fees:* £15.00 per day. Weekly ticket £45.00. Under 15's half price. *Eating facilities:* three-quarters-of-a-mile from MacGregor's Road House and Craignure Inn. *Visitors:* always welcome, except for Club inter-match days - please phone for details. Clubs, trolleys for hire, balls for sale. *Society Meetings:* welcome, discounts available. Secretary: David Howitt (01680 300402 mobile: 07799744908).

TOBERMORY. **Tobermory Golf Club**, Tobermory PA75 6PG. *Location:* situated on the cliffs above the town to the north west. Panoramic views of Sound of Mull; beautifully maintained and challenging course. 9 holes, 4921 yards, 4362 metres. S.S.S. 64. Practice ground. *Green Fees:* information not available. *Eating facilities:* Club licence. Catering April–Oct. Green Fee ticket includes temporary membership. *Visitors:* unrestricted except for some competition days. Membership available, contact Secretary. Club and trolley hire available. *Society Meetings:* welcome. Secretary: Mr John Weir (01688 302338; Fax: 01688 302140).
e-mail: secretary@tobermorygolfclub.com
website: www.tobermorygolfclub.com

ORKNEY

KIRKWALL. **Orkney Golf Club,** Grainbank, Kirkwall KW15 1RD (01856 872457). *Location:* half-a-mile west of Kirkwall. Parkland with good views over Kirkwall Bay and North Isles. 18 holes, 5411 yards, 4964 metres. S.S.S. 67. Practice area. *Green Fees:* information not available. *Eating facilities:* bar lunches during summer months. *Visitors:* welcome at all times, restrictions only during competitions. *Society Meetings:* welcome, booking advised. Secretary: Jim Robertson (07788 530689).*
website: www.orkneygolfclub.co.uk

STROMNESS. **Stromness Golf Club Ltd**, Ness, Stromness KW16 3DU (01856 850772). *Location:* situated at south end of town. Seaside course bordering Hoy Sound. 18 holes, 4762 yards. S.S.S 63. *Green Fees:* £15.00 per day. *Eating facilities:* clubhouse with full facilities. *Visitors:* welcome, no restrictions. Bowling and tennis. *Society Meetings:* welcome by arrangement through Secretary. Secretary: G.A. Bevan (01856 850885).
website: www.stromnessgc.co.uk

WESTRAY. **Westray Golf Club,** Westray, Orkney Islands KW17 2DH (01857 677373). *Location:* half a mile from Pierowall Village. Seaside links course. 9 holes, 2316 yards, 2084 metres. S.S.S. 33. *Green Fees:* information not available. *Visitors:* welcome anytime. Secretary: Mr John Cable (01857 677287).*

SHETLAND

LERWICK. **Shetland Golf Club**, Dale Gott, Shetland ZE2 9SB (01595 840369). *Location:* four miles north of Lerwick on the A970. Parkland. 18 holes, 5776 yards, 5279 metres. S.S.S 68. Driving range two miles away. Two practice nets, pitching area. *Green Fees:* information not available. *Eating facilities:* bar with sandwiches, snacks available. *Visitors:* welcome, no restrictions except on club competition days. Club hire. *Society Meetings:* contact Clubhouse Manager- C. White. Secretary: Mr E. Groat.*

WHALSAY. **Whalsay Golf Club**, Skaw Taing, Whalsay ZE2 9AL (01806 566259). *Location:* five miles from Symbister ferry terminal - ferries run from Laxo to Symbister. Seaside course with wonderful scenery and birdlife in abundance - Britain's most northerly 18 holes. 18 holes, 6009 yards. S.S.S. 68. Changing rooms. *Green Fees:* information not available. *Eating facilities:* lunch/dinner available by arrangement. *Visitors:* welcome. Saturday/Sunday competitions, check before travelling. Secretary: Charles Hutchison (01806 566450) and Harry Sandison (01806 566481).*

SKYE

SCONSER. **Isle of Skye Golf Club**, Sconser IV48 8TD (01478 650414). *Location:* on A87 halfway between Broadford and Portree, 20 miles from Skye Bridge. Seaside course with spectacular views to Isle of Raasay and North Skye. 9 holes (18 tees), 4677 yards, 4277 metres. S.S.S. 64. *Green Fees:* £16.00 per day. *Eating facilities:* tearoom serving light snacks. *Visitors:* welcome at all times. Changing and toilet facilities, trolleys and clubs for hire, small shop. *Society Meetings:* welcome. Secretary: I. Macmillan (01478 650414).
e-mail: Isleofskye.golfclub@btinternet.com
website: www.uk-golf.com/clubs/isleofskye

SKEABOST BRIDGE. **Skeabost Golf Club**, Skeabost House Hotel, Skeabost Bridge IV51 9NP (01470 532202; Fax: 01470 532454). *Location:* A850 Portree to Dunvegan Road. Wooded course. 9 holes, 3114 yards. S.S.S. 59 (for 18 holes). *Green Fees:* £13.00 daily. *Eating facilities:* buffet lunch, evening meals in hotel; bar food in public bar. *Visitors:* welcome, under 13s must be accompanied by an adult. *Society Meetings:* accepted. Club Captain: D. Sutherland. Secretary: D.J. Matheson (01470 532319).

SOUTH UIST

LOCHBOISDALE. **Askernish Golf Club**, Askernish, Lochboisdale. *Location:* off South Uist main road B888. Seaside, undulating, designed by Tom Morris Senior 1891. 9 holes, 18 tees, 5042 yards. S.S.S. 68. *Green Fees:* information not available. *Visitors:* welcome. Secretary: Neil Elliot (01878 700298).
e-mail: askernish.golf.club@cwcom.net

TIREE

SCARINISH. **Vaul Golf Club**, Scarinish, Isle of Tiree PA77 6XH. *Location:* two miles from Scarinish and half a mile from Lodge Hotel, ferry from Oban four hours and plane from Glasgow 45 minutes. Links course with crystal white beaches to north and south with beautiful views on all sides. 9 holes, 5674 yards (18 holes). S.S.S. 68 (18 holes). *Green Fees:* information not available. *Visitors:* welcome, no restrictions. Enquiries and fees to R. Omand, Royal Bank of Scotland, Scarinish. Secretary: Mrs S. Sweeney (01879 220729). *

Golf in Wales

WHERE TO PLAY • WHERE TO STAY

N O T E

All the information regarding Golf Clubs in this guide is given in good faith in the belief that it is correct. However, the publishers cannot guarantee the facts given in these pages, neither are they responsible for changes in ownership or facilities, such as green fees, that may take place after the date of going to press. Readers should always satisfy themselves that the facilities they require are available and that the terms, if quoted, still apply.

WELSH HISTORIC INNS

Enjoy Golf in North Wales...

and stay in these individual and historic Inns,
which reflect their locality and unique Welsh history.
They all offer quality, value for money and a friendly atmosphere.

Play at Llangefni Golf Course and stay at
The Bull Hotel, Llangefni

The Bull Hotel is situated in the centre of Llangefni, in a region of
outstanding natural beauty, and an ideal base to explore the beautiful
and varied North Wales area, with rugged mountains, peaceful lakes
and forests. The views over the Menai Straits and the panorama of
Snowdonia Mountains are attractions not to be missed.

The Bull Hotel, Bulkley Square, Llangefni, Anglesey LL77 7LR
Tel: 01248 722119 • Fax: 01248 750488
E-mail: bullhotel@welsh-historic-inns.com

Enjoy a round at Bala Golf Club
The White Lion Royal Hotel, Bala

The White Lion Royal Hotel is situated in Bala, an attractive and
lively historic market town within the boundaries of Snowdonia
National Park (designated an Area of Outstanding Natural Beauty).
Ideally situated, within an hour's spectacular drive of most of the
coastal resorts of Mid and North Wales, not to mention the
innumerable beauty spots and magnificent views within the interior
of this beautiful region.

The White Lion Hotel, High Street, Bala, Gwynedd LL23 7AE
Tel: 01678 520314 • Fax: 01678 521798
E-mail: whitelion@welsh-historic-inns.com

Take a Golf Break at
Royal Town of Caernarfon Golf Club
The Black Boy Inn, Caernarfon

Dating back to 1522, The Black Boy Inn is situated within the
historic town walls of the Royal Borough of Caernarfon, a
market town with an open air market every Saturday and a
World Heritage Site with both Roman and Edwardian history.
With its wooden panelling, low ceilings, and thick wooden
support beams it generates a cosy 'Olde Worlde' atmosphere.
Caernarfon is the most welsh speaking town in all of Wales and
you will receive a warm welcome in both languages.

The Black Boy Inn, Northgate Street, Caernarfon, Gwynedd LL55 1RW
Tel: 01286 673604 • Fax: 01286 674955
E-mail: blackboy@welsh-historic-inns.com

Three-Centre breaks available, start a Golf Break at Bala, progress to Caernarfon and finish at Llangefni.

Welsh Historic Inns, Caeathro, Caernarfon, Gwynedd LL55 2SS
Tel: 01286 676115 • Fax: 01286 674831
E-Mail: office@welsh-historic-inns.com
Website: www.welsh-historic-inns.com

WELSH HISTORIC
INNS

Anglesey & Gwynedd

ABERDOVEY. **Aberdovey Golf Club**, Aberdovey LL35 0RT (01654 767493; Fax: 01654 767027). *Location*: west end of Aberdovey on A493, adjacent to railway station. Seaside links, easy walking. 18 holes, 6445 yards, 5893 metres. S.S.S. 71. Practice ground, limited. *Green Fees*: weekdays from £24.00 per round; weekends from £29.00 per round, subject to review. Concessions for parties over 12 and for guests at local hotels. *Eating facilities*: restaurant, bar and lounge. *Visitors*: welcome on production of Handicap Certificate, restrictions some weekends. *Society Meetings*: catered for by prior arrangement (not August or Bank Holidays). Professional: John Davies (01654 767602). Secretary: J.M. Griffiths (01654 767493; Fax: 01654 767027).

ABERSOCH. **Clwb Golff Abersoch,** Golf Road, Abersoch LL53 7EY (01758 712622; Fax: 01758 712777). *Location:* A55 to Bangor, coast road to Abersoch. Parkland and seaside links course. 18 holes, 5671 yards. S.S.S. 68, Par 69. Practice area, putting green. *Green Fees:* weekdays from £22.50, weekends from £27.00. *Eating facilities:* full catering and bar service. *Visitors:* welcome, Ladies' day Thursdays, Gents' competition day Sundays. Handicap Certificate required. Shop. Buggies, carts. *Society Meetings:* welcome by prior arrangement. Professional/Manager: Alan Drosinos Jones (01758 712622; Fax: 01758 712777).
e-mail: pro@abersochgolf.co.uk
website: www.abersochgolf.co.uk

ANGLESEY. **Baron Hill Golf Club Ltd**, Beaumaris, Anglesey LL58 8YW (01248 810231). *Location:* turn left on approach to Beaumaris from Menai Bridge on A545. Moorland course with panoramic view of Snowdonia and Menai Straits. 9 holes, 5570 metres. S.S.S. 69. *Green Fees:* £15.00, £10.00 with a member. *Eating facilities:* comprehensive menu (closed Mondays). *Visitors:* welcome, competitions most Sundays, Ladies' Day on Tuesday mornings. *Society Meetings:* welcome by prior arrangement - special rates and packages available. Secretary: Alwyn Pleming.

ANGLESEY. **Bull Bay Golf Club Ltd**, Bull Bay, Amlwch, Isle of Anglesey LL68 9RY (01407 830213). *Location:* one mile west of Amlwch on A5025 coastal road towards Cemaes Bay and Holyhead. Coastal heathland championship course; Wales' northernmost golf course. 18 holes, 6217 yards. S.S.S. 70. Practice ground and putting green. *Green Fees:* £22.00 per day weekdays; £27.00 per day weekends and Bank Holidays. Discount for parties of 12 and over. *Eating facilities:* bar snacks, dining room; limited facilities on Mondays. *Visitors:* welcome, competitions permitting; advance bookings advised. All visitors should have current Handicap Certificates or satisfy Professional of competence to play. Snooker and pool. *Society Meetings:* welcome, booking essential. Professional: John Burns (01407 831188). Secretary/Manager: (01407 830960; Fax: 01407 832612).

ANGLESEY. **Penrhyn Golf Complex,** Llanddaniel - Fâb LL60 6NN (01248 421150). *Location:* A5 turn off at Star Crossroads taking Llanddaniel road. Follow Brown Tourism signs from the village. Parkland with some small hills. 9 holes, Par 3. 14 bay covered and floodlit driving range and putting area. *Green Fees:* £3.50. Pay as you play course. Special rates weekdays 10am - 5pm for 18 holes. *Visitors:* no restrictions. Professional: Paul Lovell (Visiting). Owner: Mr W.R. Carter.

BALA. **Bala Golf Club,** Penlan, Bala LL23 7YD (01678 520359; Fax: 01678 521361). *Location:* turn right before coming to Bala Lake on the main Bala-Dolgellau road. Upland course with superb views in the Snowdonia National Park. 10 holes, 4970 yards, 4512 metres. S.S.S. 64. *Green Fees:* information not available. *Eating facilities:* bar with snacks available. *Visitors:* welcome all year, some restrictions Bank Holidays and weekends. Snooker table and small golf shop. *Society Meetings:* very welcome by prior arrangement. Professional: Tony Davies (visiting). Secretary: G. Rhys Jones.*

BANGOR. **St Deiniol Golf Club,** Penybryn, Bangor LL57 1PX (01248 353098; Fax: 01248 370792). *Location:* at A5/A55 Junction 11 intersection, follow A5122 for one mile to eastern outskirts of Bangor. Parkland course with magnificent views. 18 holes, 5654 yards, 5068 metres. S.S.S. 67. *Green Fees:* weekdays £16.00, weekends £20.00. *Eating facilities:* two bars; full catering Mondays excepted. *Visitors:* welcome without reservation, restrictions at weekends. *Society Meetings:* welcome by prior arrangement. Secretary: Bob Thomas M.B.E. e-mail: secretary@stdeiniol.fsbusiness.co.uk

BEAUMARIS. **The Princes' Course,** Henllys Hall, Beaumaris, Anglesey LL58 8HU (01248 811717; Fax: 01248 811511). *Location:* quarter of a mile through Beaumaris town centre. Parkland course. 18 holes,

6062 yards, S.S.S. 70. Practice ground. *Green Fees:* information not available. *Visitors:* welcome, please telephone beforehand. Tuition from PGA Professionals available. Professionals: Peter Maton/David Gadsby (01248 811717; Fax: 01248 811511). Director of Golf: Peter Maton. *
e-mail: henllys@HPBsite.com

BRYNTEG. **Storws Wen Golf Club**, Brynteg LL78 8JY (01248 852673). *Location:* one-and-three-quarter miles along the B5108 from Benllech to Brynteg. Parkland course with a stream, three lakes and spectacular views. 9 holes, 5002 yards. S.S.S. 64. *Green Fees:* £12.00 per 18 holes, weekends £18.00 per 18 holes. *Eating facilities:* clubhouse with full facilities. *Visitors:* always welcome. *Society Meetings:* welcome, terms on request. Hon. Secretary: R. Perry.

CAERNARFON. **Royal Town of Caernarfon Golf Club,** Aberforeshore, Llanfaglan, Caernarfon LL54 5RP (01286 678359; Fax: 01286 672535). *Location:* less than a mile from the historic Royal town of Caernarfon. Parkland course in superb sea and mountain setting. 18 holes, 5891 yards. S.S.S. 68. *Green Fees:* summer – Monday £15.00 per round, Tuesday to Friday £22.00; Saturday £28.00, Sunday £25.00. *Eating facilities:* excellent catering and bar facilities, except Mondays. *Visitors:* welcome with no restrictions except Saturdays, please contact Professional or Secretary to reserve tee time. Tuition, shop. *Society Meetings:* welcome, subject to pre-arranged bookings. Professional: Mr Aled Owen (01286 678359). Secretary: Mr Gren Jones (01286 673783).

CRICCIETH. **Criccieth Golf Club**, Ednyfed Hill, Criccieth LL52 0PH (01766 522154). *Location:* in High Street (A497) turn right past Memorial Hall, keep going up lane to Club. 18 holes, 5755 yards. S.S.S. 68. *Green Fees:* information not available. *Eating facilities:* light meals available April to September. *Visitors:* welcome without reservation. *Society Meetings:* catered for with prior reservation. Secretary: M.G. Hamilton (01766 522697).*

DOLGELLAU. **Dolgellau Golf Club,** Pencefn Road, Dolgellau LL40 2ES (01341 422603). *Location:* half-a-mile from town centre. Parkland with panoramic views. 9 holes and alternate tees, 4671 yards. S.S.S. 63. Driving range and putting green. *Green Fees:* information not available. *Eating facilities:* catering facilities available. *Visitors:* welcome without reservation. Self-catering accommodation available for groups of 12-20 persons. *Society Meetings:* catered for. Special packages available. Secretary: Jennifer May (01341 422603).
e-mail: dolgellaugolf@netscapeonline.co.uk
website: www.dolgellaugolf.co.uk

FFESTINIOG. **Clwb Golff Ffestiniog**, Y Cefn, Ffestiniog (01766 762637). *Location:* located on B4391, one mile from Ffestiniog village. Upland course. 9 holes, 4570 yards. S.S.S. 66. *Green Fees:* weekdays £10.00, weekends £10.00. *Eating facilities:* available by prior arrangement. *Visitors:* welcome at any time, some restrictions mainly at weekends during club competitions. *Society Meetings:* by prior arrangement. Secretary: Andrew Roberts (Tel & Fax: 01766 831829).

HARLECH. **Royal St. David's Golf Club**, Harlech LL46 2UB (01766 780203). *Location:* A496 lower Harlech road. Championship links course. 18 holes, 6571 yards. S.S.S. 73. Large practice ground. *Green Fees:* weekdays £40.00 per round; weekends £50.00 per round (subject to review); reduced rates in winter months. *Eating facilities:* full catering and bar facilities available. *Visitors:* must be members of bona fide golf clubs with Handicap - booking essential. *Society Meetings:* catered for by prior arrangement. Professional: John Barnett (01766 780857). Secretary: D.L. Morkill (01766 780361; Fax: 01766 781110).
e-mail: secretary@royalstdavids.co.uk
website: www.royalstdavids.co.uk

LLANFAIRFECHAN. **Llanfairfechan Golf Club**, Llannerch Road, Llanfairfechan LL33 0EB (01248 680144). *Location:* signposted off old A55, 300 yards west of traffic lights. Hillside parkland. 9 holes, 3119 yards. S.S.S. 57. *Green Fees:* £10.00 per day. *Eating facilities:* no eating facilities, bar open weekends and weekday evenings. *Visitors:* welcome anytime except Sundays. *Society Meetings:* by arrangement, weekdays only in Summer. Secretary: M.J. Charlesworth (01248 680524).

LLANGEFNI. **Llangefni Public Golf Course**, Clai Road (B5111), Llangefni, Isle of Anglesey LL77 8YQ. Parkland course, eight Par 3s, one Par 4. 9 holes, 1467 yards, 1342 metres. Practice net. *Green Fees:* information not available. *Eating facilities:* light refreshments only. *Visitors:* welcome at all times, no restrictions. Fully stocked Discount Golf Shop. Professional: Paul Lovell (01248 722193).

MORFA BYCHAN. **Porthmadog Golf Club,** Morfa Bychan, Porthmadog LL49 9UU (01766 512037; Fax: 01766 514638). *Location:* turn in Porthmadog High Street at Woolworths towards Black Rock Sands, club on left hand side of road one mile west. Part parkland, part seaside links. 18 holes, 6363 yards. S.S.S. 71. Two practice grounds. *Green Fees:* per round £25.00 weekdays, £30.00 weekends and Bank Holidays; £32.00 and £37.00 for day tickets. Discounts available for larger parties. *Eating facilities:* new clubhouse with lounge bar, golfers' bar and large restaurant. *Visitors:* welcome, no restrictions except for competition days. Snooker room. *Society Meetings:* catered for by prior arrangement. Bookings via Secretary. Professional: Peter L. Bright (01766 513828). Office Manager: Åse Richardson (01766 514124).
e-mail: secretary@porthmadog-golf-club.co.uk
website: www.porthmadog-golf-club.co.uk

NEFYN. **Nefyn and District Golf Club,** Golf Road, Morfa Nefyn, Pwllheli LL53 6DA (Fax: 01758 720476). *Location:* north coast of Lleyn Peninsula, two miles west of Nefyn. Seaside course. 27 holes. Main Course - 18 holes, 6548 yards. S.S.S. 71. Practice area. *Green Fees:* weekdays £27.00 per round, £33.00 per day; weekends and Bank Holidays £32 .00 per round, £38.00 per day. 10% discount for parties of 12 or more players. *Eating facilities:* full restaurant facilities and two bars. *Visitors:* welcome without reservation, except club competition days. Snooker. *Society Meetings:* catered for by arrangement with Secretary. Professional: John Froom (01758 720102). Secretary: J. B. Owens (01758 720966).

PENMAENMAWR. **Penmaenmawr Golf Club,** Conwy Old Road, Penmaenmawr LL34 6RD (01492 623330). *Location:* A55 expressway three miles west of Conwy. Parkland with panoramic views. 9 holes (18 tees), 5306 yards. S.S.S. 67. Two practice areas. *Green Fees:* £12.00 weekdays, £18.00 weekends. *Eating facilities:* bar and bar snacks, meals available daily except Tuesdays. *Visitors:* welcome anytime except Saturdays. *Society Meetings:* welcome by arrangement (not Saturdays). Secretary: Mrs J. Dryhurst Jones (01492 623330).

PWLLHELI. **Pwllheli Golf Club,** Golf Road, Pwllheli LL53 5PS (01758 701644). *Location:* A499 from Caernarvon (20 miles). Parkland/seaside links. 18 holes, 6108 yards. S.S.S. 70. Two practice areas and putting green. *Green Fees:* weekdays £25.00 per day, weekends £30.00 per day. Discounts for parties of 10 or more. *Eating facilities:* two large lounge bars and diningroom. Steward: (01758 701633). *Visitors:* welcome without reservation. Pro shop. *Society Meetings:* welcome. Professional: S. Pilkington (01758 612520). General Manager: Mrs Michele Nash (01758 701644).
e-mail: admin@pwllheligolfclub.co.uk
website: www.pwllheligolfclub.co.uk

visit the FHG golf website on
www.uk-golfguide.com

RHOSNEIGR. **The Anglesey Golf Club Ltd**, Station Road, Rhosneigr, Anglesey LL64 5QX (Tel & Fax: 01407 811202; Club House 01407 810219). *Location:* turn south off A5 between Gwalchmai and Bryngwram onto A4080. In about three miles turn right at Llanfaelog church about one mile from course. Flat links course with sand dunes and heathland. 18 holes, 6300 yards. S.S.S. 70. *Green Fees:* please phone for current prices. *Eating facilities:* catering facilities available all day. *Visitors:* welcome, advanced booking advisable. Dress restrictions. *Society Meetings:* club societies welcome, for further information please contact the manager. Professional: Steve Elliot (01407 811202). Manager: Mr Vaughn Musgrave (Tel & Fax: 01407 811127).
e-mail: info@theangleseygolfclub.com
website: www.theangleseygolfclub.com

TREARDDUR BAY. **Holyhead Golf Club**, Trearddur Bay, Anglesey LL65 2YL (Tel & Fax: 01407 763279). *Location:* A55 to Holyhead, turn left at roundabout on B4545 for 1 mile, left for Trearddur Bay. Heathland, heavy gorse cover, superb sea views. Course designed by James Braid. 18 holes, 6058 yards. S.S.S. 70. *Green Fees:* weekdays £22.00 per day, weekends £29.00 per day. *Eating facilities:* restaurant/bar. *Visitors:* welcome. *Society Meetings:* catered for weekdays. Dormy House accommodation available for up to 14. Professional: Steve Elliot (01407 762022). Secretary/Manager: John Williams
e-mail: MgrSec@aol.com
website: www.holyheadgolfclub.co.uk

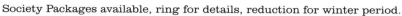

North Wales

ABERGELE. **Abergele Golf Club**, Tan-y-Gopa Road, Abergele, Conwy LL22 8DS (01745 824034; Fax: 01745 824772). *Location:* A55 from Chester. Below Gwrych Castle, Abergele. Parkland in scenic setting. 18 holes, 6256 yards. S.S.S. 70. Practice ground and indoor practice nets. *Green Fees:* £28.00 weekdays; £32.00 weekends and Bank Holidays. *Eating facilities:* restaurant and bar. *Visitors:* welcome, avoid Tuesdays (Ladies' Day) and Saturdays difficult due to club competitions. Buggy hire available, trolleys. *Society Meetings:* visiting party packages available. Professional: Iain R. Runcie (Tel & Fax: 01745 823813). Secretary: Chris Langdon (01745 824034; Fax: 01745 824772).

BETWS-Y-COED. **Betws-y-Coed Golf Club**, The Clubhouse, Betws-y-Coed LL24 0AL (01690 710556). *Location:* take Railway Museum Road in centre of the village. Parkland, flat scenic course on valley floor of River Conwy. 9 holes, 18 tees, 4998 yards. S.S.S. 63. *Green Fees:* Summer weekdays £18.00, weekends £22.00, Winter weekdays £10.00, weekend £15.00. *Eating facilities:* bar open from 12 noon onwards. *Visitors:* no restrictions provided there are no club competitions. *Society Meetings:* welcome. Secretary: P. Rowley.
e-mail: info@golf-betws-y-coed.co.uk
website: www.golf-betws-y-coed.co.uk

BODELWYDDAN. **Kinmel Park Golf Complex**, Abergele Road, Bodelwyddan LL18 5SR (01745 833548; Fax: 01745 833502). *Location:* Junction 25 off A55 Expressway at the famous White Marble church. Flat parkland course. 9 holes, 1550 yards. S.S.S. 58. 25 bay undercover and floodlit driving range. Practice chipping and putting green. *Green Fees:* Pay and Play course £4.00 weekdays, £5.00 weekends. Subject to review. *Visitors:* welcome. Golf lessons available. *Society Meetings:* Welcome, special rates. Professional: Andrew Barnett PGA. Director: Mrs Fetherstonhaugh.

CHESTER near. **Northop Country Park Golf Club**, Northop, Near Chester CH7 6WA (01352 840440; Fax: 01352 840445). *Location:* travel west on M56, follow signs for North Wales. A494/A55 for Northop. Parkland course set amongst 300 year old oak trees, designed by John Jacobs. 18 holes, 6735 yards, 6128 metres. S.S.S. 74. Practice range and academy. *Green Fees:* information not available. *Eating facilities:* clubroom for snacks, club restaurant for full meals. *Visitors:* welcome. St David's Park Hotel only five minutes away for accommodation. *Society Meetings:* welcome depending on availability. Professional: Matthew Pritchard. Director of Golf: Neil Sweeney.

CHIRK. **Chirk Golf Club**, Chirk, Near Wrexham LL14 5AD (01691 774407; Fax: 01691 773878). *Location:* just off A5 towards Llangollen. Generally flat course. 18 holes, 6541 yards. S.S.S. 72. 9 hole Par 3 course,

15 bay driving range. *Green Fees:* weekdays £18.00; weekends £19.00. *Eating facilities:* bar and restaurant. *Visitors:* welcome seven days a week. *Society Meetings:* all welcome. Professional: M. Maddison (01691 774407).

COLWYN. **Old Colwyn Golf Club,** The Clubhouse, Woodland Avenue, Old Colwyn LL29 9NL (01492 515581). *Location:* signposted at main Abergele road, Old Colwyn. Parkland. 9 holes (x 2), 5263 yards. S.S.S. 68. Practice area. *Green Fees:* information not available. *Eating facilities:* bar and meals by arrangement. *Visitors:* welcome except Saturday afternoons or Wednesday evenings. *Society Meetings:* welcome by arrangement with Secretary. Secretary: D.A. Jones. *

CONWY. **Conwy (Caernarvonshire) Golf Club,** Morfa, Conwy LL32 8ER (01492 593400). *Location:* follow signs for Conwy Marina off A55. Seaside links. 18 holes, 6647 yards. S.S.S. 72. Practice facilities. *Green Fees:* Winter package (coffee on arrival, 18 holes plus meal) - weekdays £26.00, weekends £30.00; Summer (April to October) - weekdays £40.00 per day, £35.00 per round, weekends and Bank Holidays £48.00 per day, £40.00 per round. *Eating facilities:* available daily April to October. *Visitors:* welcome with reservation, restrictions at weekends. *Society Meetings:* catered for on application to Secretary. Professional: Peter Lees (Tel & Fax: 01492 593225). Secretary: Mr D.L. Brown (01492 592423; Fax: 01492 593363).
e-mail: secretary@conwygolfclub.co.uk
website: www.conwygolfclub.co.uk

DENBIGH. **Denbigh Golf Club**, Henllan Road, Denbigh LL16 5AA (01745 816669. Fax: 01745 814888). *Location:* one mile from Denbigh town centre on the B5382 road. Parkland with excellent views. 18 holes, 5712 yards. S.S.S. 68. *Green Fees:* weekdays £27.50, weekends £32.50. Subject to review. *Eating facilities:* catering daily, bar. *Visitors:* welcome. *Society Meetings:* by arrangement. Professional: M.D. Jones (01745 814159). Secretary: Christine Hewitt.
e-mail: secretary@denbighgolfclub.com

DENBIGH near. **Bryn Morfydd Hotel Golf Club**, Llanrhaeadr, Near Denbigh LL16 4NP (01745 890280; Fax: 01745 890488). *Location:* off A525 between Denbigh and Ruthin. Mature parkland course overlooking the Vale of Clwyd. Two courses. The Duchess Course - 9 holes, 1146 yards. Par 27; The Duke's Course - 18 holes, 5685 yards. S.S.S. 67, Par 70. Practice area. *Green Fees:* information not available. *Eating facilities:* courses attached to three star Hotel, two restaurants, two bars, clubhouse. *Visitors:* welcome by arrangement. Hotel accommodation – 30 rooms en suite. *Society Meetings:* welcome by arrangement all year. Secretary/Director of Golf: Richard Hughes. Proprietor: D. & S. Frith.

FLINT. **Flint Golf Club**, Cornist Park, Flint CH6 5HJ (01352 732327). *Location:* A548 coast road, one mile from town centre. Hilly parkland. 9 holes, 5927 yards. S.S.S. 69. Practice area. *Green Fees:* £12.00 per day. *Eating facilities:* full bar and catering 11am to 11pm. *Visitors:* welcome except Sundays. *Society Meetings:* welcome by arrangement. Secretary: Mr Geoff Hughes (01352 735245).

HAWARDEN. **Hawarden Golf Club,** Groomsdale Lane, Hawarden CH5 3EH (01244 531447. Fax: 01244 536901). *Location:* A55, left at Ewloe interchange, follow Hawarden signs. Undulating parkland. 18 holes, 5842 yards, 5340 metres. S.S.S. 69, Par 69. *Green Fees:* information not available. *Eating facilities:* full bar and catering. *Visitors:* welcome by arrangement. Some restrictions Wednesday (Ladies' Day). *Society Meetings:* catered for by prior arrangement. Summer and Winter packages available. Professional: Alex Rowlands (01244 520809). Secretary: Malcolm Coppack. *

HOLYWELL. **Holywell Golf Club**, Brynford, Near Holywell CH8 8LQ (01352 713937). *Location:* turn off A55 at Springfield Hotel onto A5026, turn left at traffic lights, up hill for one and a half miles, turn right at crossroads. Flat natural terrain, links type course, a good test of golf. 18 holes, 6100 yards. S.S.S. 70. *Green Fees:* weekdays £18.00; weekends and Bank Holidays £23.00. Special rates between November and March. *Eating facilities:* full bar facilities and catering. *Visitors:* welcome weekdays without reservation; Bank Holidays and weekends by prior arrangement with Secretary. Snooker table. *Society Meetings:* by prior arrangement with Secretary. Professional: Matthew Parsley (01352 710040). Hon Secretary: John F Snead (Tel & Fax: 01352 713937). e-mail: holywell_golf_club@lineone.net

HOLYWELL **Kinsale Golf Course**, Llanerchymor, Holywell CH8 9DX (01745 561080; Fax: 01745 561079). *Location:* A55 expressway, Holywell to A548; opposite White Ship Abakham Textiles. Magnificent view over Dee Estuary towards the Wirral. 9 holes, 5944 yards. S.S.S. 69. Driving range. *Green Fees:* information not available. *Eating facilities:* snacks in clubhouse, bar and restaurant at Kinsale Hall Hotel. *Visitors:* always welcome; pay as you play course. *Society Meetings:* welcome seven days. Director of Golf/Professional/Secretary: Alan Norwood.*

LLANDUDNO. **Llandudno Golf Club (Maesdu) Ltd**, Hospital Road, Llandudno LL30 1HU (01492 876450; Fax: 01492 871570). *Location*: Llandudno General Hospital. A55 and then A470. Parkland. 18 holes, 6545 yards. S.S.S. 72. Practice ground. *Green Fees*: weekdays £25.00 per round, £30.00 per day; weekends and Bank Holidays £30.00 per round, £35.00 per day. *Eating facilities*: full catering, bar (large) available. *Visitors*: welcome, must book. Buggies, electric trolleys for hire. *Society Meetings*: must be booked. Professional: S. Boulden (01492 875195). Secretary: George Dean (01492 876450)

LLANDUDNO. **North Wales Golf Club Ltd**, 72 Bryniau Road, West Shore, Llandudno LL30 2DZ. *Location*: two miles off the A55 expressway on the A470 Junction. Seaside links with wonderful views of Conwy estuary and mountains. 18 holes, 6287 yards, S.S.S. 71. Practice ground. *Green Fees*: Summer – weekdays £30.00 per day, weekends and Bank Holidays £36.00 per day; Winter – weekdays £20.00 per round, weekends and Bank Holidays £25.00 per round. Single rounds reduced rate after 3pm. *Eating facilities*: full bar and catering facilities. *Visitors*: welcome after 9.30am weekdays, 10.30am weekends. Current Handicap Certificate required. No entrance fee payable for membership. Buggies, carts and clubs for hire. *Society Meetings*: catered for by arrangement. Professional: R.A. Bradbury (01492 876878; Fax: 01492 872420). General Manager: Gordon Downs (01492 875325; Fax: 01492 873355). e-mail: golf@nwgc.freeserve.co.uk website: www.northwalesgolfclub.co.uk

LLANDUDNO. **Rhos-on-Sea Residential Golf Club**, Penrhyn Bay, Llandudno LL30 3PU (01492 549100). *Location:* A55 to Colwyn Bay follow signs to Rhos-on-Sea, one mile past Rhos-on-Sea on coast road in Penrhyn Bay. Flat seaside parkland course. 18 holes, 6064 yards. S.S.S. 69. *Green Fees:* weekdays £22.00; weekends £30.00. *Eating facilities:* bar meals 12 - 2pm, teas, coffees, snacks available all day. Evening meals by arrangement. Licensed bar open 11am - 3pm lunch, 5.30pm - 11pm evenings; Sundays 12 - 2pm lunch, 7pm - 10.30pm evenings. *Visitors:* all welcome any time, prior booking required particularly weekends. 18 bedrooms, two full size snooker tables, small TV lounge. One £100 jackpot fruit machine. Trolley hire available. *Society Meetings:* all welcome. Professional: Mike Macara (01492 548115). Secretary: John Leigh (01492 549100).

THE APPEARANCE OF AN ASTERISK (*)
AT THE END OF A CLUB OR COURSE
ENTRY INDICATES THAT
UP-TO-DATE INFORMATION
HAS NOT BEEN SUPPLIED

LLANGOLLEN. **Vale of Llangollen Golf Club Ltd.,** The Clubhouse, Llangollen LL20 7PR (Tel & Fax: 01978 860906). *Location:* one and a half miles east of town on the A5. Course is set on the valley floor bordered by the River Dee. 18 holes, 6656 yards, 6086 metres. S.S.S. 73. Practice ground. *Green Fees:* weekdays £30.00 per round, £40.00 per day; weekends £35.00 per round, £45.00 per day. Subject to review. *Eating facilities:* full catering service. *Visitors:* welcome any day subject to availability, handicap certificate essential. *Society Meetings:* welcome. Professional: David Vaughan (01978 860040). Secretary: David Bluck (Tel & Fax: 01978 860906).

MOLD. **Mold Golf Club,** Cilcain Road, Pantymwyn, Mold CH7 5EH (01352 741513; Fax: 01352 741517). *Location:* 14 miles west of Chester. Take A55 from Chester for Mold. Follow Pantymwyn signs from Mold. Uplands course offering extensive views of Cheshire, Liverpool, Peak District. 18 holes, 5628 yards. S.S.S. 67. Practice ground and practice green. *Green Fees:* information not available. *Eating facilities:* extensive restaurant and bar facilities. *Visitors:* welcome by prior arrangement. Tee bookings advised at weekends. Trolley hire. *Society Meetings:* welcome, subject to tee availability. Professional: Mark Jordan (01352 740318) (Lessons by appointment). Secretary: P. Mather (01352 741513; Fax: 01352 741517). e-mail: info@moldgolfclub.co.uk).

MOLD. **Padeswood and Buckley Golf Club,** The Caia, Station Lane, Padeswood, Near Mold CH7 4JD (01244 550537). *Location:* A5118 Chester - Mold, one mile west of Castle Cement Works, half a mile off main road. Flat parkland; river, lakes. 18 holes, 5982 yards. S.S.S. 69. Practice ground. *Green Fees:* weekdays £20.00 per round, £25.00 per day; Saturdays only, £25.00 per round. *Eating facilities:* bar all day every day, catering daily. *Visitors:* welcome except on Sundays. Buggies, carts for hire; two snooker tables. *Society Meetings:* welcome, enquiries through Secretary; packages available. Professional: David Ashton (01244 543636). Secretary: J.M. Conway (01244 550537).

PADESWOOD. **Old Padeswood Golf Club Ltd**, Station Road, Padeswood, Near Mold CH7 4JD (01244 547701). *Location:* off A5118 Chester to Mold road, eight miles from Chester and three miles from Mold. Situated in the beautiful Alyn Valley - nine holes flat parkland, nine holes slightly undulating. 18 holes, 6668 yards, 6079 metres. S.S.S. 72/Ladies 73. Practice ground. *Green Fees:* weekdays £20.00, with member £10.00; weekends £25.00, with member £13.00. *Eating facilities:* diningroom, bar meals - two bars. *Visitors:* welcome anytime subject to tee availability. *Society Meetings:* welcome, written applications to Co-Secretary. Professional: Tony Davies (01244 547401). Co-Secretary: Mrs B. Jones (01244 550414; Fax: 01244 545082). Hon. Secretary: Mr B. Slater (01244 816573; Fax: 01244 545082). e-mail: oldpad@par72.fsbusiness.co.uk website: www.oldpadeswoodgolfclub.co.uk

PRESTATYN. **Prestatyn Golf Club**, Marine Road East, Prestatyn LL19 7HS (01745 854320). *Location*: A548, on approaching Prestatyn from Chester direction turn right at sign for Pontins Holiday Village and follow club sign. Seaside links Championship course. 18 holes, 6564 yards, 5959 metres. S.S.S. 72. Practice areas. *Green Fees*: £25.00 weekdays; £30.00 Sundays and Bank Holidays. *Eating facilities*: full catering available, bar. *Visitors*: must have Handicap Certificates. *Society Meetings*: special "all-in" arrangement for 27 holes. Professional: D. Ames (01745 854320). Manager: Girvin Palfrey (01745 888353; Fax: 01745 888327). e-mail: prestatyngcmanager@freenet.co.uk website: www.prestatyngc.co.uk

PRESTATYN. **St Melyd Golf Club**, The Paddock, Meliden Road, Prestatyn LL19 9NB (01745 854405; Fax: 01745 856908). *Location:* on main Prestatyn to Rhuddlan road, just outside Meliden. Parkland course with tight fairways and varied greens, set twixt the hills and the sea. 9 holes, 5811 yards. S.S.S. 68. *Green Fees:* information not available. *Eating facilities:* full range of catering facilities except Tuesdays which is by arrangement. *Visitors:* welcome without reservation but advise phone call first in summer season. Restriction Saturdays Competition Day; Thursdays Ladies' Day. Snooker room. *Society Meetings:* catered for by arrangement with Secretary (various golf packages). Maximum 40. Administrator: Ken Woodward.* e-mail: info@stmelydgolf.co.uk website: www.stmelydgolf.co.uk

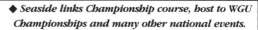

RHUDDLAN. **Rhuddlan Golf Club**, Meliden Road, Rhuddlan LL18 6LB (01745 590217). *Location*: leave A55 at St Asaph for Rhuddlan, clubhouse 100m from roundabout at Prestatyn end of Rhuddlan. Gently undulating, parkland course with natural hazards; set amid splendid scenery with fine views of the Clwydian Hills. 18 holes, White 6473 yards. S.S.S. 71; Yellow 6291 yards, S.S.S. 70; Ladies 5768 yards, Par 70. Extensive practice ground. *Green Fees*: £25.00 - £30.00 per round. *Eating facilities*: full restaurant facilities daily. *Visitors*: welcome at all times when course demand permits. Sundays with member only. No denim. Snooker table. *Society Meetings*: weekdays only, maximum 50. Professional: Andrew Carr (01745 590898). Secretary: Bryn Jones (01745 590217; Fax: 01745 590472). e-mail: golf@rhuddlangolfclub.fsnet.co.uk website: www.rhuddlangolfclub.co.uk

RHYL. **Rhyl Golf Club,** Coast Road, Rhyl LL18 3RE (01745 353171; Fax: 01745 360007). *Location:* situated alongside A548, the Rhyl/ Prestatyn coast road. Flat links. 9 or 18 holes, 6220 yards. S.S.S. 70. Practice ground. *Green Fees:* information not available. *Eating facilities:* dining room, catering and bar snacks available. *Visitors:* always welcome; some restrictions when club competitions in play. Trolleys for hire. Buggies available. *Society Meetings:* welcome, maximum 40; discounts for 10 or more. Professional: Tim Leah (01745 360007). Secretary: Mr Ian St. C. Doig (01745 353171). e-mail: rhylgolfclub@hotmail.com website: www.rhylgolfclub.com

RUTHIN. **Ruthin Pwllglas Golf Club,** Pwllglas, Near Ruthin LL15 2PE (01824 702296). *Location:* Corwen Road (A494), two miles south of Ruthin. Hilly parkland. 10 holes, 5418 yards. S.S.S. 66. Practice area. *Green Fees:* weekdays £14.00, weekends and Bank Holidays £20.00. *Eating facilities:* Bar. Secretary can arrange catering for visiting parties. *Visitors:* welcome without reservation, phone call advisable in high season and at weekends. *Society Meetings:* catered for. Hon. Secretary: Eric Owen (01824 702383 after 6pm).

WREXHAM. **Moss Valley Golf Club**, Moss Road, Wrexham LL11 6HA (Tel & Fax: 01978 720518). Private members' club. *Location:* off A541 from Wrexham roundabout. Parkland course meandering through wooded valley. 9/18 holes (twin tees on every hole), 2531 yards. S.S.S. 67. *Green Fees:* weekdays: 9 holes £8.00, 18 holes £10.00. Weekends and Bank Holidays: 9 holes £9.00, 18 holes £12.00. Membership £225.00 plus £25.00 joining fee. *Visitors:* welcome, booking required at weekend. *Society Meetings:* contact in advance. Manager/ Secretary: John Parry.
e-mail: info@mossvalleygolf.com
website: www. mossvalleygolf.com

visit the FHG golf website on
www.uk-golfguide.com

WREXHAM. **Plassey Golf Course,** Eyton, Wrexham LL13 0SP (01978 780020; Fax: 01978 781397). *Location:* 4 miles south east of Wrexham. Follow brown "Tourist Attraction" signs to "Plassey" from A483 Wrexham by-pass. Undulating parkland course. 9 holes, 4961 yards, Par 66. Practice area, driving net, pitch and putt. *Green Fees:* April to September – midweek £9.50 9 holes, £16.00 18 holes; weekends £11.00 9 holes, £17.50 18 holes. October to March – midweek £6.50 9 holes, £7.50 18 holes; weekends £9.00 9 holes, £12.50 18 holes. *Visitors:* most welcome. Please book start times at weekends. Full bar and catering facilities. Golf course is part of Plassey Leisure Park which includes shops, boutiques, craft centre, brewery, garden centre, blacksmith and award winning Caravan & Campsite. *Society Meetings:* most welcome (please book start times at weekends). Proprietor/Professional: Simon Ward (PGA Qualified).
website: www.plasseygolf.co.uk

WREXHAM. **Wrexham Golf Club**, Holt Road, Wrexham LL13 9SB (01978 351476; Fax: 01978 364268). *Location:* A543 north east of Wrexham. 18 holes, 6263 yards. S.S.S. 70. Practice facilities. *Green Fees*: weekdays £25.00; weekends £30.00. *Eating facilities*: daily. *Visitors*: welcome, subject to competitions and Society bookings. *Society Meetings*: catered for Monday, Wednesday, Thursday and Fridays only. Professional: P. Williams (01978 351476). Secretary: Jim Johnson (01978 364268).

MOSS VALLEY GOLF CLUB
Moss Road, Moss, Wrexham LL11 6HA • Tel & Fax: 01978 720518

Established in the late 1980s the 9 hole course was designed by Golf Architects in a beautiful parkland setting just 5 minutes' drive from the centre of Wrexham. The scenery can be compared with any part of North Wales and some of the views from the course are quite breathtaking. Every hole is different in character, providing a good test of golf for both beginners and the experienced. Various categories of membership are available and the club actively encourages youngsters to become involved in the club. 9/18 holes. Twin tees on every hole.

**website: www.mossvalleygolf.com
e-mail: info@mossvalleygolf.com**

See also Colour Advertisement on page 56

Carmarthenshire

AMMANFORD. **Glynhir Golf Club**, Glynhir Road, Llandybie, Ammanford SA18 2TF (Tel & Fax: 01269 851365). *Location:* seven miles from end of M4, between Ammanford and Llandybie on the A483. Turn right up Glynhir Road and proceed for about two miles. Undulating wooded parkland course. 18 holes, 6010 yards. S.S.S. 70. *Green Fees:* £16.00 weekdays (inclusive of personal insurance), weekends on request. *Eating facilities:* full catering available. *Visitors:* welcome. B&B available for six, subject to availability. *Society Meetings:* welcome anytime by prior arrangement with the Secretaries (special rates available). Professional: Duncan Prior (01269 851010). Joint Secretaries: D.J.E. Kenchington, K. Williams (01269 851365). e-mail: glynhir.golfclub@virgin.net http://freespace.virgin.net/glynhir.golfclub/

CARMARTHEN. **Carmarthen Golf Club**, Blaenycoed Road, Carmarthen SA33 6EH (01267 281214). *Location:* four miles north-west of town. Undulating heathland - a good test of golf. 18 holes, 6210 yards. S.S.S. 71. Large practice ground. *Green Fees:* weekdays £20.00, weekends £25.00. *Eating facilities:* catering every day, limited Wednesdays. *Visitors:* welcome with proof of Handicap, telephone call advisable at weekends. *Society Meetings:* by arrangement. Professional: Pat Gillis (01267 281493). Secretary: Jonathan Coe (01267 281588). e-mail: jonathanseccgc@aol.com website: www.carmarthengolfclub.com

CARMARTHEN. **Derllys Court Golf Club**, Llysonnen Road, Carmarthen SA33 5DT (Tel. & Fax: 01267 211575). *Location:* three miles west of Carmarthen on A40, signposted. Gently undulating parkland. 18 holes, 5650 yards. Practice area. *Green Fees*: information not available. *Eating facilities:* bar/lounge and restaurant. *Visitors:* welcome at all times. Equipment hire available. *Society Meetings:* welcome by prior arrangement. Secretary: Rhian Walters.*
e-mail: derllys@hotmail.com
website: www.derllyscourtgolfclub.co.uk

KIDWELLY/LLANELLI. **Glyn Abbey Golf Club**, Trimsaren, Kidwelly SA17 4LB (01554 810278; Fax: 01554 810889). *Location*: five miles north west of Llanelli on the B4317 between Trimsaran and Carway. Parkland course with spectacular views, Hawtree design, mature woodland. 18 holes, 6173 yards, Par 70. S.S.S. 70. *Green Fees*: £14.00 midweek, £17.00 weekends. *Eating facilities*: fully licensed clubhouse and restaurant. *Visitors*: welcome at all times with no restrictions. Advisable to phone ahead and book. *Society Meetings*: always very welcome by prior arrangement. Managing Director: Martin Lane (01554 810304). e-mail: course-enquiries@glynabbey.co.uk website: www.glynabbey.co.uk

---

The Mill at Glynhir, Llandybie, Carmarthenshire SA18 2TE

Tastefully converted 17th century Mill. All bedrooms en suite with spa baths. Good food. Licensed bar. Indoor heated swimming pool. Special arrangements with Glynhir Golf Club and 8 others. No under 11s.

Tel: 01269 850672 • www.glynhir.co.uk • e-mail: millatglynhir@aol.com

---

GLYNHIR GOLF CLUB

Glynhir Road, Llandybie, Ammanford SA18 2TF
Tel & Fax: 01269 851365
e-mail: glynhir.golfclub@virgin.net
http://homepage.virgin.net/glynhir.golfclub

This 18-hole parkland course is set in idyllic surroundings. Clubhouse and locker rooms refurbished. Whole day package with 9 holes in the morning, lunch, 18 holes in the afternoon followed by an evening meal. Pre-booking essential by contacting *K. Williams (01269 592345) or D. Kenchington (01269 842583)*.

SUMMER SPECIAL (April to October)
Reduced Green Fee £10.50 Monday and Friday with tee times available until 4pm. Reservations only through the *Professional: Duncan Prior (01269 851010)*

VISITORS AND SOCIETIES WELCOME

See also Colour Advertisement on page 57

 FHG For full details of clubs and courses, plus convenient accommodation, visit the FHG golf website on **www.uk-golfguide.com**

LLANDYSUL. **Saron Golf Course**, Penwern, Saron, Llandysul SA44 5EL (01559 370705). *Location*: midway between Carmarthen and Newcastle Emlyn on the A484. Parkland course in the Teifi Valley set in 50 acres. 9 holes 18 tees. 9 holes 2091 yards, 18 holes 4412 yards. *Green Fees*: 9 holes £7.00, under 15s £5.00, 18 holes £9.00, under 15s £6.00. *Visitors*: welcome at all times. Three cottages on course, sleeping six/ four/two. *Society Meetings*: welcome. Secretary: Mrs M.B.L. Searle (01559 370705). e-mail: c9mbl@sarongolf.freeserve.co.uk website: www.saron-golf.com

LLANELLI. **Ashburnham Golf Club**, Cliffe Terrace, Burry Port SA16 0HN (01554 832466). *Location:* south side of A484, four miles west of Llanelli. Seaside links with Championship status. 18 holes. S.S.S. 73. Practice area. *Green Fees:* £27.50 to £40.00. *Eating facilities:* catering except Mondays, two bars. *Visitors:* welcome, starting times available from the Secretary. Handicap Certificates. Carts. *Society Meetings:* by arrangement with Secretary. Professional: Robert A. Ryder (01554 833846). Secretary: D.K. Williams (01554 832269).

THE APPEARANCE OF AN ASTERISK * AT THE END OF A CLUB OR COURSE ENTRY INDICATES THAT UP-TO-DATE INFORMATION HAS NOT BEEN SUPPLIED

Ceredigion

ABERYSTWYTH. **Aberystwyth Golf Club,** Brynymor Road, Aberystwyth SY23 2HY (01970 615104; Fax: 01970 626622). *Location:* north end of Promenade, access near to cliff railway. Undulating meadowland designed by Harry Vardon. 18 holes, white - 6119 yards. S.S.S. 71. Practice ground. *Green Fees:* Summer: £20.00 weekdays; £25.00 weekends. 50% reduction for Juniors. *Eating facilities:* restaurant and bar. *Visitors:* welcome at all times, pre-booking helpful. *Society Meetings:* welcome, Special Deals available. Professional: (01970 625301). Secretary: (01970 615104).

BORTH. **Borth and Ynyslas Golf Club Ltd,** Borth, Ceredigion SY24 5JS (Tel & Fax: 01970 871202). *Location:* A487 Machynlleth to Aberystwyth, turn off to Borth. Gently undulating links. 18 holes, 6116 yards. S.S.S. 70 men, 72 ladies. Practice ground. *Green Fees:* information not available. *Eating facilities:* full catering and bar. *Visitors:* welcome at all times except during competitions – check with Professional. *Society Meetings:* by prior arrangement with the Secretary, 20% discount weekdays. Professional: J.G. Lewis (Tel & Fax: 01970 871557). Secretary: Mr G.J. Pritchard (01970 871202). e-mail: secretary@borthgolf.co.uk website: www.borthgolf.co.uk

CARDIGAN. **Cardigan Golf Club,** Gwbert-on-Sea, Cardigan SA43 1PR (01239 612035). *Location*: three miles from Cardigan. Seaside links course. 18 holes, 6687 yards. S.S.S. 73. **Green Fees**: weekdays £22.50, weekends and Bank Holidays £27.50. *Eating facilities*: catering and bar facilities available. *Visitors*: welcome. Tee reserved for members 1pm–2pm. *Society Meetings*: very welcome. Reductions on application. Professional: Mr Colin Parsons (01239 615359). Secretary: Mr J. Jones (Tel & Fax: 01239 621775). e-mail: golf@cardigan.fsnet.co.uk website: www.cardigangolf.co.uk

LAMPETER. **Cilgwyn Golf Club,** Llangybi, Lampeter SA48 8NN (01570 493286). *Location:* five miles north-east of Lampeter, off A485 Tregaron Road at Llangybi. Flat parkland course with natural hazards. 9 holes, 5309 yards, S.S.S. 66. Large practice ground and putting green. *Green Fees:* information not available. *Eating facilities:* full bar and catering. *Visitors:* welcome without restrictions – please telephone at weekends April to September. Golf shop, trolley hire, pool table, TV. Caravan parking and golf for Caravan Club members. Bungalow in club grounds sleeps 6, Bargain Breaks available. *Society Meetings:* welcome Wednesdays and Fridays by prior arrangement. Package deals for parties of six or more. Secretary: J.D. Morgan (01570 423226).

LLANDYSUL. **Cwmrhydneuadd Golf Club**, Pentregat, Llandysul SA44 6HD (01239 654933). *Location:* follow the Aberystwyth to Cardigan A487 trunk road to the village of Pentregat, then follow signs to golf club. Parkland course set in picturesque, secluded valley, surrounded by wooded hills. Includes three small lakes. 9 holes, 4061 yards. S.S.S. 62. *Green Fees:* information not available. *Eating facilities:* club house; home-made snacks, meals. *Visitors:* welcome, no restrictions. *Society Meetings*: welcome. Professional: S. Parsons. Secretary: J. Curry (01559 362253). *

LLANRHYSTYD. **Penrhos Golf and Country Club,** Llanrhystyd SY23 5AY (01974 202999; Fax: 01974 202100). *Location:* nine miles south of Aberystwyth on A487. Parkland and meadowland with lakes and panoramic views of the Welsh countryside. 18 holes, 6641 yards. S.S.S. 73. Practice ground, 9 holes Par 3, Par 4. *Green Fees:* information not provided. *Eating facilities:* bar meals and à la carte restaurant. *Visitors:* welcome at all times. Accommodation in en suite hotel on site and mobile homes, full leisure facilities. *Society Meetings:* welcome all week by appointment. Professional: Paul Diamond. Secretary: R. Rees-Evans. e-mail: info@penrhosgolf.co.uk website: www.penrhosgolf.co.uk

Aberystwyth Golf Club
Brynymor Road, Aberystwyth SY23 2HY

Set above the picturesque town of Aberystwyth, this championship 18-hole course was designed by Harry Vardon and was formed in 1911. It provides both exciting and challenging golf for all players, as well as offering the most picturesque and panoramic views of Cardigan Bay and the mountains of Snowdonia. It is also the ideal venue for Corporate and Society golf days and provides flexible packages to suit individual requirements. Our resident PGA Golf Professional is on hand to assist with your golfing needs. Our friendly bar and clubhouse is managed by our resident Steward, and our restaurant caters for a variety of palates, from simple bar snacks to à la carte. You will be sure of a friendly welcome at Aberystwyth Golf Club.

Tel: 01970 615104• website: www.aberystwythgolfclub.com • e-mail: aberystwythgolf@talk21.com

See also Colour Advertisement on page 57

www.cliffhotel.com

The Cliff Hotel

- Access to Cardigan Golf Course
- On site 9 hole course
- Bars & Restaurants
- 72 luxury bedrooms
- Sauna, games room, heated pool
- Stay & play golf packages
- AA 3 ★★★
- Par 72, 6426 yds

One of Wales' hidden gems!
Overlooking Cardigan Bay on the Pembrokeshire Heritage Coastline

The Cliff Hotel at Cardigan Golf Club

Cardigan is one of the finest all weather golf courses in Wales with challenging holes on this championship Par 72 course.

The Cliff Hotel, Gwbert on Sea, Cardigan, SA43 1PP Tel: 01239 613241

See also Colour Advertisement on page 53

FHG

FHG PUBLICATIONS
publish a large range of well-known accommodation guides. We will be happy to send you details or you can use the order form at the back of this book.

Pembrokeshire

FISHGUARD/HAVERFORDWEST. **Priskilly Forest Golf Club**, Castlemorris, Haverfordwest SA62 5EH (Tel & Fax: 01348 840276). *Location*: A40 Haverfordwest to Fishguard road, left turn at Letterston B4331 towards Mathry. Picturesque undulating parkland surrounded by rhododendrons, etc – a challenging course. 9 holes, 5874 yards. S.S.S. 69. Practice net and ground, trolleys and buggy for hire. *Green Fees*: £10.00 for 9 holes, £16.00 for 18 holes, £18.00 per day. Special winter rates/packages available. *Eating facilities*: licensed bar, light refreshments. *Visitors*: welcome. Accommodation with golf inclusive packages on site in 3 Star country house. Buggies for hire £15.00 for 18 holes. *Society Meetings*: welcome. Secretary: P. Evans.
e-mail: jevans@priskilly-forest.co.uk
website: www.priskilly-golfclub.co.uk

HAVERFORDWEST. **Haverfordwest Golf Club**, Arnolds Down, Haverfordwest SA61 2XQ (01437 763565). *Location:* one mile east of town on A40 trunk road. A parkland course set in Pembrokeshire National Park – challenging but easy walking. 18 holes, 5973 yards. S.S.S. 69. Practice area and putting green. *Green Fees:* weekdays £22.00 per day, £12.00 with a member; weekends £27.00 per day, £15.00 with a member. *Eating facilities:* dining room, bar snacks 11am to 9pm. *Visitors:* welcome. *Society Meetings:* welcome by arrangement. Professional: Alex Pile (01437 768409). Secretary: Mike LeClair (01437 764523; Fax: 01437 764143).

MILFORD HAVEN. **Dawn till Dusk Golf Club**, Furze Hill Farm, Rosemarket, Milford Haven SA73 1JY (01437 890281). *Location*: from Haverfordwest Bypass take A4076 as far as Johnston, turn left, signposted Rosemarket, one and a quarter miles to crossroads, turn right, 1 mile on left side of road. Flat parkland course. 9 holes (18 tees), 6373 yards, S.S.S. 71. Putting green, bunkers. *Green Fees*: 9 holes £5.00, 18 holes £8.00. *Visitors*: welcome at all times. *Society Meetings*: welcome, rates negotiable for larger groups. Grass airstrip available, by prior arrangement.

MILFORD HAVEN. **Milford Haven Golf Club Ltd,** Woodbine House, Clay Lane, Hubberston, Milford Haven SA72 3RX (01646 697762). *Location:* one mile west of Milford Haven on Dale Road. Parkland overlooking magnificent harbour. 18 holes, 6035 yards. S.S.S. 70. Practice area. *Green Fees:* weekdays £17.50 per day; weekends and Bank Holidays £22.50. Subject to review. *Eating facilities:* bar and restaurant facilities. *Visitors:* welcome at all times, please ring Pro shop to check availability. *Society Meetings:* welcome, special rates available. Professional: Martin Stimson (Tel & Fax: 01646 697762). Secretary: Mr W.S. Brown. Administrator: Mr C. Pugh (01646 697822).
e-mail: enquiries@mhgc.co.uk
website: www.mhgc.co.uk

Haverfordwest Golf Club
Arnoldstown, Haverfordwest, Pembrokeshire SA61 2XQ

Set near the Pembrokeshire National Park and boasting magnificent views of the Preseli Hills, Haverfordwest Golf Club offers a real challenge to golfers of all abilities. Easily reachable on the A40 one mile east of Haverfordwest, this course is located in majestic parkland, and despite being an easy walk, there are a few holes that test the golfer's skill. The clubhouse, built in 1994, has excellent facilities including locker rooms, lounge, bars and full catering facilities, with a wide selection of home-cooked cuisine.

• **Club founded 1904** • **18 holes** • **Parkland** • **5973 yards** • **Par 70**

• Societies welcome by arrangement • Green Fee Visitors Welcome • Special Winter Rate Packages
Contact: **Alex Pile or Peter Lewis on 01437 768409 or 01437 764523** • Fax: 01437 764143

See also Colour Advertisement on page 57

Pembrokeshire family-run caravan park, near to 18 and 9-hole golf courses and driving range. 25 luxury caravans in peaceful location. Touring pitches, super play area; pets welcome.
www.scamford.com • *e-mail: holidays@scamford.com*
Richard & Christine White (Tel/Fax: 01437 710304).
SCAMFORD CARAVAN PARK, KEESTON, HAVERFORDWEST, PEMBROKESHIRE SA62 6HN

NEWPORT. **Newport (Pembs) Golf Club Ltd,** The Golf Club, Golf Course Road, Newport SA42 0NR (01239 820244; Fax: 01239 820085). *Location:* two miles off A487 Cardigan-Fishguard at Newport, Pembrokeshire. Flat seaside links course with breathtaking views over the mountains and bay. 9 holes, 6003 yards. S.S.S. 69. Driving range. *Green Fees:* please phone the clubhouse for current rate. *Eating facilities:* full catering and bar facilities available. *Visitors:* welcome, tee times must be booked and Handicap Certificate may be required; Pro shop and buggy hire. Self-catering accommodation available in adjoining clubhouse. *Society Meetings:* welcome by arrangement, please phone Amanda Payne (01239 820244). Professional: Mr Julian Noott PGA (01239 820244). Operations Manager: Amanda Payne (01239 820244; Fax: 01239 820085) e-mail: newportgc@lineone.net

PEMBROKE. **South Pembrokeshire Golf Club,** Military Road, Pennar, Pembroke Dock SA72 6SE (01646 621453). *Location:* on hilltop overlooking Pembroke Dock and The Haven. Parkland rapidly maturing. 18 holes, 6100 yards. S.S.S. 69. Practice facilities. *Green Fees:* information not available. *Eating facilities:* bar, please book for food. *Visitors:* welcome except during club competitions, please telephone. *Society Meetings:* welcome by arrangement. Secretary: J. Gettings.*

ST DAVID'S. **St David's City Golf Club,** Whitesands Bay, St David's SA62 6QY (01437 721751). *Location:* follow signs to Whitesands Bay, on Fishguard Road out of St David's, for two miles. Car park is situated on crossroads with club sign at entrance. If you reach the beach you've gone too far! Seaside links course with spectacular panoramic views over Whitesands Bay and St David's Head. 9 holes, 6117 yards. S.S.S. 70. *Green Fees:* Summer £15.00 per day, Winter £10.00 per day. *Visitors:* welcome at all times but please check at weekends and Bank Holidays; Ladies' Day Friday afternoons, Seniors' Day Thursday afternoon. *Society Meetings:* welcome, book with Secretary. Secretary: James Wilcox (01437 721751).

TENBY. **Tenby Golf Club,** The Burrows, Tenby SA70 7NP *Location:* on A478, near Tenby Railway Station. Seaside links, Championship course, oldest in Wales. 18 holes, 6224 yards. S.S.S. 71. Practice ground. *Green Fees:* information not available. *Eating facilities:* complete dining facilities; licensed bar. *Visitors:* always welcome, subject to club competitions. Handicap Certificate required. Billiards rooms. *Society Meetings:* catered for by advance booking. Professional: Mark Hawkey PGA (01834 844447). Secretary: D. Hancock (Tel & Fax: 01834 842978). e-mail: tenbygolfclub@uku.co.uk website: www.tenbygolf.co.uk

TENBY. **Trefloyne Golf Club,** Trefloyne Park, Penally, Tenby (Tel & Fax: 01834 842165). *Location:* on edge of village of Penally, just off A4139 Tenby/Pembroke road, about 1 mile from Tenby. Men's course - 18 holes, 6635 yards, 6068 metres, S.S.S. yellow tees 72, white 73, Par 71. Ladies' course - 18 holes, 5764 yards, 5271 metres, S.S.S. 73, Par 73. Practice ground. *Green Fees:* weekdays £22.00, weekends £26.00. Special rates available to societies and via selected accommodation. *Eating facilities:* catering by arrangement. Drinks and sandwiches on sale. *Visitors:* always welcome, subject to adherence to rules and etiquette of golf and dress code. Trolleys and buggies available for hire. *Society Meetings:* welcome, minimum of 8 players. Professional: Steven Laidler. website: www.trefloynegolfcourse.co.uk

Powys

BRECON. **Brecon Golf Club,** Newton Park, Brecon LD3 8PA (01874 622004). *Location:* A40 west of town, half a mile from town centre. Flat parkland course. 9 holes, 5476 yards. S.S.S. 66, Par 68. *Green Fees:* £12.00 at all times. *Eating facilities:* bars and catering available. *Visitors:* welcome, some restriction Sundays when prior arrangement advisable. *Society Meetings:* by arrangement. Secretary: T. Barnes. (01874 622004).

BUILTH WELLS. **Builth Wells Golf Club**, Golf Club Road, Builth Wells LD2 3NF (01982 553296). *Location:* off A483, on outskirts of town on Llandovery Road. Parkland, reasonably flat. 18 holes. S.S.S. 67. Practice area. *Green Fees:* £18.00 per round, £25.00 per day weekdays; £25.00 per round, £30.00 per day weekends and Bank Holidays. Five- day ticket £85.00, seven-day ticket £125.00 – prices subject to change. *Eating facilities:* catering all day, two bars. *Visitors:* welcome. *Society Meetings:* welcome, Handicap Certificate required. Professional/Secretary: Simon Edwards (01982 553296; Fax: 01982 551064). e-mail: builthwellsgolfclub1@btinternet.com website: www.builthwellsgolfclub.co.uk

CRADOC. **Cradoc Golf Club,** Penoyre Park, Cradoc, Brecon LD3 9LP (01874 623658; Fax: 01874 611711). *Location:* about two miles north of the market town of Brecon, off B4520 Upper Chapel Road (signposted) past Brecon Cathedral. Attractive parkland course adjoining the Brecon Beacons National Park, scenic views. 18 holes, 6331 yards. S.S.S. 72. 12-bay floodlit driving range. Host of 1982 Welsh Stroke Play Championships. Home of the Welsh Brewers Champion of Champions Tournament. *Green Fees:* weekdays £22.00 per day, weekends and Bank Holidays £28.00 per day. *Eating facilities:* full catering facilities daily except Mondays. *Visitors:* welcome daily but restricted on Sundays. Electric trolley/buggy hire. *Society Meetings:* welcome any day; prior arrangement advised especially for Sundays. Special packages available. Professional: R.W. Davies (01874 625524). Secretary: Mrs E.G. Price (01874 623658). e-mail: secretary@cradoc.co.uk website: www.cradoc.co.uk

CRICKHOWELL. **Old Rectory Hotel and Golf Club**, Llangattock, Crickhowell NP8 1PH (01873 810373). *Location:* A40 to Crickhowell. Course is on a hill with spectacular views. 9 holes, 2878 yards. S.S.S. 54. *Green Fees:* information not available. *Eating facilities:* restaurant, bar meals, two bars. *Visitors:* welcome at all times, no restrictions. Accommodation available in 20 en suite bedrooms. *Society Meetings:* welcome. Secretary: G. Crawford.*

KNIGHTON. **Knighton Golf Club,** Ffrydd Wood, Knighton LD7 1DG (01547 528646). *Location:* on the A488 to Llandrindod Wells, signposted. Undulating wooded hill course with spectacular views. 9 holes, 5362 yards. S.S.S. 66. *Green Fees:* weekdays £10.00; weekends £12.00. *Eating facilities:* bar, meals available; contact Steward (01547 528646). *Visitors:* welcome, no visitors before 4.30pm on Sundays. *Society Meetings:* catered for by prior arrangement. Secretary: Mr D. B. Williams (01547 528046).

LLANDRINDOD WELLS. **Llandrindod Wells Golf Club**, The Clubhouse, Llandrindod Wells LD1 5NY (01597 823873). *Location:* signposted off A483 at south east of town. An 'Upland Links' course set in the rolling hills of mid Wales and patrolled by Red Kites and Buzzards. 18 holes, Men 5759 yards white, 5543 yards yellow, Par 69. Ladies 5143 yards, Par 72. *Green Fees:* weekdays £17.00 per round, £24.00 per day; weekends and Bank Holidays £22.00 per round, £28.00 per day. Five day ticket £70.00; seven day ticket £95.00. Year 2003 prices. Winter packages 1st November to 31st March. *Eating facilities:* full catering daily except Tuesdays when bar snacks only available, two bars. *Visitors:* welcome at all times, no restrictions. Buggy, trolley hire. *Society Meetings:* welcome any day, booking essential. Golf Shop: (01597 822247). Secretary: (Tel & Fax: 01597 823873).

LLANIDLOES. **St Idloes Golf Club,** Penrallt, Llanidloes SY18 6LG (01686 412559). *Location:* signposted from the town. Take road to Trefeglwys from Llanidloes for one mile, turn left at sharp bend before house. Meadowland and elevated course. 9 holes, 5510 yards. S.S.S. 66. Practice putting area. *Green Fees:* information not available. *Eating facilities:* snacks and meals available on most days, please telephone. *Visitors:* welcome anytime other than Sunday mornings or special competitions. *Society Meetings:* welcome, packages available. Secretary: Erys Hughes (01686 650712).*

MACHYNLLETH. **Machynlleth Golf Club,** Ffordd Drenewydd, Machynlleth SY20 8UH (01654 702000). *Location:* A489 from Newtown, left hand turn before the speed restriction sign on entering Machynlleth. Undulating meadowland course. 9 holes, 5726 yards, 5285 metres. S.S.S. 68. Small practice area. *Green Fees*: £15.00 per day. *Eating facilities:* bar. *Visitors*: welcome except during competition days. *Society Meetings*: welcome.

NEWTOWN. **St Giles Golf Club,** Pool Road, Newtown SY16 3AJ (01686 625844). *Location:* convenient to town centre, quarter-of-a-mile north east on A483 from Newtown. Challenging riverside course. 9 holes, 6012 yards. S.S.S. 70. *Green Fees:* weekdays £13.50 per day, weekends and Bank Holidays £16.00 per day. *Visitors:* welcome, with reservation Saturday afternoons and Sunday mornings. 2-Fore-1 welcome. *Society Meetings:* catered for.

RHOSGOCH. **Rhosgoch Golf Club**, Rhosgoch, Near Hay-on-Wye, Builth Wells LD2 3JY (01497 851251). *Location:* 6 miles north west of Hay-on-Wye, half-a-mile south east of the B4594. Parkland course in beautiful picturesque valley. 9 holes, 4955 yards, Par 68. S.S.S. 66. *Green Fees:* £10.00 per round. *Eating facilities:* bar/restaurant meals. *Visitors:* welcome anytime. *Society Meetings:* welcome weekdays and Saturdays. Club Steward: Andrew Davies. Secretary: Chris Dance.

WELSHPOOL. **Welsh Border Golf Club,** Bulthy Farm, Middletown, Welshpool SY21 8ER (01743 884247). *Location:* situated off the A458. Parkland course. 9 holes (x2), 6114 yards. S.S.S. 69. Driving range. *Green Fees:* information not available. *Eating facilities:* lunchtime only unless otherwise arranged. *Visitors:* welcome, but tee times must be booked. *Society Meetings:* welcome by prior arrangement. Secretary: Dennis Roberts (01743 850862/441212). *

WELSHPOOL. **Welshpool Golf Club,** Y Golfa, Golfa Hill, Welshpool SY21 9AQ (01938 850249). *Location:* A458 out of Welshpool, approximately three and a half to four miles on right. Rather hilly but spectacular views. 18 holes, 5708 yards. S.S.S. 69. *Green Fees:* weekdays £15.50 all year; weekends and Bank Holidays £15.50 1st November to 31st March, £25.50 1st April to 31st October. *Eating facilities:* open most of the day for food and drink. *Visitors:* welcome, some weekend restrictions. *Society Meetings:* welcome by arrangement, contact Don Lewis. Professional: Bob Barlow. Secretary: Don Lewis.

South Wales

ABERDARE. **Aberdare Golf Club,** Abernant, Aberdare CF44 0RY (01685 871188; Fax: 01685 872797). *Location:* half a mile from town centre. Mountain course with parkland features and view of whole Cynon Valley. 18 holes, 5875 yards. S.S.S. 69. *Green Fees:* weekdays £17.00, (with member £10.00); weekends and Bank Holidays £21.00, (with member £12.00). *Eating facilities:* bar, lounge and dining room. *Visitors:* welcome without reservation weekdays (see Professional). Saturdays and Sundays by prior arrangement with Secretary. Handicap Certificates required. Snooker room, ladies' lounge and changing room. *Society Meetings:* catered for by prior arrangement with Secretary. Professional: A. Palmer (01685 878735). Secretary: Tony Mears (01685 872797).

ABERGAVENNY. **Monmouthshire Golf Club,** Llanfoist, Abergavenny NP7 9HE. *Location*: two miles from A465 on Llanfoist to Llanellen Road (B4269). Parkland with scenic mountain views. 18 holes, 5806 yards. S.S.S. 70. Practice ground. *Green Fees*: weekdays £30.00, weekends and Bank Holidays £35.00. *Eating facilities*: bar snacks available, evening meals by arrangement. *Visitors*: welcome. Proof of membership of recognised golf club required. *Society Meetings*: catered for. Professional: Brian Edwards (Tel & Fax: 01873 852532). Secretary: R.F. Bradley (01873 852606; Fax: 01873 850470).

ABERGAVENNY. **Wernddu Golf Centre,** Old Ross Road, Abergavenny NP7 8NG (01873 856223; Fax: 01873 852177). *Location:* one and a half miles east of Abergavenny on B4521 (off A465). Sloping, well drained site with pond hazards on four holes and magnificent views. 18 holes, 5413 yards. S.S.S. 67. 24- bay covered floodlit driving range, 9 hole pitch and putt, practice putting and bunker area. *Green Fees:* £15.00. *Eating facilities:* lounge bar, light snacks. *Visitors:* welcome. *Society Meetings:* welcome. Professional: A.A. Ashmead (01873 856223; Fax: 01873 852177). Secretary: Lyn Turvey (01495 308161).

BARGOED. **Bargoed Golf Club**, Heolddu, Bargoed CF81 9GF (01443 830143). *Location:* A469 to Bargoed town centre - Moorland Road. Flat mountain top course. 18 holes, 6210 yards. S.S.S. 70. Practice area, nets, etc. *Green Fees:* £15. *Eating facilities:* full catering and bar. *Visitors:* welcome, only with member at weekends, no other restrictions. *Society*

Meetings: catered for weekdays only by prior arrangement. Professional: C Easton (01443 836411). Secretary: G. Williams (01443 830608).

BARRY. **Brynhill (Barry) Golf Club,** Port Road East, Colcot, Barry CF62 8PN (01446 720277). *Location:* leave M4 at Junction 33 (A4232), follow signs for Barry and Cardiff (Wales) Airport onto the A4050. Club on right of road, just before a roundabout. Undulating meadowland course. 18 holes, 6352 yards. S.S.S. 71. Par 72. *Green Fees:* weekdays £20.00, weekend £25.00. *Eating facilities:* Bob and Sarah extend a warm welcome, and will provide lunches between 12 noon and 2pm, afternoon teas, and dinner from 5pm. Your order prior to playing is requested. *Visitors:* welcome, except Sundays; must produce membership card and Handicap Certificate. *Society Meetings:* by arrangement with Secretary – no Sundays, must be members of a golf club. Competitive rates available. Professional: Mike Herbert (01446 720277). Joint Administrators: Rita Cook and Susan Clarke (01446 720277; Fax: 01446 740422).
website: www.brynhillgolfclub.co.uk

BARRY. **RAF St Athan Golf Club,** Clive Road, St Athan CF62 4JD (01446 751043). *Location:* eight miles from Barry, turn right through St. Athan Village. Parkland. 9 holes, 6452 yards. S.S.S. 72. Practice area and nets. *Green Fees:* information not available. *Eating facilities:* available. *Visitors:* welcome except Sundays, telephone for information. *Society Meetings:* apply through the Secretary. Secretary: P.F. Woodhouse (01446 751043; Fax: 01446 751862).

BARRY. **St Andrews Major Golf Club,** Coldbrook Road East, Near Cadoxton, Barry CF6 3BB (01446 722227; Fax: 01446 748953). *Location:* off Barry Docks Link Road, Junction 33 M4. Flat parkland course with excellent greens, full 18 holes, 5500 yards, Par 69. 12-bay floodlit driving range open 7.30am to 9.30am. *Green Fees:* £16.00 adults, £13.00 Junior/Senior. Full membership packages available to cater for all needs. *Eating facilities:* restaurant and snacks; full bar facilities, specialise in large functions up to 150 people, weddings, birthdays etc. *Visitors:* welcome anytime, but advisable to ring for bookings (especially at weekends). *Society Meetings:* we specialise in society meetings, special packages available on request. Contact Andrew Edmunds. e-mail: info@standrewsmajorgolfclub.co.uk website: www.standrewsmajorgolfclub.co.uk

BLACKWOOD. **Blackwood Golf Club**, Cwmgelli, Blackwood NP12 1EL (01495 222121/223152). *Location:* quarter of a mile north of Blackwood on A4048. 9 holes, 5350 yards. S.S.S. 67. *Green Fees:* weekdays £14.00; weekends and Bank Holidays £18.00. *Visitors:* welcome weekdays only. *Society Meetings:* by arrangement. Secretary: I. E. Power (01495 222121 or 223152).

BRIDGEND. **Coed-y-Mwstwr Golf Club**, The Clubhouse, Coychurch, Bridgend (01656 862121; Fax: 01656 864934). *Location:* Junction 35 M4, A473 towards Bridgend. Turn right into Coychurch. Parkland, south facing. 12 holes, 6144 yards. S.S.S.70. Practice nets, putting green and chipping area. *Green Fees:* weekdays £17.50, weekends £19.50. Special rates for groups of 12 or more. *Eating facilities:* bar meals and snacks. *Visitors:* members' guests only on Saturdays. *Society Meetings:* by prior arrangement. Secretary: Jim North (Tel & Fax: 01656 864934).

CAERLEON. **Caerleon Public Golf Course**, The Broadway, Caerleon, Newport NP6 1AY (01633 420342). *Location:* three miles off M4 at turnoff for Caerleon. Flat parkland. 9 holes, 3000 yards. S.S.S. 34 yellow, 35 white. Driving range, putting green. *Green Fees:* information not available. *Eating facilities:* bar, light meals (kitchen facilities) available all day. *Visitors:* welcome, must have a booking to tee off. *Society Meetings:* welcome. PGA Teaching Professional: Mark Phillips. Secretary: P. Inker (01633 667249).*

CAERPHILLY. **Caerphilly Golf Club,** Pencapel, Mountain Road, Caerphilly CF83 1HJ (029 2088 3481). *Location:* seven miles north of Cardiff on A469, 250 yards south of both railway and bus stations opposite Magistrates' Court. Mountainside course with undulating features and wooded areas. 13 holes, 6028 yards. S.S.S. 71 Increasing to 18 holes 2003. Limited practice facilities. *Green Fees:* weekdays £24.00 per round, £12.00 with a member; weekends only if playing with a member £15.00. *Eating facilities:* men's bar, ladies' lounge, mixed lounge, dining room. *Visitors:* welcome weekdays (not Bank Holidays); weekends with member only. *Society Meetings:* only a limited number by arrangement. Professional: Joel Hill (029 2086 9104). Secretary: R.J. Neill (029 2086 3441).

CAERPHILLY. **Castell Heights Golf Club,** Blaengwynlais, Caerphilly CF83 1NG (029 2088 6686). *Location:* 5 minutes from Junction 32 on M4. Flat parkland, plenty of trees. 9 holes, 2688 yards. *Green Fees:* information not available. *Eating facilities:* snacks, lunches and afternoon tea available. *Visitors:* welcome anytime, only members can book times. Professional: S. Bebb (029 2088 6666). Secretary: D. Rooney (029 2086 1128; Fax: 029 2086 9030).*

CAERPHILLY. **Mountain Lakes Golf Club,** Blaengwynlais, Caerphilly CF83 1NG (029 2086 1128). *Location:* take exit 32, M4. Last exit of roundabout "Tongwynlais", right at Lewis Arms, past Castell Coch, three miles up road on left. Part parkland, part wooded, undulating. 20 water hazards, large penncross greens. 18 holes, 6500 yards. S.S.S. 73. *Green Fees:* information not available. *Visitors:* welcome at all times but must have registered Handicap. *Society Meetings:* welcome at all times but must book. Professional: Sion Bebb (029 2088 6666). Director of Golf: P. Page (029 2086 1128; Fax 029 2086 9030).*

CAERPHILLY. **Ridgeway Golf Club**, Thornhill, Caerphilly CF83 1LY (029 2088 2255). *Location:* driving out of Cardiff towards Caerphilly over Caerphilly mountains, take first left after Traveller's Pub. Mountain course but not too steep. 9 holes, 2314 yards. S.S.S. 64. Driving range. *Green Fees:* information not available. *Eating facilities:* bar with snacks available. *Visitors:* welcome but must be member of recognised golf club. *Society Meetings:* weekdays only by arrangement. Professional: Jack Taylor. Secretary: N. Amos. *
e-mail: amos@cardiff.ac.uk.

CAERPHILLY. **Virginia Park Golf Club**, Virginia Park, Caerphilly CF83 3SW (029 2086 3919). *Location:* off Pontygwindy Road, near Caerphilly recreation centre. Flat parkland, Easy walking but challenging. 9 holes, 4661 yards, S.S.S. 63. 20 bay covered, floodlit, driving range. Practice putting green. *Green Fees:* on application. *Eating facilities:* catering available every day. *Visitors:* welcome but must observe dress code. Function room. *Society Meetings:* Telephone bookings. Professional: Joel Hill. Members' Secretary: Carol Lewis (029 2086 7891). *

CARDIFF. **Cardiff Golf Club**, Sherborne Avenue, Cyncoed, Cardiff (029 2075 3067). *Location:* two miles north of city centre or M4, A48 or A48M from east to Pentwyn exit on Eastern Avenue, and take Pentwyn Industrial Road to top of hill at Cyncoed Village, turn left at Spar shop into Sherborne Avenue. Undulating parkland, all greens bunkered. 18 holes. S.S.S. 70. *Green Fees:* £40.00. *Eating facilities:* catering and bars available from 11am every day. *Visitors:* welcome; Saturdays must play with a member. Snooker. *Society Meetings:* by arrangement - dining facility for up to 130 people. Professional: Terry Hanson (029 2075 4772). Secretary: Kenvyn Newling (029 2075 3320; Fax: 029 2068 0011).

CARDIFF. **Cottrell Park Golf Club**, St Nicholas, Cardiff CF5 6JY (01446 781781; Fax: 01446 781187). *Location*: four miles west of Cardiff on A48 main road. Two parkland courses. Driving range (20 bays) - clubhouse. Two courses: Mackintosh- 18 holes, 6377 yards. S.S.S. 72; Button - 18 holes, 6138 yards. S.S.S. 72. *Green Fees*: weekdays £25.00, weekends £35.00. *Eating facilities*: all day. *Visitors*: welcome anytime. Professional: Steve Birch.

CARDIFF. **Creigiau Golf Club**, Llantwit Road, Creigiau, Cardiff CF15 9NN (029 2089 0263). *Location:* seven miles north-west of Cardiff, two miles off A4199, M4 Junction 34 two miles. 18 holes, 6015 yards. S.S.S. 69 (Par 71). Limited practice facilities. *Green Fees:* £30.00 per day. *Eating facilities:* bars and full catering available. *Visitors:* welcome weekdays except Tuesdays, prior phone call requested; weekends with members only. Must hold Handicap Certificate. *Society Meetings:* catered for by prior arrangement (maximum 40). Professional: Ian Luntz (029 2089 0263). Secretary: (Tel & Fax: 029 2089 0263). Caterer: (029 2089 0263).

CARDIFF. **Llanishen Golf Club**, Heol Hir, Cardiff CF14 9UD (Tel & Fax: 029 2075 5078; Steward: 029 2075 2205). *Location*: five miles north of Cardiff city centre, one mile north of Llanishen village. Wooded undulating course with spectacular views. 18 holes, 5338 yards, 4881 metres. S.S.S. 67, Par 68. *Green Fees*: £32.00. Special rates for County Cards or visitors playing with member weekdays except Bank Holidays. *Eating facilities*: full bar and catering except Mondays. New clubhouse opened April 1995. *Visitors*: welcome weekdays; weekends only with member. Handicap Certificate required. *Society Meetings*: catered for Thursday and Friday, on written application. Visitors must be bona fide members of a golf club. Professional: Adrian Jones (029 2075 5076). General Manager: Anne Gregory (Tel & Fax: 029 2075 5078).

CARDIFF. **Peterstone Lakes Golf Club & Hotel,** Peterstone, Wentloog, Cardiff CF3 2TN (01633 680009; Fax: 01633 680563). *Location:* in between Newport and Cardiff off the A48 at Castleton. Parkland/links course bordering the Bristol Channel. 18 holes, 6555 yards. S.S.S. 72. Indoor teaching academy. *Eating facilities:* lounge bar, Fairways Restaurant, Crystal Suite. *Visitors:* welcome, strongly recommend telephone enquiry for a tee time. *Society Meetings:* welcome. Professional: Paul Glynn (01633 680072; Fax: 01633 680563). Manager: Peter Millar.

CARDIFF. **Radyr Golf Club,** Drysgol Road, Radyr, Cardiff CF15 8BS (029 2084 2408). *Location:* Junction 32 M4, A470 to Merthyr Tydfil, first exit. Parkland course. 18 holes, 6015 yards. S.S.S. 70. *Green Fees:* £38.00. Special rates for societies over 20 people. *Eating facilities:* snacks, lunches and evening meals (029 2084 2735). *Visitors:* welcome. *Society Meetings:* catered for Wednesdays, Thursdays and Fridays only. Professional: Rob Butterworth (029 2084 2476; Fax: 029 2084 3914). Club Manager: Alan M. Edwards (029 2084 2408; Fax: 029 2084 3914). e-mail: manager@radyrgolf.co.uk

CARDIFF. **St Mellons Golf Club,** St Mellons, Cardiff CF3 2XS (01633 680408; Fax: 01633 681219). *Location:* Junctions 28 and 30 of M4 to A48 between Cardiff and Newport. 65 year old parkland course. 18 holes, 6225 yards. S.S.S. 70. *Green Fees:* telephone for special rates. *Visitors:* welcome weekdays only. *Society Meetings:* catered for on written or telephone application. Professional: Barry Thomas (01633 680101). Secretary: R.H. Boyce (01633 680408; Fax: 01633 681219).

St Mellons Golf Club ~ Cardiff ~ 01633 680408

First opened in 1936, St Mellons is a lovely parkland course on the eastern edge of the bustling Capital city of Cardiff. Since the course was opened, some of the world's finest players have played it including Lyle, Barnes, Torrance, James, Darcy and Antonio Garrido, who held the touring Professionals' course record for many years. Visitors are very welcome at St Mellons, which is just 15 minutes' drive from the highly rated Celtic Manor, just off Junctions 28 and 30 of the M4 and 35 minutes' from the Second Severn Crossing.

Whitchurch
(Cardiff) Golf Club
18 Holes Par 71 SSS 71   Est.1914

A parkland golf course in an urban setting with panoramic views of Cardiff.

4 miles from City Centre and 600 metres from Junction 32 of M4.
Green Fees: £35 weekdays, £40 weekends/bank holidays. £15 with member.
Visitors and societies welcome • Full Catering Facilities Available

Club Professional: Eddie Clark 029 2061 4660   Club Manager: Craig R. Innes 029 2062 0985
e-mail: secretary@whitchurchcardiffgolfclub.com

See also Colour Advertisement on page 60

CARDIFF. **Wenvoe Castle Golf Club**, Wenvoe, Near Cardiff CF5 6BE (029 2059 1094; Fax: 029 2059 4371). *Location*: exit Junction 33 M4, follow signs for Cardiff Airport. Parkland course founded in 1936, fairly open layout with hilly front 9, hosted first PGA Welsh Classic. 18 holes, 6422 yards. S.S.S. 71. Practice areas. *Green Fees:* information not available. *Eating facilities:* bar snacks and restaurant meals. *Visitors:* welcome weekdays only. *Society Meetings:* catered for weekdays only, parties of 16 or more. Professional: Jason D. Harris (029 2059 3649). Secretary: Nicola Sims (Tel & Fax: 029 2059 4371).*

CARDIFF. **Whitchurch (Cardiff) Golf Club**, Pantmawr Road, Whitchurch, Cardiff CF14 7TD (029 2062 0985). *Location*: three miles north west of Cardiff on A470, 600 metres Junction 32 M4. Parkland, undulating and easy walking with panoramic views of Cardiff. A championship course with Ian Woosnam holding course record of 62. 18 holes - white tees 6258 yards. S.S.S. 71. Practice facilities. *Green Fees*: £35.00 per day weekdays, with a member £15.00; £40.00 per day weekends and Bank Holidays, with a member £15.00. *Eating facilities*: restaurant and bars. *Visitors*: welcome please phone first. Trolleys for hire. *Society Meetings*: catered for by arrangement with Club Manager. Professional: Eddie Clark (029 2061 4660). Club Manager: Craig R. Innes (029 2062 0985; Fax: 029 2052 9860).
e-mail: secretary@whitchurchcardiffgolfclub.com

CHEPSTOW. **Dewstow Golf Club**, Caerwent, Monmouthshire NP26 5AH (01291 430444; Fax: 01291 425816). *Location*: off A48 at Caerwent, between Chepstow and Newport, five miles from the Old Severn Bridge. Two 18-hole parkland courses, special features include Totem pole, Ekki bridge, 26-bay golf range. The Valley Course - Par 72, 6100 yards, The Park Course - 6200 yards. *Green Fees*: weekdays £17.00, weekends and Bank Holidays £21.00. *Eating facilities*: restaurant, function rooms and bar snacks available all day. *Visitors*: welcome at all times. Trolley and buggy hire in season. *Society Meetings*: Society and corporate days are our speciality (from £21.00 per person). Bookings and information: Hayley Battle (01291 430444). Professional: Jonathan Skuse PGA. Golf Secretary: Dave Bradbury.
e-mail: info@dewstow.com
website: www.dewstow.com

CHEPSTOW. **Marriott St Pierre Hotel and Country Club**, St Pierre Park, Chepstow, Monmouthshire NP16 6YA (01291 625261; Fax: 01291 629975). *Location*: Junction 2 of M48, A466 Chepstow, A48 Caerwent. 400 acres of beautiful parkland, some of the rarest and oldest trees in Britain. Old Course: 18 holes, 6818 yards. S.S.S. 73 off white, 71 off yellow, 75 Ladies. Mathern Course: 18 holes, 5762 yards, S.S.S. 68. 13-bay driving range with A-Star tuition facilities. *Green Fees*: £45.00. *Eating facilities*: Trophy Bar serves light bites during day, Long Weekend Cafe Bar, private suites for groups. *Visitors*: welcome, book 10 days in advance for weekdays and 48 hours in advance for weekends. *Society Meetings*: weekdays only except when resident in hotel which has 148 bedrooms all en suite, conference rooms and extensive leisure facilities. Director of Golf: Stephen Follett.

CHEPSTOW. **Shirenewton Golf Club**, Shirenewton, Chepstow NP16 6RL (01291 641642). *Location:* A48, three miles west of Chepstow, north two and three-quarter miles Shirenewton. Undulating parkland with wonderful views. 18 holes, 6607 yards. S.S.S. 72. *Green Fees:* information not available. *Eating facilities:* dining, function room, bar snacks. *Visitors:* welcome anytime but must book. *Society Meetings:* welcome but must book. Secretary: Christine Leather.*

CWMBRAN. **Greenmeadow Golf and Country Club,** Treherbert Road, Croesyceiliog, Cwmbran NP44 2BZ (01633 869321; Fax: 01633 868430). *Location:* M4 Junction 26 north on A4042, turn right at brown tourist sign for Golf Course and Driving Range. Next to Gwent Crematorium. Parkland course with undulating fairways, mature woodlands, strategically positioned lakes and bunkers. 18 holes, 6200 yards. S.S.S. 71. 26 bay floodlit driving range (8am to 10pm), putting green, six all-weather tennis courts. *Green Fees:* please phone for details and prices as there are many different packages and options. *Eating facilities:* lounge bar, patio coffee lounge and restaurant. Private function room available if required. *Visitors:* welcome, telephone golf shop for tee time. *Society Meetings:* always welcome, bookings via our golf shop. Package deals with meals available. Professional: Dave Woodman (01633 862626). Secretary: P.J. Richardson (Fax: 01633 868430).*

CWMBRAN. **Llanyrafon Golf Course**, Llanfrechfa Way, Cwmbran NP44 8HT (01633 874636). *Location:* M4 Junction 26, A4042 to Cwmbran. Flat, parkland, wooded, river enclosed course. 9 holes, 1283 yards. Practice nets, putting green. *Green Fees:* information not available. *Visitors:* always welcome. Tuition available. Professional Golf Shop. Professional: David Woodman (01633 874636). *

DINAS POWIS. **Dinas Powis Golf Club,** Golf House, Old Highwalls, Dinas Powis CF64 4AJ (029 2051 2157). *Location:* M4 Cardiff, thereafter signposted Dinas Powis, Penarth and Barry. Mostly parkland, three holes quite hilly. 18 holes, 5486 yards. S.S.S. 67. *Green Fees:* information not available. *Eating facilities:* diningroom/bar snacks except Mondays. *Visitors:* welcome weekdays, weekends by arrangement. Separate function room with bar for large societies and charity events. *Society Meetings:* welcome except Monday or Tuesday. Professional: Mr G. Bennett (029 2051 3682). Secretary: Mrs H. Williams (Tel. & Fax: 029 2051 2727).*

GLYNNEATH. **Glynneath Golf Club**, 'Penygraig', Pontneathvaughan, Near Glynneath SA11 5UH (01639 720452). *Location:* A465 trunk road to Glynneath onto B4242 to Pontneathvaughan, one and a half miles. Picturesque course overlooking Vale of Neath, in Brecon Beacons National Park, reasonably flat, half woodland, half parkland. 18 holes - white tees 5656 yards. S.S.S. 68. *Green Fees:* weekdays £17.00; weekends £22.00. *Visitors:* welcome, trolleys available; catering; snooker. *Society Meetings:* welcome weekdays and weekends, only by

arrangement. Professional: Neil Evans (01639 720872). Secretary/ Manager: (01639 720452). e-mail: glynneathgolf@tiscali.co.uk

HENGOED. **Bryn Meadows Golf Club,** Maesycwmmer, Near Hengoed CF82 7SN (01495 225590; Fax: 01495 228272). *Location:* just off A472 near Blackwood, 15 minutes to M4 Junction 28. Parkland course, spectacular views, home of British Amputee Golf Association, new challenge from every tee. 18 holes, 6100 yards. S.S.S. 69. *Green Fees:* information not available. *Eating facilities:* full à la carte restaurant, bar snacks, etc. *Visitors:* welcome weekdays, weekends by prior arrangement only. Award-winning hotel and leisure club. *Society Meetings:* welcome weekdays, weekends by prior arrangement. Professional: Bruce Hunter (01495 221905). Secretary: Stephen Brian Mayo (Fax: 01495 228272). *
e-mail: www.brynmeadows.co.uk

HENSOL. **The Vale Hotel, Golf and Spa Resort**, **Hensol Park, Hensol, Near Cardiff CF72 8JY (01443 667800).** *Location*: **set in over 450 acres of beautiful countryside yet only three minutes from Junction 34 of M4, 20 minutes from Cardiff city centre and International airport. Home to the Welsh PGA. 2 Championship standard courses - Lake Course, 6700 yards, Par 72 and Wales National Course, 7323 yards, Par 73, water features, greens to USGA standard. 20 bay driving range, short play area.** *Green Fees*: **Lake Course £35.00, Wales National Course £60.00. Corporate and society special rates on request.** *Eating facilities*: **superb eating facilities in the clubhouse and function suite.** *Visitors*: **welcome - Handicap Certificate required. Coaching available using latest video technology; pro shop. Spike and lounge bar. Buggy and trolley hire.** *Society Meetings*: **welcome, corporate days can be offered a full management service. Accommodation available in our four-star hotel. website: www.vale-hotel.com**

KENFIG. **Pyle and Kenfig Golf Club**, Waun-y-Mer, Kenfig, Near Bridgend CF33 4PU (01656 783093; Fax: 01656 772822). *Location:* one mile off M4 at Junction 37, follow Porthcawl signs. Undulating dune and downland course. 18 holes, 6741 yards, 6162 metres. S.S.S. 73. Five practice holes, driving range nearby. *Green Fees:* information not provided. *Eating facilities:* full catering facilities. *Visitors:* welcome weekdays only. *Society Meetings:* welcome by arrangement. Professional: Robert Evans (Tel & Fax: 01656 772446). Secretary: David Fellowes (01656 783093; Fax: 01656 772822).
e-mail: secretary@pyleandkenfiggolfclub.co.uk
website: www.pyleandkenfiggolfclub.co.uk

THE APPEARANCE OF AN ASTERISK (*) AT THE END OF A CLUB OR COURSE ENTRY INDICATES THAT UP-TO-DATE INFORMATION HAS NOT BEEN SUPPLIED

LLANWERN. **Llanwern Golf Club,** Tennyson Avenue, Llanwern, Newport NP18 2DW (Tel & Fax: 01633 412029). *Location:* four miles east of Newport, one mile from M4 Junction 24. Parkland. 18 holes, 6202 yards, 5581 metres. S.S.S. 70. Large practice area. *Green Fees:* information not available. *Eating facilities:* full catering and bar. *Visitors:* welcome weekdays and Thursdays especially, must have Handicap Certificate. No casual visitors at weekends. *Society Meetings:* catered for by arrangement. Professional: S. Price (01633 413233). Secretary: (Tel & Fax: 01633 412029).

MAESTEG. **Maesteg Golf Club,** Mount Pleasant, Neath Road, Maesteg CF34 9PR (01656 732037). *Location:* half a mile out of Maesteg town centre on the Port Talbot road (B4282). Reasonably flat hilltop course with scenic views over wooded hills and valleys down to Swansea Bay. 18 holes, 5929 yards. S.S.S. 69. Practice area and putting green. *Green Fees:* weekdays £17.00; weekends £20.00. Special rates for Societies. *Eating facilities:* meals available in restaurant overlooking the course, bar meals and snacks throughout the day. *Visitors:* welcome without reservation, groups of more than 12 by arrangement. *Society Meetings:* catered for weekdays only by arrangement. Secretary: Ian McBride (01656 734106).

MERTHYR TYDFIL. **Merthyr Tydfil Golf Club,** Cloth Hall Lane, Cefn Coed, Merthyr Tydfil CF48 2NU (01685 723308). *Location:* off A470 Merthyr Tydfil to Brecon Road. Mountain top course in Brecon Beacons National Park area with outstanding views. 18 holes, 5625 yards. S.S.S. 68. *Green Fees:* £10.00 weekdays; £15.00 weekends. £7.50 and £10.00 playing with member. *Eating facilities:* available by prior arrangement. *Visitors:* welcome anytime except competition days (usually Sundays). *Society Meetings:* catered for by prior arrangement. Secretary: Vivian Price.

MERTHYR TYDFIL. **Morlais Castle Golf Club,** Pant, Dowlais, Merthyr Tydfil CF48 2UY (01685 722822). *Location:* near "Heads of Valley Road", Dowlais roundabout, follow signs for Brecon Mountain Railway. Very pleasant moorland course with excellent views. 18 holes, 6320 yards, 5744 metres. S.S.S. 71. Practice area. *Green Fees:* weekdays £16.00 per day, £10.00 with member; weekends £20.00, £16.00 with a member. *Eating facilities:* clubhouse redeveloped, now offers excellent eating facilities; lounge, bars and restaurant. *Visitors:* welcome, weekends by prior arrangement with/or by application to the Secretary. *Society Meetings:* please contact Secretary. Professional: Mr H. Jarrett (Tel & Fax: 01685 388700). Secretary: Mr Meurig Price.

MONMOUTH. **Monmouth Golf Club,** Leasbrook Lane, Monmouth NP25 3SN (01600 712212). *Location:* outskirts of town on Monmouth - Ross-on-Wye dual carriageway, left turn 100 yards from roundabout; signposted. Undulating parkland, very scenic. 18 holes, 5700 yards. S.S.S. 69. Practice area, putting green. *Green Fees:* weekdays £19.00 per round, £24.00 per day; £14.0 with member; weekends and Bank Holidays £22.00 per round. £27.00 per day, £17.00 with member; juniors £7.00 at all times. *Eating facilities:* bar snacks, dining room facilities daily. *Visitors:* welcome at all times. Trolley and buggy hire. *Society Meetings:* contact the Secretary in advance. Secretary: Mr Peter Tully (Telephone & Fax: 01600 772399).
e-mail: sec.mongc@barbox.net

MONMOUTH. **The Rolls of Monmouth Golf Club,** The Hendre, Monmouth NP25 5HG (01600 715353; Fax: 01600 713115). *Location:* B4233 old Monmouth/ Abergavenny road. Arboretum wooded, hilly parkland course on private estate. 18 holes, 6283 yards. S.S.S. 71. Practice area, putting green. *Green Fees:* weekdays £36.00; weekends £40.00. Monday Special £32.00. Subject to review. *Eating facilities:* bar and catering facilities seven days a week. *Visitors:* welcome any day. Buggies and trolleys for hire. *Society Meetings:* welcome on any day including weekends. Secretary: Mrs Sandra Orton.

MOUNTAIN ASH. **Mountain Ash Golf Club,** Cefn Pennar, Mountain Ash CF45 4DT (01443 472265). *Location:* A470 Pontypridd to Aberdare road, approximately 10 miles from Pontypridd, four miles north of Abercynon. Partly wooded course. 18 holes, 5553 yards. S.S.S. 67. *Green Fees:* weekdays £20.00, £12.00 with member, weekends and Bank Holidays £20.00 only with member. *Eating facilities:* catering at club. *Visitors:* welcome anytime without reservation. *Society Meetings:* catered for, special rates by arrangement. Professional: D. Clark (01443 488770). Secretary: Geoffrey Matthews (01443 479459).

NANTYGLO. **West Monmouthshire Golf Club,** Pond Road, Nantyglo, Brynmawr NP3 4QT (01495 310233; Fax: 01495 311361). *Location:* Heads of the Valleys Road to Brynmawr, roundabout to Nantyglo, signposted. Mountain and heathland course. Now recognised as the highest golf course in Great Britain. 18 holes, 6118 yards. S.S.S. 69. *Green Fees:* information not available. *Eating facilities:* 24 hours notice required. *Visitors:* welcome. *Society Meetings:* welcome. Special package for parties – details on request. Secretary: S.E. Williams (01495 310233).*

NEATH. **Earlswood Golf Club,** Jersey Marine, Neath SA10 6JP (01792 321578). *Location:* half a mile southeast of Jersey Marine village, take B4290 turning off A483 then first right. Scenic, gently undulating course. 18 holes, 5174 yards. S.S.S. 68. *Green Fees:* £9.00. *Visitors:* pay as you play course, all visitors welcome. *Society Meetings:* by arrangement.

NEATH. **Neath Golf Club**, Cadoxton, Neath SA10 8AH (01639 643615). *Location:* two miles from Neath town centre. Mountain course, gentle slopes. 18 holes, 6492 yards. S.S.S. 72. *Green Fees:* weekdays £21.00, £13.00 with member; weekends with member only £13.00. Special rates October to March £11.00. *Eating facilities:* full catering facilities Tuesday to Sunday. *Visitors:* welcome weekdays only, Tuesdays Ladies' Day. *Society Meetings:* welcome by arrangement with Secretary. Professional: Mr R.M. Bennett (01639 633693). Secretary: Mr D.M. Hughes (01639 632759).

NEATH. **Swansea Bay Golf Club**, Jersey Marine, Neath SA10 6JP (01792 812198). *Location:* exit 42 off M4. At 1st roundabout, take B4290 turning off A483 then first right. Seaside links. 18 holes, 6605 yards. S.S.S. 72. *Green Fees:* weekdays £17.00; weekends and Bank Holidays £24.00. *Eating facilities:* bar/catering available every day from 11.00am; dinners by arrangement. *Visitors:* welcome without reservation. *Society Meetings:* by arrangement. Professional: M. Day (01792 816159). Secretary: Mrs D. Goatcher (01792 814153).

NELSON. **Whitehall Golf Club**, The Pavilion, Nelson, Treharris CF46 6ST (01443 740245). *Location:* 15 miles north of Cardiff, take A4054 off A470. Hillside course with pleasant views. 9 holes (x2), 5666 yards. S.S.S. 68. *Green Fees:* Monday to Friday £18.00, with a member £12.00. Saturdays £18.00 with or without a member but Captain's permission must be requested. Sundays/Bank Holidays by arrangement with Hon Secretary. *Eating facilities:* available, contact Steward for cooked meals. *Visitors:* welcome weekdays, weekends with members. *Society Meetings:* by prior arrangement with Secretary. Secretary: P.M. Wilde. (01443 451357).

NEWPORT. **The Celtic Manor Resort**, Coldra Woods, Newport NP18 1HQ (Resort Enquiries 01633 413000; Fax: 01633 410269). *Location:* 90 minutes from London, off Junction 24 of the M4 motorway, five minutes from new Severn Bridge. The Resort is the home of The PGA Wales Open and the venue for the Ryder Cup in 2010. Three very different and challenging Trent Jones championship courses. Scenic Wentwood Hills, Par 72; Roman Road, Par 69 - voted best inland course in Wales; Coldra Woods, Par 59, a venue for PGA short course championships. The Golf School offers comprehensive practice and coaching, two tier, floodlit driving range, 3 coaching bays with A star video graphics, practice range, award-winning Pro Shop and short play areas. *Green Fees:* information not available. *Eating facilities:* superb dining facilities available at the Clubhouse. *Visitors:* welcome. Meeting and banqueting rooms available on site. *Society Meetings:* welcome. Full event management service for Corporate Golf Days. Accommodation available at 400 bedroom hotel. Director of Golf Operations: Chris Baron. Secretary: Shane Wesson. Golf Sales (for tee-off times): 01633 410263.

NEWPORT. **Newport Golf Club,** Great Oak, Rogerstone, Newport NP10 9FX (01633 892643; Fax: 01633 896676). *Location:* M4 Junction 27, take B4591 to RISCA, one and a half miles on right. Rolling parkland. 18 holes, white tees 6460 yards, S.S.S. 71 yellow tees 6190 yards. S.S.S. 70. Two practice areas. *Green Fees:* £35.00 weekdays, £40.00 weekends. Reduced winter rates. *Eating facilities:* full dining facilities at club. *Visitors:* welcome Saturdays with members only, welcome other days; advisable to ring in advance. *Society Meetings:* welcome weekdays except Tuesdays, book only through Secretary. Professional: Paul Mayo (01633 893271). Secretary: Graham Harris (01633 892643; Fax: 01633 896676).

NEWPORT. **Parc Golf Club.** Church Lane, Coedkernew, Newport NP10 8TU (01633 680933; Fax: 01633 681011). *Location:* Junction 28 M4, then A48 three miles from Newport. Flat parkland course. 18 holes, 5512 yards, S.S.S. 69. Golf range, putting machine and putting green. *Green Fees:* information not available. *Eating facilities:* bar, conservatory, function room (can cater for 120). *Visitors:* always welcome, must pre-book. Golf days arranged, weddings, exhibitions, etc. *Society Meetings:* all catered for, minimum 12. Professional: Gareth Edwards (01633 680933). Secretary: M.V. Cleary. Manager: C. Hicks.
e-mail: enquiries@parcgolf.co.uk
website: www.parcgolf.co.uk

NEWPORT. **Tredegar Park Golf Club Ltd**, Parc-Y-Bryn, Rogerstone, Newport NP10 9TG (01633 894433). *Location:* north of M4 between Junctions 26 and 27. Newly opened parkland course. 18 holes, 6400 yards, 5850 metres. S.S.S. 72. Practice area. *Green Fees:* information not provided. *Eating facilities:* restaurant and bar. *Visitors:* welcome, must be member of affiliated club. *Society Meetings:* groups of 16 and over catered for. Professional: Lee Pagett (01633 894517). Secretary: A.J. Trickett (01633 894433; Fax: 01633 897152).

OAKDALE. **Oakdale Golf Course**, Llwynon Lane, Oakdale NP12 0NF (01495 220044). Parkland course, 9 holes. 18 bay floodlit driving range. *Green Fees:* £5.00, Juniors £4.00. *Eating facilities:* licensed bar, snacks. Snooker table. *Visitors:* welcome. Tuition available. *Society Meetings:* welcome, please pre-book. Professional: M. Griffiths.

PENARTH. **Glamorganshire Golf Club,** Lavernock Road, Penarth CF64 5UP (Tel & Fax: 029 2070 1185). *Location:* five miles west Cardiff, one mile west Penarth Centre. Parkland course overlooking Bristol Channel. 18 holes, 6150 yards. S.S.S. 70. Practice area. *Green Fees:* weekdays £35.00, weekends £40.00. *Eating facilities:* full restaurant and bar snacks, Men's bar and mixed lounge bar. *Visitors:* welcome providing no competitions in progress and/or Societies on course. Telephone call recommended. All visitors must possess current Handicap Certificate. *Society Meetings:* applications to Secretary/Manager. Reductions for parties exceeding 20. Professional: Mr A.K. Smith (029 2070 7401). Secretary/Manager: B.M. Williams (029 2070 1185).

PENCOED. **St Mary's Golf Club**, St Mary's Hill, Pencoed CF35 5EA (01656 861100; Fax: 01656 863400). *Location*: Junction 35 of M4 and take third exit at roundabout, follow A473, take road signposted Felindre for about 300 yards, we are on left. Parkland course. 18 holes, 5291 yards. S.S.S. 66. Seven Oaks 12 hole Public Course, practice area, driving range. *Green Fees:* information not available. *Eating facilities:* restaurant, three bars. *Visitors:* welcome weekdays 9am to 4pm; weekends 1pm to 4pm. 24 bedroom hotel. *Society Meetings:* welcome weekdays, restricted times at weekends. Professional: John Peters (01656 868900). Society Secretary: Leighton Janes (01656 860280).

PONTYPOOL. **Pontypool Golf Club,** Lasgarn Lane, Trevethin, Pontypool NP4 8TR (01495 763655). *Location:* Pontypool A4042 to St. Cadoc's Church, Trevethin. Undulating hillside course, with mountain turf and fine views. 18 holes, yellow tees 5838 yards. S.S.S. 69. Practice area. *Green Fees:* weekdays £20.00, weekends £24.00. *Eating facilities:* diningroom and bar snacks. *Visitors:* welcome, must have Handicap Certificates. *Society Meetings:* catered for by arrangement. Professional: Jim Howard (01495 755544). Secretary: Les Dodd (01495 763655).
e-mail: pontypoolgolf@btconnect.com
website: www.pontypoolgolf.co.uk

PONTYPOOL. **Woodlake Park Golf and Country Club**, Glascoed, Pontypool NP4 0TE (01291 673933; Fax: 01291 673811). *Location:* three miles from Usk overlooking Llandegfedd Reservoir. Undulating parkland with superb greens built to USGA specification. 18 holes, 6400 yards. S.S.S. 72. *Green Fees:* weekdays £22.50; weekends £30.00 (summer); weekdays £15.00, weekends £18.00 (winter). *Eating facilities:* spikes bar, lounge bar. *Visitors:* welcome, no restrictions. Function room for 130, games room, snooker. *Society Meetings:* welcome, must prebook, can cater for up to 100. Professional: Leon Lancey. Secretary: D. Hawker

PONTYPRIDD. **Pontypridd Golf Club**, Ty Gwyn Road, Pontypridd CF37 4DJ (01443 402359). *Location:* east side of town, off A470, 12 miles from Cardiff. Wooded mountain course. 18 holes, 5881 yards, 5378 metres. S.S.S. 68. *Green Fees:* weekdays £25.00. *Eating facilities:* bar, restaurant (restaurant closed Thursdays, snacks available). *Visitors:* welcome weekdays, Ladies' Day Tuesdays; weekends with member only. Must be member of recognised golf club in possession of Handicap Certificate. *Society Meetings:* catered for weekdays with prior reservation. Professional: Wade Walters (01443 491210). Secretary: Vikki Hooley (01443 409904; Fax: 01443 491622).

PORTHCAWL **Grove Golf Club Ltd.**, South Cornelly, Porthcawl, Mid Glamorgan CF33 4RP (01656 788771. Fax: 01656 788414). *Location:* near the Glamorgan Heritage Coast at Porthcawl on A4229 two minutes from Junction 37 off M4. Parkland course with spectacular views. 18 holes, 6128 yards, S.S.S. 69. *Green Fees:* information not available. *Eating facilities:* Full restaurant and bar snacks from 8am daily. *Visitors:* welcome every day, bookings advisable. *Society Meetings:* welcome by arrangement. A variety of packages available. Secretary: Mr Mike Thomas (01656 788771).

PORTHCAWL. **Royal Porthcawl Golf Club**, Rest Bay, Porthcawl CF36 3UW (01656 782251; Fax: 01656 771687). *Location:* Junction 37 M4, head towards Porthcawl (three miles), club located at Rest Bay. Links course. 18 holes, 6685 yards. S.S.S. 74. 27 acre practice area. *Green Fees:* information not available. *Eating facilities:* full catering and bars. *Visitors:* accepted Monday afternoons,Tuesdays, Thursdays and Fridays; limited weekend availability. *Society Meetings:* welcome. Professional: Peter Evans (01656 773702). Secretary: J.V. Dinsdale.

PORT TALBOT. **British Steel (Port Talbot) Golf Club,** Groes Fields, Margam, Port Talbot SA13 2NF (01639 871111). *Location*: Margam Park exit from M4. Flat course. 18 holes, 4808 yards. S.S.S. 64. Practice facilities. *Green Fees*: information not available. *Eating facilities*: bar meals available. *Visitors*: welcome midweek, weekends by arrangement with Secretary. Secretary: Tony Edwards (01639 791938).*

PORT TALBOT. **Lakeside Golf Club,** Water Street, Margam, Port Talbot SA13 2PA (01639 899959). *Location:* Junction 38 of M4 Port Talbot, Margam Country Park. Flat parkland course. 18 holes, 4390 yards, S.S.S. 63. 20 bay driving range. *Green Fees:* information not available. *Eating facilities:* bar meals, restaurant. *Visitors:* welcome. *Society Meetings:* welcome. Professional: Matthew Wootten (01639 888400). Secretary: Brian Channell.

RAGLAN. **Raglan Parc Golf Club**, Parc Lodge, Raglan NP5 2ER (01291 690077; Fax: 01291 690075). *Location:* near junction A40 and A449. 18 holes, 6604 yards, Par 73. *Green Fees:* weekdays £16.00, weekends £24.00. *Visitors:* welcome. *Society Meetings:* welcome; packages available. Professional: Gareth Gage. e-mail: golf@raglanparc.freeserve.co.uk

RHONDDA. **Rhondda Golf Club**, Golf House, Penrhys, Ferndale, Rhondda CF43 3PW (01443 433204). *Location:* on the Penrhys road joining Rhondda Fach and Rhondda Fawr. Mountain course. 18 holes, 6206 yards. S.S.S. 70. *Green Fees:* details on request. *Eating facilities:* all facilities daily except Mondays during winter months. *Visitors:* welcome. please telephone regarding availablilty. Handicap Certificate required. *Society Meetings:* welcome, please telephone for availability. Handicap Certificate required. Professional: Gareth Bebb PGA (01443 441385). Secretary: Paula Norman (01443 441384). e-mail: rhonddagolf@aol.com

RHYMNEY. **Tredegar and Rhymney Golf Club**, Cwmtysswg, Rhymney NP2 3BQ (01685 840743; Fax: 01685 843440). *Location:* A4048 Rhymney, Heads of the Valley road. Very scenic mountain course, lots of hazards. 18 holes, 6120 yards. S.S.S. 68. *Green Fees:* information not available. *Eating facilities:* bar snacks, meals by prior arrangement. *Visitors:* welcome at all times except Sunday mornings. *Society Meetings:* welcome at all times except Sunday mornings. Special rates. Secretary: Paul Kenealy (07944 843400).
e-mail: golfclub@tredegarandrhymney.fsnet.co.uk

SOUTHERNDOWN. **Southerndown Golf Club**, Ewenny, Bridgend CF32 0QP (01656 880326; Fax: 01656 880317). *Location:* three miles from Bridgend on the Ogmore Road. Downland overlooking Bristol Channel. 18 holes, 6449 yards. S.S.S. 72. Practice area. *Green Fees:* £35.00 weekdays; £45.00 weekends. *Eating facilities:* full dining room and bar facilities. *Visitors:* welcome any time except on competition days (check with Secretary). Handicap Certificate required. *Society Meetings:* catered for by arrangement with Secretary. Special rates dependent on number. Professional: D. McMonagle (01656 880326). Secretary: (01656 880476).
e-mail: southerndowngolf@btconnect.com

SWANSEA. **Allt-y-Graban Golf Club**, Allt-y-Graban Road, Pontlliw, Swansea SA4 1DT (01792 885757). *Location:* two miles from Junction 47 M4 turn left off A48 towards Pontarddulais, half mile past Glamorgan Arms. Parkland course. 9 holes, 4486 yards. S.S.S. 63. *Green Fees:* weekdays £8.00 for 9 holes, £12.00 for 18 holes; weekends and Bank Holidays £9.00 for 9 holes, £13.00 for 18 holes. *Eating facilities:* full club house facilities including licensed bar and meals. *Visitors:* welcome. Secretary: S. Holston.

SWANSEA. **Clyne Golf Club,** 120 Owls Lodge Lane, The Mayals, Swansea SA3 5DP (01792 401989; Fax: 01792 401078). *Location:* west of Swansea, right off Mumbles Road, signposted. Moorland course with extensive sea views. 18 holes, 6334 yards. S.S.S. 72. Large practice area, indoor and outdoor driving nets and chipping and putting green. *Green Fees:* weekdays £26.00; weekends £32.00. Winter offer - £20.00 including two course meal. *Eating facilities:* full catering facilities, fully licensed. *Visitors:* welcome except during competition days - check with Secretary. *Society Meetings:* welcome by application. Professional: Jonathan Clewett (01792 402094). Manager: Ray Thompson.
e-mail: clynegolfclub@supanet.com
website: www.clynegolfclub.com

SWANSEA. **Fairwood Park Golf Club Ltd**, Blackhills Lane, Upper Killay, Swansea SA2 7JN (01792 203648). *Location:* A4118 road - follow signs to "Sketty" and "Killay"; road to club opposite Swansea Airport. Parkland Championship course. 18 holes, 6754 yards. S.S.S. 73. Practice field and net. *Green Fees:* £25.00 per day weekdays; £30.00 per day weekends and Bank Holidays. *Eating facilities:* every day all day full range, from bar snacks to three course meals in restaurant, two licensed bars. *Visitors:* always welcome. *Society Meetings:* always welcome. Apply to Steward Mr Alan Dykes (01792 203648). Professional: Mr Gary Hughes (Tel & Fax: 01792 299194). Secretary: Mrs C.J. Beer (01792 297849).

SWANSEA. **Gower Golf Club**, Cefn Goleu, Three Crosses, Swansea (01792 872480). *Location:* Junction 47 follow signs to Gowerton. Signposted in Gowerton and Three Crosses. Rolling parkland course. 18 holes, 6441 yards. S.S.S. 72. Practice facilities. *Green Fees:* weekdays from £15.00 18 holes; weekends from £20.00 18 holes. *Eating facilities:* licensed bar, full catering facilities. *Visitors:* welcome, members start times 10am to 11am. 4 star Wales Tourist Board accommodation available for visitors. Bookings via Pro Shop (01792 879905). Tuition area. *Society Meetings:* welcome, packages arranged. Professional: Alan Williamson.

SWANSEA. **Gowerton Golf Centre**, Victoria Road, Gowerton, Swansea SA4 3AB (01792 875188; Fax: 01792 874288). Flat wooded course with rivers and bunkers. 9 holes, 1000 yards, S.S.S. 27. *Green Fees:* information not available. *Eating facilities:* Diner, hot and cold meals available. *Visitors:* open to the public. Lessons available. *Society Meetings:* welcome, group discounts. Professional: Mike Hobbs. Secretary: Steve Bromham.*
e-mail: stevenbromham@beeb.net
website: www.gowertongolf-range.com

SWANSEA. **Inco Golf Club**, Clydach, Swansea SA6 5QR (01792 841257. *Location:* easily accessible from M4. Two minutes from Junction 24 on A4067 towards Pontardawe. A flat easy-walking parkland course bordered by the meandering River Tawe. 18 holes, 6064 yards. S.S.S 69. *Green Fees:* weekdays £18.00, weekends £23.00. *Eating facilities:* full catering facilities. *Visitors:* welcome at all times. *Society Meetings:* welcome, group discounts. Secretary: D.E. Jones (01792 842929).

SWANSEA. **Langland Bay Golf Club,** Langland Bay Road, Langland, Swansea SA3 4QR (01792 361721). *Location:* Swansea A4067 to Mumbles, followed by Langland Bay. Parkland/seaside course. 18 holes, 5857 yards. S.S.S. 69. *Green Fees:* £30.00. *Eating facilities:* full catering and refreshment service provided – limited on Mondays (01792 366023). *Visitors:* welcome best to check for availability. *Society Meetings:* parties over 12 are required to book in advance. Professional: Mark Evans (01792 366186). Secretary: Mrs Lynne Coleman (01792 361721; Fax: 01792 361082).
e-mail: golf@langlandbay.sagehost.co.uk
website: www.langlandbaygolfclub.com

SWANSEA. **Morriston Golf Club,** 160 Clasemont Road, Morriston, Swansea SA6 6AJ (01792 771079). *Location:* off Junction 46 M4, turn first left and follow road for one mile, clubhouse on left hand side of road. Parkland course, rather difficult. 18 holes, 5755 yards. S.S.S. 68. Practice area. *Green Fees:* weekdays £18.00; weekends and Bank Holidays £30.00. Reduced rates playing with a member. Special rates for parties of 20 or over with prior notice. *Eating facilities:* restaurant and three bars. *Visitors:* welcome most days on application. Trolleys for hire. *Society Meetings:* welcome. Professional: D.A. Rees (01792 772335). Secretary: W.V. Thomas (Tel & Fax: 01792 796528).

SWANSEA. **Palleg Golf Club,** Lower Cwmtwrch, Swansea SA9 2QQ (01639 842193). *Location:* off A4067 (A4068) north of Swansea 14 miles, 25 miles Brecon. Meadowland course. 9 holes, 3045 yards (development ongoing for 18 holes). S.S.S. 72. *Green Fees:* information not available. *Eating facilities:* to be arranged with steward. *Visitors:* welcome through week, check with Secretary for weekends. *Society Meetings:* welcome if arranged. Secretary: Mr C. Percival.*

SWANSEA. **Pennard Golf Club,** 2 Southgate Road, Southgate, Swansea SA3 2BT (01792 233131; Fax: 01792 234797). *Location:* eight miles west of Swansea A4067, B4436. Seaside links. 18 holes, 6265 yards. S.S.S. 71. Practice areas. *Green Fees:* information not available. Eating facilities: dining room and two bars. *Visitors:* welcome at any time. Snooker room. *Society Meetings:* catered for weekdays only. Professional: M.V. Bennett (01792 233451). Secretary: E.M. Howell (01792 233131).

SWANSEA. **Pontardawe Golf Club**, Cefn Llan, Pontardawe, Swansea SA8 4SH (01792 863118). *Location:* four miles north of M4 Junction 45 on A4067 Swansea-Brecon road. Wooded course. 18 holes, 6038 yards. S.S.S. 70. *Green Fees:* £18.00. *Eating facilities:* restaurant open daily except Mondays. *Visitors:* welcome, weekends by prior arrangement only. Handicap Certificate required. *Society Meetings:* catered for by application/ appointment, parties of 20 or more - £16.00 per person for 18 holes. Professional: G. Hopkins (Tel & Fax: 01792 830977). Secretary: Keith Davey. Administrator: Mrs M. Griffiths (01792 863118; Fax: 01792 830041).

TALBOT GREEN. **Llantrisant and Pontyclun Golf Club**, Talbot Green, Pontyclun CF72 8HZ (01443 222148). *Location:* 10 miles north of Cardiff, two miles north of Junction 34 M4. Parkland. 18 holes, 5418 yards. S.S.S. 66. *Green Fees:* weekdays £20.00. Societies £17.50. *Eating facilities:* available. *Visitors:* welcome weekdays. *Society Meetings:* catered for by arrangement. Professional: Mark Phillips (01443 228169).Manager: W. Rowsell (01443 224601). e-mail: lpgc@barbox.net

USK. **Alice Springs Golf Club**, Kemeys Commander, Usk NP15 1JY (Fax: 01873 881075). *Location*: three miles north of Usk on B4598. Undulating parkland course with beautiful views across the Usk Valley. Monnow Course: 18 holes, 6185 yards. S.S.S. 72. Usk Course: 18 holes, 6041 yards. S.S.S. 69. Driving range. *Green Fees*: information not available. *Eating facilities*: restaurant facilities all day; à la carte restaurant; function room. *Visitors*: welcome at all times; telephone for tee time. *Society Meetings*: catered for, special packages available. Professional: (01873 880914). Secretary: Mr K. Morgan (01873 880708; Fax: 01873 881075).

Golf in Ireland
WHERE TO PLAY • WHERE TO STAY

Northern Ireland

ANTRIM

ANTRIM. **Massereene Golf Club**, 51 Lough Road, Antrim BT41 4DQ (028 9442 9293). *Location:* one mile S.W. of town, 3 miles from Aldergrove Airport, situated alongside the shores of Lough Neagh. 18 holes, 6602 yards. S.S.S. 72. *Green Fees:* information not available. *Eating facilities:* full catering facilities 12 noon till 9pm. *Visitors:* welcome. *Society Meetings:* catered for. Professional: Jim Smyth (028 9446 4074). Secretary: Mrs Stephanie Greene (028 9442 8096). *

BALLYCASTLE. **Ballycastle Golf Club,** Cushendall Road, Ballycastle BT64 6QP (028 2076 2536). *Location:* approximately 50 miles along the coast road west of Larne Harbour. Seaside links/undulating. 18 holes, 5744 yards, 5228 metres. S.S.S. 69. *Green Fees:* weekdays £20.00 (with member £10.00); weekends and Public Holidays £30.00 (with member £15.00). Subject to review. *Eating facilities:* catering available. *Visitors:* welcome weekdays and afternoons at weekends. *Society Meetings:* by arrangement. Professional: I. McLaughlin (028 2076 2506). Hon. Secretary: B.J. Dillon (028 2076 2536; Fax: 028 2076 9909).

BALLYCLARE. **Ballyclare Golf Club,** 25 Springvale Road, Ballyclare BT39 9JW (028 9332 2696/2352). *Location:* one and a half miles north of Ballyclare. Parkland, lakes and river. 18 holes, 6289 yards. S.S.S. 71. Practice ground. *Green Fees:* weekdays £20.00; weekends £25.00. *Eating facilities:* catering available. *Visitors:* welcome weekdays except Thursday. *Society Meetings:* catered for. Special rates for 20 plus. Secretary: H. McConnell (028 9332 2696).

BALLYCLARE. **Greenacres Golf Club**, 153 Ballyrobert Road, Ballyclare BT39 9RT (028 9335 4111; Fax: 028 9335 4166). *Location:* three miles from Corrs Corner on B56. Parkland course, 18 holes. Par 71. S.S.S. 68. Floodlit driving range. *Green Fees:* information not available. *Eating facilities:* bar and catering available.*

visit the FHG golf website on
www.uk-golfguide.com

BALLYMENA. **Ballymena Golf Club**, 128 Raceview Road, Ballymena BT42 4HY (028 2586 1207). *Location:* two miles north east of town on A42. Flat/parkland/ heathland. 18 holes, 5299 metres. S.S.S. 67. *Green Fees:* information not available. *Eating facilities:* restaurant and bar snacks. *Visitors:* welcome at all times, except Tuesdays and Saturdays. *Society Meetings:* catered for except Tuesdays and Saturdays.. Professional: Ken Revie (028 2586 1652). Secretary: Carl McAuley (Tel & Fax: 028 2586 1487). *

BALLYMENA. **Galgorm Castle Golf Club**, Galgorm Castle, Ballymena BT42 1HL (028 2564 6161; Fax: 028 2565 1151). *Location:* 1 mile south of Ballymena on A42 to Galgorm village. Mature parkland course in the grounds of one of Ireland's most historic castles. 18 holes, 6736 yards, S.S.S. 72. Driving range, practice area. *Green Fees:* £30.00 weekdays, £35.00 weekends and Bank Holidays. *Eating facilities:* full restaurant and bar. *Visitors:* welcome. Accommodation and tuition available. *Society Meetings:* welcome, special rates available. Professional: Phil Collins (028 2564 6161; Fax: 028 2565 1151). Secretary: Barbara McGeown (028 2565 0210).
e-mail: golf@galgormcastle.com
website: www.galgormcastle.com

BALLYMONEY. **Gracehill Golf Club**, 141 Ballinlea Road, Stranocum, Ballymoney BT53 8PX (028 2075 1209; Fax: 028 2075 1074). *Location:* Ballymoney; International Airport (40 minutes). Parkland. Opened May 1995 with American-style water hazards. 18 holes, 6525 yards. S.S.S. 73. Practice area. *Green Fees:* Monday to Friday £20.00, Saturday/Sunday £25.00. *Eating facilities:* restaurant/bar. *Visitors:* telephone for tee time. *Society Meetings:* all welcome. Secretary: Mr D. Kennedy.
website: www.gracehillgolfclub.co.uk

BELFAST. **Cliftonville Golf Club**, 44 Westland Road, Belfast BT14 6NH (028 9074 4158). Parkland with rivers bisecting three fairways. 9 holes, 6210 yards, 5672 metres. S.S.S. 70. Practice fairway and nets. *Green Fees:* weekdays £16.00; weekends £20.00. *Eating facilities:* bars, catering on request. *Visitors:* no visitors after 5pm weekdays until 6pm on Saturdays, and until 1.30 pm Sundays. *Society Meetings:* very welcome, especially by arrangement. Professional: Peter Hannah. Hon. Secretary: E. Lusty O.B.E (028 9074 6595).

Galgorm Castle Golf & Country Club

Galgorm Castle, Galgorm Road, Ballymena, Co. Antrim, Northern Ireland BT42 1HL
A mature parkland course in the grounds of one of Ireland's most historic castles.
Visitors always welcome • Tel: 028 2564 6161 • Fax: 028 2565 1151
Website: www.galgormcastle.com • e-mail: golf@galgormcastle.com

BELFAST. **Dunmurry Golf Club,** 91 Dunmurry Lane, Dunmurry, Belfast BT17 9JS (028 9061 0834; Fax: 028 9060 2540). *Location:* off M1 at Dunmurry, to village, turn left past Tesco, one and a half miles on right. Parkland, partially wooded. 18 holes, 6080 yards. S.S.S. 69. Practice area. *Green Fees:* weekdays £27.00; Sundays £37.00. Subject to review. *Eating facilities:* restaurant (not Mondays) and bar. *Visitors:* welcome by arrangement; not Fridays (Ladies' Day) and not Saturdays. Trolleys available. *Society Meetings:* welcome by written application; 20 or more £23.00. Professional: John Dolan (028 9062 1314; Fax: 028 9060 2540). Golf Manager: Tony Cassidy (028 9061 0834; Fax: 028 9060 2540).

BELFAST. **Fortwilliam Golf Club,** Downview Avenue, Belfast BT15 4EZ (028 9077 6798). *Location:* one mile Fortwilliam Junction M2. Parkland. 18 holes, 6030 yards. S.S.S. 69. *Green Fees:* weekdays £22.00; weekends £29.00. *Eating facilities:* excellent catering and bar. *Visitors:* welcome every day except Saturdays. *Society Meetings:* catered for Tuesdays and Thursdays, special rates available. Professional: Peter Hanna (Tel & Fax: 028 9077 0980). Secretary: M. Purdy (028 9037 0770; Fax: 028 9078 1891).

BELFAST. **Gilnahirk Golf Club**, Manns Corner, Upper Braniel Road, Gilnahirk, Belfast BT5 7TX (028 9044 8351). *Location:* two miles from city centre, east Belfast. Parkland. 9 holes, 5398 metres. S.S.S. 68. Practice area and putting green. *Green Fees:* information not available. *Eating facilities:* Saturdays only. *Visitors:* welcome, no restrictions. Club hire *Society Meetings:* all welcome. Professional: Mr K. Gray (028 9044 8477). Secretary: Mr A. Carson (028 9065 9653).*

BELFAST. **Malone Golf Club**, 240 Upper Malone Road, Dunmurry, Belfast BT17 9LB (028 9061 2758; Fax: 028 9043 1394). *Location:* five miles south of Belfast city centre, opposite Lady Dixon Park. Parkland, wooded course with large lake. 18 holes, 6599 yards. S.S.S. 71. 9 holes, 6320 yards. S.S.S. 70 (9 holes x 2). Practice ground, putting green. *Green Fees:* £40.00 weekdays, Ladies £30.00; £45.00 weekends and Bank Holidays, Ladies £35.00. *Eating facilities:* bar, bar snacks and restaurant. *Visitors:* welcome weekdays except Tuesdays (Ladies' Day); time sheet on weekends. Dress code observed on course and in clubhouse. Golf carts for hire. *Society Meetings:* welcome by arrangement Mondays and Thursdays. Professional: Michael McGee (Tel & Fax: 028 9061 4917). Manager: J.N.S. Agate (028 9061 2758; Fax: 028 9043 1394).

CARRICKFERGUS. **Carrickfergus Golf Club**, 35 North Road, Carrickfergus BT38 8LP (028 9336 3713; Fax: 028 9336 3023). *Location:* North Road, one mile from main shore road. Fairly flat parkland course, partially wooded. 18 holes, 5768 yards. S.S.S. 68. *Green Fees:* information not available. *Eating facilities:* full catering and bar facilities. *Visitors:* welcome except on Friday afternoons and weekends. *Society Meetings:* catered for on weekdays but not after 1pm on Fridays. PGA Professional: M. Stanford PGA (028 9336 3713; Fax: 028 9336 3023). Manager: John Thomson (028 9336 3713; Fax: 028 9336 3023).

CARRICKFERGUS. **Greenisland Golf Club,** 156 Upper Road, Greenisland, Carrickfergus BT38 8RW (028 9086 2236). *Location:* situated at the foot of Knockagh Hill and on the edge of Carrickfergus town, one of the best features is the scenic view over Belfast Lough. Parkland course. 9 holes, 5624 metres. S.S.S. 69. *Green Fees:* weekdays £12.00; weekends £18.00. 50% off fees if playing with a member. *Eating facilities:* lunch and evening meals available, bar snacks. *Visitors:* welcome; Saturdays not before 5.30pm. *Society Meetings:* welcome by prior arrangement. Hon. Secretary: W.J. McLaughlin.

CARRICKFERGUS. **Whitehead Golf Club**, McCrea's Brae, Whitehead, Carrickfergus BT38 9NZ (028 9337 0822). *Location:* Whitehead, 15 miles from Belfast, 10 miles from Larne. 18 holes, 6050 yards. S.S.S. 69. *Green Fees:* weekdays £20.00, £11.00 with a member; weekends with member only. *Eating facilities:* by arrangement with Caterer. *Visitors:* welcome Monday to Friday, weekends with member only. *Society Meetings:* by prior arrangement. Professional: C. Farr (028 9337 0821. Secretary/Manager: (028 9337 0820 9am - 5pm; Fax: 028 9337 0825). Caterer (028 9337 0823).

CUSHENDALL. **Cushendall Golf Club,** 21 Shore Road, Cushendall BT44 0NG (028 2177 1318). *Location:* 25 miles north on Antrim coast road from Larne Harbour. Seaside wooded course; river comes into play in seven out of nine holes. 9 holes, 4384 metres. S.S.S. 63. *Green Fees:* weekdays £13.00 per day, weekends and Bank Holidays £18.00; £5.00 concession if playing with member. *Eating facilities:* normal bar hours, bar snacks, full catering by arrangement. *Visitors:* welcome without reservation, avoid Wednesday afternoons, Thursday Ladies' Day, time sheet in operation on Sundays. *Society Meetings:* welcome. Hon. Secretary: Shaun McLaughlin (028 2175 8366).

LARNE. **Cairndhu Golf Club Ltd,** 192 Coast Road, Ballygally, Larne BT40 2QG (Tel & Fax: 028 2858 3324). *Location:* three miles north of Larne on the famous Antrim Coast road leading to the Glens of Antrim. Parkland course with stunning views. 18 holes, 5611 metres. S.S.S. 69. Practice area, driving range. *Green Fees:* Monday to Friday £20.00, Sunday £25.00. *Eating facilities:* restaurant and bar. *Visitors:* welcome except Saturdays. *Society Meetings:* welcome. Professional: Bob Walker (Tel & Fax: 028 2858 3324). General Manager: Michael Corsar.

LARNE. **Larne Golf Club**, 54 Ferris Bay Road, Islandmagee, Larne BT40 3RT (028 9338 2228; Fax: 028 9338 2088). *Location:* six miles north of Whitehead on Browns Bay Road. Part links, part parkland. 9 holes, 6288 yards. S.S.S. 70. Practice ground. *Green Fees:* weekdays £10.00, with a member £5.00; weekends £18.00, with a member £9.00. *Eating facilities:* bar, restaurant. *Visitors:* welcome Mondays to Thursdays, and Sundays. Snooker table. *Society Meetings:* welcome on application (not Friday or Saturday). 10% reduction for societies of 20 or more. Secretary: R.I. Johnston.

LISBURN. **Lisburn Golf Club,** Blaris Lodge, 68 Eglantine Road, Lisburn BT27 5RQ (028 9267 7216; Fax: 028 9260 3608). *Location:* three miles south of Lisburn on A1. Parkland. 18 holes, 6647 yards. S.S.S. 72. Practice area. *Green Fees:* £30.00 weekdays; weekends and Bank Holidays £35.00. *Eating facilities:* bar and restaurant. *Visitors:* welcome weekdays, Tuesdays Ladies have preference. Saturday after 5.30pm only, Sundays with member only. Snooker room. *Society Meetings:* Mondays and Thursdays only. Professional: S. Hamill (028 9267 7217). Manager: G.E. McVeigh (028 9267 7216). e-mail: lisburngolfclub@aol.com

MAZE. **Down Royal Park Golf Course**, 6 Dunygarton Road, Maze BT27 5RT (Tel & Fax: 028 9262 1339). *Location:* Belfast – Hillsborough road. Lisburn – Moira road. Heathland. 18 holes, 6824 metres. S.S.S. 72. *Green Fees:* weekdays £17.00, weekends £20.00. Off peak rates: weekdays £12.00 starts after 1pm , weekends £15.00 starts after 1pm. *Eating facilities*: available. *Visitors*: G.U.I. dress code applies. Budget accommodation available. *Society Meetings*: all welcome.

NEWTOWNABBEY. **Ballyearl Golf and Leisure Centre**, 585 Doagh Road, Newtownabbey BT36 8RZ (028 9084 8287; Fax: 028 9084 4896). *Location:* eight miles north of Belfast, 15 miles south of Larne. From Belfast follow signs to Larne via M2 (A8), turn right to Mossley approximately one miles from Corrs Corner Pub. Ballyearl is one mile on left. Parkland. 9 holes, 2402 yards, 2196 metres. Par 3. 27 bay covered floodlit driving range, outdoor grass teeing area. *Green Fees:* information not provided. *Eating facilities:* snacks available in Squash Club bar. *Visitors:* no restrictions – pay and play. Squash courts, hi-tech fitness suite and arts theatre. Golf lessons available by appointment, golf equipment tailored to individual requirements and can be tested on driving range. Professional: Richard Johnston (028 9084 0899).

PORTBALLINTRAE. **Bushfoot Golf Club,** 50 Bushfoot Road, Portballintrae BT57 8RR (028 2073 1317). *Location:* off Ballaghmore Road, Portballintrae. Seaside links course. 9 holes, 6075 yards. S.S.S 67. *Green Fees:* weekdays £15.00; weekends £19.00. *Eating facilities:* full dining room, bars. *Visitors:* welcome, restrictions weekends July to September. *Society Meetings:* all welcome weekdays. Secretary/Manager: J. Knox Thompson.

PORTRUSH. **Rathmore Golf Club,** Bushmills Road, Portrush BT56 8JG (028 7082 2285). *Location:* north east coast - six miles from Coleraine, beside roundabout on road to Bushmills. Royal Portrush Golf Club (valley links). Flat seaside links. 18 holes, 6304 yards. S.S.S. 70. *Green Fees:* information not available. *Eating facilities:* bar but no eating facilities. *Visitors:* Saturday and Sunday 1.30 to 2.30pm, Monday to Friday no restrictions except Tuesday after 11am September to March and Thursday from 5-6pm May to August. *Society Meetings:* must register at Royal Portrush Golf Club and pay green fees before commencement of play. Professional: Gary McNeill (R.P.G.C.) (028 7082 2311). Secretary: Derek Ross Williamson (Tel & Fax: 028 7082 2996).*

visit the FHG golf website on

www.uk-golfguide.com

PORTRUSH. **Royal Portrush Golf Club,** Dunluce Road, Portrush BT56 8JQ (028 7082 2311). *Location:* one mile from Portrush on the main Portrush/Bushmills Road. Dunluce Course-natural seaside links. 18 holes, 6845 yards. S.S.S. 73. Valley Course - flat seaside links. 18 holes, 6304 yards. S.S.S 71. Two practice grounds. *Green Fees:* information not available. *Eating facilities:* three bars, restaurant with snacks and à la carte. *Visitors:* Dunluce Course: must contact Secretary prior to visit. Restrictions Wednesday and Friday afternoons and Saturday and Sunday mornings. Valley Course: welcome weekdays, plus limited tee times at weekends. *Society Meetings:* accepted with prior bookings. Professional: Gary McNeill (028 7082 3335). Secretary: Miss W. Erskine (028 7082 2311; Fax: 028 7082 3139).*
e-mail: info@royalportrushgolfclub.com

TEMPLEPATRICK. **Hilton Templepatrick Golf Club,** Paradise Walk, Castle Upton Estate, Templepatrick BT39 0DD (02894 435542; Fax: 02894 435511). *Location:* 5 miles from Belfast International Airport, 15 miles from Belfast city centre. Parkland course - USGA greens. 18 holes, 7010 yards. S.S.S. 71. Driving range and putting green. Host to Ulster PGA Championship 2000 and 2001. *Green Fees:* £40.00 weekdays, £45.00 weekends. Discounts for groups over 12. *Eating facilities:* à la carte Restaurant and Bar Brasserie in 4 star hotel. *Visitors:* welcome. 130 bedroomed hotel, Livingwell Health Club, Tuition package. *Society Meetings:* welcome, no restrictions. Professionals: Eamonn Logue/Lynn McCool (02894 435542; Fax: 02894 435511). Director of Leisure: Bill Donald: (02894 435510; 02894 435511).
e-mail: Bill_donald@hilton.com

ARMAGH

ARMAGH. **County Armagh Golf Club**, 7 Newry Road, Armagh BT60 1EN (028 3752 2501). *Location:* Armagh/Newry road. Parkland course. 18 holes, 6212 yards. S.S.S. 69. Practice area available. *Green Fees:* £15.00 weekdays, £20.00 weekends. November to February (incl.) reduction of £1.00. *Eating facilities:* diningroom/bar meals Tuesdays to Sundays, bar facilities daily. *Visitors:* welcome by arrangement. Not Saturdays or Thursdays. Carts and buggies. *Society Meetings:* welcome by arrangement except Saturdays or Thursdays. Professional: Alan Rankin (Tel & Fax: 028 3752 5864). Secretary: June McParland (Tel & Fax: 028 3752 5861).

CRAIGAVON. **Craigavon Golf and Ski Centre**, Turmoyra Lane, Lurgan, Craigavon (028 3832 6606; Fax: 028 3834 7272). *Location:* half a mile from motorway, one mile from town centre, adjacent to ski slope. Parkland/wooded. 18 holes, 5901 meters. S.S.S. 72. 9 hole Par 3. 12 hole pitch and putt. Driving range. *Green Fees:* information not available. *Eating facilities:* full restaurant facilities. *Visitors:* always welcome. Modern clubhouse, showers and lockers. *Society Meetings:* welcome - book beforehand. Professional: D. Paul. *

CRAIGAVON. **Edenmore Golf and Country Club**, Edenmore House, 70 Drumnabreeze Road, Magheralin, Craigavon BT67 0RH (028 9261 9241; Fax: 028 9261 3310). *Location:* take main road for Lurgan, coming off M1 at Moira Exit. Signposted from village of Magheralin on main Moira – Lurgan Road. Undulating, parkland course with panoramic views. Well drained. 18 holes, 6244 yards. S.S.S. 70. Practice facilities, putting green. *Green Fees:* weekdays £16.00, weekends £20.00. *Eating facilities:* Bailies restaurant. *Visitors:* Edenmore is a friendly, welcoming club. Visitors at all times except Saturdays before 3pm. Tuition on request. *Society Meetings:* welcome. Ring to book. Secretary: Kenneth Logan (028 9261 1310; Fax: 028 9261 3310). e-mail: info@edenmore.com website: www.edenmore.com

CULLYHANNA. **Ashfield Golf Club,** Freeduff, Cullyhanna, Newry (028 3086 8180; Fax: 028 3086 8611). *Location:* A29 road, from Newry to Crossmaglen, 15 miles distance. Parkland course, lake, water hazard, bunkers. 18 holes, 5616 yards. S.S.S. 67. Par 69. Driving range. *Green Fees:* information not available. *Eating facilities:* licensed restaurant. *Visitors:* welcome at all times except before 11am on Sundays. *Society Meetings:* welcome, special rates available. Professional: Erill Maney. Secretary: Pearse Maginnis. *

LURGAN. **Lurgan Golf Club**, The Demesne, Lurgan, Craigavon BT67 9BN (028 3832 2087; Fax: 028 3831 6166). *Location:* one mile from motorway, half a mile from town centre. Parkland. 18 holes, 5895 metres. S.S.S. 69. Small practice area, putting green. *Green Fees:* weekdays £15.00; weekends £20.00. Reductions if playing with a member. Students £10.00, under 18s £5.00. *Eating facilities:* restaurant and lounge bar. Caterer: (028 3832 2087). *Visitors:* welcome Monday to Friday, and Sundays after 3pm. *Society Meetings:* welcome as per visitors. Professional: Des Paul (028 3832 1068). Secretary: Muriel Sharpe (028 3832 2087; Fax: 028 3831 6166).

PORTADOWN. **Portadown Golf Club**, 192 Gilford Road, Portadown BT63 5LF (028 3835 5356). *Location:* on main Gilford Road out of Portadown. Parkland. 18 holes, 5649 metres. S.S.S. 69 off white tees; 68 off green tees, 72 off red tees. *Green Fees:* weekdays £18.00; weekends and Bank Holidays £23.00. *Eating facilities:* Contact caterer on 028 3835 2214. *Visitors:* welcome at all times except Tuesdays and Saturdays. Squash, indoor bowling and snooker. *Society Meetings:* catered for by booking. Professional: Paul Stevenson (028 3833 4655). Secretary: Mrs Lily Holloway (028 3835 5356).

TANDRAGEE. **Tandragee Golf Club,** Markethill Road, Tandragee, Craigavon BT62 2ER (028 3884 1272; Fax: 028 3884 0664). *Location:* approximately five miles from Portadown on road to Newry and Dublin. Hilly parkland and wooded. 18 holes, 5754 metres. S.S.S. 70, Par 71. Practice ground and net. *Green Fees:* weekdays £15.00 for men, £11.00 for ladies; weekends £20.00 for men, £18.00 for ladies. Juniors £5.00. *Eating facilities:* full catering except Mondays; two lounges. *Visitors:* welcome all days except Thursdays (Ladies' Day) and Saturdays (competition day). Carts and buggies available. *Society Meetings:* welcome by arrangement. Professional: D. Keenan (028 3884 1761). Secretary/ Manager: David Clayton. e-mail: office@tandragee.co.uk website: www.tandragee.co.uk

Co. DOWN

ARDGLASS. **Ardglass Golf Club,** 4 Castle Place, Ardglass BT30 7TP (028 4484 1219; Fax: 028 4484 1841). *Location:* nearest town – Downpatrick. Situated on the coast 30 miles due south of Belfast. Seaside links. 18 holes, White markers - 6231 yards. S.S.S. 70, Par 70. *Green Fees:* weekdays £30.00; weekends £42.00. Subject to review. *Eating facilities:* bar and dining room. *Visitors:* welcome all week. *Society Meetings:* welcome except Saturdays, advance booking necessary. Professional: Philip Farrell (028 4484 1022). Club Manager: Miss Deborah Polly (028 4484 1219; Fax: 028 4484 1841). e-mail: info@ardglassgolfclub.com website: www.ardglassgolfclub.com

BALLYNAHINCH. **Spa Golf Club,** 20 Grove Road, Ballynahinch BT24 8PN (028 9756 2365; Fax: 028 9756 4158). *Location:* Ballynahinch half mile, 11 miles south of Belfast. Parkland, wooded course with panoramic views. 18 holes, 5938 yards. S.S.S. 72. Practice area. *Green Fees:* weekdays £15.00; weekends £20.00. *Eating facilities:* bar snacks/ restaurant service. *Visitors:* welcome except Saturdays. *Society Meetings:* welcome, discount for large parties. Secretary: T.G. Magee (028 9756 2365).

BANBRIDGE. **Banbridge Golf Club,** Huntly Road, Banbridge BT32 3UR. *Location:* half-a-mile from town centre on the Huntly Road. Parkland. 18 holes, 5590 yards. S.S.S. 67. Practice ground. *Green Fees:* weekdays £17.00, with a member £10.00; weekends £22.00, with a member £12.00. Societies £14.00 weekdays, £17.00 Sundays. *Eating facilities:* full catering and bar facilities. *Visitors:* welcome, restrictions on Ladies' Day (Tuesdays) and men's competition day (Saturdays). *Society Meetings:* catered for; arrange with Secretary/Manager: Mrs J.A. Anketell (028 4066 2211).
e-mail: info@banbridge-golf.freeserve.co.uk

BANGOR. **Bangor Golf Club,** Broadway, Bangor BT20 4RH (028 9127 0922; Fax: 028 9145 3394). *Location:* one mile from town centre off Donaghadee Road. Parkland. 18 holes, 6424 yards. S.S.S. 71. Practice facilities. *Green Fees:* information not available. *Eating facilities:* dining room (booking essential), lunches and evening meals, bar snacks. *Visitors:* welcome except Saturdays; Tuesday is Ladies' Day. Trolleys. *Society Meetings:* advance booking necessary. Professional: Michael Bannon (028 9146 2164). Secretary: David J. Ryan.

BANGOR. **Blackwood Golf Centre,** 150 Crawfordsburn Road, Bangor BT19 1GB (028 9185 2706). *Location:* west of Bangor. Two 18-hole courses. Driving range. *Green Fees:* on application. *Visitors:* welcome.

BANGOR. **Carnalea Golf Club**, Station Road, Bangor BT19 1EZ (028 9146 5004). *Location:* one minute walk from Carnalea Railway Station. Seaside parkland. 18 holes, 5574 yards. S.S.S. 67. *Green Fees:* weekdays £17.50; weekends £22.00. *Eating facilities:* full restaurant and two bars. *Visitors:* welcome without reservation. *Society Meetings:* catered for. Golf Shop (028 9127 0122). Professional: Tom Loughran (028 9127 0122). Secretary: G. Steele (028 9127 0368; Fax: 028 9127 3989).

BANGOR. **Helen's Bay Golf Club**, Golf Road, Helen's Bay, Bangor BT19 1TL (028 9185 2815). *Location:* A2 from Belfast - 9 miles. Parkland. 9 holes, 5161 metres. S.S.S. 67. *Green Fees:* weekdays £17.00; Friday, Sunday, Bank and Public Holidays £20.00. *Eating facilities:* available - full restaurant, bar and lounge bar (028 9185 2816). *Visitors:* welcome Sunday, Monday, Wednesday and Friday; Tuesday is Ladies' Day. *Society Meetings:* catered for by prior booking confirmed by the Secretary Manager (maximum 40). Secretary Manager: (Tel & Fax: 028 9185 2815).

BELFAST. **Balmoral Golf Club Ltd**, 518 Lisburn Road, Belfast BT9 6GX (028 9038 1514). *Location:* M1 from Belfast exit Balmoral, turn right at lights Lisburn Road, quarter mile on left beside Kings Hall or two/three miles south of Belfast on main Lisburn Road next to Kings Hall. A flat undulating course with 30 plus bunkers and a stream to contend with. Excellent greens, approached by tree-lined fairways. 18 holes, 6034 metres. S.S.S. 70 Medal, 69 regular. Practice ground and nets. *Green Fees:* information not available. *Eating facilities:* restaurant, lunch,

dinner, snacks à la carte, two bars. *Visitors:* welcome except Saturdays; restricted on Sundays. *Society Meetings:* Mondays, Thursdays and Sunday afternoons. Professional: Geoff Bleakley (028 9066 7747). Chief Executive: Terry Graham (028 9038 1514; Fax: 028 9066 6759).*

BELFAST. **Belvoir Park Golf Club,** 73/75 Church Road, Newtownbreda, Belfast BT8 7AN (028 9049 1693; Fax: 028 9064 6113). *Location:* three miles from city centre, Saintfield Road. Parkland, well wooded. 18 holes, 6501 yards, 5943 metres. S.S.S. 71. Practice area. *Green Fees:* information not available. *Eating facilities:* full catering and bar. *Visitors:* welcome except Saturday. *Society Meetings:* by prior booking only. Director of Golf: M. Kelly (028 9064 6714). Secretary: Ann Vaughan (028 9049 1693).*

BELFAST. **Knock Golf Club**, Summerfield, Dundonald, Belfast BT16 2QX (028 9048 2249; Fax: 028 9048 7277). *Location:* Upper Newtownards Road in east of the city of Belfast. Parkland with huge trees, large bunkers and a stream running through the course. 18 holes, 6435 yards. S.S.S. 71. Practice ground. *Green Fees:* weekdays £20.00, weekends and Bank Holidays £25.00. Subject to review. *Eating facilities:* full catering and bar facilities available. *Visitors:* welcome except Saturday but it is advisable to ring Professional first. Trolleys available. *Society Meetings:* catered for Mondays and Thursdays. Advance booking required; parties up to 40 £18.00 each, over 40 £15.00 each. Professional: G. Fairweather (028 9048 3825). Secretary/Manager: Mrs A. Armstrong (028 9048 3251).

BELFAST. **Ormeau Golf Club,** 50 Park Road, Belfast BT7 2FX (028 9064 0700; Fax: 028 9064 6250). *Location:* Belfast south/east; Ravenhill Road. Flat, parkland wooded course. 9 holes, 2678 yards, 2447 metres. S.S.S. 66. *Green Fees:* information not available. *Eating facilities:* bars and restaurant. *Visitors:* welcome, restrictions on Tuesdays and Saturdays. Snooker. *Society Meetings:* welcome most days. Shop Manager: Mr B. Wilson (028 90 640999). Manager: Mr W. Lynn (028 9064 0700). Caterer: (028 9064 1999).

BELFAST. **Shandon Park Golf Club**, 73 Shandon Park, Belfast BT5 6NY (028 9079 3730). Parkland. 18 holes, 5714 metres. S.S.S. 70. *Green Fees:* information not available. *Eating facilities:* restaurant facilities, bar snacks. *Visitors:* welcome except Saturdays subject to advance clearance by Professional. *Society Meetings:* Mondays and Fridays only. Professional: Barry Wilson (028 9079 7859). Secretary/Manager: Mr David Jenkins (028 9040 1856; Fax: 028 9040 2773). *

DONAGHADEE. **Donaghadee Golf Club**, 84 Warren Road, Donaghadee BT21 0PQ (028 9188 8697). *Location:* five miles south of Bangor on main coast road. Part links and inland park with scenic views over Copeland Islands and Scottish coast. 18 holes, 6000 yards, 5561 metres. Par 71, S.S.S. 69. Practice ground and putting green. *Green Fees:* weekdays £22.00; Sundays £25.00. *Eating facilities:* full catering available, seven days in summer, Tuesday to Sunday in winter. *Visitors:* welcome on any weekday and Sundays; Members only on Saturdays. Ladies welcome on Tuesdays. Juveniles must be accompanied by an adult. Pro shop. Club and trolley hire. Lessons available by prior arrangement. *Society Meetings:* welcome any day except Saturday. Special rates available. Professional: Gordon Drew (028 9188 2392). General Manager: Ron Thomas (028 9188 3624; Fax: 028 9188 8891) e-mail: deegolf@freenet.co.uk.

DOWNPATRICK. **Bright Castle Golf Club**, 14 Coniamstown Road, Bright, Downpatrick BT30 8LU (028 4484 1319). *Location:* turn right off the main Downpatrick/Killough road after approx. 4 miles (turn right a further 1 mile along this road). 18-hole parkland course, well wooded, features one of the longest holes in the British Isles (16th, 615 yards). 7110 yards. S.S.S. 74. *Green Fees:* £12.00 weekdays, £14.00 weekends. *Eating facilities:* Excellent new clubhouse opened March 2002 with full bar and restaurant. *Visitors:* very welcome, no restrictions. *Society Meetings:* very welcome, tee must be reserved. Secretary: Thomas Johnston (028 4482 8428).

DOWNPATRICK. **Downpatrick Golf Club**, 43 Saul Road, Downpatrick BT30 6PA (028 4461 5947; Fax: 028 4461 7502). *Location:* one and a half miles from town centre, south-east direction. Parkland, challenging upland course. 18 holes, 6120 yards. S.S.S. 69. Practice area and putting area. *Green Fees:* weekdays £20.00; weekends and Bank Holidays £25.00. *Eating facilities:* two lounges and diningroom. Catering: (028 4461 5244). *Visitors:* welcome, but advisable to make arrangements in advance for weekends. Snooker room. *Society Meetings:* welcome by prior arrangement. Professional: Robert Hutton (028 4461 5167). Finance Manager/Administrator: Barbara-Ann Hitchens.

HOLYWOOD. **Holywood Golf Club**, Nuns Walk, Demesne Road, Holywood BT18 9LE (028 9042 3135/2138; Fax: 028 9042 5040). Parkland. 18 holes, 5430 yards. S.S.S. 68. *Green Fees:* information not available. *Eating facilities:* bars and restaurant. *Visitors:* welcome, Thursday is Ladies' Day. *Society Meetings:* welcome Mondays, Tuesdays, Wednesdays and Fridays and between 8am and 9am Sundays. Professional: Paul Gray (028 9042 5503; Fax: 028 9042 5040). Secretary: (028 9042 3135; Fax: 028 9042 5040).*

HOLYWOOD. **The Royal Belfast Golf Club**, Station Road, Craigavad BT18 0BP (028 9042 8165; Fax: 028 9042 1404). *Location:* two miles past Holywood, off main Belfast to Bangor Road. Mainly parkland, bordering shores of Belfast Lough. 18 holes, 5961 yards. S.S.S. 69. Practice ground. *Green Fees:* information not available. *Eating facilities:* full catering and bar facilities. *Visitors:* with letter of introduction and by arrangement only. *Society Meetings:* by arrangement. Professional: C. Spence (028 9042 8586). Secretary/Manager: Mrs S.H. Morrison (028 9042 8165).*

KILKEEL. **Kilkeel Golf Club,** Mourne Park, Kilkeel BT34 4LB (028 4176 2296; Fax: 028 4176 5579). *Location:* Kilkeel to Newry road approximately three miles from Kilkeel. Parkland situated at the foot of Mourne Mountains. 18 holes, 6615 metres. S.S.S. 72. Practice area available. *Green Fees:* weekdays £20.00, weekends £25.00. *Eating facilities:* restaurant and bar. *Visitors:* welcome, club competitions on Tuesday, Thursday and Saturday. Booking for Saturday late afternoons and Sundays. *Society Meetings:* catered for by prior arrangement. General Manager: Seamus Rooney (Tel & Fax: 028 4176 5095).

KILLYLEAGH. **Ringdufferin Golf Course**, 36 Ringdufferin Road, Toye, Killyleagh BT30 9PH (Tel & Fax: 028 4482 8812). *Location*: 2 miles north of Killyleagh on Comber Road. Drumlin course. 18 holes, 5113 yards, 4641 metres, S.S.S. 66. Practice facilities. *Green Fees*: weekdays 9 holes £7.00, 18 holes £10.00; weekends 9 holes £8.00, 18 holes £12.00. *Eating facilities*: licensed restaurant. *Visitors*: welcome at all times. *Society Meetings*: welcome, 18 holes £9.00 weekdays, £11.00 weekends. Secretary: Helen Lindsay (Tel & Fax: 028 4482 8812).

KNOCKBRACKEN. **Mount Ober Golf and Country Club**, 24 Ballymaconaghy Road, Knockbracken, Belfast BT8 6SB (028 9079 5666; Fax: 028 9070 5862). *Location:* 15 minutes from centre of Belfast; Saintfield Road, Cairnshill Road, Four Winds Roundabout. Parkland on undulating ground. 18 holes, 5615 yards, S.S.S. 66. Golf academy, floodlit driving range. *Green Fees:* information not available. *Eating facilities:* full catering and bar service at all times; excellent restaurant. *Visitors:* welcome anytime, except Saturdays before 3pm. *Society Meetings:* welcome except Saturdays before 3pm. Professional: Geoff Loughrey (028 9070 1648; Fax: 028 9070 5862). Secretary: Ena Williams (028 9040 1811; Fax: 028 9070 5862). *
e-mail: mt.ober@ukonline.co.uk

NEWCASTLE. **Royal County Down Golf Club**, Newcastle BT33 0AN. *Location:* adjacent to north side of Newcastle, approach from town centre. Championship Course: 18 holes, 7065 yards, S.S.S. 74. Annesley Links Course: 18 holes, 4681 yards. S.S.S. 66. *Green Fees:* information not available. *Eating facilities:* light lunches and bar, weekdays only. *Visitors:* welcome with prior reservation. *Society Meetings:* catered for. Professional: Kevan J. Whitson (028 4372 2419). Secretary: J.H. Laidler (028 4372 3314; Fax: 028 4372 6281).
website: www.royalcountydown.org

NEWTOWNARDS. **Clandeboye Golf Club,** Tower Road, Conlig, Newtownards BT23 3PN (028 9127 1767). *Location:* Conlig village off A21 between Bangor and Newtownards. Wooded, undulating parkland/heathland. Two courses: Dufferin – 18 holes, 6559 yards, S.S.S. 71. Ava – 18 holes, 5755 yards, S.S.S. 68. Practice ground. Host to the Irish Seniors 2001. *Green Fees:* information not available. *Eating facilities:* full catering and bar. *Visitors:* welcome weekdays; no play before 3pm Saturdays, before 10.30am Sundays. Visitors changing facility. *Society Meetings:* welcome weekdays except Thursdays. Professional: Peter Gregory (028 9127 1750). Admin Manager: Rhonda Eddis (028 9127 1767; Fax: 028 9147 3711).*

NEWTOWNARDS. **Kirkistown Castle Golf Club**, 142 Main Road, Cloughey, Newtownards (028 4277 1233). *Location:* approximately 45 minutes from Belfast, 16 miles from Newtownards on the A2. 18 holes, Par 69, S.S.S. 70. *Green Fees:* £20.75 weekdays; £27.75 weekends and Public Holidays. Tourists 10% discount in approved accommodation. *Eating facilities:* full catering and snacks. *Visitors:* welcome. *Society Meetings:* outings welcome by arrangement. Secretary/ Manager: Rosemary Coulter (028 4277 1233). Professional: Jonathan Peden (028 9177 1004). Caterer: Marion Smyth (028 4277 2395; Fax: 028 4277 1699).
e-mail: kirkistown@supanet.com
website: www.kcgc.org

NEWTOWNARDS. **Mahee Island Golf Club,** Mahee Island, Comber, Newtownards BT23 6ET (028 9754 1234). *Location:* Comber/Killyleagh Road. After half a mile turn left signposted Ardmillan/Mahee Island. Keep left for six miles to course. Parkland course set on an island with magnificent views over Strangford Lough. 9 holes, 5822 yards, 5108 metres. S.S.S. 70. Par 71 over 18 holes. Putting green and pitching area. *Green Fees:* weekdays £10.00; weekends £15.00. *Eating facilities:* eating by prior arrangement with caterer (028 97 484038). *Visitors:* welcome, restricted Saturdays until 5pm. *Society Meetings:* welcome, by prior arrangement.. Professional: (Shop) Archie McCracken (028 9754 1234). Secretary: Mervyn Marshall (028 9145 7385).

NEWTOWNARDS. **Scrabo Golf Club,** 233 Scrabo Road, Newtownards BT23 4SL (028 9181 2355). *Location:* approximately 10 miles from Belfast off main Belfast to Newtownards dual carriageway, follow signs to Scrabo Country Park. Upland course. 18 holes, 5699 metres. S.S.S. 71. Practice area. *Green Fees:* information not available. *Eating facilities:* full catering (closed Mondays). *Visitors:* welcome except Saturdays and avoid Wednesdays 4.30pm to 6.30pm. *Society Meetings:* over 20 players, welcome. Professional: Paul McCrystal (028 9181 7848) General Manager: John Thomson (028 9181 2355; Fax: 028 9182 2919).

WARRENPOINT. **Warrenpoint Golf Club,** Lower Dromore Road, Warrenpoint BT34 3LN (028 4175 3695; Fax: 028 4175 2918). *Location:* five miles south of Newry on coast road. Parkland. 18 holes, 5700 metres. S.S.S. 70. Practice ground. *Green Fees:* information not available. *Eating facilities:* full catering and bar facilities. *Visitors:* welcome Sunday, Monday, Thursday, Friday. Snooker facilities available. *Society Meetings:* catered for by prior arrangement. Professional: Nigel Shaw (Tel & Fax: 028 4175 2371). Secretary: Marian Trainor. *

FERMANAGH

ENNISKILLEN. **Castle Hume Golf Club**, Belleek Road, Enniskillen BT93 7ED (028 6632 7077; Fax: 028 6632 7076). *Location:* on A46 Donegal/Belleek Road. Championship course situated within grounds of old Ely Estate, surrounded by Castle Hume Lake and Lower Lough Erne. Hosted the Ulster PGA Championships in 1996, 1997 & 1998 and also Ulster Lakeland Pro-Am 2002. 18 holes, 5932 metres. New 5-booth driving range. *Green Fees:* weekdays £20.00, 35 euros; weekends and Bank Holidays £25.00, 40 euros. *Eating facilities:* New Colonial style clubhouse opened May 2002 with public bar, licensed restaurant, conference room and pro shop. *Visitors:* always welcome. Open Days every Wednesday in May, June, July and August. Open Week first week in July. *Society Meetings:* always welcome, reduced rates for 12+. Tuition available from resident PGA Professional: Shaun Donnelly.

ENNISKILLEN. **Enniskillen Golf Club,** Castlecoole, Enniskillen BT74 6HZ (028 6632 5250). *Location:* off Enniskillen to Tempo Road on outskirts of town. Scenic parkland course with views of market town of Enniskillen on front nine, many mature trees on back nine. 18 holes, 6189 yards. S.S.S. 69. *Green Fees:* information not available. Reduction if playing with member. *Eating facilities:* bar snacks daily, full catering by arrangement. *Visitors:* welcome at all times; some restriction on Tuesdays (Ladies' Day) and weekends. *Society Meetings:* welcome at all times, special rates available. Hon. Secretary: Russell Ferguson (028 6632 5250).*

LONDONDERRY

CASTLEROCK. **Castlerock Golf Club,** 65 Circular Road, Castlerock, Coleraine BT51 4TJ (028 7084 8314). *Location:* A2, six miles west of Coleraine. Seaside links, stream in play at four holes. 18 holes, 6687 yards, S.S.S. 73. 9 holes, 2457 metres. S.S.S. 67. Practice area. *Green Fees:* weekdays £35.00 per round, £50.00 day ticket (Monday to Friday only); weekends and Bank Holidays £60.00. Subject to review. *Eating facilities:* full restaurant facilities, two bars. *Visitors:* welcome weekdays Monday to Thursday and weekends by arrangement. *Society Meetings:* welcome Monday to Thursday. Professional: Ian Blair (028 7084 9424). Secretary: Mark Steen (028 7084 8314; Fax: 028 7084 9440).

COLERAINE. **Brown Trout Golf and Country Club,** 209 Agivey Road, Aghadowey, Near Coleraine BT51 4AD (028 7086 8209; Fax: 028 7086 8878). *Location:* on A54 between Kilrea and Coleraine. Parkland course, heavily wooded, crossing water seven times in nine holes. 9 holes, 2755 metres. S.S.S. 68. *Green Fees:* information not available. *Eating facilities:* à la carte restaurant, bar snacks, barbecues. *Visitors:* always welcome. 15 new luxurious en suite bedrooms

and four new five-star cottages available. *Society Meetings:* welcome. Professional: Ken Revie. Secretary/ Manager: Bill O'Hara. *
e-mail: bill@browntroutinn.com
website: www.browntroutinn.com

LIMAVADY. **Benone Golf Course,** 53 Benone Avenue, Benone, Limavady BT49 0LQ (028 7775 0555). *Location:* situated on the A2 coast road, 12 miles from Limavady. Parkland course. 9 holes, 1458 yards, 1334 metres. S.S.S. 27. Practice range, putting green. *Green Fees:* information not available. *Eating facilities:* coffee shop open July/ August, restaurant and bars within one mile. *Visitors:* welcome. Club hire available. *Society Meetings:* welcome. Secretary: M. Clark (028 7775 0555; Fax: 028 7775 0919).

LIMAVADY. **Roe Park Golf Club,** Radisson SAS Roe Park Hotel and Golf Resort, Roe Park, Limavady BT49 9LB (028 7772 2222; Fax: 028 7772 2313). *Location:* on main A2 Londonderry-Limavady road, 16 miles from Londonderry and one mile from Limavady. (028 777 60105). Parkland. 18 holes, 6318 yards. S.S.S. 69. Floodlit driving range; putting green; equipment hire. *Green Fees:* midweek £20.00, weekend £25.00. *Eating facilities:* Coach House Brasserie. *Visitors:* welcome with some restrictions at weekend. *Society Meetings:* welcome; society packages available. Accommodation on site. Professional: Seamus Duffy. Secretary: Don Brockerton.

LONDONDERRY. **Foyle International Golf Centre,** 12 Alder Road, Londonderry BT48 8DB (028 7135 2222; Fax: 028 7135 3967). *Location:* one-and-a-half miles from Foyle Bridge heading towards Moville, Co Donegal. Parkland Championship standard Par 72, notable holes with water coming into play as third Par 3, 10th and 11th. 18 holes, 6678 yard, 6164 metres. S.S.S. 71, Par 72. 9 hole course, Par 3. Indoor floodlit driving range, putting greens. *Green Fees:* weekdays £12.00; weekends £15.00. 10% discount for groups over 12. *Eating facilities:* Pitchers Wine Bar and Restaurant within club house. *Visitors:* welcome anyday, anytime. Buggies, carts, caddies available. Golf academy with video analysis teaching system. *Society Meetings:* welcome. Professional: Kieran McLaughlin. Secretary: Margaret Lapsley.
e-mail: mail@foylegolf.club24.co.uk
website: www.foylegolfcentre.co.uk

MAGHERAFELT. **Moyola Park Golf Club,** 15 Curran Road, Castledawson, Magherafelt BT45 8DG (028 7946 8468; Fax: 028 7946 8626). *Location:* 35 miles north of Belfast on M2; off middle of Main Street, Castledawson. Attractive, spacious mature parkland. 18 holes, 6519 yards. S.S.S. 71. Practice ground, putting green. *Green Fees:* information not available. *Eating facilities:* bars and restaurant. *Visitors:* welcome weekdays except Wednesdays; Sundays (12 to 1.15pm) must be pre-booked. *Society Meetings:* welcome with prior notice. Professional: Mr Bob Cockcroft (028 7946 8830). Secretary/Manager: Tony McGuire.

PORTSTEWART. **Portstewart Golf Club**, Strand Road, Portstewart, BT55 7PG (028 7083 2015; Fax: 028 7083 4097). *Location:* north from Coleraine. Coastal links. No 1 Strand - 18 holes, 6784 yards, S.S.S. 73. No 2 Riverside - 9 holes, 2622 yards. No 3 Old - 18 holes, 4733 yards, S.S.S. 64. Practice area. *Green Fees:* information not available. *Eating facilities:* meals available - advance orders; no catering on Mondays. *Visitors:* welcome Mondays to Fridays; limited Wednesdays. Prior booking essential on Strand. Enquire about special rates for parties. *Society Meetings:* catered for by arrangement. Professional: Alan Hunter (Tel & Fax: 028 7083 2601). Secretary: Michael Moss (028 7083 2015; Fax: 028 7083 4097).* e-mail: michael@portstewartgc.co.uk.

PREHEN. **City of Derry Golf Club**, 49 Victoria Road, Prehen BT47 2PU (028 7134 6369). *Location:* three miles from city centre on the road to Strabane - follow the River Foyle. Parkland, wooded. 18 holes, 5877 metres. S.S.S. 71, Par 71. Also 9 hole (Dunhugh) course, 4305 metres. Par 66. Practice area. *Green Fees:* please contact Secretary's office. *Eating facilities:* catering and bar facilities available. *Visitors:* welcome on weekdays up to 4.30pm, weekends please contact Professional. Convenient for hotels and guest houses. *Society Meetings:* welcome, please contact Manager's Office. Professional: Mr Michael Doherty (028 7131 1496). Hon. Secretary: Mr G. Mills (028 7134 6369). Secretary: Noreen Allen (028 7134 6369).*

TYRONE

COOKSTOWN. **Killymoon Golf Club**, 200 Killymoon Road, Cookstown BT80 8TW (Tel & Fax: 028 8676 3762). *Location:* private road off A29. Signposted at Dungannon end of town opposite Drum Road. Mainly flat parkland. 18 holes, 5481 metres. S.S.S. 69. Practice ground. *Green Fees:* information not available. *Eating facilities:* full catering at club (large groups please book). *Visitors:* welcome, after 4pm Saturdays, Thursday is Ladies' Day. Booking essential. *Society Meetings:* welcome. Booking essential. Professional: Gary Chambers (Tel & Fax: 028 8676 3460); Secretary: Tom Doonan (Tel & Fax: 028 8676 3762). Club Manager: Valerie Wilson (028 8676 3762).*

DUNGANNON. **Dungannon Golf Club,** 34 Springfield Lane, Dungannon BT70 1QX (028 8772 2098; Fax: 028 8772 7338). *Location:* a short distance from Dungannon along Donaghmore Road. Flat first 9, hilly second 9. Parkland course with some water hazards newly positioned. 18 holes, 5861 yards. S.S.S. 69. *Green Fees:* weekdays £18.00; weekends and Bank Holidays £22.00. As a guest of a member £12.00 weekdays, £14.00 weekends. *Eating facilities:* bar snacks and licensed restaurant. *Visitors:* always welcome but please telephone first; precluded by timesheets at weekends, Ladies' Day Tuesdays. *Society Meetings:* welcome by prior arrangement; apply in writing. Professional: Vivian Tate. Secretary: S.T. Hughes.

FINTONA. **Fintona Golf Club,** 1 Kiln Street, Ecclesville Demesne, Fintona BT78 2BJ (Tel & Fax: 028 8284 1480). *Location:* eight miles south of Omagh, county town of Tyrone. An attractive parkland course, its main features being a trout stream; rated one of the top nine hole courses in the Province. 9 holes, 5765 metres. S.S.S. 70. Putting green. *Green Fees:* information not available. *Eating facilities:* bar snacks, meals on request. *Visitors:* welcome weekdays, weekends by arrangement. *Society Meetings:* welcome weekdays, book in advance.*

NEWTOWNSTEWART. **Newtownstewart Golf Club,** 38 Golf Course Road, Newtownstewart, Omagh BT78 4HU (028 8166 1466; Fax: 028 8166 2506). *Location:* signposted from Strabane Road (A57) at Newtownstewart, two miles west of Newtownstewart on B84. Parkland and wooded course. 18 holes, 5869 yards, 5341 metres. S.S.S. 69. Practice ground. *Green Fees:* weekdays £12.00; weekends and Bank Holidays £17.00. *Eating facilities:* available. *Visitors:* welcome at all times except during club competitions. Accommodation available in chalets beside clubhouse. Buggies and carts available. *Society Meetings:* all welcome but must be affiliated to G.U.I. Special packages available. Golf Shop: (028 8166 2242; Fax: 028 8166 2506). Secretary: Mrs Diane Cook (028 8166 1466; Fax: 028 8166 2506). e-mail: newtown.stewart@lineone.net website: www.globalgolf.com/newtownstewart

OMAGH. **Omagh Golf Club,** 83a Dublin Road, Omagh BT78 1HQ (Tel & Fax: 028 8224 3160). *Location:* one mile from Omagh town centre on Belfast/Dublin Road. Parkland. 18 holes, 5379 metres. S.S.S. 68. *Green Fees:* information not available. *Eating facilities:* snacks and bar facilities. *Visitors:* welcome any day except Tuesday and Saturday. *Society Meetings:* welcome. Hon. Secretary: Joseph A. McElholm. Secretary: Florence E.A. Caldwell (Tel & Fax: 028 8224 3160).*

STRABANE. **Strabane Golf Club**, 33 Ballycolman Road, Strabane BT82 9PH (028 7138 2271/2007; Fax: 028 7188 6471). *Location:* A5 half mile from Strabane towards Omagh. Parkland. 18 holes, 5610 metres. S.S.S. 69. *Green Fees:* information not available. *Eating facilities:* two bars, catering by arrangement. *Visitors:* welcome, except Saturdays. Practice putting green and chipping area. *Society Meetings:* by arrangement. Secretary: Gerry Glover (028 7138 2007). *

THE APPEARANCE OF AN ASTERISK * AT THE END OF A CLUB OR COURSE ENTRY INDICATES THAT UP-TO-DATE INFORMATION HAS NOT BEEN SUPPLIED

Republic of Ireland

COUNTY CARLOW

BORRIS. **Borris Golf Club**, Deer Park, Carlow (059 9773310; Fax: 059 9773750). Scenic parkland course with tree lined fairways and modern sandbased greens. 10 holes, 5680 yards, S.S.S. 69. Practice area and putting green. *Green Fees*: weekdays 20 euros, 13 Euros with member; weekends 20 euros with member only. *Eating facilities*: bar meals available. *Visitors*: welcome weekdays by prior arrangement, restrictions Thursdays and weekends. *Society Meetings*: welcome by prior arrangement. Secretary: Nollaig Lucas (059 9773310; Fax: 059 9773750).

CARLOW. **Carlow Golf Club**, Deer Park, Carlow (0503 31695; Fax: 0503 40065). *Location*: N9 2.5 miles north of Carlow town. Parkland, undulating, sandy sub-soil. 18 holes, 5974 metres. S.S.S. 71. Practice ground. New 9 hole golf course. *Green Fees*: weekdays 45 euros; weekends 60 euros. Society rates (20+) weekdays 40 euros; weekends 50 euros. 9 hole course, 18 holes for 20 euros . *Eating facilities*: bar and restaurant. *Visitors*: always welcome, weekends difficult, pre-booking advisable. Carts, caddies and club hire. *Society Meetings*: must be pre-booked with Secretary. Professional: Andrew Gilbert (0503 41745; Fax: 0503 40065). General Manager: Donard MacSweeney (0503 31695; Fax: 0503 40065).
e-mail: carlowgolfclub@eircom.net
website: www.carlowgolfclub.com

COUNTY CAVAN

BALLYCONNELL. **Slieve Russell Hotel & Golf Club**, Ballyconnel (049 952 5090; Fax: 049 952 6640). Mature parkland European tour Championship course on 350 acres. 18 holes, 7053 yards, 6412 metres. Driving range and practice ground. *Green Fees*: information not available. *Eating facilities*: Summit Bar and restaurant. *Visitors*: welcome everyday, pre-booking essential. Limited availablity on Saturdays. 4 Star Hotel on site. *Society Meetings*: welcome, please contact for details. Professional: Liam McCool. Golf Director: Ivan Hewson (049 952 6458; Fax: 049 952 6640).*
e-mail: slieve-golf-club@quinn-hotels.com
e-mail: hewsoni@quinn-hotels.com

BELTURBET. **Belturbet Golf Club,** Erne Hill, Belturbet (049 952 2287). *Location*: quarter-of-a-mile from Belturbet town centre on main Cavan-Dublin road. Parkland with elevated greens. 9 holes, 5204 yards. S.S.S. 65. Practice area and putting green. *Green Fees*: 15 euros. *Eating facilities*: catering and bar in clubhouse. *Visitors*: welcome at all times. Club hire available. *Society Meetings*: welcome, reductions available. Secretary: Liam McElgunn (049 952 2287).

BLACKLION. **Blacklion Golf Club**, Toam, Blacklion, via Sligo (071 985 3024). *Location*: Blacklion/Belcoo on Enniskillen to Sligo Road. Flat parkland, wooded copses, lake partially in play, scenic. 9 holes, 6175 yards, 5614 metres. S.S.S. 69. *Green Fees*: information not available. *Eating facilities*: full catering available. *Visitors*: welcome. Course surrounded on four holes by Loch McNean. Safe swimming in lake. Scenic hill walks. *Society Meetings*: by arrangement. Hon. Secretary: Pat Gallery.

CAVAN. **County Cavan Golf Club**, Aranmore House, Drumelis, Cavan (049 4331283). *Location:* on Killeshandra road from Cavan. Parkland course. 18 holes, 5634 metres. S.S.S 69. Practice area, driving range. *Green Fees:* information not provided. *Eating facilities:* full catering facilities including bar snacks. *Visitors:* welcome; limited availblility on Wednesdays and weekends. *Society Meetings:* on application to Norman Cinnamond (Tel & Fax: 049 4331541). Professional: Bill Nobel (049 4331388). Hon. Secretary: Brian Fitzsimons (Tel & Fax: 049 4331541).

COUNTY CLARE

CLONLARA. **Clonlara Golf and Leisure**, Clonlara (061 354141; Fax: 061 354143). *Location:* 7 miles from Limerick on Corbally to Killaloe road. Parkland. 12 holes. S.S.S.67. *Green Fees:* information not available. *Eating facilities:* fully licensed bar with bar food. *Visitors:* welcome. *Society Meetings:* welcome. No walkers, caddies, or children under 14 allowed on the course. Tennis courts, sauna, children's play area, crazy golf. Self-catering apartments available. Secretary: Ms A. O'Grady (061 354141; Fax: 061 354143).*
e-mail: tmcmahon@circom.net

DOONBEG. **Doonbeg Golf Club**, Doonbeg (353 65 9055246; Fax: 353 65 9055247). *Location*: The highly acclaimed Doonbeg Golf Club is situated between two of Ireland's greatest Links courses - Ballybunion and Lahinch. Designed by Greg Norman and host of the 2002 Palmer Cup matches, it is set along 1.5 miles of crescent-shaped beach encircling Doughmore Bay, providing magnificent views. Links course. 18 holes, 6885 yards, par 72. Practice green, putting green. *Green Fees*: information on request. *Eating facilities*: restaurant. *Visitors*: welcome. On site accommodation expected 2005.
e-mail: links@doonbeggolfclub.com

ENNIS. **Ennis Golf Club**, Drumbiggle, Ennis (065 6824074; Fax: 065 6841848). *Location:* half a mile from Ennis town centre. Parkland course set in rolling hills with five challenging Par 3s. 18 holes, 6150 yards, 5592 metres. Par 71. *Green Fees:* 35 euros. Groups rates on request. *Eating facilities:* full catering facilities and bar. *Visitors:* Monday,

Thursday, Saturday with some restrictions Tuesday and Wednesday. New Club House. Carts, clubs and caddies available. *Society Meetings:* welcome; 30 euros. Professional: Martin Ward (065 6820690). General Manager: Niall O'Donnell (065 6824074; Fax: 065 6841848).
e-mail: egc@eircom.net
website: http://golfclub.ennis.ie/EnnisGolfclub.com

ENNIS. **Woodstock Golf and Country Club**, Shanaway Road, Ennis (00353 656 829463; Fax: 00353 656 820304). *Location:* from Ennis town take Lahinch Road, 18 miles Shannon Airport. Parkland course. 18 holes, 5879 metres. S.S.S. 71. *Green Fees:* weekdays £35.00, weekends and Bank Holidays £40.00. *Eating facilities:* bar food served daily, The Tenth Tee Bar, G/B's Restaurant (065 44430). *Visitors:* welcome at all times, telephone in advance advisable at weekends. Hotel on site. *Society Meetings:* all welcome, special rates available. Secretary: Seamie Kelly (+ 353 65 682 9463; Fax: + 353 65 682 0804; mobile: 0868293652).
e-mail: woodstock.ennis@eircom.net
website: www.woodstockgolfclub.com

KILKEE. **Kilkee Golf Club,** East End, Kilkee (065 9056048; Fax: 065 9056977). *Location:* right on seafront at end of promenade. Seaside course with many cliff top tees and greens. 18 holes, 5960 metres. S.S.S. 71. *Green Fees:* 30 euros. *Eating facilities:* fully licensed restaurant and bar. *Visitors:* very welcome every day. Golf shop. *Society Meetings:* Society outings welcome, special reduced rates. Secretary/Manager: Michael Culligan (065 9056048; Fax: 065 9056977).
e-mail: kilkeegolfclub@eircom.net
website: www.kilkeegolfclub.ie

KILRUSH. **Kilrush Golf Club**, Kilrush (065 905 1138; Fax: 065 905 2633). *Location:* On main Ennis/Kilrush Road - 1km from Kilrush. Parkland course. 18 holes, 5960 yards. S.S.S. 70. *Green Fees:* information not available. *Eating facilities:* full bar and catering facilities. *Visitors:* always welcome - please book in advance. *Society Meetings:* welcome. Professional: Sean O'Connor. Secretary/Manager: Denis F. Nagle (065 905 1138).

LAHINCH. **Lahinch Golf Club**, Lahinch (065 7081003). *Location:* 32 miles north west of Shannon Airport, 200 yards from Lahinch Village on Lisconner Road. Links course. Old Course - 18 holes, 6950 yards. S.S.S. 74; Castle Course - 18 holes, 5594 yards. S.S.S. 67. *Green Fees:* Old Course 125 euros, Castle Course 50 euros. *Eating facilities:* bar and restaurant. *Visitors:* welcome. *Society Meetings:* catered for by arrangement. Professional: Robert McCavery (065 7081003). Secretary: Alan Reardon (065 7081003; Fax: 065 7081592).
e-mail: info@lahinchgolf.com

MILTOWN MALBAY. **Spanish Point Golf Club**, Spanish Point, Miltown Malbay (065-708 4198). *Location*: two miles south of Miltown Malbay at Spanish Point Beach. Links course. 9 holes, 2312 metres, S.S.S. 63. Practice facilities. *Green Fees*: information not available. *Eating facilities*: bar snacks. *Visitors*: welcome at all times, not before

noon on Sundays. *Society Meetings*: welcome weekdays excluding July and August. Secretary: David Fitzgerald (065- 708 4219).*
e-mail: david@spanish-point.com
e-mail: dkfitzgerald@tinet.ie
website: www.spanish-point.com

SHANNON. **Shannon Golf Club**, Shannon (061 471849; Fax: 061 471507). *Location:* from Limerick take Airport road, course is 200 yards past Airport. Parkland. 18 holes, 6271 yards. S.S.S. 72. Practice area, club hire, buggy hire. *Green Fees:* information not available. *Eating facilities:* full bar and catering services. *Visitors:* welcome with prior booking. *Society Meetings:* welcome. Professional: Artie Pyke (061 471551). General Manager: Michael Corry. *

COUNTY CORK

BANDON. **Bandon Golf Club**, Castlebernard, Bandon (023 41111; Fax: 023 44690). *Location:* one mile west of Bandon town centre. Undulating parkland course with scenic views of West Cork. 18 holes, 6421 yards, 5780 metres. S.S.S. 70. Practice ground. *Green Fees:* information not available. *Eating facilities:* available, menu at bar. *Visitors:* welcome, restriction at weekends. Clubs, buggies and carts for hire. *Society Meetings:* welcome except Wednesdays and Sundays. Professional: Paddy O'Boyle (023 42224; Fax: 023 44690). Secretary: Mr John McGinley.
e-mail: bandongolfclub@eircom.net

BANTRY. **Bantry Bay Golf Club**, Bantry, West Cork (353 (0) 27 50579/53773/53790; Fax: 353 (0) 27 53790). *Location:* approximately 1 mile from Bantry on N71 Killarney road. Clifftop parkland championship course to USGA standards. 18 holes, 6500 yards, 5910 metres. S.S.S. 72. *Green Fees:* 30 euros to 50 euros. *Eating facilities:* bar and restaurant open all year. *Visitors:* welcome, with restrictions at weekend. *Society Meetings:* rates on request. Secretary: John O'Sullivan.
e-mail: info@bantrygolf.com
website: www.bantrygolf.com

CARRIGALINE. **Fernhill Golf & Country Club**, Carrigaline (021 437 2226; Fax: 021 437 1011). *Location*: 30 minutes from Cork city, 15 minutes from Cork Airport, 5 minutes from Ringaskiddy Ferry Port. From city/airport follow sign to Ringaskiddy Ferry Port until roundabout with sign for Carrigaline - take Ringaskiddy exit, 2nd right, club is on this road. 18 holes, 5766 yards, S.S.S. 67. *Green Fees*: information not available. *Eating facilities*: clubhouse serves food and drink daily. *Visitors*: welcome anytime except Saturday and Sunday from 9am to 10.15am, or 9am to 10.15am Thursdays. Reservation advised for weekend golf. 18 bedroom hotel on site, tennis court, indoor pool and sauna. Golf packages available. *Society Meetings*: welcome if booked in advance, please telephone for details. General Manager: Mr Alan Bowes.
e-mail: fernhill@iol.ie
website: www.fernhillgolfhotel.com

CARRIGTWOHILL. **Fota Island Golf Club,** Carrigtwohill (021 4883700; Fax: 021 4883713). *Location*: take N25 east from Cork City (9 miles), turn off for Fota and Cobh. Gently undulating parkland bordered by mature woodland, very traditional in design. Voted 'Golf Course of the Year' 2002 by the Irish Golf Tour Operators. 18 holes, 6980 yards, 6329 metres, S.S.S. 73. Practice range and putting green. *Green Fees*: from £54.00 to £98.00. *Eating facilities*: restaurant and bar. *Visitors*: welcome everyday, telephone for tee times. Metal spikes not allowed. Buggies, carts and caddies available. *Society Meetings*: welcome everyday, but limited availability on weekends. Professional: Kevin Morris (021 4883710; Fax: 021 4883713). Venue for the 2001 and 2002 Murphy's Irish Open, one of the most prestigious events of the European Tour.
e-mail: reservations@fotaisland.ie
website: www.fotaisland.com

CASTLETOWNBERE. **Berehaven Golf Links and Amenity Park**, Filane, Castletownbere, Beara (027 70700). *Location*: on main Castletownbere - Glengarriff Road, three miles from Castletownbere. Scenic course overlooking Bantry Bay. 9 holes, 2598 metres, S.S.S. 65. *Green Fees*: information not available. *Eating facilities*: bar and restaurant. *Visitors*: welcome at all times. Tennis, crazy golf, sauna, caravan park. Club hire available. *Society Meetings*: welcome by appointment, special rates. Hon. Secretary: Bernie Twomey or Mike & Julie O'Neill (027 70700).

See also Colour Advertisement on page 95

CHARLEVILLE. **Charleville Golf Club**, Charleville (063 81257; Fax: 063 81274). *Location*: Two kilometres west of Charleville town which is on main Cork/Limerick road. Parkland, heavily wooded. 27 holes. 18 holes 6430 yards. S.S.S. 70. 9 holes 6902 yards S.S.S. 73. Two practice areas. *Green Fees*: information not available. *Eating facilities*: full eating facilities and bar. *Visitors*: welcome, weekends by appointment. *Society Meetings*: welcome. Special rates apply. Professional: David Keating (063 81257). Hon Secretary: James A. Murphy.
e-mail: charlevillegolf@eircom.net
website: www.charlevillegolf.com

COBH. **Cobh Golf Club**, Ballywilliam, Cobh (021-481 2399; Fax: 021-481 2615). Parkland course. 9 holes, 5006 yards, 4576 metres, S.S.S. 64. *Green Fees:* 16 euros. *Eating facilities:* available. *Visitors:* welcome mid week, restricted weekends and Tuesdays (Ladies' Day). Hon. Secretary: David Sloane (021-4812882).

DONERAILE. **Doneraile Golf Club**, Doneraile (022 24137). *Location:* three-and-a-half miles off main Cork/Limerick Road. Parkland, mature trees. 9 holes, 3500 yards. S.S.S.67. *Green Fees:* information not available. *Eating facilities:* by request. *Visitors:* welcome weekdays. *Society Meetings:* welcome Saturdays and weekdays. Secretary: Jimmy O'Leary (022 24379).*

DOUGLAS. **Douglas Golf Club**, Douglas (021 4891086; Fax: 021 4895297). *Location:* Douglas is on the main road from Cork to ferry port at Ringaskiddy, three miles south of Cork City. Beautifully maintained flat parkland course – the views from the Clubhouse are some of the most panoramic in the country. 18 holes, 6669 yards, 5972 metres. S.S.S. 71. Practice ground. *Green Fees:* 45 euros all week. Groups of 20 or more 40 euros. Subject to review. *Eating facilities:* full restaurant and bar available from 11am. *Visitors:* Monday, Wednesday, Thursday, Friday (mornings preferably); Saturday and Sunday after 2pm. Advisable to check in advance. *Society Meetings:* welcome but bookings should be made by end of January each year. Professional: Gary Nicholson (021 4362055). Secretary/Manager: Brian Kiely (Tel & Fax: 021 4895297).

FERMOY. **Fermoy Golf Club**, Corrin, Fermoy (025 32694; Fax: 025 33072). *Location:* 2km from Dublin to Cork main route. Parkland, wooded course. 18 holes, 5847 metres. S.S.S. 68. Practice ground. *Green Fees:* weekdays 25 euros; weekends 35 euros. Groups 25 euros weekdays, 35 euros weekends. *Eating facilities:* full bar and restaurant. *Visitors:* welcome, Mondays very limited, weekends by reservation. Caddies. *Society Meetings:* welcome, booking essential. Professional: Brian Moriarty (025 31472; Fax: 025 33072). Secretary: Kathleen Murphy. e-mail: fermoygolfclub@eircom.net

GLENGARRIFF. **Glengarriff Golf Club**, Glengarriff (027 63150). Parkland course. 9 holes, Par 33. *Green Fees:* information not available. *Eating facilities:* light snacks available in the clubhouse. *Visitors:* welcome at all times. *Society Meetings:* welcome. Secretary: Noreen Deasy (027 50315). *

KINSALE. **Kinsale Golf Club**, Farrangalway, Kinsale (021 4774722; Fax: 021 4773114). *Location:* beautifully situated in meadowland and parkland. Two courses. 18 holes and 9 holes. *Green Fees:* 35 euros midweek; 50 euros weekends. Subject to review for 2003. *Eating facilities:* full bar and catering. *Visitors:* welcome. e-mail: office@kinsalegolf.com website: www.kinsalegolf.com

KINSALE. **Old Head Golf Links**, Kinsale (+353 (0) 21 4778444; Fax: +353 (0) 214778022). *Location:* from Cork Airport follow R600 from Cork to Kinsale on to Old Head. 15 minutes south, signposted. Spectacular links course at an elevation of 100-200 ft. Practice ground, putting green, chipping green. 18 holes, 7300 yards. S.S.S. 72. *Green Fees:* 250 euros. *Eating facilities:* full bar and restaurant facilities. *Visitors:* no restrictions. *Society Meetings:* welcome subject to availability, Special rates available for groups over 24. Course closed November to March. Golf Operations: Danny Brasil. General Manager: Jim O'Brien.

Please mention
'THE GOLF GUIDE'
when enquiring about clubs or accommodation.

Charleville Golf Club
Charleville, Co. Cork, Ireland   Tel: 063 81257; Fax: 063 81274

Two challenging and enjoyable tests for all golfers, an 18-hole championship course and custom-designed 9-hole course set in the heart of Ireland's Golden Vale.

A warm welcome is extended to Irish and overseas visitors alike, with special rates for society and corporate meetings.

Professional: David Keating (063 81257).

See also Colour Advertisement on page 93

Cork Golf Club was founded in 1888 and designed in 1927 by Alister MacKenzie. It has matured to become one of the finest courses in the country.

Many Amateur and Professional championships have been hosted here.

The course is always in immaculate condition and playable all year round.

For further information regarding green fees, please contact Matt Sands, General Manager, at:

CORK GOLF CLUB

Little Island, Co. Cork, Ireland
Tel: 00 353 21 4353451 • Fax: 00 353 21 4353410
e-mail: corkgolfclub@eircom.net
www.corkgolfclub.ie

See also Colour Advertisement on page 95

LITTLE ISLAND. **Cork Golf Club**, Little Island (021 4353451; Fax: 021 4353410). *Location:* five miles east of Cork City N25, signposted. Parkland, very scenic championship course. 18 holes, 6065 metres. S.S.S. 72, 70. Practice ground. *Green Fees:* information not available. *Eating facilities:* full catering facilities, bar. *Visitors:* welcome Mondays, Tuesdays, Wednesdays and Fridays except 12.30 to 2pm; Thursdays, weekends ring in advance. *Society Meetings:* catered for, arrange with General Manager. Professional: Peter Hickey (021 4353421). General Manager: Matt Sands (021 4353451; Fax: 021 4353410). e-mail: corkgolfclub@eircom.net website: www.corkgolfclub.ie

LITTLE ISLAND. **Harbour Point Golf Club**, Clash Road, Little Island (021 4353094; Fax: 021 4354408). *Location:* follow signs for Rosslare from Cork City and then take exit for Little Island (approx 6 miles from city). Parkland course by banks of River Lee. 21 bay floodlit range and fully stocked golf store. 18 holes, 6163 metres. S.S.S. 72. 21 bay floodlit driving range. *Green Fees:* 33 euros weekdays, 38 euros weekends (Fridays to Sundays). Earlybird fee 25 euros before 11am Monday, Wednesday, Thursday and Friday (32 euros on Friday, April to September inclusive. *Eating facilities:* full bar and catering facilities. *Visitors:* welcome anytime, please book tee times. Carts, buggies and caddies for hire. *Society Meetings:* very welcome, special rates available. Professional: Mr Morgan O'Donovan. General Manager: Aylmer Barrett (021 4353094; Fax: 021 4354408). e-mail: hpoint@iol.ie website: www.harbourpointgolfclub.com

MACROOM. **Macroom Golf Club**, Lackaduv, Macroom. (026 41072; Fax: 026 41391). *Location:* through castle gates at town centre. Parkland. 18 holes, 5574 metres. S.S.S. 70. *Green Fees:* weekdays 25 euros, weekends 30 euros. Early bird Monday to Thursday from 9am to 11am 15 euros. *Eating facilities:* full catering with restaurant and bar. *Visitors:* welcome, booking essential. *Society Meetings:* welcome March to October, booking essential. Manager: Cathal O'Sullivan.

MALLOW. **Mallow Golf Club**, Ballyellis, Mallow (022 21145; Fax: 022 42501). *Location*: 1 mile from town, east, on the Killavullen road. Parkland course. 18 holes, 5960 metres, S.S.S.72. *Green Fees*: contact club for current fees. *Eating facilities*: available. *Visitors*: welcome Monday to Friday, restrictions on weekends and public holidays, please check for details. *Society Meetings*: welcome, please telephone for details. Professional: Sean Conway (022 43424). Secretary/ Manager: David Curtin (022 21145; Fax: 022 42501). e-mail: golfmall@gofree.indigo.ie

MIDLETON. **East Cork Golf Club**, Gortacrue, Midleton (021 631687; Fax: 021 613695). *Location:* two miles off main Waterford to Cork road. Exit at Midleton 13 miles west of Cork city. Parkland course. 18 hole, 5491 yards. S.S.S. 67. Driving range. *Green Fees:* information not available. *Visitors:* welcome all year round. *Society Meetings:* special rates available. Professional: Don MacFarlane (021 633667). Secretary: Maurice Maloney. *

MITCHELSTOWN. **Mitchelstown Golf Club**, Limerick Road, Gurrane, Mitchelstown (025 24072). *Location:* one kilometre from Mitchelstown (main Dublin/Cork route). Flat parkland. 18 holes, 6008 metres. S.S.S. 70. Practice area. *Green Fees:* information not available. *Eating facilities:* bar food evenings/weekends. *Visitors:* welcome. Caddie car hire. *Society Meetings:* welcome. Secretary: D. Stapleton. (025 24072).*

MONKSTOWN. **Monkstown Golf Club**, Parkgarriff, Monkstown (021 4841376; Fax: 021 4841722). *Location:* 7 miles from Cork city, just 10 minutes' drive from the Cork/Swansea Ferry. Demanding parkland course for golfers of all levels and the greens have been noted for being amongst the best in the country. 18 holes, 5640 metres. S.S.S. 69. Practice ground. *Green Fees:* Monday to Thursday: 37 euros (day), Friday to Sunday 44 euros (day). *Eating facilities:* full bar and restaurant available. *Visitors:* welcome, avoid Tuesday (Ladies' Day) and Bank Holiday Mondays. Phone at weekends. *Society Meetings:* welcome with restrictions. General Manager/Secretary: Hilary Madden e-mail: office@monkstowngolfclub.com

MUSKERRY. **Muskerry Golf Club**, Carrigrohane (021 4385297; Fax: 021 4516860). *Location:* seven and a half miles north west of Cork City, two and a half miles from Blarney. Parkland/wooded, two rivers. 18 holes, 5785 metres. S.S.S. 71. *Green Fees:* weekdays 35 euros; weekends 40 euros if available. *Eating facilities:* available. *Visitors:* welcome; Monday and Tuesday all day, Wednesday up to 10.30am, Thursday after 1.30pm and Friday up to 3.30pm; weekends as available. Members' hour weekdays 12.30pm to 1.30pm. *Society Meetings:* welcome; 30 euros weekdays, 35 euros weekends. Professional: W.M. Lehane (021 4381445). Manager: Hugo Gallagher (021 4385297; Fax: 021 4516860).

OVENS. **Lee Valley Golf Club**, Clashanure, Ovens (Tel & Fax: 353 21 7331721). *Location:* eight miles from Cork on N22, turn right at Dan Sheehans. Parkland. 18 hole championship golf course designed by Ryder Cup star Christy O'Connor Jnr. 6725 yards. Par 72. 15 bay floodlit, indoor driving range, outdoor practice facilities. *Green Fees:* 30 euros weekdays, 35 euros weekends. *Eating facilities:* bar and full restaurant. *Visitors:* welcome. Club shop, tuition; club hire, caddy car hire and caddies and buggies available. *Society Meetings:* welcome. Corporate days. Lee Valley Bus available to cater for all your transport needs. Professional: John Savage. Proprietor: Jerry Keohege. e-mail: leevalleygolfclub@eircom.net website: www.leevalleygcc.ie

SCHULL. **Coosheen Golf Club**, Coosheen, Schull (028 28182). *Location:* one mile from Schull. Seaside parkland. 9 holes, 2023 metres. S.S.S. 58. Club hire, trolley hire. *Green Fees:* information not available. *Eating facilities:* seasonal bar and daily lunches. *Visitors:* welcome. *Society Meetings:* welcome. Secretary: A. Good or Donal Morgan. *

YOUGHAL. **Youghal Golf Club**, Knockaverry, Youghal (024 92787; Fax: 024 92641). *Location:* N25 main road from Rosslare to Cork. Seaside course with panoramic views of Youghal Bay/Blackwater Estuary. 18 holes, 5626 metres. S.S.S. 69. *Green Fees:* earlybird 15 euros before 10am, weekdays 25 euros, weekends 32 euros . *Eating facilities:* full bar and restaurant facilities. *Visitors:* welcome mid-week, phone re weekends and Wednesdays (Ladies' Day). *Society Meetings:* welcome, please phone. Special rates available. Professional: Liam Burns (024 92590). Secretary: Margaret O'Sullivan.

THE APPEARANCE OF AN ASTERISK (*)
AT THE END OF A CLUB OR COURSE
ENTRY INDICATES THAT
UP-TO-DATE INFORMATION
HAS NOT BEEN SUPPLIED

COUNTY DONEGAL

BALLYLIFFIN. **Ballyliffin Golf Club**, Ballyliffin, Clonmany (00 353 74 93 76119; Fax: 00 353 74 93 76672). *Location:* Carndonagh from Derry, Buncrana from Letterkenny. Traditional links. Glashedy; 18 holes, 7250 yards. S.S.S. 72. Old Links; 18 holes, 6612 yards. S.S.S. 71. Practice ground and three practice holes. *Green Fees:* information not available. *Eating facilities:* bar and restaurant. *Visitors:* Welcome, booking advisable. *Society Meetings:* concessions for groups of 16 and over. Manager: Cecil Doherty (00 353 74 93 76119; Fax: 00 353 74 93 76672.)
e-mail: info@ballyliffingolfclub.com
website: www.ballyliffingolfclub.com

BUNCRANA. **Buncrana Golf Club**, Ballymacarry, Buncrana (077-20749). *Location*: on entry to Buncrana town take first left after Inishowen Gateway Hotel. Links course. 9 holes, 4250 metres, S.S.S. 62. *Green Fees*: Men 13 euros, Ladies 8 euros, Juveniles 5 euros. *Visitors*: welcome Monday to Friday, weekends by prior arrangement. *Society Meetings*: welcome. Professional: J. Doherty (077-62279). Secretary: Francis McGrory (077-20749).

BUNDORAN. **Bundoran Golf Club**, Great Northern Hotel, Bundoran (072 41302; Fax: 072 42014). *Location:* 22 miles north of Sligo on edge of Bundoran Town. Parkland, seaside; not wooded. 18 holes, 5688 metres. S.S.S. 70. Practice ground. *Green Fees:* weekdays 35 euros, weekends 45 euros. *Eating facilities:* soup, tea, coffee and sandwiches in bar. *Visitors:* anytime with due notice but preferably Monday to Thursday. Buggies and carts. *Society Meetings:* very welcome with due notice. Professional: David T. Robinson (072 41302). Secretary: John McGagh.

DONEGAL. **Donegal Golf Club**, Murvagh, Laghey (074 9734054; Fax: 074 9734377). *Location:* N15 off main Donegal/Ballyshannon Road. Seaside links course, Murvagh Peninsula. 18 holes, 6874 yards, 6249 metres. S.S.S. 73. Practice area. *Green Fees:* 50 euros Monday to Thursday; 65 euros Friday to Sunday and Bank Holidays. *Eating facilities:* restaurant and bar. *Visitors:* welcome, restrictions weekends and Mondays. Buggies, carts available, caddies on request. Administrator: (074 9734054; Fax: 074 9734377).
e-mail: info@donegal-golfclub.ie

DOWNINGS **Rosapenna Hotel & Golf Links**, Rosapenna, Downings (074 55301; Fax: 074 55128). *Location:* 25 miles from Letterkenny. Links course, designed by Old Tom Morris. 18 holes, 6271 yards, 5735 metres. S.S.S. 71. New 18 holes to open June 2003. *Green Fees:* information not available. *Eating facilities:* available at hotel. *Visitors:* welcome all times. Four star Hotel on course. *Society Meetings:* welcome, must have Club Handicap. Secretary:Kevin Mooney. Hotel and Course Manager: Frank T. Casey.

DUNFANAGHY. **Dunfanaghy Golf Club**, Kill, Dunfanaghy, Letterkenny (074 9136335; Fax: 074 9136684). *Location:* on main Letterkenny to Dunfanaghy Road - N56. Seaside links course overlooking Sheephaven Bay and overshadowed by Horn Head. 18 holes, 5000 metres. S.S.S. 66. Practice net. *Green Fees:* weekdays 25 euros, weekends 30 euros *Eating facilities:* bar snacks - soup, tea and sandwiches. *Visitors:* welcome weekends or most days. Time sheet in operation at weekends. Buggies, carts and caddies by request. *Society Meetings:* all welcome. Club Secretary: Sandra McGinley (074 9136335). Hon Secretary: Michael McGinley. e-mail: dunfanaghygolf@eircom.net

FAHAN. **North West Golf Club**, Lisfannon, Fahan (077 61027; Fax: 077 63284). *Location:* eight miles north west of Derry, one mile Buncrana - main Derry/Buncrana Road. Traditional links course, established 1891 founder member of G.U.I. 18 holes,

5968 yards. S.S.S. 70. Putting green. *Green Fees:* weekdays 25 euros; weekends 30 euros. Society rates on request. *Eating facilities:* full bar and restaurant; bar snacks. *Visitors:* welcome anytime, phone in advance for weekends and Wednesdays. Caddies, carts available. *Society Meetings:* all welcome, booking essential. Professional: Seamus McBriarty (077 61715). Hon. Secretary: Dudley Coyle.

KINCASSLAGH. **Cruit Island Golf Club**, Cruit Island, Kincasslagh (074 9543296). *Location:* five miles north of Dunglue, turn off opposite Daniel O'Donnell's Viking House Hotel, three miles to the clubhouse. Seaside links with 9 holes, spectacular views hugging ragged coastline. 9 holes, 4860 metres. S.S.S. 66. Practice green. *Green Fees:* 20 euros; special discounts for groups. *Eating facilities:* full menu available if pre-booked. *Visitors:* welcome all year. Secretary: Dermot Devenney (074 9548872).

LETTERKENNY. **Letterkenny Golf Club**, Barnhill, Letterkenny (074 21150). *Location:* Off Ramelton Road out of Letterkenny. Parkland/wooded course by the river. Practice area, putting green. 18 holes, 6239 yards. S.S.S. 71. *Green Fees:* information not available. *Eating facilities:* bar snacks; full à la carte menu available. *Visitors:* always welcome. *Society Meetings:* special reduced rates available, please phone for details. Secretary: Barry Ramsey (074 24491).*

PORTNOO. **Narin and Portnoo Golf Club**, Narin, Portnoo (Tel & Fax: 074 45107). *Location:* 6 miles north of Ardara adjacent to Blue Flag beach. Links course. 18 holes, 5396 metres. *Green Fees:* weekdays 26 euros, weekends 32 euros. *Eating facilities:* bar meals and snacks available. *Visitors:* welcome Monday to Friday, restrictions at weekends, please ring for a tee time. *Society Meetings:* society rates available. Secretary: Enda Bonner (Tel & Fax: 074 45107). e-mail: nairnportnoo@eircom.net

PORTSALON. **Portsalon Golf Club**, Portsalon, Fanad (074 9159459; Fax: 074 9159919). *Location:* 22 miles north of Letterkenny via Rathmelton. Seaside links. 18 holes, white markers 6185 metres. S.S.S. 72, par 72. *Green Fees:* weekdays 35 euros; weekends and Bank Holidays 40 euros. Subject to review. Phone for special rates. *Eating facilities:* diningroom and bar in clubhouse. *Visitors:* phone in advance. *Society Meetings:* welcome weekdays and some weekends, must book in advance - contact Cathal. Secretary: Peter Doherty (074 9159459; Fax: 074 9159919).

RATHMULLAN. **Otway Golf Club**, Saltpans, Rathmullan (074 9158319). *Location*: From Rathmullan take road to Portsalon, course is two miles out on right. Seaside links course. 9 holes, 4234 yards. S.S.S. 64. *Green Fees:* 20 euros. *Eating facilities*: bar. *Visitors:* always welcome. *Society Meetings*: by arrangement. Secretary: Gerry McGivern (074 9158593; Fax: 02890 599178). e-mail: gmcgivern@ntlworld.com

REDCASTLE. **Redcastle Golf Club**, Redcastle (077 82073; Fax: 077 82214). *Location:* 4 miles from Moville on Londonderry Road. Parkland. 9 holes, 6152 yards, 5700 metres. S.S.S. 69. *Green Fees:* information not available. *Eating facilities:* Redcastle Hotel. *Visitors:* Always welcome. *Society Meetings:* special group rates if pre-booked. 35 bedroom 3 star hotel. Secretary: Danny McCartney (077 82328).*

COUNTY DUBLIN

BALBRIGGAN. **Balbriggan Golf Club**, Blackhall, Balbriggan (8412173; Fax: 8413927). *Location:* quarter of a mile south of Balbriggan on main Belfast/Dublin Road. Parkland course with fine views of Cooley Peninsula and Mourne Mountains. 18 holes, 5922 metres. S.S.S. 71. *Green Fees:* 34 euros weekdays; 37 euros weekends. Early Bird - Monday, Wednesday, Thursday and Friday: 23 euros to 10am (includes full Irish Breakfast). *Eating facilities:* full restaurant facilities and bar. *Visitors:* welcome, Tuesday Ladies' Day, Saturdays and Sundays not good as club competitions take place. *Society Meetings:* catered for Mondays, Wednesdays, Thursdays and Fridays. Secretary: Michael O'Halloran (8412229).

BALLYBOUGHAL. **Hollywood Lakes Golf Club**, Ballyboughal (8433407; Fax: 8433002). *Location*: 15 minutes north of Dublin via N1 and the R129 to Ballyboughal, right at 'T' junction then two miles on right. Parkland course with water features on 11 holes. 18 holes, 5763 metres, S.S.S. 71. Practice ground, putting greens. *Green Fees:* weekdays 35 euros, weekends and Bank Holidays 45 euros. *Eating facilities:* bar and restaurant. *Visitors:* welcome, not before 1pm at weekends, not after 4pm on Wednesday. *Society Meetings*: welcome, rates negotiable. Secretary: Sid Baldwin PGA (8433407; Fax: 8433002).

BRITTAS. **Scade Valley Golf Club**, Lynch Park, Brittas (01-458 2783; Fax: 01-458 2784). *Location*: signposted from Saggart Village (approx. 4 miles). Parkland course with spectacular views over Dublin City. 18 holes, 5960 yards, 5457 metres, Par 69, S.S.S. 68. Putting green, driving net. *Green Fees:* information not available. *Eating facilities*: bar/ restaurant. *Visitors*: welcome weekdays. Professional available for lessons. *Society Meetings*: welcome weekdays - rates negotiable. Professional: John Dignam. Secretary: Michael Downes.*

CASTLEKNOCK. **Luttrellstown Castle Golf and Country Club**, Castleknock, Dublin 15 (353 1 8089988; Fax: 353 1 8089989). *Location:* six miles from Dublin City. 18 holes Championship parkland course with magnificent lakes and well manicured greens. 18 holes, 7091 yards, 6384 metres. S.S.S. 72. Practice ground. *Green Fees:* Sunday to Thursday 85 euros, Friday and Saturday 95 euros. Reductions for groups over 25 in number. *Eating facilities:* restaurant and bar. *Visitors:* some tee times reserved for members, please phone in advance. Accommodation available at Luttrellston Castle and in stable yard apartments. *Society Meetings:* welcome subject to availability. Professional: Edward Doyle.

DONABATE. **Beaverstown Golf Club**, Donabate (00 353 1 843 6439/843 6721; Fax: 00 353 1 843 5059). *Location:* on the shores of Rogerstown Estuary in North Dublin, 6km north of Dublin Airport. Attractive course set in 140 acres of lush parkland, with orchards bordering the tees and fairways. Water comes into play on 12 holes. 18 holes, 5972 metres. S.S.S. 72, Par 72. Practice facilities. *Green Fees:* weekdays 52 euros, with member 15 euros; weekends and Bank Holidays 68 euros, with member 20 euros. (2003 rates). *Eating facilities:* bar, catering. *Visitors:* welcome. Please contact Club Manager in advance. Ladies' Day Tuesday. *Society Meetings:* welcome most Saturdays. Contact Club Manager for details. Secretary: Eric Smyth (00 353 1 843 6439). e-mail: manager@beaverstown.com website: www.beaverstown.com

THE ISLAND

Golf Club
Tel: +353 (0)1843 6205
Fax: +353 (0)1843 6860

Established 1890   Corballis, Donabate, Co. Dublin, Ireland

OPEN QUALIFYING COURSE FOR 2005-2010

For sheer awe — the kind inspired by 25 foot-high dunes, vaguely lunar crevasses running through the terrain and challenging greens — the best choice is The Island Golf Club. This classic championship links course is less than 15 minutes from Dublin airport, yet the members have kept it a great secret since 1890. It is one of the best courses in Ireland and is definitely the best golf course you have never heard of.
Par 71, SSS 73, 6,857 yds. €110 (£75 approx) visitor green fee. All visitors ensured of warm and friendly welcome.

See also Colour Advertisement on page 99

DONABATE. **Balcarrick Golf Club**, Corballis, Donabate (8436957; Fax: 8436228). *Location:* from Dublin take the M1 motorway north past Dublin Airport and Swords and take the first exit signposted Donabate/Skerries/Lusk; turn right in the village of Donabate, travel 1.5km and turn right again, Balcarrick is 1km on the right hand side. Parkland course. 18 holes, 6191 metres. Par 72. *Green Fees:* weekdays 32 euros, weekends 40 euros. *Eating facilities:* full catering and bar facilities available. *Visitors:* welcome, please telephone Professional for time sheet details. *Society Meetings:* welcome. Professional: Stephen Rayfus (8434034).

DONABATE. **Corballis Golf Links**, Donabate (8436583). *Location:* main Dublin to Belfast Road. Links course. 18 holes, 4971 yards. S.S.S. 64. Putting green. *Green Fees:* information not available. *Eating facilities:* snack food. *Visitors:* welcome anytime. Carts available. *Society Meetings:* welcome. Manager: Austin Levins.*

DONABATE. **The Island Golf Club,** Corballis, Donabate (00 353 (01)1 843614; Fax: 00 353 (01)1 8436860). *Location:* 15 minute drive from Dublin Airport, across the estuary from the village of Malahide. Links course with challenging greens. 18 holes, 6857 yards, S.S.S. 73, Par 71. *Green Fees:* 110 euros. *Visitors:* warmly welcomed.
e-mail: islandgc@iol.ie
website: www.theislandgolfclub.com

DUBLIN. **Deer Park Hotel and Golf Courses**, Howth, Co. Dublin (832 2624; Fax: 839 2405). *Location:* Deer Park Hotel, nine miles east of the city centre. Parkland with panoramic sea views. 18 holes, 6830 yards, Par 77; two 9 hole courses each (3100 yards and 3370 yards) Par 3, and 12-hole Par 36. Pitch and putt. *Green Fees:* information not available. *Eating facilities:* full à la carte restaurant, bistro and bar; meal bookings required at weekends. *Visitors:* welcome at all times, Sunday mornings expect delays. 80 bedroomed hotel, swimming pool, special golf holidays available. Clubs and carts for hire. *Society Meetings:* welcome. Hotel: (832 2624; Fax: 839 2405). Golf Shop: (839 8777).
e-mail: sales@deerpark.iol.ie
website: www.deerpark-hotel.ie

DUBLIN. **Dublin City Golf Club**, Ballinascorney (01451 6430/2082; 01459 8445). *Location:* take Exit 12 off M50, head west and turn left along R114 at The Old Mill pub, course is two miles further on. Gently sloping parkland. 18 holes, 5800 yards. S.S.S. 69. *Green Fees:* information not available. *Eating facilities:* excellent clubhouse facilities. *Visitors:* welcome, phone in advance. *Society Meetings:* welcome 7 days. Buggy, club and trolley hire. Secretary: Francis Bagnall.
e-mail: info@dublincitygolf.com
website: www.dublincitygolf.com

DUBLIN. **Edmondstown Golf Club**, Edmondstown Road, Rathfarnham, Dublin 16 (493 2461; Fax: 493 3152). *Location*: south west suburbs of Dublin city. Parkland. 18 holes, 6011 metres. S.S.S. 73 Par 71. Practice facilities available. *Green Fees*: weekdays 55 euros, weekends and state holidays 65 euros. Group rates on application. *Eating facilities*: bar and restaurant. *Society Meetings*: welcome. Professional: Andrew Crofton (494 1049). Secretary: Selwyn S. Davies (493 1082).
e-mail: info@edmondstowngolfclub.ie
website: www.edmondstowngolfclub.ie

DUBLIN. **Elm Park Golf and Sports Club**, Nutley House, Donnybrook, Dublin 4 (2693438; Fax: 2694505). *Location:* between R.T.E. and St. Vincent's Hospital. Flat parkland course. 18 holes, 5929 yards, 5422 metres. S.S.S. 68. *Green Fees:* information not available. *Eating facilities:* full bar and dining facilities. *Visitors:* welcome but must telephone to arrange times with Professional. *Society Meetings:* by special arrangement. Professional: S. Green (2692650). Secretary: A. McCormack.*

DUBLIN. **The Royal Dublin Golf Club**, North Bull Island, Dollymount, Dublin 3 (8336346). *Location:* three and a half miles north east of city centre on coast road to Howth. Seaside links. 18 holes, 6309 metres. S.S.S. 73, Par 72 Championship course. 18 holes, 6002 metres, S.S.S. 71 Medal course. Large practice ground. *Green Fees:* weekdays 100 euros (excluding Friday); weekends 115 euros (including Friday). *Eating facilities:* grill room, restaurant, two bars. *Visitors:* Monday, Tuesday, Thursday, Friday, Saturday from 4pm in Summer and Sunday 10.30am to 12 noon. Carts with green fee, caddies by arrangement. *Society Meetings:* catered for, written application must be made. Senior Professional: Christy O'Connor Snr (8339833). Professional: Leonard Owens (8336477). Secretary: John Lambe (8336346; Fax: 353 1 8336504).
e-mail: info@theroyaldublingolfclub.com
website: www.theroyaldublingolfclub.com

DUN LAOGHAIRE. **Dun Laoghaire Golf Club**, Eglinton Park, Tivoli Road, Dun Laoghaire (280 3916; Fax: 280 4868). *Location:* half a mile from town centre and ferry port. Parkland. 18 holes, 5313 metres. S.S.S. 68. *Green Fees:* 55 euros. *Eating facilities:* full bar and restaurant facilities. *Visitors:* welcome anyday but only after 5pm Saturdays. Local accommodation available. *Society Meetings:* welcome by prior arrangement. Professional: Vincent Carey (280 1694). General Manager: Dennis Peacock (280 3916; Fax: 280 4868).
e-mail: dlgc@iol.ie

KILLINEY. **Killiney Golf Club**, Ballinclea Road, Killiney (Tel. & Fax: 01 2852823). *Location:* south Dunlaoghaire. Parkland. 9 holes, 5655 metres. S.S.S. 70. *Green Fees:* 50 euros. *Eating facilities:* snacks available. *Visitors:* welcome with restrictions. Professional: P. O'Boyle. Secretary: M.F. Walsh.

KILSALLAGHAN. **Corrstown Golf Club**, Corrstown, Kilsallaghan (01 864 0533/4; Fax: 01 864 0534). *Location*: 10 minutes north of Dublin Airport. Parkland course. 27 holes. Practice green and nets. *Green Fees*: weekdays 35 euros, weekends 45 euros. *Eating facilities*: full bar and restaurant. *Visitors*: welcome Monday to Friday; Saturday and Sunday when available. *Society Meetings*: welcome. Professional: Pat Gittens (01 864 3322; Fax: 01 864 0537). Secretary: Jason Kelly (01 864 0533; Fax: 01 864 0537).
e-mail: info@corrstowngolfclub.com
website: www.corrstowngolfclub.com

KILTERNAN. **Kilternan Golf Club**, Kilternan (295 2986). *Location:* off N11 Silver Tassie Pub. Hill/parkland course. 18 holes, 4952 metres. S.S.S 66. Practice ground. *Green Fees:* weekdays 25 euros, weekends and Bank Holidays 34 euros. *Eating facilities:* clubhouse. *Visitors:* welcome anytime except Saturday and Sunday mornings, subject pre-booking tee time. Buggies and carts available. *Society Meetings:* day groups. Secretary: Jimmy Kinsella (2955559; Fax: 2955670).
e-mail: kgc@kilternan-hotel.ie

MALAHIDE. **Malahide Golf Club**, Beechwood, The Grange, Malahide (8461611; Fax: 8461270) *Location:* 15 minutes from Dublin city, three miles from Dublin Airport. Parkland. 27 holes, 6066 metres. S.S.S. 71. Practice area, Proshop. *Green Fees:* weekdays 55 euros, weekends 90 euros; Group rates available. *Eating facilities*: top class restaurant and bar. *Visitors:* welcome, must book in advance. *Society Meetings:* all welcome. Professional: John Murray (8460002; Fax: 8461270). Secretary: P. J. Smyth.
e-mail: malgc@clubi.ie

PORTMARNOCK. **Portmarnock Hotel & Golf Links**, Strand Road, Portmarnock (8461800; Fax: 8461077). *Location:* 8 miles north east of Dublin, 15 minutes from Dublin Airport. Seaside links designed by Bernhard Langer. 18 holes, 6223 metres. S.S.S. 73. Pitching area with bunker and putting green. *Green Fees:* information not available. *Eating facilities:* two restaurants and three bars. *Visitors:* no restrictions. Four star deluxe hotel, 103 bedrooms and conference facilities. *Society Meetings:* group rates and corporate packages available on request. Golf Director: Moira Cassidy.
e-mail: golfers@portmarnock.com
website: www.portmarnock.com

RATHCOOLE. **Beech Park Golf Club**, Johnstown, Rathcoole (4580522; Fax: 4588365). Flat parkland course. 18 holes, 5762 metres. S.S.S. 70. *Green Fees:* 38 euros per round. *Eating facilities:* bar and restaurant. *Visitors:* welcome Monday to Friday. *Society Meetings:* welcome Monday, Thursday, Friday. General Manager: Paul Muldowney
e-mail: info@beechpark.ie
website: www.beechpark.ie

THE APPEARANCE OF AN ASTERISK (*) AT THE END OF A CLUB OR COURSE ENTRY INDICATES THAT UP-TO-DATE INFORMATION HAS NOT BEEN SUPPLIED

The Royal Dublin Golf Club
DOLLYMOUNT, DUBLIN 3 , IRELAND
Situated three and a half miles north-east of the city centre on the coast road to Howth.
Seaside links. 18 hole championship links – Championship 6309 metres. SSS 73; Medal Course 6002 metres, SSS 71. Grill room, restaurant, bars.
Visitors welcome; Society meetings catered for.

Clubhouse: 833 7153 • Secretary/Manager 833 6346
Professional: 833 6477 • Caterer: 833 3370 • Fax: 833 6504
• e-mail: info@theroyaldublingolfclub.com • website: www.theroyaldublingolfclub.com

See also Colour Advertisement on page 98

www.halpinsprivatehotels.com

50-56 Merrion Road, Ballsbridge, Dublin 4, Ireland
Direct Dial: +353 1 2838155   Fax: +353 1 2837877
E-mail: halpins@iol.ie

• *Luxury Edwardian 4**** Properties*
• *Dublin South City Centre*
• *Superb location in exclusive Ballsbridge*
• *Beside Four Seasons Hotel and Embassy District*
• *Close to Stephens Green & Trinity College*
• *Elegant spacious air conditioned rooms*
• *Suites with Four poster & spa baths*
• *Fine Food & modern comforts*
• *Private parking and Gardens*
• *Airport Luxury coach link*
• *On Dart and bus route*
• *Golf, city and country tours arranged*

Merrion
Hall
Dublin

Aberdeen
Lodge
Dublin

Blakes
Townhouse
Dublin

Halpins
Hotel

Kilkee, Co Clare, close to Shannon Airport,
Cliffs of Moher, Burren Region and Ring of Kerry

N O T E

All the information regarding Golf Clubs in this guide is given in good faith in the belief that it is correct. However, the publishers cannot guarantee the facts given in these pages, neither are they responsible for changes in ownership or facilities, such as green fees, that may take place after the date of going to press. Readers should always satisfy themselves that the facilities they require are available and that the terms, if quoted, still apply.

RATHFARNHAM. **Stackstown Golf Club**, Kellystown Road, Rathfarnham, Dublin 16 (01-494 2338; Fax: 01-493 3934). *Location*: one mile from Exit 13 on M50 towards Rathfarnham. Parkland course situated on slopes of Dublin mountains. 18 holes, 6152 yards, S.S.S. 70. Practice fairway, putting green, driving nets. *Green Fees*: weekdays 30 euros, weekends 38 euros. *Eating facilities*: full catering and bar facilities. *Visitors*: welcome everyday except Tuesday (Ladies' Day), Wednesday afternoons and Saturday until 4pm. Professional tuition available. Fully stocked shop, clubs, trolley and cart hire. *Society Meetings*: welcome Monday, Thursday, Friday and Sunday, special rates available. Professional: Michael Kavanagh (01-494 4561; Fax: 01-493 3934). Secretary: Paul Kennedy (01 494 1993; Fax: 01-493 3934). e-mail: stackstowngc@eircom.net website: www.stackstowngolfclub.com

ST MARGARET'S. **St Margaret's Golf and Country Club**, St Margaret's, Dublin (8640400; Fax: 8640289). *Location:* beside Dublin Airport and just 7 miles north of Dublin City Centre. Parkland, championship course, ultra-modern design by Craddock and Ruddy. 18 holes, 6649 yards. S.S.S. 73. Putting and practice areas. *Green Fees:* information not available. *Eating facilities:* full bar and restaurant facilities. *Visitors:* welcome at all times. Cobra Golf Academy. *Society Meetings:* welcome. Professional: David O'Sullivan. *
e-mail: sales@stmargarets.net
website: www.st-margarets.net

ST MARGARET'S. **The Open Golf Centre**, Newtown House, St Margarets (8640324; Fax: 8341400). *Location:* 2km from Dublin Airport, adjacent to N2 (Derry road). Inviting parkland course, three lakes feature prominently. 27 holes, 9500 yards. S.S.S. 69/31. 20 bay driving range. *Green Fees:* information not available. *Eating facilities:* coffee shop. *Visitors:* welcome everyday. Teaching auditorium. *Society Meetings:* welcome. Professional: R. Machin (8640324; Fax: 8341400). Secretary: R. Yates (8640324 Fax: 8341400).*

SKERRIES. **Skerries Golf Club**, Hacketstown, Skerries (01 8491567: Fax: 01 8491591). *Location:* east of Dublin/Belfast road, approximately six miles. Parkland course close to sea with undulating fairways. 18 holes, 6081 metres. S.S.S. 72. Practice ground. *Green Fees:* weekdays 50 euros; weekends 60 euros. *Eating facilities:* restaurant, snack bar, bar, lounge. *Visitors:* welcome Mondays, Thursdays, Fridays; weekends by arrangement. *Society Meetings:* welcome. Professional: Jimmy Kinsella (01 8490925). Secretary: Aiden Burns (01 8491567; Fax: 01 8491591).

SUTTON. **Howth Golf Club**, St. Fintan's, Carrickbrack Road, Sutton, Dublin 13 (8323055; Fax: 8321793). *Location:* one and a half miles from Sutton Cross on city side of Hill of Howth. Moorland course with scenic views of Dublin Bay - very hilly. 18 holes, 5672 metres. S.S.S. 69. Practice ground. *Green Fees:* 50 euros. *Eating facilities:* restaurant facilities every day from mid-day. *Visitors:* welcome weekdays except Wednesdays. Carts. *Society Meetings:*

bookings accepted by arrangement with Secretary. Reduced rates for large groups. Professional: John McGuirk (8392617). Secretary: Mrs Ann MacNeice.

SWORDS. **Swords Open Golf Course**, Balheary Avenue, Swords (Tel & Fax: 01 8409819). *Location:* three miles west of Swords. Parkland. Broadmeadow river divides course. No climbing, flat course. 18 holes, 5631 metres. S.S.S. 70. Putting green. *Green Fees:* information not available. *Eating facilities:* coffee shop. *Visitors:* any time, very welcome. *Society Meetings:* very welcome. Secretary: Orla McGuinness.

COUNTY GALWAY

ATHENRY. **Athenry Golf Club,** Palmerstown, Oran More (091 794466; Fax: 091 794971). *Location:* 8 miles from Galway city. Parkland. 18 holes, 5687 metres. Par 70, S.S.S. 70. Practice ground. *Green Fees:* midweek Monday to Thursday 30 euros per day, weekend Friday to Sunday 35 euros per round. *Eating facilities:* full bar and catering. *Visitors:* welcome except Sunday. Deals available with local hotels. Club hire and tuition. *Society Meetings:* welcome. Pro shop (091 790599). Professional: R. Ryan. Secretary/Manager: Padraig Flattery. e-mail: athenrygc@eircom.net

ANNAGHVANE. **Connemara Isles Golf Club**, Annaghvane, Lettermore (091 572498). *Location:* Take the coast road from Galway City, at Casla (Costello) take the first right after the Texaco Station. Continue on that road for four and a half miles until you pass "An Hooker Bar" (on a bend). The golf course is 500 metres ahead. Seaside links Championship course. *Green Fees:* contact club for details. *Visitors:* always welcome. *Society Meetings:* welcome. Manager Anthony Lynch.*

BALLINASLOE. **Ballinasloe Golf Club**, Rossgloss, Ballinasloe (0905 42126; Fax: 0905 42538). *Location:* 2 miles from Ballinasloe town on Portumna side. Ballinasloe on main Dublin-Galway Road, two hours from Dublin. Mature parkland course. 18 holes, 5865 metres, Par 72. Practice area, putting green. *Green Fees:* weekdays 22 euros, weekends 28 euros. Juniors 12 euros, Husband & Wife 10 euros Concession. *Eating facilities:* full bar and catering facilities. Buggy and cart hire. *Society Meetings:* welcome Monday-Saturday, group rate 20 euros per person weekdays, 25 euros per person weekends. Special midweek rates also offered. Secretary: Dr Conor Corr (0905 42126). e-mail: ballinasloegolfclub@eircom.net website: www.ballinasloegolfclub.com

CLIFDEN. **Connemara Golf Club**, Ballyconneely, Near Clifden (095 23502/23602; Fax: 095 23662). *Location:* from Clifden to Ballyconneely, 4 miles on the right. Seaside links Championship course. 27 holes, 6611 metres. S.S.S. 73. 220 yard Par 3 13th is feature hole. Practice fairway, putting green and driving net. *Green Fees:* weekdays 50 euros, weekends 55 euros, society rate available. *Eating facilities:* full restaurant and bar facilities. *Visitors:* always welcome. Fully equipped Pro Shop. *Society Meetings:* groups of 20 or more welcome. Professional: Hugh O'Neill. Secretary: Richard Flaherty.
e-mail: links@iol.ie

GORT. **Gort Golf Club**, Kilmacduagh Road, Gort (Tel & Fax: 091 632244). *Location:* two miles south-west of Gort on Castlequalter edge of Burren Mountains. Undulating parkland. 18 holes, 5979 metres. S.S.S.71. *Green Fees:* information not available. *Eating facilities:* full bar and restaurant. *Visitors:* welcome all year, restrictions at weekends. *Society Meetings:* welcome with prior booking. Secretary: James B. Hannigan (091 632244). Designer: Christy O'Connor Jnr.*
e-mail: gortgolf@eircom.net
website: www.gortgolf.com

LOUGHREA. **Loughrea Golf Club**, Craigue, Loughrea (091 841049). *Location:* one and a half miles north east of town, on New Inn Road. Parkland, undulating, with beautiful views of town and Slieve Aughty Mountains in background. 18 holes, 5261 yards. Par 67. Practice area. *Green Fees:* information not available. *Eating facilities:* tea, coffee, sandwiches at bar. New clubhouse with full catering under construction. *Visitors:* welcome weekdays and weekends with advance booking. *Society Meetings:* welcome, please telephone. Secretary: Vinny Ryan. *

ORANMORE **Galway Bay Golf and Country Club Hotel**, Renville, Oranmore (091 790500; Fax: 091 790510). *Location:* seven miles from Galway City, through Oranmore Village. Parkland by the sea, many water hazards with the Atlantic Ocean surrounding on three sides. 18 holes, 7144 yards, 6533 metres. S.S.S. 73. Putting green, chipping green, practice area, indoor practice bays. *Green Fees:* information not available. *Eating facilities:* restaurant, spike bar, cocktail bar. *Visitors:* welcome daily. Four Star Hotel on site. *Society Meetings:* welcome daily, reduced rates for groups. Professional: Eugene O'Connor (091 790503). Director of Golf: Anne Hanley (091 790503). *
website: www.gbay-golf.com

OUGHTERARD. **Oughterard Golf Club**, Gortreevagh, Oughterard (091 552131; Fax: 091 552733). *Location:* 15 miles west of Galway City on N57 to Connemara. Parkland, newly re-modelled with Greens to USPGA Standards. 18 holes, 5876 metres. S.S.S. 70. Practice area and putting green. *Green Fees:* information not available. *Eating facilities:* full dining facilities during daylight hours. *Visitors:* welcome, booking advisable. *Society Meetings:* welcome. For group rates contact secretary. Professional: Michael Ryan. Admin: Tonya McDonagh.

SALTHILL. **Galway Golf Club,** Blackrock, Salthill (091 522033; Fax: 091 529783) *Location:* three miles west of Galway city. Parkland. 18 holes, 5832 metres. S.S.S. 71. *Green Fees:* 45 euros weekdays, 50 euros weekends. *Eating facilities:* full bar and catering facilities. *Visitors:* welcome, avoid Tuesdays and weekends. *Society Meetings:* all welcome. Professional: Don Wallace (091 523038) Secretary: Padraic Fahy (091 522033; Fax: 091 529783).

Connemara Golf Club
Ballyconneely, Clifden, Co. Galway
Tel: 095 23502/23602 • Fax: 095 23662
e-mail: links@iol.ie

Opened in 1973, the links course is bounded on three sides by the Atlantic Ocean, with, on the inland side, superb views of the Twelve Bens.

27 holes • practice range • pitching green • putting green

Green Fees: weekdays 50 euros, weekends 55 euros

Clubs, caddie cars, golf carts and caddies for hire.

See also Colour Advertisement on page 99

FHG PUBLICATIONS
publish a large range of well-known accommodation guides. We will be happy to send you details or you can use the order form at the back of this book.

COUNTY KERRY

BALLYBUNION. **Ballybunion Golf Club**, Sandhill Road, Ballybunion (068 27146; Fax: 068 27387). *Location:* 20 miles from Tralee, 10 miles from Listowel. Links course established 1893, ranked in top ten in world. Two courses - Old and Cashen. 36 holes, 6800 yards. S.S.S. 71. *Green Fees:* 2003 - Old Course 110 euros per round, Cashen Course 75 euros per round, both courses same day 135 euros. Subject to review. *Eating facilities:* full bar and catering facilities. *Visitors:* welcome weekdays, some weekends; telephone bookings in advance. Carts and caddies for hire. *Society Meetings:* catered for. Professional: Brian O'Callaghan. Secretary: Jim McKenna.

BALLYFERRITER. **Ceann Sibeal (Dingle) Golf Club**, Ballyferriter (066 915 6255/6408; Fax: 066 915 6409). *Location:* turn right quarter of a mile after Ballyferriter, 40 miles Tralee, 10 miles Dingle. Traditional links, most westerly golf course in Europe. 18 holes, 6696 yards. S.S.S. 70. Practice ground. *Green Fees:* information not available. *Eating facilities:* full bar and dining room. *Visitors:* welcome at all times, book in advance. Hotel adjacent. *Society Meetings:* all welcome. Secretary: Steve Fahy (066 9156255; Fax: 066 9156409).*
e-mail: dinglegc@iol.ie

CASTLEGREGORY. **Castlegregory Golf Club**, Stradbally, Castlegregory (066 7139444). *Location:* main Tralee Conor pass Dingle Road. Scenic links course with water features. 9 holes, 5264 metres, S.S.S. 67. Putting green. *Green Fees:* information not available. *Eating facilities:* tea and snacks available. *Visitors:* welcome at all times. *Society Meetings:* welcome, 20 euros per person.

GLENBEIGH. **Dooks Golf Club**, Glenbeigh (066 9768205; Fax: 066 9768476). *Location:* on the N70 between Killorglin and Glenbeigh. Links course. 18 holes, 6071 yards. S.S.S. 68. Putting green. *Green Fees:* 48 euros. *Eating facilities:* bar and restaurant. *Visitors:* welcome Monday to Saturday. *Society Meetings:* welcome with advance booking. Secretary/Manager: Declan Mangan.
e-mail: office@dooks.com
website: www.dooks.com

KENMARE. **Kenmare Golf Club**, Kenmare (064 41291; Fax: 064 42061). *Location:* turn left at top of Main Street in town, on main Cork/Kilgarvan Road. Partly links, partly parkland surrounded by some breathtaking views. 18 holes, 6083 yards. S.S.S. 69. Putting green, driving net. *Green Fees:* information not available. *Eating facilities:* snacks in bar only. *Visitors:* welcome at all times, enquire for weekends. Always ring in advance for booking. Club hire, pull-cart hire. *Society Meetings:* welcome, must book well in advance and deposit required. Secretary: Donna Harrington. Manager: Simon Duffield.

KILLARNEY. **Beaufort Golf Club**, Churchtown, Beaufort, Killarney (064 44440; Fax: 064 44752). *Location:* seven miles west of Killarney town, just off the N72. Parkland course in unique setting surrounded by the Kerry Mountains. 18 holes, 6587 yards, 6023 metres. S.S.S. 72. Practice facilities. *Green Fees:* 45 euros weekdays, 55 euros weekends. *Eating facilities:* large bar and full food menu. *Visitors:* welcome seven days except 1pm to 2pm, but please pre-book. Electric buggies, carts, caddies by appointment. *Society Meetings:* welcome. Special rates available on request. Professional: Hugh Duggan (087 2383930). Secretary: Colm Kelly (064 44404).

KILLARNEY. **Dunloe Golf Club**, Gap of Dunloe, Kilarney (00353 64 44578). *Location:* 10 minutes from Killarney town. Take N72 (main Killarney/Killorglin Road); first left after passing Hotel Europe. Outstanding parkland layout with beautiful views of Killarney's lakes and mountains. 9 holes. Par 34. *Green Fees:* information not available. *Eating facilities:* snack bar from 8am to 9pm (from 10am in winter). Professional: Kieran P. Crehan. *
e-mail: dunloegc@gofree.indigo.ie

KILLARNEY. **Killarney Golf and Fishing Club**, Mahony's Point, Killarney (64 31034; Fax: 64 33065). *Location:* Killarney town, two miles west on Ring of Kerry road. Undulating parkland courses - lakeside. Mahony's Point: 18 holes, 6152 metres. S.S.S. 72. Killeen: 18 holes, 6474 metres. S.S.S. 73. Lackabane Course, 18 holes, 6410 metres. Practice area. *Green Fees:* information on request. *Eating facilities:* available all day. *Visitors:* welcome at all times, reservations in advance, Handicap Certificate required. *Society Meetings:* welcome. Professional: T. Coveney (64 31615). Secretary: T. Prendergast.
e-mail: reservations@killarney-golf.com
website: www.killarney-golf.com

KILLARNEY. **Ross Golf Club**, Ross Road, Killarney (064-31125; Fax: 064-31860). *Location:* from town centre follow signs to Muckross House, take first right on Muckross Road to Ross Castle and Ross Golf Club. Parkland, wooded course. 9 holes, 6450 yards, S.S.S. 73. Practice area and putting green. *Green Fees:* information not available. *Eating facilities:* full bar and snack bar serving soup and sandwiches. *Vistors:* welcome. PGA tuition and accommodation can be arranged. *Society Meetings:* welcome, special rates available. Professional & Secretary: Alan O'Meara (064 31125; Fax: 064 31860). *
e-mail: info@rossgolfclub.com
website: www.rossgolfclub.com

KILLORGLIN. **Killorglin Golf Club**, Stealroe, Killorglin (066 9761979; Fax: 066 9761437). *Location:* just 20 minutes from Killarney and from Kerry Airport, three kilometres from the bridge at Killorglin on N70 road to the county town of Tralee. Parkland course overlooking Dingle Bay. 18 holes, 6464 yards. S.S.S. 71. *Green Fees:* weekdays 25 euros; weekends 30 euros, 9 holes 16 euros. Group rates

available on request. *Eating facilities:* bar and restaurant facilities all day. *Visitors:* always welcome, booking necessary at weekends. Accommodation can be arranged; all major credit cards accepted. *Society Meetings:* all welcome, rates on request. Manager: Billy Dodd.
e-mail: kilgolf@iol.ie

SNEEM. **Parknasilla Golf Club**, Parknasilla, Sneem (064 45122; Fax: 064 45323). *Location:* on the Ring of Kerry route, two miles east of Sneem Village. Hilly seaside course, wooded. 12 holes, 5284 metres. S.S.S. 67. Practice ground. *Green Fees:* 30 euros; guests staying at the Great Southern Hotel 20 euros. *Eating facilities:* available at Great Southern Hotel, 10 minutes' walk. *Visitors:* welcome, no restrictions. Caddy cars available. *Society Meetings:* contact 064 45122. Secretary/Manager: Maurice Walsh (064 45233).

TRALEE. **The Kerries Golf Club**, Kerries East, Tralee (667 122112; Fax: 667 120085). *Location:* one mile from Tralee town. Parkland, overlooking Tralee Bay. 9 holes. S.S.S. 68. *Green Fees:* 9 holes 15 euros, 18 holes 25 euros. *Eating facilities:* snacks and wine bar . *Visitors:* welcome daily except Sundays 8am - 12.30 pm. *Society Meetings:* groups over 20 - 9 holes £10.00, 18 holes £15.00. Secretary: Helen Barrett.

TRALEE. **Tralee Golf Club**, West Barrow, Ardfert, Tralee (066 7136379; Fax: 066 7136008). *Location:* Tralee to Barrow via the Spa and Churchill. Seaside links. 18 holes, 5939 metres, S.S.S. 71. *Green Fees:* 130 euros May to October. *Eating facilities:* bar and restaurant. *Visitors:* welcome except Wednesdays of June, July and August. Other months Wednesdays 7.30 - 10.30pm, Saturdays 11.00am - 1.24pm, Bank Holidays 11.30am to 12.54pm, no visitors on Sundays. General Manager: Anthony Byrne.
e-mail: info@traleegolfclub.com
e-mail: reservations@traleegolfclub.com
website: www.traleegolfclub.com

WATERVILLE. **Waterville House and Golf Links**, Waterville (066 9474102; Fax: 066 9474482). *Location:* one mile from Waterville, 50 miles from Killarney on the Ring of Kerry. Seaside links course, surrounded by the Atlantic Ocean and Inny River with mountain views to the background. 18 holes Championship Course. 7225 yards. S.S.S. 74. Driving range and putting green; golf clinics from Professional. *Green Fees:* Mondays to Thursdays 125 euros, 75 euros before 8am and after 4pm. Fridays, weekends and Bank Holidays 125 euros. *Eating facilities:* full catering facilities and bar. *Visitors:* welcome; course open all year round, may depend on availability. Accommodation available at Waterville House and access to fishing in private lakes and rivers. *Society Meetings:* all welcome. Professional: Liam Higgins (066 9474102; Fax: 066 9474482). Secretary/Manager: Noel Cronin (066 9474102; Fax: 066 9474482.
e-mail: wvgolf@iol.ie
website: www.watervillegolflinks.ie

COUNTY KILDARE

CARBURY. **Highfield Golf Course**, Carbury (Tel & Fax: 0405 31021). *Location*: 10km from N4, nearest major town is Edenderry. Flat parkland course set in quiet countryside. 18 holes, 6292 yards, 5720 metres, S.S.S. 70. Open air driving range, pitch and putt green, bunkers. *Green Fees*: 35 euros weekends, 25 euros midweek. *Eating facilities*: full bar and restaurant. *Visitors*: welcome, not before 11am on Sundays. Tuition available. *Society Meetings*: welcome. Secretary Damien Cullen.
e-mail: hgc@indigo.ie
website: www.highfield-golf.ie

CURRAGH. **The Curragh Golf Club**, Curragh, Newbridge (045 441238; Fax: 045 442476). *Location:* three miles south of Newbridge. Hilly parkland course. 18 holes, 6035 metres. S.S.S. 71. Practice ground. *Green Fees:* weekdays 32 euros per round, with member 15 euros; weekends and Bank Holidays 37 euros, with member 20 euros. *Eating facilities:* bar and restaurant. *Visitors:* restricted, please check in advance for course availability. *Society Meetings:* by appointment. Professional: Gerry Burke (045 441896). Secretary: Ann Culleton (045 441714; Fax: 045 442476).
e-mail: curraghgolf@eircom.net

DONADEA. **Knockanally Golf and Country Club**, Donadea, North Kildare (Tel & Fax: 045 869322). *Location:* three miles off N4 between Enfield and Kilcock. Parkland, home of the Irish International Professional Championship. 18 holes, 6495 yards. S.S.S. 72. *Green Fees:* weekdays 30 euros, weekends 50 euros. *Eating facilities:* bar and restaurant. *Visitors:* welcome, no restrictions. *Society Meetings:* by arrangement. Professional: Martin Darcy (045 869322). Secretary: Noel A. Lyons (045 869322).

KILKEA. **Kilkea Castle Hotel & Golf Club**, Kilkea, Castledermot (00353 503 45555). *Location:* southbound on N7, onto M9, then N78 to Athy. Before entering Athy look for Ford garage on right. Kilkea is signposted on the left. 18 holes. Par 70. *Green Fees:* information not available. *Eating facilities:* available all day. Award-winning restaurant.*
e-mail: kilkeagolf@eircom.net

KILL. **Killeen Golf Club**, Kill (045 86603; Fax: 045 875881). *Location:* North from Dublin on N7, turn right at Kill village. Parkland course with abundant wildlife. 18 holes, 6200 yards, 5561metres. S.S.S. 71. *Green Fees:* information not available. *Eating facilities:* restaurant and bar. *Visitors:* welcome. *Society Meetings:* welcome. For bookings contact Maurice Kelly/ Marian Farry.*

NAAS. **Craddockstown Golf Club,** Blessington Road, Naas (045 897610; Fax: 045 896968). *Location:* off the southbound N7 turn left before Naas and take Blessington road, club one mile on right. Parkland and easy walking, built 1994 with sand-based greens and ample challenges to the best of golfers. 18 holes, 6200 yards, 5645 metres. S.S.S. 69. Practice area. *Green Fees:* information not available. *Eating facilities:* Full

catering service available. *Visitors:* weekdays with restrictions at weekend and Bank Holidays. *Society Meetings*: welcome. Contact club office.

NAAS. **Naas Golf Club**, Kerdiffstown, Naas (045 897509; Fax: 045 896109). *Location*: turn left at traffic lights on N7 from Dublin and on right, one-and-a-half miles up that road. Parkland. 18 holes,6232 yards. S.S.S. 69. Practice ground. Public driving range within 200 metres. *Green Fees*: information not available. *Eating facilities:* 10.30am - 11.00 pm. *Visitors:* welcome on Mondays, Wednesdays, Fridays and Saturday afternoons. Contact club in advance. Dress code applies. *Society Meetings*: contact club office to book. Manager: John Coughlan (045 874644).

NAAS. **Woodlands Golf Club**, Coill Dubh, Cooleragh (045 860777; Fax: 045 860988). *Location:* From Naas, main Road to Sallins on to Clane village, left onto prosperous village, on to public house (Dagwelds) then turn right one mile ahead. Parkland, wooded with seven lakes. 18 holes. Putting green plus 9 hole pitch & putt course. *Green Fees:* weekdays 25 euros, weekends 30 euros. *Visitors:* welcome except Saturday pm and Sunday am. Always phone in advance. *Society Meetings:* always welcome, rates depend on number playing. Secretary: Kieron Savage (01-6298013; Fax: 01-6298041).
e-mail: woodlandsgolf@eircom.net

SALLINS. **Bodenstown Golf Club**, Sallins (045 897096). *Location:* Naas dual carriageway, turn right at Kill. 36 holes. S.S.S. 72. Practice green. *Green Fees:* 18 euros. *Eating facilities:* full catering and bar. *Visitors:* welcome, no restrictions. *Society Meetings:* please telephone. Secretary: Bernadette Curtin (045 897096).

STRAFFAN. **Castlewarden Golf and Country Club**, Castlewarden, Straffan (3531 4589254; Fax: 3531 4588972). *Location:* on the N7 Dublin to Naas road, take the second right after Blackchurch Inn. Parkland. 18 holes, 6690 yards. S.S.S. 71. Practice area and putting green. *Green Fees:* information not available. *Eating facilities:* full catering and bar. *Visitors:* welcome, booking advisable. *Society Meetings:* welcome. Professional: Gerry Egan (3531 4588219). Secretary: Fiona Kane (3531 4589838). *
e-mail: castlewarden@clubi.ie
website: www.castlewardengolfclub.com

STRAFFAN. **The K Club**, Straffan, Co. Kildare (6017300; Fax: 6017399). *Location:* N7 south of Dublin to Kill, turn right, five miles from Junction. Signposted. Parkland course with trees, lakes, River Liffey – absolute Championship course. 18 holes, 7178 yards. S.S.S.76. Driving range. *Green Fees:* 265 euros non-residents, 105 euros residents. *Eating facilities:* Legends Restaurant and Bar, The Arnold Palmer Room, Snack Bar and Members' Restaurant. *Visitors:* members' hours Winter 11am to 1pm; Summer 1.30pm to 3.30pm weekdays. Golf shop, trolleys, clubs and shoe hire. The Kildare Hotel (within complex) AA 5 Red Star; 69 bedrooms. Professional: John McHenry (6017321: Fax: 6017399). Director of Golf: Paul Crowe.
e-mail: golf@kclub.ie
website: www.kclub.ie

THE KILDARE HOTEL & GOLF CLUB

at Straffan, Co. Kildare, Ireland

The 4th Green of the new South Course,
opened July 2003

"Luxurious comfort, superb facilities"

The 550-acre grounds of The K Club are nestled amid lush
green woodlands, just 17 miles from Dublin, Ireland's capital city.
Already acclaimed as one of the finest in the world, this magnificent 5 star Hotel
offers you the highest standards of comfort and service combined with the elegance
and unique charm of an Irish country house.

You can relax and be lavishly pampered or indulge in any of the quality leisure
activities available, including our two championship golf courses,
both designed by Arnold Palmer.

95 bedrooms, all individually appointed to the highest standard.
Be it for business or pleasure, The K Club is the most rewarding place to stay.

For further information and Reservations:
Hotel: Tel: 353 (0)1 601 7200 • Fax: 353 (0)1 601 7299 Reservations
Golf: Tel: 353 (0)1 601 7300 • Fax: 353 (0)1 601 7399 Golf Reservations
E-mail: golf@kclub.ie E-mail: sales@kclub.ie • Web: www.kclub.ie

Home to The Smurfit European Open
HOST TO THE RYDER CUP IN 2006

See also Colour Advertisement on page 100

COUNTY KILKENNY

CALLAN. **Callan Golf Club**, Geraldine, Callan (056 25136/25949; Fax: 056 55155). *Location*: One mile from Callan on the Knocktopher Road. Parkland course with many water features. 18 holes, 6400 yards. S.S.S. 70. Practice area. *Green Fees*: 25 euros weekdays; 30 euros Saturday and Sunday.. *Eating facilities*: food available all day, bar. *Visitors*: welcome - best to check with Golf Shop in advance. *Society Meetings*: all welcome. Professional: John O'Dwyer. Secretary/Manager: Liam Duggan (056 25136).
e-mail: info@callangolfclub.com
website: www.callangolfclub.com

CASTLECOMER. **Castlecomer Golf Club**, Drumgoole, Castlecomer (Tel & Fax: 00 353 564 441139). *Location*: Main Castlecomer/Kilkenny Road. Parkland course beside the River Deen. 18 holes, 6175 metres. S.S.S. 72. Par 72. Practice ground. *Green Fees*: weekdays 40 euros, weekends 50 euros. *Eating facilities*: catering available. *Visitors*: always welcome. *Society Meetings*: welcome, society and group rates available. Secretary: Matt Dooley (00 353 567 727480).
e-mail: castlecomergolf@eircom.net
website: www.castlecomergolf.com

KILKENNY. **Kilkenny Golf Club**, Glendine, Kilkenny (056 65400; Fax: 056 23593). *Location:* off Castlecomer Road two kilometres from centre of city. Parkland. 18 holes, 6500 yards. S.S.S. 70. Practice area. *Green Fees:* weekdays 35 euros, weekends 40 euros. *Eating facilities:* available. *Visitors:* welcome, weekends by arrangement. *Society Meetings:* welcome, by arrangement. Professional: Jimmy Bolger (056 61730). Secretary: Anne O'Neill (056 65400; Fax: 056 23593).

THOMASTOWN. **Mount Juliet Golf Club**, Thomastown (056 73000; Fax: 056 73078). *Location:* Thomastown - on main Dublin to Waterford Road. Parkland, designed by Jack Nicklaus, home of the 1993-95 Irish Open. Home of the American Express World Golf Championship 2002 won by Tiger Woods. Voted Golf Course of the Year 2003. 18 holes, 7112 yards. S.S.S. 74, 72, 69. Golf academy and driving range. *Green Fees:* information not available. *Eating facilities:* hotel, spike bar, President's bar, two restaurants. *Visitors:* welcome, no restrictions but please book in advance. Handicap Cards essential. 59 bedroom de luxe Hotel. *Society Meetings:* please book in advance. Professional: Sean Cotter.

COUNTY LAOIS

ABBEYLEIX. **Abbeyleix Golf Club**, Rathmoyle, Abbeyleix (0502 31450; Fax: 0502 30108). *Location*: quarter mile outside town of Abbeyleix on Ballyroan Road. Parkland course with many water features. Practice chipping and putting green. 18 holes, 6020 yards. S.S.S. 70. *Green Fees*: information not available. *Eating facilities*: bar/restaurant (by arrangement). *Visitors*: welcome weekdays, weekends after 5pm. Secretary: Michael Martin (0502 31546).*
website: www.abbeyleixgolfclub.com

MOUNTRATH. **Mountrath Golf Club**, Knockanina, Mountrath (0502 32558 (Public) or 0502 32643 (Office). or Fax: 0502 56735). *Location:* one kilometre off Dublin/Limerick Road, turn left outside Mountrath, signposted. Undulating parkland course with river flowing through it. 18 holes, 6100 yards, 5518 metres. S.S.S. 69. Putting green, chipping green and practice area. *Green Fees:* 20 euros. *Eating facilities:* available everyday and by arrangement. Bar everyday. *Visitors:* welcome weekdays, and weekends after 4pm, phone beforehand. *Society Meetings:* welcome, contact office. Secretary: Dinah Kingsley.

PORTLAOISE. **The Heath Golf Club**, The Heath, Portlaoise (0502 46045; Fax: 0502 48666). *Location:* three-and-a-half miles northeast of Portlaoise, off main Dublin road. Relatively flat with furze, gorse and three lakes. 18 holes, 5736 metres. S.S.S. 71. 10 bay all-weather floodlit driving range and practice area. *Green Fees:* weekdays 16 euros, weekends 30 euros. *Eating facilities:* full bar and catering facilities available. *Visitors:* welcome at all times but advance booking required for weekends and Public Holidays. *Society Meetings:* welcome by prior arrangement. Professional: Mark O'Boyle.

PORTLAOISE. **Rathdowney Golf Club**, Rathdowney, Portlaoise (0505 46170 or Tel & Fax: 0505 46065 office). *Location*: half a mile from Rathdowney, signposted from the square. Parkland course with gentle sloping hills; good test for most golfers (second 9 holes opened June 1997). 18 holes, 5894 metres, S.S.S. 70, Par 71. *Green Fees:* weekdays 20 euros; weekends and Public Holidays 25 euros. *Eating facilities*: bar open daily (afternoon), catering by prior arrangement. *Visitors:* welcome any time during the week, Sundays after 4.30pm, Saturday mornings reserved for societies. *Society Meetings:* welcome by appointment through Hon. Secretary. Hon. Secretary: Sean Bolger.

COUNTY LEITRIM

BALLINAMORE. **Ballinamore Golf Club**, Ballinamore (078 44346). *Location:* one-and-a-half miles north-west of town alongside Shannon/Erne waterway. Parkland. 9 holes, 6142 yards, 5514 metres. S.S.S.68. *Green Fees:* information not available. *Eating facilities:* bar with snacks. *Visitors:* welcome with some restrictions on certain weekends. *Society Meetings:* welcome with restrictions on certain weekends. Captain: Michael Moran (2002) (078 45951). Secretary: Martin McCartin (2002).*

COUNTY LIMERICK

ABBEYFEALE. **Abbeyfeale Golf Club**, Dromtrasna Collins, Abbeyfeale (068 32033). *Location*: two miles from Abbeyfeale. Parkland. 9 holes, 4072 yards. S.S.S. 64. 20 bay indoor driving range, practice putting green. *Green Fees*: information not available. *Eating facilities*: by appointment. *Visitors*: welcome everyday. *Society Meetings:* societies/companies/groups always welcome. Professional: John Sugrue (068 32033). Hon. Secretary: Conleth Dillon (068 31454).
e-mail: abbeyfealegolf@hotmail.com.

ARDAGH. **Newcastle West Golf Club**, Ardagh (00-353-6976500; Fax: 00-353-6976511). *Location:* Off N21 roadway linking Shannon, Limerick and Killarney beyond Rathkeale. Parkland course. 18 holes, 6400 yards. S.S.S. 72. Flood-lit driving bays, practice green and bunker. *Green Fees:* information not available. *Eating facilities:* Bar and restaurant. *Visitors:* welcome except Sundays. *Society Meetings:* welcome - Green Fee reductions. Professional: Tom Murphy (Tel & Fax: 00-353-6976500) Secretary: Paddy Lyons (Tel & Fax: 00-353-6976500).

BALLYNEETY. **Limerick County Golf and Country Club**, Ballyneety (061 351881; Fax: 061 351384). *Location:* five miles from Limerick City, R512 direction of Lough Gur/Kilmallock. Championship standard, parkland course with water hazards bordering 8 holes. 18 holes, 6116 metres. S.S.S. 73. Driving range, putting greens, 3 hole short game area, golf school with professional tuition. *Green Fees:* information not available. *Eating facilities:* excellent restaurant serving international cuisine, light snacks, lunch and dinner menus, full bar service. *Visitors:* always welcome, telephone in advance to assure tee space. Play and Stay packages available. *Society Meetings:* welcome. Professional: Donal McSweeney (061 351881). Manager: Gerry McKeon (061 351881; Fax: 061 351384).
e-mail: lcgolf@iol.ie
website: www.limerickcounty.com

CASTLETROY. **Castletroy Golf Club**, Castletroy (061 335261; Fax: 061 335373). *Location:* three miles from Limerick City on N7 (Dublin Road). Parkland with numerous trees. 18 holes, 5854 metres. S.S.S. 70. *Green Fees:* weekdays 40 euros, weekends and Bank Holidays 50 euros. *Eating facilities:* full catering service, bar. *Visitors:* welcome all week. Tuesday is Ladies' Day - advisable to phone. Golf Shop (061 330450). *Society Meetings:* welcome Mondays, Wednesdays and Fridays, group rates available. Golf Shop: (061 330450). Secretary: Laurence Hayes (061 335753; Fax: 061 335373). General Manager: Patrick Keane.

LIMERICK. **Limerick Golf Club**, Ballyclough, Limerick (061 414083; Fax: 061 319219). *Location*: five km from Limerick city on Fedamore Road. Parkland. 18 holes, 5932 metres. S.S.S. 71. *Green Fees:* 50 euros Monday to Thursday, 60 euros Friday to Sunday and Bank Holidays. *Eating facilities:* full bar and dining facilities. *Visitors*: welcome Mondays, Wednesdays, Thursdays, Fridays up to 4pm. *Society Meetings*: advance booking required. Professional: Lee Harrington (061 412492). General Manager: Pat Murray (061 415146).

NEWCASTLE WEST. **Killeline Golf Club**, Newcastle West (069 61600; Fax: 069 77428). *Location:* quarter-of-a-mile off the main Limerick to Kerry road on Drumcollier road. Flat parkland. 18 holes, 7000 metres. S.S.S. 72. *Green Fees:* information not available. *Eating facilities:* two bars and restaurant. *Visitors:* welcome. *Society Meetings:* welcome. Leisure facilities include swimming pool, sauna, gymnasium. 32 bedroom lodge. Secretary: Paul O'Toole. Director of Golf: Kevin Dorrian.*

COUNTY LONGFORD

LONGFORD. **County Longford Golf Club**, Glack, Dublin road, Longford (043 46310; Fax: 043 47082). *Location:* one mile from centre of town on Dublin road. 18 holes, 6044 yards. S.S.S. 69. Practice ground. *Green Fees:* 18 euros weekdays, 23 euros weekends. Special rates for groups over 20. Course is currently under redevelopment, completion scheduled for June 2004. Rates will be reviewed at that time. *Eating facilities:* full catering and bar. *Visitors:* welcome at all times subject to availability. Buggies and carts available. *Society Meetings:* all welcome. Secretary: Dan Rooney.

COUNTY LOUTH

ARDEE. **Ardee Golf Club**, Townparks, Ardee (041 6853227; Fax: 041 6856137). Parkland, wooded course with beautiful mature trees. 18 holes, 6348 yards, S.S.S. 71. Large practice area. *Green Fees:* information not available. *Eating facilities:* restaurant and bar. *Visitors:* welcome weekdays except Wednesdays, weekends by appointment only. Carts for hire, caddies by arrangement. *Society Meetings:* welcome Mondays to Saturdays. Professional: Scott Kirkpatrick (041 6857472). Hon Secretary: B. Healy. Secretary/Manager: M.P. Conoulty (041 6853227; Fax: 041 6856137).*

DROGHEDA. **County Louth Golf Club**, Baltray, Drogheda (041 9881530; Fax: 041 9881531). *Location:* Drogheda, five miles north east. Championship links course. 18 holes, 6932 yards. S.S.S. 72. *Green Fees:* weekdays 90 euros; weekends 110 euros. *Eating facilities:* restaurant, coffee shop and bar. *Visitors:* welcome weekdays except Tuesdays on application, weekends restricted. Residential accommodation available for 20 persons. *Society Meetings:* on application. Professional: Paddy McGuirk (041 9881536). Secretary: Michael Delany (041 9881530; Fax: 041 9881531).

DROGHEDA. **Seapoint Golf Club**, Termonfeckin, Drogheda (041 982333; Fax: 041 982331). *Location:* Dublin–Belfast–Drogheda to Termonfeckin Road. Links course. 18 holes, 6339 metres. S.S.S. 74. Practice range and putting green. *Green Fees:* information not available. *Eating facilities:* restaurant and bar. *Visitors:* welcome at all times; members' tee times 1-2pm daily and up to 10.30am weekends. *Society Meetings:* welcome, discounts available. Trolleys and caddies available. Professional: David Carroll. Secretary: Kevin Carrie.
e-mail: info@seapointgolfclub.com
website: www.seapointgolfclub.com

DUNDALK. **Dundalk Golf Club**, Blackrock, Dundalk (042 9321731; Fax: 042 9322022). *Location:* Dundalk coast road to Blackrock, two miles. Championship parkland course with tree-lined fairways. Hosted All Ireland Finals in 1997 and 2000. Attracts country's top players to Senior Scratch Cup. Hosts major PGA Pro-Am and Ladies' Home Internationals. Celebrates Centenary in 2005. 18 holes, 6776 yards, 6160 metres. S.S.S. 72 (Par 72). Six acre field practice ground. *Green Fees:* 55 euros (15 euros with a member). *Eating facilities:* full restaurant and bar. *Visitors:* welcome Mondays, Wednesdays, Thursdays and Fridays, restrictions weekends and Tuesday Ladies' Day. *Society Meetings:* welcome by appointment. Professional: Leslie Walker (042 9322102). Secretary/Manager: Terry Sloane (042 9321731; Fax: 042 9322022).
e-mail: dkgc@iol.ie
website: www.eiresoft.com/dundalkgc/

GREENORE. **Greenore Golf Club**, Greenore (042 93 73212/73678; Fax: 042 9383898). *Location:* Dundalk/ Newry, Dundalk 15 miles, Newry 12 miles. Flat semi-links course with heathland features, pine trees, rivers, ponds – very scenic, Carlingford Mountains and Mountains of Mourne. 18 holes, 6647 yards. S.S.S. 73. *Green Fees:* weekdays 32 euros; weekends and Bank Holidays 45 euros; subject to review. *Eating facilities:* full catering and bar facilities (daylight hours). *Visitors:* always welcome, prior booking advisable. Caddies on request, trolley and golf buggy available for hire. *Society Meetings:* very welcome by prior arrangement. Secretary: Connie O'Connor (042 9373678).
e-mail: greenoregolfclub@eircom.net
website: www.greenoregolf.com

KILLIN. **Killin Park Golf & Country Club**, Killin, Dundalk (00353 42 9339303). *Location:* two miles west of Dundalk. Undulating parkland with mature trees. The 4th and 6th holes are surrounded by the Castletown River. 18 holes. Par 69. *Green Fees:* weekdays 20 euros, weekends and Bank Holidays 25 euros. *Eating facilities:* available from dawn till dusk.

COUNTY MAYO

ACHILL. **Achill Golf Club**, Keel, Achill Island (098 43456). *Location:* N59 from Westport and R319 from Mulranny to Achill. Flat seaside links in scenic setting. 9 holes, 2947 yards, 2689 metres. S.S.S. 67. *Green Fees:* information not available. *Visitors:* welcome at all times, no restrictions. *Society Meetings:* by prior arrangement. Secretary: Sean P. Connolly.*

BALLINA. **Ballina Golf Club**, Mossgrove, Shanaghy, Ballina (Tel & Fax: 096 21050). *Location:* on Bonniconlon Road. Parkland course. 18 holes, 6103 yards. S.S.S. 69. *Green Fees:* weekdays 30 euros, weekends 40 euros. *Eating facilities:* bar, snacks. *Visitors:* welcome every day, Sundays 11am to 1.30pm. *Society Meetings:* weekdays to 4pm, Saturdays 10am to 12 noon, Sundays 11am to 1.30pm. Secretary: Padhraig Connolly (096 21050; Fax: 096 2178).
e-mail: ballinagc@eircom.net
website: www.ballinagolfclub.com

BALLINROBE. **Ballinrobe Golf Club**, Cloonacastle, Ballinrobe (092 41118; Fax: 092 41889). *Location:* off N84 at Ballinrobe onto the R331 to Claremorris. Parkland course with trees and man-made lakes. 18 holes, 6857 yards, 6234 metres. S.S.S. 73. Practice ground, golf range. *Green Fees:* information not available. *Eating facilities:* catering and bar facilities. *Visitors:* welcome at all times but is advisable to book tee times in advance. Buggies, carts and caddies available. Excellent shooting and beside two of the best trout fishing lakes in Europe. *Society Meetings:* welcome by arrangement. Professional: David Kearney. Secretary: Tom Feerick.*

BELMULLET. **Carne Golf Links,** Belmullet (097 82292; Fax: 097 81477) *Location:* on N59 three km from centre of Belmullet town. Pure links course - feature holes 9th, 14th and 18th. 18 holes, 6119 metres. Medal S.S.S 72; Championship. S.S.S 72, Par 72. Practice ground and putting green. *Green Fees:* 45 euros weekdays; 50 euros per round weekends and Bank Holidays. *Eating facilities:* full restaurant and bar facilities. *Visitors:* very welcome at all times. Buggies and caddies available. *Society Meetings:* by arrangement. Secretary/Manager: James O'Hara (097 82292; Fax: 097 81477).
e-mail: carngolf@iol.ie
website: www.carnegolflinks.com

CASTLEBAR. **Castlebar Golf Club**, Rocklands, Castlebar (353 94 21649; Fax: 353 94 26088). *Location:* situated on the Galway road out of town. Championship, parkland course with abundance of water and trees. 18 holes, 6500 yards, S.S.S. 70. *Green Fees:* 25 euros Monday to Thursday, 32 euros Friday to Sunday. *Eating facilities:* full catering facilities. *Visitors:* welcome every day, except Sunday before 1.30pm. *Society Meetings:* welcome every day except Sunday. Secretary: Jim McGovern (353 87 2267936).

CLAREMORRIS. **Claremorris Golf Club**, Claremorris (094 71527). *Location:* on N17, Galway 35 miles, Claremorris two miles, Knock airport 20 miles. Parkland/wooded course designed by Tom Craddock; numerous water hazards and excellent sand-based greens. 18 holes, 7000 yards. S.S.S. 72. Practice ground. *Green Fees:* information not available. *Visitors:* welcome weekdays, weekends on request.

Society Meetings: welcome, booking required. Admin Manager: Christina Rush (087 6441204) *
e-mail: claremorrisgc@ebookireland.com
website: www.ebookireland.com

SWINFORD. **Swinford Golf Club**, Brabazon Park, Swinford (094 92 51378). *Location:* on Kiltimagh Road beside Swinford town. Parkland. 9 holes, S.S.S. 68. Practice green and pitching area. *Green Fees:* 15 euros. *Eating facilities:* bar with catering by arrangement. *Visitors:* welcome with some restrictions. *Society Meetings:* Golf societies welcome, prices on application. Secretary: Tom Regan (094 92 51502).
e-mail: regantommy@eircom.net

WESTPORT. **Westport Golf Club**, Carrowholly, Westport (098 28262/27070; Fax: 098 27217). Parkland championship course. 18 holes. Practice area. *Green Fees:* weekdays 38 to 40 euros, weekends 45 to 50 euros. *Eating facilities:* bar and restaurant. *Visitors:* welcome with restrictions. *Society Meetings:* welcome. Professional: Alex Mealia. Secretary: Margaret Walsh. Manager: Paul O'Neil.
e-mail: wpgolf@eircom.net

COUNTY MEATH

ASHBOURNE. **Ashbourne Golf Club**, Archerstown, Ashbourne (00 353 (0)1835 2005 or 2562). *Location:* 12 miles from Dublin, on the road to Derry. Parkland course to USGA standards. 18 holes. Par 71. *Green Fees:* weekdays 35 euros, weekends 45 euros. *Eating facilities:* from 10am to 11pm (noon to 4pm during winter). Professional: John Dwyer.
e-mail: ashgc@iol.ie
website: www.ashgc@iol.ie

BETTYSTOWN. **Laytown and Bettystown Golf Club**, Bettystown, Drogheda. *Location:* 25 miles north of Dublin. A traditional links golf course, a good test for any golfer, excellent conditions. 18 holes, 5697 metres. S.S.S. 72. *Green Fees:* weekdays 45 euros; weekends 55 euros. *Eating facilities:* full bar and catering facilities. *Visitors:* welcome but make reservation. *Society Meetings:* welcome; make reservation. Professional: Robert J. Browne (041 9828793). Secretary: Helen Finnegan (041 9827170; Fax: 041 9828506).

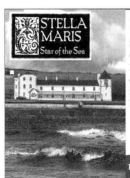

DUNSHAUGHLIN. **Black Bush Golf Club**, Thomastown, Dunshaughlin (01-8250021; Fax: 01-8250400). *Location*: situated on the Navan Road, Dunshaughlin. Lush fairways bordered by mature trees with sand based greens. 27 holes, played in a combination. Course A + B 6849 yards, S.S.S. 72; B + C 6434 yards, S.S.S. 70; C + A 6599 yards, S.S.S. 71. *Green Fees*: weekdays from 30 euros; weekends from 45 euros. *Visitors*: welcome weekdays, limited tee times on Saturday and Sunday, Tuesday is Ladies Day. Tuition available. *Society Meetings*: welcome, 35 euros Monday to Thursday, includes a 6.50 euros meal voucher; Friday and Saturday 50 euros with meal voucher. Professional: Shane O'Grady (01-8250793). Secretary: Michael Connellan.

KELLS. **Headfort Golf Club**, Kells (046 40146; Fax: 046 49282). *Location*: on N3 from Dublin, bypass Navan and half-a-mile from Kells. Parkland. 18 holes x 2, 6007 metres. S.S.S. 71. Practice area. *Green Fees*: information not available. *Eating facilities*: bar and full catering. *Visitors*: welcome weekdays. *Society Meetings*: welcome by prior arrangement. Professional: Brendan McGovern (Tel. & Fax: 046 40639). Admin. Secretary: Nora Murphy (046 82001).

KILCOCK. **Kilcock Golf Club**, Gallow, Kilcock (01 628 7592 / 628 4074). *Location:* off main Dublin to Galway motorway at Kilcock. Parkland with undulating fairways, light rough, and fast greens. Practice area. 18 holes, 5801 metres. S.S.S.71. *Green Fees:* 30 euros weekdays, 35 euros weekends. *Eating facilities:* catering available. *Visitors:* welcome but some restrictions at weekends. *Society Meetings:* welcome but must book. Secretary: Brendan Tyrrell (01 604 2683). Secretary: Sean Dowling (01 628 7592 / 628 7283).

NAVAN. **Royal Tara Golf Club**, Bellinter, Navan (+353 46 25244/25508/26868). *Location*: 25 miles north of Dublin off National Primary Route N3 - close to Hill of Tara. Parkland, private course. 18 hole course, 6457 yards, S.S.S. 71. 9 hole course 3184 yards, S.S.S. 35. Practice ground. *Green Fees*: 18 holes course - 35 euros weekdays, 40 euros weekends; 9 hole course - 15 euros weekdays and weekends. *Eating facilities*: full catering facilities all day every day. *Visitors*: welcome, Ladies' Day Tuesdays, please check with club in advance. Carts and caddies on request. *Society Meetings*: welcome except Tuesdays and Sundays. Professional: Mr Adam Whiston (+353 46 902 6009). Hon Secretary: Mr Paddy O'Brien. General Manager: Larry Clarke (+353 46 902 5508; Fax: +353 46 902 6684). e-mail: info@royaltaragolfclub.com website: www.royaltaragolfclub.com

COUNTY MONAGHAN

CARRICKMACROSS. **Mannan Castle Golf Club**, Donaghmoyne, Carrickmacross ((42) 9663308). *Location:* 3 miles from Carrickmacross on Crossmaglen Road. Wooded parkland course. 18 holes, 5795 yards. S.S.S. 71. *Green Fees:* information not available. *Eating facilities:* Full restaurant in operation. *Visitors:* welcome any day except Sunday before 4.00pm. *Society Meetings:* especially welcome, contact Sheila for details.* e-mail: mannancastlegc@eircom.net

CARRICKMACROSS. **Nuremore Hotel & Country Club**, Carrickmacross (042 9661438). *Location:* 50 miles north of Dublin on N2. *Green Fees:* 35 euros midweek, 40 euros weekends. *Eating facilities:* bar and catering facilities in hotel and clubhouse. *Visitors:* welcome at all times. Opening hours - daylight hours. All hotel facilities. Professional: Maurice Cassidy (042 9664016; Fax: 042 9661853). e-mail: nuremore@eircom.net website: www.nuremore-hotel.ie

CASTLEBLAYNEY. **Castleblayney Golf Club**, Onomy, Hope Castle Estate, Castleblayney (042 9749485). *Location:* N2 road, Hope Castle Estate, 500 yards from town centre. Scenic parkland course with lakes and forest in centre of Leisure Park. 9 holes, 5345 yards. S.S.S. 66. *Green Fees:* weekdays 12 euros, weekends 15 euros. *Eating facilities:* snacks and bar. *Visitors:* welcome at all times except during major competitions at weekends. Accommodation in Hope Castle Complex. *Society Meetings:* welcome. Secretary: Raymond Kernan (Tel & Fax: 042 9740451).

CLONES. **Clones Golf Club**, Hilton Demesne, Clones (047 56017). *Location:* three miles from Clones on the Scotshouse Road. Parkland course. 18 holes, 5600 metres. Par 69. S.S.S. - White 69, Yellow 67. Practice area and putting green. *Green Fees:* 25 euros all week or 15 euros with a member. *Eating facilities:* full catering facilities all year round. *Visitors:* welcome at all times, advance booking necessary at weekends. Caddy cars and buggy hire available. *Society Meetings:* welcome. Hon. Secretary: Martin Taylor (049 5552354). e-mail: clonesgolfclub@eircom.net

MONAGHAN. **Rossmore Golf Club**, Cootehill Road, Monaghan (047 81316). *Location:* 2 km from Monaghan town. Parkland. 18 holes, 5600 metres. S.S.S. 69. *Green Fees:* weekdays 25 euros, weekends and Bank Holidays 35 euros. *Eating facilities:* available. *Visitors:* always welcome. *Society Meetings:* welcome. Professional: Gareth McShea (047 71222). Secretary: Jimmie McKenna.

THE APPEARANCE OF AN ASTERISK * AT THE END OF A CLUB OR COURSE ENTRY INDICATES THAT UP-TO-DATE INFORMATION HAS NOT BEEN SUPPLIED

COUNTY OFFALY

Fax: 0506 55021)
e-mail: info@eskerhillsgolf.com
website: www.eskerhillsgolf.com

BIRR. **Birr Golf Club**, "The Glenns", Birr (0509 20082; Fax: 0509 22155). *Location*: approximately two miles from Birr on the Banagher Road. Parkland/wooded, carved out of natural woodlands, with undulating fairways. The course was originally part of the Estate of the Earl of Rosse, who still lives in Birr Castle. 18 holes, 6317 yards, 5754 metres. S.S.S. 70. Driving range. *Green Fees*: information not available. *Eating facilities*: available; bar. *Visitors*: always welcome; some restrictions on Sundays only. Golf shop (0509 21606). *Society Meetings*: all welcome. Secretary: Mary O'Gorman.*

EDENDERRY. **Edenderry Golf Club**, Kishawanny, Edenderry (0469 731072; Fax: 0469 733911). *Location*: outside Edenderry, quarter of a mile on Dubin Road then turn left after half a mile, on left hand side. Wooded course. 18 holes, S.S.S. 72. *Green Fees*: weekdays 30 euros, weekends 35 euros. *Eating facilities*: catering available. *Visitors*: welcome Monday, Tuesday, Wednesday and Friday, please telephone for booking. *Society Meetings*: welcome, please book in advance. Hon. Secretary: Pat O'Connell (044 22211).
e-mail: enquiries@edenderrygolfclub.com
website: www.edenderrygolfclub.com

OFFALY. **Castle Barna Golf Club**, Daingean (0506 53384; Fax: 0506 53077). *Location*: ten miles east of Tullamore and 8 miles south of main N6 Dublin to Galway road. Parkland with mature trees. 18 holes, 6200 yards. S.S.S. 69. *Green Fees*: weekdays 20 euros, weekends 27 euros. *Eating facilities*: meals available. *Visitors*: welcome except Sundays before noon. *Society Meetings*: welcome.

TULLAMORE. **Esker Hills Golf Club**, Tullamore (0506 55999; Fax: 0506 55021). *Location*: 3 miles from Tullamore, off the Tullamore/Clara Road (N80 Route). Parkland course with a distinct links feel. 18 holes, 6618 metres. S.S.S.71. Putting green, practice nets. *Green Fees*: weekdays 35 euros; weekends 45 euros. *Eating facilities*: available. *Visitors*: welcome. Golf buggies available for hire at 25 euros per buggy. *Society Meetings*: welcome. Group rates on request. Secretary: Caroline Guinan (0506 55999;

TULLAMORE. **Tullamore Golf Club**, Brookfield, Tullamore (0506 21439 Fax: 0506 41806). *Location*: from Dublin take N4 to Kinnegad then N6 to Kilbeggan, then N52 to Tullamore then three kilometres south of town towards Kinnity. Parkland. 18 holes, 6434 yds, 5885 metres. S.S.S. 71. Practice area. *Green Fees*: 37 euros weekdays, 48 euros weekends. 25 euros with member. *Eating facilities*: full bar and dining service, order meals before play. *Visitors*: welcome; restrictions Tuesdays; no visitors on a Sunday, consult Professional. Local accommodation available. *Society Meetings*: welcome, contact Secretary. Professional: Donagh McArdle (Tel & Fax: 0506 51757). Secretary: Jo Barber-Loughnane (0506 21439) or Ann Marie Cunniffe.

COUNTY ROSCOMMON

ATHLONE. **Athlone Golf Club**, Hodson Bay, Athlone (0902 92073 Fax: 0902 94080). *Location*: off the Roscommon road close to the Hodson Bay Hotel. Parkland championship standard course with mature trees and undulating fairways. 18 holes, 5854 metres. S.S.S.71. Practice ground. *Green Fees*: information not available. *Eating facilities*: restaurant and bar. *Visitors*: welcome Monday to Saturday, contact club in advance. *Society Meetings*: welcome. Professional: Martin Quinn. Administrative Secretary: I. Dockery.*

CARRICK-ON-SHANNON. **Carrick-on-Shannon Golf Club**, Woodbrook, Carrick-on-Shannon (07196 67015). *Location*: four miles west of Carrick-on-Shannon adjacent to N4. Parkland course overlooking River Shannon, a fine test of golf for low/ high handicappers. 18 holes, 5787 metres. S.S.S. 68. *Green Fees*: winter – weekdays 25 euros, weekends 30 euros; summer – weekdays 30 euros, weekends 35 euros. *Eating facilities*: full catering facilities available. *Visitors*: welcome midweek and weekends, please phone in advance. *Society Meetings*: welcome by arrangement. Secretary: Liz (07196 67015). e-mail: ckgc3@eircom.net

ROSCOMMON. **Roscommon Golf Club**, Mote Park, Roscommon (0903 26382; Fax: 0903 26043). *Location*: half a mile mile south of Roscommon town. Rolling parkland, special feature 13th hole over lake Par 3. 18 holes, 6059 metres. S.S.S. 71. Practice ground, putting green. *Green Fees*. information not available. *Eating facilities*: full bar and restaurant. *Visitors*: welcome, restrictions Sundays (competition day). Carts, caddies. *Society Meetings*: welcome with restrictions as for visitors. Secretary: Noreen O'Grady (0903 26382).
e-mail: rosgolfclub@eircom.net

COUNTY SLIGO

BALLYMOTE. **Ballymote Golf Club**, Ballinascarrow, Ballymote (071 9183504/9183089). *Location:* 15 miles south of Sligo town, 12 miles west of Boyle. Undulating parkland with pleasant views. 9 holes, 2651 metres. S.S.S. 67 (for 18 holes). *Green Fees:* information not available. *Visitors:* welcome at all times (some restrictions July and August). Carts available 3 euros rental. *Society Meetings:* please telephone. Secretary: Damien Mullaney.*

ENNISCRONE. **Enniscrone Golf Club**, Enniscrone (096 36297 three lines; Fax: 096 36657). *Location:* on coast road from Sligo to Ballina, about 13 km from Ballina. Championship links course - host to the Irish Close Championship 1993 - host to West of Ireland Championship 1997-1999 - host to Senior Inter Provincials 1999. 18 holes, 6857 yards. Par 73. Practice area and putting green. *Green Fees:* information not available. *Eating facilities:* bar and full catering facilities. *Visitors:* welcome, please phone beforehand. Professional: Charlie McGoldrick (096 36666). Hon. Secretary: Brian Casey (096 36414). Administrator: Anne Freeman. Secretary/Manager: Mick Staunton. Rated number 66 in Top 100 Courses in Great Britain and Ireland - Golf World. *
e-mail: enniscronegolf@eircom.net
website: www.enniscronegolf.com

ROSSES POINT. **County Sligo Golf Club**, Rosses Point (071 77134; Fax: 071 77460). *Location:* 8km west of Sligo city at Rosses Point village. Championship links course which has hosted all of Ireland's major championships - rates No 24 in Golf World's 100 Best Courses. 18 holes, 6037 metres. S.S.S. 72. Large practice area. *Green Fees:* Monday to Thursday 60 euros; Friday, Saturday and Sunday 75 euros. Subject to review. *Eating facilities:* full 80 seat restaurant, spacious lounge bar. *Visitors:* welcome seven days. No fourballs. Tuesdays Ladies' Day. Additional 9 holes Par 35. Ten electric buggies available at 40 euros per round. *Society Meetings:* welcome. Professional: Mr Jim Robinson (071 77171; Fax: 071 77460). Manager: Jim Ironside (071 77134; Fax: 071 77460). Reservations: Teresa Banks (071 77186).

COUNTY TIPPERARAY

CAHIR. **Cahir Park Golf Club**, Kilcommon, Cahir (052 41474; Fax: 052 42717). *Location:* half-a-mile from Cahir town on Clogheen road. Parkland. 18 holes, 5740 metres. S.S.S. 71. *Green Fees:* information not available. *Eating facilities:* meals available, bar, dining room in new clubhouse. *Visitors:* welcome. Practice area. Locker rooms. Buggy available for hire.*Society Meetings:* welcome. Hon Secretary: M.J. Costello (052 41474). *

CARRICK-ON-SUIR. **Carrick-on-Suir Golf Club**, Garravoone, Carrick-on-Suir (051 640047; Fax: 051 640558). *Location:* one mile from Carrick-on-Suir on Dungarvan Road. Parkland course set against the backdrop of the Comeragh Mountains on one side and the Suir Valley on the other. 18 holes, 6061 yards. S.S.S. 70, Par 72. *Green Fees:* information not available. *Eating facilities:* full facilities, bar open 9am to 11.30pm. *Visitors:* welcome thoughout the week except during competition times on Wednesday, Tuesday and Sunday. Sean Kelly's (cyclist) home club. One buggy for hire and carts. *Society Meetings:* all welcome by prior arrangement. Secretary/Manager: Aidan Murphy (051 640047). *

CLONMEL. **Clonmel Golf Club**, Lyreanearla, Mountain Road, Clonmel (052 24050/21138; Fax: 052 83349). *Location:* three miles up the mountain road from Clonmel town. Parkland set on the scenic slopes of the Comeragh Mountains. 18 holes, 6347 (white), 6068 (green) yards. S.S.S. 71 white, 70 green. Practice area. *Green Fees:* mid-week 30 euros, weekend (including Friday) 35 euros. *Eating facilities:* bar, sit-down meals available on request. *Visitors:* always welcome but contact Secretary/ Manager re weekends. Ladies' Day Wednesdays. Golf Buggy available for hire, contact professional. *Society Meetings:* welcome, contact Secretary/ Manager for weekends. Course information (052 83344). Professional: Robert Hayes (052 24050). Secretary/ Manager: Ms Aine Myles Keating (052 24050; Fax: 052 83349).
e-mail: cgc@indigo.ie
website: www.clonmelgolfclub.com

MONARD. **Ballykisteen Golf and Country Club**, Monard, Tipperary (052 51439; Fax: 052 33668). *Location:* on the M24 20 minutes drive from Limerick City, two miles from Tipperary town. 4 Star rated Championship Course. 18 holes, 6765 yards, Par 73. Driving range; practice green. *Green Fees:* information not available. *Eating facilities:* Full restaurant and bar facilities. *Visitors:* welcome at all times. *Society Meetings:* all welcome. Professional: David Reddan (052 33333). Secretary: Brian Begley.*

THE APPEARANCE OF AN ASTERISK (*) AT THE END OF A CLUB OR COURSE ENTRY INDICATES THAT UP-TO-DATE INFORMATION HAS NOT BEEN SUPPLIED

TEMPLEMORE. **Templemore Golf Club,** Manna South, Templemore (0504 31400; Fax: 0504 31913). *Location:* beside N62 (South) half-a-mile from town centre. Flat parkland course, short distance between greens and tees, easy to walk. 9 holes, 5443 metres. S.S.S. 68. *Green Fees:* weekdays 15 euros, weekends 20 euros. *Visitors:* welcome at all times, some restrictions Sundays. *Society Meetings:* welcome. Secretary: John Hackett (086 8338896).

THURLES. **Thurles Golf Club,** Turtulla, Thurles (0504 21983; Fax: 0504 24647). *Location:* one mile from town centre on Cork Road. Sloping parkland course. 18 holes, 6465 yards. S.S.S.71. *Green Fees:* 30 euros. *Eating facilities:* restaurant and bar. *Visitors:* welcome except Tuesday and Sunday. *Society Meetings:* welcome, special rates available. Professional: Sean Hunt. Hon. Secretary: Michael Holohan (0504 24599; Fax: 0504 24647).

COUNTY WATERFORD

DUNGARVAN. **Dungarvan Golf Club,** Knocknagranagh, Dungarvan (0035358 43310 /41605; Fax: 0035358 44113). *Location:* four kilometres east of Dungarvan on N25 to Waterford. Parkland course adjacent to Dungarvan Bay. 18 holes, 6785 yards, 6204 metres. S.S.S. 73. Practice ground. *Green Fees:* weekdays 45 euros per 18 holes, weekends 35 euros per 18 holes. *Eating facilities:* Full bar and catering services available. *Visitors:* welcome but booking advisable. *Society Meetings:* welcome, special rates. Professional: David Hayes (0035358 44707). Manager: Irene Howell.
e-mail: dungarvangc@eircom.net
website: www.dungarvangolfclub.com

DUNGARVAN. **Gold Coast Golf Club**, Ballinacourty, Dungarvan (Tel & Fax: 00 353 58 44055). *Location:* 45 miles east of Cork city, 30 miles south of Waterford city, on N25, 2 miles from Dungarvan town, on the coast. Scenic and challenging course bordering the Atlantic Ocean with unrivalled panoramic views of Dungarven Bay and Comeragh Mountains. 18 holes, 6788 yards, 6171 metres. S.S.S. 72. *Green Fees:* weekdays 35 euros, weekends 45 euros; reductions for hotel residents. Subject to review. *Eating facilities:* full hotel and leisure facilities. *Visitors:* welcome anytime. *Society Meetings:* welcome, special rates available. Secretary: Tom Considine (Tel & Fax: 00 353 58 44055).
e-mail: info@goldcoastgolfclub.com
website: www.goldcoastgolfclub.com

DUNGARVAN. **West Waterford Golf & Country Club**, Dungarvan (058 43216/41475; Fax: 058 44343). *Location:* 4km west of Dungarvan, off N25 bypass on Aglish Road. Challenging parkland course with natural water hazards, mature trees, abundant wildlife. 18 holes, 6712 yards. S.S.S. 72 blue. Large practice area and putting green. *Green Fees:*

weekdays 30 euros; weekends and Bank Holidays 40 euros. Discounts for groups and societies. *Eating facilities:* full restaurant and catering facilities. *Visitors:* always welcome, but reservations are necessary. *Society Meetings:* always welcome, pre-booking essential. Secretary: Tom Whelan (058 43216; Fax: 058 44343).
e-mail: info@westwaterfordgolf.com
website: http://westwaterfordgolf.com

DUNMORE EAST. **Dunmore East Golf Club**, Dunmore East (Tel. & Fax: 00 353 51 383151). *Location:* at the entrance to Dunmore village take first left to Strand and follow signpost to Club. Seaside parkland. 18 holes, 6070 metres. S.S.S. 70. *Green Fees:* weekdays 25 euros, weekends 30 euros. *Eating facilities:* full bar and catering facilities. *Visitors:* always welcome. *Society Meetings:* welcome, prices on request. Distance membership available. Club Professional: James Kane-Wash Secretary: M. Skehan (Tel & Fax: 00 353 51 383151). e-mail: dunmoreeastgolfclub@dunmoreeastgolfclub.ie
website: www.dunmoreeastgolfclub.ie

LISMORE. **Lismore Golf Club**, Ballyin, Lismore (058 54026; Fax: 058 53338). *Location:* one kilometre north of Lismore Heritage Town, just off the N72. Undulating parkland with mature trees, course surrounded by woodlands. 9 holes, 5291 metres. S.S.S. 67. *Green Fees:* information not available. *Eating facilities:* tea, coffee, snacks. *Visitors:* welcome weekdays, restriction may apply on Wednesday (Ladies' Day) and weekends. *Society Meetings:* welcome except Wednesday. Secretary: Bernard Dooley.*

TRAMORE. **Tramore Golf Club**, Newtown Hill, Tramore (051 386170; Fax: 051 390961). *Location:* seven miles from Waterford city. Parkland. 18 holes, 5918 metres. S.S.S. 72. *Green Fees:* information not available. *Eating facilities:* full catering and bar. *Visitors:* welcome Monday to Saturday. No visitors on Sundays. *Society Meetings:* welcome on application. Professional: Derry Kiely (087 2398856). Club Manager: James Cox. •

WATERFORD. **Faithlegg Golf Club**, Faithlegg House, Waterford (051 382241; Fax: 051 382664). *Location:* from Waterford city turn off main Dunmore East road towards Cheekpoint. Parkland course with undulating fairways, contoured greens and a number of lakes to put a premium on shot-making. 18 holes, 6629 yards. S.S.S. 72. Practice ground and putting green. *Green Fees:* mid-week (Monday to Thursday) 40 euros, Friday to Sunday and Bank Holidays 55 euros. Subject to review. *Eating facilities:* full bar and restaurant facilities available every day. *Visitors:* always welcome. Ranked in the top ten best new courses in Britain and Ireland by Golf World Magazine in December 1993. *Society Meetings:* always welcome. Professional: Derry Kiely (051 382241; Fax: 051 382664). General Manager: Paul McDaid.
e-mail: golf@faithlegg.com
website: www.faithlegg.com

WATERFORD. **Waterford Castle Golf Club**, The Island, Ballinakill, Waterford City (00 353 51 871633; Fax: 00 353 51 871634). *Location*: one mile east of Waterford City on the R683. A unique island course surrounded by River Suir and accessed by private ferry. Parkland course, internal water features, mature woodlands and a Swilken Bridge. 18 holes, 6814 yards, 6231 metres. S.S.S. 73. Driving range, practice ground, chipping area. *Green Fees*: information not available. *Eating facilities*: full bar and bar food. *Visitors*: welcome, no restrictions subject to availability. Accommodation available at five star Waterford Castle Hotel with all its facilities including all weather tennis courts and heated swimming pool. Golf buggies, trolleys available. *Society Meetings*: welcome, special rates available. Director of Golf: Michael Garland (051 871633).
e-mail: directorofgolf@waterfordcastle.com
e-mail: golf@waterfordcastle.com
website: www.waterfordcastle.com

COUNTY WESTMEATH

ATHLONE. **Glasson Golf and Country Club**, Glasson, Athlone (090 6485120; Fax: 090 6485444). *Location*: take the N55 from Athlone to Glasson village and turn left. Parkland course bordering Lough Ree and the Shannon – spectacular scenery and 555 yard 14th hole. 21 holes, 7120 yards. S.S.S. 74. 3 hole golf academy. *Green Fees*: Monday to Thursday 48 euros; Friday and Sunday 55 euros; Saturday 65 euros. Group rates on request. *Eating facilities*: restaurant, spike bar, snack bar and private rooms available. *Visitors*: welcome every day. *Society Meetings*: welcome, no restrictions, all facilities available. Office: Fidelma Reid (090 6485120; Fax: 090 6485444).
e-mail: info@glassongolf.ie
website: www.glassongolf.ie

MOATE. **Mount Temple Golf Club**, Mount Temple Village, Moate (09064 81841/81545; Fax: 09064 81957). *Location:* four miles off N6 Dublin/Galway road signposted to Mount Temple village. Parkland. 18 holes, 5927 metres. S.S.S. 72. Three hole practice area. *Green Fees:* weekdays 33 euro, weekends 38 euro. Special rates for groups over 30. *Eating facilities:* wine licence; pub 100 yards serving snacks, lunches, and dinner by arrangement. *Visitors:* welcome but possible restrictions at weekends. *Society Meetings:* welcome. Professional: David Keenan (044 44728). Secretary: Sean Donaghue (0506 32263; mobile: 086 1736339).
e-mail: mttemple@iol.ie
website: www.mounttemplegolfclub.com

COUNTY WEXFORD

ENNISCORTHY. **Enniscorthy Golf Club**, Knockmarshal, Enniscorthy (054 33191; Fax: 054 37637). *Location:* one mile from Enniscorthy town on New Ross Road. Parkland course, renowned for excellent greens. 18 holes, 6115 metres. S.S.S. 72. Practice ground. *Green Fees:* information not available. *Eating facilities:* bar and restaurant facilities. *Visitors:* welcome. Please telephone for bookings. Golf buggies available, must be pre-booked. Carts available. *Society Meetings:* welcome, must be pre-booked. Professional: Martin Sludds (054 37600). Secretary: Sean O'Leary (054 33191; Fax: 054 37637).

GOREY. **Seafield Golf and Country Club**, Ballymoney, Gorey (055 24777; Fax: 055 24837). *Location:* in the north Wexford coastal village of Ballymoney. Challenging parkland course with mature woodland and water features. 18 holes, 6814 yards, Par 72. *Green Fees:* on application. *Visitors:* welcome.
e-mail: info@seafieldgolf.com
website: www.seafieldgolf.com

THE APPEARANCE OF AN ASTERISK (*) AT THE END OF A CLUB OR COURSE ENTRY INDICATES THAT UP-TO-DATE INFORMATION HAS NOT BEEN SUPPLIED

ROSSLARE. **Rosslare Golf Club**, Rosslare Strand, Wexford (053 32203; Fax: 053 32263). *Location:* 6 miles from ferry terminal at Rosslare Harbour. 10 miles south of Wexford. Seaside links course, beside Irish Sea. Old Course – 18 holes, 6608 yards. S.S.S. 72. New Course – 12 holes, 3983 yards. S.S.S. 70. Practice ground. *Green Fees:* Old Course weekdays 35 euros; weekends and Bank Holidays 50 euros. New Course 17 - 20 euros for 12 holes. Reductions for Societies. Subject to review. *Eating facilities:* available all day. *Visitors:* welcome, telephone for booking. *Society Meetings:* welcome, telephone for booking. General Manager: J.P. Hanrick (053 32203). e-mail: office@rosslaregolf.com

ROSSLARE HARBOUR. **St Helen's Bay Golf Resort,** St Helens, Kilrane, Rosslare Harbour (053 33234; Fax: 053 33803). *Location:* two miles from Rosslare Harbour, first left in village of Kilrane. Part links, part parkland with several water features. 27 holes. *Green Fees:* from 30 to 45 euros. *Eating facilities:* full bar and restaurant facilities. *Visitors:* always welcome with no restrictions. Advisable to book in advance, especially in high season. Self catering cottage accommodation on site. *Society Meetings:* always welcome. Secretary: Kevin Doherty.

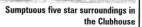

COUNTY WICKLOW

ARKLOW. **Coollattin Golf Club**, Shillelagh, Arklow (055 29125; Fax: 055 29930) *Location*: Take N11 from Dublin to Rathnew, then travel to Rathdrum, Aughrim, Tinahely and Coollattin. Parkland with large oak trees being a special feature of the course. 18 holes, 5831 yards, par 70. S.S.S. 68. *Green Fees:* information not available. *Eating facilities*: full bar and catering facilities. *Visitors*: by arrangement with Professional. *Society Meetings*: by arrangement with Dave Masterson. Professional: Peter Jones. Secretary: Denis Byrne (054 77314).

BALTINGLASS. **Baltinglass Golf Club**, Stratford Lodge, Baltinglass (059 6481350; Fax: 059 6482842). *Location:* just outside Baltinglass on main Dublin road (N81). Picturesque course with mature trees and breathtaking views. 18 holes, 5912 metres. Par 71. *Green Fees:* rates available on request. *Eating facilities:* bar and catering facilities available. *Visitors:* welcome. *Society Meetings:* booking now for 2004. Contact Hon. Secretary, Genevieve or Patricia at Club Office.
e-mail: baltinglassgc@eircom.net
website: www.baltinglass.com

BLAINROE. **Blainroe Golf Club**, Blainroe (0404 68168; Fax: 0404 69369). *Location:* three miles south of Wicklow town on coast road. Parkland terrain with extensive views of the sea. 18 holes, 6175 metres, S.S.S. 72. Practice area, putting green. *Green Fees:* weekdays 48 euros; weekends 63 euros. Special rates for groups/outings. *Eating facilities:* full bar and restaurant facilities. *Visitors:* welcome Tuesday to Friday; weekends and Bank Holidays by previous booking. Carts and caddies available. *Society Meetings:* welcome. Professional: John McDonald (0404 66470). Secretary: Mr William O'Sullivan.

BLESSINGTON. **Tulfarris Golf Club**, Blessington Lakes, Blessington (045-867555/867600; Fax: 045 867561/867565). *Location*: through Blessington village take N81, 4 miles outside town, turn left after Poulaphuca House. Parkland course built on 3 peninsulas, surrounded by Poulaphuca Lake. 18 holes, 7116 yards, S.S.S. 72. Practice range, chipping area, practice bunker, putting green. *Green Fees*: information not available. *Eating facilities*: full catering facilities. *Visitors*: welcome, except Sunday before 11.30am. 4 Star hotel on site. Tuition available. *Society Meetings*: welcome, rates available on request. Professional/Secretary: Adrian Williams (045 867600/867644; Fax: 045 867565/045 867000). *
e-mail: golf@tulfarris.com
website: www.tulfarris.com

BRAY. **Old Conna Golf Club**, Ferndale Road, Bray (01282 6055; Fax: 01282 5611). *Location:* two miles from Bray town, 12 miles south of Dublin route N11. Parkland course set in wooded hillside terrain with panoramic views of Irish Sea and Wicklow. 18 holes, 6650 yards. S.S.S 72. *Green Fees:* on application. *Eating facilities:* full catering facilities. *Visitors:* welcome, Tuesdays Ladies' Day, semi open Wednesdays. Hire of clubs/caddy car. *Society*

Glenview Hotel & Leisure Club
AA/RAC ★★★★

- 70 De luxe en suite bedrooms
- 5 ★ Leisure Centre with indoor pool
- Beauty treatments and therapies
- Award-winning Woodlands Restaurant
- Conservatory Bar
- Snooker room
- Woodland walks and gardens. Golf nearby

e-mail: sales@glenviewhotel.com
www.glenviewhotel.com

GLEN OF THE DOWNS, DELGANY, CO. WICKLOW
TEL: 00353 1287 3399

See also Colour Advertisement on page 103

Meetings: society outings welcome Mondays, Thursdays and Fridays. Professional: Ciaran Carroll (01272 0022; Fax: 01282 5611). General Manager: Tom Sheridan.

BRAY. **Woodbrook Golf Club,** Dublin Road, Bray (003531 2824799; Fax: 003531 2821950). *Location:* Bray, Co Wicklow. Flat parkland course on the cliff above Bray harbour. 18 holes, 6800 yards, S.S.S. 72. *Green Fees:* information not available. *Eating facilities:* bar/restaurant. *Visitors:* welcome Monday, Tuesday and Friday. *Society Meetings:* welcome Monday, Tuesday and Friday. Professional: Billy Kinsella (0035312 820205). Secretary: Jim Melody. *
e-mail: woodbrook@internet-ireland.ie
website: www.woodbrook.ie

BRITTAS BAY. **The European Club**, Brittas Bay, Wicklow (0404 47415). *Location:* one mile south of main Brittas Bay beach on coast road, 40 miles south of Dublin City Centre. Rolling linksland overlooking Arklow Bay, designed and owned by Pat Ruddy. Ranked No. 5 among Ireland's 30 greatest golf courses by Irish Golf Institute (1999); 24th Greatest Golf Course of the 20th Century (Golfer's Companion Jan. 2000). 18 holes, 7323 yards. S.S.S. 73. Extensive practice areas. *Green Fees:* 2003 rates 100 euros summer, 75 euros winter. Subject to review. *Eating facilities:* full services. *Visitors:* welcome to all golfers, advisable to book. *Society Meetings:* welcome. Secretary: Sidon Ruddy (0404 47415; Fax: 0404 47449).
e-mail: info@theeuropeanclub.com

DELGANY. **Delgany Golf Club**, Delgany (01287 4536; Fax: 01287 3977). *Location:* turn off N11 one mile after the Glenview Hotel (going from Dublin to Wexford, 20 miles from Dublin). Parkland, wooded course with good views, one or two hills. 18 holes, 5474 metres. S.S.S. 68. *Green Fees:* 35 euros for 2003 weekdays; 40 euros for 2003 weekends and Bank Holidays. *Eating facilities:* bar snacks, dining room, lounge. Mondays bar snacks only. *Visitors:* welcome Mondays, Wednesday mornings until 9am, Thursdays and Fridays. Carts for hire, caddies when available (school holidays only), three motor buggies. *Society Meetings:* welcome. Professional: Gavin Kavanagh (01287 4697; Fax: 01287 3977). General Manager: Peter Ribeiro.
e-mail: delganygolf@eircom.net

DUNLAVIN. **Rathsallagh Golf Club**, Dunlavin (045 403316; Fax: 045 403295). *Location:* take M7 south from Naas, exit onto M9 southbound, turn left eight miles south of Kilcullen. Set on 270 acres of mature rolling parkland of which the golf course takes up 252 acres, surrounded by thousands of trees, water on five holes. 18 holes, 6920 yards. S.S.S. 72. Practice tees, putting green, driving range. *Green Fees:* Monday to Thursday 60 euros per person; Friday, Saturday, Sunday and Bank Holidays 75 euros per person. *Eating facilities:* full bar and restaurant. *Visitors:* welcome all week. Reservation essential, no handicap required. 29 bedrooms. Golf Academy. *Society Meetings:* welcome all week. Club Professional: Brendan McDaid (045 403316; Fax: 045 403295). Secretary: Joe O'Flynn (045 403316; Fax: 045 403295).
e-mail: info@rathsallagh.com
website: www.rathsallagh.com

ENNISKERRY. **Powerscourt Golf Club**, Powerscourt Estate, Enniskerry (2046033; Fax: 2761303). *Location:* 12 miles south of Dublin just off N11, south of Bray adjacent to Enniskerry village. Follow signposts to Powerscourt Gardens. Two parkland courses with links characteristics, exceptional tiered greens and stunning views. West Course - 18 holes, 6403 metres, S.S.S. 72, Par 72. East Course - 18 holes, 6410 metres. S.S.S. 72, Par 72. Practice range, short game practice area. *Green Fees:* 100 euros. Special rates for groups and corporates. *Eating facilities:* restaurant and bar food available, full bar facilities. Five studio apartments (sleeping two/three per apartment) available. Buggies, carts and caddies available. *Visitors:* welcome daily; 8am to 6pm summer, 8.30am to 12.30pm winter. *Society Meetings:* groups and corporate meetings welcome every day. Professional: Paul Thompson. Manager: Bernard Gibbons.
e-mail: golfclub@powerscourt.ie
website: www.powerscourt.ie

GREYSTONES. **Charlesland Golf and Country Club,** Greystones. *Location*: 45 minutes south of Dublin just off the N11. Charlesland boasts a magnificent location beside the sea, in the shadow of the Wicklow mountains. 18 hole parkland Championship Course 6169 metres. S.S.S. 72. Large practice area, putting green, public driving range available within 500 metres. *Green Fees*: rates from 35 euros. Early bird rates before 10am Monday to Friday. *Eating facilities*: restaurant and bar food available. Full bar facilities. *Visitors*: welcome daily. Please make prior booking. Neat dress essential. Buggies and handcarts for hire from our well-stocked Golf Shop. 12 en suite bedrooms. Boardroom and Conference facilities. For reservations phone (01-2878200; Fax: 01-2870078). *Society Meetings*: Corporate, society and group rates available on request. For golf bookings phone (01-2874350; 01-2874360). General Manager: Patrick Bradshaw.
e-mail: teetimes@charlesland.com
website: www.charlesland.com

GREYSTONES. **Greystones Golf Club**, Whitshed Road, Greystones (01-287 4136; Fax: 01-287 3749). Parkland course. 18 holes, 5322 metres, S.S.S. 69. Practice facilities. *Green Fees*: information not available. *Eating facilities*: full catering available. *Visitors*: welcome Monday, Tuesday, Friday and Sunday. *Society Meetings*: especially welcome, please contact the Secretary for details. Professional: Karl Holmes (01-287 5308). Secretary: Jim Melody (01-287 4136).*
e-mail: secretary@greystonesgc.com
website: www.greystonesgc.com

KILCOOLE. **Kilcoole Golf Club**, Kilcoole (01 2872066; Fax: 01 2010497). *Location:* two miles from Greystones off N11. Flat course one mile from sea. 9 holes, 5506 metres. S.S.S. 69. Practice area. *Green Fees:* 30 euros midweek, 35 euros weekends. *Eating facilities:* bar with meals available. *Visitors:* welcome, booking advisable. *Society Meetings:* welcome, special rate available. Secretary/Manager: Eddie Lonergan.

GREYSTONES GOLF CLUB
Greystones, Co. Wicklow, Ireland Tel: 01-2874136
website: www.greystonesgc.com

Enjoy the challenge of our 18-hole parkland course, complemented by the panoramic views of Wicklow's dramatic coastline from Lambay Island to Wicklow Head. Our club is bright and spacious, providing excellent facilities including a bar, locker rooms, golf shop, snacks and full dining for our visitors.

See also Colour Advertisement on page 102

PLEASE MENTION **THE GOLF GUIDE** WHEN YOU WRITE
OR PHONE TO ENQUIRE ABOUT CLUBS OR ACCOMMODATION.

NEWTOWNMOUNTKENNEDY. **Druids Glen Golf Club**, Newtownmountkennedy (00 353 1287 3600; Fax: 00 353 1287 3699). *Location:* 20 miles south of Dublin. Two great championship courses: Druids Glen and Druids Heath. 18 holes, par 71. New golf academy. *Green Fees:* from 110 euros. *Eating facilities:* available. *Visitors:* welcome. Five-star hotel on site. Professional: Eamon Darcy. General Manager: Donal Flinn.

RATHDRUM. **Glenmalure Golf Club**, Greenan, Rathdrum (0404 46679). *Location:* two miles west of Rathdrum - signposted. Parkland, hilly course. 18 holes, 5500 yards. S.S.S. 66. *Green Fees:* information not available. *Eating facilities:* full facilities. *Visitors:* welcome, no restrictions. Self catering Scandinavian Lodges available. Buggies, carts available, caddy on notice. *Society Meetings:* welcome weekdays and Saturdays. Secretary: Kathleen Byrne (0404 46679).

REDCROSS. **Millbrook Golf Course**, Redcross (0404 41647). *Location:* in Redcross village, two miles off N11, eight miles from Wicklow. Parkland, Par 3 course. 18 holes, 2009 yards. S.S.S 55. *Green Fees:* information not available. *Eating facilities:* restaurant, takeaway, coffee bar and wine bar. Clubs for hire. River Valley Caravan and Camping park with mobile homes and houses to let; many other facilities also available.

WICKLOW. **Wicklow Golf Club**, Dunbur Road, Wicklow. *Location:* Wicklow Town, off N11. Parkland course by the seaside. 18 holes, 5695 metres. S.S.S. 70. *Green Fees:* information not available. *Eating facilities:* full facilities available. *Visitors:* welcome; avoid Wednesday and Thursday evenings and all day Sunday. Caddy cars. *Society Meetings:* welcome. Professional: Darren McLoughlin (0404 66122). Secretary: Joe Kelly (0404 69386).

visit the FHG golf website on
www.uk-golfguide.com

Isle of Man

DERBYHAVEN. **Castletown Golf Club,** Castletown Golf Links Hotel, Fort Island, Derbyhaven IM9 1UA (01624 822201). *Location:* five minutes from Ronaldsway Airport and 20 minutes from Douglas, the capital. Championship links course voted No. 73 in the UK by 'Golf World' magazine. 18 holes, 6711 yards. S.S.S. 72. *Green Fees:* information not available. *Eating facilities:* table d'hôte/à la carte restaurants with bar snacks available day and evening. *Visitors:* most welcome but must be pre-booked. Open 12 months of the year for accommodation; facilities include swimming pool, sauna, and two snooker tables. *Society Meetings:* catered for, must be pre-booked. Professional: Mr M. Crowe (01624 822211) tuition available. Hotel Manager: Mr Paddy Gobbett.*
e-mail: golflinks@manx.net
website: www.golfiom.com

DOUGLAS. **Douglas Golf Club**, Pulrose Park, Douglas IM2 1AE (01624 675952). *Location:* one mile out of Douglas near Pulrose Power Station. Parkland - 17th hole tee off 200ft above green (214 yards). 18 holes, 5922 yards. S.S.S. 68. Practice and putting area. *Green Fees:* information not available. *Eating facilities:* bar meals always available. *Visitors:* welcome, but not before 10am Sundays. Dress code in bar, no jeans. *Society Meetings:* catered for by arrangement with Pro Shop (01624 661558). Manager/Professional: Mike Vipond. Secretary: Elaine Vincent. *

DOUGLAS. **Pulrose Golf Course**, Pulrose Park, Douglas IM2 1AE (01624 675952). *Location:* one mile from town centre. Undulating parkland with memorable 17th hole. 18 holes, 5922 yards. S.S.S. 68. Putting and practice area. *Green Fees:* information not available. *Eating facilities:* bar; snacks available at all times. *Visitors:* welcome, not before 10am on Sundays. Dress code in bar - no jeans. *Society Meetings:* by arrangement with Professional: Mike Vipond (01624 661558).*

ONCHAN. **King Edward Bay Golf Club**, Groudle Road, Howstrake, Onchan (01624 672709). *Location:* north headland of Douglas Bay. Stunning views from Headland links course. Watered greens, excellent fairways. 18 holes, 5450 yards. S.S.S. 67. Practice area. *Green Fees:* information not available. *Eating facilities:* full catering available (except Mondays), three bars. *Visitors:* welcome without reservation but not before 9.30am Sundays. *Society Meetings:* most welcome by arrangement. Special rates. Professional: Donald Jones (01624 672709). Secretary: Cyril Kelly (01624 827726; Fax: 01624 827724).

PEEL. **Peel Golf Club,** Rheast Lane, Peel IM5 1BG (01624 842227). *Location:* outskirts of Peel on main Douglas Road. Combination of links and heathland. 18 holes, 5850 yards. S.S.S. 69. Practice ground. *Green Fees:* information not available. *Eating facilities:* full bar service and meals. *Visitors:* welcome, but check in advance for weekend availability. *Society Meetings:* catered for, check in advance. Pro Shop. Professional: Murray Crowe (01624 844232). Secretary/Manager: Michael N.D. Robinson (01624 843456).*

PORT ERIN. **Rowany Golf Club**, Rowany Drive, Port Erin IM9 6LN (Tel & Fax: 01624 834072). *Location:* off the Promenade, five minutes from Port Erin. Hilly setting and meadowland. 18 holes, 5774 yards. S.S.S. 69. Practice ground. *Green Fees*: weekdays £16.00 per round, weekends £20.00 per round. *Eating facilities:* restaurant and bar meals. *Visitors:* welcome by arrangement, few restrictions. Accommodation can be arranged. *Society Meetings:* welcome. Secretary: Mr A.Q. Bashforth. General Manager: Mr C.A. Corrin (Tel & Fax: 01624 834072).

PORT ST MARY. **Port St Mary Golf Club**, Point Road, Port St Mary (01624 834932). *Location:* clearly signposted after entering Port St Mary. Seaside links with beautiful panoramic views. 9 holes, 2754 yards. S.S.S. 67. *Green Fees:* weekdays £10.00; weekends £15.00. Twilight or with member £9.00. 10% discount for Societies. *Eating facilities:* restaurant and bar open all day. *Visitors:* welcome at all times, only restrictions weekends between 8am to 10.30am. Handicap Certificate required. Secretary: Mrs M. Boyle (01624 837231; 07624 497387).).

RAMSEY. **Ramsey Golf Club,** Brookfield, Ramsey (01624 812244; Fax: 01624 815833). *Location:* west boundary of Ramsey. Parkland. 18 holes, 5982 yards. S.S.S. 69. Practice area. *Green Fees:* weekdays £20.00; weekends: £28.00. £2.00 reduction for parties of 12 or more. *Eating facilities:* bar and restaurant. *Visitors:* welcome. *Society Meetings:* welcome weekdays only. Professional: Andrew Dyson (01624 814736). Secretary/Manager: Michael Horton (01624 812244).

SANTON. **Mount Murray Golf Club**, Mount Murray, Santon (01624 661111; Fax: 01624 661116). *Location:* three miles from Douglas on the Castletown road. Wooded parkland set on hills with panoramic views. 18 holes, 6715 yards. S.S.S. 73. 24-bay driving range, two-tier putting green. *Green Fees:* information not available. *Eating facilities:* full hotel catering, bistro, dining room, two bars. *Visitors:* welcome at any time by arrangement with the Professional. 90 bedroomed four star hotel. *Society Meetings:* welcome at any time by arrangement with the Secretary. Professional: Andrew Dyson. *

> THE APPEARANCE OF AN ASTERISK (*)
> AT THE END OF A CLUB OR COURSE
> ENTRY INDICATES THAT
> UP-TO-DATE INFORMATION
> HAS NOT BEEN SUPPLIED

The Channel Islands

ALDERNEY. **Alderney Golf Club**, Route des Carrieres, Alderney (01481 822835; Fax: 01481 823609). *Location:* one mile east of St Annes. Seaside links with sea views from every hole. 9 holes, 2528 yards. S.S.S. 65. Putting green and practice range. *Green Fees:* available on request. *Eating facilities:* friendly lounge bar with bar meals all day. *Visitors:* welcome all year, tees reserved for competitions only. *Society Meetings:* welcome by arrangement. Hon. Secretary: Barbara Dale.*

GUERNSEY. **La Grande Mare Golf Club**, Vazon Bay, Castel, Guernsey GY5 7LL (01481 255194; Fax: 01481 255194). *Location:* on west coast main road. Parkland course. 18 holes, 5112 yards. S.S.S. 67. *Green Fees:* information not available. *Eating facilities:* full hotel facilities, restaurant, bar, leisure club. *Visitors:* welcome at most times by prior booking. La Grande Mare Hotel. Changing facilities and Pro Shop. Trolleys, clubs for hire. *Society Meetings:* welcome. Professional: Matt Groves (01481 253432; Fax: 01481 255194). Secretary: Jaine Vermeulen (01481 253544; Fax: 01481 255194). *

GUERNSEY. **Royal Guernsey Golf Club**, L'Ancresse, Vale, Guernsey GY3 5BY (01481 247022). *Location:* three miles north of St. Peter Port. Seaside links. 18 holes, 6206 yards. S.S.S. 70. Driving range. *Green Fees:* information not available. *Eating facilities:* restaurant and bar. *Visitors:* welcome except Thursday and Saturday afternoons and Sundays unless playing with a member. Must have Handicap Certificate. Professional: Norman Wood (01481 245070). Secretary: Mike De Laune (01481 246523; Fax: 01481 243960). *

GUERNSEY. **St Pierre Park Golf Club**, Rohais, St. Peter Port, Guernsey (01481 727038; Fax: 01481 712041). *Location:* 10 minutes drive from town centre. Wooded parkland with numerous lakes. 9 holes, 1323 yards, 1210 metres. S.S.S. 50. Driving range, putting green. *Green Fees:* information not available. *Eating facilities:* two restaurants and two bars. *Visitors:* welcome, all times bookable. Subject to rules and regulations on display. Hotel accommodation in 135 luxurious rooms and suites. Tennis. Pro Shop/Club Manager: R. Corbet. *

JERSEY. **Jersey Recreation Grounds**, Greve d'Azette, St. Clement, Jersey (01534 721938). *Location:* inner coast road near St. Helier. Flat course with some water hazards. 9 holes, 2149 yards. S.S.S. 30. Practice green and putting green. *Green Fees:* information not available. Clubs available to hire. *Eating facilities:* licensed buffet. *Visitors:* welcome at all times. *Society Meetings:* welcome. Manager: H. Cooper.

JERSEY. **La Moye Golf Club,** St Brelade, Jersey JE3 8GQ (01534 743401; Fax: 01534 747289). *Location:* on road to Corbiere Lighthouse at La Moye, St Brelade. Turn right at airport crossroads, right again at crossroads traffic lights. Seaside links championship course. 18 holes, 6664 yards. S.S.S. 72. Practice ground. *Green Fees:* weekdays £45.00; weekends £50.00. *Eating facilities:* full restaurant/snack facilities, three bars. *Visitors:* weekdays 9.30 to 11am and 2 to 3.30pm, weekends 2.30pm onwards. Must have Handicap Certificate. *Society Meetings:* by prior appointment only. Professional: Mike Deeley (01534 743130; Fax: 01534 7499565). Secretary: Chris Greetham (01534 743401). Course Ranger's Office: (01534 747166).

JERSEY. **Les Ormes Golf & Leisure Club,** Mont à la Brune, St. Brelade JE3 8FL (01534 497000; Fax: 01534 499122). *Location:* on top of Mont à la Brune, adjacent to the airport. Attractive elevated course with beautiful coastal views. 9 hole course, 2509 yards, S.S.S. 65 white, 63 yellow. 17 bay covered driving range, practice bunker. *Green Fees:* information not available. *Eating facilities;* restaurant and bar with terrace and swimming pool. *Visitors:* welcome, pre-booking advisable. Health and fitness complex, eight indoor tennis courts and LTA qualified coaches. Hair and Beauty salon on site. *Society Meetings:* welcome by arrangement. Professional: Andrew Chamberlain (01534 744464). General Manager: Mike Graham (01534 497002). *

JERSEY. **Royal Jersey Golf Club**, Grouville, Jersey JE3 9BD (01534 854416; Fax: 01534 854684). *Location:* take coast road from St. Helier, head towards Gorey. Seaside links course. 18 holes, 6100 yards. S.S.S. 70. *Green Fees:* information not available. *Eating facilities:* restaurant and bar. *Visitors:* welcome weekdays between 10am and 12 noon or 2pm to 4pm; weekends after 2.30pm. Handicap Certificate required. *Society Meetings:* welcome by prior arrangement. Professional: D Morgan (01534 852234; Fax: 01534 854684). Secretary: D.J. Attwood. *

THE APPEARANCE OF AN ASTERISK (*) AT THE END OF A CLUB OR COURSE ENTRY INDICATES THAT UP-TO-DATE INFORMATION HAS NOT BEEN SUPPLIED

JERSEY. **Wheatlands Golf Course and Country Hotel**, Off Old Beaumont Hill, St Peter, Jersey JE3 7ED (01534 888844; Fax: 01534 69880). *Location:* Le Vieux Beaumont, which is road forking off to right by Cannon, and then first right at top of hill. Jersey's only inland/parkland course; undulating setting with pond features and extensive countryside views. Home of the Jersey Professional Short Course Championship. 9 holes (18 tees), 2767 yards, S.S.S. 54. Practice nets. *Green Fees:* information not available. *Eating facilities:* "Tenth Hole Bar", "Garden Terrace" - snacks and meals. *Visitors:* always welcome. Accommodation available in 20 en suite rooms. Hire equipment available - clubs, shoes, carts; VAT free shop. Professional tuition. *Society Meetings:* welcome. Professional: Terry Le Brocq. *

JERSEY. **Les Mielles Golf and Country Club**, St Ouen's Bay, Jersey JE3 7FQ (01534 482787; Fax: 01534 485414). *Location:* centre of St Ouen's Bay. Set in an American styled seaside parkland course with "bent grass" greens and fairways of "dwarf rye". The 18 hole course plays 5758 yards, Par 70 gents, 5253 yards, Par 71 ladies. Other facilities include: 30 bay covered driving range, practice putting green, 75 yard short hole practice hole, Europe's premier 18 hole miniature golf course. *Green Fees:* please refer to our website or telephone for 2004 prices. *Eating facilities:* Rocco's on site 110 seater restaurant, 44 seater La Rocco private function room, Rocco's bar and seasonal patio area. *Visitors:* always welcome, pre-booking necessary. Smart golfing attire required; no jeans. VAT Free Pro Shop, miniature golf, laser clay pigeon shooting, hire equipment available - carts, buggies, clubs. *Society Meetings:* welcome, packages available. Professionals: Wayne Osmand and Lee Elstone (01534 483252). Head of Administration/ Corporate Bookings Administrator: Michelle Harris (01534 485984).*
e-mail: enquire@lesmielles.co.je
website & online booking: www.lesmielles.com

Golf in France
WHERE TO PLAY • WHERE TO STAY
By Michael Gedye

France is deservedly a highly popular holiday destination. Within easy reach, with the added advantage of being able to travel in your own car, and with more than 500 attractive, inexpensive and seriously underplayed golf courses available throughout the country, it has all a visiting player could require. The golf clubs are relaxed and welcoming with relatively few restrictions, although it is advisable to have your handicap certificate with you. The courses are eminently playable, with some of true championship quality, and many are laid out in naturally beautiful surroundings. Wherever you choose to go in this spacious country, you will find places to play - all imbued with that particular casual ambience and sense of style that typifies France. Some of the courses along the Channel coast can be played on a day visit. Most form an ideal reason for a long weekend or short break. Even southern France is reachable in a day on excellent motorways. With fine, warmer weather, particularly south of the Loire, you will feel at home on familiar fairways, many designed by British architects or along classic lines. Make sure to sample local produce and vintages; every region has its specialities - and leave room in the boot for some excellent value shopping to take home, including a few cases of wine.

In this section, we have shown those courses with most appeal to the holiday golfer. All have fine facilities, offer good value and a warm welcome. They are listed under seven regions. Just across the narrowest Channel crossing is the NORTH, which includes the areas of Pas-de-Calais, Picardy and Normandy. You can choose between the historic holes of Le Touquet, Wimereux, Hardelot or elegant Deauville or test yourself over recent arrivals Belle Dune and Champ de Bataille.

The NORTH-WEST covers the traditionally popular areas of Brittany and the Western Loire. For golf in a coastal breeze, play Pleneuf Val Andre, Brest Iroise and St Jean de Monts. Should chateaux country and wooded parkland be more to your taste, visit La Freslonnière near Rennes and the well-established favourites of La Bretesche, La Baule and Sablé Solesmes.

If the charms of PARIS are on your agenda, with its sights, shopping and nightlife, be assured there is also plenty of accessible golf. Contrast the championship test of Golf National with Golf des Yveline's gentle parkland or even the course at Disneyland.

WEST and CENTRE encompasses the heartland of France, with the regions of Poitou Charentes, Limousin, Auvergne and the Loire Valley. There is a good choice of excellent golf, including the picturesque Château des Sept Tours, demanding Les Bordes set in discreet woodland and the magnificent sweeping fairways of Golf de Royal, 'Augusta-by-the-sea' .

The area to the EAST is quite the largest, covering Champagne-Ardennes, Lorraine, Alsace, Burgundy, Franche-Compte, French Alps and the Rhone Valley. This is a region of snow-capped mountains, crystal lakes, classic wines and rich, world-famous cuisine.

Serious holiday golfers, aiming to test their skills around the most concentrated cluster of quality golf in France, head for the SOUTH-WEST. Here in Aquitaine, running from the fabled vineyards of Bordeaux down the pine-lined Atlantic coast to Biarritz and beyond, are some of the finest (as well as the oldest) courses in the country. French golf had its origins here in Pau (1856), followed later by Biarritz du Phare (1888), Chiberta, La Nivelle and Hossegor. The modern era can offer golf with fine wine round the 36 holes of Golf du Médoc or Château des Vigiers. The coastal pines influence Golf du Pessac, Gujan Mestras and Moliets, while further south lie the fine examinations of Seignosse, Arcangues and Makila - more than enough for even the most devoted player.

The SOUTH follows the curve of the Mediterranean coast from Languedoc Roussillon in the west, through Provence and on to the famed Côte d'Azur and Monte Carlo. History and fashion go hand in hand here, with golf at Cap d'Agde, La Grande Motte, Nîmes and Massane leading to the craggy slopes of Golf de Frégate and the gentler parkland of Esterel and Royal Mougins. Not too far away is Sperone, the dramatic island layout on nearby Corsica.

NORTH

BAYEUX. **Golf d'Omaha Beach**, Ferme St. Sauveur, 14520 Port-en-Bessin (02 31.22.12.12; Fax: 02 31.22.12.13). *Location:* from Paris, A13 towards Caen. Don't go into the city, take the ring road towards Bayeux, follow signs to Port-en-Bessin. Hilly course; 9 holes on the sea, above the cliffs and beaches that witnessed the landing of the allied forces in June 1944. 18 holes, 6216 metres. S.S.S. 70; 9 holes, 2693 metres. S.S.S. 36. Driving range, practice area, pitch and putt course. *Green Fees:* information not available. *Eating facilities:* available at the clubhouse. *Visitors:* welcome. Professional: M. Marc Eve, M. Julien Thomas. Secretary: Stephanie Cornil, Laure Tancoigne (02 31.22.12.12; Fax: 02 31.22.12.13). *

BOULOGNE. **Golf de Wimereux**, Route d'Ambleteuse, 62930 Wimereux (03 21.32.43.20). *Location:* just off motorway A16 between Calais and Boulogne, North of Wimereux on the D940, seven km north of Boulogne. Venerable Scottish-style links course with broad fairways between sea and dunes. 18 holes, 6150 metres, Par 72. Two practice grounds, putting green, training bunker. *Green Fees:* information not available. *Eating facilities:* bar and restaurant (not open Mondays in July and August). *Visitors:* welcome. Trolley and buggy hire. *Society Meetings:* welcome weekdays, special rates. Professional: Alan White. Office Secretary: L. Hector and N. Bouzin (03 21.32.43.20; Fax: 03 21.33.62.21).* e-mail: golf.wimereux@wanadoo.fr

CAEN. **Golf de Caen**, Le Vallon, 14112 Bieville Beuville (02 31.94.72.09; Fax: 02 31.47.45.30). *Location:* follow road to Guistreham car ferries, first on your right to Château de Beauregard. A hilly course, wooded. 18 holes, 6155 metres, Par 72; 9 holes, 2950 metres, Par 36. Practice area, putting green. *Green Fees:* information not available. *Eating facilities:* available except Tuesdays. Pro shop. Professional: Christian Carle (02 31.95.17.70). Secretaries: Corinne/Elizabeth (02 31.94.72.09).*

DEAUVILLE. **Golf Barrière de Deauville**, Le Mont Canisy, BP 63500, Saint-Arnoult, 14803 Deauville (02 31.14.24.24; Fax: 02 31.14.24.25). *Location:* on the south-western side of Deauville with the sea to the north. A scenic and varied course, hilly in part with fast greens. 18 holes, 5951 metres, Par 71. 9 holes, 3038 metres, Par 36. Practice ground and putting green. *Green Fees:* weekdays 9 holes 32 euros, 18 holes 48 euros; weekends 9 holes 40 euros, 18 holes 80 euros. *Eating facilities:* bar and restaurant in clubhouse; all facilities at the adjoining Golf Hotel. *Visitors:* welcome, Handicap Certificates required. Reservations 24 hours in advance. Pro shop; cart and trolley hire. Professional: C. Hausseguy (02 31.14.24.24). Secretary: J Paul Oudin.

DEAUVILLE. **Golf de St Gatien Deauville**, Le Mont Saint Jean, 14130 Saint Gatien des Bois (02 31.65.19.99; Fax: 02 31.65.11.24). *Location:* about eight km inland and eight km east of Deauville. An interesting course with 9 holes, sloping steeply through woodland, plenty of sand and strategic water. Three 9 hole courses Par 72 (18 holes), 3044 metres (White), 3228 metres (Red), 3035 metres (Yellow). Practice facilities, putting, bunkers. *Green Fees:* information not provided. *Eating facilities:* bar and restaurant in rustic 18th century clubhouse (02 31.65.48.97). *Visitors:* welcome. Pro shop; cart, trolley and club hire. *Society Meetings:* welcome, special rates available. Three professionals. *

GRANVILLE. **Golf de Granville - Baie du Mont Saint Michel**, Route de la Plage, 50290 Breville-sur-Mer (02 33.50.23.06; Fax: 02 33.61.91.87). *Location:* near Granville, towards Coutances and Cherbourg. Seaside links. 18 holes, 5834 metres, Par 71. 9 holes, 2186 metres, Par 33. Driving range, putting green. *Green Fees:* information not available. *Eating facilities:* bar and restaurant in clubhouse. Pro shop; trolley and club hire. *Visitors:* welcome, no restrictions. Special rates for groups over 10. * e-mail: granville@best-channel-golfs.com www.best-channel-golfs.com/granville/acces.htm

HARDELOT. **Golf d'Hardelot "Les Dunes"**, 3 Avenue du Golf, 62152 Hardelot (03 21.91.90.90; Fax: 03 21.83.24.33). *Location:* at Hardelot Plage, 15km south of Boulogne. Gently sloping dunes with attractive pine trees. 18 holes, 6031 metres, Par 73. Golf academy, practice facilities. *Green Fees:* information not available. *Eating facilities:* available. *Visitors:* welcome. Handicap Certificate required. *Society Meetings:* welcome. Professionals: Louis Maisonnave/ David Amat (06.83.34.70.62/ 06.87.45.72.27). Secretary: B. Blampain (03 21.83.73.10; Fax: 03 21.83.24.33). Director of Golf: Ken Strachan. * e-mail: hardelot@opengolfclub.com website: www.opengolfclub.com

HARDELOT. **Golf d'Hardelot "Les Pins"**, 3 Avenue du Golf, 62152 Hardelot (02 21.83.73.10; Fax: 03.21.83.24.33). *Location:* the beach-resort of Hardelot Plage is 15 km south of Boulogne. Attractive course carved through a pine forest. 18 holes, 5926 metres, Par 73. Practice ground, putting green. *Green Fees:* information not provided. *Eating facilities:* clubhouse with bar and fine restaurant. Handicap Certificate required. Pro shop; club and trolley hire. Professionals: Louis Maisonnave/David Amat (03 21.91.89.80/06.87.45.72.27). Secretary: B. Blempain (03 21.83.73.10; Fax: 03 21.83.24.33). Director of Golf: Ken Strachan. * e-mail: hardelot@opengolfclub.com website: www.opengolfclub.com

LAON. **Golf de l'Ailette**, 02860 Cerny-en-Laonnois (03.23.24.79.10). *Location:* about 12km south of Laon, autoroute A26 exit Laon. An interesting course laid out on the edge of a forest flanked by large areas of water. 18 holes, 6127 metres, Par 72. 9 holes, 1753 metres, Par 32. Practice ground, pitch and putt, putting green. *Green Fees:* information not available. *Eating facilities:* bar and restaurant. *Visitors:* welcome. Handicap required (maximum 35). *Society Meetings:* welcome, 20% to 30% discount for groups. Professional: Eric Censier. Secretaries: Miss Sylvie Dolat and Mrs Marie Christine Harant (03.23.24.83.99; Fax: 03.23.24.84.66). *

LE TOUQUET. **Golf du Touquet,** Avenue du Golf - BP41, 62520 Le Touquet (03 21.06.28.00; Fax: 03 21.06.28.01). *Location:* 20km from Boulogne, on the coast, 3km from Le Touquet centre. La Forêt Course created in 1904 set in the heart of an old pine forest - 18 holes, 5659 metres, S.S.S. 69.8, Par 71. La Mer Course, designed by Harry S. Colt (1931), is a championship links course laid out amongst wild sand dunes - 18 holes, 6275 metres. S.S.S 74.9, Par 72. Le Manoir Course is perfect for beginners - 9 holes, 2817 metres, S.S.S. 35, Par 35. Practice range and putting green. *Green Fees:* information not available. *Eating facilities:* bar and restaurant in clubhouse. *Visitors:* welcome. Maximum Handicaps: La Forêt Course 35, La Mer Course 24 Gentlemen, 28 Ladies; no Handicap required for Le Manoir Course. *Society Meetings:* welcome. Pro Shop; carts, caddies. Accommodation available in Le Manoir Hotel (3 Star) located in the centre of La Forêt course. Professionals: J.P. Harismendy and Pierre Philippon. Manager: Gilles Grattepanche.

LILLE. **Golf de Bondues**, Château de la Vigne, BP 54, 59587 Bondues Cedex (03 20.23.20.62). *Location:* about 10km north of Lille, west of the N17. In the grounds of an 18th century chateau, the courses have well protected greens with deep bunkers and several water hazards. 18 holes, 6163 metres, Par 73. 18 holes, 6009 metres, Par 72. Driving range, putting green. *Green Fees:* information not available. *Eating facilities:* bar and restaurant in clubhouse. *Visitors:* welcome. Closed Tuesdays. Trolley hire. Lessons available. Professional: (03 20.23.13.87). Secretary: (03 20.23.20.62; Fax: 03 20.23.24.11). *
e-mail: golfdebondues@nordnet.fr

NEUBOURG. **Golf Club du Champ de Bataille**, 27110 Le Neubourg (02 32.35.03.72; Fax: 02 32.35.83.10). *Location:* south west of Rouen, about 28km north west of Evreux. A fine test of golf attractively laid out through the wooded estate of the elegant château. Par 3 holes. 18 holes, 6575 yards, 5983 metres, Par 72. Driving range, putting green. *Green Fees:* information not available. *Eating facilities:* bar and restaurant. *Visitors:* welcome, no restrictions. Pro shop; cart, trolley and club hire. Guest rooms available in the château. New clubhouse built on the edge of the wood, independent of the Château, offering a wide range of services. *Society Meetings:* welcome. Secretary: Ingrid Thommerel. *

ROUEN. **Golf du Vaudreuil**, 27100 le Vaudreuil (02 32.59.02.60; Fax: 02.32.59.43.88). *Location:* 30km south-east of Rouen, east of the RN15 and the A13, 5 km from Louviers. A flat course, designed by Hawtree in 1961 in wooded parkland. 18 holes, Par 73. Driving range, buggies, trolleys, clubs. *Green Fees:* information not available. *Eating facilities:* beautiful clubhouse with bar and restaurant. On course Hotel du Golf (Two star) offers special Hotel and Golf packages (02.32.59.02.94; Fax: 02 32.59.67.39).*

SAINT-JULIEN-SUR-CALONNE. **Golf & Country Club de Saint-Julien,** B.P. 76, 14130 Pont l'Eveque, S.S.S 10 (02.31.64.30.30; Fax: 02.31.64.12.43). *Location:* A13 leaving Pont l'Eveque, near Deauville (Normandy). Hilly 18 and 9 hole courses in the heart of the Pays d'Auge in Normandy. 18 hole course 6670 yards, 6065 metres, S.S.S. 72; 9 hole course 2500 yards, 2275 metres, S.S.S. 33. Driving range, putting green, bunker and approach green. *Green Fees:* information not available. *Eating facilities:* Restaurant open from 12 noon to 4pm from April to September. Bar facilities available. *Visitors:* welcome every day. *Societies:* welcome every day, special rates for groups of more than ten. Driving range, buggies, carts, caddies, trolleys available. Professional: Alain Quibeuf (02.31.64.99.58; mobile: 06.07.01.64.27). Manager: J. M. Bonnet. *

ST OMER. **Aa Saint-Omer Golf Club**, Chemin des Bois, Acquin-Westbécourt 62380 Lumbres (03.21.38.59.90; Fax: 03.21.93.02.47). *Location:* from Calais take A26 Autoroute, Junction 3 St Omer, right onto RN42 Expressway, first exit Acquin/Lumbres (30 minutes from Calais). Undulating parkland and mature trees overlooking the valley of the River Aa. La Haute Drève: 9 holes 2015 metres, Par 31; Le Val 18 holes 5979 metres, Par 73. Practice ground and putting green. *Green Fees:* information not available. *Eating facilities:* clubhouse bar and restaurant. *Visitors:* welcome all year, no restrictions. Golf and accommodation packages on request. Pro shop; trolley, buggy and club hire. Course selected by the European Tour. *Society Meetings:* welcome, special packages available. Professional: Sylvain Raout. Manager: Sandrine Grevet. *
e-mail: aa-st-omer.golf@najeti.com
website: www.aa-st-omer-golfclub.com

Please mention
'THE GOLF GUIDE'
when enquiring about
clubs or accommodation.

NORTH WEST

ANGERS. **Anjou Golf and Country Club**, Route de Cheffes, 49330 Champigne (02 41.42.01.01; Fax: 02 41.42.04.37). *Location:* about 20km north of Angers, from Paris A11, exit Durtal. Flat course with a few lakes and trees. 18 holes, 6227 metres, Par 72. Short 6 hole course, 750 metres, Par 19. Practice facilities. *Green Fees:* information not available. *Eating facilities:* "Le Prince Noir" traditional catering; "L'Auberge de Mozé" gastronomic catering. *Visitors:* welcome. Starting times must be booked in advance. Pro shop; cart, trolley and club hire; flats to rent at golf course. Professional/Director: Stephane Guguen. Secretaries: Christelle, Gaëlle, Valérie. * e-mail: info@anjougolf.com

ANGERS. **Golf de Sablé-Solesmes**, Domaine de l'Outinière, Route de Pincé, 72300 Sablé-sur-Sarthe (02 43.95.28.78; Fax: 02 43.92.39.05). *Location:* east of the A11, exit 10 (Sablé La Flèche), about 40km north of Angers, south-east of Le Mans. Three totally different 9s - Forest and River: 18 holes, 6189 metres, Par 72; Waterfall: 9 holes, 3069 metres, Par 36, radiate from the large clubhouse. Testing and spectacular with park, woodland and lakeside holes. Driving range, putting green. *Green Fees:* information not available. *Eating facilities:* bar and restaurant in clubhouse. Pro shop; cart, trolley and club hire. Professional: Christian Blanc. Director: Yves Pironneau.

AURAY. **Golf de Baden**, Kernic, 56870 Baden (02 97.57.18.96; Fax: 02 97.57.22.05). *Location:* between the village of Baden and the sea, south of the RN 165 at Auray exit. Undulating course partly through pine woods and around lakes. 18 holes, 6112 metres, Par 72. 3 hole, 535 metres pitch and putt course. Practice area, putting green, approach green. *Green Fees:* information not available. *Eating facilities:* bar and restaurant. Pro shop; trolley and club hire; club repair. Neighbouring hotels "Le Gavrinis" and "du Loch" offer year-round golfing breaks. *Society Meetings:* welcome, special rates. Professional: J. F. Le Gall. Secretaries: Mme. Le Quilliec, Mme. Burguin. Director: Mr O. Charmont.*

AURAY. **Golf de Saint Laurent**, 56400 Ploemel, Auray (02 97.56.85.18; Fax: 02 97.56.89.99). *Location:* about 10 km west of Auray and not far from Carnac with its ancient standing stones. High quality championship course, undulating through mature trees. 18 holes, 6112 metres, Par 72. 9 hole course, 2705 metres, Par 35. Driving range. *Green Fees:* information not available. *Eating facilities:* bar and restaurant in on-course Fairway Hotel St Laurent; also on-course "Maeva" self-catering cottages available. *Visitors:* welcome. Pro shop; cart, trolley and club hire. Professionals: Mr D. Jouan and Mr A. Brien.

BENODET. **Golf de l'Odet**,Benodet Menez Groas, Clohars-Fouesnant, 29950 Benodet (02.98.54.87.88; Fax: 02.98.54.61.40). *Location:* 12km south of Quimper, towards the sea at Benodet. An undulating partly wooded course. 18 holes, 6235 metres, Par 72.

9 holes, 1100 metres, Par 27. Driving range, putting green, pitching green, short game area. *Green Fees:* information not available. *Eating facilities:* bar, restaurant and on-site Hotel Eurogreen, whose residents have reduced green fees. *Visitors:* welcome, no restrictions but advisable to book tee times. Other accommodation nearby. Pro shop; cart, trolley and club hire. Professional: C. Olivard. Secretary: Christophe Bodere (02.98.54.87.88; Fax: 02.98.52.61.40)*

BREST. **Golf de Brest Iroise**, Parc de Loisirs de Lann Rohou, 29800 Landerneau (02 98.85.16.17; Fax: 02 98.85.19.39). *Location:* 10 miles east of Brest, three miles south of Landerneau. A tough course, open to the breeze in a beautiful natural setting. 18 holes, 5672 metres, Par 71. 9 holes, 3329 metres, Par 37. 22 bay driving range, 2 putting greens. *Green Fees:* High Season: Weekdays 18 holes 37 euros, 9 holes 22 euros. Weekends 18 holes 42 euros, 9 holes 26 euros. Low Season: Weekdays 18 holes 28 euros, 9 holes 19 euros. Weekends 18 holes 34 euros, 9 holes 22 euros. *Eating facilities:* bar and restaurant and all facilities at the Golf Hotel d'Iroise. *Visitors:* welcome. Pro shop; cart, trolley and club hire. Golf/Hotel packages. *Society Meetings:* welcome. Professional: J-F Pega. Secretary: Guylene.

LA BAULE. **Golf de la Bretesche**, 44780 Missillac (02 51.76.86.86; Fax: 02 40.88.36.28). *Location:* 20km and 20mm north-east of La Baule; 50km and 30mm north of Nantes on the N167. In a wooded and magnificent forest (2600 acres), large fairways and superb greens cover an area of 480 acres and borders the picturesque Chateau de la Bretesche surrounded by a vast lake. 18 holes, 6700 yards, S.S.S. 72. Practice ground, putting green, training bunker. *Green Fees:* information not available. *Eating facilities:* two bars and two restaurants. *Visitors:* welcome. Pro shop, cart, club and trolley hire. *Society Meetings:* welcome. Professional: Thierry Mathon. Manager: Fabrice Gicquiand. Secretary: Stephane Harouard/Francoise Desmarches (02 51.76.86.86; Fax: 02 40.88.36.28). *

LA BAULE. **Golf International Barrière La Baule**, 44117 St-André-des-Eaux (02.40.60.46.18; Fax: 02.40.60.41.41). *Location:* to the east of La Baule, 3 km from St André des Eaux. Three parkland courses with interesting water features. Red Course: 18 holes, 6055 metres, Par 72. Green Course, 2961 metres, Par 36. Blue Course 18 hole, 6301 metres, Par 72. Golf Academy: designed by Jack Nicklaus. *Green Fees:* information not available. *Eating Facilities:* bar and restaurant. *Visitors:* welcome by reservation booked the day before. Pro shop; cart, club and trolley hire; target and putting green, approach zone, training bunker and coaching studio. *Society Meetings:* welcome by arrangement. e-mail:golfinterlabaule@lucienbarriere.com website: www.lucienbarriere.com

---

LA ROCHE-SUR-YON. **Golf Club de la Domangère**, Route de la Rochelle, 85310 Nesmy (02 51.07.65.90; Fax: 02 51.07.65.95). *Location:* approximately 10km south of La Roche-sur-Yon west of the D747. A long and majestic course with plenty of strategic water, mature trees and bordered by the River Yon. 18 holes, 6480 metres, Par 72. 4 hole practice course, driving range, putting green. *Green Fees:* information not available. *Eating facilities:* bar, grill-room. *Visitors:* welcome. Club, cart and trolley hire. Hotel apartments. *Society Meetings:* welcome, booking required. Professional: Mr A. Stephane.

LORIENT. **Golf du Val Quéven,** Kerrousseau RD 6, 56530 Quéven (02 97.05.17.96: Fax: 02 97.05.19.18). *Location*: nearest main road RN194, Quéven situated between Lorient and Pont Scorff. Offering an impressive and diversified landscape built around 100 year old trees, the course is very challenging and is one of the best in western France. 18 holes, 6140 metres, Par 72. Driving range, putting green. *Green Fees*: information not available. *Eating facilities*: bar and restaurant. Visitors: welcome. Pro shop; club and trolley hire. *Society Meetings*: welcome. Professional: Mario Zimmermann (02 97.05.17.96; Fax: 02 97.05.19.18). Secretaries: Anita Le Basseau and M. Frédéric Dellsperger (02 97.05.17.96; Fax: 02 97.05.19.18). Director: Jean Luc Leroux. *

LORIENT. **Parcours Formule Golf Ploemeur Ocean**, Saint Jude-Kerham, 56270 Ploemeur (02 97.32.81.82; Fax: 02 97.32.80.90). *Location:* RN165 exit Ploemeur, towards Fort Bloque. Seaside links course, huge American style greens, water hazards. 18 holes, 6517 yards, 5957 metres, S.S.S. 72. Covered driving range. *Green Fees:* information not available. *Eating facilities:* bar and restaurant. *Visitors:* welcome. Hotels in immediate surroundings. *Society Meetings:* managed by the Parcours Formule Golf. Professional: Laurent Queffelec. Manager: Jeau Luc Leroux. *

RENNES. **Golf de la Freslonnière,** 35650 Le Rheu (02 99.14.84.09; Fax: 02 99.14.94.98). *Location:* three km from Rennes towards Lorient. Woodland course with water features and banks of rhododendrons. 18 holes, 5756 metres, Par 72. Practice ground and putting green. *Green Fees:* information not available. *Eating facilities:* clubhouse, restaurant and bar (closed Mondays). *Visitors:* welcome, no restrictions. Pro shop; club, cart and trolley hire. Professional: Richard Triaire. Director: V. Spillmann. * e-mail: lafreslo@compuserve.com

RENNES. **Golf de Rennes**, St. Jacques de la Lande, 35136 Rennes (02 99.30.18.18. Fax: 02 99.31.51.04). *Location:* eight km south of Rennes, off the D177 to Redon. Set amongst mature woodland with several water hazards; a new course to enjoy. 18 holes, 6150 metres, Par 72. 9 holes, 2068 metres, Par 32. Short 9 hole course. *Green Fees:* information not available. *Eating facilities:* bar and restaurant in clubhouse. *Visitors:* welcome, no restrictions. Pro shop; trolley and club hire. Secretary: Catherine du Bel. Director: Agnes Piron.*

ST MALO. **Golf de St-Malo-le-Tronchet**, Le Tronchet, 35540 Miniac Morvan (02 99.58.96.69). *Location:* 23km south of St Malo, 12km east of Dinan, south of the N176. Rolling parkland designed on a grand scale with vast greens and sand traps, strategic water. 18 holes, 5936 metres. Par 72. 9 holes, 2684 metres, Par 36. Driving range, putting green. *Green Fees:* information not available. *Eating facilities:* bar and restaurant. *Visitors:* welcome. "Hostellerie Abbatiale" close by the course with all hotel facilities and golf holiday packages. Pro shop; trolley and club hire. *Society Meetings:* welcome, bookings required. Professional: M. Cyril Bourakhowitch. Secretary: Mme Raquel Watbot.*

ST JEAN-DE-MONTS. **Golf Club de St Jean-de-Monts**, Avenue des Pays de la Loire, 85160 St. Jean-de-Monts (02 51.58.82.73; Fax: 02 51.59.18.32). *Location:* a partly links-style course along the seaside with pine trees and dunes. On the Atlantic coast some 60/70km south-west of Nantes. 18 holes, 5962 metres, Par 72. Short 5 hole course. Practice ground and putting greens. *Eating facilities:* clubhouse with bar and restaurant. The Hotel de la Plage in nearby Notre Dame de Monts offers golfing breaks. Pro shop; cart, club and trolley hire. *

PARIS

PARIS. **Golf de Forges-les-Bains,** Rue de General Leclerc, 91470 Forges-les-Bains (01 64.91.48.18; Fax: 01 64.91.40.52). *Location:* A10 Orleans, exit Les Ulis then towards Limours and Forges-les-Bains; 35 minutes from Paris. Parkland course with a lot of variety and suitable for all levels of golfers. 18 holes, 6207 metres, Par 72. Driving range, three holes training course. *Green Fees:* information not available. *Eating facilities:* bar and restaurant in clubhouse. *Visitors:* welcome, no restrictions but reservations preferred. Special rates for groups and societies. David Leadbetter Golf Academy on site. Pro shop; trolley and club hire. Professionals: Jean Luc Poü and Yann Yver. Secretary: Philippe Wibaux.*

PARIS. **Golf de la Vaucouleurs,** 78910 Civry-la-Forêt (01.34.87.16.04). *Location:* off the A13 at the Mantes interchange, south off the road to Houdan. Two 18 hole courses. "The River" - very varied with trees, water and hills, 6138 metres, Par 73; "The Little Valley" - a links-type course, 5553 metres, Par 70. Practice ground, putting green. *Green Fees:* weekdays 89 euros, weekends 64 euros. *Eating facilities:* bar and restaurant in clubhouse; also at nearby Hotel la Dousseine at Anet. Pro shop; club and trolley hire, buggy available. Professional: Pierre Girard. Secretary: (01.34.87.62.29; Fax: 01 34.87.70.09).

PARIS. **Golf de St Quentin-en-Yvelines**, RD 912, 78197 Trappes (01.30.50.86.40; Fax: 01.34.82.88.82). *Location:* about 20km west of Paris off the D912. A very popular public facility of 36 holes. White Course - 18 holes, 6100 metres, S.S.S. 72; Red Course - 18 holes, 5700 metres, S.S.S. 69. Also 9 hole compact course, driving range, putting green. *Green Fees:* information not available. *Eating facilities:* bar and restaurant in clubhouse. Pro shop; trolley and club hire. Professional: Jean Marc Lecuona. Secretary: Jerome Lauredi. *

PARIS. **Golf des Yvelines,** Château de la Couharde, 78940 La Queue-les-Yvelines (01 34.86.48.89; Fax: 01 34.86.50.31). *Location:* about 45km west of Paris by N12, near Montfort-l'Amaury. Built around the elegant château, with fairways cut through thick woods. 18 holes, 6344 metres, S.S.S. 72. 9 holes, 2065 metres, S.S.S. 31. Practice ground, putting green. *Green Fees:* information not provided. *Eating facilities:* bar and restaurant. *Visitors:* all visitors welcome. Club and trolley hire. Professional: Jean Paul Chardonnet. Secretary: Stephane Bessette. *

PARIS. **Golf National**, 2 Avenue du Golf, 78280 Guyancourt (01 30.43.36.00; Fax: 01 30.43.85.58). *Location:* about 25km south-west of Paris off the A13/A12, six miles from Versailles. A public facility of 45 holes laid out in three courses. "The Albatross" (now the venue for the French Open) - 18 holes, 6500 metres championship course with severe water hazards and winding fairways, Par 72; "The Eagle" - 18 holes, 6000 metres, Par 72 for experienced players; "The Birdie" - 9 holes, 2100 metres beginners' course, Par 32 and driving range; "The

Par" - a warm-up, practice course. Putting greens. *Eating facilities:* on-site Hotel Novotel. Two restaurants. *Visitors:* all welcome, public course. Club and trolley hire. *

WEST & CENTRE

CHEVERNY. **Golf du Château de Cheverny**, La Rousselière, 41700 Cheverny (02.54.79.24.70; Fax: 02.54.79.25.52). *Location:* to the south of Cheverny 15km south of Blois. Built over the former hunting grounds of the Château with large well-kept greens. 18 holes, 6272 metres, Par 71. 3 hole practice course, driving range and putting green. *Green Fees:* information not available. *Eating facilities:* bar and restaurant in clubhouse. *Visitors:* welcome. Pro shop; club and trolley hire, electric carts. Swimming pool by the bar. *Society Meetings:* 20% reduction on fees. Sister Club: Letham Grange (Scotland). Professional: Pierre Raguet. *
e-mail: contact@golf-cheverny.com
website: www.golf-cheverny.com

COGNAC. **Golf du Cognac**, Saint-Brice, 16100 Cognac (05 45.32.18.17; Fax: 05 45.35.10.76). *Location:* five km east of Cognac, north of the N141 across the River Charente. Undulating fairways with views of vineyards and the river; some water hazards. 18 holes, 6142 metres, Par 72. 4 hole practice course, putting green and driving range. *Green Fees:* information not available. *Eating facilities:* clubhouse with restaurant and bar. Pro shop; cart, club and trolley hire. Professional: (05 45.32.37.60). Secretary: (05 45.32.18.17).

LOUDUN. **Golf de Loudun-Roiffe**, Domaine St Hilaire, 86120 Roiffe (05 49.98.78.06; Fax: 05 49.98.72.57). *Location:* 15km north of Loudun towards Saumur on the D147. An attractive woodland course with a few water hazards and well guarded greens. 18 holes, 6343 metres, S.S.S. 73, Par 72. 6 hole pitch and putt course, driving range, practice green and putting green. *Green Fees:* from 23 to 35 euros. Subject to review. *Eating facilities:* restaurant; bar in clubhouse. *Visitors:* welcome, no restrictions. Two-star hotel with 64 rooms and 13 self-catering apartments, seminar rooms, entertainment room. Tennis, bicycles for hire, crazy-golf, swimming pool, playground for children, marked trails. Pro shop, trolley and club hire. *Society Meetings:* welcome. Professional: Jean-Marc Warot.
e-mail: golf-france@interpc.fr
website: www.france-in.com

ORLEANS. **"Les Bordes" Golf International,** 41220 St-Laurent Nouan (02 54.87.72.13; Fax: 02 54.87.78.61). *Location:* from Paris motorway A10 exit Meung sur Loire. Laid out on a former hunting park. 18 holes, 7041 yards, 6412 metres, Par 72. Driving range, putting green. *Green Fees:* information not available. *Eating facilities:* bar and restaurant in clubhouse. *Visitors:* welcome every day. Pro shop; carts, trolleys and clubs for hire. Accommodation on site. *

POITIERS. **Golf du Haut-Poitou**, Parc de Loisirs de St Cyr, 86130 Saint Cyr (05 49.62.53.62; Fax: 05 49.88.77.14). *Location:* 20km north of Poitiers and 15km south of Chatellerault. Undulating course with a lake and water hazards and wooded hills. 18 holes, 6590 metres, S.S.S. 75. 9 holes, 1800 metres, Par 31. Practice ground, driving range, putting and pitching greens. *Green Fees:* information not available. *Eating facilities:* clubhouse with brasserie and bar; Restaurant Club 19 (05494 70056) *Visitors:* welcome without restriction. Pro shop and equipment hire. *Society Meetings:* welcome. Professional: David Maxwell. Secretaries: Catherine Marchais and Jessica Guillon (05 49.62.53.62; Fax: 05 49.88.77.14). e-mail: contact@golfduhautpoitou.com

ROYAN. **Golf de Royan**, Maine-Gaudin, 17420 St-Palais-sur-Mer (05 46.23.16.24; Fax: 05 46.23.23.38). *Location:* on the D25 coast road, nine km north-west of Royan. An exciting course with narrow fairways undulating through tall pines. Two courses. 18 holes, 5970 metres, S.S.S. 73; 6 hole, 920 metres, S.S.S. 20. Practice ground with driving range, putting green. *Green Fees:* information not available. *Eating facilities:* restaurant and bar in clubhouse. *Visitors:* welcome. Pro shop with equipment hire. *Society Meetings:* welcome by arrangement with the Secretary. Professionals: Gilles Delavallade and Christine Wenandy. Secretaries: Nathalie and Christelle (05 46.23.16.24; Fax: 05 46.23.23.38). e-mail: golfderoyan@wanadoo.fr

TOURS. **Blue Green Golf d'Ardrée**, Golf d'Ardrée Tours, 37360 Saint Antoine du Rocher (02 47.56.77.38; Fax: 02 47.56.79.96). *Location:* near Tours north, direction of le Mans, nearest town St Antoine Du Rocher. Parkland course, wooded with water and bunkers. 18 holes, 5758 metres, Par 70. Practice ground and putting green. *Green Fees:* information not available. *Eating facilities:* restaurant and bar in clubhouse. *Visitors:* welcome but it would be better to reserve the tee two or three days in advance for weekdays, and five days in advance for weekends. *Society Meetings:* welcome but reservation a month in advance please. Professional: Karl Cotteray. Secretaries: Virginie and Corinne. *

TOURS. **Golf du Château des Sept Tours,** 37330 Courcelles de Touraine (02.47.24.69.75; Fax: 02.47.24.23.74). *Location:* 30kms from Tours on the D34 between Château la Vallière and Langeais. A fairly long course but relatively flat with attractive trees and water, excellent greens. 18 holes, 6194 metres, Par 72. Practice ground and putting green. *Green Fees:* information not available. *Eating facilities:* restaurant and bistro in clubhouse. *Visitors:* 4 star Hotel, restaurant and golf club open all year. Pro shop; club and trolley hire. Professional: Pascal Petit. *

EAST

AIX-LES-BAINS. **Golf d'Aix-les-Bains**, Avenue du Golf, 73100 Aix-les-bains (04 79.61.23.35). *Location:* three km south of Aix by the Lac du Bourget. An attractive parkland course on sloping land surrounded by wooded hills. 18 holes, 5519 metres. S.S.S. 71. Practice, putting green. *Green Fees:* information not available. *Eating facilities:* restaurant (04.79.61.47.20). *Visitors:* welcome. Pro shop; trolley and club hire (04.79.61.31.56). Professional: (04 79.35.39.41). Secretary: (06 09.69.34.61; Fax: 04 79.34.06.01). * e-mail: info@golf-aixlesbains.com website: www.golf-aixlesbains.com

CHAMONIX. **Golf de Chamonix**, 35 route du Golf, Les Praz, 74400 Chamonix (04 50.53.06.28; Fax: 04 50.53.38.69). *Location:* on the N506 three km north of Chamonix. A subtle and technical course, enhanced by water obstacles and numerous bunkers. Spectacular mountain views including Mont Blanc. 18 holes, 6076 metres, S.S.S. 72. Driving range, putting green. *Green Fees:* information not available. *Eating facilities:* restaurant. *Visitors:* welcome every day with a Handicap Certificate, tee off times must be booked one day in advance. Pro shop; cart, trolley and club hire. Professional: Jean Claude Bonnaz. Director: Christophe de Carné (04 50.53.06.28; Fax: 04 50.53.38.69).

EVIAN. **Evian Masters Golf Club,** South Bank of Lake Geneva, 74500 Evian-les-Bains (04.50.75.46.66; Fax: 04.50.75.65.54). *Location:* on high ground above Evian. 8kms from Thonon, 45kms west of Geneva. Hilly fairways overlooking Lake Geneva, sloping greens guarded by deep bunkers. Evian Masters course. 18 holes, 6674 yards, 6006 metres, Par 72. Covered and uncovered practice range, two putting greens, chipping green, pitching green, training bunkers, pitch and putt. *Green Fees:* information not available. *Eating facilities:* restaurant and bar: Le Chalet du Golf. *Visitors:* welcome, Handicap 35 or course authorization. Pro shop - clubs, bags and carts. *Society Meetings:* welcome (up to 180 people). Professional: Christophe Martigniere (courses). Co-Director: Margo Perrolaz. Director: Yannic Le Hec. *

GRENOBLE. **Golf International de Grenoble**, Route de Montavie, Bresson, 38320 Eybens (04 76.73.65.00; Fax: 04 76.73.65.51). *Location:* five km south of Grenoble. A long course with winding fairways, small lakes, trees - architect Robert Trent Jones Jnr. Bresson Course 18 holes, 6343 metres, Par 73; Uriage Course 9 holes, 2005 metres. Practice ground and putting green; driving range. *Green Fees:* information not available. *Eating facilities:* clubhouse and nearby hotel. *Visitors:* welcome at all times. Professional: Loic Landoas. Manager: Herve Segrais. *

LYON. **Golf Club de Lyon,** 38280 Villette d'Anthon (04 78.31.11.33; Fax: 04 72.02.48.27). *Location:* Lyon, Rocade Est exit Meyzieu Grand Large. Brocards - flat, wooded; Sangliers - hilly, wooded. Brocards 18 holes, 6229 metres. S.S.S. 72; Sangliers 18 holes, 6727 metres. S.S.S 72. Practice ground, putting green, training centre. *Green Fees:* information not available. *Eating facilities:* bar and restaurant in clubhouse. *Visitors:* welcome anytime. No jeans, no powered trolleys. *Society Meetings:* welcome. Pro shop; equipment hire. Professionals: Raphael Reynaud and Ludovic Henninot (04.78.31.11.33; Fax: 04.72.02.48.27). Secretary: (04.78.31.11.33; Fax: 04 72.02.48.27). *

ST JULIEN (Geneva). **Golf and Country Club de Bossey**, Chateau de Crevin, Bossey, 74160 St-Julien-en-Genevois. *Location:* just near the main road between St. Julien en Genevois and Annemasse about five miles from each of these towns. Just in France on the southern outskirts of Geneva. Challenging mountain golf with fine views. Well wooded with water hazards. 18 holes, 5952 metres, Par 71. Driving range, putting green. *Green Fees:* information not available. *Eating facilities:* bar and restaurant in chateau clubhouse. *Visitors:* welcome weekdays only, maximum of three times a year. Maximum handicap 30. No jeans allowed on course. Contact General Manager for details. Pro shop; cart, trolley and club hire. *Society Meetings:* catered for, contact General Manager. Professional: Mark Cobley (04.50.43.65.66). Secretary: (04.50.43.95.50; Fax: 04.50.95.32.57). *

SOUTH WEST

ALBI. **Golf d'Albi Lasbordes**, Chateau de Las Bordes, 81000 Albi (05.63.54.98.07; Fax: 05.63.47.21.55). *Location:* three minutes from town centre, overlooking the River Tarn and offering beautiful views towards the cathedral. A championship course with trees. 18 holes, 6155 metres, Par 72. *Green Fees:* information not available. *Eating facilities:* bar and restaurant in clubhouse. *Visitors:* welcome all year. Club and trolley hire. Professional: Olivier Doan. *

ANGLET. **Golf de Chiberta**, 104 Boulevard des Plages, 64600 Anglet (05 59.63.83.20; Fax: 05 59.63.30.56). *Location:* three km from Biarritz and from Bayonne. A well-established combination of seashore and wooded parkland. 18 holes, 5650 metres, Par 71. Driving range, putting green. *Green Fees:* information not available. *Eating facilities:* bar and restaurant in clubhouse. *Visitors:* welcome, Handicap Certificate required. Pro shop; trolley and club hire. Professional: H. Brouson, P Dufourg, C. Lecuona. Secretary: (05 59.63.83.20; Fax: 05 59.63.30.56). *

ARCACHON. **Golf de Gujan Mestras**, BP 74, Route de Sanguinet, 33470 Gujan Mestras (05 57.52.73.73; Fax: 05 56.66.10.93). *Location:* autoroute Bordeaux/Bayonne, A66 in the direction of Arcachon. A spectacular course with well located water obstacles. 18 holes, 6225 metres, Par 72. 9 holes, 2630 metres, Par 35. Practice facilities and putting green. *Green Fees:* information not available. *Eating facilities:* restaurant, clubhouse and at nearby hotel. Pro shop; equipment and trolley hire. *

BAYONNE. **Golf de Moliets,** Rue Mathieu Desbieys, 40660 Moliets (05 58.48.54.65; Fax: 05 58.48.54.88). *Location:* about 30km north of Bayonne on the Atlantic coast at Moliets. Part of a leisure seaside complex with links and wooded inland holes. 18 holes, 6164 metres, Par 72. 9 holes, 1905 metres, Par 31. Practice ground, putting green. *Green Fees:* information not provided. *Eating facilities:* bar and restaurant in clubhouse and in on-site hotels. *Visitors:* welcome. Pro shop; cart, club and trolley hire; tennis. *Society Meetings:* welcome. Professionals: Franck Ducousso, Christophe Beithet.

BAYONNE. **Seignosse Golf Hotel**, Avenue du Belvedere, 40510 Seignosse (05 58.41.68.30; Fax: 05 58.41.68.31). *Location:* about 25km north of Bayonne on the D79 north of Hossegor. Very hilly, exciting and undulating course, a pleasure to look at as well as play. Ranked 21st in the top 100 European courses by 'Golf World International'. 18 holes, 6124 metres, Par 72. Practice ground. *Green Fees:* information not available. *Eating facilities:* two bars and two restaurants. *Visitors:* welcome. 3 Star Hotel. Pro

shop; cart, club and trolley hire; swimming pool. *Society Meetings:* welcome. Special golf/hotel packages available 'Golf Pass Biarritz' member. Professional: F. Martin. Secretary: Armand Gadea. Sales Manager: Lyonel Robin (05 58.41.68.30). *
e-mail: golfseignosse@wanadoo.fr
website: www.golfseignosse.com

BIARRITZ. **Golf d'Arcangues**, 64200 Arcangues (05 59.43.10.56; Fax: 05 59.43.12.60). *Location:* three km south-east of Biarritz. A fine rolling test in modern but natural style. Mounded bunkers and strategic water. 18 holes, 6142 metres, Par 72. *Green Fees:* information not available. *Eating facilities:* bar and restaurant in clubhouse. *Visitors:* welcome, no restrictions. Pro shop and equipment hire. Professional: O. Leglise. Secretary: English/French Mme Sylvie Cormier; French Mme Marie-José Dabbadie. *
e-mail: golf.arcangues@wanadoo.fr

BIARRITZ. **Golf de Biarritz Le Phare**, 2 Avenue Edith Cavell, 64200 Biarritz (05 59.03.71.80). *Location:* in Biarritz, facing the ocean with cooling breezes. A historic course (1888) with fast greens, level, many bunkers. 18 holes, 5379 metres, S.S.S. 69. Practice ground, putting green. *Green Fees:* information not available. *Eating facilities:* bar and restaurant in clubhouse, the nearby Hôtel du Palais and other hotels. Pro shop; club and trolley hire. Secretary: (05 59.03.71.80; Fax: 05 59.03.26.74).
e-mail: golf.biarritz@wanadoo.fr

BORDEAUX. **Golf de Cameyrac**, R.N. 89 Bordeaux Libourne Sortie No. 5, 33450 Cameyrac (05 56.72.96.79; Fax: 05 56.72.86.56). *Location:* 15km from Bordeaux N89 (Exit no. 5) close to the famous vineyards of St Emilion and Pomerol. Fairways run through forest, alongside ponds and vineyards. 18 holes, 5972 metres, Par 72. 9 holes, 1188 metres, Par 28. Practice ground, putting green. *Green Fees:* information not available. *Eating facilities:* bar and restaurant. *Visitors:* welcome every day. Pro shop; equipment hire. *Society Meetings:* welcome. Professionals: C. Bouchet, V Fructuoso. *

BORDEAUX. **Golf du Médoc**, Chemin de Courmateau, 33290 Le Pian Médoc (05 56 70 11 90; Fax: 05 56 11 99). *Location:* 20 minutes by car from Bordeaux International Airport. Vintage golf in Bordeaux Country. 36 holes named after Medoc Wine Chateaux. The "Chateaux Course" 6316 par 71, traditional links course, host of the French Open in 1999 (PGA European Tour), host of the European Amateur Championship in 1998. The "Vignes Course" 6220m par 71 set in a typically regional landscape winding through lakes and pine trees. Practice ground, pitching and putting greens. *Green Fees:* information not available. *Eating facilities:* clubhouse with bar and quality restaurant. *Visitors:* welcome. *Society Meetings:* please contact Secretary. Professionals: Gilles Arnaud and Christophe Praud. General Manager; Fabrice Jullienne. *
e-mail: golf.du.medoc@wanadoo.fr

BORDEAUX. **Golf de Pessac**, Rue de la Princesse, 33690 Pessac (05 57.26.03.33; Fax: 05 56.36.52.89). *Location:* on the western outskirts of Bordeaux, four km from the city and close to the airport, St. Jean d'Illiac road. A level course with large bunkers and some water. 27 holes providing alternative 9 hole layouts plus 9 hole practice course. 18 holes, 6040 metres. Par 72; 9 holes, 2911 metres. Par 36. Driving range, putting green. *Green Fees:* information not available. *Eating facilities:* restaurant and bar. *Visitors:* welcome at any time. *Society Meetings:* welcome. Pro shop; cart, club and trolley hire. Professionals: Ramuntcho Artola and Nagalie Gaillard. Secretary: Alain Egloff. *

CASTELJALOUX. **Golf de Casteljaloux**, Avenue du Lac, 47700 Casteljaloux (05.53.93.51.60; Fax: 05.53.20.90.98). *Location:* situated on the D933 facing Lake Clarens on the road to Mont-de-Marsan, 15km from the exit of the motorway, 90km from Bordeaux, 170km from Toulouse. Flat and wooded on six holes, 12 holes undulating. 18 holes, 6500 yards, 5916 metres, Par 72, S.S.S. 71. Practice holes, bunkers and tees, driving range and putting green. *Green Fees:* information not available. *Eating facilities:* bar and restaurant in clubhouse with fine views. *Visitors:* welcome. Pro shop; club and trolley hire. *Society Meetings:* by arrangement. Professional: Pierre Mengel. Director: Christopher Benson. *

DORDOGNE. **Château des Vigiers Golf and Country Club,** 24240 Monestier (05 53.61.50.00; Fax: 05 53.61.50.20). *Location:* about an hour's drive east of Bordeaux on D936, bearing right on D18 at Ste-Foy-la-Grande. Rolling past orchards, vineyards, woods, lakes surrounding new clubhouse/fitness centre. 18 holes, 6003 metres. Par 72. 6 hole practice course, driving range and putting green. *Green Fees:* information not available. *Eating facilities:* restaurant and bar. Pro shop, club, cart and trolley rental; luxury hotel. Professional: Vincent Trojani.
e-mail: reserve@vigiers.com
website: www.vigiers.com

HOSSEGOR. **Golf d'Hossegor**, Avenue du Golf, 40150 Hossegor (05 58.43.56.99; Fax: 05 58.43.98.52). *Location:* about 15km north of Bayonne just west of the A63. Fine classic test of golf over gently undulating, heavily wooded land. 18 holes, 5920 metres, Par 71. Driving range, putting green. *Eating facilities:* bar and restaurant in clubhouse. Pro shop; trolley hire. *

LACANAU-OCEAN. **Golf Hotel ★★★ 3 de Lacanau Ocean**, 33680 Lacanau Océan (05 56.03.92.98; Fax: 05 56.26.30.57). *Location:* between Lac de Lacanau and the sea, 60km west of Bordeaux. Level, within a pine and oak forest, some water hazards. 18 holes, 5900 metres, Par 72. Covered and open practice ground, putting green. *Green Fees:* information not available. *Eating facilities:* regional restaurant, snacks at clubhouse; bar. *Visitors:* welcome all year round. *Society Meetings:* welcome. Pro shop; equipment, trolley, buggy hire. Special packages with Golf–Hotel and Restaurant. Three Star Hotel, 50 rooms direct onto the course; swimming pool; cottages. (05 56.03.92.92; Fax: 05 56.26.30.57).

LAVAUR. **Golf des Etangs de Fiac,** Brazis, 81500 Fiac (05.63.70.64.70; Fax: 05.63.75.32.91). *Location:* Toulouse to Lavaur, course is 10km after Lavaur in the direction of Castres. A technically interesting course, very green, with water hazards across natural ponds. 18 holes, 5800 metres. S.S.S. 71. *Green Fees:* information not available. *Eating facilities:* bar and restaurant open all year. *Visitors:* welcome all year. Pro shop, equipment hire. Swimming pool in season (golfers only) Lessons available. Professional: Pierre Crouzet. Secretaries: J. Phillippe and Sandie. Owner: Hilda Stevens. *

MAZAMET. **Golf de Mazamet la Barouge**, 81660 Pont de l'Arn, Mazamet (05.63.61.06.72). *Location:* three km north of Mazamet. A standard course with small wooded areas, set in magnificent surroundings. Notable for tricky and long Par 3s. 18 holes, 5953 metres. Par 70. *Green Fees:* information not available. *Eating facilities:* bar and restaurant in clubhouse. *Visitors:* welcome all year. Buggy hire. Professional: Didier Charria. *

PAU. **Pau Golf Club**, Rue du Golf, 64140 Billere (05 59.13.18.56; Fax: 05 59.13.18.57). *Location:* RN 117 Commune de Billere 5km from Pau towards Bayonne. The first course in continental Europe (1856). Flat, wooded, along the River Gave. 18 holes, 5312 metres, S.S.S. 69. Practice facilities including three practice holes. *Green Fees:* information not available. *Eating facilities:* bar and restaurant in clubhouse. *Visitors:* welcome. *Society Meetings:* by arrangement. Professional: D. Loustalet (06.08.41.16.14), Ph. Heugas (06.11.03.30.57). Secretary: Sylvie Loustalet et Nilda Bellanger (05 59.32.02.33). *

SAINT-JEAN-DE-LUZ. **Golf de la Nivelle**, Place William Sharp, 64500 Ciboure (05 59.47.18.99; Fax: 05 59.47.21.16). *Location:* two km south of Saint-Jean de Luz on the banks of the River Nivelle. Classic parkland with mature trees and harbour views. 18 holes, 5513 metres, Par 70. Practice ground, putting green. *Green Fees:* information not available. *Eating facilities:* bar and restaurant in clubhouse. *Visitors:* welcome, maximum Handicap 35. Self catering flats on golf course. Pro shop; equipment hire. *

TOULOUSE. **Maeva Latitudes Toulouse Seilh**, Route de Grenade, 31840 Seilh (05 62.13.14.14; Fax: 05 61.42.34.17). *Location:* about 12km north-west of Toulouse near the A62. "Yellow" Course of moderate difficulty, 18 holes, 4202 metres, Par 64; "Red" Course of competition standard, 18 holes, 6200 metres, Par 72. Extensive practice and training facilities. *Eating facilities:* bar and restaurant in clubhouse. Pro shop; club, cart and trolley hire. A new hotel with 175 rooms and apartments is now available on site with tennis and private swimming pool (05.62.13.14.15). *
e-mail: toulouse.golf@maeva.fr
website: www.maeva.latitudes.toulouse.com

VILLENEUVE-SUR-LOT. **Golf de Castelnaud**, 47290 Castelnaud de Gratecambe (05. 53. 01. 60. 19/05. 53. 10. 75. 96; Fax: 05. 53. 01. 78. 99). *Location:* on the N21 10km north of Villeneuve, between the scenic valleys of the Lot and the Dordogne. Inland course with water and many trees. 18 holes, 6322 metres, Par 72. Debutants Ecole de Golf 6 hole course. Practice ground, putting green. *Eating facilities:* the clubhouse is an 18th century manor house with brasserie/snack restaurant. Pro shop; equipment hire.

SOUTH

AGDE. **Golf du Cap d'Agde**, 4 Avenue des Alizés, 34300 Cap d'Agde (04 67.26.54.40; Fax: 04 67.26.97.00). *Location:* autoroute A9 exit Agde. Seaside links. 18 holes, 6279 metres. S.S.S. 73. Practice ground; 9 hole pitch and putt, 800 metres, S.S.S. 27. *Green Fees:* information not available. *Eating facilities:* bar and restaurant in clubhouse. *Visitors:* welcome, no restrictions. Club, trolley and cart hire. Spikes on shoes forbidden. *Society Meetings:* welcome by reservation. Professionals: Jean Pierre Prieur, Franck Renard. Secretary: Myriam Delcayre.

AIX-EN-PROVENCE. **Golf International de Château L'Arc**, Domaine de Château L'Arc, 13710 Fuveau (04 42.53.28.38; Fax: 04 42.29.08.41). *Location:* about 15km south-east of Aix-en-Provence just south of the A8. A challenging course of varying terrain through trees, sloping fairways and water hazards. 18 holes, 6200 metres. S.S.S. 71. Driving range, putting green. *Green Fees:* information not available. *Eating facilities:* bar and restaurant in clubhouse. Pro shop; cart, trolley and club hire. *Visitors:* welcome, no restriction but it is necessary to make a reservation for weekends. Professional: Eric Follet. Secretary: Catherine Peter. *

AVIGNON. **Golf de Servanes,** Domaine de Servanes, 13890 Mouries (04 90.47.59.95; Fax: 04 90.47.52.58). *Location:* leave autoroute at Salon and head for Arles; leave at Avignon and head for St. Remy. Undulating course with serveral water hazards. 18 holes, 6121 metres. S.S.S. 72. Practice facilities. *Green Fees:* information not available. *Eating facilities:* available. *Visitors:* welcome, no restrictions. *Society Meetings:* welcome. Professional: Alain Brioland.*

BANDOL. **Golf de Fregate,** Route de Bandol, RD 559, 83270 St-Cyr-sur-Mer (04 34.29.38.00; Fax: 04 94.29.96.94). *Location:* about 4km from St-Cyr-sur-Mer on the road to Bandol on the right hand side. A dramatic new course in a vineyard setting overlooking the Mediterranean. 18 holes, 6209 metres. Par 72. Also 9 holes, 1500 metres. Par 29. Practice ground and two putting greens. *Green Fees:* information not available. *Eating facilities:* bar and restaurant. Also on-site hotel (four star, 133 rooms) by 18th green. Pro shop, club, cart and trolley hire.*

CANNES. **Golf Club de Cannes-Mandelieu**, Route du Golf, 06210 Mandelieu-la-Napoule (04 92.97.32.00; Fax: 04 93.49.92.90). *Location:* across the mouth of the small River Siagne, about seven km west of Cannes, south of the A8. A short, level course, third oldest and most popular in France. 18 holes, 5867 metres, Par 71. 9 holes, 2409 metres, Par 33. Practice ground, putting green. *Green Fees:* information not provided. *Eating facilities:* bar and restaurant in attractive clubhouse. *Visitors:* welcome. *Society Meetings:* welcome. Director: Jean Stefan Camerini.

CANNES. **Golf Country Club de Cannes-Mougins**, 175 Avenue du Golf, 06250 Mougins (04 93.75.79.13; Fax: 04 93.75.27.60). *Location:* eight km north of Cannes, near the A8. A high-class private course, undulating through wooded hills. 18 holes, 6849 yards, 6263 metres, S.S.S. 72. Driving range, two putting greens, pitching green. *Green Fees:* information not available. *Eating facilities:* restaurant, bar, snacks. *Visitors:* welcome, no restrictions. Sauna. Magasin du Golf; cart, trolley and club hire. Professionals: Michel Damiano, Patrick Lemaire, Richard Sorrell (04 93.75.53.32). Secretaries: Hugues Danjou, Maryline Eynaud (04 93.75.79.13; Fax: 04 93.75.27.60). *

CANNES. **Riviera Golf Club**, Avenue des Amazones, 06210 Mandelieu (04.92.97.67.67; Fax: 04.92.97.66.57). *Location:* less than five km west of Cannes, just south of the A8, Frèjus direction. A new 18 hole course by American master Robert Trent Jones; mostly level, some hills and lakes. 18 holes, 5736 metres, Par 72. Driving range, putting green. *Green Fees:* information not available. *Eating facilities:* in clubhouse. *Visitors:* welcome, Handicap of 35 and insurance required. Professional/Manager: Y. Lecrubier. President: R.G. Boillat. *

CORSICA. **Golf de Sperone**, Domaine de Sperone, 20169 Bonifacio (04 95.73.17.13: Fax: 04 95.73.17.85). *Location*: near Bonifacio, southern point of Corsica. Another new Trent Jones creation, part on rocky maquis inland, part overlooking the Mediterranean. 18 holes, 6106 metres. S.S.S. 72. Practice facilities. *Green Fees*: information not available. *Eating facilities*: bar and restaurant with panoramic views. *Visitors*: welcome every day, please make a reservation. The golf course is closed on Thursdays from November to March and on Thursday afternoons from April to October. Pro shop, practice area, putting green, car, club and trolley hire; rented accommodation available at course. *Society Meetings*: welcome except July and August. Chairman: J.B. Casabianca. Professional: Philippe Allain. Secretary: Céline Metier, Nafissa Bartoli. website: www.sperone.net

COTE D'AZUR. **Golf Opio-Valbonne**, Route de Roquefort Les Pins, 06650 Opio ([33] 04 93 12 00 08; Fax: [33] 04 93 12 26 00). *Location*: from Nice, A8 to Aix, out Villeneuve-Loubet, D2085, at Roquefort Les Pins, Valbonne, D204. Situated between Riviera coast and mountains, in a natural park of 530 acres. 18 holes, 5782 metres, S.S.S.73. Practice area, putting green. *Green Fees*: 65 euros all week (9 holes 45 euros). *Visitors*: welcome. Car, club and trolley hire. Instruction school.
e-mail: opiovalbonne@opengolfclub.com
website: www.opengolfclub.com

GRASSE. **Golf de la Grande Bastide**, Chemin des Picholines, 06740 Chateauneuf de Grasse (04 93.77.70.08; Fax: 04 93.77.72.36). *Location:* autoroute A8 exit Cannes towards Mougin-Valbonne-Opio. Gently rolling, of equal challenge to all grades of player. 18 holes, 6105 metres, S.S.S. 72. Driving range, putting green. *Green Fees:* information not available. *Eating facilities:* bar and restaurant in clubhouse. *Visitors:* welcome anytime. Trolley and club hire. *Society Meetings:* welcome. Professional: S. Damiano (06.07.56.31.57). Manager: Alain Decovan.*

LES BAUX. **Golf des Baux de Provence**, Domaine de Manville, 13520 Les Baux de Provence (04 90.54.40.20; Fax: 04 90.54.40.93). *Location:* 25km from Avignon, 18km from Arles, 80km from Marseilles (Airport), the course is on the D27 between Les Baux and Maussane-les-Alpilles. Designed by the British architect Martin Hawtree, the course is set between pines, olive trees and scented lavender. 9 holes, 2842 metres. Par 36. Practice, putting green. *Green Fees:* 9 holes - weekdays 30 euros, weekends 32 euros. *Eating facilities:* bar and restaurant in clubhouse. *Visitors:* always welcome. Hire of clubs, trolleys and golf carts. Professional: Joël Laggoune.

MARSEILLES. **Golf d'Aix Marseille,** Domaine de Riquetti, 13290 Les Milles (04 42.24.20.41; Fax: 04 42.39.97.48). *Location:* between Marseilles and Aix-en-Provence, west of the A51. A mature parkland course in a natural setting with a wealth of established trees. 18 holes, 6291 metres, Par 73. Driving range, putting green. *Green Fees:* information not available. *Eating facilities:* bar and restaurant in clubhouse. *Visitors:* welcome, closed Tuesdays. Pro shop; trolley and club hire. *

MARSEILLES. **Golf de Marseille La Salette,** Impasse des Vaudrans, Quartier de la Valentine, 13011 Marseille (04.91.27.12.16; Fax: 04.91.27.21.33). *Location:* Autoroute A50 exit La Valentine, follow the signs for "Valentine" then "Golf de la Salette". Hilly parkland course. 18 holes, 5436 metres. Par 71. *Green Fees:* information not available. *Eating facilities:* restaurant. *Visitors:* welcome. *Society Meetings:* welcome - conference and ballrooms available for seminars. Tennis courts and swimming pool. Golf school and buggy hire available. *

MONTE CARLO. **Monte Carlo Golf Club**, Route du Mont Agel, 06320 La Turbie (04 93.41.09.11/ 04 92 41 50 70: Fax: 04 93.41.09.55). *Location:* from Nice, take autoroute A8 Exit for La Turbie. Signpost at end of town, left turn for Mont Agel. Golf course entrance after 5 kms. Picturesque course with exceptional views of the Mediterranean sea and southern Alps. 18 holes, 5700 metres, Par 71. Driving range, practice, putting green. *Green Fees:* information not available. *Eating facilities:* bar and restaurant. *Visitors:* welcome, Handicap Certificate required. *Society Meetings:* welcome by prior arrangement. Professionals: F. Ruffier-Meray, J.M. Loustalan and Sophie Halsall. Secretary: C. Houtart. *

MONTPELLIER. **Golf de la Grande-Motte**, Club House du Golf, 34280 La Grande-Motte ((33) 04.67.56.05.00; Fax: (33) 04.67.29.18.84). *Location:* on the coast, east of Montpellier. Former marshland, now a 42 hole complex with fast greens, water, trees and bunkers. "The Pink Flamingos" - 18 competition class holes, 6161 metres, Par 72; "The Seagulls" - 3220 metres, Par 58; and 6 hole practice green, 560 metres, Par 19. Practice ground, putting green. *Green Fees:* information not available. *Eating facilities:* bar and restaurant in clubhouse and on-course Golf Hotel. Pro shop; trolley and cart hire. Professionals: V. Etchevers, P.H. Milhau, A. Schneider. Manager: J. Mathieu. *

MONTPELLIER. **Golf de Massane**, Domaine de Massane, 34670 Baillargues (04.67.87.87.89; Fax: 04.67.87.87.90). *Location:* seven km from airport, 10km from Montpellier and two km from autoroute. Tough championship layout which hosts the annual Volvo Tour qualifying. Elevated greens protected by sand and water. 18 holes, 7037 metres, Par 72. 9 hole compact course. Extensive teaching school with large driving range, pitching and putting greens. *Green Fees:* information not available. *Eating facilities:* bar, snacks and restaurant in clubhouse, hotel on course. Pro shop. Leadbetter Academy. *Visitors:* welcome all year. *Society Meetings:* welcome. Professional: Nicolas Armand (04.67.87.87.91). Secretary: M. Brunet (04.67.87.87.89). *

MONTPELLIER. **Golf Hotel de Fontcaude**, Route de Lodève, Domaine de Fontcaude 34990 Juvignac (04.67. 45.90.10; Fax: 04.67.45.90.20). *Location:* at Juvignac, six km west of Montpellier. Undulating over a rolling, scrub-covered landscape, this course provides a fair and interesting challenge. Two courses: International 18 holes, 6292 metres, Par 72. Executive 9 holes, 1290 metres, Par 29. Driving range, putting green, pitching green. *Green Fees:* information not available. *Eating facilities:* bar and restaurant in clubhouse. *Visitors:* welcome, no restrictions. Pro shop; cart, trolley and club hire. *Society Meetings:* welcome. Professional: Bruno Tancogne. Secretary: Cathy Laniboire (04 67.45.90.10). Golf Club Manager: Jean Claude Lenoire. *

NANS LES PINS. **Golf de la Sainte-Baume,** Domaine de Chateauneuf, 83860 Nans-les-Pins. (04.94.78.60.12; Fax: 04.94.78.63.52). *Location:* 40 kms from Marseilles, A8 exit Saint-Maximin. 45 kms from Aix-en-Provence. Wooded, undulating course. 18 holes, 6167 metres, Par 72. *Green Fees:* information not available. *Eating facilities:* restaurant. *Visitors:* welcome. *Society Meetings:* welcome. Golf school and pro shop, buggy hire available. Accommodation available in our 4 star Domaine de Châteauneuf "Relais et Chateaux" located in the centre of the course. Managers: Alan Batteux and Marie-Pierre Puisset.

NIMES. **Golf de Nîmes-Campagne**, Route de Saint-Gilles, 30900 Nîmes (04.66.70.17.37; Fax: 04.66.70.03.14). *Location:* close to the A54, exit

Nîmes Garons (Airport). A classic flat parkland course of championship calibre built around a superb clubhouse. 18 holes, 6135 metres, Par 72. Driving range, practice bunker, putting green. *Green Fees:* information not available. *Eating facilities:* bar and excellent restaurant. *Visitors:* welcome with reservation. Pro Shop; buggies and carts for hire. *Society Meetings:* welcome during weekdays with reservation, maximum 12/15 persons. Professionals: Marc Dolisie and Didier Behin. Secretary: Sandra Dombret. *

NIMES. **Golf de Nîmes Vacquerolles**, Route de Sauve, 30900 Nimes ((33)04.66.23.33.33; Fax: (33)04.66.23.94.94). *Location:* five minutes from Nimes, autoroute A9, exit Nimes Ouest, then Le Vigan-Sauve. Running up a valley and over steeply wooded hills. 18 holes, 6260 metres, Par 73. Practice area, putting green. *Green Fees:* weekdays 35 euros to 50 euros, weekends 44 euros to 50 euros. *Eating facilities:* bar and restaurant in clubhouse. *Visitors:* welcome. Self-catering apartments on the course. *Society Meetings:* welcome. Open Golf Club. Professionals: Eric Rossary and Emmanuel Thomas.

PERPIGNAN. **Golf de St-Cyprien**, Mas d'Huston, 66750 Saint-Cyprien Plage, Perpignan (33 04.68.37.63.63; Fax: 33 04.68.37.64.64). *Location:* just south of Perpignan, a renowned course between sea and lake with the Pyrenees mountains in the background. Challenging championship course with water hazards. 18 holes, 6480 metres, Par 73. South Course - 9 holes, 2724 metres, Par 35. *Green Fees:* weekdays 38 euros, weekends 57 euros. *Eating facilities:* bar at clubhouse. Bars, restaurants and accommodation at Le Mas d'Huston, on-course hotel. Self-catering apartments a la residence on-course also. Open all year. Pro shop, golf clinic. Professional: Patrick Lacroix. Secretary: Mandy Hogdson.

ST RAPHAEL. **Golf de l'Estérel Latitudes**, Avenue du Golf, 83700 St Raphaèl (04 94.52.68.30; Fax: 04 94.52.68.31). *Location:* inland just a few metres north of St Raphaèl, close to Golf de Valescure. Not long but rated difficult; many trees, narrow fairways and water hazards protecting beautiful greens. 18 holes, 5921 metres, Par 71. 9 holes, 1400 metres, Par 29. Driving range, 9 hole school. *Green Fees:* information not available. *Eating facilities:* bar, clubhouse and restaurant. *Visitors:* welcome. On-site Hotel Latitudes-Valescure (discounts for residents). Pro shop; club, cart and trolley hire. *Society Meetings:* welcome, pre-booking with hotel. Professional: Hugues Gioux (04.94.44.64.65). *

ST RAPHAEL. **Golf et Tennis Club de Valescure**, BP451, Route de Golf, 83700 St Raphaèl (04 94.82.40.46; Fax: 04 94.82.41.42). *Location:* about five km east of St. Raphaèl. An established course (1895), winding attractively through the umbrella pine trees. 18 holes, 5067 metres, Par 68. Driving range, putting green. *Eating facilities:* bar and restaurant in period clubhouse and at golf hotel nearby. Pro shop; trolley and club hire.*

Golf in Portugal
WHERE TO PLAY • WHERE TO STAY
By Michael Gedye

Of all the destinations abroad for winter golf in the sun, nowhere do the British feel more comfortable than in Portugal - and with good reason. There is much to relate to here, a sense of relaxed familiarity when amongst Britain's oldest ally, which is only reinforced by the golf. The game was introduced here by the British just over 100 years ago and for the last forty, it is the British who have not only built and managed many of the resort courses but also provided the bulk of the playing visitors. One of the main attractions, apart from the short flight south to verdant fairways and warm sunshine, is that virtually all the golf courses were created for a foreign holiday market. Few Portuguese play, so that golf and its well-developed infrastructure of hotels and resorts is truly international.

Nearly half of the nation's courses, and most of the vacation resort complexes, are found in the Algarve. This southern coast, sheltered below a mountain range, offers mild winter weather, remedial sunshine and a cultural history heavily influenced by North Africa. Golf only arrived here in response to foreign tourist demand and all the clubs are designed for visitors rather than members. Other excellent golf, somewhat less expensive and busy, can be found to the west and south of the central capital city, Lisbon. Visitors will also find places to play near northern Oporto and on the Atlantic islands of Madeira and the Azores.

The southern coastline of the ALGARVE has two quite distinct aspects. In summer, the long stretches of sandy beach, quaint fishing villages and wide selection of hotels appeals to a family market. Although golf is playable all year round, it only really comes into its own during the winter months. From Cape St Vincent in the west to the Spanish border in the east, there are twenty-eight courses in play and more in the planning stage. The Portuguese Open has been held here on numerous occasions - at Penina, Vilamoura Old Course, Vila Sol, Vale do Lobo and Quinta do Lago, all good championship tests for any golfer. Less demanding but laid out in undulating, pine-lined settings with stunning views are Parque da Floresta, Palmares, Vale da Pinta near Carvoeiro and Pinheiros Altos. Casual players may prefer the attractive nine-hole layouts of Quinta do Gramaco, Vale do Milho and Pine Cliffs. New arrivals include Morgado Golf and Boavista in the west and Benamor, Castro Marim and the 36 holes of Quinta da Ria to the east.

LISBON, a sophisticated city rich in history, has much excellent golf within reach, less crowded and generally less expensive. To the west, around the ageless charms of the Estoril coast and its hinterland, one can contrast the strategic subtleties of Estoril Palacio with more recent tests in Penha Longa, Belas Clube de Campo and, slightly to the north, Golden Eagle and the dramatic coastal linksland of Praia d'El Rey. Across the River Tagus south of the capital, compare the championship delights of Aroeira I & II and Quinta do Peru, cut through rolling pinewoods, with the severe windswept sandbar demands of Troia. After golf, take the time to discover the wealth of freshly caught seafood in the coastal towns of Setubal and Sesimbra.

A fair choice of courses exist in the NORTH, which is where Portuguese golf began at Oporto in 1890. There is much to enjoy here, despite less predictable weather, from ancient castles and manor houses to museums, traditional crafts and rich local cuisine, accompanied by fine wines from the Douro, vinho verde and, naturally, port. The best course is the mountainous but highly playable Ponte de Lima. Out in the Atlantic, sub-tropical MADEIRA has two courses at steep volcanic altitude, offering demanding carries and sensational views.The AZORES islands, sited in mid-ocean, have three very playable courses in floral, well established locations.

ALGARVE

ALBUFEIRA. **Golf de Salgados**, Apartado 2266, Vale Rebelho, 8200-917 Albufeira (00351 289 583030; Fax: 00351 289 591112). Location: from Faro on EN125, turn left for Vale de Parra. Next to a nature reserve. Level course carved from seamarsh with plenty of water hazards. 18 holes, 6080 metres. Par 72. Driving range, putting green. Green Fees: information not available. Eating facilities: bar and restaurant in clubhouse. Visitors: welcome. Pro shop; cart, trolley and club hire. Society Meetings: all welcome. Professional: John Wood. Director: Pedro Silvestre. *

ALBUFEIRA. **Sheraton Algarve Pine Cliffs Golf and Country Club**, PO Box 644, Praia da Falesia, 8200 Albufeira (289 500100; Fax: 289 501950). Location: seven km from Vilamoura, situated outside Olhos d'Agua. Seaside links. 9 holes, 2557 yards, 2324 metres, Par (equivalent) 67. 9 holes Par 3 course. Green Fees: information not available. Discounts for hotel guests. Eating facilities: bar, restaurant. Visitors: welcome, advance booking required. Golf academy, changing facilities. Society Meetings: all groups welcome. Professional/Golf Director: Manuel Batista. *

ALMANSIL. **San Lorenzo Golf Club**, Quinta do Lago, 8135 Almansil (00 351 89 396522; Fax: 00 351 89 396908). Location: 20km from Faro Airport towards west. Parkland with seaside view surrounded by wildlife and umbrella pine trees designed by Joseph Lee. 18 holes, 6238 metres. Par 72. Practice range, putting green and driving range. Green Fees: information not available. Eating facilities: bar and restaurant. Visitors: welcome, please reserve a day before wishing to play, Handicap Certificate required - Men 28, Ladies 36. Caddies and cart rental available. Soft spikes required. Pro shop. Society Meetings: welcome if staying in Dona Filipa Hotel. Professional: A. Rodrigues. Golf Manager: Antonio Santos (00 351 89 396534). *
website: www.lemeridien-donafilipa.com

ALMANSIL. **Sociedade do Golfe da Quinta do Lago**, Quinta do Lago, 8135 Almansil (089 390700; Fax: 089 394013). Location: 15 minutes west of Faro Airport, nearest town Almansil. Gently undulating sandy land covered with umbrella pines, wild flowers and lakes. 2 courses - Quinta do Lago and Ria Formosa. Both 18 holes, 7137 and 6850 yards, 6488 and 6205 metres. S.S.S. 72. Driving range. Green Fees: information not available. Eating facilities: pizzeria, clubhouse restaurant and bar, Casa do Lago. Visitors: welcome subject to availability, starting times 48 hours in advance. Pro Shop and golf academy, buggies, trolleys and caddies. Society Meetings: welcome subject to availability. Professional: Domingos Silva (089 390700 ext 46; Fax: 089 394013). Golf Manager: Nuno Gama (089 390700 Fax: 089 394013). *

ALMANSIL. **Vale do Lobo Golf Club**, Vale do Lobo, 8135-864 Vale do Lobo, Almansil (00 351 289 353464 Fax: 00 351 289 353003). Location: on the cliff edge, overlooking the sea, 15 minutes' drive west from Faro. 2 courses. "Ocean Course", 18 holes, 5334 metres. Par 71. "Royal Course", 18 holes, 6050 metres. Par 72. Coastline scenery with fairways lined with pine, eucalyptus and almond trees. Green Fees: information not available. Eating facilities: clubhouse with restaurant, bar and cafe. Visitors: always welcome. Society Meetings: welcome. Teaching Professional: Steve Walker. Tour Professionals: Antonio Sabrinho and Jormo Sandelin. Golf Director: Mr John Pinckney.
e-mail: golf@vdl.pt
website: www.valedolobo.com

ALVOR. **Alto Golf & Country Club**, Quinto do Alto do Poco, Apartado 1, 8501 906 Alvor - Portimao (282 460870; Fax: 282 460879). Location: in Alvor, overlooking the Atlantic Ocean and the Bay of Lagos. A parkland course designed by Sir Henry Cotton with gently undulating fairways and challenging sloping greens. Stunning views of the Monchique Mountains in the background. 18 holes, 6125 metres, S.S.S. 73. Driving range, putting green. Green Fees: high season 70 euros per round, low season 56 euros per round. Eating facilities: bar and restaurant in clubhouse. Visitors: welcome. Society Meetings: groups also welcome, Handicap Certificate required. Pro shop; cart, trolley and club hire. Professional: Robert Bridge. Resort Director: David Cudmore.
e-mail: golf@altoclub.com

BUDENS/SALEMA. **Parque da Floresta Golf and Leisure Resort**, Vale do Poco, 8650-060 Budens (+351 282 690054; Fax: +351 282 695157). *Location:* EN125, 16km west of Lagos. Located just past Budens on right. Undulating course with spectacular views; member of the Portuguese Golf Federation. 18 holes, 5670 metres. S.S.S. 72. Short game practice area, driving range, golf academy, three putting greens. *Green Fees:* information not available. *Eating facilities:* clubhouse with restaurant and bar overlooking 18th hole. *Visitors:* very welcome but advisable to book. Enquire about Special Rates. Pro shop; swimming pools, tennis court, health and beauty spa. Self-catering villas and townhouses available. *Society Meetings:* welcome, catered for by arrangement with Golf Director. PGA Professionals: Gary Silcock, Scott Catlin. Golf Director: Billy Sim. * e-mail: b.sim@vigiasa.com OR golf@vigiasa.com website: www.vigiasa.com

LAGOA. **Gramacho Course,** Pestana Golf and Resort, Carvoeiro, Apartado 1011, Praia do Carvoeiro, 8400-908 Lagoa (282 340900; Fax: 282 340901). *Location:* 2km south of Lagoa on the Estrada Nacional E125, follow road signs. Two superbly prepared golf courses undulating through olive groves. Gramacho - 18 hole course 6718 yards, 6107 metres. Par 72. David Leadbetter Golf Academy, practice putting and chipping greens, driving range. *Green Fees:* information not available. *Eating facilities:* restaurant, bar plus magnificent terrace. *Visitors:* welcome, check availability, year round. Carvoeiro Golf Clube luxury villa and apartments; international golf school, video swing analysis centre. Buggies and carts available. Pro Shop. Accommodation available locally (282 340900). *Society Meetings:* welcome by arrangement. Professional: Carlos Ribeiro (282 340440; Fax: 282 340901). Secretary: Rui Gago. Director of Golf: José Matias.

LAGOA. **Pinta Course,** Pestana Golf and Resort, Carvoeiro, Apartado 1011, Praia Do Carvoeiro, 8400-908 Lagoa (282 340900; Fax: 282 340901). *Location:* 2kms south of Lagoa on the Estrada Nacional E125, follow signs. Parkland in ancient olive groves with trees 600/700 years old. 18 holes, 6727 yards, 6152 metres. S.S.S. 71. David Leadbetter Golf Academy, buggies, trolleys, two practice putting and two chipping greens, driving range. *Green Fees:* information not available. *Eating facilities:* snack bar. *Visitors:* welcome, check availability, year round. Handicap Certificate required: men 27, ladies 35. Accommodation available locally (282 340900). Golf School, Pro shop, rental of pull trolleys, electric trolleys, clubs and buggies. *Society Meetings:* welcome anytime by arrangement. Professional: Carlos Ribeiro (282 340440; Fax: 282 340449). Secretary: Rui Gago. Director of Golf: José Matias.

LAGOS. **Palmares Golf Club,** Apartado 74, Meia Praia, Lagos (282 762953/61; Fax: 282 762534). *Location:* five km from centre of Lagos on main Meia Praia beach road. Five links type holes - very scenic and serene. Magnificent views over Lagos Bay. 18 holes, 5961 metres. S.S.S. 72, Par 71. Driving range, putting green, pitch and putt area. *Green Fees:* information not available. *Eating facilities:* Palmares Restaurant serving international and Portuguese cuisine with fresh fish. Panoramic bar and veranda with spectacular views over the Bay of Lagos. *Visitors:* open to all players with Handicap Certificate all year round. Two golf shops, trolleys, buggies and golf lessons available. *Society Meetings:* always welcome at all times. Professionals: Luis Espadinha and José Dias. Secretary: Miguel de Sousa (+351 282 790500).* e-mail: golf@palmaresgolf.com website: www.palmaresgolf.com

PORTIMAO/PENINA. **Penina Golf Club**, Le Meridien Penina Golf Resort Hotel, PO Box 146, Penina, 8501-952 Portimao (282 420200; Fax: 282 420300). *Location:* five km from Portimao, 12km from Lagos. Long, flat course with lakes, trees and bunkers. 18 holes (plus two 9 hole courses) 6935 yards, 6273 metres. S.S.S. 73. Also Resort Course - 9 holes, 3268 yards, 2987 metres. S.S.S. 35 and Academy Course - 9 holes, 2035 yards, 1851 metres. S.S.S. 31. Golf academy, putting greens. *Green Fees:* please check with hotel. *Eating facilities:* clubhouse and Hotel restaurants. *Visitors:* welcome, Handicap Certificate (28 for men and 36 for ladies) and soft spike shoes required to play all courses. *Society Meetings:* welcome. Professional: José Lourenco, Robin Liddle and José Marcelino. Director: Leonel Rio.*

QUINTA DO LAGO. **Pinheiros Altos Golf Club**, Quinta do Lago, 8135 Almansil, Algarve (289 359910; Fax: 289 394392). *Location:* south of Almansil just east of the Quinta do Lago and San Lorenzo courses, bear left on first roundabout at Quinta do Lago. Pine trees and water hazards with fast bent grass greens and the island green 17th hole. 18 holes, 6236 metres. S.S.S. 72. Driving range areas, three putting greens, two chipping/ bunker areas. *Green Fees:* information not available. *Eating facilities:* restaurant, snack bar; drinks buggy. *Visitors:* welcome, Handicap Certificate required: Men 28, Ladies 36. Buggy compulsory. Pro shop; club hire. 'A' Star equipped Golf Academy. *Society Meetings:* on request. Professionals: Eddie Charnock, Dennis Struchtrup. Director of Golf: Brian Evans. *

VILAMOURA. **Laguna Golf Course**, Lusotur Golfes SA, 8125 - 507 Vilamoura, Algarve (00 351 289 310 180; Fax: 00 351 289 310 183). *Location:* 20 kms from Faro Airport, 25 kms from Faro. Relatively flat, open course with challenging placement of bunkers and water hazards, designed by Joseph Lee. 18 holes. 6133 metres. Par 72. Practice facilities, putting green, driving range. *Green Fees:* information not available. *Eating facilities:* restaurant and bar. *Visitors:* open to players with Handicap Certificate (max. Men 28, Ladies 36). *Society Meetings:* welcome at all times. Pro shop, equipment hire. Professionals: Abilio Coelho and Joaquim Catarino (089 380724). Bookings: (00 351 289 310 333; Fax: 00 351 289 310 349). Commercial Manager: Alice Carlota. Golf Manager: Eduardo de Sousa.*
e-mail: reservas_golfe@lusotur.pt
website: www.vilamoura.net

VILAMOURA. **Millennium Golf Course, Clube de Golfe Vilamoura**, Lusotur Golfes SA, 8125 - 507 Vilamoura, Algarve (00 351 289 310 188; Fax: 00 351 289 310 183). *Location:* 20km from Faro Airport, 25km from Faro. Narrow fairways through pine woods and natural countryside. 18 holes, 6143 metres. Par 72. Practice and putting greens, driving range. *Green Fees:* information not available. *Eating facilities:* restaurant and bar. *Visitors:* course open to all players with Handicap Certificate (max. Men 24, Ladies 28). Soft spikes only. Pro shop, hire of trolleys. Professional: Abilio Coelho and Joaquim Catarino Bookings: (00 351 289 310 333; Fax: 00 351 289 310 349). Commercial Manager: Alice Carlota. Golf Manager: Eduardo de Sousa.*
e-mail: reservas_golfe@lusotur.pt
website: www.vilamoura.net

VILAMOURA. **The Old Course, Clube de Golfe Vilamoura**, Lusotur Golfes SA, 8125 - 507 Vilamoura, Algarve (00 351 289 310 341; Fax: 00 351 289 310 321). *Location:* 20km from Faro Airport, 25km from Faro. Narrow fairways through pine woods, sea views. 18 holes, 6254 metres. Par 73. Practice and putting greens; driving range. *Green Fees:* information not available. *Eating facilities:* restaurant and bar. *Visitors:* course open to all players with Handicap Certificate (max. Men 24, Ladies 28). Soft spikes only. Pro shop, equipment hire. Professional: Joaquim Sequeira. Bookings: (00 351 289 310 333; Fax: 00 351 289 310 349). Commercial Manager: Alice Carlota. Golf Manager: Eduardo de Sousa.*
e-mail: reservas_golfe@lusotur.pt
website: www.vilamoura.net

VILAMOURA. **Pinhal Golf Course**, Lusotur Golfes SA, 8125 - 507 Vilamoura, Algarve (00 351 289 310 390; Fax: 00 351 289 310 393). *Location:* 20 kms from Faro Airport. Pine wood setting and magnificent sea views, designed by Frank Pennink and Robert Trent Jones. 18 holes, 6151 metres. Par 72. Driving range and putting green. *Green Fees:* information not available. *Eating facilities:* bar and restaurant. *Visitors:* open to players with Handicap Certificate (max. Men 28, Ladies 36), all year round. *Society Meetings:* welcome at any time. Pro shop, equipment hire. Professionals: Manuel Pardal and Francisco Pontes. Bookings: (00 351 289 310 333; Fax: 00 351 289 310 349). Commercial Manager: Alice Carlota. Golf Manager: Eduardo de Sousa.*
e-mail: reservas_golfe@lusotur.pt
website: www.vilamoura.net

VILAMOURA. **Vila Sol Beach, Golf & Country Club**, Morgadinhos, Alto do Semino, 8125 Vilamoura (289 300505/522; Fax: 289 316499). *Location*: just east of Vilamoura off the road leading down to Quarteira. An excellent natural course undulating through umbrella pines with good water hazards and superb greens. 27 holes, 6320 metres - men 5935 metres, ladies 5372 metres. Par 72, S.S.S 72. Driving range, putting green, golf academy, pro shop, trolley, club hire. *Green Fees*: information not available. *Eating facilities*: bar and restaurant in clubhouse. Pro shop; cart, trolley, buggy and club hire. *Visitors*: welcome. Handicap Certificate required. Soft spikes only. (Men 27, Ladies 35). Professional: Roel Gritter. Golf Secretary: Alexandra Piedade. *
e-mail: golfsecretary@vilasol.pt
e-mail: golfreservation@vilasol.pt

LISBON

AROEIRA. **Aroeira Golf**, Herdade da Aroeira, 2815-207 Chameca de Caparica, Aroeira, Costa Lisboa (00351 21 2979110; Fax: 00351 21 2971238). *Location:* south from Lisbon across the bridge, turn right to Costa Caparica and follow signs. This well-established course remains one of Portugal's best kept secrets. Venue of Portugal Open-European Tour 1996, 1997; Portuguese Ladies' Open 2002 and 2003. A superb test through a floral pine forest by Frank Pennink; one for purists to savour. 18 holes, 6040 metres, Par 72. Practice ground with shelters for bad/hot weather. Aroeira 2 opened in 2000, designed by Donald Steel. *Green Fees:* (both courses) weekdays 46 euros, weekends 65 euros. *Eating facilities:* restaurant, snack bar, cocktail bar and lounge. *Visitors:* welcome, no restrictions; subject only to having a valid Handicap and availability of tees. New golf school specialising in intensive courses, indoor and outdoor facilities. Driving range. Buggies, electric trolleys and golf bags available for hire. Professionals: Joaquim Moura, Alexandre Daninos. Operations Director: Carlos Fonseca. Commercial Director: Francisco Pinto Leite. President: Pedro Silveira.
e-mail: golf.aroeira@clix.pt
website: www.aroeira.com

AZEITAO. **Quinta do Peru Golf Course**, Alameda da Serra 2, 2975-666 Quinta do Conde (+351 21 213 43 20: Fax: +351 21 213 43 21). *Location*: Cross the bridge "25 de Abril" and follow A2 motorway to Junction 3 (24km from Lisbon). Exit A2 at Junction 3 – pass through toll (portagem) then immediately exit right up slope, signs to "COINA"– then follow signs to Quinta do Peru – Golf. Fine new, American- shaped course laid out through rolling pine woods with lakes and fine views. 18 holes, 6036 metres. S.S.S. 72. Driving range, two putting greens, chipping and bunker practice area. *Green Fees*: weekends 88 euros, weekdays 58 euros. *Eating facilities*: restaurant and bar in clubhouse. *Visitors*: welcome. Pro shop, carts, trolleys, club hire. Professional: António Dantas. Manager: Pedro de Mello Breyner.
e-mail: play@golfquintadoperu.com
website: www.golfquintadoperu.com

AZEITAO. **Sociedade Imobiliaria e Turistica Quinta do Peru**, Alameda da Serra 2, 2975-527 Quinta do Conde (01 2134320: Fax: 2134321). *Location*: turn off A2 south of Lisbon for Azeitao; course just past Quinta do Conde on right. Fine new, American- shaped course laid out through rolling pine woods with lakes and fine views. 18 holes, 6074 metres. S.S.S. 72. Driving range, two putting greens, chipping and bunker practice area. *Green Fees*: information not provided. *Eating facilities*: restaurant and bar in clubhouse. *Visitors*: welcome. Pro shop, carts, trolleys, club hire. Professional: Antonio Dantas. Director: Joao Salazar. *

BELAS. **Belas Clube de Campo**, Estrada Nacional 117, 2745 Belas (21 962 6640; Fax: 21 962 6644). *Location:* going west from Lisbon, turn right off IC19 and follow N117 through Belas to Club on right. Very new, American designed course built on a grand scale amongst a dramatic rolling landscape. 18 holes, 6380 metres. S.S.S. 72. Pro shop, driving range, short game area, putting green. *Green Fees*: on request. *Eating facilities*: restaurant and bar in clubhouse. *Visitors*: welcome. Carts, trolleys, club hire. Professional: Keith Barret. Director: Miguel Franco de Sousa.*
e-mail: golfe@planbelas.pt
website: www.golfbelas.com

ESTORIL. **Golf Do Estoril**, Avenida Da Republica, 2765-273 Estoril (351 214 680176; Fax: 351 214 682796). *Location:* in Estoril. An undulating links course with views of the Atlantic and Sintra Mountains. 18 holes, 5238 metres. S.S.S. 69. *Green Fees:* information not available. Reductions for Estoril Palacio Hotel guests. Driving range. *Eating facilities:* Clubhouse with bar and restaurant. Professionals: Joaquim Rodrigues, Henrique Pallino, Carlos Aleixo. Director: Francisco Pinherio. *

ESTORIL. **International Golf Academy**, Estoril da Lagoa Azup, Linho, Sintra 2710 (351-1-9232461; Telex: 12624). *Location:* take the main Cascais-Sintra road and turn left at the village of Linho towards Lagoa Azul. 9 holes (18 tees), 1805 metres. S.S.S. 62. Purpose-built golf academy - practice facility, chipping greens, putting green. *Green Fees:* information not available. *Eating facilities:* restaurant

and bar. *Visitors:* no restrictions. *Society Meetings:* welcome. 10% discount for groups of eight or more players. Professionals: Ian Powell. Golf Manager: Nuno Teixeira Bastos.

ESTORIL. **Penha Longa Golf Club**, Penha Longa, Golf Resort, Estrada da Lagoa Azul, Linho, 2714-511 Sintra (21.924.9011; Fax: 21.924.9024). *Location:* half an hour west of Lisbon, just north of Estoril on the main road to Sintra. Designed by Robert Trent Jones Jnr, laid out over craggy hills, wooded slopes and valleys surrounding an ancient royal palace; the 18 holes hosted the Portuguese Open in 1994 and again in 1995. 18 holes, 6910 yards, 6290 metres. S.S.S. 73. 9 holes, 2845 yards, 2588metres, S.S.S. 35. Driving range, large putting green, chipping green with two bunkers. *Green Fees:* Atlantic 18 holes Penha Longa Hotel guests - weekdays 44.50 euros, weekends/holidays 55 euros; Visitors - weekdays 89 euros, weekends/holidays 110 euros. *Eating facilities:* three bars and four restaurants. *Visitors:* welcome, Handicap Certificate required. Five star Hotel and Country Club; eight tennis courts, squash and bicycles. Golf Academy, Pro shop, cart, trolley, club and shoe hire. Sauna, jacuzzi. No jeans. Professional: Robert Judd/Antonio Dantas. Director: Patrick Tolos.

ESTORIL. **Quinta da Marinha Conference and Golf Resort**, Quinta da Marinha, Casa 36 - 2750 Cascais (351 1 4860180; Fax: 351 1 4869032). *Location:* 3km from Cascais centre, 35km from Lisbon, near Guincho beach. Championship golf course designed by Robert Trent Jones. Open sandy course with pine trees, lakes and spectacular views over the mountains and ocean. 18 holes, 6684 yards. S.S.S. 71. Driving range, putting greens. *Green Fees:* information not available. *Eating facilities:* bar, restaurant and club house. *Visitors:* welcome. Men's Handicap 28, Ladies' Handicap 36. Club hire, trolley rental; Pro shop. Accommodation available in 70 villas or our new 200 bedroom Marinha Golf Hotel facing the course, including conference facilities, swimming pools, tennis courts and health centre. *Society Meetings:* not applicable. Professional: Derek Chad. Golf Director: Pedro Castelo Branco. *

LISBON. **Lisbon Sports Club**, Casal da Carregueira, Belas - 2745 BELAS (00 4310077). *Location:* 25 km from Lisbon. Parkland. 18 holes, 5233 metres. S.S.S. 69. *Green Fees:* information not available. *Eating facilities:* clubhouse with restaurant, bar and swimming pool, sauna. *Visitors:* welcome weekdays, Handicap Certificate required. Professional: Jose Baltazar (00 4321474). Director: Carlos Galvao (00 432 1474). *

OBIDOS. **Praia D'el Rey Golf and Country Club**, Vale de Janelas, Apartado 2, 2510 Obidos (262 905005; Fax: 262 905009). *Location:* from A8 to Obidos, take turnoff 14 to Peniche and follow EN114, turn right at course sign in Sierra D'el Rey. True links course; one of the best in Europe. 18 holes, 6467 metres. S.S.S. 72. Driving range, pitching and putting greens. *Green Fees:* information not available. *Eating facilities:* snack bar, bar, restaurant. *Visitors:* always welcome. Caddies, trolleys, equipment hire. *
e-mail: golf@praia-del-rey.com

PRAIA DE MIRAMAR. **Clube de Golf de Miramar**, Av. Sacadura Cabral, Miramar, 4405-013 Arcozelo (22 7622067; Fax: 22 7627859). *Location*: approximately 13km south of Oporto by A1, N109 direction Espinho. Flat coastal course amongst dunes alongside the beach. 9 holes, 4884 metres. S.S.S. 67. Driving range. *Green Fees*: information not available. 50% discount on green fees given by some hotels. *Eating facilities*: clubhouse with restaurant and bar. *Visitors*: welcome, Handicap Certificate required. Hotels, restaurants and casino nearby. Pro shop. Professional: Sergio Ribeiro. Secretaries: Sofia Bessa and Paula Sousa.

RIO MAIOR. **Golden Eagle Golf and Country Club**, Quinta do Brincal, Arrouquelas, 2040 Rio Maior (043 908148; Fax: 043 908149). *Location:* A1 from Lisbon to Aveiras exit, follow N366, turn right to IC2, course on right at 63km. Undulating heathland with strategic sand and water. 18 holes, 6200 metres. S.S.S. 72. Driving range, putting green. *Green Fees:* information not available. *Eating facilities:* bar, restaurant. *Visitors:* always welcome. Trolley hire available. *

TROIA. **Troia Golf Club**, Troia, Carvalhal GDL (265 494112; Fax: 265 494315). *Location:* on the Troia Peninsula, 42 km south of Lisbon. From Lisbon, A2/A12 to Setubal, then follow signs for Troia to the ferry boat; in Troia follow EN243-1 to Comporta; golf course signposted. Spectacular links, 30th on list of Europe's 100 best golf courses and a superb challenge to all golfers. Designed by Robert Trent Jones Snr; host to Portuguese Open-European Tour in 1983. 18 holes, 6320 metres Par 72. Driving range, two putting greens, practice area. *Green Fees:* information not available. *Eating facilities:* clubhouse with bar/restaurant. *Visitors:* welcome, Handicap Certificate (27 men, 35 ladies). Hotel accommodation available (265 499030). Special rates for Troia Hotels guests. Pro shop, trolley and buggy rental. Director of Golf : Henrique de Sousa. *

VIMEIRO. **Vimeiro Golf Club**, Praia de Porto Novo, Termas do Vimeiro, 2560 Torres Vedras (061 984157; Fax: 061 984621). *Location:* situated in a wonderful cliff over the Atlantic coast, next to the beach. A level course divided by a river and sheltered by rocky cliffs. 9 holes with 18 tees, 5228 yards. S.S.S. 67. *Green Fees:* information not available. *Eating facilities:* restaurant in hotel Golf Mar, three bars. Caddies and hand trolleys available. Guests at the Hotel play for free.*

MADEIRA

FUNCHAL. **Palheiro Golf Club**, Sitio do Balancal, Sao Goncalo, 9050-296 Funchal (00 351 291 792116; Fax: 00 351 291 792456). *Location:* take Camacha turn-off from airport road, straight on under bridge, past car inspection centre (I.P.O.). Follow golf signs. A Cabell Robinson design, built on a hill top overlooking Funchal. Parkland course, amazing views with superb trees and flora. 18 holes, 6086 metres. Par 72. Driving range, putting green. *Green Fees:* information not available. *Eating facilities:* bar and restaurant – excellent international cuisine. Pro shop; cart, trolley and club hire. Casa Velha, the five-star hotel, is situated on the course. Professional: Ashley Northridge PGA.

MADEIRA. **Campo de Golfe da Madeira**, Santo Antonio da Serra, 9100 Santa Cruz (091 552345; Fax: 091 552367). *Location:* main highway to Airport (Santa Cruz) Machilo. Wooded, mountainous with view over Atlantic Ocean. 27 holes, 6082 metres. Driving range, putting and chipping green. *Green Fees:* information not available. *Eating facilities:* restaurant, snack bar, lounge bar. *Visitors:* welcome to play in tournaments except PGA Madeira Island Open (January). Pro shop; cart, trolley and club hire. Professional: Joao Sousa. Secretary: Anthony Barton (acting). *

OPORTO

AMARANTE. **Amarante Golf Clube, Quinta da Deveza**, Fregim, 4600 - 593 Amarante. (+351 255 44 60 60; Fax: +351 255 44 62 02). *Location*: take A4 from Oporto heading to Vila Real, come off at Amarante Oeste, then follow signs for Fregim, the golf course is signposted from here. A true mountain course with spectacular views over surrounding peaks and valleys. 18 holes, 5035 metres. Par 68. Driving range, putting green, bunker and chipping practice area, Pro-shop, swimming pools, tennis courts. *Green Fees*: weekdays 35 euros per round; weekends and holidays 45 euros per round. *Eating facilities*: restaurant and bar in clubhouse. *Visitors*: welcome. Caddies, carts, trolleys, club hire. Hotels – Casa Da Calgaza (+351 255 410830; Fax: +351 255 426670); Hotel Navarras (+351 255 431 036; Fax: +351 255 432 991) (Professional: Paulo Teixeira. Secretary: João Silva. e-mail: sgagolfeamarante@oninet.pt

NOTE. All the information regarding Golf Clubs in this guide is given in good faith in the belief that it is correct. However, the publishers cannot guarantee the facts given in these pages, neither are they responsible for changes in ownership or facilities, such as green fees, that may take place after the date of going to press. Readers should always satisfy themselves that the facilities they require are available and that the terms, if quoted, still apply.

ESPINHO. **Oporto Golf Club**, Paramos, 4500 Espinho (02 722008; Fax: 02 726895). *Location:* 18 miles south of Oporto, one mile south of Espinho. Seaside links, few trees, founded in 1890. 18 holes, 5556 metres. Course rating 70.2; Slope rating 127; Par 71. Practice ground. *Green Fees:* 60 euros. Half price for guests of Hotels mentioned below. *Eating facilities:* bar with snacks (restaurant - members only). *Visitors:* welcome Tuesdays to Fridays (closed Mondays); weekends and Bank Holidays till 10.30am. Handicap Certificate required. Beach, hotels - Hotel Solverde, Hotel Praia - Golf, casino nearby. Professional: Eduardo Maganinho (02 7313649).

ESPOSENDE. **Golfe de Quinta da Barca**, Gemezes, Barca do Lago, 4740 476 Esposende (+351 253 966723; Fax: +351 253 969068). *Location:* 50km north of Oporto on JC 1, turn right to Esposende and before Esposende turn to Quinta da Barca. A 9 hole course but very demanding. The river, lakes, bunkers and undulating greens make it a precision test. 9 holes, 1927 metres. C.R. 62,2; S.R. 106. Driving range, putting and chipping greens, apart hotel, marina, tennis. *Green Fees*: information not available. *Eating facilities*: restaurant and bar in clubhouse. *Visitors*: welcome. Pro shop, caddies, cart, trolley, club hire. Professional: Manuel Carneiro. Director: Luis Catarino.
e-mail: lcatarino@quintabarca.com
website: www.quintabarca.com

ESTELA. **Estela Golf Club**, Rio Alto-Estela, 4490 Povoa de Varzim (52 612700/601567; Fax: 52 612701). *Location:* 30 km north of Oporto, 24 km from the international airport. Seaside links. 18 holes, 6095 metres. S.S.S. 73. *Green Fees:* information not available. *Eating facilities:* full bar and catering facilities. *Visitors:* welcome anytime when no competitions taking place. Sopete Hotel guests entitled to special privileges. *Society Meetings:* by arrangement. Professionals: Carlos Alberto, Carlos Henrique. Secretary/Manager: Salete Correia. *

PONTE DE LIMA. **Golfe de Ponte de Lima**, Quinta de Pias, Fornelos, 4990 Ponte de Lima (058 743414/5; Fax: 058 743424). *Location:* one kilometre north of Ponte de Lima on EN201. Beautiful and scenic; hilly front nine. 18 holes, 6005 metres. S.S.S. 70. Driving range, Putting green, chipping and bunker practice area. *Green Fees:* information not available. *Eating facilities*: restaurant and bar in clubhouse "Beni-Golf". *Visitors*: welcome. Pro shop, caddies, cart, trolley, club hire. Professionals: Manuel Carneiro, Paulo Teixeira. Director: Manuel Farncisco de Miguel.*

VIDAGO. **Vidago Golf Club**, Vidago 5425 (97106; Telex: 238888). *Location:* mountain valley course, in spa/resort area well inland, only 25 km from Spanish border. Short 9-hole course, 1000ft high, 2678 yards. S.S.S. 63 (18 holes). *Eating facilities:* Vidago Palace Hotel.*

THE AZORES

SAO MIGUEL. **Batalha Golf Course**, Rua do Bom Jesus, Aflitos, 9545-234 Fenais da Luz, Sao Miguel-Azores (296 498559; Fax: 296 498284). *Location:* go north from Ponta Delgada in direction Faja de Cima, turn right for Aflitos before reaching Fenais da Luz. Championship course with sweeping views over large flowing greens with wide and generous fairways. Beautiful surroundings and fabulous scenery. 18 holes, 6435 metres. S.S.S. 72. Driving range, two large putting greens, chipping area. *Green Fees:* information not available. *Eating facilities:* modern clubhouse with classic island architecture; bars and restaurant. *Visitors:* welcome. Complete range of support services. Caddies, carts, trolleys, club hire. Professional: Rui Indio. Golf Director: Luis Indio (296 498559).

SAO MIGUEL. **Furnas Golf Course**, Achada das Furnas, 9675-030 Furnas, Sao Miguel-Azores. (296 584341; Fax: 296 498284). *Location:* 40 minutes from Ponta Delgada. Designed originally by McKenzie Ross and extended by Bob Cameron. Unique style and characteristics, with fairways flanked by trees and fiendishly undulating greens. 18 holes, 6232 metres. Par 72.. *Green Fees:* information not available. *Eating facilities:* modern clubhouse; bar, restaurant. *Visitors:* always welcome. Carts, trolleys, club hire. Professional: Rui Indio. Golf Director: Luis Indio (296 584341).

TERCEIRA. **Terceira Golf Club**, Caixa Postal 15, 9760 Praia da Vitoria, Terceira (00351 295 902444/902299; Fax: 00351 295 902445). *Location:* a few kilometres from Angra do Heroismo and Praia da Vitoria on the island of Terceira in the Azores. Landscaped course through trees and low hills, with small lakes. 18 holes, 6227 metres. S.S.S. 70. Practice facilities. *Green Fees:* on request. *Eating facilities:* available. *Visitors:* always welcome. Hotel accommodation nearby. *Society Meetings:* always welcome. Professional: Eduardo Correia. General Director: Antonio P. Camara.*

> ## THE APPEARANCE OF AN ASTERISK * AT THE END OF A CLUB OR COURSE ENTRY INDICATES THAT UP-TO-DATE INFORMATION HAS NOT BEEN SUPPLIED

Golf in Spain

WHERE TO PLAY • WHERE TO STAY

By Michael Gedye

The first winter sunshine country in Europe to realise the commercial potential of golf, Spain encouraged the development of courses in coastal resort areas where, out of the high summer holiday season, golf could prove a magnet to lure northerners south in the winter months. In turn, this niche holiday market kept hotels and other commercial enterprises open and created a whole new specialised package tour programme on the back of cheap charter flights. Golfers came, liked what they saw, and developers quickly created whole resort communities around the new golf courses catering to owners of second or retirement homes.

Spain continues to be the leader in holiday golf in Europe, primarily through the winter season. With world-class courses kept in prime condition and growing demand, this colourful country can link golf to a vibrant culture, influential history, rich cuisine and an attractive climate to offer proven value.

Spanish holiday golf, for most people, means the COSTA DEL SOL. This sunshine coast, with more than forty courses the largest concentration in Europe, can be compared to the American equivalents of Palm Springs and Myrtle Beach. For simplicity, this is best sub-divided into three regions. The most westerly include the PGA Tour venues of Ballesteros-designed Novo Sancti Petri and Montecastillo. Moving east past Gibraltar, one reaches the elegant courses of San Roque and Sotogrande, the latter estate combining the first Trent Jones course in Spain (1964) and his more recent masterpiece of Valderrama, site of the 1997 Ryder Cup.

The central coast, running from Estepona past swinging Marbella to just beyond Malaga, presents more opportunities to play than any visitor could hope to achieve. From Guadalmina (1959), a comprehensive infrastructure of resort locations with top class golf courses, luxury hotels and other amenities was created. Built to international standards, they have attracted a burgeoning international clientele and generated considerable investment in related property. Such is the quality of the courses in this region that they have been the venues for two World Cups, the Ryder Cup, the annual Volvo Masters and numerous Spanish Opens. Excellent courses like Las Brisas, La Quinta and Los Arqueros contrast with the truly spectacular locations of La Cala or Monte Mayor. For something less demanding, visit Santa Maria or Rio Real. Numerous teaching academies cater to emerging as well as experienced golfers, plus driving ranges and even a course floodlit at night. East beyond Malaga, the tranquil seaside setting of Almerimar provides a pleasant contrast.

Progress northwards brings you to Europe's foremost self-contained multi-sports resort, the La Manga Club. Here one can choose between three palm-fringed courses surrounded by low hills as well as a wide spectrum of other sports, accommodation and leisure facilities all on site.

Next up is VALENCIA, home to what is arguably one of the finest public courses in the world, the genuine links challenge of El Saler by Javier Arana. Alternatively, visitors can enjoy the challenges of Golf Escorpion, Villamartin and the demanding El Bosque.

CATALONIA covers the regions of Girona and the popular Costa Brava in the north east. The pine-lined fairways of Pals present an interesting challenge and there are other fine courses here, both old and new.

The island of MAJORCA in the Balearics, has developed a reputation as a holiday centre, not least for its vibrant nightlife. It can also offer a good selection of golf courses, mostly in scenic peaceful locations. The luxury Son Vida hotel overlooks its own course and the port of Palma. Other testing opportunities include the European PGA Tour venue of Santa Ponsa, Poniente and Pollensa. All the elements for satisfying holiday golf are here - fine courses, a mild Mediterranean climate, gentle sea breezes and plenty of out-of-season sunshine.

ANDALUCIA – CENTRAL

BENAHAVIS. **La Quinta Golf and Country Club**, Urb La Quinta, s/n 29660 Nueva, Andalucia (Marbella), Malaga (95.276.23.90; Fax: 95.276.23.99). *Location:* on main road to Ronda, 3.5km from N340 coast road. Inland hilly course. 18 holes, 5517 metres, Par 72, S.S.S. 71; also 9 hole course, 2848 metres. Par 36, S.S.S. 71. *Green Fees:* information not available. *Eating facilities:* clubhouse, restaurant. *Visitors:* welcome, please book in advance. Golf Academy, Pro-shop, table tennis, squash, sauna, swimming pool, fitness centre, therapic and static centre. *Society Meetings:* welcome. Professional: Manuel Pinero. Director: D. Marcos Lería Couderc.

BENAHAVIS. **Monte Mayor Golf Club**, Los Naranjos Country Club, Nueva Andalucia, 29660 Marbella, Malaga (345 211 30 88; Fax: 345 211 30 87). *Location:* in the hills between San Pedro de Alcantara and Estepona; inland from Ctra. N-340, km. 165.6. Possibly the Costa del Sol's most spectacular course, a challenging layout over mountainous terrain for the bold and accurate. 18 holes, 5652 metres, Par 71. *Green Fees:* information not available. *Eating facilities:* bar and restaurant in clubhouse. Cart hire. Pyr Hotel, Puerto Banos - very good package for golfers (345 281 73 53; Fax: 345 281 79 07). *

BENALMADENA. **Golf Torrequebrada**, Edif Club de Golf, 29630 Benalmadena (95 244 27 42; Fax: 95 256 11 29). *Location:* Exit CN 340 at junction 222. Undulating terrain, lots of vegetation, superb views over Mediterranean Sea. 18 holes, 5852 metres, Par 72. Driving range. *Green Fees:* 84 euros. *Eating facilities:* full bar and restaurant. *Visitors:* welcome at all times. Handicap Certificate required, maximum 27 men, 35 ladies. Pro shop, changing rooms. One of the Costa's favourite golf courses, has hosted two Spanish PGA Championships. Professional: Juan Jimenez. Commercial Director: Eddie MacLean.

ESTEPONA. **Atalaya Golf & Country Club Estepona-Malaga**, Ctra de Benahavis, 29688 Estepona, Malaga (95 2882812; Fax: 95 2887897). *Location:* between Marbella and Estepona, off N340 going west, turn inland for Benahavis just past Guadalmina. Two courses Atalaya Old and New. The fairly open parkland holes are lined with eucalyptus and pine. 36 holes, 6142 metres, Par 72. Large practice ground and putting greens. *Green Fees:* information not available. *Eating facilities:* bar and restaurant in clubhouse. Pro shop; club, cart and trolley hire. Professional: (95 2882812; Fax: 95 2887897). Secretary: Maribel Martin (95 2882812/95 2882811; Fax: 95 2887897). Golf Director: Andres Sanchez.

ESTEPONA. **Golf El Paraiso**, Carretera de Cadiz-Malaga 29680 Estepona, Malaga (95.288.38.35; Fax: 95.288.58.27). *Location:* west on N340, turn right at Benavista then inland 3 km. A fine rolling parkland style course opened in 1974. The holes run over and around a hill surmounted by the El Paraiso Hotel. 18 holes, 6116 metres, Par 71. Practice ground and putting green. *Green Fees:* information not available.. *Eating facilities:* bar and restaurant. Pro shop; club, cart and trolley hire. Professional: Paul Crangle and Tomas Bellios. Secretary: Colin Christison. *

MALAGA. **Guadalhorce Club de Golf**, Ctra de Cartama, Apartado 48, 29590 Campanillas, Malaga (952 179378; Fax: 952 179372). *Location:* east towards Malaga on N340 past airport; turn right at sugar refinery taking underpass towards Bacardi distillery. A combination of classic parkland on level land with sculptured holes with raised greens and strategic water. 18 holes, 6194 metres, Par 72. Practice ground and putting green. Also 9 short holes. *Green Fees:* information not available. *Eating facilities:* bar and restaurant in classical 19th century Andalucian manor house. Pro shop; club, buggies and trolley hire. Professional: S. Bruna. Director of Golf: G Alvarez. *

MARBELLA. **Aloha Golf Club**, Nueva Andalucia, 29660 Marbella, Malaga (952-90 70 85/86; Fax: 952-81 23 89). *Location:* 3 km inland from Puerto Banus, 8km west of Marbella. Very tight driving course with tree-lined fairways and very strategically placed lakes and streams. 18 holes, 6246 metres, S.S.S. 74 (back tees). Practice area. *Green Fees:* information not available. *Eating facilities:* bar and restaurant (952-61 23 50). *Visitors:* basically a members' club, non-members may play in most weekly competitions. Pro shop; club, cart and trolley hire. Professional and Sport Director: Jose Luis Mangas (952 81 47 55; Fax: 952 81 23 89). *

MARBELLA. **Golf Rio Real**, Apartado 82, 29600 Marbella (952-76 57 33; Fax: 952-77 21 40). *Location:* 5km east from Marbella on N340, situated in a very nice valley with sea views and crossed by the Rio Real Creek. A relatively gentle test of golf. Well-cared for and closely linked to the five star Rio Real Golf Hotel. 18 holes, 6166 metres, Par 72. Practice ground and putting green. *Green Fees:* information not available. *Eating facilities:* restaurant and bar.
e-mail: golf@rioreal.com
website: www.rioreal.com

MARBELLA. **Guadalmina Club de Golf**, Urb. Guadalmina Alta, 29678 S. Pedro Alcantara, Malaga (34 5 2886522; Fax: 2883375). *Location:* turn right off N340 approximately 1km west of San Pedro de Alcantara. A development which now boasts 45 holes - the original South course, the North which is more open despite some strategic water, and a short 9 hole layout. North: 18 holes, 5825 metres, Par 71. South: 18 holes, 6021 metres, Par 72. Driving range and putting greens. *Green Fees:* information not available. *Eating facilities:* spike bar and restaurant. *Visitors:* welcome, Handicaps 27 men, 35 ladies. Pro shop; club, cart and trolley hire. Professional: Francisco Hernandez. Secretary: Alvaro Beamonte (2883455/2883375; Fax: 2883483). *

MARBELLA. **Los Naranjos Golf Club**, Apartado 64, 29660 Nueva Andalucia, Malaga (952-81 24 28; Fax: 952-81 14 28). *Location:* turn right off N340 (going west) at Puerto Banus. Pass bullring and go over hill for 2km. The front nine holes run in a quiet undulating landscape and second nine through an orange grove giving the name to the course. 18 holes, 6038 metres, Par 72. Practice ground and putting green. *Green Fees:* Information not available *Eating facilities:* bar and restaurant in new clubhouse. Pro shop, club, cart and trolley hire. *Visitors:* Handicap Certificates required. Manager: Christer Sorensson. *

MARBELLA. **Real Club de Golf Las Brisas**, Apartado 147, Nueva Andalucia, 29660 Marbella, Malaga (952-81 08 75; Fax: 952-81 55 18). *Location:* turn right off N340 at Puerto Banus. Over hill past bullring, then right and follow signs to Hotel Del Golf. A fine course which has played host to two World Cups and numerous other major Opens. Tough, with plenty of water and fast, sloping greens. 18 holes, 6163 metres, Par 72. Practice ground and putting green. *Green Fees:* as this is a members' club, green fee playing space is limited. Check availability in advance. *Eating facilities:* bar and restaurant. Pro shop; club, cart and trolley hire. *

MIJAS. **La Cala Resort**, Apdo de Correos 106, La Cala de Mijas, 29649 Mijas Costa, Malaga (34 952669000; Fax: 34 952669034). *Location:* situated between Fuengirola and Marbella, on N340 highway, turn at La Cala Village, "Cala de Mijas" 6km inland. La Cala offers elevated greens, large bunkers, playable and challenging holes and some magnificent views. 36 holes, North Course – 6187 metres, Par 73; South Course – 5966 metres, Par 72. David Leadbetter Academy, one driving range, 6 hole Executive Par 3 course, football academy. *Green Fees:* information not available. *Eating facilities:* bars and restaurants. *Visitors:* always welcome. Pro shop. Squash and tennis. La Cala Five Star Hotel. *Society Meetings:* welcome. General Manager: Alan Saunders (34 952669036; Fax: 34 952669034).

MIJAS. **Mijas Golf International**, Apartado 145, 29640 Fuengirola, Malaga (0034 52 47 6843; Fax: 0034 52 46 7943). *Location:* from Marbella on N340 take the Fuengirola bypass and turn left at underpass. Then drive for two km before turning right. Two excellent courses: Los Lagos - 18 holes, 6348 metres, Par 71; and Los Olivos - 18 holes, 5896 metres, Par 72. The former course is relatively open although the greens are well protected by sand and water; the latter is narrower with smaller greens, favouring finesse over power. Driving range and putting green. *Green Fees:* information not available. *Eating facilities:* excellent food and bars. *Visitors:* welcome at anytime subject to availability. Pro shop; club, cart and trolley hire. Secretary: Michael Lovett. *

visit the FHG golf website on
www.uk-golfguide.com

ANDALUCIA – EAST

ALMERIA. **Golf Almerimar**, Urb Almerimar, 04700 El Ejido, Almeria (950-49 74 54; Fax: 950-49 72 33). *Location:* 7 km from El Ejido, which is some 35 km from Almeria on the main Malaga road. This is a well-established course in a relatively level situation, with a wealth of trees and the chance of a breeze from the sea alongside. 18 holes, 5892 metres, S.S.S. 72. Practice ground and putting green. *Green Fees:* information not available. *Eating facilities:* snack bar and restaurant. Pro shop; club, cart and trolley hire. Professional: Juan Parron. *

RINCON DE LA VICTORIA. **Anoreta Golf**, Avda. del Golf, s/n, 29730 Rincon de la Victoria, Malaga (952-40 40 00; Fax: 952-40 40 50). *Location:* 12 km east of Malaga at Rincon de la Victoria, only second course to be built east of Malaga. Seaside/parkland course. 18 holes, 5976 metres, Par 71. Driving range and putting green. *Green Fees:* information not available. *Eating facilities:* bar and restaurant. *Visitors:* welcome, no restrictions. Pro shop; club, cart and trolley hire.*

ANDALUCIA – WEST

CADIZ. **Club de Golf Novo Sancti Petri**, Urb. Novo Sancti Petri, Playa de la Barrosa, 11130 Chiclana de la Frontera, Cadiz (0034 956 49 40 05; Fax: 0034 956 49 43 50). *Location:* end of the La Barrosa road at Chiclana. 36 holes divided into two rounds, one round bordered by trees, the other with magnificent views overlooking the Atlantic Ocean. Various water hazards. Designed by Severiano Ballesteros. Round A 6097 metres, Round B 5846 metres (yellow tees), all Par 72. Practice ground and putting green. 9 hole pitch and putt course. *Green Fees:* information not available. *Eating facilities:* bar and restaurant. *Visitors:* welcome, no restrictions.Only soft spikes to be worn. Pro shop; club, cart and trolley hire. Professionals: Chema Andrade, Pip Andrade, Peter Bronson, Jeroen Dekker, Günther Winkler, Jose Lorca, Christophe Meymat, Renger Mostert, Björn Raschovsky. Secretary: Mrs Ruiz-Cortina.*
e-mail: sales@golf-novosancti.es

CADIZ. **Montecastillo Hotel & Golf Resort**, Ctra de Arcos, 11406 Jerez de la Frontera, Cadiz ([34] 9-56 15 12 00; Fax: [34] 9-56 15 12 09). *Location:* half a mile main road, four miles Jerez, 46 miles Sevilla. A relatively level but rolling layout with a distinct links flavour. Plenty of mounds and elevated tees, vast bunkers and water. 18 holes, 6424 metres, Par 72. Driving range and putting green. *Green Fees:* information not available. *Eating facilities:* restaurant,

two coffee shops. *Visitors:* welcome. Special packages available. Tennis court, football pitches, paddle tennis courts and Montecastillo Spa, including indoor swimming pool, jacuzzi, saunas, massage rooms, gym, cafeteria and solarium. *Society Meetings:* welcome. Secretary: Immaculada Fernandez (956 151213; Fax: 956 151215). *

SAN ROQUE. **Real Club de Golf Sotogrande**, Paseo del Parque, Apartado 14, 11310 Sotogrande (956-79 50 50; Fax: 956-79 50 29). *Location:* km 130 of national road N340, turn 2.5km towards sea. Well established (1964) and a major golfing landmark in Europe. Rolling slopes and strategic water are offset by cork oak, eucalyptus, palm and pine, first golf course in Europe designed by Robert Trent Jones. A demanding golfing feast. 18 holes, 6224 metres, Par 74. Also 9 hole short course. Practice ground and putting green. *Green Fees:* information not available. *Eating facilities:* cafeteria and restaurant. *Visitors:* welcome daily from 11am to 1pm. Pro shop; club, cart and trolley hire; tennis, paddle and swimming pool. Professional: Teddoro Gonzalez (345 6795722). Secretary: Fugenio Reviriego (345 6794516). *

SAN ROQUE. **San Roque Club**, CN 340, KM 126, 11360 San Roque, Cadiz ([34] 9-56 613030/60/90; Fax: 613013). *Location:* 3km from Sotogrande towards San Roque village. Undulating first 9 holes, wooded second 9 holes, water hazards. 18 holes, 6494 metres White markers, 6134 metres Yellow, 5588 metres Blue, 5174 metres Red. S.S.S. 74, Par 72. Two-tiered, covered range (28 bays), two pitching areas, putting greens, three practice bunkers. *Green Fees:* information not available. *Eating facilities:* Snack Bar, "El Bolero" Restaurant, "Tappan Yaki" Japanese Restaurant. *Visitors:* welcome anytime but must pre-book tee times. Pro shop, locker facilities, club rental, buggy, trolley rental, golf lessons available. Golf Director: Ian F. Martin.

SAN ROQUE. **Club de Golf Valderrama**, Avda Los Cortijos, s/n, 11310 Sotogrande, Cadiz ([34] 9-56 791200; Fax: [34] 9-56 796028). *Location:* access through the main Sotogrande entrance (right of N340 going west); then 2.5 km inland. Cork oaks, rolling hills, view to the sea. Ryder Cup venue 1997 and home of the Volvo Masters. 18 holes, 6356 metres, Par 71. Practice ground and putting green. *Green Fees:* information not available. *Eating facilities:* bar and restaurant open to non members for dinner Tuesdays to Saturdays and for buffet on Sundays. *Visitors:* tee off times for visitors 12 noon to 2pm, must book in advance. Handicap maximum 24 men, 32 ladies. Soft spikes on golf shoes compulsory. Pro shop. Valderrama hosted the World Golf Championships and the American Express Championships in 1999 and 2000. *Society Meetings:* welcome by prior arrangement. Professional: Miguel Sedeno. Director General: Derek Brown. *

CATALONIA

GIRONA. **Costa Brava Golf Club**, Urb. Golf Costa Brava, "La Masia", 17246 Sta. Cristina D'Aro, Girona (972 83 70 55; Fax: 83 72 72). *Location:* from A7 highway Exit 9. 30km from Girona, five/six km from the coast. From a hilly, wooded first 9 holes with fine views, the back 9 holes slope down by the river to flatter ground. 18 holes, 5625 metres. S.S.S. 70. Putting greens and practice areas. *Green Fees:* information not provided. Special rates for groups. *Eating facilities:* restaurant, bar and snack bar. *Visitors:* welcome anytime, no restrictions. Pro shop, changing rooms. Buggies and caddy carts for hire. *Society Meetings:* welcome, discounts available. Professional: Miguel Gil Garcia (Tel & Fax: 83 50 33). Secretary: Ma. Victoria Figueras Garcia (83 71 50; Fax: 83 72 72).

GIRONA. **Club de Golf Girona**, Urbanitz. Golf Girona, 17481 Sant Julia Ramis (Girona). (00.34.972.17.16.41;Fax:00.34.972.17.16.82). *Location:* four km north of Girona town centre, near the Girona North Exit (6) of the Girona-La Jonquera Motorway (A7). An undulating course around wooded valleys and hills with three man-made lakes. 18 holes, 6100 metres. S.S.S. 72. Driving range, putting green. *Green Fees:* information not available. *Eating facilities:* bar, restaurant, golfer's menu. *Visitors:* welcome all year by arrangement. Pro shop, caddy carts for hire. *Society Meetings:* welcome by arrangement; 10% reduction. Professional: Carlos Garcia Simarro (972.17.00.11; Fax: 972. 17.16.82). *
e-mail: golfgirona@golfgirona.com

GIRONA. **Club de Golf D'Aro Mas Nou**, 17250 Playa de Aro, Costa Brava (Girona) (972 826900; Fax: 972 826906). *Location:* on the Costa Brava, between Playa de Aro and Santa Cristina, 35 km east of Girona. A scenic course with panoramic views of the Costa Brava from its situation on the Les Gavarres mountains. Trees and lakes add to the course's charm. 18 holes, 6218 metres. S.S.S. 72. 9 hole Par 3 course, practice area. *Green Fees:* information not available. *Eating facilities:* clubhouse with bar, snack bar and restaurant. Caddies. Professionals: Piter Runlus, Pedro Martinez. Secretary: Toni Hidalgo (003 4 972 826900/816727; Fax: 972 826906). Manager: Rudolf Glanzmann (003 4 972 826900). *
e-mail: golfdaromasnou@retemail.es

PALS. **Emporda Golf Club**, Ctra. Palafrugell-Torroella de Montgri, 17257 Gualta (Girona) (+37 72 76 04 50; Fax: +37 72 75 71 00). *Location:* 40km from Girona almost on the coast, between Pals and Torroella. Combination course with dunes, lakes, wooded, flat course. 27 holes. S.S.S. 71. Large driving range, chipping area. *Green Fees:* information not available. *Eating facilities:* clubhouse, restaurant, snack bar. *Visitors:* welcome anytime, no restrictions. Swimming pool. Professional: Jordi Riera. Manager: Isidre Soria. Commercial Director: Jaume Marin. *

PALS. **Golf Platja de Pals**, Ctra. del Golf, s/n, 17256 Pals, Costa Brava (34 972 667739; Fax: 34 972 637339) *Location:* on the coast at Playa de Pals beach, eight km from Begur and 40 km east of Girona. The oldest course on the Costa Brava, requires great golfing skills as its fairways are ringed by 100 year old pine trees. 18 holes, 6200 metres. S.S.S. 72/74. Par 73. Practice course with pitching, chipping and putting green areas. *Green Fees:* on application. *Eating facilities:* snack bar, dining area with spectacular golfing views. Mediterranean style menu. *Visitors:* welcome. Clubs, caddy cars and golf carts can be hired. *Society Meetings:* welcome.
e-mail: comercial@golfplatjadepals.com
website: www.golfplatjadepals.com

PALS. **Golf Serres de Pals**, Pals, Girona 17256 ([972] 637 375; Fax: [972] 667 447). *Location:* motorway to Le Bisbel, 3km from Flaça take the first turn on the left and then follow the signs for Golf Serres de Pals. Three different areas with smooth hill top and pine tree forest, and fairways between lakes. 18 holes, 6882 yards, 6263 metres. S.S.S. 72. Driving range with practice areas and three Par 3 holes. *Green Fees:* information not available. *Eating facilities:* restaurant and bar. *Visitors:* always welcome. Closed Christmas Day. Shop, golf school, changing rooms etc. Hotel accommodation on site. Hire of buggies, clubs, trolleys. *Society Meetings:* always welcome. Tailor-made packages. Secretary: Pedro Garcia Ruiz.*
e-mail: info@golfserresdepals.com
website: www. golfserresdepals.com

MURCIA

MURCIA. **La Manga Club,** Los Belones, Cartagena, 30385 Murcia (968-56 45 11; Fax: 968-56 47 50). *Location:* 330 km from Cartagena, 75 km from Murcia and 100 km from Alicante airport. Access off road to Murcia Airport. A true sporting resort in all aspects, with 54 holes of palm-lined golf backed by low hills as well as tennis, squash, bowls, health club and watersports at the Mar Menor close by. Five star La Manga Club hotel on site. Three courses: North 18 holes, 5780 metres, Par 71; South 18 holes, 6361 metres, Par 72; West 18 holes, 5971 metres, Par 72. Driving range and putting green. *Green Fees:* information not available. *Eating facilities:* bar and restaurant. Pro shop; club, cart and trolley hire. *

VALENCIA

BETERA. **Club de Golf Escorpion**, Apartado 1, 46117 Betera, Valencia (96-160 12 11; Fax: 96-169 01 87). *Location:* take the road from Valencia to Liria, turning off at San Antonio de Benageber. Go 4 km to the right in the direction of Betera. A fine private club offering parkland-style golf with a mountain backdrop. Tree-lined and interesting. 18 holes, 6319 metres, Par 72. Driving range and putting green. *Green Fees:* information not available. *Eating facilities:* bar and restaurant. Pro shop; club, cart and trolley hire. *

CHIVA. **Club de Golf El Bosque**, Carretera Godelleta, Urban. El Bosque 46370 Chiva, Valencia (96-180 8000; Fax: 96-180 8001). *Location:* take the Nacional III road (Madrid-Valencia) Exit 337, turn off for Godelleta. Wooded course, designed by Robert Trent Jones Snr. 18 holes, 6276 metres, S.S.S. 72. Driving range and putting green. *Green Fees:* information not available. *Eating facilities:* cafeteria, restaurant. *Visitors:* welcome. One, two and three bedroom flats available. Professionals: Alfonso Pinto, Ignecio Briz. *

ORIHUELA. **Campo de Golf Villamartin**, Crta Alicante - Cartagena, 03189 Orihuela, Alicante (96 6765127; Fax: 96 6765158). *Location:* 7 km from Torrevieja, 3 km from the beach and 3km from the main road N332. Two courses laid out on interesting coastal sandy land with some pines. A good test of golf, open to the breeze. 18 holes, 6132 metres, Par 72; 18 holes, 5770 metres, Par 72. Driving range and putting green. *Green Fees:* information not available. *Eating facilities:* bar, coffee shop and restaurant. *Visitors:* welcome. Pro shop; buggies and carts. *Society Meetings:* welcome, 20% discount. Professional: Emilio Rodriguez (96 6765127; Fax: 96 6765158). Secretary: Juan Miguel Buendia (96 6765051; Fax: 96 6765170).

VALENCIA. **Campo de Golf El Saler**, Parador De Turismo "El Saler", El Saler, Valencia (Tel & Fax: 96-162 73 66). *Location:* at 18km on the road from Nazaret to Oliva, right by the sea. One of the great Spanish tests of golf, with open links fairways and tight holes lined with umbrella pine; a public facility offering true seaside conditions. 18 holes, 6042 metres, Par 72. Driving range and putting green. *Green Fees:* 75 euros. *Eating facilities:* bar, restaurant and coffee shop. *Visitors:* welcome. Pro shop; club, cart and trolley and electric trolley hire. *

Please mention
'THE GOLF GUIDE'
when enquiring about
clubs or accommodation.

MAJORCA

CALA D'OR. **Club Vall D'Or Golf**, Ctra Cala d'Or a Portocolom, 07669 S'Horta (971 837068; Fax: 971 837299). *Location:* approximately 60km east of Palma on the road from Porto Colom to Cala D'Or. Undulating, winding course, with trees. 18 holes, 5824 metres. S.S.S. 71. Driving range, club hire. *Green Fees:* information not available. *Eating facilities:* clubhouse, bar and restaurant. *Visitors:* welcome with Handicap. Nearby hotels include Cala D'Or, Rocador, Rocador Playa. Professional: Antonio Gonzalez. Secretary: Barbara Denk (971 837001). *

MAGALLUF. **Golf de Poniente**, Crta. Cala Figuera S/N, 07182 Calvia (0034971 130148; Fax: 0034971 130176). *Location:* 18km west of Palma, one km from Magalluf on the Andraitx Road. The course is considered long and difficult, surrounded by trees and water, with large and fast greens. 18 holes, 6430 metres. S.S.S. 72. Driving range, putting green. *Green Fees:* information not available. *Eating facilities:* clubhouse, restaurant and bar. *Visitors:* welcome. Nearby hotels include Son Caliu, Club Galatzo. Professionals: Paco Ruiz, Brian Salter. e-mail: golf@ponientegolf.com website: www.ponientegolf.com

PALMA. **Real Golf de Bendinat**, Campoamor S/N, 07181 Bendinat Calvia (971 405200; Fax: 971 700786). *Location:* five km west from Palma centre on the road between Illetas and Portals Nous. Mixed woodland, good vistas. 18 holes, 5650 metres. S.S.S. 71. Driving range, putting green. *Green Fees:* information not available. *Eating facilities:* excellent restaurant. *Visitors:* welcome, limited numbers. Please reserve tee-off times through our Fax No: (971 700786). *Society Meetings:* welcome. Professional: Ricardo Galiano (971 405450; Fax: 971 700786). Secretary: Alison Bradshaw (971 405200; Fax: 971 700786).

PALMA. **Son Vida Golf**, Urb. Son Vida, 07013 Palma de Mallorca (34/971-79.12.10; Fax: 34/971.79.11.27). *Location:* three km from Palma centre, access via de Sinora Exit Son Rapina. Majorca's first course (1964) winding through trees and estate villas with lakes and gentle slopes. 18 holes, 5740 metres. S.S.S. 71. Driving range, Pro Shops, car, trolley and club rental. *Green Fees:* information not available. *Eating facilities:* snacks and lunches in the comfortable clubhouse, excellent restaurant El Pato (The Duck) overlooking 18th hole. *Visitors:* welcome, Handicap Certificate/Card required. Nearby hotels (discount on green fees) include Arabella Golf Hotel (5 stars), Hotel Son Vida (4 stars) on the course, Victoria Sol (4 stars), Palma, Bonanza Playa Illetas, Son Caliu. *Society Meetings:* welcome. Professionals: R. Maer, S. Ruiz. Secretary: Mrs Layda. Manager: Juan Alvarez. *

POLLENSA. **Golf Pollensa**, Ctra. Palma Pollensa, 07460 Pollensa (0034971 533216; Fax: 0034971 533265). *Location:* in the north of the island, 45 km from Palma Airport and 2 km from Pollensa. On the south side of a hill with smooth and beautiful undulations and sea views. 9 holes: White tees 5304 metres S.S.S. 68; Red tees 5116 metres S.S.S. 70, Par 70. Driving range, putting & pitching green. *Green Fees:* 30 euros 9 holes, 52 euros 18 holes. *Eating facilities:* snack bar, beautiful restaurant, excellent food, 7 days a week. *Visitors:* welcome, tee reservation recommended. Changing room. Pro shop, golf lessons, club and electric cart rental. *Society Meetings:* welcome. Professional: Carlos Insua. Director: Christina Schallock. Secretaries: Teresa Moll and Joana March.

SANTA PONSA. **Santa Ponsa Golf Club One**, Santa Ponsa, 07184 Calvia (971 690211; Fax: 971 693364). *Location:* 18km on motorway from Palma to Andraitx, turn off roundabout Santa Ponsa. Gently sloping fairways with water hazards. 18 holes, 6543 metres. S.S.S. 72 men, 73 ladies. Practice range, two putting greens. *Green Fees:* 68 euros 18 holes. *Eating facilities:* restaurant and bar in clubhouse, also small bar on golf course. *Visitors:* welcome; maximum Handicaps - 28 men, 36 ladies. Guests at the hotel receive 50% reduction on green fees. Accommodation available, swimming pool, paddling pool, tennis. *Society Meetings:* welcome. Professionals: Diego Lopez/Mark Schmidt. Director: Jose M. Gomez. Secretary: Vicky Garcia.

SANTA PONSA. **Santa Ponsa Golf Club Two**, Santa Ponza, Calvia (690211; Fax: 693364). *Location:* as Santa Ponza One. A very interesting and enjoyable course, it has a mixture of holes, some with very tight fairways and others with many water hazards. Designed by Jose Gancedo. 18 holes, 6053 metres. S.S.S. 73, Par 72. Practice range, putting green. *Green Fees:* on request. *Eating facilities:* as Santa Ponza One. *Visitors:* at moment only open for shareholders. *

SON SERVERA. **Son Servera Golf Club**, Costa de los Pinos, 07550 Son Servera (71 84.00.96; Fax: 71 84.01.60). *Location:* Palma - Manacor - Sant Lloreng - Son Servera. Fairly flat, narrow, seaside course, set among pine trees. 9 holes, 2978 metres. S.S.S. 72. *Green Fees:* information not available. *Eating facilities:* bar and restaurant. *Visitors:* welcome. Handicap Certificate required. Nearby hotels include Eurotel Golf Punta Roja, Flamenco, Royal Mediterranea, Gran Sol. Professional: Jaime Artiach. Secretary: Jose Colom.

Golf in the USA
WHERE TO PLAY • WHERE TO STAY
By Michael Gedye

The biggest single difference between holiday golfers in America and their counterparts in Europe is that the latter have to travel abroad to find winter play in the sun. Americans merely travel to another, warmer part of their homeland to enjoy an environment, food and language with which they are totally familiar. With a wide selection of highly competitive sunshine resorts in the USA, the visitor can only benefit from the force of these market pressures. By the same token, one should accept and enjoy holiday golf the American way.

Service will be impeccable and all-embracing, almost certainly including a mandatory golf cart. The courses, if a little bland and artificial, should be impressively maintained and every effort will be made, from on-course catering to clubhouse shoe cleaning, to make you feel like royalty. The inevitable slow play can be enlivened by regular refreshment stops and moderate prices. American holiday golf is social, laid back and a world of its own - enjoy it.

Taking into account existing golf travel packages on offer from Europe and the broad selection of attractive destinations, we have chosen four to recommend - fascinating Florida, the two Carolinas on the eastern seaboard and the slightly surreal luxury of Palm Springs in California. At each destination we have included some championship tests of the game. Most recognisable is the sunshine state of FLORIDA. With over a thousand courses to choose from, it has long been a favoured destination with Americans living further north and has the experience to match.We have selected the Palm Beach coast north of Miami, central Orlando and the western coast of the Gulf of Mexico. Demanding tests include Innisbrook and PGA National; for more friendly golf, try Naples Beach or Saddlebrook.

Mention NORTH CAROLINA and all thoughts turn to historic Pinehurst, venue for the 1999 US Open (and again in 2005). This well-established resort has a long and deserved reputation for its old-fashioned southern hospitality and the quality of the eight courses that radiate out under towering pines. The PGA Golf Hall of Fame nearby is well worth a visit.

Two quite different locations are on offer in SOUTH CAROLINA. The greatest concentration of holiday golf in the world is to be found at Myrtle Beach, where 110 courses, many by top designers, offer play at all levels. They follow a wooded belt just inshore from a beachfront that is a complete contrast - a lively strip of fast food, motels, bargain shopping and vibrant nightlife. All part of the U.S. popular vacation mix, but well worth a visit for the chance to play on so many courses of true class, linked by a computerised tee-time system to ensure that all can find a game. Just a short way down the coast, Hilton Head Island is a world apart, where some fine coastal resort golf exists in an atmosphere of tranquil, relaxed, upmarket isolation. Prime attraction is Harbour Town, annual venue of the Heritage Classic on the USPGA Tour.

CALIFORNIA, known for movies, oranges, non-stop sunshine and colourful excess, presents the ultimate in man-made resort living at PALM SPRINGS. Just an hour and a half east of Los Angeles, it is a totally artificial 25-mile strip of flourishing green acreage in the middle of endless sandy desert. Long the favoured retreat of Hollywood's finest since the 1920s, it offers over ninety excellent golf courses, their lush fairways lined with tall palms and many water hazards, backed by ranges of pastel-shaded mountains. On this verdant playground for the super-rich, there are also 160 hotels, 600 tennis courts and a mere 10,000 swimming pools. With virtually no humidity, a limitless underground water supply and constant sunshine, it represents the ultimate in five-star American-style holiday golf.

N O T E All the information regarding Golf Clubs in this guide is given in good faith in the belief that it is correct. However, the publishers cannot guarantee the facts given in these pages, neither are they responsible for changes in ownership or facilities, such as green fees, that may take place after the date of going to press. Readers should always satisfy themselves that the facilities they require are available and that the terms, if quoted, still apply.

FLORIDA

AVENTURA. **Turnberry Isle Resort & Club**, 19999 West Country Club Drive, Aventura, FL. 33180 (305) 932 6200; Fax: (305) 933 6922. North Miami Beach. This luxurious private resort and country club is the perfect spot for sports enthusiasts. Two Robert Trent Jones, Sr. championship courses keep resort guests and members in the swing. North 6323 yards, Par 70; South 7003 yards, Par 72. Full facilities.

BOCA RATON. **Boca Raton Resort & Club**, 501 East Camino Real, Boca Raton, Florida 33431 (561-447 3000; Fax: 561-447 5294). *Location:* 22 miles from Palm Beach. Historic golf resort which combines links with the past and contemporary luxury. 36 holes: Country Club Course 6714 yards Par 72. Resort Course 6253 yards, Par 71. Full facilities. *Eating facilities:* beverage carts, snack bars and restaurants. *Green Fees:* information not available. *Visitors:* closed to public, must be a member, guest of a member or staying at the resort. Director of Golf: Bob Coman. *

BONITA SPRINGS. **Pelican's Nest Golf Club at Pelican Landing**, 4450 Pelican's Nest Drive, Bonita Springs FL (239) (947 4600). *Location:* just inside Pelican Landing, a wonderful complement to local amenities. Two, member-owned, Tom Fazio designed, private golf courses. Gator: 18 holes, 7066 yards, Par 73, Rating 74.7. slope 137. Hurricane: 18 holes, 6894 yards, Par 72, Rating 74, slope 137. *Green Fees:* information not available. *Eating facilities:* new clubhouse.
website: www.nestgolf.com

LAKE COUNTY. **Mission Inn Golf and Tennis Resort**. *Location:* on the country side of Orlando, less than one hour from central Florida's famous attractions. Mission Inn boasts 36 holes of championship golf on two renowned courses. El Campeon: 18 holes, 6852 yards. Las Colinas: 18 holes, 6879 yards. *Green Fees:* information not available. *Visitors:* Stay & Play golf packages available inclusive of green fees, accommodation, meals, and for green fees and accommodation only. Many other resort facilities are available for guests travelling with golf enthusiasts - tennis, hydro spa, heated outdoor pool, fitness room, bicycle trails, marina, shopping, etc. Reservations made by calling Destination Golf: 0181-891 5151.

NAPLES. **Lely Resort**, 8202 Lely Resort Boulevard, Naples, Fl. 34113 (941) 793 2200; Fax: (941) 793 3963. 40 miles from Fort Myers. Great golf in substantial homesite development. Golf design by Jones, Player and Trevino. 54 holes Flamingo Course 7171 yards Par 72. Full facilities. *

NAPLES. **Naples Beach Hotel & Golf Club**, 851 Gulf Shore Boulevard North, Naples, Florida 37102 (941 2612222; Fax: 941 2617380). *Location:* 30 miles from S.W. Florida International Airport in Fort Myers. Beachside hotel and golf resort with much tradition. Very popular with British players. 18 holes 6642 yards Par 72. Full facilities. Golf school, driving range and full service spa. Professional: Larry Guntzer. *

ORLANDO. **Grenelefe Golf & Tennis Resort**, 3200 SR 546, Haines City, Fl. 33844 (941) 422 7511. 25 miles south-west of Disney World. A comprehensive golf and tennis resort in a rolling, wooded setting. Popular also for conventions. 54 holes: East 6802 yards, Par 72; South 6869 yards, Par 71; West 7325 yards, Par 72. Full facilities. *

ORLANDO. **The Villas of Grand Cypress One**, North Jacaranda, Orlando, FL 32836 (800/835 7377; Fax: 407/239 7219). *Location:* take I4 to Exit 68 right to SR 535 North. Superb resort complex. Four Courses: New Course 18 holes, 6773 yards Blue, 6181 yards White; North Course 9 holes, Gold 3521, Blue 3143, White 2912, Par 36; South Course 9 holes, Gold 3472 yards, Blue 3212 yards, White 2911 yards, Par 36; East Course 9 holes, Gold 3434 yards, Blue 3151 yards, White 2878 yards, Par 36. Driving range. *Green Fees:* $175 in season, $115 off season. *Eating facilities:* The Club restaurant and Sports Bar, Black Swan Restaurant. *Visitors:* only if guests of Villas of Grand Cypress or Hyatt Regency Grand Cypress. Locker room. Academy of Golf, Equestrian Centre and racquet club. Director of Golf: Bill Rowden (407 239 1956; Fax: 407 239 1969). Secretary: Lisa Monohan (407 239 1913; Fax: 407 239 1969).

PALM BEACH. **PGA National Golf Club**, 400 Avenue of the Champions, Palm Beach Gardens Fl 33418 (561 627 1800). 15 miles from West Palm Beach. Golf for all levels, including beginners, at a superb resort which hosted the 1983 Ryder Cup. 90 holes: Champion Course 7022 yards Par 72. Full facilities including teaching academy. *

TAMPA. **Saddlebrook Resort**, 5700 Saddlebrook Way, Wesley Chapel Tampa, Fl. 33543-4499 (813 973 1111; Fax: 813 973 4504). *Location:* 33 miles north of Tampa International Airport, take I-75 to SR54, then east one mile. 480 acres of natural countryside surrounded by tall cypress, pines, palm trees, blue lakes and rolling hills. Two courses (both designed by Arnold Palmer): Saddlebrook Course - 18 holes, 6564 yards. Par 70. Palmer Course - 18 holes, 6469 yards. S.S.S. 71. Practice green, practice range. *Green Fees:* seasonal, please enquire. *Eating facilities:* four restaurants, lounge, pool bar and sports bar. *Visitors:* welcome, open all year. Pro shop; Arnold Palmer Golf Academy; cart and club rental. *Society Meetings:* welcome. Professional: Jerry Couzynse. *

TARPON SPRINGS. **Innisbrook Hilton Resort**, 36750 US 19 N, Palm Harbor, Fl. 34684 (813 942 2000/800 456 2000). *Location:* 20 miles from Tampa International Airport. Florida's finest golf resort. The Copperhead course ranks in Florida's top five. 72 holes: Copperhead 7087 yards Par 71; Island 6999 yards Par 72. Three practice ranges. *Green Fees:* seasonal, please enquire. *Eating facilities:* seven restaurants. *Visitors:* welcome. 13 tennis courts, six pools, golf school, children's programme, fitness centre, airport shuttle. *

NORTH CAROLINA

VILLAGE OF PINEHURST. **Pinehurst Resort & Country Club**, PO Box 4000, Carolina Vista, Village of Pinehurst, North Carolina 28374 (800 487-4653). *Location*: 70 miles from Raleigh. Truly historic with great golf, an old world atmosphere and service to match. 8 courses, 24 tennis courts, croquet lawn, bowls and fitness centre. *Green Fees*: seasonal. *Eating facilities*: Carolina Dining Room, Donald Ross Grill, Mulligan's Sports Bar and Grill. *Visitors*: Pinehurst is a stay and play facility. Visitors must be a guest of the resort to play on the courses. Four practice ranges and four clubhouses. *

PALM SPRINGS

INDIAN WELLS. **Indian Wells Golf Resort**, 44-500 Indian Wells Lane, Indian Wells (00 1 760 346 4653). 36 holes of rolling holiday golf by Ted Robinson, well-watered, manicured, a handicapper's delight. 36 holes: East 6662 yards, West 6478 yards, both Par 72. Driving range, putting green. *Green Fees:* information not available. *Eating facilities:* bar/snacks in clubhouse. Pro shop; cart and club rental. Head Professional: Joe Williams.

LA QUINTA. **La Quinta Resort & Club (Dunes)**, 50-200 Avenue Vista Bonita, La Quinta, Palm Springs (00 1 619 564 7686). A fine resort course by Pete Dye with plenty of hazards. 18 holes, 6251 yards. Par 72. Driving range, putting green. *Green Fees:* information not available. *Eating facilities:* bar and restaurants in low-rise Spanish-style hotel. Pro shop; cart and club hire. Head Professional: Todd Williams.*

LA QUINTA. **La Quinta Resort & Club (Mountain)**, 50-200 Avenida Vista Bonita, La Quinta, CA 92253, Palm Springs (00 1 619 564 7686; Fax: 00 1 760 564 2757). Carved into the base of the Santa Rosa hills, these Pete Dye courses have been ranked in USA Top 100. 18 holes, 6303 yards. Par 72. Driving range, putting green. *Green Fees:* information not available. *Eating facilities:* bar and restaurants in low-rise Spanish-style hotel. Pro shop; car and club hire. Professional: Randy J. Duncan. *

LA QUINTA. **PGA West Resort Course (Nicklaus)**, 55-900 PGA Boulevard, La Quinta, Palm Springs (00 1 619 564 7170). One of Jack Nicklaus's best with rolling mounds, much sand and water. Accuracy is all. 18 holes, 6671 yards. Par 72. Driving range, putting green. *Green Fees:* information not available. Pro shop; cart and club hire. Head Professional: Billy Neal. *

LA QUINTA. **PGA West Resort Course (TPC Stadium)**, 55-900 PGA Boulevard, La Quinta, Palm Springs (00 1 619 564 7170). Highly strategic with vast mounds and steep escarpments; a Pete Dye course almost unplayable by mere mortals. 18 holes, 6836 yards. Par 72. Driving range, putting green.

Green Fees: information not available. *Eating facilities:* bar and restaurant in clubhouse. Pro shop; cart and club hire. Head Professional: Billy Neal. *

NORTH PALM SPRINGS. **Desert Dunes**, 19-300 Palm Drive, Palm Springs (00 1 619 251 5366). *Location:* north west of downtown, approaching the foothills. A course by Robert Trent Jones Jr. full of natural, savage beauty; a contrast to the norm, home from home for real golfers. 18 holes, 6614 yards. Par 72. Driving range, putting green. *Green Fees:* information not available. *Eating facilities:* bar and restaurant. Pro shop, cart and club hire. Head Professional: Tom Connelly. *

PALM DESERT. **Desert Falls Country Club**, 1111 Desert Falls Parkway, Palm Desert, CA (00 1 760 304 5646) Top ten rated course in greater Palm Springs area. Links style course with rolling terrain accented by palms, water and sand hazards. A Ron Fream designed course with panoramic views of the mountains on every hole. 18 holes, 7005 yards. Par 74, 6529 yards Par 72, 5250 yards (Ladies) Par 72. Large practice facility. *Green Fees:* information not available. *Eating facilities:* Restaurant, snackbar and lounge. Full service. Pro shop, club rental (Titleist) available. Head Professional: Terry Ferraro. *

PALM DESERT. **Marriot's Desert Springs Resort and Spa**, 74855 Country Club Drive, Palm Desert, Palm Springs (760 341 1756; Fax: 760 341 1828). Two excellent resort courses rich in tall palms and strategic yet ornamental water features and falls, with island greens by Ted Robinson, backed by vast 884 room hotel. 36 holes: Palms 6381 yards, Valley 6326 yards, both Par 72. Driving range, 18 hole putting course, John Jacobs teaching. *Green Fees:* information not available. *Eating facilities:* 5 restaurants and many bars. Pro shop; cart and club hire. Head Professional: Tim Skogen (760 341 1757). Assistant: Irma Garcia (760 341 6757). * .

RANCHO MIRAGE. **Rancho Las Palmas Country Club**, 42-000 Bob Hope Drive, Rancho Mirage, Palm Springs (00 1 619 862 4551). A 27 hole resort complex with hotel on site. Gently rolling land with many established trees. Short and tight, now 20 years old. West/South Course 18 holes, 6128 yards. Par 70. Driving range, putting green. *Green Fees:* information not available. *Eating facilities:* bar and snacks in golf clubhouse. Hotel close by. Pro shop; cart and club hire, daily golf clinics, extensive instruction programme. Head Professional: Troy Sprister. *

RANCHO MIRAGE. **Westin Mission Hills Resort Golf Club**, 71-501 Dinah Shore Drive, Rancho Mirage, Palm Springs (760 328 3198; Fax: 760 770 4984). *Location:* five miles east of Palm Springs. Pete Dye and Gary Player have built two excellent courses here, undulating past colourful shrubs and water with a mountain backdrop. Pete Dye Resort Course, 18 holes, 6706 yards S.S.S.70. Gary Player Signature Course 18 holes, 7062 yards S.S.S.70. Magnificent 15 acre driving range, putting green. *Green Fees:* information not available. *Eating facilities:* bar and restaurants in palatial Moroccan-style clubhouse. Pro-shop, cart and club hire. Professional: Alan Deck.*

SOUTH CAROLINA

HILTON HEAD. **Harbour Town Golf Links**, Sea Pines Plantation, Hilton Head Island, South Carolina (803) 842 1892. Home of the Heritage Classic and a true thoroughbred regularly ranked in US top 25. 18 holes 6912 yards Par 71. Full facilities. *

HILTON HEAD. **Port Royal Golf Club**, Hilton Head Island, South Carolina (803 686 8801). Three fine courses winding past magnolia and oak to a hospitable plantation-style clubhouse. 54 holes Robber's Row 6711 yards Par 72; Planter's Row 6520 yards Par 72; Barony 6530 yards Par 72. Full facilities.*

HILTON HEAD. **Shipyard Golf Club**, Hilton Head Island, South Carolina (803 785 2402. Plenty of water hazards on these well-established tree-lined holes near the sea. 27 holes: Galleon 3364 yards; Brigantine 3352 yards; Clipper 3466 yards, all Par 36. Full facilities. *

HILTON HEAD ISLAND. **Palmetto Dunes Resort**, Hilton Head Island, South Carolina (803 785 1161). Rolling dunes and fairways make a contrast at this popular golf and vacation resort. 54 holes: Arthur Hills Course 6651 yards, Par 72; George Fazio Course 6873 yards, Par 70; Robert Trent Jones Course 6710 yards, Par 72. Full facilities. *

MYRTLE BEACH. **Litchfield Country Club**, PO Box 379, Pawleys Island, South Carolina 29585 (843 237 3411). *Location:* 20 miles south of Myrtle Beach. Fine plantation-style golf winding past giant oaks, cypress, marshland and strategic lakes. 18 holes 6752 yards Par 70.6/119. Driving range. *Green Fees:* information not available. *Eating facilities:* full clubhouse with grill and bar. *Visitors:* always welcome. Accommodation available; carts for hire. Professional: Bob Vanderbloemen (843 237 3411). *

MYRTLE BEACH. **Pine Lakes International Country Club**, Woodside Drive, Central Myrtle Beach, South Carolina (803 449 6459). Old fashioned service and style colour every aspect of this mature Scottish-designed golf setting. 18 holes 6709 yards Par 71. Full facilities. *

MYRTLE BEACH. **Tidewater Golf Club**, 901 Little River Neck Road, North Myrtle Beach, South Carolina 29582 (800 446 5363). *Location:* from Highway 17, take Cherry Grove Exit. Stop at end of exit ramp, turn left, turn right on to Little River Neck Road (at Harbour Gate). Two miles to Tidewater. Situated on a seaside peninsula, course designed by Ken Tomlinson. 18 holes, 7150 yards Championship, 6530 yards Blue, 6000 yards Men, 5090 yards Ladies, 4665 yards Juniors. *Green Fees:* call golf course for rates. *Eating facilities:* full facilities. *Visitors:* welcome, public course. Professional: Paul Kline. *

MYRTLE BEACH. **Wild Wing Plantation**, PO Box 51090, Myrtle Beach, South Carolina 29579 (800 736 9464; Fax: 843 347 5732). *Location:* on US Highway 501, six miles west of the Intracoastal waterway. Parkland setting. Wood Stork Course - 18 holes, 7044 yards; Hummingbird Course - 18 holes, 6853 yards; Avocet Course - 18 holes, 7127 yards; Falcon Course - 18 holes. Extensive practice facility. *Green Fees:* fees vary. *Eating facilities:* Wishbones Restaurant, Players' Pub. *Visitors:* always welcome. Wild Wing School of Golf, Golf Villas/Homes (888 398 9464). Director of Golf: Timothy P. Tilma.

MYRTLE BEACH. **The Witch Golf Club**, Highway 544 between Conway and Myrtle Beach, South Carolina (803 448 1300). 5 miles from Myrtle Beach. A natural spellbinding course winding through dense forest and mangrove swamp. 18 holes 6702 yards Par 71. Full facilities. *

Golf in South Africa
By Paul Dimmock

The international golf enthusiast will find South Africa is a unique experience. Nowhere else in the world can offer the discerning and adventurous golfer such an array of challenging golf courses. The courses are surrounded by gloriously stunning panoramas which include the splendour of Table Mountain, sweeping views of the Indian Ocean, the mystique of the African bushveld and areas of beautiful lush tropical vegetation inhabited by an amazing display of wildlife. South Africa is a vibrant and emerging world golf destination, with over 400 courses. Many of the courses are championship standard and on a par with major European and North American courses. To complete the South African experience there is a full range of accommodation from luxurious 5 star hotels offering the best of international comfort and cuisine, to the game park lodge with its cultural delights. Thanks to an advantageous exchange rate the visitor from the UK will find South Africa incredible value for money.

FISH HOEK. **Clovelly Golf Club,** P.O. Box 22119, Fish Hoek 7974 (+27 21 782 1118; Fax: +27 21 782 6853). *Location*: 30 minutes drive south of Cape Town to Clovelly in the Clovelly Valley. Excellent fairways, bent grass greens - some sloping. Offers stern challenges on almost every hole. Surrounded by mountains and sand dunes. 18 holes. Men's - Par 72. 5869 metres. Ladies' - Par 73, 5156 metres. *Green Fees*: information not available. *Eating facilities*: clubhouse, light snacks, restaurant. *Visitors*: welcome, book in advance. Handicap not required. Pro shop. Tennis and bowls. Club Professional: Dave Odendaal. Club Manager: Jeremy Lindquist.
e-mail: clubhouse@global.co.za
website: www.clovelly.co.za

GEORGE. **Fancourt Golf and Country Club Estate,** P.O. Box 2266, Montagu Street, Blanco, George 6530 (+27 (0) 44 804 0000; Fax:+27 (0) 44 804070). *Location*: 440km south east of Cape Town on the N2 Garden Route in Blanco on the western boundary of the pretty village of George. Four 18 hole Gary Player designed championship courses including The Links - Home of the Presidents Cup 2003. Warm up area, putting and chipping green, driving range, 4-hole academy course. Member of "Great Golf Resorts of the World Association" and "Preferred Hotels & Resorts Worldwide". *Green Fees*: information not available. E*ating facilities:* clubhouse, light snacks, dining room and four restaurants. *Visitors:* exclusive private club, visiting players must be Fancourt Hotel Guests, advance booking essential. Tennis, swimming, spa. e-mail: golf@fancourt.co.za

MOWBRAY. **Mowbray Golf Club,** Raapenberg Road, Mowbray, P.O. Box 38003, Howard Place 7450 (+27 21 685 3018; Fax: +27 21 686 6008). *Location*: south of

Cape Town, approximately 10 km or 10 minutes from airport. Parkland course. No steep hills but plenty of trees, bent grass greens, numerous water hazards. The cross-wind on 14 holes is a real test. Beautiful views of Table Mountain, Devils Peak. Host to South Africa Open on a number of occasions. 18 holes, Par 72. Men's 6054/5760 metres, Ladies' 5049 metres. *Green Fees*: R350. *Eating facilities*: clubhouse, halfway house, restaurant. *Visitors*: advance booking necessary, maximum Handicap men 24, ladies 30. Pro Shop. Professional: Greg McDonald. Manager: Dave Duncan. Secretary: Mrs Ingrid Tait.

SOMERSET WEST. **Erinvale Country Estate and Golf Course,** Lourensford Road, Somerset West 7129 (+27 24 847 1160; Fax: +27 24 847 1901). *Location*: 35 minutes due south from central Cape Town in the heart of the winelands. Parkland, wide kikuyu fairways and penn cross greens. Front nine mainly flat with water hazards, back nine on rolling high ground. Spectacular views of False Bay. Hosted 1996 World Cup Golf. Gary Player designed course. 18 holes, Par 72. Men's 5892 metres, Ladies 5126 metres. *Green Fees*: information not available. *Eating facilities*: clubhouse, restaurant, halfway house. *Visitors*: welcome, advance booking essential. No visitors from mid December to mid January. Maximum Handicap: Men 24, Ladies 36, card required. Professional: Bruce Bain. Secretary: Andrea Arnold. *
e-mail: clubhouse@erinvale.com

SUN CITY. **Gary Player Country Club,** Sun City, Pilansberg, North Western Province (+27 14 557 1000; Fax: +27 14 657 3426). *Location*: 150km north west of Johannesburg. 18 holes, Par 72, rating 76. 6938 meters. The most demanding course in South Africa. Mainly flat but unique hole designs, water

hazards and deceptive greens. Kikuyu fairways and bent grass greens. A variety of tees can shorten the course. Venue for Million Dollar Challenge. *Green Fees*: information not available. *Eating facilities*: clubhouse, light snacks, restaurant. *Visitors*: welcome, book in advance. Part of Sun City complex, bowls and casino. *
website: www.milliondollar.co.za/course.asp

WOODBRIDGE ISLAND. **Milnerton Golf Club**, Bridge Road, Woodbridge Island, Milnerton 7441 (+27 21 552 1047; Fax: +27 21 551 5897). *Location*: ten miles due north (Otto du Plessis Drive) from Cape Town. Only true Links course in Western Cape. Nestled between Atlantic Ocean and a lagoon, spectacular views of Table Mountain. Wind direction plays a major role, first nine downwind, second nine almost directly into the wind. 18 holes, Par 72. Men's 5721 metres, Ladies' 5022 metres. *Green Fees*: information not available. *Visitors*: welcome, book in advance. *Eating facilities*: halfway house, Maestro's Restaurant. Pro Shop. Professional: Stuart Howard. Manager: Gideon Hitchcock.
e-mail: milgolf@intekom.co.za

WYNBERG. **Royal Cape Golf Club**, 174 Ottery Road, Wynberg 7800 (+27 21 761 6551; Fax: +27 21 797 5246). *Location*: southern suburbs of Cape Town. 15 minute drive from city centre and 15 minutes from international airport. Flat parkland course. Narrow tree-lined kikuyu fairways. Dominant Bent greens, water on six holes, 58 bunkers. Wind plays a major part on some holes. Host to the South Africa Open 11 times. The oldest golf club in South Africa. Spectacular views. 18 holes, Par 72. Men's 6121 metres, Ladies' 5288 metres. *Green Fees*: information not available. *Eating facilities*: clubhouse, light snacks and restaurant. *Visitors*: welcome, advance booking necessary. Pro Shop. Professionals: Craig Ross and Barbara Pestana.
e-mail: manager@royalcapegolf.co.za
　　　　bookings@royalcapegolf.co.za
website: www.royalcapegolf.co.za

Golf in Dubai

Dubai is a thriving commercial centre with magnificent hotel and leisure amenities which now include unique opportunities for serious business and holiday golf. The Emirates Club, The Dubai Golf and Racing Club and the Dubai Creek Golf and Yachting Club all have unrivalled facilities for visiting golf, including the Dubai Golf Pass. Details from The Secretary, PO Box 6302, Dubai, United Arab Emirates.

DUBAI. **Dubai Creek Golf and Yacht Club**, PO Box 6302, Dubai (009714 2956000; Fax: 009714 2956044). *Location:* beside the Al Garhoud Bridge, close to the city centre and airport. Long, rolling course with green dunes and palm trees, man-made lakes and large sandy wastes. 18 hole championship course, 6958 yards. S.S.S. 73 and floodlit 9 hole Par 3 course. Two ended driving range. *Green Fees:* information not available. *Eating facilities:* Lakeview, Legends Steakhouse, Aquarium Restaurant and Boardwalk. *Visitors*: welcome. Golf carts compulsory. Swimming pool, gym, yacht club and marina. Host venue for the Dubai Desert Classic 1999 and 2000. Professional: Alan McKenzie. Secretary: Craig Skimming.

DUBAI. **Emirates Golf Club**, PO Box 24040, Dubai (971-4-3473222; Fax: 971-4-3472888). *Location*: on the Dabai - Abu Dhabi Highway junction 5. Two Championship standard 18-hole, Par 72 courses. Home of the Dubai Desert Classic. Majlis Course: 7101 yards with palm-edged fairways, lakes and immaculate greens. Wadi course: 7000 yards with water hazards and bunkers. Two driving ranges (one floodlit), 3 hole Academy course, pitching/putting greens. Academy of Golf with three PGA qualified professionals. *Green Fees:* information not available. *Eating facilities:* Five star Le Classique restaurant, Spike Bar and The Terrace. *Visitors:* welcome. Tennis, squash, swimming and gym available. Golf Operations Manager: Adrian Flaherty. *
e-mail: booking@dubaigolf.com

DUBAI. **Nad Al Sheba Club**, PO Box 52872, Nad Al Sheba, Dubai (971-4-3363666; Fax: 971-4-3363717). *Location:* Nad Al Sheba Racecourse, a few kilometres from the city centre. A links-type course with undulating fairways, heavily bunkered and water comes into play on 14 holes. 18 holes, 6428 yards S.S.S. 71. Fully floodlit. Golf clinics, floodlit driving range, practice area, chipping and putting. *Green Fees:* on application. *Eating facilities:* well equipped clubhouse with licensed steak house and spike bar. *Visitors:* welcome; overseas pass available, open daily. Lessons available. Golfing attire and Handicap Certificates required. General Manager: Jerry Kilby. See website for full details.
website: www.nadalshebaclub.com

Golf in Thailand

WHERE TO PLAY • WHERE TO STAY

By Michael Gedye

Thailand fulfils, in so many respects, every holiday golfer's dream. For the time being, however, it remains the great undiscovered secret. From November through to March, the temperatures are reasonable, the sun shines and there is no rain. You can choose from nearly two hundred lush, green courses, all well-manicured, with many of genuine world-class. The majority, particularly close to vacation resort areas, were designed by leading international names in golf architecture and constructed during the last fifteen years to very high standards, with levels of floral display that can prove a genuine distraction.

Despite Thailand having a thriving market of domestic golfers, there is ample room to play, especially in holiday areas and midweek near the cities. You can play at bargain basement prices with levels of service from inexpensive but highly experienced young lady caddies and clubhouse staff that is unmatched anywhere. With a number of good value travel packages available, this is a wonderful winter season holiday destination; an historic ancient kingdom, with a colourful exotic culture - a great place to visit for a hundred excellent reasons that also just happens to be a great destination for golf.

The country experienced a golfing boom some fifteen years ago, when more new courses of genuine quality were constructed than anywhere else outside the United States. Subsequently the economy suffered a temporary downturn but the golf courses remain, well-kept but underplayed, with green and caddie fees a mere fraction of holiday courses elsewhere. Expect typical Thai touches such as palatial clubhouses like luxury hotels, armies of attentive lady caddies and floral touches that turn golf courses into colourful gardens. All clubs have buggies, modern golf sets, even shoes and umbrellas for hire, plus refreshing drinks' shelters every three holes.

We have listed the selected golf under five regions, three within a relatively short driving distance of the capital city, Bangkok, and two more in resort areas just a short internal flight away. Many are near the sea or backed by mountains, with a good selection of 4 and 5-star hotels plus local shopping and sightseeing.

PHUKET is a very popular southern island with superb beaches and excellent golf, including the 36 holes of Blue Canyon, built around a former tin mine.

The city of Bangkok and the region to the west of it, is covered by CENTRAL. Visit The Rose Garden for delightfully floral golf and a unique cultural show. Slightly to the north-west lies Kanchanaburi, with golf near the infamous bridge over the River Kwai. The best selection of true resort golf lies just inland from the coastal stretch of Cha-Am and Hua Hin, ably supported by many excellent hotels, fresh seafood restaurants and a gentle, relaxed, seaside ambience backed by wooded hills.

The NORTH-EASTERN region lies two hours' drive from Bangkok, an area of dramatic wooded mountains with sensational views. There is a good choice of golf plus the Khao Yai National Park, where you can see undisturbed wildlife in its natural jungle habitat.

Down the south-east edge of the Gulf of Siam, well served by the fast super-highway from Bangkok, is the EASTERN region. Embracing the coastal cities of Chonburi, Pattaya and Rayong, it offers the greatest concentration of modern resort golf in Thailand. The verdant rolling courses have tall palms, vivid tropical flora and much strategic water. Top tests are arguably Laem Chabang (by Jack Nicklaus) and Natural Park Hill (by Ronald Fream), but there are some twenty others to also examine your game, as well as a variety of international restaurants and vibrant nightlife.

Somewhat cooler than the rest of the country, especially in the winter season, is the mountainous NORTH. Here you can discover the historic ancient cities of Chiang Mai and Chiang Rai, colourful hill tribes, delicate handicrafts and a number of fine golf courses including Chiangmai Lamphun, Royal Chiangmai and the absolute manicured perfection of the testing Robert Trent Jones Jr. layout of Saniburi.

PHUKET

LAGUNA PHUKET. **Banyan Tree Golf Club**, 34 Moo 4, Tambon Cherngtalay, Amphur Talang, Phuket 83110 (66 76-324 350; Fax: 66 76-324 351). *Location*: part of the Laguna resort complex, 20 minutes south west from Phuket airport. Pleasant, not too demanding modern resort course by Max Wexler and David Abell. Palm trees and water hazards open to the sea breeze. 18 holes, 6768 yards. Par 71. Pro shop, teaching professionals, driving range, chipping areas, putting greens. *Green Fees*: information not available. *Eating facilities*: restaurant and bar in clubhouse. *Visitors*: welcome. Club, shoe, umbrella, chair hire. *
e-mail: golf-phuket@banyantree.com

PHANG-NGA. **Thai Muang Beach Golf & Marina**, 157/12 Moo 9, Limdul Road, Tambon Thai Muang, Amphur Thai Muang, Phang-Nga 82120 (66 76 571 533/5; Fax: 66 76 571 214). *Location*: off Highway 4, 40 km (30 minutes drive) north of Phuket Airport over road bridge into Phang-Nga. Created by Dye Designs, this is the only true seaside course along the Andaman Sea. Demanding layout in a relaxed, remote setting. 18 holes, 7019 yards. Par 72. Pro shop, driving range, putting green. *Green Fees*: information not available. *Eating facilities*: restaurant and bar in clubhouse. Beach chalet accommodation available. Reservations and Information: (66 76 571 533/4; Fax: 66 76 571 214). Refreshment kiosks on course. *Visitors*: welcome. Carts, club, shoe, umbrella and chair hire. *
website: www.thaimuanggolf.com

PHUKET. **Blue Canyon Country Club**, 165 Moo 1, Thepkasattri Road, Maikaw, Thalang, Phuket 83110 (66 76 328 088; Fax: 66 76 328 068). *Location:* just 5 minutes drive south of Phuket International Airport. One of the premier golf resorts in Asia. Two dramatic 18-hole courses built around a former tin mine with some spectacular carries and kept in excellent condition. Twice venue of Johnnie Walker Classic. Clubhouse hotel overlooks course from crest of hill. Canyon Course: 18 holes, 7179 yards, Par 72. Lakes Course: 18 holes, 7129 yards, Par 72. Blue Canyon Golf School, driving range, putting greens. *Green Fees:* available on request. Playing rights open only to residents of clubhouse hotel and guests of members. *Eating facilities:* Canyon Restaurant, Golfers' Terrace, Lobby Lounge, Members' Lounge. *Visitors:* only by invitation or as hotel guest. Caddies, club hire.
e-mail: reservation@bluecanyonclub.com
website: www.bluecanyonclub.com

PHUKET. **Loch Palm Golf Club Phuket**, 38 Moo 5, Vichitsongkram Road, Kathu District, Phuket 83120 (076 321 930; Fax: 076 321 927/8). *Location:* in kathu village about 7km from Phuket town and 40 minutes drive from Phuket Airport. Laid out around a large lake on the site of a former tin mine, this is a pleasant course with palm trees and encircled by wooded hills. 18 holes, 6434 yards, Par 72. Pro shop, driving range, chipping and putting green. *Green Fees:* information not available. *Eating facilities:* lakeside restaurant in temporary clubhouse. Four refreshment kiosks on course. *Visitors:* welcome. Cart, club, shoe, umbrella, chair hire.

PHUKET. **Phuket Country Club**, 80/1 Vichitsongkram Road, Katu, Phuket 83120 (076 321 038; Fax: 076 321 721). *Location*: 30 minutes from Phuket Airport on main road (4020) to Patong Beach. Two very interesting and well-kept courses. (18 and 9 holes) with plenty of water hazards. Scenic, with mature flowering shrubs and palms in location of former tin mine. Surrounded by wooded hills. Old Course 18 holes, 6483 yards, Par 72. Country Club Course 9 holes, 3575 yards, S.S.S. 37. Pro shop, driving range, putting green. *Green Fees:* weekdays and weekends Baht 2,350 per round; caddie fee Baht 200 per round. *Eating facilities:* restaurant and bar terrace in clubhouse. Refreshment kiosks on course. *Visitors:* welcome. Club hire. Soft spikes only. General Manager: Mr Keat Lau.
e-mail: bookings@phuketcountryclub.com
website: www.phuketcountryclub.com

CENTRAL REGION

AYUTTHAYA. **Bangsai Country Club**, 77/7 Moo 3, Bangplee, Bangsai, Ayutthaya 13190 (035 371 490-7; Fax: 035 371 490). *Location*: due north of Bangkok on Route 1 direction Ayutthaya. Near Bangsai follow signs to course. Superbly innovative 18 holes course offering a mixture of parkland and links-style golf in an inland setting. 18 holes, 6923 yards, Par 72. Pro shop, driving range, putting green. *Green Fees*: information not available. *Eating facilities*: clubhouse restaurant, refreshment kiosk on course. *Visitors*: welcome. Cart, club hire. *

BANGKOK. **Muang Ake Golf Course**, 52 Moo 7, Phaholyothin Road, Amphoe Muang, Pathum Thani (02 539 335/40; Fax: 02 539 9345). *Location:* take Vibhavadi Rangsit Road north out of the city past Don Muang Airport. Filter left before junction with Phaholyothin Road. After 2km turn left at petrol station and then bear right at fork. Pleasant, mature course on fairly compact site with many water hazards. 18 holes, 6398 yards, Par 72. Pro shop, driving range, putting green. *Green Fees:* information not available. *Eating facilities:* restaurant and bar in clubhouse. *Visitors:* welcome. Club, shoe, umbrella hire. *

CHA-AM. **Imperial Lake View Hotel and Golf Club**, 79 Moo 4, Hubkrapong-Praburi, Highway Tambol Samphraya, Cha-Am, Petchburi 76120 (032 520 178; Fax: 032 520 098). *Location:* 25 minutes north up the coast road from central Hua Hin. Very imaginative and challenging 27 holes of golf by Roger Packard. Rolling mounds, large greens, lakes and palms. 18 holes, 6915 yards, Par 72 plus new 9 holes. Hotel, pro shop, putting green. *Green Fees:* information not available. *Eating facilities:* cafe and restaurant in clubhouse. Refreshment kiosks on course. *Visitors:* welcome. Cart, club, shoe, umbrella hire. *

CHA AM. **Springfield Royal Country Club**, Springfield Village Golf and Spa, 193 Moo 6 Huay Sai Nua, Cha am, Petchaburi 76120 (+66 32593223; Fax: +66 3259 3260). *Location:* about 110 miles from Bangkok by new highway; 30 minutes north of central Hua Hin and 15 minutes from Springfield Beach resort. This is golf of true championship calibre, part of a planned 36 hole layout. The first course, designed by Jack Nicklaus and opened in 1993 is a great test with all the usual trademarks and one of the best maintained courses in Thailand. Venue of Thailand Open 2000 and 1993/2000 APGA qualifying schools. 18 holes, 7043 yards. Second course under construction). Driving range, pitching area, putting greens. *Green Fees:* 2500 baht weekday/weekend, 200 baht mandatory caddie fee. Club rental 600 baht, cart 750 baht . Hearland Golf School. Lessons and clinics available. *Eating facilities:* lounge bar and coffee shop in clubhouse. Refreshment kiosks on course. *Visitors:* welcome. Soft spikes only. 5 Star accommodation available. Director of Golf: Toni Meechai. General Manager: Lt. Col. Kittithep Krinchai. Head Professional: Michael

van Amelsvoort (66 32 593 223; Fax: 66 32 593 227). e-mail: springfieldgolf@yahoo.com
   playgolf@springfieldresort.com
website: www.springfieldresort.com

HUA-HIN. **Palm Hills Golf Resort and Country Club**, 1444 Petchakasem Highway, Cha-Am District, Petchaburi 76120 Thailand (6632 520800 11; Fax: 6632 520820). *Location:* on Petchakasem highway just 8km before Hua Hin. Links/seaside course. A most pleasant course by Max Waxler with good use of rocks and flowers to decorate holes that mostly follow the natural terrain spilling down from wooded hills behind. 18 holes (Tiff Eagle green), 6373 yards. Par 72. Pro shop, driving range, putting green. *Green Fees:* weekdays 1.400 bhat, weekends 1,800 bhat. *Eating facilities:* international restaurant and executive bar lounges in clubhouse, refreshment kiosks on course. Visitors: welcome. Cart, club, shoe, chair hire.

HUA HIN. **The Majestic Creek Country Club**, Ban Wangkoi, Thumbol Tabtai, Hua Hin District, Prachuap Klirikan (032-520162-6, Fax: 032-520477). *Location:* 25 minutes drive directly inland on Huay Mongkil Road from Hua Hin town, backing up to low hills. Plenty of streams and water hazards on this rolling, challenging but well-maintained course. 18 holes, 6961 yards. Par 72. Pro shop, driving range, putting green. *Green Fees:* from November 2003, 1800 baht. *Eating facilities:* restaurant and bar in clubhouse. Refreshment kiosks on course. *Visitors:* welcome. Cart, club, shoe, umbrella hire. Accommodation is also provided by the Majestic Creek Country Club at the Majestic Beach Resort about 25km from the golf course, by the sea. Transport can be included. (032 520162-6; Fax: 032 520 477).

HUA HIN. **Royal Hua Hin Golf Course**, Hua Hin District, Prachuapkirikhan (032 512 475: Fax: 032 513 038). *Location:* in the centre of Hua Hin town right by the railway station. Built in 1922 this is the oldest 'proper' golf course in the Kingdom. Historic, very natural golf running back into wooded hills offering sensational views. 18 holes, 6654 yards. Par 72. Pro shop, driving range, putting green. *Green Fees:* information not available. *Eating facilities:* restaurant and bar in clubhouse. Refreshment kiosks on course. *Visitors:* welcome. Club, shoe, umbrella hire.*

KANCHANABURI. **Barrington Saiyoke Sports Club,** Sing Sub-district, Saiyoke District, Kanchanaburi (034 591110; Fax: 02 9344906). *Location:*from Kanchanaburi take route 323 and fork left 6km past town. Course is right on 6km marker. Two hours from Bangkok by road. Gently mounded course by Gary Roger Baird on fairly level site with plenty of water hazards and shallow winding bunkers backed by rugged hills. 18 holes, 6605 yards, Par 72. Pro shop, driving range, putting green. *Green Fees:* information not available. *Eating facilities:* Thai and European restaurant and bar in clubhouse. *Visitors:* welcome. Cart, club and shoe hire. 98 bedroom hotel. Swimming pool, tennis court, sauna and jacuzzi. Major Credit Cards accepted. *

KANCHANABURI. **Mission Hills Golf Club**, 27/7 Moo 7, Tambon Pungtru, Amphur Tha Muang, Kanchanaburi (reservations: 02 254 8199; Fax: 02 254 8266). *Location:* about 126 km northwest of Bangkok from Bang Pong, take the left fork and continue 15km towards Tha Maka. At Route 3089 turn left and find course on left. No expense spared on this Jack Nicklaus designed course with waste bunkers, water hazards and mature palms. Course slopes gently away from clubhouse nestling under a wooded hill. 18 holes, 7042 yards. Par 72. Hotel, pro shop, putting green. *Green Fees:* information not available. *Eating facilities:* restaurant and bar in clubhouse. Turf roofed refreshment kiosks on course. *Visitors:* welcome. Club, shoe, umbrella, cart hire. *

KANCHANABURI. **Nichigo Resort & Country Club**, 106 Moo 4, Tambol Wangdong, Ampor Muang, Kanchanaburi 71000 (Tel & Fax: 034 513 334). *Location:* about 25km from Kanchanaburi town (150km north-west of Bangkok) on Ladya-Erawan Falls Road. 27 holes of superb resort golf on land skoping down either side of the Kwai Yai River. Gentle contours, shallow bunkers and few trees offer an attractive round against a backdrop of craggy rock outcrops. Three distinct nines - River, Lake and Mountain courses. Two 18 hole combinations, 7133 and 7260 yards, both Par 72. Hotel, pro shop, driving range, putting green. *Green Fees:* information not available. *Eating facilities:* bar and restaurant in clubhouse; drinks huts on course. *Visitors:* welcome. cart, club hire. *

NAKORN PATHOM. **The Rose Garden**, Km 32 Pet Kasem Highway, Sampran, Nakorn Pathom 73110 (034 322 770/1; Fax: 034 322 768). *Location:* about one hour north-west of Bangkok on Petchakasem Road Km 32. A unique gem both to visit and to play, where the overall ambience and standards of service only enhance an interesting, mature test of golf over a level site with flowering shrubs, trees and water hazards. A genuine treat – not least from the smiling assistance of over 400 knowledgeable young lady caddies. 18 holes, 7085 yards, Par 72. Riverside hotel, pro shop, driving range, putting green. *Green Fees:* information not available. *Eating facilities:* international restaurant in clubhouse includes shushi bar; refreshment kiosks on course. *Visitors:* welcome. Club, cart, shoe, umbrella hire. *

> **THE APPEARANCE OF AN ASTERISK (*) AT THE END OF A CLUB OR COURSE ENTRY INDICATES THAT UP-TO-DATE INFORMATION HAS NOT BEEN SUPPLIED**

NORTH REGION

CHIANGMAI. **Chiangmai-Lamphun Golf Club**, San Kamphaeng-Banthi Road, Chiangmai 50130 (66 (0) 5388 0880-4; Fax: 66 (0) 5388 0888). *Location:* about half-an-hour's drive south-east of Chiangmai. Sheltered in the golden teak valley with delightful trees and many hazards. 18 holes, 6919 yards, Par 72. Golf shop, driving range, putting green. *Green Fees:* information not available. *Eating facilities:* restaurant and bar in clubhouse. *Visitors:* welcome. Cart, club, shoes and umbrella hire. *

CHIANGMAI. **Royal Chiangmai Golf Resort**, 169 Moo 5, Chiangmai-Phrao Road 26km, Maefak, Sansai, Chiangmai 50290 (053 849301-6; Fax: 053 849310). *Location:* a little north-east of Chiangmai city towards Chiangrai. Attractive course laid out in a valley surrounded by wooded hills. 18 holes, 6969 yards, Par 72. Golf shop, driving range, putting green. *Green Fees:* information not available. *Eating facilities:* restaurant and bar in clubhouse. *Visitors:* welcome. Cart, club hire. Five star 56 room hotel with swimming pool, fitness centre, massage and sauna, snooker, karaoke and function rooms. *
e-mail: rcgc@cm.ksc.co.th
e-mail:golf1@cm.ksc.co.th
website: www.royalchiangmai.co.th

CHIANG RAI. **Santiburi Country Club**, 12 Moo 3, Huadoi-Sadpao Road, Wiang-Chai District, Chiang Rai 57210 (053 662821-6; Fax: 053 717377). *Location:* about twenty minutes drive north-east of Chiang Rai. Elegant course laid out in rolling land backed by wooded mountains. Always in superb condition. 18 holes, 6981 yards, Par 72. Pro shop, putting green. *Green Fees:* information not available. *Eating facilities:* restaurant and bar in clubhouse; refreshment kiosks on course. *Visitors:* welcome. Cart, club and umbrella hire. *

CHIANG RAI. **Waterford Valley Chiangrai Golf Course & Resort**, 333 Moo 5, Tamboon Pasang, Amphur Wiangchai, Chiangrai 57210 (053 953 425-7; Fax: 053 953 447). *Location:* about 40 minutes' drive west from Chiang Rai. A well-established course combining holes falling steeply down from the hilltop clubhouse with more level, lake country. 18 holes, 6961 yards, Par 72. Golf shop, driving range, putting green. *Green Fees:* information not available. *Eating facilities:* clubhouse restaurant; refreshment kiosks on course. *Visitors:* welcome. Club, cart hire. *

FHG For full details of clubs and courses, plus convenient accommodation, visit the FHG golf website **www.uk-golfguide.com**

N. EASTERN REGION

NAKHON RATCHASIMA. **Mission Hills Khao Yai Golf Club**, 151 Moo 5, Tambon Musi, Amphur Pakchong, Nakhon Ratchasima (reservation: 02 391 9346/8; Fax: 02 221 3736). *Location:* up Friendship Highway from Bangkok; turn to Thanaratch (Km 165) then turn right at Km 20 before Khao Yai National Park. Designed by Jack Nicklaus, this gently undulating course, part of a luxurious prestige resort, is protected by dramatic forested crags and hills. Mature trees and some water. 18 holes, 7058 yards, Par 72. Hotel, pro shop, putting green. *Green Fees:* information not available. *Eating facilities:* coffee shop and restaurant in clubhouse. *Visitors:* welcome as hotel or member's guest. Cart, club hire. *

NAKHON RATCHASIMA. **The Country Club Khao Yai**, Km 23 Thanaratch Road, Pakchong District, Nakhon Ratchasima (reservation: 02 255 3979; Fax: 02 255 2168). *Location:* take Friendship Highway from Bangkok; to Pakchong District, turn to Thanaratch Road at Km 165 to Khao Yai National Park. Open nearly five years and designed by Jack Nicklaus, there is plenty of sand and water in this demanding valley course surrounded by wooded mountain environment. 18 holes, 7102 yards, Par 72. Pro shop, putting green. *Green Fees:* information not available. *Eating facilities:* coffee shop and restauraunt in clubhouse. *Visitors:* welcome. Cart, club, shoe hire. *

EASTERN

CHONBURI. **Laem Chabang International Country Club**, 106/8 Moo 4, Beung, Sriracha, Chonburi 20230 (038 372 273; Fax: 038 372 318). *Location:* just 120km from Bangkok by the new highway and 30 minutes north of Pattaya. On new Chonburi-Pattaya Road 32km. Three superb nine hole loops by Jack Nicklaus - Lake, Valley and Mountain - of championship quality. Satisfying from the normal tees; tough off the back. Plenty of variety of terrain, plus strategic sand and water. Three x 9 holes, Lake 3472, Valley 3608, Mountain 3486 yards, all Par 36. Golf lodge, pro shop, driving range, putting greens. *Green Fees:* information not available. *Eating facilities:* international restaurant and coffee shop in clubhouse; refreshment kiosks around course. *Visitors:* welcome. Cart, club, shoe, umbrella, chair hire. Swimming pool. *

CHONBURI. **Natural Park Hill Golf Club**, 159/1 Moo 2, Saensuk-Bangpra Road, Ban Muang, Chonburi 20131 (038 393 001/18; Fax: 038 393 019). *Location:* turn left at third exit of Chonburi bypass onto route 36 (keep right onto flyover). At 6km

market, turn right and follow road to course. A fine rolling natural design by Ronald Fream, spilling downhill from the clubhouse set against a wooded hill past mature mango trees and palms to several strategic lakes. 18 holes, 6807 yards, Par 72. Pro shop, driving range (irons), putting green. *Green Fees:* information not available. *Eating facilities:* restaurant and bar lounge in clubhouse; refreshment kiosks around course. *Visitors:* welcome. Carts, club, shoe hire. *

CHONBURI. **Natural Park Resort Golf Club**, 502 Moo 10, Bangpra, Sriracha, Chonburi 20210 (038 349 370/80; Fax: 038 349 383). *Location:* take routes 34 and 3 from Bangkok through Chonburi (bypass). Course is on left of main road at 109km marker. Well-established 27-hole layout with much use of flowering shrubs, rocks, waterfalls as decoration. Level site with interesting but not overly demanding holes defined by palms and water. 27 holes, A 3526, B 3483, C 3480 yards, all Par 36. Pro shop, driving range, putting green. *Green Fees:* information not available. *Eating facilities:* coffee shop in clubhouse; refreshment kiosks around course. *Visitors:* welcome. Pro-shop, cart, club, shoe, umbrella, chair hire; sports club, fitness centre, Golf Lodge. *

CHONBURI. **Noble Place Golf Resort & Country Club**, 88/8 Moo 6, Tambon Klongkiew Banbung, Chonburi 20220 (for information: 02 391 3161; Club: 01-982 0382; Fax: 01 940 3250). *Location:* leave Bangkok on Bangna-Trad Road, then turn to by-pass 344 and after right on to 331. Club is on left after 5km. Another example of the natural style of Peter Thomson and Michael Wolveridge. Rolling slopes, gentle mounds, pot bunkers and wild grasses create a seaside feel to a palm lined 27 hole course backed by wooded hills. 27 holes - A 3500, B 3500 and C 3565 yards, all Par 72. Pro shop, driving range, putting green, sand bunker practice area. *Green Fees:* information not available. *Eating facilities:* restaurant in clubhouse. *Visitors:* welcome. Cart, club, shoe, umbrella hire. Managing Director: Ekapol Chakshuraksha. *
website: www.babadoogolf.com

CHONBURI. **Plutaluang Navy Golf Course**, Plutaluang, Sattahip, Chonburi (Tel & Fax: 038 701843). *Location:* about 30km south of Pattaya towards Rayong. Take route 331 across 36 and 332, turning right under bridge at 5km, fork left, then right. Established since 1969, the course, 36 holes, is managed by the Royal Thai Navy. Well-established trees and fairly traditional design make for interesting and challenging golf on well-maintained holes in a most attractive setting. 36 holes - South 3274, East 3175, North 3374 and West 3353 yards, all Par 36. Pro shop, putting green. *Green Fees:* weekdays 450 baht, weekends 750 baht. *Eating facilities:* restaurant in clubhouse. *Visitors:* welcome. Cart, club hire.
e-mail: plutaluang1969@thailand.com
        aree1960@hotmail.com

RAYONG. **Eastern Star Country Club**, 241/5 Moo 3, Ban Chang District, Rayong 21130 (038 630 410/7; Fax: 038 630 418). *Location:* take the Bangna-Trad highway towards Rayong and route 3 all the way to 193 km marker, 58 km south of Pattaya and 2 km short of Ban Chang. Enjoyable, gently undulating course by Robert Trent Jones Jr edged with mature palms. Sand is not too penal but some strategic water hazards. 18 holes, 7134 yards, Par 72. Pro shop, driving range, putting green. *Green Fees:* information not available. *Eating facilities:* restaurant and bar in clubhouse, refreshment kiosks on course. *Visitors:* welcome. Cart, club hire. *

RAYONG. **Rayong Green Valley Country Club**, 23 Moo 7, Banchang, Rayong 21130 (038 893 838-42, 01 940 8181, 01 940 8228; Fax: 038 893 845). *Location:* club is 25 km from North Pattaya. Drive from the end of the Bang Na Expressway to Km15 on highway 36. Wonderfully natural golf created on sloping terrain by Peter Thomson and Michael Wolveridge. Low hills and lush foliage frame the links-style contouring of an interesting layout. 18 holes, Pro 7264 yards Yellow 6856 yards, Am 6835 yards, Ladies 5685 yards. Par 72. Pro shop, driving range, putting green. *Green Fees:* visitors weekday 1000 baht, weekend 2000 baht; member's guests weekday 500 baht, weekend 1000 baht. Caddie 200 baht (18 hole), 100 baht (9 hole). *Eating facilities:* international menu in clubhouse restaurant. *Visitors:* welcome. Cart, club, shoe, umbrella hire.

SRIRACHA. **Sriracha International Golf Club**, 284-285 Moo 6, Sukhumvit 7, Sriracha, Chonburi 20230 (038 338 375/8; Fax: 038 338 379). *Location:* 40km north-east of Pattaya. From Benga-Trad Highway from Bangkok, turn left onto 3241 at Sriracha, soon after Chonburi. Club on right. Host to the 1996 Thailand Open, this course designed by Gary Player follows relatively level land below the hillside clubhouse. Plenty of mature trees; watch out for the Par 3 3rd hole, 180 yards over a crocodile filled lake! 18 holes, 6227 yards, Par 72. Hotel, pro shop, driving range, putting green. *Green Fees:* information not available. *Eating facilities:* restaurant and lounge in clubhouse. *Visitors:* welcome. Cart, club, shoe hire. *

Please mention
'THE GOLF GUIDE'
when enquiring about clubs or accommodation.

Driving Ranges – England

LONDON

CHINGFORD. **Chingford Golf Range**, Waltham Way, Chingford E4 8AQ (020 8529 2409). *Location:* two miles south of Junction 26 M25. 23 bay floodlit, covered two tier driving range. *Fees:* information not provided. *Opening hours:* 8am to 10pm. Practice putting green, practice bunker; new multi-level practice mat; video, tuition available at all times. Professional: Gordon Goldie PGA (020 8529 2409).

LONDON. **Dukes Meadows Golf Club and Chiswick Bridge Golf Range**, Dukes Meadows, Great Chertsey Road, London W4 2SH (020 8995 0537; Fax: 020 8995 5326). *Location:* Next to Chiswick Bridge on A316, 1 mile south of the Hogarth Roundabout. Golf Range with 50 covered, floodlit bays and practice bunker. *Fees:* £4.00 for 50 balls. *Eating facilities:* bar restaurant area. *Opening hours:* weekdays from 9am to 10pm, weekends 8.30am to 10pm. Twelve PGA teaching professionals. Indoor digital tuition studio, individual group and on-course tuition. 9 hole, Par 3 course. Dress code in operation. Practice, putting green. Promenade Suite function room - catering up to 300 people. Professional: Malcolm Henbery (020 8995 0537). General Manager: Scott Margetts (020 8994 3314).

LONDON. **Ealing Golf Range**, Rowdell Road, Northolt, Middlesex UB5 6AG (Tel & Fax: 020 8845 4967). *Location:* A40 Target roundabout, Northolt. Golf range with 35 floodlit, covered bays. Bunker. Artificial putting green. *Fees:* information not available. *Eating facilities:* bar and snack bar. *Opening hours:* 9.30am to 10pm. Five professionals, video tuition, large golf shop, repair shop. Head Professional: Paul O'Brien (Tel & Fax: 020 8845 4967).*
e-mail: pob.golf@cwco.net

NORTHOLT. **Lime Trees Park Golf Club**, Ruislip Road, Northolt UB5 6QZ (020 8845 3180). *Location:* 500 yards south of Polish War Memorial roundabout off A40, two miles inside M25. 20 bay covered, floodlit, grassed driving range. *Fees:* information not available. *Eating facilities:* two bars and bistro (bar open 11am to 11pm). *Opening Hours:* 10am to 10pm. Two PGA Professionals, 'Geoff Buddis' golf superstore, public golf course. Social club with pool and snooker; functions catered for. Professional: Neil MacDonald. Secretary: Adam Phelps (020 8842 0442; Fax: 020 8842 2097).*

NORTHOLT. **London Golf Centre**, Ruislip Road, Northolt UB5 6QZ (020 8845 3180). *Location:* 500 yards south of Polish War Memorial roundabout off A40, two miles inside M25. 20 bay covered, floodlit, grassed driving range. *Fees:* information not available. *Eating facilities:* full bar and catering facilities (bar open 11am to 11pm). *Opening Hours:* daybreak to sunset. Two PGA Professionals, golf superstore, public golf course. Social club with pool and snooker; functions catered for.*

STANMORE. **Brockley Hill Golf Park**, Brockley Hill, Stanmore HA7 4LR (020 8420 6222; Fax: 020-8420-6333). *Location:* 200 yards down on right hand side from Royal Orthopaedic Hospital, (A5). 38 bay covered floodlit driving range. *Fees:* information not available. *Eating facilities:* sandwiches and soft drinks available. *Opening hours:* Monday to Friday 8am-10pm every day. Group lessons and academy programmes available. Professionals: James Reynolds (Head), Martyn Shoulder and Andrew Stubbs. *

BEDFORDSHIRE

DUNSTABLE. **Tilsworth Golf Centre**, Dunstable Road, Tilsworth, Near Leighton Buzzard LU7 9PU (01525 210721). *Location:* two miles north of Dunstable, off A5 Tilsworth turn. 30 bay covered floodlit range. *Fees:* information not available. *Eating facilities:* restaurant and bar (extensive menu), function suite. *Opening hours:* 10am to 10pm. Large Pro shop, repairs, tuition and group lessons. 18 hole golf course open to public. *Society Meetings:* catered for; prior reservation essential. Professional: Nick Webb (01525 210721; Fax: 01525 210465).*

LEIGHTON BUZZARD. **Aylesbury Vale Golf Club**, Stewkley Road, Wing, Leighton Buzzard LU7 0UJ (01525 240196). *Location:* four miles west of Leighton Buzzard between the villages of Wing and Stewkley. 9 bay covered, floodlit range.18 hole golf course, 6622 yards, Par 72. *Fees:* £1.50 per bucket. *Eating facilities:* downstairs bar and restaurant, first floor bar and balcony. *Opening hours:* Daylight hours. Please telephone. Group and individual lessons. Professional: James Pugh (077 7175 2143). Secretary/Manager: Chris Wright (01525 240196).

BERKSHIRE

BINFIELD. **Blue Mountain Golf Centre**, Wood Lane, Binfield, Bracknell RG42 4EX (01344 300 200; Fax: 01344 360 960). *Location:* two miles from M4 near Bracknell/Wokingham. 33 bay covered floodlit range. Parkland course with numerous lakes. 18 holes, 6097 yards. S.S.S 70. *Eating facilities:* fully licensed restaurant/bar. New Blues Bar with live jazz and food. New Spike Bar. *Opening hours:* please call for details. Manager: Jeremy Henry (01344 300220).*

MAIDENHEAD. **Bird Hills Golf Centre**, Drift Road, Hawthorn Hill, Near Maidenhead SL6 3ST (01628 771030). *Location*: on A330 Ascot to Maidenhead road. 36 covered, floodlit bays. 18 hole "pay and play"course. Professional's tuition. *Fees*: information not available. *Opening hours*: 7.30am to 10pm daily. *Eating facilities:* "Racecourse Restaurant" and Golfers Bar and terrace.*

WARGRAVE. **Hennerton Golf Club**, Crazies Hill Road, Wargrave RG10 8LT (01189 401000; Fax: 01189 401042). *Location*: halfway between Maidenhead and Reading off the A321 to Henley. Scenic course overlooking the Thames valley. 9 holes, 5460 yards. S.S.S. 67. *Visitors:* welcome. Driving range. *Eating facilities:* clubhouse with full facilities. Fully stocked Pro shop. Professional/ Manager: William Farrow (01189 404778).*

WOKINGHAM. **Downshire Golf Complex**, Easthampstead Park, Wokingham RG11 3DH (01344 302030; Fax: 01344 301020). *Location*: between Bracknell and Wokingham, off the Nine Mile Ride. 30 bay covered floodlit driving range. *Fees*: information not available. *Eating facilities:* bar and restaurant, bar snacks available. *Opening hours*: 7.30am to 10pm. Tuition, 18 hole course, 9 hole pitch and putt; golf superstore. Societies welcome. Golf Manager: Paul Stanwick.*
e-mail: downshiregc@bracknell-forest.gov.uk
website: www.bracknell-forest.gov.uk/downshiregc/

BUCKINGHAMSHIRE

AYLESBURY. **Aylesbury Golf Centre**, Hulcott Lane, Bierton, Aylesbury HP22 5GA (01296 393644). *Location*: north of Aylesbury on the A418 Leighton Buzzard road. 30 bay covered, floodlit driving range. *Fees*: information not available. *Eating facilities*: bar, bar snacks 11am to 11pm. *Opening hours*: weekdays 8am to 10pm; weekends 7am to 10pm. Professional coaching. 18 hole golf course. General Manager: Kevin Partington. Professional: A Saary.*

COLNBROOK. **Colnbrook Golf Range**, Galleymead Road, Colnbrook SL3 0EN (01753 682670). *Location*: one mile from Junction 5 M4, one mile Junction 14 M25. 27 bay floodlit, grassed range; 14 covered bays. *Fees*: information not available. *Opening hours*: 9am to 6pm. Professional: Alistair McKay. Full tuition, video assisted lessons given. *

MILTON KEYNES. **Kingfisher Country Club**, Buckingham Road, Deanshanger MK19 6DG (01908 562332; Fax: 01908 260857). *Location*: Between Milton Keynes and Buckingham on A422 opposite Shires Motel. 10 bay covered, grassed driving range. *Fees*: information not available. *Eating facilities:* full clubhouse and lodge facilities. *Opening hours:* 7.30am to 7.30pm Monday to Sunday. Professional tuition by request. Director Golf & Leisure: Major D. M. Barraclough (01908 562332; Fax: 01908 260857).*

MILTON KEYNES. **Windmill Hill Golf Centre**, Tattenhoe Lane, Bletchley, Milton Keynes MK3 7RB (01908 630660; Fax: 01908 630034; Tee reservations: 01908 631113. 7 days in advance). *Location*: M1 South Junction 14/M1 North Junction 13, A421 towards Buckingham. 23 bay covered floodlit driving range, 7 grassed bays. Two putting greens; practice area; two pool tables. *Fees*: information not available. *Eating facilities:* carvery restaurant, cafeteria, two bars, function room. *Opening hours*: 7.30am till dusk. *Society Meetings:* welcome (after 11am weekends and Bank Holidays). Three teaching Professionals, tuition, Pro shop. Professional: Colin Clingan (01908 378623; Fax: 01908 271478). Secretary: Brian Smith (Tel & Fax: 01908 366457).*

STOKE POGES. **Lanes Golfing Academy,** Stoke Road, Stoke Poges (01753 554840). *Location*: half-a-mile from Slough Railway Station in direction of Stoke Poges. 18 bay covered, floodlit driving range. Parkland course ideal for the less experienced player. 9 holes. 2400 yds. S.S.S. 62 (18 holes). *Eating facilities:* small lounge area with snack facilities. *Opening hours*: contact for details. Clubs for hire. Expert tuition available. A Golf Foundation starter centre. Professional: P. Warner (01753 554840). *

STOWE. **Silverstone Golf Club**, Silverstone Road, Stowe MK18 5LH (01280 850005; Fax: 01280 850156). Location: A43 Oxford-Northampton opposite Grand Prix Circuit. 11 bay covered range. *Fees*: information not available. *Eating facilities:* Restaurant/bar. *Opening hours*: dawn to dusk. Tuition by teaching professional is available - group or private. Corporate packages with motor sport. Contact - General Manager. Professional: Rodney Holt. General Manager: Bryan Major. *

CAMBRIDGESHIRE

CAMBRIDGE. **Cambridge Golf Club,** Station Road, Longstanton, Cambridge CB4 5DR (01954 789388). *Location*: 10 minutes from city, off A14 at Bar Hill, turn right to Longstanton B1050. 9 bay floodlit driving range. Parkland course. 18 holes, 6736 yards, S.S.S. 72. 9 holes pitch and putt. *Fees*: information not available. *Eating facilities:* clubhouse. *Opening hours*: contact for details. Buggies and trolleys for hire. Society meetings catered for. Professional: Geoff Hugget. *

HUNTINGDON. **Edrich Driving Range and Old Nene Golf and Country Club**, Muchwood Lane, Bodsey, Ramsey PE26 2XQ (01487 813519). *Location:* halfway between Ramsey and Ramsey Mereside, three quarters of a mile north of Ramsey, half a mile from Rainbow Supercentre. 24 bay driving range, 12 covered, 24 floodlit. *Fees*: information not available. *Eating facilities:* at adjoining club house, open to all. *Opening hours:* summertime, dawn to 9pm, winter to 7pm weekends. Private and group instruction arranged on 9 hole (18 tee) golf course. Coarse fishing on half acre lake and barbecues for summer months arranged. Ramsey Miniature Car Racing Club meetings at weekends. Professional: Ian Galloway. Secretary/Director: P.B. Cade.*

PETERBOROUGH. **Thorney Golf Centre,** English Drove, Thorney, Peterborough PE6 0TJ (01733 270570). *Location*: A47 Leicester to Wisbech, turn left in Thorney, first right out of village. 13 bay covered, floodlit, grassed range. Two 18 hole courses. *Fees*: £2.00 for 55 balls. *Eating facilities*: full bar and restaurant open to public. *Opening hours*: 8am to 9.30pm seven days.*

ST NEOTS. **Abbotsley Golf Hotel & Country Club,** Eynesbury, Hardwicke, St Neots PE19 4XN (01480 474000; Fax: 01480 471018). *Location*: A428 St Neots bypass to Abbotsley, south east of St Neots Junction 13 M11. 21 bay floodlit driving range, 300 yard grass driving range. Two 18 hole courses, 9 hole par 3 course. Abbotsley course is regarded by many as one of the finest golf courses in the county and combines the best of both parkland and woodland features. Excellent drainage makes it an ideal venue for all year round corporate and society days. Home of the Denise Hastings School of Golf. *Fees*: information not available. *Visitors:* welcome, golf breaks from £55.00. 42 room hotel, gym, squash courts, beauty salon.

CHESHIRE

CHESTER. **Carden Park Golf Hotel Resort and Spa,** Chester CH3 9DQ (01829 731000; Fax: 01829 731599). *Location*: on A543 east of Wrexham. Golf School. 13 bay covered driving range and short game area. *Eating facilities*: Full Clubhouse facilites and 192 bedroom four star hotel. Nicklaus Course - 7045 yards. Cheshire Course - 6653 yards. Azelea Course 9 hole, Par 3. Professional: Paul Hodgson (01829 731000).

MACCLESFIELD. **Adlington Golf Centre,** Sandy Hey Farm, Adlington, Macclesfield SK10 4NG (01625 850660). *Location*: 2 miles south of Poynton off A523, via Adlington Industrial Estate. 24 bay covered, floodlit driving range. *Fees*: Information not available. *Eating facilities*: tea and coffee available. *Opening hours*: 9am to 10.00pm Monday to Friday, 8.30am to 9.00pm weekends. 9 hole Par 3 course plus 9 hole Academy Course. Reductions for Senior Citizens/Juniors. Tuition available all the time. Professionals: Chad Goldstraw, John Watson and Dave Jeffery. Proprietor: David Moss (01625 850660).*

NORTHWICH. **Hartford Golf Range,** Burrows Hill, Hartford, Northwich CW9 3AP. *Location*: off A556 Northwich, near ICI. 26 bay floodlit driving range. Golf shop. 9 hole pay as you play course now open. Professional: (01606 871162; Fax: 01606 872182).*

STOCKPORT. **Cranford Golf Centre,** Harwood Road, Heaton Mersey, Stockport SK4 3AW (0161-432 8242; Fax: 01625 827365). *Location*: five minutes from M60 and M56 motorways. 43 all-weather covered tees, fully floodlit. Two indoor bunkers, 9 hole indoor putting course. *Fees*: £3.00 per bucket (50 balls); £5.50 100 balls. No booking or membership required. School, Junior and group concessions. *Eating facilities*: drinks and snacks

available. *Opening hours:* Monday to Thursday 10am to 10pm, Friday to Sunday 10am to 9.30pm. Changing rooms and golf shop. Group facilities and lessons available. Custom club fitting and repair centre now open. Professional: Terry Gilbert. Director: Jeffrey S. Yates

STYAL. **Styal Golf Driving Range and Par 3 Academy Course,** Home of Cheshire Golf Academy, Styal Golf Club, Station Road, Styal SK9 4JN (Office: 01625 530063; Golf Booking Line: 01625 531359; Pro: 01625 528910). *Location*: five minutes from Manchester Airport. Junction 5 M56, near Wilmslow. 24 bay covered floodlit range plus 12 outdoor bays. 10 bays on the existing range have been fitted with power tee self loading ball dispensers. *Fees*: £3.00 for 50 balls, £5.00 for 100 balls. *Eating facilities:* drinks and snacks available. *Opening hours:* 7.30am to 9.30pm midweek, 7am to 8.30pm weekends. Cheshire Golf Academy, tuition available for beginners and established players. Range is fully carpeted with target greens and two-piece premium golf balls. Latest hi-tec teaching and practice facilities. 9 hole deluxe par 3 course, USGA spec greens, 1242 yards, par 27. Professional: Simon Forrest. Secretary: Bill Higham. Golf Director: Glynn Traynor.
e-mail: gtraynor@styalgolf.co.uk
website: www.styalgolf.co.uk

CORNWALL

NEWQUAY. **Merlin Golf Course and Driving Range,** Mawgan Porth, Newquay TR8 4DN (01841 540222; Fax: 01841 541031). *Location*: on coast road between Newquay and Padstow, after Mawgan Porth take St. Eval Road, golf course and range on right. 6 bay covered, floodlit driving range. *Fees*: information not available. *Eating facilities*: use of the club facilities. *Opening hours*: 8am till dark. Secretary: Mrs Margaret Oliver.*

REDRUTH. **Radnor Golf and Ski Centre,** Radnor Road, Redruth TR16 5EL (01209 211059). *Location*: follow signs from Old Redruth by-pass (A3047) or crossroads at north country. Covered driving range. *Fees*: information not available. *Eating facilities*: coffee, tea etc. *Opening hours*: 8.30am to dusk daily. PGA Approved. Teaching, club repairs, shop. Indoor ski machine, snooker. 9 hole Par 3 course.*

SALTASH. **China Fleet Country Club,** Saltash PL12 6LJ (01752 848668). *Location*: one mile from Tamar Bridge. Parkland course with beautiful river views. 18 holes, 6551 yards, S.S.S. 72. 28 bay floodlit driving range. *Fees:* information not available. *Eating facilities:* bars and bar meals, full restaurant facilities, coffee shop. *Visitors:* welcome, Handicap Certificate required. Other facilities include large Pro Shop, full leisure facilities and 42 self contained apartments. *Society Meetings:* welcome, minimum number 12 persons. Professional: Nick Cook (01752 848668 extension 460; Fax: 01752 848456). Golf Manager: Linda Goddard (01752 848668 extension 657; Fax: 01752 848456). *

TRURO. **Killiow Golf Club & Driving Range**, Kea, Truro TR3 6AG (01872 270246; Fax: 01872 240915). *Location*: take A39 Truro to Falmouth Road. Turn right into club at first playing place roundabout (2½ miles). 18 hole golf course (Par 69). All weather floodlit driving range. *Opening hours*: 8am to 9pm weekdays; weekends till 6pm. *Eating facilities*: bar and restaurant. *Visitors*: only restricted by competitions – phone for availability. Secretary: John Crowson (01872 266876).

CUMBRIA

CARLISLE. **The Eden Golf Course**, Crosby-on-Eden, Carlisle CA6 4RA (01228 573003; Fax: 01228 818435). *Location*: M6 Junction 44, A689 to Crosby-on-Eden village. 16 bay floodlit range. *Fees:* information not available. *Eating facilities*: modern clubhouse, Fairway restaurant. *Opening hours:* 8am to 9pm. Professional tuition. Junior school of excellence. 18 hole parkland course, tree lined fairways and numerous water hazards. *Society Meetings:* welcome. Discounts for societies, company days, etc. Professional/Manager: Steven Harrison (01228 573003).

DERBYSHIRE

BRAILSFORD. **Brailsford Golf Centre**, Pools Head Lane, Brailsford, Near Ashbourne DE6 3BU (01335 360096). *Location*: on the main A52 Derby to Ashbourne road, Derby 6 miles, Ashbourne 5 miles. 15 covered, floodlit bays with bunkers. 9 hole parkland course. 6219 yards (18 holes), S.S.S. 70. Practice facilities. *Fees*: information not available. *Eating facilities*: available. *Opening hours*: dawn till 9.30pm. Tuition available. Professional: David McCarthy (01335 360096). Secretary: Mr K. Wilson (01332 553703). *

BUXTON. **Peak Practice Golf**, Barms Farm, Fairfield, Buxton SK17 7HW (01298 74444; Fax: 01298 78692). *Location:* approximately one mile north of Buxton off A6 on right hand side. Same drive as for Barms Farm Guesthouse. 300 metre floodlit public driving range offering 20 covered bays, 12 outdoor bays, sand bunker and putting green. Top quality two-piece balls and mats used, clubs for hire. *Fees*: £2.75 for 50 balls, £4.60 for 100 balls (Discounted rates for PPG range members). *Eating facilities*: drinks and snacks available. *Opening hours*: Monday to Friday 10am to 9pm, Saturday and Sunday 9.30am to 6pm. Five PGA Professionals available for individual and group tuition. Societies very welcome with advance notification.
e-mail: peakpracticegolf@aol.com
website: www.peakpracticegolf.co.uk

CHESTERFIELD. **Grassmoor Golf Centre**, North Wingfield Road, Grassmoor, Chesterfield S42 5EA (01246 856044; Fax: 01246 853486). *Location*: 4 miles M1 Junction 29 or A61 near Chesterfield. 26 bay covered, floodlit range, grass landing areas and target greens. 18 hole pay as you play course. 5723yds Par 69. *Fees*: information not available. *Eating facilities:* Bar & Restaurant open daily 8am to 10pm. *Opening hours:* seven days a week 8am to 10pm. Coaching available. Club Membership also available. Societies welcome, must book in advance. Discount Golf Superstore. Professional: Gary Hagues. Club Manager: Helen Hagues.*
website: www.grassmoorgolf.co.uk

DEVON

ILFRACOMBE near. **Ilfracombe & Woolacombe Golf Range**, Woolacombe Road, Near Ilfracombe EX34 7HF (01271 866222; Fax: 01271 342939). *Location*: Woolacombe Road (B3343). 12 grassed bays, 6 floodlit bays. *Fees*: information not available. *Eating facilities*: snacks. *Opening hours:* 10am - 7pm Summer, 11am - 5pm Winter. Facilities include tuition, tennis and bowls. PGA Professional: Jimmy McGhee.*
e-mail: DCWRanger@aol.com

IVYBRIDGE. **Dinnaton Golf Club,** Dinnaton Sporting and Country Club, Ivybridge PL21 9HU (01752 892512; Fax: 01752 698334). *Location*: leave A38 at Ivybridge, follow signs for Dinnaton Golf Club. Six bay covered driving range. *Fees*: information not available. *Eating facilities*: coffee lounge. *Opening Hours*: dawn till dusk. Professional, 9 hole course, squash, table tennis, gymnasium, sauna, solarium, steam room, 25 metre heated indoor pool, tennis court, aerobics. Conference facilities available. Professional: Douglas Gray. Secretary: David Trevarthen.*

DORSET

SHAFTESBURY. **Twyford Golf Range**, Twyford, Shaftesbury SP7 0JN (Tel & Fax: 01747 811356). *Location*: situated 4½ miles south of Shaftesbury between Twyford and Bedchester, 14 bay grassed range, 6 covered. 310 yards long with markers, flags and sand bunker. *Fees*: information not available. *Opening hours:* open every day dawn until dusk.*

DURHAM

STOCKTON-ON-TEES. **Knotty Hill Golf Centre**, Sedgefield, Stockton-on-Tees TS21 2BB (01740 620320; Fax: 01740 622227). *Location*: A1 (M) Junction 60, one mile north of Sedgefield on A177. Indoor Golf Academy, tuition and video range, 20 bay covered, floodlit range, 14 tees open and grassed, chipping and putting greens, practice bunker, target golf. *Fees*: small baskets £2.00, large basket £3.00 (two-piece balls). *Eating facilities*: restaurant and coffee shop. *Opening hours*: 8am to 9pm. Professional tuition. Secretary: Mrs J. Reynolds (01740 620320).

ESSEX

BRAINTREE. **Towerlands Driving Range**, Panfield Road, Braintree CM7 5BJ (01376 326802; Fax: 01376 552487). *Location*: take A120 into Braintree then B1053. 6 grassed bays. *Fees*: information not available. *Eating facilities:* full bar and restaurant. *Opening hours*: 8.30am till dark. 9 hole course, professional tuition, indoor bowls, squash, full sports hall and equestrian facilities.*

CHADWELL HEATH. **Warren Park Golf Centre**, Whalebone Lane North, Chadwell Heath, Romford RM6 6SB (020 8597 1120; Fax: 020 8590 5457). *Location*: on A12 opposite "Moby Dick" public house. 37 bay covered, floodlit driving range. *Fees*: information not available. *Eating facilities:* bar and snacks; function suite. *Opening hours*: 9am to 9.45pm Monday to Friday, 9am to 8.45pm Saturday and Sunday. Warren Park is a JJB Golf Centre. Seven PGA Professionals. Fully stocked golf shop, golf club repair facilities. Two piece range balls and astroturf mats. *

COLCHESTER. **Colchester Golf Range**, Old Ipswich Road, Ardleigh, Colchester (01206 230974). *Location*: next to the Crown Inn, Old Ipswich Road. Covered, floodlit range, 12 bays. Professional tuition available. Fully stocked Pro shop and repair centre. *Fees*: information not available. *Opening hours*: weekdays 10am to 9pm, weekends 10am to 6pm. *Eating facilities:* The Crown Inn, 50 yards from golf range. *

COLCHESTER. **The Essex Golf and Country Club**, Earls Colne, Colchester CO6 2NS (01787 224466; Fax: 01787 224410). *Location:* A1124 signed from A1124 and B1024. 22 bay covered floodlit driving range. Indoor bunker range. 18 hole and 9 hole courses. *Fees*: information not available. *Eating facilities:* Sports Brasserie and bar facilities. *Opening hours*: weekdays 7am to 11pm, weekends 8am to 9pm. Tuition available from 3 professional teachers. Video studio, Leisure centre - swimming pool, gym, sun beds, aerobics, beauty parlour, spa bath. Six indoor tennis courts and three all-weather outdoor courts. Full day nursery facilities. Sports injury clinic. Hairdresser. Conference and banqueting facilities. 42 bedroom hotel. Professional: Lee Cocker. Golf Secretary: David Clark.*

COLCHESTER. **Lexden Wood Golf Club**, Bakers Lane, Colchester CO3 4AU (01206 843333; Fax: 01206 854775). *Location*: one mile north west of Colchester off A133. 24 bay driving range (floodlit and covered). *Eating facilities:* home-cooked food and snacks are always available. *Fees*: information not available. *Opening hours*: weekdays 7.30am to 9pm; weekends 7am to 7.30pm. Tuition available. 9 hole Par 3 course and 18 hole main course playing over many water features. Brand new golf superstore now open. *Society Meetings*: welcome by appointment. Professional/Centre Director: Phil Grice.

ILFORD. **Fairlop Waters**, Forest Road, Barkingside, Ilford IG6 3JA (020 8500 9911). *Location*: two miles north of Ilford, half a mile from A12, one and a half miles from southern end of M11. Covered, floodlit range, 36 bays. 18 hole golf course, 9 hole Par 3 course. Individual or group tuition available. *Fees*: information not available. *Opening hours*: 7am to 10pm. *Eating facilities:* bars and diner. Banqueting facilities and conferences. 38 acre sailing lake, 25 acre country park, children's play area. Professional: Paul Davies (020 8501 1881).*

MALDON. **Five Lakes Resort**, Colchester Road, Tolleshunt Knights, Maldon CM9 8HX. *Location*: eight miles from Colchester on the B1026. 10 bay grassed, covered driving range. Mats. *Fees*: information not available. *Eating facilities*: full catering, bar snacks. *Opening hours*: 7.30am to 10pm weekdays; 7am to 10pm weekends. Lessons given to non-members, group lessons. Professional: Gary Carter.*

GLOUCESTERSHIRE

BRISTOL. **Europro Golf Centre**, Hambrook Golf Range, Common Mead Lane, Filton Road, Bristol BS16 1QQ (0117-970 1116; Fax: 0117-970 1118). *Location*: by the side of Holiday Inn Hotel on A4174 by Junction 1 of M32. 24 bay covered, floodlit range with power tees. *Fees*: £3.00 for 54 balls. *Eating facilities:* coffee shop. *Opening hours*: weekdays 9am to 10pm; weekends 9am to 8pm. Astroturf putting green, bunker and chipping green. 7 PGA Professionals available for group and individual lessons. Award-winning golf shop with club repair facilities.

CHURCHDOWN. **Brickhampton Court Golf Complex,** Cheltenham Road, Churchdown GL2 9QF (01452 859444; Fax: 01452 859333). *Location:* midway between Cheltenham and Gloucester on B4063 within Brickhampton Court Golf Complex. 26 bays floodlit and covered Driving Range and Ping Custom Fit Centre.. Adjacent practice bunker and putting green. Part of Brickhampton Court Golf Complex which includes 18 hole, par 71 and 9 hole par 31 courses. *Fees*: 30 balls £2.00, 60 balls £3.00, 90 balls £4.00. *Eating facilities*: full catering facilities at Clubhouse. *Opening hours*: weekdays 9am to 9pm; weekends 9am to 5.30pm. PGA. qualified teaching staff available for group and individual lessons. Two fully stocked Pro shops.
website: www.brickhampton.co.uk

GLOUCESTER. **Ramada Hotel & Resort Gloucester**, Robinswood Hill, Matson Lane, Gloucester GL4 6EA (01452 525653). 12 bays covered and floodlit. *Fees:* information not available. *Opening Hours*: 10am to 8.45pm. *Eating facilities*: available. Five professional instructors, private and group tuition available. Sebastian Coe Health Park, dry ski slope, golf course, indoor swimming pool, sauna, solarium, gymnasium, 5 squash courts, two tennis courts, snooker, pool, etc.*

TEWKESBURY. **Sherdons Golf Centre**, Tredington, Tewkesbury GL20 7PB (01684 274782; Fax: 01684 275358). 26 bays; 20 covered, 6 grassed. Floodlit. Bunker, putting, 9 hole golf course. *Fees*: information not available. *Opening Hours:* April to October inclusive 8am to 9 pm. October to March weekdays 8am to 9pm; weekends 8am to 6pm. *Eating facilities*: coffee, bar, pies and pasties. Group and individual tuition, Golf Foundation junior coaching. Professionals: Philip Clark/John Parker. Secretary: Richard Chatham.*

HAMPSHIRE

BORDON near. **Kingsley Golf Club**, Main Road, Kingsley, Near Bordon GU35 9NG (01420 489478). *Location*: B3004 off A325 Farnham to Petersfield road. 9 hole course; driving range. *Fees*: information not available. Professional/Acting Secretary: G.W. Doggrell. *

ROMSEY. **Paultons Golf Centre**, Old Salisbury Road, Ower, Near Romsey SO51 6AN (023 8081 3992). *Location*: off M27 at Junction 2, A36 towards Salisbury, at first roundabout take first exit then first right at the Vine Public House. 24-bay covered floodlit driving range. *Fees*: information not available. *Eating facilities:* full bar and restaurant. *Opening hours:* 8am until 9pm. Full Professional shop and teaching facilities. 27 holes.*

SOUTHAMPTON. **Chilworth Golf Club**, Main Road, Chilworth, Southampton SO16 7JP (02380 740544). *Location*: on the A27. 22 floodlit bays, 11 grassed, covered driving range. Bunker practice. *Fees*: information not available. *Eating facilities*: bar. *Opening hours*: Monday to Friday 7.30am till 9.00pm, Saturday and Sunday 7.30am till 6.00pm. Tuition available. Professional: Garry Stubbington (02380 740544). *

HEREFORDSHIRE

LEOMINSTER. **Grove Golf Centre**, Fordbridge, Leominster HR6 0LE (01568 610602). *Location*: adjacent to Leominster Golf Club three miles south of Leominster on A49. 18 bay floodlit driving range, four outdoor bays. 9 hole putting green, practice bunker. *Fees*: information not available. *Eating facilities:* full bar and catering facilities every day. *Visitors:* welcome anytime. *Opening hours:* 8am to 9pm. Professional: Phil Brookes (01568 615333).*

> **THE APPEARANCE OF AN ASTERISK (*)**
> **AT THE END OF A CLUB OR COURSE**
> **ENTRY INDICATES THAT**
> **UP-TO-DATE INFORMATION**
> **HAS NOT BEEN SUPPLIED**

ROSS-ON-WYE. **South Herefordshire Golf Club**, Twin Lake, Upton Bishop, Ross-on-Wye HR9 7UA (01989 780535; Fax: 01989 740611). *Location:* end roundabout at M50. At Ross take B4221 to Upton Bishop. At Upton Bishop turn right half a mile. 16 bay covered, floodlit, grassed driving range. Top quality mats and two piece balls. *Fees:* information not available. *Eating facilities:* fully licensed bar serving snacks and full meals. *Opening hours:* 8.30am to last balls 9pm. 9 hole Par 3 also for practice. 18 hole Par 71, S.S.S. 72 Course. Fully qualified PGA Professional, club fitting centre, Pro shop. Free junior training Saturday mornings, group lessons available. Manager: Edward Litchfield.*
e-mail: shgc.golf@clara.co.uk.

HERTFORDSHIRE

BROXBOURNE. **The Hertfordshire Golf & Country Club**, Broxbournebury Mansion, Broxbourne EN10 7PY (01992 466666; Fax: 01992 470326). *Location*: 10 minutes north on A10 from Junction 25 of M25 take Broxbourne Exit, third left Bell Lane, over A10 right hand side. Driving range with 30 covered floodlit bays and 25 grassed bays. *Fees*: information not available. *Eating facilities:* Spike Bar, Cocktail Bar. Health club, indoor pool, indoor and outdoor tennis courts, golf academy. 18 hole "Nicklaus" design course set around a Grade II Listed country house. 18 holes 6400 yards. Professionals: Adrian Shearn and David Smith. *

ROYSTON. **Whaddon Golf Centre**, Whaddon, Royston SG8 5RX (01223 207325). *Location*: four miles north of Royston off A1198, nine miles south of Cambridge off A603. 14 bays covered, floodlit, and 9 grassed. Putting green and Par 3 9 hole course. *Fees*: £1.50 for 40 balls. £3.00 per round, £3.50 weekends. *Eating facilities:* available. *Opening hours*: 8am to 9pm daily. Video, group and individual tuition available daily. Crazy golf. Professional: Geoff Huggett (01223 207325).

WARE. **Whitehill Golf Centre**, Dane End, Ware SG12 0JS (01920 438495; Fax: 01920 438891). *Location*: turn at 'Raj Villa', High Cross four miles north of Ware. 25 bays covered, floodlit, grassed. *Fees:* information not available. *Eating facilities:* full catering facilities 8am to 6pm. *Opening hours*: Monday to Friday 7am to 10pm, Tuesday 10am to 10pm, weekends 7am to dusk. Professional tuition, 18 hole golf course, practice bunkers, snooker. Professional: Matthew Belsham (01920 438326). Secretary: Andrew Smith.*

WATFORD. **Topgolf Game Centre**, Bushey Mill Lane, Watford WD24 7AB (01923 222045; Fax: 01923 222885). *Location*: off Junction 5 on M1. The latest in golf driving ranges. 44 heated bays with screens giving instant feedback on how far you hit each shot and a points score – thanks to a microchip inside each and every Maxfli XS Tour golf ball. *Eating Facilities:* Café/bar. American Golf Discount Centre and David Leadbetter Golf Academy. As seen on Sky Sports Golf Extra and Tomorrow's World.*
website: www.topgolf.co.uk

WELWYN GARDEN CITY. **Gosling Golf Range**, Gosling Sports Park, Stanborough Road, Welwyn Garden City AL8 6XE (01707 331056). *Location:* A1(M) Junction 4, follow signs for Welwyn Garden City. 22 bays covered floodlit driving range. *Fees:* information not available. *Opening hours:* 10am to 10pm weekdays, weekends 9am to 8pm. *Eating facilities:* extensive bar/catering within Sports Park. Resident Professional, tuition and shop. Extensive facilities with ski-ing, tennis, athletics, bowls, cycling, badminton. Health suite, etc. Brochure available.*

KENT

ASHFORD. **Ashford Great Chart Golf & Leisure Complex**, Great Chart, Ashford (01233 645858; Fax: 01233 663550). *Location:* signposted from Great Chart, Ashford. 26 bay covered floodlit driving range, 9 hole full course, 9 hole Par 3 course, Beach soccer, volleyball. *Fees:* information not available. *Eating facilities:* bar/cafe. *Opening hours:* 10am to 10pm 7 days a week. Par 3 course, tuition, video tuition, shop, practice bunkers. Juniors and families welcome. Professional: Cameron Cowie. Secretary: Grant Kay/John Kay.*

ASHFORD. **The Homelands Bettergolf Centre**. Ashford Road, Kingsnorth, Ashford TN26 1NJ (01233 661620; Fax: 01233 720934). *Location:* take exit 10 off M20. Signed to international passenger station, at second roundabout turn left, course signposted through Kingsnorth. 14 bay covered floodlit range. 4 grassed bays. 9 hole parkland course. Practice ground; bunker, pitching, chipping and putting green. 4 hole junior academy course. *Fees:* information not available. *Eating facilities:* licensed bar and bar snacks. *Opening hours:* 8am to 10pm. Close-circuit TV Sportsview system. Accredited as a National Junior Starter Centre by the England Junior Golf Committee. Professional: Tony Bowers. Secretary: Ian S. Johnson.

CHATHAM. **Chatham Golf Centre,** Street End Road, Chatham ME5 0BG. *Location:* five minutes' drive from Rochester Airport. Covered, floodlit range, 30 bays. Tuition available. *Fees:* £3.00 per 65 balls. *Opening hours:* 10am to 10pm. *Eating facilities:* vending area. Fully stocked Pro Shop. Competitive prices. Professional: Colin Bentley (01634 848925). Secretary: R. Burden (01634 848907).

CHISLEHURST. **World of Golf**, A20 Sidcup Bypass, Chislehurst BR7 6RP (020 8309 0181; Fax: 020 8308 1691). *Location:* six miles from Junction 3 on M25 heading towards London on A20. 54 bay floodlit driving range, Golf School and coaching studio. Par 3 9 hole course, floodlit short game practice area, putting green and bunker, golf shop, club repair service. Adventure putting course, tennis courts, cafe/bar. JJB Sports Golf Store. Eating facilities: licensed cafe/bar. Visitors: welcome, no restrictions. *Opening hours:* 9am to 10.30pm weekdays; 8am to 10pm weekends. Head Golf Professional: David Young. Centre Manager: Colin Payne.

DARTFORD. **Birchwood Park Golf Centre**, Birchwood Road, Wilmington, Dartford DA2 7HJ (01322 660554; Fax: 01322 667283). *Location:* Take Junction 3 off M25 onto B2173 towards Sidcup, turn right into Birchwood Road at Vauxhall Garage. 41 bay floodlit driving range. *Fees:* information not available. *Eating facilities:* snacks and bar food always available, dining/function room also available. *Visitors:* very welcome. 18 hole course and 9 hole course available. Teaching Professionals: Cranfield Golf Academy (Fax: 01322 667283). Manager: Julie Carter (01322 660554; Fax: 01322 667283). *

GRAVESEND. **Thamesview Golf Centre at Gravesend**, Thong Lane, Gravesend DA12 4LG (01474 335002; Fax: 01474 335004). *Location:* only one and a half miles from the A2. 30 bay floodlit, covered driving range. *Opening hours:* 9am to 10pm daily. Thamesview Golf School 9 hole Par 3 golf course, practice putting green, floodlit short game practice area, golf shop, club repair service. Head Teaching Professional: Chris Lightfoot. *

MAIDSTONE. **Maidstone Golf Centre**, Sutton Road, Langley, Maidstone ME17 3NQ (Tel & Fax: 01622 863163). *Location:* south of Maidstone on A274, first turning after Park Wood Industrial Estate. 26 covered, floodlit bays. *Fees:* information not available. *Opening hours:* 10am to 10pm weekdays, 9.30 am to 7.30 pm weekends. PGA tuition, video coaching, putting green. Professional: Robert Head.*

ORPINGTON. **Ruxley Park Golf Centre**, Sandy Lane, St Pauls Cray, Orpington BR5 3HY (01689 871490; Fax: 01689 891428). *Location:* off old A20 at Ruxley Corner. 24 bays, covered, floodlit, grassed. *Fees:* information not available. *Opening hours:* 9am to 10.30pm. *Eating facilities:* breakfast, lunch available, bar open all day. 18 hole, Par 71 golf course. *

RAMSGATE. **Manston Golf Course**, Manston Road, Manston, Ramsgate CT12 5BE (01843 590005). *Location:* quarter of a mile east of Manston village. 20 floodlit bays, grassed and covered. New 9 hole course open to the public, 2505 yards. Par 33. *Fees:* £2.00 for 48 balls. *Eating facilities:* snacks, coffee, tea, etc. *Opening hours:* 8am till 8pm weekends, 9am till 10pm midweek. Fundamental Golf School. Specialised teaching unit and short game practice area with real greens and bunkers. Absolute beginners welcome. Five PGA qualified teaching Professionals. Professional /Manager: Philip Sparks. website: www.manstongolf.com

RAMSGATE near. **Stonelees Golf Centre**, Ebbsfleet Lane, Near Ramsgate CT12 5DJ (01843 823133; Fax: 01843 850569). *Location:* near junction of A256 and B2048. 22 bay covered floodlit/carpeted range. Animated and jackpot range targets. 2 piece balls. Practice bunker, putting green and chipping area. *Fees:* 30 balls £1.25, 60 balls £2.50. Golf course club member discount. *Eating facilities:* licensed bar/restaurant. *Opening hours:* Centre - 8am to 10pm. Range - weekdays 10am to 10pm, weekends 9am to 10pm. Open every day except Christmas Day. PGA Approved teaching centre. Smart golf simulator. Golf course members' competitions and social activities. Professional: David Bonthron. Secretary: Dr Peter Nicholson.

SITTINGBOURNE. **The Oast Golf Centre Ltd,** Church Road, Tonge, Sittingbourne ME9 9AR (01795 473527). *Location*: one mile north A2 between Faversham and Sittingbourne, take the turning to Tonge at Bapchild. 17 bay covered floodlit driving range. *Fees*: information not available. *Eating facilities:* sandwiches, rolls. *Opening hours*: Range 8.30am to 10pm; Par 3 Course 8.30am to dusk. Par 3 approach course, 9 holes £5.00; 18 holes £7.00. Tuition available, golf shop. Two short mat bowls facility. Functions room available for business or social purpose. *Society Meetings*: welcome. Professional: David Chambers. Secretary: Sally Chambers. *
e-mail: mail@oastgolf.co.uk

SWANLEY. **Olympic Golf Range**, Beechenlea Lane, Swanley BR8 8DR (01322 615126). *Location*: Junction 3 M25, take Swanley exit then first on right. 17 covered, 8 open air bays, all floodlit. Putting green and practice bunker. *Green Fees*: information not available. *Eating facilities:* bar, restaurant and sun terrace, all open to the public. *Opening hours*: 10am to 10pm. Extensive group tuition by PGA qualified staff. Also snooker centre, bowling green and conference rooms.

SWANLEY. **Pedham Place Golf Centre**, London Road, Swanley BR8 8PP (01322 867000; Fax: 01322 861646). *Location:* off Junction 3 of M25, A20 towards Brands Hatch. 40-bay floodlit driving range, putting green, practice facilities.18-hole and 9-hole golf courses. *Fees:* information not available. *Eating facilities:* bar; food available daily. *Opening hours:* weekdays 8am to 10pm, weekends 8am to 9pm.*
e-mail: golf@ppgc.co.uk
website: www.ppgc.co.uk

TONBRIDGE. **Hilden Golf Centre**, Rings Hill, Hildenborough, Tonbridge TN11 8LX (01732 833607; Fax: 01732 834484). *Location*: take exit off A21 for Tonbridge North/Hildenborough; take second turning right (Watts Cross Road), follow road past station to bottom of the hill, golf centre is on the left. 36 bay covered, floodlit and grassed driving range. *Fees:* information not available. *Eating facilities:* fully licensed bistro bar serving food until 9pm. *Visitors:* open to the public all day every day, memberships available. Health and leisure centre, creche (9.30am to 11.20am weekdays), French boules - Petanque. Teaching academy and large golf discount store stocking all the top brands at discount prices. *Society Meetings:* welcome. Professional: Nicky Way (01732 834404; Fax: 01732 834484). Secretary: Vicki Brett (01732 834404; Fax: 01732 834484).*

LANCASHIRE

BLACKBURN. **Blackburn Golf Driving Range**, Queens Park Playing Fields, Haslingden Road, Blackburn BB2 3HQ. *Location*: east side of Blackburn, one mile from town centre. 27 bay covered, floodlit range. Two bunkers and two greens for outdoor practice. *Fees*: £3.85 for 100 balls, £2.25 for 55 balls. *Opening hours*: 9am to 9pm weekdays; 9am to 5pm weekends. PGA Professional: Simon Eaton. Owner: Jim Gornall (01254 581996).

BLACKPOOL. **De Vere Herons' Reach Golf Club**, East Park Drive, Blackpool FY3 8LL (01253 766156; Fax: 01253 798800). Location: leave M55 at Junction 4, follow signs for Stanley Park and Victoria Hospital. Testing championship course with 10 man-made lakes - all year round play course. Herons Reach Course - 18 holes, 6461 yards, S.S.S. 72. 18 bay floodlit driving range, putting and chipping green. *Fees:* information not available. *Eating facilities:* spikes bar serving from 7am to 6pm daily, leisure bar and Cairolis open seven days. *Visitors:* welcome. Handicap Certificate required. 164 bedroomed hotel with extensive conference and banqueting facilities for up to 600 plus leisure complex. *Society Meetings:* welcome. Secretary: Mr P. Heaton. *

LEICESTERSHIRE

BOTCHESTON. **Forest Hill Golf Club**, Markfield Lane, Botcheston LE9 9FJ (01455 824800; Fax: 01455 828522). *Location*: M1 junction 22, take Leicester exit on A50, at first roundabout turn right towards Desford, 3 miles on left. 25 bay floodlit, grassed driving range. 18 hole course. *Fees*: information not available. *Eating facilities*: food available all day. *Society Meetings*: welcome Monday to Thursday. Professional: Phil Harness (01455 824800). Secretary: G.D. Hyde (01455 824800; Fax: 01455 828522).*
e-mail: gerry@hyde14.fsnet.co.uk

COALVILLE. **Discovery Golf & Leisure**, Ashby Road, Coalville LE67 3LG (01530 811622). *Location:* follow the signs to Snibston Discovery Park at Coalville. 30 bay driving range, 18 covered, floodlit, 12 grassed. *Fees*: information not available. *Eating facilities:* licensed bar and bar food available. *Opening hours*: 10am to 10pm weekdays, 9am to 10pm weekends and Bank Holidays. Group bookings available. Golf shop, tuition, repairs. 9 hole Par 3 golf course, mini-putt. PGA Professional. Director: Michael W. Moore. *

---

visit the FHG golf website on
www.uk-golfguide.com

LINCOLNSHIRE

GRIMSBY. **Great Grimsby Golf Centre** (incorporating **Willow Park Golf Club**), Cromwell Road, Grimsby DN31 2BH (01472 250555; Fax: 01472 267447). *Location:* two miles from A180 and A46. Four-and-a-half miles from A16. Adjacent to Grimsby Leisure Centre/Auditorium. 27 bay covered, floodlit range. *Fees:* information not available. *Opening Hours:* 9am to 9.30 pm. *Society Meetings:* welcome by prior arrangement. 2500 sq ft golf superstore. All club repairs undertaken. Pay and Play and Membership available for Willow Park Golf Club. Reductions for Juniors and Seniors. European Tour Professional: Stephen Bennett. Secretary: B.J. Hoggett. *

GREATER MANCHESTER

KEARSLEY. **Kearsley Golf Driving Range**, Moss Lane, Kearsley, Bolton BL4 8SF (01204 575726). *Location:* Two miles north on A666 from Junction 16 on M60. Driving range, 10 covered, 15 grassed tees. Fees: £2.90 for 50 balls. *Opening hours:* weekdays 11am to 9.30pm; weekends 11am to 4pm. *Visitors:* welcome. Bar. Small 3 hole pitch and putt with practice sand bunker. Open to the public. Professional/Owner: E. Raymond Warburton PGA. 18 hole pay as you play course immediately adjacent.

ROCHDALE. **Castle Hawk Driving Range**, Chadwick Lane, Castleton, Rochdale OL11 3BY (01706 659995). *Location:* five minutes from exit 20 M62. 20 bay covered, floodlit, grassed driving range. 27 hole course. *Fees:* information not available. *Eating facilities:* restaurant available at club. *Opening hours:* 9am to 7.30pm. Professional tuition available. Professionals: Frank Accleton and Craig Bowring.*
e-mail: teeoff@castlehawk.co.uk
website: www.castlehawk.co.uk

MERSEYSIDE

MORETON. **Moreton Hills Golf Centre**, Tarran Way, Moreton, Wirral CH46 4TP (0151-677 6606; Fax: 0151-678 4359). *Location:* off Pasture Road, opposite Cadbury's factory. 30 bay covered floodlit driving range. *Fees:* information not available. *Eating facilities:* not available. *Opening hours:* 8am to 9pm. 6 hole golf course, 27 hole putting green, practice bunkers, golf shop, PGA Professionals, golf lessons in an indoor academy. *

NORTHAMPTONSHIRE

CHURCH BRAMPTON. **Brampton Heath Golf Centre**, Sandy Lane, Church Brampton, Northampton NN6 8AX (01604 843939; Fax: 01604 843885). *Location:* 2 miles north east of Kingsthorpe off A5009 (Welford Road). 18 bay covered floodlit driving range. *Fees:* information not available. *Eating facilities:* Spike bar/restaurant. *Opening Hours:* Summer: weekdays 8am to 10pm. Weekends 7.30am to 9pm. Winter: 8am to 9pm. Weekends 8am to 8.30pm. Group/individual tuition available. 9 hole Par 3 academy course. Professional: Richard Hudson. Manager: Simon Lawrence (Fax: 01604 843885). *

NORTHAMPTON. **Delapre Golf Complex**, Eagle Drive, Nene Valley Way, Northampton NN4 7DU (01604 764036; Fax: 01604 706378). *Location:* two miles from Junction 15 M1 on A45 towards Wellingborough. 40 bay covered, floodlit range (30 grassed bays). 27 holes main course, 2x9 hole Par 3 courses, 9 hole pitch and putt course, bunkers and practice putting greens. *Fees:* £1 for 30 balls. *Eating facilities:* Public restaurant 9am to 9.30pm. Public bar during licensing hours. *Opening hours:* 7am to 10.30pm daily. PGA qualified teaching staff available for private or group tuition; golf schools - video, etc. Delapre Park Golf Complex is a facility provided by Northampton Borough Council. Professional/Secretary: John Corby.

NOTTINGHAMSHIRE

CALVERTON. **Ramsdale Park Golf Centre**, Oxton Road, Calverton NG14 6NU (0115 965 5600). *Location:* north east Nottingham city, on B6386 Oxton Road. 25 bay covered floodlit range. 18 hole main course and 18 hole Par 3 course. *Fees:* information not available. *Eating facilities:* bar, restaurants. Food all day. Function room. *Opening hours:* 7.30am to 11pm. Professional tuition, PGA video teaching bay and custom-fit centre. Manager: N.R. Birch.

LONG EATON. **Trent Lock Golf Centre**, Lock Lane, Sawley, Long Eaton, Nottingham NG10 2FY (0115 946 4398; Fax: 0115 9461183). *Location:* 2 miles from M1 motorway Junction 24 or 25. 23 bay covered, floodlit driving range. 18-hole and 9 hole golf course. *Fees:* information not available. *Eating facilities:* à la carte restaurant, 200 capacity function suite, bar and bar food area. *Opening hours:* 8am until midnight. Professional tuition available, five PGA staff. River trips and walking available. Professional: Mark Taylor (01159 464398; Fax: 01159 461183). *

NEWARK. **Rufford Park Golf & Country Club,** Rufford Lane, Rufford, Newark (01623 825253; Fax: 01623 825254). *Location:* situated 400 yards off A614, two miles south of Ollerton Roundabout - map available on request. 16 bay floodlit driving range. 18 hole golf course. Practice greens. *Eating facilities:* large function suite and clubhouse available for social functions, restaurant with spectacular views offering a warm and genuine welcome to all who enjoy superb food. *Opening hours:* 7.30am to 9.00pm. Tuition available from both professionals. 8 buggies for hire. Corporate hospitality and Society days a speciality. Meeting rooms available. Professionals: James Thompson/John Vaughan. Secretary: Kay Whitehead.

NOTTINGHAM. **Cotgrave Place Golf and Country Club**, Cotgrave, Near Stragglethorpe, Radcliffe-on-Trent, Nottingham NG12 3HB (0115 933 3344; Fax: 0115 933 4567). *Location:* two minutes from A52 to Grantham from Nottingham city centre. 10 bay covered, floodlit range. *Fees:* information not available. *Eating facilities:* food available all day in the golf clubhouse. *Opening hours:* 8am to dusk seven days a week. Professional tuition. 36 holes of golf. Ideal for all standards. Buggies available. Golf clinics. Professional: Robert Smith (0115 933 3344; Fax: 0115 933 4567. General Manager: Mike Evans.* e-mail: cotgrave@americangolf.com

OXFORDSHIRE

DRAYTON. **Drayton Park Golf Course,** Steventon Road, Drayton, near Abingdon OX14 2RR (01235 528989). *Location:* A34 Didcot turn off, through Steventon to Drayton. 21 bay covered floodlit driving range. 18 hole Par 67 Golf Course. 9 hole Par 3 course. *Fees:* information not available. *Eating facilities:* full facilities available. *Opening hours:* 8am to 9pm. Fully qualified PGA Professional. Societies, groups and individual golfers welcome. Professional: Martin Morbey *

HORTON-CUM-STUDLEY. **Studley Wood Golf Club**, The Straight Mile, Horton-cum-Studley, Oxford OX33 1BF (01865 351122; Fax: 01865 351166). *Location:* 4 miles east of Oxford. 15 bay covered driving range. *Fees:* information not available. *Eating facilities:* full Clubhouse facilities; bar, bistro, function room. *Opening hours:* 9am to dusk. Four teaching professionals, short game academy plus practice putting green. Eight target greens complete with bunkers, fully irrigated grass practice tee and target greens. Professional: Tony Williams. Competitions Secretary: Richard Booth.* e-mail: admin@swgc.co.uk website: www.studleywoodgolf.co.uk

OXFORD. **Oxford Golf Centre**, Binsey Lane, Botley Road, Oxford OX2 0EX (01865 721592). *Location:* within city boundary, past railway station, fourth turn on right going south. 26 bay covered floodlit driving range. *Fees:* information not available. *Eating facilities:* light refreshments. *Opening Hours:*

weekdays 10am to 9pm, weekends 10am to 8pm. Two professionals, group and individual tuition available. Shop and video room. Professional: Simon Walker.*

OXFORD. **Waterstock Golf Club Driving Range**, Thame Road, Waterstock, Oxford OX33 1HT (01844 338093). *Location:* on Junction 8 M40, one mile from Wheatley, four miles from Oxford, three miles from Thame. 22 bay covered, fully floodlit, open grassed driving range. *Fees:* information not available. *Eating facilities:* full bar and catering facilities. *Opening hours:* weekdays 7.30am to 10pm, Saturdays 7am to 9pm, Sundays 7am to 8pm. Resident Professional offers tuition; large junior and adult golf academy; Pro shop with many demonstration clubs; 18-hole golf course; clubhouse with full social facilities (societies and functions catered for).

WITNEY. **Witney Lakes Golf Club**, Witney Lakes Resort, Downs Road, Witney OX29 0SY (01993 893011; Fax: 01993 778866). *Location:* two miles west of Witney town centre, turn into Downs Road. from B4095. 22-bay floodlit covered driving range. *Fees:* information not available. *Opening hours:* 7am to 9pm. *Eating facilities:* Greens Sportsbar and Greens Restaurant, Function/ Conference room. Health and fitness club includes swimming pool, gymnasium and sauna. Large well-stocked golf shop, 3 teaching Professionals. Head Professional: Adam Souter (01993 893011; Fax: 01993 778866). Secretary: (01993 893005; Fax: 01993 778866). e-mail: golf@witneylakes.co.uk website: www.witney-lakes.co.uk

SHROPSHIRE

NEWPORT. **Aqualate Golf Centre**, Stafford Road, Newport TF10 9DB (01952 811699). *Location:* On A518 two miles east of Newport town centre and 400 yards from junction with A41. 20 floodlit bay driving range. *Fees:* information not available. *Opening hours:* weekdays 9.00am to 10.00pm, weekends and Bank Holidays 7.30am to 9.00pm. *Eating facilities:* coffee bar. PGA Professional tuition available by appointment - group and/or personal lessons. Golf Club Memberships available. 9 hole, 18 tee golf course - Pay and Play golf available. Visitors welcome. No handicap restrictions. Professional: Kevin Short. Manager: H. Brian Dawes. *

OSWESTRY. **Oswestry Golf Driving Range**, Mile End, Oswestry SY11 4JE (01691 671246; Fax: 01691 670580). *Location:* signposted "Mile End Golf Club" off A5, one mile south-east of Oswestry. 11 bay covered, floodlit driving range. *Fees:* £1.00 for 30 balls. *Eating facilities:* bar/catering available to members and green fee paying visitors who adhere to dress code. *Opening hours:* Summer: 8.00am until dusk daily; Winter: 8.00am to 8pm weekdays, 8.00am to 6pm weekends. Group bookings welcome. Many "Try before you buy" demo days. Professional tuition available, fully stocked Pro shop. Par 71 18 hole golf course. Professional: Scott Carpenter (01691 671246). Proprietor: Richard Thompson.

TELFORD. **The Shropshire**, Granville Park, Muxton, Telford TF2 8PQ (01952 677800; Fax: 01952 677622). *Location:* Take B5060 off M54/A5 heading for Donnington. Take third exit at Granville roundabout. 30 bay covered, floodlit driving range. *Fees:* information not available. *Eating facilities:* Greenkeeper Bar open from 8am serving food. *Opening hours:* 7am to 10pm. 27 hole golf course, 12 hole Par 3 course, 2 putting greens, retail shop. Entertainment nights, seven function suites, and conference facilities available. *Society Meetings:* welcome. Professional: Andrew Holmes (07866 721956). *

SOMERSET

BRISTOL. **Mendip Spring Golf Club**, Honeyhall Lane, Congresbury, Bristol BS49 5JT (01934 852322). *Location:* between A370 and A38. 15 bay covered, floodlit driving range with a grassed area. Practice bunker and putting green. *Fees:* information not available. *Eating facilities:* none at range but restaurant/bar facilities available at the clubhouse. *Opening hours:* 7.30am to 8pm. Tuition available from our team of professionals. Buggies for hire April to September. There is also an active members' social club. Societies welcome by arrangement.*

LANGPORT. **Long Sutton Golf Club**, Langport TA10 9JU (01458 241017; Fax: 01458 241022). *Location:* three miles north of A303 from Podimore roundabout on A372 to Langport and Taunton. 12 bay covered, floodlit, grassed range. 18 hole golf course and large practice putting green. *Fees:* information not available. *Eating facilities:* snacks in bar, restaurant. *Opening hours:* 8am till dusk. Tuition from Michael Blackwell by appointment. Secretary: G. C. Bennett.*

TAUNTON. **Oake Manor Driving Range**, Oake Manor Golf Club and Range, Oake, Taunton TA4 1BA (01823 461993). *Location:* Junction 26 M5, take A38 to Taunton, follow signs to Oake, only seven minutes from motorway. 11 bay covered range. *Fees:* information not available. *Eating facilities:* adjacent bar/lounge, food available seven days all day long. *Opening hours:* 8am to dark. *Visitors:* welcome. 18 hole course, tuition by appointment, new golf academy and 3 practice holes; Pro shop, 4 PGA Professionals; club fitting centre - free equipment advice service and demo clubs.*
e-mail: golf@oakemanor.com
website: www.oakemanor.com

TICKENHAM. **Tickenham Golf Club**, Clevedon Road, Tickenham BS21 6RY (01275 856626). *Location:* M5 Junction 20, follow Nailsea signs, Centre on left after Tickenham village. 9 hole course, 24 bay covered, floodlit driving range. Power tees. Practice bunkers. *Fees:* 40 balls for £2.00. Members' discount half-price. *Eating facilities:* 19th hole licensed bar, hot and cold food. *Opening hours:* 8.30am to 8.30pm daily. Professionals available for tuition, group lessons, etc.

STAFFORDSHIRE

BURTON-ON-TRENT. **The Craythorne**, Craythorne Road, Stretton, Burton-on-Trent DE13 0AZ (01283 564329). *Location:* Stretton, one and a half miles north of Burton – A5121/A38 Junction. 14 bay covered floodlit driving range. *Fees:* £1.00 per bucket. *Eating facilities:* 80 cover restaurant open to public every day, two bars. *Opening Hours:* weekdays 7.30am to 10pm. *Society Meetings:* welcome, rates available. Conference and function facilities available; discounts at local hotels. Professional (PGA): Steve Hadfield. Managing Director: A.A. Wright.
website: www.craythorne.co.uk

SUFFOLK

HALESWORTH. **Halesworth Golf Club**, Bramfield Road, Halesworth IP19 9XA (01986 875567; Fax: 01986 874565). *Location:* A12, A144 to and through Bramfield, over crossroads and then first right. 13 bays floodlit (10 covered). *Fees:* information not available. *Opening hours:* 8am until dusk. Professional tuition and fully equipped Pro shop; 27-hole golf course, putting and chipping greens. Professional: Simon Harrison. Secretary: Mr D. Cotton. *

IPSWICH. **Fynn Valley Golf Club,** Witnesham, Ipswich IP6 9JA (01473 785463; Fax: 01473 785632). *Location:* two miles due north of Ipswich on B1077. 23 bays floodlit (10 covered). Practice green and bunker. 9 hole par 3 course. 18 hole course. *Fees:* information not available. *Opening hours:* 9am to 9pm Monday to Friday and 8am to 6pm Saturday and Sunday. *Eating facilities:* meals available every lunchtime. Evening meals Tuesday to Saturday. *Societies:* welcome. Professional tuition, group lessons, etc. Golf shop. Golf range membership available. Professionals: Kelvin Vince, Paul Wilby, Alex Lucas, Simon Dainty. Secretary: Mr. A. Tyrrell.
e-mail: enquiries@fynn-valley.co.uk
website: www.fynn-valley.co.uk

WOODBRIDGE. **Seckford Golf Club**, Seckford Hall Road, Great Bealings, Near Woodbridge IP13 6NT (01394 388000; Fax: 01394 382818). *Location:* signposted from A12 near Woodbridge. 12 bay fixed mats driving range. *Fees:* information not available. *Eating facilities:* available. *Opening Hours:* dawn - dusk. Golf lessons available from qualified PGA staff using GASP video analysis system as seen on Sky TV. Hire equipment available. Professionals: Simon Jay, Nic Grundtvig.*

THE APPEARANCE OF AN ASTERISK (*) AT THE END OF A CLUB OR COURSE ENTRY INDICATES THAT UP-TO-DATE INFORMATION HAS NOT BEEN SUPPLIED

SURREY

CHESSINGTON **Chessington Golf Centre,** Garrison Lane, Chessington KT9 2LW (020 8391 0948). *Location*: off A243, 500 yards from Chessington World of Adventure. Opposite Chessington South Station, Junction 9 M25. Covered, floodlit range, 18 bays. 9 hole course. Private and group tuition available. *Fees*: information not available. *Opening hours*: 8am to 10pm. *Eating facilities*: bar and catering. Tuition, public course.*

COBHAM. **Silvermere Driving Range,** Redhill Road, Cobham KT11 1EF (01932 584300; Fax: 01932 584301). *Location*: half-a-mile from Junction 10 on M25 at A3; 30 minutes from central London. Covered, floodlit range, 34 bays. Public golf course. *Fees*: information not available. *Eating facilities*: full service available. *Opening hours*: 8.30am to 9.30pm. Tuition available. Telephone bookings taken. Administrator: Claire Wheeley (01932 584300; Fax: 01932 584301).

CROYDON. **Croydon Driving Range Ltd,** 175 Long Lane, Addiscombe, Croydon CR0 7TE (020 8656 1690; Fax: 020 8654 7859). *Location*: on A222 about two miles east of Croydon. 24 bay covered, floodlit, driving range. *Fees*: £3.00 for 50 balls, £5.50 for 100 balls. *Eating facilities*: snacks/coffee. *Opening hours*: weekdays 9am to 10pm, weekends 9am to 8pm. *Visitors*: very welcome at all times, open to public. Lessons from 3 PGA qualified instructors, and club repairs available. Professional: Bill Woodman (020 8656 1690; Fax: 020 8654 7859).

ESHER. **Sandown Golf Centre,** More Lane, Esher KT10 8AN (01372 461234). *Location*: signposted from A3, centre of Sandown Park Racecourse. 33 bay covered floodlit driving range, plus grassed area. Three golf courses. *Fees*: on application. *Eating facilities*: bar and restaurant. *Opening hours*: 8am to 10pm weekdays; 7am to 8pm weekends. Cranfield Golf Acadamy *Visitors*: visitors and societies welcome. General Manager: David Parr (01372 461234; Fax: 01372 461203).

GODALMING. **Broadwater Park Golf Club,** Guildford Road, Farncombe, Near Godalming GU7 3BU (01483 429955). 16 bay covered, floodlit driving range. *Fees*: information not available. *Eating facilities*: licensed bar. *Opening hours*: 8am to 10pm. Professional, tuition and 9 hole Par 3 course. Professional: Kevin Milton.*

LEATHERHEAD. **Pachesham Park Golf Centre,** Oaklawn Road, Leatherhead KT22 0BT (01372 843453; Fax: 01372 844076). *Location*: half-a-mile outside Leatherhead, just off A244. Junction 9 M25. 33 bay covered floodlit range. 9 hole golf course. *Fees*: 25 balls £2.00, 50 balls £3.00, 75 balls £4.00, 125 balls £5.00. Discount range ball cards available. *Eating facilities*: available. *Opening hours*: weekdays 9am to 10pm, weekends 9am to 9pm. PGA teaching professionals, video lessons available. Club membership also available.

NEWDIGATE. **Rusper Golf Club and Driving Range,** Rusper Road, Newdigate RH5 5BX (01293 871871; Fax: 01293 871456). *Location*: Dorking-Horsham A24, Beare Green roundabout, left to Newdigate, in village turn right to Rusper, club approximately one mile on right hand side. 12 bay covered driving range. 18 hole golf course. *Fees*: please contact the club. *Eating facilities*: fresh food and daily specials available every day; bar. *Opening hours*: dawn till dusk. Qualified professional tuition by arrangement; club hire. Membership available, monthly payments. Professional: Janice Arnold.

NEW MALDEN. **World of Golf at Beverley Park,** Beverley Way, New Malden KT3 4PH (020 8949 9200; Fax: 020 8336 2856). *Location*: leave the A3 northbound at B282, follow sign to A3 London, entrance on left before rejoining A3. Southbound exit A3 at A298, follow A3 London from roundabout. 60 bay floodlit, covered driving range, easy tee system. Golf School, two coaching studios, floodlit putting green and bunker, JJB Golf Store, club repair service, cafe/bar. *Opening hours*: 8am to 11pm daily.

OLD WOKING. **Hoebridge Golf Centre,** Woking Road, Old Woking GU22 8JH (01483 722611; Fax: 01483 740369). *Location*: on outskirts of Woking on the Woking to Byfleet Road. 36 bay covered, floodlit range. Two 18 hole courses and 9 hole course. *Fees*: information not available. *Eating facilities*: full catering available. *Opening hours*: 8am to 11pm. Individual and group tuition. Fully equipped video bay available. *Society Meetings*: welcome. **Professional**: Tim Powell. Centre Manager: Patrick Dawson.

REDHILL. **Redhill Golf Centre,** Canada Avenue, Redhill RH1 5BT (01737 770204). *Location*: in the grounds of East Surrey Hospital, one-and-a-half miles south of Redhill. 37 bay covered, floodlit driving range. 9-hole golf course. *Fees*: information not available. *Eating facilities*: available at Causeway Pub. *Opening hours*: 8.00am to 1.00pm; weekends 9.00am. Sponsored by Golf Foundation to give free junior coaching. Lessons available from PGA qualified instructor. Private and group tuition available. Repairs service. Hot and cold drinks available. *Society Meetings*: welcome. Professional: James Edgar. Secretary: Steven Furlonger.*

EAST SUSSEX

HELLINGLY. **Wellshurst Golf and Country Club,** North Street, Hellingly BN27 4EE (01435 813456). *Location*: two miles from the A22 London to Eastbourne Road on A267. 16 bay covered, floodlit range. 18 hole course, two sand bunker bays. *Fees*: £2.00 per large bucket of quality two piece balls. *Eating facilities*: full bar and catering facilities available at all times. *Opening hours*: 7.30am to 9.30pm. Full leisure and conference facilities. Full professional staff for lessons, well stocked pro shop.

HORAM. **Horam Park Golf Course and Floodlit Driving Range**, Chiddingly Road, Horam TN21 0JJ (01435 813477, Fax: 01435 813677). *Location:* 13 miles north of Eastbourne, 7 miles east of Uckfield. Covered, floodlit, Astroturf range. 15 bays. 3 PGA golf Professionals, lessons and tuition available. Golf shop. *Fees:* information not available. *Eating facilities:* restaurant bar and spike bar, seven days, children welcome. All day food and golf prices available. *Opening hours:* 7.30am to 10.30pm. Home of the East Sussex School of Golf. Professional: G. Velvick. *

SEDLESCOMBE. **Sedlescombe Golf Club**, Kent Street, Near Battle TN33 0SD (01424 871700). *Location:* 1066 country, five miles north of Hastings on the A21, three miles from Battle. Home of The James Andrews School of Golf. 24 bay floodlit driving range, 14 covered. Residential golf school with two, three and five day intensive courses for all ages and abilities. Five PGA Professionals. Facilities include indoor video and computer analysis centre, on-site hotel, golf shop and tennis courts. *Eating facilities:* Greens bar and restaurant open seven days. *Opening hours:* 7am to 9.30pm. Group coaching and individual lessons available daily, Residential Golf School (01424 871717). Head Professional: James Andrews (01424 871701).*

WEST SUSSEX

BURGESS HILL. **The Burgess Hill Golf Academy**, Cuckfield Road, Burgess Hill RH15 8RE (01444 258585; Fax: 01444 247318). *Location:* on the B2036 north of Burgess Hill, on the Burgess Hill to Cuckfield road. 28 bay undercover, grassed, floodlit driving range. 9 hole short course. New practice bunker, synthetic grass tees (first in UK), Augusta style putting green. *Fees:* information not available. *Eating facilities:* Bar and restaurant. Tea and coffee. *Opening Hours:* seven days a week 8am to 9pm. Well stocked golf shop. PGA teaching academy including video tuition. Professional: Mark Collins (01444 258585 Fax: 01444 247318). Secretary: Mark Collins.

CHICHESTER. **Chichester Golf Club**, Hunston Village, Chichester PO20 6AX (01243 533833). *Location:* take B2145 off A27 to Selsey, golf club is on the left after Hunston Village. 27 bay covered, floodlit, grassed driving range. Two 18 hole golf courses, 9 hole Par 3 minigolf. *Fees:* information not available. *Eating facilities:* fully licensed clubhouse. *Opening hours:* 7.30am to 9.30pm. *Society Meetings:* welcome seven days a week. Video teaching academy. Membership available. Professional: John Slinger. *

CRAWLEY. **Gatwick Manor Golf Club**, Gatwick Manor Hotel, London Road, Lowfield Heath, Crawley RH10 2ST (01293 526301 (Hotel); 01293 538587 (Club)). *Location:* A23 Crawley to Gatwick Airport on London Road on right. 9 grassed tees. *Fees:* information not available. *Eating facilities:* hotel facilities at Gatwick Manor. *Opening hours:* 9am to 8.00pm seven days a week. *

RUSTINGTON. **Rustington Golf Centre**, Golfers Lane, Angmering, BN16 4NB (01903 850790; Fax: 01903 850982). *Location:* on A259 at Rustington, between Worthing and Littlehampton. 9 holes with 18 tees, 5735 yards. Par 70. 9 hole par 3 course, 3 hole golf academy course, putting green, 30 Bay floodlit driving range. Two golf academies work from the facility. *Green Fees:* information not available. *Opening hours:* 8.30am - 9.00pm, 7 days a week. *Eating facilities:* coffee shop and licensed bar. *Visitors:* welcome at all times. Two golf academies available for tuition of all standards. *Society Meetings:* societies and corporate days welcome. Centre Manager: Gary Salt (01903 850790; Fax: 01903 850982).*

TYNE & WEAR

NEWCASTLE-UPON-TYNE. **Parklands**, High Gosforth Park, Newcastle-upon-Tyne NE3 5HQ (0191-236 4480). *Location:* off A1 for Gosforth Park. 45 bay covered, floodlit range. *Fees:* £3 per 80 balls. *Eating facilities:* bar and restaurant. *Opening hours:* 8am to 10.30pm. Professional tuition, 18 hole golf course, 9 hole pitch and putt.

WASHINGTON. **George Washington Golf and Country Club**, Stone Cellar Road, High Usworth, District 12, Washington NE37 1PH (0191 4029988; Fax: 0191 4151166). *Location:* just off A1(M), take A194 then exit A195 Washington. 21 bay covered, floodlit, grassed range. 9 hole pitch and putt. *Fees:* information not available. *Eating facilities:* Bunkers Bar - hours vary, serves snacks. Buffets etc by arrangement. Tuition available. Golf buggies. Leisure club with sauna, pool, solarium, multi gym, spa and squash. Professional: David Paterson (0191 417 8346). *

WARWICKSHIRE

COVENTRY. **John Reay Golf Centres**, Sandpits Lane, Keresley, Coventry CV7 8NJ (024 7633 3920). *Location:* three miles from Coventry city centre along A51 Tamworth Road. Covered, floodlit driving range. 60 bays. Golf club repair facility. Teaching professionals using latest video techniques. *Fees:* information not available. *Opening hours:* daily 9am to 10pm. *Eating facilities:* Hogan's Bar & Bistro open every day. *Visitors:* open to the public. Large Golf Shop with all the leading brands of golf equipment. Professional: John Reay (024 7633 3920/3405).*

WARWICK. **Warwick Golf Centre**, The Racecourse, Warwick CV34 6HW (01926 494316). *Location:* A46 off the M40 (middle of Warwick). 25 bay covered, floodlit range. 9 hole golf course (Par 34) open to the public. *Fees:* information not available. *Eating facilities:* bar only. *Opening hours:* driving range 10am to 9pm, 9 hole golf course 8am to 9pm. Professional tuition. Professional: Phil Sharp. Secretary: Roma Dunkley.*

WEST MIDLANDS

DUDLEY near. **Swindon Ridge Golf Driving Range, Shop & Golf Club**, Bridgnorth Road, Swindon, Near Dudley DY3 4PU (01902 896191). *Location:* B4176 Bridgnorth/Dudley Road, three miles from Himley A449 Junction. 27 bay floodlit range (22 covered). *Fees:* information not available. *Opening hours:* 9am to 9.30pm weekdays, 8.30am to 6pm weekends. *Eating facilities:* licensed bar and restaurant. 18 hole private golf club on site plus 9 hole Par 3. Snooker table in bar.*

SUTTON COLDFIELD. **Lea Marston Hotel & Leisure Complex**, Haunch Lane, Lea Marston, Sutton Coldfield B76 0BY (01675 470468; Fax: 01675 470871). *Location:* From Junction 9 of M42, take A4097 towards Kingbury for just over one mile, take second right into Haunch Lane, right after 150 yards approximately. 27 floodlit bays. 9 hole Marston Lakes Par 31 and 9 hole Par 3 pay and play course. *Fees:* information not available. *Eating facilities:* Adderley Restaurant, Sportsman's Lounge Bar and Conservatories. *Visitors:* welcome. Professional tuition available. Golf simulator with 20 courses including Valderrama and the Belfry's Brabazon. Fully stocked golf shop. 83 bedroom hotel, leisure facilities including indoor swimming pool. *

WOLVERHAMPTON. **Three Hammers Golf Complex**, Old Stafford Road, Coven WV10 7PP (01902 790428). *Location:* Junction 2 M54 north on A449, one mile on right. 24 covered floodlit bays. *Fees:* information not available. *Eating facilities:* bookings taken from 10.30am, details on (01902 791917). *Opening hours:* weekdays 9.30am to 10pm, weekends 9.30am to 9pm. 18 hole Par 3 course, two teaching Professionals.

WILTSHIRE

SWINDON. **Broome Manor Golf Complex**, Pipers Way, Swindon SN3 1RG (01793 532403). *Location:* two miles from Junction 15 of M4, follow signs for Golf Complex. 34 bays, 27 covered, seven uncovered, floodlit range (astroturf). *Fees:* information not available. *Eating facilities:* full service available. *Opening hours:* Summer 8am to 10pm, Winter 8am to 9pm. Five PGA professionals - group and individual lessons always available. 18 hole courses, 9 hole course and nearby pitch and putt course. Restaurant available for functions and conferences.*

WESTBURY near. **Thoulstone Park Golf Club and Driving Range,** Chapmanslade, Near Westbury BA13 4AQ (01373 832825; Fax: 01373 832821). *Location:* three miles north-west of Warminster on A36. 20 bay covered, floodlit range. *Fees:* information not available. *Eating facilities:* Clubhouse open 11am to 3.30pm for food and 11.00am to 9.00pm for drinks. *Opening hours:* weekdays and Saturdays 8am to 9pm, Sundays 8am to 6pm. Professional available for lessons, Pro shop (8.00am to 7.30pm weekdays and Saturdays; 7.30am to 6.00pm Sundays). 18 hole course. Professional: T. Isaacs (01373 832808). *

WORCESTERSHIRE

REDDITCH. **The Abbey Hotel, Golf and Country Club**, Hither Green Lane, Dagnell End Road, Redditch B98 7BD (01527 63918; Fax: 01527 584112). *Location:* leave M42 at Junction 2, take A441 towards Redditch, at end of dual carriageway turn left still keeping on the A441, at petrol station turn left into Dagnell End Road (A4101) - hotel and golf club are approximately 600 yards on right. 12 bay range. *Fees:* information not available. *Eating facilities:* extended Bramblings Restaurant and Tawnys Bar. *Opening hours:* 7:00am until 8:30pm in summer, 7:30am until dusk in winter. Fully stocked golf shop. Golf & Leisure Complex . Professional tuition available. Professional: Rob Davies.

WORCESTER. **Bromsgrove Golf Centre**, Stratford Road, Bromsgrove B60 1LD (01527 575886; Course Reception: 01527 570505; Conference & Restaurant 01527 579179). *Location:* easily located at the roundabout junction of the A38 and A448, one mile from Bromsgrove town centre. Just five minutes drive from junctions 4 and 5 of the M5 and junction 1 of the M42 (exit west bound only). 35 bay floodlit driving range, new teaching studio complete with state of the art computerised video systems. Large multi level putting green. *Golf and Professional Fees:* wide range of tuition available with resident P.G.A. professionals, 'on' course, video tuition etc - tuition fees list available on request. 18 hole "Pay and Play" course (Hawtree and Son design). Large fully stocked Terry Matthews Golf Shop. *Eating facilities:* friendly clubhouse with full bar and restaurant facilities. Bar snacks or 'Daily Specials' available in spacious bar/lounge. Sky TV. *Opening hours:* weekdays 8am to 9pm, Saturdays, 7am to 9pm, Sundays 7am to 5pm (Sunday lunch 12 noon to 4pm).

WORCESTER. **Worcester Golf Range**, Weir Lane, Lowerwick WR2 4AY (01905 748788/421213). *Location:* Junction 7 M5 off Malvern Road next to Lowerwick Swimming Pool. 26 bay covered, floodlit, golf range. 9 hole pitch and putt. *Fees:* 25 balls £1.40, 45 balls £2.30, 90 balls £4.60. *Eating facilities:* cold drinks, free coffee, confectionery and sandwiches. *Opening hours:* 9.30am to 10pm Monday - Friday, 9.30am to 6pm Saturday and Sunday. Three fully qualified PGA professionals always available for teaching. Swimming pool next door. Professional: Mark Dove.

EAST YORKSHIRE

BEVERLEY. **Cherry Burton Golf Club**, Leconfield Lane, Cherry Burton, Beverley HU17 7RB (Tel & Fax: 01964 550924). *Location*: off the B1248 3 miles north of Beverley. 6 bay covered, grassed, floodlit driving range. One bunker. *Fees*: information not available. *Eating facilities*: licensed bar with snacks. *Opening hours*: dawn to dusk. James Calam Golf Academy. Professional: James Calam (01964 550924 or 07979 596134; Fax: 01964 550924). *
website: www.cherryburtongolfclub.co.uk

SCUNTHORPE. **Grange Park Golf Range**, Butterwick Road, Messingham, Scunthorpe DN17 3PP (01724 764478). *Location*: five miles south of Scunthorpe between Messingham and East Butterwick, four miles south of Junction 3 of M180. 20 bay covered floodlit driving range. 9 hole pay and play course on site. *Fees*: £1.80 for 50 balls. *Opening hours*: 9am to 9.30pm weekdays, 9am to 8.30pm weekends. Large Pro shop and exclusive golf ladies' wear shop. Smart Golf indoor simulator. Professional available.

NORTH YORKSHIRE

HARROGATE. **Rudding Park Golf**, Rudding Park, Harrogate HG3 1JH (01423 872100; Fax: 01423 873011). *Location*: lies just off the A658 linking the A61 from Leeds to the A59 York Road. Parkland course designed to USGA specifications. 18 holes, 6871 yards. Par 72. 24 bay floodlit driving range with four professionals. *Fees*: information not available. *Eating facilities*: Clubhouse open all day everyday, spike bar. *Visitors*: welcome at all times, must have a handicap certificate. Shop and buggies available all year round with all year weather buggy tracks, caddies on request. Society and corporate days welcome. Professional: Mark Moore (01423 873400). e-mail: golf.admin@ruddingpark.com

SALTBURN. **Hunley Hall Golf Club & Hotel**, Brotton, Saltburn TS12 2QQ (01287 676216; Fax: 01287 678250). *Location:* off A174 at St. Margarets Way in Brotton. Signposted through housing estate, approximately half-a-mile to club. 12 bay floodlit driving range, large practice and chipping area. Picturesque 27 hole coastal courses adjacent to Heritage Coast. *Fees:* £3.50 per 100 balls. *Eating facilities:* excellent facilities including two restaurants, lounge bar, spike bar, golfers' bar; quality food available all day, every day. *Opening hours:* Summer - 8am to 8pm, 6pm weekends and Bank Holidays. Winter - 8am till dusk, floodlit Wednesday, Thursday and Friday to 7.30pm. Two Star Hotel on site. Club hire, buggy hire and tuition available. *Society Meetings:* welcome Monday to Saturday, packages available. Golfing Holidays available. Professional: Andrew Brook (Tel & Fax: 01287 677444). Secretary: Liz Lillie (01287 676216; Fax: 01287 678250). e-mail: enquiries@hunleyhall.co.uk e-mail: asbrook-golf@18global.co.uk website: www.hunleyhall.co.uk

WEST YORKSHIRE

BRADFORD. **Shay Grange Golf Centre**, Long Lane, off Bingley Road, Bradford BD9 6RX (01274 491945). *Location:* take the A650 Bradford to Bingley road, turn left at Cottingley lights, the Centre will be found on the left after two miles. 32 bay covered, floodlit, grassed range. *Fees:* information not available. *Eating facilities:* fully licensed bar and catering facilities. *Opening hours:* weekdays 9am to 9pm, weekends and Bank Holidays 7am to 9pm. 9 hole (Par 29) course, Golf Academy, all weather putting green, sand bunker, grass short game area.Tuition. Golf clinics - Juniors, Senior Citizens, Ladies. Golf shop staffed by qualified PGA professionals. Manager: T. Grunwell.*

BRIGHOUSE. **Willow Valley Golf and Country Club**, Highmoor Lane, off Walton Lane, Clifton, Brighouse HD6 4JB (01274 878624; Fax: 01274 852805). *Location:* Junction 25 off M62 to Brighouse A644, right at roundabout A643, 2 miles on right. 24 bay, covered, floodlit, grassed driving range. 18 hole and 9 hole courses. *Fees:* information not available. *Eating facilities:* fully licensed bar and catering. Junior Golf Foundation courses and 3 hole floodlit golf course. Professional: Julian Haworth. *
website: www.wvgc.co.uk

HUDDERSFIELD. **Stadium Golf Driving Range**, The Alfred Macalpine Stadium, Stadium Way, Huddersfield HD1 6PG (01484 452564; Fax: 01484 452540). *Location:* off A62 centre of Huddersfield, signposted the Macalpine Stadium. 30 bay covered, floodlit driving range, range grassed. *Fees:* information not available. *Eating facilities:* snack bar serving sandwiches, etc., licensed bar. *Opening hours:* Weekdays 9am to 10pm (last balls 9.30pm). Weekends 9am to 7pm (last balls 6.30pm). State of the art Panasonic split screen video lessons with PGA qualified instructors. Corporate and group evenings a speciality. Team and video golf fun for juniors to seniors and all in between. Well stocked shop with all major brands. An excellent place to learn golf. Professional: Simon Roberts.*

LEEDS. **Leeds Golf Centre**, Wike Ridge Lane, Shadwell, Leeds LS17 9JW (0113 2886000; Fax: 0113 2886185). *Location:* two miles north of Leeds between A61 and A58 at the village of Wike. 19 bay covered, floodlit range. *Fees:* basket of balls £2.50. *Eating facilities:* bar/brasserie open 8.30am to 10pm. *Opening hours:* 7am to 10pm. 3 resident teaching professionals, 18 hole championship course, 12 hole Par 3 course. Professional: Mark Pinkett. Managing Director: Robert Bailey.

Driving Ranges – Scotland

ABERDEEN. BANFF & MORAY

ABERDEEN. **Kings Links Golf Centre**, Golf Road, Aberdeen AB24 1RZ (01224 641577; Fax: 01224 639410). *Location:* behind Pittodrie Stadium, on the Kings Links, by the beach. 58 covered bays on two tiers, floodlit range. *Fees:* information not available. *Eating facilities:* vended drinks and snacks. *Opening hours:* 9am to 10pm weekdays, 9am to 6pm weekends. Adjoins Kings Links Golf Course, PGA qualified Professionals for tuition and club repair. Short game area and putting green. Concessions available for Senior Citizens and under 14s. 3000 sq ft golf superstore with indoor short game centre and specialist Callaway shop. State of the art video academy. Beginners welcome. PGA Professional: David McDowell.*

AYRSHIRE & ARRAN

DAILLY. **Brunston Castle Golf Course**, Dailly, Girvan KA26 9GD (01465 811471). *Location:* five miles north of Girvan on B471. *Fees:* information not available. *Eating facilities:* full bar and restaurant facilities. *Opening hours:* 8am to 11pm (Summer). 18 hole championship course in most scenic part of Ayrshire. Driving range. Full PGA tuition by professional, full practice facilities. PGA Professional: Stephen Forbes.*
website: www.brunstoncastle.co.uk

DUMFRIES & GALLOWAY

GRETNA. **Gretna Golf Course**, Gretna DG16 5HD (01461 337362). *Location:* half-a-mile south west of M74 and A75 junction, half-a-mile on west side of Gretna. 14 bay covered driving range, 7 bays grassed. 9 hole golf course. *Fees:* information not available. *Eating facilities:* available. *Opening Hours:* 10am to dark. *

DUNDEE & ANGUS

DUNDEE. **Ballumbie Castle Golf Club,** 3 Old Quarry Road, Off Ballumbie Road, Dundee DD4 0SY (01382 730026; Fax: 01382 730008). *Location:* one and a half miles north of Claypotts Junction, less than 2 miles from Dundee City Centre. 22 bay floodlit driving range, putting green, chipping green. 18 hole course. *Fees:* information not available. *Eating facilities:* clubhouse facilities with menu and full bar. Public house licence. *Opening hours:* 9am to 9pm

weekdays, 9am to 7pm weekends. Tuition available. *Society Meetings:* welcome, please telephone for details. Professional: Lee Sutherland (01382 770028).*
e-mail: ballumbie2000@yahoo.com
website: www.ballumbiegolf.com

EDINBURGH & LOTHIANS

EDINBURGH. **Braid Hills Shop and Golf Range**, 91 Liberton Drive, Edinburgh EH16 6NS (0131-658 1111; Fax: 0131-672 1411). *Location:* leave Edinburgh bypass at Straiton Junction, head towards city centre, take left turn at second set of traffic lights, proceed half-a-mile along Liberton Drive. 32 bay covered, floodlit astroturf range. *Fees:* information not available. *Opening Hours:* 10am to 9pm weekdays, 9am to 6pm weekends. Scotland's top Professionals available for group and individual tuition. S.A.S video tuition. Professionals: Ian Young, Colin Brooks, Sandy Stephen, Mark Berrie, Paul Malone. *

EDINBURGH. **Port Royal Golf Driving Range**, Eastfield Road, Ingliston, Edinburgh EH28 8TR (0131-333 4377). *Location:* situated next to Edinburgh Airport. Recently refurbished to cater for golfers of every ability. 25 covered, floodlit practice bays, 17 outside bays, double teaching studio with swing analysis software, 100 square yard Himalayan putting green, 9 hole Par 3 golf course.PGA Professionals and tuition. *Fees:* information not available. *Eating facilities:* licensed cafe/bar area, snacks served all day. *Opening hours:* 10am to 10pm summer, 10am to 9pm winter. Open all year. General Manager/Head Professional: Keith Pickard. *

EDINBURGH near. **Melville Golf Centre, Golf Course, Range & Shop**, Lasswade EH18 1AN (0131-663 8038; Fax: 0131-654 0814). *Location:* south of Edinburgh, three minutes from City Bypass on A7 South (signposted). 22 floodlit, covered bays plus 12 bays. 300 yards long. *Fees:* £2.50 per 50 balls and concessions. Happy hour 5-6pm every day. *Eating facilities:* hot and cold vended drinks, sandwiches, crisps, etc. *Opening hours:* weekdays 9am to 10pm, weekends 9am to 8pm. Full equipment and shoe hire. Repairs. Golf shop fully stocked, ladies, gents, and juniors; professional tuition; practice bunker, putting green, 4 hole practice area, pay & play 9-hole golf course, par 66. Children under 14 must be accompanied by an adult. A Golf Foundation Starter Initiative Centre. Professional: Gary Carter. Owners Mr and Mrs MacFarlane.
e-mail: golf@melvillegolf.co.uk
website: www.melvillegolf.co.uk

FIFE

ST ANDREWS. **St Andrews Links Trust Golf Practice Centre**, St Andrews, KY16 9SF (01334 474489; Fax: 01334 479555). *Location:* situated parallel to the Old Course, just 10 minutes' walk from the town centre. 12 floodlit indoor bays, 32 outdoor bays, 12 floodlit bays. *Fees:* information not available. *Eating facilities:* light refreshments and seated viewing area. *Opening hours:* 7am to 9pm daily from 1st May - 31st August; 8am to 9pm from 1st September - 30 April. Pitching, putting, bunker area using own balls. Golf club hire available. Locker rooms. Centre Manager: Brendan Duffy (01334 474489).*

GLASGOW

UDDINGSTON. **Clydeway Golf Centre**, Blantyre Farm Road, Uddingston G71 7RR (0141-641 8899). *Location:* near Glasgow Zoo. 25 covered floodlit bays. *Fees:* information not available. Professional tuition. Group rates for parties, schools, colleges, works, offices, etc. Now incorporates Nevada Bob's golf discount superstore, target golf competition. *

HIGHLANDS

INVERNESS. **Loch Ness Golf Course**, Castle Heather, Inverness IV2 6AA (01463 713335; Fax: 01463 712695). *Location:* on the southern outskirts of Inverness, heading west along the new ring road. 20 bay covered, floodlit driving range. 18 hole, par 73 golf course. 6493 yards yellow, 6772 yards white. *Fees:* information not available. *Eating facilities:* Restaurant and lounge bar. *Opening hours:* Monday to Saturday 8am to 10pm daily. *Visitors:* welcome, buggies, carts and caddies available. *Society Meetings:* welcome by prior arrangement. Professional tuition. Professional: Martin Piggot. Secretary: Neil D. Hampton. *
e-mail: info@golflochness.com
website: www.golflochness.com

PERTH & KINROSS

BLAIRGOWRIE. **Strathmore Golf Centre Driving Range**. Leroch, Alyth, Blairgowrie PH11 8NZ (01828 633322; Fax: 01828 633533). *Location:* one mile south of Alyth, (off the A926 Alyth-Kirriemuir Road). 10 bay floodlit driving range. *Fees:* information not available. *Eating facilities:* restaurant and bar at Clubhouse . *Opening hours:* dawn to 10pm. 18 and 9 hole courses available. Managing Director: Pat Barron.*
e-mail: enquiries@strathmoregolf.com
website: www.strathmoregolf.com

MIDDLEBANK. **Middlebank Golf Range**, Middlebank, Errol PH2 7SX (01821 670320). *Location:* midway between Perth and Dundee on the A90. 23 bay floodlit driving range; 7 covered, 16 grassed. *Fees:* information not available. *Eating facilities:* coffee, sandwiches, etc. available. *Opening Hours:* Summer 9am to 9pm 7 days, Winter 9am to 5pm 7 days. PGA professional for tuition by appointment, and well stocked golf shop. *

SCONE. **Murrayshall Golf Range**, Murrayshall Hotel & Golf Courses, Scone PH2 7PH (01738 554804; Fax: 01738 552595). *Location:* 3 miles outside Perth (NE) off A94. 18 bay covered, floodlit driving range, 11 grassed, bunkers. Two 18 hole golf courses. *Fees:* £2.00 for 50 balls. Discount Multi Cards £17.50 for 10 x 50 balls. *Eating facilities:* 4 Star Hotel and golf clubhouse on site. *Opening hours:* Daylight until 9:30pm. Video analysis tuition. Professional: Alan Reid
e-mail: golf@murrayshall.co.uk
website: www.murrayshall.co.uk

RENFREWSHIRE

RENFREW. **John Mulgrew Normandy Golf Centre**, Inchinnan Road, Renfrew PA4 9EG (0141-886 7477; Fax: 0141-885 0786). *Location:* take M8, then take Glasgow Airport turn-off, then take Renfrew Road one mile away. 20 bays covered, 5 bays short game area. *Fees:* £2.00 for 50 balls, £4.00 for 100 balls. *Opening hours:* 9.30am to 9pm Mon-Fri, 9.30am to 6pm weekends (last token 30 mins before closing). *Eating facilities:* full hotel facilities. Professional, assistants, tuition anytime. Adjacent to Renfrew Golf Club. Large comprehensive stock of all leading golf equipment. Director: N. Carlin.

FHG

Visit the FHG website
www.holidayguides.com
for details of the wide choice of accommodation
featured in the full range of FHG titles

Driving Ranges – Wales

ANGLESEY & GWYNEDD

ANGLESEY. **Penrhyn Golf Complex,** Llanddaniel - Fâb LL60 6NN (01248 421150). *Location:* A5 turn off at Star Crossroads taking Llanddaniel road. Follow Brown Tourism signs from the village. *Course:* 14 bay covered and floodlit driving range, 9 hole golf course. *Fees:* 100 balls £3.50, 50 balls £2.50. *Visitors:* no restrictions. Professional: Paul Lovell (Visiting). Owner: Mr W.R. Carter.

PWLLHELI. **Llyn Golf Centre**, Pen-y-Berth, Penrhos, Pwllheli LL53 7HG (01758 701200). *Location:* Situated off the A499 between Pwllheli and Abersoch. 15 covered floodlit bays and bunker practice area. Hire clubs available. *Fees:* information not available. *Eating facilities:* coffee shop. *Opening hours:* open daily from 9am until 7pm during the summer; 9am to 5pm during the winter. Discount golf shop. Professionals from local clubs available for tuition (ie Nefyn, Abersoch, Pwllheli).

NORTH WALES

CHESTER near. **Bannel Golf Driving Range**, Mold Road, Penymynydd, Near Chester CH4 0EN (01244 544639). *Location:* A5118 Penymynydd to Mold road, 7 miles from Chester. 10 bay covered floodlit range; three bays open. *Fees:* information not available. *Eating facilities:* light refreshments available. *Opening hours:* 10am to 9pm weekdays, 10am to 6pm weekends. 9 hole putting green, golf shop. Lessons from PGA Professional by appointment. Proprietors: L.J. & J. Povey (01244 544639).*

ST ASAPH. **North Wales Golf Driving Range and 9 hole Course**, Llannerch Park, St Asaph LL17 0BD (01745 730805). *Location:* on the A525 between St Asaph and Trefnant, one-and-a-quarter miles from St Asaph Cathedral. 14 bay covered, floodlit driving range. *Fees:* £1.00 for 30 balls. *Eating facilities:* refreshments, hot and cold drinks, sweets, biscuits, crisps. *Opening hours:* 10am to 9pm seven days a week during Summer, early closing in Winter 5pm Friday to Monday. Lessons with non-resident Professional by arrangement £9.00 per half hour. 9 hole course also on site - £3.00 pay and play. Non-membership Complex. Secretary: Lily Gresley Jones.

POWYS

CRADOC. **Cradoc Golf Club**, Penoyre Park, Cradoc, Brecon LD3 9LP (01874 623658; Fax: 01874 611711). *Location:* about two miles north of the market town of Brecon, off B4520 Upper Chapel Road (signposted) past Brecon Cathedral. 12-bay undercover floodlit driving range. *Fees:* information not available. *Eating facilities:* full catering facilities daily except Mondays. *Opening hours:* 8.00am till 8.45pm. Tuition, 18 hole golf course. Professional: R.W. Davies (01874 625524). Secretary: Mrs E.G. Price (01874 623658).*
e-mail: secretary@cradoc.co.uk
website: www.cradoc.co.uk

SOUTH WALES

ABERGAVENNY. **Wernddu Golf Centre**, Old Ross Road, Abergavenny NP7 8NG (01873 856223; Fax: 01873 852177). *Location:* one and a half miles east of Abergavenny on B4521 (off A465). 26 bay floodlit driving range. *Fees:* information not available. *Eating facilities:* lounge bar, bar snacks. *Opening hours:* 7.30am to 10.30pm. *Visitors:* welcome. Professional tuition, 9 hole pitch and putt and 18 hole Par 67 golf course.

BARRY. **South Wales Golf Range and Course**, Port Road East, Barry (Range: 01446 742434; Mobile: 07986 738744). *Location:* A4050 road Cardiff to Barry. 16 covered floodlit bays. *Fees:* information not available. *Opening hours:* weekdays 9am to 8pm; weekends 9am to 6pm. Professional tuition available from Simon Cox (three times Welsh Champion); 9-hole Par 3 course.

CAERPHILLY. **Virginia Park Golf Club**, Virginia Park, Caerphilly CF8 1LP (029 2086 7891). *Location:* off Pontygwindy Road, next to recreation centre. 20 bay covered, floodlit, grassed driving range. *Fees:* information not available. *Eating facilities:* licensed bar in clubhouse, full catering. Coffee shop in driving range. *Opening hours:* Weekdays 10.30am to 10pm. Weekends 7am to 7pm seven days a week. Professional: Richard Barter. Secretary: Carol Lewis.*

CHEPSTOW: **Dewstow Golf Club**, Caerwent, Chepstow NP6 4AQH (01291 430444; Fax: 01291 425816). *Location:* Off A48 at Caerwent, between Chepstow and Newport, four miles from Severn Bridge. 20 bay floodlit, covered golf range. Two 18 hole courses. *Fees:* information not available. *Eating facilities:* restaurant, bars. *Opening hours:* on application. *Society Meetings:* welcome weekdays. Limited weekends. Professional: Kim Dobson. Golf Secretary: Eric Tose (01291 430444; Fax: 01291 425816). Booking Secretary: Hayley Battle.*

visit the FHG golf website on

www.uk-golfguide.com

COEDKERNEW. **Parc Golf Club**, Church Lane, Coedkernew NP1 9TU (01633 680933). *Location:* Junction 28 M4, then A48 towards Cardiff. 38 bay covered, floodlit driving range. *Fees:* information not available. *Eating facilities:* excellent full facilities. *Opening Hours:* weekdays 7.30am to 10pm, weekends 7.30am to 8.30pm. Three Professionals, individual and group tuition, excellent shop. Function suite, corporate and society days organised. Weddings, seminars, private parties catered for. *

CWMBRAN. **Greenmeadow Golf and Country Club**, Treherbert Road, Croesyceiliog, Cwmbran NP44 2BZ (01633 869321; Fax: 01633 868430). *Location:* M4 Junction 26 five miles north on A4042. Turn right at brown tourist sign. Golf Course & Range next to Gwent Crematorium. 26 bay covered floodlit driving range. *Fees:* please phone for details and prices as there are many different packages and options. *Eating facilities:* lounge bar, patio coffee lounge and restaurant, private function room. *Opening hours:* 8am to 10pm all year. *Visitors:* welcome. Professional tuition by appointment. Six floodlit all-weather tennis courts, 18 hole parkland golf course, putting green. Range situated with panoramic views, facing easterly. Professional: Dave Woodman (01633 862626. Fax: 01633 868430). Secretary: P. Richardson (01633 869321).*

SWANSEA. **Gowerton Golf Range**, Victoria Road, Gowerton, Swansea, SA4 3AB (01792 875188; Fax: 01792 874288). 20 covered bays, 8 grassed, all floodlit. Bunker. *Fees*: £3.50 for 70 balls. *Eating facilities*: diner, hot and cold meals available. *Opening hours*: 10am to 9pm, closed at 7pm winter weekends. Tuition available. Putting green, golf course. Professional: Mike Hobbs.
e-mail: stevenbromham@beeb.net
website: www.gowertongolfrange.com

Please mention
'THE GOLF GUIDE'
when enquiring about
clubs or accommodation.

Other specialised
FHG PUBLICATIONS
Published annually: available in all good bookshops or direct from the publisher.

PETS WELCOME! £7.99
Recommended **COUNTRY HOTELS OF BRITAIN** £6.99
Recommended **COUNTRY INNS & PUBS** £6.99
Recommended **SHORT BREAK HOLIDAYS IN BRITAIN** £6.99

FHG PUBLICATIONS LTD,
Abbey Mill Business Centre, Seedhill, Paisley PA1 ITJ
Tel: 0141-887 0428 • Fax: 0141-889 7204
e-mail: fhg@ipcmedia.com • website: www.holidayguides.com

PLEASE MENTION THIS GUIDE WHEN YOU WRITE OR PHONE TO ENQUIRE ABOUT CLUBS OR ACCOMMODATION.

Driving Ranges – Ireland

NORTHERN IRELAND

ANTRIM

NEWTOWNABBEY. **Ballyearl Golf and Leisure Centre**, 585 Doagh Road, Newtownabbey BT36 8RZ (028 9084 0899). *Location:* from Belfast take M2 then A8 to Larne, half a mile through second roundabout following exit from motorway turn right to Mossley. Ballyearl one mile on left. 24 bay covered, floodlit range, large grassed area. *Fees:* information not available. *Eating facilities:* squash club with bar facilities. *Opening hours:* 9.30am to 9.30pm. 9 hole Par 3 course, PGA Golf Professional, tuition, fully stocked golf shop, repairs. Squash court, fitness suite, arts theatre.*

ARMAGH

CRAIGAVON. **Craigavon Golf and Ski Club**, Turmoyra Lane, Lurgan, Craigavon (028 3832 6606; Fax: 028 3834 7272). *Location:* half a mile from motorway, one mile from town centre, adjacent to ski slope. Driving range. 18-hole course, 9-hole par 3 course, 12-hole pitch and putt. *Fees:* information not available. *Eating facilities:* full restaurant facilities. *Visitors:* always welcome. Modern clubhouse, showers and lockers. *Society Meetings:* welcome - book beforehand. Professional: D. Paul. *

Co. DOWN

KNOCKBRACKEN. **Mount Ober Golf and Country Club**, 24 Ballymaconaghy Road, Knockbracken, Belfast BT8 6SB (028 9079 5666; Fax: 028 9070 5862). *Location:* outskirts of Belfast, approximately three miles from the centre along Ormeau Road to "Four Winds" public house and restaurant. 36 bays covered, floodlit, and grassed. *Fees:* £3.90 for 100 balls, £2.90 for 70 balls, £2.00 for 35 balls. *Eating facilities:* bar open seven days a week during normal opening hours, catering available seven days a week 11am to 10pm. *Opening hours:* 10am to11pm. Tuition available at Golf Academy by PGA professionals. Snooker, playing machines. Professional: (028 9070 1648). Secretary: (028 9079 5666).
e-mail: mt.ober@ukonline.co.uk

WARRENPOINT. **Pat Trainor's Golf Academy,** Milltown Street, Burren, Warrenpoint BT34 3RJ (028 4177 3247). *Location:* six miles south of Newry, at Warrenpoint roundabout turn left for Burren: approximately one mile. Driving range - 10 covered, 20 grassed bays, all floodlit. 9 hole pitch and putt course. *Fees:* £3.00 for 50 balls, £3.50 for 80 balls, £4.00 for 120 balls. *Opening hours:* weekdays 10am to 10pm; weekends 10am to 8pm. Tuition available at all times for individuals, groups and schools. Owner/ Professional: Pat Trainor.

FERMANAGH

ENNISKILLEN. **Ashwoods Golf Centre**, Sligo Road, Enniskillen (028 6632 5321; Fax: 028 6632 5874). *Location:* one and a half miles west of Enniskillen on main Sligo Road. 7 bay covered, floodlit range. *Fees:* information not available. *Eating facilities:* none on site, available 300 yards away. *Opening hours:* 9am to 10pm summer, 9am to 7pm winter. Professional lessons. Professional golf shop stocking full range of clubs, clothes and all golf accessories.*

LONDONDERRY

LIMAVADY. **Roe Park Golf Club**, Radisson SAS Roe Park Resort, Roe Park, Limavady BT49 9LB (028 777 6015; Fax: 028 7772 2313). *Location:* on main A2 Londonderry-Limavady Road, 16 miles from Londonderry and one mile from Limavady. 10 covered, floodlit, astroturfed and 6 uncovered bays. 18 hole parkland course. *Fees:* information not available. *Eating facilities:* Coach Brasserie. *Opening hours:* 8am until 10pm, golf course open from 8am until 8pm. PGA Tuition available. Professional: Seamus Duffy. Secretary: Don Brockerton.

LONDONDERRY. **Foyle International Golf Centre**, 12 Alder Road, Londonderry BT48 8DB (028 71 352222; Fax: 028 71 353967). *Location:* one and a half miles from Foyle Bridge towards Moville, Co Donegal. 25 bay covered, floodlit driving range. 18 hole, par 72 course and 9 hole par 3 course. *Fees:* information not available. *Eating facilities:* Pitchers Wine Bar and Restaurant. *Opening hours:* 8.00am to 10.00pm. Tuition available. Professional indoor video analysis. Professional: Kieran McLaughlin (028 71 352222; Fax: 028 71 353967).*
e-mail: mail@foylegolf.club24.co.uk
website: www.foylegolfcentre.co.uk

REPUBLIC OF IRELAND

COUNTY CORK

CARRIGTWOHILL. **Fota Island Golf Club,** Carrigtwohill (021 883700; Fax: 021 883713). *Location:* take the N25 east from Cork City, turn off Carrigtwohill/Cobh exit. Follow sign for Fota (100m). Grassed range. Venue for the 2002 Murphy's Irish Open. 18 hole championship course. Voted golf course of the year on 2002 by the Irish Golf Tour Operators. *Fees:* information not available. *Eating facilities:* full bar and restaurant. *Opening hours:* daylight only. PGA professional plus assistants available for tuition, practice putting/chipping green. Professional: Kevin Morris.
e-mail: reservations@fotaisland.ie
website: www.fotaisland.com

COUNTY DUBLIN.

FOXROCK. **Leopardstown Driving Range**, Foxrock (2895341). *Location:* five miles south of Dublin city centre situated in Leopardstown race course. 38 indoor, 38 outdoor floodlit bays. *Opening hours:* 9am to 10pm. *Eating facilities:* restaurant. Tuition available from three PGA Professionals - practice green. 18 hole golf course. *Fees:* information not available. Manager: Michael Hoey.*

CHANNEL ISLANDS.

ST OUEN'S. **Les Mielles Golf and Country Club**, St Ouen's Bay, Jersey JE3 7PQ (01534 482787; Fax: 01534 485414). *Location:* centre of St Ouen's Bay. 30 bay covered driving range. *Fees:* information not available. *Opening hours:* dawn till dusk. *Eating facilities:* restaurant, alfresco eating, kiosk. Public golf facility. Putting green; golf shop. Professional: Lee Elstone (01534 483699; Fax: 01534 485414). Director of Golf: J.A. Le Brun.*

ST MARGARET'S. **The Open Golf Centre,** Newtown House, St Margaret's (010 3531 8640324; Fax: 010 3531 8341400). *Location:* 2kms from Dublin Airport, adjacent to N2 (Derry road). 16 bay floodlit, grassed range. *Fees:* information not available. *Eating facilities:* coffee shop. *Opening hours:* 7.30am to dusk. Nine golf professionals on site, groups organised, video, lecture room and club fitting room.*

COUNTY MONAGHAN

CARRICKMACROSS. **Nuremore Golf Club**, Nuremore Hotel and Country Club, Carrickmacross (042 61438). *Location:* 50 miles from Dublin on N2. *Fees:* on request. *Eating facilities:* bar and catering facilities in new clubhouse and hotel. *Opening hours:* daylight hours. PGA Professional, all hotel facilities.

WATERFORD

DUNGARVAN. **Gold Coast Golf Club**, Ballinacourty, Dungarvan (058 44055; Fax: 058 43378). *Location:* from Waterford left of N25 two miles before Dungarvan. Parkland bordered by Atlantic. 18 holes, 6788 yards, 6171 metres. S.S.S. 72. *Green Fees:* information not available. *Eating facilities:* full hotel and leisure facilities. *Visitors:* welcome. *Society Meetings:* welcome, special rates available. Secretary: Tom Considine (Tel & Fax: 058 44055). *
e-mail: info@clonea.com
website: www.clonea.com

PORTUGAL

ESTORIL. **Quinta da Marinha Golf Conference and Golf Resort**, Quinta da Marinha Hotel Village Resort, Casa 36, 2750 Cascais, Portugal (01 4869881/9; Fax: 4869032). *Location:* motorway to Cascais from Lisbon. Grassed driving range. *Fees:* information not available. *Eating facilities:* club restaurant and bar. Opening hours: 7.45am to 9pm. Professional tuition for driving range and lessons. Driving range also available for rental. 18-hole golf course, two putting greens. Six tennis courts and two swimming pools, conference rooms and banqueting facilities. Accommodation available in 70 villas or the new 200 bedroom Marinha Golf Hotel facing the course. Professional: Keith Ashdown. Secretary: Maria Pinto Coelho. *

Index of Clubs and Courses

Index of Advertisers

OTHER FHG TITLES FOR 2004

FHG Publications have a large range of attractive holiday accommodation guides for all kinds of holiday opportunities throughout Britain. They also make useful gifts at any time of year. Our guides are available in most bookshops and larger newsagents but we will be happy to post you a copy direct if you have any difficulty. POST FREE for addresses in the UK. We will also post abroad but have to charge separately for post or freight.

The original
Farm Holiday Guide to COAST & COUNTRY HOLIDAYS in England, Scotland, Wales and Channel Islands. Board, Self-catering, Caravans/Camping, Activity Holidays.

BED AND BREAKFAST STOPS
Over 1000 friendly and comfortable overnight stops. Non-smoking, Disabled and Special Diets Supplements.

BRITAIN'S BEST HOLIDAYS
A quick-reference general guide for all kinds of holidays.

Recommended
WAYSIDE AND COUNTRY INNS of Britain
Pubs, Inns and small hotels.

Recommended
COUNTRY HOTELS
of Britain
Including Country Houses, for the discriminating.

PETS WELCOME!
The original and unique guide for holidays for pet owners and their pets.

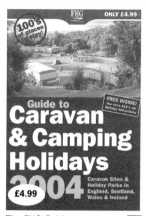

CHILDREN WELCOME! ☐
Family Holidays and Days
Out guide.
Family holidays with details of
amenities for children and
babies.

The FHG Guide to
CARAVAN & CAMPING ☐
HOLIDAYS,
Caravans for hire, sites and
holiday parks and centres.

SELF-CATERING ☐
HOLIDAYS
in Britain
Over 1000 addresses
throughout for self-catering
and caravans
in Britain.

Recommended
SHORT BREAK HOLIDAYS in Britain
"Approved" accommodation for quality bargain breaks.

£6.99

☐

Tick your choice and send your order and payment to

FHG PUBLICATIONS, ABBEY MILL BUSINESS CENTRE,
SEEDHILL, PAISLEY PA1 1TJ
TEL: 0141- 887 0428; FAX: 0141- 889 7204
e-mail: fhg@ipcmedia.com
Deduct 10% for 2/3 titles or copies; 20% for 4 or more.

FHG

Send to: NAME ....
           ADDRESS ....
           ....
           ....
           POST CODE ....
I enclose Cheque/Postal Order for £ ....
           SIGNATURE..DATE ....

Please complete the following to help us improve the service we provide. How
did you find out about our guides?:

☐Press   ☐Magazines   ☐TV/Radio   ☐Family/Friend   ☐Other

SHETLAND ISLANDS

A B C D E F 1

ORKNEY
ISLANDS
MAINLAND
Stromness
Kirkwall

HOY

YELL

MAINLAND

Lerwick

2

Sumburgh

0 10 20 30 40 50 Kilometres
0 10 20 30 Miles
Grid interval is 30 miles

Durness
Bettyhill
Tongue
Thurso
John o'Groats

LEWIS

Scourie
Wick

WESTERN
ISLES

Lochinver

Lairg
Helmsdale
Golspie
Ullapool
Bonar Bridge
Dornoch
Gairloch Poolewe
Tain

Portree
Cullen Banff Fraserburgh
Dingwall
Rosemarkie Elgin Fochabers
SKYE
Fortrose Nairn Forres Keith Turriff Peterhead
Beauly Kilravock Castle
Kyle of Lochalsh Croy
Inverness Huntly Methlick
Broadford Dornie Daviot
Kyleakin Grantown-on-Spey Inverurie
Carrbridge Tomintoul
HEBRIDES
Mallaig Fort Augustus Kingussie *ABERDEENSHIRE* Aberdeen
Aviemore
HIGHLAND *MORAY* CITY OF
ABERDEEN

Braemar Banchory
Stonehaven

Fort William *ANGUS*
Kinlochleven Kinloch Brechin
Tobermory Ballachulish Glencoe Rannoch Pitlochry
Aberfeldy Montrose
MULL Oban Dunkeld Forfar
Taynuilt Killin Blairgowrie Arbroath
Dalmally Lochearnhead Monifieth Carnoustie
Inveraray Crianlarich Perth Dundee
Strathyre Crieff 1. CITY OF DUNDEE
Arrochar Callander Cupar St Andrews 2. CLACKMANNANSHIRE
ARGYLL & BUTE Tarbet Aberfoyle Auchterarder 3. FALKIRK
Lochgilphead Luss *STIRLING* Kinross *FIFE* 4. WEST LOTHIAN
JURA Drymen 5. CITY OF EDINBURGH
Ardrishaig Dunoon Balloch North 6. MIDLOTHIAN
Gourock Dumbarton Stirling Kirkcaldy Berwick 7. EAST LOTHIAN
Tarbert Greenock Glasgow Dunfermline *EDINBURGH*
ISLAY Rothesay Paisley Dalkeith Haddington Eyemouth
Largs Hamilton Lauder Chirnside
Beith Lanark Peebles Duns Berwick upon Tweed
NORTH AYRSHIRE Fenwick Biggar Galashiels Coldstream Cornhill-on-Tweed
Brodick Ardrossan Kilmarnock *SCOTTISH BORDERS* Wooler Damburgh
KINTYRE Lamlash Irvine *EAST* Selkirk Kelso Seahouses
Troon *AYRSHIRE* Abington Jedburgh
Campbeltown Prestwick Hawick Alnwick
ARRAN Ayr
Maybole Moffat
New Beattock
Cumnock *NORTHUMBER-*
Girvan *LAND* Morpeth
SOUTH Langholm Bellingham
AYRSHIRE *DUMFRIES & GALLOWAY* Whitley
New Galloway Dumfries Gretna Bay
Stranraer Newton Stewart Castle Douglas Annan Longtown Newcastle-upon-Tyne
Portpatrick Crocketford Greenhead Hexham Corbridge
Wigtown Gatehouse of Fleet Silloth Carlisle
Port William Kirkcudbright *CUMBRIA* Alston Durham

8. INVERCLYDE
9. RENFREWSHIRE
10. WEST DUNBARTONSHIRE
11. EAST DUNBARTONSHIRE
12. NORTH LANARKSHIRE
13. CITY OF GLASGOW
14. EAST RENFREWSHIRE

Bassenthwaite Penrith

A B C D E F G

Map 1

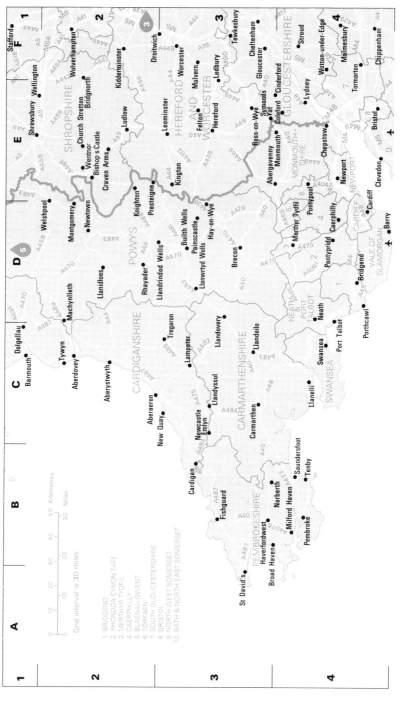

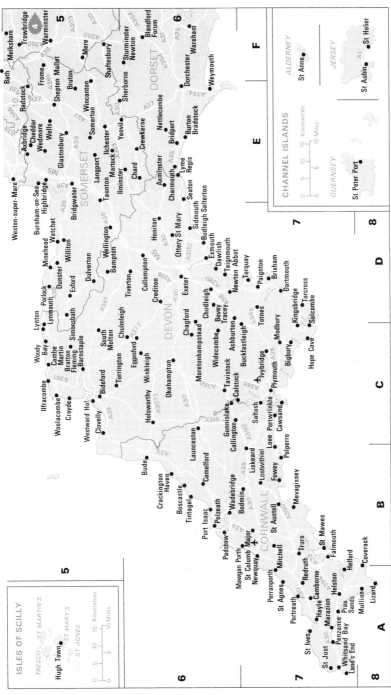

Map 2

ISLES OF SCILLY

TRESCO   ST MARTIN'S
          ST MARY'S
          ST AGNES

Hugh Town

0   5   10   15 Kilometres
0   5   10 Miles

CHANNEL ISLANDS

ALDERNEY

St Anne

GUERNSEY

St Peter Port

JERSEY

St Aubin   St Helier

0   5   10   15 Kilometres
0   5   10 Miles

GEOprojects (U.K.) Ltd
Crown Copyright Reserved

Map 3

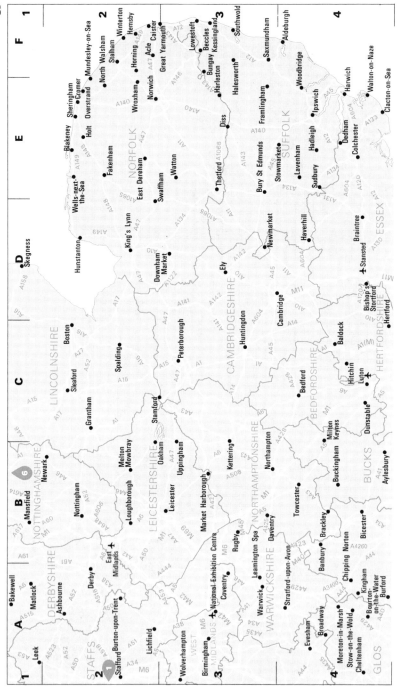

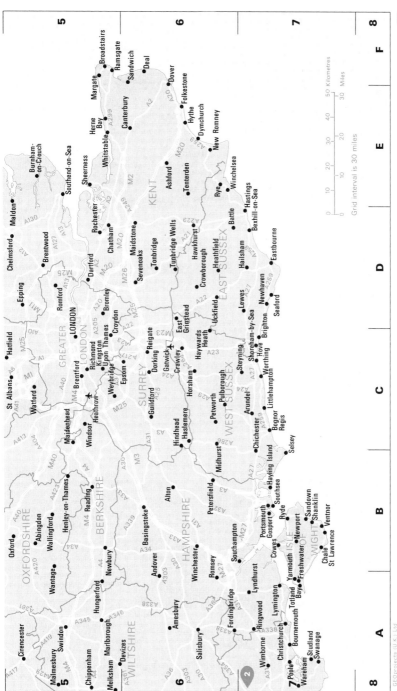

Map 4

Grid interval is 30 miles

50 Kilometres
30 Miles

GEOprojects (U.K.) Ltd
Crown Copyright Reserved

Map 5

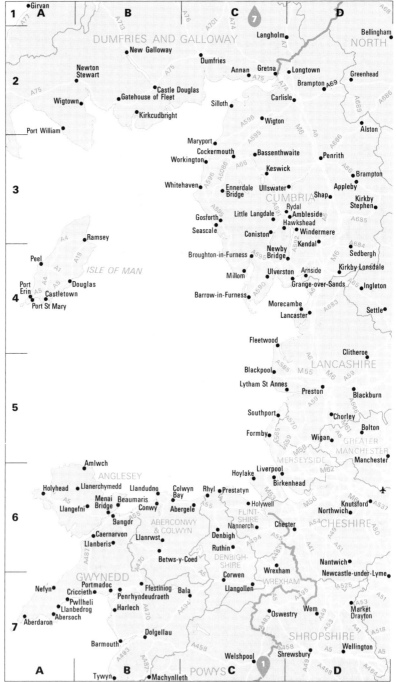

Girvan

1 A B C **7** D

DUMFRIES AND GALLOWAY

Langholm
Bellingham
NORTH

New Galloway
Dumfries

Newton
Stewart

2
Annan Gretna Longtown
Brampton Greenhead

Castle Douglas
Gatehouse of Fleet
Carlisle

Wigtown
Silloth

Kirkcudbright
Wigton
Alston

Port William
Maryport
Cockermouth Bassenthwaite Penrith

Workington
Keswick Brampton

3
Whitehaven Ennerdale Ullswater Shap
Bridge CUMBRIA Kirkby
Stephen

Rydal
Gosforth Little Langdale Ambleside
Hawkshead

Seascale Windermere
Coniston Kendal

Ramsey
Newby Sedbergh
Broughton-in-Furness Bridge

Peel
Millom Kirkby Lonsdale

ISLE OF MAN
Ulverston Arnside
Ingleton

Port
Erin Douglas
Grange-over-Sands

4
Castletown
Barrow-in-Furness Settle
Port St Mary
Morecambe
Lancaster

Fleetwood
Clitheroe

Blackpool LANCASHIRE

Lytham St Annes
Preston Blackburn

5
Southport Chorley
Bolton

Formby
Wigan
GREATER
MANCHESTER
Manchester

Amlwch
MERSEYSIDE
Hoylake Liverpool

ANGLESEY
Birkenhead

Holyhead Llanerchymedd Llandudno Colwyn Rhyl Prestatyn
Bay Knutsford

Menai Beaumaris Holywell
Llangefni Bridge Conwy Abergele Northwich

6
Bangor ABERCONWY FLINT-
& COLWYN SHIRE
Caernarvon Llanrwst Nannerch Chester CHESHIRE

Llanberis Denbigh
Betws-y-Coed Ruthin DENBIGH-
SHIRE Nantwich
Newcastle-under-Lyme

GWYNEDD
Wrexham
WREXHAM

Nefyn Portmadoc Corwen
Criccieth Ffestiniog Bala Llangollen Wem
Penrhyndeudraeth Market

7
Pwllheli Harlech Drayton
Llanbedrog Oswestry
Aberdaron Abersoch SHROPSHIRE

Dolgellau Wellington

Barmouth POWYS
Welshpool Shrewsbury

A B Tywyn Machynlleth **C** **D**

GEOprojects (U.K.) Ltd
Crown Copyright Reserved

Map 6

E | F | G | H | 1

Morpeth

UMBERLAND
A696

Whitley
Bay
Tynemouth
Corbridge
TYNE
South Shields
Newcastle
upon-Tyne
AND
Hexham
WEAR
Sunderland

2

Durham

0 10 20 30 40 50 Kilometres
0 10 20 30 Miles
Grid interval is 30 miles

1. STOCKTON-ON-TEES
2. MIDDLESBROUGH
3. KINGSTON UPON HULL
4. NORTH EAST LINCOLNSHIRE

DURHAM
HARTLEPOOL

Bishop Auckland
Redcar
Middleton-in-Teesdale
Middlesbrough
Saltburn-by-the-Sea
REDCAR & CLEVELAND
Barnard Castle
Darlington
Guisborough
Whitby
A66
Stokesley

3

Richmond

Hawes
Leyburn
A684
Northallerton
Scarborough
Middleham
Leeming Bar
Cayton Bay
Thirsk
Helmsley
Pickering
Ayton
Filey
NORTH YORKSHIRE
A170
Flamborough
Ripon
Castle
Howard
Malton
Grassington
Huby
Sledmere
Bridlington
Driffield
Skipton
Harrogate
York
A166
Keighley
Ilkley
YORK
EAST RIDING
OF YORKSHIRE
Hornsea
Bingley
Bradford
Leeds
Selby
Beverley
Heptonstall
WEST
Halifax
YORKSHIRE
M62
Hull
Withernsea
Huddersfield
Goole

4

5

Barnsley
NORTH
LINCOLNSHIRE
Glossop
Doncaster
Scunthorpe
Grimsby
SOUTH
Cleethorpes
YORKSHIRE
Sheffield
Gainsborough
Louth
Worksop
Mablethorpe
Buxton
Chesterfield
Alford
Macclesfield
Lincoln
Horncastle
Bakewell
Congleton
Skegness
Leek
Matlock
NOTTINGHAM-
SHIRE
LINCOLNSHIRE
Stoke-on-Trent
Ashbourne
Newark
DERBYSHIRE
Sleaford
Boston
Nottingham
STAFFORDSHIRE
Derby
Grantham
Stafford
East
Midlands
Burton-upon-Trent
Loughborough
Melton
Mowbray
Spalding
Lichfield
LEICESTERSHIRE
Stamford
M54
Oakham
Leicester
Uppingham
Peterborough

6

7

E | F | G | H

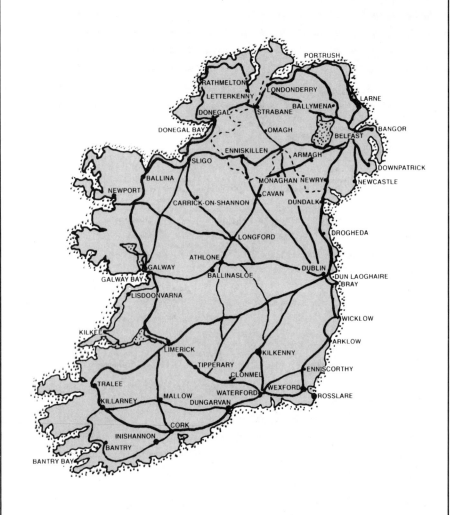

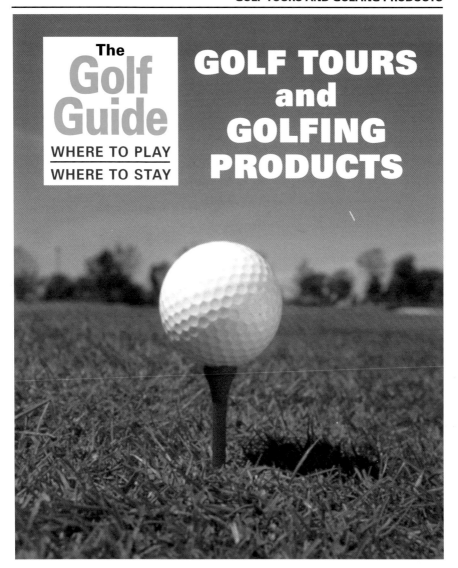

Publisher's Note

While every effort is made to ensure accuracy, we regret that FHG Publications cannot accept responsibility for errors, omissions or misrepresentations in our entries or any consequences thereof. We will follow up complaints but cannot act as arbiters or agents for either party.

take the shock out of golf...

Greenhill Leisure Products, the world's leading designer of electric golf trolleys, are proud to present their new electric golf trolley

The GreenMaster 600S

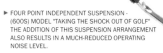

Incorporating Greenhill's new unique independent suspension system

▸ FOUR POINT INDEPENDENT SUSPENSION - (600S) MODEL "TAKING THE SHOCK OUT OF GOLF" THE ADDITION OF THIS SUSPENSION ARRANGEMENT ALSO RESULTS IN A MUCH-REDUCED OPERATING NOISE LEVEL.

▸ IMPROVED HANDLING COMFORT BY MINIMISING TRANSMISSION OF SHOCKS AND VIBRATION FROM THE WHEELS TO THE USER.

▸ QUIET POWERFUL ELECTRIC MOTOR 250WATT (0.35hp)

▸ ULTRA LOW - NOISE MOTOR-GEAR BOX FOR RELIABLE PERFORMANCE.

▸ EASY GRIP MOULDED HANDLE HAS VARIABLE SPEED CONTROL AND ON-OFF SWITCH FOR EFFICIENT ECONOMY.

▸ MAINTENANCE FREE EXTRA HIGH CAPACITY 500 CYCLES SEALED BATTERY (28Ah) SONNENSCHEIN.

▸ ADVANCED ELECTRONIC 12V 4A BATTERY CHARGER INCLUDED.

▸ PUNCTURE FREE TYRES AS STANDARD.

▸ THE LIGHTWEIGHT ALUMINIUM FRAME WEIGHS LESS THAN 8 kilos (without battery) 17½lbs, REQUIRES NO ASSEMBLY AND WILL STAND UPRIGHT.

▸ BOX SECTION CHASSIS DESIGN FOR EXTRA MECHANICAL STRENGTH.

▸ THE ORIGINAL ONE PIECE "Z" FOLDING-ASSEMBLY FOR EASY STORAGE.

▸ THE SMALLEST, MOST COMPACT, POWER TROLLEY ON THE MARKET WITH 'NEW' FOLD UNDER FRONT WHEEL FOR MAXIMUM COMPACTNESS 67cm x 60cm x 26cm

▸ EXTRA HIGH STABILITY TOP BAG SUPPORT WITH QUICK RELEASE STRAPS WILL HOLD ALL SIZES OF GOLF BAG

▸ AIR CONDITIONING COMES AS STANDARD

greenhill▸ **Designed and Engineered in Great Britain**

Greenhill Leisure Products, Leyburn Business Park, Leyburn, North Yorkshire DL8 5QA Phone 01969 624324 Fax 01969 625124 www.green2hill.co.uk

Patent pending

The
Golf Guide
WHERE TO PLAY
WHERE TO STAY

OVERSEAS GOLF TOURS

NOTE

All the information regarding Golf Clubs in this guide is given in good faith in the belief that it is correct. However, the publishers cannot guarantee the facts given in these pages, neither are they responsible for changes in ownership or facilities, such as green fees, that may take place after the date of going to press. Readers should always satisfy themselves that the facilities they require are available and that the terms, if quoted, still apply.

DRIVETIME swings to the town's success

Ask Managing Director Ed Norris why **DRIVETIME** is swinging all hours and he'll give you a simple answer. It's not just he 12 years of work they've put in to make a great golf centre and conference venue for the region - it's as much to do with the massive success **Warrington** has been enjoying recently.

When we started, we were on to something new - there was a novelty about a practice centre, and it was still the domain of the serious golfer or the keenest junior.

Now we're opening doors to whole new groups of customer who can come down any time without membership and get right into what is no longer an elitist game.

For that we have to partly thank the likes of Tiger Woods, but it also says something about how well the town is doing too," Ed says. "Tiger's a great ambassador and role model in his cool gear, attracting hundreds of youngsters nto the game. And it's also down to the success of the town, the companies here, and the local community."

Capable of hosting events for up to 100 at a time, Drivetime's package of golf centre and conference venue within minutes of the town centre has seen companies as large as BP and United Utilities join the client list, and with plans to add a designated short game area to the remodelled practice centre, more are likely to follow.

Accommodation can be arranged with nearby hotels, and all sorts of fun or more intense golf packages put on for clients, and Ed is also particularly pleased at the American Golf superstore at Drivetime - another link with a successful local company.

The reasons we get the serious golfer coming to practice are easy to see - decent facilities and equipment throughout, from the balls and mats to the way we position our targets. For beginners, it's more about the easy to understand the teaching they get from our professionals, and that everything is so accessible, and they can relax and get a bite to eat."

Ladies too are regular customers, often encouraged by the word of mouth of others who've visited. And on the Drivetime side, too, female staff have played a key role in the development of the centre, few more than function manager Donna Beswick, who has been with the team for years, building up services to offer everything from light snacks and refreshments to whole banquets.

"It's great to see the way we've developed," says Ed, "and I guess one of the greatest successes we've seen is on the coaching side, with Adrian Fryer and Alan Clark here from the start and now widely recognised for their work with so many.

Tel: 01925 234800 • Fax: 01925 240053
www.drivetimeuk.com